Cryptography

Cryptography

Algorithms, Protocols, and Standards for Computer Security

Zoubir Mammeri

Library of Congress Cataloging-in-Publication Data:
Names: Mammeri, Zoubir, author. | John Wiley & Sons, publisher.
Title: Cryptography : algorithms, protocols, and standards for computer
    security / Zoubir Mammeri.
Description: Hoboken, New Jersey : JW-Wiley, [2024] | Includes
    bibliographical references and index.
Identifiers: LCCN 2023030470 | ISBN 9781394207480 (hardback) |
    ISBN 9781394207497 (pdf) | ISBN 9781394207503 (epub) | ISBN 9781394207510 (ebook)
Subjects: LCSH: Cryptography. | Computer security.
Classification: LCC QA268 .M34 2024 | DDC 005.8/24--dc23/eng/20230807
LC record available at https://lccn.loc.gov/2023030470

Cover Design: Wiley
Cover Image: © zf L/Getty Images

Set in 9.5/12.5pt STIXTwoText by Integra Software Services Pvt. Ltd, Pondicherry, India

Contents

Preface

For millennia, human beings have used multiple forms of codes to protect their oral communications, entries of castles, their messages, and other belongings. Indeed, cryptography existed early in human history and civilizations, before the event of computers. Cryptography has been developed and improved over the centuries, in particular for protecting military secrets and spying on enemies, then for protecting industrial and economical secrets, then for protecting recent applications made possible with the use of the internet, and ultimately for protecting the privacy of electronic devices' users. In a highly computerized world, cryptography is the pillar of security. Encrypting and signing are the most performed cryptographic operations in the digital world.

Cryptography provides services to secure websites, electronic transmissions, and data repositories. For more than three decades, public-key cryptography has been enabling people, who never met before, to securely communicate and trust each other. Cryptography is not only used over the internet, but also in phones, bank cards, televisions, cars, aircrafts, door locks, implants, and a variety of other devices. Without cryptography, hackers could get into victims' emails, listen to their phone conversations, tap into their cable companies and acquire free cable services, or break into their bank accounts.

Cryptography is the discipline at the intersection of computer science and mathematics. It provides algorithms for guaranteeing confidentiality, integrity, authentication, and non-repudiation for parties that share data or exchange messages to perform operations and transactions in cyberspace. For example, customers' bank accounts or citizens' votes must remain confidential and not altered by any unauthorized third party. E-merchants, as well as clients, must be protected from each other; a customer, who ordered an article, could not deny ordering; and a merchant, who has been paid, could not deny having been. A person, who digitally signed an agreement or a contract, cannot deny having signed. Such protections, and many others, are provided thanks to cryptography.

Cryptography standards are needed to enable interoperability in cyberspace. In general, standard protocols follow rigorous procedures of testing before their adoption. Therefore, it is highly recommended to use only standard security protocols to build information security systems. Security, in general, and cryptography, in particular, have evolved at a rapid pace in the past two decades. Security technology has gone through tremendous changes in terms of protocols and standards. The continuous evolution of information technology, on one hand, and the discovery of vulnerabilities in standards, on the other hand, motivate the development of new standards. In the last 15 years, cryptography standards made tremendous advances that are not included in existing books. Some standards have become obsolete and others have recently been recommended. This book aims at providing a comprehensive description of recent advances in cryptographic protocols. The focus is on the NIST (National Institute for Standards and Technology, US) and IETF (Internet Engineering Task Force) standards, which are commonly used in the internet and networking applications.

This book, also, aims at providing a comprehensive description of notions, algorithms, protocols, and standards in the cryptographic field. It addresses algorithms through examples and problems, highlights vulnerabilities of deprecated standards, and describes in detail algorithms and protocols recommended in recent standards. In addition, it focuses on the basic notions and methods of security analysis and cryptanalysis of symmetric ciphers. The book is designed to serve as a textbook for undergraduate and graduate students, as well as a reference for researchers and practitioners in cryptography.

Definitions Used in the Book

Definitions included in this book are inspired by NIST and IETF glossaries [1,2]. They are not formal definitions. Rather, they are provided to summarize the basic notions of cryptography and facilitate the learning of algorithms and protocols.

1) Paulsen C, Byers RD. Glossary of Key Information Security Terms. NIST; 2019.
2) Shirey R. Internet Security Glossary, RFC 4949. Internet Engineering Task Force; 2007.

Organization of the Book

Chapter 1: This chapter introduces aims at introducing the main issues and notions of security in computer-based systems. The main properties of security (namely confidentiality, integrity, authenticity, and non-repudiation) are introduced. A taxonomy of attacks on digital assets is provided. Multiple components and practices, required to address from different perspectives the security of computer-based systems, are introduced in this chapter. The main technical components of security include cryptography, which is the focus of the remainder of the book.

Chapter 2: Cryptography has developed and improved over time. Chapter 2 aims at providing a brief history of cryptography and presenting its main notions and techniques. Breaking cryptographic codes is a very ancient activity to disclose secrets. An overall categorization of attacks on modern cryptographic algorithms is discussed in this chapter. There exist two main categories of cryptographic systems: symmetric and asymmetric (also called public-key) cryptosystems. The design differences between both categories are briefly discussed. Message digest, digital signature, and digital certificate are of prime importance to establish trust between parties that share data and exchange messages. These notions are introduced in Chapter 2.

Chapter 3: This chapter aims at reviewing and presenting, with examples and exercises, the mathematical background useful to address cryptography algorithms. In particular, modular arithmetic and finite fields are of prime importance to understand the design of cryptographic algorithms. Fundamental theorems for cryptography are provided. In addition, to mathematical notions, computation algorithms (such as Extended Euclidean algorithm, square-and-multiply method to perform modular exponentiation, modular multiplication, Gauss's algorithm to solve congruence systems, Tonelli-Shanks's algorithm to find modular square roots, and Rabin's algorithm to test irreducibility of polynomials), which are often used in cryptographic algorithms, are introduced with examples and exercises. Readers who have a sufficient background in the reminded notions and algorithms can skip this chapter.

Chapter 4: Shift and substitution ciphers have been used in written text transmission; and dominated the art of secret writing for at least two millenniums. The most known historical ciphers in this category include Caesar's, Vigenere's, Affine, One Time Pad, and Enigma ciphers. All those ciphers are original inventions, with ideas and principles that inspired authors of modern cryptographic algorithms. Before presenting modern cryptographic algorithms, Chapter 4 aims at providing an overview of historical ciphers and their ingenious ideas. Methods used to break historical ciphers have widely been exploited to design modern ciphers.

Chapter 5: This chapter introduces three notions of cryptography: hash functions, message authentication codes, and digital signature. All of them are of paramount importance for providing integrity and authentication guarantees. Hash functions produce digital fingerprints, also called message tags, which are mainly used to verify the integrity of messages and files, to generate and verify digital signatures, and to generate random numbers. Approaches to design hash functions and standard hash functions (i.e. SHA-1, SHA-2, and SHA-3) and standard Message Authentication Codes (i.e. HMAC and KMAC) are described in detail. Common attacks against MAC algorithms and digital signatures are discussed.

Chapter 6: Stream ciphers are symmetric ciphers that encrypt and decrypt bits individually. They are used, in particular, to secure communications in wireless and cellular networks. Stream ciphers are well-suited to hardware implementation and they are generally faster than block ciphers. They also are well-suited to encrypt and decrypt continuous data at high rate and when devices have limited memory to store long messages. Often, stream ciphers are designed using LFSRs (Linear-Feedback Shift Registers) combined with nonlinear filtering functions. Chapter 6 aims at providing a discussion of the design principles of LFSRs and stream ciphers to produce keystream bits, used to encrypt plaintexts and decrypt ciphertexts. It also provides a detailed description of the most known and standard stream ciphers: A5/1, E0, SNOW 3G, ZUC, Chacha20, RC4, Trivium, and Enocoro.

Chapter 7: This chapter addresses block ciphers, which are the most used algorithms to secure data and messages. Data or messages are split into blocks of a fixed size (e.g. 128 bits) and plaintext blocks are encrypted individually to generate ciphertext blocks of the same bit-length than that of a plaintext block. In addition to ciphering, block ciphers can be used to generate pseudorandom numbers or to build hash functions and MACs (Message Authentication Codes). A huge number of block ciphers are published in literature. However, a very small number of them are standards that are used in operational cryptosystems. This chapter introduces the basics of construction of block ciphers and presents in detail the standard block ciphers, currently in use, namely TDEA (Triple Data Encryption Algorithm) and AES (Advanced Encryption Standard). Known attacks against block ciphers are discussed.

Chapters 8 and 9: A block cipher, such as AES or TDEA, takes a fixed-size plaintext block and returns a ciphertext block of the same size. However, in many applications, a plaintext (e.g. a text file or an image) is composed of several (maybe in thousands or even more) blocks. When plaintext blocks are repeated in the same data or message and identically encrypted, an attacker may infer some information regarding the ciphertexts that he/she intercepted. In addition, in many applications, the recipient of a message may need to authenticate the message sender. Chapter 8 addresses standard operation modes of block ciphers to guarantee confidentiality. The NIST recommends 11 modes (ECB, CBC, CBC-S1, CBC-S2, CBC-S3, OCB, CTR, CFB, FF1, FF-3, and XTS-AES) for guaranteeing confidentiality. Chapter 9 focuses on modes of operation of block ciphers to provide either authentication or confidentiality and authentication. NIST recommends three modes (CMAC, GMAC, and Poly1305-AES), for authentication-only, and six modes (CCM, GMAC, AED-ChaCha20-Poly1305, KW, KWP, and TKW) for authentication and confidentiality. All the 20 operation modes recommended by NIST are addressed in detail in Chapters 8 and 9. Known attacks against operation modes are also discussed.

Chapter 10: Modern cryptographic security relies on the computational difficulty to break ciphers rather than on the theoretical impossibility to break them. If adversaries have enough resources and time, they can break any cipher. The security analysis of block ciphers and their modes of operation is a wide field in cryptanalysis. It aims at finding bounds on the amount of data to encrypt with the same key without compromising the security of encrypted data. Chapter 10 introduces security analysis in which adversaries are given black boxes that simulate block ciphers or their modes of operation. Then, adversaries query black boxes, receive ciphertexts, plaintexts, or tags, and try to guess some information about the used keys or to forge signatures or message tags. Secure ciphers are those ciphers for which the advantage of adversaries is negligible if their resources and time remain below some limits. The analysis of different scenarios of attacks is an approach to assess the security of ciphers from a probabilistic point of view.

Chapter 11: Cryptanalysis is the science and techniques of analyzing and breaking cryptographic algorithms and protocols. It is a very exciting and challenging field. There exist hundreds of cryptanalysis attack variants. Chapter 11 aims at presenting the most known cryptanalysis attacks against symmetric ciphers, namely memory-time trade-off attacks, linear cryptanalysis, differential cryptanalysis algebraic cryptanalysis, cube attacks, divide-and-conquer attacks, and correlation attacks.

Chapter 12: The turning point in modern cryptography occurred in 1976–1977, when Diffie and Hellman on one side and Rivest, Shamir, and Adleman, on the other, proposed original schemes to secure systems without requiring a unique cipher key shared by both parties. The proposed schemes were and are still used to design public-key cryptosystems. The latter provide support to secure communications worldwide between people who do not a priori know each other. The first and still most widely used public-key cryptosystem is with no doubt RSA. Modern cryptography is founded on the idea that the key used to encrypt messages can be made public, while the key used to decrypt messages must be kept private. Chapter 12 aims to describe public-key algorithms and protocols, for providing confidentiality, integrity, and authentication guarantees. They include RSA, Diffie-Hellman key exchange, Menezes-Qu-Vanstone, and ElGamal cryptosystems. The security of public-key cryptosystems is based on either the integer factorization problem or the discrete logarithm problem over cyclic groups. Those problems are known to be computationally infeasible for large numbers; and they are discussed in this chapter. Known attacks against addressed algorithms are introduced.

Chapter 13: The second generation of public-key cryptosystems are based on elliptic curve theory. Elliptic curve (EC) cryptography algorithms entered wide use in 2004. After a slow start, EC-based algorithms are gaining popularity and the pace of adoption is accelerating. EC cryptosystems have been adopted by Amazon, Google, and many others to secure communications with their customers. EC cryptosystems amply outperform RSA-based cryptosystems. Until 2015, the NSA (National Security Agency, US) recommended 256-bit EC cryptography for protecting classified information up to the secret level and 384-bit for Top-secret level. Since 2015, the NSA has recommended 384-bit for all classified information. IETF standards have been proposed to support EC for Transport Layer Security. Chapter 13 aims at addressing different forms of EC-based algorithms, such as ECDSA, to provide confidentiality, integrity, and authenticity guarantees. Compared to RSA, EC-based algorithms make use of more difficult mathematical operations, which are addressed in this chapter.

Chapter 14: Keys are owned and used by entities that interact with each other to perform specific operations in different fields of activities. These keys are analogous to the combination of a safe. If adversaries know the combination of a safe, then the latter does not provide any security against attacks, even it is very complex. Keys are the most valuable items in computer security. Therefore, their protection is of paramount importance. Chapter 14 focuses on key management, which provides functions to secure cryptographic keys throughout their lifetime. It mainly includes key generation, storage, distribution, recovery, suspension, and withdrawal. This chapter aims at introducing the main mechanisms and protocols for key generation, key agreement, key transport, and key distribution over unsecure channels.

Chapter 15: Parties, which exchange encrypted messages over the internet, need to trust each other to secure their operations and transactions in e-commerce, e-banking, e-voting, etc. In addition, parties that exchange messages or access encrypted data inside a company or an institution, where messages/data are encrypted using symmetric keys, need to securely share their keys. Chapter 15 addresses both situations and presents different notions, including key distribution center, digital certificate, certification authority, and Public-key infrastructures (PKIs). PKIs are of paramount importance to establish trust between partners that do not a priori trust each other in the open digital world. Today, digital certificates are used by billions of end-entities, including web servers and their clients, to authenticate each other. The main protocol to secure communications over the internet is with no doubt TLS (Transport Layer Security); it is introduced in this chapter.

Chapter 16: Modern cryptography is fundamentally based on large random and prime numbers. In particular, keys should be generated using large random numbers; and RSA keys are generated using large prime numbers. Any weakness (in term of randomness) in a selected key may result in damage of data and messages protected by that weak key. Chapter 16 addresses algorithms and methods recommended to generate random and prime numbers. True random numbers are hard to produce by computer. In consequence, deterministic random number generators (DRNGs) are of common use in cryptography. However, it is of prime importance to use only DRNGs recommended by NIST and IETF. DRNGs cannot guarantee that generated integers are prime. Therefore, algorithms for testing primality are of common use in cryptography. When prime numbers are required, only provable and probable primes should be used. Probable primes are those integers shown to be prime by probabilistic tests. Both types of primes are discussed in this chapter.

Appendix: A series of 200 multiple choice questions (with answers), relating to computer security in general and to cryptography in particular, are proposed for knowledge testing. These MCQs were collected from various sources, including questions for job applicants, course certification, and exams in IT security field.

Using the Book as a Course

Some chapters are independent of each other, while some chapters are grouped into blocks, because they share notions, objectives, or mathematical background. Chapter blocks are marked with dotted lines. Therefore, the book may be used in different ways, depending on the audience. In particular, chapters focusing on symmetric-key algorithms are independent of those addressing public-key algorithms. Various learning paths are suggested in the figure below, where single arrows show the recommended sequential reading order of chapters, while double arrows indicate that the reader can focus on chapter blocks in any order.

Chapters 1 and 2 are introductive. Therefore, it is recommended to read them. Chapter 3 recalls mathematical background. It could be skipped and, at any time, the reader can return to this chapter to learn about mathematical notions used in the other chapters. For readers not familiar with modular arithmetic and algebra notions, it is recommended to take time to address the exercises given in Chapter 3.

Chapter 4 is a review of historical ciphers. It is recommended in order to learn some roots of modern cryptography. Chapter 5 presents notions relevant to both symmetric and asymmetric cryptosystems.

The two big chapter blocks (i.e. symmetric and asymmetric algorithms, protocols, and standards), may be addressed in any order. However, we recommend finishing a block before starting the other one. Chapters 10 and 11 focus on advanced notions in cryptanalysis of symmetric ciphers. Therefore, they are recommended for graduate students.

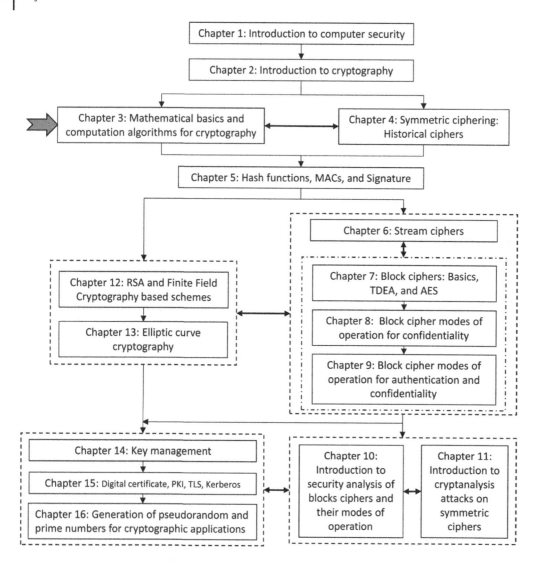

For feedback, contact the author at
zoubir.mammeri@irit.fr or zoubir.mammeri11@gmail.com

1

Introduction to Computer Security

Information and computer technologies (ICT), or simply IT technologies, are everywhere, in all fields of activities (business, commerce, transportation systems, health, leisure, education, administration, national security, army, etc.). Nowadays, human beings are more than ever dependent on IT technologies. Therefore, IT security became a paramount concern for any owner or user of electronic devices.

Since the early stage of computers, cyberattacks have never stopped. Worse, statistics provided annually by cybercrime observers and experts often show increases in attacks worldwide. In particular, ransom attacks have become the most lucrative criminal activities in the cyberspace. Partial or total shutdown of systems, as long as ransoms are not paid, results in losses in billions of dollars for companies, hospitals, e-merchants, banks, and individuals.

This chapter aims at providing an introduction to the main issues and notions of security in computer-based systems and tries to answer the following questions:

- What are the security issues and requirements?
- Why and how do security attacks occur?
- How to face security attacks? That is, what are the countermeasures to security attacks?

Security techniques encompass at least two distinct domains:

- Technical domain, including hardware and software design to address security;
- Organizational domain, including education, staff training, and laws to make involved people aware of IT security.

This book addresses security from a technical point of view only; in particular, it addresses cryptography. However, it should be clear that technology alone is not enough to address security. Imagine that you use a sophisticated alarm system in your home, but the code to access the system is "1234"; or if a teenager in your family does not protect the house alarm code when he/she is at school or at sport club; or even worse, he/she forgets switching on the alarm system when he/she leaves your home. Therefore, organizational issues (including education to security) are of prime importance.

Several books (including [1–9] and journal papers [10, 11]) addressed in detail IT security. This chapter aims only to present the notions of IT security, in particular the security services that can be supported by cryptographic algorithms.

1.1 Introduction

1.1.1 Why Do Attacks Occur?

Since the dawn of time, evil behavior of human beings have emerged: stealing or destroying belongings of others, injuring or even killing others, having interest in details or even disclosing the private life of others, etc.

Different human's defaults result in misbehaving; they include:

- Ego (i.e. Be the best and the center of the world).
- Greediness (i.e. Own all or the maximum of things/goods).
- Curiosity (i.e. Know private details about the others).
- Revenge (i.e. Having been mistreated, seek revenge without going through justice).

Cryptography: Algorithms, Protocols, and Standards for Computer Security, First Edition. Zoubir Mammeri.
© 2024 John Wiley & Sons, Inc. Published 2024 by John Wiley & Sons, Inc.

- Competition (i.e. Be the first in sport, business, science, ...).
- Beliefs (religion) (i.e. Having some religious beliefs, do not agree with those of others or worse hate and fight them).
- Opinions (politics, ideology) (i.e. same reasons as those for religious beliefs).

Therefore, there is no unique profile (or reason) for potential attackers and criminals to act. Attacks on computer-based systems are one of the evil facets of humanity. We would say, times change, but the original flaws remain. Attacks can be prevented, detected, and handled to mitigate their effects. We cannot ignore them or naïvely hope that they will definitely cease. From ICT point of view, attacks may be classified as:

- Theft of private or confidential data.
- Data disclosure regarding privacy of individuals (their home, their beliefs, ...) or disclosing industrial and business secrets of companies, strategies of governments, and national defense secrets.
- Threats and ransoms (via email) to extort secrets (in case of spying) or money.
- Sabotage of ICT resources, which may be data alteration to force the use of erroneous/false/fabricated data, data deletion to prevent data owners to access their data, or computer shutdown or slowing down to make it unusable by its users.
- Sabotage of physical equipment (such as cars, trains, satellites, antennas, factories, smart grids, smart homes, nuclear plants, hospitals, patients...), for example, exploiting vulnerabilities of wireless communications and/or viruses.

When we disregard security issues, all of us are convinced that computers and the internet would be a revolution never seen before. Using Internet, communications between people and between devices became easy and worldwide. Communication borders between people have been deeply transformed and abolished to some extent. Internet has transformed earth into a village, from the communication point of view. Using Internet has so many benefits in almost all domains: industry, economy, society, health, learning, leisure, politics, democracy, etc.

Unfortunately, when security is of concern, the internet is probably the worst technology that harms computer-based assets. Internet became a haven for hackers, cyberterrorists, government-sponsored espionage agencies, etc., allowing attackers to operate from anywhere on earth, in particular from hostile countries or countries without deterrent and applicable laws.

1.1.2 Are Security Attacks Avoidable?

A drastic solution was suggested by Gene Spafford: "The only truly secure system is one that is powered off, cast in a block of concrete and sealed in a lead-lined room with armed guards," quoted in [12]. Unfortunately, Spafford's solution prevents any use of computers or systems. In practice, using a computer (or any other electronic device) is risky for any user.

The objectives of security techniques are to minimize the risks at reasonable cost. For example, protection of one's family pictures and the protection of national security and defense systems do not involve similar risks or similar costs. One thing should be clearly understood: there is no 100% secure and reliable system, which is human-made and (directly or indirectly) accessible to attackers. In practice, many risks are taken into consideration only when attacks are reported. In preference, the attacks should first affect others, and we are happy to learn from their misfortunes (credit card stealing, lock of cars, shutdown of hospital services, etc.).

1.1.3 What Should Be Protected in Cyberspace?

Definition 1.1 Cyberspace: *it is the space composed of electromechanical devices, computers, communication links, and applications servers where humans interact using the provided facilities.*

Cyber comes from *Cybernetics*, which is a large discipline including control systems, electrical theory, mechanical engineering, logic modeling, and others. The main component of cybernetics is the computer. Starting from the 1960s most of engineering studies in cybernetics have been specialized and became computer science, electronics, automation, telecommunications, and so on.

From security point of view, protections focus on:

- *Physical entities*: including plants, labs, stores, parking areas, loading areas, warehouses, offices, machines, robots, vehicles, products, materials, etc. At this level, the protection is physical (e.g. protect doors, PCs, cables, etc.).

- *People*: protect life, health, the privacy of staff members, customers, and guests.
- *Data*: protect files, databases, messages, programs, servers...

This book focuses on data protection only. However, before focusing on data protection, below is a brief introduction to barriers used for physical protection to enforce data protection.

i) Physical barriers

They are used to deter the potential attackers; they include:

- Guards: deploy security agents in and around vulnerable areas.
- Fences: build high and impassable fences and walls.
- Restricted access technologies (alarms, locks): deploy alarm systems to detect intrusions and highly-resistant locks to prevent unauthorized access.

ii) Physical access restrictions

They are used to deter attacks; they include:

Isolation of computers or networks to make them inaccessible.
Encryption of removable media and storage in restricted-access areas.
Use remote storage systems (e.g. cloud servers) to store data in secure locations or to store copies of data to download in the event of damage of the original copies.

iii) Personnel security practices

They participate in improving data protection; they include:

- Limited access zones: according to the criticality of zones, different access rights must be granted to staff, personnel, customers, and visitors.
- Biometrics and badges: use biometrics and badges to enforce identification and authentication.
- Faraday cages: in some (critical) situations, Faraday's cages are used to enforce data protection. There is no communication interception, when communicating devices are inside a Faraday's cage.
- Training: security training includes awareness regarding the good practices, awareness regarding the abnormal behavior reporting, and enforcement of the spirit of loyalty and patriotism.

Notes

- Physical access barring is the first defense line and it is deterrent against attackers. Without physical protection measures, it is very unlikely that data protection would be assured.
- Physical protection comes with high costs; and it is mainly deployed by institutions and companies. The costs depend on the required protection level.

1.1.4 Security vs Safety

There are two different properties (or functional requirements) regarding ICT systems: safety and security. Unfortunately, those two terms are sometimes mixed up and used interchangeably.

- *Safety*: it aims at addressing the issues to protect systems against risks and threats that come with *technology*, including hardware failures, software errors, communication interferences, etc.
- *Security*: it aims at addressing the issues to protect systems against *human attacks* on computers, servers, and data.

To better understand the difference between safety and security, let's take the case of home security. We use robust materials to build safe houses regarding flood, fire, heat, rain, snow, and wind; it is the safety concern. We use robust locks, cameras, and alarms to make houses secure regarding thieves; it is the security concern.

1.1.5 Cybersecurity vs IT Security

Often, the three terms *cybersecurity, IT security*, or simply *security* are used interchangeably in the information technology and science fields. However, there exists some difference between those terms, as stated by the NIST [1] [13].

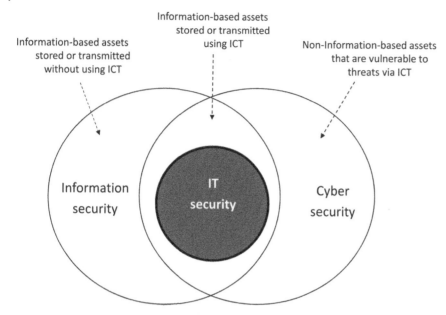

Figure 1.1 IT security vs cybersecurity.

- *Information security* is defined as: the protection of information and information systems from unauthorized access, use, disclosure, disruption, modification, or destruction in order to provide confidentiality, integrity, and availability.
- *Cybersecurity* is defined as: the ability to protect or defend the use of cyberspace from cyberattacks. Cybersecurity is about securing devices (computers, mobile devices, applications, and data) that are accessible through ICT.

In practice, cybersecurity term is often used by people not directly involved or specialized in computer science (e.g. police officers, judges, presidents, and mayors) to talk about attacks made via Internet. Whereas IT security or simply security terms are used by those people directly involved in computers and software. In this book, *security* is used to designate *IT security*. Figure 1.1 provides an overall comparison of *IT security* to *Cybersecurity*, where:

- *Information* (of a company, country, or an individual) includes digital and non-digital (i.e. papers, frames, books, films, etc.). Non-digital information is not under the control of computers, while digital information is. Information security is concerned by the security of information whatever is the support and ways of access.
- *Cyberspace* is composed of computers and by other equipment (e.g. trains, cars, grid installations, robots, and water provisioning equipment). All those categories of equipment are vulnerable to attacks through ICT. Their protection requires specific methods and techniques; some of them are out of the computer field (e.g. smart grids and industrial equipment). Cybersecurity is concerned with the security of any assets vulnerable because they are connected to ICT systems.
- Intersection of information and cyberspace security is the IT security focusing on digital data, which are vulnerable to threats via ICT.

1.2 Security Terms and Definitions

1.2.1 Assets and Attackers

Three fundamental notions are at the core of security: asset, adversary, and attack vector.

Definition 1.2 Asset*: it refers to any resource to protect. Assets to secure include hardware (laptops, work stations, disks, USB keys, routers, switches, cables, antennas), software (operating systems, libraries, applications, severs), and data (files, databases, messages).*

Definition 1.3 Adversary: *it is any entity that attacks or that is a potential threat to a system. It is also called attacker or threat agent.*

Definition 1.4 Attack vector: *it refers to any path or means by which an attacker can gain access to an asset. The adversary uses attack vectors (such as email, web servers, physical access, etc.) to gain access to protected assets.*

1.2.2 Vulnerabilities, Threats, and Risks

Definition 1.5 Vulnerability: *it refers to a known weakness of an asset that can be exploited by attackers.*

Example 1.1

– No password change for years, open account with no user in a company, and secret data stored in a place easy to access are examples of vulnerabilities.
– No update of phone software with recent security recommendations and a web camera with code 1234 are other examples of vulnerabilities.

Any entities, including the following, using computer-based systems are vulnerable:

• Companies, banks, and financial institutions
• Internet service providers and Telecom operators
• Hospitals, museums, and universities
• Government and defense agencies
• Smart cities and smart grids
• Industrial installations and factories
• Nuclear plants

Definition 1.6 Attack surface: *it is defined as the set of all vulnerability points of an asset, a system, or a network.*

The larger the attack surface is, the more difficult the protection is.

Definition 1.7 Threat: *it refers to any incident that has the potential to harm a system. A threat is something that may or may not happen; but if happens, it has the potential to cause serious damage.*

Threats depend on targets, for example:

• Threats on hardware: theft and sabotage.
• Threats on software: deletion, server access blocking, theft, alteration of functions or configurations, content change of web pages, and web server hacking.
• Threats on data: theft of private data, theft of intellectual properties, file deletion, file access blocking, and data alteration.

Definition 1.8 Risk: *It is defined as the potential for loss or damage, if a threat exploits a vulnerability.*

Example 1.2   Financial lofsses, loss of privacy, reputational damage, legal implications, and even loss of life are examples of security risks.

Figure 1.2 summarizes the relationships between the main terms of security:

– The legitimate owner of assets needs protection of his/her assets.
– The adversary threatens to use, alter, or destroy the assets.
– The assets have vulnerabilities, which may be exploited by the adversary.
– Vulnerabilities are loopholes for the adversary to design and mount attacks.
– The owner deploys countermeasures to minimize the risks relevant to the threats.

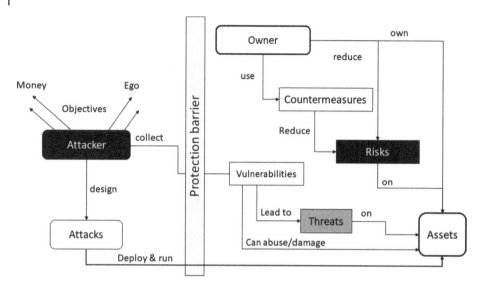

Figure 1.2 Relationships between basic security terms.

1.3 Security Services

The three basic security services are referred to as the *CIA triad*. *CIA* stands for Confidentiality-Integrity-Availability. Sometimes, CIA are called basic properties of *security*. In addition to CIA, authentication, authorization, and non-repudiation are services often required in the cyberspace. Depending on the asset owner's needs, a single, two, or several services may be required. Figure 1.3 summarizes the main security services used to protect assets.

1.3.1 Confidentiality and Privacy

Confidentiality aims at guaranteeing that private or confidential information is not made available or disclosed to unauthorized entities. *Secrecy* is a term usually used synonymously with confidentiality.

Privacy is a specific case of confidentiality. Privacy protection aims at preventing disclosure of private-life data (see Section 1.7).

Example 1.3   The following are examples of information that require confidentiality protection:
– industrial secrets of companies
– business agreements
– defense secrets
– health data, bank accounts, and private meetings of individuals

1.3.2 Integrity

Asset integrity is a property whereby asset content and/or behavior have not been modified in an unauthorized manner after being created, updated, maintained, stored, or transmitted. According to the category of asset, three types of integrity are distinguished: data, system/software, and hardware integrity.

Data integrity: it is a property whereby data has not been modified in an unauthorized manner after being created, stored, or transmitted. Data modification includes the insertion, deletion, and substitution of data.

System/software integrity: it is a property whereby a system (e.g. a web server) or a software (e.g. a library) has not been modified in an unauthorized manner after being created, stored, or transmitted. Software modification includes deletion and alteration of some functions or some configuration parameters. System/software integrity aims at guaranteeing that a system or the software performs its intended functions in an unimpaired manner, free from deliberate or inadvertent unauthorized manipulations of system or software.

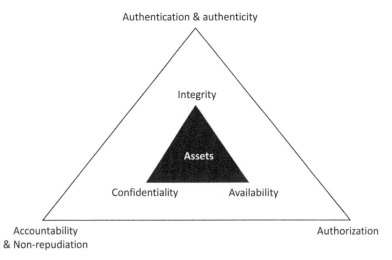

Figure 1.3 Overview of security services.

Hardware integrity: it is a property whereby a hardware component (e.g. a camera, a sensor, or a card reader) has not been modified in an unauthorized manner after being created and acquired or after maintenance operation.

Example 1.4 Examples of assets that require integrity guarantees:

− Your ID: if your ID is modified, you become somebody else.
− Web servers: if web server pages are modified, visitors would see inappropriate content or worse they would be asked to enter confidential data.
− Braking system of a car: if car brakes are sabotaged, then passengers and driver could be injured.

1.3.3 Availability

Asset availability is a property whereby asset content or services are available to be used by its legitimate users. An asset may become temporarily or definitely inaccessible, thus unavailable because of attacks. In a similar way to integrity, according to asset category, three types of availability are distinguished: data, system/software, and hardware availability.

Data availability: it is a property whereby data (i.e. files and databases) is accessible whenever requested by legitimate users. Both data deletion and data server blocking impact data availability.

System/software availability: it is a property whereby the function/service of a system (e.g. a web server) or a software is not slowed down or stopped by an attack. Therefore, it is not denied to authorized users. For example, a web server should process legitimate requests and not be blocked (totally or partially) by fraudulent requests.

Hardware availability: it is a property whereby a hardware component is available for use.

Notes

− Attacks targeting asset availability are frequent in today's Internet. In general, after stopping partially or entirely a system, attackers demand a ransom.
− Attacks against asset availability are the most difficult to address.

1.3.4 Authentication and Authenticity

Two types of authentication services are of interest in the IT security field: identity authentication and source authentication.

Identity authentication service is used to provide assurance of the identity of an entity interacting with a system. The question addressed by identity authentication is the following: Is the entity presenting an ID really the entity it claims to be?

Source authentication service is used to verify the identity of the entity that created a data and sent a message, that contains that data, is the one included, as a source, in the message. The question addressed by source authentication is the following: is the sender of a message really the entity that created the data included in the message?

Identity authentication and source authentication are very similar, but have different purposes. The first authentication aims at controlling access to services, while the second aims at verifying the authenticity of a message. The latter is the property whereby the recipient of a message has guarantees that the message was generated and sent by a trusted source.

1.3.5 Non-repudiation and Accountability

Non-repudiation of electronic operations (such as bank transactions, e-shopping, and e-voting) is of paramount importance in the cyberspace. A digital signature, which is similar to handwritten signature, is used to provide assurance of authenticity of the sender; and therefore, the signing individual cannot deny he/she was the signer. For example, when a person electronically signs a house sale agreement; he/she cannot, one month later, deny having accepted to sell his/her house.

The accountability service provides capabilities to trace the responsible entity in case of a security incident or action in order to protect against denial by one of the parties in a communication or a transaction. Authentication and accountability services are commonly used in e-commerce: i) the buyer must provide multiple proofs, including name, card number, and date of birth to be authenticated by the seller, and ii) the transaction is confirmed by a third party (e.g. e-commerce platform) and a receipt is provided; thus, none of the buyer and seller could deny the transaction.

1.3.6 Authorization

Authorization is concerned with providing permissions to perform specific operations or activities on assets; for example, read or copy files, use specific printers, or access some rooms or factories in a company. In general, authorization follows authentication; i.e. the person identity is authenticated, and then, the requesting person is granted some rights to access assets.

1.4 Attacks

Figure 1.4 summarizes the most common attacks in the cyberspace.

1.4.1 Taxonomy of Attacks

This section provides three criteria to categorize attacks in the cyberspace. Overall, the main objectives of attacks on digital assets are to delete data, steal data, block a system, and prepare context for future attacks with malicious software.

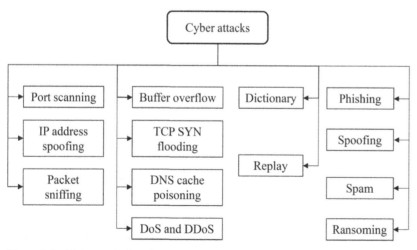

Figure 1.4 Main attacks in cyberspace.

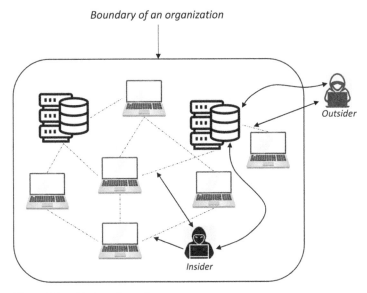

Boundary of an organization

Outsider

Insider

Figure 1.5 Origins of attacks.

1.4.1.1 Attacks According to Their Origin

The first criterion of attack categorization is related to the origin of attack. Attacks can be triggered by outsiders (external people) or by insiders (company personnel, friends, etc.). Figure 1.5 illustrates attack origins, where the solid arrows denote message interception, data or message modification, and unauthorized accesses.

In general, it is harder to address attacks when they come from staff, personal, family members, and friends.

1.4.1.2 Passive vs Active Attacks

The second criterion attack categorization is related to how the attacks act on the assets: active and passive attacks.

1.4.1.2.1 Passive Attacks

Attacks in this category are made through the interceptions of messages via a network or any other means (access to unsecured areas and cupboards). Attacker may:

- Use the data internally (i.e. attacker knows your private data, your intellectual property, etc.).
- Use the stolen data to withdraw money and make payment while e-shopping.
- Release the content (private-life detail, industrial secrets, ...) to enemies or competitors to harm.

The main variant of passive attacks is referred to as *eavesdropping*, which is the act of secretly (stealthily or permanently) listening to private conversations or communications of others without their consent. Such a practice is widely regarded as unethical, and in many jurisdictions, it is illegal. Different methods are known as eavesdropping in ICT security; they include port scanning, packet sniffing, phone call interception, etc.

Note. As passive attacks do not leave traces in ICT systems, they are difficult to detect. When they are detected, it is already too late. With education of asset owners and users, passive attacks could be prevented or at least their number minimized.

1.4.1.2.2 Active Attacks

Active attacks modify or destroy assets. They have different forms including:

- Manipulation of communications (i.e. alteration of messages while being transmitted).
- Masquerade: forge identity and pretend to be someone known and access assets.
- Modification: change the content of an asset (e.g. change a bank account balance).
- Replay: this is mixture of two attacks, capture passively and then replay a part of what has been captured.
- Denial of service: it is one of the common attacks in the internet to prevent a system, a server or a network to work properly.
- Deny: once a transaction has been validated, the attacker may deny having participated in the transaction.

1.4.1.3 Attacks According to Their Objectives

The third criterion of attack categorization is related to attacker's objectives, which may be basic (e.g. find open TCP ports) or complex (e.g. spying or ransoming). In other words, the objectives of attacks can be understood only by people with skills in computers or also by the general public. For example, TCP connection hacking does not provide understandable concern to general public, while ransoming does.

1.4.1.3.1 Basic (or Generic) Attacks

Basic attacks are building blocks of complex attacks. For example, searching open TCP ports may be used to install ransoming code, and then ask the victim to pay. They include the following attacks commonly discussed in literature:

i) Port scanning attacks

Port scanning is one of the very basic attacks. It targets the status of ports[2] of computers. Its main goal is to find out open, closed, and filtered[3] ports. When open ports are detected, attackers can exploit their vulnerabilities to mount specific attacks (e.g. install viruses). Closed and filtered ports prevent attacks relying on port scanning.

ii) IP source address spoofing attacks

In general, unwanted users or websites are blocked by firewalls using their IP addresses. IP source address spoofing refers to an attack where the adversary forges an IP address trusted by the targeted computers. Using a trusted IP address, the attacker misleads the victims and steals or alters their data.

iii) TCP SYN flooding attacks

TCP SYN flooding attack takes advantage of the vulnerabilities of TCP (Transmission Control Protocol) to perform Denial of service attacks. TCP is available on almost all devices connected to the internet. Roughly, in normal operation to establish a TCP connection between computers A and B: computer A sends a TCP segment with bit SYN=1; computer B responds with a TCP segment with bits SYN=1 and ACK=1; and computer A sends a segment with bit ACK=1. A hostile user sends, at a high rate, TCP segments with bit SYN=1 on distinct open ports and never sends any segment with bit ACK=1. The result is that the attacked computer loses time in waiting segments that will never arrive, which prevents it establishing connections with legitimate computers. To imagine what TCP SYN flooding would look like, consider a shop. A group of people, who do not want to buy any article, enter the shop and take a long time asking the merchant about many details. When some individuals of the group leave the shop, other people from the group, with the same objectives, enter in the shop and sustain discussions with the merchant. When this situation lasts for a long time, the shop is full and no honest client can enter.

iv) Packet sniffing attacks

Packet sniffing is a passive attack aiming to intercept and collect packets transmitted over a network, a channel, or a connection. Many tools, such as tcpdump and wireshark, are available to help network and legitimate system administrators to perform monitoring and traffic analysis. Such tools are exploited by attackers to collect packets for malicious purposes.

v) Dictionary attacks

Dictionary attacks are mainly used to disclose passwords or other secrets. In a dictionary attack, the attacker builds a large table (the table is called a dictionary) containing potential passwords based on what is known about the targeted individuals (their first names, family names, occupations, animals, preferred films and music, etc.). Then, attacker tries many passwords before probably succeeding. Weak passwords are generally easily disclosed by dictionary attacks; that is why it is highly recommended to use long and complex passwords, without information that could be exploited by attackers (i.e. the name, the pseudo-name, the birthday, the city, etc.).

vi) DNS cache poisoning attacks

DNS (Domain Name Server) is a server available on most of devices connected to the internet. It translates human readable domain names (for example, www.bmw.de) to machine readable IP addresses (for example, 160.46.252.15). In general, the various client applications (such as mail clients, web browsers, etc.) maintain their own DNS caches (i.e. the IP addresses and names of the recently used domains). *DNS cache poisoning* attack aims to alter the local cache of a victim in order to redirect the flows to fake domains. The redirection of web browsers to fake websites also is called *pharming*.

vii) Buffer overflow attacks

Some applications use dynamic memory allocation to serve requests. In case the maximum amount of the memory is used, any additional request (which requires memory to store relevant data) can result in a buffer overflow. When buffer overflow is handled correctly, only exceptions are raised and an adequate procedure is executed. When it is not handled correctly, the attacked system may stop and must be restarted, which is a kind of denial-of-service. Worse than that, the attacker can write in protected memory zones, delete data, or upload a virus. Notice that well-coded applications are not vulnerable to buffer overflow at tacks.

viii) DoS and DDoS attacks

With Denial-of-Service (DoS) attack, the attacker seeks to make a server, a computer, a router, or a network unavailable to its intended users, by temporarily or indefinitely disrupting its services. DoS is typically accomplished by flooding the targeted system or resource with superfluous requests; for example, using TCP SYN flooding. In DDoS (Distributed DoS) attack, the incoming traffic flooding the victim originates from multiple sources. Several infected computers, and monitored by the attacker, work together to overload the attacked system with massive amounts of forged traffic and do so to such an extent that the attacked system becomes unusable by its legitimate users. This effectively makes it impossible to stop the attack by blocking a single hostile computer. It is worth noticing that DDoS attacks are the most difficult to thwart.

ix) Replay attacks

In a replay attack, the cybercriminal intercepts messages and then he/she resends all or some of the intercepted messages to the recipient. When no mechanism is used to detect retransmissions, some functions or data of the recipient may be compromised. For example, imagine that an encrypted software is sent, with the replay attack the content of the software is altered on the recipient side, which may lead to erroneous executions of the software. Another example, imagine that the sent messages include encrypted financial transactions. If a replay attack succeeds, the recipient records more transactions than those sent by the legitimate sender. Last example, imagine that the attacker captured two encrypted messages, one to lock a door and the other to unlock it. With a replay attack, if the encrypted messages are always the same, the attacker can unlock the door without knowing the encryption key. Replay attacks are easy to perform because they do not require any decryption operation from the attacker.

1.4.1.3.2 *Attacks with Objectives Understandable to General Public*
They include the following attacks commonly discussed in literature.

i) Phishing

Phishing is an online fraud that attempts to steal sensitive information such as usernames, passwords, and credit card numbers. When phishing is directed to a specific individual (or organization), it is referred to as *spear phishing*. In general, phishing is a form of social engineering where the attacker attempts to fraudulently retrieve licit user sensitive information, by imitating electronic communication from a trusted organization (for example, from a bank or from an administration). It is typically carried out by emails or instant messaging. It often directs users to enter personal information on fake website. Notice that phishing is the main form of attacks currently encountered in the cyberspace.

ii) Spoofing

Spoofing is similar to phishing, where the attacker steals the identity of a licit user and pretends to be the hacked user, in order to breach the system security or to steal data. Spoofing is a kind of identity theft, while phishing is not. There are various types of spoofing attacks such as IP spoofing, Email spoofing, URL spoofing, and MAC spoofing, which mask the IP address, user email, the URL, the MAC address, respectively.

iii) Spam

With no doubt, the most prevalent inconvenience that any computer user must face is reception of unsolicited messages, known as spams. There are two categories of spams. In the first spam category, messages may be sent by honest individuals or organizations with advertising or news purposes; we lose time to open and delete them. In the second category, the messages are issued by malicious individuals or organizations (imitating banks, government administrations, etc.) and include links to launch phishing attacks. Those spams are dangerous. The use of spam filters (i.e. tools for statistical analysis of emails to decide whether or not they are spams) is recommended. However, even with spam filters, users should remain watchful, because ingenuity of cybercriminals sometimes exceeds the detection capabilities of spam filters.

iv) Ransom attacks

The objective of ransom attacks is to require that an amount of money must be paid by the attacked individual or organization. Ransom attacks can be categorized into two classes. In the first class of attacks, the attacker sends an email to the victim pretending that he/she possesses compromising pictures, videos, or SMSes; the victim must pay or the compromising information will be disclosed to friends, family, and colleagues of the victim. In the second category, the attacker installs a code (called ransomware) on a system of an individual or an organization; when the ransomware is launched, the attacked system is blocked partially or entirely; then, the attacker sends an email to the attacked individual or organization, asking to pay a ransom; otherwise, their system remains blocked, or worse, data and software will be infected or deleted starting from a given date.

Notice that in the first category of ransom attacks, it is often unlikely that the attacker possesses any compromising information, while in the second class, the effects of the attack are clearly visible to victims.

1.4.1.3.3 New Complex Attacks

The fraudsters' ingenuity has no limit and new forms of attacks will appear in the future. The war is not ended and may never end. In particular, new and complex attacks have been recently proposed. Such attacks would dominate in the future; and they include the following:

- *AI-generated fake video and audio*: using machine learning techniques, attackers may forge videos and audios and threaten people. Example, you receive a fabricated video of your mother asking you to do something (e.g. send money). For more on the topic, refer to [14–16].
- *Poisoning AI defenses*: using machine learning, the attacker forges scenarios (i.e. data), which, once introduced in the defense system, makes this system unable to detect the attack. In other words, this attack makes the defense system unaware of the attacker. For more on the topic, refer to [17–19].
- *Hacking smart contracts* (attacks on blockchains): in a blockchain, transactions between people are written in a register, with a reputation to be tamper-proof. Some new attacks on blockchains have been reported [20]. Blockchains (in particular private ones) are strong but not perfectly. For example, a transaction indicating Bob has purchased the house of Eve and paid $300k? Then, Eve (who is assumed to be expert in blockchain breaking) deletes the transaction.
- *Breaking encryption using quantum computers*: quantum computers (which are still in prototype stage) have computation capacities never seen before. Some attacks have been published to describe how the quantum power may be used to break an RSA cyphering in a reasonable time (in hours) compared to the required time to break RSA with conventional computers (in hundreds of centuries) [21, 22].
- Attacking from the computing cloud (e.g. Amazon and Google cloud, Edge computing...): attackers install servers in a worldwide manner and then mount their attacks using the IP addresses of legal cloud servers.

1.4.2 Taxonomy of Attackers

Attackers can be categorized depending on their objectives and harmfulness capacities:

- *Amateurs* (not malicious crackers): they attack just for fun or vanity.
- *Hackers*: a hacker is someone who uses his/her skills and knowledge to find vulnerabilities in computer systems and helps improve and patch those vulnerabilities. The hackers are often hired to locate and identify system vulnerabilities. In practice, it is not easy to distinguish hackers from other malicious attackers.
- *Crackers*: a cracker is an individual who attempts to access computer systems without authorization. These individuals are often malicious, as opposed to hackers, and have many means at their disposal for breaking into a system. Crackers are motivated by vanity, ego, and money. Crackers also are called *black hats*.
- *Cybercriminals*: they are individuals or teams who use technology to commit malicious activities on servers or networks, with the intention of stealing sensitive information of organizations or personal data and generating profit. They include cyberterrorists, organized crime syndicates, and state-supported information warriors.

Cybercrime organizations are the most sophisticated structures and the most dangerous. They may be structured according to multiple roles as in conventional organizations:

- IT experienced staff:
  - Programmers who write codes or programs used by cybercriminal organizations. They may be IT engineers or data scientists and have strong skills.

- IT experts who maintain a cybercriminal organization IT infrastructure, such as servers, encryption technologies, and databases. Very experienced IT engineers are employed by cybercrime organizations.
- Hackers who exploit systems, applications, and network vulnerabilities.
- Fraudsters who create and deploy schemes like spam and phishing.
- Distributors who distribute and sell stolen data to associated cybercriminals.
- System hosts and providers, which host sites that possess illegal contents.

- Business and finance experienced staff (who usually lack technical knowledge):

  - Cashiers who provide account names to cybercriminals and control drop accounts.
  - Money mules who manage bank account wire transfers.
  - Tellers who transfer and launder illegal money by using digital and foreign exchange facilities.
  - Leaders who are often connected to big bosses of large criminal organizations. They assemble and direct cybercriminal teams.

Figure 1.6 summarizes the motivations of common attackers and cyberterrorists. Starting from the bottom, which is the lowest complexity of organization:

- Insider threats that come from employees who are not happy because of salary, position, tasks, or simply because they have been fired. It also can come from jealous friends or classmates.
- Thrill-seekers who want to show to others (friends and colleagues) that they at the top of their field and can act on anything.
- Hacktivists who are guided by ideology (politics and other) and who try to spread their points of view through fake news and sabotage of web servers.
- Terrorist groups that are guided by ideological violence (in other words, anyone who does not agree with their believes should pay).
- Cybercriminals, whose objective is profit.
- Government-sponsored: for economical and/or geopolitical reasons some (may be all but with different capacities) countries use their citizens or foreign cybercriminals to collect data to disclose industry secrets, to threaten or worse to attack other countries.

1.4.3 Malware Taxonomy

Definition 1.9 Malware*: it stands for MALicious soft-WARE. It is any software intentionally designed to cause damage to a computer, server, or network.*

Malware is an umbrella term for any type of malicious software that is designed to infiltrate devices of others without their knowledge. There are many types of malware, which include viruses, worms, spyware, botnets, trojans, rootkits, and ransomware. Each works differently depending on its goals; however, all malware variants share two defining traits: they are sneaky and are actively working against interests of their targets.

All malware variants follow the same basic pattern: exploit a vulnerability to download and/or install a malicious code, then infect the target device or system. Emails, web links, free software, free music and movies, and corrupted storage devices (such as USB keys) are usual vectors that enable attackers to download and/or install their malware. Figure 1.7 shows the common malware variants. It is worth noticing that malware variants are not disjoint. Rather, some malware variants use entirely or partially other variants to design more complex attacks. In the sequel, the main distinctive features of malware variants are presented. For more on malware, refer to [23–25].

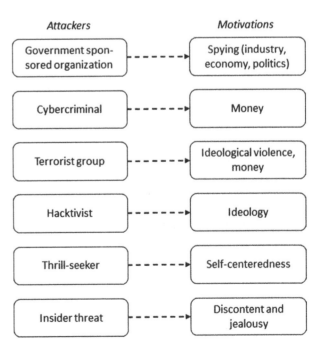

Figure 1.6 Categorization of cybercrime motivations.

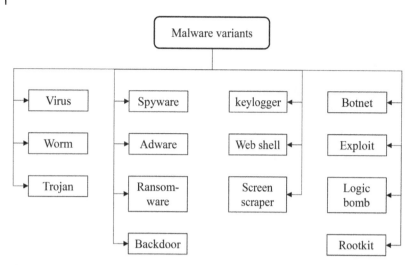

Figure 1.7 Malware variants.

1.4.3.1 Virus

Virus is the most known term of cyberattack. A virus is a program (often referred to as malicious code) that can link itself to the executable files of a computer. It can replicate itself or modify the files to which it is attached and seek the other programs appended to those files. It then infects other programs simultaneously.

Viruses in ICT inherited their name from biology. In biology, a virus infects a plant, an animal, or a human being and compromises the health or the life of the infected host. The virus can spread quickly from host to another. In ICT, a virus attacks digital assets to compromise their contents and can duplicate itself locally or via the network.

1.4.3.2 Worm

A worm is a self-replicating code that resides in the memory of an infected computer. Worm differs from a virus in the way it is triggered. A worm is self-contained; i.e. it does not need to attach itself to another program. A worm is able to replicate itself locally or send copies of itself to other machines. A worm triggers itself without relying on human actions.

1.4.3.3 Trojan

Trojan is a term derived from the ancient Greek story of the deceptive Trojan horse, which permitted the fall of the city of Troy. Trojan is any malware, which misleads users about its true intents. Generally, Trojans are spread by some form of social engineering (including emails, images, music, etc.). Therefore, a trojan may be embedded in a piece of code that actually does something useful, but with a hidden malicious part, which is intended to perform compromising or destructive actions.

Trojans may allow attackers to access personal information of victims, such as passwords or IDs. They can delete files or infect other devices connected to the network. Finally, they can create connections between infected system and the attacker, to monitor some activities of infected devices (e.g. any captured image or keystroke on keyboard can be made known to attackers).

1.4.3.4 Ransomware

Ransomware is a type of malware that threatens to publish victim's data or perpetually blocks access to it unless a ransom is paid. It is a means of performing ransom attacks.

1.4.3.5 Spyware and Adware

Spyware aims to gather information about a person (e.g. his/her credit card or health file) or an organization (e.g. industrial and business secrets) and sends such information to other entities, without the owner's consent.

Adware is the contraction of ADvertizing softWARE. Today, multiple forms of advertising, over the internet, are used to generate revenues to software and website developers. Developers provide free content (including games, movies, courses, etc.), which are consumed daily by millions of users worldwide. Unfortunately, adware may become spyware; i.e. some of free software and websites may include links, which are used to collect private data. Therefore, before clicking any link, be aware that, may be, somebody is collecting data about you somewhere.

1.4.3.6 Botnet

Botnet is the contraction of roBOT NETwork. A botnet is a set of compromised computers or electronic devices used to create and send spams or viruses or to flood a network or a server. Any equipment in a botnet is called *bot*. Trojans or other malware variants are used to infect a large network of computers or devices. Then, all infected computers (which become bots) are monitored remotely by a supervisor under the control of a single attacker or a group of cybercriminals. In general, bots are not used to collect data from the infected computers; rather, they are used by cybercriminals to commit attacks, such as DDoS or to monitor specific areas, using for example infected cameras.

Any device or computer connected to the internet may become a member of a botnet. Often, the bots consume few resources (computation and bandwidth), because they operate very infrequently. Therefore, infected devices and computers cannot be easily detected by legitimate users when they just observe their computers. Fortunately, most antiviruses can help detect infected computers.

1.4.3.7 Keylogger, Screen Scraper, and Web Shell

Keylogger also is referred to as keylogging or keyboard capturing. It is the action of recording keystrokes on a keyboard. Using a keylogger, the attacker can know some of the actions the users is performing.

Screen scraper is a malicious code to record and collect contents displayed on monitors of victim users. Using a screen scraper, the attacker can see exactly the content seen by a victim.

Web shell is a malicious code, which can be uploaded to a web server to allow remote access to the web server and manipulate its service.

1.4.3.8 Exploit, Logic Bomb, Backdoor, and Rootkit

Exploit is a generic term to designate any piece of software or a sequence of commands that takes advantage of a vulnerability to cause an unanticipated behavior to occur on a system.

Logic bomb is a generic term to designate any piece of code intentionally inserted into a software system that will initiate a malicious function on the attacked system, when specified conditions are met.

Backdoor is a typically covert method of bypassing normal authentication or encryption in a system. Roughly speaking, there exist two categories of backdoors; those installed by attackers using trojans or other methods and those installed by the manufacturers of the software and hardware. In today's international ICT business competition, backdoors raise much disputes (e.g. between USA and China regarding 5G infrastructures). Regarding the second category of backdoors, the question is how one can trust the manufacturers of the software and hardware components? Hard question to answer.

Rootkit is any collection of malicious software installed by an attacker on a computer. It is designed to enable access to some components of the computer that are not otherwise allowed; and it often masks its existence. Rootkits include keystroke logging and recording of other user activities. In general, rootkits provide partial or full access to infected computers.

1.4.4 Daily Awareness to IT Security

Most daily activities require the use of electronic devices and access to the internet. Therefore, there is a high probability to be a victim of cybercriminals each day, if some basic vigilance rules are ignored. Each click may get you in troubles. Much of attacks presented above can be prevented, if the following common-sense rules are observed:

- Do not be naïve and believe that someone somewhere in the world you never met before would offer you money (in million dollars).
- Never send your personal/private data unless you really trust the recipient.
- Carry out e-commerce transactions only via secured websites with double authentication.
- Do not open any suspicious file attached to an email.
- Do not click on links in suspicious emails (even if the emails are forwarded by people you trust).
- Do not download files from suspicious websites. Some websites provide you opportunity to download files. Unfortunately, some files may contain malware.
- Do not open folders and files in storage devices (such USB keys) unless the devices are checked by an antivirus tool.
- Use strong passwords and change them periodically.
- Limit your private data shared on social networks. A picture or a comment that you think innocuous can cause you big problems some years later.

- Install security updates on your computer as soon as possible after being notified.
- Use the up-to-date antivirus software.
- Update your software regularly (outdated software have vulnerabilities).
- Use software certified, or at least approved, by trusted parties.
- Any new installed device (e.g. a webcam or a home alarm) should be secured by changing the default password.

1.5 Countermeasures/Defenses

This section provides an overview of defense actions, commonly called *countermeasures*.

1.5.1 Very Old Roots of Countermeasures

Most defense actions have been inspired by very old actions taken to protect castles in the middle ages. Technologies differ, but objectives and roots of techniques are similar as illustrated by Table 1.1.

Let us see similarities between protecting castles and protecting IT systems:

- Castles are placed in specific locations, with natural obstacles (hills, mountains, islands, and so on). In the same way, IT systems are located in locked rooms and spaces, with restricted access.
- Castle architectures are based on heavy doors, strong walls and gates, high towers, and no (or few) windows on the external walls. In addition, guards are posted at vulnerable points. In the same way, IT systems use specific hardware such as cameras, strong cables and boxes, firewalls, and proxies.
- Secret words and specific material (such as seals) were used for authentication to enter castles or to know confidential information. In the same way, IT systems encompass mechanisms such as encryption techniques, authentication with (passwords and biometric material), and deflection mechanisms (called honeypots to escape attacks).

1.5.2 Methods for Defense

There exist different criteria to categorize security defense methods out of which three are discussed in the sequel.

1.5.2.1 Prevention/Detection/Reaction Methods

Methods of defense are categorized into three classes: prevention, detection, and reaction methods.

Prevention methods: they are preferred and most effective methods (when possible). They aim to prevent attacks by blocking vulnerability points, and consequently making the system secure. Two approaches can be deployed:

- Deter attacks by making them impossible (e.g. deploying a permanent and armed guard team in front of the entrance of a bank deters almost all the thieves!)
- Deter attacks with an ingenious idea based on the use of resources imitating the resource to protect (i.e. lures) to draw attackers' attention. Fake systems used to deter attacks are often referred to as *honeypots*.

Table 1.1 Defense of castles vs defense of IT system.

Castles in middle ages	*IT systems*
- Location with natural obstacles	- Locked rooms and spaces
- Surrounding moats	- Hardware (cameras, strong cables, and boxes...)
- Heavy doors and strong walls	
- Strong gates and high towers	- Firewalls, Proxies
- No (or very few) windows, Guard	- VPN, NAT, IDS, IPS...
- Secret words to enter	- Encryption
- Specific material to enter (seal...)	- Authentication (Passwords, biometrics)
	- Deflection mechanisms (honeypot)

The cost of prevention methods may be high, which prevents their use. For example, a university cannot pay to have a permanent guard in front of each lab and each classroom.

Detection methods: these methods are based on the ability to detect attacks when they occur. Intrusion detection systems are commonly used as tools to detect attacks.

Reaction methods: it is the capability to deploy mitigation actions including recovery actions. For example, database management systems store multiple copies of the DB and the list and dates of transactions. Whenever an attack is detected, the stored data is used to recover the operational database. Depending on the attack, some of transactions may be irretrievably lost. The mitigating actions aim at minimizing the data loss and unavailability.

Example 1.5   Let us take a simple example to see what security defense actions could be. The example is a simplified version of e-shopping activities. The threat of interest in this example is: someone may steal your money.

- Prevention: multiple countermeasures are used in nowadays e-commerce: encrypt your order and card number, enforce merchants to do some extra checks, use PIN and trusted tier (example banks), and do not send your card number in cleartext via an insecure channel.
- Detection: be careful and check periodically your account to detect any unauthorized transaction appearing on your credit card statement.
- Reaction: in the event of a fraud, notify your bank and complain, dispute and prosecute, ask for a new card number or pay and forget (because you were not careful and you disclosed your data through social networks or by any other channel; it is your mistake!).

1.5.2.2   Level of Automation of Defense Methods

Approaches of defense may also be categorized according to their level of automation. Automation of defense actions means how they are implemented. There are three levels:

- Security is fully supported by ICT (software and hardware). In practice, the full automation of security is unrealistic in most cases, because of its costs.
- Security is entirely manual. That is, human beings are permanently involved in detection and mitigation actions. Such an approach is unrealistic when current IT systems are of concern, because of the frequency of attack occurrences and their complexity of detection.
- The last class is the most used now: some actions are fully automated and others are manually done. Human being's involvement is still required. Nevertheless, it is clear that human actions are less and less admitted, because they are error-prone and require a lot of attention at all times. In future, machine learning–based security systems would be more likely to perform better than human beings.

1.5.2.3   Design Orientations of Defense Methods

The third classification criterion is related to when and how security components are designed regarding the applications/services to protect. There exist three main ways to address security:

- *Separation* approach: the most (and still) used approach is based on two layers: applications are designed apart from security services and it is assumed that they will be protected. There is a collection of security services expected to protect almost all applications. Therefore, this approach is based on two separate layers: application layer and security layer.
- *Secure-by-default* approach: the principle is that each application sets up configuration parameters such that the system is very likely to be secure. The system has clear limits; for example:

  - No more than one transaction per hour (thus, DoS attack becomes ineffective).
  - No client data storage (thus, it is impossible to steal client data from a server).
  - No private data of clients manipulated (thus, confidentiality does not matter).
  - Use of resilient and secure material (best material used to deter attackers).

It should be noticed that secure-by-default approach suffers from severe weaknesses, because of three main factors: 1) the capabilities of the system are willingly limited; thus, such a system cannot react to unexpected conditions, 2) the parameter limits are hard to set up (e.g. why two transactions per minute and not four?), and 3) the cost of the security material.

- *Secure-by-design* approach: for a long time, application software developers and security components developers did not collaborate; and the end-users buy and deploy applications and security components separately. Recently, both communities understood that IT security would be more efficient when they work in tandem. Consequently, application software developers learn from security software developers and vice versa. Such a collaboration is more likely to dominate in the future. It is more dynamic and efficient than secure-by-default approach. In secure-by-design approach, each component of an application follows guidelines and methodology of vulnerability investigation. The security requirements are taken into consideration throughout the life cycle of application development. For example, many OS functions (such as *gets* or TCP socket use) have been identified as system vulnerabilities. Therefore, the application developer should not use them, if he/she is not aware of their vulnerabilities.

  Secure-by-design approach implies inclusion of security procedures in all the steps of software engineering (from requirements specification to software maintenance). Secure-by-design does not mean that conventional security components are no more useful. Rather, it means that in each step of software development, developers should 1) produce attack resistant codes 2) determine which security components to use and which security components to include in the system if they are not present. For more on security-by-design, refer [6, 26, 27].

Finally, remember what we mentioned regarding castle's security. Castles were designed according to the secure-by-design approach. Castle architects did not follow an orientation such as built smart, spacious, and all-round view castles. They had important requirements from the king, which may be summarized in one requirement: the first concern is to deter enemies.

1.5.3 Overview of Security Countermeasures

There are two categories of countermeasures: organizational and technical. Organizational measures to security are only hovered up in this book; the focus is on the technical countermeasures.

1.5.3.1 Organizational Measures

The organizational security measures refer mainly to the following:

- *Manager awareness*: ensuring that business leaders and those in charge of IT systems are aware of the security risks associated with their assets, and the laws, regulations, and policies, which they must obey.
- *Education to good practices*: users should be trained to assess the safety of their actions to prevent manipulations. In particular, training should focus on the impacts of social engineering on the security of IT systems. Indeed, many viruses and confidential data disclosure are due to social interactions between company or institution personal and external parties (friends, family, and followers). Another aspect to teach is to do not bring inside their organization files on untrusted key storage found outside.
- *Awareness to loyalty and patriotism*: loyalty and patriotism are at the heart of confidential data protection, whatever the IT system. Even if it is expected that nobody should deviate from the ethics of his/her organization, it is of prime importance to deploy strategies to check the behavior of staff regarding confidentiality. The access rights of any member leaving the organization should be immediately withdrawn.
- *Staff's liability*: any individual acting on assets should be aware of his/her liability. In the event of security violation, internal sanctions or even legal prosecutions should be applied. Liability is one of the keys to build secure systems.
- *Physical protection*: areas (including rooms and spaces) where critical and sensitive data are either stored or processed should be physically protected. None is allowed to enter an area without explicit authorization.
- *Security assessment*: periodically check vulnerabilities of the assets and search new vulnerabilities. CVC (Common Vulnerabilities Exposure) is a very valuable association, which regularly publishes vulnerabilities in operating systems, in protocols, in web servers, etc. CVC vulnerability list should be accessed periodically by the security managers to assess the security of their organization.
- *Risk assessment*: periodically incurred risks should be evaluated to make decisions regarding how to enforce the security system. A compromise between investment costs in IT security and risk costs should be revised periodically. For example, the manager of a hospital who learned that the IT systems of some other hospitals have been blocked and ransoms required, should immediately invest to secure his/her hospital against the emerging attacks.
- *Auditing policy*: actions that may have an impact on security should be logged and secured. Then, recorded logs are used for monitoring, detection, and analysis of security violations.

- *Contingency plans*: define the procedures to resume normal operation for each attack likely to occur. Train people to do local and remote (cloud) backups.
- *Certification label*: for some organizations (e.g. banking, cloud services, stock exchange, and e-commerce), which store and manipulate client data, it is more and more required that those organizations should have provable high-level security systems. To reassure their clients, those organizations must receive and explicitly show a certification regarding their good security practices. There exist specialized companies, which provide security certification services.

1.5.3.2   Technical Countermeasures

The basic technical countermeasures (or building blocks) to design a security system include the following:

- *Identification*: an identity is a document/info/card used to prove a person's identity. Identification of any entity trying to access a resource is the first and basic service to guarantee security. Identification may be formulated as a question: who are you?
- *Authentication*: it is the process of verifying that a user trying to access a system holds the provided identity. Authentication may be formulated as a question: prove that you are who you are pretending to be. Authentication is addressed in more detail in Chapter 15.
- *Access control*: it is the function of specifying access rights/privileges (i.e. read, write, append, delete, close, open, etc.) to system resources. It is used jointly with authentication.
- *Encryption*: it is the mechanism focusing on data and message ciphering to appear as noise for unauthorized readers. Encryption is the fundamental mechanism to guarantee confidentiality and integrity. It is the pillar of security. Encryption algorithms are the main objective of this book.
- *Message digest*: it is a fixed size numeric representation of the contents of a message or data; it is computed by a *hash function*. To one chunk of data is associated one digest. Message digest is not used for providing confidentiality guarantees. Rather, it is for guaranteeing data integrity. It is commonly admitted that it is not computationally feasible to forge a message, which corresponds to a known digest. Message digest is addressed in more detail in Chapter 5.
- *Intrusion detection*: it aims at monitoring a network or system for malicious activity or policy violations. Any malicious activity is reported either to an administrator or collected centrally using a security information and event management system. Depending on the nature of attacks, detection may be done online (i.e. while the attack is running) or offline (i.e. using log files that record the system activities). Notice that it is hard (or even very hard) to decide to mark a behavior as a security violation if the behavior is occurring for the first time. Only known intrusions can be marked easily. Suspecting any action makes the system slow and consequently unacceptable for its legitimate users. Suspecting only few actions makes the system a strainer; and consequently untrusted by its legitimate users. In modern intrusion detection systems, machine learning techniques are used as follows (in a simplified form): there is a step called learning in which the detection system processes a dataset containing different forms of system activities where some of them are marked as intrusions. Then, in a second step, called prediction, the detection system decides whether the current action is an intrusion or not.
- *Antiviruses*: the antiviruses are well-known tools of security. They are used to detect and remove viruses. Many antiviruses exist today.

1.5.4   Security Penetration Testing Tools

Tools that are very helpful for continuous security monitoring are called *security penetration testing tools* (SPTTs). They are useful to simulate attacks and test if a system is resistant in detecting (some) attacks. Multiple functions can be provided by SPTTs:

- Scanning of networks and discovery of servers, and firewalls.
- Traffic capturing and analysis.
- Evaluation of systems security against older vulnerabilities.
- Discovering vulnerabilities.
- Monitoring host or service uptime and performing mapping of network attack surfaces.
- Managing security evaluations and formulating defense methodologies.

Popular SPTTs include *Wireshark, Aircrack-n, John the Ripper, Burpsuite, Metasploit, Nmap, Nessus, and pwnie express*.

1.6 Overview of Defense Systems

Figure 1.8 illustrates the main defense systems to deal with intrusions (i.e. attacks) made easy by communication networks. They include firewalls, IDSs (Intrusion Detection Systems), IPSs (Intrusion Protection Systems), honeypots, proxies, Network Address Translation (NAT), and VPNs (Virtual Private Networks). The ultimate objectives of defense systems are to continuously monitor incoming/outgoing traffic in order to prevent and detect intrusions and to limit their impacts. The main objectives and characteristics of those systems are briefly discussed in this section.

Definition 1.10 Intrusion detection*: it is the process of monitoring the events occurring in a computer system or network and analyzing them for signs of possible intrusions (incidents).*

Definition 1.11 Intrusion prevention*: it is the process of discarding any suspicious traffic to avoid intrusions.*

Definition 1.12 Packet filtering*: it is a method to inspect packets and to reject packets issued by untrusted hosts or users.*

Definition 1.13 Content filtering*: it is a method that allows blocking internal users from receiving some types of content.*

In general, "Is a traffic an intrusion or not?" is a hard question. To address intrusions, some knowledge or assumptions should be considered:

- System activities are observable (i.e. the defense systems should know the activities of the assets to protect);
- Attacker behavior is (sufficiently) different from legitimate user behavior. In other words, the actions of the attackers should exhibit some signs to detect them. Is any person entering a shop is a thief? Definitely not. However, any armed person entering a shop is very likely to be an attacker.
- In practice, there exist overlaps between legitimate and illegal actions:
  - Some legitimate behavior may appear malicious. For example, when the number of requests per second entering a web server is beyond a given limit, should we immediately conclude that there is a DoS attack?
  - Intruders can attempt to disguise their behavior as that of legitimate users. For example, forged mails are very similar to those sent by the bank of the victim or any other entity known to him/her.
- Asset owners should assess intrusion detection risks: what would be the risks if intrusions were not detected?

1.6.1 Firewalls

Firewalls are the most commonly used defense systems in IT security. Like security guards at the entrance of a building and specific areas, firewalls monitor and control incoming and outgoing packets based on predetermined *security rules*. A firewall provides a central *choke point* for all traffic entering and exiting the system. Therefore, it provides perimeter defense, aiming the following:

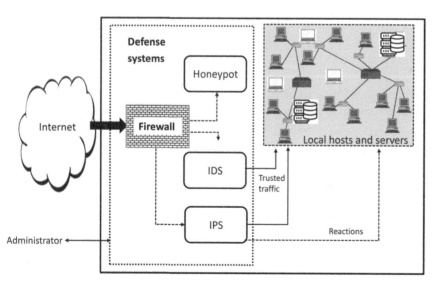

Figure 1.8 Big picture of defense systems.

- Service control: what services can be accessed (inbound or outbound)?
- Behavior control: how services are accessed, so that attacks can be detected (e.g. what information to use for spam and web content filtering)?

Therefore, firewalls are valuable to (partially) face multiple forms of attacks: illicit remote login, operation of backdoors, denial of service, spams, trojans, phishing, etc. In firewalls, packet filtering is mainly based on transport-layer information:

- IP source address and/or IP destination address.
- Protocol header (TCP, UDP, ICMP, etc.).
- TCP or UDP source and/or destination ports.
- TCP Flags.
- Other IP and/or TCP fields.

Firewall configuration refers to:

- Specification of a security policy (what/why/how to defend).
- Specification of actions to apply to incoming/outgoing packets
  - *Forward*: packet is forwarded
  - *Drop*: packet is dropped
  - *Log*: packet appearance is logged
  - *Alarm*: packet appearance triggers an alarm
- Specification of default policies for firewalls (e.g. reject any packet coming from unknown hosts).
- Description of rules in terms of logical expressions based on packet fields.

Example 1.6   Below are examples of configuration rules (in a high-level language)

– Rule 1: remote host with name Zebra is denied any access and all its packets must be dropped.
– Rule 2: if local port is 25, then accept and forward packets.
– Rule 3: if local port is greater than 1024, then reject packets.

1.6.2   Proxy Overview

The second category of defense systems is that of *proxies*, which are frequently used to protect application servers (as illustrated by Figure 1.9). The proxy acts as an intermediary agent between its client and the server. A proxy acts as *cache server* or as a firewall. No request is directly received by application servers. The requests must first be checked by the proxy. The application servers are hidden from the clients; thus, they are protected from attacks based on the names or IP addresses of hosts.

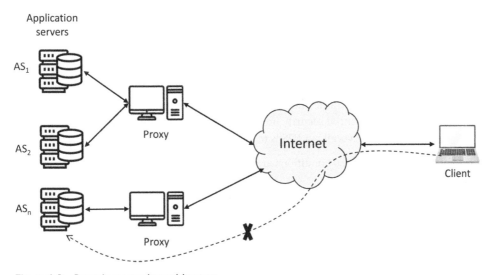

Figure 1.9   Proxy in a security architecture.

The main services/roles provided by proxies are the following:

- The first, and the most important, role of a proxy is authentication and access control. It checks if remote clients are authorized to access local application services. The authentication process may rely on the IP addresses of clients or on a protocol of authentication (discussed in Chapter 15).
- The second role of proxy is to control the requests of local users to prevent them accessing some specific (may be prohibited) websites.
- The third role of proxy is providing anonymous communications to local users. In such a case, the proxy hides internal users from the external network behind the proxy IP address. Notice that anonymity is partial because the proxy IP address is known.
- The fourth role of proxy is the improvement of performance either for clients (which can use cached data) or for severs (which can optimize resource utilization).
  - Optimize local server activities: a server may take time (due to computations, database access, etc.) before delivering a result associated with a query. To avoid performing the same tasks, for multiple requests, the proxy may cache the outputs of frequent queries; and it replies to remote clients without involving new computations by the server. Such an optimization is of paramount importance for some servers (such as those used in weather forecasting, in newspapers, etc.).
  - Optimize bandwidth: when local users access remote services, the proxy acts as local cache. If the requested data is in the cache, it is immediately returned to the local client. Otherwise, the proxy sends the request to the remote server, waits for response, and then delivers the received data to the local client.

  To achieve the fourth role, i.e. optimization, proxies use statistics (regarding visited webpages, for example) and algorithms (some of them are based on machine learning) to cache the appropriate contents.

- The last role of proxies is to anticipate system saturations (due to legitimate or malicious requests). For example, a proxy may deny service when the bandwidth utilization rate is close to 90%.

Depending on the security requirements of each institution, company or individual, different types of proxies may be deployed, including web proxy, FTP proxy, HTTP proxy, SMTP proxy, SOCKS proxy, and anonymous proxy.

> **Notes**
>
> – A firewall aims at filtering and discarding packets, while a proxy aims at controlling requests to access application services and caching data to improve performance.
> – A proxy may be a software installed on a computer, which performs multiple functions or a computer entirely dedicated to proxy functions.
> – One or multiple proxy servers can be deployed in the same private network.
> – It is important not to confuse *device* with *service*. A *router* may implement (at the same time) routing, filtering, and proxy services. Filtering (firewall) and proxy services may be implemented on the same device, which may be called *Firewall* or *Proxy*.

1.6.3 Intrusion Detection Systems

Definition 1.14 Intrusion detection system (IDS): *it is defined as the tools, methods, and resources to help identify, assess, and report unauthorized or unapproved network activities.*

An IDS aims to detect specific types of malicious network traffic and computer usages that cannot be detected by firewalls and proxies. IDSs are passive in nature. They detect potential security breaches, log the intrusion information, and signal alerts; any reaction is taken by human administrators. Overall, an IDS is made of three main components:

- Sensors, which generate security events (when predefined conditions are met).
- Console to monitor events and alerts and control the sensors.
- Engines, which record events logged by the sensors in a database and use a system of rules to generate alerts from security events received.

Figure 1.10 illustrates the overall operation of IDS:

- First, an IDS has two databases:
  - One database containing the traffic models (which describe *intrusion signatures*).
  - Decision rules, which are generally *if-then-else* rules, to specify the reactions regarding received packets.

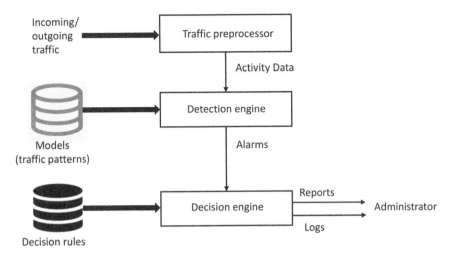

Figure 1.10 Components of IDS.

- Second, the IDS has three processing modules:
  - Traffic pre-processor, which summarizes the traffic activity (in terms of packet volumes, source addresses, ports, etc.).
  - Detection engine: traffic models and activity data provided by pre-processor are used to trigger events or alarms.
  - Decision engine, which decides what to do regarding detected events or alarms; it logs the events and alarms; and generates reports to be used by human administrators.

Example 1.7 The following situations may be marked as potential intrusions:

  - Emails with a subject including *Lottery winner*.
  - Emails with attachment of an executable file.
  - Users that read files in other users' personal directories.
  - Users that write in other users' files.
  - Users who login often and copy a huge number of files.
  - Users who open disk devices directly and do not make use higher-level OS utilities.
  - Resources used simultaneously by too many remote processes.
  - Users who make copies of system programs.
  - The rate of bandwidth utilization exceeds 90% for a long period.

There exist three main approaches to intrusion detection: signature-based approach, anomaly-based approach, and stateful protocol analysis approach.

Signature-based approach. An intrusion signature is like a footprint left behind the predators. For example, the following is retrieved in the log of a system: scan directory, copy password file, try some passwords, access some accounts; and later the security administrator concludes that an intrusion has succeeded in stealing some confidential data. To tackle intrusions people learn from each one another. When, in a given system, an intrusion is detected, a signature is associated with it. Then, the new signature is broadcast to the community and included in IDSs. The easiest intrusion signatures to detect are those relating to emails including executable files or links to malicious websites. The set of collected intrusion signatures are used as training models to IDSs.

Anomaly-based approach. In this approach, the security administrator must first describe what is normal and what is abnormal. There are multiple forms of anomaly-based detection depending on how normal and abnormal activities have been described:

- Use of performance metrics (e.g. bandwidth utilization, frequency of requests, interval between remote logins, duration of sessions, number of login failures) and thresholds associated with metrics.
- Use of the frequency of occurrence of specific events, within a specific period of time (e.g. activities during weekends).
- Use of traffic profile and deviation from a user-specific baseline.
- Sample network activity to compare to traffic that is known to be normal. When measured activity is outside baseline parameters, IDS triggers an alert. For example, DoS results in abnormal bursts of packets received by the victim.

Stateful protocol analysis approach. Any standard protocol follows a predefined order of actions. IDS can store the states of a session running a protocol. Deviation of states of a session from the normal states of the used protocol may be considered as intrusion. The basic example in this category is an IDS that checks how the segments received over a TCP connection deviate from the normal operation of TCP. For example, when too many connections are opened without sending data and these connections are not closed, there is a high probability of DoS attack.

1.6.4 Intrusion Protection Systems

IPS (Intrusion Protection System) is an IDS enhanced with reaction capacities. When an intrusion is detected, the reaction to restore a secure state of the assets is performed by the IPS and may be with the assistance of human administrators. The forms of reactions to perform include:

- Terminate the network connection or user that is being used by attacker.
- Block access to the target service/host/data.
- Stop a host or a service.
- Save a database.
- Replace attacked file.
- Remove a file (including a virus).
- Remove or replace malicious portions of an attack material to make it benign (e.g. discard an infected file attachment from an email).
- Reconfigure a device (such as firewall, router, or switch) to prevent a similar attack in the future.

The scope of reactions depends on the level of automation of the security system. There are three alternatives to perform reactions:

- *Full automatic*: IPS decides what actions to undertake and launches them.
- *Manual*: IPS suggests the actions to undertake and human operators launch them.
- *Semi-automatic*: mixture of manual and fully-automatic reactions, depending on the complexity and/or the risks of executing some specific countermeasures.

Today's fully-automated security systems are known to be more efficient to react to intrusions than human beings are. It is worth noticing that artificial intelligence in general and machine learning in particular are the core components of emerging IDSs and IPSs [28–30].

1.6.4.1 Performance Requirements Regarding IDSs and IPSs

IDSs and IPSs are used in real-time to check incoming (and may be outgoing) traffic and actions on the assets to protect. Therefore, both defense systems may jeopardize the entire performance of the protected system, which may become slow to perform legitimate actions. In all fields, excessive control is known to influence the utilization of resources. Therefore, some requirements must be addressed to design or to setup IDSs and IPSs, including:

- High-speed monitoring (i.e. do not impact response times).
- Large volume monitoring (i.e. collect as much data as possible on objectives of traffics).
- Real-time notification (i.e. react immediately when an intrusion is suspected).
- Mechanisms separated from policy (i.e. define the decision rules separately from the mechanisms used to react, for modularity, extensibility and maintenance reasons).
- Broad detection coverage (i.e. detect nearly all intrusions, even those considered as exceptional!).
- Economy in resource usage (i.e. optimize resource utilization and find a compromise between detection costs and risks).
- Resilience to attacks against IDS and IPS, because both IDS and IPS can be attacked.

1.6.5 Honeypots

One defense system of interest is *honeypot*. It is used in infrastructures requiring a high level of security. The basic principle is to deploy (in parallel to assets to protect) fake assets to lure potential attackers. Instead of accessing genuine assets, the attackers are deviated to fake assets that imitate the original ones. For example, make a copy of customer accounts with fake data and lure the attackers to steal the fake copy. With the honeypot:

- Attackers cannot see the genuine data.
- Operations of the attackers may be monitored by the honeypot (to some extent, the spy is being spied!).
- Since honeypot is not legitimate, any access to the honeypot is suspicious (thus, activity and traffic filtering is easier when the traffic goes through honeypot).

Depending on the costs to bear, database, computers, servers, and networks can be deployed to form a honeypot. There are two main potential locations for deploying honeypots:

- Honeypot is installed before firewalls:
  - It can easily help detecting attempted connections to unused IP addresses and port scanning.
  - There is no risk of compromised systems behind the firewall, since the traffic is defected to fake environment.
  - However, it does not protect from internal attackers.
- When a honeypot is installed after firewalls
  - It helps catching internal attacks.
  - It can detect firewall misconfigurations/vulnerabilities (owing to a second check of traffic).

1.6.6 Network Address Translation

Another technique widely used for intrusion prevention is NAT (Network Address Translation). NAT is a router function, where IP addresses (and possibly port numbers) of IP datagrams are replaced at the boundary of a private network to hide the packet source. NAT may be used for:

- Security needs; i.e. hide resources or hosts, so that the names or the IP addresses of accessed servers are not visible outside the private network.
- As a solution to the problem of the depletion of IPv4 addresses. For example, local IP addresses: 10.0.0.0-10.255.255.255; 172.16.0.0-172.32.255.255; 192.168.0.0-192.168.255.255 are replaced by global addresses (many locals to one global).
- Load balancing between local servers and server fault tolerance: by using redundant servers with the same IP address, one can improve response time and availability of provided services.

The basic operation of NAT may be summarized as follows:

- Private network is managed using a private address space; thus, the same addresses may be duplicated and used in different private networks.
- NAT device, located at the boundary between the private network and the public internet, manages a pool of public IP addresses.
- When a host from the corporate network sends an IP packet to a remote host, the NAT device picks a public IP address from the address pool, and binds this address to the private address of the host.
- IP address biding may be static or dynamic.
- NAT device also may change the port numbers.

> **Notes**
>
> - It is important to emphasize similarities and differences between proxy and NAT. Both proxy and NAT use address translation. However, proxy operates at application layer (as proxies are associated with application services), while NAT operate at TCP/IP level.
> - NAT server should be in a secure location; otherwise, attackers can know the addresses of local hosts; and therefore, their protection would be no more guaranteed.

1.6.7 Virtual Private Networks

A Virtual Private Network (VPN) provides a secure channel between two private networks through a backbone, often Internet. It provides authentication and encryption to secure the messages, to participate in videoconferences or in call conferences or to work remotely. VPN is an emulation of a secure point-to-point link, as if the partners were connected via a direct (point-to-point) link. As illustrated by Figure 1.11, VPN client and VPN server functions are deployed on the routers of both private networks of partners. VPN clients and servers perform authentication, encryption, and decryption functions.

VPNs are set up by network administrators of companies and institutions, Telecom operators, and Internet access providers.

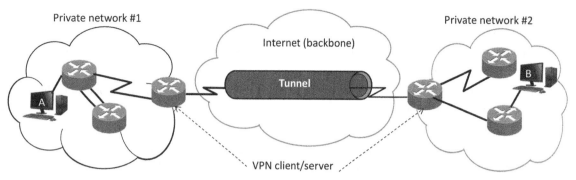

Figure 1.11 VPN is a secure channel between private networks.

There exist four main scenarios of VPN usage:

- Private networks interconnection: for example, interconnecting local networks of a bank, where agencies are located worldwide. With VPNs, local networks form a kind of large and secure local network. In this use case, the VPN is (nearly) permanent.
- Private network interconnection with specific routing: to speed up and secure traffic, a VPN may be used to route packets from/to local networks. In this use case, the VPN is (nearly) permanent.
- Connection of mobile-PC to router: when people are traveling, they can use VPNs to securely access to their corporate network, to their local work station... In this use case, VPNs are used on a per-session basis.
- PC-to-firewall and router-to-firewall: when the link between a firewall and a PC or a router is considered not sufficiently secure, a VPN may be deployed. In this use case, the VPN is (nearly) permanent.

Tunneling. The fundamental mechanism used to install VPNs is called tunneling. The latter is the process of encrypting data and keeping it separate from other traffic on the internet. The main tunneling mechanisms include:

- Encapsulation and decapsulation of packets.
- Selection of a path connecting end-users providing the required QoS level (in terms of bandwidth, etc.).
- Setup of encryption keys between endpoints.
- Encryption and decryption of packets.

1.6.8 Layered-Security Architecture

Last but not the least point to highlight is the notion of *layered-security system* based on multiple security barriers or obstacles that attackers must skip to reach the sensitive assets, as illustrated by Figure 1.12. The external prevention may be composed of firewalls. Then, a barrier composed of specialized firewalls or other filtering equipment. Then, a sophisticated intrusion detection system; some of detected intrusions may be either stopped or redirected to fake environment (to let the attacker think he/she has succeeded in attacking). Last, when some intrusions reach the sensitive data, mitigating actions are undertaken either while the intrusion is progressing or offline. It is worth noticing that most operation security systems are built according to the layered-security notion, because a single security component is not enough to address the huge variety of potential attacks.

1.7 Introduction to Privacy Protection

1.7.1 Overview of Privacy Issues

With the advent and daily usages of the internet, social networks, GPS, and smartphones in particular, privacy has never been more threatened. Personal data are disclosed daily and sometimes sold. The boundaries and content of what is considered private differ among cultures and individuals. In addition, for national security reasons, almost all government security agencies collect data about their citizens and also about foreigners (even in their country). There is no doubt, the internet, smartphones, web cameras, and many other electronic devices are significantly impacting people's privacy.

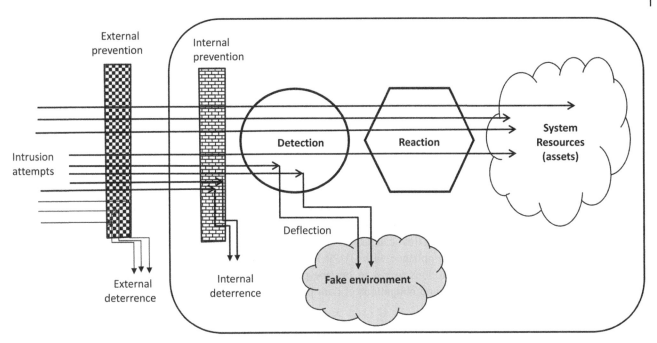

Figure 1.12 Layered-security structure for IT systems.

Definition 1.15 Privacy*: it refers to the ability of individuals to isolate themselves, or information about themselves, and thereby express themselves selectively.*

Definition 1.16 Data protection*: it refers to legislation that is intended to protect the right to privacy of individuals and to ensure that their personal data is used appropriately by organizations that may have it.*

Definition 1.17 Data consent*: it is any freely given, specific, informed, and unambiguous indication of the data owner's wishes by which he/she, by a statement or by a clear affirmative action, signifies agreement to the processing of personal data relating to him/her.*

Every day, each of us is receiving messages relating to commercial advertising he/she never asked for or worse he/she receives threats regarding his/her privacy or ransom messages. In the same way, companies and institutions are attacked via Internet. Consequently, citizens request protection laws to preserve their privacy and business. Roughly, protection laws should clearly state:

- Who can use data of citizens?
- Who can store data and where data must be stored?
- How to file a complaint for damages?

Today's picture of legislation may be seen at two levels:

- Protection inside a country: the protection is good to average depending on countries. National laws are applied when the attacker and victim are in the same country and all the means used to deploy the attack are deployed entirely in the same country. Federal (e.g. in USA), national (e.g. in France), or country union laws exist.
- Today's laws for inter-countries protection are bad or even worse in some situations. There are multiple reasons, including cultural, geostrategic, or competition reasons. Some attacks are considered as minor or meaningless if they occur in other countries; and other attacks are encouraged by some hostile countries against others.

Notice that protecting private data in any country is required, but it is insufficient, because attackers can connect from outside and mount their attacks. Therefore, worldwide collaboration is required. For more on privacy, refer to [7, 31].

1.7.2 Introduction to the GDPR Directive

One of the significant collaborative work done in the arena of cybersecurity has been achieved in European Union to protect privacy of European citizens. The work has resulted in the GDPR (General Data Protection Regulation); its application started in May 2018. Very similar directives and laws have been promulgated and/or adopted in US, Canada, Japan, etc.

The objectives of GDPR are to support rights of individuals, which include rights [32, 33]:

- to be informed
- to rectification
- of access
- of erasure
- to restrict processing
- to object to processing
- to data portability
- to be forgotten

The GDPR states (and clarifies) the responsibilities of data processors (i.e. any entities which store and/or process citizen data). First, the GDPR provides guidelines to comply with GDPR (i.e. what should the data processors do to comply with GDPR?). Second, the GDPR specifies, in general terms, the incurred penalties when the GDPR is violated: up to €20M or 4% of the global turnover for the preceding financial year in case of violation; national courts have responsibility to fix penalties. It should be noticed that the compliance with GDPR has just started and it would take a long time to be fully observed in Europe. GDPR defines notions useful to privacy protection, including concept of personal data, acts of processing, data protection principles, and obligations of data processors. A brief presentation of the above concepts is given below.

1.7.2.1 Personal Data and Acts of Processing

Personal data is any information that can be used to identify a natural person, including

- Name, date of birth, address, and photographs.
- Phone number, email address, and IP address.
- Membership number (of associations, political parties...).
- etc.

Some categories of information are defined as *special categories of personal data*. They require more stringent measures of protection:

- Religion
- Ethnicity
- Sexual orientation
- Trade union membership
- Medical information

Acts on data that need protection awareness include:

- Collecting, recording, organizing, structuring, and storing data.
- Adapting, combining, updating, retrieving, consulting, and using data.
- Disclosing and disseminating data.
- Authorizing/restricting access to data.
- Erasing and destroying data.
- Migration of data from a location to another.

1.7.2.2 Principles of Data Protection

The main principles of data protection specified by GDPR to observe are the following:

- Data collection: collect data for specified, explicit, and legitimate purposes (i.e. specify a clear procedure for data collection and do not mislead citizens).
- Data minimization: collect adequate, relevant, and limited amount of data to what is necessary.
- Data accuracy: collect accurate and, where necessary, keep up to date.
- Data storage limitation: keep data for no longer than necessary for the specified purpose(s).

General-purpose obligations are provided to data processors:

- Lawfulness, fairness, and transparency of processing of data.
- Any data processing action must be agreed upon based on consent.

- Legitimate interest in the collected data; for example, a bank (which controls some of client data) has legitimate interest to transmit client data (e.g. client phone numbers) to its partners (e.g. credit companies). The balance between citizen rights and the business or interest to data processors is far from being clearly understood by concerned parties; much effort remains to do.
- Integrity and confidentiality, which means processing data while ensuring appropriate security.
- Accountability, which means keeping necessary records to demonstrate compliance, when requested by citizens or by courts.

It should be noticed that the principles above are hard to verify in practice, because:

- It is not easy for citizens with few skills in IT systems to understand the risks when they accept data collection.
- Is the data collector fully complying with the principles? Who can check the compliance with principles at a fine granularity? Hard question to answer.
- Nowadays, there is an atmosphere of mistrust regarding current usages of IT technologies by companies, and worse by governments. Citizens are watched and tracked in their daily life. Not all what is considered as conspiracy is wrong or false. Much work remains to be done to reassure citizens.

1.8 Concluding Remarks

This chapter provided an overview of IT security, which is a complex discipline, because of several reasons, including:

- The top issue is related to the malicious nature of human beings, which is limitless in terms of creativity.
- Users and managers are often unaware of the value of computing resources to decide which ones to protect. Frequently, it is only when a confidential information is disclosed or destroyed that the owner becomes aware of its value. Example, one may lose just an SMS, which would cause a disaster (in private life) some years later.
- Deploying a security architecture comes with a cost. Return on investment of security deployment is difficult to assess. Therefore, users invest little. However, the way of addressing security investment is changing in recent years, because of attacks that spread and affect all sectors; even hospitals have been blocked by cybercriminals requiring ransoms.
- Legal definitions are often vague or nonexistent in many countries. Therefore, legal prosecution is difficult even when the attacker and the victim are in the same country. Legal prosecution becomes (nearly) impossible when the attacker is hosted by an unfriendly state.
- Finally, from the technical point of view, many subtle technical issues to address and master, including protocols, algorithms, infrastructures, and tools. Attack techniques are constantly changing and users and security managers have to adapt all the time.

The objectives of this book are to address a fundamental field of security that is cryptography.

1.9 Exercises and Solutions

1.9.1 List of Exercises

Exercise 1.1
List some good practices to prevent identity theft.

Exercise 1.2
Consider a shop owner and show why some CIA properties are required. The assets are products (e.g. electronic devices), agreements with suppliers, client invoices, and cash register.

Exercise 1.3
Consider six assets: a medical file, a university website, an aircraft design document, home camera, a video-surveillance camera in a city, and a camera in a ski station (that broadcasts pictures). Use a table and show which CIA properties are required for each type of asset.

Exercise 1.4
Cite some threats against e-voting system.

Exercise 1.5

Suggest actions of protection against ransomware attacks, virus infection, and spam attacks.

Exercise 1.6

You receive an email with the name of your bank as sender name. The message looks like a message from your bank, which asks you to use a link in order to update your profile. The message may be genuine or fake. What do you do?

Exercise 1.7

Why DDoS attacks are (nearly) impossible to block?

Exercise 1.8

Somebody has subscribed to four free online magazines that belong to a unique company, but the subscribers do not know the companies owning the magazines. To activate the subscription, the first magazine asked for the name, the second asked for the birthday date, the third asked for the complete mailing address, and the fourth asked for the phone number. What threat do you infer from this situation? How to prevent the identified threat?

1.9.2   Solutions to Exercises

Exercise 1.1

Below are some of good practices to prevent identity theft:
– Use well-constructed and unique password to access each server
– Avoid sharing confidential information on social networks
– Limit commercial transactions to known and trusted websites
– Install the latest versions of antiviruses
– Update your browser when you receive update notification

Exercise 1.2

Examples of requirements:
– Confidentiality: the content of the cash register is confidential; agreements (including prices of articles) with suppliers are confidential.
– Integrity: the products on the shelves must not be damaged or altered by visitors or clients; customer invoices must not be altered.
– Availability: no blockage of shop entrance to prevent business with customers; no blockage of the invoice-editing server.

Exercise 1.3

	Confidentiality	Integrity	Availability
Medical file	High	High	High
University website	No	High	Medium
Aircraft design document	High	High	High
Home camera	High	High	Medium
City video surveillance camera	No	High	High/Medium
Ski station camera	No	High	Medium/Low

Exercise 1.4

The following are threats on an e-voting system:
– Preventing citizens to vote after a given hour
– Inclusion of votes of unregistered people
– Disclosing votes
– Double voting
– Tampering the results
– Blocking access to the results

Exercise 1.5

Below are some protection actions

- Against ransomware attacks: regular back up of critical data in safe location; set up backup computers and internet connections.
- Against virus infection: be aware of any file download; run antivirus regularly.
- Against spams: verify the source of any message that asks to click on a link or to send private data; do not blindly trust any email attachments.

Exercise 1.6

- First of all, banks do not, in general, ask their clients to provide personal data using links included in emails. Rather, they ask clients to connect to their account (using credentials and codes) and then perform actions. Therefore, an email including a link, and with a bank as sender, is very likely to be a spam.
- If you can call your bank, do it to know more about the received message.
- In the extended header of the email, you can see the original source IP address of the sender. Copy the IP address and use an online IP address locator, which helps you to see on a map the location of the IP address, say location X. Compare location X to one of the website of your bank. Often, the location of the original source IP address of an attacker is very different from that of your bank. For example, the attacker is located in a Russian city, while your bank is located in Spain. Be careful, some attackers may use a cloud server located in the same zone than that of your bank to send their email.

Exercise 1.7

DDoS attacks are (nearly) impossible to block, because they do not exploit vulnerabilities of the victim; they do not install a malware on the attacked system. The requests from the attacking hosts are similar to legitimate requests. The more widely distributed is a DDoS attack, the more difficult it is to distinguish legitimate requests from those that are not. The harmfulness power of DDoS attacks relies only on the number of requests and the number and locations of attacking hosts. One solution would be to increase the local resources to absorb the traffic and wait until the storm ends. Another solution would be to use secondary resources, unknown to the attacker, and activate them when DDoS attack on the primary resources is detected.

Exercise 1.8

If the publishing company is malicious, it can combine the four data provided by the subscriber and then either sell them (to whom may be interested in the provided profile) or worse use them for identity theft.

To prevent the threat above, never provide personal data when you feel it is not necessary or to entities, you do not personally trust. In the considered scenario, there is no legitimate need for an online magazine to know the complete mailing address, the phone number, and the birthday date.

Notes

1 NIST: national institute of standards and technology, US.
2 Ports refer to TCP/UDP ports used at the transport layer.
3 A port is said to be filtered, if the incoming packets are processed by a firewall or another equipment to reject the packets issued by suspicious sources.

References

1 Bidgoli, H. (2006). *Handbook Information Security*. John Wiley and Sons.
2 Bressler, S.E. and Grantham, C.E. (2000). *Communities of Commerce: Building Internet Business Communities to Accelerate Growth, Minimize Risk, and Increase Customer Loyalty*. Mc Graw Hill.
3 Horton, M. and Mugge, C. (2003). *Hacknotes: Network Security - Portable Reference*. McGraw Hill.
4 Schneier, B. (2003). *Beyond Fear: Thinking Sensible about Security in an Uncertain World*. Copernicus Books.
5 Weaver, R. (2006). *Guide to Network Defense and Countermeasure*. Thomson.
6 Griffor, E. (2016). *Handbook of System Safety and Security*. Syngress.
7 Stallings, W. (2020). *Information Privacy Engineering and Privacy*. Addison Wesley.

8 Pfleeger, C.P. (1997). *Security in Computing*. Prentice Hall.

9 Russel, D. and Gangemi, G.T. (1991). *Computer Security Basics*. O Reilly.

10 Pongle, P. and Chavan, G. (2015). Real time intrusion and wormhole attack detection in internet of things. *International Journal of Computer Applications* 121 (9): 1–9.

11 Abomhara, M. (2015). Cyber security and the internet of things: vulnerabilities, threats, intruders and attacks. *Journal of Cyber Security and Mobility* 4 (1): 65–88.

12 Dewdney, A.K. (1989). Computer recreations of worms, viruses and core war. *Scientific American* 260 (3): 110–113.

13 NIST. Glossary terms and definitions. [Online]. Cited 2023 April. Available from: https://csrc.nist.gov/glossary.

14 Agarwal, S., Farid, H., Gu, Y. et al. (2019). Protecting world leaders against deep fakes. In: *Computer Vision and Pattern Recognition Workshops*, 38–45. Long Beach, CA: IEEE Xplore.

15 Verdoliva, L. (2020). Media forensics and deepfakes: an overview. *IEEE Journal of Selected Topics in Signal Processing* 14 (5): 910–932.

16 Chesney, R. and Citron, D.K. (2019). Deep fakes: a looming challenge for privacy, democracy, and national security. *California Law Review* 107: 1753–1820.

17 Jagielski, M., Oprea, A., Biggio, B. et al. (2018). Manipulating machine learning: poisoning attacks and countermeasures for regression learning. In: *IEEE Symposium on Security and Privacy*, 19–35. San Francisco: IEEE Xplore.

18 Chen, S., Xue, M., Fan, L. et al. (2018). Automated poisoning attacks and defenses in malware detection systems: an adversarial machine learning approach. *Computer & Security* 73: 326–344.

19 Li, M., Sun, Y., Lu, H. et al. (2020). Deep reinforcement learning for partially observable data poisoning attack in crowdsensing systems. *IEEE Internet of Things* 7 (7): 6266–6278.

20 Sayeed, S., Marco-Gisbert, H., and Caira, T. (2020). Smart contract: attacks and protections. *IEEE Access* 8: 24416–24427.

21 Shankland, S. Quantum computers could crack today's encrypted messages. That's a Problem. [Online]. Cited 2023 April. Available from: https://www.cnet.com/tech/computing/quantum-computers-could-crack-todays-encrypted-messages-thats-a-problem.

22 Deign, J. Quantum computers will crack your encryption - maybe they already have. [Online]. Cited 2023 April. Available from: https://newsroom.cisco.com/c/r/newsroom/en/us/a/y2022/m03/is-2022-the-year-encryption-is-doomed.html.

23 Creutzburg, R. (2016). *Handbook of Malware - A Wikipedia Book*. Wikipedia.

24 Monnappa, K.A. (2018). *Learning Malware Analysis*. Packt.

25 Sikorski, M. and Honig, A. (2012). *Practical Malware Analysis*. No Starch Press.

26 Vehent, J. (2018). *Securing DevOps: Security in the Cloud*. Manning.

27 Johnson, D.B., Deogun, D., and Sawano, D. (2017). *Secure by Design*. Manning.

28 Raza, S., Wallgren, L., and Svelte:, V.T. (2013). Real-time intrusion detection in the Internet of things. *Ad Hoc Networks* 11 (8): 2661–2674.

29 Meidan, Y., Bohadana, M., Mathov, Y. et al (2018). N-BaIoT: network-based detection of IoT botnet attacks using deep autoencoders. *IEEE Pervasive Computing* 17 (3): 12–22.

30 Liu, H. and Lang, B. (2019). Machine learning and deep learning methods for intrusion detection systems: a survey. *Applied Sciences, MDPI* 9 (20): 1–28.

31 Richards, N. (2021). *Why Privacy Matters*. Oxford University Press.

32 EU (2016). Protection of natural persons with regard to the processing of personal data and on the free movement of such data, and repealing Directive 95/46/EC (General Data Protection Regulation) - Regulation (EU) 2016/679. European Union Parliament.

33 Taal, A. (2021). *The GDPR Challenge: Privacy, Technology, and Compliance in an Age of Accelerating*. CRC Press.

2

Introduction to Cryptography

For millennia, human beings used multiple forms of cryptographic codes to protect their oral communications, entries of castles, their messages (in particular between armies and their commanders), their money, etc. Therefore, cryptography had existed very early in human history and civilizations, before the advent of computers.

Since the early times, Human beings were in need to communicate, share information, and communicate selectively. These two needs gave rise to the art of message coding (i.e. encrypting) in such a way that only the intended people could have access to the information.

Cryptography has been developed and improved over centuries; in particular for military and defense reasons (protection of military secrets and spying of enemies), then for industrial reasons (protection of industrial secrets), afterward for securing the recent applications made possible thanks to the internet (e-banking, e-commerce, bitcoins, ...), and ultimately for protecting the privacy of electronic devices' users.

In modern digitalized society, cryptography is the pillar of security. Cryptography is used to protect data while in transit over unsecure channels and data on storage devices (i.e. USB devices, disks, etc.). Encryption is everywhere in the cyberspace. Encrypting and signing are the most performed cryptographic operations. Cryptography secures websites and makes electronic transmissions safe. In particular, public-key cryptography enables people (e.g. a client and a merchant), who never met before, to securely communicate and trust each other. Cryptography is not only used over the internet, but also in phones, television, cars, aircrafts, door locks, implants, and a variety of other devices. Without cryptography, hackers could get into users' emails, listen to their phone conversations, tap into their cable companies and acquire free cable service, or break into their bank accounts.

As cryptographic algorithms protect sensitive data, they have been (and still they are) the target of attackers. Who can imagine what would happen if suddenly the cryptographic techniques used in the cyberspace were to be broken?

In Chapter 1, we saw that confidentiality, integrity, non-repudiation, and authentication services are of paramount importance for IT security. Cryptographic algorithms and protocols provide all those services. This chapter succinctly introduces the terminology, notions, algorithms, and attacks relating to cryptography, which will be addressed in more detail in the subsequent chapters.

2.1 Definitions of Basic Terms

2.1.1 Cryptography, Cryptanalysis, and Cryptology

The word *cryptography* is the contraction of two Greek words, *kryptós*, which means *hidden* or *secret* and *graphein* which means *write*.

Cryptography may be defined as the art, techniques, and science of concealing the data and messages to include secrecies, which protect data and messages from unwanted usages [1–4]. In other words, cryptography enables to store sensitive information or to transmit it across insecure channels, so that it cannot be read by anyone except the intended recipient(s). Cryptography not only protects sensitive data from disclosure or alteration, but also enables user and message authenticity verification.

Cryptography: Algorithms, Protocols, and Standards for Computer Security, First Edition. Zoubir Mammeri.
© 2024 John Wiley & Sons, Inc. Published 2024 by John Wiley & Sons, Inc.

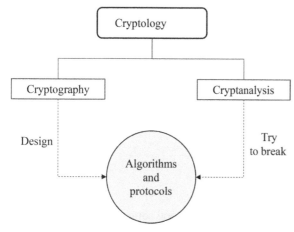

Figure 2.1 Cryptology = Cryptography + Cryptanalysis.

Definition 2.1 Cryptosystem: *it is an implementation of cryptographic techniques to provide information security services (such as confidentiality and integrity).*

Cryptanalysis is the science and technique of analyzing and breaking cryptographic algorithms and protocols. Cryptanalysts are also called attackers, who may be categorized into two groups. The first category of cryptanalysts intensively analyzes any new cryptographic algorithm to find vulnerabilities. When the algorithm is broken (sometimes under very specific conditions), the result of analysis is published, which helps improving the security of the proposed algorithm or recommending not to use it. The second category is more dangerous; this type of cryptanalysts search vulnerabilities and exploit them to design attacks and disclose sensitive data.

Cryptology is the discipline of cryptography and cryptanalysis combined, as illustrated by Figure 2.1.

2.1.2 Brief History of Cryptography

Since the beginning of time, multiple techniques have been used to make messages secret. Different forms of ingenious ideas were used depending on four factors:

- The worth of the message to protect: is the cost of message protection reasonable compared to the value of the message?
- The available resources (technological or not) to encrypt and decrypt.
- The period to keep a message secret: how long the message should remain secret? Almost all secrets were/will be disclosed over time.
- The power (capabilities) of potential attackers against messages. Any secret message may be broken when required resources to break are available.

The art of cryptography was (certainly) born when secrets during battles had to be protected; including number of soldiers, weapons, troop positions, attack and pullback orders had to be protected. Modern cryptography techniques have many roots in ancient civilizations: Egyptian, Greek, and Roman. Below is a brief of major inventions and highlights in cryptography.

Ancient Egypt. The earliest known encrypted text found in Egypt dates back to (nearly) 1900 BC. Hieroglyphics on pharaohs and dignitaries tombs had been hiding secrets, and were disclosed (nearly) four millennia later. Secrets were represented as symbols (i.e. hieroglyphics), unreadable to those who did not (and still do not) know the hieroglyphics alphabet.

Greece. In 500s BC, Greeks developed cylinder messages. The cipher made use of a baton (called scytale). Each baton round had the capacity to write k letters. k represents the secret key. First, a parchment was wound up in spiral around the baton. Second, the text to be encrypted was written on the parchment in straight lines (in rows). Third, the parchment was unrolled; and it represented the ciphertext. The recipient of the ciphertext was required to possess a baton (with the same diameter than that of the sender) on which the received parchment was wound up to recover the plaintext. Figure 2.2 illustrates an example of a message encryption using the Greek scytale. The plaintext is TWO THOUSAND SOLDIERS ONSITE ON SATURDAY; spaces are removed before writing the plaintext on a parchment wound up around a baton with a diameter of six letters. When the parchment is unrolled, the yielded ciphertext is TUOSEUWSLOOROADNNDTNISSAHDEIAYOSRTT.

Rome. With no doubt, the most known cipher was developed in Rome 2000 years ago, and referred to as Caesar's cipher. The code was mainly used to secure communications between commanders and troops on battlefields or between Rome and provincial governors. Caesar's cipher is a substitution cipher, where a letter is shifted by some fixed position number; i.e. letter at position i in alphabet is replaced by letter at position $i + k \bmod 26$. This number, k, was the secret key of the cipher. Caesar's cipher is presented in more detail in Section 4.2.

Vigenere's cipher. In the 1500s, Blaise de Vigenere made improvements to Caesar's cipher. A 26-by-26 table is used to substitute letters, so that the same letter is not always replaced by the same letter as Caesar's cipher does. This is the base concept of polyalphabetic ciphers, which are harder to break than Caesar's cipher. Vigenere's cipher is presented in more detail in Section 4.4.

Jefferson's wheel cipher. In the late 1700s, Thomas Jefferson came up with a cipher system similar to that of Vigenere, but with higher security, because it has much more combinations to select keys. As illustrated by Figure 2.3, Jefferson's cylinder is composed of 36 disks (or wells), stacked on top of each other around an axle. The 26 Latin letters are randomly inscribed on each disk. The disks are numbered; they are removable and can be mounted on the axle in any desired order. The order of disk mounting represents the secret key. Both the sender and receiver of a message had to mount the disks in the same way.

The message to encrypt is split into 36-letter fragments. To encrypt a 36-letter fragment, the sender rotates each disk, so that the fragment appears on a horizontal row parallel to the rotation axis. Then, he/she chooses any row parallel to the plaintext row and sends it as ciphertext. Upon reception of a ciphertext, the recipient rotates the disks so that the ciphertext appears on a horizontal row parallel to the rotation axis; then, looks for the row, which contains the plaintext. There is a very low probability that the recipient keeps a row, which does not correspond to the correct plaintext. Jefferson's wheel cipher may be considered as the ancestor of the Enigma machine presented below.

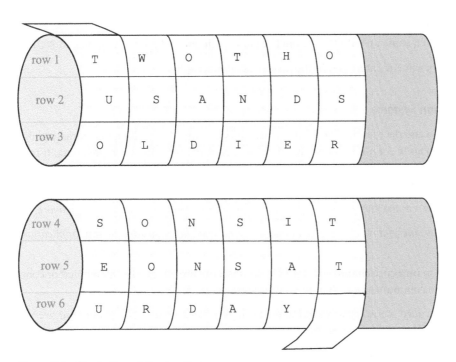

Figure 2.2 Illustration of Greek cylinder message.

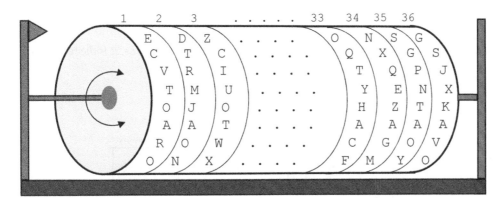

Figure 2.3 Overall structure of Jefferson's wheel cipher.

Enigma machine. The Enigma machine, invented during World War I and improved during World War II, was mainly used by the army of the third Reich. Enigma is one of the first electromechanical devices used for encryption and decryption; and the most used in practice at that time. It is a very sophisticated version of Jefferson's cylinder. Enigma was very hard to break; but Alan Turing did it. Enigma machine is presented in more detail in Section 4.5.

Vernam's cipher. In 1917, the one-time pad (OTP) cipher was (re)invented by Gilbert Vernam and patented in the US. OTP cannot be cracked, because a single-use random key is required for each message, and the key must be at least of the same bit-length than that of the message to encrypt. Vernam's cipher was a cipher that combined a message with a key read from a paper tape or pad; hence, the word *pad* in the name of the cipher. OTP was used in limited number of applications, including military applications, because a new key is required for each message. OTP is discussed in more detail in Section 4.6.

Modern cryptography. Much progress has been achieved since the early 1970s and many cryptographic algorithms were proposed; they are discussed in this book. From our point of view, the following six steps are the most prominent in the modern cryptography:

- In the early 1970s, IBM developed Lucifer cipher, which became the Data Encryption Standard (DES) in 1976.
- In 1976, Whitfield Diffie and Martin Hellman introduced the principle of public-key cryptography.
- In 1977, Ronald Rivest, Adi Shamir, and Leonard Adleman came up with the RSA algorithm.
- In 1987, Neal Koblitz proposed elliptic curves to design public-key ciphers.
- In 1995, the first Secure Hash Algorithm (SHA1) was approved by the NIST.
- In 1998, Joan Daemen and Vincent Rijmen came up with the symmetric cipher Rijndael, which became AES in 2001.

| **Note.** [5] is an excellent book for readers who are interested in the history of cryptography.

2.1.3 Basic Terms Related to Encryption Systems

Confidentiality is supported by encryption and decryption algorithms, which process three basic elements, namely plaintext, ciphertext, and key, as illustrated by Figure 2.4. Channel is any unsecure means to access the encrypted data. It may be a communication network (e.g. Internet, a private network, or a cellular network) or storage device (e.g. a USB key). The attacker can listen to the channel or read the storage device.

Definition 2.2 Plaintext *(or cleartext): it is a data either on a storage device or in transit over a communication network.*

Definition 2.3 Ciphertext*: it is data after encryption; it is not readable for human beings or usable by any application, without possession of the decryption key.*

A ciphertext is either transmitted over an unsecure channel or stored in an unsecure area. It can be intercepted or compromised by anyone who has access to the communication channel or the storage area.

Definition 2.4 Cryptographic key *(also called secret key or simply key): it is a parameter used by encryption and decryption algorithms. It is the most critical material.*

Static keys are intended to be used for a long period of time (e.g. the PIN code to access a bank account), while *ephemeral keys* are used for a very limited time (e.g. to encrypt one message).

Definition 2.5 Encryption algorithm *(also called enciphering): it is the process of creating a ciphertext. It makes use of a key to scramble the input (i.e. the plaintext), so that the result (i.e. the ciphertext) looks like a noise for any observer who does not know the decryption key.*

Definition 2.6 Decryption algorithm*: it is the process of transforming a ciphertext into a plaintext; i.e. it is the reverse process of encryption.*

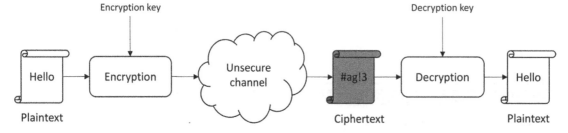

Figure 2.4 Main components of encryption/decryption chain.

Definition 2.7 Encryption key: *it is a secret value that is known to the sender.*

Definition 2.8 Decryption key: *it is a value that is known to the receiver. The decryption key is related to the encryption key, but it is not always identical to it.*

Definition 2.9 Cipher *(also called encryption system): encryption and decryption algorithms form together a cipher.*

2.1.4 Symmetric and Asymmetric Cryptographic Systems

There exist two types of cryptosystems: symmetric-key encryption and asymmetric-key encryption. The main difference between those two cryptosystems is the relationship between the encryption and the decryption keys. In any cryptosystem, it is practically impossible to decrypt a ciphertext with the key that is unrelated to the encryption key.

2.1.4.1 Symmetric Cryptosystems

Till the late 1970s, all cryptosystems were symmetric. Even today, symmetric cryptosystems are used extensively in many cryptosystems, in particular to encrypt and decrypt data. Collectively, the algorithms used in symmetric cryptosystems are referred to as *symmetric cryptography*. The well-known symmetric algorithms include AES (Advanced Encryption Standard) and DES (Digital Encryption Standard).

As illustrated by Figure 2.5, in symmetric cryptosystems, the entity, which encrypts a data, and the entity that decrypts an encrypted data share the same key. Before any cryptographic operation, both entities need to exchange the key using a secure channel. In addition, a shared key should be changed periodically or after encrypting a given amount of data to prevent some attacks.

If a group of n people need to securely exchange encrypted data, $n * \dfrac{n-1}{2}$ keys are required, because each member shares a key with each of the other $n-1$ members. Example, for 1000 staff members, nearly half a million keys are required to be generated, exchanged, and periodically changed.

In general, symmetric cryptography has two restrictive challenges:

- *Key establishment*: agreement on a secret symmetric key requires to make use of secure channel (e.g. a phone call, a bag, post mail, etc.) or a specific key-agreement protocol.
- *Trust*: since both parties (i.e. sender and recipient) use the same key, there is an implicit requirement that they trust each other. If an attacker exploits the weaknesses of one party to recover the key, the other party is not informed and continues to send sensitive data, which would be easily disclosed by the attacker. Symmetric cryptography alone is not practical to provide security when parties do not belong to the same circle. For example, in e-shopping, the client does not trust the merchant and vice versa.

2.1.4.2 Asymmetric Cryptosystems

In the late 1970s, asymmetric cryptosystems were invented to overcome the limitations of symmetric cryptography. Asymmetric cryptosystems are considered as a turning point in cryptography history. Encryption and decryption keys are distinct, a private key, which must remain secret, and a public key. Both keys are linked by a mathematical relationship relying on one-way functions, i.e. given a key, it is impossible (in practice) to disclose the second key.

When the owner of the private key, say A, needs to receive encrypted data from a party, B, the latter encrypts messages, using A's public key; and the receiver decrypts using his/her/its private key. When party A wants to sign a message, he/she/it generates the signature using his/her/its private key; and the recipient verifies the signature using A's public key. The overall structure of asymmetric ciphers is illustrated by Figure 2.6.

Public-key cryptography is divided into three classes:

1) Integer factorization cryptography, which mainly incudes RSA cryptosystem, addressed in detail in Chapter 12.
2) Finite field Cryptography, which is based on computations over finite fields, addressed in detail in Chapter 12.
3) Elliptic curve cryptography, which is based on computations over elliptic curves, addressed in detail in Chapter 13.

2.1.4.3 Symmetric vs Asymmetric Cryptosystems and Their Combination

As we will see in this book, there exist many symmetric ciphers, while only a few asymmetric algorithms exist. The primary advantage of symmetric-key algorithms is that they are often significantly faster than asymmetric-key algorithms.

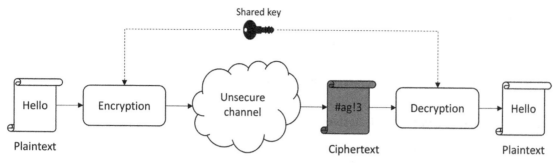

Figure 2.5 Overall structure of symmetric-key cryptosystem.

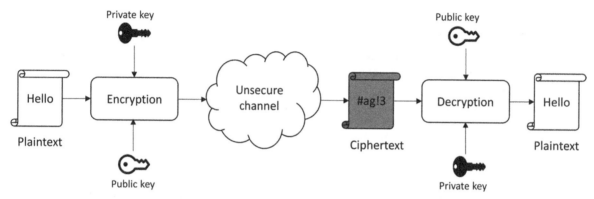

Figure 2.6 Overall structure of asymmetric-key cryptosystem.

The second advantage is that symmetric keys are shorter in length for the same security strength. The key length may be an important consideration, if memory for storing the keys or the bandwidth for transporting the keys are limited. In addition, advances in cryptanalysis and computational efficiency have tended to reduce the level of protection provided by public-key cryptography more rapidly than that provided by symmetric-key cryptography. The third advantage of symmetric-key algorithms is that they are based on simple bit operations (substitution, XORing, shifting, swapping), while public-key algorithms are based on mathematical notions (modular arithmetic and operations over finite fields). In the next chapter, we introduce the useful theorems and facts before going in depth in cryptography. Public-key cryptography has, at least, two advantages compared to symmetric cryptography:

1) Increased security of private keys: unlike symmetric cryptosystems, the private keys never need to be transmitted or shared with anyone, when public-key cryptosystems are used.
2) Asymmetric cryptography provides digital signatures, so that authentication of message can be assured. In addition, using digital certificates and signature provides non-repudiation assurance.

In operational security systems, symmetric and asymmetric algorithms are combined to provide performant security services. Roughly, public-key algorithms are used to generate shared session keys, to sign messages and verify signatures, and to authenticate users, while symmetric-key algorithms are used to encrypt and decrypt messages using shared session keys.

2.1.4.4 Trapdoor Functions

Definition 2.10 One-way function: *let $f: \{0,1\}^m \rightarrow \{0,1\}^n$ be function, which receives m-bit input and returns n-bit output. f is said to be one-way, if it is easy to compute $f(x) = y$ for $x \in \{0,1\}^m$, but it is computationally infeasible to find a preimage $x = f^{-1}(y)$ given $y \in \{0,1\}^n$.*

Example 2.1 Below are examples of one-way functions:

– Given two large primes a and b, it is easy to find the product $p = a * b$, while given p, it is not easy to find a and b, such that $a * b = p$. This problem is referred to as factorization problem.
– Given three integers a, k, and n, it is easy to compute b, such that $a^k \bmod n = b$, while it is not easy to find k, such that $a^k \bmod n = b$, when a, b, and n are given. This problem is referred to as discrete logarithm problem.

– Any hash function H is a one-way function, because given a, it is easy to compute t, such that $H(a) = t$, while given t, it is not easy to find a, such that $H(a) = t$.

Definition 2.11 Trapdoor function*: it is a one-way function for which the inverse direction is easy if some useful information is known, but difficult otherwise.*

Generally, public-key cryptosystems are based on trapdoor functions. The public key gives information about the particular instance of the function; and the private key gives information about the trapdoor. Anyone who knows the trapdoor can compute the function easily in both directions, but anyone who does not know the trapdoor can only easily perform the function in the forward direction. In public-key cryptosystems, the forward direction (i.e. the public key) is used for encryption and signature verification; the inverse direction (i.e. the private key) is used for decryption and signature generation.

Note. Public-key cryptosystems used in practice are based on functions that are believed to be one-way. However, no function has been mathematically proven to be so.

2.2 Cryptographic Primitives

Definition 2.12 Cryptographic primitive*: it is a basic cryptographic algorithm used to build computer security systems.*

Over millennia, cryptography has focused on keeping messages and data confidential. Today's cryptography is more than encryption and decryption. Data integrity, authentication, digital signature, and non-repudiation are security services provided by cryptography. Common cryptographic primitives may be categorized into six classes (as illustrated by Figure 2.7):

- Encryption/decryption primitives
- Hash functions
- Message authentication codes
- Digital signatures
- Shared-secret generation
- Pseudorandom number generation

Table 2.1 summarizes the security services provided by each cryptographic primitive.

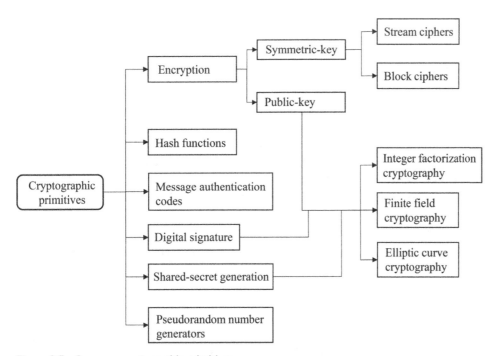

Figure 2.7 Common cryptographic primitives.

Table 2.1 Cryptographic primitives and services.

	Primitives			
Service	Encryption[1]	Hash function	MAC[2]	Digital signature[3]
Confidentiality	Yes	No	No	No
Integrity	No	No[4]	Yes	Yes
Availability	No	No	No	No
Message authentication	No	No	Yes	Yes
Entity authentication	No	No	No	Yes
Non-repudiation	No	No	No	Yes

2.2.1 Encryption

The main objective of encryption primitives is to assure confidentiality. Scrambling data makes it unusable (i.e. looks like a noise) by those who do not know the decryption key. There exist two families of symmetric ciphers: block and stream ciphers.

- *Stream ciphers* are encryption algorithms that apply encryption algorithms on a bit-by-bit basis (one bit at a time) to plaintext using a keystream. If P is the plaintext and S is the keystream (of the same length than the plaintext), then the ciphertext C is defined by $C = P \oplus S$, where $\oplus$ is the bitwise XOR operator. Inversely, $P = C \oplus S$. Therefore, encryption and decryption are identical operations. In general, stream ciphers are by far faster than block ciphers.
- *Block ciphers* are encryption algorithms that encrypt/decrypt plaintexts of a fixed size (e.g. 128 bits), called blocks. The encryption (or decryption) operation works in the form of a series of sequential rounds. Each round makes use of substitutions and permutations of fragments of its input (initial plaintext, secret key, and output of the preceding round). In general, the decryption operation performs substitutions and permutations operations in the inverse order of encryption. Two of the most known and used blocks ciphers are DES and AES. To encrypt plaintexts longer than a single block, modes of operation are used to split a plaintext into blocks, and then call the block cipher to encrypt each block. Blocks of ciphertext and plaintext may be combined to prevent some attacks.

The main public-key encryption algorithms include RSA, ElGamal, and ECIES (Elliptic Curve Integrated Encryption Scheme) cryptosystems.

2.2.2 Hash Functions and Data Integrity

Encryption provides assurance regarding confidentiality. However, encryption alone cannot protect against alterations (i.e. add, delete, or modify bits) of the ciphertext, which result in a decrypted plaintext that differs from the original one. To protect the integrity of data, one-way functions, called *hash functions*, are used to produce digital fingerprints, also called *digests* or *tags*. A hash function takes a variable-length data (maybe in hundred gigabytes) and produces a fixed-length digest (of a few hundred bits). The data and its tag are stored or sent together. As illustrated by Figure 2.8, to check the integrity of data, the recipient computes a digest of the received data and compares it to the received tag. If both tags are identical, the recipient accepts the received data. Otherwise, the data is rejected. The two fundamental properties of hash functions are:

1) If one or a few bits of data are changed, a completely different tag is produced.
2) If one knows a tag associated with a data, he/she cannot find another data which maps to the same tag; that is why the term fingerprint is used in cryptography.

2.2.3 Message Authentication Codes

Message authentication code (MAC) algorithms are cryptographic algorithms used to provide message source authentication and integrity. They produce authentication tags, also called MACs. In general, MACs can be generated by:

Figure 2.8 Principle of integrity verification using a hash function.

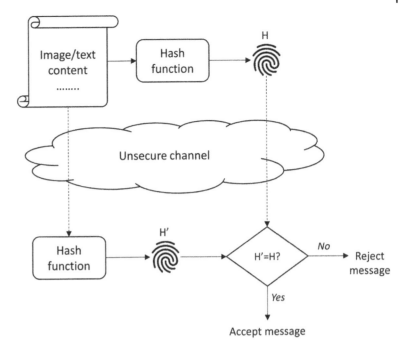

- Algorithms that rely on hash functions and a key; that is why they are called hash MAC (or HMAC) or keyed-hash functions. The data and the key are hashed together to produce a MAC, which is then stored or transmitted with data.
- Algorithms based on stream ciphers, where the final state of internal cipher registers contain the MAC.
- Algorithms based on block ciphers, where data is encrypted block by block and the ciphertext of each block is used to encrypt the next block. The encryption of the final block represents the MAC.

The sender generates a MAC using data to protect and a key shared with the recipient. At reception of a pair (data, MAC), the recipient computes a MAC using the received data and the shared key and then compares it to the received MAC. If both are equal, the recipient concludes that the received data has not been altered (i.e. integrity verification) and it has been sent by an entity that shares the secret key (i.e. source authentication).

2.2.4 Digital Signature

Definition 2.13 Digital signature: *it is a message hash encrypted with a private key; and used to authenticate the message source.*

As illustrated by Figure 2.9, a digital signature is obtained as follows: the data to sign is hashed to yield a tag, then the tag is encrypted with the private key of the signer; the signed tag is called *digital signature*. When a message-signature pair is received, the recipient computes a tag H of the received data, decrypts the received signature, and obtains a tag H'. If both tags are identical, the recipient concludes that the data was signed by the entity owning the private key associated with the used public key and the message was not altered in transit. In the event the data or the signature is altered, the authentication fails. Therefore, digital signature provides assurance regarding the message integrity as well as the authenticity of message.

Both digital and handwritten signatures rely on the fact that it is very hard to find two people with the same signature. While the handwritten signature is the same on all the signed documents, a distinct digital signature is associated with each signed message. Handwritten signatures can be reproduced (mimicked), which results in fraudulent documents. Unlike handwritten signatures, digital signatures are very unlikely to be mimicked. Therefore, they are considered as foolproof. In addition, handwritten signatures do not protect the integrity of a signed document (the fraudster can change a picture, words or letters, while keeping the authentic signature), while any alteration of the original data results in an invalid signature.

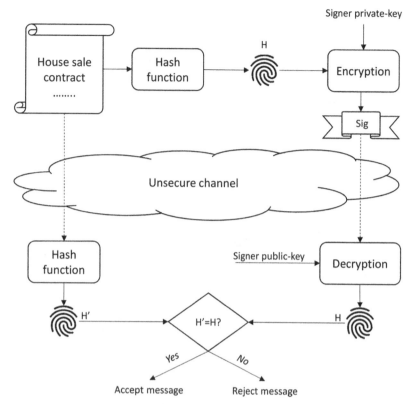

Figure 2.9 Integrity protection provided by digital signature.

2.2.5 Digital Certificates and Non-Repudiation

***Definition 2.14 Digital certificate** or **public-key certificate**: it is an electronic document used to prove the ownership of a public key.*

Public-key cryptosystems have one primary challenge; the recipient of a signed message needs to trust that the public key that he/she/it is using to authenticate the message is really owned by the entity who signed the message and not stolen by a malicious adversary. The trust can be established using *digital certificate*. The latter is an electronic document signed by using the private key of a trusted authority, called Certificate authority, to certify that the name of the entity on the certificate owns the public key included in the certificate. A digital certificate functions like a physical certificate, such as a passport delivered by an administrative authority. Two entities (individuals or organizations) with distinct names and IP addresses cannot have the same certificate.

Digital certificates are used in the cyberspace to prevent malicious entities (individuals or organizations) impersonate others and receive sensitive data or send fake data to their target. They allow verification of the claim that a specific public key does in fact belong to a specific individual or organization. To verify a signature included in a message, the recipient requests the signer to send his/her/its certificate. Then, he/she/it makes use of the public key in the certificate to verify the signature.

In addition to data integrity and message authentication, digital certificates provide a second service, which is of prime importance for electronic transactions (e-shopping, e-banking, e-voting, etc.). It is non-repudiation assurance. Since it is assumed that only the entity owning a key-pair (private and public) can sign using his/her/its private key, he/she/it can only create unique signature on a given data. Thus, the recipient can present data and the digital signature to a third party as evidence if any dispute arises in the future. The legitimate signer cannot deny having signed the message.

2.2.6 Shared-Secret Generation

One major progress in cryptography is due to Whitfield Diffie and Martin Hellman, who proposed a protocol, called Diffie-Hellman exchange protocol, which enables two parties to agree on a shared secret. The parties make use of their public keys to agree on a shared secret that does not need to be sent over a network. Then the shared secret can be used as a session key (to encrypt data) or used to derive a session key. Key derivation is a method, which takes an input, performs specific operations, such as hashing, and then truncates the hash function result to yield a key. This issue is addressed in detail in Chapter 14.

2.2.7 Pseudorandom Number Generation

Random numbers are used in a wide variety of cryptographic operations, such as key generation and key agreement protocols. A random number generator (RNG) is a function that outputs a sequence of numbers, such that at any point, the next number cannot be predicted based on the previous numbers. Unfortunately, true random number generation is difficult to realize on computers, which are deterministic. Instead of true RNs, pseudorandom RNs (PRNGs) are used in many cryptographic algorithms. A PRNG produces a sequence of numbers that is very likely to appear as random. With each distinct initialization value (called seed), a PRNG generates a distinct sequence of numbers.

As discussed in Chapter 26, in general, PRNGs are based on hash functions. It is worth noticing that the security of cryptographic algorithms relies on the randomness in the sequence of random numbers used. If an attacker can predict the next values to be produced by a PRNG, he/she can infer secret information.

2.3 Fundamental Properties of Cryptographic Algorithms

2.3.1 Should Cryptographic Algorithms Be Secret or Not?

In the past, some cryptographic algorithms or mechanisms were kept secret and the security they provide relies on the assumption that the attackers do not know the details of targeted cryptosystems. Modern cryptographic algorithms are publicly known. Keeping an algorithm secret may act as a significant barrier to honest cryptanalysts who could discover its weaknesses and would suggest mechanisms to make it secure. Without involvement of honest cryptanalysis, a cryptographic algorithm would be the target of only malicious cryptanalysts, who could take advantage of the discovered weaknesses to attack IT systems using the algorithm. Keeping the algorithms secret is possible only when they are used in a very limited circle and are not expected to operate at a large scale.

In 1883, Auguste Kerckhoffs, a Dutch cryptograph, stated a fundamental principle for the design of cryptographic systems: "a cryptosystem should be secure even if everything about the system, with the exception of the key, is public knowledge." Cryptographic algorithms used in the current (civilian) cyberspace are based on Kerckhoffs's principle.

2.3.2 Models of Security Proof

One of the most important properties of cryptographic algorithms is the proof of their security. The models of security proof include two classes: unconditional security and computational security.

- *Unconditional security* (also called *information-theoretic security*): a system is said to have unconditional security, if it is secure against attackers with unlimited computing resources (memory space and time).
- *Computational security* refers to the amount of computational resources needed to break an algorithm using the best known attack. Most of the currently used algorithms fall in this class. *Computationally secure algorithm* is any algorithm that cannot be broken using reasonable computing resources.

2.3.2.1 Computational Infeasibility

In theory, any algorithm can be broken, if the attacker has an infinite amount of computation resources (processors, memory, and bandwidth). In practice, any attacker has a limited capacity to perform an attack and the attack would take a time depending on the deployed resources.

An attack is said to be *computationally infeasible*, if the required amount of resources is beyond the capacity of any attacker (with probably the exception of governmental agencies). Currently, an attack that requires at least 2^{90} operations is considered as computationally infeasible. Notice that the strength level of 80 bits (i.e. the required number of operations is of at least 2^{80}) is no more considered secure.

2.3.2.2 Provable Security

As far as we know, no cryptographic algorithms used in practice have been mathematically proven to be entirely secure. In general, under specific and restrictive conditions, an algorithm can be declared secure. Since the key space is finite, the probability to recover a secret key is not 0, even if the key bit-length is large. In addition, some plaintexts (e.g. bank transactions or personal communications) have a format known to attackers, who can infer, using traffic analysis, information that could help breaking the encryption algorithm. Therefore, the security of cryptographic algorithms is based on probabilistic approach; and not on a formal proof.

In practice, given a cryptographic algorithm and a set of talented cryptanalysts, if none of them can break it after a long time, using reasonable computation resources, users of the algorithm can reasonably assume that it is secure. After the publication of a weakness that resulted in breaking (partially[5] or totally) an algorithm, the use of the algorithm should be stopped as soon as possible.

One of the best citations regarding proof of security was stated by Brice Schneier, who wrote, "*Anyone, from the most clueless amateur to the best cryptographer, can create an algorithm that himself can't break. It's not even hard. What is hard is creating an algorithm that no one else can break, even after years of analysis. And the only way to prove that is to subject the algorithm to years of analysis by the best cryptographer around*" [6].

The lifetime cycle of a cryptographic algorithm may be summarized in four steps:

1) A talented cryptograph publishes a new algorithm, either spontaneously or to participate to a call[6] for new algorithms. He/she believes that the algorithm is secure. Publishing a new cryptographic algorithm is understood as a challenge for cryptanalysts, as *try to break my algorithm*. Sometimes, organizations, such as the NIST, publish security challenges, with rewards for those who succeed in breaking the algorithms.
2) Worldwide talented cryptanalysts deeply analyze the robustness of the published algorithm regarding known attacks.
3) When a weakness is discovered by cryptanalysts, the algorithm is updated as soon as possible; and a new version is published.
4) If the discovered weakness is critical (i.e. no cure exists without deeply redesigning the algorithm), the algorithm is deprecated.

2.3.3 Perfect Secrecy

Perfect secrecy (or *information-theoretic security*) property means that the ciphertext conveys no information about the content of the plaintext. In other words, no matter how much ciphertexts the attacker has, they do not convey anything about what the plaintexts and the key were. In terms of probability, perfect secrecy property means that the probability distribution of the possible plaintexts is independent of the ciphertexts. More formally,

> *An encryption scheme over plaintext space $\mathcal{M}$ has the perfect secrecy property, if for every probability distribution over $\mathcal{M}$, every message $m \in \mathcal{M}$, and every ciphertext $c \in \mathcal{C}$, for which $Pr[C = c] > 0$,*
>
> $$Pr[M = m \mid C = c] = Pr[M = m] \tag{2.1}$$
>
> *where M and C are random variables associated with plaintext and ciphertext, respectively.*

The probability distribution of ciphertexts is defined by:

$$\forall c \in \mathcal{C}, Pr[C = c] = \sum_{m \in \mathcal{M}} Pr[C = c \mid M = m] * Pr[M = m] \tag{2.2}$$

Example 2.2 Consider the Caesar's cipher, where 26 keys (from 0 to 25) can be used equally (i.e. with a probability of 1/26) to encrypt one letter of the Latin alphabet. Each plaintext letter is encrypted with a key randomly selected. Observing a ciphertext of one letter does not provide any information about the encrypted letter. Therefore, the cipher has the perfect secrecy property.

Perfect forward secrecy (PFS) property: a cryptosystem is said to have the PFS property, if the compromise of long-term keys does not allow an attacker to obtain past session keys. In other words, PFS property protects past sessions against future compromises of long-term keys. In addition, by generating a unique session key for every session initiated by a party, the compromise of a single session key will not affect any data other than that exchanged in the specific session protected by that particular session key.

We will see in Chapter 14 that Diffie-Hellman exchange protocol and its variants have the PFS property.

Example 2.3 At time t, a client and a server make use of the following protocol to agree on a session key. The client sends its public key to the server. The latter computes a session key, encrypts it using the client public key, and sends it to the client, over an unsecure channel. No other entity, with the exception of the client, can read the session key. Next, parties exchange messages encrypted using the session key and terminate the session. An attacker listening to the channel, copies all the encrypted messages, but he/she cannot decrypt them. Sometime later (may be after months), the same attacker recovers the public key of the client. He/she decrypts the message containing the encrypted session key, and then discloses all the messages he/she intercepted some time ago. The key agreement protocol above has not the PFS property. That is, a compromise of the long-term public-key of the client results in disclosing ciphertexts sent in the past.

2.3.4 Security Strength of Cryptographic Algorithms

Security strength is expressed in the total amount of computations an attacker needs to perform in order to break an algorithm (i.e. disclose a plaintext, recover the key, forge a message tag, etc.). It also is referred to as the *computational complexity*.

In current recommended cryptographic algorithms, the security strength is specified in number of bits (e.g. 112, 128, 192, 256, and 512). At the security strength of 256 bits, an attacker would require a computation of roughly 2^{255} or more bit operations to compromise security. The security strength of a system is the minimum of the bit-lengths of its components (private key, public key, signatures, random generator, etc.). For example, if the security strength is 256 bits for all components except one, which has a security strength of 128 bits, then the security strength of the whole system is 128 bits.

2.4 Attacks Against Cryptographic Algorithms

In Chapter 1, we presented cyberattacks, including phishing, spam, DDoS, and ransoming. Those attacks mainly aim to collect sensitive and personal data, block system access, threaten private life, and demand ransoms. Most of those attacks exploit vulnerabilities due to naivety, recklessness, and greed of users, weaknesses of operating systems, and broadcasting and dissemination capacities provided by networks. They are launched by cybercriminals who, in general, are not cryptanalysts. Attacks discussed in this section address weaknesses of cryptographic algorithms; they mainly aim:

- To disclose one or several plaintexts associated with known ciphertexts.
- To forge a tag or a signature without knowledge of the secret key.
- To recover the secret key (used to encrypt, to compute MAC, or to sign).
- To infer a partial internal state of a cipher (e.g. a key round used in block cipher or a fragment of keystream of a stream cipher).

Malleability is the ability to transform a ciphertext into a different ciphertext that will produce a new and different plaintext when decrypted in the recipient side. It also is the ability to transform a data, while keeping the same tag or signature, so that the recipient will consider the data authentic, while it is not. Malleability is generally an undesirable property. For example, a bit-flipping attack takes advantage of the malleability of stream ciphers.

Attacks against cryptographic algorithms are designed and performed by cryptanalysts. They take advantage of the design weaknesses of algorithms, their implementation, and/or their usages. In particular, social networks are used by attackers to infer some useful information regarding targeted individuals (or organizations). For example, from discussions between individuals, attackers may infer some parts of encrypted plaintexts (infer names, greetings, and discussion topics) and then use the inferred knowledge to disclose more information about targeted individuals.

2.4.1 What Is Cryptanalysis?

Cryptanalysis is considered as the flip side of cryptography. It is the science and technique to break cryptographic algorithms. Academic cryptanalysts, national security agencies (in US, Europe, Japan, etc.) cryptanalysts, and cyberterrorists have been intensively involved in this field. Since the emergence of modern cryptography, governments have employed staff and hired code cracker services for studying encryption and breaking codes. Wars and spying (in many domains including industry, agriculture, health, finance, and politics) have been the main vectors of cryptanalysis development.

Cryptanalysis relies on knowledge of the design details of encryption algorithms (in particular, algorithms for civilian applications are often public knowledge) and information about the structure of the plaintexts (such as the structure of e-banking transactions and administrative documents). The efficiency of cryptanalysis mainly depends on computation resources, plaintexts, and ciphertexts available to the attackers.

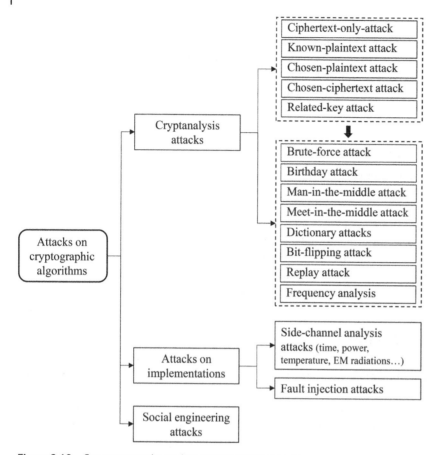

Figure 2.10 Common attacks against cryptographic algorithms.

Figure 2.10 summarizes the common attacks on cryptographic algorithms. In the following chapters, we only focus on cryptanalysis attacks.

Note. Cryptanalysis is not always a malicious activity. Indeed, all the standard cryptographic algorithms currently in use have been improved and secured due to the valuable involvement of cryptanalysts worldwide.

2.4.2 Categorization of Cryptanalysis Attacks

Cryptanalysis attacks may be categorized according to two main criteria:

- What information is available to attackers?
- What techniques are used to design the attacks?

Note. Cryptanalysis attacks are not exclusive; rather, they are commonly combined to design powerful attacks.

2.4.2.1 First Categorization of Cryptanalysis Attacks

One common approach to categorize cryptanalysis attacks is based on the kind of information available to attackers. Availability of ciphertexts or plaintexts is either obtained by intercepting messages in transit or by accessing storage devices containing encrypted and signed files. The amount of available information depends on when the attackers can collect information, i.e. permanently or at specific times (weekends, working times, etc.). The larger the collected information is, the higher the probability of attack success is. It is worth noticing that wireless technologies (in particular Wi-Fi) make message interception very easy, while interception through wired networks is much harder. In addition, stealing or copying storage devices (such as USB keys) give access to all ciphertexts.

There exist five types of attacks, when the information availability criterion is considered: ciphertext-only, known-plaintext, chosen-plaintext, chosen-ciphertext, and related-key attacks.

Ciphertext-only attack (COA): in this type of attack, the adversary has access to a subset or all ciphertexts; but, he/she has no access to plaintexts. The attacker tries to disclose some or all plaintexts from known ciphertexts or to recover the encryption key. COA is the easiest attack to mount in practice, because ciphertexts can be collected easily when wireless communications are used. However, COA alone is very unlikely to succeed, because the attacker lacks useful information on plaintexts.

Known-plaintext attack (KPA): in this attack type, the adversary has access to limited number of pairs of plaintexts and the corresponding ciphertexts. The KPA aims to recover the key. For example, spies can collect plaintext–ciphertext pairs and try to recover the key in order to disclose other plaintexts. Different methods (such as linear cryptanalysis) can be used to guide the key search.

Chosen-plaintext attack (CPA): in general, this attack type is used to identify the vulnerabilities of an algorithm. CPA assumes that the adversary has access to a black box (called *oracle*) which implements or emulates the algorithm to be analyzed. The attacker randomly chooses some plaintexts and queries the oracle to process the plaintexts. The returned result may be a ciphertext or signature, depending on the algorithm. Then, the adversary makes use of the collected plaintext–ciphertext pairs or data–tag pairs in order to recover the key or to generate message tags without knowing the key (so that a forged message–tag pair is validated by the recipient, which compromises the security of the authentication service). The adaptive CPA is a specific variant of the generic CPA, where the adversary selects the subsequent plaintexts to be processed by the oracle, depending on what has been learned from the previous queries. Examples of adaptive CPA are discussed in Chapter 10.

Chosen-ciphertext attack (CCA): like CPA, this attack type is used to identify vulnerabilities of a cryptographic algorithm. CCA assumes that the adversary has access to an oracle, which implements or emulates the algorithm to be analyzed. The attacker randomly chooses some ciphertexts or message tags and queries the oracle to process them. The returned result may be plaintexts or a signature validation results (i.e. the input tags are valid with regard to the provided messages), depending on the algorithm. Then, the adversary makes use of the collected plaintext–ciphertext pairs or data–tag pairs in order to recover the key or to generate message tags without knowing the key. The adaptive CCA is a specific variant of the generic CCA, where the adversary selects the subsequent ciphertexts or data–tag pairs to be processed by the oracle, depending on what has been learned from the previous queries.

Related-key attack: in this attack type, it is assumed that the adversary has access to a set of ciphertexts produced for the same plaintext, using two or several unknown keys (e.g. the attacker intercepted the traffic generated in several sessions; and in each session, a new key is used to encrypt a subset of plaintexts known to the adversary). In addition, the adversary knows that the keys have some mathematical relationships (for example, keys are generated with the same pseudorandom number generator,[7] which is initialized one time for all the sessions; or more naïvely, the session keys are generated with a linear function, i.e. $K_i = f(K_{i-1})$, where f is a linear function). The adversary tries to infer the key currently in use from the known plaintext–ciphertext pairs and relationships between keys. Notice that related-key attack is unrealistic against commonly used algorithms, mainly because key generation does not yield keys that have linear relationships.

2.4.2.2 Second Categorization of Cryptanalysis Attacks

The second categorization criterion refers to how the available information is processed to perform attacks. The naïve technique is to try everything in the search space; the other techniques aim to limit the resources (especially, computation time), while keeping high the success probability of attacks.

*Brute-force attack (also called *exhaustive search attack*)*: in this attack model, every possible key is tried until the correct one is found. For example, if the bit-length of the key is 128, the attacker has to try $2^{128} \approx 10^{13}$ keys. The attacker is assumed to have access either to plaintext–ciphertext pairs or to plaintexts and ciphertexts without known association. In the first case, the attacker considers each pair and encrypts the known plaintext with each possible key and compares it to the corresponding ciphertext, until the correct key is recovered. Depending on the cipher,[8] one or several pairs are needed to disclose the correct valid key. In the second case, each ciphertext is decrypted with each possible key and the decryption result is compared to the known plaintexts, until the correct key is recovered. Like the first case, more than one ciphertext may be considered before recovering the correct key. If no ciphertexts known to the attacker map to the known plaintexts, the attack cannot succeed.

Almost all cryptographic algorithms are vulnerable to brute-force attack. Fortunately, brute-force attack is computationally infeasible against cryptosystems used in practice. One fundamental requirement for any cryptographic algorithm to be used in operational cryptosystems is that brute-force attack must be computationally infeasible against the algorithm. However, an algorithm considered secure against brute-force attack at a given period may be no more secure some years later, because of advances in computer technologies.

Birthday attack: it refers to the *birthday paradox* (see Section 3.4), which states that given a group of persons, if one picks randomly $1.18 * \sqrt{365} \approx 23$ persons, the probability to have two persons with the same birthday date is close to ½. Intuitively, one may think that more persons are required to get two individuals with the same birthday date at a probability of ½. In cryptanalysis, birthday attack is a variant of brute-force technique, which is mainly used against hash functions and signature algorithms. For example, given a 128-bit signature algorithm, when the attacker knows a signature S for a message M, he/she can find, with a probability of ½, another message M', among 2^{64} messages, distinct from M, such that M and M' have the same signature S. Then, he/she can send a signed message, which will be validated by the recipient, while the message has never been signed by a legitimate user. Brute-force attack requires trying in average 2^{127} messages, while birthday attack requires $\sqrt{2^{128}} = 2^{64}$, which results in a significant reduction of the search space.

Meet-in-the-middle attack: it is another variant of brute-force attack, which drastically reduces the effort to perform a brute-force attack. It is a compromise (hence the term *meet in the middle*) between memory space and computation time. For example, a brute-force attack that requires 2^{192} time can be reduced to 2^{96} time and 2^{96} memory space. We'll see in Section 7.2.3.3 how the meet-in the middle attack was used to break block ciphers. Notice that meet-in-the-middle attack has no similarity with man-in-the-middle attack.

Man-in-the-middle attack: it is one of the most known attacks, which targets mainly public-key algorithms. In this attack, it is assumed that the attacker can intercept and modify messages exchanged between two legitimate users. Such an assumption is realistic in wireless networks and when the attacker can take control of routers. To illustrate how the attack works, consider the following scenario: a user A wants to receive encrypted messages from user B (see Figure 2.11). User A sends his/her public key to B. The attacker intercepts A's public key and instead sends his/her public key to B. Upon reception of a public key, user B is misled, thinking he/she is communicating with user A. User B encrypts messages with attacker's public key, and not with that of A. The attacker intercepts and reads any message sent to A; and can encrypt the received plaintexts using A's public key and send them to A or alternatively, he/she can relay fake messages. Notice that digital certificates, when available, prevent the attack above, because the attacker cannot modify the certificate of A to include his/her public key.

Dictionary attacks: there exist many variants referred to as dictionary attacks, among which:

- Build a list of passwords that are likely to be used by the target. Then, try one by one the selected passwords to log into the attacked system.
- Build a table (also called dictionary), which contains all the pairs of plaintext–ciphertext learned over a long period. Then, for each intercepted ciphertext, search in the table the corresponding plaintext. This attack is efficient when the vocabulary of plaintexts is limited.
- Build a subset of the key space composed of the keys that are the most likely to be used by the attacked entity. Then, for each intercepted ciphertext, try each key in the subset to recover the correct key. The probability of success depends on how the key subset is selected.

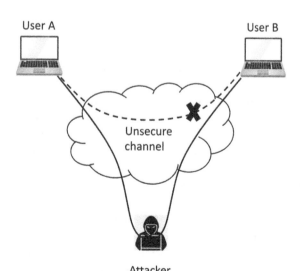

User A   User B

Unsecure channel

Attacker

Figure 2.11 Illustration of Man-in-the-middle attack.

Replay attack: it is a variant of man-in-the-middle attack, where the attacker intercepts messages sent to the victim. Then, he/she resends some or all messages to the victim, in such a way that the victim receives multiple copies of some fragments of the original traffic, which results in undertaking inconsistent actions, thus compromising integrity. Imagine that the attacker knows an intercepted message, which corresponds to money transfer to his/her account. He/she can resend several times the same message to the bank to have his/her account credited multiple times. Fortunately, protocols used by banks are resistant to replay attacks; they use techniques such as assigning a unique number (such as a timestamp) to each transaction.

Bit-flipping attack: it is an attack against stream ciphers in which the attacker changes one or several bits in the ciphertext, at specific positions, in such a way that the plaintext changes at the same positions. The attacker cannot control the resulting plaintext, if he/she does not know the original plaintext format. However, if he/she knows the message format and

Table 2.2 Relative frequency of letters in English texts (from Wikipedia).

Letter	%	Letter	%	Letter	%	Letter	%
E	12.70%	D	4.25%	Y	1.97%	J	0.15%
T	9.06%	L	4.03%	P	1.93%	X	0.15%
A	8.17%	C	2.78%	B	1.49%	Q	0.10%
O	7.51%	U	2.76%	V	0.98%	Z	0.07%
I	6.97%	M	2.41%	K	0.77%		
N	6.75%	W	2.36%				
S	6.33%	F	2.23%				
H	6.09%	G	2.02%				
R	5.99%						

the content of the bits to change, he/she can control the modified plaintext, because the ciphertext in stream ciphers is yielded by XORing the plaintext with the key. For example, if the attacker knows the format of a bank transaction, which contains the value 50 in bits at positions 100 to 120, he/she can change the value to 50+1024. Another example is discussed in Problem 4.9.

Frequency analysis: it is an attack particularly efficient when the attacker tries to disclose ciphertexts corresponding to texts in a natural language. The attacker exploits the frequency of letters in texts, the frequency of the first letter in words, the repetitions of words and spaces in texts; all these features differ from a language to another. For example, Table 2.2 shows the relative frequency of letters in English texts. When the same letter is always mapped to the same code, the attacker can compute the frequency of each code in the ciphertext, and then assumes that the code with the highest frequency is space, then the next is letter E, etc. In World War II, this technique (partially) helped to disclose some messages encrypted with the Enigma machine.

2.4.3 Attacks on Implementations of Cryptographic Algorithms

Implementation-oriented attacks are not performed against the design of cryptographic algorithms, but against their implementations. They are more difficult to perform, because the attacker material needs (in general) to be very close to the attacked system. The attacker needs to know all about the attacked cryptosystem (in particular characteristics of processors and software implementation of cryptographic operations); and he/she needs to have very accurate probes to get measurements. In general, implementation-oriented attacks are performed by attackers with excellent skills in electronics and by security agencies.

The two most popular categories of implementation attacks are side-channel analysis and fault injection attacks [7]. The attacks in the first category are passive; and exploit the information leakage related to cryptographic device internals through side channels. The attacks in the second category are (in general) invasive. Both categories can be combined to design powerful attacks.

2.4.3.1 Side-Channel Attacks

Side-channel attacks mainly include timing, power, electromagnetic radiation emission, and temperature analysis. These attacks are non-invasive; thus, they cannot be detected by attack systems.

Timing attacks: this type of attacks exploits the fact that different computations take different times, depending on the used processor. By measuring such times, it is possible to infer that a processor is carrying out some specific computations. For example, if the encryption takes a longer time, it indicates that the secret key is long. Another example is that the time taken by a multiplication varies significantly depending on the operands (e.g. multiplication by a power of 2 is performed by a left shift rather than a series of multiplications and additions). From the time taken by a modular exponentiation, used for example in RSA, the attacker may infer the number of 1s in the private key.

Power analysis attacks: they are effective ways to extract the content of cryptographic devices, such as smartcards [8]. With power analysis, the variation in power consumption of a device is used to infer some useful information about the secret content of devices. There exist two types of power analysis (PA): simple PA and differential PA. In the simple PA, the attacker observes the device's current consumption over a period of time. Different operations (e.g. multiplication and additions) exhibit different power profiles. In addition, when transferring data from a memory to CPU, the ratio of 1s vs 0s is reflected in the power profile. Therefore, the attacker can infer what type of function is being performed at any given time and what data pattern is being transferred or processed. Devices protected against simple PA create noise (by performing random computations) to avoid collecting the correct physical traces. Differential PA is a statistical method for analyzing power consumption to identify data-dependent correlations in order to improve the quality of information inferred by the attacker. It is more difficult to thwart than simple PA.

Electromagnetic emission attacks: these attacks exploit the electromagnetic radiations emitted by the attacked device, while running cryptographic code. Codes and their execution are characterized by electromagnetic radiation emission profiles. From the electromagnetic emission traces, the attacker can infer useful information on attacked device.

Temperature attacks: these attacks exploit the observed temperatures of the attacked device, while running cryptographic code. Codes and their execution are characterized by temperature profiles. From the temperature traces, the attacker can infer useful information on attacked device.

2.4.3.2 Fault-Injection Attacks

Fault-injection attacks rely on specialized hardware (such as laser beam) to inject faults on devices, such as smartphones, during the execution of a cryptographic algorithm. The voltage and clock frequency alterations are frequent attacks in this category. For example, the attacker can inject faults to disturb the last round of a block cipher or to erase data currently in use by the algorithm. Then, he/she observes the outputs of the device and derives useful information to recover a key or other secret data.

2.4.4 Practicality of Cryptanalysis Attacks

The attacks on cryptosystems described in this chapter are highly academic, as majority of them come from the academic community. Academic attacks are often against weakened versions of cryptographic algorithms (such as stream and block ciphers, message authentication code generation algorithms, and signature algorithms). In fact, many academic attacks involve quite unrealistic assumptions about application context as well as the capacities of attackers. For example, in some chosen-ciphertext attacks, the attacker needs an impractical number of plaintext–ciphertext pairs. Another example of unrealistic assumptions is to break a block cipher with 8 rounds, while in practice 16 rounds are required; and it is known that the time complexity of an attack grows (near) exponentially with the number of rounds. However, any probably realistic attack is carefully considered to improve the attacked algorithm. Another assumption is the availability of an oracle that implements or emulates the algorithm to attack. Under such assumption, the attacker can collect as much plaintext–ciphertext pairs and message–tag pairs as he/she wants. Chosen-plaintext and chosen-ciphertext attacks are likely to be used when testing the earlier versions of an algorithm rather than for attacking it in a real application.

Some attacks assume that the implementation or usage of cryptographic algorithms are not complying with standards. For example, a cryptosystem makes use of secret keys, which were not generated by a recommended pseudorandom number generation, or with small prime numbers. Under such assumption, keys become easy to recover. Some cryptographic algorithms, such as DES, have been deprecated without a clear proof that the block cipher has been entirely broken in practice, and sensitive data disclosed.

Cryptanalysis methods from governmental security and spying agencies are not public and make use of much more resources than those of academic cryptanalysts to break algorithms. Even if security agencies are able to break codes used by millions of people, they do not publish anything about their findings. Worse, most countries prohibit the civil use of cryptographic techniques beyond a certain key-size limit, or even prohibit the transfer of cryptographic technologies, which reduces the number of cryptosystems that could be attacked in practice. Therefore, the entire list of cryptographic algorithms, broken in practice, is not a public knowledge. As a precaution, immediately following a suspicion about the vulnerability of a cryptographic algorithm, the standardization bodies deprecate it.

Finally, it is worth noticing that cryptanalysis in the future (starting in the 2030s) would rely on quantum computers, which would have computation speeds surpassing those of current computer technologies. Attacks that are currently considered computationally infeasible would be easily feasible with quantum computers. For example, the recovery of RSA private key that would take (thousands or even more) years of computations using the current technologies would take minutes using quantum computers. Waiting for the massive arrival of quantum computers, the cryptographic algorithms currently used in civil applications are considered robust against known attacks, made by nongovernmental organizations. For more on security and quantum computers, refer to [9].

2.5 Steganography

The last section is a brief overview of *steganography*, which is another complex and ingenious category of techniques to hide contents. Unlike cryptography where intruders are aware that sensitive data is being communicated, because they can see the scrambled messages, in steganography, an unintended recipient or an intruder is unaware of the fact that observed data or message contains hidden information. With steganography, people not only want to protect the secrecy of an information by concealing it, but they also want to make sure any unauthorized person gets no evidence that the information even exists.

Steganography may be defined as the art and techniques of information hiding in other contents, referred to as containers. It existed before the advent of computers. Containers used by steganography may be texts, images, videos, audio files, etc. Since the early 2000s, steganography is used by spying and security agencies and by terrorists to disseminate messages through the internet. Before discussing some examples, it is worth noticing the limitations of steganography:

- Steganography results in a high overhead, because hiding a secret at an undetectable position in a container is not easy; and it requires time for the receiver to retrieve the hidden secret.
- Steganography requires some genius of concealment for both parties, the sender and the receiver of a content. Steganography applications are easy to understand once explained, but they are (very) difficult to design.
- Steganography looks like a symmetric cipher. Therefore, the sender and recipient must agree on the container to use and locations to retrieve the hidden secret.

2.5.1 Examples of Secret Hiding Without Using Computer

The first example is a steganography text, exchanged during World War II. A German spy sent to his hierarchy a secret in a telegram. In literature, the story is narrated in two message versions.

First version:

```
President's embargo ruling should have immediate notice. Grave situation affecting
international law. Statement foreshadows ruin of many neutrals. Yellow journals uni-
fying national excitement immensely.
```

Second version:

```
Apparently, neutral's protest is thoroughly discounted and ignored. Isman hard hit.
Blockade issue affects pretext for embargo on by-products, ejecting suets and veg-
etable oils.
```

Tacking the first letter (in first message) or second letter (in second message), the following message emerges: `Pershing sails from NY June I`. (*Pershing* was the name of a warship of US.)

The second example is to hide secrets in paintings. The technique consists of hiding letters in trees, people's hair, flowers, etc. Then, by retrieving and grouping the letters, texts are discovered.

2.5.2 Examples of Secret Hiding Using Computer

The first example consists of hiding a secret in a binary image file of an image (e.g. in a file.png). The technique takes advantage of how pixels are coded using three bytes to code RGB (Red, Green, and Blue) colors. It is used to adapt the least significant bits (say two bits) of each byte to insert the secret. The image recipient extracts the two least-significant bits of each byte to reconstruct the secret. When observed by people not suspecting any hidden secret, both pictures are similar, just a difference in pixel brightness.

The second example consists of hiding a secret in an audio file. A typical WAV (Waveform Audio File) represents one audio sample with a 16-bit number. A person could split up the secret message into bits and embed them, one at a time, into each audio sample; thus changing only the amplitude of the sample by 1 at maximum. Human ear is far from detecting this change. In this manner, the secret is embedded in the audio file without noticeable change and without altering the file size. When people not suspecting any hidden secret listen to both versions of the WAV, they are unable to detect any difference.

The story of the third example is linked to Joe Biden's inauguration, in 2020; but, the technique could have been used in other contexts. The white house website presented the main events of the ceremony with a picture of the president and other details. Some hours after posting the content, crackers published on social networks, a message to explain how white house services have included call-for-hackers. The included secret was in an HTML comment line and says: `<!-- If you're reading this, we need your help building back better >`. The lesson to learn from this example is that comment lines in a code (of any programming language) may be used to hide secrets without affecting the code itself. This form of steganography is the easiest technique to hide secrets, which can reach not only a single person, but also a wider public in a country or worldwide.

The last example is related to the terrorist attack of September 11, 2001. Many people claim that the terrorist attack was planned using steganography over Internet. On February 5, 2001, *USA Today* reported the following: "Lately, al-Qaeda operatives have been sending hundreds of encrypted messages that have been hidden in files on digital photographs on the auction site eBay.com." The lesson to be learned from this example is that banal web pages can serve as vectors for the dissemination of messages, thus escaping security agencies that can break ciphers with very large keys.

2.6 Exercises and Problems

2.6.1 List of Exercises and Problems

Exercise 2.1
How many distinct keys can be generated?
- using five distinct Latin letters
- using five Latin letters
- using 10 decimal digits

Exercise 2.2
What is the primary difference between Meet-in-the-middle and Man-in-the-middle attacks?

Exercise 2.3
Explain why a cipher designed according to Kerckhoffs's principle is very likely to be stronger than one that does not follow the same principle.

Exercise 2.4
What is the main drawback of One-time pad cipher?

Exercise 2.5
How computational security differs from unconditional security? Which one is realistic when we consider existing cryptographic algorithms?

Exercise 2.6
Assuming that an attacker can test, per second, 2^{20} keys of a bit-length of 50. How long would a brute-force attack take?

Problem 2.1
Consider the following cryptosystem:
- Plaintext space: $\mathcal{M} = \{a, b, c\}$
- Ciphertext space: $\mathcal{C} = \{1, 2, 3\}$
- Key space: $\mathcal{K} = \{k_1, k_2, k_3\}$

With the following probability distributions:
- Probability distribution of plaintexts: $Pr[M = a] = 1/2$, $Pr[M = b] = 1/3$, $Pr[M = c] = 1/6$
- Probability distribution of keys: $Pr[K = k_i] = 1/3$, for $i \in \{1, 2, 3\}$.

The encryption matrix is as follows:

	a	b	c
k_1	3	2	1
k_2	1	3	2
k_3	2	1	3

Does the cryptosystem as defined above satisfy the perfect secrecy condition?

Problem 2.2

Consider the following cryptosystem:

Plaintext space: $\mathcal{M} = \{a, b, c\}$

Ciphertext space: $\mathcal{C} = \{1, 2, 3, 4\}$

Key space: $\mathcal{K} = \{k_1, k_2, k_3\}$

With the following distributions:

- Probability distribution of plaintexts: $Pr[M = a] = 1/2$, $Pr[M = b] = 1/3$, $Pr[M = c] = 1/6$.

- Probability distribution of keys: $Pr[K = k_i] = 1/3$, for $i \in \{1, 2, 3\}$.

The encryption matrix is as follows:

	a	b	c
k_1	1	2	3
k_2	2	3	4
k_3	3	4	1

Does the cryptosystem as defined above satisfy the perfect secrecy condition?

Problem 2.3

Consider the following cryptosystem:

Plaintext space: $\mathcal{M} = \{0, 1, 2\}$

Ciphertext space: $\mathcal{C} = \{0, 1, 2\}$

Key space: $\mathcal{K} = \{k_1, k_2, k_3, k_4\}$

With the following distributions:

- Probability distribution of plaintexts: $Pr[M = 0] = 1/3$, $Pr[M = 1] = 1/4$, $Pr[M = 2] = 5/12$

- Probability distribution of keys: $Pr[K = k_i] = 1/4$ for $i \in \{1, 2, 3, 4\}$.

The encryption operation is defined by $E_{k_i}(m) = 2m + i \bmod 3$, for $m \in \{0, 1, 2\}$ and $i \in \{1, 2, 3, 4\}$.

Does the cryptosystem as defined above satisfy the perfect secrecy condition?

Problem 2.4

Prove that One-time pad cipher satisfies the perfect secrecy condition. Assume that all plaintexts and ciphertexts have the same probability distribution of 2^{-n}, where n denotes the bit-length of plaintext (or ciphertext). Also assume that each plaintext is encrypted using a distinct $2n$-bit key.

Problem 2.5

Consider a cryptosystem where messages of two Latin letters are encrypted using Caesar's cipher; both letters of a message are encrypted with the same key. Prove that the cryptosystem does not satisfy the perfect secrecy condition. Assume that all letters and all keys (0 to 25) have the same probability distribution.

2.6.2 Solutions to Exercises and Problems

Exercise 2.1

- $26 * 25 * 24 * 23 * 22$ keys can be generated using five distinct letters.
- 26^5 keys can be generated using five letters.
- 10^{10} keys can be generated using 10 decimal digits.

Exercise 2.2

The primary difference between Man-in-the-middle and Meet-in-the-middle attacks is that the first one is interactive (i.e. the attacker participates online in the communication), while the second one is not (i.e. the attacker collects some plaintext–ciphertext pairs, prepares some encryption or decryption operations, and stores them in memory, and then tries a set of keys to disclose the correct one).

Exercise 2.3

Kerckhoffs's principle states that "a cryptosystem should be secure even if everything about the system, with the exception of the key, is public knowledge." This means that the only secret that the adversary can discover is the key. If the design of a cipher does not fulfill Kerckhoffs's principle, it means that some design features (e.g. computation formulas, constants, format of data) are hidden because they increase the security of the cipher. Therefore, the cipher has multiple points of weaknesses, and discovering each point provides more information to the attacker to break the cipher. In addition, when the design of a cipher is public, the honest cryptanalysts may participate in its analysis and then address any discovered weakness to make the cipher stronger. However, when the internal design of a cipher is hidden, only malicious cryptanalysts may be interested in breaking the cipher and disclose sensitive data.

Exercise 2.4

The main drawback of OTP cipher is that it is impractical when a huge number of messages are to be encrypted. Each message requires to use a distinct key, which is communicated to the recipient before sending the encrypted message.

Exercise 2.5

Unconditional security means that whatever the resources used by adversaries, the cryptographic algorithm cannot be broken, while computational security means that the code cannot be broken, assuming that the adversaries make use of limited and reasonable resources. All existing cryptographic algorithms used in practice are (assumed to be) computationally secure.

Exercise 2.6

The key space has 2^{50} elements. The time required to test all keys is $2^{50}/2^{20}$ seconds. $\dfrac{2^{30}}{60*60*24*365} \approx 34$ years.

Problem 2.1

In general, given the plaintext probability distribution (i.e. $Pr[M=m]$ is known for each $m \in \mathcal{M}$), the probability distribution of a ciphertext $c \in \mathcal{C}$ yielded by any key $k \in \mathcal{K}$ using a plaintext space $\mathcal{M}$ is defined by:

$$Pr[C=c] = \sum_{k \in \mathcal{K}} \left(Pr[K=k] * Pr[M=D_k(c)] \right)$$

where $\mathcal{M}$, $\mathcal{C}$, and $\mathcal{K}$ denote the plaintext, ciphertext, and key spaces, respectively; M, C, and K denote the random variables associated with plaintext, ciphertext, and key, respectively. $D_k(c)$ denotes the decryption of ciphertext c using the key k. Compute the probability distribution of the ciphertexts:

$$Pr[C=1] = Pr[K=k_2]*Pr[M=a)] + Pr[K=k_3]*Pr[M=b)] +$$
$$Pr[K=k_1]*Pr[M=c)] = \frac{1}{3}*\frac{1}{2}+\frac{1}{3}*\frac{1}{3}+\frac{1}{3}*\frac{1}{6}=\frac{1}{3}$$

$$Pr[C=2] = \frac{1}{3}*\frac{1}{2}+\frac{1}{3}*\frac{1}{3}+\frac{1}{3}*\frac{1}{6}=\frac{1}{3}$$

$$Pr[C=3] = \frac{1}{3}*\frac{1}{2}+\frac{1}{3}*\frac{1}{3}+\frac{1}{3}*\frac{1}{6}=\frac{1}{3}.$$

Compute the conditional probability distribution of the plaintexts

$$Pr[M=a\,|\,C=1] = \frac{Pr[M=a]*Pr[C=1\,|\,M=a]}{Pr[C=1]} = \frac{\frac{1}{2}*\frac{1}{3}}{\frac{1}{3}} = \frac{1}{2}$$

$$Pr[M=a\,|\,C=2] = \frac{Pr[M=a]*Pr[C=2\,|\,M=a]}{Pr[C=2]} = \frac{\frac{1}{2}*\frac{1}{3}}{\frac{1}{3}} = \frac{1}{2}$$

$$Pr[M=a\,|\,C=3] = \frac{Pr[M=a]*Pr[C=3\,|\,M=a]}{Pr[C=3]} = \frac{\frac{1}{2}*\frac{1}{3}}{\frac{1}{3}} = \frac{1}{2}$$

$$Pr[M=b\,|\,C=1] = \frac{\frac{1}{3}*\frac{1}{3}}{\frac{1}{3}} = \frac{1}{3} \qquad Pr[M=b\,|\,C=2] = \frac{\frac{1}{3}*\frac{1}{3}}{\frac{1}{3}} = \frac{1}{3}$$

$$Pr[M=b|C=3]=\frac{\frac{1}{3}*\frac{1}{3}}{\frac{1}{3}}=\frac{1}{3} \quad Pr[M=c|C=1]=\frac{\frac{1}{6}*\frac{1}{3}}{\frac{1}{3}}=\frac{1}{6}$$

$$Pr[M=c|C=2]=\frac{\frac{1}{6}*\frac{1}{3}}{\frac{1}{3}}=\frac{1}{6} \quad Pr[M=c|C=3]=\frac{\frac{1}{6}*\frac{1}{3}}{\frac{1}{3}}=\frac{1}{6}.$$

The cryptosystem satisfies the perfect secrecy condition.

Problem 2.2

We reuse the solution to Problem 2.1 (which provides the general formula to compute the probability distribution of ciphertexts):

$$Pr[C=1]=\frac{1}{3}*\frac{1}{2}+\frac{1}{3}*\frac{1}{6}=\frac{2}{9}$$

$$Pr[C=2]=\frac{1}{3}*\frac{1}{2}+\frac{1}{3}*\frac{1}{3}=\frac{5}{18}$$

$$Pr[C=3]=\frac{1}{3}*\frac{1}{2}+\frac{1}{3}*\frac{1}{3}+\frac{1}{3}*\frac{1}{6}=\frac{1}{3}$$

$$Pr[C=4]=\frac{1}{3}*\frac{1}{3}+\frac{1}{3}*\frac{1}{6}=\frac{1}{6}.$$

Compute the conditional probability distribution of the plaintexts

$$Pr[M=a|C=1]=\frac{Pr[M=a]*Pr[C=1|M=a]}{Pr[C=1]}=\frac{\frac{1}{2}*\frac{1}{3}}{\frac{2}{9}}=\frac{3}{4}$$

$$Pr[M=a|C=2]=\frac{Pr[M=a]*Pr[C=2|M=a]}{Pr[C=2]}=\frac{\frac{1}{2}*\frac{1}{3}}{\frac{5}{18}}=\frac{3}{5}$$

$$Pr[M=a|C=3]=\frac{Pr[M=a]*Pr[c=3|M=a]}{Pr[C=3]}=\frac{\frac{1}{2}*\frac{1}{3}}{\frac{1}{3}}=\frac{1}{2}$$

$$Pr[M=a|C=4]=\frac{Pr[M=a]*Pr[C=4|M=a]}{Pr[C=4]}=\frac{\frac{1}{2}*0}{\frac{1}{6}}=0$$

$$Pr[M=b|C=1]=\frac{\frac{1}{3}*0}{\frac{2}{9}}=0 \quad Pr[M=b|C=2]=\frac{\frac{1}{3}*\frac{1}{3}}{\frac{5}{18}}=\frac{2}{5}$$

$$Pr[M=b|C=3]=\frac{\frac{1}{3}*\frac{1}{3}}{\frac{1}{3}}=\frac{1}{3} \quad Pr[M=b|C=4]=\frac{\frac{1}{3}*\frac{1}{3}}{\frac{1}{6}}=\frac{2}{3}$$

$$Pr[M = c \mid C = 1] = \frac{\frac{1}{6} * \frac{1}{3}}{\frac{2}{9}} = \frac{1}{4} \qquad Pr[M = c \mid C = 2] = \frac{\frac{1}{6} * 0}{\frac{5}{18}} = 0$$

$$Pr[M = c \mid C = 3] = \frac{\frac{1}{6} * \frac{1}{3}}{\frac{1}{3}} = \frac{1}{6} \qquad Pr[M = c \mid C = 4] = \frac{\frac{1}{6} * \frac{1}{3}}{\frac{1}{6}} = \frac{1}{3}.$$

The cryptosystem does not satisfy the perfect secrecy condition.

Problem 2.3

Matrix of encryption is as follows:

	0	1	2
k_1	1	0	2
k_2	2	1	0
k_3	0	2	1
k_4	1	0	2

We reuse the solution to Problem 2.1 (which provides the general formula to compute the probability distribution of ciphertexts):

$$Pr(C = 0) = \frac{1}{4} * \frac{1}{3} + \frac{1}{4} * \frac{1}{4} + \frac{1}{4} * \frac{1}{4} + \frac{1}{4} * \frac{5}{12} = \frac{5}{16}$$

$$Pr(C = 1) = \frac{1}{4} * \frac{1}{3} + \frac{1}{4} * \frac{1}{3} + \frac{1}{4} * \frac{1}{4} + \frac{1}{4} * \frac{5}{12} = \frac{1}{3}$$

$$Pr(C = 2) = \frac{1}{4} * \frac{1}{3} + \frac{1}{4} * \frac{1}{4} + \frac{1}{4} * \frac{5}{12} + \frac{1}{4} * \frac{5}{12} = \frac{17}{48}.$$

Compute the conditional probability distribution of the plaintexts

$$Pr[M = 0 \mid C = 0] = \frac{Pr[M = 0] * Pr[C = 0 \mid M = 0]}{Pr[C = 0]} = \frac{\frac{1}{3} * \frac{1}{4}}{\frac{5}{16}} = \frac{4}{15}$$

$$Pr[M = 0 \mid C = 1] = \frac{Pr[M = 0] * Pr[C = 1 \mid M = 0]}{Pr[C = 1]} = \frac{\frac{1}{3} * 2 * \frac{1}{4}}{\frac{1}{3}} = \frac{1}{2}$$

$$Pr[M = 1 \mid C = 2] = \frac{Pr[M = 1] * Pr[C = 2 \mid M = 1]}{Pr[C = 2]} = \frac{\frac{1}{4} * \frac{1}{4}}{\frac{17}{48}} = \frac{3}{17}.$$

None of the three pairs above satisfies the perfect secrecy condition. Notice that a single pair is sufficient to state that the cryptosystem does not satisfy the perfect secrecy condition.

Problem 2.4

Let $\mathcal{M}$, $\mathcal{C}$, and $\mathcal{K}$ denote the plaintext, ciphertext, and key spaces, respectively. Let M, C, and K denote the random variables associated with plaintext, ciphertext, and key, respectively. Let $m \in \mathcal{M}$ be a plaintext and $c \in \mathcal{C}$, a ciphertext. Let n denote the bit-length of plaintext, ciphertext, and key.

By definition of OTP cipher, given c and m, $\exists k \in \mathcal{K} \mid m \oplus k = c$.

Since all plaintexts and ciphertexts have the same probability of 2^{-n} and each plaintext is encrypted using a distinct key,

$$Pr[C = c \mid M = m] = Pr[M \oplus K = c \mid M = m]$$

$$= Pr[m \oplus K = c] = Pr[K = m \oplus c] = 2^{-n}. \tag{a}$$

Using the conditional probability:

$$Pr[M = m \mid C = c] = \frac{Pr[M = m] * Pr[C = c \mid M = m]}{Pr[C = c]} \tag{b}$$

$$Pr[C = c] = \sum_{m' \in \mathcal{M}} \left(Pr[C = c \mid M = m'] * Pr[M = m'] \right). \tag{c}$$

Using (a), (b), and (c)

$$Pr[M = m \mid C = c] = \frac{Pr[M = m] * 2^{-n}}{\sum_{m' \in \mathcal{M}} \left(2^{-n} * Pr[M = m'] \right)} =$$

$$\frac{Pr[M = m]}{\sum_{m' \in \mathcal{M}} \left(Pr[M = m'] \right)} = \frac{Pr[M = m]}{1}.$$

Therefore, the OTP cipher satisfies the perfect secrecy condition.

Problem 2.5
To prove that a Caesar's cipher where both letters of the same message are encrypted using the same key does not satisfy

the perfect secrecy condition (2.1), we need just to find a counterexample. By Bayes's theorem, condition (2.1) becomes:

$$\frac{Pr[C = c \mid M = m] * Pr[M = m]}{Pr[C = c]} = Pr[M = m].$$

Take a plaintext $m = "AC"$ and a ciphertext $c = "ZZ"$. When all the plaintexts have the same probability distribution,

$Pr[M = "AC"] = \frac{1}{26 * 26}.$

$Pr[C = "ZZ" \mid M = "AC"] = 0$, because no key can associate the ciphertext $"ZZ"$ with the plaintext $"AC"$. Therefore,

$Pr[M = "AC" \mid C = "ZZ"] = \frac{0 * Pr[M = m]}{Pr[C = c]} = 0 \neq \frac{1}{26 * 26}$, which contradicts condition (2.1). Therefore, the considered

Caesar's cipher does not satisfy the perfect secrecy condition.

Notes

1 Both symmetric and asymmetric cryptography.

2 Symmetric cryptography only.

3 Asymmetric cryptography only.

4 Integrity is verified only if either data or tag may be altered, but not both.

5 For example, some ciphers have been deprecated because attackers had broken the cipher assuming 8 rounds, while the cipher makes use of 14 rounds. It is a partial breaking.

6 Some standard cryptographic algorithms have been selected after a call (e.g. NIST calls).

7 We'll see in Chapter 16 that the initialization value of pseudorandom number generator (PRNG) must be secret, because PRNGs used in practice are deterministic. If the adversary knows the initialization value of a PRNG, then he/she can compute the sequence of generated random numbers.

8 We'll see later in the book that some plaintexts may be mapped to the same ciphertext using more than a single key.

References

1 Katz, J. and Lindell, Y. (2007). *Introduction to Modern Cryptography*. CRC Press.

2 Menezes, A., van Oorschot, P., and Vanstone, S. (2001). *Handbook of Applied Cryptography*. CRC Press.

3 Paar, C. and Pelzl, J. (2010). *Understanding Cryptography*. Springer.

4 Trappe, W. and Washington, L.C. (2020). *Introduction to Cryptography with Coding Theory*. Pearson.

5 Singh, S. (2000). *The Code Book: The Evolution of Secrecy from Ancient Egypt to Quantum cryptography*. Anchor books.

6 Schneier, B. (2003). *Beyond Fear: Thinking Sensible about Security in an Uncertain World*. Copernicus Books.

7 Shepherd, C., Markantonakis, K., van Heijningen, N. et al. (2021). Physical fault injection and side-channel attacks on mobile devices: a comprehensive analysis. *Elsevier Computer & Security* 111: 1–31.

8 Mangard, S., Oswald, E., and Popp, T. (2007). *Power Analysis Attacks, Revealing the Secrets of Smart Cards*. Springer.

9 NIST. Post-Quantum Cryptography. [Online]. Available from: https://csrc.nist.gov/projects/post-quantum-cryptography (Cited 2023 April).

3

Mathematical Basics and Computation Algorithms for Cryptography

Cryptography is a discipline that requires a background in mathematics. All encryption, decryption, and signature algorithms are based on notions and theorems known in number theory, modular arithmetic, and abstract algebra. Before we start the presentation and analysis of cryptographic algorithms, we need to review basics from number theory and abstract algebra. This chapter aims to review and present, with examples and exercises, the mathematical background to address cryptography algorithms. Seminal theorems are given with the names of their authors. Proofs of theorems are not included in this chapter and can be found in many books and papers on the topics [1–6].

To make attacks against cryptosystems computationally infeasible, numbers used in cryptographic algorithms are very large (in magnitude of $2^{160}, 2^{256}, 2^{2048}$, etc.). Therefore, optimized (in term of execution time) computation methods are needed. In addition to mathematical basics, algorithms commonly used to do fast computations in cryptographic algorithms are addressed in this chapter. Finally, the birthday paradox is presented; it is useful for the analysis of attack complexity.

According to the mathematics and computation algorithms skills of the reader, he/she may:

- Skip this chapter and address directly cryptographic algorithms.
- Learn basics, move to cryptographic algorithms, and return to this chapter to retrieve the needed facts and results.
- Learn the basics and theorems and deepen through the examples and exercises included, then move to cryptographic algorithms.

3.1 Number Theory Notations, Definitions, and Theorems

Notations
$\mathbb{N}$: set of natural numbers $\{0, 1, 2, 3, \ldots\}$
$\mathbb{Z}$: set of integers $\{\ldots, -3, -2, -1, 0, 1, 2, 3, \ldots\}$
$\mathbb{D}$: set of decimal numbers
$\mathbb{Q}$: set of rational numbers
$\mathbb{R}$: set of real numbers
$x \mid y$: x divides y (or y is a multiple of x)
$exp1 \mid exp2$: $exp1$ such that $exp2$ holds
$\lfloor x \rfloor$: greatest integer less than or equal to x
$\lceil x \rceil$: least number greater than or equal to x
$GCD(a, b$: greatest common divider of a and b
$LCM\ (a, b$: least common multiplier of a and b
$\vee$: logical operator *or*
$\wedge$: logical operator *and*
$\neg$: logical operator *not*
(Continued)

Cryptography: Algorithms, Protocols, and Standards for Computer Security, First Edition. Zoubir Z. Mammeri.
© 2024 John Wiley & Sons Inc. Published 2024 by John Wiley & Sons Inc.

$\mathbb{Z}_n$: set of positive integers less than n, i.e. $\mathbb{Z}_n = \{0, 1, 2, ..., n-1\}$

$\mathbb{Z}_n^*$: set of invertible elements of $\mathbb{Z}_n$, i.e. $\mathbb{Z}_n^* = \{a \in \mathbb{Z}_n \mid GCD(a,n) = 1\}$

F_p: finite field with p prime

F_{q^m}: finite field with power prime q^m

F_p^*: set of nonzero elements of a field, i.e. $F_p^* = F_p - \{0\}$

$\langle g \rangle$: group generated by generator g

$F[x]$: set of polynomials over the field F

$F_{p^m}[x]$: set of polynomials of degree less than m with coefficients in $\mathbb{Z}_p$

$F_{2^m}[x]$: set of polynomials of degree less than m with coefficients in $\mathbb{Z}_2$

$F_{2^m}[x]/f(x)$: field F_{2^m} under the reduction polynomial $f(x)$

3.1.1 Basic Terms and Facts of Number Theory

Definition 3.1 Greatest common divider: *a positive integer c is the greatest common divider of two integers a and b if*

i) $(c \mid a) \wedge (c \mid b)$

ii) $\forall c' \mid (c' \mid a) \wedge (c' \mid b) \Rightarrow (c' \mid c) \wedge (c \geq c')$

Example 3.1

$GCD(15, 100) = 5 \quad GCD(150, 700) = 50$

Definition 3.2 Least common multiplier: *a positive integer m is the least common multiple of two integers, a and b, if*

i) $(a \mid m) \wedge (b \mid m)$

ii) $\forall m' \mid (a \mid m') \wedge (b \mid m') \Rightarrow (m \mid m') \wedge (m \leq m')$

Example 3.2

$LCM(15, 100) = 300 \quad LCM(150, 700) = 2100$

Definition 3.3 Prime: *a prime is an integer greater than 1 that is not a product of two (or more) smaller integers.*

Example 3.3

$3, 11, 47, 73, 97$, and 103 are primes.

Definition 3.4 Coprime or **relatively prime**: *two positive integers a and b are coprime (also called relatively prime) if* $GCD(a,b) = 1$.

Example 3.4 $(12, 49)$ and $(39, 32)$ are two pairs of coprimes.

Definition 3.5 Prime power: *a prime power is an integer that can be expressed as* p^m, *where p is a prime and m a positive integer.*

Example 3.5 $2^2, 2^8, 5^4, 101^4$ are prime powers.

$12^3, 25^4$, and 100^3 are not prime powers, because 12, 25, and 100 are not prime.

Definition 3.6 Integer factorization and **composite number**: *every integer $N > 2$ can be written as a product of powers, i.e. $N = p_1^{n_1} * p_2^{n_2} * ... * p_k^{n_k}$, where $p_1, p_2, ..., p_k$ are distinct prime factors of N and $n_1, n_2, ..., n_k$ are positive integers. For every integer N, the factorization is unique (the order of the primes in the product does not matter). A number is said to be composite if it has at least two factors.*

Example 3.6

$91476 = 2^2 * 3^3 * 7 * 11^2.$

2, 3, 7, and 9 are primes and are factors of the composite number 91476.

Definition 3.7 Euler's totient function *(or **Euler's phi function**): for an integer $N \geq 1$, the number of integers in the interval $[1, N]$ which are coprime to N is denoted $\varphi(N)$. φ is called Euler totient function (or Euler phi function).*

Example 3.7 $\varphi(n) = ?$

- $n = 12$: integers in range $[1, 12]$, which are relatively prime to 12, are 1, 5, 7, and 11. Hence, $\varphi(12) = 4$.
- $n = 9$: integers in range $[1, 9]$, which are relatively prime to 9, are 1, 2, 4, 5, 7, and 8. Hence, $\varphi(9) = 6$.
- $n = 7$: integers in range $[1, 7]$, which are relatively prime to 7, are 1, 2, 3, 4, 5, and 6. Thus, $\varphi(7) = 6$.

Theorem 3.1 **Euler totient function properties**

Let N, a, b, p, k, p_1, p_2, ..., p_k, n_1, n_2, ..., and n_k be nonnegative integers.
  i) If p is a prime, then $\varphi(p) = p - 1$.
 ii) If $GCD(a,b) = 1$, then $\varphi(a * b) = \varphi(a) * \varphi(b)$.
iii) If $N = p_1^{n_1} * p_2^{n_2} * ... * p_k^{n_k}$ and $\forall i, j \in (1, k)$ with $i \neq j$, $p_i \neq p_j$, and p_i is prime $\forall i \in (1, k)$, then
$\varphi(N) = (p_1^{n_1} - p_1^{n_1 - 1})(p_2^{n_2} - p_2^{n_2 - 1})...(p_k^{n_k} - p_k^{n_k - 1}).$

Theorem 3.2   For integers a, b, c if $a|c$ and $b|c$ and a and b are coprime, then $ab|c$.

Example 3.8   Let $a = 7$, $b = 12$, and $c = 420$; a and b are coprime. The following hold:

$7 | 420$, because 420 is multiple of 7. $12 | 420$, because 420 is a multiple of 12.

$(7 * 12) | 420$, because 420 is a multiple of 84.

3.1.2 Sets

Definition 3.8 Set:

 i) *A set is a collection of elements.*
ii) *A finite set is a set that has a finite number of elements.*

Example 3.9

$S_1 = \{0, 1, 2, 3, 4, 5, 6, 7, 8, 9\}$ is a finite set composed of 10 integers.

$S_2 = \{..., -2, -1, 0, 1, 2, 3, ...\}$ is an infinite set of negative and positive integers.

Definition 3.9 Order *(or **cardinality**): the order, also referred to as cardinality, of a set S is the number of elements of S. It is denoted $|S|$ or $ord(S)$.*

Example 3.10

$S_1 = \{0, 1, 2, 3, 4, 5, 6, 7, 8, 9\} \Rightarrow ord(S_1) = |S_1| = 10.$

3.1.3 Modulo Operator and Equivalence Class

Definition 3.10 Congruence: *let a, b, and n be three positive integers. a is congruent to b modulo n, which is denoted $a \equiv b \bmod n$, if $n | (a - b)$. In other words, $a \equiv b \bmod n \Rightarrow \exists k \in \mathbb{Z} | a = b + kn$. In the congruence relation $a \equiv b \bmod n$, n is called the modulus and b the residue (or the remainder).*

The congruence also is denoted $a \equiv b \pmod{n}$. The remainder b is such $|b| < n$. In the usual convention, b is the least positive residue. Negative residue also can be used.

Example 3.11

$17 \equiv 2 \bmod 5$, which is the same as $17 \equiv -3 \bmod 5$.
$17 \equiv 1 \bmod 8$, which is the same as $17 \equiv -7 \bmod 8$.

In general, computations in cryptography algorithms make use of least positive residues.

Definition 3.11 Congruence class (*or* ***residue class***): *the congruence class modulo n of an integer $a \in \mathbb{Z}$, such that $|a| < n$, is the set of all integers x that have the same residue modulo n: $\{x \in \mathbb{Z} \mid x \equiv a \bmod n\}$. An equivalence class is an infinite set. All elements of an equivalence class mod n are equivalent, i.e. they are congruent to the same value mod n. Congruence class of integer a modulo n is denoted $\bar{a}_n$. It also is called* ***residue class*** *or simply residue of integer a.*

Example 3.12

– $\bar{1}_9 = \{\ldots, -17, -8, 1, 10, 19, 28, 37, \ldots\}$ is the congruence class $\bmod\ 9$ associated with element 1.
– $\overline{13}_{17} = \{\ldots, -21, -4, 13, 30, 47, 64, 81, \ldots\}$ is the congruence class $\bmod\ 17$ associated with element 13.

3.1.4 Basic Properties of Modular Arithmetic

Let a, b, k, and n be integers. The following are properties of modular arithmetic:

i) Reflexivity: $a \equiv a \bmod n$
ii) Symmetry: if $a \equiv b \bmod n$, then $b \equiv a \bmod n$
iii) Transitivity: if $a \equiv b \bmod n$ and $b \equiv c \bmod n$, then $a \equiv c \bmod n$
iv) Compatibility with translation: if $a \equiv b \bmod n$, then $a + k \equiv (b + k) \bmod n$
v) Compatibility by scaling: if $a \equiv b \bmod n$, then $k * a \equiv k * b \bmod n$
vi) Compatibility with exponentiation: if $a \equiv b \bmod n$, then $a^k \equiv b^k \bmod n$
vii) If $a_i \equiv b_i \bmod n$, for $i = 1, 2, \ldots, m$, then:
 • Compatibility with addition: $\sum_{i=1}^{m} a_i \equiv \sum_{i=1}^{m} b_i \bmod n$
 • Compatibility with multiplication: $\prod_{i=1}^{m} a_i \equiv \prod_{i=1}^{m} b_i \bmod n$
 • Compatibility with subtraction: $a_j - a_i \equiv b_j - b_i \bmod n, 1 \le i \le m, 1 \le j \le m$
viii) Compatibility with polynomial evaluation: If $a \equiv b \bmod n$ and $p(x)$ is any polynomial, then $p(a) \equiv p(b) \bmod n$.

The following lemma is very useful to reduce the amount of calculations. It is a direct consequence of property vii) above.

> **Lemma 3.1[1]** ***Modular arithmetic exponentiation rule:*** if a, n, and k are positive integers, then:
> $a^k \bmod n \equiv (a \bmod n)^k \bmod n$.

> **Lemma 3.2[2]** Let N be a product of primes $n_1, n_2, \ldots, n_k$. If $x \equiv a \bmod n$, then $x \equiv a \bmod n_i$ for $1 \le i \le k$.

3.1.5 $\mathbb{Z}_n$: Integers Modulo n

The set of integers *modulo n* is denoted $\mathbb{Z}/n\mathbb{Z}$, $\mathbb{Z}/n$, or simply $\mathbb{Z}_n$ and is defined by: $\mathbb{Z}_n = \{0, 1, 2, \ldots, n-1\}$. $\mathbb{Z}_n$ operations (such as addition and multiplication) are defined *modulo n*.

Example 3.13

– $\mathbb{Z}_2 = \{0,1\}$: $100 \bmod 2 = 4 \bmod 2 = 1000 \bmod 2 = 0$
– $\mathbb{Z}_{12} = \{0, 1, 2, 3, \ldots, 11\}$: $1 \bmod 12 = 13 \bmod 12 = 25 \bmod 12 = 1$. $\mathbb{Z}_{12}$ may be used to represent the set of hours of day).

3.1.6 Multiplicative Inverse

Definition 3.12 Modular multiplicative inverse[3]: *let $a \in \mathbb{Z}_p$. The modular multiplicative inverse of a, if it exists, is an element $a^{-1} \in \mathbb{Z}_p$ such that $a * a^{-1} \equiv 1 \bmod p$.*

Example 3.14

– In $\mathbb{Z}_9$: $2^{-1} = 5$, because $2*5 \equiv 1 \, mod \, 9$
– In $\mathbb{Z}_{23}$: $2^{-1} = 12$, because $2*12 \equiv 1 \, mod \, 23$

Definition 3.13 Invertible element: *an element $a \in \mathbb{Z}_p$ is said to be invertible if its multiplicative inverse exists in $\mathbb{Z}_p$.*

Theorem 3.3 ***Existence of multiplicative inverse:*** an element $a \in \mathbb{Z}_n$ has a multiplicative inverse *modulo n* if and only if $GCD(a,n) = 1G$.

Definition 3.14 $\mathbb{Z}_n^*$: *the multiplicative group of $\mathbb{Z}_n$ denoted $\mathbb{Z}_n^*$ is the set of invertible elements of $\mathbb{Z}_n$. Formally,* $\mathbb{Z}_n^* = \{a \in \mathbb{Z}_n \mid GCD(a,n) = 1\}$.

Lemma 3.3[4] ***Cardinality of*** $\mathbb{Z}_n^*$: $\left|\mathbb{Z}_n^*\right| = \varphi(n)$.

Theorem 3.4 ***Euler's theorem:*** if $a \in \mathbb{Z}_n^*$, then $a^{\varphi(n)} \equiv 1 \, mod \, n$.

Theorem 3.5 ***Fermat's little theorem:*** if p is a prime and a is a positive integer coprime with p, then $a^{p-1} \equiv 1 \, mod \, p$.

Fermat's little theorem is a special case of Euler's theorem. If p is a prime, by Euler's totient function properties, $\varphi(p) = p - 1$.

| **Note.** Euler's and Fermat's little theorems are of prime importance to cryptography.

3.1.7 Modular Square Roots

Definition 3.15 Modular square root: *a modular square root r of an integer a modulo n is an integer greater than 1 such that:* $r^2 \equiv a \, mod \, n$.

Definition 3.16 Quadratic residue: *an integer a is called quadratic residue of n, if there exists an integer r, such that* $r^2 \equiv a \, mod \, n$. *Otherwise, a is called a quadratic* ***nonresidue***.

Theorem 3.6 ***Modular square root:*** if a square $r \, mod \, n$ exists, then there exists a second square root $-r$ modulo n.

Example 3.15

– 5 is a modular square root of 4 *mod* 7, because $5^2 \equiv 4 \, mod \, 7$. Thus, -5, which is equal to 2 *mod* 7, also is a modular square root of 4 *mod* 7, because $2^2 \equiv 4 \, mod \, 7$.
– 9 is a modular square root of 3 *mod* 13, because $9^2 \equiv 3 \, mod \, 13$. Thus, -9, which is equal to 4 *mod* 13, also is a modular square root of 3 *mod* 13, because $4^2 \equiv 3 \, mod \, 13$.

3.1.7.1 Square Root of Primes

Let p be a prime. With the exception of integer 2, all primes are odd. Thus, $\frac{p-1}{2}$ is an integer, for $p > 2$. In addition, $\varphi(p)$, the Euler totient of p, is equal to $p - 1$. Given two integers a and p, $r^2 \equiv a \, mod \, p$ may have a solution or not. Before trying to find a square root, one must first check if a solution exists. Given below is the condition to square root existence. Suppose $r^2 \equiv a \, mod \, p$ has a solution. Raising both sides to power $\frac{p-1}{2}$ results in:

$$(r^2)^{\frac{p-1}{2}} \equiv a^{\frac{p-1}{2}} \, mod \, p$$

$$r^{p-1} \equiv a^{\frac{p-1}{2}} \, mod \, p.$$

By Euler-Fermat theorem (Theorem 3.5), $r^{p-1} \equiv 1 \, mod \, p$. Hence, $a^{\frac{p-1}{2}} \equiv 1 \, mod \, p$. Therefore, if $r^2 \equiv a \, mod \, p$ has a solution, then $a^{\frac{p-1}{2}} \equiv 1 \, mod \, p$.

Theorem 3.7 *Euler's criterion:* given two integers a and p, such that $p > 2$ and a and p are coprime,

i) $a^{\frac{p-1}{2}} \equiv 1 \bmod p$, if there exists r such that $r^2 \equiv a \bmod p$

ii) $a^{\frac{p-1}{2}} \equiv -1 \bmod p$, if there does not exist r such that $r^2 \equiv a \bmod p$.

Definition 3.17 Legendre symbol: *let p be a prime greater than 2 and a an integer, Legendre symbol, denoted $\left(\dfrac{a}{p}\right)$, is defined by:*

$$\left(\frac{a}{p}\right) = \begin{cases} 0 & \text{if} & \mathrm{GCD}(a,p) \neq 1 \\ +1 & \text{if} & a \text{ is quadratic residue} \\ -1 & \text{if} & a \text{ is quadratic nonresidue} \end{cases}.$$

Example 3.16

$\left(\dfrac{1}{7}\right) = 1$, because $1^3 \equiv 1 \bmod 7$ $\left(\dfrac{2}{7}\right) = 1$, because $2^3 \equiv 1 \bmod 7$

$\left(\dfrac{3}{7}\right) = -1$, because $3^3 \not\equiv 1 \bmod 7$ $\left(\dfrac{4}{7}\right) = 1$, because $4^3 \equiv 1 \bmod 7$

$\left(\dfrac{5}{7}\right) = -1$, because $5^3 \not\equiv 1 \bmod 7$ $\left(\dfrac{6}{7}\right) = -1$, because $6^3 \not\equiv 1 \bmod 7$

$\left(\dfrac{7}{7}\right) = 0$, because $\mathrm{GCD}(7,7) \not\equiv 1$.

The Euler's criterion tells us that $r^2 \equiv a \bmod p$ has a solution if and only if $a^{\frac{p-1}{2}} \equiv 1 \bmod p$. However, it does not tell us how to find the solution.

Example 3.17

– Does $r^2 \equiv 3 \bmod 13$ have a solution?

Since $3^{\frac{13-1}{2}} = 3^6 \equiv 1 \bmod 13$, there are two solutions to $r^2 \equiv 3 \bmod 13$.

– Does $r^2 \equiv 31 \bmod 83$ have a solution?

Since $31^{\frac{83-1}{2}} = 31^{41} \equiv 1 \bmod 83$, there are two solutions to $r^2 \equiv 31 \bmod 83$.

Lemma 3.4[5]

if p is a prime greater than 2, then $\frac{p-1}{2}$ elements of $\mathbb{Z}_p^*$ are quadratic residues; and $\frac{p-1}{2}$ are quadratic nonresidues.

Example 3.18   Let $p = 7$.

$$p = 7 \Rightarrow \frac{p-1}{2} = 3.$$

$\mathbb{Z}_7^* = \{1, 2, 3, 4, 5, 6\}$.

Check using the Euler's criterion (Theorem 3.7):

$1^3 \equiv 1 \bmod 7$ $2^3 \equiv 1 \bmod 7$ $4^3 \equiv 1 \bmod 7$

$3^3 \equiv -1 \bmod 7$ $5^3 \equiv -1 \bmod 7$ $6^3 \equiv -1 \bmod 7$.

Hence, three (i.e. the half) elements in $\mathbb{Z}_7^*$ are square residues and three are square nonresidues.

The Euler's criterion is used to test if a solution exists. However, it does not tell us how to find the solution. Therefore, we need to do some (not easy) work. Given a prime p, there are three[6] alternatives to address: $p = 2$, $p \equiv 1 \bmod 4$, and $p \equiv 3 \bmod 4$.

i) *Case p = 2*

In such a case, $a \equiv 0 \bmod 2$ or $a \equiv 1 \bmod 2$.

$r = 0$, if $a \equiv 0 \bmod 2$ and $r = 1$, if $a \equiv 1 \bmod 2$.

ii) *Case $p \equiv 3 \bmod 4$*

Lemma 3.5[7] If p is a prime such that $p \equiv 3 \bmod 4$ and a is a quadratic residue of p, then a solution to $r^2 \equiv a \bmod p$ is given by $r = a^{\frac{p+1}{4}}$.

Example 3.19 $p = 83$ and $a = 4$

By the Euler's criterion, $4 \bmod 83$ has a solution, because $4^{\frac{83-1}{2}} \equiv 1 \bmod 83$.

The modular square roots of $4 \bmod 83$ are $\pm 4^{\frac{83+1}{4}} \bmod 83$, i.e. $+81$ and -81.

Check: $81^2 \equiv 4 \bmod 83$. $-81 \bmod 83 = 2$. Hence, $2^2 \equiv 4 \bmod 83$. Thus, 2 and 81 are square roots of $4 \bmod 83$.

iii) *Case $p \equiv 1 \bmod 4$*

The hardest case to find a modular square root is that when $p \equiv 1 \bmod 4$. The most commonly used algorithm to find square roots in such a case is *Tonelli-Shanks algorithm*, which is described in Section 3.3.5.1.

3.1.7.2 Square Roots for Multiple Primes

In case n is a product of k primes denoted n_1, n_2, ..., n_k, finding a square root to $r^2 \equiv a \bmod n$ requires much more effort. The method to solve such a problem is based on two well-known algorithms, Tonelli-Shanks's and Gauss's algorithms, which are presented in Sections 3.3.4 – 3.3.5.1.

3.1.8 List of Exercises and Problems

Exercise 3.1

Determine the integers, which are coprime with N, and then apply the Euler's totient function $\varphi()$ to check the result. Consider $N = 17, 42, 25$.

Exercise 3.2

1) Find the additive and multiplicative inverses of 27 in $\mathbb{Z}_{100}^*$.
2) Find the Euler totient: $\varphi(101)$, $\varphi(102)$, and $\varphi(500)$.

Exercise 3.3

1) Find an integer x such that $3^x \equiv 13 \bmod 17$.
2) Show that there does not exist an integer x such that $4^x \equiv 5 \bmod 31$.
3) In general, how hard is it to find $x \mid a^x \equiv b \bmod n$ with known integers a, b, and n?

Exercise 3.4

Apply Euler's theorem (Theorem 3.4) to find modular inverses of integers from 1 to 8 in $\mathbb{Z}_9^*$.

Exercise 3.5

Use (if applicable) theorems of Euler and Fermat (Theorems 3.4 and 3.5) to find $a^{-1} \bmod n$:

1) $a = 6$, $n = 7$
2) $a = 7$, $n = 15$
3) $a = 19$, $n = 101$. Hint: $19^{25} \equiv 1 \bmod 101, 19^{19} \equiv 5 \bmod 101$, and $19^5 \equiv 84 \bmod 101$
4) $a = 97$, $n = 100$. Hint: $97^{20} \equiv 1 \bmod 100$ and $97^{19} \equiv 33 \bmod 100$.

Exercise 3.6

Find x such that:

$x \equiv 4^{100} \bmod 17$

$9^x \equiv 13 \bmod 17$

$5^x \equiv 13 \bmod 17$

$7^x = 11 \bmod 13$

Problem 3.1

Prove Lemma 3.1.

Problem 3.2

Prove Lemma 3.2.

Problem 3.3

Prove Lemma 3.3.

Problem 3.4

1) Prove that if p is even, then any even integer has no multiplicative inverse in $\mathbb{Z}_p^*$.
2) Prove that the cardinality of $\mathbb{Z}_{2^m}^*$ is at most 2^{m-1}.

Problem 3.5

Let $p = 11$. Show that $\frac{p-1}{2}$ elements of $\mathbb{Z}_p^*$ are square residues and $\frac{p-1}{2}$ are square nonresidues.

Problem 3.6

Prove Lemma 3.4.

Problem 3.7

Prove Lemma 3.5.

Problem 3.8

Let u be an element $\mathbb{Z}_p^*$. Prove that:

1) $a = u^{(p-1)/2}$ is a square root of 1
2) $u^{(p-1)/2}$ is 1 or -1.

Problem 3.9

Prove the following lemma:

Given two distinct primes p and q, $p\left(p^{-1} mod\ q\right) + q\left(q^{-1} mod\ p\right) = pq + 1$.

3.2   Basic Algebraic Structures

3.2.1   Groups and Rings and Their Properties

3.2.1.1   Groups and Rings

Definition 3.18 Group: *a group, denoted $(G, \circ)$, is a set equipped with an operation $\circ$, which is usually the addition or the multiplication modulo n, satisfying the following properties for all elements x, y, $z \in G$:*

  i)   *Closeness: the group operation $\circ$ is closed. That is: $x \circ y = c, c \in G$*
 ii)   *Neutral element (also called identity): there exists an element e in G such that $e \circ x = x \circ e = x$*
iii)   *Inverse: for every $x \in G$ there exists $x' \in G$ such that $x \circ x' = x' \circ x = e$*
iv)   *Associativity of operation $\circ$: $x \circ (y \circ z) = (x \circ y) \circ z$*

Definition 3.19 Abelian group: *a group G is said to be abelian (or commutative) if $x \circ y = y \circ x$, $\forall x \in G$, $\forall y \in G$.*

Definition 3.20 Subgroup: *H, a subset of a group G, is called a subgroup of G if H is a group with respect to the operation $\circ$ over G.*

Definition 3.21 Additive and multiplicative groups: *if a group G is equipped with the addition operation (+), it is called additive group and denoted $(G, +)$ and its neutral element is 0. If a group G is equipped with the multiplication operation $(\times)$,[8] it is called multiplicative group and denoted $(G, \times)$ and its neutral element is 1.*

Definition 3.22 Order of a group: *the order of a group G, denoted $|G|$, is the number of elements in G. A group G is infinite if $|G|$ is infinite.*

Example 3.20

- $\mathbb{R}$ (the set of real numbers) is a group under the addition operation as well as under the multiplication operation. Any number $x \in \mathbb{R}$ has an additive inverse (i.e. $-x \in \mathbb{R}$) and a multiplicative inverse (i.e. $x^{-1} \in \mathbb{R}$).
- $\mathbb{N}$ (the set of positive integers) is neither a group under the addition operation nor a group under multiplication operation, because additive inverses are negatives and multiplicative inverses of most integers are not integers.
- $\mathbb{Z}_p$ (the set of integers modulo p) is a group under the addition operation, but it is not a group under multiplication operation, because some multiplicative inverses do not exist in $\mathbb{Z}_p$ when p is not prime.

Definition 3.23 Order of element: *the order of an element $a \in G$, denoted $ord(a)$, is the smallest positive integer k such that $a^k = a \circ a \circ \ldots \circ a \equiv e$, where e is the neutral element of G. If no such k exists, the element a is said to have an infinite order.*

Theorem 3.8

Let G denote a group $(\mathbb{Z}_p, *)$ and $a \in G$. If $a^k \equiv 1 \bmod p$, then $a^{m*k} \equiv 1 \bmod p$ for any positive integers m and k.

Theorem 3.8 is very useful to compute modular exponentiation. For example, one can immediately find that $2^6 = 64 \equiv 1 \bmod 9$. However, finding $2^{66666666666666} \bmod 9$ is more complex without using Theorem 3.8. Indeed, since the exponent is a multiple of 6 and $2^6 \bmod 9$ is known, by the previous theorem, one can easily find that $2^{66666666666666} \bmod 9 = 1$.

Example 3.21

- Let $(\mathbb{Z}_7, +)$ denote the group over the set $\{0, 1, 2, 3, 4, 5, 6\}$ equipped with the addition operation. $(\mathbb{Z}_7, +)$ is a finite group. Its cardinality is $|\mathbb{Z}_7| = 7$. The order of element 4 is 3, because $4 * 4 * 4 = 1 \bmod 7$.
- Let S denote the set $\{1, 2, 3, 4, 5, 6, 7, 8\}$. Let us check if S is a finite group under the multiplication operation. We have to check if all elements have inverses:

$$1 * 1 \equiv 1 \bmod 9 \qquad 2 * 5 \equiv 1 \bmod 9 \qquad 4 * 7 \equiv 1 \bmod 9$$
$$5 * 2 \equiv 1 \bmod 9 \qquad 7 * 4 \equiv 1 \bmod 9 \qquad 8 * 8 \equiv 1 \bmod 9$$

Elements 3 and 6 have no multiplicative inverses. Therefore, the set S is not a finite group under the multiplication operation, while $S' = \{1, 2, 4, 5, 7, 8\}$ is.
- Let $G = \{1, 2, 4, 5, 7, 8\}$ be a finite group under the multiplication operation. We check if all element orders are finite:

$ord(1) = 1$, because $1 * 1 = 1 \bmod 9$
$ord(2) = 6$, because $2 * 2 * 2 * 2 * 2 * 2 = 1 \bmod 9$
$ord(4) = 3$, because $4 * 4 * 4 = 1 \bmod 9$
$ord(5) = 6$, because $5 * 5 * 5 * 5 * 5 * 5 = 1 \bmod 9$
$ord(7) = 3$, because $7 * 7 * 7 = 1 \bmod 9$
$ord(8) = 2$, because $8 * 8 = 1 \bmod 9$

Therefore, all the elements of the group have an order less or equal to 6, which is the order of the group.

Definition 3.24 Ring: *a ring, denoted $(R, +, \times)$, is a set R equipped with two operations, addition and multiplication, satisfying the following properties:*

i) $\langle R, + \rangle$ *is an abelian group*
ii) *Associativity of operation $\times$: $a \times (b \times c) = (a \times b) \times c$*
iii) *Distributivity: $a \times (b + c) = (a \times b) + (a \times c)$ and $(b + c) \times a = (b \times a) + (c \times a)$*
iv) *Multiplicative identity: there exists an element $1 \in R \mid a \times 1 = 1 \times a = a$.*

Definition 3.25 Commutative ring: *a commutative ring, denoted $(R, +, \times)$, is a ring satisfying the following property: Commutativity of operation $\times$: $a \times b = b \times a$, for all $a, b \in R$.*

3.2.1.2 Cyclic Groups

Definition 3.26 ***Cyclic group***: *a cyclic group is a finite group that is generated by a single element g, called* **generator** *(or* **primitive element***) of the group.*

Properties of elements of a cyclic group

Let g be a generator of a cyclic group G with elements in $\mathbb{Z}_p$. Each element $a \in G$ can be written:

i) as a multiple of g in $(\mathbb{Z}_p, +)$ group:

$\forall a \in \mathbb{Z}_p, \exists k, (k \in \mathbb{N}) \mid k * g \equiv a \bmod p$

Alternatively, we can write:

$G = \{a \equiv k * g \bmod p, 0 \leq k \leq \varphi(p) - 1)\} = \{0, g, 2g, 3g, (\varphi(p) - 1)g\}$

ii) as a power of $g \in (\mathbb{Z}_p^*, *)$ group, i.e. with the multiplication operation:

$\forall a \in \mathbb{Z}_p^* \exists k, (k \in \mathbb{N}) \mid g^k \equiv a \bmod p$

Alternatively, we can write:

$G = \{g^k \equiv a \bmod p, 0 \leq k \leq \varphi(p) - 1)\} = \{1, g, g^2, ..., g^{\varphi(p)-1}\}$

Property of a generator of a multiplicative group

If p is a prime and g is a prime and a generator of the group $\mathbb{Z}_p^*$, then $g^{p-1} \equiv 1 \bmod p$. Such a property is a result of Fermat's little theorem.

Definition 3.27 ***Primitive root modulo n***: *a number α is called primitive root modulo n, if every number coprime to n is congruent to a power of α modulo n. Formally, α is a primitive root if for any integer a such that GCD(a,n) = 1, there exists an integer k such that $\alpha^k \equiv a \bmod n$.*

Theorem 3.9 *Primitive root conditions and properties:*

i) Primitive root *mod n* exists only
   - if n is 2 or 4
   - or if $n = p^k$, with p a prime ≥ 3 and k a positive integer ≥ 1
   - or if $n = 2p^k$, with p a prime ≥ 3 and k a positive integer ≥ 1.

ii) Given an integer n, if primitive roots *mod n* exist, then the number of primitive roots *mod n* is equal to $\varphi(\varphi(n))$.

iii) If α is a primitive root *mod n*, then the smallest k such that $\alpha^k \equiv 1 \bmod n$ is equal to $\varphi(n)$.

Theorem 3.10 For every prime p, $\mathbb{Z}_p^*$ is an abelian finite cyclic group under the multiplication operation.

Properties of cyclic group $(\mathbb{Z}_p^*, *)$

i) If g is a generator of a cyclic group G, then the order of g is equal to the cardinality of group G. Formally: $ord(g) = |G|$.

ii) For any element a in a cyclic group G: $a^{|G|} \equiv 1 \bmod p$.

iii) Any generator of a cyclic group $G = \langle \mathbb{Z}_p^*, * \rangle$ is a primitive root *mod p*.

iv) For any element $a \in G$, the set of powers of a forms a group H, which is a subgroup of G:
   $H = \{b = a^i, 0 \leq i \leq ord(a) - 1\} = \{1, a, a^2, ..., a^{ord(a)-1}\}$.

v) For any element a in a cyclic group G: $ord(a)$ *divides* $|G|$.

vi) Every cyclic group is an abelian group.

vii) Every finitely generated abelian group is a direct product of cyclic groups. The direct product is an operation that takes two groups G_1 and G_2 and constructs a new group G, such that $G = G_1 \times G_2$.

viii) Every cyclic group of prime order is a group, which cannot be broken down into smaller groups. Cyclic groups of prime order (also called elementary groups) are the building blocks from which all groups can be built.

Theorem 3.11 *Lagrange's theorem:*

If G is a finite group and H is a subgroup of G, $|H|$ divides $|G|$.

Corollary 3.1 $\forall a \in G$, $ord(a)$ divides $|G|$.

Corollary 3.2 If $|G|$ is prime, then $\forall a \in G$, $a \neq e$, $ord(a) = |G|$.

Example 3.22

– Let $G = (\mathbb{Z}_{11}, +)$ be a cyclic group. Elements of G are $\{0, 1, 2, 3, 4, 5, 6, 7, 8, 9, 10\}$. Element 5 is a generator of $\mathbb{Z}_{11}$, because:

$0 * 5 \equiv 0 \ mod \ 11 \quad 9 * 5 \equiv 1 \ mod \ 11 \quad 7 * 5 \equiv 2 \ mod \ 11$

$5 * 5 \equiv 3 \ mod \ 11 \quad 3 * 5 \equiv 4 \ mod \ 11 \quad 5 * 1 \equiv 5 \ mod \ 11$

$10 * 5 \equiv 6 \ mod \ 11 \quad 8 * 5 \equiv 7 \ mod \ 11 \quad 6 * 5 \equiv 8 \ mod \ 11$

$4 * 5 \equiv 9 \ mod \ 11 \quad 2 * 5 \equiv 10 \ mod \ 11$

– Let $G = (\mathbb{Z}_{11}^*, *)$ be a cyclic group. Elements of G are $\{1, 2, 3, 4, 5, 6, 7, 8, 9, 10\}$. Element 2 is a generator of G, since all its elements are generated as follows:

$2^0 \equiv 1 \ mod \ 11 \quad 2^1 \equiv 2 \ mod \ 11 \quad 2^8 \equiv 3 \ mod \ 11$

$2^2 \equiv 4 \ mod \ 11 \quad 2^4 \equiv 5 \ mod \ 11 \quad 2^9 \equiv 6 \ mod \ 11$

$2^7 \equiv 7 \ mod \ 11 \quad 2^3 \equiv 8 \ mod \ 11 \quad 2^6 \equiv 9 \ mod \ 11$

$2^5 \equiv 10 \ mod \ 11$

– Let $G = (\mathbb{Z}_{11}^*, *)$ be a cyclic group. Let us check if the orders of all elements of $\mathbb{Z}_{11}^*$ divide $|\mathbb{Z}_{11}^*|$, which is equal to 10:

$ord(1) = 1$, because $1^1 \equiv 1 \ mod \ 11$ $\quad ord(2) = 10$, because $2^{10} \equiv 1 \ mod \ 11$

$ord(3) = 5$, because $3^5 \equiv 1 \ mod \ 11$ $\quad ord(4) = 5$, because : $4^5 \equiv 1 \ mod \ 11$

$ord(5) = 5$, because $5^5 \equiv 1 \ mod \ 11$ $\quad ord(6) = 10$, because $6^{10} \equiv 1 \ mod \ 11$

$ord(7) = 10$, because $7^{10} \equiv 1 \ mod \ 11$ $\quad ord(8) = 10$, because $8^{10} \equiv 1 \ mod \ 11$

$ord(9) = 5$, because $9^5 \equiv 1 \ mod \ 11$ $\quad ord(10) = 2$, because $10^2 \equiv 1 \ mod \ 11$

Hence, the orders of the elements of $\mathbb{Z}_{11}^*$ are all dividers of $|\mathbb{Z}_{11}^*|$. It should be noticed that the elements 2, 6, 7, and 8 have an order of 10 (which is equal to $|\mathbb{Z}_{11}^*|$). So, they are all generators of $\mathbb{Z}_{11}^*$.

3.2.2 Fields

Definition 3.28 Field: *a field F is a set of elements[9] together with two operations, Addition (+) and Multiplication (×), satisfying the following properties:*

i) *$(F, +)$ is an abelian group with a neutral element denoted 0 such that $a + b = b + a$ and $a + 0 = a$, $\forall a$, $\forall b \in F$.*
ii) *$(F - \{0\}, \times)$ is a commutative group under the multiplication operation with an identity element $1 : a \times b = b \times a$ and $a \times 1 = a$, $\forall a$, $\forall b \in F$. $F - \{0\}$ is often denoted F^*.*
iii) *Associativity: $(a + b) + c = a + (b + c)$, $(a \times b) \times c = a \times (b \times c)$, $\forall a$, $\forall b$, $\forall c \in F$.*
iv) *Distributivity: $a \times (b + c) = a \times b + a \times c$, for $a, b, c \in F$.*
v) *Every nonzero element $a \in F$ has a multiplicative inverse $a^{-1} \in F \mid a \times a^{-1} = 1$.*

In other words, a commutative ring where all nonzero elements have multiplicative inverses is a field.

3.2.2.1 Prime Finite Fields

Definition 3.29 Finite field: *a finite field F_p, also called **Galois** field and denoted $GF(p)$, is a field with a finite number of elements p. It is a set with two operations, addition (+) and multiplication (×), which are both commutative and associative.*

Notations:
Finite field with prime p is denoted F_p, $F(p)$, or $GF(p)$.
Finite field with prime power p^m is denoted F_{p^m}, $F(p^m)$, or $GF(p^m)$.
F^* is the set of nonzero elements of finite F (i.e. $F^* = F - \{0\}$).

Theorem 3.12 *Finite field:* a field F_p is finite if and only if p is prime or a prime power.

Theorem 3.13 If F_p is finite field, then the group $F_p^\times$ is cyclic.

Definition 3.30 Prime field: *any field F_p, also denoted[10] $\mathbb{Z}_p$, with prime p, is unique and called prime field.*

Operations over prime finite fields

Let $a, b, c,$ and h be elements of F_p.

- Addition and subtraction modulo p
  - $a + b = c \bmod p$
  - $a - b \bmod p \triangleq a + (-b) \bmod p = d$: subtraction is defined as an addition of the negative of b
- Multiplication: $a * b = h \bmod p$
- Division: $\frac{a}{b} \bmod p \triangleq a * b^{-1} \bmod p$, where b^{-1} is the inverse of b. Division is defined as a multiplication by the inverse.

Theorem 3.14 *Multiplicative inverse property in prime fields:* let a be an element of a prime field F_p and g a generator of F_p. Element a and its multiplicative inverse $a^{-1} \in F_p$ are linked by the following property:

$$a \in F_p, a \neq 0, \exists i \in \mathbb{N}, 0 \leq i \leq p-2 \mid g^i \equiv a \bmod p \text{ and } g^{p-i-1} \equiv a^{-1} \bmod p$$

Note. Theorem 3.14 is very useful to quickly compute multiplicative inverses.

Example 3.23

- $3 - 5 \bmod 7 = 3 + 2 = 5$, because $-5 \equiv 2 \bmod 7$
- $\frac{3}{5} \bmod 7 = 3 \times (5^{-1}) = 2$, because 3 is the multiplicative inverse of 5 mod 7.

Example 3.24

$\mathbb{Z}_7$, under the usual addition and multiplication operations $+$ and $*$ is a finite field, because:

- The number of elements of $\mathbb{Z}_7$ is finite.
- $(\mathbb{Z}_7, +)$ and $(\mathbb{Z}_p^*, *)$ are commutative groups.
- Each nonzero element of $\mathbb{Z}_7$ has its multiplicative inverse in $\mathbb{Z}_7$. Below is the table of computations for $\mathbb{Z}_7$:

+	0	1	2	3	4	5	6
0	0	1	2	3	4	5	6
1	1	2	3	4	5	6	0
2	2	3	4	5	6	0	1
3	3	4	5	6	0	1	2
4	4	5	6	0	1	2	3
5	5	6	0	1	2	3	4
6	6	0	1	2	3	4	5

*	0	1	2	3	4	5	6
0	0	0	0	0	0	0	0
1	0	1	2	3	4	5	6
2	0	2	4	6	1	3	5
3	0	3	6	2	5	1	4
4	0	4	1	5	2	6	3
5	0	5	3	1	6	4	2
6	0	6	5	4	3	2	1

a	$-a$	a^{-1}
0	0	-
1	6	1
2	5	4
3	4	5
4	3	2
5	2	3
6	1	6

Example 3.25

- $\mathbb{Z}_{100}$, with the usual addition and multiplication operations $+$ and $*$, is not a finite field, because some elements (i.e. even elements and multiples of 5) have no multiplicative inverse mod 100. Recall that the multiplicative inverse of $a \in \mathbb{Z}_p$ exists only if $GCD(a, p) = 1$.

– $\mathbb{Z}_8$, with the usual addition and multiplication operations + and * is not a finite field, because even elements (i.e. 2, 4, and 6) have no multiplicative inverse *mod* 8. However, $\mathbb{Z}_8$ can be written as F_{2^3} and by Theorem 3.12, $\mathbb{Z}_8$ should be a field. To make $\mathbb{Z}_8$ a field, we need to redefine addition and multiplication (see Section 3.2.3).

Example 3.26 Elements of the field F_{23} are $\{0, 1, 2, 3, ..., 21, 22\}$. Element 5 is a generator of F_{23}^*, since its powers give all the elements of F_{23}^*, as follows:

$5^0 \equiv 1 \bmod 23$	$5^1 \equiv 5 \bmod 23$	$5^2 \equiv 2 \bmod 23$	$5^3 \equiv 10 \bmod 23$
$5^4 \equiv 4 \bmod 23$	$5^5 \equiv 20 \bmod 23$	$5^6 \equiv 8 \bmod 23$	$5^7 \equiv 17 \bmod 23$
$5^8 \equiv 16 \bmod 23$	$5^9 \equiv 11 \bmod 23$	$5^{10} \equiv 9 \bmod 23$	$5^{11} \equiv 22 \bmod 23$
$5^{12} \equiv 18 \bmod 23$	$5^{13} \equiv 21 \bmod 23$	$5^{14} \equiv 13 \bmod 23$	$5^{15} \equiv 19 \bmod 23$
$5^{16} \equiv 3 \bmod 23$	$5^{17} \equiv 15 \bmod 23$	$5^{18} \equiv 6 \bmod 23$	$5^{19} \equiv 7 \bmod 23$
$5^{20} \equiv 12 \bmod 23$	$5^{21} \equiv 14 \bmod 23$	$5^{22} \equiv 1 \bmod 23$	

Example of inverse calculation based on the generator of F_{23}:

$6^{-1} = 4 \bmod 23$, since $6 * 4 = 1 \bmod 23$. Since 5 is a generator of F_{23} and $5^{18} = 6 \bmod 23$, $6^{-1} = 5^{23-18-1} = 5^4 = 4$.

Properties of prime fields

i) The set of elements of field F_p is $\{0, 1, 2, ..., p-1\}$.

ii) The order of field F_p, with prime p, is the number of the elements in the field and it is denoted $|F_p|$ and it is equal to p.

iii) Adding p copies of any element of F_p results in zero, i.e. for any $a \in \mathbb{Z}_p$, $p * a \equiv 0 \bmod p$.

iv) Every nonzero element in F_p has a multiplicative inverse in F_p.

v) $F_p - 0$, denoted F_p^*, is a cyclic group of order $p-1$.

3.2.3 Extension Fields F_{p^m}

Definition 3.31 Extension field: *a field F is said to be an extension of a field E, if E is a subfield of F. That is denoted F / E or F over E. An extension field also is called extended field.*

Definition 3.32 Characteristic of extension field: *if F_{p^m} is an extension of field F_p, it has a characteristic of p. That is, adding p copies of any elements of F_{p^m} results in adding the neutral element 0.*

Example 3.27

– $\mathbb{R}$, the set of real numbers, is an extension of $\mathbb{Q}$, the set of rational numbers, and $\mathbb{Q}$ is an extension of $\mathbb{Z}$, the set of integers.

– $F_{2^3} = \{0, 1, 2, 3, 4, 5, 6, 7\}$ is an extension field of $\mathbb{Z}_2$. It has a characteristic of 2. Hence, $\forall a \in F_{2^3}, a + a = 0$, because addition is done *modulo* 2.

– $F_{3^2} = \{0, 1, 2, 3, 4, 5, 6, 7, 8\}$ is an extension field of $\mathbb{Z}_3$. It has a characteristic of 3. Hence, $\forall a \in F_{3^2}, a + a + a = 0$, because addition is done *modulo* 3.

To do operations on elements of extension fields F_{p^m}, we need to represent them as polynomials. That is, any element of an extension field is a polynomial with coefficients in a subfield F_p.

3.2.3.1 Basics of Modular Polynomial Arithmetic

Definition 3.33 Polynomial: *a polynomial $P(x)$ of degree d is an expression of the form $P(x) = c_{d-1}x^{d-1} + c_{d-2}x^{d-2} + \cdots + c_1x^1 + c_0$, where $c_i, i = 0, 1, ..., d-1$ are called **coefficients** and are elements of some field F. x is called the **unknown**.*

Example 3.28

Let $A(x) = x^3 + x^2 + x + 1$ and $B(x) = x^2 + 1$.

– Computations over $\mathbb{Z}_5$:

  $A(x) + B(x) = x^3 + 2x^2 + x + 2$

  $A(x) * B(x) = x^5 + x^4 + 2x^3 + 2x^2 + x + 1$

– Computations over $\mathbb{Z}_2$:

  $A(x) - B(x) = x^3 + x$

  $A(x) * B(x) = x^5 + x^4 + x + 1$

Notation:

$G[x]$ denotes the set of polynomials over the group G.

Definition 3.34 Polynomial congruence: *let $A(x)$, $P(x)$, and $R(x)$ be polynomials with coefficients in some field F. $A(x)$ is said to be congruent to $R(x)$ modulo $P(x)$, if $P(x)$ divides $A(x) - R(x)$. The congruence relation is denoted $A(x) \equiv R(x) \bmod P(x)$.*

Example 3.29

– $(x^2 + 1) \equiv ? \bmod (x + 1)$ in $\mathbb{Z}_2[x]$

  Since $(x + 1) * (x + 1) = x^2 + 2x + 1$, $(x^2 + 1) \equiv 0 \bmod (x + 1)$

– $(x^2 + 1) \equiv ? \bmod (x + 1)$ in $\mathbb{Z}_3[x]$

  Since $(x - 1) * (x + 1) + 2 = x^2 + 1$, $(x^2 + 1) \equiv 2 \bmod (x + 1)$

– $(x^3 + 11x^2 + x + 7) \equiv (?) \bmod (x^2 + 2x + 9)$ in $\mathbb{Z}_{101}[x]$

  $(x^2 + 2x + 9) * (x + 9) = x^3 + 11x^2 + 27x + 81$

    $= x^3 + 11x^2 + x + 7 + (26x + 74)$

  Hence, $(x^3 + 11x^2 + x + 7) \equiv -(26x + 74) \bmod (x^2 + 2x + 9)$

– $(x^3 + 11x^2 + x + 7) \equiv (?) \bmod (x^2 + 2x + 9)$ in $\mathbb{Z}_{13}[x]$

  In $\mathbb{Z}_{13}$, $-(26x + 74) = -(2 * 13x + 5 * 13 + 9) \equiv -9 \bmod 13 = 4$

  Hence, $(x^3 + 11x^2 + x + 7) \equiv 4 \bmod (x^2 + 2x + 9)$

Properties of polynomial congruence

Let $A(x), B(x), C(x), A_1(x), B_1(x), \ldots, A_k(x), B_k(x)$, and $P(x)$ be polynomials and k a positive integer. The following properties hold:

  i) $A(x) \equiv A(x) \bmod P(x)$

  ii) If $A(x) \equiv B(x) \bmod P(x)$, then $B(x) \equiv A(x) \bmod P(x)$

  iii) If $A(x) \equiv B(x) \bmod P(x)$ and $B(x) \equiv C(x) \bmod P(x)$, then $A(x) \equiv C(x) \bmod P(x)$

  iv) If $A(x) \equiv A_1(x) \bmod P(x)$ and $B(x) \equiv B_1(x) \bmod P(x)$, then

    $A(x) + B(x) \equiv (A_1(x) + B_1(x)) \bmod P(x)$ and

    $A(x) * B(x) \equiv (A_1(x) * B_1(x)) \bmod P(x)$

  v) If $A_i(x) \equiv B_i(x) \bmod P(x)$, for $i = 1, 2, \ldots, k$, then

    $\sum_{i=1}^{k} A_i(x) \equiv \sum_{i=k}^{k} B_i(x) \bmod P(x)$

    $\prod_{i=1}^{k} A_i(x) \equiv \prod_{i=1}^{k} B_i(x) \bmod P(x)$

    $A_j(x) - A_i(x) \equiv B_j(x) - B_i(x) \bmod P(x), 1 \le i \le k, 1 \le j \le k$

Definition 3.35 Polynomial root: *$a \in \mathbb{Z}_p$ is a root of polynomial $f(x)$, if $f(a) = 0$. Therefore, if a is a root of $f(x)$, there exists a polynomial $g(x)$ of degree less than that of $f(x)$, such that $f(x) = (x - a) * g(x)$.*

Definition 3.36 Irreducible polynomial: *a polynomial $f(x)$ is said to be irreducible in $\mathbb{Z}_p$ if it does not factor as a product of two or more polynomials with coefficients in $\mathbb{Z}_p$ each of degree less than that of $f(x)$.*

In other words, an irreducible polynomial over $\mathbb{Z}_p$ has no root in $\mathbb{Z}_p$. Irreducible polynomials are counterpart of primes: irreducible polynomials cannot be expressed as a product of two other polynomials like primes cannot be factorized. Therefore, irreducible polynomials are used as polynomial moduli to construct finite fields.

Theorem 3.15 *Irreducibility conditions:* let $f(x)$ be a polynomial over $\mathbb{Z}_p$. Then,

  i) if $f(x)$ has a root $a \in \mathbb{Z}_p$, then $f(x)$ is reducible over $\mathbb{Z}_p$.
  ii) if $f(x)$ has no roots and its degree is 2 or 3, then it is irreducible.

In general, if a polynomial has no root, it does not necessarily mean that it is irreducible. For example, in $\mathbb{Z}_3$, $x^4 + 2x^2 + 1$ can be written as a product $(x^2 + 1)(x^2 + 1)$. Therefore, it is reducible, but it has no roots in $\mathbb{Z}_3$, because $(x^2 + 1)$ has no roots in $\mathbb{Z}_3$.

Example 3.30

– Reducible polynomial over F_2: $P(x) = x^2 + 1$.
 Since $P(1) = 0$, 1 is a root; and $P(x)$ can be written as a product, i.e. $x^2 + 1 = (x - 1)(x - 1)$.
– Reducible polynomial over F_5:
 $P(x) = x^4 + 2x^3 + 3x + 1$.
 Since $P(3) = 145 \equiv 0 \bmod 5$, 3 is a root; and $P(x)$ can be written as a product, i.e.
 $(x - 3)(x^3 + 3) = (x + 2)(x^3 + 3) = x^4 + 2x^3 + 3x + 6 = x^4 + 2x^3 + 3x + 1$.
– Irreducible polynomials over F_2
 $P(x) = x^2 + x + 1$: $P(0) = 1$ and $P(1) = 1$. Thus, $P(x)$ has no root over F_2. Hence, by Theorem 3.14, $P(x)$ is irreducible.
 $P(x) = x^4 + x + 1$: check if there exist two polynomials $Q(x)$ and $R(x)$ of degree less than 4 such that $P(x) = Q(x) * R(x)$: candidate polynomials for $Q(x)$ and $R(x)$ are: $x + 1, x^2 + 1, x^2 + x + 1, x^3 + 1, x^3 + x + 1$, and $x^3 + x^2 + x + 1$. No product of a pair of candidate polynomials results in $P(x)$. Therefore, the latter is irreducible.

3.2.3.2 Representation of Finite Fields as Polynomials

The general representation of elements of a field F_{p^m}, with prime p, is a polynomial basis representation, in which a distinct polynomial of degree less than m is associated with each element of the field F_{p^m}. That is, each element $a \in F_{p^m}$ has a unique polynomial $A(x)$ with degree less than m. For example, $a = 2 \in F_{2^4}$ and $b = 13 \in F_{2^4}$ are represented by $A(x) = x$ and $B(x) = x^3 + x^2 + 1$, respectively, because $2 = 2^1$ and $13 = 2^3 + 2^2 + 2^0$.

Let $F_{p^m}[x]$ denote the set of polynomials of degree less than m with coefficients in F_p.

Theorem 3.16 Let $f(x)$ be an irreducible polynomial of degree m with coefficients in F_p. $F_{p^m}[x] / f(x)$ is a finite field of order p^m.

Note. $F_{p^m}[x] / f(x)$ denotes the set of polynomials yielded by operations modulo $f(x)$ on polynomials in the set $F_{p^m}[x]$. Addition of two polynomials is done by usual polynomial addition with modulo p on the coefficients. Multiplication of two polynomials is performed with modulo $f(x)$ on the usual product of two polynomials.

Definition 3.37 *Reduction polynomial*: the irreducible polynomial $f(x)$ used to reduce the product of polynomials in $F_{p^m}[x]$ is called reduction polynomial.

Theorem 3.17 *Uniqueness of finite fields:*

for every prime power p^m, there exists a unique finite field of order p^m.

Theorem 3.18 *Existence of reduction polynomial:*

for prime power p^m, there exists at least one irreducible polynomial of degree m over F_p.

Example 3.31

– $F_{2^3} = \{0, 1, 2, 3, 4, 5, 6, 7\}$ is represented by the set of polynomials $F_{2^3}[x] = \{0, 1, x, x + 1, x^2, x^2 + 1, x^2 + x, x^2 + x + 1\}$.
 With the reduction polynomial $f(x) = x^3 + x + 1$ over F_2, examples of operations are:
$$(x^2 + x) + (x^2) + (1) = x + 1$$
$$(x^2 + 1)(x + 1) \bmod f(x) = (x^3 + x^2 + x + 1) \bmod f(x) = x^2$$

- $F_{3^2} = \{0,1,2,3,4,5,6,7,8\}$ is represented by the set of polynomials $F_{3^2}[x] = \{0,1,2,x,x+1,x+2,2x,2x+1,2x+2\}$.

  With the reduction polynomial $f(x) = x^2 + 1$ over F_3, examples of operations are:

  $(x+2)+(x+2) = 2x+1$

  $(x+2)(2x+2)\ mod\ f(x) = (2x^2 + 6x + 4)\ mod\ f(x) = 2.$

3.2.3.3 Construction of Finite Fields as Polynomials

Definition 3.38 Primitive polynomial: *$f(x)$, a polynomial of degree m, irreducible in $F_p[x]$, and with coefficients in F_p, is said to be primitive polynomial if it has a root $\alpha \in F_{p^m}$ such that $\{0,1,\alpha,\alpha^2,\alpha,^3 \ldots, \alpha^{p^{m-2}}\}$ is the entire field F_{p^m}. In other words, a root of a primitive polynomial is a field generator.*

Example 3.32   Below is a non-comprehensive list of primitive polynomials with degree up to 32.

Degree	Polynomial	Degree	Polynomial
2	$x^2 + x + 1$	13	$x^{13} + x^{12} + x^{11} + x^8 + 1$
3	$x^3 + x^2 + 1$	14	$x^{14} + x^{11} + x^6 + x + 1$
4	$x^4 + x^3 + 1$	15	$x^{15} + x^4 + 1$
5	$x^5 + x^3 + 1$	16	$x^{16} + x^{12} + x^7 + x^2 + 1$
6	$x^6 + x^5 + 1$	17	$x^{17} + x^6 + 1$
7	$x^7 + x^6 + 1$	18	$x^{18} + x^{11} + 1$
8	$x^8 + x^6 + x^5 + x^4 + 1$	19	$x^{19} + x^{18} + x^{17} + x^{14} + 1$
9	$x^9 + x^5 + 1$	20	$x^{20} + x^{17} + 1$
10	$x^{10} + x^7 + 1$	30	$x^{30} + x^{23} + x^2 + x + 1$
11	$x^{11} + x^9 + 1$	31	$x^{31} + x^3 + 1$
12	$x^{12} + x^5 + 1$	32	$x^{32} + x^{22} + x^2 + x + 1$

Theorem 3.19 *Properties of primitive polynomials*:   let $f(x)$ be a primitive polynomial of degree m, with coefficients in F_p.

i) If $\alpha \in F_{p^m}$ is a root of $f(x)$, then all the roots of $f(x)$ are given by elements $\alpha,\ \alpha^p, \alpha^{p^2}, \ldots, \alpha^{p^{m-1}}$.

ii) $f(x)$ divides $x^k - 1$ for $k = p^m - 1$ and for no smaller positive integer k.

The consequence of Theorem 3.19 is that given a root α of a primitive polynomial $f(x)$ of degree m and with coefficients in F_p, we can generate all elements of the extension field F_{p^m} as powers of α modulo $f(x)$.

Example 3.33   Let $f(x) = x^3 + x + 1$ be a primitive polynomial over $F_2[x]$. According to Theorem 3.19, $f(x)$ has three roots α, α^2, and α^4 in $F_{2^3}[x]$. By definition of a root, if α is a root of $f(x)$, then $f(\alpha) = \alpha^3 + \alpha + 1 = 0$ in $F_{2^3}[x]/f(x)$.

Let us show that if $\alpha = 2$ is a root, then α^2 and α^4 are roots, too.

Since operations in extension fields are done modulo the reduction polynomial $f(x)$, $x^3 + x + 1 \equiv 0\ mod\ f(x)$.

Since $\alpha = x$, $f(\alpha^2) = (x^2)^3 + x^2 + 1 = x^6 + x^2 + 1 \equiv 0\ mod\ f(x)$. Hence, α^2 is a root to $f(x)$.

$f(\alpha^4) = (\alpha^4)^3 + \alpha^4 + 1$.

Since $\alpha = x$, $f(\alpha^4) = (x^4)^3 + x^4 + 1 = x^{12} + x^4 + 1 \equiv 0\ mod\ f(x)$. Hence, α^4 is a root to $f(x)$. Notice that: $x^4 \equiv x^2 + x\ mod\ f(x)$.

Polynomials x, x^2, and $x^2 + x$ represent elements 2, 4, and 6 in F_{2^3}, respectively.

Let us check the roots above:

$f(2) = 2^3 + 2 + 1 = 11$ is represented by polynomial $x^3 + x + 1$. Since, $x^3 + x + 1 \equiv 0\ mod\ f(x)$, $f(2) = 0$.

$f(4) = 4^3 + 4 + 1$ is represented by polynomial $x^6 + x^2 + 1$. Since, $x^6 + x^2 + 1 \equiv 0\ mod\ f(x)$, $f(4) = 0$

$f(6) = 6^3 + 6 + 1$ is represented by polynomial $(x^2 + x)^3 + (x^2 + x) + 1 = x^6 + x^5 + x^3 + x^3 + x^2 + x + 1$. Since $x^6 + x^5 + x^3 + x^3 + x^2 + x + 1 \equiv 0\ mod\ f(x)$, $f(6) = 0$.

Definition 3.39 Polynomial basis: *given a polynomial $f(x)$ of degree m and irreducible in F_p and α a root of $f(x)$ and α a primitive element in F_{p^m}, the set of polynomials $\{1, \alpha^1, \ldots, \alpha^{m-2}, \alpha^{m-1}\}$ is called polynomial basis of F_{p^m}.*

Theorem 3.20 Any element $a \in F_{p^m}$ can be expressed as a linear combination of elements of the polynomial basis. That is, $a = a_{m-1}\alpha^{m-1} + a_{m-2}\alpha^{m-2} + \cdots + a_1\alpha + a_0$, with $a_i \in F_p$ for $0 \le i \le m-1$.

Alternatively, $a \in F_{p^m}$ can be expressed as a power of $f(x)$ root. That is,

$\forall a \in F_{p^m}, \exists k \in \mathbb{N}, 0 \le k \le p^m - 2 \mid \alpha^k \equiv a \bmod f(x)$. Therefore, $F_{p^m} = \left\{0, 1, \alpha^1, \ldots, \alpha^m, \ldots, \alpha^{p^m - 2}\right\}$

Lemma 3.6[11]: It is not true that a root α of any polynomial $f(x)$ of degree m, irreducible over F_p, can generate all elements of field F_{p^m}.

Example 3.34 Let us consider the extension field F_{2^3} under the irreducible polynomial $f(x) = x^3 + x + 1$ and check that $\left\{1, \alpha, \alpha^2\right\}$ is a polynomial basis to F_{2^3}.

The eight elements of the binary field F_{2^3} over F_2, in polynomial and binary representations, are as follows:

$$0 \ (000) \qquad 1 \ (001) \qquad x \ (010) \qquad x+1 \ (011)$$
$$x^2 \ (100) \qquad x^2+1 \ (101) \qquad x^2+x \ (110) \qquad x^2+x+1 \ (111)$$

Since α is a root of $f(x)$, $\alpha^3 + \alpha + 1 = 0 \Rightarrow \alpha^3 = -\alpha - 1 = \alpha + 1$.

The powers, till $2^3 - 2$, of α give:

$$\alpha^0 = 1 \qquad \alpha^1 = \alpha \qquad \alpha^2 = \alpha^2 \qquad \alpha^3 = \alpha + 1$$
$$\alpha^4 = \alpha(\alpha+1) = \alpha^2 + \alpha \qquad \alpha^5 = \alpha(\alpha^2 + \alpha) = \alpha^2 + \alpha + 1$$
$$\alpha^6 = \alpha(\alpha^2 + \alpha + 1) = \alpha^2 + 1.$$

Hence, F_{2^3} can be written in three forms:

$$
\begin{aligned}
F_{3^2} &= \left\{0, \ 1, \ 2, \ 3, \quad 4, \ 5, \quad\ 6, \quad\ 7 \qquad\quad\right\}\\
&= \left\{0, \ \alpha^0, \ \alpha^1, \ \alpha^3, \quad \alpha^2, \ \alpha^6, \quad \alpha^4, \quad \alpha^5 \qquad\right\}\\
&= \left\{0, \ 1, \quad \alpha, \quad \alpha+1, \ \alpha^2, \ \alpha^2+1, \ \alpha^2+\alpha, \ \alpha^2+\alpha+1\right\}
\end{aligned}
$$

To see polynomials in unknown x, we have just to replace α by x. Since α can generate all nonzero elements of F_{2^3}, $\left\{1, \alpha, \alpha^2\right\}$ is a polynomial basis.

3.2.4 Extension Fields

First of all, it is worth noticing that in cryptography, F_{2^m} fields are often used. In computers, data is represented as bit strings spanning one or multiple words. For example, a positive integer may be represented as a 64-bits word. Hence, it is of interest to consider fields built over binary set $\{0, 1\}$.

In Example 3.25, it is shown that $\mathbb{Z}_{2^3}$ is not a finite field under the usual addition and multiplication operations $\bmod\, 8$. In general, $\mathbb{Z}_{2^m}$ is not a field under the usual addition and multiplication operations, because even numbers have no multiplicative inverses $\bmod\, 2^m$. Thus, there exist two alternatives: i) use only $\mathbb{Z}_p$, with prime p or ii) redefine the addition and multiplication operations to make F_{2^m} a finite field for any positive integer m. It is worth noticing that computations are faster in F_{2^m} than in $\mathbb{Z}_p$. For example, F_{2^m} uses the XOR bitwise operation, while $\mathbb{Z}_p$ makes use of addition $\bmod\, m$.

3.2.4.1 Special Case: F_2

F_2 field is the smallest field. The set of elements of field F_2 is $\{0, 1\}$.

Addition operation: $0+0 = 0$, $1+0 = 1$, $0+1 = 1$, $1+1 = 0$. Therefore, the addition operation in F_2 is the binary *XOR* operation (denoted $\oplus$).

Multiplication operation: $0*0 = 0$, $1*0 = 0$, $0*1 = 0$, $1*1 = 1$. Therefore, the multiplication operation in F_2 is the binary *AND* operation (denoted $\wedge$).

Additive inverse: $1+1 = 0$. Thus, 1 is the additive inverse of 1; and $0+0 = 0$; so, 0 is the additive inverse of 0.

Multiplicative inverse: $1*1 = 1$. Thus, 1 is the multiplicative inverse of 1. 0 has no multiplicative inverse.

3.2.4.2 Representation and Construction of F_{2^m} Fields

Definition 3.40 **Binary polynomial**: *a binary polynomial is a polynomial over F_2, i.e. with coefficients in $\{0,1\}$.*

Definition 3.41 **Binary field**: *a field of the form F_{2^m} is called binary field and it has exactly 2^m elements, which are usually represented as m-bit strings $(a_{m-1}a_{m-2}\ldots a_1 a_0)$ ranging from $(000\ldots000)$ to $(111\ldots111)$.*

Each element $a \in F_{2^m}$ is commonly represented as an m-bit string $(a_{m-1}a_{m-2}\ldots a_1 a_0)$ and a polynomial $A(x) = (a_{m-1}x^{m-1} + a_{m-2}x^{m-2} + \cdots + a_1 x^1 + a_0) \in F_{2^m}[x]$ is associated with it.

$F_{2^m}[x]$ denotes the set of F_{2^m} polynomials defined by:

$$F_{2^m}[x] = \left\{ a_{m-1}x^{m-1} + a_{m-2}x^{m-2} + \cdots + a_1 x^1 + a_0 \right\}, \text{ where } a_{i=0,\ldots,m} \in \{0,1\}.$$

Definition 3.42 **Polynomial basis of F_{2^m}** : *the set of polynomials $\left\{ x^{m-1}, x^{m-2}, \ldots, x^1, 1 \right\}$ forms a basis to the field F_{2^m}.*

Corollary 3.3 Existence of binary reduction polynomial: for every field F_{2^m}, there exists at least one polynomial of degree m irreducible over F_2.

Corollary 3.3 is a consequence of Theorem 3.18.

Operations over field F_{2^m}

Let a, b, and c be elements in F_{2^m} and their respective polynomials:

$$A(x) = a_{m-1}x^{m-1} + a_{m-2}x^{m-2} + \cdots + a_1 x^1 + a_0; \, A(x) \in F_{2^m}[x]$$
$$B(x) = b_{m-1}x^{m-1} + b_{m-2}x^{m-2} + \cdots + b_1 x^1 + b_0; \, B(x) \in F_{2^m}[x]$$
$$C(x) = c_{m-1}x^{m-1} + c_{m-2}x^{m-2} + \cdots + c_1 x^1 + c_0; \, C(x) \in F_{2^m}[x]$$

- Addition: $A(x) + B(x) = C(x)$, where $c_i = (a_i + b_i) \, mod \, 2 = a_i \oplus b_i$.
- Subtraction: $A(x) - B(x) = C(x)$, where $c_i = (a_i + b_i) \, mod \, 2 = a_i \oplus b_i$. Subtraction is the same as addition over F_2.
- Multiplication: $A(x) * B(x) = R(x) = r_{m-1}x^{m-1} + r_{m-2}x^{m-2} + \cdots + r_1 x^1 + r_0$; $R(x)$ is the remainder of the polynomial product $A(x) * B(x)$ divided by the reduction polynomial $f(x)$.
- Multiplicative inverse: if $a \in F_{2^m}$ (a is a nonzero element), then the multiplicative inverse of a is denoted a^{-1}, such that: $A(x) * A^{-1}(x) \equiv 1 \, mod \, f(x)$, where $A^{-1}(x) = d_{m-1}x^{m-1} + d_{m-2}x^{m-2} + \cdots + d_1 x^1 + d_0$ is a polynomial in $F_{2^m}[x]$.

3.2.4.3 Generator of Field F_{2^m}

By definition 3.38, a primitive polynomial of an extension field F_{2^m} is of degree m, with coefficients in F_2, and irreducible in $F_2[x]$.

Definition 3.43 **Field generator** or **primitive element**: *given a field F_{2^m} and a primitive polynomial $f(x)$ of degree m, an element $g \in F_{2^m}$ is called generator (or primitive element) of F_{2^m} if and only if g is a root of $f(x)$ in F_{2^m} and every nonzero element of F_{2^m} can be uniquely written as a power of g.*

Theorem 3.21 **Multiplicative inverse property in field F_{2^m}:**

let a and g be elements of F_{2^m} and $A(x)$ and $G(x)$ their respective polynomials and g be a generator of F_{2^m}. a and its multiplicative inverse $a^{-1} \in F_{2^m}$ are linked by the following property:

$$a \in F_{2^m}, a \neq 0, \exists i \in \mathbb{N}, (0 \leq i \leq 2^m - 2) \mid (G(x))^i \equiv A(x) \, mod \, f(x)$$
$$\text{and } (G(x))^{2^m - i - 1} \equiv A^{-1}(x) \, mod \, f(x).$$

Theorem 3.22 **Generator property in field F_{2^m}:**

if g is a generator of field F_{2^m}, then, $(G(x))^{2^m - 1} \equiv 1 \, mod \, f(x)$.

Lemma 3.7 **Property of primitive polynomial in F_{2^m}:** if $f(x)$ is a primitive polynomial of degree m, with coefficients in F_2, and a root in F_{2^m}, then $f(x)$ divides $x^{2^m - 1} + 1$.

The two theorems above are very useful to quickly calculate multiplicative inverses and exponentiation with large exponents.

> **Theorem 3.23** Number of generators of F_{2^m} **field**: The number of primitive elements (or generators) of field F_{2^m} is $\varphi(2^m - 1)$.

> **Theorem 3.24** Given a positive integer m, if $2^m - 1$ is prime, then any element of F_{2^m}, with the exception of elements 0 and 1, is a generator of F_{2^m}.

***Corollary* 3.4** By Theorems 3.22 and 3.24, if $2^m - 1$ is prime, then the square root of any element $x \in F_{2^m}$ is $\sqrt{x} = x^{2^{m-1}}$.

Example 3.35 Verification of Lemma 3.7 with an example.

$P(x) = x^4 + x^3 + 1$ is a primitive polynomial in F_{2^4}.
$x^{15} + 1 = (x^4 + x^3 + 1)(x^4 + x^3 + x^2 + x + 1)(x^4 + x + 1)(x^2 + x + 1)(1 + x)$ over F_2. Therefore, $x^4 + x^3 + 1$ divides $x^{15} + 1$.

Example 3.36 The eight elements of the binary field F_{2^3} over F_2 are as follows in polynomial and binary representations:

$$0 \ (000) \qquad 1 \ (001) \qquad x \ (010) \qquad x+1 \ (011)$$
$$x^2 \ (100) \quad x^2+1 \ (101) \quad x^2+x \ (110) \quad x^2+x+1 \ (111)$$

$2^3 - 1$ is prime. Therefore, by Theorem 3.23, F_{2^3} has six generators, which are $2, 3, 4, 5, 6, 7$.
Let $f(x) = x^3 + x + 1$, which is an irreducible polynomial, be the reduction polynomial for field F_{2^3}.

– Example of addition over F_{2^3}: $(111) + (100) = (011)$
  In polynomial form over $F_{2^3}[x]$: $(x^2 + x + 1) + (x^2) = x + 1$
– Example of multiplication over F_{2^3}: $(100) * (011) = (111)$ explained as follows:
  $(x^2) * (x + 1) \bmod f(x) = (x^3 + x^2) \bmod (x^3 + x + 1) = x^2 + x + 1$
– One of the generators of F_{2^3} is the element 6, which can be checked as follows:
  Generator 6 is represented by polynomial $x^2 + x$
  $(x^2 + x)^0 \bmod (x^3 + x + 1) = 1$, which represents element 1
  $(x^2 + x)^1 \bmod (x^3 + x + 1) = x^2 + x$, which represents element 6
  $(x^2 + x)^2 \bmod (x^3 + x + 1) = x$, which represents element 2
  $(x^2 + x)^3 \bmod (x^3 + x + 1) = x^2 + x + 1$, which represents element 7
  $(x^2 + x)^4 \bmod (x^3 + x + 1) = x^2$, which represents element 4
  $(x^2 + x)^5 \bmod (x^3 + x + 1) = x^2 + 1$, which represents element 5
  $(x^2 + x)^6 \bmod (x^3 + x + 1) = x + 1$, which represents element 3
  $(x^2 + x)^7 \bmod (x^3 + x + 1) = 1$, which represents element 1
  Therefore, all nonzero elements of F_{2^3} are powers of $6 \bmod (x^3 + x + 1)$.
– Example of inverse calculation: calculate 3^{-1}
  Calculation without Theorem 3.21: one has to find a polynomial $Q(x)$ of degree less than 3 such that: $(x + 1) * Q(x) \bmod (x^3 + x + 1) = 1$. $Q(x) = x^2 + x$ is the appropriate polynomial to fulfill the previous condition. $Q(x)$ represents the bit string (110). Thus, the inverse of 3 in F_{2^3} is 6.
  Calculation using Theorem 3.21 under generator $g = 6$: Element 3 is generated by g power 6. Hence, by Theorem 3.21, 3^{-1} is given as follows:
  $$(x^2 + x)^{2^3 - 6 - 1} \bmod (x^3 + x + 1) = x^2 + x.$$
  Since $x^2 + x$ is the polynomial associated with the element 6, the inverse of 3 in F_{2^3} is 6.

Example 3.37 The 16 elements of the binary field F_{2^4} over F_2 are as follows in polynomial and binary representations:

$$0 \ (0000) \qquad x^2+1 \ (0101) \qquad x^3+x \ (1010)$$
$$1 \ (0001) \qquad x^2+x \ (0110) \qquad x^3+x+1 \ (1011)$$
$$x \ (0010) \quad x^2+x+1 \ (0111) \qquad x^3+x^2 \ (1100)$$
$$x+1 \ (0011) \qquad x^3 \ (1000) \quad x^3+x^2+1 \ (1101)$$
$$x^2 \ (0100) \qquad x^3+1 \ (1001) \quad x^3+x^2+x \ (1110)$$
$$x^3+x^2+x+1 \ (1111)$$

By Theorem 3.1, $\varphi(16-1) = \varphi(5) * \varphi(3) = 4 * 2 = 8$. By theorem 3.23, F_{2^4} has $\varphi(16-1) = 8$ generators. Let $f(x) = x^4 + x + 1$, which is an irreducible polynomial over F_2, be the reduction polynomial for field F_{2^4}.

- Example of addition: $(1101) + (1000) = (0101)$
  In polynomial form over F_{2^4} : $(x^3 + x^2 + 1) + (x^3) = 2x^3 + x^2 + 1 = x^2 + 1$.
- Example of multiplication over F_{2^4} : $(1110) * (1000) = (1001)$ explained as follows:
  $(x^3 + x^2 + x) * (x^3) \bmod f(x) = (x^6 + x^5 + x^4) \bmod (x^4 + x + 1) = (x^3 + 1)$.
- One of the generators of F_{2^4} is the element 2, which can be checked as follows (element 2 is represented by polynomial x):

	Polynomial	Binary	Decimal
$x^0 \bmod f(x)$	1	0001	1
$x^1 \bmod f(x)$	x	0010	2
$x^2 \bmod f(x)$	x^2	0100	4
$x^3 \bmod f(x)$	x^3	1000	8
$x^4 \bmod f(x)$	$x+1$	0011	3
$x^5 \bmod f(x)$	$x^2 + x$	0110	6
$x^6 \bmod f(x)$	$x^3 + x^2$	1100	12
$x^7 \bmod f(x)$	$x^3 + x + 1$	1011	11
$x^8 \bmod f(x)$	$x^2 + 1$	0101	5
$x^9 \bmod f(x)$	$x^3 + x$	1010	10
$x^{10} \bmod f(x)$	$x^2 + x + 1$	0111	7
$x^{11} \bmod f(x)$	$x^3 + x^2 + x$	1110	14
$x^{12} \bmod f(x)$	$x^3 + x^2 + x + 1$	1111	15
$x^{13} \bmod f(x)$	$x^3 + x^2 + 1$	1101	13
$x^{14} \bmod f(x)$	$x^3 + 1$	1001	9
$x^{15} \bmod f(x)$	1	0001	1

- Example of inversion calculation: calculate 3^{-1} (3 is represented by polynomial $x + 1$):
  Calculation without using the inverse property (i.e. Theorem 3.21): one has to find a polynomial $Q(x)$ of degree less than 4, such that: $(x + 1) * Q(x) \bmod (x^4 + x + 1) = 1$. $Q(x) = x^3 + x^2 + x$ is the appropriate polynomial to fulfill the previous condition. $Q(x)$ represents the bit string (1110). Thus, the inverse of 3 in F_{2^4} is 14.
  Calculation using Theorem 3.21 with generator $g = 2$:
  Element 3 is generated by g power 4. Thus, by Theorem 3.21, 3^{-1} is equal to
  $$x^{16-4-1} \bmod (x^4 + x + 1) = x^{11} \bmod (x^4 + x + 1) = x^3 + x^2 + x.$$
  Since $x^3 + x^2 + x$ is the polynomial associated with element 14, the inverse of 3 in F_{2^4} is 14.

3.2.4.4 Selection of Reduction Polynomial for Field F_{2^m}

By Theorem 3.18, given a prime power $q = 2^m$, there always exists at least one reduction polynomial $f(x)$ of degree m over F_2 to construct the field F_{2^m}. Notice that the set of elements of a finite field is the same, whatever is the selected reduction polynomial. However, the calculations (i.e. addition, subtraction, multiplication, and multiplicative inverse) on elements yield different results under different reduction polynomials.

To simplify the Euclidian division, the polynomial $f(x)$ usually selected is a trinomial of the form $x^m + x + 1$ or, if all trinomials are reducible, select pentanomials of the form $x^m + x^{k3} + x^{k2} + x^{k1} + 1$, with $k1, k2, k3 \in (1, m-1)$ [7].

For real cryptosystem implementation, the standard X9.142 [8] recommends the following reduction polynomials depending on q:

- If $q = 2^{233}$, then use $f(x) = x^{233} + x^{74} + 1$.
- If $q = 2^{283}$, then use $f(x) = x^{283} + x^{12} + x^7 + x^5 + 1$.
- If $q = 2^{409}$, then use $f(x) = x^{409} + x^{87} + 1$.
- If $q = 2^{571}$, then use $f(x) = x^{571} + x^{10} + x^5 + x^2 + 1$.

3.2.5 List of Exercises and Problems

Exercise 3.7 What is the order of each of the following groups? $\mathbb{Z}_7^*$, $\mathbb{Z}_{101}^*$, and $\mathbb{Z}_{18}^*$.

Exercise 3.8 What is the order 2, 5, and 6, which are elements in $\mathbb{Z}_{13}^*$?

Exercise 3.9
1) Calculate $\dfrac{2}{5}$ in $\mathbb{Z}_8^*$.
2) Is $\mathbb{Z}_6^*$ (i.e. set of invertible elements $mod\ 6$) a cyclic group?
3) Is $\mathbb{Z}_8^*$ (i.e. set of invertible elements $mod\ 8$) a cyclic group?

Exercise 3.10 Compute $99^{707^{411}} \ mod\ 100$.

Exercise 3.11 How many elements are generators of $\mathbb{Z}_{29}^*$?

Exercise 3.12 Build the multiplication table of the extension field F_{2^3} with the irreducible polynomial $f(x) = x^3 + x^2 + 1$.

Exercise 3.13 Do the following computations over the extension field F_{3^2} with the irreducible polynomial $f(x) = x^2 + 2x + 2$:
1) $4 + 5$
2) $3 * 2$
3) $4 * 5$
4) 8^2

Exercise 3.14 Do the following computations over the extension field F_{2^4} under the irreducible polynomial $f(x) = x^4 + x + 1$:
1) x^{-1} and x^{-3}
2) $x^2 / (x^3 + x^2 + 1)$
3) $(x^3 + x^2 + x) / (x^2 + x + 1)$
4) Which of the computation results (obtained for the three previous questions) change if $f(x) = x^4 + x^3 + 1$?

Exercise 3.15 Check if the following polynomials are reducible in F_2

1) $f_1(x) = x^6 + x^4 + x^2$
2) $f_2(x) = x^3 + 1$
3) $f_3(x) = x^4 + x^3 + x + 1$
4) $f_4(x) = x^4 + x^2 + 1$

Exercise 3.16 Let α be a root of polynomial $f(x) = x^2 + x + 2$, which is irreducible over F_3. Check that α can generate all nonzero elements of F_{3^2}.

Exercise 3.17 Let $f(x) = x^2 + x + 2$ be a polynomial irreducible over F_3. Let α be a root of $f(x)$ in F_{3^2}. Assume that α is the element 3. Using the properties of a root α, compute the following over F_{3^2}:
1) 3^{-1}
2) 3^7
3) 3^{7k} (k integer greater than 1)
4) $6 * 7$

Exercise 3.18 Let $x^4 + x + 1$ be a polynomial irreducible over F_2 associated with the field F_{2^4}. Assuming that 2 is a generator, do the following operations over F_{2^4}:
1) $9 * 6$
2) 9^{-1} (hint: use Theorem 3.21)
3) $(9+1)^{357}$ (hint: do not compute usual addition and use 2 as generator)

Exercise 3.19 The 256 elements of field F_{2^8} are represented as polynomials $F_{2^8}[x]\ mod\ f(x)$, where $f(x) = x^8 + x^4 + x^3 + x + 1$.

1) Calculate the sum of 01010011 and 11001010.
2) Calculate the product of 01010011 and 11001010.
3) Find the multiplicative inverse of 00000010.

Problem 3.10 Let g be a generator of $\mathbb{Z}_p^*$. Prove that g^{-1} also is a generator of $\mathbb{Z}_p^*$.

Problem 3.11 Prove the correctness of Lemma 3.6 by counterexamples:
1) Show that a root α of the irreducible polynomial $f(x) = x^2 + 1$ cannot generate all nonzero elements of the field F_{3^2}.

2) Show that a root α of the irreducible polynomial $f(x) = x^3 + 2x + 2$ cannot generate all nonzero elements of field F_{3^3}.

Problem 3.12

1) Let $g_1, g_2, ..., g_m$ be the generators of $\mathbb{Z}_p^*$, with $p > 3$. Prove that

$$\prod_{i=1}^{i=k} g_i \equiv 1 \bmod p.$$

2) Let F_p be a prime field. Prove that $\sum_{u \in F_p} u \equiv 0 \bmod p$.

Problem 3.13   Show that $\mathbb{Z}_4$ is not a field.

Problem 3.14   Consider field F_{2^5} with reduction polynomial $f(x) = x^5 + x^2 + 1$. Show that $g = x$ is a generator of F_{2^5}.

Problem 3.15   Let $f(x) = x^4 + x + 1$ be an irreducible polynomial over F_2. $f(x)$ is used for computations over field F_{2^4}. Solve the following linear equations:

1) $3y = 4$
2) $9y + 3 = 2$

3.3   Computation Algorithms

The previous sections presented theorems and lemmas, which are of paramount importance to cryptographic algorithms. Often, computations are needed to find elements (e.g. multiplicative inverses, square roots, etc.). Such computations are time consuming in particular when large numbers are of concern. Many algorithms exist in literature aiming to optimize computations in general and in cryptosystems in particular. This section presents the most commonly used algorithms to speed up computations in cryptographic algorithms. They include Extended Euclidean algorithm to find the greatest common divider and multiplicative inverse, Square-and-multiply method to perform modular exponentiation, Montgomery multiplication to compute modular multiplication, Gauss's algorithm to solve congruence systems, Tonelli-Shanks algorithm to find modular square roots, and Rabin's algorithm to test irreducibility of polynomials.

3.3.1   Euclidean and Extended Euclidean Algorithms

3.3.1.1   Euclidean Algorithm
The Euclidean algorithm is the most known and used method for computing the greatest common divider (*GCD*) of two integers. There exist different ways to describe the Euclidean algorithm. Below is a pseudocode for the description of the Euclidean algorithm:

```
function Euclidean_Algorithm_GCD(a, b)
  # a and b are integers such that a ⩾ b
  while b ≠ 0 do
    t = b; b = a mod b; a = t
  return a
```

3.3.1.2   Extended Euclidean Algorithm

Theorem 3.25   Bezout's theorem (also called **Bezout's identity**): for every pair of two non-negative integers a and b, there exist two integers x and y, such that $\mathrm{GCD}(a,b) = ax + by$.

In addition to the *GCD* computation, the Extended Euclidean algorithm computes two coefficients (called Bezout's identity coefficients) x and y, such that $ax + by = GCD(a,b)$. The pseudocode of the extended Euclidean algorithm is as follows:

```
function Extended_Euclidean_Algorithm (a, b)
  # a and b are integers such that a ⩾ b
  r = a; r1 = b; x = 1; x1 = 0; y = 0; y1 = 1
  while r1 ≠ 0 do
    Q = r div r1 (quotient)
    aux = r1; r1 = r - Q*r1; r = aux
```

```
    aux = x1; x1 = x - Q*x1; x = aux
    aux = y1; y1 = y - Q*y1; y = aux
    return "Bezout coefficients:", (x, y), "GCD:", r
```

3.3.1.3 Finding Multiplicative Inverse

Finding multiplicative inverse in $\mathbb{Z}_p^*$, with p a prime, is a very frequent operation in cryptography. Below, two methods, often used to find multiplicative inverses, are introduced. They differ in terms of time computation.

3.3.1.3.1 Finding Multiplicative Inverse Using Euler's Theorem

Euler's theorem states that if a and p are two coprime positive integers, then $a^{\varphi(p)} \equiv 1 \bmod p$, where $\varphi(p)$ is the Euler's totient.

Multiply both sides of the congruence by a^{-1} yields $a^{\varphi(p)} * a^{-1} \equiv a^{-1} \bmod p$.

Hence, $a^{\varphi(p)-1} \equiv a^{-1} \bmod p$, which means that the multiplicative inverse is obtained by exponentiation.

We know, by Theorem 3.1, that if p is a prime, then $\phi(p) = p - 1$. Hence, $a^{\varphi(p)-1} = a^{p-2} \equiv a^{-1} \bmod p$, if p is prime.

Example 3.38

– Compute modular inverse of 2 in $\mathbb{Z}_{11}^*$
  By Theorem 3.1, $p = 11$ is prime $\Rightarrow \varphi(11) = 1C$ $2^{-1} \equiv 2^{11-2} \bmod 9 = (2^4) * (2^5) \bmod 11 = 6$
  Check: $2 * 2^{-1} \bmod 11 = 2 * 6 \bmod 11 = 1$
– Compute modular inverse of 2 in $\mathbb{Z}_{23}^*$
  By Theorem 3.1, $p = 23$ is prime $\Rightarrow \varphi(23) = 22$
  $2^{-1} \equiv 2^{23-2} \bmod 9 = 12$
  Check: $2 * 2^{-1} \bmod 9 = 2 * 12 \bmod 23 = 1$

3.3.1.3.2 Finding Multiplicative Inverse Using Extended Euclidean Algorithm

The Extended Euclidean algorithm finds x and y such that $ax + by = GCD(a,b)$. Let us see why the Extended Euclidean algorithm is appropriate to compute the multiplicative inverse. By definition of a multiplicative group $\mathbb{Z}_n^*$, any element $\alpha \in \mathbb{Z}_n^*$ is less than n and has an inverse $\alpha^{-1} \in \mathbb{Z}_n^*$. Since α is invertible in $\mathbb{Z}_n^*$, $GCD(p, \alpha) = 1$.

By definition of multiplicative inverse:

$$\alpha * \alpha^{-1} \equiv 1 \bmod n \Rightarrow \exists k \in \mathbb{Z}_n \mid \alpha * \alpha^{-1} = 1 + k * n.$$

Thus, $\alpha * \alpha^{-1} - k * n = n * (-k) + \alpha * (\alpha^{-1}) = 1 = GCD(n, \alpha)$.

Hence, given α and n, applying the Extended Euclidean algorithm to $n * (-k) + \alpha * (\alpha^{-1}) = 1$ returns $-k$ and α^{-1}. In other words, we substitute n to a, α to b, $-k$ to x, and α^{-1} to y in the equality $ax + by = GCD(a, b)$ and keep the returned value for y.

3.3.2 Modular Exponentiation: Square-and-Multiply

Some cryptographic algorithms, such as RSA, make use of modular exponentiation to encrypt or decrypt messages. Since cryptographic algorithms use very large numbers (in magnitude of thousands of bits), it is of paramount importance to use efficient modular exponentiation algorithms to get messages encrypted or decrypted in reasonable time to not jeopardize the performance of cryptosystems.

Square-and-Multiply algorithms are useful to compute large integer powers of a number, for example $7^{3110190717} \bmod 1001$. The most known and used algorithm in the Square-and-Multiply algorithm family is called *right-to-left*[12] *binary exponentiation algorithm*, or simply *binary exponentiation algorithm*. To better understand the Square-and-Multiply method, recall the following rules of modular arithmetic:

For any positive integers a, a_1, b, b_1 k, m:

- If $(a \equiv a_1 \bmod n) \wedge (b \equiv b_1 \bmod n) \Rightarrow (a * b) \bmod n \equiv (a_1 * b_1) \bmod n$
- $a^k \bmod n \equiv (a \bmod n)^k \bmod n$

In the congruence $a^m \bmod n$, a is called the base, m the exponent, and n the modulus. To compute $a^m \bmod n$, the *right-to-left binary exponentiation method* is based on the reuse of powers of 2 of a. Let us see an example to show computation principle of the method:

$5^{11} \bmod 14 \equiv ?$

$5^{11} = 5^{4*2+2+1}$ (11, the power of 5, is expressed as a sum of powers of 2.)

$5^{11} \bmod 14 \equiv \left[\left(\left(5^2\right)^4\right)*\left(5^2\right)*5\right] \bmod 14$.

By the modular arithmetic rules recalled above:

$5^{11} \bmod 14 \equiv \left[\left(5^2 \bmod 14\right)^4 *\left(5^2 \bmod 14\right)*\left(5 \bmod 14\right)\right] \bmod 14$.

Replace $5^2 \bmod 14 \equiv 11$ and $5 \bmod 14 \equiv 5$ in the previous equation:

$5^{11} \bmod 14 \equiv (11)^4 *(11)*(5) \bmod 14 \equiv \left(11^5 * 5\right) \bmod 14$

$11^5 \bmod 14 \equiv \left[\left(11^2 \bmod 14\right)^2 * 11\right] \bmod 14 \equiv (9)^2 * 11 \bmod 14 \equiv 9$.

Thus, $5^{11} \bmod 14 \equiv 9 * 5 \bmod 14 \equiv 3$.

The right-to-left binary exponentiation method computes $a^k \bmod n \equiv b$ as follows:

1) Convert k in binary notation $k = k_{L-1}k_{L-2}\cdots k_0$, $k_i \in \{0,1\}$, $(0 \leq i \leq L-1)$.

2) Thus, $k = \sum_{i=0}^{i=L-1} 2^i * k_i$.

3) a^k is considered as a product of powers of 2: $a^k = a^{\left(\sum_{i=0}^{i=L-1} 2^i * k_i\right)} = \prod_{i=0}^{i=L-1}\left(a^{k_i}\right)^{2^i}$.

4) For i from 0 to $L-1$: $b_i \equiv \left(a^{k_i}\right)^{2^i} \bmod n$.

5) $b \equiv \left(\prod_{i=0}^{i=L-1} b_i\right) \bmod n$.

One of the most efficient pseudocodes proposed in literature to implement the right-to-left exponentiation is as follows:

```
function Right_to_Left_Binary_Exponentiation
  input a: base; n: modulus; k: exponent
  output res
  res = 1; a = a mod n
  while k > 0 do
    if (k mod 2 == 1) then res = res*a mod n
    k = ⌈k/2⌉; a = a*a mod n
  return res
```

3.3.3 Fast Modular Multiplication and Montgomery's Multiplication

Given three positive integers a, b, and n, the modular multiplication $a*b \bmod n$ finds an integer r such that: $\exists q \in \mathbb{N} \mid a*b = q*n+r$. If a and b are less than N, then the product $a*b$ is less than or equal to $(n-1)^2$.

In regular modular multiplication, the bit-length of arguments a, b, and n are assumed to be less than or equal to w, the word bit-length of the underlying hardware. Often, w is 32 or 64. If arguments a and b have a bit-length less than or equal to w, then the naïve modular multiplication is performed with four basic operations: a multiplication $P_1 = a*b$, a division $q = \left\lceil \dfrac{P_1}{n} \right\rceil$, a multiplication $P_2 = q*n$, and a subtraction $r = P_1 - P_2$.

It is commonly admitted that division is an expensive operation (in time computation) and numbers used in cryptography are (very) large integers, which have bit-length in hundreds or in thousands (128, 512, 1024, 2048, etc.). Consequently, cryptographic numbers may be composed of several machine words and the naïve modular multiplication results in excessive computation time. That would jeopardize the performance of cryptosystems. Therefore, to implement cryptographic algorithms, specific computation techniques are required. This chapter presents the Montgomery multiplication [9], which is the most known and fast used modular multiplication method in cryptographic algorithm implementation. The efficiency of Montgomery multiplication comes from the avoidance of expensive division operations.

3.3.3.1 Single-precision Montgomery Multiplication Algorithm

Basic Montgomery multiplication is applicable if single-precision arguments, i.e. a, b, and n take values less than 2^w, where w denotes the word bit-length of the underlying hardware. When properly implemented, the Montgomery multiplication reduces the computation time due to division and consequently it accelerates modular multiplication. The main principle behind Montgomery multiplication is to change the representation of arguments a and b and change the modular multiplication accordingly. The Montgomery multiplication does not directly compute $a * b \bmod n$. Instead, it computes $M(a, b) = \left(\left(\left(a * R \bmod n\right) * \left(b * R \bmod n\right)\right)\right) * R^{-1} \bmod n$ for a carefully chosen integer R, which is called *Montgomery radix*. When Montgomery multiplication is used in cryptosystems, R is chosen to be equal to a power of 2, greater than n, and coprime to N. For example, if $n = 103$, R may be 128, 256, etc.

Definition 3.44 Montgomery reduction: *let n and R be two integers such that $R > n$ and $\mathrm{GCD}(n, R) = 1$. For any integer T, such that $0 \leq T < n * R$, the Montgomery reduction of T, denoted $REDC(T)$ modulo n w.r.t. R is defined by:* $REDC(T) = T * R^{-1} \bmod n.$

Montgomery reduction function described below enables to quickly compute $T * R^{-1} \bmod N$ from T:

---

function *REDC*
  input T: integer such that $0 \leq T < R * n$
       n, n', R: integers
  output t
  1. $m = \left(T \bmod R\right) * n' \bmod R$
  2. $t = \dfrac{T + m * n}{R}$
  3. **if** $t \leq n$ **then** $t = t - n$
  4. **return** t (# $t = T * R^{-1} \bmod n$)

Next, the Montgomery reduction function *REDC* is used to compute the modular multiplication $a * b \bmod N$ as follows:

---

function *Modular Multiplication $\_with_{REDC}$* a, b, n)
  1. # Choose R such that $\mathrm{GCD}(n, R) = 1$ and $n < R = 2^k \leq 2^w$
  2. # Compute $n' = -n^{-1} \bmod R$
  3. # Compute the Montgomery transforms of a and b
     $\tilde{a} \equiv a * R \bmod n; \tilde{b} \equiv b * R \bmod n$
  4. # Compute the Montgomery reductions c' and c:
     $c' \equiv REDC\left(\tilde{a} * \tilde{b}\right); c \equiv REDC\left(c'\right)$
  5. **return** c

Note. The correctness of the Montgomery multiplication is discussed in Problem 3.17.

Example 3.39   We make use of the Montgomery reduction to find $a * b \bmod n$ with $a = 43$, $b = 56$, and $n = 97$.

$n = 97$ is less than 2^7, we can pick $R = 128 = 2^7$.
$n^{-1} \bmod R = 97^{-1} \bmod 2^7 = 33$, $-n^{-1} = 95$.
Montgomery conversion of arguments a and b:
$\tilde{a} \equiv 43 * 2^7 \bmod 97 = 72$, $\tilde{b} \equiv 56 * 2^7 \bmod 97 = 87$
$c' \equiv REDC(\tilde{a} * \tilde{b}) = REDC(6264) = 55$
$c \equiv REDC\left(c'\right) = 80$, which is equal to $43 * 56 \bmod 97$.

Why does Montgomery's method speed up the modulation multiplication?

1) First, in cryptosystems that use Montgomery multiplication, R, R^{-1}, n^{-1}, and n' are computed once and used in several modular multiplications. Therefore, their computation time has a negligible impact on the cryptosystem performance. For example, in RSA the modulus n is computed from two large primes, then the public and private keys are computed and the same pair (public and private keys) is used to encrypt and decrypt messages for a long time (maybe in months).

2) Second, when R is a power of 2, multiplication and division by R are efficiently performed with left and right bit-shifting, which are very fast operations in hardware. Therefore, t in line 2 of DECR is computed with a w-right-shift.

3) Third, in line 1 of DECR function, *mod R* is used instead of *mod n*. Since R is a power of 2, *mod R* can be efficiently computed with shifting operations as follows: for any integer x, $x \equiv z \bmod R \equiv z \bmod 2^w$. By definition of modulo $z = x - \left\lfloor \dfrac{x}{2^w} \right\rfloor * 2^w$. Therefore, z is computed by a w-right-shift (i.e. $q = \left\lfloor \dfrac{x}{2^w} \right\rfloor$), a w-left-shift (i.e. $p = q * 2^w$), and a subtraction (i.e. $z = x - p$).

3.3.3.2 Multi-precision Montgomery Multiplication Algorithm

A large integer X is represented as an array of l w-bit-words $(x_0, ..., x_{l-1})$ such that:

$$X = \sum_{i=0}^{l-1} x_i * (2^w)^i = \sum_{i=0}^{l-1} x_i * B^i, \quad (0 \leq x_i < B, \ i = 0, ..., l-1)$$

where $B = 2^w$ is called *representation basis*. For example, in hexadecimal format,
$X = 112233445566778899AABBCCDDEEFF00$ is represented as:
two 64-bit words: $x_0 = 1122334455667788$ et $x_1 = 99AABBCCDDEEFF00$
or alternatively, as four 32-bit words: $x_0 = 11223344$, $x_1 = 55667788$, $x_2 = 99AABBCC$, $x_3 = DDEEFF00$.

Large integers are called multi-precision integers and arithmetic operations on large integers are said to be multi-precision operations. One multi-precision operation requires multiple simple-precision operations to be performed. Multi-precision addition, subtraction, and multiplication are introduced.[13]

---

function MultiprecisionAddition
    input X, Y : two large integers $X = (x_0, ..., x_{l-1})$ and $Y = (y_0, ..., y_{l-1})$
           # Integer with less than l words is left-padded with zero-words
           B: base (in cryptography, B is a power of 2)
    output S # sum represented in base B as $S = (s_0, ..., s_l)$
    1. $c = 0$ # c is the carry digit. It is 0 or 1.
    2. **for** i = 0 **to** $l-1$ **do**
        $s_i = (x_i + y_i + c) \bmod B$
        if $(x_i + y_i + c) < B$ **then** $c = 0$ **else** $c = 1$
    3. $s_l = c$
    4. **return** (S)

---

function MultiprecisionSubtraction
    input X, Y: two large integers $X = (x_0, ..., x_{l-1})$ and $Y = (y_0, ..., y_{l-1})$
           # Integer with less than l words is left-padded with zero-words
           # To simplify the function, assume $X \geq Y$
           B: base (in cryptography, B is a power of 2)
    output D # difference represented in base B as $D = (d_0, ..., d_{l-1})$
    1. $c = 0$ # c is the carry digit. It is 0 or -1
    2. **for** i=0 **to** $l-1$ **do**
        $d_i = (x_i - y_i + c) \bmod B$
        if $(x_i - y_i + c) \geq 0$ **then** $c = 0$ **else** $c = -1$
    4. **return** (D)

---

function MultiprecisionMultilpication
    input X, Y: two large integers $X = (x_0, ..., x_{l-1})$ and $Y = (y_0, ..., y_{k-1})$
           # $k \leq l$ (arguments are ordered to reduce operations)
           B: base (in cryptography, B is a power of 2)

```
output P # Product represented in base B as P = (d_0,...,d_{l+k-1})
1. for i=0 to (l + k − 1) do P_i = 0
2. for i=0 to k − 1 do
   2.1 r = 0
   2.2 for j = 0 to l − 1 do
       V = p_{i+j} + x_j * y_i + r  # Multiplication in base B
       r = leftWord (V)
   2.3 p_{i+l} = r
3. return (P)
```

When computing modular multiplication $X * Y \bmod n$ over large integers, the Montgomery multiplication is valuable to speed up computations. The modulus n and arguments and X and Y are represented as l words in base B:

$$n = \sum_{i=0}^{l-1} n_i * \left(B\right)^i, \ X = \sum_{i=0}^{l-1} x_i * \left(B\right)^i, \ Y = \sum_{i=0}^{l-1} y_i * \left(B\right)^i.$$

Arguments are padded on the left with zero-words if needed.

The Montgomery radix R is chosen such that n is coprime to R and $n < R = B^l$ (in cryptography $R = 2^{l*w}$ where w denotes the word bit-length). Before performing modular multiplication, $n' = -n^{-1} \bmod B$ is computed. Notice that $\bmod B$ is used and not $\bmod R$ (as in single-precision Montgomery reduction). R and n' are computed once and used in several modular multiplications with the same modulus n. Pseudocode of the multi-precision Montgomery multiplication is as follows:

```
function MultiprecisionMontgomeryMultiplication
   input n, X, Y : l-word integers; n is an odd integer
         n': one-word integer
         B: base (in cryptography, B is a power of 2)
         l: word-length of arguments n, X, Y, R
         # Condition: R = B^l, R > n and GCD(R, n) = 1
   output X * Y * R^{-1} mod n
   1. A = 0 # A = (a_{l-1}, a_{l-2},..., a_0), where a's are words in base B.
   2. for i=0 to l − 1 do
      A = A + x_i * Y;  q = A * n' mod B;  A = (A + n * q) / B
   3. if A ≥ n then A = A − n
   4. return A
```

The multi-precision Montgomery multiplication computes $X * Y * R^{-1} \bmod n$. Therefore, to find the modular multiplication, the returned result is multiplied by R.

Note. The multi-precision Montgomery multiplication makes use of multi-precision addition, subtraction, and multiplication. In addition, division by n' and $\bmod B$ operations are performed using shift operations.

Example 3.40 $n = 50021$ (n is a prime), $X = 15063$, $Y = 37551$, Base $B = 100$
X is three 2-decimal-digit-words: $X = \left(01, 50, 63\right)$.
We choose $R = 100^4$, which meets the conditions $R > n$ and $GCD\left(R, n\right) = 1$.
$R = 100^4 = 100^l \Rightarrow l = 4$
Compute $n' = -n^{-1} \bmod B$
$\quad n' = -50021^{-1} \bmod 100 = -81 \bmod 100 = 19.$
Below are the computations in multi-precision Montgomery multiplication:

i	x_i	$A + x_i * Y$	$q = A * n' \bmod B$	$A = \left(A + n * q\right) / B$
0	63	2365713	47	47167
1	50	1924717	23	30752
2	01	68303	57	29195
3	00	29195	5	2793

The multi-precision Montgomery multiplication returns 2793, which represents $X**R^{-1} \bmod n$. Multiplying by R yields $\left(X*Y*R^{-1}\right)*R \bmod n \equiv X*Y \bmod n$.

Thus, $2793*100^4 \bmod 50021 = 15063*37551 \bmod 50021 \equiv 43266$.

3.3.4 Chinese Remainder Theorem and Gauss's Algorithm

The Chinese remainder theorem (CRT) was introduced in the 3rd century. It provides a powerful tool for solving problems involving congruences. In particular, the CRT helps solving congruences including large numbers (see Exercise 3.26).

> **Theorem 3.26** Chinese remainder theorem: if k integer numbers $n_i, i = 1, \ldots, k$, are pairwise coprime and greater than 1, and if k numbers $a_1, \ldots, a_k$ are such that $0 \le a_i < n_i$ for every i, then there is one and only one integer x such that:
>
> $0 \le x < \prod_{i=1}^{i=k} n_i$ and $x \equiv a_i \bmod n_i$, for every $i \in [1, k]$.

Example 3.41

$$\begin{cases} x \equiv 1 \bmod 5 \\ x \equiv 2 \bmod 7 \\ x \equiv 3 \bmod 9 \\ x \equiv 4 \bmod 11 \end{cases}$$

In the equation system above, $n_1 = 5$, $n_2 = 7$, $n_3 = 9$, $n_4 = 11$, $a_1 = 1$, $a_2 = 2$, $a_3 = 3$, and $a_4 = 4$. All n_i's are pairwise coprime and $0 \le a_i < n_i$ for every i. $x = 1731$ is a solution, since:

i) $1731 < 5*7*9*11 = 3465$

ii) $1731 \equiv 1 \bmod 5 \qquad 1731 \equiv 2 \bmod 7 \qquad 1731 \equiv 3 \bmod 9 \qquad 1731 \equiv 4 \bmod 11$

Gauss's algorithm

The Chinese remainder theorem says that there is a unique solution when some conditions are met, but it does not say how to find it. This is usually done using Gauss's algorithm.

Given a system of k congruence equations that fulfill the conditions of application of Chinese remainder theorem, Gauss's algorithm finds the solution to the congruence equation system as follows:

> 1) Compute the common modulus $N = \prod_{i=1}^{i=k} n_i$
>
> 2) Let $N_i = \dfrac{N}{n_i}$, for $1 \le i \le k$
>
> 3) Compute N_i^{-1} the modular inverse of $N_i \bmod n_i$, for $1 \le i \le k$
>   i.e. $N_i * N_i^{-1} \equiv 1 \bmod n$, for $1 \le i \le k$
>
> 4) The solution to the congruence equation system is
>
> $$x = \left(\sum_{i=1}^{k} \left(a_i * N_i * N_i^{-1} \right) \right) \bmod N$$

Example 3.42 Find x for the following congruence equation system using Gauss's algorithm.

$$\begin{cases} x \equiv 1 \bmod 5 \\ x \equiv 2 \bmod 7 \\ x \equiv 3 \bmod 9 \\ x \equiv 4 \bmod 11 \end{cases}$$

The constants of the congruence equation system are:

$n_1 = 5, n_2 = 7, n_3 = 9, n_4 = 11$

$a_1 = 1, \ a_2 = 2, \ a_3 = 3, \ a_4 = 4$

All n_i's are pairwise coprime and $a_i < n_i$, for every i. Therefore, the conditions to use the Chinese remainder theorem are met.

Steps of calculation of x using Gauss's algorithm:

- Common modulus $N = 5 * 7 * 9 * 11 = 3465$

- $N_1 = \dfrac{3465}{5} = 693,\ N_2 = \dfrac{3465}{7} = 495,\ N_3 = \dfrac{3465}{9} = 385,\ N_4 = \dfrac{3465}{11} = 315$

- Multiplicative inverses:

  $N_1^{-1} * N_1 \equiv 1\ mod\ 5 \Rightarrow N_1^{-1} = 2 \quad N_2^{-1} * N_2 \equiv 1\ mod\ 7 \Rightarrow N_2^{-1} = 3$

  $N_3^{-1} * N_3 \equiv 1\ mod\ 9 \Rightarrow N_3^{-1} = 4 \quad N_4^{-1} * N_4 \equiv 1\ mod\ 11 \Rightarrow N_4^{-1} = 8$

- $x = \left(\displaystyle\sum_{i=1}^{4} \left(a_i * N_i * N_i^{-1} \right) \right) mod\ N$

  $= \left((1 * 693 * 2) + (2 * 495 * 3) + (3 * 385 * 4) + (4 * 315 * 8) \right) mod\ 3465$

  $= 19056\ mod\ 3465 = 1731$

- Check of correctness:

  $1731 = 346 * 5 + 1 \equiv 1\ mod\ 5$

  $1731 = 247 * 7 + 2 \equiv 2\ mod\ 7$

  $1731 = 192 * 9 + 3 \equiv 3\ mod\ 9$

  $1731 = 157 * 11 + 4 \equiv 4\ mod\ 11.$

3.3.5 Finding Modular Square Roots

3.3.5.1 Tonelli-Shanks Algorithm for Finding Modular Square Roots of Primes

The most commonly used algorithm to find modular square roots, i.e. to solve congruence of the form $r^2 \equiv a\ mod\ p$, when $p \equiv 1\ mod\ 4$ is Tonelli-Shanks algorithm [10]. Pseudocode of the latter is as follows:

---

function Tonelli_Shanks

    input p, a: prime p and integer a, with $0 < a < p$

    output $r: r \in \mathbb{Z}_p^*$ such that $r^2 \equiv a\ mod\ p$

    1. # Use Euler's criterion to check that a square root exists and stop,

       # if it does not exist.

    2. # Find q and s such that: $p = 2^s q + 1$ and q is odd.

    3. # In $\mathbb{Z}_p^*$, select[14] a quadratic nonresidue u.

    4. # Variable initialization

       $m = s; \quad c = u^q\ mod\ p\,; t = a^q\ mod\ p\,; R = a^{\frac{q+1}{2}}\ mod\ p.$

    5. **loop**

       5.1. **if** $t = 1$, **then return** $r = R$

       5.2. **else**

          i. $k = 0$

          while $\boldsymbol{not}\left(t^{2^k} \equiv 1\ mod\ p\right)$ **do**: $k = k + 1$

             # the loop above is to find the least k, such that $t^{2^k} \equiv 1\ mod\ p$.

          ii. # Variable update

             $b = c^{2^{(m-k-1)}}\ \boldsymbol{mod}\ p\,; m = k; c = b^2\ mod\ p$

             $t = t * b^2\ mod\ p\,; \quad R = R * b\ mod\ p$

Example 3.43 Find the square roots of $111\ mod\ 113$.

– Check, by Euler's criterion (Theorem 3.7), that a square root exists:

$111^{\frac{113-1}{2}}\ mod\ 113 = 111^{56}\ mod\ 113 = \left((-2)^{56} \right) mod\ 113 = 1$. Thus, there exists a solution.

- $113 = 2^4 * 7 + 1$. Thus, $s = 4$ and $q = 7$.
- Selection of a quadratic nonresidue u using an iterative search:

    Check element 1: $1^{\frac{113-1}{2}}$ $mod\ 113 = 1$. Thus, 1 is a quadratic residue.

    Check element 2: $2^{\frac{113-1}{2}}$ $mod\ 113 = 1$. Thus, 2 is a quadratic residue.

    Check element $2^{\frac{113-1}{3}}$ $mod\ 113 = -1$. Thus, 3 is a quadratic nonresidue. We keep $u = 3$.

- Initialization

    $m = 4$

    $c = 3^7\ mod\ 113 = 40$

    $t = 111^7\ mod\ 113 = 98$

    $R = 111^{\frac{7+1}{2}}\ mod\ 113 = 16$

- Loop

    a) Iteration 1: t is not equal to 1. Hence, computations continue

    $98^{2^2} \equiv 1\ mod\ 113$. Thus, $k = 2$

    $b = 40^{2^{(4-2-1)}}\ mod\ 113 = 40^2\ mod\ 113 = 18$

    $m = 2$

    $c = 18^2\ mod\ 113 = 98$

    $t = 98 * 18^2\ mod\ 113 = 112$

    $R = 16 * 18\ mod\ 113 = 62$

    b) Iteration 2: t is not equal to 1. Hence, computations continue

    $112^{2^1} \equiv 1\ mod\ 113$. Thus, $k = 1$.

    $b = 98^{2^{(2-1-1)}}\ mod\ 113 = 98^{2^0}\ mod\ 113 = 98$

    $m = 1$

    $c = 98^2\ mod\ 113 = 112$

    $t = 112 * 98^2\ mod\ 113 = 1$

    $R = 62 * 98\ mod\ 113 = 87$.

    c) Iteration 3: t is equal to 1. Thus, return $r = 87$.

    Hence, the solutions to $111\ mod\ 113$ are 87 and 26 (i.e. $-87\ mod\ 113$).

3.3.5.2 Finding Square Roots of Multiple Primes

This subsection considers the following problem:

Find the solutions to $y^2 \equiv a\ mod\ n$, with n a multiple of two or more primes.

3.3.5.2.1 Case of Two Primes

Let us start with the following example: find solutions to $r^2 \equiv 29\ mod\ 35$.

In such a scenario, $N = 35$ is a product of two primes 5 and 7.

By Lemma 3.2, if there exists r such that $r^2 \equiv 29\ mod\ 35$, then $r^2 \equiv 29\ mod\ 5$ and $r^2 \equiv 29\ mod\ 7$.

$r^2 \equiv 29\ mod\ 5$ is equivalent to $r^2 \equiv 4\ mod\ 5$.

$r^2 \equiv 29\ mod\ 7$ is equivalent to $r^2 \equiv 1\ mod\ 7$.

$4\ mod\ 5$ has two quadratic squares: 2 and 3.

$1\ mod\ 7$ has two quadratic squares: 1 and 6.

Thus, there are four congruence systems to solve:

$$S_1 = \begin{cases} x \equiv 2\ mod\ 5 \\ x \equiv 1\ mod\ 7 \end{cases} \qquad S_2 = \begin{cases} x \equiv 2\ mod\ 5 \\ x \equiv 6\ mod\ 7 \end{cases}$$

$$S_3 = \begin{cases} x \equiv 3\ mod\ 5 \\ x \equiv 1\ mod\ 7 \end{cases} \qquad S_4 = \begin{cases} x \equiv 3\ mod\ 5 \\ x \equiv 6\ mod\ 7 \end{cases}$$

Recall that the commonly used method to solve congruence systems is Gauss's algorithm. Below are calculations to solve S_1 system:

The constants of the congruence equation system are: $n_1 = 5$, $n_2 = 7$, $a_1 = 2$, $a_2 = 1$.
Common modulus is $N = 5 * 7 = 35$

$$N_1 = \frac{35}{5} = 7, \ N_2 = \frac{35}{7} = 5.$$

Multiplicative inverses: $N_1^{-1} * N_1 \equiv 1 \ mod \ 5 \Rightarrow N_1^{-1} = 3$

$N_2^{-1} * N_2 \equiv 1 \ mod \ 7 \Rightarrow N_2^{-1} = 3$

$$x = \left((2 * 7 * 3) + (1 * 5 * 3) \right) mod \ 35 = 22.$$

Applying Gauss's algorithm to the four congruence systems yields the following:

$x = 22$ is a solution to S_1

$x = 27$ is a solution to S_2

$x = 8$ is a solution to S_3

$x = 13$ is a solution to S_4

Now, check that the values are square roots of $29 \ mod \ 35$

$x = 22 : 22^2 = 484 \equiv 29 \ mod \ 35$

$x = 27 : 27^2 = 729 \equiv 29 \ mod \ 35$

$x = 8 : 8^2 = 64 \equiv 29 \ mod \ 35$

$x = 13 : 13^2 = 169 \equiv 29 \ mod \ 35$

Thus, $29 \ mod \ 35$ has four square roots.

3.3.5.2.2 General Case (2 or More Primes)

When n is a product of k primes denoted $n_1, n_2, ..., n_k$, the commonly used method to find the square roots of $a \ mod \ n$ is composed of two steps:

Step 1: Find the square roots of prime moduli

i) From congruence $a \ mod \ n$, derive congruences $a_1 \ mod \ n_1, ..., a_k \ mod \ n_k$, where $a_i \equiv a \ mod \ n_i$, for $1 \leq i \leq k$.

ii) Then, find the square roots to each of congruences $a_i \ mod \ n_i$, $1 \leq i \leq k$. The result is a set of k pairs $(r_i, -r_i)$, where $r_i^2 \equiv a_i \ mod \ n_i$, $1 \leq i \leq k$. At this step, depending on each n_i, either Lemma 3.5 or Tonelli-Shanks algorithm should be used to find square roots to $r_i^2 \equiv a_i \ mod \ n_i$.

Step 2: Solve a set of congruence systems

iii) Build a set of $2k$ distinct congruence systems denoted $S_1, S_2, ..., S_{2^k}$ such that each congruence system is composed of exactly k congruences (a congruence for each of the k primes) as follows:

$$S_1 = \left\{ r_1 \ mod \ n_1, \ r_2 \ mod \ n_2, \ ..., \ r_{k-1} \ mod \ n_{k-1}, \ r_k \ mod \ n_k \right\}$$

$$S_2 = \left\{ r_1 \ mod \ n_1, \ r_2 \ mod \ n_2, \ ..., r_{k-1} \ mod \ n_{k-1}, -r_k \ mod \ n_k \right\}$$

$$S_3 = \left\{ r_1 \ mod \ n_1, \ r_2 \ mod \ n_2, \ ..., -r_{k-1} \ mod \ n_{k-1}, \ r_k \ mod \ n_k \right\}$$

...

$$S_{2^k} = \left\{ -r_1 \ mod \ n_1, -r_2 \ mod \ n_2, \ ..., -r_{k-1} \ mod \ n_{k-1}, -r_k \ mod \ n_k \right\}$$

iv) Use Gauss's algorithm to find the solutions to each of the 2^k congruence systems. The 2^k found solutions represent the square roots to $a \ mod \ n$.

3.3.6 Test of Irreducibility

In cryptography, before using a polynomial $f(x)$ of degree m over a field F_p as a reduction polynomial to construct a field F_{p^m}, one must first check that p is prime and $f(x)$ is irreducible over F_p. Hence, algorithms for testing irreducibility are needed in cryptography. There exist two approaches to test if a polynomial $f(x)$ of degree m over a finite field F_p is irreducible: naïve approach and Rabin's test for irreducibility.

3.3.6.1 Naïve Approach

Take each element in $\{0, 2, ..., p-1\}$ and check if $f(0), f(1), ..., f(p-1)$ is equal to 0. When the first element a such that $f(a) = 0$ is found, stop testing, because there exists at least a root of $f(x)$ and $f(x)$ can be factorized as $f(x) = (x-a) * q(x)$, with $q(x)$ a polynomial of degree less than m, and consequently $f(x)$ is reducible.

Example 3.44   Test irreducibility of $f(x) = x^4 + x^2 + x + 1$ over F_2:

$F_2 = \{0,1\}$. Thus, the check is:

$$f(0) = 0^4 + 0^2 + 0 + 1 \bmod 2 = 1 \qquad f(1) = 1^4 + 1^2 + 1 + 1 \bmod 2 = 0.$$

Therefore, $f(x)$ is reducible and can be expressed as $(x+1)(x^3 + x^2 + 1)$.

Irreducibility test of $f(x) = x^4 + x^3 + x + 1$ over F_5:

$F_5 = \{0,1,2,3,4\}$. Thus, the check is:

$$f(0) = 0^4 + 0^3 + 0 + 1 \bmod 5 = 1 \qquad f(1) = 1^4 + 1^3 + 1 + 1 \bmod 5 = 4$$

$$f(2) = 2^4 + 2^3 + 2 + 1 \bmod 5 = 2 \qquad f(3) = 3^4 + 3^3 + 3 + 1 \bmod 5 = 2$$

$$f(4) = 4^4 + 4^3 + 4 + 1 \bmod 5 = 0.$$

Hence, $f(x)$ is reducible and can be expressed as $(x-4)(x^3 + 1)$, which is the same as $(x+1)(x^3 + 1)$ over F_5.

Such a naïve method is easy to understand and implement. Unfortunately, it suffers two weaknesses: 1) it does not scale (remember that in cryptography very large numbers are used) and 2) a polynomial may be reducible even if it has no roots. For example, in field F_3, $x^4 + 2x^2 + 1$ can be written as a product $(x^2 + 1)(x^2 + 1)$. Therefore, it is reducible, but it has no roots in $\mathbb{Z}_3$, because $(x^2 + 1)$ has no roots in F_3.

3.3.6.2 Efficient Approach (Rabin's Test of Irreducibility)

One of well-known algorithms for testing the irreducibility of polynomials over $\mathbb{Z}_p$ is the Rabin's test [11], which results from the following theorem:

Theorem 3.27. *Rabin test's of irreducibility:*   let $f(x)$ be a polynomial of degree m over F_p. Then, $f(x)$ is irreducible over F_p if and only if:

$f(x)$ divides $x^{p^m} - x$ and $\mathrm{GCD}\left(f(x), x^{p^{\left[\frac{m}{n_i}\right]}} - x\right) = 1$, for each n_i that is prime divisor of m.

Pseudocode of Rabin's test of irreducibility is as follows:

---

function Rabin_Irreducibilility_Test
    input $f(x)$: polynomial of degree m over a field F_q
            $m_1, m_2, \ldots, m_k$ are all distinct prime dividers of m
    output "Reducible" or "Irreducible"
    1. **for** j=1 **to** k **do** $p_j = m / m_j$
    2. **for** j=1 **to** k **do**
        2.1 $h(x) = x^{q^{p_j}} - x \bmod f(x)$
        2.2 $g(x) = \mathrm{GCD}\,(f(x), h(x))$
        2.3 **if** $g(x) \neq 1$, **then return** "Reducible"}
    3. $g(x) = x^{q^m} - x \bmod f(x)$
    4. **if** $g(x) = 0$, **then return** "Irreducible"
    5. **else return** "Reducible"

Example 3.45

– Check of irreducibility of $f(x) = x^4 + x^2 + x + 1$ over F_2

$m = 4$, so the prime divider of m is 2.

$$p_1 = \frac{4}{2} = 2$$

Iteration #1 (test of prime divider 2, i.e. $p_1 = 2$):

$$x^{2^2} = x^4 \equiv x^2 + x + 1 \bmod f(x)$$

$$h(x) = x^2 + x + 1 - x \bmod f(x) = x^2 + 1$$

$$g(x) = \mathrm{GCD}(f(x), h(x)) = x + 1$$

$g(x) \neq 1$; thus, $f(x)$ is irreducible over F_2 as it was checked by the naïve method (see Example 3.44). Stop the algorithm.

– Check of irreducibility of $x^3 + x + 1$ over F_2

$m = 3$ is a prime. Thus, the prime divider of m is 3.

$$p_1 = \frac{3}{3} = 1$$

Iteration #1 (test of prime divider 3, i.e. $p_1 = 1$):

$$h(x) = x^2 - x \ mod \ f(x) = x^2 + x$$
$$g(x) = GCD(f(x), h(x)) = 1$$

$g(x) = 1$; hence, the algorithm continues.

Second step of the algorithm

$$g(x) = x^{2^3} - x = x^8 + x \ mod \ f(x) = 0.$$

Thus, $f(x)$ is irreducible.

3.3.7 List of Exercises and Problems

Exercise 3.20 Use the Euclidean algorithm to compute the *GCD* of:
1) 726 and 1144
2) 2184 and 16170
3) 113 and 13

Exercise 3.21 Use the Extended Euclidean algorithm to find $GCD(654, 123)$ and to find integers u and v such that $654u + 123v = GCD(654, 123)$.

Exercise 3.22 Find the multiplication inverse of the following using the Extended Euclidean algorithm
1) $13^{-1} \ mod \ 31$
2) $111^{-1} \ mod \ 4111$

Exercise 3.23
1) Compute $147^{165} \ mod \ 23$ with the right-to-left binary exponentiation method.
2) Use Fermat's little theorem to reduce the number of iterations in the right-to-left binary exponentiation method.

Exercise 3.24

Compute $X * Y \ mod \ n$, using the Montgomery multiplication with:

$n = 50021 \ (50021$ is a prime$)$, $X = 15063$, $Y = 37551$, Base $= 16$.

Exercise 3.25 Find x for the following congruence equation system using Gauss's algorithm:

$$S = \begin{cases} x \equiv 3 \ mod \ 5 \\ x \equiv 1 \ mod \ 7 \\ x \equiv 6 \ mod \ 8 \end{cases}$$

Exercise 3.26 Use Gauss's algorithm and Lemma 3.1 to compute $113^{72\,000\,000\,000\,013} \ mod \ 105$.

Exercise 3.27 Use the Tonelli-Shanks algorithm to find the square roots of:
1) $37 \ mod \ 43$
2) $36 \ mod \ 43$
3) $53 \ mod \ 97$

Exercise 3.28 Find the solution(s) to $y^2 \equiv 3 \ mod \ 143$.

Exercise 3.29 Find the solution(s) to $y^2 \equiv 421 \ mod \ 693$.

Exercise 3.30 Check the irreducibility of $f(x) = x^{10} + x^3 + 1$ over F_2 using Rabin's test of irreducibility.

Exercise 3.31 Check that $f(x) = x^5 + x^4 + x^3 + x^2 + x - 1$ is irreducible over F_3 using Rabin's test of irreducibility.

Problem 3.16

1) Compute $147^{155} \ mod \ 23$ using Fermat's little theorem.
2) How many iterations are needed to compute $147^{155} \ mod \ 23$ with the right-to-left binary exponentiation? What do you conclude?

Problem 3.17

1) Prove the correctness of the Montgomery reduction function REDC, i.e. prove that $t = T * R^{-1} \bmod n$.
2) Prove the correctness of the Montgomery multiplication algorithm based on REDC.

Problem 3.18   Prove the correctness of Gauss's algorithm.

Problem 3.19   Prove Lemma 3.8, which is stated as follows:

If $a^{(n-1)/2} \not\equiv \pm 1 \bmod n$, with n coprime to a, then n must be composite.

3.4 Birthday Paradox and Its Generalization

First of all, it is worth noticing that Birthday paradox is used to find the complexity of some attacks against cryptographic algorithms that will be discussed in next chapters.

Birthday paradox, also referred to as *Birthday problem*, is relating to the probability that, in a set of n randomly chosen people, a pair of them will have the same birthday. In a group of 23 people, the probability of a same birthday exceeds 50%, while a group of 70 has a 99.9% chance of a same birthday. Birthday problem is a paradox, because it first appears counter-intuitive that with 23 people, there is 50% chance that two people share the same birthday.

Proof:

It is assumed that all 365 birthdays have the same probability of occurrence.

Let $P(n)$ represent the probability that at least a pair among the n people have the same birthday.

$\overline{P}(n) = 1 - P(n)$ represents the probability that no pair among the n people have the same birthday. It is obvious to deduce that $\overline{P}(n) = 0$, if $n \geq 365$.

Let us consider $n < 365$:

Without loss of generality, assume that persons are numbered from 1 to n.

$$\overline{P}(n) = \overline{p}(1) * \overline{p}(2) * \overline{p}(3) * \ldots * \overline{p}(n-1)$$

$\overline{p}(1)$ is the probability that person 2 does share birthday with person 1 and $\overline{p}(k)$ is the probability that person $k+1$ does share birthday with the other k persons.

$$\overline{P}(n) = \left(\frac{365-1}{365}\right) * \left(\frac{365-2}{365}\right) * \left(\frac{365-3}{365}\right) * \ldots * \left(\frac{365-(n-1)}{365}\right).$$

After some arrangements,

$$\overline{P}(n) = \frac{365!}{365^n (365-n)!}.$$

Thus, $P(n) = 1 - \dfrac{365!}{365^n (365-n)!}$ $\square$

For $n = 23$, $P(n) \cong 50.07\%$ For $n = 30$, $P(n) \cong 70.06\%$
For $n = 50$, $P(n) \cong 97\%$ For $n = 70$, $P(n) \cong 99.97\%$

The generalization of the birthday paradox to any set of M values with a uniform distribution is relating to the probability that two values among n values from the set M are equal. Such a probability is

$$P(n, M) = 1 - \frac{M!}{M^n (M-n)!}.$$

In cryptography field, $P(n, M)$ is called *collision probability*.

Approximation and bounds to collision probability

The following two approximations are proposed in literature to compute the number n of required people given M, the size of the population, and the expected probability of success $P(n)$:

- $n \approx \sqrt{2 * M * P(n)}$, which works well for $P(n)$ less or equal to 0.5.

- $n \approx \sqrt{2 * M * ln(\dfrac{1}{1 - P(n)})}$, where ln is the napierian logarithm.

Using the approximation below, to have 50% chance that at least a pair of persons have the same birthday, $n \approx \sqrt{2 * 365 * \dfrac{1}{2}} \approx 20$ and $n \approx \sqrt{2 * 365 * ln(2)} \approx 23$ for the first and second approximations, respectively.

If $P(n) = 0.5$, the first approximation results in $n \approx \sqrt{M}$ and the second in $n \approx \sqrt{2 * M * ln(2)} \approx 1.18\sqrt{M}$.

In [12] and other references in literature, the following bounds have been proven to delimit the collision probability $P(n, M)$. The first upper bound is as follows:

$$P(n, M) \leq \frac{n(n-1)}{2M}$$

If is large, may n is large, $n^2 - n$ may be approximated by n^2. Thus, a second upper bound is used:

$$P(n, M) \leq \frac{n^2}{2M}.$$

The upper bound to probability of no collision $\bar{P}(n, M)$ is

$$\bar{P}(n, M) \leq e^{-\frac{q(q-1)}{2N}}.$$

Thus, the lower bound to $P(n, M)$ becomes

$$1 - e^{-\frac{q(q-1)}{2N}} \leq P(n, M).$$

The following property holds for any real number $x \in [0, 1]$:

$$(1 - e^{-1}) * x \leq 1 - e^{-x} \leq x.$$

Finally, using the property above, the lower bound to $P(n, M)$ can be approximated as:

$$0.316 * \frac{q(q-1)}{N} \leq P(n, M).$$

3.5   Solutions to Exercises and Problems

Exercise 3.1

Pro perties of Euler's totient function are given by Theorem 3.1.
1) $N = 17$ is a prime. Hence, all the 16 integers in range $[1, 16]$ are coprime to 17. l7 *is prime* $\Rightarrow \varphi(17) = 17 - 1 = 16$.
2) $N = 42$:

   12 integers, which are coprime to 42, are: $1, 5, 11, 13, 17, 19, 23, 25, 29, 31, 37, 41$.

   $42 = 7 * 3 * 2 \Rightarrow \varphi(42) = (7 - 1)(3 - 1)(2 - 1) = 12$.
3) $N = 25$:

   20 integers, which are coprime to 25, are: $1, 2, 3, 4, 6, 7, 8, 9, 11, 12, 13, 14, 16, 17, 18, 19, 21, 22, 23, 24$

   $25 = 5^2 \Rightarrow \varphi(25) = (5^2 - 5) = 20$.

Exercise 3.2

1) More generally, a' is the additive inverse of a modulo p if $a' + a \equiv 0 \bmod p$ and a^{-1} is the multiplicative inverse of a modulo p if $a * a^{-1} \equiv 1 \bmod p$. The additive inverse of 27 is 73, because if $27 + 73 \equiv 0 \bmod 100$ and its multiplicative inverse is 63, because if $27 * 63 = 1701 \equiv 1 \bmod 100$.
2) By properties of Euler's phi function (Theorem 3.1):
   - 101 is prime. Thus, $\varphi(101) = 100$
   - $102 = 2 * 3 * 17$. Thus, $\varphi(102) = \varphi(2) * \varphi(3) * \varphi(17) = 1 * 2 * 16 = 32$
   - $500 = 2^2 * 5^3$. Thus, $\varphi(500) = (2^2 - 2^1)(5^3 - 5^2) = 200$.

Exercise 3.3

1) Find x such that $3^x \equiv 13 \, mod \, 17$: we can use a trial-and-error method and find $x = 4$.

$$3^4 = 81 = 4*17 + 13 \Rightarrow 3^4 \, 13 \, mod \, 17$$

2) If $x \leq 5$, there is no solution to $4^x \equiv 5 \, mod \, 31$, because $4^1, 4^2, 4^3, 4^4$, and 4^5 are not congruent to $5 \, mod \, 31$. In particular, $4^5 \equiv 1 \, mod \, 31$.

If x is greater than 5, it can be written as $x = 5k + x'$, for some positive integer k and x', an integer less than 5. Thus,

$4^x \, mod \, 31 \equiv \left(4^5\right)^k \left(4\right)^{x'} mod \, 31 \equiv \left(1\right)^k \left(4\right)^{x'} mod \, 31 \equiv 4^{x'} mod \, 31$.

Since x' is less than 5, $4^{x'} \not\equiv 5 \, mod \, 31$. Therefore, there does not exist x such that $4^x \equiv 5 \, mod \, 31$.

3) In general, the modular exponentiation is an invertible function. It is what is called Discrete Logarithm Problem.

Exercise 3.4

By definition of multiplicative inverse, a has an inverse modulo n, if and only if $GCD(a,n) = 1$. Thus, $\mathbb{Z}_9^*$ has only six elements; $\mathbb{Z}_9^* = \{1, 2, 4, 5, 7, 8\}$.

Euler's theorem (Theorem 3.4 states that if $a \in \mathbb{Z}_n^*$, then $a^{\varphi(n)} \equiv 1 \, mod \, n$, which can be written as $a * a^{\varphi(n)-1} \equiv 1 \, mod \, n$. Using the definition of multiplicative inverse, we deduce that $a^{\varphi(n)-1}$ is the inverse of a.

By definition of Euler's totient (Theorem 3.1), $\varphi(9) = \left(3^3 - 3\right) = 6$. Therefore, using Euler's theorem, the inverses are computed and checked as follows:

$1^{-1} \equiv 1^5 \, mod \, 9 \equiv 1$. Check: $1*1 \equiv 1 \, mod \, 9$

$2^{-1} \equiv 2^5 \, mod \, 9 \equiv 5$. Check: $2*5 = 10 \equiv 1 \, mod \, 9$

$4^{-1} \equiv 4^5 \, mod \, 9 \equiv 7$. Check: $4*7 = 28 \equiv 1 \, mod \, 9$

$5^{-1} \equiv 5^5 \, mod \, 9 \equiv 2$. Check: $5*2 = 10 \equiv 1 \, mod \, 9$

$7^{-1} \equiv 7^5 \, mod \, 9 \equiv 4$. Check: $7*4 = 28 \equiv 1 \, mod \, 9$

$8^{-1} \equiv 8^5 \, mod \, 9 \equiv 8$. Check: $8*8 = 64 \equiv 1 \, mod \, 9$.

Let us try to find 3^{-1} using Euler's theorem:

$3^{-1} \equiv 3^5 \, mod \, 9 \equiv 0$, which is incongruous, since 0 is not the inverse of any other integer. Therefore, Euler's theorem is applicable only if a and n are coprime.

Exercise 3.5

If n is prime and n and a are coprime, then Fermat's little theorem states that $a^{n-1} \equiv 1 \, mod \, n$, which can be rewritten as $a * a^{n-2} \equiv 1 \, mod \, n$. Using the definition of inverse, we deduce that a^{n-2} is the inverse of a. Euler's theorem states that if $a \in \mathbb{Z}_n^*$, then $a^{\varphi(n)} \equiv 1 \, mod \, n$, which can be written as $a * a^{\varphi(n)-1} \equiv 1 \, mod \, n$. Using the definition of inverse, we deduce that $a^{\varphi(n)-1}$ is the inverse of a.

1) $a = 6, n = 7$:

7 is prime and coprime to 6. Thus, Fermat's little theorem is applicable.

$6^{-1} \equiv 6^5 \, mod \, 7 \equiv 6$. Check: $6*6 \equiv 1 \, mod \, 7$.

2) $a = 7, n = 15$:

15 is not prime. Thus, Fermat's little theorem is not applicable. We use Euler's theorem.

By Theorem 3.1, $\varphi(15) = (5-1)(3-1) = 8$

$7^{-1} \equiv 7^{8-1} \, mod \, 15 \equiv 13$.

Check: $7*13 \, mod \, 15 \equiv 1$

3) $a = 19, n = 101$:

101 is prime and coprime to 19. Thus, Fermat's little theorem is applicable.

$19^{-1} \equiv 19^{99} \, mod \, 101$

$19^{-1} \equiv \left(19^{3*25}\right)\left(19^{19}\right)\left(19^5\right) mod \, 101 \equiv 1*5*84 \, mod \, 101 \equiv 16$.

Check: $19*16 \, mod \, 101 \equiv 1$

4) $a = 97, n = 100$:

100 is not prime. Thus, Fermat's little theorem is not applicable. We use Euler's theorem.

By theorem 3.1, $\varphi(100) = (25 - 5)(4 - 2) = 40$

$97^{-1} \equiv 97^{39} \, mod \, 100 \equiv \left(97^{20} * 97^{19}\right) mod \, 100 \equiv 33$.

Check: $97*33 \, mod \, 100 \equiv 1$

Exercise 3.6

1) $x \equiv 4^{100} \ mod \ 17$

   $4^2 \equiv -1 \ mod \ 17$

   Thus, $4^{100} \equiv mod \ 17 \equiv 4^{2*50} \ mod \ 17 \equiv (-1)^{50} \ mod \ 17 \equiv 1$.

   Therefore, $x = 1$.

2) $9^x \equiv 13 \ mod \ 17$

   $9^2 \equiv 13 \ mod \ 17$. Therefore, $x = 2$

3) $5^x \equiv 13 \ mod \ 17$

   $5^2 \equiv 8 \ mod \ 17$

   $(5^2)*(5^2) \equiv 8*8 \ mod \ 17 = 13$. Therefore, $x = 4$

4) $7^x \equiv 11 \ mod \ 13$

   $(7^2)*(7^2)*(7^1) \equiv 10*10*7 \ mod \ 13 = 9*7 \ mod \ 13 = 11$.

   Therefore, $x = 5$.

Exercise 3.7

By definition, the order of a group is the number of the group elements.

1) $\mathbb{Z}_7^*$: 7 is prime. Thus, $\left|\mathbb{Z}_7^*\right| = 7$.

2) $\mathbb{Z}_{101}^*$: 101 is prime. Thus, $\left|\mathbb{Z}_{101}^*\right| = 101$.

3) $\mathbb{Z}_{18}^*$: 18 is not prime. Thus, we need to identify the invertible elements that belong to $\mathbb{Z}_{18}^*$. In general, an integer $a \in \mathbb{Z}_n^*$, if and only if $GCD(a,n) = 1$. Thus, $\mathbb{Z}_{18}^* = \{1, 5, 7, 11, 13, 17\}$ and $\left|\mathbb{Z}_{18}^*\right| = 6$.

Exercise 3.8

By definition, the order of an element $a \in \mathbb{Z}_n^*$ is the smallest integer k such that

1) $a^k \equiv 1 \ mod \ n$.

2) $2^{12} \equiv 1 \ mod \ 13$. Thus, $ord(2) = 12$.

3) $5^4 \equiv 1 \ mod \ 13$. Thus, $ord(5) = 4$.

4) $3^3 \equiv 1 \ mod \ 13$. Thus, $ord(3) = 3$.

Exercise 3.9

1) Calculate $\dfrac{2}{5}$ in $\mathbb{Z}_8^*$

   $\dfrac{2}{5} = 2 * 5^{-1}$

   $5 * 5 \equiv 1 \ mod \ 8$; hence, $5^{-1} = 5$

   Hence, $\dfrac{2}{5} = 2 * 5 = 2$ in $\mathbb{Z}_8^*$.

2) Is $\mathbb{Z}_6^*$ a cyclic group?

   Recall that an integer b has a multiplicative inverse $mod \ p$ if and only if $GCD(b,p) = 1$. Thus, $\mathbb{Z}_6^* = \{1,5\}$.

   Recall that a cyclic group is a finite group that is generated by a single element g, called generator.

   $5^0 \equiv 1 \ mod \ 6$, $5^1 \equiv 5 \ mod \ 6$.

   Hence, 5 is a generator for $\mathbb{Z}_6^*$. Therefore, $\mathbb{Z}_6^*$ is a cyclic group.

3) Is $\mathbb{Z}_8^*$ a cyclic group?

   $\mathbb{Z}_8^* = \{1,3,5,7\}$

   $3^0 \equiv 1 \ mod \ 8$, $3^1 \equiv 3 \ mod \ 8$ $3^2 \equiv 1 \ mod \ 8$ $3^3 \equiv 3 \ mod \ 8$ ...

   $5^0 \equiv 1 \ mod \ 8$, $5^1 \equiv 5 \ mod \ 8$ $5^2 \equiv 1 \ mod \ 8$ $5^3 \equiv 5 \ mod \ 8$ ...

   $7^0 \equiv 1 \ mod \ 8$, $7^1 \equiv 7 \ mod \ 8$ $7^2 \equiv 1 \ mod \ 8$ $7^3 \equiv 7 \ mod \ 8$ ...

   No element in $\mathbb{Z}_8^*$ can generate $\mathbb{Z}_8^*$. Therefore, $\mathbb{Z}_8^*$ is not a cyclic group.

Exercise 3.10

$99^{707^{411}} \ mod \ 100 = (100-1)^{707^{411}} \ mod \ 100$.

By Lemma 3.1, for integers a, m, and n, $a^m \ mod \ n = (a \ mod \ n)^m \ mod \ n$.

Thus, $99^{707^{411}} \ mod \ 100 = (-1)^{707^{411}} \ mod \ 100$.

The exponent 707^{411} is odd. Thus, there exists k such that $707^{411} = 2k + 1$.

$99^{707^{411}} \ mod \ 100 = (-1)^{2k} * (-1) \ mod \ 100 = 99$.

Exercise 3.11

More generally (by Theorem 3.9), if p is a prime number, then Z_p^* has $\varphi(\varphi(p))$ generators (also called primitive roots), where $\varphi()$ is the Euler's totient function. By Theorem 3.1, since 29 is prime, $\phi(29) = 28$. Integers between 1 and 28, which are coprime with 28, are $\{1, 3, 5, 9, 11, 13, 15, 17, 19, 23, 25, 27\}$. Thus, $\phi(28) = 12$. Therefore, by Theorem 3.9, $\mathbb{Z}_{29}^*$ has 12 generators.

Exercise 3.12

In general, to build the multiplication table of a finite field F_{p^m} with an irreducible polynomial $f(x)$:

  i) associate with each element $i \in F_{p^m}$ a polynomial $P_i(x)$ of degree m and with coefficients in F_p.

 ii) compute $R_{i,j}(x) \equiv \left(P_i(x) * P_j(x)\right) \bmod f(x)$ for all pairs of elements i and j in F_p^m.

iii) Let *MulTab* be the multiplication table of 8 rows by 8 columns. $MulTab[i, j] = \sum_{k=0}^{m-1}(2^k * r_{i,j,k})$, $\forall i \in [0, m-1]$, $\forall j \in [0, m-1]$, where $r_{i,j,k}$, $k = 0, \ldots, m-1$, are the binary coefficients of the polynomial $R_{i,j}(x)$.

Now, build the multiplication table of field F_{2^3} with the irreducible polynomial $f(x) = x^3 + x^2 + 1$:
$F_{2^3} = \{0, 1, 2, 3, 4, 5, 6, 7\}$.

Polynomial representation of field elements:

$$P_0(x) = 0 \qquad P_1(x) = 1 \qquad P_2(x) = x \qquad P_3(x) = x+1 \qquad P_4(x) = x^2$$
$$P_5(x) = x^2 + 1 \quad P_6(x) = x^2 + x \quad P_7(x) = x^2 + x + 1$$

$P_i(x)$ denotes the polynomial associated with element i of F_{2^3}.

Recall that the multiplication is commutative in finite fields.

$P_0(x) * P_j(x) \bmod f(x) \equiv 0, \forall j \in F_{2^3}$

$P_1(x) * P_j(x) \bmod f(x) \equiv P_j(x), \forall j \in F_{2^3}$

$P_2(x) * P_2(x) \bmod f(x) \equiv x^2 \Rightarrow 2 * 2 = 4$

$P_2(x) * P_3(x) \bmod f(x) \equiv x^2 + x \Rightarrow 2 * 3 = 6$

$P_2(x) * P_4(x) \bmod f(x) \equiv x^3 \bmod f(x) \equiv x^2 + 1 \Rightarrow 2 * 4 = 5$

$P_2(x) * P_5(x) \bmod f(x) \equiv x^3 + x \bmod f(x) \equiv x^2 + x + 1 \Rightarrow 2 * 5 = 7$

$P_2(x) * P_6(x) \bmod f(x) \equiv x^3 + x^2 \bmod f(x) \equiv 1 \Rightarrow 2 * 6 = 1$

$P_2(x) * P_7(x) \bmod f(x) \equiv x^3 + x^2 + x \bmod f(x) \equiv x + 1 \Rightarrow 2 * 7 = 3$

$P_3(x) * P_3(x) \bmod f(x) \equiv x^2 + 1 \bmod f(x) \equiv x^2 + 1 \Rightarrow 3 * 3 = 5$

$P_3(x) * P_4(x) \bmod f(x) \equiv x^3 + x^2 \bmod f(x) \equiv 1 \Rightarrow 3 * 4 = 1$

$P_3(x) * P_5(x) \bmod f(x) \equiv x^3 + x^2 + x + 1 \bmod f(x) \equiv x \Rightarrow 3 * 5 = 2$

$P_3(x) * P_6(x) \bmod f(x) \equiv x^3 + x \bmod f(x) \equiv x^2 + x + 1 \Rightarrow 3 * 6 = 7$

$P_3(x) * P_7(x) \bmod f(x) \equiv x^3 + 1 \bmod f(x) \equiv x^2 \Rightarrow 3 * 7 = 4$

$P_4(x) * P_4(x) \bmod f(x) \equiv x^4 \bmod f(x) \equiv x^2 + x + 1 \Rightarrow 4 * 4 = 7$

$P_4(x) * P_5(x) \bmod f(x) \equiv x^4 + x^2 \bmod f(x) \equiv x + 1 \Rightarrow 4 * 5 = 3$

$P_4(x) * P_6(x) \bmod f(x) \equiv x^4 + x^3 \bmod f(x) \equiv x \Rightarrow 4 * 6 = 2$

$P_4(x) * P_7(x) \bmod f(x) \equiv x^4 + x^3 + x^2 \bmod f(x) \equiv x^2 + x \Rightarrow 4 * 7 = 6$

$P_5(x) * P_5(x) \bmod f(x) \equiv x^4 + 1 \bmod f(x) \equiv x^2 + x \Rightarrow 5 * 5 = 6$

$P_5(x) * P_6(x) \bmod f(x) \equiv x^4 + x^3 + x^2 + x \bmod f(x) \equiv x^2 \Rightarrow 5 * 6 = 4$

$P_5(x) * P_7(x) \bmod f(x) \equiv x^4 + x^3 + x + 1 \bmod f(x) \equiv 1 \Rightarrow 5 * 7 = 1$

$P_6(x) * P_6(x) \bmod f(x) \equiv x^4 + x^2 \bmod f(x) \equiv x + 1 \Rightarrow 6 * 6 = 3$

$P_6(x) * P_7(x) \bmod f(x) \equiv x^4 + x \bmod f(x) \equiv x^2 + 1 \Rightarrow 6 * 7 = 5$

$P_7(x) * P_7(x) \bmod f(x) \equiv x^4 + x^2 + 1 \bmod f(x) \equiv x \Rightarrow 7 * 7 = 2$

Finally, the multiplication table of F_{2^3} with irreducible polynomial $f(x) = x^3 + x^2 + 1$ is as follows:

*	0	1	2	3	4	5	6	7
0	0	0	0	0	0	0	0	0
1	0	1	2	3	4	5	6	7
2	0	2	4	6	5	7	1	3
3	0	3	6	5	1	2	7	4
4	0	4	5	1	7	3	2	6
5	0	5	7	2	3	6	4	1
6	0	6	1	7	2	4	3	5
7	0	7	3	4	6	1	5	2

Notice that all the nonzero elements of F_{2^3} appear seven times in the table.

Exercise 3.13

Elements of field F_{3^2} are $\{0, 1, 2, 3, 4, 5, 6, 7, 8\}$.

$f(x) = x^2 + 2x + 2$ is irreducible over field F_3.

Note that in F_3: $-1 \equiv 2 \bmod 3$ and $-2 \equiv 1 \bmod 3$.

Also note that coefficients in polynomial representation of elements of F_{3^2} are in $\{0, 1, 2\}$. Polynomial representation of the elements of field F_{3^2}:

$$P_0(x) = 0 \quad P_1(x) = 1 \quad P_2(x) = 2$$
$$P_3(x) = x \quad P_4(x) = x + 1 \quad P_5(x) = x + 2$$
$$P_6(x) = 2x \quad P_7(x) = 2x + 1 \quad P_8(x) = 2x + 2$$

$P_i(x)$ denotes the polynomial associated with element i of field F_{3^2}.

1) $4 + 5$:
   $(x + 1) + (x + 2) = 2x + 3 = 2x + x = 3x = 0$. Therefore, $4 + 5 = 0$.
2) $3 * 2$:
   $(x) * (2) \bmod f(x) \equiv 2x$. Therefore, $3 * 2 = 6$.
3) $4 * 5$:
   $(x + 1) * (x + 2) = x^2 + 3x + 2 = x^2 + 2$
   $x^2 + 2 \bmod (x^2 + 2x + 2) \equiv -2x = x$. Therefore, $4 * 5 = 3$.
4) 8^2:
   $(2x + 2) * (2x + 2) = 4x^2 + 8x + 4 = x^2 + 2x + 1 \bmod f(x)$
   $x^2 + 2x + 1 \bmod f(x) \equiv -1 \equiv 2$. Therefore, $8^2 = 2$.

Exercise 3.14

Recall that adding/subtracting twice the same element with coefficients in F_2 is equivalent to adding/subtracting 0, which has no effect.

Let $f(x) = x^4 + x + 1$ be the irreducible polynomial used in multiplication over F_{2^4}.

1) Compute x^{-1} and x^{-3}
   $(x) * (x^3 + 1)) \bmod (x^4 + x + 1) \equiv 1 \Rightarrow x^{-1} = x^3 + 1$
   $((x^3) * (x^3 + x^2 + x + 1)) \bmod (x^4 + x + 1) \equiv 1 \Rightarrow x^{-3} = x^3 + x^2 + x + 1$.
2) Compute $(x^2) / (x^3 + x^2 + 1) = (x^2) * (x^3 + x^2 + 1)^{-1}$
   First, compute the inverse of $(x^3 + x^2 + 1) \bmod (x^4 + x + 1)$
   $(x^3 + x^2 + 1) * x^2 = x^5 + x^4 + x^2 = x^5 + x^4 + x^2 + (x - x) + (1 - 1)$
   $= x(x^4 + x + 1) + (x^4 + x + 1) + 1$
   $(x^3 + x^2 + 1) * x^2 \bmod (x^4 + x + 1) \equiv 1$.
   Thus, $(x^3 + x^2 + 1)^{-1} \bmod (x^4 + x + 1) \equiv x^2$.

Second, compute $(x^2)*x^2 \bmod (x^4+x+1)$

$(x^4) \bmod (x^4+x+1) \equiv x+1.$

Therefore, $(x^2)/(x^3+x^2+1)=x+1.$

In numeric form, $\frac{4}{13}=3.$

3) Compute $(x^3+x^2+x)/(x^2+x+1)$

First, compute the inverse of $(x^2+x+1) \bmod f(x)$

$(x^2+x+1)*(x^2+x)=x^4+x^3+x^2+x^3+x^2+x=x^4+x$

$(x^2+x+1)*(x^2+x) \bmod (x^4+x+1) \equiv 1.$

Thus, $(x^2+x+1)^{-1} \bmod (x^4+x+1) \equiv (x^2+x).$

Second, compute $(x^3+x^2+x)*(x^2+x) \bmod (x^4+x+1)$

$(x^3+x^2+x)*(x^2+x)=(x^5+x^2)$

$(x^5+x^2) \bmod (x^4+x+1) \equiv x .$

Therefore, $(x^3+x^2+x)/(x^2+x+1)=x.$

In numeric form, $\dfrac{14}{7}=2.$

4) All the previous computations make use of multiplication in a finite field, which—by design—is based on a computation modulo $f(x)$. Therefore, if $f(x)$ changes, the computation results change.

Exercise 3.15

Check of polynomial reducibility in field F_2. Recall that adding twice the same polynomial with coefficients in F_2 is equivalent to adding 0.

1) $f_1(x)=x^6+x^4+x^2=x^2(x^4+x^2+1)$. Hence, $f_1(x)$ is reducible in F_2.

2) $f_2(x)=x^3+1=x^3+(2x^2)+1=(x+1)(x^2+x+1)$. Hence, $f_2(x)$ is reducible in F_2.

3) $f_3(x)=x^4+x^3+x+1=x(x^3+1)+(x^3+1)=(x+1)(x^3+1)$. Hence, $f_3(x)$ is reducible in F_2.

4) $f_4(x)=x^4+x^2+1=(x^2+x+1)^2$. Hence, $f_3(x)$ is reducible in F_2.

Exercise 3.16

Let us consider the extension field F_{3^2} under polynomial $f(x)=x^2+x+2$ irreducible over F_3. α is a root of $f(x)$.

Thus, $\alpha^2+\alpha+2=0 \Rightarrow \alpha^2=-\alpha-2=2\alpha+1.$

The powers, till 3^2-2, of α give:

$\alpha^0=1 \qquad\qquad \alpha^1=\alpha$

$\alpha^2=2\alpha+1 \qquad\quad \alpha^3=\alpha(2\alpha+1)=2\alpha+2$

$\alpha^4=\alpha(2\alpha+2)=2 \qquad \alpha^5=\alpha(2)=2\alpha$

$\alpha^6=\alpha(2\alpha)=\alpha+2 \qquad \alpha^7=\alpha(\alpha+2)=\alpha+1.$

Thus, α can generate all nonzero elements of F_{3^2}. The latter can be written in three forms:

$$F_{3^2}=\{0, \quad 1, \quad 2, \quad 3, \quad 4, \quad 5, \quad\quad 6, \quad 7, \quad\quad 8\}$$
$$=\{0, \quad \alpha^0, \quad \alpha^4, \quad \alpha^1, \quad \alpha^7, \quad \alpha^6, \quad\quad \alpha^5, \quad \alpha^2, \quad\quad \alpha^3\}$$
$$=\{0, \quad 1, \quad 2, \quad \alpha, \quad \alpha+1, \quad \alpha+2, \quad 2\alpha, \quad 2\alpha+1, \quad 2\alpha+2\}.$$

Exercise 3.17

$\alpha=3$ is a root of $f(x)=x^2+x+2$ over F_{3^2}.

1) Compute 3^{-1}

   $f(\alpha) = \alpha^2 + \alpha + 2 = \alpha(\alpha + 1) + 2 = 0 \Rightarrow \alpha(\alpha + 1) = -2 = 1$.

   Thus, $(\alpha + 1)$ is the inverse of α. Therefore, $3^{-1} = 4$ over $F_{3^2} / (x^2 + x + 2)$.

2) Compute 3^7

   Since α is a root of $f(x)$, $f(\alpha) = \alpha^2 + \alpha + 2$. Thus, $\alpha^2 = -\alpha - 2 = 2\alpha + 1$

   $(\alpha)^7 = \alpha^2 * \alpha^2 * \alpha^2 * \alpha = \left((2\alpha + 1)^2 * (2\alpha + 1) \right) * \alpha$

   $= \left((\alpha^2 + \alpha + 1)(2\alpha + 1) \right) * \alpha = \left((2)(2\alpha + 1) \right) * \alpha$

   $= (\alpha + 2) * \alpha = \alpha^2 + 2\alpha = 2\alpha + 1 = 1$

   Thus, $3^7 = 1$.

3) Compute 3^{7k}

   $(3)^{7k} = (3^7)^k = (1)^k = 1$

4) Compute $6 * 7$

   $6 = 2\alpha$, $7 = 2\alpha + 1$

   $2\alpha * (2\alpha + 1) = 4\alpha^2 + 2\alpha = \alpha^2 + 2\alpha = 2\alpha + 1 + 2\alpha = \alpha + 1$.

   Thus, $6 * 7 = 4$.

Exercise 3.18

Let $x^4 + x + 1$ be a polynomial irreducible over F_2 associated with the field F_{2^4}.
Do the following operations over F_{2^4}:

1) $9 * 6 = ?$

   9 is represented by polynomial $x^3 + 1$ and 6 by $x^2 + x$.

   $(x^3 + 1)(x^2 + x) \bmod (x^4 + x + 1) = x + 1$.

   Thus, $9 * 6 = 3$ over field F_{2^4}.

2) $9^{-1} = ?$

   9 is represented by polynomial $x^3 + 1$ and 2 by x.

   $x^i \equiv x^3 + 1 \bmod (x^4 + x + 1) \Rightarrow i = 14$.

   Let $A^{-1}(x)$ denote the polynomial associated with 9^{-1}.

   By Theorem 3.21, $(x)^{16-14-1} \equiv A^{-1}(x) \bmod f(x) \Rightarrow A^{-1}(x) = x$.

   Hence, $9^{-1} = 2$.

3) $(9 + 1)^{357} = ?$

   9 is represented by polynomial $x^3 + 1$ and 1 by constant polynomial 1. Thus, the addition over F_{2^4}, is $(x^3 + 1) + (1) = x^3$.

   2 is chosen as generator, which is represented by polynomial x. By Theorem 3.22, $x^{2^4 - 1} = x^{15} \equiv 1 \bmod f(x)$.

   $(9 + 1)^{357}$ is represented by polynomial $x^{3*357} = x^{(15*71)+6}$.

   Thus, $x^{3*357} \equiv (1^{71})(x^6) \bmod f(x) = x^3 + x^2$.

   Hence, $(9 + 1)^{357} = 12$.

Exercise 3.19

1) Addition in field binary F_{2^8} is an XOR operation.

   $01010011 + 11001010 = 10011001$.

2) Find the product of $01010011 * 11001010$ over F_{2^8} with reduction polynomial $f(x) = x^8 + x^4 + x^3 + x + 1$.

   Represent bit strings as polynomials, then find the $\bmod f(x)$:

   $01010011 \rightarrow A(x) = x^6 + x^4 + x + 1$

   $11001010 \rightarrow B(x) = x^7 + x^6 + x^3 + x$

   $01010011 * 11001010 = C \mid C(x) = A(x) * B(x) \bmod f(x)$

   $A(x) * B(x) = x^{13} + x^{12} + x^{11} + x^{10} + x^9 + x^8 + x^6 + x^5 + x^4 + x^3 + x^2 + x$

   $A(x) * B(x) \bmod f(x) = 1 \cdot$

   Thus, $01010011 * 11001010 = 00000001$.

3) Find the multiplicative inverse of 00000010, in field F_{2^8} with reduction polynomial $f(x) = x^8 + x^4 + x^3 + x + 1$.

   $a = 00000010$ is represented by polynomial $A(x) = x$.

By definition of the multiplicative inverse, if a' is the multiplicative inverse of x, then $A(x) * A'(x) \equiv 1 \bmod f(x)$, where $A(x)$ and $A'(x)$ are the polynomials associated with a and a', respectively. $f(x)$ can be written as follows:

$$f(x) = x^8 + x^4 + x^3 + x + 1 = x * (x^7 + x^3 + x^2 + 1) + 1$$

Thus, $(x^7 + x^3 + x^2) * x \equiv 1 \bmod f(x)$.

Hence, the multiplicative inverse of $x \bmod (x^8 + x^4 + x^3 + x + 1)$ is $x^7 + x^3 + x^2 + 1$. In binary representation, the multiplicative inverse of 00000010 is 10001101.

Exercise 3.20

The Euclidean algorithm is based on the principle that the *GCD* of two numbers does not change if the larger number is replaced by its difference with the smaller number. The algorithm is iterative and stops when the remainder is zero and the returned value of *GCD* is the remainder of the last but one step.

1) Steps of computation of GCD(1144, 726) are shown in Figure 3.1. The remainder of the 5th step, i.e. 22, is the *GCD* of 1144 and 726.

1st step: 1144 = 726 * 1 + 418

2nd step: 726 =   418 * 1 + 308

3rd step: 418 =   308 * 1 + 110

4th step: 308 =   110 * 2 + 88

5th step: 110 =   88 * 1 + (22)

6th step: 88   22 * 4 + 0

Figure 3.1   Computation of GCD(1144, 726) using Euclidean algorithm.

2) Steps of computation of GCD(16170, 2184) are shown in Figure 3.2. The remainder of the 3rd step, i.e. 42, is the *GCD* of 16170 and 2184.

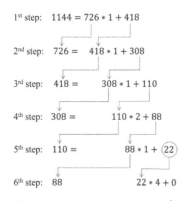

1st step: 16170   = 2184 * 7 + 882

2nd step: 2184 =   882 * 2 + 420

3rd step: 882 =   420 * 2 + (42)

4th step: 420 =   42 * 10 + 0

Figure 3.2   Computation of GCD(16170, 2184) using Euclidean algorithm.

3) Steps of computation of GCD(113, 13) are shown in Figure 3.3. The remainder of the 3rd step, i.e. 1, is the *GCD* of 113 and 13.

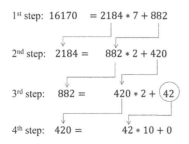

1st step: 113   = 13 * 8 + 9

2nd step: 13 =   9 * 1 + 4

3rd step: 9 =   4 * 2 + (1)

4th step: 4 =   4 * 1 + 0

Figure 3.3   Computation of GCD(113, 13) using Euclidean algorithm.

Exercise 3.21

The steps of computation of $\text{GCD}(654, 123)$ are as follows:

1st step: $654 = 123 * 5 + 39$

2nd step: $123 = 39 * 3 + 6$

3rd step: $39 = 6 * 6 + 3$ 4th step: $6 = 3 * 2 + 0$

Thus, $\text{GCD}(654, 123) = 3$.

To find u and v such that $654u + 123v = \text{GCD}(654, 123)$, do backward calculations starting from the result of the 3rd step:

$$3 = 39 - 6 * 6$$
$$= (654 - 123 * 5) - 6 * (123 - 39 * 3)$$
$$= (654 - 123 * 5) - 6 * 123 + (39 * 18)$$
$$= (654 - 123 * 5) - 6 * 123 + 18 * (654 - 123 * 5)$$
$$= 654 * 19 + 123 * (-5 - 6 - 90)$$
$$= 654 * 19 + 123 * (-101)$$

Hence, $u = 19$ and $v = -101$.

Exercise 3.22

Use the Extended Euclidean algorithm to find multiplicative inverse of $a \bmod n$. We need to find u and v such that $n * u + a * v = 1$. Then, $v = a^{-1} \bmod n$.

1) $13^{-1} \bmod 31 = ?$

 The steps of computation of $\text{GCD}(31, 13)$ are as follows:

 1st step: $31 = 13 * 2 + 5$

 2nd step: $13 = 5 * 2 + 3$

 3rd step: $5 = 3 * 1 + 2$

 4th step: $3 = 2 * 1 + 1$

 5th step: $2 = 2 * 1 + 0$

 Thus, $\text{GCD}(31, 13) = 1$

 To find u and v such that $31u + 13v = 1$, do backward calculations starting from the result of the 4th step:

 $$1 = (3) - (2) = (13 - 2 * 5) - (2) = (13 - 2 * (31 - 2 * 13)) - (2)$$
 $$1 = (5 * 13 - 2 * 31) - (2) = (5 * 13 - 2 * 31) - (5 - 3)$$
 $$1 = (5 * 13 - 2 * 31) - ((31 - 2 * 13) - (3))$$
 $$1 = (5 * 13 - 2 * 31) - ((31 - 2 * 13) - (13 - 2 * 5))$$
 $$1 = (5 * 13 - 2 * 31) - ((31 - 2 * 13) - (13 - 2 * (31 - 2 * 13)))$$
 $$1 = 31 * (-5) + 13 * (12)$$

 Hence, $13^{-1} \bmod 31 = 12$

2) $111^{-1} \bmod 4111 = ?$

 The steps of computation of $\text{GCD}(4111, 111)$ are as follows:

 1st step: $4111 = 111 * 37 + 4$

 2nd step: $111 = 4 * 27 + 3$

 3rd step: $4 = 3 * 1 + 1$

 4th step: $1 = 1 * 1 + 0$

 Thus, $\text{GCD}(4111, 111) = 1$.

 To find u and v such that $4111u + 111v = 1$, do backward calculations starting from the result of the 3rd step:

 $$1 = (4) - (3) = (4111 - 111 * 37) - (111 - 4 * 27)$$
 $$1 = (4111 - 111 * 37) - (111 - (4111 - 111 * 37) * 27)$$
 $$1 = (28) * (4111) + (-38 - 37 * 27) * 111$$
 $$1 = (28) * (4111) + (-1037) * 111.$$

 Hence, $111^{-1} \bmod 4\,111 = -1037 \bmod 4\,111 = 3074$.

Exercise 3.23

1) $147^{165} \ mod \ 23 \equiv ?$

$165 = 128 + 32 + 4 + 1 = 2^7 + 2^5 + 2^2 + 2^0$

$L = 8, \ k_7 = 1, \ k_6 = 0, \ k_5 = 1, \ k_4 = 0, \ k_3 = 0, \ k_2 = 1, \ k_1 = 0, \ k_0 = 1$

$b_0 \equiv \left(147^1\right)^{2^0} \ mod \ 23 \equiv 147 \ mod \ 23 \equiv 9$

$b_1 \equiv \left(147^0\right)^{2^1} \ mod \ 23 \equiv 1$

$b_2 \equiv \left(147^1\right)^{2^2} \ mod \ 23 \equiv 147^4 \ mod \ 23 \equiv \left(147 \ mod \ 23\right)^4 \ mod \ 23 \equiv 6$

$b_3 \equiv \left(147^0\right)^{2^3} \ mod \ 23 \equiv 1$

$b_4 \equiv \left(147^0\right)^{2^4} \ mod \ 23 \equiv 1$

$b_5 \equiv \left(147^1\right)^{2^5} \ mod \ 23 \equiv 147^{32} \ mod \ 23 \equiv \left(147 \ mod \ 23\right)^{32} \ mod \ 23 \equiv 18$

$b_6 \equiv \left(147^0\right)^{2^6} \ mod \ 23 \equiv 1$

$b_7 \equiv \left(147^1\right)^{2^7} \ mod \ 23 \equiv 137^{128} \ mod \ 23 \equiv \left(147 \ mod \ 23\right)^{32*4} \ mod \ 23 \equiv 4$

$147^{165} \ mod \ 23 \equiv 9 * 1 * 6 * 1 * 1 * 18 * 1 * 4 \ mod \ 23 \equiv 3888 \ mod \ 23 \equiv 1.$

2) Fermat's little theorem states that if p is prime and a is an integer not divisible by p, then $a^{p-1} \equiv 1 \ mod \ p$.
By Fermat's little theorem, $147^{22} \ mod \ 23 \equiv 1$, because 147 is not divisible by 23.
Also, $147^{22*7} \ mod \ 23 \equiv 1$.

Thus, $147^{165} \ mod \ 23 \equiv \left(147^{22*7}\right)\left(147^{165-22*7}\right) \ mod \ 23 \equiv 1^7 * 147^{11} \ mod \ 23$.

Then, solve $147^{11} \ mod \ 23$ using the right-to-left binary exponentiation method.

$11 = 8 + 2 + 1 = 2^3 + 2 + 1$

$L = 4, \ k_3 = 1, \ k_2 = 0, \ k_1 = 1, \ k_0 = 1$

$b_0 \equiv \left(147^1\right)^{2^0} \ mod \ 23 \equiv 147 \ mod \ 23 \equiv 9$

$b_1 \equiv \left(147^1\right)^{2^1} \ mod \ 23 \equiv \left(9\right)^2 \ mod \ 23 \equiv 12$

$b_2 \equiv \left(147^0\right)^{2^2} \ mod \ 23 \equiv 1 \ mod \ 23$

$b_3 \equiv \left(147^1\right)^{2^3} \ mod \ 23 \equiv \left(12\right)^4 \ mod \ 23 \equiv 13$

$147^{165} \ mod \ 23 \equiv 9 * 12 * 1 * 13 \ mod \ 23 \equiv 1.$

Therefore, using Fermat's little theorem before applying the binary exponentiation algorithm reduces significantly the number of squaring and multiplication operations.

Exercise 3.24

$n = 50021$, $X = 15063$, $Y = 37551$, Base $B = 16$.

Hexadecimal representation of arguments:

$n = 50021_{10} = C365_{16}$

$X = 15063_{10} = 3AD7_{16}$, $Y = 37551_{10} = 92AF_{16}$

X is four 16-bit words: $X = \left(3, 10, 13, 7\right)$. Words are in decimal representation to make the computations by hand easy.

We keep $R = 16^4$, which meets the conditions $R > n$ and $GCD\left(R, n\right) = 1$.

$R = 16^4 = 16^l \Rightarrow l = 4$.

Compute $n' = -n^{-1} \ mod \ B$: $n' = -50021^{-1} \ mod \ 16 = -13 \ mod \ 16 = 3$.

Below are the computations in multi-precision Montgomery multiplication:

i	x_i	$A + x_i * Y$	$q = A * n' \bmod B$	$A = (A + n * q) / B$
0	7	262857	11	50818
1	13	538981	15	80581
2	10	456091	1	31632
3	3	144285	7	30902

The multi-precision Montgomery multiplication returns 30902, which represents $X * Y * R^{-1} \bmod n$. Multiplying by R yields $\left(X * Y * R^{-1}\right) * R \bmod n \equiv X * Y \bmod n$.

Thus, $30902 * 16^4 \bmod 50021 = 15063 * 37551 \bmod 50021 \equiv 43266$.

Exercise 3.25

Let us consider the following congruence system:

$$S = \begin{cases} x \equiv 3 \bmod 5 \\ x \equiv 1 \bmod 7 \\ x \equiv 6 \bmod 8 \end{cases}$$

The constants of the congruence equation system are:

$n_1 = 5, \ n_2 = 7, \ n_3 = 8 \qquad a_1 = 3, \ a_2 = 1, \ a_3 = 6$.

All n_i's are pairwise coprime and $a_i < n_i$, for $i = 1,2,3$. Thus, the conditions to use the Chinese remainder theorem are met. Steps of calculation of x using Gauss's algorithm:
Common modulus $N = 5 * 7 * 8 = 280$.

$N_1 = \frac{280}{5} = 56, \ N_2 = \frac{280}{7} = 40, \ N_3 = \frac{280}{8} = 35$

Multiplicative inverses:

$N_1^{-1} * N_1 \equiv 1 \bmod 5 \Rightarrow N_1^{-1} = 1 \qquad N_2^{-1} * N_2 \equiv 1 \bmod 7 \Rightarrow N_2^{-1} = 3$

$N_3^{-1} * N_3 \equiv 1 \bmod 8 \Rightarrow N_3^{-1} = 3$

$x = \left(\sum_{i=1}^{3} \left(a_i * N_i * N_i^{-1}\right)\right) \bmod N$

$= \left((3 * 56 * 1) + (1 * 40 * 3) + (6 * 35 * 3)\right) \bmod 280$

$= 918 \bmod 280 = 78$.

Check: $78 \equiv 3 \bmod 5, 78 \equiv 1 \bmod 7, 78 \equiv 6 \bmod 8$

Exercise 3.26

$105 = 3 * 5 * 7$
- $113 \equiv 2 \bmod 3$
  By Lemma 3.1:

  $103^{72\,000\,000\,000\,013} \equiv (2)^{72\,000\,000\,000\,013} \bmod 3$

  $\equiv (2^1) * (2^2)^{\frac{72\,000\,000\,000\,012}{2}} \bmod 3$

  $\equiv 2 * (1)^{\frac{72\,000\,000\,000\,012}{2}} \bmod 3 = 2$ (because $2^2 \equiv 1 \bmod 3$)

- $113 \equiv 3 \bmod 5$
  By Lemma 3.1:

  $113^{72\,000\,000\,000\,013} \bmod 5 \equiv (3)^{72\,000\,000\,000\,013} \bmod 5$

  $\equiv (3^1) * (3^4)^{\frac{72\,000\,000\,000\,012}{4}} \bmod 5$

  $\equiv 3 * (1)^{\frac{72\,000\,000\,000\,012}{4}} \bmod 5 = 3$ (because $3^4 \equiv 1 \bmod 5$)

- $113 \equiv 1 \; mod \; 7$.

  By Lemma 3.1:

  $113^{72\,000\,000\,000\,013} \; mod \; 7 \equiv (1)^{72\,000\,000\,000\,013} \; mod \; 7 = 1.$

- Thus, we have the following congruences:

  $113^{72\,000\,000\,000\,013} \equiv 2 \; mod \; 3$

  $113^{72\,000\,000\,000\,013} \equiv 3 \; mod \; 5$

  $113^{72\,000\,000\,000\,013} \equiv 1 \; mod \; 7.$

  There exist two positive integers k and $x < 105$, such that $113^{72\,000\,000\,000\,013} = k*105 + x$. Thus, from the congruences above, we derive the following congruence equation system:

$$S = \begin{cases} x \equiv 2 \; mod \; 3 \\ x \equiv 3 \; mod \; 5 \\ x \equiv 1 \; mod \; 7 \end{cases}$$

The constant of the congruence system above are: $n_1 = 3$, $n_2 = 5$, $n_3 = 7$, $a_1 = 2$, $a_2 = 3$, and $a_3 = 1$. All moduli are pairwise coprime and $a_i < n_i$, for $i = 1,2,3$. Therefore, the conditions to use the Chinese remainder theorem are met. Hence, according to the CRT there exists a unique value of $x \; mod \; 3*5*7$ that satisfies the three congruences. The solution to the congruence equation system is as follows:

$N \equiv 3*5*7 = 105$

$N_1 = 5*7 = 35 \qquad N_2 = 3*7 = 21 \qquad N_3 = 3*5 = 15$

$N_1^{-1} = 2 \qquad\qquad N_2^{-1} = 1 \qquad\qquad N_3^{-1} = 1$

$x = \left((2*35*2) + (3*21*1) + (1*15*1) \right) mod \; 105 = 8.$

Exercise 3.27

1) First, use the Euler's criterion (Theorem 3.7) to test if $37 \; mod \; 43$ has a solution.

   $37^{(43-1)/2} \equiv 42 \; mod \; 43 = -1$. Therefore, no solution exists.

2) First, use the Euler's criterion to test if $36 \; mod \; 43$ has a solution.

   $36^{(43-1)/2} \equiv 1 \; mod \; 43$. Thus, two solutions exist.

   The steps of Tonelli-Shanks algorithm are as follows:

   $43 = 2^1 * 21 + 1$. Thus, $s = 1$ and $q = 21$.

   Find a square nonresidue modulo 43. $u = 2$ is a square nonresidue.

   Initialization: $m = 1$; $c = 2^{21} \; mod \; 43 = 42$; $t = 36^{21} \; mod \; 43 = 1$

   $\qquad\qquad\qquad R = 36^{(21+1)/2} \; mod \; 43 = 6.$

   Loop: the algorithm stops at the first iteration, because $t = 1$, and returns $r = 6$.

   Check: $(\pm 6)^2 \equiv 36 \; mod \; 43$.

3) First, use the Euler's criterion to test if $53 \; mod \; 97$ has a solution.

   $53^{(97-1)/2} \equiv 1 \; mod \; 97$. Thus, two solutions exist.

   The steps of Tonelli-Shanks algorithm are as follows:

   $97 = 2^5 * 3 + 1$. Thus, $s = 5$ and $q = 3$.

   Find a square nonresidue modulo 97: $u = 5$ is a square nonresidue.

   Initialization: $m = 5$; $c = 5^3 \; mod \; 97 = 28$; $t = 53^3 \; mod \; 97 = 79$

   $\qquad\qquad\qquad R = 53^{(3+1)/2} \; mod \; 97 = 93.$

   Loop:

Iteration #1:

$79^{2^4} \equiv 1 \bmod 97$. Thus, $k = 4$.

$b = 28^{2^0} \bmod 97 = 28$

$m = 4$

$c = 28^2 \bmod 97 = 8$

$t = 79 * 28^2 \bmod 97 = 50$

$R = 93 * 28 \bmod 97 = 82$

Iteration #2:

$50^{2^3} \equiv 1 \bmod 97$. Thus, $k = 3$.

$b = 8^{2^0} \bmod 97 = 8$

$m = 3$

$c = 8^2 \bmod 97 = 64$

$t = 50 * 8^2 \bmod 97 = 96$

$R = 82 * 8 \bmod 97 = 74$

Iteration #3:

$96^{2^1} \equiv 1 \bmod 97$. Thus, $k = 1$.

$b = 64^2 \bmod 97 = 22$

$m = 1$

$c = 22^2 \bmod 97 = 96$

$t = 96 * 22^2 \bmod 97 = 1$

$R = 74 * 22 \bmod 97 = 76$

Iteration #4:

$t \equiv 1 \bmod 97$. Hence, stop and return $r = 76$.

Check: $(\pm 76)^2 = 53 \bmod 97$.

Exercise 3.28

Find the solution(s) to $y^2 \equiv 3 \bmod 143$.

143 has two prime factors 13 and 11.

Step 1: Find the square roots of prime moduli.

From congruence $3 \bmod 143$, two congruences are derived using Lemma 3.1:

$3 \bmod 11$ and $3 \bmod 13$.

$3 \bmod 11$ has two square roots: $r_1 = 5$ and $-r_1 = 6$

$3 \bmod 13$ has two square roots: $r_2 = 4$ and $-r_2 = 9$.

Step 2: Solve a set of congruence systems.

Build a set of 2^2 distinct congruence systems denoted S_1, S_2, S_3, and S_4 as follows:

$$S_1 = \begin{cases} x \equiv 5 \bmod 11 \\ x \equiv 4 \bmod 13 \end{cases} \qquad S_2 = \begin{cases} x \equiv 5 \bmod 11 \\ x \equiv 9 \bmod 13 \end{cases}$$

$$S_3 = \begin{cases} x \equiv 6 \bmod 11 \\ x \equiv 4 \bmod 13 \end{cases} \qquad S_4 = \begin{cases} x \equiv 6 \bmod 11 \\ x \equiv 9 \bmod 3 \end{cases}.$$

Use Gauss's algorithm to find the solutions to each of the four congruence systems. Below, only the calculations to solve S_1 are included.

The constants of congruence equation system S_1 are: $n_1 = 11$, $n_2 = 13$, $a_1 = 5$, $a_2 = 4$.

Common modulus is $N = 11 * 13 = 143$.

$N_1 = \frac{11*13}{11} = 13$, $N_2 = \frac{11*13}{13} = 11$.

Multiplicative inverses: $N_1^{-1} * N_1 \equiv 1 \bmod 11 \Rightarrow N_1^{-1} = 6$

$N_2^{-1} * N_2 \equiv 1 \bmod 13 \Rightarrow N_2^{-1} = 6$

$x = ((5 * 13 * 6) + (4 * 11 * 6)) \bmod 143 = 82 \cdot$

Applying Gauss's algorithm to the four congruence systems yields the following:

$x = 82$ is a solution to S_1

$x = 126$ is a solution to S_2

$x = 17$ is a solution to S_3

$x = 61$ is a solution to S_4.

Now, check that the four values are square roots of 3 *mod* 143

$x = 82 : 82^2 = 6724 \equiv 3 \ mod \ 143$

$x = 126 : 126^2 = 15876 \equiv 3 \ mod \ 143$

$x = 17 : 17^2 = 289 \equiv 3 \ mod \ 143$

$x = 61 : 61^2 = 2304 \equiv 3 \ mod \ 143.$

Thus, 3 *mod* 143 has four square roots.

Exercise 3.29

Find the solution(s) to $y^2 \equiv 421 \ mod \ 693$.

Since $693 = 7*9*11$ is a product of three primes, there should exist 2^3 square roots. Procedure to find the square roots in case of multiple primes is composed of two steps:

Step 1: Find the square roots of prime factors.

By Lemma 3.2:

$$x \equiv 421 \ mod \ 693 \begin{cases} x \equiv 421 \ mod \ 7 \Rightarrow x \equiv 1 \ mod \ 7 \\ x \equiv 421 \ mod \ 9 \Rightarrow x \equiv 7 \ mod \ 9 \\ x \equiv 421 \ mod \ 11 \Rightarrow x \equiv 3 \ mod \ 11 \end{cases}$$

Find square roots for each of the three congruences above:

1 *mod* 7 has two square roots: $r_1 = 1$ and $-r_1 = 6$.

7 *mod* 9 has two square roots: $r_2 = 4$ and $-r_2 = 5$.

3 *mod* 11 has two square roots: $r_3 = 5$ and $-r_3 = 6$.

Step 2: Find solutions to congruence systems.

From the squares roots of the primes factoring 693, eight congruence systems are derived:

$$S_1 = \begin{cases} x \equiv 1 \ mod \ 7 \\ x \equiv 4 \ mod \ 9 \\ x \equiv 5 \ mod \ 11 \end{cases} \quad S_2 = \begin{cases} x \equiv 1 \ mod \ 7 \\ x \equiv 4 \ mod \ 9 \\ x \equiv 6 \ mod 11 \end{cases}$$

$$S_3 = \begin{cases} x \equiv 1 \ mod \ 7 \\ x \equiv 5 \ mod \ 9 \\ x \equiv 5 \ mod \ 11 \end{cases} \quad S_4 = \begin{cases} x \equiv 1 \ mod \ 7 \\ x \equiv 5 \ mod \ 9 \\ x \equiv 6 \ mod \ 11 \end{cases}$$

$$S_5 = \begin{cases} x \equiv 6 \ mod \ 7 \\ x \equiv 4 \ mod \ 9 \\ x \equiv 5 \ mod \ 11 \end{cases} \quad S_6 = \begin{cases} x \equiv 6 \ mod \ 7 \\ x \equiv 4 \ mod \ 9 \\ x \equiv 6 \ mod \ 11 \end{cases}$$

$$S_7 = \begin{cases} x \equiv 6 \ mod \ 7 \\ x \equiv 5 \ mod \ 9 \\ x \equiv 5 \ mod \ 11 \end{cases} \quad S_8 = \begin{cases} x \equiv 6 \ mod \ 7 \\ x \equiv 5 \ mod \ 9 \\ x \equiv 6 \ mod \ 11 \end{cases}$$

Gauss's algorithm is used to find solutions to the eight congruence systems. Below are calculations to solve S_1 system:

The constants of the congruence equation system are $n_1 = 7$, $n_2 = 9$, $n_3 = 11$, $a_1 = 1$, $a_2 = 4$, $a_2 = 5$.

Common modulus is $N = 7*9*11$

$$N_1 = \frac{7*9*11}{7} = 99, \ N_2 = \frac{7*9*11}{9} = 77, \ N_3 = \frac{7*9*11}{11} = 63.$$

Multiplicative inverses:

$N_1^{-1} * N_1 \equiv 1 \ mod \ 7 \Rightarrow N_1^{-1} = 1$

$N_2^{-1} * N_2 \equiv 1 \ mod \ 9 \Rightarrow N_2^{-1} = 2$

$N_3^{-1} * N_3 \equiv 1 \ mod \ 11 \Rightarrow N_3^{-1} = 7$

$x = \left((1*99*1) + (4*77*2) + (5*63*7) \right) mod \ 693 = 148.$

Applying the SRT to the eight congruence systems yields the following:

$x = 148$ is a solution to S_1 $x = 589$ is a solution to S_2
$x = 302$ is a solution to S_3 $x = 50$ is a solution to S_4
$x = 643$ is a solution to S_5 $x = 391$ is a solution to S_6
$x = 104$ is a solution to S_7 $x = 545$ is a solution to S_8.

Check if the eight solutions to the congruence systems are square roots of $421 \bmod 693$:

$x = 148 : 148^2 = 21904 \equiv 421 \bmod 693$
$x = 589 : 589^2 = 346921 \equiv 421 \bmod 693$
$x = 302 : 302^2 = 91204 \equiv 421 \bmod 693$
$x = 50 : 50^2 = 2500 \equiv 421 \bmod 693$
$x = 643 : 643^2 = 413449 \equiv 421 \bmod 693$
$x = 391 : 391^2 = 152881 \equiv 421 \bmod 693$
$x = 104 : 104^2 = 10816 \equiv 421 \bmod 693$
$x = 545 : 545^2 = 297025 \equiv 421 \bmod 693$.

Finally, notice that

$-148 \bmod 693 = 545$ $-545 \bmod 693 = 148$
$-589 \bmod 693 = 104$ $-104 \bmod 693 = 589$
$-302 \bmod 693 = 391$ $-391 \bmod 693 = 302$
$-50 \bmod 693 = 643$ $-643 \bmod 693 = 50$.

Thus, $421 \bmod 693$ has exactly eight square roots: four roots and their negatives.

Exercise 3.30

Note that to do computations with large numbers, a tool implementing the polynomial extended Euclidean algorithm is required.

In the following, $-ax \bmod p$ is replaced by $(p-a)x \bmod p$.
Check the irreducibility of $f(x) = x^{10} + x^3 + 1$ over F_2.
Degree of $f(x)$ is $m = 10$. The prime dividers of 10 are 5 and 2.

$$p_1 = \frac{10}{5} = 2, \ p_2 = \frac{10}{2} = 5.$$

Iteration #1 (test of prime divider 5, i.e. $p_1 = 2$):

$x^{2^2} \equiv x^4 \bmod f(x)$
$h(x) = x^4 - x \bmod f(x) = x^4 + x$
$g(x) = \text{GCD}(f(x), h(x)) = 1$ $g(x) = 1$; hence, the algorithm continues.

Iteration #2 (test of prime divider 2, i.e. $p_2 = 5$):

$x^{2^5} \equiv (x^8 + x^5 + x^4 + x^2 + x) \bmod f(x)$
$h(x) = x^8 + x^5 + x^4 + x^2 + x - x \bmod f(x) = x^8 + x^5 + x^4 + x^2$
$g(x) = \text{GCD}(f(x), h(x)) = 1$
$g(x) = 1$; hence, the algorithm continues.

Second step of the algorithm

$g(x) = x^{2^{10}} - x \bmod f(x) = 0$.
Thus, $x^{10} + x^3 + 1$ is irreducible over F_2.

Exercise 3.31

Note that to do computations with large numbers, a tool implementing the polynomial extended Euclidean algorithm is required.

In the following, $-ax \bmod p$ is replaced by $(p-a)x \bmod p$.

Let $f(x) = x^5 + x^4 + x^3 + x^2 + x - 1$.

First, notice that, over F_3, $f(0) = 2$, $f(1) = 1$, and $f(2) = 1$. Hence, $f(x)$ has no roots in F_3. Since $f(x)$ is of degree 5, we cannot conclude that $f(x)$ is irreducible. Thus, let us check $f(x)$ irreducibility using Rabin's test.

The given polynomial is of degree 5. Thus, only one prime divider is to be considered.

$$p_1 = \frac{5}{5} = 1.$$

Iteration #1 (test of prime divider 5, i.e. $p_1 = 1$):

$$x^{3^1} = x^3 \equiv x^3 \bmod f(x)$$

$$h(x) = x^3 - x \bmod f(x) = x^3 + 2x \bmod f(x)$$

$$\text{GCD}(f(x), h(x)) = 1.$$

Hence, the algorithm continues.

Second step of the algorithm

$$g(x) = x^{3^5} - x \bmod f(x) = 2x^2 + 2x + 1$$

Thus, $f(x) = x^5 + x^4 + x^3 + x^2 + x - 1$ is irreducible over F_3.

Indeed, $x^5 + x^4 + x^3 + x^2 + x + 2 = (x^2 + 2x + 2)(x^3 + 2x^2 + x + 1)$.

Problem 3.1 (Proof of Lemma 3.1)

Lemma 3.1 states that if a, n, and k are positive integers, then $a^k \bmod n \equiv (a \bmod n)^k \bmod n$.

By definition, for any integers a and b: $a * b \bmod n \equiv (a \bmod n) * (b \bmod n) \bmod n$.

Thus, $a * a \bmod n \equiv (a \bmod n)^2 \bmod n$.

Then, $a * a * a \bmod n \equiv (a \bmod n)^3 \bmod n$, which may be generalized to $a^k \bmod n \equiv (a \bmod n)^k \bmod n$ for any integer $k > 2$. $\square$

Problem 3.2 (Proof of Lemma 3.2)

$x \equiv a \bmod N = a \bmod (n_1 * n_2 * \ldots * n_k)$.

Thus, there exists an integer u such that $x = a + u * (n_1 * n_2 * \ldots * n_k)$.

Let $N_i = \dfrac{u * N}{n_i}$, for $1 \le i \le k$. N_i is an integer because n_i is a factor of N.

x can be expressed as $x = a + N_i * n_i$, for $1 \le i \le k$.

$a + N_i * n_i \equiv a \bmod n_i \Rightarrow x \equiv a \bmod n_i$ for $1 \le i \le k$. $\square$

Problem 3.3 (Proof of Lemma 3.3)

By definition, $\varphi(n)$ is the number of elements of $\mathbb{Z}_n$, which are coprime with n. By Theorem 3.3, all the $\varphi(n)$ elements have multiplicative inverse *mod n*. Therefore, they are elements of $\mathbb{Z}_n^*$. Hence, $\left|\mathbb{Z}_n^*\right| = \varphi(n)$. $\square$

Problem 3.4

1) By definition of multiplicative inverse, given two elements x and x' of $\mathbb{Z}_p^*$, if x' is a multiplicative inverse of x, then $x * x' \equiv 1 \bmod p$.

    Let a be an even integer less than p. There exists a positive integer m such that $a = 2m$. a', the multiplicative inverse of a, does not exist because the condition $a * a' \equiv 1 \bmod p$ cannot be satisfied, if p is even, which is proven as follows:

    If a' was the multiplicative inverse of a, then:

$$a * a' \equiv 1 \bmod p \Rightarrow \exists k \,|\, 2m * a' = k * p + 1. \tag{a}$$

Since p is even, there exists q such that $p = 2q$.

Statement (a) becomes:

$$a * a' \equiv 1 \ mod \ p \Rightarrow \exists k \mid 2m * a' = k * 2q + 1$$

$$2(m * a') = 2(k * q) + 1. \tag{b}$$

Statement (b) cannot hold because the left side of equality is even while the right one is odd. Thus, no even integer is an element of $\mathbb{Z}_p^*$ if p is even.

2) $\mathbb{Z}_{2^m}^*$ means $\mathbb{Z}_p^*$ with $p = 2^m$. Since p is even, $\mathbb{Z}_p^*$ does not include any even elements, because their multiplicative inverses do not exist in $\mathbb{Z}_{2^m}^*$. Thus, $\mathbb{Z}_{2^m}^*$ includes only odd elements. Hence, its cardinality can be at most $\frac{2^m}{2} = 2^{m-1}$.

Problem 3.5

$$\mathbb{Z}_{11}^* = \{1, 2, 3, 4, 5, 6, 7, 8, 9, 10\}$$

$$p = 11 \Rightarrow \frac{p-1}{2} = 5 \text{ and } -1 = 10 \ mod \ 11.$$

Check by Euler's criterion (Theorem 3.7):

$$1^5 \equiv 1 \ mod \ 11, 3^5 \equiv 1 \ mod \ 7, 4^5 \equiv 1 \ mod \ 11, 5^5 \equiv 1 \ mod \ 11, 9^5 \equiv 1 \ mod \ 11$$

$$2^5 \equiv -1 \ mod \ 11, 6^5 \equiv -1 \ mod \ 11, 7^5 \equiv -1 \ mod \ 11, 8^5 \equiv -1 \ mod \ 11, 10^5 \equiv -1 \ mod \ 11.$$

Thus, five (i.e. $\frac{11-1}{2}$) of elements in $\mathbb{Z}_{11}^*$ are square residues and five elements are square nonresidues.

Problem 3.6 (Proof of Lemma 3.4)

$$\mathbb{Z}_p^* = \{1, 2, ..., p-1\}.$$

Since p is a prime greater than 2, the number of elements of $\mathbb{Z}_p^*$ is even.

By definition of $\mathbb{Z}_p^*$, if $-a \in \mathbb{Z}_p^*$, then $-a \in \mathbb{Z}_p^*$ (i.e. any element and its additive inverse are elements of $\mathbb{Z}_p^*$). Any element of $\mathbb{Z}_p^*$ has one and only one additive inverse.

$$\mathbb{Z}_p^* = \{1, 2, ..., p-1\} = \left\{1, 2, ..., \frac{p-1}{2}, \frac{p+1}{2}, ..., p-2, p-1\right\}.$$

By definition of the additive inverse (or negative):

$$-1 = p - 1 \ mod \ p, \qquad -2 = p - 2 \ mod \ p, ..., -\frac{p-1}{2} = p - \frac{p-1}{2} \ mod \ p = \frac{p+1}{2}$$

Thus, $\mathbb{Z}_p^* = \{1, 2, ..., p-1\} = \left\{1, 2, ..., \frac{p-1}{2}, -\frac{p-1}{2}, ..., -2, -1\right\}.$

The squares that are elements of $\mathbb{Z}_p^*$ are: $1^2, (-1)^2, 2^2, (-2)^2, ..., \left(\frac{p-1}{2}\right)^2, \left(-\frac{p-1}{2}\right)^2$. Since $\forall a \in \mathbb{Z}_p^*$, $a^2 = (-a)^2$, there exist $\frac{p-1}{2}$ distinct squares. It is easy to prove that if a and b are two distinct elements in $\mathbb{Z}_p^*$, with $b \neq -a$, then $a^2 \ mod \ p$ and $b^2 \ mod \ p$ are two distinct elements. By definition, an element $a \in \mathbb{Z}_p^*$ is a quadratic residue if there exists $y \in \mathbb{Z}_p^*$ such that $y^2 \equiv a \ mod \ p$. Since there are exactly $\frac{p-1}{2}$ distinct squares in $\mathbb{Z}_p^*$, the number of square residues is $\frac{p-1}{2}$. Hence, the remaining $\frac{p-1}{2}$ elements are square nonresidues. □

Problem 3.7 (Proof of Lemma 3.5)

Since a is a quadratic residue of p, we know by Euler's criterion (Theorem 3.7) that $a^{\frac{p-1}{2}} \equiv 1 \ mod \ p$. Thus, if $r = a^{\frac{p+1}{4}}$, then $r^2 = a^{\frac{p+1}{2}} = a * a^{\frac{p-1}{2}} \Rightarrow r^2 \equiv a * (1) \ mod \ p = a.$ □

Problem 3.8

By definition, $\mathbb{Z}_p^* = \{a \in \mathbb{Z}_p \mid \text{GCD}(a, p) = 1\}$.

Let u be any element of $\mathbb{Z}_p^*$.

- $a = u^{(p-1)/2} \Rightarrow a^2 = u^{(p-1)}$.
  By Fermat's little theorem (Theorem 3.5), $u^{(p-1)} \equiv 1 \bmod p$.
  Thus, $a^2 \equiv 1 \bmod p$. Hence, a is a square root of 1.

- From answer to question 1, we know that $u^{(p-1)/2}$ is a square root of $1 \bmod p$. Thus, $u^{(p-1)/2}$ is 1 or -1 in modulo p.

Problem 3.9

Prove that: *given two distinct primes p and q:*

$$q\left(q^{-1} \bmod p\right) + p\left(p^{-1} \bmod q\right) = pq + 1.$$

Let $N = q\left(q^{-1} \bmod p\right) + p\left(p^{-1} \bmod q\right)$. $\hfill \text{(a)}$

By definition of multiplicative inverse:

$$p\left(p^{-1} \bmod q\right) \equiv 1 \bmod q \Rightarrow \exists k \in \mathbb{N} \mid p * p^{-1} = k * q + 1 \hfill \text{(b)}$$

$$q\left(q^{-1} \bmod p\right) \equiv 1 \bmod p \Rightarrow \exists k' \in \mathbb{N} \mid q * q^{-1} = k' * p + 1. \hfill \text{(b')}$$

By substitution of (b) and (b') in (a):

$$N = q\left(q^{-1} \bmod p\right) + k * q + 1 \Rightarrow N \equiv 1 \bmod q \hfill \text{(c)}$$

$$N = k' * p + 1 + p\left(p^{-1} \bmod q\right) \Rightarrow N \equiv 1 \bmod p. \hfill \text{(c')}$$

Since p and q are coprime, from (c) and (c'):

$$N \equiv 1 \bmod p * q \hfill \text{(d)}$$

All integers $\left(p, \; p^{-1}, \; q, \; q^{-1}\right)$ in (a) are greater than 1, so:

$$N \geq 2. \hfill \text{(e)}$$

By definition of modulo:

$$p^{-1} \bmod q \leq q - 1 \Rightarrow p\left(p^{-1} \bmod q\right) < p * q \hfill \text{(f)}$$

$$q^{-1} \bmod p \leq p - 1 \Rightarrow q\left(q^{-1} \bmod q\right) < q * p. \hfill \text{(f')}$$

From (a), (e), (f), and (f'):

$$2 \leq N < 2 * p * q. \hfill \text{(g)}$$

The unique value of N, which fulfills (d) and (g), is $p * q + 1$.

Therefore, $q\left(q^{-1} \bmod p\right) + p\left(p^{-1} \bmod q\right) = 1 + p * q$.

Problem 3.10

Let q be the order of $\mathbb{Z}_p^*$ and 1 its neutral element.

If g is a generator of $\mathbb{Z}_p^*$, then elements of $\mathbb{Z}_p^*$ can be expressed as powers of g:

$$\mathbb{Z}_p^* = \left\{1, g, g^2, \ldots, g^{q-1}\right\}.$$

Since g is a generator of $\mathbb{Z}_p^*$ and $\left|\mathbb{Z}_p^*\right| = q$, $g^q \equiv 1 \bmod p$.
By definition of multiplicative inverse: $g * g^{-1} = 1$.

Then, $\left(g * g^{-1}\right)^q = 1 \Rightarrow g^q * \left(g^{-1}\right)^q = 1 \Rightarrow 1 * \left(g^{-1}\right)^q = 1 \Rightarrow \left(g^{-1}\right)^q = 1.$

Since the order of g^{-1} is q, g^{-1} is a generator of $\mathbb{Z}_p^*$.

Problem 3.11 (Proof of Lemma 3.6)

To prove that Lemma 3.6 is correct, we need to prove that the statement "any irreducible polynomial of degree m can generate all the elements of field F_{p^m}" is false. The two following scenarios are counterexamples to the statement above.

1) Let $f(x) = x^2 + 1$ and α its root over field F_{3^2}.

   Since α is a root of $f(x)$, then $\alpha^2 + 1 = 0 \Rightarrow \alpha^2 = -1 = 2.$

   Let us see how powers of α generate elements of field F_{3^2}:

   $\alpha^0 = 1 \qquad \alpha^1 = \alpha$

   $\alpha^2 = 2 \qquad \alpha^3 = \alpha\left(\alpha^2\right) = 2\alpha$

   $\alpha^4 = \alpha(2\alpha) = 2\,\alpha^2 = 1$

   $\alpha^5 = \alpha(1) = \alpha \qquad \alpha^6 = \alpha(1) = 2.$

   Thus, α cannot generate all the eight nonzero elements of F_{3^2}. Hence, α, which represents the element 3, is not a primitive element in F_{3^2}.

2) Let $f(x) = x^3 + 2x + 2$ and α its root over field F_{3^3}.

	$x^i \bmod f(x)$	Element		$x^i \bmod f(x)$	Element
α^0	1	1	α^9	$\alpha + 2$	5
α^1	α	3	α^{10}	$\alpha^2 + 2\alpha$	15
α^2	α^2	9	α^{11}	$2\alpha^2 + \alpha + 1$	22
α^3	$\alpha + 1$	4	α^{12}	$\alpha^2 + 1$	10
α^4	$\alpha^2 + \alpha$	12	α^{13}	1	1
α^5	$\alpha^2 + \alpha + 1$	13	α^{14}	α	3
α^6	$\alpha^2 + 2\alpha + 1$	16	α^{15}	α^2	9
α^7	$2\alpha^2 + 2\alpha + 1$	25	α^{16}	$\alpha + 1$	4
α^8	$2\alpha^2 + 2$	20	...	...	...

Root α can generate only 12 nonzero elements among the 26 nonzero elements of F_{3^3}.

Both examples above prove (by counterexamples) that not all polynomials of degree m and irreducible over field F_p have a root α that can generate all elements of a field F_{p^m}. $\qquad\square$

Problem 3.12

1) If g_i is a generator, then its multiplicative inverse g_i^{-1} also is a generator.

   By definition of multiplicative inverse: $g_i * g_i^{-1} \equiv 1 \bmod p$.

   Let q be the number of generators of $\mathbb{Z}_p^*$ and G the set of $\mathbb{Z}_p^*$ generators denoted $\{g_1, g_2, \cdots, g_q\}$. Each element in G has its multiplicative inverse in G. Without loss of generality, assume that, if q is even, the set G is organized into two halves

   such that g_k, $1 \le k \le \dfrac{q}{2}$, is the inverse of g_{q-k+1}, i.e. $G = \left\{g_1, g_2, \cdots, g_{\frac{q}{2}}, g_{\frac{q}{2}}^{-1}, \cdots, g_2^{-1}, g_1^{-1}\right\}.$

   The product $\prod_{i=1}^{i=k} g_i = g_1 * g_2 * \cdots * g_q$ may be rewritten as

   $$\prod_{i=1}^{i=k} g_i = \left(g_1 * g_1^{-1}\right) * \left(g_2 * g_2^{-1}\right) * \cdots * \left(g_{\frac{q}{2}} * g_{\frac{q}{2}}^{-1}\right).$$

   Thus, $\prod_{i=1}^{i=k} g_i \equiv 1 * 1 * \cdots * 1 \equiv 1 \bmod p.$

If q is odd, G is organized as $\left\{ g_1, g_2, ..., g_{\frac{q-1}{2}}, g_{\frac{q+1}{2}}, g_{\frac{q-1}{2}}^{-1}, g_2^{-1}, g_1^{-1} \right\}$. Since, the elements in the subset of G on the right of

$g_{\frac{q+1}{2}}$ and the elements on its left are pairwise inverses, $g_{\frac{q+1}{2}} = g_{\frac{q+1}{2}}^{-1}$. Hence, $\prod_{i=1}^{i=k} g_i \equiv 1*...1...*1 \equiv 1 \ mod \ p$.

2) Let F_p be a prime field. Thus, $F_p = \{0, 12, ..., p-1\}$. Each element $u \in F_p$ has one and only one additive inverse $u' \in F_p$, such that $u + u' = 0$. The elements of F_p can be organized as follows: $\left\{ 0, 1, -1, 2, -2, ..., \frac{p-1}{2}, -\left(\frac{p-1}{2}\right) \right\}$. Therefore,

$$\sum_{u \in F_p} u \equiv (0) + (1-1) + (2-2) + ... + \left(\frac{p-1}{2} - \frac{p-1}{2}\right) mod \ p = 0.$$

Problem 3.13

$\mathbb{Z}_4 = \{0, 1, 2, 3\}$ is not a field, because 0 and 2 have no multiplicative inverse in $\mathbb{Z}_4$.

Problem 3.14

Consider field F_{2^5} with reduction polynomial $f(x) = x^5 + x^2 + 1$. Show that $g = x$ is a generator of F_{2^5}.
The set of elements of F_{2^5} is $\{0, 1, 2, ..., 30, 31\}$.

By definition, if g is a generator of a field F_{2^m}, then every nonzero element of F_{2^m} can be uniquely written is a power of g.
That is: $F_{2^m}^* = F_{2^m} - \{0\} = \{2^m, 0 \le i \le 2^m - 2\}$.

$g = x$ is it a generator of F_{2^5}?

In this problem $2^m = 32$. Thus, we have to check the powers of x from 0 to 30.

$x^0 \ mod \ f(x) = 1 = (00001) = 1 \qquad x^1 \ mod \ f(x) = x = (00010) = 2$

$x^2 \ mod \ f(x) = x^2 = (00100) = 4 \qquad x^3 \ mod \ f(x) = x^3 = (01000) = 8$

$x^4 \ mod \ f(x) = x^4 = (10000) = 16 \qquad x^5 \ mod \ f(x) = x^2 + 1 = (00101) = 5.$

From power 5, we make use of the following rule of modular arithmetic:

$(A(x) * B(x)) mod \ P(x) = ((A(x) mod \ P(x)) * (B(x) mod \ P(x))) mod \ P(x)$
for any polynomials $A(x)$, $B(x)$, and $P(x)$

$x^6 \ mod \ f(x) = ((x \ mod \ f(x)) * (x^5 \ mod \ f(x))) mod \ (fx)$

$= x * (x^2 + 1) mod \ f(x) = x^3 + x = (01010) = 10$

$x^7 \ mod \ f(x) = ((x^2 \ mod \ f(x)) * (x^5 \ mod \ f(x))) mod \ (fx)$

$= x^2 * (x^2 + 1) mod \ f(x) = x^4 + x^2 = (10100) = 20$

$x^8 \ mod \ f(x) = ((x^3 \ mod \ f(x)) * (x^5 \ mod \ f(x))) mod \ (fx)$

$= x^3 * (x^2 + 1) mod \ f(x) = x^3 + x^2 + 1 = (01101) = 13$

$x^9 \ mod \ f(x) = ((x^1 \ mod \ f(x)) * (x^8 \ mod \ f(x)))$

$= x * (x^3 + x^2 + 1) = x^4 + x^3 + x = (11010) = 26$

$x^{10} \ mod \ f(x) = ((x^1 \ mod \ f(x)) * (x^9 \ mod \ f(x)))$

$= x * (x^4 + x^3 + x) mod \ f(x) = x^4 + 1 = (10001) = 17$

$x^{11} \ mod \ f(x) = ((x^1 \ mod \ f(x)) * (x^{10} \ mod \ f(x)))$

$= x * (x^4 + 1) mod \ f(x) = x^2 + x + 1 = (00111) = 7$

$x^{12} \ mod \ f(x) = ((x^1 \ mod \ f(x)) * (x^{11} \ mod \ f(x)))$

$= x * (x^2 + x + 1) mod \ f(x) = x^3 + x^2 + x = (001110) = 14$

$$x^{13} \bmod f(x) = \left(\left(x^1 \bmod f(x)\right) * \left(x^{12} \bmod f(x)\right)\right) = (11100) = 28$$

$$x^{14} \bmod f(x) = \left(\left(x^1 \bmod f(x)\right) * \left(x^{13} \bmod f(x)\right)\right) = (11101) = 29$$

$$x^{15} \bmod f(x) = \left(\left(x^1 \bmod f(x)\right) * \left(x^{14} \bmod f(x)\right)\right) = (11111) = 31$$

$$x^{16} \bmod f(x) = \left(\left(x^8 \bmod f(x)\right) * \left(x^8 \bmod f(x)\right)\right) \bmod (fx) = (11011) = 27$$

$$x^{17} \bmod f(x) = (10011) = 19 \qquad x^{18} \bmod f(x) = (00011) = 3$$

$$x^{19} \bmod f(x) = (00110) = 6 \qquad x^{20} \bmod f(x) = (01100) = 12$$

$$x^{21} \bmod f(x) = (11000) = 24 \qquad x^{22} \bmod f(x) = (10101) = 21$$

$$x^{23} \bmod f(x) = (01111) = 15 \qquad x^{24} \bmod f(x) = (11110) = 30$$

$$x^{25} \bmod f(x) = (11001) = 25 \qquad x^{26} \bmod f(x) = (10111) = 23$$

$$x^{27} \bmod f(x) = (01011) = 11 \qquad x^{28} \bmod f(x) = (10110) = 22$$

$$x^{29} \bmod f(x) = (01001) = 9$$

$$x^{30} \bmod f(x) = \left(\left(x^{16} \bmod f(x)\right) * \left(x^{14} \bmod f(x)\right)\right) \bmod f(x)$$

$$= \left(x^4 + x^3 + x + 1\right) * \left(x^4 + x^2\right)^2 \bmod f(x) = x^4 + x = (10010) = 18.$$

Problem 3.15

Let $f(x) = x^4 + x + 1$ be an irreducible polynomial over F_2. $f(x)$ is used for computations over field F_{2^4}. Solve the following linear equations:

1) $3y = 4$

   $y = 4 * 3^{-1}$.

   Operations are done using polynomial representation.

   $$3^{-1}: (x+1)\left(x^3 + x^2 + x\right) \bmod \left(x^4 + x + 1\right) = 1 \Rightarrow 3^{-1} = 14$$

   $$4 * 3^{-1}: \left(x^2\right)\left(x^3 + x^2 + x\right) \bmod \left(x^4 + x + 1\right) = x^3 + x^2 + 1.$$

   Hence, $y = 13$

2) $9y + 3 = 2$

   $y = (2 - 3) * 9^{-1}$.

   Operations are done with polynomial representation.

   $2 - 3: x - x - 1 = -1 = 15$

   $$9^{-1}: \left(x^3 + 1\right)(x) \bmod \left(x^4 + x + 1\right) = 1 \Rightarrow 9^{-1} = 2$$

   $$(2 - 3) * 9^{-1}: 15x \bmod \left(x^4 + x + 1\right) = 15x = -x$$

   Hence, $y = -2 = 14$.

Problem 3.16

$147^{155} \bmod 23 \equiv ?$

1) Fermat's little theorem states that given two positive integers m and p, such that p is prime and m is not divisible by p, then $m^{p-1} \equiv 1 \bmod p$.

   In this problem $m = 147$ and $p = 23$. m and p are coprime. Thus, Fermat's little theorem is applicable. Thus, $147^{22} \equiv 1 \bmod 23$ is used to reduce the computations as follows:

$$147^{155} \ mod \ 23 \equiv 147^{7*22+1} \ mod \ 23 \equiv \left(147^{22}\right)^{7} * \left(147\right) \ mod \ 23$$

$$\equiv \left(1\right)^{7} * \left(147\right) \ mod \ 23 \equiv 9.$$

To use the right-to-left binary exponentiation method, we need to represent the exponent as a sum of powers of 2:

$$155 = 128 + 16 + 8 + 2 + 1 = 2^{7} + 2^{4} + 2^{3} + 2^{1} + 2^{0}.$$

The number of iterations of the right-to-left binary exponentiation method depends on the rank of the leftmost significant bit of the exponent. If the exponent is 155, the number of iterations of the algorithm is 8 (i.e. 7+1). Consequently, when applicable, Fermat's little theorem is a very fast method to perform modular exponentiation.

Problem 3.17

1) We need to prove that $t * R = T \ mod \ n$, $0 \le t < n$ (because a residue is less than the modulus), and t is an integer.

$$t * R = T \ mod \ n? \tag{a}$$

In line 2, $t = (T + m * n) / R$. Multiplying both sides by R yields $t * R = (T + m * n) \equiv T \ mod \ n$, because adding $m * n$ does not change the residue. Therefore, condition (a) holds.

$$0 \le t < n? \tag{b}$$

From line 3, the returned result is either $t < n$ or $t = t - n$. Therefore, we need to prove that $t < 2n$. From definition in line 1, $0 \le m < R$. Thus, $0 \le n * m < n * R$. By definition 3.44, $0 \le T < n * R$. Thus, $0 \le T + n * m < 2 * n * R$. Dividing the inequality by R yields $0 \le (T + n * m) / R < 2 * n$. Thus, condition (b) holds.

$$t \ \text{is it an integer?} \tag{c}$$

Multiplying both sides in line 1 by n yields $n * m = n * T * n' = T * \left(-n * n^{-1}\right) = -T \ mod \ R$. Therefore, there exists some integer k such that $n * m = k * R - T$ and hence $t = \frac{T + m * n}{R} = \frac{k * R}{R}$ is an integer. $\square$

2) We need to prove that $c \equiv a * b \ mod \ n$, where c denotes the result of the Montgomery multiplication. We proceed by substitution starting from the definition of c:

$$c \equiv REDC(c') \equiv c' * R^{-1} \ mod \ n \equiv \left(REDC\left(\tilde{a} * \tilde{b}\right)\right) * R^{-1} \ mod \ n$$

$$\equiv \left(\left(\tilde{a} * \tilde{b}\right) * R^{-1}\right) * R^{-1} \ mod \ n$$

$$\equiv \left(\left(\left(a * R \ mod \ n\right) * \left(b * R \ mod \ n\right)\right) * R^{-1}\right) * R^{-1} \ mod \ n$$

$$\equiv \left(\left(\left(a * R * R^{-1} \ mod \ n\right) * \left(b * R * R^{-1} \ mod \ n\right)\right)\right) mod \ n \equiv a * b \ mod \ n. \qquad \square$$

Problem 3.18 *(Proof of Gauss's algorithm)*

Gauss's algorithm is correct if and only if the returned value of x satisfies all the congruence equations. Recall that to apply the Chinese remainder theorem, the moduli in congruence equations must meet the following condition:

For $1 \le i \le k$, n_i is coprime with n_j, for $i \ne j$ and $1 \le j \le k$.

Proof:

By construction, $N_i = \dfrac{\prod_{i=1}^{i=k} n_i}{n_i}$, for $1 \le i \le k$. Thus,

i) Since the n_i's are pairwise coprime and N_i does not have a factor equal to n_i, $GCD(N_i, n_i) = 1$. Thus, the multiplicative inverse of $N_i \ mod \ n_i$, for every i in $[1, k]$, exists.

ii) For every j in $(1, k)$, $N_j \equiv 0 \ mod \ n_i$ for every i in $[1, k]$ and $j \ne i$, because n_i is a factor of N_j.

From i) and ii), for i and j in $[1, k]$:

$$\left(a_j * N_j * N_j^{-1}\right) mod \ n_i = 0 \text{ if } j \ne i \text{ (because } n_i \text{ is a factor of } N_j\text{)}.$$

$$\left(a_i * N_i * N_i^{-1}\right) mod \ n_i = a_i \ mod \ n_i \text{ (because } \left(N_i * N_i^{-1}\right) mod \ n_i = 1\text{)}.$$

$$\Rightarrow \left(\sum_{i=1}^{k}\left(a_i * N_i * N_i^{-1}\right)\right) mod\ n_i = a_i\ mod\ n_i, \forall i \in [1,k].$$

By construction: $x = \left(\sum_{k}^{i=1}\left(a_i * N_i * N_i^{-1}\right)\right) mod\ N$. Hence, there exists a positive integer m such that

$$x = \sum_{k}^{i=1}\left(a_i * N_i * N_i^{-1}\right) - m * N$$

$$\Rightarrow x\ mod\ n_i = \left(\sum_{i=1}^{k}\left(a_i * N_i * N_i^{-1}\right) - m * N\right) mod\ n_i.$$

Since N is a multiple of n_i,

$$x\ mod\ n_i = \left(\sum_{i=1}^{k}\left(a_i * N_i * N_i^{-1}\right)\right) mod\ n_i = a_i\ mod\ n_i, \forall i \in [1,k]. \qquad \square$$

Problem 3.19 (Proof of Lemma 3.8)

First, we need to prove that if n and x are integers such that $1 < x < n$ and $x^2 \equiv 1\ mod\ n$, then n is composite.

Proof. $x^2 \equiv 1\ mod\ n \Rightarrow x^2 - 1 \equiv 0\ mod\ n \Rightarrow (x+1)(x-1) \equiv 0\ mod\ n$. If $x \neq 1$ and $x \neq n-1$, n must be composite because $(x+1)$ and $(x-1)$ are less than n and their product is a multiple of n. For example, $5^2 \equiv 1\ mod\ 24$, $(5+1)(5-1) \equiv 0\ mod\ 24$, and 24 is composite.

Second, let n and a be integers such that $GCD(a,n) = 1$ and $a^{\frac{n-1}{2}} \not\equiv \pm 1\ mod\ n$. Either $a^{n-1} \not\equiv 1\ mod\ n$ or $a^{n-1} \equiv 1\ mod\ n$ holds. By Fermat's little theorem, if $a^{n-1} \equiv 1\ mod\ n$, then n must be composite. $a^{n-1} \equiv 1\ mod\ n$ is the same as $(a^{(n-1)/2})^2 \equiv 1\ mod\ n$, which means that $a^{(n-1)/2}$, which is different from 1 and -1, is a square root of 1 $mod\ n$. Therefore, by the fact proven above, n must be composite. $\qquad \square$

Notes

1 See Problem 3.1 for proof of Lemma 3.1.

2 See Problem 3.2 for proof of Lemma 3.2.

3 In the sequel, multiplicative inverse or simply inverse is used instead of modular multiplicative inverse, because we only consider calculations in modular arithmetic.

4 See Problem 3.3 for proof of Lemma 3.3.

5 See Problem 3.6 for proof of Lemma 3.4.

6 It is easy to prove that if p is a prime and greater than 2, then $p \not\equiv 0\ mod\ 4$ and $p \not\equiv 2\ mod\ 4$.

7 See Problem 3.7 for proof of Lemma 3.5.

8 The multiplication operation $\times$ may refer or not to the usual integer multiplication operation denoted "$*$" $mod\ n$. Unless explicitly redefined, $\times$ means $*$.

9 Elements of a field can be (integer or real) numbers, booleans, literals, strings, etc. In this book, field elements are integers.

10 If p is prime, F_p and $\mathbb{Z}_p$ have exactly the same elements $\{0,1,2, ...,p-1)$.

11 See Problem 3.11 for proof of Lemma 3.6.

12 There exists a second variant of binary exponentiation, called left-to-right binary exponentiation, which proceeds in the inverse direction of the bit rank, i.e. form the most significant bit to the least significant bit of the exponent. Both methods have equivalent complexity.

13 Multi-precision division is not given, because it is not used in the sequel.

14 Comments for selection: i) The half of $\mathbb{Z}_p^*$ elements are quadratic nonresidue. ii) Depending on the implementation of the algorithm, the selection of a candidate element in $\mathbb{Z}_p^*$ may be at random or by starting from 1 and incrementing. iii) Candidate elements can be tested by Euler's criterion. iv) Stop the selection when the first quadratic nonresidue element is found.

References

1 McEliece, R.J. (2011). *Finite Fields for Computer Scientists and Engineers*. Kluwer Academic Publishers.

2 Hachenberger, D. and Jungnickel, D. (2020). *Topics in Galois Fields*. Springer.

3 Mullen, G.L. and Panario, D. (2013). *Handbook of Finite Fields*. CRC Press.

4 Stein, W. (2009). *Elementary Number Theory: Primes, Congruences, and Secrets: A Computational Approach*. Springer.

5 Rosen, K.H. (1984). *Elementary Number Theory and Its Applications*. Addison Wesley.

6 Tattersall, J.J. (2005). *Elementary Number Theory in Nine Chapters*. Cambridge University Press.

7 Blake-Wilson, S., Bolyard, N., Gupta, V. et al. (2006). *Elliptic Curve Cryptography (ECC) Cipher Suites for Transport Layer Security (TLS) - RFC 4492*. Internet Engineering Task Force (IETF).

8 ANSI. (2020). *Financial Services - Public Key Cryptography for the Financial Services Industry: The Elliptic Curve Digital Signature Algorithm - ECDSA - ANSI X9.142*. American National Standard Institute.

9 Montgomery, P.L. (1985). Modular multiplication without trial division. *Mathematics of Computation* 44 (170): 519–521.

10 Shanks, D. (1972). Five number-theoretic algorithms. In *Second Manitoba Conference on Numerical Mathematics*. Winnipeg, MB, Canada: American Mathematical Association, 51–70.

11 Rabin, M.O. (1980). Probabilistic algorithms in finite fields. *SIAM (Society for Industrial Applied Mathematics) Journal of Computing* 9 (2): 273–280.

12 Katz, J. and Lindell, Y. (2007). *Introduction to Modern Cryptography*. CRC Press.

4

Symmetric Ciphering

Historical Ciphers

Shift and substitution ciphers have been used for written text transmission and dominated the art of secret writing for at least two millenniums (and maybe more). The most known historical ciphers in this category, include Caesar's, Vigenere's, affine, OTP, and Enigma ciphers. With the advent of computers, shift and substitution ciphering were abandoned, because it has become easy to break them. However, it is important to learn them since they had inspired the modern cryptography. The material below is mostly collected from [1–5].

4.1 Definitions

Definition 4.1 Alphabet: *it is a set of elements, which may be letters, words, or any other form of bit strings that are used to generate plaintexts and ciphertexts.*

In the sequel, the alphabet elements are either Latin letters or bits.

Definition 4.2 Substitution cipher: *it is a cipher in which an alphabet element is replaced by another alphabet element to yield a ciphertext.*

Definition 4.3 Shift cipher: *it is a special type of substitution cipher in which a letter is replaced by another letter located a few positions away.*

Definition 4.4 Monoalphabetic cipher: *it is a cipher in which the letters of the plaintext are mapped to ciphertext letters based on a single substitution key and each letter is always replaced by the same letter. The transformation is bijective.*

Definition 4.5 Polyalphabetic cipher: *it is a cipher, which makes use of multiple alphabets and a letter may be replaced by many other letters depending on its position in the plaintext. It makes use of multiple keys. The transformation is not bijective.*

Definition 4.6 Information-theoretic secure cipher: *a cipher is information-theoretic secure if it cannot be broken even if the adversary has unlimited computation resources.*

4.2 Caesar's Cipher

One of the most known shift ciphers is Caesar's cipher used in the Roman Empire to encrypt messages exchanged between Roma (i.e. the emperor and his attorneys) and roman armies around the world. At ancient Rome, the romans had an intelligence system comparable to the one in today's USA.

A message to encrypt is a string of letters over an alphabet A of m letters. Each letter has an index in interval $[0, m-1]$. Let $Ind(y)$ be a function that returns the index of a letter y in the alphabet A and $Let(c)$, a function that returns the letter of index c. Caesar's cipher may be formulated as follows:[1]

Cryptography: Algorithms, Protocols, and Standards for Computer Security, First Edition. Zoubir Mammeri.
© 2024 John Wiley & Sons, Inc. Published 2024 by John Wiley & Sons, Inc.

Encryption: given a key k ($k \ni \mathbb{N}$, $k < m$) and l a letter to encrypt, the encryption is a shift right to yield the encrypted letter l'. Formally:

$$Enc(l) = l' = Let\ (\mathcal{A}((Ind\,(l) + k)\ mod\ m)).$$

Decryption: It is a shift left. Formally,

$$Dec(l') = l = Let\ (\mathcal{A}((Ind\,(l') - k)\ mod\ m)).$$

Example 4.1   Let $\mathcal{A}$ be the Latin alphabet, $m = 26$, and $k = 3$.
The encryption table would be:

A	B	C	D	E	F	G	H	I	J	K	L	M	N	O	P	Q	R	S	T	U	V	W	X	Y	Z
D	E	F	G	H	I	J	K	L	M	N	O	P	Q	R	S	T	U	V	W	X	Y	Z	A	B	C

The decryption table would be:

A	B	C	D	E	F	G	H	I	J	K	L	M	N	O	P	Q	R	S	T	U	V	W	X	Y	Z
X	Y	Z	A	B	C	D	E	F	G	I	H	J	K	L	M	N	O	P	Q	R	S	T	U	V	W

Encryption of plaintext *CAESAR* is yielded as follows:

$$l_1' = Let\ (\mathcal{A}((Ind(C) + 3)\ mod\ 26)) = Let\ (\mathcal{A}(5)) = F$$

$$l_2' = Let\ (\mathcal{A}((Ind(A) + 3)\ mod\ 26)) = Let\ (\mathcal{A}(3)) = D$$

$$l_3' = Let\ (\mathcal{A}((Ind(E) + 3)\ mod\ 26)) = Let\ (\mathcal{A}(7)) = H$$

$$l_4' = Let\ (\mathcal{A}((Ind(S) + 3)\ mod\ 26)) = Let\ (\mathcal{A}(21)) = V$$

$$l_5' = Let\ (\mathcal{A}((Ind(A) + 3)\ mod\ 26)) = Let\ (\mathcal{A}(3)) = D$$

$$l_6' = Let\ (\mathcal{A}((Ind(R) + 3)\ mod\ 26)) = Let\ (\mathcal{A}(20)) = U$$

Therefore, the encrypted message is *FDHVDU*.

The decryption is performed as follows:
$$l_i = Let\ (\mathcal{A}((Ind(l_i') - 3)\ mod\ 26)),\ \text{for } i = 0, 1, ..., 25.$$ Therefore, the plaintext is the same as the original message.

Caesar's chipper security

Caesar's ciphering was very robust at Roman time. It required frequent changes of the secret (i.e. the key k) to prevent attacks. For example, during a secured mission that could not be jeopardized by enemies, a list of keys was transmitted to the governors of districts and then the keys were used for specific periods and for specific communicating entities (e.g. one key for each exchange between Roma and any other location in the empire).

Caesar's cipher had been used for centuries because computer did not exist at that time. Unfortunately, Caesar's cipher has two flaws. First, since there are only 26 letters in Latin alphabet, there exist 25 shifts ($k = 0$ or 26 results in no shift). Second, since frequency of letters in human readable texts is dependent on the language in use (e.g. "E" is more frequent than "X") and since each letter is always encrypted with the same letter once the key is fixed, the distribution of letters in ciphertexts is the same as the one in plaintexts. Therefore, Caesar's cipher is vulnerable to frequency-analysis attacks. Hence, with the event of computers, Caesar's cipher can be easily broken either with brute-force attack or by frequency analysis (see Problem 4.1).

4.3   Affine Ciphers

In affine ciphers, each letter is encrypted using an affine substitution based on indices of letters in the alphabet. Formally:

Encryption: $Enc(x) = a * x + b\ mod\ m = y$.
Decryption: $Dec(y) = a^{-1} * (y - b)\ mod\ m = x$.

where:
  pair (a, b) denotes the key of substitution
  m denotes the number of letters in alphabet
  a^{-1} is the multiplicative inverse of $a \bmod m$
  l denotes the letter in plaintext and x, its index in alphabet; i.e. $x = Ind(l)$
  l' denotes the letter in ciphertext and y, its index in alphabet; i.e. $l' = Let(y)$.

The intercept b can be any value in the interval $[0, m-1]$. The decryption operation makes use of multiplicative inverse a^{-1}. Therefore, not all values in $[1, m-1]$ can be used for slope a. Indeed, a must be an element of $\mathbb{Z}_m^*$. Recall that an element a belongs to $\mathbb{Z}_m^*$ if and only if $GCD(m, a) = 1$.

| **Note.** Shift ciphers, including Caesar's cipher, are affine ciphers with $a = 0$.

Example 4.2   Let $\mathcal{A}$ be the Latin alphabet. Thus, $m = 26$.

$$\mathbb{Z}_{26}^* = \{1, 3, 5, 7, 9, 11, 15, 17, 19, 21, 23, 25\}.$$

Therefore, the slope a can take distinct 12 values. For each element of $\mathbb{Z}_{26}^*$ there exists a multiplicative inverse in $\mathbb{Z}_{26}^*$ as shown in the following table:

a	1	3	5	7	9	11	15	17	19	21	23	25
a^{-1}	1	9	21	15	3	19	7	23	11	5	17	25

Let CAT be the plaintext, $a = 5$, and $b = 7$.
The encryption is done as follows:

$$l' = Let(\mathcal{A}((Ind(C) * 5 + 7) \bmod 26)) = Let(\mathcal{A}(17)) = R$$

$$l_2' = Let(\mathcal{A}((Ind(A) * 5 + 7) \bmod 26)) = Let(\mathcal{A}(7)) = H$$

$$l_3' = Let(\mathcal{A}((Ind(T) * 5 + 7) \bmod 26)) = Let(\mathcal{A}(24)) = Y.$$

Resulting ciphertext is RHY. The decryption is done as follows:
  First letter:

$$x_1 = 5^{-1} * (y_1 - 7) \bmod 26 = 21(17 - 7) \bmod 26 = 2$$

$$l_1 = Let(2) = C.$$

  Second letter:

$$x_2 = 5^{-1} * (y_2 - 7) \bmod 26 = 21(7 - 7) \bmod 26 = 0$$

$$l_2 = Let(0) = A.$$

  Third letter:

$$x_3 = 5^{-1} * (y_3 - 7) \bmod 26 = 21(24 - 7) \bmod 26 = 19$$

$$l_3 = Let(19) = T.$$

Affine cipher security
The total number of key combinations is $\left| \mathbb{Z}_m^* \right| * m$, where m denotes the cardinality of the alphabet and $\left| \mathbb{Z}_m^* \right|$, the cardinality of the group $\mathbb{Z}_m^*$. For example, with Latin alphabet, the number of keys is $12 * 26 = 312$. Even if an affine cipher provides more keys than Caesar's cipher, it has the same flaws when computers are used in attacks.

4.4 Vigenere's Cipher

To make attacks based on frequency analysis harder, polyalphabetic ciphers have been invented in the 16th century. One of the most famous polyalphabetic ciphers is the one invented by Blaise de Vigenere.

Vigenere's cipher was proposed in the middle of the 16th century and it resisted all attempts to break it for three centuries. Vigenere's cipher is an improvement of Caesar's cipher. It makes use of several Caesar's ciphers in sequence with different shift values. A table T, called Vigenere's table, is defined as follows (see Figure 4.1): the first row is composed of the 26 letters of the Latin alphabet, the second row is one-position circular left shifting of the first row, ..., the 26th row is one-position left circular shifting of the 25th row. Letters and table columns and rows are numbered from 0 to 25.

	0	1	2	3	4	5	6	7	8	9	10	11	12	13	14	15	16	17	18	19	20	21	22	23	24	25
0	A	B	C	D	E	F	G	H	I	J	K	L	M	N	O	P	Q	R	S	T	U	V	W	X	Y	Z
1	B	C	D	E	F	G	H	I	J	K	L	M	N	O	P	Q	R	S	T	U	V	W	X	Y	Z	A
2	C	D	E	F	G	H	I	J	K	L	M	N	O	P	Q	R	S	T	U	V	W	X	Y	Z	A	B
	...	...	...	...	...	...	...	...	...	...	...	...	...	...	...	...	...	...	...	...	...	...	...	...	...	...
24	Y	Z	A	B	C	D	E	F	G	H	I	J	K	L	M	N	O	P	Q	R	S	T	U	V	W	X
25	Z	A	B	C	D	E	F	G	H	I	J	K	L	M	N	O	P	Q	R	S	T	U	V	W	X	Y

Figure 4.1 Vigenere's table.

Encryption:

1) Before any encryption operation, the sender and receiver of message M must agree on a secret key word k.
2) Key expansion K: the key word k is repeated until the size of the expanded key equals the size of the message M to encrypt.
3) For each letter M_j ($j = 0, ..., len(M) - 1$) of message M, Vigenere's table T is used for substitution as follows:

Let $Ind(M_j)$ be the index of letter M_j and $Ind(K_j)$, the index of the jth letter of the expanded key. Then, the encryption is

$$Enc(M_j) = M_j' = T(K_j, Ind(M_j)).$$

Decryption:

For each letter M_j' ($j = 0, ..., len(M') - 1$) of the received message M', the decryption is performed as follows:

Go to raw K_j of Vigenere's table, locate the column of letter M_j' on raw K_j, say c_j. Then, use the letter $T(0, c_j)$.

Formally, $Dec(M_j') = M_j = T(0, Col(K_j, M_j'))$ where $Col(i,l)$ is a function that returns the column of letter l in raw i of table T.

The original version of Vigenere's ciphering is based on a table (see Figure 4.1), because encryption and decryption were carried out by hand. With computers, the implementation of both operations does no more require the table. Indeed, Vigenere's ciphering may be described without using a table as follows:

– Letters are ordered from $0\,(A)$ to $25\,(Z)$.
– Encryption of jth letter of message M, denoted M_j, is:
$M_j' = (M_j + K_j)\,mod\,26$ (K_j is the jth letter of the expanded key).
– Decryption of the jth letter encrypted message M', denoted M_j', is:
$M_j = (M_j' - K_j)\,mod\,26$.

The second description of Vigenere's cipher makes it an extension of Caesar's cipher.

Example 4.3 Let HORSE and LEAVEHOUSE be the shared secret and the plaintext, respectively. Key expansion yields HORSEHORSE, which is of the same length as the plaintext. Then, the indices of expanded key letters are

$$Ind(K_0)=7 \quad Ind(K_1)=14 \quad Ind(K_2)=17 \quad Ind(K_3)=18 \quad Ind(K_4)=4$$
$$Ind(K_5)=7 \quad Ind(K_6)=14 \quad Ind(K_7)=17 \quad Ind(K_8)=18 \quad Ind(K_9)=4.$$

- Encryption and decryption using Vigenere's table

Encryption

$$M_0 = L \rightarrow M_0' = T(7,11) = S \qquad\qquad M_5 = H \rightarrow M_5' = T(7,7) = O$$
$$M_1 = E \rightarrow M_1' = T(14,4) = S \qquad\qquad M_6 = O \rightarrow M_6' = T(14,14) = C$$
$$M_2 = A \rightarrow M_2' = T(17,0) = R \qquad\qquad M_7 = U \rightarrow M_7' = T(17,20) = L$$
$$M_3 = V \rightarrow M_3' = T(18,21) = N \qquad\qquad M_8 = S \rightarrow M_8' = T(18,18) = K$$
$$M_4 = E \rightarrow M_4' = T(4,4) = I \qquad\qquad M_9 = E \rightarrow M_9' = T(4,4) = I$$

Thus, the ciphertext is SSRNIOCLKI.

Decryption

$$M_0' = S \rightarrow M_0 = T(0,Col(7,S)) = L \qquad\qquad M_5' = O \rightarrow M_5 = T(0,Col(7,O)) = H$$
$$M_1' = S \rightarrow M_1 = T(0,Col(14,S)) = E \qquad\qquad M_6' = C \rightarrow M_6 = T(0,Col(14,C)) = O$$
$$M_2' = R \rightarrow M_2 = T(0,Col(17,R)) = A \qquad\qquad M_7' = L \rightarrow M_7 = T(0,Col(17,L)) = U$$
$$M_3' = N \rightarrow M_3 = T(0,Col(18,N)) = V \qquad\qquad M_8' = K \rightarrow M_8 = T(0,Col(18,K)) = S$$
$$M_4' = I \rightarrow M_4 = T(0,Col(4,I)) = E \qquad\qquad M_9' = I \rightarrow M_9 = T(0,Col(4,I)) = E$$

Thus, the plaintext is LEAVEHOUSE.

- Encryption and decryption without Vigenere's table

Encryption

$$M_0 = L \rightarrow M_0' = Let(11+7) = S \qquad\qquad M_5 = H \rightarrow M_5' = Let(7+7) = O$$
$$M_1 = E \rightarrow M_1' = Let(4+14) = S \qquad\qquad M_6 = O \rightarrow M_6' = Let(14+14) = C$$
$$M_2 = A \rightarrow M_2' = Let(0+17) = R \qquad\qquad M_7 = U \rightarrow M_7' = Let(20+17) = L$$
$$M_3 = V \rightarrow M_3' = Let(21+18) = N \qquad\qquad M_8 = S \rightarrow M_8' = Let(18+18) = K$$
$$M_4 = E \rightarrow M_4' = Let(4+4) = I \qquad\qquad M_9 = E \rightarrow M_9' = Let(4+4) = I$$

Thus, the ciphertext is SSRNIOCLKI.

Decryption

$$M_0' = S \rightarrow M_0 = Let(18-7) = L \qquad\qquad M_5' = O \rightarrow M_5 = Let(14-7) = H$$
$$M_1' = S \rightarrow M_1 = Let(18-14) = E \qquad\qquad M_6' = C \rightarrow M_6 = Let(2-14) = O$$
$$M_2' = R \rightarrow M_2 = Let(17-17) = A \qquad\qquad M_7' = L \rightarrow M_7 = Let(11-17) = U$$
$$M_3' = N \rightarrow M_3 = Let(13-18) = V \qquad\qquad M_8' = K \rightarrow M_8 = Let(10-18) = S$$
$$M_4' = I \rightarrow M_4 = Let(8-4) = E \qquad\qquad M_9' = I \rightarrow M_9 = Let(8-4) = E$$

Thus, the plaintext is LEAVEHOUSE.

Vigenere's cipher security

Vigenere's cipher makes use of a repeated key of length L. If the key length is known to adversary, the number of keys to test is 26^L, which is the space size of keys taken in the Latin alphabet. The adversary tests each candidate key either using a known pair of plaintext and ciphertext or using only a ciphertext until a clear and comprehensible text is found. When the adversary knows the upper bound of key length, denoted Γ, he/she tries all the combinations of keys with length less than $\Gamma - 1$ until a key matching with a known pair or a comprehensible text is discovered. In the worst case, the number of keys to test is $\sum_{i=1}^{\Gamma} 26^i$. If the upper bound of key length is unknown to the adversary, the number of keys

to test is $\sum_{i=1}^{\max(len(M))} 26^i$, where $\max(len(M))$ denotes the maximum message length.

With a key length of 3, there exist $1.75 * 10^4$ keys; and $9.5 * 10^{16}$ keys, with a length of 12. That is why Vigenere's cipher was unbreakable by brute-force attack until the era of computers.

4.5 Enigma Machine

The first modern cyphering machine, which had been widely used, is with no doubt the *Enigma machine*. Many modern ciphering algorithms were inspired by Enigma machine design, whose internal structure looks like a symmetric ciphering algorithm.

A German engineer (Arthur Scherbius) at the end of World War I invented enigma machine; it had been used commercially from the early 1920, and was adopted by Nazi Germany before and during World War II (WW2). Enigma has played a significant role in 3rd Reich domination. However, when the ciphering technique of Enigma has been broken by the British (with the support of the mathematician Alan Turing), the fall of Nazi army started. Most of secret messages transmitted by Nazi commandment were disclosed by the English and allies secrecy agencies. For more detail on the story of Enigma, refer to [6].

Enigma machine is an electromechanical design of a polyalphabetic substitution cipher. It consists of multiple elements, among which six are of prime importance to understand how encryption and decryption are performed (see Figure 4.2[2]):

- Batteries for power supply of bulbs.
- Keyboard for keying plaintext and ciphertext.
- Lamp panel in which the letter resulting from the encryption or decryption of a keyed letter is illuminated.

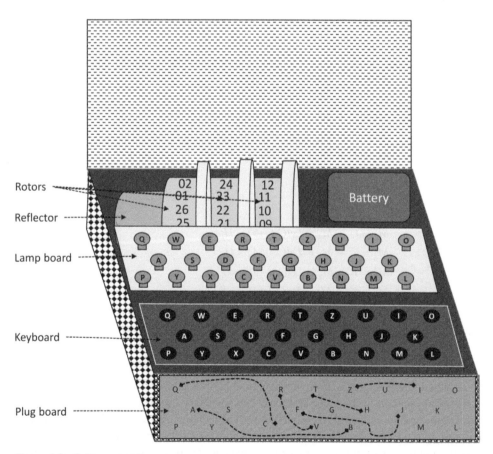

Figure 4.2 Enigma machine.

- Three or four rotors selected out of five or eight.
- Plug board to swap letters.
- Reflector, which is a component that sends electrical impulses that have reached it from the rotors back in reverse order through those rotors.

4.5.1 Principle of Secure Communication Using Enigma

Enigma machines were not connected to any network. Any long messages were fragmented into smaller messages sent separately. A message to encrypt is a text entered by an operator using the Enigma keyboard. When a key, say A, is pressed on the keyboard, one of the 26 bulbs just above the keyboard lights up and illuminates a letter, say T. Then, the operator writes on a piece of paper letter T. If the same letter A is pressed again, another letter is illuminated, say G. For example, a message AABBCCA would be encrypted as XTYGFEK. Thereby, the same letter in plaintext may take 25 distinct encryptions in the produced ciphertext. Therefore, frequency analysis attacks become infeasible using the computation resources available in WW2.

Once all the letters of message keyed, the operator stops the encryption process. Then, the ciphertext written on paper is delivered to a radio operator for transmission. Another operator, at the message destination, receives the encrypted message by radio, writes it on a piece of paper, and delivers it to an Enigma operator. The latter keys one by one the letters of received message and writes on a piece of paper each illuminated key. Once all the letters of the encrypted message keyed, a full plaintext, written on a piece of paper, is delivered personally to whom it may concern.

Enigma machines were produced in thousands and sent worldwide to German army. Some earliest versions of Enigma were commercially available before the beginning of WW2 and several Enigma machines were found or stolen by British, American, spy agencies, etc. In modern cryptosystems, the security does not rely on used algorithms (such as RSA, AES, etc.), because they are public, but on secret keys. In the same way, the security of Enigma machine does not rely on its internal electromechanical structure, but on secret keys. With Enigma, the secret key is formed by the settings of the rotors and the plug board connections. Therefore, the operator who decrypts a message must have exactly the same machine settings as the operator who encrypted the message.

4.5.2 Rotors and Reflector

Enigma machine is delivered with three, five, or eight rotors, also called wheels, numbered from I to VIII (see Figure 4.3a) and two reflectors (numbered B and C). Depending on the machine model, three or four rotors are inserted in the machine every day at midnight. Each rotor has a specific cross-wiring that maps letters of alphabet to wiring to connect the pressed key to a bulb (see Figure 4.3b). Each rotor has 26 internal connections, which differ from a rotor to another. In addition, the order to insert the rotors in the machine is important (because of their internal wiring).

Before insertion of a rotor in the Enigma machine, its wiring must be setup; the operation is called rotor setting and it enables to change the positions of the internal wiring relative to the rotor. Changing the rotor settings modifies the

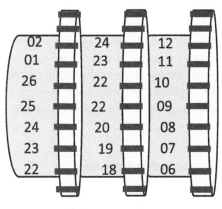
(a) Three rotators aligned together

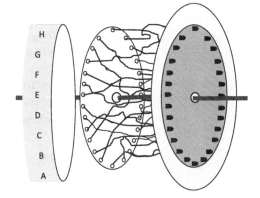
(b) Internal cross-wiring of rotor

Figure 4.3 Rotors of Enigma machine.

positions of the wiring relative to the turnover-point and start position. With three rotors selected out of five, there exist $5*4*3 = 60$ permutations to fit the rotors.

The reflector receives a signal coming from the keyboard and propagates it toward the lamp board to illuminate the appropriate bulb.

When a letter is pressed on the keyboard, a bulb lights up and the rightmost wheel makes a single step (one-contact move position). Each rotor has a notch[3] on its left side at a specific location (from 1 to 26). When the rightmost rotor makes a full turn (after 26 pressed keys), its notch triggers the stepping motion, by engaging a pawl, of the rotor to the left, which makes a single step, and so on until the leftmost rotor makes a single step. Therefore, 26^3 keystrokes are needed to the Enigma machine to return to its start position (see Problem 4.7).

4.5.3 Plug Board

The plug board is a technique to scrambling letters. The plug board has 26 sockets that are marked with the letters (see Figure 4.4). Each 2-pins-socket associated with a letter can be connected to another socket. Therefore, letters are swapped in pairs. A cable is used to connect two letters. Plug board connections do not change after pressing keys. Figure 4.4 shows some connection settings: Q↔X, R↔P, Z↔L, I↔H, and V↔N.

4.5.4 Machine Setting

To enforce the security level, sending a message requires two keys, called daily key and message key.

Daily key
Each operator receives monthly a table (called codebook), which specifies, for each day:

1) Model of reflector to use (B or C)
2) Numbers (from I to VIII) of rotors to install and order of rotor insertion into machine
3) Settings of each rotor
4) List of pairs of letters to swap on the plug board
5) Identification groups

Figure 4.5 shows a piece of Enigma codebook. The operator selects accordingly the reflector and the rotors, performs the settings of each rotor, and then inserts the rotors inside the Enigma machine. Once an Enigma machine is configured, it becomes ready for encrypting and decrypting messages.

On battlefields, some encrypted messages may be delayed and delivered to Enigma operators after one or maybe several days after being sent. To enable operators apply the settings of the transmission day of delayed messages, a list of codes (3-letters strings) are used to identify each day in the codebook. The identification groups are unique for each day in the month.

Notice that one of vulnerabilities of Enigma-based security is its codebook, which can be intercepted by enemies. In the event of loss of a codebook, a radio message was sent to stop using the current codebook and a new codebook was immediately sent to groups.

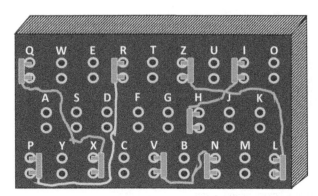

Figure 4.4 Enigma plug board.

Message key
During the same day, a lot of messages may be encrypted. Sending all the encrypted messages of the day is insecure, because the adversary may exploit some features to break the code. To strengthen the ciphering security, each message is encrypted with a distinct random start position called message key.

4.5.5 Encryption and Decryption Procedures

Recall that any encryption or decryption may be performed only when the Enigma machine has been configured according to the settings of the day.

Tag	UKW	Walzenlage			Ringstellung			Steckerverbindungen	Kenngruppen			
31	C	I	III	V	21	19	06	AW BG CZ DJ FO HT KP MX QY SV	WWP	OSB	ZQX	NWQ
30	B	II	V	III	10	03	13	AD FGP HO IX JZ KU LN MS PV QW	HQG	AXV	WDY	RQB
29	C	IV	I	V	01	12	21	AR BY CI DX EN FV GW HO JQ KT	QGL	IXI	VIT	SGU
28	B	II	IV	I	26	03	21	AD BP CY FL GI HS KM OU RZ VX	UGZ	DMD	OTV	PPL
27	B	II	III	IV	26	22	04	AD BP CE FK CY HQ JO LV NW SZ	SYI	CGY	NBY	RHC

Heading of sheet: GEHEIM!   SONDER-MASHINENSCHUSSEL : DARWIN ENIGMA C   JANUAR 1942

Figure 4.5 Example of a piece of Enigma codebook. *Tag*: day in month (the first day of month is located on bottom of the sheet, because the operators are required to cut off and destroy expired settings), *UKW*: model of reflector—*Walzenlage*: roller position (rotor numbers and order). *Ringstellung*: rotor settings—*Steckerverbindungen*: connections on the plug board. *Kenngruppen*: Identification groups.

A *start position* is a string of three or four letters each associated with one and only rotor. For example, in case of three rotors, the start position WXZ means the leftmost rotor should be placed on letter W, the middle rotor on letter X, and the rightmost on letter Z.

Enigma encryption

1) If not yet done, install the Enigma machine according to the settings of the day.
2) Let M be the message content to encrypt.
3) Select randomly a start position, say WXZ, and a message key, say XTS, and write both values on paper.
4) Turn the rotors to the start position WXZ and encrypt the message key XTS and write the encrypted message key, say ASV, on paper.
5) Change the start position to the message key XTS.
6) Encrypt message content and write the resulting letters on paper. Let M' be the encrypted message content.
7) Form a key identification as follows: select two random letters, say FE and select one of the strings in the identification groups from the settings of the day, say CGY.
8) Write on paper an encrypted message $\mathfrak{M}$ of four parts: key identification (FECGY), start position (WXZ), encrypted message key (ASV), and the encrypted message content (M').
9) Deliver the encrypted message $\mathfrak{M}$ to the radio operator for transmission.

Enigma decryption

1) If not yet done, install the Enigma machine according to the settings of the day.
2) Let $\mathfrak{M}$ be the encrypted message, which is received by the radio operator. The latter delivers the encrypted message to Enigma operator. $\mathfrak{M}$ is composed of four fields: identification group (in clear), say FECGY, start position (in clear), say WXZ, encrypted message key, say ASV, and encrypted message content.
3) The first task of the operator is to check message freshness. If the message has been encrypted in the current day, identification group (in our example, CGY) in the message header appears in the identification groups of the current day (in the codebook). Otherwise, the message had been received within a delay exceeding one day and the operator must inspect the codebook to find the day associated with the received identification group and then select and reinstall the rotors accordingly.
4) Set rotors in start position WXZ and decrypts ASV (the encrypted message key) to yield the message key XTS.
5) Set rotors in start position XTS and decrypts M' (the encrypted message content) to yield the message content M. Write on paper, one by one, the illuminated letters.
6) Deliver the plaintext M to whom it may concern.

Example 4.4 Figure 4.5 shows a piece of codebook of Enigma settings for five days.
Assume that the current day is 29. The operator selects reflector C, and rotors IV, I, and V. Then, Rotor IV is set on position 01, rotor I on position 12, and rotor V on position 21. Reflector and rotors are inserted in the machine. Next, letters are interconnected on the plug board: A↔R, B↔Y, C↔I, D↔X, E↔N, F↔V, G↔W, H↔O, J↔Q, K↔T. If a message is received with identification group in {QGL, IXI, VIT, SGU} the message is decrypted with the settings of the current day.

If a message is received with identification group equal to `SYI`, the operator must reconfigure the machine according to the settings of day 27 to decrypt.

4.5.6 Enigma Decryption Correctness

Without loss of generality, we consider configurations with three rotors.

Encryption

In Figure 4.6, letter Z is swapped with I; and letter O with M. It shows the electrical flow from letter Z to the bulb, which illuminates letter M. Electrical connections are established in the following order:

Z in keyboard → Z in plug board → I in plug board →
G of rightmost rotor (right side) → V of rightmost rotor (left side) →
H of middle rotor (right side) → W of middle rotor (left side) →
P of leftmost rotor (right side) → R of leftmost rotor (left side) →
Q of reflector input → I of reflector output →
H of leftmost rotor (left side) → J of leftmost rotor (left side) →
F of middle rotor (left side) → N of middle rotor (right side) →
D of rightmost rotor (left side) → O of rightmost rotor (right side) →
M on plug board → M on lamp board.

Decryption

When letter M is keyed, the Enigma machine has exactly the same configuration as the one used when Z is keyed at encryption stage. Therefore, connections between the rotors and between the leftmost rotor and the reflector are the same. Recall that the internal wiring of rotors does not change. Figure 4.7 shows the electrical flow from letter M to the bulb, which illuminates letter Z. Therefore, the encryption and decryption of a letter follow the same electrical path but in opposite directions.

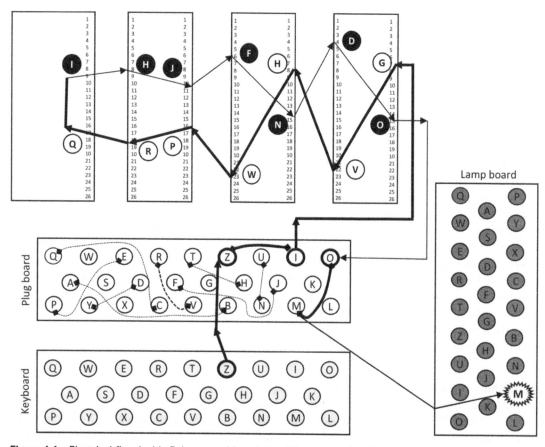

Figure 4.6 Electrical flow inside Enigma machine—Letter Z is encrypted to M.

Formal modeling of encryption and decryption

Encryption

Formally, the encryption of a letter $x \in \{A,B,C,\dots,Z\}$ can be expressed as:

$$x' = Enc(x, s_x) = P^{-1}\left(L^{-1}\left(M^{-1}\left(R^{-1}\left(U\left(L\left(M\left(R\left(P(x)\right)\right)\right)\right)\right)\right)\right)\right) \tag{4.1}$$

where:

x' is the encryption output, i.e. the illuminated letter on the lamp board.

t_x denotes the time when letter x is pressed.

s_x denotes the state of the Enigma configuration at time t_x:

$s_x = (u, p, r(t_x), m(t_x), l(t_x))$, where u denotes the reflector model, p, the matrix of connections on plug board, and $r(t_x)$, $m(t_x)$, and $l(t_x)$, the positions of rightmost, middle, and leftmost rotor at time t_x, respectively.

$R(z)$, $M(z)$, and $L(z)$ denote the substitutions yielded by rightmost, middle, and leftmost rotors, respectively, if the input from the right rotor side is z and the state of Enigma machine is s_x. For example, in Figure 4.6, letter I is connected to letter G of the rightmost rotor whose output is letter V. Thus, $R(I) = V$.

$R^{-1}(z)$, $M^{-1}(z)$, and $L^{-1}(z)$ denote the substitutions yielded by rightmost, middle, and leftmost rotors, respectively, if the input from the left rotor side is z and the state of Enigma machine is s_x. For example, in Figure 4.7, letter J of leftmost rotor is connected to letter F of the middle rotor whose output is letter N. Thus, $M^{-1}(J) = N$.

$P(z)$ denotes the swapping of pressed letter z to enter the ciphering components. For example, $P(Z) = I$.

$P^{-1}(z)$ denotes the swapping of letter z to exit the ciphering components (toward the lamp board or keyboard). For example, $P^{-1}(I) = Z$.

$U(z)$ denotes the substitution yielded by the reflector.

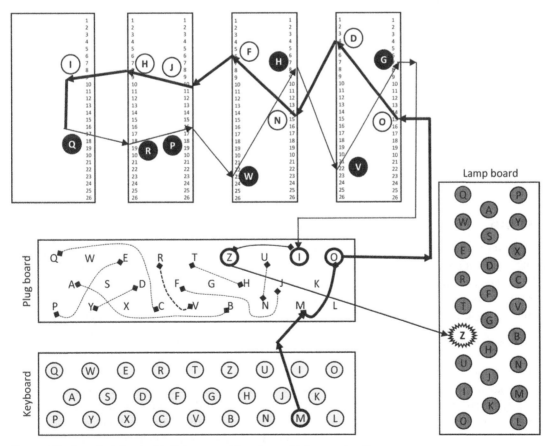

Figure 4.7 Electrical flow inside Enigma machine—Letter M decrypted to Z.

Decryption

The decryption is correct if and only if the encryption of an encrypted letter yields the initial letter, i.e. $Enc(Enc(x,s_x), s_x) = x$, for any letter x in the plaintext. Let $x' = Enc(x,s_{x'})$ and $t_{x'}$, the time when letter x' is pressed. x'' denotes the illuminated letter resulting from x' encryption. To decrypt, operators on both sides are required to use same Enigma state (i.e. same deflector, same connections on plug board, and same rotor positions). Thus, $s_{x'} = s_x$. By definition of Enigma encryption:

$$x'' = Enc(x,s_x) = P^{-1}\left[R^{-1}\left[M^{-1}\left(L^{-1}\left(U\left(L\left(M\left(R\left(P(x')\right)\right)\right)\right)\right)\right)\right]\right] \tag{4.2}$$

$P(.)$, $P^{-1}(.)$, and $U(.)$ depend only the initial machine settings. Thus, $U(U(z)) = z$ and $P^{-1}(P(z)) = z$, for any letter z.

During the encryption of a letter, the state of the Enigma machine remains unchanged. It changes at the end of encryption process. Therefore, inverting the result of a rotor transformation is equivalent to not transforming the input. That is, $\mathcal{F}^{-1}(\mathcal{F}(z)) = z$, for $\mathcal{F} \in \{R,M,L\}$. Below are the substitutions of (4.1) in (4.2), starting from the innermost function,

$$P(x') = R^{-1}\left[M^{-1}\left(L^{-1}\left(U\left(L\left(M\left(R\left(P(x)\right)\right)\right)\right)\right)\right)\right]$$

$$R(P(x')) = M^{-1}\left(L^{-1}\left(U\left(L\left(M\left(R\left(P(x)\right)\right)\right)\right)\right)\right)$$

$$M\left(R\left(P(x')\right)\right) = L^{-1}\left(U\left(L\left(M\left(R\left(P(x)\right)\right)\right)\right)\right)$$

$$L\left(M\left(R\left(P(x')\right)\right)\right) = U\left(L(M\left(R\left(P(x)\right)\right))\right)$$

$$U\left(L\left(M\left(R\left(P(x)\right)\right)\right)\right) = L\left(M\left(R\left(P(x)\right)\right)\right)$$

$$L^{-1}\left(U\left(L\left(M\left(R\left(P(x')\right)\right)\right)\right)\right) = M\left(R\left(P(x)\right)\right)$$

$$M^{-1}\left(L^{-1}\left(U\left(L\left(M\left(R\left(P(x)\right)\right)\right)\right)\right)\right) = R(P(x))$$

$$R^{-1}\left[M^{-1}\left(L^{-1}\left(U\left(L\left(M\left(R\left(P(x)\right)\right)\right)\right)\right)\right)\right] = P(x)$$

$$P^{-1}\left[R^{-1}\left[M^{-1}\left(L^{-1}\left(U\left(L\left(M\left(R\left(P(x)\right)\right)\right)\right)\right)\right)\right]\right] = x = x''.$$

Hence, encrypting twice a letter results in the same letter. Therefore, Enigma decryption is correct.

4.5.7 Complexity Analysis

The Enigma cipher generates a polyalphabetic substitution cipher with a period, which was much longer than any message, or even a set of messages, sent with the same key. (see Problem 4.7.) The strength of the security provided by Enigma is the product of multiple choices of machine settings.

Let R be the number of rotors delivered with an Enigma machine and r the number of rotors to insert in the Enigma machine, with $R \geq 3$ and $3 \leq r \leq 4$. The rotors have distinct wirings and their order inside the machine matters. Therefore, there exist $\dfrac{R!}{(R-r)!}$ arrangements to install the rotors; each rotor has 26 positions. Therefore, there exist $\dfrac{R! * 26^r}{(R-r)!}$ distinct configurations to setup the rotors.

In addition to rotors, Enigma machine makes use of a plug board to letter swapping, which results in letter scrambling that is difficult to guess by adversary. Let c be the number of connections to set on the plug board; in practice c was 10. There are 26 letters in the alphabets and the operator has to connect c letters to c other letters and the connections are symmetric (i.e. connect A to Q is the same as connect Q to A). Therefore, the total number of distinct configurations of the plug board is $\dfrac{26!}{(26-2c)! * c! * 2^c}$.

Table 4.1 Number of distinct settings of Enigma machine.

Security strength level	1	3	4
Reflectors	1 out of 2	1 out of 2	1 out of 2
Rotors	3 out of 3	3 out of 5	4 out of 8
Letter swapping	6	10	10
Settings	$2*1.059*10^{16}$	$2*1.589*10^{20}$	$2*1.157*10^{23}$
	$\cong 2^{54}$	$\cong 2^{68}$	$\cong 2^{77}$

Finally, the operator selects one of the reflectors. Therefore, the number of distinct settings that an Enigma machine may have as a whole is $2*\dfrac{R!}{(R-r)!}*\dfrac{26!}{(26-2c)!*c!*2^c}$.

Table 4.1 shows the number of settings depending on the strength level of security to guarantee. Strength levels 2 and 3 were the most deployed by Nazi army from 1940 onward, which had an equivalent of security strength of 68 and 77 bits of modern digital ciphers. In WW2, breaking a 77-bits code was very difficult though Turing did it.

4.5.8 Breaking Enigma Code

Enigma settings space was very large (see Table 4.1), which made pure brute-force attack to disclose the daily or message key infeasible with the computational resources available in WW2. In addition, the average messages encrypted with Enigma were only a few hundred letters. Therefore, the alphabet never repeated in an Enigma message. That is what made Enigma very hard to break with frequency analysis.

Huge efforts were made to break Enigma code. Hundreds (or even more) of mathematicians, electronic engineers, mechanical engineers, chess players, spies, and secret intelligence services in Europe (in particular Great Britain and Poland) and USA were committed to break Enigma code. Several ideas and devices were proposed based on real Enigma machines or only on traffic analysis. Some intercepted messages had been decrypted. Unfortunately, till Turing's machine, key searching took too much time (around ten days or more), which made the disclosed keys or content of message useless in a context of war. Recall that the keys were changed daily or even per-message.

The most known machine that had a paramount effect to break Enigma is with no doubt the Bombe machine [7]. The first version of Bombe machine was built by Rejewski, a Polish mathematician, and it reproduced six[4] Enigma machines, without plug board, operating in parallel. Unfortunately, Rejewski's machine was limited to the earliest versions of Enigma machines that were abandoned by Nazi army during the WW2. Turing, a British mathematician, and his team improved the Bombe machine to make it capable of breaking the Enigma machines used during WW2 within 20 minutes. Turing's Bombe machine reproduced 36 Enigma machines operating in parallel.

The efforts to break the Enigma machine have long story and took around two decades (before and during WW2). In this chapter, we only present the main principles of Turing's Bombe machine, which widely helped the allies to break Enigma code and then to win the war.

4.5.8.1 Weaknesses, Practices, and Other Features that had been Exploited
To reduce the search space, cryptanalysts tried to discover weaknesses in the Enigma design, message contents, practices of Enigma operators, and German language.

4.5.8.1.1 Enigma Design Weaknesses
The first cryptanalysts focused on the Enigma design, which had multiple weaknesses that could be used to disclose the keys (daily and message keys). The following had been the most exploited weaknesses:

- A letter could be never encrypted to itself. Because of the reflector, the electrical pathways of a letter and its encryption are always distinct (see Figures 4.6 and 4.7). This was the biggest weakness of Enigma.
- Regular stepping of the rotors: after 26, 26^2, and 26^3, the 1st, 2nd, and 3rd rotor, respectively, returns to its initial position. In addition, turnover notches on rotors were distinct, but at fixed (and known) positions, and some rotors make steps triggered by two turnover notches. This weakness helped cryptanalysts to derive when some rotors made steps and guessed initial positions of some rotors.

- The plug board connections are reciprocal. Therefore, for example, if T is connected to F on the plug board, then pressing TFTFFTTTFF... results in an output where T and F are never present.

4.5.8.1.2 *Practices of Enigma Operators*

Weaknesses relating to Enigma operators were harder to identify and exploit compared to weaknesses related to Enigma wirings. Weaknesses in Enigma operator practices included many aspects and required huge resources and time to discover them. Spies and captured or surrendered Enigma operators provided valuable information including codebooks and practices. However, guessing the plaintext for a message to decode was a highly skilled task. Broadly speaking, from the known (i.e. intercepted plaintexts, origin and destination of messages, the time of message transmission, the conditions of war at specific places, etc.), the keyword selection task was to decide which keyword would be likely to appear in the message under analysis. Among the weaknesses in practices of Enigma operators, the following ones had contributed to break the Enigma code:

- A letter is swapped with the same letter for 24 hours or not swapped at all. The number of connections that could be fixed on the plug board is 13. In practice, only 10 or worst 6 connections were mandatory. Such a limitation resulted in a reduction of connection combinations and consequently less effort was needed to break the code.
- Messages had a standard format, which enabled cryptanalysis to address each part of ciphertext with appropriate technique (for example, techniques for guessing a 3-letters message key or guessing a person name in the ciphertext were different).
- The first messages of a day often included the weather of the day ("sunny", "rain", "snow", "wind", etc. appeared in the first messages of day).
- Numbers were written in letters, which helped guessing them.
- Some expressions were included under specific context (e.g. "Nothing to report", "Attack enemy", "cross bridge", etc.).
- Some messages were retransmitted from a location to another in an identical form.
- Like weak passwords in today's systems, operators used weak message keys (e.g. ABC, AAA, XYZ, etc.), easy to disclose, or repeated the message keys.

4.5.8.1.3 *Frequency Analysis of German Language*

German language has its specific frequency of letters. Some letters are often doubled in words. Most German plaintexts contained roughly 20% of repeated letters.

4.5.8.2 **Crib-based Attack**

The term *Crib* was introduced by the British to denote a fragment of plaintext. Crib-based attack (i.e. plaintext attack) includes three main steps: crib selection, ciphertext fragment selection, and settings identification.

Step 1: Crib selection

The crib task was to decide which keyword was (very) likely to appear in the message being decoded. As mentioned previously, keywords such as "nothing to report", "significant damage", "weather report", "sunny", "cloudy", "twenty", etc. may be included in plaintext. It is worth noticing that guessing the portion of plaintext given a ciphertext was a highly skilled task and the success to break the code depends on the selected crib (or keyword). Several keywords may be tried in parallel depending on the context (the weather of the day, the attacks of the troops and their locations, etc.).

Assume the following scenario: the sending operator encrypted a message including WETTER SONNENTAG UND HOHE TEMPERATUR (Weather sunny day and high temperature) and the associated ciphertext was OYWMMGJQKBHMEOCKOMAJUYS XPGLVIKKU. The intercepted message was the first message of a hot day in July. From what was already known, the crib team suggested HOHE TEMPERATUR (high temperature) as a crib to break the code.

Step 2: Selection of ciphertext portions

Once the crib had been selected, the next task was the identification of fragments in the ciphertext that could match the crib. Let *s* be the length of the crib. Crib letters are pairwise compared to letters at positions 1 to *s* in the ciphertext. If the fragment under check is complying with Enigma encryption, i.e. a letter is never encrypted to itself and double letters never encrypted to the same letter, the fragment is kept as a candidate for next step. Then, the first letter of the ciphertext is removed (or shifted to the left) and the next fragment is checked. When all the fragments are checked, the second step ends. Figure 4.8 shows the comparison process. Any ciphertext fragment with a cell in black is discarded. For example, QKBHMEOCKOMAJU is discarded, because letter E in plaintext is encrypted to itself.

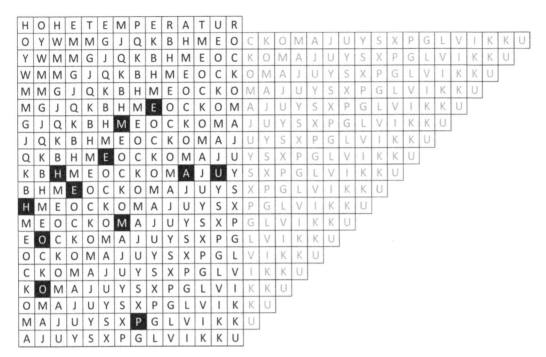

Figure 4.8 Example of tests of matching between ciphertext and crib. Letters in black boxes denote non-compliance with Enigma encryption. Letters in gray denote letters that are not yet checked.

The number of candidate fragments depends on many factors including the length of the crib and its chance to appear in the plaintext and the distribution of letters in the plaintext.

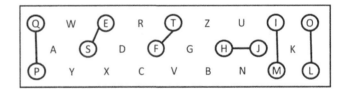

Figure 4.9 Example of connection settings to guess.

Step 3: Identification of Enigma settings

Each ciphertext fragment identified in step 2 was assumed to be associated with the crib and it is a candidate for guessing the Enigma settings. However, only one candidate had helped to break the code. If a selected fragment was the right one and the selected crib was included in the encrypted message, then, there was a high probability for Bombe machine to disclose the Enigma settings.

First assume that rotor settings are correct and try to guess six (the same approach is used for 10) connections on the plug board. Figure 4.9 shows an example of the plug board connections of the sender's Enigma machine that Bombe machine tries to guess.

The processing of any ciphertext fragment, which does not match the crib, may take a long time and ends without recovering the Enigma settings. Thus, a huge number of combinations are tested before a potential conclusive result.

To show how the settings are guessed, assume that the crib is HOHETEMPERATUR. Then, let the ciphertext fragment to test be AJUYSXPGLVIKKU, which is the right one. Assume that the rotor settings are correct and let us see how plug board connections can be guessed using two examples.

First attempt:

1) Start with the 1st letter of the ciphertext, which is A, and decide to connect letters W and A. Then, press letter A and identify on Bombe machine on which letter the signal from the rightmost rotor returns to the plug board, say J. If the connection A↔W is correct, then J must be connected to the 1st letter of the crib, i.e. H. Then, keep connections A↔W and J↔H.

2) Continue with the 2nd letter of the ciphertext, which is J. Letter J is already connected to H. Then, press J and identify on which letter the signal from the rightmost rotor returns to the plug board, say L. If the previous decisions were right, L must be connected to the 2nd letter of the crib, i.e. O. Then, keep connection L↔O.

3) Continue with the 3rd letter of the ciphertext, which is U, and decide to connect letters U and R. Then, press U and identify on which letter the signal from the rightmost rotor returns to the plug board, say K. Therefore, letter K needs to be

connected to letter H, which is already connected to J. Such a situation is called contradiction. Therefore, the previous decisions were wrong and the work must restart from the first letter of the ciphertext fragment.

Second attempt:

1) Start with the first letter of the ciphertext, which is A, and decide to not connect letter A. Then, press letter A and identify, on Bombe machine, on which letter the signal from the rightmost rotor returns to the plug board, say J. From letter J on plug board, the signal has to travel to letter H on the lamp board. Therefore, keep connection J↔H.

2) Continue with the 2nd letter of the ciphertext, which is J. Letter J is already connected to H. Then, press J and identify on which letter the signal from the rightmost rotor returns to the plug board, say L. If the previous decisions were correct, L must be connected to the 2nd letter of the crib, i.e. O. Therefore, keep connection L↔O.

3) Continue with the 3rd letter of the ciphertext, which is U, and decide to not connect letter U. Then, press U and identify on which letter the signal from the rightmost rotor returns to the plug board, say J. Since letter J is already connected to H, no new connection is guessed.

4) Continue with the 4th letter of the ciphertext, which is Y, and decide to not connect letter Y. Then, press Y and identify on which letter the signal from the rightmost rotor returns to the plug board, say S. If the previous decisions were right, S must be connected to the 4th letter of the crib, i.e. E. Therefore, keep connection E↔S.

5) Continue with the 5th letter of the ciphertext, which is S that is already connected to E. Then, press S and identify on which letter the signal from the rightmost rotor returns to the plug board, say F. If the previous decisions were right, F must be connected to the 5th letter of the crib, i.e. T. Then, keep connection F↔T.

6) Continue with the 6th letter of the ciphertext, which is X, and decide to not connect letter X. Then, press X and identify on which letter the signal from the rightmost rotor returns to the plug board, say S. Therefore, no new connections are guessed.

7) Continue with the 7th letter of the ciphertext, which is P, and decide to connect P to Q. Then, press P and identify on which letter the signal from the rightmost rotor returns to the plug board, say I. If the previous decisions were right, I must be connected to letter of the crib, i.e. M. Therefore, keep connection P↔Q and I↔M.

8) At this stage, six connections have been guessed. The remaining letters of the ciphertext fragment do not raise contradictions and no connections are added: when G is pressed, the signal returns via Q and then goes to P; when L is pressed, the signal returns via S and then goes to E; when V is pressed, the signal returns to R; when I is pressed, the signal returns to A; when K is pressed, the signal returns via F and then goes to T; when the second K is pressed, the signal returns to U; when U is pressed, the signal returns to R.

Guessing the right connections requires a huge number of attempts before success. If a contradiction occurs while addressing the ith letter of ciphertext fragment, take another decision (not connect the ith letter or connect it to a not-yet tested letter). If all decisions regarding the ith letter lead to a contradiction, return to i-1th letter and take another decision. If all the decisions regarding the first letter of the chosen ciphertext fragment lead to contradictions, then select another ciphertext fragment in the list of candidates and retry. If all the fragments lead to contradictions, change the rotor settings (the position of rightmost rotor is changed first). If all the settings of rotors lead to contradictions, then change the crib and retry.

4.5.8.3 Improvement of Settings Identification Process

In addition to parallelization of computations in the Bombe machine, Turing (but also some other cryptanalysts) proposed useful approaches to optimize to settings identification process in order to break Enigma code within an acceptable time. In particular, the following techniques greatly reduced the search time:

- The initial settings of rotors before starting to guess plug board connections are of paramount importance. Using a ciphertext, Bombe machine tests several configurations (i.e. rotor types, positions, and settings) of Enigma machine. If the tested configuration is close to the sender's configuration, then the result of decryption provides a text, which is not the original plaintext, but with indications such as repetitions of letters. Then, after frequency analysis, the promising configurations are changed a little and results observed. The most promising configuration is kept and used to guess plug board connections.

- In the process of identification of plug board connections, Turing noticed that when a decision regarding a letter in the ciphertext fragment leads to a contradiction, all the following decisions are wrong and they are no more made. Then, he built the Bombe machine with electric circuits in such a way that when a letter of ciphertext fragment is tested all the wrong connections appear instantaneously, thus reducing the space and time of search.

4.6 One-time Pad

Definition 4.7 One-time pad: *it is a symmetric encryption technique impossible to break in which each message is encrypted with a unique random key no smaller than the plaintext.*

The principle of OTP was first used, in the 19th century, to secure communications in telegraphy. It has been improved in the 20th century using the progress in electronics and computer engineering. The principle of OTP is as follows:

- *Encryption*

  For each plaintext M to encrypt, select a random key K, at least as long as the plaintext. Then, each element (bit or character) of message M is encrypted using a transformation T. Formally, $C = Enc(M, K)$, where $C_i = T(M_i, K_i)$, $i = 1, ..., |M|$. M_is, K_is, and C_is are bits of M, K, and C, respectively.

- *Decryption*

  Given a ciphertext C and a shared secret key K, the plaintext is yielded as:
  $M = Dec(C, K)$, where $M_i = T^{-1}(C_i, K_i)$, $i = 1, ..., |C|$.

With modern electronics, the transformations T and T^{-1} are a bitwise XOR operation.

Assuming that the channel for key exchange is secure, the one-time pad cipher is impossible to break because of the following:

- The key is at least as long as the plaintext.
- The key is random and independent of the plaintext.
- The key is used only once.

In the 1940s, Claude Shannon, one of the fathers of information theory, provided a proof that OTP (which he called *perfect secrecy*) is unbreakable in the sense that the ciphertext gives absolutely no additional information about the plaintext. Shannon stated that given a plaintext M in the plaintext space $\mathcal{M}$ and ciphertext C in the ciphertext space $\mathcal{C}$, if C is yielded by a key K randomly[5] selected in the key space $\mathcal{K}$, which is larger than plaintext space $\mathcal{M}$, then K binds M to C as one-time pad. In other words, when the ciphering key is randomly selected in a key space larger than the message space, the entropy[6] of the plaintext, denoted $H(M)$, is equal to the conditional entropy[7] of the plaintext given the ciphertext, denoted $H(M|C)$.

Drawbacks of OTP in practice

The property of unbreakability makes the OTP a perfect cipher from the security point of view. However, in practice, OTP suffers the following:

- Imagine that a 10 GB video is to be sent. To use OTP, the parties must share a key of at least 10 GB. Another alternative is to fragment the file into 10 000 pieces of 1 MB each and the parties must share 10 000 distinct keys of at least 1 MB each. Thereby, OTP is impractical.
- To provide perfect secrecy, true random selection of keys is required. Unfortunately, generating true random values requires time in practice. Imagine the time needed for a coin flipping procedure to generate a secret key for a message larger than 1 M bytes. This is a second reason for OTP impracticability.
- Being a symmetric cipher, OTP is as secure as the protocol for key exchange and destruction.

Only a few fields of applications, such as military and spying communications, made use of OTP. For example, before moving to battle field, the troop commander receives a list of secret keys (on paper) to use in a specified order. Then, in the field, the received messages are decrypted with secret keys and each key is used once.

4.7 Exercises and Problems

4.7.1 List of Exercises and Problems

Exercise 4.1
OTP is known to be unconditionally secure. However, it is uncommon in modern ciphering systems. Discuss some of the reasons, which make OTP impracticable.

Exercise 4.2

Explain why brute-force attack cannot succeed in breaking an OTP-based security system even if infinite computational resources are available to the adversary.

Exercise 4.3

If the most repeated letter in a long ciphertext encrypted by an affine cipher $y = ax + b$ is S, what are the most likely values for a and b such that $0 < a < 4$ and $b \leq 10$? Assume an English plaintext.

Exercise 4.4

An affine cipher with modulus 31 encrypts 3 as 22 and 7 as 11. Determine the secret key.

Exercise 4.5

An adversary intercepted a text encrypted with an affine cipher. The ciphertext starts with *LSRB*; and the adversary knows that the plaintext starts with DEAR. Assume that only lowercase Latin letters and space are in the text and space has index 0, A, index 1, ..., and Z, index 26.

1) Determine the encryption key.
2) Use the recovered key to decrypt the ciphertext.

Problem 4.1

1) How many attempts are required to brute-force attack to disclose a message encrypted with Caesar's cipher?
2) Assume a sender that encrypts people's names using Caesar's cipher with $k = 3$. Also, assume that hundreds of ciphertexts are known to an adversary, who also knows the frequency of letters in names as shown by the table below. Explain how the adversary could try to recover the name contained in the encrypted message PDUWLQ.

A	B	C	D	E	F	G	H	I	J	K	L	M	N	O	P	Q	R	S	T	U	V	W	X	Y	Z
9	2	4	6	10	3	0	4	5	6	2	6	5	6	5	4	1	4	6	5	1	1	1	0	1	0

Problem 4.2

Consider an affine cipher $y = (ax + b) \bmod 26$, where $a \in \mathbb{Z}_{26}^*$. Using Euler's theorem (Theorem 3.4) show that a^{-1} used in decryption (see Section 4.3) is derived as $a^{-1} \equiv a^{11} \bmod 2$.

Problem 4.3

Assume that an affine cipher is used and brute-force attack is done by hand. Show that widening an alphabet may jeopardize its resistance to brute-force attack. In other words, larger alphabets are not always more brute-force-attack-resistant than smaller alphabets.

Problem 4.4

An adversary knows that a sender encrypted a plaintext with a Vigenere's cipher using the plaintext as a key. Can the plaintext be recovered?

Problem 4.5

Assume that the following ciphertext has been produced by an affine cipher and it includes a message written in English.

   KAR KRPYREFKNER DH ADXA. KAR FMFHJF IRFE MRUK KAR IMNR PVNSKFDS F TRRJ FXV FSO PVQRO
KV KAR EDQRE. DK UDHARH HFMPVS.

Make use of frequency analysis to recover the plaintext. The table of letter frequency used in English is given in Table 2.2.

Problem 4.6

How many pairs of letters (plaintext and ciphertext) are required to recover the key of the following ciphers?

1) Caesar's cipher
2) Affine cipher
3) Vigenere's cipher, assuming a key length of L

Problem 4.7

What is the period of Enigma alphabet?
Hint: a rotor may have one or two notches to trigger its step-rotation.

Problem 4.8

It is recommended to never use the same OTP key to encrypt two distinct messages. However, by mistake a user can encrypt more than one plaintext with the same key. Such a mistake has been reported in cryptography literature. Show how an adversary can break the code if two ASCII-coded English texts, with space character, are encrypted with the same key.

Problem 4.9

1) Show that OTP suffers malleability vulnerability, i.e. an adversary can change the content of the original plaintext, thus impacting its integrity. Notice that malleability attack is applicable in man-in-the-middle context.
2) Assume that Eve knows the format of Bob's plaintext and she knows that the plaintext includes an amount of $1000, located at position p in the plaintext, which indicates a penalty that Eve should pay to Alice. Show how Eve can lower her penalty to $10.

4.7.2 Solutions to Exercises and Problems

Exercise 4.1
OTP is known to be unconditionally secure. However, OTP is not used in practice for many reasons among which:

- The size of the encryption key is the same as (or even greater than) that of the data to encrypt. It would be infeasible in practice to generate OTP keys, store, and send them to the receivers, when large amounts of data are of concern. For example, secure transfer of multiple-terabyte database or secure periodic remote data sensing based on OTP would be impracticable.
- Even if one can generate very large OTP keys, their secure exchange would be difficult in almost all commonly used applications and services over digital networks. For example, spies, diplomatic staff, and armies in the field receive the keys in hand via diplomatic bag or dedicated persons. Such key exchange protocols would jeopardize the performance of any modern cryptosystem.
- OTP key generation requires secure random generators with capacity of generating long keystreams without periodicity. If not enough secure, the algorithm used to generate the OTP keys would be a vulnerability of the security system.

Exercise 4.2
An OTP key is random and with the same length as (or even longer than that of) the plaintext and each message is encrypted with a distinct randomly generated key. Therefore, there is no information in the ciphertext (such as letter frequency) that the adversary could use to recover the plaintext/key. Also, even if enough resources are available to the adversary to apply a brute-force attack, where the adversary decrypts the ciphertext with all possible keys, the adversary would have no way in knowing which plaintext is the original plaintext. This is because a brute-force attack would produce many potential plaintexts that make sense to the adversary.

Exercise 4.3
The most common letter in English texts is E. Therefore, letter E is likely to be replaced by S in the ciphertext under consideration.

In Latin alphabet, letters A, E, and S have indices 0, 4, and 18, respectively. Substitution in equation $y \equiv ax + b \bmod 26$ yields $18 \equiv a*4 + b \bmod 26$.

There exist two solutions $a = 2, b = 10$ and $a = 3, b = 6$.

Exercise 4.4
By definition of an affine cipher, a plaintext P is encrypted as $C = a*P + b$, where (a,b) is the key. Two plaintexts and their ciphertexts are known. Therefore, we have two equations:

$$22 = a*3 + b \bmod 31$$

$$11 = a*7 + b \bmod 31$$

Combining the equations yields:

$$-11 = a*4 \bmod 31 \Rightarrow a = 20*4^{-1} \bmod 31$$

$$\Rightarrow a = -11*8 \bmod 31 \Rightarrow a = 5$$

$$22 = 5*3 + b \bmod 31 \Rightarrow b = 7$$

Therefore, the key of the affine cipher is $(5,7)$.

Exercise 4.5
An affine cipher maps an integer x to an integer $y = ax + b \bmod N$, with $y < N$. Let $Idx(l)$ denote the integer representing letter l.

1) Key recovery:

Since the adversary knows that the plaintext starts with *DEAR*, we get the following congruences

$$Idx(L) = 12 \equiv a * Idx(D) + b \bmod 27 = a * 4 + b \bmod 27$$

$$Idx(S) = 19 \equiv a * Idx(E) + b \bmod 27 = a * 5 + b \bmod 27$$

$$Idx(R) = 18 \equiv a * Idx(A) + b \bmod 27 = a * 1 + b \bmod 27$$

$$Idx(B) = 2 \equiv a * Idx(R) + b \bmod 27 = a * 18 + b \bmod 27$$

Take the following congruences:

$$12 \equiv a * 4 + b \bmod 27$$

$$19 \equiv a * 5 + b \bmod 27$$

Subtracting the first congruence from the second yields $a = 7$, then $b = 11$.

2) Decryption with the recovered key:

Make substitution in the formula $y = ax + b \bmod N$:

$$y \equiv 7x + 11 \bmod 27$$

$$-7x \equiv -y + 11 \bmod 27$$

$$x \equiv (y - 11) * 7^{-1} \bmod 27$$

$$x = 4y + 10 \bmod 27$$

Now, decrypt:

$$y = 12 \Rightarrow x = 4 * 12 + 10 \bmod 27 = 4 \Rightarrow \text{letter is } D$$

$$y = 19 \Rightarrow x = 4 * 19 + 10 \bmod 27 = 5 \Rightarrow \text{letter is } E$$

$$y = 18 \Rightarrow x = 4 * 18 + 10 \bmod 27 = 1 \Rightarrow \text{letter is } A$$

$$y = 2 \Rightarrow x = 4 * 2 + 10 \bmod 27 = 18 \Rightarrow \text{letter is } R$$

Problem 4.1

1) The key used to shift letters in Caesar's cipher is a value in the interval $[1, 25]$. Therefore, the adversary should try each of the 25 keys to retrieve the plaintext. Given a ciphertext, 25 distinct texts are found, but only one matches the original plaintext.

2) Since the letter substitution is bijective when Caesar's cipher is used, the adversary builds a similar frequency table for ciphertext letters as follows:

A	B	C	D	E	F	G	H	I	J	K	L	M	N	O	P	Q	R	S	T	U	V	W	X	Y	Z
0	1	0	9	2	4	6	10	3	0	4	5	6	2	6	5	6	5	4	1	4	6	5	1	1	1

When likelihood is high, the adversary makes association between plaintext letters and ciphertext letters as follows:

Ciphertext	Plaintext
H	E, A
D	E, A
G, M, O, Q, V	D, J, L, N, S
...	...

Assume the adversary receives the ciphertext PDUWLQ. The letter with the highest frequency is D. Now, the adversary assumes that D results from either E or A and the key is either 25 or 3, respectively.

First, try key = 25:

$$l_1 = \mathcal{A}((Ind(P) - 25) \bmod 26) = O$$

$$l_2 = \mathcal{A}((Ind(D) - 25) \bmod 26) = E$$

$$l_3 = \mathcal{A}((Ind(U) - 25) \bmod 26) = T$$

$$l_4 = \mathcal{A}((Ind(W) - 25) \bmod 26) = V$$

$$l_5 = \mathcal{A}((Ind(L) - 25) \bmod 26) = K$$

$$l_6 = \mathcal{A}((Ind(Q) - 25) \bmod 26) = P$$

Guessed name is OETVKP, which does not sound as a name. Therefore, the adversary tries the second key = 3:

$$l_1 = \mathcal{A}((Ind(P) - 3) \bmod 26) = M$$

$$l_2 = \mathcal{A}((Ind(D) - 3) \bmod 26) = A$$

$$l_3 = \mathcal{A}((Ind(U) - 3) \bmod 26) = R$$

$$l_4 = \mathcal{A}((Ind(W) - 3) \bmod 26) = T$$

$$l_5 = \mathcal{A}((Ind(L) - 3) \bmod 26) = I$$

$$l_6 = \mathcal{A}((Ind(Q) - 3) \bmod 26) = N$$

The second guessed name is MARTIN, which is widespread name. Therefore, the adversary may stop searching or try other alternatives starting with Q, which may result from D, J, L, N, or S.

Problem 4.2

Euler's theorem states that if $a \in \mathbb{Z}_n^*$, then $a^{\varphi(n)} \equiv 1 \bmod n$, which can be written as $a * a^{\varphi(n)-1} \equiv 1 \bmod n$. Using the definition of multiplicative inverse, we can derive that $a^{\varphi(n)-1}$ is the inverse of a.

By definition of Euler's totient (Theorem 3.1), $\phi(26) = (13 - 1)(2 - 1) = 12$.

Therefore, using Euler's theorem (Theorem 3.4), $a^{-1} \equiv a^{12-1} \bmod 26 \equiv a^{11} \bmod 26$.

Problem 4.3

Recall that in affine ciphers, letters are mapped to integers, which represent letter indices in the alphabet. In order to decrypt, affine ciphers do calculations over multiplicative group $\mathbb{Z}_m^*$, where m denotes the number of letters in alphabet. An affine function is defined by: $y = ax + b$; the slope $a \in |\mathbb{Z}_m^*|$ and the intercept $b \in \{0, 1, ..., m-1\}$. A key is a pair (a, b). Therefore, the number of distinct keys is $|\mathbb{Z}_m^*| * m$.

Assume that we start with an alphabet of 13 letters. Hence, $m = 13$. Since 13 is prime, the cardinality of $\mathbb{Z}_{13}^*$ is of 12. Therefore, the slope a can take any of the 12 values of $\mathbb{Z}_{13}^*$, i.e. $a \in \{1, 2, 3, ..., 12\}$. The intercept b is any value in $\{0, 1, 2, 3, ..., 12\}$. Therefore, the number of combinations of the key is $12 * 13 = 156$.

Now, assume that we widen the alphabet to 18 letters. First, compute $\mathbb{Z}_{18}^*$. (See how to find the elements of a multiplicative finite field in Section 3.2.2): $\mathbb{Z}_{18}^* = \{1, 5, 7, 11, 13, 17\}$.

With the second alphabet, the slope a can take any of the six values of $\mathbb{Z}_{18}^*$, while the intercept b can take any value in $\{0, 1, 2, 3, ..., 17\}$. Hence, the number of combinations of the key is $6 * 18 = 108$.

Therefore, the number of attempts, in a brute-force attack, is larger with a smaller alphabet.

Problem 4.4

Let M_j and K_j denote the jth letter of the plaintext and the jth letter of expanded key, respectively.

If the plaintext is used as a key in Vigenere's ciphering, then $K_j = M_j$, for $0 \le j \le length(M)$. Vigenere's encryption for letter M_j is

$$M_j' = (M_j + K_j) \bmod 26 = (2M_j) \bmod 26$$

Therefore, $M_j = 2^{-1} * M_j' \bmod 26$ is used as decryption function by the adversary to recover the plaintext.

In general, it is recommended not to use English texts as keys when encrypting with Vigenere's cipher.

Problem 4.5

Let the ciphertext be

```
KAR KRPYREFKNER DH ADXA. KAR FMFHJF IRFE MRUK KAR IMNR PVNSKFDS F TRRJ FXV FSO PVQRO KV
KAR EDQRE. DK UDHARH HFMPVS.
```

Frequencies of letters in ciphertext are:

Letters	Frequency	Letters	Frequency
R	15/92	M, P, S	4/92
F, K	10/92	N	3/92
A	7/92	I, J, O, Q, U, X	2/92
D	6/92	T, Y	1/92
E, H, V	5/92	B, C, G, L, W, Z	0/92

Using the frequency of letters in English texts, the search should start with the highest-frequency letters, that is:

Letter	Frequency	Letter	Frequency
e	12.02	i	7.31
t	9.10	n	6.95
a	8.12	s	6.28
o	7.68	r	6.02

In the ciphertext, the guessed letters are in lower cases. Since there is lot of attempts before disclosing the plaintext, we only show the guesses that lead to recover the plaintext:

- e, t, or a could be R, F, or K.

  Associations R↔e and K↔t lead to

  "tAe tePYeEFtNEe DH ADXA. tAe FMFHJF IeFE MeUt tAe IMNe PVNStFDS F TeeJ FXV FSO PVQeO tV tAe EDQeE. Dt UDHAeH HFMPVS".

- Since two sentences start with tAe, there is a high probability that A is associated with h. F is alone; it is likely to be associated with article a. Associations A↔h and F↔a lead to

  "the tePYeEatNEe DH hDXh. the aMaHJa IeaE MeUt the IMNe PVNStaDS a TeeJ aXV aSO PVQeO tV the EDQeE. Dt UDHheH HaMPVS".

- Next high-frequency letter is o. It may be associated with D, E, H, or V. Association V↔o leads to

  "the tePYeEatNEe DH ADXh. the aMaHJa IeaE MeUt the IMNe PoNStaDS a TeeJ aXo aSO PoQeO to the EDQeE. Dt UDHheH HaMPoS".

- Next high-frequency letter is i. It may be associated with D, because Dt at the beginning of a sentence is likely to be it. Association D↔i leads to

  "the tePYeEatNEe iH hiXh. the aMaHJa IeaE MeUt the IMNe PoNStaiS a TeeJ aXo aSO PoQeO to the EiQeE. it UiHheH HaMPoS".

- The next high frequency letters are n, s, and r; they may be associated with E, H, M, P, and S. Associations E↔r, H↔s, and S↔n lead to

  "the tePYeratNre is hiXh. the aMasJa Iear MeUt the IMNe PoNntain a TeeJ aXo anO PoQeO to the riQer. it Uishes saMPon".

- It is likely that aXo is ago and anO is and. Associations X↔g and O↔d lead to

  "the tePYeratNre is high. the aMasJa Iear MeUt the IMNe PoNntain a TeeJ ago and PoQed to the riQer. it Uishes saMPon".

- From "the tePYeratNre is high" it is likely that P is m, Y is p, and N is u. Associations P↔m, Y↔p, and N↔u lead to

  "the temperature is high. the aMasJa Iear MeUt the IMue mountain a TeeJ ago and moQed to the riQer. it Uishes saMmon".

- The remaining letters have low frequency; hence, many attempts are to do before recovering the plaintext.

  If "Uishes" is "fishes", then "saMmon" is "salmon." Associations U↔f and M↔l lead to

  "the temperature is high. the alasJa Iear left the Ilue mountain a TeeJ ago and moQed to the riQer. it fishes salmon". "moQed to the riQer" is likely to be "moved to the river",

  Associations Q↔v leads to

  "the temperature is high. the alasJa Iear left the Ilue mountain a TeeJ ago and moved to the river. it fishes salmon".

  From the words river, fishes, and salmon, we can guess Alaska and week by associations J↔k and T↔w. The last words to guess are bear and blue.

Therefore, the plaintext was: "the temperature is high. the alaska bear left the blue mountain a weeJ ago and moved to the river. it fishes salmon"., which has been encrypted with an affine cipher $y = 3x + 5$.

Problem 4.6

1) In Caesar's cipher, any letter x is replaced by a letter y using formula $y = x + k \bmod 26$. Therefore, a single letter x_1 and its encrypted letter y_1 are enough to recover Caesar's cipher key k. That is, $k = y_1 - x_1 \bmod 26$.

2) In affine cipher, any letter x is replaced by a letter y using formula $y = x + k \bmod 26$, where $a \in \mathbb{Z}_{26}^*$ and $b \in \mathbb{Z}_{26}$. Therefore, two distinct letters x_1 and x_2 and their encrypted letters y_1 and y_2 are enough to recover an affine cipher key (a,b). That is, given two equations $y_1 = ax_1 + b \bmod 26$ and $y_2 = ax_2 + b \bmod 26$, a and b are unique.

3) In Vigenere's cipher, any letter M_j of message M is encrypted using letter K_j of the expanded key, as $M'_j = (M_j + K_j) \bmod 26, 0 \le j < len(M)$. Thus, $M'_j - M_j = K_j \bmod 26$. Therefore, L distinct pairs of letters and their encryptions are enough to recover a Vigenere's cipher key of length L.

Problem 4.7

Let n be the number of rotors installed in an Enigma machine, where $n = \{3, 4\}$. Let r_n and r_1 denote the leftmost and rightmost rotors, respectively.

If all rotors have a single notch, then each rotor r_{i+1} makes a step when rotor r_i finishes a full revolution. Therefore, Enigma returns to its start position after pressing 26^n keys.

As mentioned previously, some rotors may have two (or even more) notches. If a rotor r_i has two notches, then in a full revolution, it triggers two steps of rotor r_{i+1}. Thus, rotor r_{i+1} makes a full revolution after 13 full revolutions of rotor r_i. Therefore, the period of ciphering alphabet of Enigma with n rotors is $\dfrac{26^n}{\prod_{i=1}^{n-1} c_i}$, where $c_i \in \{1, 2\}$ denotes the number of notches of rotor r_i. Therefore, doubling the notches on rotors reduces the security strength of ciphering.

Problem 4.8

Let (M_1, C_1) and (M_2, C_2) be two pairs of plaintext–ciphertext. The same OTP key k is used to encrypt both plaintexts. Hence, $C_1 = M_1 \oplus k$ and $C_2 = M_2 \oplus k$. C_1 and C_2 are known to the adversary. Thus, the latter can compute:

$$C_1 \oplus C_2 = (M_1 \oplus k) \oplus (M_2 \oplus k)$$
$$= (M_1 \oplus M_2) \oplus (k \oplus k) = M_1 \oplus M_2$$

Notice that to recover both plaintexts, the latter must be of the same bit-length.

Let $M_{1,i}$ and $M_{2,i}$ denote letter i in plaintexts M_1 and M_2, respectively. Also, let $left3(l)$ denote the three leftmost bits of a 7-bit ASCII letter l.

Without loss of generality, we only focus on uppercase letters and space. Recall the ASCII codes (in Hexadecimal): space $\to 20_{16}$, $A \to 41_{16}$, $B \to 42_{16}$, $O \to 4F_{16}$, $\to 50_{16}, \ldots,$ $\to Y59_{16}$, $Z \to 5A_{16}$. The ASCII code has some characteristics that can serve the adversary to speed up the attack (i.e. recover plaintexts):

- If $M_{1,i} \oplus M_{2,i} = 00$, then $M_{1,i} = M_{2,i}$. Therefore, recovering a letter in one ciphertext results in recovering the same letter in the other ciphertext.
- Space code is 20_{16}, having a single 1-bit, and the codes of uppercase letters are greater than 41_{16}. If $M_{1,i}$ and $M_{2,i}$ are two letters, then $M_{1,i} \oplus M_{2,i} < 1A_{16}$. If $M_{1,i} \oplus M_{2,i} > 20_{16}$, then either $M_{1,i}$ or $M_{2,i}$ is a space. Hence, $(M_{1,i} \oplus M_{2,i}) \oplus 20_{16}$ is a letter included in one plaintext; and the other plaintext has a space at the same position. Example, $5A_{16} \oplus 20_{16} = 3A_{16} > 20_{16}$. Therefore, one plaintext has a letter Z and the other has a space. Such a property is very useful to speed up the attack, since spaces are very frequent in English text (nearly 19% of characters are spaces). In addition, spaces are unlikely to occur at the same positions in distinct plaintexts, which results in more letters recovered in both ciphertexts.
- Codes of letters A to O start with 100, while codes of letters P to Z start with 101. If $left3(M_{1,i} \oplus M_{2,i}) = 000$, then both letters $M_{1,i}$ and $M_{2,i}$ are in the same half of alphabet, i.e. either in $[A,O]$ or in $[P,Z]$. If $left3(M_{1,i} \oplus M_{2,i}) = 001$, then letters $M_{1,i}$ and $M_{2,i}$ are not in the same half of alphabet. Such property is useful while testing different letters.

The adversary takes advantage of the ASCII characteristics to automatically recover some letters. Then, he/she applies a crib dragging technique, i.e. guess some words likely to be in the original plaintexts, XOR them with the ciphertexts and derive a part of the key, which, in turn, serves to recover a word in the other ciphertext. Repeat the guess until both plaintexts are recovered.

Problem 4.9

1) Indeed, OTP suffers malleability vulnerability under the man-in-the-middle attack, which can be shown as follows:
   Bob sends a ciphertext $C_1 = M_1 \oplus k$ to Alice.
   Eve, the adversary, intercepts ciphertext C_1 and computes $C' = C_1 \oplus M'$, where M' is either a random or a specific plaintext chosen by Eve.
   When Alice receives the ciphertext C', she obtains, after decryption, a plaintext M_2:
   $M_2 = C' \oplus k = C_1 \oplus M' \oplus k = M_1 \oplus k \oplus M' \oplus k = M_1 \oplus M'$
   M_2 is distinct from M_1. Therefore, integrity is no more assured to Alice.

2) In the ciphertext C intercepted by Eve, a value of $1000_{10} = 001111101000_2$ is included starting from bit-position p. Eve forges a ciphertext as follows:
   Copy the ciphertext: $C' = C$

   Change bits at locations p to $p+11$:

   $$N = (001111101000_2) \oplus (000000001010_2) = (001111100010_2)$$

   $$C' = C[1,p-1] \parallel C[p,p+11] \oplus N[1,12] \parallel C[p+12, len(C)]$$

   Send C' to Alice. $s[i,i+k]$ denotes bits i to $i+k$ of any bit-string s.
   At reception, Alice decrypts as follows:

   $$M_2 = C' \oplus k = M_{2,1} \parallel M_{2,2} \parallel M_{2,3}, \text{ with}$$

   $$M_{2,1} = C'[1,p-1] \oplus k[1,p-1] = M_1[1,p-1]$$

   $$M_{2,2} = C'[p,p+11] \oplus k[p,p+11]$$

   $$= C[p,p+11] \oplus N[1,12] \oplus k[p,p+11]$$

   $$= (C[p,p+11] \oplus k[p,p+11]) \oplus N[1,12]$$

   $$= M_1[p,p+11] \oplus N[1,12]$$

   $$= (001111101000_2) \oplus (001111100010_2) = 000000001010_2$$

   $$M_{2,3} = C'[p+12, len(C)] \oplus k[p+12, len(C)] = M_1[p+12, len(C)]$$

Therefore, Alice concludes that penalty is of \$10 instead of \$1000.

Notes

1 Congruence was discovered in the 18th century and Caesar's ciphering made use of tables. Congruence is used in this chapter to formalize the idea of Caesar's cipher.

2 Genuine pictures of ENIGMA are available from several national army museums and websites including Wikipedia and Cryptomuseum.com.

3 Rotors numbered VI, VII, and VIII have two, or even more, turnover notches; thus, they trigger two (or more) steps for the rotor on their left after a full revolution. It has been shown that it was not a good idea from security point of view, because double stepping of the rotor on the left reduces the substitution alphabet period.

4 "Six" is the number of rotors arrangements in the earliest versions of Enigma machine.

5 "Randomly selected" means that any key K has a probability of $\frac{1}{|\mathcal{K}|}$ to be selected.

6 In the information theory, the *entropy* of a random variable X, denoted $H(X)$, is the average level of *uncertainty* inherent in the variable possible outcomes (see Chapter 16).

7 In the information theory, the *conditional entropy*, denoted $H(M \mid C)$, quantifies the amount of information needed to describe the outcome of a random variable M given that the value of another random variable C is known.

References

1 Katz, J. and Lindell, Y. (2007). *Introduction to Modern Cryptography*. CRC Press.

2 Menezes, A., van Oorschot, P., and Vanstone, S. (2001). *Handbook of Applied Cryptography*. CRC Press.

3 Trappe, W. and Washington, L.C. (2020). *Introduction to Cryptography with Coding Theory*. Pearson.

4 Singh, S. (2000). *The Code Book: The Evolution of Secrecy from Ancient Egypt to Quantum Cryptography*. Anchor Books.

5 Stallings, W. (2020). *Information Privacy Engineering and Privacy*. Addison Wesley.

6 Web1. *Cryptanalysis of the Enigma*. [Online]. (Cited 2023 April). Available from: https://en.wikipedia.org/wiki/Cryptanalysis_of_the_Enigma.

7 Hodges, A. (2014). *Alain Turing: The Enigma*. Princeton University Press.

5

Hash Functions, Message Authentication Codes, and Digital Signature

This chapter introduces three aspects of cryptography, namely hash functions, Message Authentication Codes, and Digital signature. All of them are of paramount importance for providing integrity and authentication guarantees. Hash functions produce digital fingerprints, also called Message Authentication Codes (MAC), which are used to meet multiple needs:

- Verifying integrity of messages and files: a hash works like a fingerprint, which uniquely represents data. Thus, any change in an email, a file, a software, an image, and so on, results in a hash, which does not match the hash generated by the sender.
- Generating and verifying digital signatures,[1] which enable to verify the authenticity of a message. If the encrypted hash is altered, the verification fails and if the message is altered, the hash computed by the recipient does not match the message. In both cases, the message is rejected.
- Facilitating secure password storage and verification: instead of storing and exchanging passwords, hashes of passwords are stored and used to control local and remote logins.
- Since hashes look like random values, hash functions may be used as pseudorandom bit generators.

It is worth noticing that MAC algorithms provide stronger assurance of data integrity than a checksum or an error detecting code. The verification of a checksum or an error detecting code is designed to detect only accidental modifications of data, while MAC is designed to detect intentional, unauthorized modifications of data, as well as accidental modifications.

MACs can be generated either by hash functions alone or by block ciphers. The first category of MACs is addressed in this chapter, while block cipher modes of operation that generate MACs are addressed in Chapter 9.

5.1 Hash Functions

Definition 5.1 Hash function*: it is a mathematical function that takes an arbitrary data input and produces a fixed-size output called a hash value, digest, hash code, or just hash. A hashing algorithm[2] is an algorithm founded on a hash function and implements hashing operations.*

Formally, a hash function $H()$ is defined by: $H : \{0,1\}^N \rightarrow \{0,1\}^n$, where $\{0,1\}^N$ is the set of input space and $\{0,1\}^n$ the set of output space. N and n are the bit-lengths of spaces. $H(x)$ is the hash or digest of input x. In practice n is between 160 and 512, while N may be very large.[3]

Since the input space is much larger than the output space, two distinct inputs x and x' may result in the same output, which is a circumstance called *collision*. The larger the number of possible hashes, the smaller the chance that two values will create the same hash. In existing hash functions, collisions are unavoidable, but the probability of collision occurrence should be minimized.

5.1.1 Properties of Hash Functions

In order not to compromise either the security or the performance of the underlying systems, hash functions should possess the following properties:

Cryptography: Algorithms, Protocols, and Standards for Computer Security, First Edition. Zoubir Mammeri.
© 2024 John Wiley & Sons, Inc. Published 2024 by John Wiley & Sons, Inc.

- *Determinism*: the same input always results in the same output.
- *Efficiency*: the computation of hash value should be low.
- *Security*: hash functions should be practically irreversible (i.e. one-way) in order to be attack resistant.

Preimage resistance

This property means given a hash value z, it should be computationally infeasible to find an input value x that hashes to z. Formally:

$$\forall\, z \in \{0,1\}^n\,,\; Pr(\text{Finding } x \,|\, x \in \{0,1\}^N,\, H(x)=z) \cong 0$$

$Pr()$ denotes probability. Preimage resistance property of hash function protects against an attacker who has a hash and wants to find the associated data. For example, the attack would be the recovery of a password from the hash of the password.

Second preimage resistance (also referred to as *weak collision resistance*)

This property means given an input x_1, it is computationally infeasible to find an input x_2 distinct from x_1 with the same hash. Formally:

$$\forall\, x_1 \in \{0,1\}^N\,,\; Pr\!\left(\text{Finding } x_2 \mid x_2 \in \{0,1\}^N,\quad x_1 \neq x_2,\quad H(x_1)=H(x_2)\right) \cong 0$$

Second preimage resistance property of hash function protects against an attacker who has an input value and its hash and wants to substitute a forged value to the original input value. In other words, pre-image resistance preserves data integrity.

Collision resistance

This property means it should be computationally infeasible to find any two inputs that result in the same hash. Formally:

$$Pr\!\left(\text{Finding } x_1,\, x_2 \mid x_1,x_2 \in \{0,1\}^N,\, H(x_1)=H(x_2)\right) \cong 0$$

Notice that if a hash function is collision-resistant, then it is second preimage resistant (see Problem 5.7). Collision resistance prevents from creating two distinct data or messages with the same hash. For example, in password management systems, hashes are associated with passwords. Passwords are supplied to users when they register and hashes are stored in the password file in the authentication system. When a user tries to log in the system, he/she provides his/her password, then the verification system computes the hash of the password entered by the user and compares it to the one stored in the password hash file. Consequently, distinct hashes should be associated to distinct passwords; otherwise, a user may be admitted to access a service granted to another user.

Even the hash functions, which have been considered secure for a long time, may have collisions. For example, Figure 5.1 shows a collision attack against MD5, a hash function widely used in the past. Two documents, File1.ps and File2.ps, with distinct contents have the same MD5 hash.

The output of hash functions used in operational cryptosystems looks like[4] a random string and any small change (of one bit or one byte) results in entirely different hash. Below are three examples of hashes produced by SHA256 algorithm associated with two strings "Hello" and "hello" which have major differences:

SHA256("Hello") = 185f8db32271fe25f561a6fc938b2e264306ec304eda518007d1764826381969
SHA256("hello") = 2cf24dba5fb0a30e26e83b2ac5b9e29e1b161e5c1fa7425e73043362938b9824

5.1.2 Generic Attacks Against Hash Functions

A generic attack is an attack that tries to break hash functions without any knowledge of their internal structure. In other words, generic attacks apply to all hash functions, while specific attacks take advantage of the internal structure of hash functions. By internal structure, we mean for example the number of rounds and the forms of block transformation operations.

Attacks against hash functions are directly linked to resistance properties. Thus, attacks against hash functions are categorized into three classes:

1) Collision attacks aiming to find a hash collision.
2) Preimage attacks aiming to recover a data given its hash (for example, recovering a password once its hash has been intercepted).
3) Second preimage attacks aiming to alter the content of message while keeping its hash.

The number of steps[5] of a generic attack is the number of hash function tries before breaking the hash function. The best known generic (second) preimage attack is brute-force attack, which requires 2^n steps and the best known collision attack is birthday attack, which requires $2^{(n+1)/2}$ steps, where 2^n denotes the cardinality of the hash space. Proof of attack complexity is addressed in Problems 5.13 and 5.14.

It is worth noticing that in literature, $2^{(n+1)/2} = 2^{1/2} * 2^{n/2}$ is often approximated by $2^{n/2}$, when n is large. Therefore, the security strength of hash functions to resist to all three forms of generic attacks is $\min\left(2^{n/2}, 2^n\right) = 2^{n/2}$.

5.1.3 Overall Operation Principle of Hashing Algorithms

There are many hashing algorithms used by services and applications with different security and performance requirements. The most popular hashing algorithms include:

- SHA family (SHA-0, SHA-1, SHA-2, SHA-3)
- MD family (MD2, MD3, MD4, MD5, MD6)
- Blake family (Blake1, Blake2, Blake3)
- RIPEMD, Tiger, Whirlpool, etc.

MD5 (Message Digest 5) was the most popular and widely used hash function for many years. It was adopted as an internet standard. In 2004, collisions were found in MD5. Published collision-attacks showed that MD5 is not entirely secure and hence it is no longer recommended. Figure 5.1 shows an example of MD5 collision.

> Julius. Caesar
> Via Appia 1
> Rome, The Roman Empire
>
> May, 22, 2005
>
> To Whom it May Concern:
>
> Alice Falbala fulfilled all the requirements of the Roman Empire intern position. She was excellent at translating roman into her gaul native language, learned very rapidly, and worked with considerable independence and confidence.
>
> Her basic work habits such as punctuality, interpersonal deportment, communication skills, and completing assigned and self-determined goals were all excellent.
>
> I recommend Alice for challenging positions in which creativity. reliability, and language skills are required.
>
> I highly recommend hiring her. If you'd like to discuss her attributes in more detail, please don't hesitate to contact me.
>
> Sincerely,
>
> Julius Caesar

> Julius. Caesar
> Via Appia 1
> Rome, The Roman Empire
>
> May, 22, 2005
>
> Order:
>
> Alice Falbala is given full access to all confidential and secret information about GAUL.
>
> Sincerely,
>
> Julius Caesar

Figure 5.1 Example of collision attack against MD5. MD5(File1.ps) = a25f7f0b29ee0b3968c860738533a4b9. MD5(File2.ps) = a25f7f0b29ee0b3968c860738533a4b9. *From*: http://web.archive.org/web/20071226014140 /http://www.cits.rub.de/MD5Collisions.

5.1.3.1 Merkle-Damgård Construction

Most hashing algorithms, including MD5, SHA-1, and SHA-2, are designed according to model known as Merkle-Damgård construction [1, 2], which operates as follows (see Figure 5.2):

- Padding bytes are appended to the data so that the length of padded data is multiple of a chosen block bit-length L. Padding bits are appended to the end of the initial data in a format known to both parties; so that the verifier of the hash uses the same padding bits. There exist different ways to encode the data length in the padding field depending on hash functions. Then, padded data to hash is divided into m blocks B^1, B^2, ..., B^m of equal length L.
- Each block is hashed separately with additional input as follows:
  Block B^1: the hash function takes a combination of B^1 and an initialization value, also known as initialization vector (IV), and returns a hash value H^1. Block i ($i = 2, ..., m$): the hash function takes a combination of B^i and the hash value H^{i-1} and returns hash value H^i.
- The hash function is a series of rounds and each round is made of a series of transformations (bit string additions, permutations, etc.).
- The output of the final round of the last block of message is the hash to the entire message. Hash bit-length is denoted n.

If any block or the final hash is altered, the final hash computed by the data integrity verifier does not match the data. Hash bit-length n is a parameter of hashing algorithms. In existing hashing functions, parameter n takes its value form the set $\{128, 160, 192, 224, 256, 384, 512\}$. The security and performance of the hashing algorithm are dependent on the hash length. The larger the hash length is, the lower the collision probability is. The larger the hash length is, the higher the hash computation time is.

5.1.3.2 Vulnerability to Length Extension Attack

Some cryptographic algorithms using hash functions based on Merkle-Damgård construction are vulnerable to a specific attack called *length extension attack*. In the latter, the adversary knows a message M, a hash $H(key \| M)$, and the length of key, $len(key)$, but the value of the key is unknown. Problem 5.15 discusses why the key length is required. For example, after signing a message, the sender transmits the message and the signature, but the private key used to sign is not sent. In a similar way, when MAC (message authentication code) is used, the sender transmits the message and its MAC, but not the key used to generate the MAC. If the three items (M, $H(key \| M)$, and $len(key)$) are available to an adversary, he/she can extend the original message and generate a hash without using the key. Upon reception, the verifier validates the (forged) message as if it were generated by a legitimate party using the appropriate key.

Below is how the length extension attack can be realized:

When the legitimate party generates $H(key \| M)$ using the key known to him/her, a padding string P is appended at the end of the string $key \| M$. The length of padding string P is such that $len(key \| M \| P)$ is a multiple of the block length L of the hash function H (e.g. $L = 1024$ in case of SHA-2). Then, before hashing, the string $key \| M \| P$ is represented as a sequence of m blocks (B^1, B^2, ..., B^m) with equal length L.

Recall that in hash functions based on Merkle-Damgård construction (see Figure 5.2), block B^1 and initialization vector IV, which also is referred to as H^0, are used by the hash function to produce H^1, then H^1 and B^2 are used to produce H^2, ..., and finally, H^m represents the hash of the entire message.

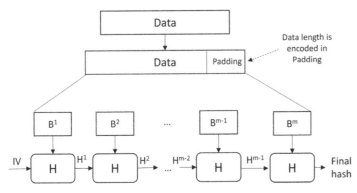

Figure 5.2 Overall operation of hashing algorithm.

Length extension attack assumes that the length of the key is known to the adversary. Thus, the latter can easily compute the padding string P and forges a string $\mathcal{F}$ starting with P and continuing with a fake data string f of interest to him/her. The forged message is $M' = M \| P \| \mathcal{F}$.

Length extension attack takes advantage of the design of Merkle-Damgård construction to adapt[6] the hash function H, such that H_0 is not the constant initialization vector, rather it takes the value of $H(key \| M \| P)$, which is known to the adversary Thus, hashing block(s) of f looks like a continuation of blocks of string $key \| M \| P$ and the resulting hash $H(\mathcal{F})$ matches the hash $H(key \| M \| P \| \mathcal{F})$ that would be produced by a normal hash function.

Proof of correctness

Let P' be the padding string to append to fake data $\mathcal{F}$, such that $len(\mathcal{F} \| P')$ is a multiple of the block size L and K, the number of blocks of the string $\mathcal{F} \| P'$.

Let M' be the bit string $M \| P \| \mathcal{F}$ that the recipient receives.

Let $\mathbb{h}(B,v)$ denote a one-block hash function, which hashes one block B using an initialization vector v and returns a hash.

Let $\left(B^1, B^2, ..., B^m\right)$ be the sequence of blocks representing the string $key \| M \| P$ and $\left(B^{m+1}, B^{m+2}, ..., B^{m+K}\right)$ be the block sequence representing the string $\mathcal{F} \| P'$.

By design of Merkle-Damgård construction–based hash functions, given a bit-string X of N blocks $B^1, B^2, ..., B^N$, the hash function $H()$ is defined by:

$H(X,IV) = H^N$, such that:

$H^k = \mathbb{h}\left(B^k, H^{k-1}\right)$, $1 < k \leq N$

$H^1 = \mathbb{h}\left(B^1, IV\right)$, where IV denotes the initialization vector.

Upon reception of padded message M', the legitimate verifier computes the following hash:

$$H\left((Key \| M \| P \| \mathcal{F} \| P'), IV\right) = H\left(\left(B^1, B^2, ..., B^m, B^{m+1}, B^{m+2}, ..., B^{m+K}\right), IV\right)$$

$$= H\left(\left(B^{m+1}, B^{m+2}, ..., B^{m+K}\right), H\left(\left(B^1, B^2, ..., B^m\right), IV\right)\right)$$

$$= H\left(\mathcal{F} \| P', H((key \| M \| P), IV)\right)$$

The adversary knows the hash v computed by the legitimate sender, $v = H\left(key \| M \| P, IV\right)$. He/she modifies the hash function to use a chosen initialization vector and computes $H(\mathcal{F} \| P', v)$. Thus, the hash computed by the adversary is the same as the one computed by the verifier; and the received message M' is validated. $\square$

5.2 Secure Hash Algorithms (SHA)

SHA algorithm family is the most used hashing algorithms in current cryptosystems and it is very likely to dominate in the next decade(s). SHA family is a set of NIST standards named SHA-0, SHA-1, SHA-2, and SHA-3. The most popular algorithm is SHA-1. SHA-0 was published in 1993, SHA-1 in 1995, SHA-2 in 2002, and SHA-3 in 2015. SHA-0 was replaced by SHA-1, which in turn was attacked with success, but still used. Current and future cryptosystems are either using or moving to SHA-2 or SHA-3.

Each subfamily may have more than one variant. SHA variants differ in terms of maximum message size, hash size, block size, and number of rounds (see Table 5.1). SHA-1 and SHA-2 are similar in design, while SHA-3 relies on different design principles. SHA-1 and SHA-2 make use of Merkle-Damgård hash construction model [1, 2], while SHA-3 makes use of sponge construction model [3, 4].

SHA-2 and SHA-3 offer the same set of hash lengths and the same security strengths levels. Main characteristics of SHA variants are summarized in Table 5.1. It is worth noticing that the most important characteristic, when security is of concern, is the message digest size.

5.2.1 SHA-1 and SHA-2 Algorithms

The first version of SHA-1 was published in 1995 [5]. The last revisions of SHA-1 and SHA-2 algorithms were published in 2012 under the name of SHS (Secure Hash Standard) [6]. SHS includes seven variants: SHA-1, SHA-224, SHA-256, SHA-384, SHA-512, SHA-512/224, and SHA-512/256. Notice that SHA-2 is not used alone in certificates, instead its variants are used. In the sequel, SHA-x denotes one of the seven SHS variants.

The following principles are common to all SHA-1 and SHA-2 variants:

- *Input and output*
  Input of SHA-x is a bit string of an arbitrary size. However, the maximum message size is fixed (see Table 5.1). SHA-x produces hashes with fixed length (see Table 5.1).

Table 5.1 Main characteristics of SHA algorithms.

Algorithm	Message size (bits)	Block size (bits)	Message digest (bits)	Number of rounds
SHA-1	$< 2^{64}$	512	160	80
SHA-224	$< 2^{64}$	512	224	64
SHA-256	$< 2^{64}$	512	256	64
SHA-384	$< 2^{128}$	1024	384	80
SHA-512	$< 2^{128}$	1024	512	80
SHA-512/224	$< 2^{128}$	1024	224	80
SHA-512/256	$< 2^{128}$	1024	256	80
SHA3-224	No limit[7]	1152[8]	224	24
SHA3-256	No limit	1088	256	24
SHA3-384	No limit	832	384	24
SHA3-512	No limit	576	512	24

- *Data representation*
  - Hashing algorithms manipulate words of either 32 or 64 bits. An integer between 0 and $2^{32} - 1$ (or $2^{64} - 1$) is represented by a word of 32 or 64 bits, respectively. The least significant bits of an integer are rightmost bits of the word.
  - Message to hash is split into blocks with a fixed size of either 512 or 1024 bits.
  - Blocks of the message to hash are labeled $B^1, \ldots, B^m$, where m is the number of blocks of the message including padding bits.
  - To be processed, each block B^i is stored in 16 words labeled $B_0^i, B_1^i, \ldots, B_{15}^i$.
- *Message padding*
  The purpose of padding is to ensure that the bit-length of the padded message is a multiple of block size. Padding bits are appended to the end of the initial message in a format known to both parties. Let l denote the bit-length of the message M to hash. Two distinct padding methods are used:

  Padding in SHA-1, SHA-224, and SHA-256 is done as follows: append a bit "1" at the end of message M, followed by k zero bits, where k is the smallest positive integer such that $l + 1 + k \equiv 448 \bmod 512$, then append the binary value of l represented on 64 bits.

  Padding in SHA-384, SHA-512, SHA-512/224, and SHA-512/256 is done as follows: append a bit "1" at the end of message M, followed by k zero bits, where k is the smallest positive integer such that $l + 1 + k \equiv 896 \bmod 1024$, then append the binary value of l represented on 128 bits.
- *Bit operations used by SHA-x*
  Bitwise operations used by SHA-x are: $\wedge$ (and), $\vee$ (or), $\oplus$ exclusive or, and $\neg$ (complement).
  The sum of integers x and y is $z = (x + y) \bmod 2^{32}$ (or $\bmod \, 2^{64}$).
  $ROTL^n(x)$ denotes the circular shift (i.e. rotation) of a word x by n bit-positions to the left.
  $ROTR^n(x)$ denotes the circular shift (i.e. rotation) of a word x by n bit-positions to the right.
  $SHR^n(x)$ denotes the right shift of a word x by n bit-positions.
- *Logical functions and constants*
  SHA variants make use of logical functions and constants to brew the blocks. Constants appear as random values and are in hexadecimal representation.

5.2.1.1 SHA-1 Algorithm

- *SHA-1 sizes, constants, and logical functions*
  SHA-1 processes 512-bit blocks. It uses a schedule of 80 rounds and five 32-bit working variables a, b, c, d, and e. 32-bit round words are labeled $W_0, \ldots, W_{79}$. 32-bit words of hash value of block B^i are labeled $H_0^i, H_1^i, H_2^i, H_3^i, H_4^i$ (i.e. 5*32 bits = 160 bits). SHA-1 uses a sequence of eighty constant 32-bit words, $K_0, K_1, \ldots, K_{79}$ defined by:

$$K_i = 5a827999 \text{ if } 0 \leq i \leq 19 \qquad K_i = 6ed9eba1 \text{ if } 20 \leq i \leq 39$$
$$K_i = 8f1bbcdc \text{ if } 40 \leq i \leq 59 \qquad K_i = ca62c1d6 \text{ if } 60 \leq i \leq 79$$

SHA-1 uses a sequence of functions $f_0, f_1, ..., f_{79}$. Each function f_i operates on three 32-bit words and produces a 32-bit word as output. The computation of logical functions depends on their index as follows:

$$f_i(x,y,z) = Ch(x,y,z) = (x \wedge y) \oplus (\neg x \wedge z) \qquad \text{if } 0 \leq i \leq 19$$
$$f_i(x,y,z) = Parity(x,y,z) = x \oplus y \oplus z \qquad \text{if } 20 \leq i \leq 39$$
$$f_i(x,y,z) = Maj(x,y,z) = (x \wedge y) \oplus (x \wedge z) \oplus (y \wedge z) \quad \text{if } 40 \leq i \leq 59$$
$$f_i(x,y,z) = Parity(x,y,z) = x \oplus y \oplus z \qquad \text{if } 60 \leq k \leq 79$$

- *SHA-1 initialization*

$$H_0^0 = 67452301 \qquad H_1^0 = efcdab89 \qquad H_2^0 = 98badcfe$$
$$H_3^0 = 10325476 \qquad H_4^0 = c3d2e1f0$$

- *Computing message hash*

For each block $B^i (i = 1, ..., m)$ of padded message do:

1) Prepare the message schedule words $W_0, W_1, ..., W_{79}$:

$$W_t = \begin{cases} B_t^i & 0 \leq t \leq 15 \\ ROTL^1 \left(W_{t-3} \oplus W_{t-8} \oplus W_{t-14} \oplus W_{t-16} \right) & 16 \leq t \leq 79 \end{cases}$$

2) *Initialize the five working words*:

$$a = H_0^{i-1}, \; b = H_1^{i-1}, \; c = H_2^{i-1}, \; d = H_3^{i-1}, \; e = H_4^{i-1}$$

3) *Process 80 rounds*:

for $t = 0$ to 79 do

$$Tmp = ROTL^5(a) + f_i(b,c,d) + e + K_t + W_t$$
$$e = d; \quad d = c; \quad c = ROTL^{30}(b); b = a; \quad a = Tmp$$

4) *Compute the hash of block* i:

$$H_0^i = a + H_0^{i-1}; \quad H_1^i = b + H_1^{i-1}; \quad H_2^i = c + H_2^{i-1}$$
$$H_3^i = d + H_3^{i-1}; \quad H_4^i = e + H_4^{i-1}$$

5) After processing block B^m, $H_0^m \| H_1^m \| H_2^m \| H_3^m \| H_4^m$ is the 160-bit string representing the hash of the entire message.

5.2.1.2 SHA-256 Algorithm

- *SHA-256 sizes, constants, and logical functions*

SHA-256 processes 512-bit blocks. It uses a schedule of 64 rounds and eight 32-bit working variables a, b, c, d, e, f, g, and h. 32-bit round words are labeled $W_0, ..., W_{63}$. Words of hash value of block B^i are labeled $H_0^i, H_1^i, H_2^i, H_3^i, H_4^i, H_5^i, H_6^i, H_7^i$ (i.e. 8*32 bits = 256 bits).

A sequence of six logical functions are used in SHA-224 and SHA-256. Each function operates on one or three 32-bit words and produces a 32-bit word as output. Those functions are defined by:

$$Ch(x,y,z) = (x \wedge y) \oplus (\neg x \wedge z)$$
$$Maj(x,y,z) = (x \wedge y) \oplus (x \wedge z) \oplus (y \wedge z)$$
$$\sum_0^{\{256\}}(x) = ROTR^2(x) \oplus ROTR^{13}(x) \oplus ROTR^{22}(x)$$
$$\sum_1^{\{256\}}(x) = ROTR^6(x) \oplus ROTR^{11}(x) \oplus ROTR^{25}(x)$$
$$\sigma_0^{\{256\}}(x) = ROTR^7(x) \oplus ROTR^{18}(x) \oplus SHR^3(x)$$
$$\sigma_1^{\{256\}}(x) = ROTR^{17}(x) \oplus ROTR^{19}(x) \oplus SHR^{10}(x)$$

SHA-224 and SHA-256 use the same sequence of 64 constant 32-bit words, $K_0^{\{256\}}$, ..., $K_{63}^{\{256\}}$, defined as follows, from the left to the right:

428a2f98	71374491	b5c0fbcf	e9b5dba5	3956c25b	59f111f1
923f82a4	ab1c5ed5	d807aa98	12835b01	243185be	550c7dc3
72be5d74	80deb1fe	9bdc06a7	c19bf174	e49b69c1	efbe4786
0fc19dc6	240ca1cc	2de92c6f	4a7484aa	5cb0a9dc	76f988da
983e5152	a831c66d	b00327c8	bf597fc7	c6e00bf3	d5a79147
06ca6351	14292967	27b70a85	2e1b2138	4d2c6dfc	53380d13
650a7354	766a0abb	81c2c92e	92722c85	a2bfe8a1	a81a664b
c24b8b70	c76c51a3	d192e819	d6990624	f40e3585	106aa070
19a4c116	1e376c08	2748774c	34b0bcb5	391c0cb3	4ed8aa4a
5b9cca4f	682e6ff3	748f82ee	78a5636f	84c87814	8cc70208
90befffa	a4506ceb	bef9a3f7	c67178f2		

- *SHA-256 Initialization*

  $H_0^0 = 6a09e667 \quad H_1^0 = bb67ae85 \quad H_2^0 = 3c6ef372$

  $H_3^0 = a54ff53a \quad H_4^0 = 510e527f \quad H_5^0 = 9b05688c$

  $H_6^0 = 1f83d9ab \quad H_7^0 = 5be0cd19$

- *Computing message hash*

  For each block B^i ($i = 1, ..., m$) of padded message do:

  1) *Prepare the message schedule words* W_0, W_1, ..., W_{63}:

  $$W_t = \begin{cases} B_t^i & 0 \le t \le 15 \\ \sigma_1^{\{256\}}\left(W_{t-2}\right) + W_{t-7} + \sigma_0^{\{256\}}\left(W_{t-15}\right) + W_{t-16} & 16 \le t \le 63 \end{cases}$$

  2) *Initialize the five working words*:

  $a = H_0^{i-1}; \quad b = H_1^{i-1}; \quad c = H_2^{i-1}; \quad d = H_3^{i-1}$

  $e = H_4^{i-1}; \quad f = H_5^{i-1}; \quad g = H_6^{i-1}; \quad h = H_7^{i-1}$

  3) *Process 64 rounds*:

  for $t = 0$ to 63 do

  $Tmp1 = h + \sum_1^{\{256\}}(e) + Ch(e, f, g) + K_t^{\{256\}} + W_t$

  $Tmp2 = \sum_0^{\{256\}}(a) + Maj(a, b, c)$

  $h = g; g = f; f = e$

  $e = d + Tmp1; d = c; c = b; b = a; a = Tmp1 + Tmp2$

  4) *Compute the hash of block* i:

  $H_0^i = a + H_0^{i-1}; \quad H_1^i = b + H_1^{i-1}; \quad H_2^i = c + H_2^{i-1}; \quad H_3^i = d + H_3^{i-1}$

  $H_4^i = e + H_4^{i-1}; \quad H_5^i = f + H_5^{i-1}; \quad H_6^i = g + H_6^{i-1}; \quad H_7^i = h + H_7^{i-1}$

  5) After processing block B^m, $H_0^m \parallel H_1^m \parallel H_2^m \parallel H_3^m \parallel H_4^m \parallel H_5^m \parallel H_6^m \parallel H_7^m$ is the 256-bit string representing the hash of the entire message.

5.2.1.3 SHA-224 Algorithm

SHA-224 is defined exactly as SHA-256, with two exceptions:

- The constants used in the initialization step are as follows:

$$H_0 = c1059ed8 \quad H_1 = 367cd507 \quad H_2 = 3070dd17 \quad H_3 = f70e5939$$
$$H_4 = ffc00b31 \quad H_5 = 68581511 \quad H_6 = 64f98fa7 \quad H_7 = befa4fa4$$

- The message hash is obtained by keeping only 7 words of the final block hash, i.e. $H_0^m \parallel H_1^m \parallel H_2^m \parallel H_3^m \parallel H_4^m \parallel H_6^m$.

5.2.1.4 SHA-512 Algorithm

- *SHA-512 sizes, constants, and logical functions*

  SHA-512 processes 1024-bit blocks. Blocks of padded message are labeled B^1, B^2, ..., B^m, where m is the number of blocks of padded message. Each block B^i is represented as sixteen 64-bit words labeled B_t^i ($0 \le t \le 15$).

  SHA-512 uses a schedule of 80 rounds and eight 64-bit working variables a, b, c, d, e, f, g, and h. 64-bit round words are labeled $W_0, ..., W_{79}$. Words of hash value of block B^i are labeled $H_0^i, H_1^i, H_2^i, H_3^i, H_4^i, H_5^i, H_6^i, H_7^i$ (i.e. $8 * 64$ bits = 512 bits).

  A sequence of six functions are used in SHA-3, SHA-512, SHA-512/224, and SHA-512/256. Each function operates on one or three 64-bit words and produces a 64-bit word as output. Those functions are defined by:

$$Ch(x,y,z) = (x \wedge y) \oplus (\neg x \wedge z)$$
$$Maj(x,y,z) = (x \wedge y) \oplus (x \wedge z) \oplus (y \wedge z)$$
$$\sum\nolimits_0^{\{512\}}(x) = ROTR^{28}(x) \oplus ROTR^{34}(x) \oplus ROTR^{39}(x)$$
$$\sum\nolimits_1^{\{512\}}(x) = ROTR^{14}(x) \oplus ROTR^{18}(x) \oplus ROTR^{41}(x)$$
$$\sigma_1^{\{512\}}(x) = ROTR^1(x) \oplus ROTR^8(x) \oplus SHR^7(x)$$
$$\sigma_1^{\{512\}}(x) = ROTR^{19}(x) \oplus ROTR^{61}(x) \oplus SHR^6(x)$$

SHA-384, SHA-512, SHA12/224, and SHA-512/256 use the same sequence of 80 constant 64-bit words, $K_0^{\{512\}}$, ..., $K_{79}^{\{512\}}$, defined as follows, from left to right:

428a2f98d728ae22	7137449123ef65cd	b5c0fbcfec4d3b2f	e9b5dba58189dbbc
3956c25bf348b538	59f111f1b605d019	923f82a4af194f9b	ab1c5ed5da6d8118
d807aa98a3030242	12835b0145706fbe	243185be4ee4b28c	550c7dc3d5ffb4e2
72be5d74f27b896f	80deb1fe3b1696b1	9bdc06a725c71235	c19bf174cf692694
e49b69c19ef14ad2	efbe4786384f25e3	0fc19dc68b8cd5b5	240ca1cc77ac9c65
2de92c6f592b0275	4a7484aa6ea6e483	5cb0a9dcbd41fbd4	76f988da831153b5
983e5152ee66dfab	a831c66d2db43210	b00327c898fb213f	bf597fc7beef0ee4
c6e00bf33da88fc2	d5a79147930aa725	06ca6351e003826f	142929670a0e6e70
27b70a8546d22ffc	2e1b21385c26c926	4d2c6dfc5ac42aed	53380d139d95b3df
650a73548baf63de	766a0abb3c77b2a8	81c2c92e47edaee6	92722c851482353b
a2bfe8a14cf10364	a81a664bbc423001	c24b8b70d0f89791	c76c51a30654be30
d192e819d6ef5218	d69906245565a910	f40e35855771202a	106aa07032bbd1b8
19a4c116b8d2d0c8	1e376c085141ab53	2748774cdf8eeb99	34b0bcb5e19b48a8
391c0cb3c5c95a63	4ed8aa4ae3418acb	5b9cca4f7763e373	682e6ff3d6b2b8a3
748f82ee5defb2fc	78a5636f43172f60	84c87814a1f0ab72	8cc702081a6439ec
90befffa23631e28	a4506cebde82bde9	bef9a3f7b2c67915	c67178f2e372532b
ca273eceea26619c	d186b8c721c0c207	eada7dd6cde0eb1e	f57d4f7fee6ed178
06f067aa72176fba	0a637dc5a2c898a6	113f9804bef90dae	1b710b35131c471b
28db77f523047d84	32caab7b40c72493	3c9ebe0a15c9bebc	431d67c49c100d4c
4cc5d4becb3e42b6	597f299cfc657e2a	5fcb6fab3ad6faec	6c44198c4a475817

- *SHA-512 initialization*

$$H_0^0 = 6a09e667f3bcc908 \qquad H_1^0 = bb67ae8584caa73b$$
$$H_2^0 = 3c6ef372fe94f82b \qquad H_3^0 = a54ff53a5f1d36f1$$
$$H_4^0 = 510e527fade682d1 \qquad H_5^0 = 9b05688c2b3e6c1f$$
$$H_6^0 = 1f83d9abfb41bd6b \qquad H_7^0 = 5be0cd19137e2179$$

- *Computing message hash*

For each block B^i $(i = 1, ..., m)$ of padded message do:

1) *Prepare the message schedule W_0, W_1, ..., W_{79}:*

$$W_t = \begin{cases} B_t^i & 0 \le t \le 15 \\ \sigma_1^{\{512\}}(W_{t-2}) + W_{t-7} + \sigma_0^{\{512\}}(W_{t-15}) + W_{t-16} & 16 \le t \le 63 \end{cases}$$

2) *Initialize the five working words:*

$$a = H_0^{i-1}; \quad b = H_1^{i-1}; \quad c = H_2^{i-1}; \quad d = H_3^{i-1}$$
$$e = H_4^{i-1}; \quad f = H_5^{i-1}; \quad g = H_6^{i-1}; \quad h = H_7^{i-1}$$

3) *Process 80 rounds:*

for $t = 0$ to 79 do

$$Tmp1 = h + \sum_1^{\{512\}}(e) + Ch(e, f, g) + K_t^{\{512\}} + W_t$$
$$Tmp2 = \sum_0^{\{512\}}(a) + Maj(a, b, c)$$
$$h = g; g = f; f = e; e = d + Tmp1; d = c; c = b; b = a$$
$$a = Tmp1 + Tmp2$$

4) *Compute the hash of block i:*

$$H_0^i = a + H_0^{i-1}; \quad H_1^i = b + H_1^{i-1}; \quad H_2^i = c + H_2^{i-1}; \quad H_3^i = d + H_3^{i-1};$$
$$H_4^i = e + H_4^{i-1}; \quad H_5^i = f + H_5^{i-1}; \quad H_6^i = g + H_6^{i-1}; \quad H_7^i = h + H_7^{i-1}$$

5) After processing block B^m, $H_0^m \parallel H_1^m \parallel H_2^m \parallel H_3^m \parallel H_4^m \parallel H_5^m \parallel H_6^m \parallel H_7^m$ is the 256-bit string representing the hash of the entire message.

5.2.1.5 SHA-384, SHA-512/224, and SHA-512/256 Algorithms

SHA-384, SHA-512/224 algorithms are defined exactly as SHA-512 algorithm with the following exceptions:

- Initialization values are as follows:
  - SHA-384 initialization

$$H_0^0 = cbbb9d5dc1059ed8 \qquad H_1^0 = 629a292a367cd50$$
$$H_2^0 = 9159015a3070dd17 \qquad H_3^0 = 152fecd8f70e5939$$
$$H_4^0 = 67332667ffc00b31 \qquad H_5^0 = 8eb44a8768581511$$
$$H_6^0 = db0c2e0d64f98fa7 \qquad H_7^0 = 47b5481dbefa4fa4$$

  - SHA-512/224 initialization

$$H_0^0 = 8c3d37c819544da2 \qquad H_1^0 = 73e1996689dcd4d6$$
$$H_2^0 = 1dfab7ae32ff9c82 \qquad H_3^0 = 679dd514582f9fcf$$

$$H_4^0 = 0f6d2b697bd44da8 \qquad H_5^0 = 77e36f7304c48942$$

$$H_6^0 = 3f9d85a86a1d36c8 \qquad H_7^0 = 1112e6ad91d692a1$$

– SHA-512/256 initialization

$$H_0^0 = 22312194fc2bf72c \qquad H_1^0 = 9f555fa3c84c64c2$$

$$H_2^0 = 2393b86b6f53b151 \qquad H_3^0 = 963877195940eabd$$

$$H_4^0 = 96283ee2A88effe3 \qquad H_5^0 = be5e1e2553863992$$

$$H_6^0 = 2b0199fc2c85b8aa \qquad H_7^0 = 0eb72ddc81c52ca2$$

- After processing block B^m, the message hash is obtained by truncation as follows:

  – SHA-384 keeps six 64-bit words, $H_0^m \parallel H_1^m \parallel H_2^m \parallel H_3^m \parallel H_4^m \parallel H_5^m$
  – SHA-512/224 keeps three 64-bit words and the left half of the fourth 64-bit word, $H_0^m \parallel H_1^m \parallel H_2^m \parallel left\_half\left(H_3^m\right)$
  – SHA-512/256 keeps four 64-bit words, $H_0^m \parallel H_1^m \parallel H_2^m \parallel H_3^m$

5.2.1.6 SHA-1 Security

In 2005, a method was proposed for finding SHA-1 collisions under restrictive conditions; the number of rounds was 53 instead of 80 in the standard SHA-1. From that time, SHA-1 security became doubtful, but no formal proof of its insecurity was provided. As of 2020, attacks against SHA-1 have become practical. As such, it is recommended to withdraw SHA-1 from existing products as soon as possible and use SHA-2 or SHA-3 instead. As far as we know, the most efficient attack against SHA-1 has been published in 2020 [7]. It belongs to chosen-prefix collision attacks. In the designed attack, the adversary starts with two prefixes P and P', then computes two parts M and M', such that $H(P \parallel M) = H(P' \parallel M')$. Chosen-prefix collision attack has a complexity of $2^{63.4}$ and is far from the brute-force attack that has a complexity of $2^{160/2}$.

5.2.2 SHA-3 Functions

SHA-3 is based on an instance of Keccak[9] algorithm, which was selected as the winner of SHA-3 public cryptographic hash algorithm competition, initiated by NIST in 2007, after serious attacks were published against SHA-1. SHA-3 was published in 2015 [8]. The security strength levels provided by SHA-3 are the same as the ones of SHA-2.

Four hash functions, namely SHA3-224, SHA3-256, SHA3-384, and SHA3-512 along with two extendable-output functions, Shake128 and Shake256, form the SHA-3 family. Shake128 and Shake256 are not hash functions, but can be specialized to hash functions. They are not described in the sequel. The four SHA-3 functions are based on the sponge construction model [3, 4] in which the main component is the Keccak permutation.

Notation:
SHA-3 function specification makes use of polymorphic functions. To be used in a specific context, a polymorphic function ϕ must first be instantiated to produce a concrete function, which in turn is called at multiple times to return a result. In $\phi[I_1, I_2, ...](c_1, c_2, ...)$, $I_1, I_2, ...$ denote the instantiation parameters and $c_1, c_2, ...$ denote the call (or input) parameters. For example, *Sponge* function is instantiated to produce a hash function of a cryptosystems, then the produced hash function is used to return hash digests (see Section 5.2.2.2).

5.2.2.1 Keccak-p Permutation

A Keccak-p[10] permutation is denoted $Keccak\_p[b, N_r]$, where b is the input bit-string size and N_r the number of rounds. Input string size b is any value in $\{25, 50, 100, 200, 400, 800, 1600\}$ and N_r is any positive integer. $Keccak\_p$ provides foundations to design a large variety of hash functions to fulfill specific application requirements. However, the current SHA-3 standard chose a single pair of value parameters $b = 1600$ and $N_r = 24$.

A round consists of a sequence of five transformations, which are called step mappings labeled θ, ρ, π, χ, and τ.

5.2.2.1.1 State Array

Bit strings manipulated by Keccak-p transformations are represented as 3-dimensional arrays of bits, called *state arrays*. Any string used in a permutation is represented as a 3D array, $5 \times 5 \times w$ array of bits, where $w = b/25$. The 2D sub-arrays are called *sheets*, *planes*, and *slices*; and 1D sub-arrays are called *rows*, *columns*, and *lanes* (see Figure 5.3). Thus, the state array

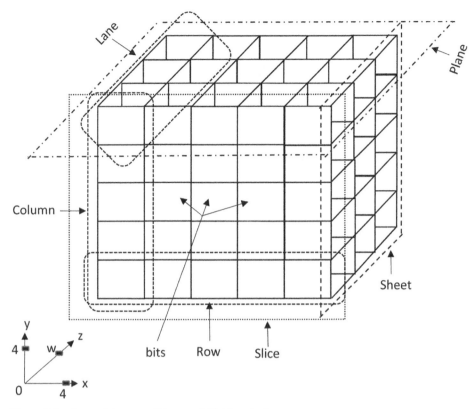

Figure 5.3 Parts of the state 3D-array (100-bit string).

Table 5.2 Keccak-p permutation (width *b* and related quantities, *w* and *l*).

b	25	50	100	200	400	800	1600
w	1	2	4	8	16	32	64
l	0	1	2	3	4	5	6

associated with a bit string of a bit-length of *b* is composed as follows: five planes, five sheets, and *w* slices. Two quantities, labeled *w* and *l*, are associated with each bit string length *b* (see Table 5.2). They are used in transformation specification.

Rules for conversion

1) A string *S* of size *b*, whose bits are labeled $S[0]$, $S[1]$, ..., $S[b-1]$ is converted into a state array *A* as follows:
   For all triples (x, y, z) such that $0 \leq x < 5, 0 \leq y < 5, \ 0 \leq z < w$ do:

$$A[x, y, z] = S[w(5y + x) + z]$$

2) A state array *A* is converted into a bit string *S* of size *b*, whose bits are as follows:

$$S = Plane(0) \parallel Plane(1) \parallel Plane(2) \parallel Plane(3) \parallel Plane(4)$$

where:

$$Plane(j) = Lane(0, j) \parallel Lane(1, j) \parallel Lane(2, j) \parallel Lane(3, j) \parallel Lane(4, j), 0 \leq j < 5$$

$$Lane(i, j) = A[i, j, 0] \parallel A[i, j, 1] \parallel A[i, j, 2] \parallel ... \parallel A[i, j, w-1], 0 \leq i < 5 \text{ and } 0 \leq j < 5$$

$S[80]$	$S[84]$	$S[88]$	$S[92]$	$S[96]$
$S[60]$	$S[64]$	$S[68]$	$S[72]$	$S[76]$
$S[40]$	$S[44]$	$S[48]$	$S[52]$	$S[56]$
$S[20]$	$S[24]$	$S[28]$	$S[32]$	$S[36]$
$S[0]$	$S[4]$	$S[8]$	$S[12]$	$S[16]$

Slice 1

$S[81]$	$S[85]$	$S[89]$	$S[93]$	$S[97]$
$S[61]$	$S[65]$	$S[69]$	$S[73]$	$S[77]$
$S[41]$	$S[45]$	$S[49]$	$S[53]$	$S[57]$
$S[21]$	$S[25]$	$S[29]$	$S[33]$	$S[37]$
$S[1]$	$S[5]$	$S[9]$	$S[13]$	$S[17]$

Slice 2

$S[82]$	$S[86]$	$S[90]$	$S[94]$	$S[98]$
$S[62]$	$S[66]$	$S[70]$	$S[74]$	$S[78]$
$S[42]$	$S[46]$	$S[50]$	$S[54]$	$S[58]$
$S[22]$	$S[26]$	$S[30]$	$S[34]$	$S[38]$
$S[2]$	$S[6]$	$S[10]$	$S[14]$	$S[18]$

Slice 3

$S[83]$	$S[87]$	$S[91]$	$S[95]$	$S[99]$
$S[63]$	$S[67]$	$S[71]$	$S[75]$	$S[79]$
$S[43]$	$S[47]$	$S[51]$	$S[55]$	$S[59]$
$S[23]$	$S[27]$	$S[31]$	$S[35]$	$S[39]$
$S[3]$	$S[7]$	$S[11]$	$S[15]$	$S[19]$

Slice 4

Figure 5.4 Mapping of a 100-bit string to a state array.

Example 5.1

Let $b = 100$.

Any string of 100 bits is organized into four slices of 25 bits each. Figure 5.4 shows the location of each bit on the four slices.

5.2.2.1.2 Step Mappings

A round is composed of five step mappings (i.e. transformations) denoted by θ, ρ, π, χ, and τ. With the exception of the mapping τ, the input A and output A' of step mappings are state arrays. Step mappings are defined as follows.

Step mapping θ

The effect of θ is to XOR each bit of the state with the parities of two column in the array. More formally, θ is specified as follows:

– For all pairs (x,z) such that $0 \leq x < 5$ and $0 \leq z < w$ do:

$$C[x,z] = A[x,0,z] \oplus A[x,1,z] \oplus A[x,2,z] \oplus A[x,3,z] \oplus A[x,4,z]$$

– For all pairs (x,z) such that $0 \leq x < 5$ and $0 \leq z < w$ do:

$$D[x,z] = C[(x-1)\bmod 5, z] \oplus C[(x+1)\bmod 5, (z-1)\bmod w]$$

– For all triples (x,y,z) such that $0 \leq x < 5$, $0 \leq y < 5$, and $0 \leq z < w$ do:

$$A'[x,y,z] = A[x,y,z] \oplus D[x,z]$$

Step mapping ρ

The effect of ρ is to rotate the bits of each lane by a length, called offset, which depends on x and y coordinates of the lane. More formally, mapping ρ is specified as follows:

– For all z such that $0 \leq z \leq w$ do: $A'[0,0,z] = A[0,0,z]$

– $(x,y) = (1,0)$

– For $t = 0$ to 23 do:
  i) For z such that $0 \leq z < w$ do: $A'[x,y,z] = A[x,y,(z-(t+1)(t+2)/2) \bmod w]$
  ii) $(x,y) = (y, (2x+3y) \bmod 5)$

Step mapping π

The effect of π is to rearrange the positions of the lanes. More formally, mapping π is specified as follows:

For all triples (x,y,z) such that $0 \leq x < 5$, $0 \leq y < 5$, and $0 \leq z < w$ do:

$$A'[x,y,z] = A[(x+3y) \bmod 5, y, z]$$

Step mapping χ

The effect of χ is to XOR each bit with a nonlinear function. More formally, mapping χ is specified as follows:
   For all triples (x,y,z) such that $0 \le x < 5, 0 \le y < 5$, and $0 \le z < w$ do:

$$A'[x,y,z] = A[x,y,z] \oplus \left(A[(x+1) \bmod 5, y, z] \oplus 1 \right) \wedge \left(A[(x+2) \bmod 5, y, z] \right)$$

Step mapping τ

The effect of τ is to modify some of the bits of $Lane(0,0)$ in a manner depending on the index of the round. The input of τ is a pair (A, i_r), where A is a state array and i_r a round index; its output is a state array A'. More formally, mapping τ is specified as follows:
- For all triples (x,y,z) such that $0 \le x < 5, 0 \le y < 5$, and $0 \le z < w$ do: $A'[x,y,z] = A[x,y,z]$
- $RC = 0^w$ (RC is a string of w 0-bits)
- $l = \log_2(b/25)$
- For $j = 0$ to l do: $RC[2^j - 1] = rc(j + 7i_r)$
- For all z such that $0 \le z < w$ do: $A'[0,0,z] = A'[0,0,z] \oplus RC[z]$

Function $rc(t)$ is specified as follows:
- If $t \bmod 255 = 0$, then return 1
- $R = 10000000$ (R is an array of eight bits)
- For $i = 1$ to 255 do:

$$R = 0 \| R \qquad R[0] = R[0] \oplus R[8] \qquad R[4] = R[4] \oplus R[8]$$

$$R[5] = R[5] \oplus R[8] \qquad R[6] = R[6] \oplus R[8]$$

$$R = Trunc_8[R] \text{ (keep the eight leftmost bits of } R)$$

- Return R

5.2.2.1.3 Keccak_p[b, N_r] Permutation

$Keccak\_p[b, N_r]$ permutation takes a string S of a bit-length of b, and a number of rounds N_r and returns a bit string S' of the same length b. The permutation consists of N_r rounds. More formally, $Keccak\_p[b, N_r]$ is specified as follows:
- Convert the input bit string S into a state array A.
- $l = \log_2(b/25)$
- For $i_r = 12 + 2l - N_r$ to $12 + 2l - 1$ do: $A = \tau\left(\chi\left(\pi\left(\rho(\theta(A)) \right) \right), i_r \right)$
- Convert the final state array A into a bit string S'.

5.2.2.1.4 Keccak_f[b] Permutation

$Keccak\_f[b]$ permutation is a specialization of the generic $Keccak\_p$ permutation, where the number of rounds N_r is omitted, since it is fixed at 24.
   $Keccak\_f[b]$ is equivalent to $Keccak\_p[b, 12 + 2\log_2(b/25)]$.
   $Keccak\_p[1600, 24]$ is the underlying permutation to all SHA-3 functions and it is equivalent to $Keccak\_f[1600]$.

5.2.2.2 Sponge Construction

Sponge construction is a framework for specifying functions of binary data with arbitrary output length [3, 4]. The functions that the framework produces are called *sponge functions*. The latter are denoted by $Sponge[f, Padding, r]$ where: f is a function that takes a string of length b and returns a string with the same length, r is called rate, and $Padding$ is a padding rule.

   A sponge function takes as inputs, a bit string N and an output bit-length d; and it returns a string Z of length d (see Figure 5.5).

   In its generic form, given two inputs x and m, $Padding(x,m)$ returns a sequence of padding bits with a length such that $m + len(Padding(x,m))$ is a multiple of x. In sponge construction $x = r$ and $m = len(N)$.

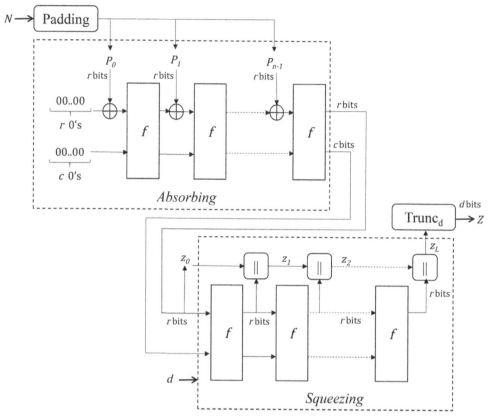

Figure 5.5 Sponge construction.

Bit string N is concatenated with the padding bits produced by *Padding* function to yield a sequence of bit strings $P_0, P_1, P_0, ..., P_{n-1}$. Each bit string $P_i, 0 \le i \le n-1$, has a fixed length of r bits. n, the number of strings, is equal to bit-length of padded input by r, i.e. $n = (len(N) + len(Padding(r, len(N))))/r$. Notice that bit strings $P_0, P_1, P_0, ..., P_{n-1}$ are equivalent to blocks $B^1, B^2 ...$ in SHA-1 and SHA-2.

Sponge function is composed of two stages: *absorbing* and *squeezing*. In absorbing stage, the transformation of each bit string $P_i, 1 \le i \le n-1$, is yielded by function f whose input is P_i and the result of transformation of bit string P_{i-1}. The bit string S yielded by the absorbing stage is used as input to the squeezing stage in which function f is applied L times and in each iteration, the r most-left bits of the result of function f are appended to a bit string Z initialized to empty string. The number of iterations of squeezing stage is $L = \left\lceil \dfrac{d}{r} \right\rceil$.

The algorithm of $Sponge[f, Padding, r](N, d)$ is specified as follows:

1. $P = N \parallel Padding(r, len(N))$
2. $n = len(P)/r$ (by construction, $len(P)$ is a multiple of r)
3. Let $P_0, P_1, P_0, ..., P_{n-1}$ be a sequence of strings of length r such that $P = P_0 \parallel P_1 \parallel ... P_{n-1}$
4. $c = b - r$ (r is always less than b)
5. $S = 0^b$ (S is a sequence of b 0-bits)
6. **for** $i = 0$ **to** $n-1$ **do** $S = f\left(S \oplus \left(P_i \parallel 0^c\right)\right)$
7. Let Z be the empty string
8. $Z = Z \parallel Trunc_r(S)$ (keep the r most-left bits of string S)
9. **if** $d \le len(Z)$, **then return** $Trunc_d(Z)$; **else** continue
10. $S = f(S)$
11. **go to** step 8

5.2.2.3 SHA-3 Functions

When the sponge function is specialized for hashing, N represents the message, d the hash length, and Z the message digest. In SHA-3 hashing algorithms, the underlying function f is a $Keccak\_p$ permutation. Thus, the generic form of hashing functions produced by sponge construction is:

$$H(N,d) \overset{\text{def}}{=} Sponge\big[Keccak\_p[b, N_r], Padding, r\big](N,d)$$

b, the length of bit string size manipulated by $Keccak\_p$ permutation, is greater than d, the hash size. $c = b - r$ is called the capacity of the sponge function.

SHA-3 standard made the following choices:

- $b = 1600$: the size of state arrays manipulated by mapping steps of Keccak-p permutation is 1600. The rationale of choice is that all SHA-3 variants have the same implementation support and 1600 is a multiple of 64 and 32; hence, $Keccak\_p[1600,.]$ favors 64-bit CPUs and remains efficient on 32-bit CPUs.
- $c = 2d$: with such a capacity, there are no generic attacks with expected complexity below 2^d.
- $r = 1600 - 2d$: since by design $b = r + c$, $r = 1600 - 2d$.
- $N_r = 24$: 24 rounds are estimated sufficient to provide resistance against potential attacks.
- SHA-3 *Padding* function is labeled $"pad10*1"$. It returns a string equal to $"1 \| 0^j \| 1"$, where $j = ((-len(N) - 2) \bmod r$ and 0^j is a sequence of j 0-bits. $pad10*1$ is easy to specify and implement, while providing compliance regarding the randomness of padding bits.

Concrete sponge function model used to specify SHA-3 functions is labeled $Keccak[c]$, where c is the capacity of the sponge function:

$$Keccak[c] \overset{\text{def}}{=} Sponge\big[Keccak\_p[1600, 24], pad\ 10*1, 1600 - c\big]$$

Given an input bit string N and an output length d, $Keccak[c](N,d)$ produces a bit string of length d, which is a hash of N.

SHA-3 standard specified four hash functions based on sponge function whose capacity is the double of the hash bit-length:

- SHA3-224 $(M) = Keccak[448](M \| 01, 224)$
- SHA3-256 $(M) = Keccak[512](M \| 01, 256)$
- SHA3-384 $(M) = Keccak[768](M \| 01, 384)$
- SHA3-512 $(M) = Keccak[1024](M \| 01, 512)$

Notice the two additional paddings bits are appended to message M before launching the sponge function.

5.3 Message Authentication Codes

Message signature and message authentication codes (MACs) are the main applications of hash functions. Both mechanisms produce a key-based message digest for guaranteeing message integrity and authenticity. MACs differ from digital signatures as MAC values are both generated and verified using the same secret, while signatures may be generated by private keys and validated by public keys (see next chapters).

5.3.1 Objectives and Properties of MACs

A *message authentication code* (MAC) is a piece[11] of information associated with a message, which is used to authenticate message sender and to protect the integrity of message transmitted over an insecure network. MACs are used between two parties that share a secret. MAC algorithms have two parameters: a secrete key k, used to verify authenticity, and a hash function H, used to produce message digests (see Figure 5.6). A MAC system is composed of three components (or functions):

- A key generation algorithm, which selects keys from the key space uniformly at random and periodically refreshed.
- A tag generation algorithm, which returns a tag given the key and a message.
- A verifying algorithm, which verifies the authenticity of the message given the key and the tag. If the hash computed by the receiver is identical to the received one, the message is accepted. Otherwise, it is rejected.

This chapter focuses on the second component, i.e. generation of tags. The other components depend on the underlying cryptosystems either symmetric or asymmetric. In symmetric systems, the shared secret is used to encrypt and to sign. In public key cryptosystems, specific methods are used to generate private and public key and to generate signatures using hash functions and verifying them (see Chapters 12 and 13).

MAC Properties:

1) P1: MAC systems should adapt to a large number of applications. Thus, they should accept arbitrary length of message, while producing a fixed length output.
2) P2: preserve the integrity of message.
3) P3: authenticate the message sender.

P1 and P2 properties are fulfilled by hash functions, while P3 is provided by using a shared secret key. It is worth noticing that MACs do not provide the property of non-repudiation assured by signatures, because any user who share the secret key can verify and generate MACs. In contrast to MAC, a digital signature is generated using the private key of a user. Since this private key is only accessible to its holder, a digital signature proves that a message was signed by none other than that private keyholder.

There exist two main standard categories of MACs:

1) Hash function-based MACs, which are addressed in this chapter.
2) Block cipher-based MACs, which are addressed in Chapter 9.

5.3.2 Hash Function-based MACs

The naïve, but simple, idea to designing MAC algorithms is to use the concatenation of key k and message M as input to the hash function leading to two design alternatives:

$MAC(M,k) = H(k \| M)$, called secret prefix MAC.
$MAC(M,k) = H(M \| k)$, called secret suffix MAC.

Secret prefix MACs, when used alone, are known to be vulnerable, while secrete suffix are not (see Problem 5.18). MAC algorithms used in practice, such as HMAC or KMAC, include additional mechanisms to provide secure MACs. Both HMAC and KMAC are called *keyed hash functions* and make use of a secret key, known as *MAC key*.

5.3.2.1 HMAC
HMAC is the acronym for either *keyed-hash message authentication code* or *hash-based message authentication code*. HMAC was originally proposed by Bellare, Canetti, and Krawczyk [9] and then adopted by the IETF in 1997 [10]. HMAC is widely used in particular jointly with SHA-1 or SHA-2. Before being broken, MD5 also was widely used in HMAC implementations.

HMAC is a MAC family parameterized with the underlying hash function. HMAC instances are denoted HMAC-H, where H may be any hash function including SHA-1, MD5, SHA-256, SHA3-512, etc. HMAC takes two parameters M, the message, and k, the secrete key, and generates a digest $HMAC(M,k)$ of a length of n bits, which is the same as the hash function output bit-length. HMAC can be used with any secret key length. However, secret keys with length less than the length of block size processed by the hash function are strongly discouraged, because they would decrease the security strength of the HMAC as a whole. Figure 5.7 illustrates the diagram of HMAC. HMAC is a double hashing method to provide resistant MACs.

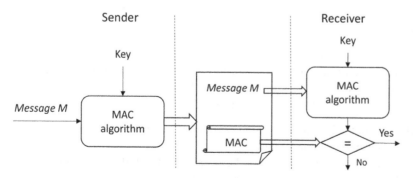

Figure 5.6 Overall diagram of MAC algorithms.

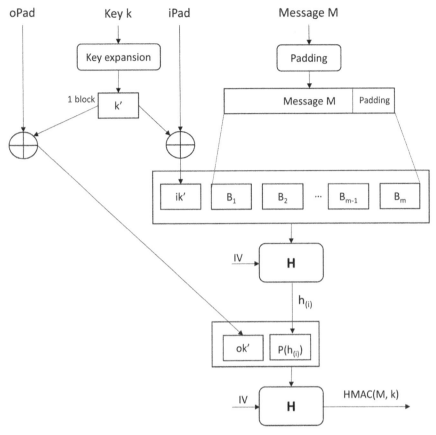

Figure 5.7 HMAC diagram.

ik' denotes the block yielded after XORing the expanded key k' with $iPad$ block.

ok' denotes the block yielded after XORing the expanded key k' with $oPad$ block.

$h_{(i)}$ denotes the inner hash and $P(h_{(i)})$, the block yielded after padding $h_{(i)}$.

Given a message M and a secret key k, the yielded MAC is expressed as:

$$HMAC(M,k) = H\big((k' \oplus oPad) \,\|\, \big(H(k' \oplus iPad \,\|\, M)\big)\big)$$

which is computed with the following procedure:

$HMAC(M,k)$ description

Notations:

- M is the message for which integrity and authentication are required.
- n and L denote the output bit-length and the block size of the underlying hash function H, respectively.
- $len(k)$ denotes the bit-length of the secret key.
- $iPad^{12}$ is a constant byte string of length $L/8$ bytes all equal to $0x36$.
- $oPad$ is a constant byte string of length $L/8$ bytes all equal to $0x5C$.

1) *Secret key expansion*:

   If $len(k)$ is less than L, then append zeros to the end of key k to produce an expanded key k' with length of L bits.

   If $len(k)$ is greater than L, then first hash the key k to produce a hash $H(k)$. Then append zeros to the end of $H(k)$ and use the resulting bit-string as expanded key k' of a bit-length of L bits.

2) *Inner hash computation*: $h_{(i)} = H(k' \oplus iPad \,\|\, M)$

3) *Outer hash computation*: $h_{(o)} = H\big(k' \oplus oPad \,\|\, h_{(i)}\big)$

4) $h_{(o)}$ is the MAC of message M.

Security of HMAC

The security of HMAC depends on the security strength of the underlying hash function H, which in turn depends on the size of hash function output. HMAC is resistant to common attacks against MAC, including recovering the private key or altering the message content. In HMAC, the inner hash (i.e. $h_{(i)}$) would be vulnerable to length-extension attack, while the outer hash (i.e. $HMAC(M,k)$) is not (see Problem 5.19).

5.3.2.2 KMAC

KMAC is the acronym for *Keccak Message Authentication Code*. It is based on Keccak function of SHA-3 [11]. Two variants exist, KMAC-128 and KMAC-256. Notice that 128 and 256 in KMAC variants refer to the capacity of the sponge function (see Section 5.2.2.3). KMAC functions take the following parameters:

- K, a key of a variable bit-length, which depends on the required security strength, but $len(K)$ is at most 2^{2040}.
- M, a message of a variable bit-length.
- L, the requested bit-length of the output (i.e. the tag length), with $L < 2^{2040}$.
- S, an optional customization bit-string, which may be empty, of length $len(S) < 2^{2040}$.

Let $KMAC\langle m\rangle$ denote either $KMAC128$ or $KMAC256$. $KMAC\langle m\rangle$ is defined by:

---

function $KMAC\langle m\rangle(K,M,L,S)$

1. **if** $m = 128$, **then** $R = 168$ **else** $R = 136$
2. $X' = BytePad(EncodeString(K),R) \parallel M \parallel RightEncode(L)$
3. $T = BytePad\big(EncodeString("KMAC") \parallel EncodeString(S),R\big)$
4. $Res = Keccak[2*m](T \parallel X' \parallel 00, L)$
5. **return** Res

KMAC internal functions

---

function $EncodeString(Y)$

1. $Y' = LeftEncode(len(Y)) \parallel Y$
2. **return** Y'

function $RightEncode(x):$

\# encode integer x as byte-string ending with the byte-length of x:
1. n is the smallest positive integer such that $2^{8n} > x$
2. Let $x_1 x_2 \ldots x_n$ be the representation of x in base 256, i.e. $x = \sum_{i=1}^{n}\big(x_i * 2^{8(n-i)}\big)$
3. **for** $i = 1$ **to** n **do** $O_i = enc8(x_i)$ $(^{13})$
4. $O_{n+1} = enc8(n)$
5. **return** $\big(O_1 \parallel O_2 \parallel \ldots \parallel O_{n+1}\big)$

function $LeftEncode(x):$

\# encode integer x as byte-string starting with the byte-length of x:
1. n is the smallest positive integer such that $2^{8n} > x$
2. Let $x_1 x_2 \ldots x_n$ be the representation of x in base 256
3. **for** $i = 1$ **to** n **do** $O_i = enc8(x_i)$
4. $O_0 = enc8(n)$
5. **return** $\big(O_0 \parallel O_1 \parallel O_2 \parallel \ldots \parallel O_n\big)$

function $BytePad(Y,w):$

\# Prepend an encoding of w to the input-string bit- string Y,
\# then pad it with zeros until the new bit-string is multiple of w
1. $z = LeftEncode(w) \parallel Y$

---

2. **while** $len(z)$ *mod* $8 \neq 0$ **do** $z = z \parallel 0$
3. **while** $len(z) / 8$ *mod* $w \neq 0$ **do** $z = z \parallel 0000\,0000$
4. **return** z

5.3.2.3 Generic Attacks Against Hash Function-based MAC Algorithms

MAC systems may be a target for attacks either to recover the secret key or to forge messages. More specifically, the common generic attacks against MACs include:

- A1: Recover the secret key.
- A2: Append fake information to the end of the original message.
- A3: Substitute a fake message for the original one.
- A4: Existential forgery: it is the ability of the adversary to create a message and its MAC that have not been generated in the past by the legitimate sender.

In A1, given a message M and the keyed hash $MAC(M,k)$, the attack (without knowledge of the internal structure of the hash function) is a brute-force attack, which requires to test all potential keys concatenated to M, either on the left (in case of secret prefix MAC) or on the right (in case of secret suffix MAC) of k. Thus, the resistance to attack A1 depends on the length of the secret key.

In A2, given a message M and the keyed hash $MAC(M,k)$, adversary can append fake data to M and generate a keyed hash without knowledge of the secret key if the secret prefix MAC approach is used, i.e. $MAC(M,k) = H(k \parallel M)$. (see Section 5.1.3.2 and Problem 5.18).

In A3, given a message M and the keyed hash $MAC(M,k)$, to substitute M' to $k \parallel M$ or to $M \parallel k$, without controlling the content of M', the adversary must find a second preimage collision, which is known to be computationally infeasible.

In A4, the adversary has to find a collision, which is known to be computationally infeasible. In addition, MAC algorithms, such as HMAC, make use of two hash function calls (producing inner and outer hashes), which makes them very secure regarding collision attacks (see Problem 5.19).

5.3.3 Block Cipher-based MACs

Modes of operation of block ciphers have been standardized by the NIST to provide methods for authenticated encryption and MAC generation. They include CMAC (Cipher MAC), CCM (Counter with Cipher block chaining-MAC), GCM (Galois/Counter MAC), GMAC (Galois MAC), and AES-GCM-SIV. All those MAC generation methods will be addressed in Chapter 9.

5.4 Digital Signature

Digital signature algorithms are the most important application of hash functions in the cyberspace.

5.4.1 Digital Signature in Public Key World

In paper documents, the issuer manually signs his/her documents to provide proof of authenticity that can be checked by document recipients. In the digital space (or cyberspace), data included in messages are used for Internet shopping, banking, stock exchange, voting, company transactions, etc. Public key cryptosystems evolve in a world where messages and unencrypted data (including public keys) are not hidden to observers. The big question is: how can the recipient trust the sender? Message signature is the answer to this question.

A digital signature (or simply signature) is a cryptographic transformation, which is similar to handwritten signature to provide assurance of authenticity of the sender. Digital signature also is used for *non-repudiation*: the signing individual cannot deny he/she has not been the signer. For example, one may electronically sign a car rental contract, which states he/she must pay monthly $500. Then, he/she cannot claim either the amount to pay is $400 or worse, he/she has never signed the contact. Non-repudiation is of paramount importance in the cyberspace. Digital signature also is a means of guaranteeing integrity. If a message is altered during transport, the signature will no more match the received message and the received message is rejected. Two digital signature methods exist:

- *Signature with appendix*[14]: given a message M, the signer generates a signature S from the hash of message and sends a pair (S, M). The verifier decrypts the signature S to yield a hash H', computes H, the hash of the received message, then compares both hashes (see Figure 5.8).
- *Signature with message recovery*: given a message M, all or some of message M is embedded in the signature S. When the message is entirely embedded, the verification procedure requires only the signature S and recovers M from the signature.

In symmetric cryptosystems, the same key, which is shared by both parties, is used for generating and verifying signature. In asymmetric cryptosystems, the signer makes use of his/her private key to generate the signature, while the verifier makes use of the public key of the signer to verify the signature.

Digital signature algorithms include:

- RSASSA (RSA Signature Scheme with Appendix), presented in Section 12.2.6.
- DSA (Digital Signature Algorithm), presented in Section 12.4.
- ElGamal signature algorithm, presented in Section 12.3.4.2.
- ECDSA (Elliptic Curve Digital Signature Algorithm) and EdDSA (Edwards Elliptic Curve Digital Signature Algorithm), presented in Sections 13.5.5–13.5.6.

All those algorithms make use of hash functions. They are addressed in detail in Chapters 12–14 when the foundations of the underlying public key are introduced. Then, attacks against digital signatures produced by public key algorithms are discussed.

5.4.2 Attacks Against Digital Signature Schemes

Hand signature is approximately the same in all documents signed by a given person. The difficulty in forging a hand signature is directly linked to the graphic pattern elaborated, thanks to the ingenuity of the signer. Some hand signatures are easy to reproduce, while others are too complex requiring a high level of imitation to reproduce them. Hand signatures may be imitated even carefully designed by their owners. To enforce signature, public notaries play a third party role. It is commonly considered that a document, double-checked and signed by a notary, includes an authentic signature.

In the cyberspace, digital signature is a cryptographic transformation. Consequently, the difficulty in forging signatures is linked to the mathematical foundations used to design digital signature schemes. Thus, digital signatures are by far more difficult to forge than hand signatures.

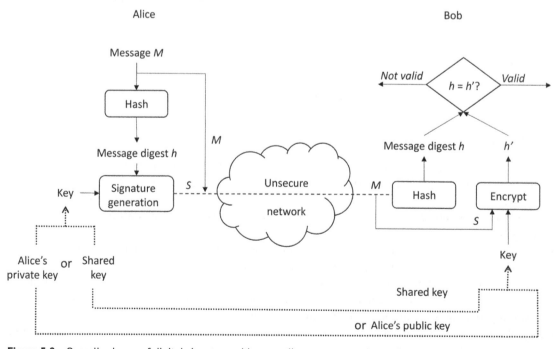

Figure 5.8 Overall scheme of digital signature with appendix.

Attacks against digital signature may be categorized into three groups:

- Universal forgery: adversary is able to recover the private key of the signer and then signs any message on behalf of the legitimate key owner.
- Selective forgery: adversary is able to create valid signatures for messages of his/her choice.
- Existential forgery: adversary can generate a pair composed of a signature and a message without controlling the message content.

5.5 Concluding Remarks

Digital signature and MACs are used for guaranteeing message integrity and authentication. MAC algorithms do not provide non-repudiation service because the secret used to produce MACs may be shared by more than two users; and even with two users, both can produce MACs. Whereas with digital signatures, each key is private to each user; hence, there is non-repudiation as only the private keyholder can sign with his/her key.

It is worth noticing that message authentication and user authentication are distinct services. Message authentication, also called message origin authentication, enables the receiver to check that the MAC accompanying a message has been generated by a user sharing a key with him/her. Whereas user authentication (also called entity authentication) enables the recipient to check if the message sender engaged in the current session is really the person who is pretending to be. Let us take the following two scenarios to show the difference between both authentications.

Alice, Bob, and Eve share a secret. Bob computes the MAC of a message, then sends the message and its MAC to Alice. Alice forwards the message and the MAC to Eve, who can verify that the message was originated by a holder of the shared secret. However, Eve is not communicating with Bob; thus, she cannot authenticate him.

Alice and Eve know the public key of Bob. Bob signs a message and sends the message and its signature to Alice. Alice forwards the message and signature to Eve, who can verify that the message was signed by Bob. However, Eve is not communicating with Bob; thus, she cannot authenticate him. Thus, used alone, neither MACs nor signatures provide entity authentication. Other mechanisms are required to provide user authentication (see Chapter 15).

5.6 Problems

5.6.1 List of Problems

Problem 5.1
Fundamental security properties include confidentiality, integrity, authenticity, and non-repudiation.

1) Which of the above properties are provided by digital signature?
2) Which of the above properties are provided by MACs?

Problem 5.2
Hashing and encryption are two cryptographic functions, which manipulate inputs to produce a kind of random output. What is the fundamental difference between those functions from a security point of view?

Problem 5.3
Discuss why the following functions cannot be used as hash functions regarding preimage and collision resistance properties:

1) $H_1(x)$ is a function that returns the parity bit of x.
2) $H_2(x)$ is defined by $H_2(M) = P(M) \ mod \ g(x)$
where $P(M)$ is a polynomial associated with M such that $P(M) = m_i.x^i + m_{i-1}.x^{i-1} + m_1.x^1 + m_0$, where $m_i, ..., m_0$ are bits of M and $g(x)$ is a given polynomial of degree k.

Problem 5.4
Discuss the hash function properties of the following function for generating MACs.
Let X be a bit-string; $X = X_1 \ || \ X_2 \ || ... || \ X_m$, where $X_{i=1,...,m}$ are 128-bit blocks.
Given a 128-bit key K, the MAC is generated as follows:

$$MAC(X,k) = C_m + K \ mod \ 2^{128}$$

where: $C_0 = 99$ and $C_i = C_{i-1} \oplus X_i, i = 1, ..., m$

Problem 5.5

Discuss why CRC (Cyclic Redundancy Check), used to protect against transmission errors, is not appropriate for use as hash functions? Which hash function properties are not fulfilled with CRCs?

Problem 5.6

Why collision-free hash functions do not exist?

Problem 5.7

Prove that a collision-resistant hash function also is second-preimage resistant.

Problem 5.8

Let $H_1: \{0,1\}^{2m} \to \{0,1\}^m$ be a collision-resistant hash function.

Define $H_2: \{0,1\}^{4m} \to \{0,1\}^m$ as follows:

$H_2(x_1 \| x_2) = H_1\big(H_1(x_1) \| H_1(x_2)\big)$, where $x_1 \in \{0,1\}^{2m}$ and $x_2 \in \{0,1\}^{2m}$

Prove that H_2 also is collision-resistant.

Problem 5.9

Let $H_1()$ be a collision-resistant hash function. Do the following constructions provide collision-resistant hash functions?

1) $H_2(x) = H_1(x) \| x$
2) $H_3(x) = H_1(x \oplus 1)$
3) $H_4(x) = H_1(x \oplus c)$, c is a constant integer less than $\max(x)$.

Problem 5.10

One of the applications of hash functions is the protection of passwords in authentication systems. Instead of storing the passwords in clear, only password hashes are stored. To authenticate a user, his/her password is hashed and the resulting hash is compared to that stored on the authentication system. Therefore, even if the password file is stolen, the passwords are very hard to recover. Assume that the hash function used by an attacked authentication system is known to the adversary.

1) Is it secure to use a hash bit-length of 10 to protect 500 passwords?
2) Assume that an adversary has access to 1000 hashes of 8-byte passwords. Is it difficult, from the computational feasibility point of view, for the adversary to gain access to the system as a legitimate user with a brute-force attack?
3) Assume that each of 1000 passwords is concatenated to a random input called *salt* so that the appended password has a bit-length of 512. The authentication system stores the 128-bit hashes of passwords in a file and the salts in another file. Consider an adversary who has access to the hash file but not the salt file. Can the adversary gain access to the system?

Problem 5.11

Assume that the hash function used by Alice manipulates blocks with a length of 512 bits and the maximum size of data to hash is 1 G bytes. Alice has an album of 1000 pictures each of 1 M bytes. She has two alternatives to send her album to Bob: either hash and send each picture separately or zip the album, then hash and send the hashed zipped file.

1) What is the most attack-resistant alternative?
2) Assume that the second preimage is feasible but at a high cost for the adversary. Which alternative is preferred if integrity is of interest?

Problem 5.12

Deterministic generic attacks are attacks that break hash resistance whatever is the hash function. What is the maximum number of steps required for a generic deterministic attack to succeed in finding a preimage, a second preimage or a collision? Assume that no dictionary is built in advance.

Problem 5.13

Prove that the number of steps required to preimage brute-force-attack to succeed (at a probability close to 1) is approximately 2^n, where n is the hash bit-length. Use Taylor's approximation of e^x, which states that: $e^x \approx 1 + x$, when $|x| \ll 1$.

Problem 5.14

1) Prove that the number of steps required for a collision birthday attack to succeed at a 50% probability is approximately $2^{n/2}$, where n is the hash bit-length. Birthday paradox is presented in Section 3.4.
2) Infer that the number of steps required to collision birthday attack to succeed at a probability close to 1 is approximately $2^{n/2}$.

Problem 5.15
Why key length is required in length extension attack?

Problem 5.16
Length extension attack is introduced in Section 5.1.3.2.

1) Explain why SHA-512/224 and SHA-512/256 are not vulnerable to length extension attack.
2) Explain why SHA-3 is not vulnerable to length extension attack.

Problem 5.17
Imagine that a journalist and an editor use a MAC algorithm for message authentication. Then the editor posts a content sent by the journalist who claims he/she never authored the posted content. In case of legal dispute, who is the winner? In security terms, do MACs provide non-repudiation service?

Problem 5.18
In length extension attack (see Section 5.1.3.2), the adversary takes advantage of the internal operation of Merkle-Damgård construction, to append fake data at the end of the original and to generate a MAC without knowledge of the secret key.

1) Show that secret prefix MAC is vulnerable to length extension attack.
2) Assume that the MAC algorithm includes the length of message in the hash computation, i.e. $MAC(M,k) = H(key \| len(Message) \| Message)$. Does the length extension attack still work against secret prefix MAC, designed with such a hash function, under the assumption the key length is known to adversary?
3) Show that secret suffix MAC is not vulnerable to length extension attack.

Problem 5.19
Explain why HMAC inner hash is vulnerable to length extension attack, while the outer hash is not vulnerable.

5.6.2 Solutions to Problems

Problem 5.1
Fundamental security properties include confidentiality, integrity, authenticity, and non-repudiation.

1) Digital signature provides guarantees regarding integrity, authenticity, and non-repudiation. However, if the plaintext is not encrypted, the digital signature cannot provide confidentiality.
2) MACs provide integrity and message authenticity guarantees. They do not guarantee confidentiality, if the message is not encrypted. They do not provide non-repudiation guarantees, as well.

Problem 5.2
Hashing and encryption are two distinct cryptographic functions. Encryption is something used to convert plaintext (readable) into ciphertext (indecipherable). Decryption is done either with the same ciphering key, which is a secret, in symmetric systems or with a key mathematically related to the encryption key in asymmetric systems. In asymmetric systems, messages are encrypted with public keys and then decrypted with private keys. Hashing is a technique used to produce a fingerprint to characterize uniquely a data, while it does not hide data. In hashing, nothing is secret. Encryption is for ensuring confidentiality, while hashing is for ensuring integrity.

Problem 5.3
1) $H_1(x)$ is a function that returns the parity bit of x.
   Given a value of parity bit (i.e. 0 or 1), the half of the input space matches the chosen value. Thus, H_1 is not preimage resistant.
   The probability of collision is 50%. Thus, H_1 is not collision-resistant.
2) $H_2(x)$ is defined by $H_2(M) = P(M) \mod g(x)$.
   Let k denote the degree of polynomial $g(x)$, L denote the degree of polynomial $P(M)$, and $Q(x)$ a polynomial of degree $L-k$.
   Given a hash z, any message M such that $P(M) = g(x) * Q(x) + P(z)$ matches the chosen hash z. $P(z)$ denotes the polynomial associated with the bit string representing z. Thus, H_2 is not preimage-resistant.
   All message M' such that $P(M') = g(x) * Q(x) + r(x)$, where $r(x)$ is a polynomial of degree less than k, have the same hash, which is $r(x)$. Thus, H_2 is not collision-resistant.

Problem 5.4

With the given function, the MAC is computed as: $MAC(X,K) = C_m + K \bmod 2^{128}$

$$C_m = C_{m-1} \oplus X_m = \left(C_{m-2} \oplus X_{m-1}\right) \oplus X_m = C_0 \oplus X_1 \oplus X_2 \oplus \ldots \oplus X_m.$$

The function defined above does not match any hash function property.

No collision resistance: it is easy to find collisions. For example, all permutations of three blocks have the same MAC. That is:

$$MAC\left(X_1 \parallel X_2 \parallel X_3, K\right) = MAC\left(X_2 \parallel X_1 \parallel X_3, K\right) = MAC\left(X_3 \parallel X_1 \parallel X_2, K\right) = \ldots$$

No preimage resistance: given a MAC h, it is easy to find a preimage. For example, a preimage with a single block X_1 can be easily found, if C_0 and K are known, by the congruence relationship: $h = \left(C_0 \oplus X_1\right) + K \bmod 2^{128}$

No second preimage resistance: given a bit string X and its MAC h, it is easy to find another bit string X' with the same MAC. For example, we can replace blocks X_1 and X_2 in X to obtain X' with the same MAC:

$$h = C_m + K \bmod 2^{128} = \left(C_m \oplus 0\right) + K \bmod 2^{128} = \left(C_m \oplus B \oplus B\right) + K \bmod 2^{128}$$

$$= C_0 \oplus \left(X_1 \oplus B\right) \oplus \left(X_2 \oplus B\right) \oplus \ldots \oplus X_m + K \bmod 2^{128} = MAC\left(X', K\right)$$

where B is an arbitrary 128-bit block.

Problem 5.5

Recall that CRC-based technique to detect transmission operates as follows:

Let S denote a bit string to transmit. A polynomial $S(x)$ is associated with the string S, where the polynomial coefficients are the bits of S. A generator polynomial $G(x)$ of degree n (n is the number of bits of CRC) is used to compute the CRC as:

$$CRC(x) \equiv \left(S(x) * x^n\right) \bmod G(x).$$

For example, compute a 3-bit CRC for string 10111 with $G(x) = x^3 + x + 1$.

$$CRC(x) \equiv \left(\left(x^4 + x^2 + x + 1\right) * x^3\right) \bmod \left(x^3 + x + 1\right) = x + 1.$$

Thus, the CRC is 011.

CRC-based functions cannot be securely used as hash functions, because of the following:

No collision resistance: it is easy to find collisions, because any pair of bit strings S_1 and S_2 such that $S_1(x) = S_2(x) + q(x) * G(x)$ or $S_2(x) = S_1(x) + q'(x) * G(x)$, where $q(x)$ and $q'(x)$ are two polynomials with binary coefficients, have the same CRC.

No preimage resistance: it is easy to find the preimage given a CRC C, because any bit string S such that $S(x) = C(x) + q(x) * G(x)$ is a preimage to C, where $q(x)$ is a polynomial.

No second preimage resistance: it is easy to change a bit string S_1 to another bit string S_2 while keeping the original hash C, if $S_2(x) = S_1(x) + q'(x) * G(x)$.

Problem 5.6

Collisions are intrinsic to all existing hash functions. Collison-free hash functions do not exist for, at least, the following reasons:

In practice, the input space is much larger than the input space. Thus, the same output value is an image for multiple input values. In mathematics, the *pigeonhole principle* states that if N items are put into m containers, with $N > m$ then at least one container must contain more than one item.

Even if the output space size is equal or greater than the input space size, the probability of collision in all existing hash functions is not zero. In addition, increasing the size of the hash function output results in more consumption or storage and communication resources.

Problem 5.7

Recall that attack-resistance of hash functions qualifies the difficulty, from the computational point of view, of finding collisions or preimage and not the property that collisions do not exist or that preimage can never be found. The statement to prove is: a collision-resistant hash function also is second-preimage resistant. The suggested proof is by contradiction. Assume that a hash function H is collision-resistant but not second-preimage resistant. If H is not second-preimage resistant, then, given an input x, one can find an input x' such that $x \neq x'$ and $H(x) = H(x')$. However, if one can find two distinct inputs with the same hash, he/she can prove that H is not collision-resistant, which is a contradiction with the hypothesis that H is collision-resistant.

Problem 5.8

Let $H_1: \{0,1\}^{2m} \rightarrow \{0,1\}^m$ be a collision-resistant hash function.
Let $H_2: \{0,1\}^{4m} \rightarrow \{0,1\}^m$ be a hash function defined by:

$$H_2(x_1 \| x_2) = H_1(H_1(x_1) \| H_1(x_2)).$$

The suggested proof of H_2 collision-resistance is by contradiction.

If H_2 is not collision-resistant, then one can find two pairs (x_1, x_2) and (x_1', x_2') such that $x_1 \neq x_1'$ or $x_2 \neq x_2'$ ("or" is inclusive) and $H_2(x_1 \| x_2) = H_2(x_1' \| x_2')$.

By substitution:

$$H_1(H_1(x_1) \| H_1(x_2)) = H_1(H_1(x_1') \| H_1(x_2')).$$

Since H_1 is collision-resistant, it is computationally infeasible to find two bit strings $H_1(x_1) \| H_1(x_2)$ and $H_1(x_1') \| H_1(x_2')$ that have the same hash. In consequence, H_2 also is collision-resistant.

Problem 5.9

Let $H_1()$ be a collision-resistant hash function.
1) $H_2(x) = H_1(x) \| x$
   If H_2 is not collision-resistant, then one can find $x_1 \neq x_2$ such that

   $$H_2(x_1) = H_2(x_2).$$

   By substitution, the equality becomes:

   $$H_1(x_1) \| x_1 = H_1(x_2) \| x_2$$

   Since H_1 is collision-resistant, if $x_1 \neq x_2$, then $H_1(x_1) \neq H_1(x_2)$.
   Thus, the bit strings $H_1(x_1) \| x_1$ and $H_1(x_2) \| x_2$ are distinct. Hence, H_2 is collision-resistant.
2) $H_3(x) = H_1(x \oplus 1)$.
   Let z be a bit string and x_1 and x_2 two bit strings starting with z and ending with distinct bits, i.e.

   $$x_1 = z \| 0 \text{ and } x_2 = z \| 1$$

   $$x_1 \oplus 1 = (z \| 0) \oplus 1 = z \| 0$$

   $$x_2 \oplus 1 = (z \| 1) \oplus 1 = z \| 0$$

   By construction of H_3:

   $$H_3(x_1) = H_1(x_1 \oplus 1) = H_1(z \| 0)$$

   $$H_3(x_2) = H_1(x_2 \oplus 1) = H_1(z \| 0)$$

   Thus, a collision is found and consequently H_3 is not collision-resistant.
3) $H_4(x) = H_1(x \oplus c)$, c is a constant integer less than x.
   Let $c_0, c_1, ..., c_{k-1}$ be the bits of constant c.

Let x_1 and x_2 be two bit strings that differ at least by one bit at position i such that $0 \leq i \leq k-1 : x_1 = z \| 0 \| y$ and $x_2 = z \| 1 \| y$

If $c_i = 1$, then $x_1 \oplus c = x_2 \oplus c = z \| 0 \| y$.

By construction of H_4:

$$H_4(x_1) = H_1(x_1 \oplus c) = H_1(z \| 0 \| y)$$
$$H_4(x_2) = H_1(x_2 \oplus c) = H_1(z \| 0 \| y)$$

Thus, a collision is found and consequently H_4 is not collision-resistant.

Problem 5.10

1) With a hash bit-length of 10, the hash space is of 2^{10}. If the number of hashed passwords is 500, any randomly chosen password, whatever is its length, has a chance of $\frac{500}{2^{10}} \approx \frac{1}{2}$ to have a hash, which is present in the authentication system list. Therefore, using small hash length is not secure to protect passwords.

2) The password space is of 2^{8*8}. Computing the hashes of all potential passwords is computationally feasible. The number of hash computations is 2^{64}, which is low compared to the bound of 2^{90} (i.e. the limit of computationally feasibility with current technologies). Then, the adversary builds an attack dictionary of 1000 entries each containing a valid hash (i.e. a hash that is included in the list stolen by the adversary) and the corresponding passwords. Then, the adversary selects a password to log in the system.

3) The space of passwords with salt is of 2^{512} and that of hashes is of 2^{128} but only 1000 passwords were hashed. The probability to pick a random password and a random salt such that the resulting hash is in the system list is $\frac{1000}{2^{128}} \approx \frac{1}{2^{118}}$.

Computing the hashes of 2^{512} distinct passwords is computationally infeasible. Therefore, adding salt and using large hash bit-length make the authentication system resistant to hash file theft.

Problem 5.11

1) Attack-resistance means resistance to preimage, second preimage, and collision attacks. The security strength of a hash function depends on the hash size and not on the size of the hashed data size. Thus, from the hash attack perspective, both alternatives are equivalent.

2) *Integrity* means integrity of pictures received by Bob. In the first alternative, if a picture is second-preimage attacked, Bob receives a fake picture (but he does know it is a fake picture!). In the second alternative, if the entire album is second-preimage attacked, Bob receives a fake album (but he does know it is a fake album!). Finding a fake image for each of the 1000 pictures takes more time than finding one fake image for the entire album. Therefore, the first alternative provides more chance to Bob to receive authentic pictures.

Problem 5.12

A deterministic attack provides absolute guarantees that the searched information is found when the attack ends. Let 2^n be the hash space size and S the size of the input space. In generic deterministic attack, the adversary tests one by on each element in the input space and stops when the searched element is found.

Let $C(i)$, $0 \leq i \leq 2^n$, be the number of elements, which hash to i.

Let $E(i)$, $0 \leq i \leq 2^n$, be the set of input elements, which hash to i.

Deterministic preimage attack:

The worst case to the deterministic preimage attack is when the given hash z has the lowest value of $C(i)$, i.e. $C(z) = \min_{0 \leq i \leq 2^n} C(i)$, and the elements of the subset $E(z)$ are last to be tested. The attack ends when the first element of $E(z)$ is tested. Thus, the worst case of test number for a deterministic preimage attack is: $S - \left(\min_{0 \leq i \leq 2^n} C(i) - 1 \right)$.

Deterministic second-preimage attack:

The worst case to the deterministic second-preimage attack is when the given element x hashes to z, which has the lowest value of $C(i)$, i.e. $C(z) = \min_{0 \leq i \leq 2^n} C(i)$, and the elements of subset $E(z) - \{x\}$ are last to be tested. The attack ends when the first element of $E(z) - \{x\}$ is tested. Thus, the worst case of test number for a deterministic second-preimage attack is: $S - \left(\min_{0 \leq i \leq 2^n} C(i) - 1 - 1 \right)$.

Deterministic collision attack:

The attack may be history-aware (i.e. the adversary caches the hashes already computed) or memoryless (i.e. adversary does not cache the hashes already computed). In memoryless attack, the adversary selects randomly an input element and tries to find another input element with the same hash. The worst-case test number is the same as for the second-preimage attack. In case of history-aware, the worst case for testing occurs when all the first 2^n input elements have distinct hashes. Thus, the worst-case test number is $2^n + 1$ for history-aware collision-attack.

Problem 5.13

Preimage brute-force attack takes as input a hash h and tries to find a message x that hashes to h. The adversary takes a random message and compares its hash to h. If hashes are distinct, he/she tries another message until the calculated hash matches the given hash h. Let $P(N)$ denote the probability that the hash of the Nth message matches the given hash h.

$\overline{P}(N) = 1 - P(N)$ denotes that the probability that no matching hash is found with the N tested (distinct) messages. Since there exist 2^n hash values, given a random message M, the probability[15] that $H(M) \neq h$ is $1 - \dfrac{1}{2^n}$. Thus, $\overline{P}(N) = \left(1 - \dfrac{1}{2^n}\right)^N$.

$\dfrac{1}{2^n}$ is a very small value. Therefore, we can use Taylor's formula for exponentiation approximation: $e^{-\frac{1}{2^n}} \approx 1 - \dfrac{1}{2^n}$

By substitution and simplification:

$$\overline{P}(N) \approx \left(e^{-\frac{1}{2^n}}\right)^N = e^{-\frac{N}{2^n}}$$

$$e^{-\frac{N}{2^n}} \approx 1 - P(N)$$

$$e^{\frac{N}{2^n}} \approx \frac{1}{1 - P(N)}$$

$$\ln\left(e^{\frac{N}{2^n}}\right) \approx \ln\left(\frac{1}{1 - P(N)}\right)$$

$$N \approx 2^n * \ln\left(\frac{1}{1 - P(N)}\right)$$

In the previous formula, $P(N) = 1$ cannot be used. Thus, the probability of success is $1 - \varepsilon$. $N \approx 2^n * \ln\left(\dfrac{1}{\varepsilon}\right)$. At $\varepsilon = 0.01$, $\ln\left(\dfrac{1}{\varepsilon}\right) = 3.0$ and at $\varepsilon = 10^{-20}$, $\ln\left(\dfrac{1}{\varepsilon}\right) = 6.79$. Thus, when n is large, 2^n is a good approximation of N.

Problem 5.14

1) In the basic birthday paradox, the problem is to find the minimum number of people such that at least a pair among them share the same birthday. When collision attack is of concern, the birthday problem may be reformulated as: find the number of input elements so that two elements have the same hash. In case of collision birthday attack, input elements are selected randomly and hashes are associated with them. The hash is the equivalent of the birthday in the basic paradox. Hence, the input space is the hash space. The attack terminates when two hashes are equal. In Section 3.4, three approximations of the number of elements to use for finding two elements with the same value are presented. In the general case, two formulas may be used to approximate the required number of elements: $N \approx \sqrt{2S * P(N)}$ or $N \approx \sqrt{2S * ln(1/(1 - P(N)))}$ where S denotes the cardinality of the input space and $P(N)$ the probability of finding two equal elements among N randomly selected elements. In case of collision birthday attack, S is the cardinality of the input hash space function of 2^n, where n is the hash bit-length. By substitution with $P(N) = 0.5$:

First approximation yields: $N \approx \sqrt{2 * 2^n * 0.5} = \sqrt{2^n} = 2^{n/2}$

Second approximation yields: $N \approx \sqrt{S * 2 * \ln(2)} = 2^{n/2} * 1.77 < 2^{(n+1)/2}$.

2) "always succeed" means finding a collision with a probability of 1. Approximation $N \approx \sqrt{2S * P(N)}$ may be used with $P(N) = 100\%$ and results in $N \approx 2^{1/2} * 2^{n/2}$, which may be approximated by $2^{n/2}$ when n is large.

Approximation $\sqrt{2S * \ln(1/(1 - P(N))}$ cannot be used with $P(N) = 100\%$, but with $P(N) = 1 - \varepsilon$, where ε is a positive integer very close to 0. Thus, the approximation becomes: $N \approx \sqrt{S * 2 * \ln\left(\dfrac{1}{\varepsilon}\right)} = 2^{n/2} * \sqrt{2 * \ln\left(\dfrac{1}{\varepsilon}\right)}$.

At $\varepsilon = 0.01$, $\sqrt{2 * \ln\left(\dfrac{1}{\varepsilon}\right)} = 3.0$ and at $\varepsilon = 10^{-10}$, $\sqrt{2 * \ln\left(\dfrac{1}{\varepsilon}\right)} = 6.7$. Thus, when n is large, $2^{n/2}$ is a good approximation of N.

Problem 5.15

Given a message M, the adversary easily computes the length of padding string for M. However, the sender computes the padding string for string $key \parallel M$ to generate $H(key \parallel M)$. Without knowing the length of key, the adversary is unable to compute the length for padding string $key \parallel M$. Therefore, he/she cannot run the length extension attack.

Problem 5.16

1) In SHA-384, SHA-512/224, and SHA-512/256, the initialization hash H^0 and the block hashes H^i, $i = 1, ..., N$, are represented as eight words of 64 bits. But, the message hash is produced by truncation of H^N, the hash of the last block. From the later, SHA-384 keeps six 64-bit words, SHA-512/224 keeps three 64-bit words and the left half of the fourth 64-bit word, and SHA-512/256 keeps four 64-bit words. Message hash and initialization hash H^0 have different lengths. Consequently, the message hash cannot be used as H^0 to enable the adversary extend the original message. In other words, hash obtained by truncation prevents the hash function from length extension attack.

2) In SHA-3, the hash function output length d is the half of Keccak-p permutation capacity c. Inside the sponge function, Keccak-p permutation takes an input of b bits, called state array, with $b > c$. In squeezing step, the message hash is produced by truncation. Consequently, the message hash intercepted by the adversary cannot be substituted to the initial state array to realize a length extension attack.

Problem 5.17

Recall that non-repudiation is the assurance that a message originator cannot deny having sent the message (e.g. denying having sent a newspaper article). First, since MACs do not address confidentiality, messages with MACs can be checked by more than one receiver and any user who share the secret with the sender(s) can produce valid MACs. For example, a pool of journalists shares the same secret with their editor. Second, in case the sender is malicious (e.g. a malicious editor), he/she can generate a MAC and then claims he/she received it from a journalist. Consequently, if the sender and receiver get involved in a dispute over message origination, MACs cannot provide a proof that a message was indeed sent by the designated sender.

Problem 5.18

Length extension means appending a bit string F to the end of the original message. Without loss of generality, assume that the length of string F is a multiple of the block length of the targeted hash function.

1) In secret prefix MAC, $MAC(M, key) = H(key \parallel M)$.

The input bit string $key \parallel M \parallel P$ are structured into a sequence $\left(B^1, B^2, ..., B^n\right)$ of blocks of fixed size L, which is a parameter of the hash function. P denotes the padding bits added so that the length of $key \parallel M \parallel P$ is a multiple of the block length of the hash function.

$$MAC(M, key) = H\left(key \parallel M \parallel P\right) = H\left(B^1 \parallel B^2 \parallel ... \parallel B^n\right)$$

In Merkle-Damgård construction, block B^1 and initialization vector, which also is referred to as H^0, are used as inputs of the hash function to produce H^1, then H^1 and block B^2 are used to produce H^2, etc. and finally, H^n represents $H(key \parallel M \parallel P)$. Length extension attack takes advantage of the design of Merkle-Damgård construction to adapt the hash function H, such that H^0 is not a constant vector, rather it takes the value of $H(key \parallel M \parallel P)$. Hashing block(s) of fake data F with $H^0 = H(key \parallel M \parallel P)$ looks like a continuation of blocks of the string $key \parallel M \parallel P$, and the resulting hash $H(key \parallel M \parallel P \parallel F)$ is a MAC that would be produced by a legitimate party. Consequently, secret prefix MACs are vulnerable to length extension attack.

2) The hash available to the adversary is $H(key \parallel len(M) \parallel M \parallel P)$.

Let B be the sequence of blocks $\left(B^1, B^2, ..., B^n\right)$ such that

$$B^1 \parallel B^2 \parallel ... \parallel B^n = key \parallel len\left(M\right) \parallel M \parallel P$$

Let F be the bit string appended by the adversary. Upon reception of the forged message, the verifier computes the hash as $H(key \parallel (len(M) + len(F)) \parallel M \parallel F \parallel P')$, where P' is the padding bits for the string $key \parallel (len(M) + len(F)) \parallel M \parallel F$.

Let A be the sequence of blocks $\left(A^1, A^2, ..., A^n, ..., A^{n+d}\right)$ such that

$A^1 \parallel A^2 \parallel \ldots \parallel A^{n+d} = key \parallel (len(M) + len(F)) \parallel M \parallel F \parallel P'$, where d depends on the bit-length of string F.

The sequences B and A start with the same blocks, which represent the *key*. Then, after hashing the *key* block(s), both sequences are distinct; sequence B continues with a block including $len(M)$, while sequence A continues with a block including $len(M) + len(F)$. Consequently, $H(A^1 \parallel A^2 \parallel \ldots \parallel A^{n+d})$ computed by the verifier with $H^0 = IV$ is distinct from $H(F)$ computed by the adversary with $H^0 = H(B^1 \parallel B^2 \parallel \ldots \parallel B^n)$. Since the hash known to the adversary is computed with the original message and the adversary has no means to find a new hash computed with the lengths of the original message and the appended data F, the length extension attack cannot succeed.

3) In secret suffix MAC, $MAC(M, key) = H(M \parallel P \parallel key)$.

The hash available to the adversary is $H(M \parallel P \parallel key)$. Suppose that the adversary appends a string F. The verifier computes the hash as $H(M \parallel P \parallel F \parallel key)$ with $H^0 = IV$, and the adversary computes $H(F)$ with $H^0 = H(M \parallel P \parallel key)$. The input hash of the verifier when he/she starts hashing blocks of F is $H(M \parallel P)$, while the input state used by the adversary is $H(M \parallel P \parallel key)$. Those two hashes are distinct. Thus, the adversary cannot realize a length extension attack.

Problem 5.19

Inner hash of HMAC is $h_{(i)} = H(k' \oplus iPad \parallel M)$ and its outer hash is $h_{(o)} = H(k' \oplus oPad \parallel h_{(i)})$. The outer hash is the output of HMAC algorithm.

The inner hash is designed according to the secret prefix MAC; hence, it is vulnerable to length extension attack (see Problem 5.18).

Assume that the adversary appends a fake string F to the original message M. Let $M' = M \parallel F$. The length extension attack works like if the first part of M', i.e. M, is hashed at sender and the second part, i.e. F, is hashed at adversary as a continuation using the hash produced by the sender. However, the inner hash is not available to the adversary and the output of HMAC is a hash of a hash combined with the key. Hence, the adversary has no means to use a hash output to substitute to initialization vector to continue hashing. Thus, HMAC algorithm is not vulnerable to length extension attack.

Notes

1 Digital signature is an encrypted hash.

2 Sometimes, hash function and hashing algorithm are used interchangeably.

3 The maximum value of N depends on the used hash function.

4 Such a property is called *avalanche effect*.

5 The time complexity of attacks refers to the same issue than the number of steps.

6 Here "adapt" means changing the implantation of the hash function to make the attack feasible.

7 SHA-3 standard does not fix any bound on the message size.

8 SHA-3 transformation functions manipulate blocks with a fixed length of 1600 bits divided into two parts: $1600 - 2d$ bits are message bits and $2d$ bits are bits specific to the permutation function at the core of SHA-3. d is the hash bit-length, a value in $\{224, 256, 384, 512\}$.

9 Keccak is the name of the research team who proposed the hash functions based on sponge construction.

10 "p" is used in Keccak-p permutation to distinguish it from other types of Keccak permutations.

11 Sometimes MAC is referred to as *tag* or *cryptographic checksum*.

12 *iPad* and *oPad* stand for inner and outer pads.

13 For an integer z in $[0, 255]$, $enc8(z)$ is the byte-encoding of z, with bit 0 being the low-order bit of the byte.

14 In the three digital signature standards currently in use, namely RSASSA, DSA, and Elliptic-curve-based DSA, only signature with appendix is supported.

15 Assuming that the hash values are uniformly distributed.

References

1 Merkle, R. (1989). One way hash functions and DES. *9th Annual International Cryptology Conference, Advances in Cryptology - CRYPTO'89*, 428–446. Santa Barbara, California: Springer, LNCS 435.

2 Damgard, I. (1989). A design principle for hash functions. *9th Annual International Cryptology Conference, Advances in Cryptology - CRYPTO'89*, 416–427. Santa Barbara, California: Springer, LNCS 435.

3 Bertoni, G., Daemen, J., Peeters, P. et al. (2007). Sponge functions. *ECRYPT Hash Functions Workshop*, 1–22. Barcelona, Spain.

4 Bertoni, G., Daemen, J., Peeters, P. et al. (2008). On the indifferentiability of the sponge construction. *27th Annual International Conference on the Theory and Applications of Cryptographic Techniques, Advances in Cryptology*, 181–197. Istanbul, Turkey: Springer, LNCS 4965.

5 NIST. (1995). *Secure hash standard - FIPS PUB 180-1*. National Institute of Standards and Technology.

6 NIST. (2015). *Secure hash standard - FIPS PUB 180-4*. National Institute of Standards and Technology.

7 Leurent, G. and Peyrin, T. (2020). SHA-1 is a shambles: first chosen-prefix collision on SHA-1 and application to the PGP web of trust. *29th USENIX Security Symposium*, 1839–1856. Boston, US: Unix Association.

8 NIST. (2015). *SHA-3 Standard: Permutation-Based Hash and Extendable-Output Functions - FIPS PUB 202*. National Institute of Standards and Technology.

9 Bellare, M., Canetti, R., and Krawczyk, H. (1996). Keying hash functions and message authentication. *Annual International Cryptology Conference, Advances in Cryptology - Crypto'96*, 1–15. Santa Barbara, California: Springer, LNCS 1109.

10 Krawczyk, H., Bellare, M., and Canetti, R. (1997). *HMAC: Keyed-Hashing for Message Authentication - RFC 2104*. Internet Engineering Task Force.

11 Kelsey, J., Chang, S., and Perlner, R. (2016). *SHA-3 Derived Functions: cSHAKE, KMAC, TupleHash and ParalleHash, Special Publication 800-185*. National Institute for Standards and Technology (NIST).

6

Stream Ciphers

Stream ciphers are symmetric ciphers that encrypt and decrypt bits individually. They are used to secure communications in wireless and cellular networks. Stream ciphers are well-suited to hardware implementation and they are generally faster than block ciphers. They also are well-suited to encrypt and decrypt continuous data (e.g. phone communication) at high rate and when devices have limited memory to store long messages. That is why, stream ciphers are often used in telecommunication networks, such as 3G, 4G, and 5G.

ChaCha20 stream cipher is an Internet standard; it is recommended as a cipher in TLS protocol to secure communications between clients and web servers [1]. Most common stream ciphers are built around linear feedback shift registers, which makes them easy to implement in hardware.

This chapter aims at presenting the principles and standard algorithms related to stream ciphers.

6.1 Stream Ciphers

6.1.1 Principles of Stream Ciphers

*Definition 6.1 **Stream cipher**: it is a symmetric cipher where plaintext bits are pairwise combined with bits of a key stream. Each bit of ciphertext is yielded by a bitwise XOR operation.*

*Definition 6.2 **Initialization vector (IV)**: it is a bit string computed for each plaintext (or for a set of plaintexts) and used jointly with the secret key to generate the keystream.*

There are two main reasons to use and frequently change initialization vectors: 1) long sequences of keystream require periodic synchronization of encryption and decryption processes (because of transmission errors) and 2) encrypting distinct plaintexts with the same key is insecure. Therefore, initialization vectors is a solution to generate different pseudorandom sequences without necessarily changing the secret key.

*Definition 6.3 **Key-Scheduling Algorithm (KSA)**: it is the operation of mixing the secret key and the Initialization vector to yield a key, which is then used to encrypt/decrypt a single plaintext.*

As shown in Figure 6.1, the main building block of cipher stream is the keystream generator. The latter is a PRNG (pseudo random number generator), which generates a stream of bits given a secret key and an initialization vector.

Stream ciphers were inspired by One-time pad cipher (see Section 4.6). Unlike OTP cipher, in which the key stream is at least as long as the data to encrypt, stream ciphers make use of periodic PRNGs.

The secret key is shared by both parties. Therefore, the keystream generators on both sides generate the same sequence of keystream bits. Encryption and decryption operations are very simple. Let a_i and s_j be the current plaintext and keystream bits, respectively. Formally,

Encryption is: $c_i = a_i \oplus s_j \ mod \ 2$
Decryption is: $a_i = c_i \oplus s_j \ mod \ 2$

Cryptography: Algorithms, Protocols, and Standards for Computer Security, First Edition. Zoubir Mammeri.
© 2024 John Wiley & Sons, Inc. Published 2024 by John Wiley & Sons, Inc.

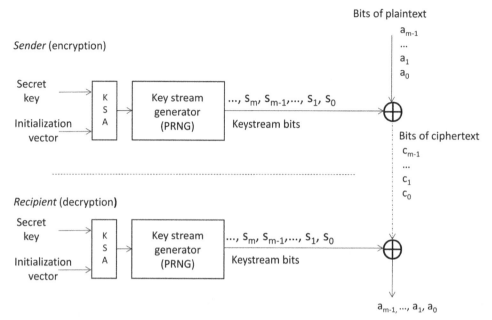

Figure 6.1   General structure of stream cipher (synchronous model).

where $\oplus$ denoted the XOR bitwise[1] operation.

Since the keystream generator produces a keystream, which is periodic, the same keystream may be used to encrypt (or decrypt) more than one plaintext (or ciphertext). That is why two distinct indices i and j are used.

It is very easy to check that the decryption process is correct:

$$c_i \oplus s_j \ mod \ 2 = \left(a_i \oplus s_j \ mod \ 2\right) \oplus s_j \ mod \ 2 = a_i \oplus s_j \oplus s_j \ mod \ 2 = a_i$$

In binary field, adding twice an element is equivalent to adding 0.

Example 6.1

Encryption

Plaintext	1100110101001110
Keystream	$\oplus$ 1000011111001011
Ciphertext	0100101010000101

Encryption

Ciphertext	0100101010000101
Keystream	$\oplus$ 1000011111001011
Plaintext	1100110101001110

6.1.2   Synchronous vs Self-synchronized Keystream Generators

To decrypt correctly, both parties must use the same keystream to encrypt and recover the same plaintext bit. Therefore, both parties need to be synchronized when using keystream bits. There exist two types of keystream generators: synchronous and self-synchronized.

Definition 6.4 Synchronous stream cipher*: it is a cipher in which the keystream is generated independently of the plaintext and of the ciphertext.*

Definition 6.5 Self-clocking stream cipher*: it is a cipher in which the keystream is generated from a key function and a fixed number of previous ciphertext bits.*

6.1.2.1 Synchronous Stream Ciphers

In a synchronous stream cipher, both parties initialize one time (per session or message) their keystream with the same values (i.e. secret key and initialization vector) and then encrypt and decrypt bits until the end of session or message. Formally, encryption and decryption may be described as follows:

Let $Init(K, IV)$ be a function that initializes the keystream cipher using a secret key K and an initialization vector IV and $Next()$ a function, which yields the next state of the keystream generator. In section 6.1.4, $Next()$ function will be addressed in detail. Let σ_i denote the state and $g(\sigma_i)$, the output of the keystream generator at cycle i, $i = 0, 1, \ldots$ Then, encryption and decryption can be described as:

# Encryption side	# Decryption side
$\sigma_0 = Init(K, IV)$	$\sigma_0 = Init(K, IV)$
for each plaintext bit i **do**	**for** each ciphertext bit i **do**
$s_i = g(\sigma_i)$	$s_i = g(\sigma_i)$
$c_i = a_i \oplus s_j \bmod 2$	$a_i = c_i \oplus s_j \bmod 2$
$\sigma_{i+1} = Next(\sigma_i)$	$\sigma_{i+1} = Next(\sigma_i)$

Synchronous stream ciphers have at least two advantages and one drawback.

Advantages: i) If a bit is modified but not deleted, the process of decryption continues to correctly decrypt the remaining bits. Therefore, synchronous stream ciphers are not error-propagation sensitive. ii) If some bits are inserted, by an adversary, the receiver will lose synchronization and the forged bits as well as the remaining bits are very likely to be discarded. Therefore, synchronous stream ciphers are more prone to support the detection of some attacks.

Drawback: if a bit is lost (because of transmission error), the receiver is desynchronized and the decryption may fail starting from the missing bits if no re-synchronization mechanism is used.

Therefore, synchronous stream ciphers are very useful to encrypt streaming media (voice, audio, and video) where the speed of data-traffic is more important than the integrity of the data (e.g. loss of a few pixels or images in video streaming is not damaging).

It is worth noticing that synchronous stream ciphers are the most common in practice. To alleviate the drawback above, the common approach, is to reinitialize the keystream generator each limited-length message.

6.1.2.2 Self-synchronized Stream Ciphers

As mentioned previously, stream ciphers are well-suited to secure continuous-flow communication such as voice in which a continuous message is encrypted bit per bit. Transmission errors may occur while bits are transmitted through the channel. Can you imagine phone subscribers accepting phone call breaks because of loss of one bit? Self-synchronizing stream ciphers are a solution to prevent desynchronization due to bit loss or fraudulent insertion. They are suited to flows (such as voice of video) that tolerate bit loss. One simplest way to describe self-synchronizing stream ciphers is given below.

Self-synchronizing stream ciphers rely on a synchronization window of length l bits. At the beginning of cycle i (i.e. cycle of processing the plaintext bit a_i), the synchronization window denoted C_i is the set of the l most recent ciphertext bits, i.e. $C_i = (c_{i-l}, c_{i-l+1}, \ldots, c_{i-1})$. A function $\omega(C_i, K)$ computes the output s_i of the keystream generator at cycle i using the synchronization window bits and the secret key K (see Figure 6.2). If neither bit loss nor bit insertion occur, the set C_i is the same on both sides. Therefore, both sides compute the same keystream bit s_i. Now, let us consider two scenarios: bit loss and bit insertion.

Bit loss. In the event of transmission error,[2] no ciphertext bit is correctly received during cycle i. Thus, the receiver has no valid ciphertext bit to append to the synchronization window set. Rather, it appends the undefined binary value denoted $\mathcal{O}$. Therefore, it cannot correctly compute the keystream bits for bits from $i+1$ to $i+l$. The synchronization resumes at bit $i+l+1$. One strategy, under the assumption that the application is loss-tolerant, is to discard l bits starting from bit i. Thus, self-synchronizing stream ciphers have the advantage of limiting the propagation of transmission errors to a few bits of a continuous flow. Example 6.2 illustrates how the self-synchronization is reestablished.

Bit insertion.[3] By adversary: assume that bit c_i is replaced by bit c_i'. In such a case, the set C_{i+1} at sender differs from the set C_{i+1} at receiver, which results in distinct keystream bits for bits $i+1$ to $i+l$, which results in a decryption error. The synchronization resumes at bit $i+l$. Example 6.2 illustrates how the self-synchronization is reestablished.

Self-synchronizing stream ciphers have the advantage of limiting the propagation of transmission errors and malicious bit alterations to a few bits of a continuous flow. Below is the pseudocode of self-synchronizing stream cipher operations.

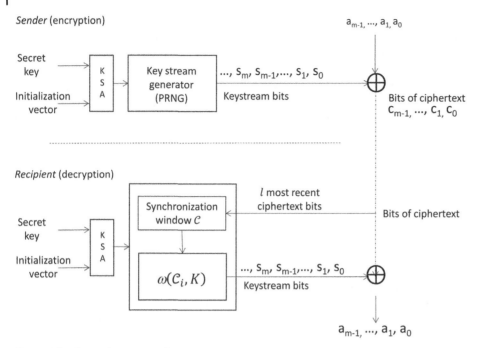

Figure 6.2 General structure of self-synchronizing stream cipher.

# Encryption side	# Decryption side
$C_0 = Init(IV)$	$C_0 = Init(IV)$
for each cycle i **do**	**for** each cycle i **do**
$\quad s_i = \omega(C_i, K)$	$\quad$ **if** $Tx\_err()$
$\quad c_i = a_i \oplus s_j \bmod 2$	$\quad\quad$ **then** $\{C_{i+1} = Update(C_i, \mathcal{O})\}$
$\quad C_{i+1} = Update(C_i, c_i)$	$\quad\quad$ **else** $\{s_i = (C_i, K)$
	$\quad\quad\quad a_i = c_i \oplus s_j \bmod 2$
	$\quad\quad\quad C_{i+1} = Update(C_i, c_i)\}$

Tx_err is a function, which returns *True*, in the event of a bit-transmission error.

$Update(C_i, e)$ is a function that removes the oldest element of set C_i and adds element e.

Example 6.2

– Bit loss

Assume that l, the length of synchronization window, is 5 and a transmission error occurs on bit i. The table below shows the synchronization window bits at each cycle on both sides. At, cycle i, both parties have the same bit set, but the receiver cannot decrypt the errored bit. Therefore, it includes the undefined value $\mathcal{O}$ in its set. Next, from cycle $i+1$ to cycle $i+5$, the receiver has a distinct synchronization window set and consequently, it cannot not decrypt correctly. Next, staring from cycle $i+6$, both parties have the same set and the decryption resumes correctly.

Cycle	Sender synchronization window	Receiver synchronization window	Synchro
i	$(c_{i-5}, c_{i-4}, c_{i-3}, c_{i-2}, c_{i-1})$	$(c_{i-5}, c_{i-4}, c_{i-3}, c_{i-2}, c_{i-1})$	Yes
$i+1$	$(c_{i-4}, c_{i-3}, c_{i-2}, c_{i-1}, c_i)$	$(c_{i-4}, c_{i-3}, c_{i-2}, c_{i-1}, \mathcal{O}))$	No
$i+2$	$(c_{i-3}, c_{i-2}, c_{i-1}, c_i, c_{i+1})$	$(c_{i-3}, c_{i-2}, c_{i-1}, \mathcal{O}, c_{i+1})$	No
$i+3$	$(c_{i-2}, c_{i-1}, c_i, c_{i+1}, c_{i+2})$	$(c_{i-2}, c_{i-1}, \mathcal{O}, c_{i+1}, c_{i+2})$	No
$i+4$	$(c_{i-1}, c_i, c_{i+1}, c_{i+2}, c_{i+3})$	$(c_{i-1}, \mathcal{O}, c_{i+1}, c_{i+2}, c_{i+3})$	No
$i+5$	$(c_i, c_{i+1}, c_{i+2}, c_{i+3}, c_{i+4})$	$(\mathcal{O}, c_{i+1}, c_{i+2}, c_{i+3}, c_{i+4})$	No
$i+6$	$(c_{i+1}, c_{i+2}, c_{i+3}, c_{i+4}, c_{i+5})$	$(c_{i+1}, c_{i+2}, c_{i+3}, c_{i+4}, c_{i+5})$	Yes

– Bit insertion

Assume that l, the length of synchronization window, is 4 and a bit i has been altered by an adversary. Let c_i' denote the received ciphertext bit. The table below shows the synchronization window bits at each cycle on both sides. At cycle i, both parties have the same bit set, but the receiver decrypts an altered bit and updates its synchronization set with c_i'. Next, from cycle $i+1$ to cycle $i+4$, the parties have two distinct synchronization sets. Therefore, their keystream bits are distinct resulting in bits of plaintext that are different from the decrypted bits. Starting from cycle $i+5$, both parties have the same set and the decryption resumes correctly. Notice that the receiver has no means, at this stage, to know that a bit had been altered.

Cycle	Sender synchronization window	Receiver synchronization window	Synchro
i	$(c_{i-4}, c_{i-3}, c_{i-2}, c_{i-1})$	$(c_{i-4}, c_{i-3}, c_{i-2}, c_{i-1})$	Yes
$i+1$	$(c_{i-3}, c_{i-2}, c_{i-1}, c_i)$	$(c_{i-3}, c_{i-2}, c_{i-1}, c_i')$	No
$i+2$	$(c_{i-2}, c_{i-1}, c_i, c_{i+1})$	$(c_{i-2}, c_{i-1}, c_i', c_{i+1})$	No
$i+3$	$(c_{i-1}, c_i, c_{i+1}, c_{i+2})$	$(c_{i-1}, c_i', c_{i+1}, c_{i+2})$	No
$i+4$	$(c_i, c_{i+1}, c_{i+2}, c_{i+3})$	$(c_i', c_{i+1}, c_{i+2}, c_{i+3})$	No
$i+5$	$(c_{i+1}, c_{i+2}, c_{i+3}, c_{i+4})$	$(c_{i+1}, c_{i+2}, c_{i+3}, c_{i+4})$	Yes

6.1.3 How to Generate Random Keystream Bits?

Keystream generators are the core of stream ciphers. They are Pseudo Random Bit Generators. There exist two main approaches to design the keystream generators: linear congruential generators (LCG) and Linear-feed-back-shift-register-based generators. Most common stream ciphers belong to the second category, which is addressed in detail in the next section. This subsection just surveys the linear congruential generators.

In general, a linear congruential generator is defined as a process that produces random values as follows:

Let A, B, m, and z_0 be parameters of the generator. The number generated at cycle i, denoted z_i, is defined by: $z_i = A * z_{i-1} + B \bmod m$. It is easy to find A and B with plaintext attack (see Problem 6.2).

If the LCG is used in a stream cipher, its output z_i is a string of $\lceil log_2 m \rceil$ bits used for encryption and decryption. At least A and B must be secret. Like affine cipher presented in Section 4.3, stream ciphers relying on LCG are vulnerable to plaintext attacks. $3 * \lceil log_2 m \rceil$ bits of plaintext and their corresponding ciphertext bits are enough to recover the secret key formed by A and B (see Problem 6.3).

6.1.4 Linear-Feedback Shift Registers (LFSRs)

6.1.4.1 LFSR Principle and Properties

Linear-feedback shift registers (LFSRs) are building blocks for a wide variety of applications including cryptography, cyclic redundancy check (CRC), and pseudorandom number generators. When cryptography is of concern, LFSRs provide key streams to encryption and decryption operations of stream ciphers.

An LFSR is a register composed of m flip-flop[4] elements (also called cells or simply bits) driven by a clock; i.e. at each clock impulse the state of register changes. The output of each element i, denoted FF_i, is the current output value in the element. The rightmost element of the LFSR is the register output.

Figure 6.3 shows a simplified structure of shift register without feedback, where ρ denotes the register output. The m flip-flop (FF) elements of the register are initialized to a selected value, called *seed*, say 10…10. That is, the first register

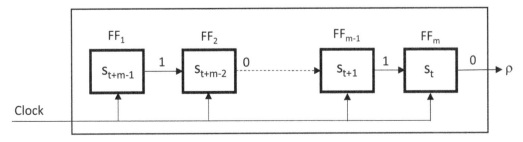

Figure 6.3 General structure of no-feedback shift register.

output is $s_t = 0$. Then, at next clock impulse, the register elements are one-position right-shifted and the second register output $s_{t+1} = 1$. At the $m - 1^{th}$ clock impulse, the register output is $s_{t+m-1} = 1$. Then, the register output does not change (i.e. all register elements are zeros).

If a non-feedback register has enough bits, it can be used to deliver the key in one-time pad cipher. Unfortunately, since the secret key is at least as long as the message and messages may have a long length, non-feedback shift registers are not appropriate to implement OTP ciphers in hardware.

Shift registers, used in hardware implementation of stream ciphers, are characterized by feedback; that is why they are called Feedback Shift Registers. That is, the output of some or all flip-flop elements are used to generate an input to the first element. Not all the elements are required to generate feedback. Thus, binary coefficients, denoted $c_m, c_{m-1}, ...,$ and c_1, indicate if the output of flip-flop elements are used or not. In Figure 6.4, the operation $\otimes$ denotes binary multiplication (i.e. the output of FF_i participates in the feedback only if $c_i = 1$). The flip-flops that impact the feedback are called *taps* or *feedback coefficients*. The feedback is yielded by a linear function; that is why LFSRs are called linear. There exist other LFSRs that are not linear. The operation of an LFSR can be described as follows:

---

m: number of elements (or bits) of register
c: vector of feedback coefficients
FF: vector of element states
Seed: a vector of booleans for register initialization
m: number of elements (or bits) of the register
$\left(FF_m, FF_{m-1}, ..., FF_2, FF_1\right) = Seed$
$\rho = FF_m$
At each clock impulse:

$$f = \left(\sum_{i=1}^{m} \left(c_i * FF_i\right)\right) mod\ 2$$

Register right-shift: $FF_j = FF_{j-1} \ \forall j = m, ..., 2$
Input the feedback: $FF_1 = f$
Deliver the register output: $\rho = FF_m$

The state of an LFSR at time t, denoted $\sigma(t)$, is the product of the states of its flip-flop elements. That is, $\sigma(t) = \left(FF_m(t), FF_{m-1}(t), ..., FF_1(t)\right)$, where $FF_i(t)$ denotes the state of flip-flop i at time t. In bit representation, the state of LFSR is a bit string ranging from $000...001$ to $111...111$.

At each clock impulse, the LFSR delivers a bit and register elements are right-shifted. Therefore, the register output is a bit stream that starts with string $s_{t+m-1}, s_{t+m-2}, ..., s_{t+1}, s_t$. The first bit produced by the LFSR is s_t. The next bits of the keystream are computed as follows:

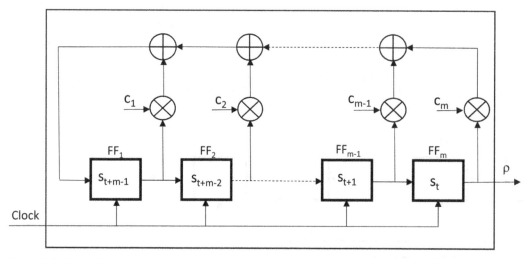

Figure 6.4 General structure of Linear-Feedback Shift Register.

$$s_{t+m} = s_{t+m-1}c_1 \oplus s_{t+m-2}c_2 \oplus \ldots \oplus s_{t+1}c_{m-1} \oplus s_t c_m = \left(\sum_{j=0}^{m-1} s_{t+j}c_{m-j}\right) mod\ 2$$

$$s_{t+m+1} = s_{t+m}c_1 \oplus s_{t+m-1}c_2 \oplus \ldots \oplus s_{t+2}c_{m-1} \oplus s_{t+1}c_m = \left(\sum_{j=0}^{m-1} s_{t+j+1}c_{m-j}\right) mod\ 2$$

...

$$s_{t+m+i} = s_{t+m+i-1}c_1 \oplus s_{t+m+i-2}c_2 \oplus \ldots \oplus s_{t+i+1}c_{m-1} \oplus s_{t+i}c_m = \left(\sum_{j=0}^{m-1} s_{t+j+i}c_{m-j}\right) mod\ 2 \tag{6.1}$$

> **Lemma 6.1[5]**
> An LFSR with m flip-flop elements can generate N distinct states such that $N \leq 2^m - 1$. N is called *cycle* (or period) of LFSR.

Properties of LFSRs

i) The output of LFSR, which has N distinct states, is a bit string, which repeats every N bits. Therefore, the state of flip-flop i at time $t + kN$, with k a positive integer, is the same as at time t.

ii) An LFSR with n flip-flops is said to be maximal-length LFSR, if it has exactly $2^n - 1$ distinct states.

iii) An LFSR, which reaches a state where all flip-flop states are 0s, has a constant[6] output equal to 0.

Example 6.3

Figure 6.5 shows an example of LFSR with four FF elements. To simplify the LFSR structure, an equivalent representation is used; if $c_i = 1$, then the output of element FF_i is connected to the XOR feedback line; and there is no connection otherwise.

The initial state of the LFSR is 1100. t denotes clock impulses. It is worth noticing that the first LFSR has only 6 distinct states, while the second has 15 distinct states. The second LFSR is maximal-length. Table 6.1 shows the state changes of the considered LFSR.

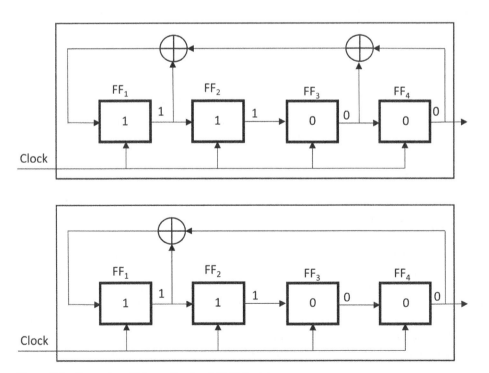

Figure 6.5 Examples of Linear-Feedback Shift Registers.

Table 6.1 Example of LFSR state changes.

t	Register state (Figure 6.5a)	t	Register state (Figure 6.5b)
0	1 1 0 0	0	1 1 0 0
1	1 1 1 0	1	1 1 1 0
2	0 1 1 1	2	1 1 1 1
3	0 0 1 1	3	0 1 1 1
4	0 0 0 1	4	1 0 1 1
5	1 0 0 0	5	0 1 0 1
6	1 1 0 0	6	1 0 1 0
7	1 1 1 0	7	1 1 0 1
8	0 1 1 1	8	0 1 1 0
9	0 0 1 1	9	0 0 1 1
10	0 0 0 1	10	1 0 0 1
11	1 0 0 0	11	0 1 0 0
12	1 1 0 0	12	0 0 1 0
13	1 1 1 0	13	0 0 0 1
14	0 1 1 1	14	1 0 0 0
15	0 0 1 1	15	1 1 0 0
16	0 0 0 1	16	1 1 1 0

6.1.4.2 Feedback Polynomial of LFSRs

To build stream ciphers, LFSRs with m cells are commonly used under computations over either extension fields (i.e. fields of the form F_{2^m}) or prime fields (i.e. fields of the form F_p, with p prime). Most common stream ciphers based on LFSRs rely on extension fields. In such a case, an LFSR with feedback coefficients c_i, $i = 1, ..., m$, where m is the number of register bits and $c_{i=1,...,m} \in \{0,1\}$, can be represented as a polynomial, called *feedback polynomial*, $\mathcal{F}(x)$, defined by:

$$\mathcal{F}(x) = 1 + \left(\sum_{i=1}^{m} c_i x^i \right) \bmod 2 \tag{6.2}$$

In Example 6.1, $\mathcal{F}(x) = x^4 + x^3 + x + 1$; in Figure 6.5a and $\mathcal{F}(x) = x^4 + x + 1$ in Figure 6.5b. Polynomial and diagram representations are equivalent. That is, from a feedback polynomial, the structure of LFSR can be drawn; and from a structure of an LFSR, the feedback polynomial can be derived. Polynomial representation is used when mathematical analysis is of concern.

Lemma 6.2

Given a m-bit linear-feedback shift register R represented with a feedback polynomial $\mathcal{F}(x)$ and initialized with a nonzero binary vector, if $\mathcal{F}(x)$ is a primitive polynomial, then R is a maximal-length LFSR (i.e. with a period of $2^m - 1$).

A proof of Lemma 6.2 is given in [2]. Recall that a primitive polynomial $p(x)$, of degree m, is a polynomial irreducible in $\mathbb{Z}_2$ that can generate all elements of a field F_{2^m} (see Section 3.2.4). For any integer $m \geq 2$, there exists at least one primitive polynomial of degree m to generate a field F_{2^m}. The number of distinct primitive polynomials of degree m grows quasi-exponentially with m. Therefore, there exist multiple combinations of tags to build LFSRs with a cycle of $2^m - 1$. To reduce the hardware implementation of LFSRs (i.e. reduce the number of connections and XOR circuits due to tags), sparse primitive polynomials of degree m, i.e. with the least number of monomials, are preferred.

Table 6.2 [3] provides a list of examples of feedback polynomials with minimal cost (i.e. with minimum electronic circuits) to build LFSRs with 2 to 32 bits.

Table 6.2 Feedback polynomials of LFSR with 2 to 20 and 32 bits.

Number of bits	Cycle length	Feedback Polynomial Example 1	Feedback Polynomial Example 2
2	3	x^2+x+1	
3	7	x^3+x^2+1	x^3+x+1
4	15	x^4+x^3+1	x^4+x+1
5	31	x^5+x^3+1	x^5+x^2+1
6	63	x^6+x^5+1	x^6+x+1
7	127	x^7+x^6+1	x^7+x+1
8	255	$x^8+x^6+x^5+x^4+1$	$x^8+x^6+x^5+x+1$
9	511	x^9+x^5+1	x^9+x^4+1
10	1 023	$x^{10}+x^7+1$	$x^{10}+x^3+1$
11	2 047	$x^{11}+x^9+1$	$x^{11}+x^2+1$
12	4 095	$x^{12}+x^5+1$	$x^{12}+x^3+1$
13	8 191	$x^{13}+x^{12}+x^{11}+x^8+1$	$x^{13}+x^4+x^3+x+1$
14	16 383	$x^{14}+x^{11}+x^6+x+1$	$x^{14}+x^8+x^6+x+1$
15	32 767	$x^{15}+x^4+1$	$x^{15}+x+1$
16	65 535	$x^{16}+x^{12}+x^7+x^2+1$	$x^{16}+x^{12}+x^3+x+1$
17	131 071	$x^{17}+x^6+1$	$x^{17}+x^3+1$
18	262 143	$x^{18}+x^{11}+1$	$x^{18}+x^7+1$
19	524 287	$x^{19}+x^{18}+x^{17}+x^{14}+1$	$x^{19}+x^6+x^5+x+1$
20	1 048 575	$x^{20}+x^{17}+1$	$x^{20}+x^3+1$
32	4 294 967 295	$x^{32}+x^{22}+x^2+x+1$	

6.1.5 LFSRs for Building Stream Ciphers

LFSRs are common building blocks to design and implement stream ciphers. In such a case, the seed of initialization of LFSR is the secret key shared between parties. Unfortunately, a single LFSR is vulnerable to plaintext attacks (see Problem 6.7). Therefore, it is not recommended to use a single LFSR.

There exist two basic approaches to use LFSRs to build stream cipher. The first is to use several LFSRs in parallel and combine their outputs in a secure way (i.e. hard to attack) to generate the key stream. Such generators are called combination generators. The second approach is to use a single LFSR, then apply a nonlinear function to its output to generate the key stream. The registers in the second category are called *filter generators*. Both approaches can be mixed to yield highly secure stream ciphers. Therefore, the recommended approach to build LFSR-based stream ciphers is to mix several LFSRs that run in parallel and combine their outputs.

A huge number of solutions have been proposed to design LFSR-based stream ciphers. They differ regarding how the LFSRs are clocked and how their outputs are combined. As shown in Figure 6.6, the LFSR-based stream ciphers are characterized by two components: Logic of clocking and logic of output combination. Thus, LFSR-based stream cipher design approaches can be classified according to their components.

i) Clocking technique
 – *Regular clocking*: all the LFSRs are clocked at the same rate to produce their output.
 – *Irregular clocking*: only LFSRs that match a given condition are clocked. In general, the output or some specific bits of certain LFSRs are used to clock other LFSRs. Figure 6.7 shows an example of irregular clocking. $LFSR_3$ is clocked only if both outputs of $LFSR_1$ and $LFSR_2$ are 1, and $LFSR_4$ is clocked only if the output of $LFSR_2$ is 0. The standard E0, which is presented in 6.2.1, is based on irregular clocking.

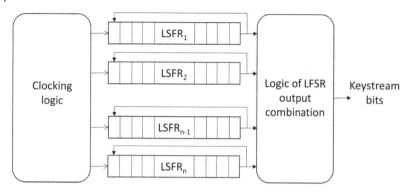

Figure 6.6 General architecture for building LFSR-based stream ciphers.

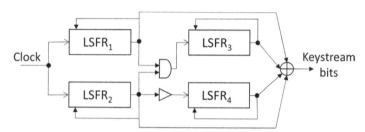

Figure 6.7 Example of irregular clocking of LFSRs.

ii) Combination of LFSR outputs

There exist two main approaches:

– Use of a nonlinear function F to combine the outputs of the LFSRs. Since a function is used to filter outputs, the generators are called *filtering generators*. In Figure 6.8, the output of the keystream generator is a nonlinear combination of four LFSRs. Let s_i denote the output of $LFSR_i$. Therefore, the output of the entire keystream generator is $F(1,2,3,4) = \left(\neg s_1 \wedge s_2\right) \oplus \left(\neg\left(s_3 \oplus s_4\right)\right)$.

– Use of Finite state machine (FSM): to increase nonlinearity, function F may be designed as an FSM. With FSM, the keystream generator makes use of past computations to produce keystream bits, thus reinforcing the security level. Most standard stream ciphers, including SNOW 3G and ZUC presented in 6.2, rely on FSM.

Note. Since mathematical proofs of security of LFSR-based keystream generators are not yet known, such generators can only be deemed as computationally secure.

6.2 Examples of Standard Keystream Generators

Several stream ciphers have been proposed and some of them have been standardized and widely used in operational networks. Recall that standardization organizations involved in networks and telecommunications are mainly IEEE,[7] 3GPP,[8] ETSI,[9] IETF,[10] and ISO,[11]

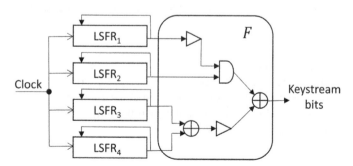

Figure 6.8 Example of nonlinear combination generator.

Standard stream ciphers include A5/1, E0, SNOW 3G, ZUC, Chacha20, and RC4, which are presented in the sequel.

Note. In the sequel, the presentation of keystream generators preserves the notations of standards. Therefore, different notations for numbering cells and states will be used depending on the standard.

6.2.1 A5/1 Keystream Generator

A5/1 is a cipher stream used to secure communications between mobile phones and base stations in GSM networks (i.e. 2G cellular networks). Billions of phones used A5/1 to protect communications while propagating over the air.

A5/1 relies on a key stream generator composed of three LFSRs with irregular clocking and defined by feedback polynomials:

$$\mathcal{F}_1(x) = x^{19} + x^{18} + x^{17} + x^{14} + 1 \qquad \mathcal{F}_2(x) = x^{22} + x^{21} + 1$$
$$\mathcal{F}_3(x) = x^{23} + x^{22} + x^{21} + x^8 + 1$$

Therefore, in total, $19 + 22 + 23$ bits are used to deliver a key stream. The registers are initialized using a key of 64 bits stored on the mobile phone.

A5/1 output is an XOR of the output of the three registers. In each register, a specific bit, called clocking bit, is used to know when the shift operation is to perform. In Figure 6.9, bit 8 is the bit clocking of the first and second registers and bit 10 is the bit clocking of the third register. At each cycle, the clocking bits of the three registers are examined. A register is clocked (i.e. a clock signal is delivered to the register; thus, it shifts its cells to the right) if the current state of its clocking bit agrees with the majority of clocking bits. Therefore, at each cycle, two or three register shifts are performed. The state of register of which the clocking bit differs from the clocking bits of the other registers does not change.

The irregularity of register clocking was a countermeasure against plaintext attacks against LFSR (see attack against LFSR, Problem 6.7). Unfortunately, even with irregular clocking of registers, several attacks succeeded and showed that A5/1 was not secure. From then on, A5/1 was no longer a solution for cellular networks.

Another countermeasure was proposed in A5/2 cipher, with four registers, but it is no more recommended, because of reported attacks.

6.2.2 E0 Keystream Generator

E0 is a stream cipher used to encrypt and decrypt data packets between two Bluetooth devices [4]. E0 makes use of a key stream generator composed of four LFSRs defined by feedback polynomials:

$$\mathcal{F}_1(x) = x^{25} + x^{20} + x^{12} + x^8 + 1 \qquad \mathcal{F}_2(x) = x^{31} + x^{24} + x^{16} + x^{12} + 1$$
$$\mathcal{F}_3(x) = x^{33} + x^{28} + x^{24} + x^4 + 1 \qquad \mathcal{F}_4(x) = x^{39} + x^{36} + x^{28} + x^4 + 1$$

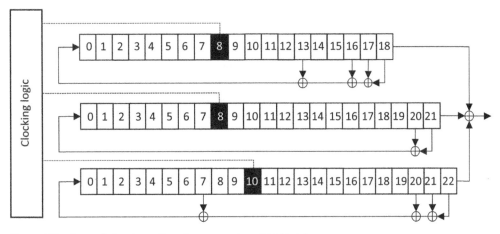

Figure 6.9 General structure of random generator of A5/1 cipher.

Therefore, in total 128 ($= 25 + 31 + 33 + 39$) bits are used to deliver a key stream. The output of LFSRs is combined with a state machine called summation combiner (see Figure 6.10).

In addition to the four registers, E0 cipher makes use of two internal 2-bit-words denoted c_{t-1} and c_t initialized to 00. The main steps of E0 cipher are Generation of key stream and Initialization.

Generation of key stream bits

Let the start time be $t = 0$.
Let x_t^k denote the output of register k ($k = 1, 2, 3, 4$) at time t.
Let c_{t-1}^1 and c_t^1 denote the left bit of words c_{t-1} and c_t, at time t, respectively.
Let c_{t-1}^0 and c_t^0 denote the right bit of words c_{t-1} and c_t, at time t, respectively.
Let $\left(w_t^0, w_t^1\right)$ denote the two bits of a 2-bit-word w.

The output of the key stream generator is performed as:

1) Compute the sum over integers:

$$y_t = x_t^1 + x_t^2 + x_t^3 + x_t^4. \text{ Thus, } 0 \leq y_t \leq 4.$$

2) The output of the entire keystream generator is $z_t \in \{0, 1\}$, where

$$z_t = x_t^1 \oplus x_t^2 \oplus x_t^3 \oplus x_t^4 \oplus c_t^0$$

$$c_{t+1} = \left(c_{t+1}^1, c_{t+1}^0\right) = s_{t+1} \oplus T_1[c_t] \oplus T_2[c_{t-1}]$$

$$s_{t+1} = \left(s_{t+1}^1, s_{t+1}^0\right) = \left\lfloor \frac{y_t + c_t}{2} \right\rfloor.$$

$T_1[.]$ and $T_2[.]$ are two linear functions defined by:

$$T_1 : \left(c_t^1, c_t^0\right) \mapsto \left(c_t^1, c_t^0\right); \quad T_2 : \left(c_{t-1}^1, c_{t-1}^0\right) \mapsto \left(c_{t-1}^0, c_{t-1}^1 \oplus c_{t-1}^0\right).$$

Initialization of LFSRs (Key Scheduling Algorithm)
Before starting the generation of key stream bits, the four LFSRs and the two 2-bit words, c_{-1} and c_0, are initialized using four inputs: an encryption key K_{enc}, 128 publicly known random bits, a 48-bit Bluetooth device address, and 26 central's clock bits. All the initialization inputs (i.e. $len(K_{enc}) + 128 + 48 + 26$ bits) enter the four registers, in a specific order, and keystream generator is clocked without producing key stream bits. Then, after some cycles of registers, the entire key stream generator becomes ready to deliver the first bit of the key stream. The encryption key K_{enc} is derived by a function called E3 using the link key exchanged during the authentication step performed by Bluetooth devices.

6.2.3 SNOW 3G Keystream Generator

SNOW 3G is keystream generator chosen by 3GPP for confidentiality and integrity guarantees in 3G cellular networks [5]. SNOW 3G also is included in the ISO/IEC 18033-4 standard [6]. Unlike A5/1 and E0 keystream generators, in which LFSR elements are bits, SNOW 3G is a word-keystream generator. That is, the elements (also called stages) of SNOW 3G LFSR are 32-bit words. At every clock tick, SNOW 3G produces a 32-bit word of output, which is then used to encrypt/decrypt 32 bits of data. SNOW 3G is composed of two components: an LFSR of sixteen 32-bit stages and an FSM of three 32-bit registers (see Figure 6.11). FSM registers are not LFSRs; they are updated using substitutions.

6.2.3.1 Formal Description of SNOW 3G

LFSR of SNOW 3G is defined over field[12] $F_{2^{32}}$. The 32-bit elements of LFSR are denoted $s_{15}, s_{14}, ..., s_0$ (see Figure 6.11). Notice that stage s_0 is the rightmost element of the LFSR. Hence, the feedback polynomial of SNOW 3G is defined by:

$$\mathcal{F}(x) = \alpha x^{16} \oplus x^{14} \oplus \alpha^{-1} x^5 + 1 \in F_{2^{32}}[x]$$

The feedback word, at cycle $t + 1$, is recursively computed as:

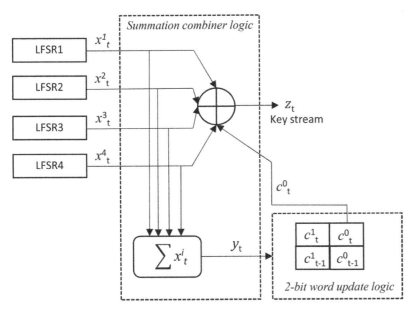

Figure 6.10 General structure of random generator of E0 cipher.

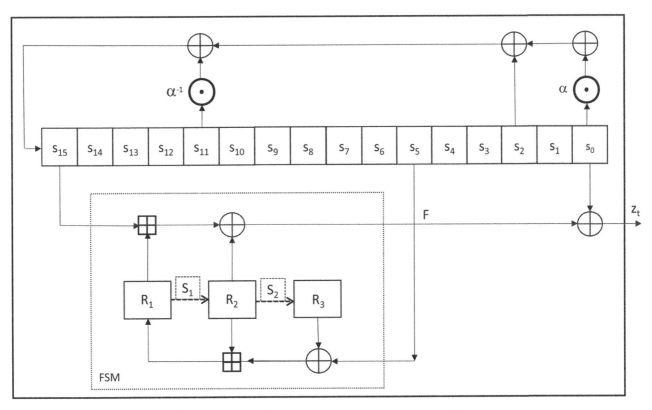

$\boxplus$ Addition modulo 2^{32} $\odot$ Multiplication by α or α^{-1} over field $F(2^{32})$ S_i Substitution using S-box i

Figure 6.11 SNOW 3G keystream generator.

$$s_{15}^{t+1} = \alpha^{-1} * s_{11}^{t} \oplus s_{2}^{t} \oplus \alpha * s_{0}^{t}$$

where:

s_i^t denotes the state, at cycle t, of stage i ($i = 0, 1, ..., 15$),

$\alpha \in F_{2^{32}}[x]$ is a root of $F_{2^8}[x]$ polynomial $x^4 + \beta^{23}x^3 + \beta^{245}x^2 + \beta^{48}x + \beta^{239}$,

$\beta \in F_{2^8}[x]$ is a root of $F_2[x]$ polynomial $x^8 + x^7 + x^5 + x^3 + 1$

α^{-1} is the multiplicative inverse of α over $F_{2^{32}}$.

For detail on finite fields F_{2^m}, see Section 3.2.4.

The output of FSM, at cycle t, denoted F^t, is computed as: $F^t = \left(s_{15}^t + R_1^t\right) \oplus R_2^t$.

The update of FSM registers, at cycle t, is defined by:

$$R_1^t = R_2^{t-1} + \left(R_3^{t-1} \oplus s_5^{t-1}\right); \quad R_2^t = S_1\left(R_1^{t-1}\right); \quad R_3^t = S_2\left(R_2^{t-1}\right)$$

where S_1 and S_2 are two 32-bit to 32-bit substitution boxes. S_1 and S_2 s-boxes make use of two small 8-bit s-boxes S_R and S_Q. S_R is the well-known s-box used in AES cipher (see Section 7.3).

After the initialization step, the output of the SNOW 3G keystream generator, at cycle t, is $z^t = z^t \oplus s_0^t$.

Before starting the generation of the first bit of the keystream in cycle t_s, the value of $s_{15}^{t_s}$ is $s_{15}^{t_s} = \alpha^{-1} * s_{11}^{t_s-1} \oplus s_2^{t_s-1} \oplus \alpha * s_0^{t_s-1} \oplus F^{t_s-1}$.

6.2.3.2 Algorithmic Description of SNOW 3G

SNOW 3G relies on a series of functions, substitution boxes, and clocking modes, which are presented below.

6.2.3.2.1 *Notations and Functions of SNOW 3G*

Notations

0_X: hexadecimal notation of an 8-bit value (i.e. a byte).

$0_X \ll_n t$: t-bit left shift of an n-bit register; t is the number of shifting positions.

V, c: 8-bit values. W: 32-bit word

$W = W_0 \| W_1 \| W_2 \| W_3$: 32-bit word, with W_0 the most and W_3 the least significant byte.

s_i: element i of LFSR, $i = 0, ..., 15$ $s_{i,k}$: byte k ($k = 0,1,2,3$) of element s_i

R_j: register R_j ($j = 1,2,3$) of the FSM

$\oplus$: addition *modulo 2* $\boxplus$: addition *modulo* 2^{32}

SNOW 3G makes uses of four functions:

1) *MULx* function: maps eight bits to eight bits as follows:

$$MULx(V,c) = \begin{cases} (V \ll_8 1) \oplus c & \text{if} \quad \text{the most significant bit of } V = 1 \\ (V \ll_8 1) & \text{otherwise} \end{cases}$$

For example, $MULx(0x2A, 0x12) = 0x54$; $MULx(0xA2, 0x12) = 56$.

2. *MULxPOW* function: recursively maps eight bits to eight bits as follows:

$$MULxPOW(V,i,c) = \begin{cases} V & \text{if} \quad i = 0 \\ MULx\left(MULxPOW(V,i-1,c),c\right) & \text{otherwise} \end{cases}.$$

3. MUL_α function: maps eight bits to 32 bits as follows:

$$MUL_\alpha(c) = MULxPOW(c, 23, 0xA9) \| MULxPOW(c, 245, 0xA9) \|$$

$$MULxPOW(c, 48, 0xA9) \| MULxPOW(c, 239, 0xA9).$$

4. DIV_α function: maps eight bits to 32 bits as follows:

$$DIV_\alpha(c) = MULxPOW(c, 16, 0xA9) \| MULxPOW(c, 39, 0xA9) \|$$

$$MULxPOW(c, 6, 0xA9) \| MULxPOW(c, 64, 0xA9)$$

6.2.3.2.2 *Substitution Boxes of SNOW 3G*

SNOW 3G makes use of two substitution boxes S_1 and S_2.

Given a word W, S-box S_1 returns a result $S_1(W) = r_0 \| r_1 \| r_2 \| r_3$ defined as follows:

$$r_0 = MULx\left(S_R\left(W_0\right), 0x1B\right) \oplus S_R\left(W_1\right) \oplus S_R\left(W_2\right) \oplus MULx\left(S_R\left(W_3\right), 0x1B\right) \oplus S_R\left(W_3\right)$$
$$r_1 = MULx\left(S_R\left(W_0\right), 0x1B\right) \oplus S_R\left(W_0\right) \oplus MULx\left(S_R\left(W_1\right), 0x1B\right) \oplus S_R\left(W_2\right) \oplus S_R\left(W_3\right)$$
$$r_2 = S_R\left(W_0\right) \oplus MULx\left(S_R\left(W_1\right), 0x1B\right) \oplus S_R\left(W_1\right) \oplus MULx\left(S_R\left(W_2\right), 0x1B\right) \oplus S_R\left(W_3\right)$$
$$r_3 = S_R\left(W_0\right) \oplus S_R\left(W_1\right) \oplus MULx\left(S_R\left(W_2\right), 0x1B\right) \oplus S_R\left(W_2\right) \oplus MULx\left(S_R\left(W_3\right), 0x1B\right)$$

where S_R, which is called Rijndael's s-box, is a table of 256 8-bit-constants that, given $u = i*16 + j$ (i and j are row and column numbers of a cell in Rijndael's table), returns a 8-bit constant. For example, $S_R(17) = S_R(0x11) = 0x63$, $S_R(127) = S_R(0x7F) = 0xD2$, $S_R(255) = S_R(0xFF) = 0x16$.

Given a word W, S-box S_2 returns a result $S_2(W) = r_0 \parallel r_1 \parallel r_2 \parallel r_3$ defined as follows:

$$r_0 = MULx\left(S_Q\left(W_0\right), 0x69\right) \oplus S_Q\left(W_1\right) \oplus S_Q\left(W_2\right) \oplus MULx\left(S_Q\left(W_3\right), 0x69\right) \oplus S_Q\left(W_3\right)$$
$$r_1 = MULx\left(S_Q\left(W_0\right), 0x69\right) \oplus S_Q\left(W_0\right) \oplus MULx\left(S_Q\left(W_1\right), 0x69\right) \oplus S_Q\left(W_2\right) \oplus S_Q\left(W_3\right)$$
$$r_2 = S_Q\left(W_0\right) \oplus MULx\left(S_Q\left(W_1\right), 0x69\right) \oplus S_Q\left(W_1\right) \oplus MULx\left(S_Q\left(W_2\right), 0x69\right) \oplus S_Q\left(W_3\right)$$
$$r_3 = S_Q\left(W_0\right) \oplus S_Q\left(W_1\right) \oplus MULx\left(S_Q\left(W_2\right), 0x69\right) \oplus S_Q\left(W_2\right) \oplus MULx\left(S_Q\left(W_3\right), 0x69\right)$$

where S_Q is a second table of 256 8-bit-constants used in the same way as table S_R, but with distinct arrangements of constants inside the tables. For example, $S_Q(17) = S_Q(0x11) = 0x25$, $S_Q(127) = S_Q(0x7F) = 0x5A$, $S_Q(255) = S_Q(0xFF) = 0x86$.

6.2.3.2.3 SNOW 3G Clocking
Clocking the LFSR

Two modes of LFSR clocking are distinguished:

1) LFSR clocking in initialization mode

   LFSR receives a 32-bit word F from the FSM, then performs the following:

$$v = \left(s_{0,1} \parallel s_{0,2} \parallel s_{0,3} \parallel 0x00\right) \oplus MUL_\alpha\left(s_{0,0}\right) \oplus s_2 \oplus$$
$$\left(0x00 \parallel s_{11,0} \parallel s_{11,1} \parallel s_{11,2}\right) \oplus DIV_\alpha\left(s_{11,3}\right) \oplus F.$$

   Shift LFSR elements using the feedback v
   $$s_i = s_{i+1}, \text{for } i = 0, \ldots, 14; \qquad s_{15} = v$$

2) LFSR clocking in keystream mode
   It performs the following:

$$v = \left(s_{0,1} \parallel s_{0,2} \parallel s_{0,3} \parallel 0x00\right) \oplus MUL_\alpha\left(s_{0,0}\right) \oplus s_2 \oplus$$
$$\left(0x00 \parallel s_{11,0} \parallel s_{11,1} \parallel s_{11,2}\right) \oplus DIV_\alpha\left(s_{11,3}\right)$$

   Shift LFSR elements using feedback v
   $$s_i = s_{i+1}, \text{for } i = 0, \ldots, 14; \qquad s_{15} = v$$

Clocking the FSM
FSM is clocked to produce a 32-bit word denoted F as follows:

- $F = \left(s_{15} \boxplus R_1\right) \oplus R_2$
- Update registers: $r = R_2 \boxplus \left(R_3 \oplus s_5\right); R_3 = S_2\left(R_2\right); R_2 = S_1\left(R_1\right); R_1 = r.$

6.2.3.2.4 Operation of SNOW 3G
Initialization (Key Scheduling Algorithm)
SNOW 3G is initialized with a key K composed of four 32-bit words, denoted K_1, K_2, K_3, and K_4 and an initialization variable IV composed of four 32-bit words, denoted IV_1, IV_2, IV_3, and IV_4. LFSR element initialization is as follows (where $\Omega = 0xFFFFFFFF$):

$s_{15} = K_3 \oplus IV_0$	$s_{14} = K_2$	$s_{13} = K_1$	$s_{12} = K_0 \oplus IV_1$
$s_{11} = K_3 \oplus \Omega$	$s_{10} = K_2 \oplus \Omega \oplus IV_2$	$s_9 = K_1 \oplus \Omega \oplus IV_3$	$s_8 = K_0 \oplus \Omega$
$s_7 = K_3$	$s_6 = K_2$	$s_5 = K_1$	$s_4 = K_0$
$s_3 = K_3 \oplus \Omega$	$s_2 = K_2 \oplus \Omega$	$s_1 = K_1 \oplus \Omega$	$s_0 = K_0 \oplus \Omega$

The FSM registers R_1, R_2, and R_3 are all set to 0. Then, the following two steps are repeated 32 times:

1) FSM is clocked to produce a 32-bit word F.
2) LFSR is clocked according to initialization mode using word F.

Generation of keystream
First, the FSM is clocked once and its output is discarded. Then, the LFSR is clocked according to the keystream mode. After that, keystream 32-bit words are produced by repeating the following steps as long as keystream bits are needed to encrypt/decrypt messages:

1) FSM is clocked to produce a 32-bit word F.
2) The next keystream word is produced as $z_t = F \oplus s_0$.
3) LFSR is clocked according to the keystream mode.

| **Note.** For interested readers, some issues regarding the resynchronization mechanism of SNOW 3G are discussed in [7].

6.2.4 ZUC Keystream Generator

6.2.4.1 Principle of ZUC Keystream Generator

ZUC[13] is stream cipher proposed in China for support of security in cellular networks [8]. ZUC also is an ETSI standard [9]. There exist two ZUC versions: ZUC-128 for 4G/LTE and ZUC-256 for 5G networks. The structure and operations of both versions are the same; they differ in the length of the key and the initialization vector and in the register initialization phase. ZUC-128 is 128-bit key-based, while ZUC-256 is 256-bit key-based. Therefore, ZUC-256 provides a higher security strength. In the sequel, ZUC description refers to ZUC-128.

ZUC is organized into three logical layers: LFSR, bit reorganization, and an FSM (see Figure 6.12). It is worth noticing that the bit reorganization layer extracts halves of eight LFSR stages, which are then used in a nonlinear function F. Such a design makes (till now) the standard cryptanalysis against common stream ciphers not directly applicable to break ZUC cipher.

Like SNOW 3G, ZUC is a word-keystream cipher. It takes a key of 128 bits and an initialization vector of 128 bits to deliver a 32-bit word of keystream bits used to encrypt/decrypt data.

ZUC has an LFSR of sixteen 31-bit stages denoted s_0, s_1, ..., s_{14}, s_{15}.

The design of ZUC differs from common stream ciphers, such as SNOW 3G, which are defined only over extension fields, i.e. F_2, F_{2^8}, and F_{2^m}. Rather, the LFSR of ZUC is defined over a prime field F_p, with $p = F_{2^{31}-1}$, while the FSM registers[14] are defined over extension field $F_{2^{32}}$.

The feedback word, at cycle $t + 1$, is recursively computed as:

$$s_{15}^{t+1} = 2^{15} * s_{15}^t + 2^{17} * s_{13}^t + 2^{21} * s_{10}^t + 2^{20} * s_4^t + \left(1 + 2^8\right) * s_0^t \ mod \left(2^{31} - 1\right).$$

LFSR feedback polynomial of ZUC is:

$$\mathcal{F}(x) = x^{16} - \left(2^{15} x^{15} + 2^{17} x^{13} + 2^{21} x^{10} + 2^{20} x^4 + \left(1 + 2^8\right)\right).$$

6.2.4.2 ZUC Algorithm

| **Notes**
| – In ZUC, addition and multiplication of LFSR stages are over prime field $F_{2^{31}-1}$.
| – If $s_{15}^{t+1} = 0$, then s_{15}^{t+1} is replaced by $2^{31} - 1$ (because in F_p, p and 0 are equivalent).
| – Any element $a \in F_{2^{31}-1}$ can be written as $a = \sum_{i=0}^{30} a_i 2^i$, $a_{i=0,...,30} \in \{0,1\}$. Then, $\forall x \in F_{2^{31}-1}$, $k < 31$, $2^k * x := x \lll_{31} k$. This makes implementation of ZUC quite efficient. $x \lll_{31} k$ denotes a left circular shift of 31-bit element by k positions.

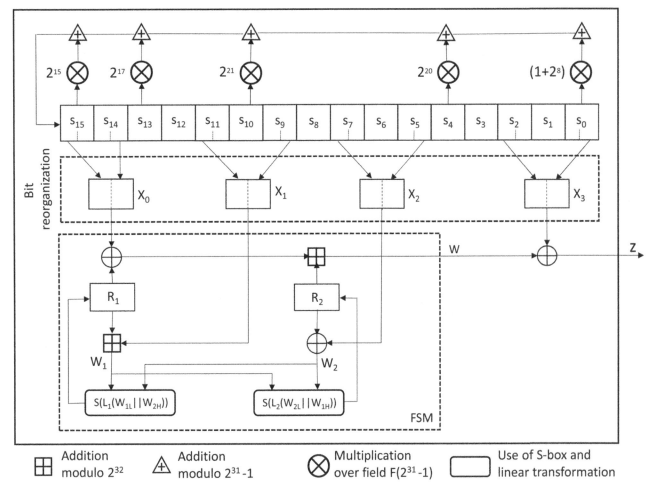

Figure 6.12 SNOW 3G keystream generator.

6.2.4.2.1 ZUC LFSR Modes

Stages of LFSR are 31-bits. Like in SNOW 3G, the LFSR of ZUC operates in two modes: Initialization and keystream generation.

1) LFSR Initialization mode (Key Scheduling Algorithm)

   In LFSR initialization mode, ZUC performs the following:

   Receive a 32-bit word W from the nonlinear function.

   $u = W \gg 1$ (i.e. remove the rightmost bit of W to match LFSR stage length)

   $$v = 2^{15} s_{15} + 2^{17} s_{13} + 2^{21} s_{10} + 2^{20} s_4 + \left(1 + 2^8\right) s_0 \ mod \left(2^{31} - 1\right)$$

   $$T = \left(u + v\right) mod \left(2^{31} - 1\right)$$

   If $T = 0$, then $T = 2^{31} - 1$

   $$\left(s_1, s_2, ..., s_{14}, s_{15}, T\right) \rightarrow \left(s_0, s_1, ..., s_{14}, s_{15}\right) \text{(i.e. shift stages).}$$

2) LFSR work mode

   In LFSR initialization mode, ZUC performs the following:

   $$T = 2^{15} s_{15} + 2^{17} s_{13} + 2^{21} s_{10} + 2^{20} s_4 + \left(1 + 2^8\right) s_0 \ mod \left(2^{31} - 1\right)$$

   If $T = 0$, then $T = 2^{31} - 1$

$$\left(s_1, s_2, ..., s_{14}, s_{15}, T\right) \rightarrow \left(s_0, s_1, ..., s_{14}, s_{15}\right)$$

6.2.4.2.2 ZUC Bit Reorganization

From the stages of the LFSR, four 32-bit words are formed as follows:

$$X_0 = s_{15H} \parallel s_{14L} \qquad X_1 = s_{11L} \parallel s_{9H} \qquad X_2 = s_{7L} \parallel s_{5H} \qquad X_3 = s_{2L} \parallel s_{0H}$$

where s_{iL} and s_{iH} denote the leftmost and rightmost 16 bits of stage i, respectively.

6.2.4.2.3 ZUC Nonlinear Function F

The core of the FSM of ZUC is a nonlinear function denoted F, which makes use of two 32-bit registers R_1 and R_2 and the three words yielded by bit reorganization to deliver a 32-bit word W as follows:

$$F\left(X_0, X_1, X_2\right):$$
$$\left\{ W = \left(X_0 \oplus R_1\right) \boxplus R_2; \qquad W_1 = R_1 \boxplus X_1; \qquad W_2 = R_2 \oplus X_2; \right.$$
$$\left. R_1 = S\left(L_1\left(W_{1L} \parallel W_{2H}\right)\right); \; R_2 = S\left(L_2\left(W_{2L} \parallel W_{1H}\right)\right) \right\}$$

S is a 32-bit substitution box, which is defined by four juxtaposed 8-bit s-boxes similar (but with distinct ordering of 16-bit constant) to Rijndael's table used in SNOW 3G.

L_1 and L_2 are two 32-bit linear transforms defined by:

$$L_1(X) = X \oplus \left(X \lll_{32} 2\right) \oplus \left(X \lll_{32} 10\right) \oplus \left(X \lll_{32} 18\right) \oplus \left(X \lll_{32} 24\right)$$

$$L_2(X) = X \oplus \left(X \lll_{32} 8\right) \oplus \left(X \lll_{32} 14\right) \oplus \left(X \lll_{32} 22\right) \oplus \left(X \lll_{32} 30\right)$$

where $a \lll_n k$ denotes the k-bit cyclic left-shift of the n-bit register a.

6.2.4.2.4 ZUC Initialization

Let $K = K_0 \parallel K_1 \parallel ... \parallel K_{14} \parallel K_{15}$ be the secret key and $IV = IV_0 \parallel IV_1 \parallel ... \parallel IV_{14} \parallel IV_{15}$ the initialization vector. Each K_i or IV_i, $i = 0, ..., 15$, is an 8-bit value. The secret key and the initialization vector are expanded to sixteen 31-bit values to initialize the LFSR stages as follows:

$s_i = K_i \parallel d_i \parallel IV_i$, $i = 0,1, ..., 15$, where $d_{i=0,...,15}$ are 15-bit constants defined by:

$$d_0 = 0\text{x44D7} \quad d_1 = 0\text{x26BC} \quad d_2 = 0\text{x626B} \quad d_3 = 0\text{x135E}$$
$$d_4 = 0\text{x5789} \quad d_5 = 0\text{x35E2} \quad d_6 = 0\text{x7135} \quad d_7 = 0\text{x09AF}$$
$$d_8 = 0\text{x4D78} \quad d_9 = 0\text{x2F13} \quad d_{10} = 0\text{x6BC4} \quad d_{11} = 0\text{x1AF1}$$
$$d_{12} = 0\text{x5E26} \quad d_{13} = 0\text{x3C4D} \quad d_{14} = 0\text{x789A} \quad d_{15} = 0\text{x47AC}$$

Perform the following steps:
- $R_1 = R_2 = 0$
- Run *Bit reorganization*
- $W = F(X_0, X_1, X_2)$
- Run *LFSR initialization mode* with $w \gg 1$. ($w \gg 1$ denotes 1-bit right shift of w).

6.2.4.2.5 Keystream Generation

After the initialization phase, execute once the following steps and discard the output of function F:

- Run *Bit reorganization*
- $w = F\left(X_0, X_1, X_2\right)$
- Run *LFSR work mode.*

Then, ZUC enters in phase of generation of keystream bits. At each cycle, a 32-bit word Z is produced as an output of the ZUC keystream generator as follows:

- Run *Bit reorganization*
- $Z = F(X_0, X_1, X_2) \oplus X_3$
- Run *LFSR work mode.*

6.2.5 ChaCha20 Stream Cipher

ChaCha20[15] is a stream cipher designed by D. Bernstein [10]. It is an IETF standard [11] recommended in particular as a cipher in TLS protocol [1].

Some performance analyses showed that ChaCha20 is around three times fast as AES (the standard block cipher, presented in the next chapter), when both are software-only implemented. Another interesting property of ChaCha20 is that it is not sensitive to timing attacks. ChaCha20 takes a 256-bit key, a 32-bit counter, and a 96-bit nonce; and generates a 64-byte keystream block.

6.2.5.1 ChaCha20 State

The state of Chacha20 is composed of sixteen 32-bit words, denoted $S_0, ..., S_{15}$, generally organized in a matrix, as illustrated by Figure 6.13.

The initial state of Chacha20 is set as shown in Figure 6.14:

- The first matrix row is initialized using four constants:

$$S_0 = \alpha_0 = 0x61707865 \qquad S_1 = \alpha_1 = 0x3320646e$$
$$S_2 = \alpha_2 = 0x79622d32 \qquad S_3 = \alpha_3 = 0x6b206574$$

- The second and third matrix rows are initialized using a 256-bit key K (represented by eight 32-bit integers, denoted K_0, $K_1, ..., K_7$).
- The fourth matrix row is initialized using a 32-bit counter, denoted C, and a 96-bit nonce (represented by three 32-bit integers, denoted N_0, N_1, N_2).

$$\begin{bmatrix} S_0 & S_1 & S_2 & S_3 \\ S_4 & S_5 & S_6 & S_7 \\ S_8 & S_9 & S_{10} & S_{11} \\ S_{12} & S_{13} & S_{14} & S_{15} \end{bmatrix}$$

Figure 6.13 ChaCha20 state structure.

$$\begin{bmatrix} \alpha_0 & \alpha_1 & \alpha_2 & \alpha_3 \\ K_0 & K_1 & K_2 & K_3 \\ K_4 & K_5 & K_6 & K_7 \\ C & N_0 & N_1 & N_2 \end{bmatrix}$$

Figure 6.14 ChaCha20 initial state.

6.2.5.2 ChaCha20 Quarter Round

The basic function of the ChaCha20 algorithm is the quarter-round, denoted *QRound*; it takes four 32-bits integers a, b, c, and d; and it performs the following operations:

```
function QRound
    input a,b,c,d # four 32-bit words
    output a,b,c,d
    # n ⋘ₘ denotes m-bit left-rotation of a 32-bit integer n
    1. a = a + b mod 2³²; d = d ⊕ a; d = d ⋘₁₆
    2. c = c + d mod 2³²; b = b ⊕ c; b = b ⋘₁₂
    3. a = a + b mod 2³²; d = d ⊕ a; d = d ⋘₈
    4. c = c + d mod 2³²; b = b ⊕ c; b = b ⋘₇
    5. return (a,b,c,d)
```

6.2.5.3 ChaCha20 Keystream Block Generation

To generate a 512-bit keystream block, ChaCha20 takes an initial state. Then, ten series of quarter-rounds are performed. Each series is composed of eight quarter-rounds; therefore, in total 80 quarter-rounds (i.e. 20 full rounds) are run to yield one keystream block. As shown in Figure 6.15, quarter-round operating on words of the same column are called *column quarter-rounds*; and those operation on words in four distinct columns are called *diagonal quarter-rounds*. Figure 6.15 also shows the order in which the state words are used to form inputs of quarter-rounds. Using such a scanning of state words, ChaCha20 realizes a very fast diffusion.

The full pseudocode of the Keystream block generation function is given below.

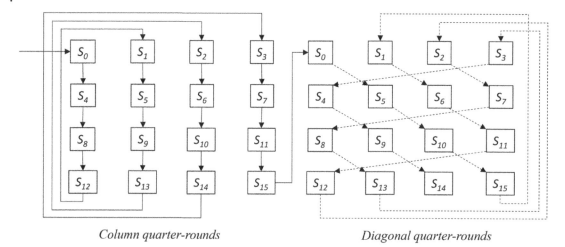

Column quarter-rounds   Diagonal quarter-rounds

Figure 6.15 Order in which state words are used to form one 8-quarter-round series.

---

function KeyStreamBlock_Generation
    input K: 256-bit key; Ctr: 32-bit counter; *Nonce*: 96-bit nonce
    output *Kstr*: 64-byte keystream
    1. *Constants* = 0x61707865 || 0x3320646e || 0x79622d32 || 0x6b206574
    2. *InitState* = *Constants* || K || *Ctr* || *Nonce*
    3. S = *InitState*
    4. **for** i=1 **to** 10 **do**
        # perform four column quarter-rounds
        $Qround\left(S[0], S[4], S[8], S[12]\right); Qround\left(S[1], S[5], S[9], S[13]\right)$
        $Qround\left(S[2], S[6], S[10], S[14]\right); Qround\left(S[3], S[7], S[11], S[15]\right)$
        # perform four "diagonal" quarter-rounds
        $Qround\left(S[0], S[5], S[10], S[15]\right); Qround(S[1], S[6], S[11], S[12])$
        $Qround\left(S[2], S[7], S[8], S[13]\right); Qround\left(S[3], S[4], S[9], S[14]\right)$
    # After 80 quarter-rounds
    5. *Kstr* = *null*
    # add the initial state to the current
    6. **for** i=0 **to** 15 **do**
        $S[i]$ = $S[i]$ + *InitState*[i] # (addition *mod* 2^{32})
        Kstr = *Kstr* || *LittleEndianEncode* ($S[i]$)
    7. **return** *Kstr* # Bit-length of *Kstr* is of 512 bits

---

6.2.5.4 Plaintext Encryption and Decryption Using ChaCha20

A nonce is associated with each plaintext. Then, the plaintext is split into 64-byte blocks. An initial counter C is associated with the first plaintext block; the counter is incremented for each plaintext block. A 512-bit keystream is XORed with each plaintext block to yield a ciphertext block. If the plaintext byte-length is not a multiple of 64 bytes, the last plaintext block is a non-complete block; only a portion of the last generated keystream block is used to yield the last ciphertext block.

   Below is the pseudocode of ChaCha20 plaintext encryption. The decryption is identical to the encryption (only the input and output differ). $Blen\left(P\right)$ means the byte-length of byte-string P.

---

function ChaCha20_Encryption
    input K: 256-bit key; C: 32-bit counter; *Nonce*: 96-bit nonce
           P: variable-length plaintext
    output *Ciphertext*: bit-string
    1. *Ciphertext* = *null*
    2. $m = \lfloor Blen(P) / 64 \rfloor - 1$ # m + 1 is the number of full 64-byte blocks

```
3. for j = 0 to m do
       Kstr = KeyStreamBlock_Generation (K, C+j, nonce)
       Ciphertext= Ciphertext || (P[j * 64 : j * 64 + 63] ⊕ Kstr)
4. if (ByteLen(P) mod 64 ≠ 0) then
       j = ⌊ByteLen(P) / 64⌋; r = Blen(P) − j * 64
       Kstr = KeyStreamBlock_Generation(K, C + j, nonce)
       Blk = P⌊j*64: Blen(P)-1⌋
       Ciphertext = Ciphertext || (Blk ⊕ Kstr[0: r − 1])
5. return Ciphertext
```

6.2.6 RC4 Stream Cipher

RC4 (also known as Rivest Cipher 4) is a stream cipher, initially protected by US patent. After the discovery of its internal operation, it became public and widely used as building block in many services including SSL (secure socket layer), TLS ((transport layer security), SSH (Secure Shell), Wired Equivalent Privacy (WEP), and Wi-Fi Protected Access (WPA). However, because of flaws discovered, the IETF has banned the use of RC4 since 2015 in almost all security services. Some vulnerabilities of RC4 are discussed in [12].

RC4 is presented in this chapter for pedagogical purpose as it is a well-known cipher not based on LFSRs and which is easy to implement in software [13].

RC4 does not rely on LFSRs. It makes use of a permutation vector S of 256 elements denoted $S[0]$, $S[1]$, $S[2]$, ..., $S[255]$. Each element $S[i]$ is a byte. Vector S contains all the values from 0 to 255, stored in a random way. Therefore, taking one element of vector S looks like a generation of a random number between 0 and 255.

6.2.6.1 RC4 Key-scheduling Algorithm

RC4 takes a key K of a variable-length ranging from 1 to 256 bytes. In initialization phase, called key scheduling algorithm, RC4 produces the first permutation S as follows:

```
for i=0 to 255 do S[i] = i
j = 0
for i=0 to 255 do
    j = (j + S[i] + K[i mod len(K)]) mod 256
    Swap(S[i], S[j])
```

$K[i]$ denotes byte i of key K, with $i = 0,1, ..., len(K)$ and $len(K)$ denotes the byte-length of key K. Swap(S[i], S[j]) is a function to swap the contents of elements *S[i]* and *S[j]*.

If the length of key K is 256, key K is used once. Otherwise, it is used many times.

6.2.6.2 Keystream Generation Phase

Keystream generation of RC4 is depicted on Figure 6.16. From two current variables i and j, do the following: swap elements $S[i]$ and $S[j]$, then deliver $S[S[i]+S[j] \bmod 256]$ as keystream output.

The pseudocode of RC4 keystream generation is as follows:

```
i, j = 0
while (GeneratingOutput) do
    i = (i + 1) mod 256
    j = (j + S[i]) mod 256
    Swap(S[i], S[j])
    Z = S[(S[i] + S[j]) mod 256]
    output Z
```

The encryption and decryption with RC4 are XOR operations.

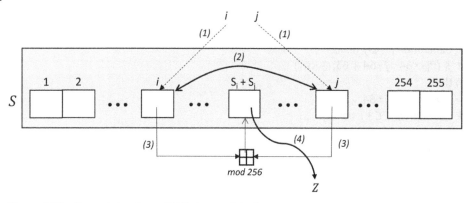

Figure 6.16 General structure of RC4 stream ciphering.

6.2.7 Lightweight Cryptography Stream Ciphers

Lightweight cryptography (LWC) is a vital and fast growing field in today's world where billions of IoT (Internet of Things) devices (including RFIDs, sensors, and actuators) need to communicate wirelessly. Such devices have limited resources (memory, CPU, and battery) and require light techniques to secure their communications. LWC is a collection of solutions of encryption techniques that features low computational complexity devices. It is aimed at expanding the applications of cryptography to limited-resource devices, while providing a high level of security.

Many companies and laboratories proposed various solutions to secure limited-resource-devices. Almost all the LWC ciphers make use of nonlinear feedback shift registers (NLFSR).

From the standardization perspective, the ISO/IEC 29192-3 standard [14] specified two LWC stream ciphers, *Trivium* and *Enocoro v2*, which are presented in this subsection.

6.2.7.1 Trivium Stream Cipher

Trivium is a synchronous stream cipher inspired by the design of block ciphers [15, 16]. It takes an 80-bit key and an 80-bit IV and generates a keystream of length up to 2^{64} bits. 2^{64} bits represent the number of bits transmitted at 1 Gbps over 2^{34} seconds. The period of the keystream generator output is $2^{93} - 1$, which makes Trivium secure against cryptanalysis. As shown on Figure 6.17, Trivium architecture makes use of three NLFSR registers of variable length, providing a total of 288 bits. The three registers are connected with nonlinear functions.

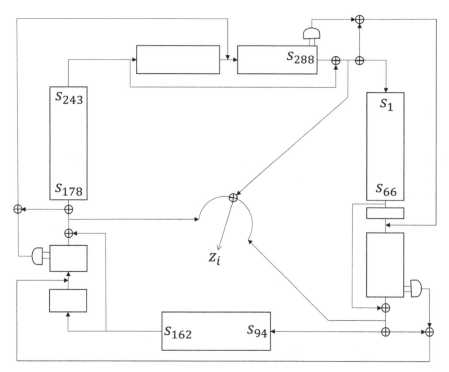

Figure 6.17 Internal structure of Trivium keystream generator.

i) *Keystream generation*

Trivium interval state is composed of 288 register bits, denoted s_1, s_2, ..., s_{288}, among which 15 bits are iteratively used to generate N keystream bits, $N \leq 2^{64}$, as follows:

---

for $i = 1$ **to** N **do**
    1. # Compute one bit of the keystream
        $t_1 = s_{66} \oplus s_{93}$; $t_2 = s_{162} \oplus s_{177}$; $t_3 = s_{243} \oplus s_{288}$; $z_i = t_1 \oplus t_2 \oplus t_3$
    2. # Update the internal state
        $t_1 = t_1 \oplus (s_{91} \wedge s_{92}) \oplus s_{171}$; $t_2 = t_2 \oplus (s_{175} \wedge s_{176}) \oplus s_{264}$
        $t_3 = t_3 \oplus (s_{286} \wedge s_{287}) \oplus s_{69}$
        $(s_1, s_2, ..., s_{93}) \leftarrow (t_3, s_1, s_2, ..., s_{92})$
        $(s_{94}, s_{95}, ..., s_{177}) \leftarrow (t_1, s_{94}, s_2, ..., s_{176})$
        $(s_{178}, s_{179}, ..., s_{288}) \leftarrow (t_3, s_{178}, s_{179}, ..., s_{287})$

---

ii) *Initialization*

The internal state of Trivium is initialized using 80-bit key K and 80-bit IV as follows:

---

1. # Load the key and IV into the registers
    $(S_1, S_2, ..., S_{93}) \leftarrow (K_1, K_2, ..., K_{80}, 0, 0, 0, 0, 0, 0, 0, 0, 0, 0, 0, 0, 0)$
    $(S_{94}, S_{95}, ..., S_{177}) \leftarrow (IV_1, IV_2, ..., IV_{80}, 0,0,0,0,0,0,0,0,0,0,0,0,0,0)$
    $(S_{178}, S_{179}, ..., S_{288}) \leftarrow (0,0, ..., 0,1,1,1)$
2. # Make four full rotations of the three registers as follows:
    for $k = 1$ **to** 4 **do**
      for $i = 1$ **to** 288 **do**
        $t_1 = t_1 \oplus (s_{91} \wedge s_{92}) \oplus s_{171}$; $t_2 = t_2 \oplus (s_{175} \wedge s_{176}) \oplus s_{264}$
        $t_3 = t_3 \oplus (s_{286} \wedge s_{287}) \oplus s_{69}$; $(s_1, s_2, ..., s_{93}) \leftarrow (t_3, s_1, s_2, ..., s_{92})$
        $(s_{94}, s_{95}, ..., s_{177}) \leftarrow (t_1, s_{94}, s_2, ..., s_{176})$
        $(s_{178}, s_{179}, ..., s_{288}) \leftarrow (t_3, s_{178}, s_{179}, ..., s_{287})$

6.2.7.2 Enocoro Stream Cipher

Enocoro stream cipher family consists of two algorithms, Enocoro-80, which has a key length of 80 bits and Enocoro-128v2, which has a key length of 128 bits [17]. Enocoro-80 is obsoleted because of its weak security level. In the sequel, Enocoro implicitly refers to Enocoro-128v2.

Enocoro has a reduced hardware circuit size. Compared to AES, the current de facto standard for data encryption, Enocoro achieves the encryption process with about 1/10 of the amount of power consumption.

Enocoro keystream generator (KSG) consists of an initialization function, an output function, and a finite state machine. The latter consists of an internal state $S^{(t)}$, which is updated by a function *Next* at each clock step. *Init* function generates the first state $S^{(0)}$. *Output* function generates the keystream bit $Z^{(t)}$.

The internal state of Enocoro KSG has two parts: a state a and a buffer (NLFSR) b (see Figure 6.18). The state a is composed of two bytes denoted a_0 and a_1. Buffer b is composed of n_b bytes denoted b_0, ..., b_{n_b-1}.

Enocoro is a byte-keystream cipher. Thus, the operations are byte-oriented. Addition is the XOR bitwise operation and the multiplication is performed over the extension field F_{2^8}, under the primitive polynomial $\varphi_8(x) = x^8 + x^4 + x^3 + x^2 + 1$.

At time t, the content of state a is denoted $a^{(t)}$ and that of the buffer, $b^{(t)}$. The update function *Next* is composed of two functions denoted ρ and λ. Thus, Enocoro may be specified as follows:

$$S^{(0)} = Init\left(Key,\ IV\right)$$

$$Z^{(t)} = Output\left(S^{(t)}\right) = a_1^{(t)}$$

$$S^{(t+1)} = \left(a^{(t+1)},\ b^{(t+1)}\right) = Next\left(S^{(t)}\right) = \left(\rho\left(a^{(t)},\ b^{(t)}\right),\ \lambda\left(a^{(t)},\ b^{(t)}\right)\right)$$

Enocoro family has 11 parameters denoted:

- n_b: byte-length of the buffer.
- q_1, p_1, q_2, p_2, q_3, and p_3: numbers of buffer elements (boxes) used in λ function.
- k_1, k_2, k_3, and k_4: numbers of buffer elements used in ρ function.

Different choices of the parameters result in different internal structures. In the standard Enocoro 128-v2, the parameters are fixed as follows:

- $n_b = 32$
- $q_1 = 2,\ p_1 = 6,\ q_2 = 7,\ p_2 = 15,\ q_3 = 16,\ p_3 = 28$
- $k_1 = 2,\ k_2 = 7,\ k_3 = 16,\ k_4 = 29$

Function ρ

It takes four elements of buffer b, numbered 2, 7, 16, and 29, to update the a-state bytes as follows:

$$u_0 = a_0^{(t)} \oplus S\left[b_2^{(t)}\right] \quad u_1 = a_1^{(t)} \oplus S\left[b_7^{(t)}\right] \quad (v_0, v_1) = L(u_0, u_1)$$
$$a_0^{(t+1)} = v_0 \oplus S\left[b_{16}^{(t)}\right] \quad a_1^{(t+1)} = v_1 \oplus S\left[b_{29}^{(t)}\right]$$

where L is a linear transformation over finite field F_{2^8}, defined by:

$$\begin{pmatrix} v_0 \\ v_1 \end{pmatrix} = L(v_0,\ v_1) = \begin{pmatrix} 1 & 1 \\ 1 & d \end{pmatrix}\begin{pmatrix} u_0 \\ u_1 \end{pmatrix},\ \text{where } d = 0\text{x}02$$

S is a substitution box, which maps eight bits to eight bits to provide nonlinearity to operation of the KSG.

Function λ

It rotates buffer b and then updates three bits of the buffer as follows:

$$b_i^{(t+1)} = b_{i-1}^{(t)},\ i \neq 0,3,8,17 \qquad \text{(partial shifting of register)}$$
$$b_0^{(t+1)} = b_{31}^{(t)} \oplus a_0^{(t)} \qquad\qquad b_3^{(t+1)} = b_2^{(t)} \oplus b_6^{(t)}$$
$$b_8^{(t+1)} = b_7^{(t)} \oplus b_{15}^{(t)} \qquad\qquad b_{17}^{(t+1)} = b_{16}^{(t)} \oplus b_{28}^{(t)}$$

Initialization

For each encryption, a distinct pair (Key, IV) is selected. The *Init* function takes a 128-bit key K and a 64-bit initialization vector IV and performs the following:

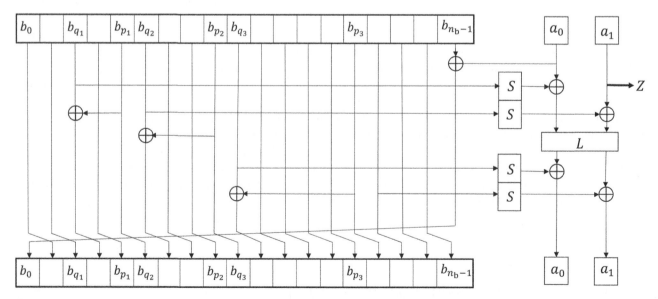

Figure 6.18 Internal structure of Enocoro keystream generator [17].

$$b_i^{(-96)} = K_i, \quad 0 \le i \le 16$$

$$b_{i+16}^{(-96)} = IV_i, \quad 0 \le i < 8$$

$$b_{24}^{(-96)} = 0\text{x}66 \qquad b_{25}^{(-96)} = 0\text{x}e9$$

$$b_{26}^{(-96)} = 0\text{x}4b \qquad b_{27}^{(-96)} = 0\text{x}4d$$

$$b_{28}^{(-96)} = 0\text{x}ef \qquad b_{29}^{(-96)} = 0\text{x}8a$$

$$b_{30}^{(-96)} = 0\text{x}2c \qquad b_{31}^{(-96)} = 0\text{x}3b$$

$$a_0^{(-96)} = 0\text{x}88 \qquad a_1^{(-96)} = 0\text{x}4c$$

After initialization of the state (i.e. a and b) using the key, the initialization vector, and constants, the state is updated with 96 iterations of two functions (namely, XORing the iteration counter and register element b_{31} followed by *Next* function). The iteration counter is initialized by 0x01 and incremented by the multiplication by 0x02 over the extension field F_{2^8}, under the primitive polynomial $\varphi_8(x)$. Then, the KSG delivers the first byte of the keystream, which is used to encrypt or decrypt one byte.

6.3 Exercises and Problems

6.3.1 List of Exercises and Problem

Exercise 6.1
Let R be an LFSR defined with the following parameters:
  Seed: $FF_1 = 0, FF_2 = 0, FF_3 = 1$
  Feedback coefficients: $c_1 = 1, c_2 = 0, c_3 = 1$
  Show the states of R in the eight first clock impulses. What is the cycle of the register?

Exercise 6.2
Show the table of states of the following LFSRs for nine clock impulses:
1) First LFSR: feedback polynomial $\mathcal{F}_1(x) = x^3 + 1$ and seed $= (0, 1, 0)$
   Second LFSR: feedback polynomial $\mathcal{F}_2(x) = x^3 + x^2 + 1$ and seed $= (0, 1, 0)$
2) Why the second LFSR has more states?

Exercise 6.3
1) What is the maximum byte-length of plaintexts that can be encrypted with ChaCha20?
2) What is the maximum amount of data that can be encrypted with the same ChaCha20 key?

Problem 6.1
1) Consider a self-synchronizing stream cipher (S3C) with a large synchronization window. Discuss why synchronous stream ciphers (S2Cs) are less impacted by transmission errors than S3Cs.
2) Consider a self-synchronizing stream cipher (S3C) with a short synchronization window. Discuss why it is more difficult to detect bit deletion or insertion with S3Cs than with S2C.

Problem 6.2
1) Show that it is easy to recover the parameters A and B of a linear congruential generator if three outputs and the modulus m, which is a prime, are known.
2) Assume that three LCG values are known: $z_1 = 13, z_2 = 6$, and $z_3 = 5$ and the modulus m is 20. Find parameters of LCG.
3) Assume that three LCG values are known: $z_1 = 6, z_2 = 5$, and $z_3 = 2$ and the modulus m is 20. Find parameters of LCG.
4) What do you conclude?

Problem 6.3
1) Show that it is easy to recover the secret key (A, B) of a stream cipher based on a linear congruential generator if $3n$ bits of plaintext and their cipher bits and the modulus m of the LCG are known. Assume that $m = 2^n - 1$ is a prime. Assume that the known bits are the first bits of a message. Hint: use the result of Problem 6.2.
2) Find the secret key (A, B), if $n = 3$ and the known plaintext is $a = 101010101$ and the ciphertext $c = 000100111$.

Problem 6.4

Let R be an LFSR defined by feedback polynomial $\mathcal{F}(x) = x^4 + x + 1$. Show that the output sequence of R is defined by the initial entries and the recursion $s_{4+i} = s_{3+i} + s_i$.

Problem 6.5

In the feedback of SNOW 3G, there are two multiplications one by α and one by α^{-1}. α is an element of extension field $F_{2^{32}}$ and α^{-1} is its multiplicative inverse. The field $F_{2^{32}}$ is generated by α, which is a root of $F_{2^8}[x]$ polynomial $P4(x) = x^4 + \beta x^{23} x^3 + \beta^{245} x^2 + \beta^{48} x + \beta^{239}$. $\beta \in F_{2^8}[x]$ is a root of $F_2[x]$ polynomial $P8(x) = x^8 + x^7 + x^5 + x^3 +$. How x^{-1} can be expressed using β?

Hint: check with parameters of DIV_α function.

Problem 6.6

Prove Lemma 6.1.

Problem 6.7

Assume that the adversary knows $2m$ bits of plaintext (for example, he/she knows the header of a message) and their ciphertext. He/she also knows that the sender is using a stream cipher based on an LFSR with m bits. Assume that known bits of plaintext are located at the beginning of a message. Show that LFSR-based ciphers are vulnerable to plaintext attack.

Problem 6.8

A plaintext $M = 1001\ 0010\ 0110\ 1101\ 1001\ 0010\ 0110$ is encrypted with an LFSR-based stream cipher and the ciphertext is $C = 1011\ 1100\ 0011\ 0001\ 0010\ 1011\ 0001$. Assume that the pair (M, M') is given and the period of the keystream generator is less than 15.

1) What is the period of the keystream generator used to encrypt M?
2) What is its degree, initialization value, and feedback polynomial?

Problem 6.9

Consider a keystream generator with a period of L bits. The adversary can intercept all the traffic. All the encrypted messages start with a content (e.g. an application protocol header) of k bits known to adversary. No other characteristics of the code are known.

What is the potential vulnerability of the considered encryption system (i.e. under which conditions the code can be broken)?

Problem 6.10

Consider a user who has a series of documents to encrypt with a stream cipher and then store them. All documents are English texts including only uppercase letters and space in 7-bit ASCII code. Given the large size of the documents, the user decides to restart (with the same initial value) the keystream generator to encrypt each document. Show that if the number of documents is enough large, an adversary, who has copies of the encrypted documents, can recover partially or entirely all the documents.

Problem 6.11

Imagine a text-source sending a text in natural language. In such a case, some portions of plaintext are likely to be the same. The adversary can take advantage of plaintext redundancy to derive relations between keystream bits, which contribute to recover the key. Consider a simple stream cipher composed of an LFSR with feedback polynomial $x^3 + x + 1$ and a key $K = (K_0, K_1, K_2) = (0,0,1)$, as illustrated by Figure 6.19. Show how an adversary who knows the positions, denoted i and j, of two portions of plaintext of L-bit length, $L \geq 3$, can recover the key.

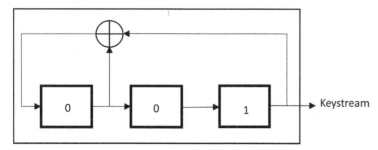

Figure 6.19 Simple LFSR.

6.3.2   Solutions to Exercises and Problems

Exercise 6.1

Seed: $FF_1 = 0, FF_2 = 0, FF_3 = 1$. Feedback coefficients: $c_1 = 1$, $c_2 = 0$, $c_3 = 1$.
Below are the states of LFSR R in the 9 first clock impulses.

Clock	FF_1	FF_2	FF_3
0	0	0	1
1	1	0	0
2	1	1	0
3	1	1	1
4	0	1	1
5	1	0	1
6	0	1	0
7	0	0	1
8	1	0	0

From the table above, we see that the register has a cycle of 7. Another way to find the register cycle is to inspect the feedback polynomial, which is equal to $x^3 + x + 1$. Such a polynomial of degree 3 is a primitive polynomial (see Table 6.2). Therefore, the register is maximal-length, with a cycle of $2^3 - 1$.

Exercise 6.2

1) Below are the state tables for both LFSRs.

$\mathcal{F}_1(x) = x^3 + 1$					$\mathcal{F}_2(x) = x^3 + x^2 + 1$			
Clock	FF_1	FF_2	FF_3		Clock	FF_1	FF_2	FF_3
0	0	1	0		0	0	1	0
1	0	0	1		1	1	0	1
2	1	0	0		2	1	1	0
3	0	1	0		3	1	1	1
4	0	0	1		4	0	1	1
5	1	0	0		5	0	0	1
6	0	1	0		6	1	0	0
7	0	0	1		7	0	1	0
8	1	0	0		8	1	0	1
9	0	1	0		9	1	1	0

2) $\mathcal{F}_2(x)$ is a primitive polynomial. By Lemma 6.2, the LFSR is a maximal-length LFSR; it has a cycle of $2^3 - 1$. The polynomial $\mathcal{F}_1(x)$ is reducible in F_2. That is, $x^3 + 1 = (x+1)(x^2 + x + 1)$. $\mathcal{F}_1(x)$ cannot be a primitive polynomial; thus, the first LFSR has a cycle less than $2^3 - 1$.

Exercise 6.3

1) The same ChaCha20 key and nonce are used to encrypt each plaintext. Up to 2^{32} counter values can be used with the same nonce to generate a maximum of 2^{32} keystream blocks. Each keystream block is used to encrypt a 64-byte plaintext block. Therefore, the maximum byte-length of any plaintext is of 2^{38} bytes (i.e. 256 Gb).

2) The same ChaCha20 key can be used with up to 2^{96} nonces; and each nonce can be used with up to 2^{32} counter values to generate a maximum of $2^{96} * 2^{32}$ keystream blocks. Each keystream block is used to encrypt a 64-byte plaintext block. Therefore, the maximum amount of data that can be encrypted with the same ChaCha20 key is of 2^{134} bytes.

Problem 6.1

Let n be the number of bits in the synchronization window of a self-synchronized (S3C).

1) Assume that n is large and a transmission error occurs when transmitting bit i. With a synchronous stream cipher (S2C), the receiver just discards the bit i. With an S3C, the receiver cannot correctly decrypt n bits, starting with bit i. For example, if the continuous flow being transmitted is composed of pixels represented with eight bits, with an S2C, a single pixel is discarded, while $\lceil n/8 \rceil$ pixels are discarded with an S3C.

2) Assume that n is low and a few bits have been inserted or deleted by an adversary. In the S2C, the receiver loses synchronization and the forged bits as well as the remaining bits are very likely to be discarded. This helps in detecting attacks because of inconsistency between the message content before and after the alteration. In S3C, only bits altered in synchronization window may be discarded, which reduces the chance to detect attacks. For example, imagine that the adversary changes an amount 10 to 1000 in a text. On the receiver side, in S2C, it is very likely that the part of the message starting from the altered amount will be entirely different from the original one and the receiver has chance to detect the attack. In the S3C, only the amount and may be a few other characters in encrypted message will be different from the characters in decrypted message. Therefore, the receiver has less chance to detect the attack.

Problem 6.2

1) Assume that three successive outputs, denoted z_1, z_2, and z_3, of a linear congruential generator are known as well as the modulus m.

In the following, computations are over $\mathbb{Z}_m^*$ (i.e. the set of invertible elements of $\mathbb{Z}_m$). By definition of LCG, the following equalities hold:

$$z_2 = A * z_1 + B \bmod m$$

$$z_3 = A * z_2 + B \bmod m$$

Thus,

$$B = z_2 - A * z_1 \bmod m$$

$$B = z_3 - A * z_2 \bmod m$$

$$z_2 - A * z_1 \bmod m = z_3 - A * z_2 \bmod m$$

$$\Rightarrow A = (z_2 - z_3)(z_1 - z_2)^{-1} \bmod m$$

Since z_1, z_2, and z_3 are known, A and B can be easily derived in $\mathbb{Z}_m^*$.

2) Make substitutions in the last equation:

$$A = (6 - 5)(13 - 6)^{-1} \bmod 20$$

$$= (7)^{-1} \bmod 20 = 3$$

Then, $B = 6 - 3 * 13 \bmod 20 = -33 \bmod 20 = 7$.

3) Make substitutions in the last equation:

$$A = (5 - 2)(6 - 2)^{-1} \bmod 20$$

$$= 3 * (4)^{-1} \bmod 20$$

Since 4 and 20 are not coprime, $4^{-1} \bmod 20$ does not exist. Thus, A and B cannot be recovered.

4) From the previous example, we conclude that if the modulus m is not a prime, some elements of $\mathbb{Z}_m$ do not belong to $\mathbb{Z}_m^*$. In particular, $(z_1 - z_2)^{-1}$ may not exist in $\mathbb{Z}_m^*$ and consequently, the 3-known-value attack may fail to recover A and B. Therefore, a non-prime modulus is preferred when security is of concern.

Problem 6.3

1) Let the known bits be $a_{3n}, a_{3n-1}, ..., a_2, a_1$ and their corresponding cipher bits be $c_{3n}, c_{3n-1}, ..., c_2, c_1$. The modulus $2^n - 1$ of the linear congruential generator (LCG) also is known. Each LCG output is of a length of n bits. Thus, LCG output k ($k = 1,2,3$) can be written as $z_k = (z_{k,n}, z_{k,n-1}, ..., z_{k,1})$.

Assume that the known bits are the first bits of a message. Therefore, the keystream bits used to encrypt them form the first three outputs of LCG, i.e. $z_1, z_2,$ and z_3. From the plaintext and ciphertext, keystream bits can be derived as follows:

$z_{1,i} = a_i \oplus c_i$, for $i = 1, ..., n$.
$z_{2,i} = a_{i+n} \oplus c_{i+n}$, for $i = 1, ..., n$.
$z_{3,i} = a_{i+2n} \oplus c_{i+2n}$, for $i = 1, ..., n$.

Then, once the three values $z_1, z_2,$ and z_3 are computed, it easy to recover the key (A,B) as in Problem 6.2.

2) Find the secret key (A,B), if the modulus is $m = 7$ and the known plaintext is $a = 101010101$ and the ciphertext $c = 000100111$. From the known elements, keystream bits are derived as:

$z_{1,1} = 1 \oplus 1 = 0 \qquad z_{1,2} = 0 \oplus 1 = 1 \qquad z_{1,3} = 1 \oplus 1 = 0$
$z_{2,1} = 0 \oplus 0 = 0 \qquad z_{2,2} = 1 \oplus 0 = 1 \qquad z_{2,3} = 0 \oplus 1 = 1$
$z_{3,1} = 1 \oplus 0 = 1 \qquad z_{3,2} = 0 \oplus 0 = 0 \qquad z_{3,3} = 1 \oplus 0 = 1$

Thus, $z_1 = 2, z_2 = 6,$ and $z_3 = 5$
By design of LCG:

$6 = A * 2 + B \bmod 7$

$5 = A * 6 + B \bmod 7$

Hence,

$1 = -A * 4 \bmod 7$

$A = (-1) * 4^{-1} \bmod 7 = -2 \bmod 7 = 5$

$B = 6 - 2 * A \bmod 7 = -4 \bmod 7 = 3$

Problem 6.4

R is an LFSR defined by feedback polynomial $\mathcal{F}(-1) = x^4 + x + 1$. Hence, its feedback coefficients are $c_1 = 1, c_2 = 0, c_3 = 0, c_4 = 1$. The property of the output sequence of R is proven by induction.

$i = 1, s_{4+1} = s_4 c_1 \oplus s_3 c_2 \oplus s_2 c_3 \oplus s_1 c_4 = s_4 \oplus s_1$

$i = 2, s_{4+2} = s_5 c_1 \oplus s_4 c_2 \oplus s_3 c_3 \oplus s_2 c_4 = s_5 \oplus s_2$

$i = n, s_{4+n} = s_{4+n-1} c_1 \oplus s_{4+n-2} c_2 \oplus s_{4+n-3} c_3 \oplus s_n c_4 = s_{4+n-1} \oplus s_n$

Assume that the recurrence is valid for $i = n$. Then,

$i = n+1, s_{4+n+1} = s_{4+n} c_1 \oplus s_{4+n-1} c_2 \oplus s_{4+n-2} c_3 \oplus s_{n+1} c_4 = s_{4+n} \oplus s_{n+1}$

Therefore, the output sequence of LFSR R is defined by the recurrence $s_{4+i} = s_{3+i} + s_i$ for any positive integer i.

Problem 6.5

Since $\alpha \in F_{2^{32}}[x]$ is a root of $F_{2^8}[x]$ polynomial $P4(x) = x^4 + \beta^{23} x^3 + \beta^{245} x^2 + \beta^{48} x + \beta^{239}$, the field $F_{2^{32}}$ is equivalent to the set $\{0, 1, \alpha^1, \alpha^2, ..., \alpha^{32-2}\}$. Any element of $F_{2^{32}}$ can be represented by a polynomial of degree less than 32 with coefficients in $\{0,1\}$ or as a polynomial of degree less than 4 with coefficients in F_{2^8}.

By definition of a field F_{2^m} generated with a primitive polynomial $P(x)$, multiplication of two elements a and b, represented by their polynomials $a(x) * b(x)$ and $b(x)$, is the element c, such that $c(x)$ is the remainder of the Euclidean division of $a(x) * b(x)$ by $p(x)$.

Since $x^{-1} \in F_{2^{32}}[x]$, $x^{(-1)}(x)$ is represented by a polynomial $c_3 x^3 + c_2 x^2 + c_1 x + c_0$, with $c_{i=0,1,2,3} \in F_{2^8}$.

By definition of multiplicative inverse, $\forall a \in F_{2^{32}}, aa^{-1} = 1$. Thus, $x * x^{-1} = 1 = x(c_3 x^3 + c_2 x^2 + c_1 x + c_0) \bmod P4(x)$

The Euclidean division of $(c_3 x^4 + c_2 x^3 + c_1 x^2 + c_0 x)$ by $x^4 + \beta^{23} x^3 + \beta^{245} x^2 + \beta^{48} x + \beta^{239}$ returns a remainder equal to

$$\left(c_2 - c_3\beta^{23}\right)x^3 + \left(c_1 - c_3\beta^{245}\right)x^2 + (c_0 - c_3\beta^{48})x - c_3\beta^{239} = 1$$

By Theorem 3.22, since $\beta \in F_{2^8}[x]$ is a root of $x^8 + x^7 + x^5 + x^3$; so, $\beta^{2^8-1} = \beta^{255} = 1$
To match the remainder equation, we need:

$$\begin{aligned}
c_3\beta^{239} = 1 = \beta^{255} &\Rightarrow c_3 = \beta^{16}\\
\left(c_2 - c_3\beta^{23}\right) = 0 &\Rightarrow c_2 = \beta^{39}\\
\left(c_1 - c_3\beta^{245}\right) = 0 &\Rightarrow c_1 = \beta^6\\
\left(c_0 - c_3\beta^{48}\right) = 0 &\Rightarrow c_0 = \beta^{64}
\end{aligned}$$

Therefore, x^{-1} is expressed by polynomial $\beta^{16}x^3 + \beta^{39}x^2 + \beta^6 x + \beta^{64}$.
Check: in function DIV_∞, which is an implementation of multiplication by x^{-1}, the constants $16, 39, 6$, and 64 are present.

Problem 6.6

LFSR state is the content of a register of m bits. The maximum number of distinct values of an m-bit register is 2^m. If an LFSR reaches a state with all flip-flops at 0, it will no more change its state. Therefore, the maximum of non-zero states is $2^m - 1$.

Let $\sigma_t = \left(s_t^1, s_t^2, ..., s_t^m\right)$ denote the initial state of the register and s_t^i the state of each element i, respectively. After N iterations, the register returns to its initial state. Therefore, $\sigma_{t+N} = \left(s_{t+N}^1, s_{t+N}^2, ..., s_{t+N}^m\right) = \left(s_t^1, s_t^2, ..., s_t^m\right)$, then after one iteration, $\sigma_{t+N+1} = \left(s_{t+N+1}^1, s_{t+N+1}^2, ..., s_{t+N+1}^m\right) = \left(s_{t+1}^1, s_{t+1}^2, ..., s_{t+1}^m\right)$, etc. until $t+2N$, where $\sigma_{t+2N} = \left(s_{t+2N}^1, s_{t+2N}^2, ..., s_{t+2N}^m\right) = \left(s_t^1, s_t^2, ..., s_t^m\right)$.

The same repeats after kN iterations (k is a positive integer). Thus, the output of LFSR follows a cyclic pattern of bits with a period of N. $\square$

Problem 6.7

Assume that the adversary knows $2m$ bits of plaintext (for example, he/she knows the header of a message) and their ciphertext. He/she also knows that the sender is using a stream cipher based on an LFSR with m bits.

Without loss of generality, assume that known bits of plaintext are located at the beginning of a message and denoted $a_{2m-1}, a_{2m-2}, ..., a_1, a_0$. The ciphertext bits are denoted $a'_{2m-1}, a'_{2m-2}, ..., a'_1, a'_0$. By definition of a stream cipher, given a plaintext and its ciphertext, it is easy to compute the key bit string $\left(s_{2m-1}, s_{2m-2}, ..., s_1, s_0\right)$. That is,

$$s_{2m-1} = a'_{2m-1} \oplus a_{2m-1}$$

$$s_{2m-2} = a'_{2m-2} \oplus a_{2m-2}$$

...

$$s_m = a'_m \oplus a_m$$

$$s_{m-1} = a'_{m-1} \oplus a_{m-1}$$

...

$$s_0 = a'_0 \oplus a_0$$

With equation (6.1), and $t = 0$, we build a system of m linear equations:

$$\begin{cases}
s_m = a'_m \oplus a_m = \left(\sum_{j=0}^{m-1} s_j c_{m-j}\right) mod\ 2\\[2ex]
s_{m+1} = a'_{m+1} \oplus a_{m+1} = \left(\sum_{j=0}^{m-1} s_{j+1} c_{m-j}\right) mod\ 2\\[2ex]
...\\[2ex]
s_{2m-1} = a'_{2m-1} \oplus a_{2m-1} = \left(\sum_{j=0}^{m-1} s_{j+m-1} c_{m-j}\right) mod\ 2
\end{cases}$$

Feedback coefficients $c_m, c_{m-1}, ..., c_1$ are given by solving the linear equation system above.

Example:

The LFSR output is given by the rightmost bit. As shown on Figure 6.5b, the first eight outputs of LFSR R defined by polynomial $x^4 + x + 1$ are $(1, 0, 1, 1, 1, 1, 0, 0)$; they represent the key bit string of the stream cipher. Hence, $s_7 = 1$, $s_6 = 0$, $s_5 = 1$, $s_4 = 1$, $s_3 = 1$, $s_2 = 1$, $s_2 = 1$, and $s_0 = 0$.

Let $a = (1, 1, 0, 1, 1, 1, 0, 0)$ be the plaintext. The ciphertext yielded by a stream cipher relying on LFSR R is $a' = (0, 1, 1, 0, 0, 0, 0, 0)$. Given the plaintext and ciphertext, the adversary derives the keystream bits as follows:

$$a_0' = 0 = s_0 \oplus a_0 \wedge a_0 = 0 \Rightarrow s_0 = 0$$
$$a_1' = 0 = s_1 \oplus a_1 \wedge a_1 = 0 \Rightarrow s_1 = 0$$
$$a_2' = 0 = s_2 \oplus a_2 \wedge a_2 = 1 \Rightarrow s_2 = 1$$
$$a_3' = 0 = s_3 \oplus a_3 \wedge a_3 = 1 \Rightarrow s_3 = 1$$
$$a_4' = 0 = s_4 \oplus a_4 \wedge a_4 = 1 \Rightarrow s_4 = 1$$
$$a_5' = 1 = s_5 \oplus a_5 \wedge a_5 = 0 \Rightarrow s_5 = 1$$
$$a_6' = 1 = s_6 \oplus a_6 \wedge a_4 = 1 \Rightarrow s_6 = 0$$
$$a_7' = 0 = s_7 \oplus a_7 \wedge a_5 = 1 \Rightarrow s_7 = 1$$

By definition of LFSR with $m = 4$, s_{i+4} is yielded by feedback polynomial using s_{i+3}, s_{i+2}, s_{i+1}, s_i. Hence, we can build the following linear equation system:

$$\begin{cases} s_4 = s_3 c_1 \oplus s_2 c_2 \oplus s_1 c_3 \oplus s_0 c_4 = c_1 \oplus c_2 = 1 \\ s_5 = s_4 c_1 \oplus s_3 c_2 \oplus s_2 c_3 \oplus s_1 c_4 = c_1 \oplus c_2 \oplus c_3 = 1 \\ s_6 = s_5 c_1 \oplus s_4 c_2 \oplus s_3 c_3 \oplus s_2 c_4 = c_1 \oplus c_2 \oplus c_3 \oplus c_4 = 0 \\ s_7 = s_6 c_1 \oplus s_5 c_2 \oplus s_4 c_3 \oplus s_3 c_4 = c_2 \oplus c_3 \oplus c_4 = 1 \end{cases}$$

The previous linear equation system can be easily solved with Gaussian elimination, which yields the solution: $c_1 = 1$, $c_2 = 0$, $c_3 = 0$, $c_4 = 1$.

Problem 6.8

$$M = 1001\ 0010\ 0110\ 1101\ 1001\ 0010\ 0110 \text{ and}$$

$$C = 1011\ 1100\ 0011\ 0001\ 0010\ 1011\ 0001.$$

1) Period and degree of the keystream generator
   The keystream used to encrypt M is:

   $$1001\ 0010\ 0110\ 1101\ 1001\ 0010\ 0110 \oplus$$

   $$1011\ 1100\ 0011\ 0001\ 0010\ 1011\ 0001 =$$

   $$0010\ 1110\ 0101\ 1100\ 1011\ 1001\ 0111$$

   We observe that the repeated keystream pattern is either 0010111 or 00101110010111.
   Therefore, the period of the keystream generator is either 7 or 14.
2) Degree of the keystream generator
   By Lemma 6.1, an LFSR with m bits can have a maximum period of $2^m - 1$. Therefore, the LFSR under consideration cannot have less than $m = 3$ bits. Therefore, the degree is $m \geq 3$. Notice that at this point, we are not yet sure that the degree is $m = 3$ or $m = 4$.
3) Initialization vector and feedback polynomial
   If the degree is 3, then the keystream bits generated in the first period are:

   $$\left(s_0 = 0,\ s_1 = 0,\ s_2 = 1,\ s_3 = 0,\ s_4 = 1,\ s_5 = 1,\ s_6 = 1 \right)$$

   Under the assumption that the degree is $m = 3$. The initialization vector is 100, because the m first bits (i.e. s_0, s_1, and s_2) delivered by a keystream generator are equal to the initialization vector. Then, the coefficients of the LFSR result from the following equations:

   $$s_3 = \left(s_2 c_1 \right) \oplus \left(s_1 c_2 \right) \oplus \left(s_0 c_3 \right) = \left(1 \cdot c_1 \right) \oplus \left(0 \cdot c_2 \right) \oplus \left(0 \cdot c_3 \right) = 0 \Rightarrow c_1 = 0$$

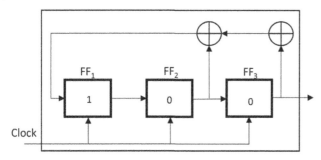

Figure 6.20 LFSR structure.

$$s_4 = (s_3 c_1) \oplus (s_2 c_2) \oplus (s_1 c_3) = (0 \cdot c_1) \oplus (1 \cdot c_2) \oplus (0 \cdot c_3) = 1 \Rightarrow c_2 = 1$$

$$s_5 = (s_4 c_1) \oplus (s_3 c_2) \oplus (s_2 c_3) = (1 \cdot 0) \oplus (0 \cdot 1) \oplus (1 \cdot c_3) = 1 \Rightarrow c_3 = 1$$

$$s_6 = (s_5 c_1) \oplus (s_4 c_2) \oplus (s_3 c_3) = (1 \cdot 0) \oplus (1 \cdot 1) \oplus (0 \cdot 1) = 1$$

Therefore, the feedback polynomial is $\mathcal{F}(x) = x^3 + x^2 + 1$, which is a primitive polynomial; that is why the period of the LFSR is $2^3 - 1 = 7$ (by Lemma 6.2). The internal structure is shown in Figure 6.20 . Now, we are able to confirm that degree is $m = 3$.

Problem 6.9

Assuming that all the encrypted messages start with a known header of k bits, an adversary can break a code based on a keystream generator with a period of L bits if the adversary can collect a set of ciphertexts such that he/she can rebuilt an entire period of the keystream generator as follows:

Let $m_1, m_2, ..., m_t$ be the intercepted messages and $I(m_i)$ denote the index of the first bit used in the keystream period to encrypt message m_i. For example, $L = 127$ and five intercepted messages of the following lengths:

$$len(m_1) = 72 \quad len(m_2) = 110 \quad len(m_3) = 40$$
$$len(m_4) = 33 \quad len(m_5) = 77$$

Thus, $I(m_1) = 0, I(m_2) = 72, I(m_3) = 55, I(m_4) = 95, I(m_5) = 1$
Assume that intercepted messages $m_{i_1}, m_{i_2} ..., m_{i_t}$ are ordered such that:

$$I(m_{i_1}) \le I(m_{i_2}) \le ... \le I(m_{i_t}).$$

If $m_{i_1} = 0, I(m_{j+1}) \le I(m_j) + k, \forall j, i_1 \le j < i_t$, and $I(m_{i_t}) + k \ge L$, then the adversary can recover all the keystream generator output in an entire period. Therefore, the code is vulnerable.

Problem 6.10

Let $C_1, C_2, ..., C_n$ be the n known encrypted documents. Each document is composed of uppercase letters and space in 7-bit ASCII code. Let $C_{i,k}$ denote the kth character of ciphertext i.

Recall ASCII codes (in Hexa): space $\to 20_{16}$, $A \to 41_{16}$, $B \to 42_{16}$, $O \to 4F_{16}$, $P \to 50_{16}$, ..., $Y \to 59_{16}$, $Z \to 5A_{16}$.

The attacker exploits two advantages: i) space character is frequent in English texts (nearly 19% characters are spaces in English texts) and ii) XORing any letter with space character returns a value greater than 20_{16} and XORing two letters returns a value less than 20_{16}. Attacker exploits all pairs of ciphertexts, and for each pair $(C_i, C_j), 1 \le i, j \le n, i \ne j$, performs the following:

K is the keystream generator output, which is the same for all ciphertexts.
Let $s = min(len(C_i), len(C_j))$.
Reduce both bit string C_i and C_j to the same bit-length s, i.e. the longer document is truncated.
XOR the ciphertexts:
$$C_i \oplus C_j = (D_i \oplus K) \oplus (D_j \oplus K) = D_i \oplus D_j$$
$$D_i \oplus D_j = (D_{i,1}, D_{i,2}, ..., D_{i,s}) \oplus (D_{j,1}, D_{j,2}, ..., D_{j,s})$$
$D_i \oplus D_j$ represents the XOR of two original documents.

Exploit the property of XORing a letter and space.

For each $k, 1 \leq k \leq s$:

If $D_{i,k} \oplus D_{j,k} \oplus 20_{16}$, then $D_{i,k}$ is a space and $D_{j,k}$ is a letter or vice versa. Check which alternative is more likely to appear in the documents under consideration and act accordingly (i.e. either confirm a letter and a space in documents or mark pending alternatives).

The more spaces are discovered, the more letters are confirmed in documents. If the number of encrypted documents is enough, and given that the spaces do not appear at the same positions in distinct English text documents, it is very likely that the attacker recovers all the documents entirely. Nevertheless, it takes time to succeed!

Problem 6.11

Since the LFSR has a primitive feedback polynomial of degree 3, it generates a periodic 7-bit sequence equal to 0111001. Assume that two portions of a plaintext P, located at positions i and j, of bit-length L, are identical, i.e. $P_{i+b} = P_{j+b}$, for $b = 0, ..., L-1$. Let C be the ciphertext associated with P. Thus,

$$C_{i+b} \oplus C_{j+b} = \left(P_{i+b} \oplus S_{i+b}\right) \oplus \left(P_{j+b} \oplus S_{j+b}\right) = S_{i+b} \oplus S_{j+b}, \text{ for } b = 0, ..., L-1.$$

Encryption step

Consider a plaintext $P = 11011001\,11011001$ composed of two identical bytes. The keystream, denoted S, used to encrypt P is composed of bits of two LFSR periods plus two bits, i.e. $S = 01\,0111001\,0111001$.

Thus, $C = P \oplus S = 10000101\,01100000$. Let P_i, C_i, and S_i, $i = 0, ..., 15$, denote bits of plaintext, ciphertext, and keystream, respectively. The first bit has index 0. After 16 clock impulses, the bits of the keystream are computed as follows:

$$S_0 = S_7 = S_{14} = K_2 = 1 \qquad S_1 = S_8 = S_{15} = K_1 = 0 \qquad S_2 = S_9 = K_0 = 0$$
$$S_3 = S_{10} = K_0 \oplus K_2 = 1 \qquad S_4 = S_{11} = \left(K_0 + K_2 + K_1\right) = 1$$
$$S_5 = S_{12} = \left(K_2 + K_1\right) = 1 \qquad S_6 = S_{13} = \left(K_0 + K_1\right) = 0$$

Attack step

The adversary builds an equation system as follows:

$$C_0 \oplus C_8 = 1 = S_0 \oplus S_8 = K_2 \oplus K_1$$
$$C_1 \oplus C_9 = 0 = S_1 \oplus S_9 = K_1 \oplus K_0$$
$$C_2 \oplus C_{10} = 1 = S_2 \oplus S_{10} = K_0 \oplus \left(K_0 \oplus K_2\right) = K_2$$

Therefore, $K_2 = 1$, $K_1 = 0$, and $K_0 = 0$.

Notes

1 Recall that $0 \oplus 0 = 0, 1 \oplus 0 = 1, 0 \oplus 1 = 1, 1 \oplus 1 = 0$.

2 "Transmission error" means that at the physical layer, the signal received cannot be sampled as 1 or 0.

3 Bit insertion means either modification or appending of bits in the original message.

4 Flip-flops are the basic building blocks of digital systems. Broadly speaking, a flip-flop circuit can be modeled as a black box, which has two stable states, 0 or 1. A flip-flop stores one bit. When it receives a clock impulse, it changes its state to the state of its input. Then, the output is the state of the flip-flop until the next clock impulse.

5 For proof of Lemma 6.1, see Problem 6.6.

6 It should be noticed that LFSRs using only XOR operation may remain in 0-state. There also exist LFSRs, which use jointly XOR and XNOR (i.e. exclusive NOR), that do not stay in 0-state.

7 IEEE: Institute of Electrical and Electronics Engineers.

8 3GPP: 3rd Generation Partnership Project.

9 ETSI: European Telecommunications Standards Institute.

10 IETF: Internet Engineering Task Force.

11 ISO: International Organization for Standardization.

12 Addition ($+$) and multiplication ($*$) are done over finite field $F_{2^{32}}$, while XOR operation ($\oplus$) is over F_2. See Chapter 3 for more on operations over finite fields.

13 ZUC acronym comes from Zu Chongzhi, a Chinese mathematician and scientist (5th century).

14 FSM registers are of 32 bits; hence, they are adapted to computations over extended field $F_{2^{32}}$.

15 ChaCha20 is an instance of ChaCha algorithm, with 20 rounds. ChaCha20 is a variant of another stream cipher, called Salsa20; both algorithms are proposed by the same author.

References

1 Rescorla, E. (2018). The transport layer security (TLS) protocol version 1.3, RFC 8446. Internet Engineering Task Force (IETF).

2 Fredricksen, H. (1982). A survey of full length nonlinear shift register cycle algorithms. *SIAM (Society for Industrial and Applied Mathematics) Review* 24 (2): 195–221.

3 Web1. Primitive polynomial list. [Online]. [Cited 2023 April]. https://www.partow.net/programming/polynomials.

4 BLE. (2021). Bluetooth core specification, Revision v5.3. Bluetooth SIG, Inc.

5 ETSI. (2006). Specification of the 3GPP confidentiality and integrity algorithms UEA2 & UIA2, document 2 – SNOW 3G specification. European Telecommunications Standards Institute.

6 ISO/IEC. (2011). Information technology security techniques – encryption algorithms – part 4: stream ciphers – ISO/IEC 18033-4. International Organization for Standardization/International Electrotechnical Commission.

7 Biryukov, A., Schmid, D.P., and Zhang, B. (2010). Analysis of SNOW 3G Resynchronization Mechanism. In *International Conference on Security and Cryptography*, 327–333. Athens, Greece: IEEE Xplore.

8 Mukherjee, C.S., Dibyendu, R., and Maitra, S. (2021). *Design and Cryptanalysis of ZUC: A Stream Cipher in Mobile Telephony*. Springer.

9 ETSI. (2011). Specification of the 3GPP confidentiality and integrity algorithms 128-EEA3 & 128-EIA3, document 2 – ZUC specification. European Telecommunications Standards Institute.

10 Bernstein, D. (2008). ChaCha, a Variant of Salsa20. [Online]. [Cited 2023 April]. http://cr.yp.to/chacha/chacha-20080128.pdf.

11 Nir, Y. and Langley, A. (2018). ChaCha20 and Poly1305 for IETF Protocols, RFC 8439. Internet Engineering Task Force (IETF).

12 Fluhrer, S., Mantin, I., and Shamir, A. (2001). Weaknesses in the key scheduling algorithm of RC4. In: *8th Annual International Workshop on Selected Areas in Cryptography*, 1–24. Toronto, Canada: Springer, LNCS 2259.

13 Schneier, B. (1996). *Applied Cryptography: Protocols, Algorithms and Code in C*. Wiley.

14 ISO/IEC. (2012). Information technology – security techniques – lightweight cryptography – part 3: stream ciphers. ISO/IEC 29192-3. International Organization for Standardization/International Electrotechnical Commission.

15 DeCanniere, C. (2006). Trivium: a stream cipher construction inspired by block cipher design principles. In: *9th International Conference ISC*, 171–186. Samos Island, Greece: Springer, LNCS 4176.

16 DeCanniere, C. and Preneel, B. (2006). Trivium specifications. [Online]. [Cited 2023 April]. https://www.ecrypt.eu.org/stream/p3ciphers/trivium/trivium_p3.pdf.

17 Hitachi. (2010). Pseudorandom number generator Enocoro, Specification Ver. 2.0. Hitachi Corporation.

7

Block Ciphers: Basics, TDEA, and AES

This chapter focuses on block ciphers, which are the most commonly used algorithms to encrypt confidential data. In addition to ciphering, block ciphers can be used as stream ciphers and pseudorandom number generators or used to build hash functions and MACs (Message Authentication Codes). Therefore, block ciphers are of prime importance to build cryptosystems.

A huge number of block ciphers are published in literature; but a very small number of them are standards used in operational cryptosystems. This chapter aims at introducing the basics of construction of block ciphers and present in detail the standard block ciphers, currently in use, namely TDEA (Triple Data Encryption Algorithm) and AES (Advanced Encryption Standard). Both ciphers are NIST (National Institute of Standards and Technology, US) standards. It is worth noticing that, because of some reported attacks (even if they are theoretical) against TDEA, AES would be the dominating block cipher in the near future and for a long time.

7.1 Construction Principles for Block Cipher Design

Definition 7.1 Block cipher*: it is an encryption–decryption scheme where a block of plaintext is treated as a single block and is used to obtain a block of ciphertext with the same size.*

Modern ciphering was inspired by mechanical ciphering machines such as Enigma, presented in Section 4.5. The most commonly used cyphers, called *block ciphers*, operate as follows (see Figure 7.1):

- The plaintext is divided into a series of fixed-length blocks ($P_1, P_2, ..., P_m$). In the standards currently in use, the block bit-length is of either 64 or 128.
- An encryption key K (with a known length of 56, 128, 192, or 256 bits).
- Encrypted blocks ($C_1, C_2, ..., C_m$) are of a fixed length, which is the same than that of plaintext blocks.
- Decryption is the inverse operation.

A block cipher is composed of two algorithms: encryption and decryption algorithms, which make use of the same secret key K. The algorithms are denoted $E_K()$ and $D_K()$, which operate on input of fixed-length and produce output with the same length. Formally:

$$E: \{0,1\}^k \times \{0,1\}^n \rightarrow \{0,1\}^n$$

$$D: \{0,1\}^k \times \{0,1\}^n \rightarrow \{0,1\}^n$$

where n is the block bit-length and k, the key bit-length.

For any block plaintext P, the following property holds: $D_K(E_K(P)) = P$.

Encryption and decryption algorithms are based on iterated operations, mainly substitutions and permutations.

Cryptography: Algorithms, Protocols, and Standards for Computer Security, First Edition. Zoubir Mammeri.
© 2024 John Wiley & Sons, Inc. Published 2024 by John Wiley & Sons, Inc.

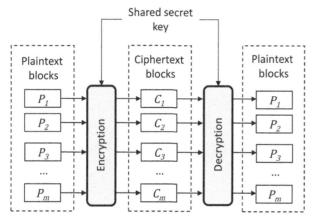

Figure 7.1   Block-based ciphering.

7.1.1   Confusion and Diffusion Properties

In the cryptography field, Claude Shannon proposed in the 1940s two fundamental properties of operation of secure ciphers called *confusion* and *diffusion* [1]. Both properties aim to make statistical-analysis-based attacks impracticable. With robust methods of confusion and diffusion, block ciphers appear as generating random ciphertexts, which are independent from the key and the plaintext.

Definition 7.2 Confusion*: it is a cipher operation where each bit of the ciphertext should depend on several bits of the key. Therefore, the statistical relationship between the plaintext and ciphertext should be hidden.*

Definition 7.3 Diffusion*: it is a cipher operation where when a single bit is changed in the plaintext, several bits in the ciphertext should change. Similarly, when a single bit changes in the ciphertext, several bits in the plaintext should change.*

Definition 7.4 Avalanche effect*: changing a few bits in the plaintext (resp. in ciphertext) results in a lot of changes in the ciphertext (resp. in plaintext), which is known as avalanche effect; i.e. a small change in either the key or the plaintext should cause a drastic change in the ciphertext.*

Affine and Caesar ciphers, presented in Sections 4.2–4.3, do not make use of diffusion and confusion methods. Therefore, they are very easy to break. In block ciphers, the common techniques to achieve confusion and diffusion are: substitution boxes, permutations, and key expansion.

7.1.1.1   Substitution Boxes

An S-Box is an array of R rows by C columns. It contains elements of a specific length; for example, TDEA S-Boxes are of a length of four bits, while those of AES are of a length of eight bits. In general, the number of rows or columns is at most 16.

   The bit-length of the elements of an S-box depends on each cipher. For example, Elements of TDEA S-boxes are of a length of four bits, while those of AES are of a length of eight bits. The element space of an S-Box is at most equal to that of the input space; otherwise, some elements of the S-Box are never used. In some ciphers, such as TDEA, some elements may be repeated in an S-Box. Figure 7.2 illustrates the access to an S-Box. The value to replace D is converted into two indexes, r and c. Then, the content of the cell, $D' = S\_Box(r,c)$, is returned as the element to replace D.

   The following properties are expected not to compromise security and to enable decryption:

i) S-Boxes include elements that appear as random sequences of elements; therefore, no relationship between elements could be inferred to design attacks. Such property is referred to as the nonlinearity of S-Boxes.
ii) S-Boxes are deterministic; i.e. the same input is always mapped to the same output.

7.1.1.2   Permutation

Definition 7.5 Permutation*: a function $E: \{0,1\}^n \rightarrow \{0,1\}^n$ is a permutation if there exists an inverse function E^{-1} such that $E^{-1}(E(x)) = x$, for any $x \in \{0,1\}^n$.*

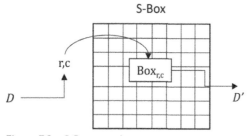

Figure 7.2   S-Box mapping.

Block ciphers make use of permutations to swap a part of a block with another, so that the diffusion is increased. In block ciphers addressed in this chapter, permutations are defined either by permutation tables or with shifting and mixing.

7.1.1.3   Key Expansion

Block ciphers are iterated ciphers, which perform the same operations at all (with some exceptions) rounds. To increase confusion in the resulting ciphertexts, instead of using the same cipher key in all the

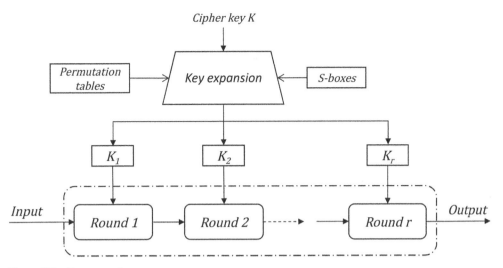

Figure 7.3 Key expansion.

rounds, each round has its own key called *round key*. The result is that the ciphers make use of r keys, where r is the number of rounds. The key expansion function, also called key schedule function, is the component of block ciphers that generates the round keys from the initial key (also called cipher key). In general, key expansion function makes use of permutations and s-boxes (see Figure 7.3).

7.1.2 Feistel Structure

Many block ciphers (including DEA, Blowfish, CAST-128, and Kasumi) are based on *Feistel network*. The latter is also called *Feistel structure*.[1] The main component of a Feistel network is the *round function F*, which takes an input block and a *round key* and returns an output of the same length than that of the input block. The round function may be invertible or not. The number of rounds, denoted n, is a setting parameter of cryptosystems; often, $n = 10, 12, 14$, or 16. The number of rounds depends on the tradeoff between the desired security level and the efficiency. The latter is measured in terms of computation time or hardware implementation complexity.

When Feistel structure is used in cryptography, each round i, $1 \leq i \leq n$ makes use of a round key K_i and performs a substitution and a permutation. Round keys are derived from the initial secret key by a key expansion function.

As shown on Figure 7.4, the data block under processing (either for encryption or for decryption) is divided into two halves, denoted L (left) and R (right), and the cipher operates only on a single half in each round of encryption or decryption. Between rounds, the left and right halves are swapped.

Below are the encryption and decryption procedures:

Encryption
> **input** B: plaintext
> **output** C: ciphertext
> 1. $(LE_0, RE_0) = B$ **#** B is the plaintext divided into two equal-length halves,
> LE_0 and RE_0. Abbreviations: L (Left), R (Right), E (encryption).
> 2. **for** $i = 1$ **to** n **do**
> $LE_i = RE_{i-1}$; $RE_i = LE_{i-1} \oplus F(RE_{i-1}, K_i)$
> 3. $C = RE_n \parallel LE_n$; **return** C

Note. The halves computed in the last round are concatenated in this order RE_n followed by LE_n to form the ciphertext block.

Decryption[2] is the same as the encryption with one difference: the round keys used in encryption are used in the reverse order.

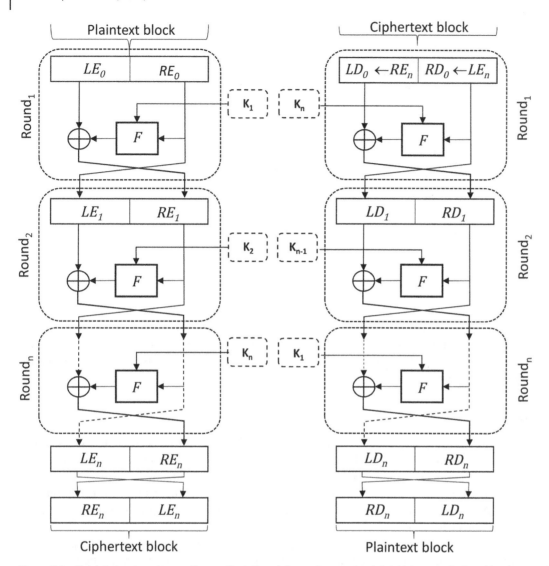

Figure 7.4 Feistel structure (encryption on the left and decryption on the right). Halves are indexed by the round number; and E and D denote encryption and decryption.

Decryption
> **input** C: ciphertext
> **output** B: plaintext
> 1. $(LD_0, RD_0) = C$ # Divide C into two equal-length halves, with
>   # abbreviations: L (Left), R (Right), D (Decryption)
>   # Thus, $LD_0 = RE_n$ and $RD_0 = LE_n$.
> 2. **for** $i = 1$ **to** n **do**
> $LD_i = RD_{i-1}$; $RD_i = LD_{i-1} \oplus F(RD_{i-1}, K_{n-i+1})$
> 3. $B = RD_n \parallel LD_n$; **return** B

Note. The halves computed in the last round are concatenated in this order RD_n followed by LD_n to form the plaintext block.

7.2 Triple Data Encryption Algorithm (TDEA)

The first version of TDEA was approved by the NIST in 2004; and the most recent revision of TDEA was published in 2017 [2]. Till now, TDEA is considered as a secure block cipher. It applies the DEA (Data Encryption Algorithm) cipher three times to each data block. To understand how TDEA works one must first understand the basics of DEA.

7.2.1 Data Encryption Algorithm (DEA)

It is worth noticing that DEA was originally specified in the Data Encryption Standard (DES[3]), which became effective in 1977 and widely used for nearly three decades. DES was proposed by IBM researchers and its internals were covered by a patent.[4] However, they became public afterward. DES is the most studied cipher; and the lessons learned from the vulnerabilities of DES contributed to the design of more secure ciphers.

However, since 2005, the last version of DES [3] is no longer recommended to be used alone, after some vulnerabilities were discovered. DES was withdrawn from NIST standards and DEA is specified as an engine of TDEA, i.e. DEA is repeated three times to encrypt or decrypt 64-bit blocks.

7.2.1.1 DEA Encryption and Decryption

DEA is a block cipher with a block length of 64 bits and a key of a bit length of 56 bits (see Figure 7.5). DEA encryption and decryption transformations are very similar:

- Both encryption and decryption run in 16 rounds numbered from 1 to 16, forming a Feistel network (see Figure 7.6).
- Each round takes a 64-bit input block and yields a 64-bit output block. Each input or output 64-bit block is split into two 32-bit halves, denoted L (left) and R (right). In encryption, the input halves of round i are denoted LE_{i-1} and RE_{i-1}; and its output halves LE_i and RE_i. In decryption, the input halves of round i are denoted LD_{i-1} and RD_{i-1}; and its output halves LD_i and RD_i.
- Each round i makes use of its 48-bit round key, denoted K_i, which is derived from a DEA key, denoted KEY, using a key schedule function KS (see Section 7.2.2.3); $K_i = KS(KEY,i)$.
- All the rounds use the same core function f (see Section 7.2.1.3) to process the right half of their input.

The algorithms of encryption and decryption differ only by the order in which the round keys are used. In more detail, the algorithms are as follows:

```
function E # DEA encryption
    input   B, KEY: 64-bit plaintext block and a 56-bit key
    output  C: 64-bit ciphertext block
    1. # The initial permutation IP is applied to the block B
            (LE₀, RE₀) = IP(B)
    2. for i = 1 to 16 do
            LEᵢ = REᵢ₋₁
            REᵢ = LEᵢ₋₁ ⊕ f(REᵢ₋₁, KS(KEY, i))
    3. # Halves of the 16ᵗʰ round are arranged to form a 64-bit block Pre_output
            Pre_output = RE₁₆ ‖ LE₁₆
    4. # The inverse initial permutation IP⁻¹ is applied to the block Pre_output
            C = IP⁻¹(Pre_output)
    5. return C
```

Figure 7.5   Overall view of DEA.

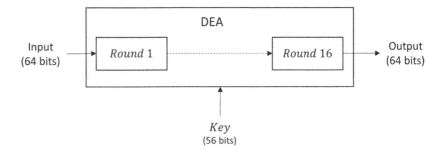

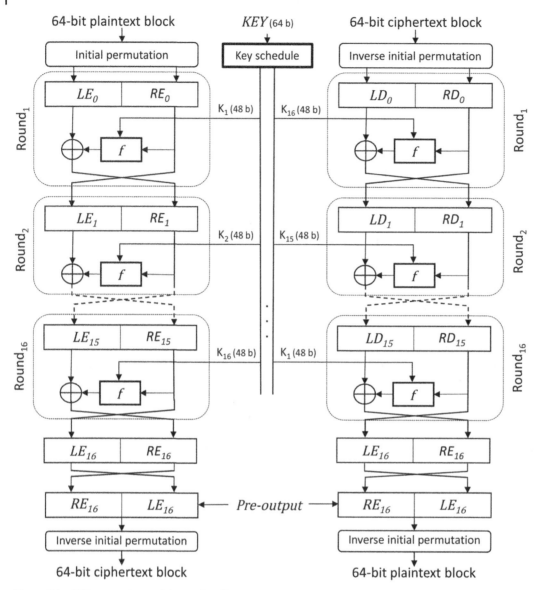

Figure 7.6 DEA encryption and decryption diagrams.

function D # DEA decryption
    input C, KEY: 64-bit ciphertext block and 56-bit key
    output B: 64-bit plaintext block
    1. # The initial permutation IP is applied to the block C
           $(LD_0, RD_0) = IP(C)$
    2. **for** $i = 1$ **to** 16 **do**
           $LD_i = RD_{i-1}$
           $RD_i = LD_{i-1} \oplus f(RD_{i-1}, KS(KEY, 16 - i + 1))$
    3. # Halves of the 16th round are arranged to form a 64-bit block *Pre_output*
           $Pre\_output = RD_{16} \parallel LD_{16}$
    4. # The inverse initial permutation IP^{-1} is applied to the block *Pre_output*
           $B = IP^{-1}(Pre\_output)$
    5. **return** B

As shown in the encryption and decryption algorithms above and in Figure 7.6, DEA makes use of specific internal components: initial permutation and its inverse, key schedule function KS, and function f; all these components are described below.

| **Note**. DEA permutation and substitution tables are two-dimension arrays. In the sequel, both rows and columns indices start with 0; $T[0,0]$ denotes the first element of any table.

7.2.1.2 Initial Permutation and Its Inverse

The input and output of the initial permutation and of its inverse are 64-bit blocks. An input block is permuted according to a predefined rule to yield the output. Both permutations are keyless and deterministic. Therefore, they only aim at making bit transpositions. In literature, it is argued that the initial permutation and its inverse were introduced to be implemented in hardware to thwart the attacks against DEA by software.

Initial permutation IP

Let $B[1:64]$ and $B'[1:64]$ be the input and output bit-vectors of permutation IP, respectively. Let *IP* (Table 7.1) be the table used by the permutation IP. Block B' is yielded from block B as follows:

$$B'[i] = B[IP[i_r, i_c]], \text{ for } i = 1, ..., 64, \text{ where } i_r = \lceil i/8 \rceil - 1 \text{ and } i_c = i - 8*i_r - 1$$

Example:

$$B'[1] = B[IP[0,0]] = B[58] \qquad B'[2] = B[IP[0,1]] = B[50]$$

$$B'[64] = B[IP[7,7]] = B[7]$$

Inverse permutation IP^{-1}

Let $C[1:64]$ and $C'[1:64]$ be the input and output bit-vectors of permutation IP^{-1}, respectively. Let IP^{-1} (Table 7.2) be the table used by the permutation IP^{-1}. Block C' is yielded from block C as follows:

$$C'[i] = C[IP^{-1}[i_r, i_c]], \text{ for } i = 1, ..., 64, \text{ where } i_r = \lceil i/8 \rceil - 1 \text{ and } i_c = i - 8*i_r - 1$$

Example:

$$C'[1] = C[IP^{-1}[0,0]] = C[40] \qquad C'[2] = C[IP^{-1}[0,1]] = C[8]$$

$$C'[64] = C[IP^{-1}[7,7]] = C[25]$$

7.2.1.3 Function f

Function f is the core of DEA, as it makes use of selection functions to scramble a 32-bit round input using a round key, an expansion operation *Exp*, and a permutation P (see Figure 7.7). The pseudocode of the function f is as follows:

```
function f
    input   R, k: 32-bit string and round key
    output  R' # 32-bit string
    1. Rxp = Exp(R) # expand R to 48 bits
    2. Z = k ⊕ Rxp
    3. Let Z[1:48] be the bit-vector representation of Z
    4. Z_i = Z[6*(i−1)+1,6*i], i = 1,...,8 # Split vector Z into 8 sub-vectors
    5. for i = 1 to 8 do
           Y_i = SF_i(Z_i) # selection function SF_i compacts Z_i to four bits
    6. Y = Y_1 || Y_2 || Y_3 || Y_4 || Y_5 || Y_6 || Y_7 || Y_8 # Concatenate the eight values
    7. R' = P(Y) # Permute the 32 bits of Y
    8. return R'
```

Table 7.1 Initial permutation *IP* table.

58	50	42	34	26	18	10	2
60	52	44	36	28	20	12	4
62	54	46	38	30	22	14	6
64	56	48	40	32	24	16	8
57	49	41	33	25	17	9	1
59	51	43	35	27	19	11	3
61	53	45	37	29	21	13	5
63	55	47	39	31	23	15	7

Table 7.2 Inverse permutation IP^{-1} table.

40	8	48	16	56	24	64	32
39	7	47	15	55	23	63	31
38	6	46	14	54	22	62	30
37	5	45	13	53	21	61	29
36	4	44	12	52	20	60	28
35	3	43	11	51	19	59	27
34	2	42	10	50	18	58	26
33	1	41	9	49	17	57	25

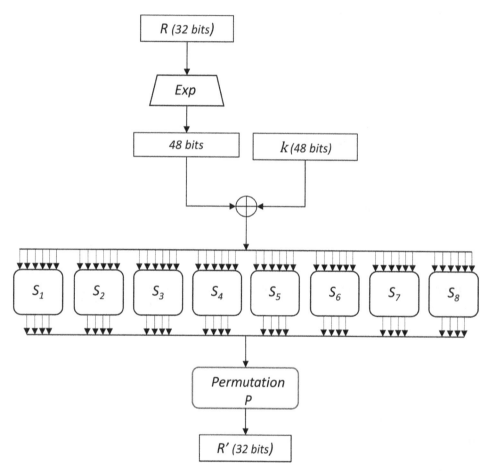

Figure 7.7 Diagram of function f of DEA.

Expansion function Exp

It takes a 32-bit string and expands it to a 48-bit string using the table E (Table 7.3). Notice that in table E, values in the rightmost two columns (i.e. 1, 4, 5, 8, 9, 12, 13, 16, 17, 20, 21, 24, 25, 28, 29, 32) are repeated, so that the number of values in the table E is 48. Given Y, a 32-bit string, the expanded bit-string $Y' = Exp(Y)$ is defined by:

$$Y'[i] = Y\left[E\left[i_r, i_c\right]\right], \text{ for } i = 1, \ldots, 48, \text{ where } i_r = \lceil i/6 \rceil - 1 \text{ and } i_c = i - 6 * i_r - 1$$

Example:

$$Y'[1] = Y\left[E[0,0]\right] = Y[32] \qquad Y'[4] = Y\left[E[0,3]\right] = Y[3]$$

$$Y'[48] = Y\left[E[7,5]\right] = Y[1]$$

Table 7.3 Table *E*.

32	1	2	3	4	5
4	5	6	7	8	9
8	9	10	11	12	13
12	13	14	15	16	17
16	17	18	19	20	21
20	21	22	23	24	25
24	25	26	27	28	29
28	29	30	31	32	1

Selection functions

Selection functions also are called *substitution boxes* (or S-boxes). They are nonlinear (see Exercise 7.4), which provide some level of security to DEA. DEA makes use of eight selection functions, denoted $SF_j, j = 1, ..., 8$, which operate like compression functions. Each selection function SF_j has a table S_j associated with it (Table 7.4). Tables of selection functions are represented as 4 rows by 16 columns matrices. Given a 6-bit value v, each selection function $SF_j, j = 1, ..., 8$, yields a 4-bit value $w_j = SF_j(v)$. $SF_j(v)$ returns the table element $S_j(v_r, v_c)$ such that v_r, the row number, is a 2-bit value formed by the first and the last bits of v; and v_c, the column number, is a 4-bit value formed by the 2nd, 3rd, 4th, and 5th bits of v.

For example, let $v = 27 = 011011_2$. Then, $v_r = 01_2$ and $v_c = 1101_2$. Hence, the reductions of $v = 27$ are:

$$SF_1(27) \to S_1(1,13) = 5 \qquad SF_2(27) \to S_2(1,13) = 9 \qquad SF_3(27) \to S_3(1,13) = 11$$
$$SF_4(27) \to S_4(1,13) = 10 \qquad SF_5(27) \to S_5(1,13) = 9 \qquad SF_6(27) \to S_6(1,13) = 11$$
$$SF_7(27) \to S_7(1,13) = 15 \qquad SF_8(27) \to S_8(1,13) = 14$$

Table 7.4 Tables of selection functions $S_1 - S_8$.

S_1	14	4	13	1	2	15	11	8	3	10	6	12	5	9	0	7
	0	15	17	4	14	2	13	1	10	6	12	11	9	5	3	8
	4	1	14	8	13	6	2	11	15	12	9	7	3	10	5	0
	15	12	8	2	4	9	1	7	5	11	3	14	10	0	6	13
S_2	15	1	8	14	6	11	3	4	9	7	2	13	12	0	5	10
	3	13	4	7	15	2	8	14	12	0	1	10	6	9	11	5
	0	4	7	11	10	4	13	1	5	8	12	6	9	3	2	15
	13	8	10	1	3	15	4	2	11	6	7	12	0	5	14	9
S_3	10	0	9	14	6	3	15	5	1	13	12	7	11	4	2	8
	13	7	0	9	3	4	6	10	2	8	5	14	12	11	15	1
	13	6	4	9	8	15	3	0	11	1	2	12	5	10	14	7
	1	10	13	0	6	9	8	7	4	15	14	3	11	5	2	12
S_4	7	13	14	3	0	6	9	10	1	2	8	5	11	12	4	15
	13	8	11	5	6	15	0	3	4	7	2	12	1	10	14	9
	10	6	9	0	12	11	7	13	15	1	3	14	5	2	8	4
	3	15	0	6	10	1	13	8	9	4	5	11	12	7	2	14

(Continued)

Table 7.4 (Continued)

S_5	2	12	4	1	7	10	11	6	8	5	3	15	13	0	14	9
	14	11	2	12	4	7	13	1	5	0	15	10	3	9	8	6
	4	2	1	11	10	13	7	8	15	9	12	5	6	3	0	14
	11	8	12	7	1	14	2	13	6	15	0	9	10	4	5	3
S_6	12	1	10	15	9	2	6	8	0	13	3	4	14	7	5	11
	10	15	4	2	7	12	9	5	6	1	13	14	0	11	3	8
	9	14	15	5	2	8	12	3	7	0	4	10	1	13	11	6
	4	3	2	12	9	5	15	10	11	14	1	7	6	0	8	13
S_7	4	11	2	14	15	0	8	13	3	12	9	7	5	10	6	1
	13	0	11	7	4	9	1	10	14	3	5	12	2	15	8	6
	1	4	11	13	12	3	7	14	10	15	6	8	0	5	9	2
	6	11	13	8	1	4	10	7	9	5	0	15	14	2	3	12
S_8	13	2	8	4	6	15	11	1	10	9	3	14	5	0	12	7
	1	15	13	8	10	3	7	4	12	5	6	11	0	14	9	2
	7	11	4	1	9	12	14	2	0	6	10	13	15	3	5	8
	2	1	14	7	4	10	8	13	15	12	9	0	3	5	6	11

Permutation P

It takes a 32-bit string and yields a bit string of the same length, using table P (Table 7.5). Table P is an 8-row by 4-colum matrix. Given a 32-bit value Y, the permuted bit-string $Y' = P(Y)$ is defined by:

$$Y'[i] = Y\big[P[i_r, i_c]\big], \text{ for } i = 1, ..., 32, \text{ where } i_r = \lceil i/4 \rceil - 1 \text{ and } i_c = i - 4 * i_r - 1$$

Example:

$$Y'[1] = Y\big[P[0,0]\big] = Y[16] \qquad Y'[4] = Y\big[P[0,3]\big] = Y[21]$$

$$Y'[32] = Y\big[P[7,3]\big] = Y[25]$$

7.2.2 TDEA Construction and Usage

7.2.2.1 Bundle and DEA Keys

In the previous section, DEA the engine of TDEA, was introduced. The next step is to discuss how secret keys are used to feed the function F with round keys.

Table 7.5 Table *P*.

16	7	20	21
29	12	28	17
1	15	23	26
5	18	31	10
2	8	24	14
32	27	3	9
19	13	30	6
22	11	4	25

A TDEA key, called *bundle key*, consists of three DEA keys, denoted Key_1, Key_2, and Key_3; i.e. $BundleKey = (Key_1, Key_2, Key_3)$. Two options are permitted:

1) The three keys are all distinct (i.e. $Key_i \neq Key_j, \forall i \neq j, i, j \in \{1,2,3\}$); in such a case, the block cipher is called three-key TDEA (and denoted 3TDEA). It is the recommended option.

2) Two keys are identical and are distinct from the third one, which is an option for legacy use only. The selection of keys shall fulfill the following condition: $Key_1 \neq Key_2$, $Key_2 \neq Key_3$, and $Key_1 = Key_3$; in such a case, the block cipher is called two-key TDEA (and denoted 2TDEA[5]).

When a DEA key is used, it has a length of 56 bits. However, when DEA keys are generated, distributed, or stored, they are represented as a 64-bit strings, where eight extra bits are odd parity bits (i.e. one odd parity bit is added on the right of every seven bits in the initial key), which may be used for error detection. Odd parity bits are dropped by the key schedule function; they have no impact on security.

Weak keys and semi-weak keys
A key *Key* is said to be *weak*, if all the round keys generated from it are identical. The bad property of a weak key is that encrypting twice a plaintext M yields M and decrypting twice a ciphertext C yields C. Formally,

$$Weak(K) \Rightarrow \left(E_K\left(E_K(M)\right) = M, \forall M \in \{0,1\}^{64}\right) \wedge \left(D_K\left(D_K(C)\right) = C, \forall C \in \{0,1\}^{64}\right)$$

The following keys are considered *weak*, when used in DEA engine, and should be avoided:

$$01010101\ 01010101_{16} \qquad \text{FEFEFEFE FEFEFEFE}_{16}$$
$$\text{E0E0E0E0 F1F1F1F1}_{16} \qquad \text{1F1F1F1F 0E0E0E0E}_{16}$$

A key *Key* is said to be *semi-weak*, if only two distinct round keys can be generated from it. If two keys key_1 and key_2 are semi-weak keys and have the same round keys, they form a pair of semi-weak keys. In other words, encryption with one of the keys in the pair is equivalent to decryption with the other (and vice versa). The bad property of a pair of weak keys is that encrypting a plaintext M with both keys in cascade yields M. Formally,

$$WeakPair\left(Key_1, Key_2\right) \Rightarrow E_{Key_1}\left(E_{Key_2}(M)\right) = M, \forall M \in \{0,1\}^{64}$$

The following six pairs are pairs of semi-weak keys and should be avoided:

$$\text{011F011F010E010E}_{16} \quad \text{and} \quad \text{1F011F010E010E01}_{16}$$
$$\text{01E001E001F101F1}_{16} \quad \text{and} \quad \text{E001E001F101F101}_{16}$$
$$\text{01FE01FE01FE01FE}_{16} \quad \text{and} \quad \text{FE01FE01FE01FE01}_{16}$$
$$\text{1FE01FE00EF10EF1}_{16} \quad \text{and} \quad \text{E01FE01FF10EF10E}_{16}$$
$$\text{1FFE1FFE0EFE0EFE}_{16} \quad \text{and} \quad \text{1FFE1FFE0EFE0EFE}_{16}$$
$$\text{E0FEE0FEF1FEF1FE}_{16} \quad \text{and} \quad \text{FEE0FEE0FEF1FEF1}_{16}$$

Finally, there is a list of 48 keys that produce only four distinct round keys when the key schedule is applied and when it should be avoided (see NIST recommendation [2]).

Problems 7.6 and 7.7 discuss examples of weak and semi-weak keys.

7.2.2.2 TDEA Encryption and Decryption

TDEA encryption of a 64-bit plaintext P is defined by:

$$E^{(TDEA)}_{(Key_3, Key_2, Key_1)}(P) = E_{Key_3}\left(D_{Key_2}\left(E_{Key_1}(P)\right)\right) = C$$

TDEA decryption of a 64-bit ciphertext C is defined by:

$$D^{(TDEA)}_{(Key_3, Key_2, Key_1)}(C) = D_{Key_1}\left(E_{Key_2}\left(D_{Key_3}(C)\right)\right) = P$$

Figure 7.8 shows an overview of how DEA is used to perform TDEA encryption and decryption. Notice that a TDEA bundle key bit-length is $3*64$ when it is stored or distributed, while its bit-length from the cryptographic perspective is $3*56$.

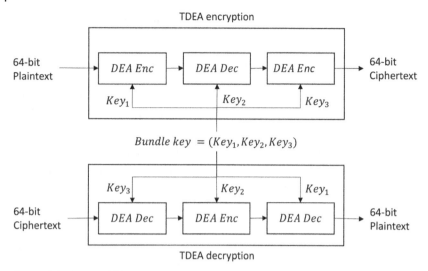

Figure 7.8 Overall TDEA encryption and decryption.

7.2.2.3 Key Schedule Function *KS*

The key schedule function *KS*, shown on Figure 7.9, generates sixteen 48-bit round keys using a 64-bit key, denoted *KEY*; $KEY \in \{Key_1, Key_2, Key_3\}$. The round keys are denoted K_i, $i \in [1,16]$. Two permutation tables, *PC1* (Table 7.6) and *PC2* (Table 7.7) are used in the *KS* function to perform compression permutations (i.e. it computes 48-bit round keys from a 64-bit key). Table *PC1* is an eight by seven matrix containing numbers from 1 to 63, but the eight odd parity bits (i.e. bits with numbers 8, 16, 24, 32, 40, 48, 56, and 64) are dropped. Table *PC1* is divided into two parts; the upper half (i.e. bits 57 to 36) to choose a 28-bit string, denoted C_0, and the lower half (bits 63 to 4) to choose a 28-bit string, denoted D_0.

Permuted choice function is used once; it takes a 64-bit key *KEY* and makes use of permutation *PC1* to compress and permute *KEY* to yield two 28-bits blocks C_0 and D_0 defined by:

$$C_0[i] = KEY\left[PC1[i_r, i_c]\right], \text{ for } i = 1, ..., 28, \text{ where } i_r = \lceil i/7 \rceil - 1 \text{ and } i_c = i - 7 * i_r - 1.$$

$$D_0[i] = KEY\left[PC1[i_r, i_c]\right], \text{ for } i = 1, ..., 28, \text{ where } i_r = \lceil (i+28)/7 \rceil - 1 \text{ and } i_c = (i+28) - 7 * i_r - 1.$$

Example:

$$C_0[1] = KEY\left[PC1[0,0]\right] = KEY[57] \qquad C_0[2] = KEY\left[PC1[0,1]\right] = KEY[49]$$

$$C_0[28] = KEY\left[PC1[3,6]\right] = KEY[36] \qquad D_0[1] = KEY\left[PC1[4,0]\right] = KEY[63]$$

$$D_0[2] = KEY\left[PC1[4,1]\right] = KEY[55] \qquad D_0[28] = KEY\left[PC1[7,6]\right] = KEY[4]$$

Compression permutation is used for each iteration i, $i = 1, ..., 16$; it takes two 28-bits blocks C_i and D_i and makes use of compression permutation *PC2* to yield the round key K_i. Each 28-bit block C_i (resp. D_i) is yielded from C_{i-1} (resp. D_{i-1}) using a left rotation by one or two positions. The number of rotation positions for each iteration is given by the vector *NLR* (Table 7.8). Pseudocode of the key scheduling function *KS* is as follows:

---

function *KS* # Key schedule
    input   *KEY*: 64-bit block
    output K_i, $i \in [1,16]$: 16 round keys
    1. $(C_0, D_0) = PermutedChoice(KEY)$ # first pair of 28-bit blocks
    2. **for** $i=1$ **to** 16 **do**
        2.1. $C_i = LeftRotate(C_{i-1}, NLR_i)$
        2.2. $D_i = LeftRotate(D_{i-1}, NLR_i)$
        2.3. # Generate the ith round key
            $K_i = CompressionPermutation(C_i \parallel D_i)$
    3. **return** K_i, $i \in [1,16]$

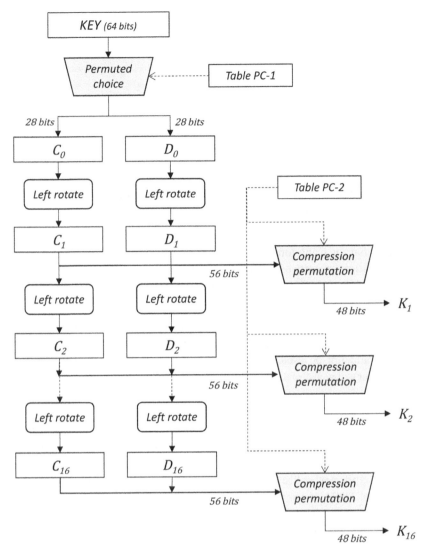

Figure 7.9 Key schedule function.

Table 7.6 Table *PC1*.

57	49	41	33	25	17	9
1	58	50	42	34	26	18
10	2	59	51	43	35	27
19	11	3	60	52	44	36
63	55	47	39	31	23	15
7	62	54	46	38	30	22
14	6	61	53	45	37	29
21	13	5	28	20	12	4

Table 7.7 Table *PC2*.

14	17	11	24	1	5
3	28	15	6	21	10
23	19	12	4	26	8
16	7	27	20	13	2
41	52	31	37	47	55
30	40	51	45	33	48
44	49	39	56	34	53
46	42	50	36	29	32

Table 7.8 NLR: Number of left rotations in KS iteration.

Iteration number	1	2	3	4	5	6	7	8	9	10	11	12	13	14	15	16
# of left rotations	1	1	2	2	2	2	2	2	1	2	2	2	2	2	2	1

7.2.3 Security Issues

7.2.3.1 Complexity of Attacks Against DES

Three main attacks against DEA key have been investigated in literature: brute-force attack, differential cryptanalysis, and linear analysis. Differential analysis and linear analysis are discussed in Chapter 11.

- Brute-force attack: given a pair of plaintext and ciphertext blocks (P,C), the adversary needs to test, in the worst case, 2^{56} keys to find a key K such that $C = E(K,P)$. Notice that the brute-force attack complexity becomes 2^{55} (i.e. reduced by a factor of $\frac{1}{2}$) if the attacker exploits the complementation property of DES (see Problem 7.5).
- Biham and Shamir [4] showed that DES could be broken with 2^{47} tests using differential cryptanalysis.
- Matsui [5] showed that DES could be broken with 2^{43} tests using linear cryptanalysis.

It is worth noticing that both bounds of Biham and Matsui are theoretical and their attacks have not been successfully experimented in practice, because of the huge amount of the required plaintext-ciphertext pairs. Therefore, DEA is vulnerable to attacks using current technologies; and should not be used alone. In 2007, an FPGA-based machine, called COPACOBANA (Cost-Optimized Parallel Code Breaker), at a cost of $10,000, broke DES in less than a week.

7.2.3.2 TDEA Security Limit

Recall that the security of data depends on the security provided for the keys used to protect data and the amount of data protected by a same key. A collision occurs when two distinct plaintext blocks map to the same ciphertext block. A collision in ciphertext blocks, once detected, may leak information about the corresponding plaintext blocks. By the birthday paradox (see Section 3.4), with a block length of 64 bits, a ciphertext collision will likely occur when about $2^{\frac{64}{2}}$ plaintext blocks are encrypted with the same key. In the 2012 revision of TDEA, it was recommended that the number of blocks should not exceed 2^{32}. In response to known security weaknesses, 2017 revision [2] lowered the 3TDEA limit to 2^{20} 64-bit data blocks per key bundle and disallows the use of TDEA alone for applying cryptographic protection to new information. Therefore, TDEA should be used with modes of operation of block cipher (such as CBC and CTR); modes of operation are introduced in the next chapter. In addition, it is worth noticing that in 2017, NIST urged all users of TDEA to migrate to AES as soon as possible.

7.2.3.3 Meet-in-the-Middle Attack Against Double DES and TDEA

Double-DES (denoted 2DES) is defined by a double encryption/decryption using two (independent) keys as follows:

Encryption: $E^{(2DE)}_{(Key_2,Key_1)}(P) = E_{Key_2}(E_{Key_1}(P)) = C$

Decryption: $D^{(2DE)}_{(Key_2,Key_1)}(P) = D_{Key_1}(D_{Key_2}(C)) = P$

where P is the plaintext, C the ciphertext, and Key_1 and Key_2, the keys.

At a first glance, one may think that the brute-force attack against 2DES has a complexity of $2^{2*56} = 2^{112}$. Therefore, doubling the key length would result in a secure cipher. Unfortunately, 2DES is insecure; therefore, it is not recommended. 2DES is insecure under the *meet-in-the-middle attack*, which is presented below. Its effective key length is $2^{57.}$

In a similar way to 2DES, the meet-in-the-middle attack reduces the complexity of TDEA, with three distinct keys, to 2^{112}. Therefore, tripling the key length of DES does not result in a security of 2^{168} as naïvely expected. However, TDEA, with three distinct keys, has an effective key length of 112. Therefore, an attack of a complexity of 2^{112} is computationally infeasible with current technologies, which makes TDEA a secure cipher.

7.2.3.3.1 Meet-in-the-Middle Attack Against Double DES

One of the well-known attacks against the key pair of double DES is the meet-in-the-middle attack described below. In general, the *meet-in-the-middle attack* (MITM attack) is a generic space-time tradeoff cryptographic attack against encryption schemes that rely on performing multiple encryption in sequence using the same cipher.

Assume that an adversary knew a plaintext–ciphertext pair (P,C) and has the capacities to compute and store the ciphertexts associated with the plaintext P encrypted with all the 2^{56} DES keys. The MITM attack takes advantage of the following observation:

$$(X = E_{Key_1}(P)) \wedge (C = E_{Key_2}(E_{Key_1}(P))) \Rightarrow D_{Key_2}(C) = X$$

The principle of MITM attack is to perform encryptions of the known plaintext with all values of Key_1 and perform decryptions of the known ciphertext with all the values of Key_2 and join both computations to find key pair candidates (K_1, K_2), such that: $E_{K_1}(P) = D_{K_2}(C)$. Hence, the notion of *meet in the middle*.

In the attack complexity analysis, it is assumed that only encryption and decryption operations, which are the most time-consuming, are of interest. The MITM attack algorithm is as follows:

---

1. **for** $K_1 = 0$ **to** $2^{56} - 1$ **do** $T[K_1] = E_{K_1}(P)$ #Encryption: build a table T
   # including the encryption of P for each of the 2^{56} keys
2. *CandidatePairList* $=$ *EmptyList*()
3. #Decryption and test:
       for $K_2 = 0$ **to** $2^{56} - 1$ **do**
           $Z = D_{K_2}(C)$ # Decrypt C
           for $K_1 = 0$ **to** $2^{56} - 1$ **do**
               if $T[K_1] = Z$, **then**
               # a candidate pair (K_2, K_1) is found
               CandidatePairList $=$ *Append.CandidatePairList*$((K_2, K_1))$
               else continue

In the attack above, the worst case of the number of encryptions is 2^{56} and that of decryptions is 2^{56}. Therefore, the attack complexity is of 2^{57}. However, only one of the key pair candidates is the real pair (Key_2, Key_1). In Problem 7.9, we address the probability of success of the MITM attack.

In the pseudocode above, the table T is a vector, where $T[i]$ contains the ciphertext of plaintext P encrypted with key i. However, when a decrypted value $Z = D(K_2, C)$ is searched in table T, the search time would be very high, because one needs, in average, to test half of the table. One optimization of the MITM attack algorithm is to use a table with two columns $T[0:2^{56} - 1, 1:2]$, where $T[i,1] = E(i,P)$ and $T[i,2] = i$. Then, sort the table on the first column. Then, a dichotomic search may be applied to reduce the computation time of the attack.

7.2.3.3.2 Meet-in-the-Middle Attack Against TDEA

TDEA encryption is defined by:

$$E^{(TDEA)}_{(Key_3, Key_2, Key_1)}(P) = E_{Key_3}(D_{Key_2}(E_{Key_1}(P))) = C$$

Like Double DES, TDEA is defined by a repetitive use of the same cipher. Therefore, it is vulnerable to MITM attack. The principle of MITM attack against TDEA is very similar to the attack against double DES. It takes advantage of the following observation:

$$\left(X = E_{Key_1}(P)\right) \wedge \left(C = E_{Key_3}\left(D_{Key_2}\left(E_{Key_1}(P)\right)\right)\right) \Rightarrow E_{Key_2}\left(D_{Key_3}(C)\right) = X$$

The MITM attack against TDEA may be formulated as follows:

1) For each of the 2^{56} values of K_1, compute $E_{K_1}(P)$ and build a 2-column table T, sorted on the values of the computed ciphertexts. That is, the first column of T contains the ciphertext and the second column the used key.
2) For each of the 2^{56*2} pairs of keys (K_3, K_2), compute $Z = E_{K_2}(D_{K_3}(C))$. Then, try to find entries $i, j, ...,$ in the table T, such that $T[i,1] = Z$, $T[j,1] = Z$, ... Each matching table entry results in a candidate triplet (K_3, K_2, K_1).
3) False alarms may occur and one or two additional plaintext–ciphertext pairs are required to get, at a probability close to 1, a key triplet identical to the real one.

In the first step attack mentioned above, 2^{56} operations are performed, while in the second step one, 2^{112} operations are performed. Therefore, the complexity of MITM attack against TDEA is of 2^{112}.

7.3 Advanced Encryption System (AES)

The Advanced Encryption Standard (AES), also known by its original name Rijndael,[6] was proposed by Daemen and Rijmen in the late 1990s. Rijndael algorithm was one of the finalists to the public call issued by the NIST in 1997 to replace DES, because of the discovered weaknesses. Rijndael algorithm was the winner and it was confirmed by the NIST as a standard in 2001, but under the name AES [6]. The only difference between Rijndael and AES is the range of supported values of block length and key length.

AES is by now the most widely used cipher in cryptosystems and it is expected to dominate for long time. In 2003, the NSA (National Security Agency) allowed AES for protection of classified data up to Top secret with keys of 192 or 256 bits.

7.3.1 Distinctive Features of AES

The main features of AES include the following:

- AES operates on 128-bit blocks using three different key bit-lengths: 128, 192, and 256 bits. Unlike DEA, no weak or semi-weak AES keys have been reported until now.
- Like DEA, AES is an iterated block cipher; the encryption or the decryption follows a sequence of Nr rounds, which depends on the key length: 10 rounds for 128-bit keys, 12 rounds for 192-bit keys, and 14 rounds for 256-bit keys (see Figure 7.10). Thus, AES may be referred to as AES-128, AES-192, and AES-256.
- AES makes use of $Nr + 1$ round keys. Before starting the first round, an initial round key is added to the input and then each round ends with an addition of its round key to the output of its last transformation. Such a design is called *key-alternating*.
- AES is a byte-oriented cipher, unlike DES, which is a bit-oriented cipher. The basic unit of processing in AES is the byte. The 128-bit input and output of rounds are organized as 4×4 arrays of bytes, which are called *states*.
- With the exception of the last round, all other rounds are identical. Each encryption round includes four transformations: byte substitution, row shifting, column mixing, and round key addition.
- Very similar steps are used in encryption and decryption. However, the encryption transformations are inversed in decryption, and, unlike DEA, two distinct algorithms are used in AES, one for encryption and another for decryption.
- Unlike DEA, AES is not based on Feistel structure even though it makes use of a substitution-permutation network structure. All the input bits of each round are processed, unlike DEA where only the right half of input is processed.
- AES computations are performed over extension fields (i.e. Galois fields, introduced in Section 3.2.4). Therefore, the design rationale and the proof of correctness of AES rely on mathematical notions.

For more detail on the design criteria and rationale of the Rijndael algorithm, the reader may refer to Daemen and Rijmen's book [7].

7.3.2 Data Representation in AES

Input and output of rounds follow specific forms of data representation, which will be addressed before going into detail of AES transformations. The basic unit of processing in AES is the byte. The input, output, and the round keys are processed as 4×4 *arrays* of bytes.

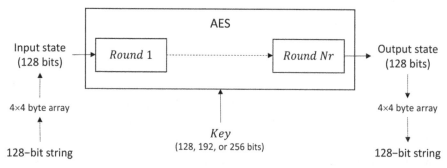

Figure 7.10 Overview of AES.

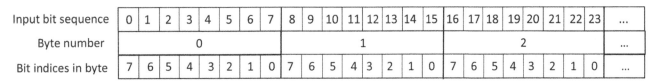

Figure 7.11 Indices for bytes and bits of data.

Let A be an input, an output, or a round key of 16 bytes. A is represented in one of the following forms:

1) byte representation: $A = A_0 A_1 \ldots A_{16}$
2) word representation: $A = W_0 W_1 W_2 W_3$, where W_{0-3} are 32-bit words
3) bit representation: $A = b_0 b_1 \ldots b_{127}$.

Bit indices of a 128-bit block are represented by Figure 7.11.

State notion

AES transformations are performed on two-dimensional arrays of bytes called *states*. A state has four rows each of four bytes (i.e. $4 * 4$ bytes $= 128$ bits). Notice that in the current version of AES, the block length is of 128 bits; it might change in the future. Therefore, the number of bytes per row should change.

Each byte within a state S is denoted $S_{r,c}$, where r, $0 \le r \le 3$, denotes the row number and c, $0 \le c \le 3$, the column number. The mapping from the cipher input to the state and from the state to the cipher output is illustrated by Figure 7.12.

The four bytes in each column of a state form a 32-bit word. Therefore, a state S can be considered as an array of four words W_0, W_1, W_2, and W_3, defined as follows:

$$W_0 = \left[S_{0,0},\ S_{1,0},\ S_{2,0},\ S_{3,0} \right] \qquad W_1 = \left[S_{0,1},\ S_{1,1},\ S_{2,1},\ S_{3,1} \right]$$

$$W_2 = \left[S_{0,2},\ S_{1,2},\ S_{2,2},\ S_{3,2} \right] \qquad W_3 = \left[S_{0,3},\ S_{1,3},\ S_{2,3},\ S_{3,3} \right]$$

7.3.3 Overall Structure of AES

The encryption and decryption follow a sequence of Nr rounds, where Nr depends on the key bit-length. Like DEA, the cipher key K is processed by the key expansion function to generate an array, called key schedule, denoted W, forming $Nr + 1$ round keys each of Nk words. Therefore, W is an array of $(Nr + 1) * Nk$ words.

Each encryption round, with the exception of the last round, consists of four transformations denoted `SubBytes` (byte substitution), `ShiftRows` (left shift of state rows), `MixColumns` (mixing three state columns), and `AddRoundKey` (i.e. XORing the round key with the output of the previous transformation). The decryption rounds are similar to those of encryption, but make use of inverse transformations (i.e. `InvSubBytes`, `InvShiftRows`, and `InvMixColumns`), and use the round keys in the inverse order of that of the encryption.

The overall structure of AES is illustrated by Figure 7.13; and the pseudocodes are given below.

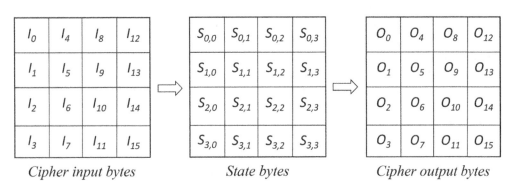

Figure 7.12 Mapping between the cipher input, output bytes, and the state bytes.

```
function E # AES Encryption
    input   P: 128-bit plaintext block; W: key schedule array
    output  C: 128-bit ciphertext block
    1. State = CopyCipherInputToStateArray(P)
    2. AddRoundKey (State, W[0,3])
    3. for Round = 1 to Nr − 1 do
            SubBytes(State); ShiftRows(State)
            MixColumns(State)
            AddRoundKey (State, W[Round * 4, (Round + 1) * 4 − 1])
    4. # Transformations of the last round
            SubBytes(State); ShiftRows(State)
            AddRoundKey(state, W[Nr * 4, (Nr + 1) * 4 − 1])
    5. C = CopyStateToCipherOutput(State)
    6. return C
```

```
function D #AES Decryption
    input   C: 128-bit ciphertext block; W: key schedule array
    output  P: 128-bit plaintext block
    1. State = CopyCipherInputToStateArray (C)
    2. AddRoundKey (State, W[Nr * 4, (Nr + 1) * 4 − 1])
    3. for Round = Nr − 1 downto 1
            InvShiftRows (State); InvSubByes(State)
            AddRoundKey(state, W[Round * 4, (Round + 1) * 4 − 1]).
            InvMixColumns (State)
    4. # Transformations of the last round
            InvShiftRows(State); InvSubBytes(State)
            AddRoundKey(state, W[0,3])
    5. C = CopyStateToCipherOutput(State)
    6. return P
```

CopyCipherInputToStateArray and *CopyStateToCipherOutput* are conversion functions to convert a bit-string (i.e. plaintext or ciphertext block) to a state array and vice versa.

7.3.4 AES Transformation Description

7.3.4.1 `SubBytes` and `InvSubBytes` Transformations

`SubBytes` transformation aims at providing optimal diffusion, which results in resistance against differential and linear cryptanalysis. It consists in using a 16×16 lookup table, called S-box (Table 7.9), to replace each of the 16 bytes of the state by another byte. Byte substitution of a byte b is performed as follows:

Let $b = b_7 b_6 b_5 b_4 b_3 b_2 b_1 b_0$ be the sequence of bits of byte b. Let $i = b_7 b_6 b_5 b_4$ be the four leftmost bits of b and $j = b_3 b_2 b_1 b_0$, its four rightmost bits. Then, i and j are used as row and column indexes to yield $b' = S\_Box(i, j)$.

`InvSubBytes` makes use of the InvS-box (Table 7.10) to yield the inverse byte substitution of that yielded by `SubBytes`.

Note. Unlike DEA, which makes use of random S-boxes, the AES s-boxes have an algebraic structure (see Section 7.3.6.2).

Example 7.1

`SubBytes` and `InvSubBytes` make use of tables S-box and InvS-box, respectively. Byte $[3c]_{16}$ is replaced by $S\_Box(3,12) = [eb]_{16}$. Byte $[eb]_{16}$ is replaced by $InvS\_Box(14,11) = [3c]_{16}$.

Byte $[75]_{16}$ is replaced by $S\_Box(7,5) = [9d]_{16}$. Byte $[9d]_{16}$ is replaced by $InvS\_Box(9,13) = [75]_{16}$.

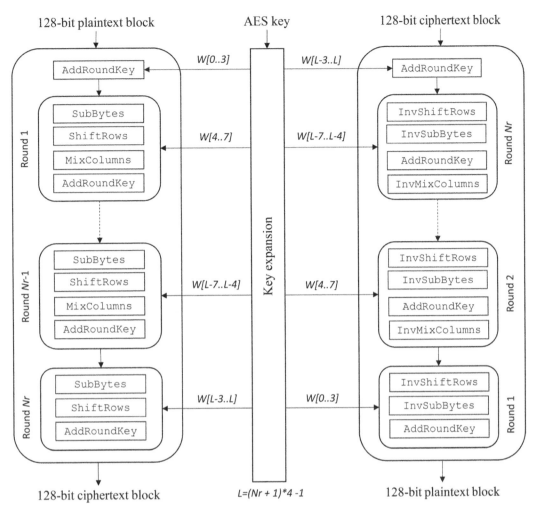

Figure 7.13 Overall structure of AES.

Table 7.9 S-box (in hexadecimal representation).

		y															
		0	1	2	3	4	5	6	7	8	9	a	b	c	d	e	f
x	0	63	7c	77	7b	f2	6b	6f	c5	30	01	67	2b	fe	d7	ab	76
	1	ca	82	c9	7d	fa	59	47	f0	ad	d4	a2	af	9c	a4	72	c0
	2	b7	fd	93	26	36	3f	f7	cc	34	a5	e5	f1	71	d8	31	15
	3	04	c7	23	c3	18	96	05	9a	07	12	80	e2	eb	27	b2	75
	4	09	83	2c	1a	1b	6e	5a	a0	52	3b	d6	b3	29	e3	2f	84
	5	53	d1	00	ed	20	fc	b1	5b	6a	cb	be	39	4a	4c	58	cf
	6	d0	ef	aa	fb	43	4d	33	85	45	f9	02	7f	50	3c	9f	a8
	7	51	a3	40	8f	92	9d	38	f5	bc	b6	da	21	10	ff	f3	d2
	8	cd	0c	13	ec	5f	97	44	17	c4	a7	7e	3d	64	5d	19	73
	9	60	81	4f	dc	22	2a	90	88	46	ee	b8	14	de	5e	0b	db
	a	e0	32	3a	0a	49	06	24	5c	c2	d3	ac	62	91	95	e4	79
	b	e7	c8	37	6d	8d	d5	4e	a9	6c	56	f4	ea	65	7a	ae	08
	c	ba	78	25	2e	1c	a6	b4	c6	e8	dd	74	1f	4b	bd	8b	8a
	d	70	3e	b5	66	48	03	f6	0e	61	35	57	b9	86	c1	1d	9e
	e	e1	f8	98	11	69	d9	8e	94	9b	1e	87	e9	ce	55	28	df
	f	8c	a1	89	0d	bf	e6	42	68	41	99	2d	0f	b0	54	bb	16

Table 7.10 InvS-box (in hexadecimal representation).

		y															
		0	1	2	3	4	5	6	7	8	9	a	b	c	d	e	f
x	0	52	09	6a	d5	30	36	a5	38	bf	40	a3	9e	81	f3	d7	fb
	1	7c	e3	39	82	9b	2f	ff	87	34	8e	43	44	c4	de	e9	cb
	2	54	7b	94	32	a6	c2	23	3d	ee	4c	95	0b	42	fa	c3	4e
	3	08	2e	a1	66	28	d9	24	b2	76	5b	a2	49	6d	8b	d1	25
	4	72	f8	f6	64	86	68	98	16	d4	a4	5c	cc	5d	65	b6	92
	5	6c	70	48	50	fd	ed	b9	da	5e	15	46	57	a7	8d	9d	84
	6	90	d8	ab	00	8c	bc	d3	0a	f7	e4	58	05	b8	b3	45	06
	7	d0	2c	1e	8f	ca	3f	0f	02	c1	af	bd	03	01	13	8a	6b
	8	3a	91	11	41	4f	67	dc	ea	97	f2	cf	ce	f0	b4	e6	73
	9	96	ac	74	22	e7	ad	35	85	e2	f9	37	e8	1c	75	df	6e
	a	47	f1	1a	71	1d	29	c5	89	6f	b7	62	0e	aa	18	be	1b
	b	fc	56	3e	4b	c6	d2	79	20	9a	db	c0	fe	78	cd	5a	f4
	c	1f	dd	a8	33	88	07	c7	31	b1	12	10	59	27	80	ec	5f
	d	60	51	7f	a9	19	b5	4a	0d	2d	e5	7a	9f	93	c9	9c	ef
	e	a0	e0	3b	4d	ae	2a	f5	b0	c8	eb	bb	3c	83	53	99	61
	f	17	2b	04	7e	ba	77	d6	26	e1	69	14	63	55	21	0c	7d

7.3.4.2 `ShiftRows` and `InvShiftRows` Transformations

In the `ShiftRows` transformation (see Figure 7.14), the row 0 of the input state S remains unchanged and each of the other three rows, $r = 1,2,3$, are rotated by r byte(s) to the left. Formally, `ShiftRows` transformation is defined by:

$$S'_{r,c} = S_{r,(c+LRotate(r,Nb)) \bmod Nb} \text{ for } 1 \le r < 4 \text{ and } 0 \le c < Nb$$

where $LRotate(r,Nb)$ operation rotates r with Nb positions to the left. Recall that when the block bit-length is 128, Nb, the number of state columns, is 4.

Note that `ShiftRows` transformation ensures that the four bits of one column are spread out to four different columns.

`InvShiftRows` transformation (see Figure 7.15) inverses the `ShiftRows` output. The row 0 of the input state S remains unchanged and each of the other three rows, $r = 1,2,3$, are rotated by r byte(s) to the right. Formally, `InvShiftRows` transformation is defined by:

$$S'_{r,c} = S_{r,(c+RRotate(r,Nb)) \bmod Nb} \text{ for } 1 \le r < 4 \text{ and } 0 \le c < Nb$$

where $RRotate(r,Nb)$ operation rotates r with Nb positions to the right.

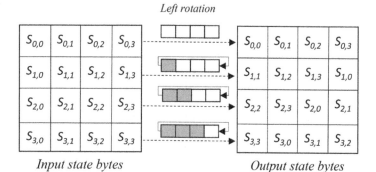

Figure 7.14 `ShiftRows` of a state.

Right rotation

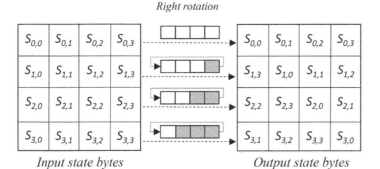

Input state bytes   Output state bytes

Figure 7.15 `InvShiftRows` of a state.

7.3.4.3 `MixColumns` and `InvMixColumns` Transformations

`MixColumns` operates on the state column-by-column using a linear function, which provides a strong diffusion. More precisely, each byte in a column of the input state is replaced by twice that byte, plus three times the next byte, plus the byte that comes next, and plus the byte that follows in the column. In each column, bytes are used in a circular way. `InvMixColumns` undoes the `MixColumns` transformation.

7.3.4.4 `AddRoundKey` Transformation

`AddRoundKey` XORes a round key with the input state, byte-by-byte. The key of round rnd, $rnd = 1, ..., Nr$, is composed of four words denoted KW_{rnd*4} to $KW_{(rnd+1)*4-1}$. The rule of transformation is defined by:

$$\left[S'_{0,c},\, S'_{1,c},\, S'_{2,c},\, S'_{3,c}\right] = \left[S_{0,c},\, S_{1,c},\, S_{2,c},\, S_{3,c}\right] \oplus \left[KW_{rnd*4+c}\right],\ \text{for } 0 \leq c < 4$$

In the encryption (resp. decryption) operation, the initial input state is added to the key words KW_0 to KW_3 (resp. KW_{Nr*4} to KW_{Nr*4+3}) before performing the first encryption (resp. decryption) round.

7.3.5 Key Expansion

Key expansion takes a key K of 128, 192, or 256 bits, and generates $Nr + 1$ round keys grouped in a 4-byte-word array, denoted W. The total number of 4-byte words of W array is of $(Nr + 1) * 4$: four words are added to the initial state input and four words for each of the Nr rounds. The four words, $W[4R]$, $W[4R + 1]$, $W[4R + 2]$, and $W[4R + 3]$, form the key of round R.

The round keys are computed recursively; i.e. the key of round R is computed from that of round $R - 1$. To simplify the key expansion description, we focus on a key length of 128 bits (i.e. $Nk = 4$),[7] which is illustrated by Figure 7.16:

1) Key K is mapped to a state of four words: $W[0]$, $W[1]$, $W[2]$, $W[3]$. Therefore, the first `AddRoundKey` call in encryption and decryption adds the cipher key to initial block.
2) The words of the key of round R is computed as:
   $$W[4 * R] = W[4(R - 1)] \oplus g(W[4R - 1])$$
   $$W[4 * R + j] = W[4R + j - 1] \oplus W[4(R - 1) + j],\ \text{for } j = 1, 2, 3$$
   The function $g(Z)$ has one-word input and output. It consists in three operations:

   - Z' is yielded using a one-byte left rotation of input Z
   - using the S-Box, substitute each byte of Z' and output Z''
   - XOR Z'' with a known round constant $Rcon[Rnd]$

Therefore, $g(Z)$ is defined by: $g(Z) \overset{\text{def}}{=} SubBytes\left(LRotate(Z) \oplus Rcon[Rnd]\right)$

The $Rcon$ is an array, which associates one 4-byte constant word with each round R as follows: $Rcon[R] = \left[x^{R-1}, 00, 00, 00\right]$, where x^{R-1} denotes a modular exponentiation in the field (see Section 3.3.2). The three rightmost bytes of $Rcon$ are zeros and the leftmost bytes are given in Table 7.11.

Pseudocode below is a specification of the key expansion function for any value of Nk (4, 6, or 8).

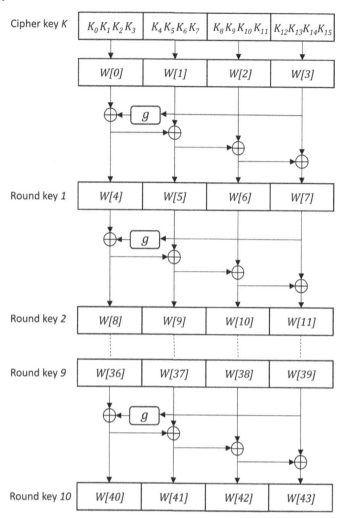

Figure 7.16 Key expansion for a key-bit length of 128.

Table 7.11 Values of the leftmost byte of the constant vector Rcon.

Round number	1	2	3	4	5	6	7	8	9	10
Rcon	01_{16}	02_{16}	04_{16}	08_{16}	10_{16}	20_{16}	40_{16}	80_{16}	$1b_{16}$	36_{16}

```
function KeyExpansion
      input   Nk: key length in 32-bit words; K: key array of Nk 32-words
      output  W: array of the round keys; W is of 4 * (Nr + 1) words
   1. for i= 0 to Nk do
            # Copy the cipher key K Nk + 1 times in the array W
            # K[j] denotes the jth byte of key K; 0 ≤ j ≤ len(K)-1
            W[i] = [K[4 * i], K[4 * i + 1], K[4 * i + 2], [4 * i + 3]]
   2. for i=Nk to 4 * (Nr + 1) -1 do
            tmp = W[i − 1]
            if (i mod Nk = 0)
                    then tmp = SubWord(RotWord(tmp)) ⊕ Rcon[i/Nk]
                    else if (Nk> 6 and i mod Nk = 4)
                        then tmp = SubWord(tmp)
            W[i] = W[i − Nk] ⊕ tmp
   3. return W
```

SubWord(Z) is a function that takes a 4-byte input word Z and applies the S-Box to each of the four bytes to yield an output word Z'. *RotWord(Z)* is a function that takes a 4-byte input word $Z = [Z_0, Z_1, Z_2, Z_3]$ and outputs the permuted word $Z' = [Z_1, Z_2, Z_3, Z_0]$. *Rcon(i)* is a constant array.

7.3.6 Mathematical Description of AES

AES computations are performed over the extension field F_{2^8}. Therefore, the design rationale and the proof of correctness of AES rely on mathematical notions. This section aims at describing AES operations using extension field computations. The proof of correctness of AES transformations is addressed in Problems 7.10 and 7.11.

The extension field F_{2^8}, also Galois field $GF(2^8)$, is the set of elements $\{0, 1, ..., 255\}$; it is used to represent and process bytes in AES transformations. *We advise the reader to refer to chapter 3 to learn the fundamentals of finite fields and to do some exercises included in that chapter.*

7.3.6.1 Data Representation and Operations on Data

7.3.6.1.1 Byte Representation and Operations on Bytes
A byte b is a concatenation of eight bits $b_7 b_6 b_5 b_4 b_3 b_2 b_1 b_0$ and it is interpreted as an element of an extension field using a polynomial representation; i.e. $b(x) = b_7 x^7 + b_6 x^6 + b_5 x^5 + b_4 x^4 + b_3 x^3 + b_2 x^2 + b_1 x + b_0$. A byte may be written in base 2 or in base 16. The notation used to write a constant in base 16 is $[..]_{16}$; for example $[21]_{16}$ represents the value 33 in base 10; and $[fd]_{16}$ the value 253.

Byte addition
Bytes are elements of the extension field F_{2^8}. Addition of elements of extension field F_{2^8} is denoted $\oplus$, which is the bitwise XOR.

Example 7.2
Let $a = 11011011$ and $b = 11100011_2$ be two bytes in binary representation. In polynomial representation, we have:

$$a(x) = x^7 + x^6 + x^4 + x^3 + x + 1 \text{ and } b(x) = x^7 + x^6 + x^5 + x + 1$$

In extension field F_{2^8}, the coefficients in the polynomials are binaries. Hence, $c = a + b$ is yielded by:
$$c(x) = a(x) + b(x) = x^5 + x^4 + x^3$$

With the bitwise XOR operation:

$$a \oplus b = (11011011_2) \oplus (11100011_2) = 00111000_2$$

Byte multiplication
Byte multiplication, denoted $\bullet$, is performed with the irreducible polynomial $m(x) = x^8 + x^4 + x^3 + x + 1$. Notice that since the irreducible polynomial $m(x)$ is of degree 8, any multiplication of two bytes results in a value represented by a byte. Any element b and its inverse b^{-1} are both elements of F_{2^8}. The irreducible polynomial used in AES has a useful property, which makes it easy to implement the operations especially in hardware.

Example 7.3
Let $a = 11011011_2$ and $b = 00000011_2$ be two bytes in binary representation.
$c = a \bullet b$ is computed as follows:

$$c(x) = a(x) * b(x) \bmod \left(x^8 + x^4 + x^3 + x + 1\right)$$
$$= (x^8 + x^6 + x^5 + x^3 + x^2 + 1) \bmod \left(x^8 + x^4 + x^3 + x + 1\right)$$
$$= x^6 + x^5 + x^4 + x^2 + x$$

$$c = 11011011_2 \bullet 00000011_2 = 01110110_2$$

Let $a' = 10000111_2$ and $b' = 01010110_2$ be two bytes in binary representation.
$c' = a' \bullet b'$ is computed as follows:

$$c'(x) = a'(x) * b'(x) \bmod \left(x^8 + x^4 + x^3 + x + 1\right)$$
$$= (x^{13} + x^{11} + x^9 + x^7 + x^5 + x) \bmod \left(x^8 + x^4 + x^3 + x + 1\right) = 1$$

$c' = 10000111_2 \cdot 01010110_2 = 00000001_2$

Notice that b' is the multiplicative inverse of $a' \bmod (x^8 + x^4 + x^3 + x + 1)$.

7.3.6.1.2 Word Representation and Operations on Words

A 4-byte word can be represented as a polynomial of degree 3 with coefficients in F_{2^8}. More precisely, a word $A = [A_0, A_1, A_2, A_3]$ is represented as a polynomial

$$A(x) = A_3 x^3 + A_2 x^2 + A_1 x + A_0, \text{ where } A_{i=0,1,2,3} \in F_{2^8}.$$

Word addition

The addition of two words $A = [A_0, A_1, A_2, A_3]$ and $B = [B_0, B_1, B_2, B_3]$ is yielded by the bitwise XOR of their coefficients. More precisely, $C = A + B$ is yielded as follows:

$$C = [A_0 \oplus B_0, A_1 \oplus B_1, A_2 \oplus B_2, A_3 \oplus B_3]$$

Alternatively, we can write: $C(x) = (A_3 \oplus B_3)x^3 + (A_2 \oplus B_2)x^2 + (A_1 \oplus B_1)x + (A_0 \oplus B_0)$.

Word multiplication

Word multiplication is not used in AES transformations. Rather, the modular product of words, denoted $\otimes$, is used instead. The modular product of two words $A = [A_0, A_1, A_2, A_3]$ and $B = [B_0, B_1, B_2, B_3]$, $D = A \otimes B$ is computed in two steps:

1) Compute the polynomial product $A(x) \cdot B(x)$:

$$\begin{aligned}
C(x) = A(x) \cdot B(x) = &\left(A_3 x^3 + A_2 x^2 + A_1 x + A_0\right) * \left(B_3 x^3 + B_2 x^2 + B_1 x + B_0\right) \\
= &\left(A_3 \cdot B_3\right) x^6 \\
&+ \left((A_3 \cdot B_2) \oplus (A_2 \cdot B_3)\right) x^5 \\
&+ \left((A_3 \cdot B_1) \oplus (A_2 \cdot B_2) \oplus (A_1 \cdot B_3)\right) x^4 \\
&+ \left((A_3 \cdot B_0) \oplus (A_2 \cdot B_1) \oplus (A_1 \cdot B_2) \oplus (A_0 \cdot B_3)\right) x^3 \\
&+ \left((A_2 \cdot B_0) \oplus (A_1 \cdot B_1) \oplus (A_0 \cdot B_2)\right) x^2 \\
&+ \left((A_1 \cdot B_0) \oplus (A_0 \cdot B_1)\right) x \\
&+ \left(A_0 \cdot B_0\right)
\end{aligned}$$

2) Reduce the polynomial $C(x)$:

   $C(x)$ is a polynomial of degree 6 and does not represent a 4-byte word. That is why a reduction with a polynomial of degree 4 is required. More precisely, the polynomial $x^4 + 1$ is used in AES:

$$D(x) = A(x) \otimes B(x) = C(x) \bmod (x^4 + 1) = D_3 x^3 + D_2 x^2 + D_1 x + D_0$$

Thus, $D(x)$ is of degree 3 and its coefficients are computed as follows:

$$\begin{aligned}
D(x) = &\left((A_3 \cdot B_0) \oplus (A_2 \cdot B_1) \oplus (A_1 \cdot B_2) \oplus (A_0 \cdot B_3)\right) x^3 \\
&+ \left((A_2 \cdot B_0) \oplus (A_1 \cdot B_1) \oplus (A_0 \cdot B_2) \oplus (A_3 \cdot B_3)\right) x^2 \\
&+ \left((A_1 \cdot B_0) \oplus (A_0 \cdot B_1) \oplus (A_3 \cdot B_2) \oplus (A_2 \cdot B_3)\right) x \\
&+ \left(A_0 \cdot B_0\right) \oplus (A_3 \cdot B_1) \oplus (A_2 \cdot B_2) \oplus (A_1 \cdot B_3)
\end{aligned}$$

The modular product $D(x) = A(x) \otimes B(x)$ can also be written in matrix[8] form as:

$$\begin{bmatrix} D_0 \\ D_1 \\ D_2 \\ D_3 \end{bmatrix} = \begin{bmatrix} A_0 & A_3 & A_2 & A_1 \\ A_1 & A_0 & A_3 & A_2 \\ A_2 & A_1 & A_0 & A_3 \\ A_3 & A_2 & A_1 & A_0 \end{bmatrix} \begin{bmatrix} B_0 \\ B_1 \\ B_2 \\ B_3 \end{bmatrix}$$

Notes

1) The polynomial $x^4 + 1$ is not an irreducible polynomial, because it has 1 as a root. Thus, the multiplicative inverse does not exist for some elements $mod\, x^4 + 1$. However, it is not important, because AES makes use of only two polynomials that both have inverses:
   - Polynomial $A(x) = [03]_{16} x^3 + [01]_{16} x^2 + [01]_{16} x + [02]_{16}$ is used in MixColumns; and its inverse is $A(x)^{-1} = [0b]_{16} x^3 + [0d]_{16} x^2 + [09]_{16} x + [0e]_{16}$. One can easily check that $A(x) * A(x)^{-1} = 1\, mod\, (x^4 + 1)$.
   - Polynomial $A(x) = x^3$ is used in key expansion; and its inverse is $A(x)^{-1} = x$, because $x^3 * x\, mod\, (x^4 + 1) = 1$.
2) AES selected the polynomial $x^4 + 1$, due to its simplicity of reduction. Indeed, it provides the following reduction: $x^i\, mod\, (x^4 + 1) = x^{i\, mod\, 4}$.

Example 7.4

– Let $W^{(1)}$ and $W^{(2)}$ be two 32-bit words such that:

$$W^{(1)} = \left[[fe]_{16}, [11]_{16}, [03]_{16}, [ab]_{16} \right] \text{ and } W^{(2)} = \left[[aa]_{16}, [c1]_{16}, [10]_{16}, [d0]_{16} \right]$$

Adding $W^{(1)}$ to $W^{(2)}$ yields $W^{(1+2)}$, computed as:

$$W^{(1+2)}(x) = \left([ab]_{16} \oplus [d0]_{16} \right) x^3 + \left([03]_{16} \oplus [10]_{16} \right) x^2 + \left([11]_{16} \oplus [c1]_{16} \right) x + \left([fe]_{16} \oplus [aa]_{16} \right)$$
$$= [7b]_{16} x^3 + [d0]_{16} x^2 + [13]_{16} x + [54]_{16}$$

Thus, $W^{(1+2)} = W^{(1)} + W^{(2)} = \left[[54]_{16}, [d0]_{16}, [13]_{16}, [7b]_{16} \right]$.

– Let $W^{(1)}$ and $W^{(2)}$ be two 32-bit words such that:

$$W^{(1)} = \left[[00]_{16}, [00]_{16}, [00]_{16}, [11]_{16} \right] \text{ and } W^{(2)} = \left[[cd]_{16}, [00]_{16}, [22]_{16}, [55]_{16} \right]$$

The modular product $W^{(1)}$ and $W^{(2)}$ yields the word, computed as follows:

○ Compute the coefficients of the polynomial $C^{(1*2)}(x) = W^{(1)}(x) * W^{(2)}(x)$:

$$C^{(1*2)}(x) = \left([11]_{16} x^3 \right) * \left([55]_{16} x^3 + [22]_{16} x^2 + [cd]_{16} \right)$$
$$= \left([11]_{16} \bullet [55]_{16} \right) x^6 + \left([11]_{16} \bullet [22]_{16} \right) x^5 + \left([11]_{16} \bullet [cd]_{16} \right) x^3$$

Compute $[11]_{16} \bullet [55]_{16}$:

$$\left(x^4 + 1 \right) \left(x^6 + x^4 + x^2 + 1 \right) mod\, x^8 + x^4 + x^3 + x + 1$$
$$= x^6 + x^5 + x^4 + x$$

Thus, $[11]_{16} \bullet [55]_{16} = [72]_{16}$

Compute $[11]_{16} \bullet [22]_{16}$:

$$(x^4 + 1)(x^5 + x)\, mod\, x^8 + x^4 + x^3 + x + 1 = x^5 + x^4 + x^2$$

Thus, $[11]_{16} \bullet [22]_{16} = [34]_{16}$

Compute $[11]_{16} + [cd]_{16}$:

$$\left(x^4 + 1 \right) \left(x^7 + x^6 + x^3 + x^2 + 1 \right) mod\, x^8 + x^4 + x^3 + x + 1$$
$$= x^7 + x^5 + x^3 + 1$$

Thus, $[11]_{16} \bullet [cd]_{16} = [a9]_{16}$.

Therefore, $C^{(1*2)}(x) = [72]_{16} x^6 + [34]_{16} x^5 + [a9]_{16} x^3$

- Reduce the polynomial $C^{(1*2)}(x)$:

$$C^{(1*2)}(x) \bmod (x^4 + 1) = [a9]_{16} x^3 + [72]_{16} x^2 + [34]_{16} x$$

- Finally, $W^{(1 \otimes 2)} = W^{(1)} \otimes W^{(2)} = \left[[00]_{16}, [34]_{16}, [72]_{16}, [a9]_{16} \right]$.

7.3.6.2 SubBytes and InvSubBytes Transformations

SubBytes is a nonlinear[9] transformation, which operates independently on each byte of the state using the S-Box; InvSubBytes is its inverse, which makes use of the InvS-Box. Both boxes are 16×16byte arrays. Row and column indexes, denoted x (4 bits) and y (4 bits), of a box cell form a byte $x \parallel y$, which is an element of the extension field F_{2^8}.

Construction of S-Box

Let a denote the concatenation of the row and column indexes of an S-Box cell. b', the content of the S-Box cell indexed[10] by a, is computed in two steps as follows:

1) Take b, the multiplicative inverse of a in the extension field F_{2^8}; that is, $b = a^{-1}$; i.e. $1 = b(x) * a(x) \bmod (x^8 + x^4 + x^3 + x + 1)$. Since the element 00 has no multiplicative inverse in any extension field, AES authors made an exception and mapped 00 to itself.
2) Apply the following affine transformation to the element b, for $0 \leq i < 8$, to yield b' such as:

$$b'_i = b_i \oplus b_{(i+4) \bmod 8} \oplus b_{(i+5) \bmod 8} \oplus b_{(i+6) \bmod 8} \oplus b_{(i+7) \bmod 8} \oplus c_i, \tag{7.1}$$

where c is a constant with the value $[63]_{16} = 01100011_2$.

Computing inverses in F_{2^8} results in a nonlinear byte substitution, which makes AES resistant against some forms of cryptanalysis attacks.

Example 7.5
- $S\_Box(0,0) = [63]_{16}$, because:
  o The inverse of $a = 00$ is $b = 00$ (by AES design)
  o By (7.1), $b'_i = c_i$. Since $c = [63]_{16}$, $b' = [63]_{16}$.
- $S\_Box(8,7) = 17$, because:
  o In extension field F_{2^8}, the inverse of $a = 87$ is $b = 56$
  o By (7.1):

$$b'_7 = 0 \oplus 0 \oplus 1 \oplus 0 \oplus 1 \oplus 0 = 0 \qquad b'_3 = 0 \oplus 0 \oplus 0 \oplus 1 \oplus 1 \oplus 0 = 0$$
$$b'_6 = 1 \oplus 1 \oplus 0 \oplus 1 \oplus 0 \oplus 1 = 0 \qquad b'_2 = 1 \oplus 1 \oplus 0 \oplus 0 \oplus 1 \oplus 0 = 1$$
$$b'_5 = 0 \oplus 1 \oplus 1 \oplus 0 \oplus 1 \oplus 1 = 0 \qquad b'_1 = 1 \oplus 0 \oplus 1 \oplus 0 \oplus 0 \oplus 1 = 1$$
$$b'_4 = 1 \oplus 0 \oplus 1 \oplus 1 \oplus 0 \oplus 0 = 1 \qquad b'_0 = 0 \oplus 1 \oplus 0 \oplus 1 \oplus 0 \oplus 1 = 1$$

In the matrix form, the affine transformation (7.1) can be specified as follows (with addition modulo 2):

$$\begin{bmatrix} b'_0 \\ b'_1 \\ b'_2 \\ b'_3 \\ b'_4 \\ b'_5 \\ b'_6 \\ b'_7 \end{bmatrix} = \begin{bmatrix} 1 & 0 & 0 & 0 & 1 & 1 & 1 & 1 \\ 1 & 1 & 0 & 0 & 0 & 1 & 1 & 1 \\ 1 & 1 & 1 & 0 & 0 & 0 & 1 & 1 \\ 1 & 1 & 1 & 1 & 0 & 0 & 0 & 1 \\ 1 & 1 & 1 & 1 & 1 & 0 & 0 & 0 \\ 0 & 1 & 1 & 1 & 1 & 1 & 0 & 0 \\ 0 & 0 & 1 & 1 & 1 & 1 & 1 & 0 \\ 0 & 0 & 0 & 1 & 1 & 1 & 1 & 1 \end{bmatrix} \begin{bmatrix} b_0 \\ b_1 \\ b_2 \\ b_3 \\ b_4 \\ b_5 \\ b_6 \\ b_7 \end{bmatrix} \oplus \begin{bmatrix} 1 \\ 1 \\ 0 \\ 0 \\ 0 \\ 1 \\ 1 \\ 0 \end{bmatrix} \tag{7.2}$$

Construction of InvS-Box

The InvS-Box is constructed in the inverse order of that of the S-Box; it is obtained by the inverse of the affine transformation used to construct the S-Box and then, by computing the multiplicative inverse.

Let α denote the concatenation of the row and column indexes of an InvS-Box cell. β', the content of the InvS-Box cell indexed by α, is computed in two steps as follows:

1) Apply the following affine transformation to the element α, for $0 \leq i < 8$, to yield

$$\alpha_i' = \alpha_{(i+2)\,mod\,8} \oplus \alpha_{(i+5)\,mod\,8} \oplus \alpha_{(i+7)\,mod\,8} \oplus d_i, \tag{7.3}$$

where d is a constant with a value of $05_{16} = 00000101_2$.

2) Take β', the multiplicative inverse of α' in the extension field F_{2^8}; that is, $\beta' = \alpha'^{-1}$.

In the matrix form, the affine transformation (7.3) can be specified as follows (with addition modulo 2):

$$\begin{bmatrix} b_0' \\ b_1' \\ b_2' \\ b_3' \\ b_4' \\ b_5' \\ b_6' \\ b_7' \end{bmatrix} = \begin{bmatrix} 0 & 0 & 1 & 0 & 0 & 1 & 0 & 1 \\ 1 & 0 & 0 & 1 & 0 & 0 & 1 & 0 \\ 0 & 1 & 0 & 0 & 1 & 0 & 0 & 1 \\ 1 & 0 & 1 & 0 & 0 & 1 & 0 & 0 \\ 0 & 1 & 0 & 1 & 0 & 0 & 1 & 0 \\ 0 & 0 & 1 & 0 & 1 & 0 & 0 & 1 \\ 1 & 0 & 0 & 1 & 0 & 1 & 0 & 0 \\ 0 & 1 & 0 & 0 & 1 & 0 & 1 & 0 \end{bmatrix} \begin{bmatrix} b_0 \\ b_1 \\ b_2 \\ b_3 \\ b_4 \\ b_5 \\ b_6 \\ b_7 \end{bmatrix} \oplus \begin{bmatrix} 1 \\ 0 \\ 1 \\ 0 \\ 0 \\ 0 \\ 0 \\ 0 \end{bmatrix} \tag{7.4}$$

Note. The elements of the S-Box and their inverses are constants; thus, they are computed one time and stored in two tables.

7.3.6.3 `ShiftRows` and `InvShiftRows` Transformations

In `ShiftRows` and `InvShiftRows`, the row 0 of the state is not shifted, while the others are left-shifted using `ShiftRows` and right-shifted using `InvShiftRows`. Therefore, for any state S, *InvShiftRows(ShiftRows(S)) = S*.

7.3.6.4 `MixColumns` and `InvMixColumns` Transformations

In the `MixColumns` transformation, each column of the state is considered as a polynomial of degree 4 with coefficients in the extension field F_{2^8} and multiplied modulo the polynomial $x^4 + 1$ by a fixed polynomial $a(x) = [03]_{16} x^3 + [01]_{16} x^2 + [01]_{16} x + [02]_{16}$. Thus, a state S is mapped to S', such that: $S'(x) = S(x) \otimes a(x)$, which can be written as a matrix multiplication, for each column $c, 0 \leq c < 4$, as follows:

$$\begin{bmatrix} S_{0,c}' \\ S_{1,c}' \\ S_{2,c}' \\ S_{3,c}' \end{bmatrix} = \begin{bmatrix} 02 & 03 & 01 & 01 \\ 01 & 02 & 03 & 01 \\ 01 & 01 & 02 & 03 \\ 03 & 01 & 01 & 02 \end{bmatrix} \begin{bmatrix} S_{0,c} \\ S_{1,c} \\ S_{2,c} \\ S_{3,c} \end{bmatrix} \tag{7.5}$$

The four bytes resulting from the multiplication are as follows:

$$S_{0,c}' = ([02]_{16} \bullet S_{0,c}) \oplus ([03]_{16} \bullet S_{1,c}) \oplus S_{2,c} \oplus S_{3,c}, \text{for } 0 \leq c < 4$$

$$S_{1,c}' = S_{0,c} \oplus ([02]_{16} \bullet S_{1,c}) \oplus ([03]_{16} \bullet S_{2,c}) \oplus S_{3,c}, \text{ for } 0 \leq c < 4$$

$$S_{2,c}' = S_{0,c} \oplus S_{1,c} \oplus ([02]_{16} \bullet S_{2,c}) ([03]_{16} \bullet S_{3,c}), \text{ for } 0 \leq c < 4$$

$$S_{3,c}' = ([03]_{16} \bullet S_{0,c}) \oplus S_{1,c} \oplus S_{2,c} \oplus ([02]_{16} \bullet S_{3,c}), \text{ for } 0 \leq c < 4$$

From the four equalities above, we observe that each byte in a column c of the input state S is replaced by twice that byte, plus three times the next byte, plus the byte that comes next, and plus the byte that follows in the column.

Example 7.6

Assume that the first column of the state S is $[[10]_{16}, [00]_{16}, [00]_{16}, [01]_{16}]$. We compute the new column yielded by `MixColumns`. The polynomial associated with the first column is: $S_{*,0}(x) = [01]_{16} x^3 + [10]_{16}$.

Compute the modular product: $S_{*,0}(x) \otimes a(x)$.

$$S_{*,0}(x) \otimes a(x) = \left([01]_{16} x^3 + [10]_{16}\right) * \left([03]_{16} x^3 + [01]_{16} x^2 + [01]_{16} x + [02]_{16}\right) mod \left(x^4 + 1\right)$$

$$= \left([03]_{16} \cdot [01]_{16}\right) x^6 + \left([01]_{16} \cdot [01]_{16}\right) x^5 + \left([01]_{16} \cdot [01]_{16}\right) x^4$$

$$+ \left([02]_{16} \cdot [01]_{16} \oplus [03]_{16} \cdot [10]_{16}\right) x^3 + \left([01]_{16} \cdot [10]_{16}\right) x^2$$

$$+ \left([01]_{16} \cdot [10]_{16}\right) x + \left([02]_{16} \cdot [10]_{16}\right) mod \left(x^4 + 1\right)$$

$$= \left([02]_{16} \cdot [01]_{16} \oplus [03]_{16} \cdot [10]_{16}\right) x^3 + \left([01]_{16} \cdot [10]_{16} \oplus [03]_{16} \cdot [01]_{16}\right) x^2$$

$$+ \left([01]_{16} \cdot [10]_{16} \oplus [01]_{16} \cdot [01]_{16}\right) x + \left([02]_{16} \cdot [10]_{16} \oplus [01]_{16} \cdot [01]_{16}\right)$$

$$= \left([02]_{16} \oplus [03]_{16} \cdot [10]_{16}\right) x^3 + \left([10]_{16} \oplus [03]_{16}\right) x^2$$

$$+ \left([10]_{16} \oplus [01]_{16}\right) x + \left([02]_{16} \cdot [10]_{16} \oplus [01]_{16}\right)$$

$$= [31]_{16} x^3 + [13]_{16} x^2 + [11]_{16} x + [21]_{16}$$

Therefore, the new first column is $\left[[21]_{16}, [11]_{16}, [13]_{16}, [32]_{16}\right]$.

In the `InvMixColumns` transformation, the columns of the state are considered as polynomials of degree 4 with coefficients in the extension field F_{2^8} and multiplied modulo the polynomial $x^4 + 1$ by a fixed polynomial $a^{-1}(x) = [0b]_{16} x^3 + [0d]_{16} x^2 + [09]_{16} x + [0e]_{16}$, the inverse modulo $x^4 + 1$ of the one used in `MixColumns`.

Thus, a state S is mapped to S', such that: $S'(x) = S(x) \otimes a^{-1}(x)$, which can be written as a matrix multiplication, for each column c, $0 \le c < 4$, as follows:

$$
\begin{bmatrix} S'_{0,c} \\ S'_{1,c} \\ S'_{2,c} \\ S'_{3,c} \end{bmatrix} =
\begin{bmatrix} 0e & 0b & 0d & 09 \\ 09 & 0e & 0b & 0d \\ 0d & 09 & 0e & 0b \\ 0b & 0d & 09 & 0e \end{bmatrix}
\begin{bmatrix} S_{0,c} \\ S_{1,c} \\ S_{2,c} \\ S_{3,c} \end{bmatrix}
\tag{7.6}
$$

The four bytes resulting from the multiplication are as follows:

$$S'_{0,c} = \left([0e]_{16} \cdot S_{0,c}\right) \oplus \left([0b]_{16} \cdot S_{1,c}\right) \oplus \left([0d]_{16} \cdot S_{2,c}\right) \oplus \left([09]_{16} \cdot S_{3,c}\right), \text{ for } 0 \le c < 4$$

$$S'_{1,c} = \left([09]_{16} \cdot S_{0,c}\right) \oplus \left([0e]_{16} \cdot S_{1,c}\right) \oplus \left([0b]_{16} \cdot S_{2,c}\right) \oplus \left([0d]_{16} \cdot S_{3,c}\right), \text{ for } 0 \le c < 4$$

$$S'_{2,c} = \left([0d]_{16} \cdot S_{0,c}\right) \oplus \left([09]_{16} \cdot S_{1,c}\right) \oplus \left([0e]_{16} \cdot S_{2,c}\right) \oplus \left([0b]_{16} \cdot S_{3,c}\right), \text{ for } 0 \le c < 4$$

$$S'_{3,c} = \left([0b]_{16} \cdot S_{0,c}\right) \oplus \left([0d]_{16} \cdot S_{1,c}\right) \oplus \left([09]_{16} \cdot S_{2,c}\right) \oplus \left([0e]_{16} \cdot S_{3,c}\right), \text{ for } 0 \le c < 4$$

7.3.6.5 `AddRoundKey` Transformation
AddRoundKey is an XOR operation between a state and the round key; it is its inverse.

7.3.7 Security of AES

Although AES was introduced in 2001, all the threats against the AES cipher remain theoretical, because of their time complexity, which remains beyond the ability of any computer system to handle. This would last for a long time. In particular, differential and linear cryptanalyses have been used to design attacks against AES; however, their time complexity is just an optimization of that of brute-force attack. Such attacks will be addressed in Chapter 11.

A major known risk to AES encryption comes from side-channel attacks. Rather than attempting brute-force or cryptanalysis-based attacks, side-channel attacks are aimed at collecting information about what a computing device does when it is performing cryptographic operations (e.g. AES permutations, substitutions, etc.). Some side-channel attacks have been proposed and took advantage of some specific hardware or software implementations. To our knowledge, the most recent side-channel attack against AES was proposed in [8]. The attack targeted AES used in OpenSSL and made strong assumptions: i) the attacker is hosted on the same processor as the attacked system and both share the same processor cache, ii) the attacker can pre-empt the victim while it is encrypting or decrypting, iii) a few blocks of plaintext or ciphertext are known. Under such assumptions, the proposed attack runs in less than a minute. In conclusion, security experts still consider that AES is secure when implemented properly.

7.4 Exercises and Problems

7.4.1 List of Exercises and Problems

Exercise 7.1

Consider the first round of the Feistel cipher encryption. Which part of the plaintext is encrypted at the end of the round?

Exercise 7.2

Select randomly six bits in a 64-bit block B and check that the permutation IP^{-1} (defined by Table 7.2) is the inverse of the initial permutation IP (defined by Table 7.1).

Exercise 7.3

What is the probability that DES encryption maps a plaintext x to a ciphertext y for a given key? For all keys?

Exercise 7.4

One property of DEA that makes TDEA secure is that the selection functions $SF_i, i \in [1,8]$, are nonlinear. Use the following three pairs of inputs and show that $SF_2(x_1) \oplus SF_2(x_2) \neq SF_2(x_1 \oplus x_2)$; i.e. show that SF_2 is nonlinear.
- $x_1 = 111111_2$ and $x_2 = 000000_2$
- $x_1 = 110110_2$ and $x_2 = 001001_2$
- $x_1 = 111000_2$ and $x_2 = 000111_2$

Exercise 7.5

1) What is the output of the first round of DEA when the plaintext and the key are both all zeros?

2) What is the output of the first round of DEA when the plaintext and the key are both all ones?

Exercise 7.6

What do you get if you left-rotate by one position the last two 28-bits blocks, i.e. C_{16} and D_{16}, in the key schedule function?

Exercise 7.7

Show that `SubBytes` and `ShiftRows` transformations of AES can be applied in either order with the same result.

Exercise 7.8

What is the output of the first round of AES when the plaintext block and the cipher key are both of a value of $1^{(128)}$; i.e. all bits are 1s?

Problem 7.1

Recall that, in a round i of Feistel network, the input is a pair of halves L_{i-1} and R_{i-1} and a round key K_i; and the output is a pair of halves L_i and R_i, defined by $L_i = R_{i-1}$ and $R_i = L_{i-1} \oplus F(R_{i-1}, K_i)$. Prove that no matter what the function F is, the round transformation is one-to-one, i.e. we can recover the old state (L_{i-1}, R_{i-1}) from the new state (L_i, R_i) and the round-key K_i.

Problem 7.2

Prove the correctness of Feistel encryption and decryption assuming that the number of rounds is 1 or 2.

Problem 7.3

Prove the correctness of Feistel cipher for an arbitrary number of rounds.

Problem 7.4

Prove the correctness of TDEA, i.e. the decryption a ciphertext block yields the original plaintext block.

Problem 7.5

1) Prove the following property called *complementation property* of DES:
$$C = E(K,M) \Rightarrow \bar{C} = E(\bar{K}, \bar{M})$$
where $\bar{x}$ is the bit-by-bit complementation of bit-string x.

2) Explain how the complementation property of DES can be used to reduce the computation time of a brute-force attack against a DES key by about a factor of 2, if the adversary knew two plaintext–ciphertext pairs, (M_1, C_1) and (M_2, C_2), such that $M_2 = \overline{M_1}$, $C_2 = \overline{C_1}$, $C_1 = E(K, M_1)$, $C_2 = E(K, M_2)$. Assume that only encryption and decryption operations are time-consuming.

Problem 7.6

1) Show that if all the round keys of DEA are identical, encrypting twice a plaintext B results in the plaintext B; i.e. $E(K, E(K, B)) = B$.

2) Discuss why the following DEA keys are weak and should be avoided $Key_1 = 0101\,0101\,0101\,0101_{16}$ and $Key_2 = \text{FEFE FEFE FEFE FEFE}_{16}$.

Problem 7.7

Let $Key_1 = 011F011F010E010E_{16}$ and $Key_2 = 1F011F010E010E01_{16}$ be a pair of DEA keys.

1) How many distinct round keys are generated for both keys?

2) Show that (Key_1, Key_2) is a pair of semi-weak keys, i.e. for any plaintext M, $E(Key_1, E(Key_2, M)) = M$.

Problem 7.8

In the DEA key scheduling function, after dropping odd parity bits, 56 bits are used to generate 48-bit round keys. Thus, at each iteration, eight bits of the key are not used. Identify which key bits are not used to generate the first round key.

Problem 7.9

In this problem, we discuss the success probability of the meet-in-the-middle attack against double-DES described in Section 7.2.3.3.

1) What is the probability of false alarm with a single known plaintext–ciphertext pair (P_1, C_1)?

2) To increase the success probability of the attack, consider the following strategy: i) The first plaintext–ciphertext pair (P_1, C_1) yields a set of key pair candidates, denoted S.
   ii) A second plaintext–ciphertext pair (P_2, C_2) also is known and it is tested, but only the key pair candidates in S are used. What is the false alarm probability with two known plaintext–ciphertext pairs?

3) What is the false alarm probability with three known plaintext–ciphertext pairs?

Problem 7.10

Using the matrix forms of construction of S-Box and InvS-Box, prove that `InvSubBytes(SubBytes(S))= S`, for any state S.

Problem 7.11

1) Prove that $[0b]_{16} x^3 + [0d]_{16} x^2 + [09]_{16} x + [0e]_{16}$ is the inverse of $[03]_{16} x^3 + [01]_{16} x^2 + [01]_{16} x + [02]_{16} \bmod (x^4 + 1)$, with coefficients in F_{2^8}.

2) Using the matrix form, prove that `InvMixColumns` is the inverse of `MixColumns`.

7.4.2 Solutions to Exercises and Problems

Exercise 7.1

Operations performed in the first round are $LE_1 = RE_0$ and $RE_1 = LE_0 \oplus F(RE_0, K_1)$.

The right half is used in the round function F, but it does not change and it is directly copied in the left part of the input to the second round.

The left half is XORed with the output of the round function F and the transformation result is copied in the right part of the input to the second round. Therefore, only the left part of the plaintext is encrypted in the first round.

Exercise 7.2

Let B, B', and B'' be 64-bit blocks presented as vectors of bits $B[1:64]$, $B'[1:64]$, and $B''[1:64]$. Let $B' = IP(B)$ and $B'' = IP^{-1}(B')$. We need to check that $B'' = B$.

Consider six bits randomly selected: $B[1], B[5], B[21], B[49], B[52], B[63]$.

Computation of $B' = IP(B)$ yields:

$$B'[1] = B[58] \qquad B'[5] = B[26] \qquad B'[21] = B[30]$$

$$B'[49] = B[61] \qquad B'[52] = B[37] \qquad B'[63] = B[15]$$

Computation of $B'' = IP^{-1}(B')$ yields:

$$B''[1] = B'[40] = B[1] \qquad\qquad B''[5] = B'[56] = B[5]$$
$$B''[21] = B'[54] = B[21] \qquad\quad B''[49] = B'[34] = B[49]$$
$$B''[52] = B'[10] = B[52] \qquad\quad B''[62] = B'[17] = B[62]$$

Exercise 7.3

DEA key length is of 56 bits; hence, there exist 2^{56} distinct keys. DEA block length is of 64 bits; hence, there exist 2^{64} distinct plaintext blocks and 2^{64} distinct ciphertext blocks. For one key, a plaintext x maps to a ciphertext y with a probability of $\frac{1}{2^{64}}$.

For 2^{56} distinct keys, a plaintext x maps to a ciphertext y with a probability of $\frac{1}{2^{64}} * 2^{56} = \frac{1}{256}$.

Exercise 7.4

Recall that given a 6-bit value v, selection function SF_j, $j = 1, ..., 8$, yields a 4-bit value $w_j = SF_j(v)$. $SF_j(v)$ returns the table element $S_j(v_r, v_c)$ such that v_r, the row number, is a 2-bit value formed by the first and the last bits of v; and v_c, the column number, is a 4-bit value formed by the 2nd, 3rd, 4th, and 5th bits of v. We compute input images and then check the nonlinearity of the selection function SF_2:

- $x_1 = 111111_2 = 63$ and $x_2 = 000000_2 = 0$

  $SF_2(63) = S_2(3,15) = 1001_2$ and $SF_2(0) = S_2(0,0) = 1111_2$

  $SF_2(63) \oplus SF_2(0) = 1001_2 \oplus 1111_2 = 0110_2 \neq SF_2(111111_2 \oplus 000000_2) = 1001_2$

- $x_1 = 110110_2 = 54$ and $x_2 = 001001_2 = 9$

  $SF_2(54) = S_2(2,11) = 0110_2$ and $SF_2(9) = S_2(1,4) = 1111_2$

  $SF_2(54) \oplus SF_2(9) = 0110_2 \oplus 1111_2 = 1001_2 \neq SF_2(110110_2 \oplus 001001_2) = 1001_2$

- $x_1 = 111000_2 = 54$ and $x_2 = 000111_2 = 7$

  $SF_2(56) = S_2(2,12) = 1001_2$ and $SF_2(7) = S_2(1,3) = 0111_2$

  $SF_2(56) \oplus SF_2(7) = 1001_2 \oplus 0111_2 = 1110_2 \neq SF_2(110110_2 \oplus 001001_2) = 1001_2$

All the checked pairs confirm the nonlinearity of SF_2. The same applies if another DEA selection function is tested.

Exercise 7.5

1) Let $B = 0^{(64)}$ and $K = 0^{(54)}$ be a plaintext and a key; both are all 0-bit strings.

   Applying the initial permutation to B yields a 64 zero-bit string. Therefore, the input of the first round is the same than B; i.e. $L_0 = 0$ and $R_0 = 0$.

   If the DEA key is $0^{(54)}$, then the key scheduling function yields 16 round keys, which are all equal to $0^{(48)}$. Application of the function F with $R_0 = 0^{(32)}$ and a round key $K_1 = 0^{(48)}$: first the expansion key yields a $0^{(48)}$ bit-string; second, the input of all the selection functions is $0^{(6)}$; therefore, all of them yield the first element of their tables: $SF_1(0) = 14$, $SF_2(0) = 15$, $SF_3(0) = 10$, $SF_4(0) = 7$, $SF_5(0) = 2$ $SF_6(0) = 12$, $SF_7(0) = 4$, $SF_8(0) = 13$.

   Thus, $f\left(0^{(32)}, 0^{(48)}\right) = P\left(11101111101001110010110001001101_2\right)$

   $$= 11011000110110001101101110111100_2$$

   Therefore, the output of round 1 is:

   $$L_1 = R_0$$
   $$R_1 = L_0 \oplus f(0,0) = 11011000110110001101101110111100_2$$
   $$= D8D8DBBC_{16}$$

2) Let $B = 1^{(64)}$ and $K = 1^{(54)}$ be a plaintext and a key; both are all 1-bit strings.

   Applying the initial permutation to B yields a $1^{(64)}$ bit string. Therefore, the input of the first round is the same than B; i.e. $L_0 = 1^{(32)}$ and $R_0 = 1^{(32)}$.

   If the DEA key is $1^{(54)}$, then the key scheduling function yields 16 identical round keys, which are all equal to $1^{(48)}$. Application of the function F with $R_0 = 1^{(32)}$ and a round key $K_1 = 1^{(48)}$: first the expansion key yields a $1^{(48)}$ bit-string; second, $Exp(R_0 \oplus K_1) = 0^{(48)}$; thus, the input of all the selection functions is $1^{(6)}$; thus, all of them yield the first element of their tables: $SF_1(0) = 14$, $SF_2(0) = 15$, $SF_3(0) = 10$, $SF_4(0) = 7$, $SF_5(0) = 2$ $SF_6(0) = 12$, $SF_7(0) = 4$, $SF_8(0) = 13$. Notice that $f(1^{(32)}, 1^{(48)})$ is the same than $f(0^{(32)}, 0^{(48)})$).

Therefore, the output of round 1 is: $L_1 = 1^{(32)}$ and $R_1 = 1^{(32)} \oplus f(1^{(32)}, 1^{(48)}) = 00100111001001110010010001000011_2$ $= 27272443_{16}$.

Exercise 7.6

All blocks C_i and D_i, $i = 1, ..., 16$, used in the key schedule function are 28-bit blocks. *NLR* (Table 7.8) vector determines the number of positions to rotate both C_i and D_i for each round i. At 16th round, the value of C_{16} (resp. D_{16}) is the initial value C_0 (resp. D_0), which has been left-rotated by a total number of positions equal to the sum of elements of vector *NLR* (i.e. $4*1 + 12*2 = 28$). Thus, if you left-rotate C_{16} (resp. D_{16}) by one position, you get C_1 (resp. D_1). Notice that $C_0 = C_{16}$ and $D_0 = D_{16}$.

Exercise 7.7

Let $Sb(S_{r,c})$ denote the substitution of byte $S_{r,c}$ (i.e. the byte of state S at row r and column c) using the S-Box. The result of `ShiftRows (SubBytes (S))` is given on the left of Figure 7.17 and that of `SubBytes(ShiftRows(S))` on the right. The results are the same. Thus, `SubBytes` and `ShiftRows` can be applied in either order in the AES encryption.

Exercise 7.8

1) The plaintext and cipher key are both of a value of $1^{(128)}$; therefore, the key expansion function yields the following two first round keys:

Key of initialization, $K_0 = (W[0], W[1], W[2], W[3])$, where $W[0] = W[1] = W[2] = W[3] = [FF, FF, FF, FF]$
Key of the first round, $K_1 = (W[4], W[5], W[6], W[7])$ computed as follows:
$W[4] = W[0] \oplus g(W[3])$, where $g(W[3])$ is yielded by three operations:

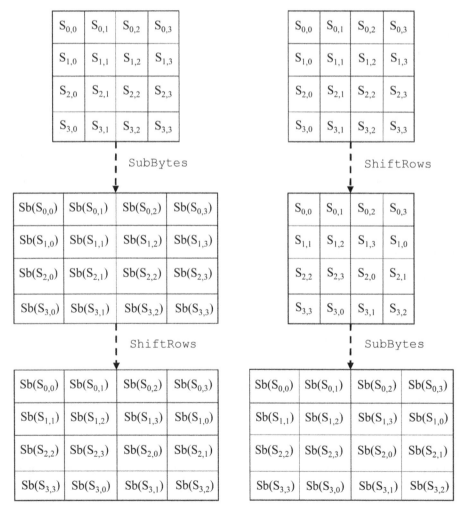

Figure 7.17 `ShiftRows` and `SubBytes` can be used in any order.

$Z = LRotate(W[3]); Z = [FF, FF, FF, FF]$, because $W[3]$ has only 1-bits.

$Z' = SubBytes(Z); Z' = [16, 16, 16, 16]$, because $S\_Box[FF] = 16$

$Z'' = [16, 16, 16, 16] \oplus Rcon[1] = [17, 16, 16, 16]$

Thus, $W[4] = [FF, FF, FF, FF] \oplus [17, 16, 16, 16] = [e8, e9, e9, e9]$

$W[5] = W[4] \oplus W[1] = [e8, e9, e9, e9] \oplus [FF, FF, FF, FF] = [17, 16, 16, 16]$

$W[6] = W[5] \oplus W[2] = [17, 16, 16, 16] \oplus [FF, FF, FF, FF] = [e8, e9, e9, e9]$

$W[7] = W[6] \oplus W[3] = [e8, e9, e9, e9] \oplus [FF, FF, FF, FF] = [17, 16, 16, 16]$

2) The transformations steps until the end of the first round are as follows:

$S1 = AddRoundKey(S) = [FF, ..., FF] \oplus [FF, ..., FF] = [00, ..., 00]$

$S1$ is an array of sixteen 0-bytes.

$S2 = SubBytes(S1) = [63, ..., 63]$; $S2$ is an array of sixteen 63-bytes.

$S3 = ShiftRows(S2) = [63, ..., 63]$; $S3$ is an array of sixteen 63-bytes.

The four columns of $S3$ are identical. The transformation of one column by *MixColumns* is computed as follows:

$$\begin{bmatrix} 02 & 03 & 01 & 01 \\ 01 & 02 & 03 & 01 \\ 01 & 01 & 02 & 03 \\ 03 & 01 & 01 & 02 \end{bmatrix} \begin{bmatrix} 63 \\ 63 \\ 63 \\ 63 \end{bmatrix} = \begin{bmatrix} 02 \cdot 63 \oplus 03 \cdot 63 \oplus 01 \cdot 63 \oplus 01 \cdot 63 \\ 01 \cdot 63 \oplus 02 \cdot 63 \oplus 03 \cdot 63 \oplus 01 \cdot 63 \\ 01 \cdot 63 \oplus 01 \cdot 63 \oplus 02 \cdot 63 \oplus 03 \cdot 63 \\ 03 \cdot 63 \oplus 01 \cdot 63 \oplus 01 \cdot 63 \oplus 02 \cdot 63 \end{bmatrix} = \begin{bmatrix} 63 \\ 63 \\ 63 \\ 63 \end{bmatrix}$$

Thus, $S4 = MixColumns(S3) = [63, ..., 63]$

$S5 = AddRoundKey(S4) =$

$\quad [63, 63, 63, 63, 63, 63, 63, 63, 63, 63, 63, 63, 63, 63, 63, 63]$

$\oplus [e8, e9, e9, e9, 17, 16, 16, 16, e8, e9, e9, e9, 17, 16, 16, 16]$

$= [8b, 8a, 8a, 8a, 74, 75, 75, 75, 8b, 8a, 8a, 8a, 74, 75, 75, 75]$

$S5$ is the output of the first round.

Problem 7.1

If L_i and R_i are known, then L_{i-1} and R_{i-1} are recovered as follows:

$$L_i = R_{i-1} \Rightarrow R_{i-1} = L_i$$

$$R_i = L_{i-1} \oplus F(R_{i-1}, K_i) \Rightarrow L_{i-1} = R_i \oplus F(R_{i-1}, K_i) = R_i \oplus F(L_i, K_i).$$

Therefore, we can recover L_{i-1} and R_{i-1} if we know L_i, R_i, and K_i, for any function F.

Problem 7.2

Feistel cipher is correct, if $Dec(Enc(B)) = B$, where B denotes a plaintext block.

1) Number of rounds $n = 1$

$B = (LE_0, RE_0)$; B is the plaintext, which is divided into two equal-size halves, LE_0 and RE_0.

Encryption
Round 1:
$LE_1 = RE_0; RE_1 = LE_0 \oplus F(RE_0, K_1)$
The ciphertext is $C = RE_1 \| LE_1$

Decryption
$C = (LE_0 \oplus F(RE_0, K_1)) \| (RE_0)$ is the ciphertext
Divide C into two equal-size halves: $C = ((LE_0 \oplus F(RE_0, K_1)), (RE_0))$

$$LD_1 = RD_0 = RE_0$$

$$RD_1 = LD_0 \oplus F(RD_0, K_1) = LE_0 \oplus F(RE_0, K_1) \ F(RE_0, K_1) = LE_0$$

$RD_1 \| LD_1 = B$. Therefore, the decryption produces the original plaintext block.

2) Number of rounds $n = 2$

$B = (LE_0, RE_0)$; B is the plaintext divided into two equal-size halves.

Encryption
Round 1:

$$LE_1 = RE_0; RE_1 = LE_0 \oplus F(RE_0, K_1)$$

Round 2:

$$LE_2 = RE_1 = LE_0 \oplus F\left(RE_0, K_1\right)$$
$$RE_2 = LE_1 \oplus F\left(RE_1, K_2\right) = RE_0 \oplus F\left(LE_0 \oplus F\left(RE_0, K_1\right), K_2\right)$$

The ciphertext is $C = (RE_0 \oplus F(LE_0 \oplus F(RE_0, K_1), K_2)) \parallel (LE_0 \oplus F(RE_0, K_1))$

Decryption:
$C = ((RE_0 \oplus F(LE_0 \oplus F(RE_0, K_1), K_2)), (LE_0 \oplus F(RE_0, K_1)))$ is the ciphertext.
Round 1:

$$LD_1 = RD_0 = LE_0 \oplus F(RE_0, K_1); RD_1 = LD_0 \oplus F(RD_0, K_2)$$

$$= (RE_0 F(LE_0 \oplus F(RE_0, K_1), K_2)) \oplus F(LE_0 \oplus F(RE_0, K_1), K_2) = RE_0$$

Round 2:

$$LD_2 = RD_1 = RE_0$$
$$RD_2 = LD_1 \oplus F(RD_1, K_1) = LE_0 \oplus F(RE_0, K_1) \oplus$$

$$\left[F((RE_0 \oplus F(LE_0 \oplus F(RE_0, K_1), K_2)) \oplus F(LE_0 \oplus F(RE_0, K_1), K_2), K_1)\right] = LE_0 \oplus F(RE_0, K_1) \oplus \left[F(RE_0, K_1)\right] = LE_0$$

$$RD_2 \parallel LD_2 = B.$$

Therefore, the decryption produces the original plaintext block. □

Problem 7.3

In Problem 7.2, we proved the correctness of Feistel cipher when the number of rounds is 1 or 2. In this problem, we address the correctness of Feistel cipher for an arbitrary number of rounds. To prove the correctness of Feistel cipher, we need to prove (by recurrence) that the computations in the decryption step have the following property:

$$\forall i, 1 \leq i \leq n, LD_i = RE_{n-i} \text{ and } RD_i = LE_{n-i}$$

The proof is made easy by the following fact: in encryption step, at round i, the right half is directly copied in left half used in round $i+1$. Hence, by Feistel design, $LE_i = RE_{i-1}$, for $i = 1, ..., n$.

The input of decryption is a ciphertext, which is equal to $RE_n \parallel LE_n$. Thus, $LD_0 = RE_n$ and $RD_0 = LE_n$.

In the following, halves computed in encryption step are used in substitutions in the calculations of halves in decryption step.

Verify the property in round 1:

$$LD_1 = RD_0 = LE_n = RE_{n-1}$$
$$RD_1 = LD_0 \oplus F\left(RD_0, K_n\right) = RE_n \oplus F\left(RE_{n-1}, K_n\right)$$
$$= \left(LE_{n-1} \oplus F\left(RE_{n-1}, K_n\right)\right) \oplus F\left(RE_{n-1}, K_n\right) = LE_{n-1}$$

Verify the property in round 2:

$$LD_2 = RD_1 = LE_{n-1} = RE_{n-2}$$
$$RD_2 = LD_1 \oplus F\left(RD_1, K_{n-1}\right) = RE_{n-1} \oplus F\left(LE_{n-1}, K_{n-1}\right)$$
$$= \left(LE_{n-2} \oplus F\left(RE_{n-2}, K_{n-1}\right)\right) \oplus F\left(RE_{n-2}, K_{n-1}\right) = LE_{n-2}$$

Assume that the property hold for round $n-1$. So,

$$LD_{n-1} = RE_{n-(n-1)} = RE_1$$
$$RD_{n-1} = LE_{n-(n-1)} = LE_1$$

Then, verify the property in round n:

$$LD_n = RD_{n-1} = LE_1 = RE_0$$
$$RD_n = LD_{n-1} \oplus F\left(RD_{n-1}, K_1\right) = RE_1 \oplus F\left(LE_1, K_1\right)$$
$$= \left(LE_0 \oplus F\left(RE_0, K_1\right)\right) \oplus F\left(LE_1, K_1\right) = \left(LE_0 \oplus F\left(RE_0, K_1\right)\right) \oplus F\left(RE_0, K_1\right) = LE_0$$

The result of the last decryption round is (RE_0, LE_0). Then, swapping the two halves yields (LE_0, RE_0), which is the original plaintext. $\square$

Problem 7.4

First, we address the correctness of DEA. Recall that DEA encryption and decryption are based on a Feistel network of 16 rounds. Let the 16-round Feistel network be modeled as a function $\mathcal{F}$ that takes a 64-bit block and a set of 16 round keys; and it yields an output of the same bit-length. DEA encryption and decryption can be written using the function $\mathcal{F}$ as follows:

Encryption: $E(K, p) = c = IP^{-1}(\mathcal{F}(\mathcal{K}_E, IP(p)))$ (a)

Decryption: $D(K, c) = p = IP^{-1}(\mathcal{F}(\mathcal{K}_D, IP(c)))$ (b)

where $\mathcal{K}_E = \{K_1, K_2, ..., K_{16}\}$ is the set of the round keys yielded by the key schedule function, using the key K; and $\mathcal{K}_D$ is the reverse set of $\mathcal{K}_E$; $\mathcal{K}_D = \{K_{16}, K_{15}, ..., K_1\}$.

$\mathcal{F}$ is proven to be correct (see the solution to Problem 7.3). Therefore, if $\mathcal{K}_E$ is a set of 16 round keys and $\mathcal{K}_D$ is its reverse, then:

$$\mathcal{F}(\mathcal{K}_E, x) = y \Rightarrow \mathcal{F}(\mathcal{K}_D, y) = x, \text{for any}\,(x, y) \in \{0,1\}^{64} \times \{0,1\}^{64}$$ (c)

Making substitution of (a) in (b) and using (c):

$$D(K, c) = IP^{-1}\left(\mathcal{F}\left(\mathcal{K}_D, IP\left(IP^{-1}\left(\mathcal{F}\left(\mathcal{K}_E, IP(p)\right)\right)\right)\right)\right)$$
$$= IP^{-1}\left(\mathcal{F}\left(\mathcal{K}_D, \mathcal{F}\left(\mathcal{K}_E, IP(p)\right)\right)\right) = IP^{-1}\left(IP(p)\right) = p$$

Second, TDEA is correct if and only if the following condition holds:

$$D_{TDEA}((Key_1, Key_2, Key_3), E_{TDEA}((Key_1, Key_2, Key_3), p)) = p$$

By TDEA construction:

$$E_{TDEA}((Key_1, Key_2, Key_3), p) = E(Key_3, D(Key_2, E(Key_1, p)))$$
$$D_{TDEA}((Key_1, Key_2, Key_3), c) = D(Key_1, E(Key_2, D(Key_3, c)))$$

Let $c_1 = E(Key_1, p)$, $c_2 = D(Key_2, c_1)$, and $c = E(Key_3, c_2)$
Make substitutions in the decryption formula:

$$D\left(Key_1, E\left(Key_2, D\left(Key_3, c\right)\right)\right)$$
$$= D\left(Key_1, E\left(Key_2, D\left(Key_3, E\left(Key_3, c_2\right)\right)\right)\right)$$
$$= D\left(Key_1, E\left(Key_2, c_2\right)\right) = \left(Key_1, E\left(Key_2, D\left(Key_2, c_1\right)\right)\right)$$
$$= D\left(Key_1, c_1\right) = D\left(Key_1, E\left(Key_1, p\right)\right) = p$$

Problem 7.5

1) Proof of the complementarity property of DES
   We need the following lemma.
   Lemma: for any pair of n-bit strings, x and y, the following holds:
   $\bar{x} \oplus y = \overline{x \oplus y}$ and $\bar{x} \oplus \bar{y} = x \oplus y$.
   Proof: let $1^{(n)}$ denote a bit string with n 1-bits.
   By definition of the bit-by-bit complementation (denoted 1-complement):
   $\bar{x} \oplus 1^{(n)} = x$ and $x \oplus 1^{(n)} = \bar{x}$.
   $\bar{x} \oplus y = \bar{x} \oplus y \oplus (1^{(n)} \oplus 1^{(n)}) = ((\bar{x} \oplus 1^{(n)}) \oplus y) \oplus 1^{(n)}$
   $\quad = (x \oplus y) \oplus 1^{(n)} = \overline{x \oplus y}$
   $\bar{x} \oplus \bar{y} = \bar{x} \oplus \bar{y} \oplus (1^{(n)} \oplus 1^{(n)}) = (\bar{x} \oplus 1^{(n)}) \oplus (\bar{y} \oplus 1^{(n)}) = x \oplus y.$ $\square$

We need the following facts, which are easy to prove:

i) Initial and final permutations and expansion operation: for any input x, $IP(\overline{x}) = \overline{IP(x)}$, $IP^{-1}(\overline{x}) = \overline{IP^{-1}(x)}$, $Exp(\overline{x}) = \overline{Exp(x)}$. Therefore, these transformation operations have no impact on the proof.

ii) Given a DES key K, the round keys generated using $\overline{K}$ are 1-complement to those generated using K.

iii) Because in function f, the round key is XORed with the input, the 1-complement is eliminated. Thus, $f(\overline{R_{i-1}},\overline{K_i}) = f(R_{i-1},K_i)$.

When $E(\overline{K},\overline{M})$ is computed, the initial halves are $\overline{L_0} = \overline{L_0}$ and $\overline{R_0} = \overline{R_0}$.

When $E(K,M)$ is computed, for any round i, $i \in [1,16]$, the rule of state change is defined by: $L_i = R_{i-1}$ and $R_i = L_{i-1} \oplus f(R_{i-1},K_i)$

We can derive the state change when $E(\overline{K},\overline{M})$ is computed as follows:

$$L_i = R_{i-1} \Rightarrow \overline{L_i} = \overline{R_{i-1}}$$

$$R_i = L_{i-1} \oplus f(R_{i-1},K_i) \Rightarrow \overline{R_i} = \overline{L_{i-1} \oplus f(R_{i-1},K_i)}$$

By the previous lemma and fact iii),

$$\overline{R_i} = \overline{L_{i-1}} \oplus f(R_{i-1},K_i) = \overline{L_{i-1}} \oplus f(\overline{R_{i-1}},\overline{K_i})$$

After the final permutation, the output of $E(\overline{K},\overline{M})$ is $(\overline{R_{16}},\overline{L_{16}})$, which is the 1-complement of $E(K,M) = (R_{16}, L_{16})$. Therefore, we can conclude that:

$$C = E(K,M) \Rightarrow \overline{C} = E(\overline{K},\overline{M}) \qquad \square$$

2) In general, when the naïve brute-force attack is applied against DES, the adversary, who knew a plaintext–ciphertext pair (M,C), needs to test each of the 2^{56} keys to find a key, which matches the known pair. In this problem, we assume that the adversary knew two plaintext–ciphertext pairs, (M_1,C_1) and (M_2,C_2), such that $M_2 = \overline{M_1}$ and $C_2 = \overline{C_1}$; i.e. $C_2 = E(K, M_2) = E(K,\overline{M_1}) = \overline{C_1} = \overline{E(K,M_1)}$.

By the complementation property, which states that $C = E(K,M) \Rightarrow \overline{C} = E(\overline{K},\overline{M})$,

$$\overline{C_2} = \overline{E(K,M_2)} = E(\overline{K},\overline{M_2}) = E(\overline{K},M_1) \tag{a}$$

Let's see the attack that takes advantage of the complementation property. The adversary tries all the 2^{55} keys whose leftmost bit is 0 (notice that the other 2^{55} keys are 1-complement of the tried keys). Let K' be one of the tried keys. The adversary makes an encryption, $C = E(K',M_1)$. If $C_1 = C$, then K' is likely to be the real key K. Otherwise, if $\overline{C_2} = C$, then, by the double equality (a), K' is likely to be the 1-complement of the real key K, i.e. $K' = \overline{K}$, because $\overline{C_2} = E(\overline{K},M_1) = E(K',M_1)$. If neither K' nor $\overline{K'}$ can be the real key K, another key is picked and tested as above. We mentioned "likely to be the real key," because false alarm may occur. Indeed, because the DES key space is of 2^{56} and the ciphertext space is of 2^{64}, the same ciphertext may be yielded by more than one key. In particular, we may have $C = E(K',M_1) = E(K'',M_1)$, while K' and K'' are two distinct keys. To reduce the probability of false alarm, more than two plaintext–ciphertext pairs should be used. In conclusion, the complementation property of DES reduces the maximum number of encryptions to 2^{55}.

Problem 7.6

1) The algorithms of DEA encryption and decryption are the same with the exception of the use of the round keys. In the encryption, the rounds keys are used from k_1 to k_{16}, while they are used in the inverse order, from k_{16} to k_1, in the decryption. If all the round keys are identical, the order does matter. Therefore, encrypting $E(K,B)$ is equivalent to a decryption. Hence, $E(K,E(K,B)) = B$. Notice that decrypting twice a ciphertext C results in the ciphertext C, i.e. $D(K,D(K,C)) = C$.

2) Take $key_1 = 0101\ 0101\ 0101\ 0101_{16}$ and drop the odd[11] parity bits. The resulting 56-bit key is $Key_{1(56)} = 00\ 0000\ 0000\ 0000_{16}$. Since all the bits of the input are 0 s in key schedule function, all the generated round keys are also 0 s. Permutation, rotation, and compression of s yield only 0 s.

Take $Key_2 = FEFE\ FEFE\ FEFE\ FEFE_{16}$ and remove the odd parity bits. The resulting 56-bit key is and $Key_{2(56)} = FF\ FFFF\ FFFF\ FFFF_{16}$. Since all the bits of the input are s, in key schedule function, all the generated round keys are also 1 s. Permutation, rotation, and compression of 1 s yield only 1 s. Taking into account the answer to the first question, both keys are weak and should be avoided, because an attacker can try all weak keys to decrypt twice an intercepted ciphertext and recover the key if the result is the same after two decryptions.

Problem 7.7

1) In the first step of the key schedule function, applying permutation PC-1 to $Key_1 = 011F011F010E010E_{16}$ yields two 28-bits blocks $C_0^{Key_1} = 0000000_{16}$ and $D_0^{Key_1} = AAAAAAA_{16}$; and applying permutation PC-1 to $Key_2 = 1F011F010E010E01_{16}$ yields two 28-bits blocks and $D_0^{Key_2} = 5555555_{16}$.

First, after left rotation of $C_0^{Key_1}$ and $C_0^{Key_2}$ both remain unchanged, because both are equal to a 28 0-bit string.

Second, since $A_{16} = 1010_2$ and $5_{16} = 0101$, left-rotating $D_0^{Key_1}$ or $D_0^{Key_2}$ yields either $AAAAAAA_{16}$ or 5555555_{16}:

$$LeftRotate(5555555_{16}, 1) = AAAAAAA_{16}$$

$$LeftRotate(AAAAAAA_{16}, 1) = 5555555_{16}$$

$$LeftRotate(5555555_{16}, 2) = 5555555_{16}$$

$$LeftRotate(AAAAAAA_{16}, 2) = AAAAAAA_{16}$$

In the last step of the key schedule function, only two distinct round keys can be generated, i.e.

$$K^{(1)} = PC\text{-}2(00000005555555_{16}) \text{ or } K^{(2)} = PC\text{-}2(0000000AAAAAAA_{16}).$$

Using the number of rotation positions given in vector (Table 7.8), the 32 round keys derived from Key_1 and Key_2 are:

$$RoundKeys(Key_1) = (K^{(1)}, K^{(2)}, K^{(2)}, K^{(2)}, K^{(2)}, K^{(2)}, K^{(2)}, K^{(2)},$$
$$K^{(1)}, K^{(1)}, K^{(1)}, K^{(1)}, K^{(1)}, K^{(1)}, K^{(1)}, K^{(2)})$$
$$RoundKeys(Key_2) = (K^{(2)}, K^{(1)}, K^{(1)}, K^{(1)}, K^{(1)}, K^{(1)}, K^{(1)}, K^{(1)},$$
$$K^{(2)}, K^{(2)}, K^{(2)}, K^{(2)}, K^{(2)}, K^{(2)}, K^{(2)}, K^{(1)})$$

2) Recall that the algorithms of DEA encryption and decryption differ only in the order in which the round keys are used. Let $K_i, i = 1, ..., 16$ be the round keys generated by the key schedule function from a key Key. The encryption algorithm makes use of K_1 in the 1st round, ..., and K_{16} in the 16th round, while the decryption algorithm makes use of K_{16} in the 1st round, ..., and K_1 in the 16th round. In the answer to question 1, the list of round keys generated from Key_1 is the reverse of that generated from Key_2. Therefore, encrypting $C = E(Key_2, M)$ using Key_1 is equivalent to decrypting C with Key_2; i.e. $E(Key_1, E(Key_2, M)) = D(Key_2, E(Key_2, M)) = M$, for any plaintext M.

Problem 7.8

Using Table PC-1, we build the first two 28-bit blocks, C_0 and D_0, used to generate the round keys. Let K^j denote the bit $j, j = 1, ..., 64$ of the key K ("64", because the key scheduling function starts with a 64-bit key and then drops odd parity bits).

$$C_0 = K^{57} K^{49} K^{41} K^{33} K^{25} K^{17} K^9 K^1 K^{58} K^{50} K^{42} K^{34} K^{26} K^{18}$$
$$K^{10} K^2 K^{59} K^{51} K^{43} K^{35} K^{27} K^{19} K^{11} K^3 K^{60} K^{52} K^{44} K^{36}$$
$$D_0 = K^{63} K^{55} K^{47} K^{39} K^{31} K^{23} K^{15} K^7 K^{62} K^{54} K^{46} K^{38} K^{30} K^{22}$$
$$K^{14} K^6 K^{61} K^{53} K^{45} K^{37} K^{29} K^{21} K^{13} K^5 K^{28} K^{20} K^{12} K^4$$

C_0 and D_0 are concatenated to form a 56-bit block. The inspection of Table PC-2 shows that at any round $i, i = 1, ..., 16$, the following bits are not used to generate the round key K_i: bits 9, 18, 22, and 25, located in C_0; and bits 35, 38, 43, and 54, located in D_0 (because all those eight numbers are not included in Table PC-2).

The first round key, K_1, is computed as follows: C_0 and D_0 are one-bit-left-rotated to yield C_1 and D_1, which are concatenated and used in the compression permutation. Therefore, the key bits that are not used to generate K_1 are: K^{50}, K^{43}, K^{11}, K^{52}, K^7, K^{46}, K^6, and K^{12}.

Problem 7.9

1) With a key bit-length of 56, there exist $2^{56} * 2^{56}$ pairs of keys $(K_i, K_j); i, j \in [0, 2^{56} - 1]$. Each pair is used to double-encrypt. We can do 2^{112} double encryptions, but the final ciphertext is an element in $\{0,1\}^{64}$. Thus, in average, each element of the ciphertext space can be yielded by $\dfrac{2^{112}}{2^{64}} = 2^{48}$ pairs. The probability to pick the real key pair is $1/2^{48}$. Therefore, the probability of false alarm is $1 - 1/2^{48}$, which is a very high probability.

2) With a space of key pairs of 2^{48} pairs, a maximum of 2^{48} ciphertexts may be yielded. Thus, in average, the number key pairs, selected in the previous step, that encrypt the same plaintext to the same ciphertext is $\dfrac{2^{48}}{2^{64}} = 2^{-16}$; this probability is also the probability of false alarm. In other words, with two known plaintext-ciphertext pairs, the probability to find the real key pair is $1 - 2^{-16} \approx 1$.

3) With three known plaintext-ciphertext pairs, the probability that three ciphertexts are yielded by the same key pair is $\dfrac{2^{-16}}{2^{64}} = 2^{-80}$. The latter is the probability of false alarm. In conclusion, three known plaintext-ciphertext pairs are enough to break double DES.

Problem 7.10

In SubBytes and SubBytes transformations, byte substitution is performed byte-by-byte, independently from each other. Therefore, to prove that InvSubBytes is the inverse of SubBytes, we need to prove that $InvS\_Box(S\_Box(b)) = b$ for any byte b. We use the matrix forms of substitution; i.e. (7.2) and (7.4):

$$b' = S\_Box(b) \Rightarrow b' = A * b \oplus c, \text{ where } c = [63]_{16}$$
$$x = InvS\_Box(b') \Rightarrow x = B * b' \oplus d, \text{ where } d = [05]_{16}$$

Then, by substitution: $x = B * (A * b \oplus c) \oplus d = ((B * A) * b) \oplus (B * c) \oplus d$
It is easy to check that $B * A$ is the identity matrix.
Then, by substitution: $x = b \oplus (B * c) \oplus d$
As shown below, $(B * c) \oplus d = 0$. Therefore, $x = b$, which confirms that $InvS\_Box(InvS\_Box(b))$ for any byte b.

$$
\begin{array}{cccc}
B & c & B*c & d \quad B*c \oplus d \\
\begin{bmatrix}
0 & 0 & 1 & 0 & 0 & 1 & 0 & 1 \\
1 & 0 & 0 & 1 & 0 & 0 & 1 & 0 \\
0 & 1 & 0 & 0 & 1 & 0 & 0 & 1 \\
1 & 0 & 1 & 0 & 0 & 1 & 0 & 0 \\
0 & 1 & 0 & 1 & 0 & 0 & 1 & 0 \\
0 & 0 & 1 & 0 & 1 & 0 & 0 & 1 \\
1 & 0 & 0 & 1 & 0 & 1 & 0 & 0 \\
0 & 1 & 0 & 0 & 1 & 0 & 1 & 0
\end{bmatrix}
\begin{bmatrix} 1 \\ 1 \\ 0 \\ 0 \\ 0 \\ 1 \\ 1 \\ 0 \end{bmatrix}
=
\begin{bmatrix} 1 \\ 0 \\ 1 \\ 0 \\ 0 \\ 0 \\ 0 \\ 0 \end{bmatrix}
\oplus
\begin{bmatrix} 1 \\ 0 \\ 1 \\ 0 \\ 0 \\ 0 \\ 0 \\ 0 \end{bmatrix}
=
\begin{bmatrix} 0 \\ 0 \\ 0 \\ 0 \\ 0 \\ 0 \\ 0 \\ 0 \end{bmatrix}
\end{array}
$$

Problem 7.11

1) $\left([0b]_{16} x^3 + [0d]_{16} x^2 + [09]_{16} x + [0e]_{16}\right) * \left([03]_{16} x^3 + [01]_{16} x^2 + [01]_{16} x + [02]_{16}\right) \bmod \left(x^4 + 1\right)$

$= ([0b]_{16} \cdot [03]_{16}) x^6 + \left([0b]_{16} \cdot [01]_{16} \oplus [0d]_{16} \cdot [03]_{16}\right) x^5$

$\quad + \left([0b]_{16} \cdot [01]_{16} \oplus [0d]_{16} \cdot [01]_{16} \oplus [09]_{16} \cdot [03]_{16}\right) x^4$

$\quad + \left([0b]_{16} \cdot [02]_{16} \oplus [0d]_{16} \cdot [01]_{16} \oplus [09]_{16} \cdot [01]_{16} \oplus [0e]_{16} \cdot [03]_{16}\right) x^3$

$\quad + \left([0d]_{16} \cdot [02]_{16} \oplus [09]_{16} \cdot [01]_{16} \oplus [0e]_{16} \cdot [01]_{16}\right) x^2$

$\quad + \left([09]_{16} \cdot [02]_{16} \oplus [0e]_{16} \cdot [01]_{16}\right) x$

$\quad + \left([0e]_{16} \cdot [02]_{16}\right) \left(\bmod x^4 + 1\right)$

$= \left([0b]_{16} \cdot [02]_{16} [0d]_{16} \cdot [01]_{16} [09]_{16} \cdot [01]_{16} [0e]_{16} \cdot [03]_{16}\right) x^3$

$\quad + \left([0d]_{16} \cdot [02]_{16} \oplus [09]_{16} \cdot [01]_{16} \oplus [0e]_{16} \cdot [01]_{16} \oplus [0b]_{16} \cdot [03]_{16}\right) x^2$

$\quad + \left([09]_{16} \cdot [02]_{16} \oplus [0e]_{16} \cdot [01]_{16} \oplus [0b]_{16} \cdot [01]_{16} \oplus [0d]_{16} \cdot [03]_{16}\right) x$

$\quad + \left([0e]_{16} \cdot [02]_{16} \oplus [0b]_{16} \cdot [01]_{16} \oplus [0d]_{16} \cdot [01]_{16} \oplus [09]_{16} \cdot [03]_{16}\right)$

$= \left([16]_{16} \oplus [0d]_{16} \oplus [09]_{16} \oplus [12]_{16}\right) x^3 + \left([1a]_{16} \oplus [09]_{16} \oplus [0e]_{16} \oplus [1d]_{16}\right) x^2$

$\quad + \left([12]_{16} \oplus [0e]_{16} \oplus [0b]_{16} \oplus [17]_{16}\right) x$

$\quad + \left([1c]_{16} \oplus [0b]_{16} \oplus [0d]_{16} \oplus [1b]_{16}\right)$

$= (0) x^3 + (0) x^2 + (0) x + 1 = 1 \bmod \left(x^4 + 1\right)$

Therefore, $[0b]_{16}x^3 + [0d]_{16}x^2 + [09]_{16}x + [0e]_{16}$ is the inverse of $[03]_{16}x^3 + [01]_{16}x^2 + [01]_{16}x + [02]_{16} \mod(x^4 + 1)$ with computations in the extension field F_{2^8}.

2) Let A and B be the matrices defined by (7.5) and (7.6). Using the matrix form of the MixColumns transformation, for any 4-byte column c, $c' = MixColumns(c)$ can be written as $c' = A * c$ and $d = InvMixColumns(c')$ can be written as $d = B * c'$. Hence, $d = (B * A) * c$. Let D be the product of matrices B by A.

$$D = B * A = \begin{bmatrix} 0e & 0b & 0d & 09 \\ 09 & 0e & 0b & 0d \\ 0d & 09 & 0e & 0b \\ 0b & 0d & 09 & 0e \end{bmatrix} \begin{bmatrix} 02 & 03 & 01 & 01 \\ 01 & 02 & 03 & 01 \\ 01 & 01 & 02 & 03 \\ 03 & 01 & 01 & 02 \end{bmatrix}$$

Since $\oplus$ is a commutative operation, we have:

$$D[1,1] = D[2,2] = D[3,3] = D[4,4]$$
$$= [0e]_{16} \cdot [02]_{16} \oplus [0b]_{16} \cdot [01]_{16} \oplus [0d]_{16} \cdot [01]_{16} \oplus [09]_{16} \cdot [03]_{16}$$
$$= [1c]_{16} \oplus [0b]_{16} \oplus [0d]_{16} \oplus [1b]_{16} = 1$$
$$D[1,2] = [0e]_{16} \cdot [03]_{16} \oplus [0b]_{16} \cdot [02]_{16} \oplus [0d]_{16} \cdot [01]_{16} \oplus [09]_{16} \cdot [01]_{16}$$
$$= [12]_{16} \oplus [16]_{16} \oplus [0d]_{16} \oplus [09]_{16} = 0$$
$$D[1,3] = [0e]_{16} \cdot [01]_{16} \oplus [0b]_{16} \cdot [03]_{16} \oplus [0d]_{16} \cdot [02]_{16} \oplus [09]_{16} \cdot [01]_{16}$$
$$= [0e]_{16} \oplus [1d]_{16} \oplus [1a]_{16} \oplus [09]_{16} = 0$$
$$\ldots$$
$$D[4,3] = [0b]_{16} \cdot [01]_{16} \oplus [0d]_{16} \cdot [03]_{16} \oplus [09]_{16} \cdot [02]_{16} \oplus [0e]_{16} \cdot [01]_{16}$$
$$= [0b]_{16} \oplus [17]_{16} \oplus [12]_{16} \oplus [0e]_{16} = 0$$

Hence, $B*A$ is the identity matrix and therefore, $d = B * A * c = c$, which confirms that InvMixColumns is the inverse of MixColumns.

Notes

1 *Feistel structure* notion was proposed in 1973 by Horst Feistel and Don Coppersmith and implemented in Lucifer cipher.
2 In literature, there exist other equivalent descriptions of Feistel decryption, which perform computations in the inverse order, i.e. from $i = n$ to $i = 0$ and start with round key K_0.
3 DEA is also referred to as the algorithmic design of DES.
4 US patent n° 3962539, which describes DES, was assigned to IBM Corporation in 1976. This patent expired in 1993.
5 Do not confuse 2TDEA with 2DES. The latter uses only two encryptions (or decryptions) in sequence.
6 Rijndael is a contraction of Rijmen and Daemen, the authors of Rijndael algorithm.
7 *Nk* denotes the number of 32-bit words of the key. That is, $Nk = 4, 6$, and 8 to denote keys of 128, 192, and 256 bits, respectively.
8 In the matrix forms discussed in the chapter, the usual addition is replaced by the XOR operation.
9 SubBytes and its inverse are the only non-linear transformation in AES.
10 "Indexed by a" means "a is split into two 4-bit halves to yield the indexes of a cell in the S-Box."
11 Odd parity works as follows: for a given set of bits, if the count of bits with a value of 1 is even, the parity bit value is set to 1 making the total count of s in the entire set (including the parity bit) an odd number. If the count of bits with a value of 1 is odd, the count is already odd; hence, the parity bit value is 0.

References

1 Shannon, C. (1949). Communication theory of secrecy systems. *Bell System Technical Journal* 28: 656–715.

2 Barker, E. and Mouha, N. (2017). *Recommendation for the Triple Data Encryption Algorithm (TDEA) Block Cipher - Special publication 800-67 (Rev. 2)*. NIST.

3 NIST. (1999). *Data Encryption Standard (DES) - FIPS publication 46-3*. National Institute for Standards and Technology.

4 Biham, E. and Shamir, A. (1991). Differential cryptanalysis of DES-like cryptosystems. *Journal of Cryptology* 4 (1): 3–72.

5 Matsui, M. (1993). Linear cryptanalysis method for DES cipher. *International Workshop on the Theory and Application of Cryptographic Techniques, Advances in Cryptology*, 386–397. Lofthus, Norway: Springer, LNCS 765.

6 NIST. (2001). *Advanced Encryption Standard (AES) - FIPS PUB 197*. National Institute for Standards and Technology.

7 Deamen, J. and Rijmen, V. (2002). *The Design of Rijndael: AES – The Advanced Encryption Standard*. Springer.

8 Ashokkumar, C., Giri, R., and Menezes, B. (2016). Highly efficient algorithms for AES key retrieval in cache access attacks. *IEEE European Symposium on Security and Privacy*, 261–275. Saarbrucken, Germany: IEEE Xplore.

8

Block Cipher Modes of Operation for Confidentiality

In the previous chapter, two standard block ciphers, namely TDEA and AES, have been presented. A block cipher takes a fixed-size plaintext block and returns a ciphertext block of the same size. However, in many applications, a plaintext (for example an image) is composed of thousands of blocks or even more. It is not desirable to use a block cipher in such a way that the encryption of the individual plaintext blocks leaks some features about the whole plaintext. In addition, in many applications, the recipient of a message may need to authenticate the message sender.

Data protection refers to confidentiality of data in transit (i.e. data exchanged via a communication network) and data on storage devices (such as CD-ROMs and USB flash drives). Like messages that may be intercepted, while being transmitted form sender to recipient, storage devices may be stolen or copied, which would result in disclosing confidential data. In addition, the advent of storage area networks has made storage devices, which are directly connected to servers, vulnerable to attacks. Therefore, protecting storage devices is (often) required. Such a protection is commonly achieved using block ciphers. Overall, encryption of data on storage devices aims at providing: data confidentiality, fast data storage and retrieval, and optimization of storage space.

It should be noticed that the protection of data in transit (i.e. messages) and that of data on storage devices differ, which results in important implications for encryption, even though the core encryption algorithms are the same:

- *Latency*: message transmission is ephemeral, while data storage is often used for a long time. In networks, the recipient follows a protocol for key establishment and authentication before encrypting/decrypting messages. Attacks against messages need that the attacker is present when messages are transmitted, while attacks against storage devices do not.
- *Key management*: in networks, the encryption key changes from a message to another. Even the public key used for signature is renewed periodically. If a key is lost, the participants run a protocol to agree on a new key. In case of storage, if the encryption key is lost, the entire encrypted data is lost.

With the exception of one mode (XTS-AES), the modes of operation presented in this chapter can be used directly to protect messages or, with some adaptions, to protect data on storage devices. This chapter addresses the standard approaches to use block ciphers to encrypt and decrypt plaintexts, while considering plaintexts of a size longer than that of a single block.

It is worth noticing that encryption alone provides confidentiality guarantees but not data integrity guarantees. Indeed, in the event an adversary alters a message or the storage device content, the decryption operation cannot detect any alteration. Therefore, message authentication codes or other techniques are required to preserve data integrity. Modes of operation that provide data authenticity are addressed in the next chapter

8.1 Introduction

8.1.1 Definitions

Definition 8.1 Mode of operation of block cipher*: it describes how to repeatedly apply a single-block cipher to provide confidentiality or authenticity. Alternatively, modes of operation are ways of using block ciphers for encrypting and decrypting multiple-block data or for providing authentication service.*

Cryptography: Algorithms, Protocols, and Standards for Computer Security, First Edition. Zoubir Mammeri.
© 2024 John Wiley & Sons, Inc. Published 2024 by John Wiley & Sons, Inc.

***Definition 8.2 Deterministic encryption**: given a key, an encryption is said to be deterministic if plaintext blocks with the same content are mapped to a same ciphertext block.*

***Definition 8.3 Probabilistic encryption**: given a key, an encryption is said to be probabilistic if any two plaintext blocks are (very likely) mapped to distinct ciphertext blocks [1].*

8.1.2 Overview of Standard Modes of Operation

To provide confidentiality and authenticity guarantees based on block ciphers, the NIST approved a set of modes of operation for block ciphers, which are presented and discussed in this chapter and the next one. They include (as shown on Figure 8.1):

- Eight modes of operation for confidentiality guarantees: Electronic Codebook (ECB), Cipher Block Chaining (CBC) and its variants, Cipher Feedback (CFB), Output Feedback (OFB), Counter (CTR), XTS-AES, FF1, and FF3 [25].
- Five modes of operation for confidentiality and authenticity guarantees: CCM, GCM, KW, KWP, and TKW.

  Two modes of operation for authenticity guarantees: CMAC and GMAC.

8.1.3 Notations and Common Basic Functions

Below are the notations and the basic functions used in the sequel to describe the modes of operation of block ciphers.

#: comment in algorithm description.
0x: prefix of a bit string, represented with hexadecimal characters.

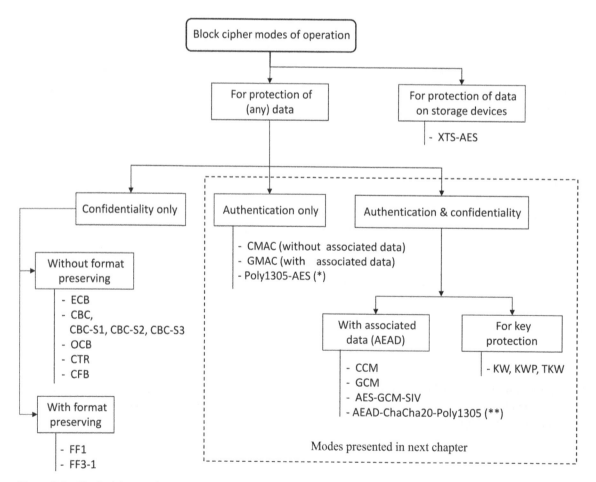

Figure 8.1 Block cipher modes of operations. (*) Poly1305-AES is not yet approved as a block cipher mode of operation. (**) ChaCha20 is a stream cipher, not a block cipher.

$\lceil x \rceil$:the least integer that is not less than the real number x.

$\lfloor x \rfloor$: the greatest integer that is not greater than the real number x.

$X \parallel Y$: concatenation of bit strings X and Y.

$X \oplus Y$: bitwise exclusive-OR of bit strings X and Y of the same length.

$\lceil x \rceil_s$: binary representation of integer x in s bits, where $0 \leq x < 2^s$.

0^s: bit string of s "0" bits.

$MSB_d(X)$: bit string consisting of the d leftmost bits of the bit string X (i.e. most significant d bits).

$LSB_d(X)$: bit string consisting of the d rightmost of the bit string X.

$X \ll 1$: one-bit left shift of bit string X.

$X \gg 1$: one-bit right shift of bit string X (the rightmost bit is dropped).

$Enc_K()$: encryption primitive of a symmetric cipher with key K.

$Dec_K()$: decryption primitive of a symmetric cipher with key K.

$len(X)$: bit-length of a bit string X.

b: block of fixed-length (in bits).

n: plaintext length (in bits).

m: number of blocks in a plaintext.

B_i: block i ($1 \leq i \leq m$)

8.1.4 Common Aspects of Modes for Confidentiality

8.1.4.1 Plaintext Length and Padding

In ECB and CBC modes, the total number of bits in a plaintext must be a multiple of the block length b, while in CBC variants, OFB, CTR, FF1, FF3-1, and XTS-AES modes, the total number of bits in a plaintext is arbitrary. In CFB mode, the total number of bits in a plaintext must be a multiple of a parameter s, with $s \leq b$.

ECB and CBC modes require a padding mechanism to fill the last block, in such a way that the padded plaintext is of a length multiple of that of a block. The other modes do not require any data padding mechanism. In OFB, CTR, and CFB modes, the last plaintext block, which may be not fully filled, is XORed with a part of the ciphertext resulting from the encryption of an initialization vector or a counter.

When padding is required, there exist different techniques to generate padding bits. For example, start the padding field with a special bit (e.g. "1") or a combination of bits (e.g. "1010"), and then add a fixed bit sequence (e.g. add zero-bits).

8.1.4.2 Initialization Vector

The objective of the initialization vector (IV) is to make the encryption probabilistic, i.e. two identical plaintexts are (very likely) to be mapped to two distinct ciphertexts. An IV must be generated for each plaintext encryption and the same IV is required in the corresponding decryption operation. Therefore, either the IV is sent to the recipient before the first ciphertext or both sides agree to use a specific function that generates the same IV for each message to encrypt/decrypt.

CBC, CFB, and OFB modes require the IV and the data block to be of the same bit-length. CTR mode requires a counter, which is similar to IV, but with some difference discussed in the sequel.

IV does not need to be secret. However, depending on the mode of operation of interest, IV must be either a nonce (i.e. an IV value should never be reused with the same key to encrypt two distinct plaintexts) or unpredictable (i.e. it must not be possible, for adversary, to predict the IV that will be associated with any plaintext). Two methods are recommended to generate unpredictable IVs:

1) First method: generate a nonce, then encrypt and send it to recipient before the first ciphertext. Since the encrypted value is an encrypted nonce, the adversary cannot derive which IV will be used for the upcoming message.
2) Second method: use a pseudorandom number generator (PRNG) with a hidden seed.[1]

The simplest way to generate a nonce is to use a counter or use addresses and current time.

8.2 ECB Mode of Operation

In the Electronic Codebook[2] (ECB) mode, the encryption and decryption operations are applied independently to each block (see Figure 8.2). ECB mode is the simplest mode of operation.

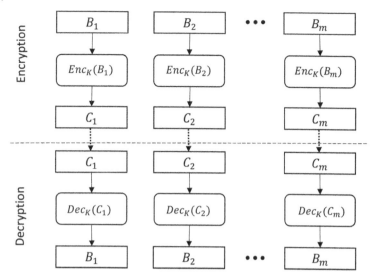

Figure 8.2 Electronic CodeBook (ECB) mode of operation.

Formally, ECB mode is defined by the following equations:

$$C_i = Enc_K(B_i), \forall i, 1 \leq i \leq m$$
$$B_i = Dec_K(C_i), \forall i, 1 \leq i \leq m$$

The first advantage of ECB is that operations on distinct blocks may be performed in parallel. The second is that ECB is error-propagation free. That is, if a ciphertext block is altered,[3] the encryption of the other ciphertext blocks is not affected (i.e. plaintexts whose ciphertexts are not altered are correctly recovered by the recipient).

However, ECB mode is not recommended, because of its vulnerability to statistical analysis and replay attacks. In ECB mode, attackers can easily find repetitions in a ciphertext and then use such a knowledge to disclose partially or entirely a plaintext.

8.3 CBC Modes of Operation

8.3.1 Basic CBC Mode

In the Cipher Block Chaining (CBC) mode, the encryption and decryption processes combine successive blocks. As shown in Figure 8.3, the first block is encrypted/decrypted using a selected initialization vector, then each block B_i ($i > 1$) is encrypted/decrypted using the ciphertext of block B_{i-1} as an Initialization Vector. With the exception of the first block, each ciphertext block depends on its predecessor.

Formally, CBC mode is defined by the following equations:

$$C_1 = Enc_K\left(B_i \oplus IV\right)$$
$$C_i = Enc_K\left(B_i \oplus C_{i-1}\right), \quad \forall i, 2 \leq i \leq m$$
$$B_1 = Dec_K\left(C_1\right) \oplus IV$$
$$B_i = Dec_K\left(C_i\right) \oplus C_{i-1}, \quad \forall i, 2 \leq i \leq m$$

Unlike ECB, in CBC and in other modes of operation, blocks with the same content are encrypted with distinct ciphertexts. In CBC, the encryption cannot be performed in parallel, but decryption can be. Indeed, when all ciphertext blocks are received, the recipient can perform parallel computations on them to recover the plaintext blocks.

CBC is not fully error-propagation free, because the decryption of ciphertext block i makes use of two ciphertext blocks i and $i-1$. In case some bits of ciphertext block i are altered, plaintext blocks i and $i+1$ cannot be recovered, but plaintext blocks with index greater than $i+1$ can be recovered correctly. CBC mode requires an initialization vector known to sender and recipient. In addition, the IV value should be unpredictable.

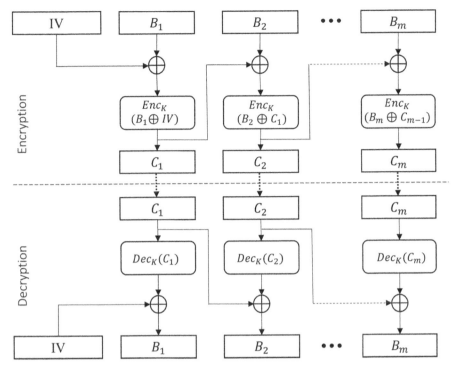

Figure 8.3 Cipher Block Chaining (CBC) mode of operation.

8.3.2 CBC Variants (CS1, CS2, CS3)

CBC is the most used mode of operation to provide confidentiality. However, padding is considered as a factor, which affects the performance[4] of CBC-based cryptosystems. To overcome padding drawback, three variants of CBC mode named CBC-CS1, CBC-CS2, and CBC-CS3 have been added to the basic CBC [4]. CS stands for ciphertext stealing.

CBC variants encrypt plaintexts of arbitrary bit-length. A plaintext B is a concatenation of m blocks: $B = B_1 \| B_2 \| ... \| B_{m-1} \| B_m^*$ with $(m-1)b + len(B_m^*) = len(B)$ and $len(B_m^*) \le b$. B_m^* may be a partial block and the other blocks are complete ones. With the ciphertext stealing technique, the ciphertext and the plaintext are of the same bit-length. The encryption and decryption of complete blocks $(B_1, ..., B_{m-2})$ and $(C_1, ..., C_{m-2})$ are the same as in the basic CBC. CS variants differ only in how they order and process the two last ciphertext blocks C_{m-1} and C_m. Ciphertext stealing has no impact on security and block ordering is only used for implementation convenience. If $len(B)$ is a multiple of the block length b, then all three variants are equivalent to the basic CBC.

8.3.2.1 CBC-CS1 Mode

In CBC-CS1 mode, padding[5] is used to encrypt. Then, the ciphertext sent to recipient and the unpadded plaintext both have the same bit-length. Encryption and decryption of CBC-CS1 are as follows (see Figure 8.4):

Encryption
- $d = len(B_m^*)$; $Pad = 0^d$
- $B_m = B_m^* \| Pad$
- Apply basic CBC encryption to the complete plaintext blocks $B_1, B_2, ..., B_{m-1}, B_m$ and obtain ciphertext blocks $C_1, C_2, ..., C_{m-1}, C_m$
- Let $C_{m-1}^* = MSB_d(C_{m-1})$, where $MSB_d(s)$ denotes the d leftmost bits of bit-string C_{m-1}.
- $C_{m-1}^{**} = LSB_{b-d}(C_{m-1})$, where $LSB_{b-d}(C_{m-1})$ denotes the $b-d$ rightmost bits of bit-string C_{m-1}.
- Then, the ciphertext is $C = C_1 \| C_2 \| ... \| C_{m-1}^* \| C_m$.

Decryption
- Receive ciphertext C and organize it into blocks such that:
  $C = C_1 \| C_2 \| ... \| C_{m-1}^* \| C_m$, with $\left(len(C_i) = b, \forall i \in [1, m] \wedge i \ne m-1 \right) \wedge \left(\left(len(C_{m-1}^* = d) \right) \wedge (d \le b) \right)$

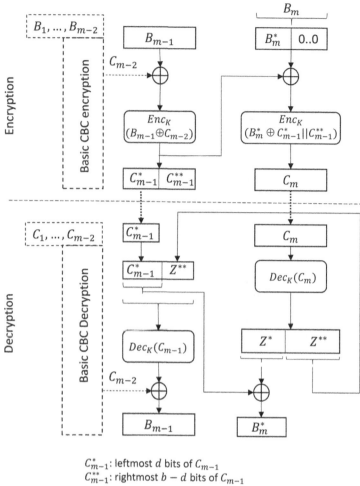

C^*_{m-1}: leftmost d bits of C_{m-1}
C^{**}_{m-1}: rightmost $b - d$ bits of C_{m-1}

Figure 8.4 CBC-CS1 mode.

- Let $Z = Dec_K\left(C_m\right)$
  $Z^* = MSB_d(Z)$
  $Z^{**} = LSB_{b-d}(Z)$
- Let $C_{m-1} = C^*_{m-1} \,\|\, Z^{**}$
- Apply basic CBC decryption to ciphertext bocks C_1, C_2, ..., C_{m-1}, using the IV, and obtain plaintext blocks B_1, B_2, ..., B_{m-1}.
- Let $B^*_m = C^*_{m-1} \oplus Z^*$.
- Then, the plaintext is $B = B_1 \,\|\, B_2 \,\|\dots\| B_{m-1} \,\|\, B^*_m$.

Note. In line 3 (of decryption), $b - d$ bits are taken from the decryption of C_m to rebuild C_{m-1}. Hence, the idea of *ciphertext stealing*.

8.3.2.2 CBC-CS2 and CBC-CS3 Modes

CBC-CS2 and CBC-CS3 are minor modifications of CBC-CS1 mode to swap the ciphertext blocks C^*_{m-1} and C_m. The most popular variant is CBC-CS3, because the ciphertext is aligned on block boundary, which makes hardware implementations simpler.

Encryption in CBC-CS2 mode:
- Apply CBC-CS1 to produce a ciphertext $C = C_1 \,\|\, C_2 \,\|\dots\| C^*_{m-1} \,\|\, C_m$.
- Conditional swapping:
  If $len\left(C^*_{m-1}\right) = b$, then $C = C_1 \| C_2 \|\dots\| C^*_{m-1} \| C_m$.
  If $len\left(C^*_{m-1}\right) < b$, then $C = C_1 \| C_2 \|\dots\| C_m \| C^*_{m-1}$.

Decryption in CBC-CS2 mode:
- Receive C.
- If $len\left(B_m^*\right) = b$, then apply CBC-CS1 to decrypt.
- If $len\left(B_m^*\right) < b$, then:
  Rearrange the ciphertext: $C' = C_1 \,\|\, C_2 \,\|\, \ldots \,\|\, C_{m-1}^* \,\|\, C_m$
  Apply CBC-CS1 to decrypt C'.

Encryption in CBC-CS3 mode:
- Apply CBC-CS1 to produce a ciphertext $C = C_1 \| C_2 \,\|\, \ldots \,\|\, C_{m-1}^* \,\|\, C_m$.
- Rearrange ciphertext as $C = C_1 \,\|\, C_2 \,\|\, \ldots \,\|\, C_m \,\|\, C_{m-1}^*$. Swapping is unconditional in CBC-CS3.

Decryption in CBC-CS3 mode:
- Receive C.
- Undo swapping: $C' = C_1 \,\|\, C_2 \,\|\, \ldots \,\|\, C_{m-1}^* \,\|\, C_m$.
- Apply CBC-CS1 to decrypt C'.

8.4 OFB Mode of Operation

OFB, CTR, and CFB modes of operation function like stream ciphers. Therefore, all of them use the same function to encrypt and decrypt. They do not directly encrypt the plaintext using the key. Instead, they compute a bit string, which is XORed with the plaintext block. The first plaintext block is XORed with the encrypted IV. Then, the latter is encrypted to produce a bit string, which is XORed with the second plaintext block, etc. (see Figure 8.5). OFB mode requires that the IV is a nonce.

OFB mode does not require padding. Indeed, if the last plaintext block is of bit-length u less than b (the block length), only the most significant u bits of the last ciphertext block are XORed with the plaintext block and the least significant $b - u$ bits are discarded. The same applies to decrypt if the last ciphertext block is of a length less than b. Such an operation is identical to that of a stream cipher.

Formally, the OFB mode is defined with the following equations:

Encryption:		Decryption:	
$I_1 = IV$		$I_1 = IV$	
$I_j = O_{j-1},$	$\forall j, 2 \leq j \leq m$	$I_j = O_{j-1},$	$\forall j, 2 \leq j \leq m$
$O_j = Enc_k\left(I_j\right),$	$\forall j, 2 \leq j \leq m$	$O_j = Enc_k\left(I_j\right),$	$\forall j, 2 \leq j \leq m$
$C_j = B_j \oplus O_j,$	$\forall j, 2 \leq j \leq m-1$	$B_j = C_j \oplus O_j,$	$\forall j, 2 \leq j \leq m-1$
$C_m = B_m \oplus MSB_u\left(O_m\right), u = len\left(B_m\right)$		$B_m = C_m \oplus MSB_u\left(O_m\right), u = len\left(C_m\right)$	

With the exception of the first plaintext block, the encryption of a plaintext block depends on the encryption of the previous plaintext block. The same applies to decryption. Therefore, neither encryption nor decryption of blocks can be performed in parallel.

Like EBC, OFB mode is error-propagation free, because one ciphertext block is used to recover one plaintext block and ciphertext blocks are not recalculated at recipient. Only the plaintext block associated with the altered ciphertext block cannot be recovered.

8.5 CTR Mode of Operation

CTR mode is similar to OFB mode with the exception that a counter is used instead of an initialization vector (see Figure 8.6). In CTR, it is required that each plaintext block is encrypted with a distinct counter.

One advantage of CTR over OFB is that encryption and decryption of distinct blocks can be performed in parallel. Formally, the OFB mode is defined by the following equations, where Cnt_1, Cnt_2, ..., Cnt_m denote the values of the counter:

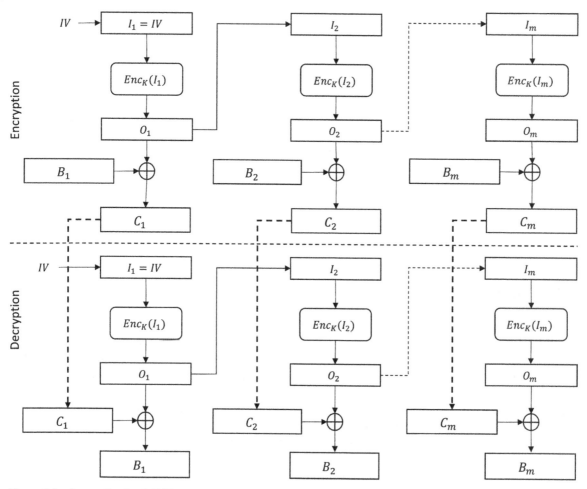

Figure 8.5 Output Feedback (OFB) mode of operation.

Encryption:

$$O_j = Enc_k\left(Cnt_j\right), \quad \forall j, 1 \le j \le m$$

$$C_j = B_j \oplus O_j, \quad \forall j, 1 \le j \le m-1$$

$$C_m = B_m \oplus MSB_u\left(O_m\right), u = len\left(B_m\right)$$

Decryption:

$$O_j = Enc_k\left(Cnt_j\right), \quad \forall j, 1 \le j \le m$$

$$B_j = C_j \oplus O_j, \quad \forall j, 1 \le j \le m-1$$

$$B_m = C_m \oplus MSB_u\left(O_m\right), u = len\left(C_m\right)$$

Counter values can be generated by any function that returns a distinct value for each call. In addition, it is required that all counter values must be distinct for all messages encrypted with the same key. To fulfill the uniqueness of counter values used with a specific key, there exist several methods, including:

- Sequential assignment of counter values, which is defined as follows:
  - $Cnt_1^1 = random()$
  - $Cnt_i^j = Cnt_{i-1}^j + 1 \bmod 2^b$, for $i = 2, \ldots, m_j, j = 1, \ldots, L$
  - $Cnt_1^j = Cnt_{m_{j-1}}^{j-1} + 1$ for $j = 2, \ldots, L$

  where Cnt_1^1 denotes the first randomly selected counter value to use with a new key, Cnt_1^j the first counter value to use for message j, Cnt_i^j, the counter value to use for block i of message j, m_j the number of blocks of message j, and L the number of messages, respectively.

- Hybrid sequential assignment of counter values, which is defined as follows:
  - Divide the counter bits into two parts of r and $b - r$ bits, where $r < b$.
  - Assign to each message j, a nonce nc^j in the interval $\left[0, 2^r - 1\right]$.
  - Assign to each block i of message j a counter block Cnt_i^j as follows:
    $v_1^j = random()$ in $\left[0, 2^{b-r} - 1\right], j = 1, \ldots, L$
    $v_i^j = v_{i-1}^j + 1 \bmod 2^{b-r}$, for $i = 2, \ldots, m_j, j = 1, \ldots, L$

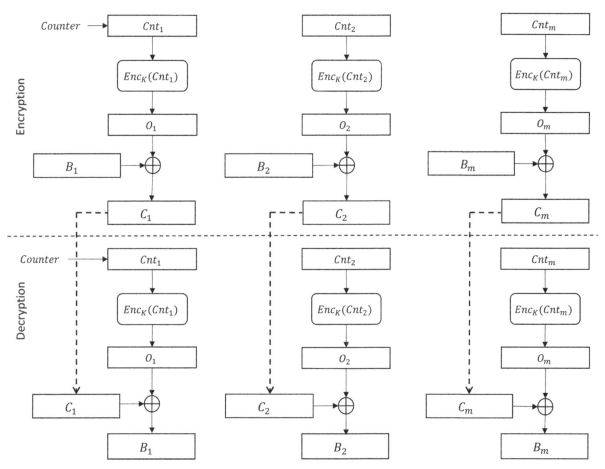

Figure 8.6 Counter (CTR) mode of operation.

$$Cnt_i^j = nc^j \,\|\, v_i^j, \text{ for } i = 1, \dots, m_j, \, j = 1, \dots, L$$

| **Note.** When CTR mode is used, a maximum of 2^b blocks can be encrypted with the same key.

8.6 CFB Mode of Operation

Like OFB, Cipher Feedback (CFB) mode operates as a stream cipher and makes use of an initialization vector and the same algorithm for encryption and decryption. In CFB mode, a feedback between successive plaintext blocks is used as in CBC mode, but in a different way (see Figure 8.7). CFB mode uses an initialization vector and a parameter s, which is an integer less than (or equal to) the block length b. The IV used in CFB must be unpredictable. Often, the name of CFB mode starts with the value of parameter s, such that $1 \leq s \leq b$. For example, CFB-8 and CFB-64 denote CFB with $s = 8$ and $s = 64$, respectively. CFB mode is said to be full-CFB if $s = b$ (i.e. a block contains one and only one segment).

CFB operates on plaintext/ciphertext segments of length s and not on blocks of length b. To distinguish segments from blocks, segments are upper-indexed with "#". CFB does not directly encrypt (with operation Enc_K) the plaintext. Instead, it uses a bitstring (which results from either the encryption of IV or a previous ciphertext) and XORes it with the plaintext to get a ciphertext. Formally, CFB mode is defined by the following equations, where m_s denotes the number of segments of the plaintext, $LSB_d(x)$ and $MSB_d(x)$ denote the d least and most significant bits of integer x, respectively:

Encryption:	*Decryption:*
$I_1 = IV$	$I_1 = IV$
$I_j = LSB_{b-s}\left(I_{j-1}\right) \,\|\, C_{j-1}^{\#}, \; \forall j, 2 \leq j \leq m\_s$	$I_j = LSB_{b-s}\left(I_{j-1}\right) \,\|\, C_{j-1}^{\#}, \; \forall j, 2 \leq j \leq m\_s$
$O_j = Enc_K\left(I_j\right), \forall j, 1 \leq j \leq m\_s$	$O_j = Enc_K\left(I_j\right), \; \forall j, 1 \leq j \leq m\_s$
$C_j^{\#} = B_j^{\#} \oplus MSB_s\left(O_j\right), \forall j, 1 \leq j \leq m\_s$	$B_j^{\#} = C_j^{\#} \oplus MSB_s\left(O_j\right), \forall j, 1 \leq j \leq m\_s$

With the exception of the first block, in CFB mode, the encryption of a block depends on the previous one. Therefore, distinct blocks cannot be encrypted in parallel. However, once all the ciphertext blocks are received, the recipient can compute the input blocks (I_2, I_3, ..., I_{m_s}) and then perform in parallel the decryption of ciphertext blocks.

Like CBC, CFB mode is not fully error-propagation free. In case a ciphertext block i is altered, plaintext blocks i and $i+1$ cannot be recovered, but plaintext blocks with index greater than $i+1$ can be recovered correctly. It should be noticed that CFB mode is the slowest mode because it processes a small portion of the data to encrypt/decrypt at each step. The number of operations depends on segment size s.

8.7 Format-Preserving Encryption Modes of Operation

8.7.1 Common Aspects to FPE Modes

FF1 and FF3-1 modes[6] of operation are called *Format-Preserving Encryption* (FPE) modes [3]. Both aim at preserving the format and the length of data in the ciphertext. For example, if the plaintext format is composed of credit card number (16 digits), CB holder name (20 characters), and expiry date (5 characters), the ciphertext must have the same format with three parts each corresponding to a CB field with the same length (see Figure 8.8).

FPE modes are useful for applications that require data in specific format without need to change data models before encrypting or decrypting. Imagine that a semi-encrypted file contains the data of thousands of bank customers (where only

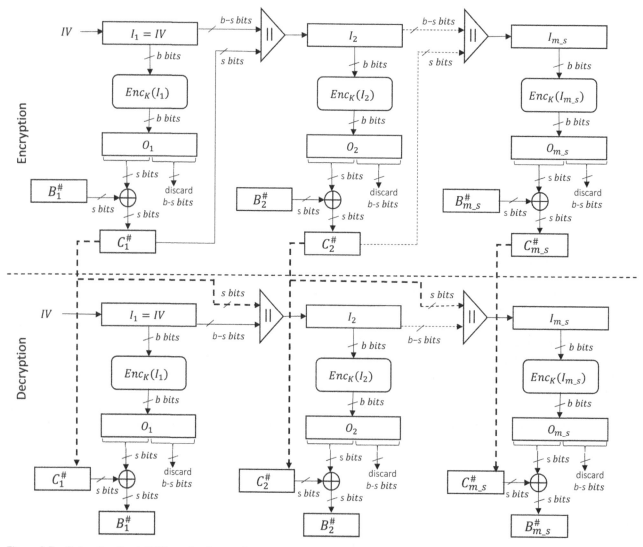

Figure 8.7 Cipher Feedback (CFB) mode of operation.

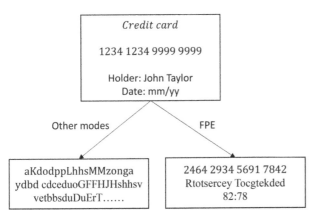

Figure 8.8 FPE encryption vs other modes of encryption (e.g. AES or TDEA).

names are in clear) and an application needs to check the expiry date of client John Taylor. Since the encryption of distinct fields are chained, it is required to decrypt a large portion of the file to retrieve the expiry date of interest, in most modes of operations. That may take a long time to decrypt. With FPE modes, applications can easily locate ciphertext portions of interest and decrypt only the required fields of data.

Currently, FF1 and FF3-1 modes are approved to be used only with AES block cipher with block length of 128 bits and key lengths of 128, 192, or 256 bits.

Data representation. FPE modes are designed to be adapted for any type of data. The number of symbols (also called characters) of an alphabet is called the base; it is denoted *radix*. The set of symbols[7] of a base *radix* is $\{0, 1, 2, ..., radix - 1\}$. A numeral is a nonnegative integer less than the base and a numeral string is a finite ordered sequence of numerals of the given base.

Example 8.1
- If *radix* = 8, then the set of characters is $\{0, 1, 2, 3, 4, 5, 6, 7\}$ in decimal representation and $\{000, 001, 010, 011, 100, 101, 110, 111\}$ in binary representation.
- If *radix* = 16, then the set of characters is $\{0, 1, 2, ..., 14, 15\}$ in decimal representation and $\{0, 1, 2, ..., E, F\}$ in hexadecimal representation.
- With *radix* = 16, $X = 12\ 13\ 5\ 7\ 2$ is a string of five numerals (i.e. 12, 13, 5, 7, and 2) in decimal representation.
- With *radix* = 2^{10}, $X = 125\ 978\ 2$ is a string of three numerals (i.e. 125, 978, and 2) in decimal representation.

For simplicity, in the sequel, we focus only on numeral data represented with decimal characters. Texts and special characters should be converted into decimal symbols before applying FPE modes. For example, lower-case Latin letters may be represented with numbers 1 to 26, upper-case letters with numbers 27 to 52, etc. Another representation would be the well-known ASCII code.

The input data of FF1 and FF3-1 modes are numeral strings. If the base is greater than 10, then numerals of a string are separated by space character. FF1 and FF3-1 use different conventions for interpreting numeral strings as numbers. For FF1, numbers are represented by strings of numerals with *decreasing* order of significance (i.e. in big-endian); for FF3-1, numbers are represented by strings of numerals in the reverse order, i.e. with *increasing* order of significance (i.e. in little-endian). For example, "0125" is a string of decimal digits that represents the number "one hundred twenty-five" for FF1 and the number "five thousand two hundred ten" for FF3-1.

Tweak. To encrypt data, FPE modes make use of a secret key and a *tweak*. The latter does not need to be secret and intends the same as an initialization vector in other modes. In CBC, OFB, and CFB modes, the IV is used to encrypt and decrypt the first block. In FPE modes, the tweak[8] is used inside a Feistel structure jointly with a key and can be regarded as a changeable part of a cipher key. Block ciphers that make use of tweaks are referred to as *tweakable block ciphers* [6]. One application of tweakable block ciphers is disk encryption, where each disc portion has an index, which is used as a tweak.

Encryption and decryption of FPE modes are based on Feistel structure presented in Section 7.1.2, with some adaptations. Specifically, instead of XOR operations in basic Feistel structure, in FPE modes, the operations are addition and subtraction modulo a power of the chosen base and the round function F_K takes a key, the bit-length of the plaintext, the tweak, and the round number.

As shown in Figure 8.9, the encryption and decryption are transformations in three steps: 1) the input is split into two parts A (left) and B (right) of lengths denoted u and v, respectively; 2) a keyed function is applied to one part of the input; and 3) the two parts are swapped and used as input of the next round.

If the length of the plaintext is even, then $u = v = len(B)/2$. Otherwise, one half has one symbol more than the other. $u = (len(B)-1)/2$ and $v = (len(B)+1)/2$. The bit-lengths u and v are taken into account when swapping a half with the other.

The number of rounds, denoted r, is of 10 for FF1 and of 8 for FF3-1. Inputs of round i ($i = 0, \ldots, r-1$) are denoted A_i and B_i.

8.7.2 Encryption and Decryption in FF1 and FF3-1 Modes

Common notations and basic functions

- $radix \in [2..2^{16}]$: range of supported bases
- X, Y: numeral[9] or bit strings. For example, 1101100010 is a bit string, while $15\,154\,13\,19$ is a numeral string in base 256 represented in base 10.
- $[minLen .. maxLen]$: range of supported plaintext length, such that $2 \leq minLen \leq maxLen < 2^{32}$ and $radix^{minLen} \geq 1\,000\,000$.
- $maxTLen$: maximum supported tweak byte-length.
- $[x]^c$: representation of integer x as a string of c bytes. For example, $[23]^1 = 00010111$.
- $len(X)$: number of bits/numerals of bit/numeral string X. For example, if $radix = 2$, then $len(1101) = 4$; if $radix = 16$, then $len(11\ 13\ 7\ 2) = 4$.
- $Num(X)$: integer that a bit string X represents in base 10 when bits are in decreasing order of significance. For example, $Num(0100001) = 33$.

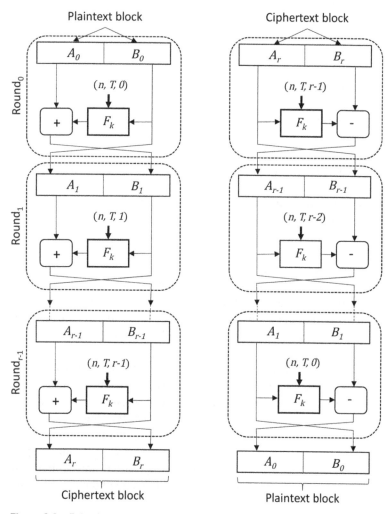

Figure 8.9 Feistel structure for building FF1 and FF3-1 modes.

- $Num_{radix}(x)$:integer that a numeral string x represents in base *radix* when numerals are in decreasing order of significance. For example, $Num_8(0100001) = 1*8^5 + 1 = 32769$.
- $Str_{radix}^m(x)$: given a positive integer x less than $radix^m$, this function returns a string of numerals in base *radix*. For example, $str_{16}^4(1957) = 07105$, because $0*16^3 + 7*16^2 + 10*16^1 + 5*16^0 = 1957$.

8.7.3 FF1 Mode

FF1 mode makes use of a pseudorandom function $PRF(X)$, which takes an input multiple of 128 bits and produces a 128-bit block. It is similar to CBC mode, with the exception that CBC produces a ciphertext block for each plaintext block, while function PRF produces a single block for a set of blocks. Function $PRF(X)$ is defined as follows:

```
function PRF # Pseudorandom function
        input X: bit string with a bit-length multiple of 128
             K: cipher key
        output y: 128-bit string
        1. Let m = len(x) / 128 # m is number of blocks in X
        # the underlying block cipher, i.e. AES, processes 128-bit blocks
        2. Let X₁ || X₂ || ... || Xₘ = X
        # X₁,...,Xₘ are the input of the block cipher
        3. Y₀ = 0¹²⁸ # Yₒ is 128 0-bit string
        4. for i=1 to m do Yᵢ = Encₖ(Yᵢ₋₁ ⊕ Xᵢ)
        5. return Yₘ
```

Figure 8.10 depicts the computations performed in each round of FF1 mode. The encryption algorithm of FF1 mode is as follows:

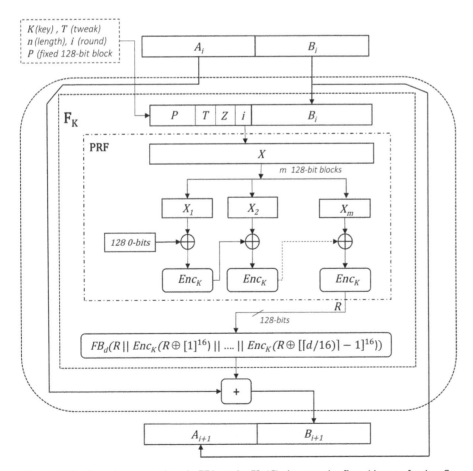

Figure 8.10 Round computations in FF1 mode. $FB_d(S)$ denotes the first d bytes of string S.

function FF1_Encryption

    input K: key; T: tweak of length t bytes; $t \in [0..maxTLen]$
        X: plaintext, a string of n numerals in base $radix$
        # $n \in [minLen..maxLen]$

    output Y: ciphertext of the same length than that of input X

1. # The input numeral string X is split into two halves A (left) and B (right).
     # If length of X is odd, then the right half has one numeral more than
     # the left. A and B are strings of numerals
   $$u = \lfloor n/2 \rfloor; v = n - u; A = X[1:u]; B = X[u+1:n]$$

2. # b and d are byte-lengths.
   2.1. # b is the number of bytes to represent numeral string B in binary
   $$b = \lceil \lceil v * log_2(radix) \rceil / 8 \rceil$$
   2.2. # d: it ensures that the output of the Feistel round function is at
       # least four bytes longer than b, which minimizes any bias in the
       # modular reduction in Step 4.3.
   $$d = 4 \lceil b/4 \rceil + 4$$

3. # P is a static-value 128-bit block used for invocation of PRF function.
   $$P = [1]^1 \| [2]^1 \| [1]^1 \| [radix]^3 \| [10]^1 \| [u \bmod 256]^1 \| [n]^4 \| [t]^4$$

4. **for** $i = 0$ **to** 9 **do** # FF1 has ten rounds
   4.1. # Encode in bytes: tweak T, substring Z, round number i, and
       # numeral string B. Z is a 0-byte string added so that the byte length
       # of Q is a multiple of 16 bytes (i.e. 128 bits, which is the AES block length.
   $$Z = [0]^{(-t-b-1) \bmod 16}; \qquad Q = T \| Z \| [i]^1 \| [Num_{radix}(B)]^b$$
   4.2. # PRF function is applied to $P \| Q$ string to produce a 128-bit block R
   $$R = PRF(P \| Q)$$
       # R is truncated or expanded to a string S of a length of d bytes.
       # If $d \leq 16$, then S is composed of the first d bytes of R. Otherwise,
       # block R is expanded (with iterative encryption of R and a constant)
       # to produce d bytes. $FB_d(S)$ denotes the first d bytes of string S.
       # S corresponds to the output of round function F_K
   $$S = FB_d \left(R \| \begin{pmatrix} Enc_K(R \oplus [1]^{16}) \| Enc_K(R \oplus [2]^{16}) \| \ldots \\ Enc_K(R \oplus [\lceil d/16 \rceil - 1]^{16}) \end{pmatrix} \right)$$
   $$y = Num(S)$$
   4.3. # To take into account the parity of X length, the computation of the
       # next value of half B is performed with $modulo\ radix^u$ if the round
       # number is even, and with $modulo\ radix^v$ otherwise,
       if i is even, **then** $m = u$, **else** $m = v$
   $$c = (Num_{radix}(A) + y) \bmod radix^m$$
       # C is a sum converted into a string of m numerals in base $radix$
   $$C = str_{radix}^m(c)$$
   4.4. # Swap of halves:
       $A = B; B = C$

5. $Y = A \| B$; **return** Y

Notes

– Why R is padded with random string in step 4.2? S, the output of round function, is obtained from R by padding with random blocks $(Enc_K(R \oplus [1]^{16}, Enc_K(R \oplus [2]^{16}, \ldots, Enc_K \left(R \oplus [\lceil d/16 \rceil - 1]^{16} \right))$ instead of padding with a constant bit sequence, which would be a potential security risk. Therefore, the round function produces a fully random output.

– Why d is greater than b by 4 at least? Given a substring A of length b, the round function must return a scrambled string of at least b bytes. In step 4.3, the sum $c = Num_{radix}(A) + y \bmod radix^m$ is composed of two parts $Num_{radix}(A)$ and y. $Num_{radix}(A)$ is less than $radix^m$, because substring A has u or v symbols in base $radix$; and $m = u$ or $m = v$. To scramble A with y, without bias we need a value of y in which all bits are random. Therefore, for y to be a fully randomized number, it must be at least equal to $radix^m$. With a bit-string S of length d, with $d = 4\lceil b/4 \rceil + 4$, we can represent integers greater than $radix^m$. Indeed, $radix^m = 2^{\log_2(radix)*m} \, 2^{8*b} < 2^{8*d}$.

Algorithm of FF1 decryption is similar to that of encryption. Both algorithms differ only in lines 4.1, 4.3, and 4.4. That is, the encryption algorithm makes use of half B to produce the bit string Q and it uses the half A and modular addition to yield C, which is copied in half B, while the decryption algorithm makes use of half A to produce the bit string Q and it uses the half B and modular subtraction to produce C, which is copied in half A.

---

function FF1_Decryption

    input K: key; T: tweak of length t bytes; $t \in [0..maxTLen]$
        X: ciphertext, a string of n numerals in base $radix$
        # $n \in [minLen..maxLen]$
    output Y: plaintext of the same length than that of X
    1. # Input numeral string X is split into two halves A (left) and B (right)
        $u = \lceil n/2 \rceil; v = n - u; A = X[1:u]; B = X[u+1:n]$
    2. # b and d are byte-lengths.
        $b = \lceil \lceil v * \log_2(radix) \rceil / 8 \rceil; d = 4\lceil b/4 \rceil + 4$
    3. $P = [1]^1 \,\|\, [2]^1 \,\|\, [1]^1 \,\|\, [radix]^3 \,\|\, [10]^1 \,\|\, [u \bmod 256]^1 \,\|\, [n]^4 \,\|\, [t]^4$

    4. **for** $i = 0$ **to** 9 **do**
        4.1. $Z = [0]^{(-t-b-1) \bmod 16}; \quad Q = T \,\|\, Z \,\|\, [i]^1 \,\|\, [Num_{radix}(A)]^b$
        4.2. $R = PRF(P \,\|\, Q)$

$$S = FB_d\left(R \,\|\, \begin{pmatrix} Enc_K(R \oplus [1]^{16}) \,\|\, Enc_K(R \oplus [2]^{16}) \,\|\, \cdots \\ Enc_K(R \oplus [\lceil d/16 \rceil - 1]^{16}) \end{pmatrix}\right)$$

        $y = Num(S)$
        4.3. **if** i is even, **then** $m = u$, **else** $m = v$
        $c = (Num_{radix}(B) - y) \bmod radix^m$
        $C = str_{radix}^m(c)$
        4.4. # Swap of halves:
        $B = A; A = C$
    5. $Y = A \,\|\, B$; **return** Y

Example 8.2

Below is a simple example to show how FF1 performs the encryption and decryption. To perform FF1 operations by hand, we need two simplifications: the number of rounds is limited to two and the $PRF(X)$ function returns six 0-bytes followed by the two rightmost bytes of input X followed by eight 0-bytes.

Let the plaintext be $X = 28750457$, a string of eight characters in base 10. Let the tweak be $T = [67]$, a string of one byte. Therefore, $t = 1$.

Encryption
– Split the input: $u = v = \dfrac{8}{2} = 4; A = 2875; B = 0457$
– $b = \lceil \lceil 4 * \log_2(10) \rceil / 8 \rceil = 2$. Two bytes are required to represent in binary each of 2875 and 0457 values.
– $d = 4\lceil 2/4 \rceil + 4 = 8$
– $P = [1]^1 \,\|\, [2]^1 \,\|\, [1]^1 \,\|\, [10]^3 \,\|\, [10]^1 \,\|\, [4]^1 \,\|\, [8]^4 \,\|\, [1]^4$

Round 0
– $Z = [0]^{(-1-2-1) \bmod 16} = [0]^{12}$
– $Q = [67] \,\|\, [0]^{12} \,\|\, [0]^1 \,\|\, [0457]^2$. $len(Q)$ is 16 bytes.

- $R = PRF(P \| Q)$. PRF receives two 128-bit blocks and returns a 128-bit block R, which depends on the key and AES encryption of the bit string $P \| Q$.

To simply, we assume that the returned value is

$$R = [0][0][0][0][0][0][0457]^2[0][0][0][0][0][0][0][0]$$

- $\lceil d/16 \rceil - 1 = \lceil 8/16 \rceil - 1 = 0$. Thus, $S = LSB_8(R) = [0][0][0][0][0][0][0457]^2$
- $y = Num(S) = 457$
- $u = v = 4$; thus, there is no need to adapt the modulo computation for each round.
- $C = str_{10}^4\left((Num_{radix}(A) + y) \bmod 10^4\right) = str_{10}^4(2875 + 457) \bmod 10^4) = 3332$
- Swap of halves: $A = 0457$; $B = 3332$

Round 1
- $Q = [1] \| [0]^{12} \| [1]^1 \| [3332]^2$.
- $R = PRF(P \| Q)$
- Assume that $R = [0][0][0][0][0][0][3332]^2[0][0][0][0][0][0][0][0]$
- $\lceil d/16 \rceil - 1 = 0$; hence, $S = LSB_8(R) = [0][0][0][0][0][0][3332]^2$
- $y = Num(S) = 3332$
- $C = str_{10}^4(0457 + 3332) \bmod 10^4) = 3789$
- Swap of halves: $A = 3332$; $B = 3789$

Finally, the returned ciphertext is $Y = 33323789$.

2. Decryption
- Let the ciphertext be $X = 33323789$.
- Split the input $u = v = \dfrac{8}{2} = 4$; $A = 3332$; $B = 3789$
- $b = \lceil \lceil 4 * \log_2(10) \rceil / 8 \rceil = 2$; $d = 4\lceil 2/4 \rceil + 4 = 8$
- $P = [1]^1 \| [2]^1 \| [1]^1 \| [10]^3 \| [10]^1 \| [4]^1 \| [8]^4 \| [1]^4$

Round 0
- $Z = [0]^{(-1-2-1) \bmod 16} = [0]^{12}$
- $Q = [67] \| [0]^{12} \| [0]^1 \| [3332]^2$.
- $R = PRF(P \| Q)$ with the chosen *PRF* function,

$$R = [0][0][0][0][0][0][3332]^2[0][0][0][0][0][0][0][0]$$

- $\lceil d/16 \rceil - 1 = \lceil 8/16 \rceil - 1 = 0$. Thus, $S = LSB_8(R) = [0][0][0][0][0][0][3332]^2$
- $y = Num(S) = 3332$
- Since $u = v = 4$, there is no need to adapt the modulo computation for each round.
- $C = str_{10}^4\left((Num_{radix}(B) - y) \bmod 10^4\right)$
  $= str_{10}^4(3789 - 3332) \bmod 10^4) = 457$
- Swap of halves: $B = 3332$; $A = 0457$

Round 1
- $Q = [67] \| [0]^{12} \| [1]^1 \| [0457]^2$.
- $R = PRF(P \| Q)$

$$R = [0][0][0][0][0][0][0457]^2[0][0][0][0][0][0][0][0]$$

- $\lceil d/16 \rceil - 1 = 0$; hence, $S = LSB_8(R) = [0][0][0][0][0][0][0457]^2$
- $y = Num(S) = 0457$
- $C = str_{10}^4(3332 - 0457) \bmod 10^4) = 2875$
- Swap of halves: $A = 3154$; $B = 0457$; $A = 2875$

Finally the returned plaintext $Y = 28750457$, which is correct.

8.7.4 FF3-1 Mode

The main differences between FF1 and FF3-1 modes are the following:

- FF3-1 is not flexible regarding the tweak length. In FF1, the tweak is an arbitrary string, which may be empty, while it must be of exactly 56 bits in FF3-1.
- FF1 runs 10 rounds, while FF3-1 runs eight rounds.
- If the length of the input string is odd, the length of the right half is one byte longer than the left half in FF1 mode and the inverse in FF3-1.
- FF1 makes use of big-endian representation, while little-endian is used in FF3-1. Therefore, FF3-1 makes use of two functions to inverse strings before performing arithmetic operations:
  - $REV(X)$: given a character string X, $REV(X)$ returns X in the reverse order. For example, $REV(1957) = 7591$.
  - $REVB(B)$: given a byte string B, $REVB(B)$ returns B in the reverse byte order. For example, $REVB\left([1]^1 \,\|\, [9]^1 \,\|\, [5]^1 \,\|\, [7]^1\right) = [7]^1 \,\|\, [5]^1 \,\|\, [9]^1 \,\|\, [1]^1$.

Figure 8.11 depicts computations performed in each round of FF3-1 encryption; conversion from symbols to integers and vice versa is not shown on the figure.

---

function FF3_1_Encryption

      input K: key; T: tweak of length of 56 bits

          X: plaintext, a string of n numerals in base *radix*

          # $n \in \left[minLen..maxLen\right]$

      output Y: ciphertext of the same length than that of input X

1. # The input numeral string X is split into two halves A (left) and B (right).
  # If length of X is odd, then the left half has one numeral more than the
  # right. A and B are strings of numerals
  $u = \lceil n/2 \rceil; v = n - u; A = X[1:u]; B = X[u+1:n]$

2. # The tweak T is partitioned into two parts, left (T_L) and right (T_R), each
  # of 32 bits (28 bits from T and four 0-bits):
  $T_L = T[0:27] \| 0^4; T_R = T[32:55] \| T[28:31] \| 0^4$

3. **for** $i = 0$ **to** 7 # FF3-1 has eight rounds

    3.1. **if** i is even, **then** $m = u; W = T_R$ **else** $m = v; W = T_L$

    3.2. # Half B is reversed and combined with the round number and a
        # tweak half to produce a 128-bit block.
        # Reverse operations (in FF3-1) are performed byte per byte.
        $P = W \oplus [i]^4 \| \left[Num_{radix}\left(REV(B)\right)\right]^{12}$

    3.3. # The byte-string P and the key K are reversed before encryption
        # and then the produced ciphertext is reversed
        $S = REVB\left(Enc_{REVB(K)}\left(REVB(P)\right)\right)$

    3.4. $y = Num(S)$

    3.5. $c = \left(Num_{radix}\left(REV(A)\right) + y\right) \bmod radix^m$

    3.6. # Before swapping, a reverse operation is performed
        $C = REV\left(str_{radix}^m(c)\right)$

    3.7. # Half swapping:
        $A = B; B = C;$

4. $Y = A \| B$; **return** Y

Algorithm of FF3-1 decryption is similar to that of encryption. Both algorithms differ only in lines 3.2 and 3.5. That is, the encryption algorithm makes use of half B to produce the bit string P and it uses the half A and modular addition to produce C, which is copied in half B, while the decryption algorithm makes use of half A to produce the bit string P and it uses the half B and modular subtraction to produce C, which is copied in half A.

---

function FF3_1_Decryption

      input K: key; T: tweak of length of 56 bits

          X: ciphertext, a string of n numerals in base *radix*

          # $n \in \left[minLen..maxLen\right]$

output Y: plaintext of the same length than that of input X

1. # The input numeral string X is split into two halves A(left) and B (right).
   1.1. $u = \lceil n / 2 \rceil; v = n - u$
   1.2. $A = X[1:u]; B = X[u+1:n]$
2. # Tweak partitioning
   $T_L = T[0:27] \| 0^4; T_R = T[32:55] \| T[28:31] \| 0^4$
3. **for** $i = 0$ **to** 7# FF3-1 has eight rounds
   3.1. **if** i is even, **then** $m = u; W = T_R$ **else** $m = v; W = T_L$
   3.2. $P = W \oplus [i]^4 \| \left[Num_{radix} \left(REV(A) \right) \right]^{12}$
   3.3. $S = REVB \left(Enc_{REVB(K)} \left(REVB(P) \right) \right)$
   3.4. $y = Num(S)$
   3.5. $c = \left(Num_{radix} \left(REV(B) \right) - y \right) mod\ radix^m$
   3.6. $c = REV \left(str_{radix}^m (c) \right)$
   3.7. # Half swapping:
       $B = A; A = C$
4. $Y = A \| B; return\ Y$

8.8 XTS-AES Mode of Operation

8.8.1 Overview of XTS-AES

The standard algorithm to protect data on storage devices is the XTS-AES mode of operation. The latter was designed to provide data confidentiality on storage devices [5]. It was not designed to secure data in transit over networks. The acronym

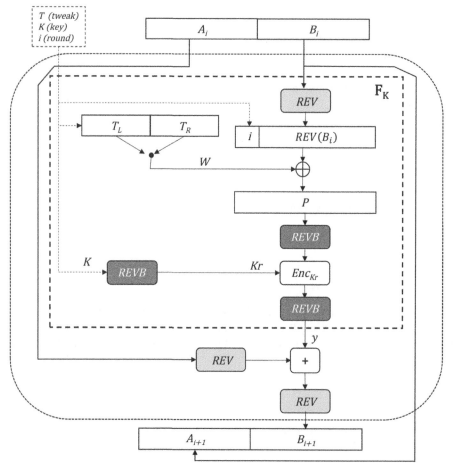

Figure 8.11 Round computations in FF3-1 mode.

XTS stands for XEX (Xor-Encrypt-Xor) Tweakable block cipher with ciphertext Stealing. XTS-AES mode also is referred to as IEEE standard 1619. It is supported by many operating systems and platforms.

XTS-AES is a format-preserving encryption mode of operation. Hence, the length and the format of plaintext and ciphertext are the same (i.e. no disk space waste). Therefore, applications do not need to change data format to encrypt or decrypt. In addition, XTS-AES encrypts individual data units resulting in independent ciphertexts. Therefore, applications are not required to decrypt all ciphertexts to retrieve a specific item of data. Rather, XTS-AES provides support to fast data random access.

XTS-AES operates with keys of bit-length of either 256 or 512. If the XTS-AES key consists of 256 bits, the encrypt/decryption procedures use 128-bit AES; if the XTS-AES key consists of 512 bits, the procedures use 256-bit AES, which differ in term of number of rounds (see Section 7.3.3).

Definition 8.4 Key scope: *it defines the stream of data encrypted by a particular key. The key scope is represented by three integers: tweak value corresponding the first data unit, the bit-length of data unit, and the number of units to be encrypted/decrypted under the control of this key.*

Definition 8.5 Data unit:[10] *it is a fixed-length bit-string within a key scope. The data unit length should be at least 128 bits. Each data unit is divided into 128-bit blocks.*

The total number[11] of 128-bit blocks of the entire data shall not exceed 2^{64} and the maximum number[12] of 128-bit blocks in a data unit shall not exceed 2^{20}. Usually the length of data unit equals the sector length of storage devices, e.g. 512 or 4k bytes.

Definition 8.6 XTS-AES Tweak value: *it is a 128-bit value representing the logical position of the data being encrypted or decrypted. Each data unit is assigned a tweak value.*

Tweak values are assigned consecutively, starting from an arbitrary value. An easy way to assign tweak values is to start with a random value T_1 and then increment it for each subsequent data unit; i.e. $T_i = T_{i-1} + 1$ for $i > 1$. Figure 8.12 illustrates the main items of XTS-AES mode of operation.

Modular multiplication: input and output of XTS-AES encryption and decryption operations are bit-string of a length of 128 bits. Such operations perform multiplication, denoted $\otimes$, over an extension field $F_{2^{128}}$ (as below) with a reduction polynomial $f(x) = x^{128} + x^7 + x^2 + x + 1$ and a primitive element α, which corresponds to polynomial x (i.e. $0000\ldots0010_2 = 0002_{10}$). For more on extension fields, see Section 3.2.3.

8.8.2 Encryption and Decryption Algorithms

Figures 8.13 and 8.14 depict the XTS-AES encryption and decryption operations. There are two encryption/decryption levels: single block and data unit encryption/decryption. To address data unit with a bit-length, which is not a multiple of 128 bits, XTS-AES makes use of ciphertext stealing as in CBC variants. Below are the algorithms of XTS-AES mode.

---

function XTS_AES_Block_Encryption
  input K: key with a length of 256 or 512 bytes
      P_x: 128-bit plaintext block; T: tweak value (a 128-bit block)
      j: sequential number for each 128-bit block inside the data unit
  output C_x: 128-bit ciphertext block
  1. # The key is split into two equal length subkeys
     Let $K = K_1 \parallel K_2$
  2. # Ciphertext block computation
     $A = AES\_Enc_{K_2}(T) \otimes \alpha^j$; $B = AES\_Enc_{K_1}(P_x \oplus A)$; $C_x = B \oplus A$
  3. **return** C_x

---

function XTS_AES_Data_unit_Encryption
  input K: key with a length of 256 or 512 bytes
      P: plaintext composed of one or more 128-bit blocks
      T: tweak value (a 128-bit block) assigned to the data unit

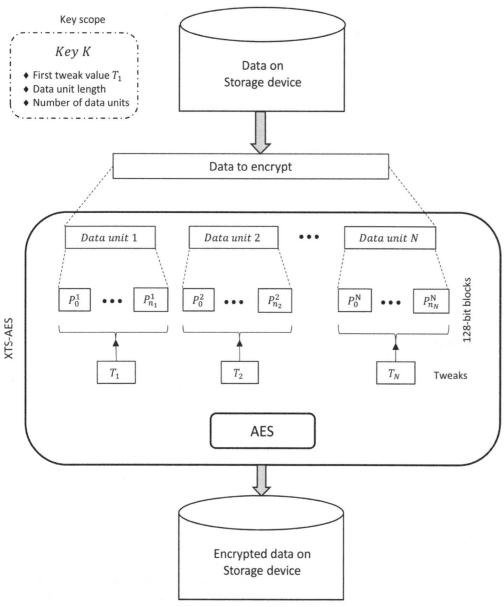

Figure 8.12 Basic items of XTS-AES cipher.

output C : ciphertext of the same bit-length than P

1. # The key is partitioned into $m+1$ blocks, where m is the largest
   # integer such that $m*128 < len(P)$. Blocks $P_0, ..., P_{m-1}$ have the
   # same length of 128 bits. The last block P_m is of a bit-length
   # between 0 and 127.
   Let $P = P_0 \parallel P_1 ... \parallel P_m$
2. # Ciphertext computation
   2.1 **for** $i = 0$ **to** $m-2$ **do**

   $\quad C_i = XTS\_AES\_Block\_Encrytion(K, P_i, T, i)$
   2.2 $b = len\left(P_m\right)$
   2.3. **if** $b = 0$, **then**

   $\quad C_{m-1} = XTS\_AES\_Block\_Encrytion(K, P_{m-1}, T, m-1)$
   $\quad C_m = Empty$
   2.4 **else**

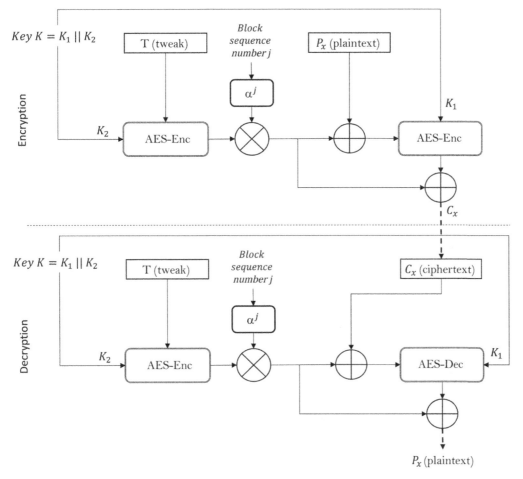

Figure 8.13 XTS-AES block encryption and decryption procedures.

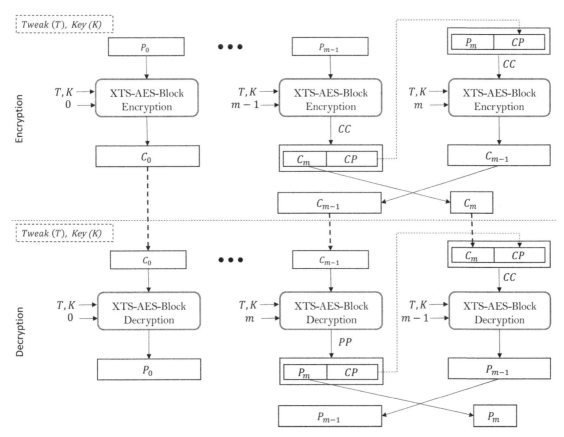

Figure 8.14 XTS-AES data unit encryption and decryption procedures.

$$CC = XTS\_AES\_Block\_Encryption(K, P_{m-1}, T, m-1)$$
$$C_m = MSB_b(CC); CP = LSB_{128-b}(CC); PP = P_m \,\|\, CP$$
$$C_{m-1} = XTS\_AES\_Block\_Encryption(K, PP, T, m)$$

3. $C = C_0 \,\|\, C_1 \ldots \|\, C_m$ **return** C

---

function XTS_AES_Block_Decryption
  input K: key with a length of 256 or 512 bytes
      C_x: 128-bit ciphertext block; T: tweak value (a 128-bit block)
      j: sequential number for each 128-bit block inside the data unit
  output P_x: 128-bit plaintext block
  1. # The key is split into two equal length subkeys
      Let $K = K_1 \,\|\, K_2$
  2. # Plaintext block computation
      $A = AES\_Enc_{K_2}(T) \oplus a^j; B = AES\_Dec_{K_1}(C_x \oplus A); P_x = B \oplus A$
  3. **return** P_x

---

function XTS_AES_Data-unit_Decryption
  input K: key with a length of 256 or 512 bytes
      C: ciphertext composed of one or more 128-bit blocks
      T: tweak value (a 128-bit block) assigned to the data unit
  output P: plaintext of the same bit-length than C
  1. # Key is partitioned into $m+1$ blocks, where is m is the largest
      # integer such that $m * 128 < len(C)$.
      # Blocks $C_0, \ldots, C_{m-1}$ have the same bit length, 128.
      # The last block C_m is of bit-length between 0 and 127.
      Let $C = C_0 \,\|\, C_1 \ldots \|\, C_m$
  2. # Ciphertext decryption
      2.1 **for** $i = 0$ **to** $m - 2$ **do**
          $P_i = XTS\_AES\_Block\_Decryption(K, C_i, T, i)$
      2.2 $b = len(C_m)$
      2.3. **if** $b = 0$, **then**
          $P_{m-1} = XTS\_AES\_Block\_Decryption(K, C_{m-1}, T, m-1)$
          $P_m = Empty$
      2.4 **else**
          $PP = XTS\_AES\_Block\_Decryption(K, C_{m-1}, T, m)$
          $P_m = MSB_b(PP); CP = LSB_{128-b}(PP); CC = C_m \,\|\, CP$
          $P_{m-1} = XTS\_AES\_Block\_Decryption(K, CC, T, m-1)$
  3. $P = (P_0 \,\|\, P_1 \ldots \|\, P_m)$; **return** P

8.8.3 Some Strengths and Weaknesses of XTS-AES

XTS-AES looks like ECB mode, because the ciphertexts are independent in both modes and encryption and decryption may be parallelized. However, with ECB, identical plaintext blocks are encrypted with the same ciphertext block, which provides some substrate for cryptanalysis attacks. With XTS-AES, due to block sequence number and tweaks, identical plaintext blocks are encrypted with distinct ciphertext blocks.

XTS-AES is more performant than CBC, when decrypting ciphertexts. In CBC, to access a specific field (or portion) in data on storage device, the decryption of the entire data is often required. With XTS-AES, only the searched field (or portion) requires decryption. Since XTS-AES is a format-preserving encryption only, it cannot provide support for data integrity. Indeed, because there is no hash or MAC (message authentication code) in the produced ciphertext, any alteration (modification, deletion or insertion), in the ciphertext, is decrypted as some (random) plaintext. There exist three main categories of potential attacks against XTS-AES:

- Randomizing a sector: an adversary with write access to the encrypted storage device can change a sector to an arbitrary value, which results in invalid data used by legitimate applications.
- Selective replay attack: an adversary with write access to the encrypted storage device can set the value of a sector to a specific value observed in past in order to corrupt some write operations. For example, consider a malicious store employee who has write access to a stock status file and who knows the index of a block, say $C_x^{current}$, associated with the number of articles A, of interest to him/her, in stock and he/she also knows that different versions of the file are encrypted with the same tweak, and finally, he/she has access to an older version of the same file. Under such conditions, the employee can replace block $C_x^{current}$ by an older block C_x^{old}. Since $C_x^{current}$ and C_x^{old} ciphertext blocks have been encrypted by the same parameters (tweak, key, and bock index), the decryption of the modified block yields the stock status of interest to the malicious employee.
- Traffic analysis: if an adversary can observe the communication between the encrypting device and the storage device, he/she can infer when some sectors are modified over time and then use such a knowledge to design an attack.

8.9 Comparison of Design Features of Modes for Confidentiality

Table 8.1 aims at summarizing some fundamental design features to compare block cipher modes of operation. The features of interest are the following:

- *Encryption determinism*: is the same plaintext block always mapped to the same ciphertext block under the same key?
- *Padding* is the plaintext length required to be a multiple of block length?
- *Initialization vector*: is IV required? If Yes, should the IV be a nonce or unpredictable?
- *Parallelization*: can the encryption or decryption of blocks be performed in parallel?
- *Ciphertext error-propagation*: does a bit error in a ciphertext block prevent[13] the recovery of the remaining plaintext blocks? "No" means only the plaintext block associated with the altered ciphertext block is unlikely to be recovered correctly; "Yes" means the plaintext block associated with the altered ciphertext block and the plaintext block that follows are unlikely to be recovered correctly.
- *IV and counter error-propagation*: in case the IV or counter is sent[14] to recipient, does bit alteration in the IV or counter impact the decryption?
- *Diffusion* property: does a modification of a bit in a plaintext block propagate in the whole ciphertext?
- *Block cipher (BC) decryption use*:[15] does the mode of operation make use of the decryption operation of the underlying block cipher to decrypt?
- *Stream cipher*[16] *construction*: can the mode of operation be used as a stream cipher?

8.10 Security of Modes of Operation for Confidentiality

When a block cipher is used for confidentiality protection, the security goal is to prevent an eavesdropper with limited computational power to learn any information about the plaintext (except for maybe its length). This eavesdropper can apply the following attacks: known-plaintext attacks, chosen-plaintext attacks, and chosen-ciphertext attacks that should be prevented by the underlying cipher.

Table 8.1 Comparison of modes of operation for confidentiality guaranteeing.

	ECB	Basic CBC	CBC-SC variants	OFB	CTR	CFB	FF1FF3-1	XTS-AES
Determinism	Yes	No	No	No	No	No	No	No
Padding	Yes	Yes	No	No	No	No	No	No
IV/counter	No	Unpr.	Unpr.	Nonce	Ctr[(a)]	Unpr.	Twk[(b)]	Twk[(c)]
Encryption parallelization	Yes	No	No	Yes[(d)]	Yes[(d)]	No	No	Yes[(e)]
Decryption parallelization	Yes	Yes	Yes[(f)]	Yes[(g)]	Yes[(g)]	Yes[(h)]	No	Yes[(i)]
Error propagation	No	Yes	Yes[(j)]	No	No	Yes[(k)]	Yes[(l)]	No[(m)]
IV/counter error propagation	n.a	No[(n)]	No[(o)]	Yes[(p)]	Yes[(q)]	Yes[(r)]	Yes[(s)]	Yes[(s)]
Diffusion	No	Yes	Yes	No	No	Yes	Yes	No
BC decrypt. algorithm use	Yes	Yes	Yes	No	No	No	No	Yes
Stream cipher	No	No	No	Yes	Yes	Yes	No	No

Unpr.: unpredictable; *n.a*: not applicable

Notes:

(a) A unique counter block for each plaintext block that is ever encrypted under a given key, across all messages, i.e. the block counter should be a nonce.
(b) A distinct tweak is used for each plaintext.
(c) A distinct tweak is used for each data unit.
(d) Under the condition that the blocks $O_1, \ldots, O_m$ are precomputed.
(e) With the exception of the two last blocks.
(f) With the exception of the two last blocks, which cannot be treated in parallel.
(g) Under the condition that the blocks $O_1, \ldots, O_m$ are precomputed.
(h) Under the condition that the blocks $I_1, \ldots, I_m$ are precomputed, upon reception of the ciphertext blocks.
(i) With the exception of the two last blocks.
(j) In CBC variants, the decryption of the last but one block steals some bits from the last ciphertext block. Therefore, if the last cipher block is altered, then the two last blocks are unlikely to be recovered correctly.
(k) If segment $C_i^{\#}$ is altered, then segments $C_i^{\#}, C_{i+1}^{\#}, \ldots,$ to $C_{i+\lfloor b/s \rfloor}^{\#}$ are unlikely to be recovered correctly.

(l) Because of the Feistel structure of FF1 and FF3-3 modes, if a ciphertext block is altered, it is very unlikely that any plaintext block could be recovered correctly.
(m) With the exception of the last but one block, because the last ciphertext block steals some bits from the block before it.
(n) Only the decryption of the first ciphertext block makes use of the IV. Therefore, only the first plaintext block is unlikely to be recovered correctly.
(o) As in basic CBC and in addition, if the ciphertext is composed of two blocks only, both blocks are unlikely to be recovered correctly.
(p) If an error occurs in the IV, then it is very unlikely that any plaintext block could be recovered correctly.
(q) If the initial counter is altered, then it is very unlikely that any plaintext block could be recovered correctly.
(r) If segment $C_i^{\#}$ is lost, then segments $C_{i+1}^{\#}, \ldots,$ to $C_{i+\lfloor b/s \rfloor}^{\#}$ are unlikely to decrypt to correct plaintext segments.

(s) If the tweak is altered in transit, then it is very unlikely that any plaintext block could be recovered correctly.

8.10.1 Vulnerability to Block Repetitions and Replay

In general, ECB is not recommended, because of the following vulnerabilities:

- A block with a same content is encrypted with the same ciphertext, if it repeats in the same message or in distinct messages. ECB mode is the only mode, which does not hide repetitions in the plaintext, which may give advantage to adversary.
- If an adversary replays ciphertexts, the recipient has no means to detect replays. For example, if a user is uploading a file on a storage server while using ECB, multiple portions of the file may be erroneously duplicated on the server in the event of a replay attack.

With the exception of ECB, the other modes (CBC, OFB, CTR, CFB, FF1, FF3-1, and XTS) do not suffer replay and plaintext repetition vulnerabilities due to the use of IV (which may be a nonce or unpredictable), counter (which is unique for each block), or tweak (which is a nonce) assuming that they are used correctly (i.e. the IV/counter/tweak is a nonce or unpredictable and the maximum number of plaintexts encrypted with the same key is not greater than the recommended limit).

8.10.2 Vulnerability to Predictable IV or Tweak

Remember that the ultimate goal for encryption algorithms is to provide confidentiality guarantees. With such a property, it is practically impossible for any adversary to infer any knowledge from the observed ciphertexts; i.e. all ciphertexts should appear as noise. For example, consider a scenario in which Alice sends a response Yes or No to answer a question from Bob. If the adversary can infer which response is sent without decrypting the response ciphertext, the secrecy is broken.

In some modes of operation, the IV (in CBC and CFB) or the tweak (in FF1, FF3-1, and XTS-AES) is required to be unpredictable because prediction of the IV/tweak may result in a break of the confidentiality property. Therefore, IV or tweak-based modes of operation are vulnerable to chosen-plaintext attacks as shown by the following attack scenario (see Figure 8.15) in which the adversary attacks a CBC oracle.

1) The adversary queries the oracle with a message m_0.
2) Since the IV is not required to be secret, the oracle returns the ciphertext $C_0 = Enc_K\left(IV_0 \oplus m_0\right)$ and the initialization vector IV_0, which has been used for encrypting message m_0.
3) Given IV_0, the adversary is assumed to be able to predict the next IV that will be used, say IV_1. He/she queries the oracle with two messages say m_1 and m_2, such that $m_1 \neq m_2$ and $m_1 = IV_1 \oplus IV_0 \oplus m_0$.
4) The oracle is assumed to process the queries in their order of arrival. The oracle returns two ciphertexts:

$$C_1 = Enc_K\left(IV_1 \oplus \left(IV_1 \oplus IV_0 \oplus m_0\right)\right) = Enc_K\left(IV_0 \oplus m_0\right) = C_0$$
$$\text{and } C_2 = Enc_K\left(IV_2 \oplus m_2\right)$$

5) The adversary can easily infer that ciphertext C_1 contains the plaintext m_1, because C_1 is identical to C_0 that has been seen before. This situation breaks the property that the adversary should not be able to distinguish between two ciphertexts to infer any knowledge.

Another example of vulnerability to predictable IV is considered in Problem 8.8.

8.10.3 Vulnerability to IV/Tweak that Is Not a Nonce

In OFB and CTR modes, if the IV is not a nonce, two messages may be encrypted with the same IV value, which may compromise confidentiality of encrypted plaintexts. Both modes are stream ciphers and the encryption of plaintext B_j is defined by $C_j = B_j \oplus O_j$, where O_j is the keystream block defined by: $O_j = Enc_k\left(I_j\right)$ for OFB mode or $O_j = Enc_k\left(Cnt_j\right)$ for CTR mode. I_1 is the IV in OFB and Cnt_1 is the initial counter in CTR.

Let B_i^1, B_i^2, C_i^1, and C_i^2, $i = 1, ..., L$, be the plaintext blocks and ciphertext blocks of message M_1 and M_2, respectively, where $L = min\left(len\left(M_1\right), len\left(M_2\right)\right)$. Since both messages are encrypted with the same IV/counter, the sequence of keystream blocks is the same. Let this sequence be $O_1, O_2, ..., O_L$.

$$C_i^1 = B_i^1 \oplus O_i \text{ and } C_i^2 = B_i^2 \oplus O_i, \text{ for } i = 1, ..., L.$$

The adversary can XOR the ciphertexts to find the following:

$$C_i^1 \oplus C_i^2 = B_i^1 \oplus O_i \oplus B_i^2 \oplus O_i = B_i^1 \oplus B_i^2, \text{ for } i = 1, ..., L.$$

Such a relationship may be used to disclose a plaintext if another is known, to find repetitions (at the same positions) in two plaintexts, or to infer other features of interest to the adversary.

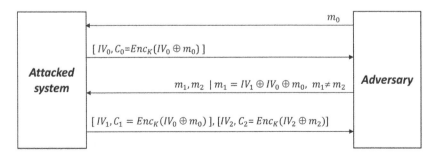

Figure 8.15 Chosen-plaintext attack against CBC under predictable IV.

Before encrypting plaintext blocks, FF1 and FF3-1 modes append to the plaintext other strings (tweak, plaintext length, round number, and constants), then a Feistel structure is applied, and bits are scrambled in each round. In the output of FF1 and FF3-1, applying $C_i^1 \oplus C_i^2$ does not help to derive $B_i^1 \oplus B_i^2$.

In XTS-AES mode, the encryption of two plaintexts M_1 and M_2, with the same tweak, results in the following decryption, for $i = 1, \ldots, \min\left(len\left(M_1\right), len\left(M_2\right)\right)$:

$$C_i^1 = Enc_{K_1}\left(B_i^1 \oplus Enc_{K_2}(T) \otimes \alpha^i\right) \oplus Enc_{(K_2)}(T) \otimes \alpha^i,$$

$$C_i^2 = Enc_{K_1}\left(B_i^2 \oplus Enc_{K_2}(T) \otimes \alpha^i\right) \oplus Enc_{(K_2)}(T) \otimes \alpha^i$$

Applying $C_i^1 \oplus C_i^2$ does not help to derive $B_i^1 \oplus B_i^2$. Therefore, FF1, FF3-1, and XTS-AES modes are not vulnerable to attacks based on reuse of tweak value.

8.10.4 Vulnerability to Birthday Attacks

If the block bit-length of the underlying cipher (i.e. AES, TDEA, etc.) is n, then by birthday paradox, the adversary needs to intercept $2^{\frac{n}{2}}$ ciphertext blocks to have (at a high probability) a collision. Such an interception is easy if the adversary has access to encrypted files. A collision may reveal some information useful to the adversary. For example, it may reveal repetition in the same plaintext or in distinct plaintexts. Notice that the exploitation of collisions in FF1 and FF3-1 modes is unlikely to help discovering any useful information about plaintexts due to the scrambling performed by modes.

In general, to avoid birthday attacks, it is recommended to encrypt less than $\alpha * 2^{\frac{n}{2}}$ blocks by the same key, with α a small constant in magnitude of 10^{-3} or even less.

8.10.5 Vulnerability to Bit-Flipping Attacks

The aim of bit-flipping attack is to change a ciphertext block at some positions in order to change the plaintext recovered by recipient at the same positions. In CBC mode, ciphertext block C_i is XORed with the decryption of block ciphertext C_{i+1} to recover plaintext B_{i+1}. OFB, CTR, and CFB modes are stream ciphers where the ciphertext block C_i is XORed with keystream block O_i to recover plaintext block B_i. Therefore, changing a bit at position j in ciphertext block C_i results in a change of the bit at position j of plaintext block B_{i+1}, in case of CBC mode, or B_i in case of OFB, CTR, and CFB modes.

If the message format is known to adversary, this can cause devastating effects, especially if the important information is located at positions known to the adversary. For example, imagine an adversary who knows that the amount of money to transfer, denoted v, is less than 100 and it is encrypted alone in block C_4 using the AES-CTR. He/she can change C_4 so that the amount to transfer is increased by 1024 as follows:

The original plaintext block is recovered by the recipient as $B_4 = C_4 \oplus Enc_k\left(Cnt_4\right)$.

Let $S = 0^{117} \parallel 10000000000$ be the bit-string representing the integer 1024 on 128 bits.

The adversary changes C_4 to $C_4' = C_4 \oplus S$. Then, the recipient decrypts as follows:

$$B_4' = C_4' \oplus Enc_k\left(Cnt_4\right) = \left(C_4 \oplus S\right) \oplus Enc_k\left(Cnt_k\right)$$

$$= \left(C_4 \oplus Enc_k\left(Cnt_k\right)\right) \oplus S = B_4 \oplus S.$$

Since the original amount v is less than 100, the bit-string B_4' represents the integer $1024 + v$.

ECB mode is not vulnerable to bit-flipping, because each ciphertext block is decrypted only with the decryption operation of the underlying block cipher, which is a pseudorandom permutation.

Given the scrambling performed in FF1 and FF3-1 rounds when encrypting or decrypting, the adversary has no control on which bits will flip in the recovered plaintext, if some bits are flipped in the ciphertext.

In the XTS-AES mode, block decryption is performed with AES-encryption followed by AES-decryption. Therefore, the adversary has no control on which bits will flip in the recovered plaintext, if some bits are flipped in the ciphertext.

8.11   Exercises and Problems

8.11.1   List of Exercises and Problems

Exercise 8.1
Consider a block cipher E, defined by the pseudorandom permutation given by the table below. Each letter is a block. Then, consider ECB and CBC as modes of operation of the block cipher E. As the XOR operation (i.e. $\oplus$) is not defined on the set $\{A, B, ..., Z\}$, the following adaptations are used:

   To encrypt a block B_i, the ciphertext C_{i-1} (or the IV) is added *modulo* 26 to B_i (e.g. $B \oplus C = D$, $K \oplus I = S$).
1) Decrypt the ciphertext OXBBJ, which was encrypted using ECB mode.
2) Decrypt the ciphertext DOLYV, which was encrypted using CBC mode with IV=K.

	0	1	2	3	4	5	6	7	8	9	10	11	12	13	14	15	16	17	18	19	20	21	22	23	24	25
P	A	B	C	D	E	F	G	H	I	J	K	L	M	N	O	P	Q	R	S	T	U	V	W	X	Y	Z
$E(K,P)$	Q	E	R	Z	X	G	N	O	P	I	C	B	V	S	J	F	W	D	H	M	T	A	Y	K	U	L

Exercise 8.2
Discuss which of ECB, CBC, CTR, and FF1 modes could provide integrity guarantees.

Exercise 8.3
How many distinct counter blocks are required to encrypt a hard disk of 16 T bytes with AES-CTR?

Exercise 8.4
Let s denote the segment length parameter of CFB mode and b the block bit-length. Show that CFB mode is the same as OFB mode if $s = b$.

Exercise 8.5
Show that ECB leaks information regarding plaintext-block repetition while CBC does not.

Problem 8.1
Consider a list of N names each of a length of 16 bytes. The name list is encrypted with four modes (ECB, CBC, OFB, and CTR) of operation of AES.
1) On transit, a ciphertext block of index $i(1 \leq i \leq N)$ is altered because of transmission errors changing some 0-bits to 1-bits and vice versa. What is the number of names that cannot be correctly recovered by the recipient for each mode of operation?
2) On transit, a ciphertext block of index $i(1 \leq i \leq N)$ is lost. What are the names that are missing in the recipient list and those that are not correctly recovered in each mode of operation?

Problem 8.2
Consider a plaintext, composed of N segments, encrypted with CFB mode.
1) On transit, a ciphertext segment of index $i\left(1 \leq i \leq N\right)$ is altered because of transmission errors changing some 0-bits to 1-bits and vice versa. What is the number of segments that cannot be correctly recovered by the recipient?
2) On transit, a ciphertext segment of index $i(1 \leq i \leq N)$ is lost. What are the plaintext segments that are missing in the recipient plaintext and those not correctly recovered? Without loss of generality, assume that the block length is a multiple of the segment length.

Problem 8.3
Show how CTR and OFB modes can be attacked if two plaintexts M_1 and M_2 are encrypted with the same initial counter or IV, respectively.

Problem 8.4
Assume that a plaintext–ciphertext pair is known. Show that keeping the IV secret in OFB mode does not make an exhaustive key search more complex, if the number of plaintext blocks is at least 2.

Problem 8.5
Consider the following scenario: in a company, a group of engineers collaborate on a project including several tasks. Some engineers are task managers and they declare, on a weekly basis, the number of hours of participation of each engineer

(including themselves) in the tasks assigned to them. Participation declarations are first securely sent to a server 1 by each task manager, and then server 1 encrypts, with ECB mode, a message for each engineer participation and sends the ciphertext to a server 2, which centralizes the engineers' participation in the project. The key shared by servers is not known to engineers. The format of the messages between both servers is composed of three fields each represented on one block: Manager identifier, participating engineer identifier, and the number of hours of participation. One malicious task manager who participates in multiple tasks and who knows the format of ECB-encrypted messages and who can intercept and modify ciphertexts between servers, wants to increase his/her amount of participation hours. He/she observed that the task managers used to send participation declarations on Friday before 6:00 p.m., but the server 1 accepts declarations up to Friday midnight. How may the malicious engineer design the attack?

Problem 8.6
Prove the correctness of CBC-CS1 mode of operation.

Problem 8.7
Prove the correctness of XTS-AES block encryption.

Problem 8.8
Consider the following context: Alice and Bob agree to use CBC mode to protect their communications. Eve has the capacity to ask Alice to encrypt messages for her (i.e. Eve is able to mount chosen-plaintext attacks) and she is able to predict the IV that will be used by Alice to encrypt her next message. Bob asks Alice to do something and she has to reply just by "Yes" or "No" in one block. Alice encrypts her response $P_{Alice} =$ 'Yes', using IV IV_0, and sends a ciphertext C_{toBob} to Bob. Eve intercepts IV_0 and C_{toBob} and she wants to know Alice's response without any knowledge about the key. Show how Eve can discover Alice's response.

8.11.2 Solutions to Exercises and Problems

Exercise 8.1
Let C_i be the ciphertext of plaintext block B_i. Let D denote the decryption operation of block cipher E.
1) Decryption of ciphertext OXBBJ using ECB mode
   The decryption using ECB mode is defined by: $B_i = D(C_i)$.
   The plaintext associated with ciphertext OXBBJ is HELLO, because:
   $D(O) = H, D(X) = E, D(B) = L, D(B) = L, D(J) = O$
2) Decryption of the ciphertext DOLYV, which was encrypted using CBC mode with IV=K
   The decryption using CBC mode is defined by: $B_i = D(C_i) \oplus C_{i-1}$, with $C_0 = IV$
   Since $\oplus$ is not defined on the letters, the decryption is transformed as follows:

$$B_i = Letter\left(Ind\left(D(C_i)\right) - Ind\left(C_{i-1}\right) mod\ 26\right)$$

Hence,

$$B_1 = Letter\left(Ind\left(D(D)\right) - Ind(K) mod\ 26\right) = Letter(17 - 10\ mod\ 26) = H$$

$$B_2 = Letter\left(Ind\left(D(O)\right) - Ind(D) mod\ 26\right) = Letter(7 - 3\ mod\ 26) = E$$

$$B_3 = Letter\left(Ind\left(D(L)\right) - Ind(O) mod\ 26\right) = Letter(25 - 14\ mod\ 26) = L$$

$$B_4 = Letter\left(Ind\left(D(Y)\right) - Ind(L) mod\ 26\right) = Letter(22 - 11\ mod\ 26) = L$$

$$B_5 = Letter\left(Ind\left(D(V)\right) - Ind(Y) mod\ 26\right) = Letter(12 - 24\ mod\ 26) = O$$

Exercise 8.2
ECB, CBC, CTR, and FF1 are algorithms aiming to provide confidentiality guarantees. As they do not make use of tags, no integrity guarantees could be provided. Any altered ciphertext is decrypted to a plaintext, which is very likely to be distinct from the original plaintext and the recipient has no means to check the integrity.

Exercise 8.3

We consider a disk of 16 T bytes encrypted with AES-CTR. 16 tera bytes are split into m 128-bit blocks, where $m = \dfrac{2^4 * 2^{40} * 2^3}{2^7} = 2^{40}$. Each plaintext block requires a distinct counter block; hence, the number of distinct counter blocks is 2^{40}.

Exercise 8.4

If the segment length s is equal to the block length b, then:

- The number of segments m_s is equal to the number of blocks m.
- For any i, $1 \leq i \leq m$, segments $B_i^{\#}$ and $C_i^{\#}$ are equal to blocks B_i and C_i, respectively.
- $LSB_{b-s}(X) = null$ and $MSB_s(X) = X$, for a bit-string of bit-length not greater than b.

With the limitations above, the CFB encryption formulas become:

$$I_1 = IV$$
$$I_j = LSB_{b-s}\left(I_{j-1}\right) \| C_{j-1}^{\#} = null \| C_{j-1}^{\#} = C_{j-1}, \quad \forall j, 2 \leq j \leq m\_s$$
$$O_j = Enc_K\left(I_j\right) = Enc_K\left(C_j\right), \qquad\qquad \forall j, 1 \leq j \leq m\_s$$
$$C_j^{\#} = B_j^{\#} \oplus MSB_s\left(O_j\right) = B_j \oplus O_j, \qquad\quad \forall j, 1 \leq j \leq m\_s - 1$$
$$C_j^{\#} = B_j^{\#} \oplus MSB_s\left(O_j\right) = B_j \oplus MSB_s\left(O_j\right), \qquad j = m\_s$$

The formulas above are the same as those of OFB encryption. The same apply to decryption. Therefore, CFB mode is identical to OFB mode if the segment length is the same as that of the block.

Exercise 8.5

Let A and B be two blocks and $P = A \| B \| B \| B$, a plaintext with three repetitions of block B. If ECB or CBC is used, then the ciphertext is $C = C_1 \| C_2 \| C_3 \| C_4$.

If ECB is used, then $C_1 = Enc_K(A), C_2 = C_3 = C_4 = Enc_K(B)$.

If CBC is used, then $C_1 = Enc_K(A \oplus IV), C_2 = Enc_K\left(B \oplus C_1\right), C_3 = Enc_K\left(B \oplus C_2\right), C_4 = Enc_K\left(B \oplus C_3\right)$.

We can see that the same ciphertext block $Enc_K(B)$ repeats three times in C. Therefore, ECB leaks information regarding plaintext repetition, while CBC does not.

Problem 8.1

1) Error-propagation resistance

- In ECB, OFB, and CTR modes, the decryption of a block is independent of that of other blocks. Therefore, if ciphertext block i is errored, only the name with index i is unlikely to be correctly recovered.
- In CBC mode, the decryption of ciphertext block k depends on ciphertext blocks k and $k-1$. Therefore, if ciphertext block i is errored, there exist two cases: a) if $i = N$, only the last name in the list is unlikely to be correctly recovered and b) if $i < N$, the names with indices i and $i+1$ are is unlikely to be correctly recovered.

2) Loss-propagation resistance

- In ECB mode, the decryption of a block is independent of that of other blocks. Therefore, if ciphertext block C_i is lost, only the name with index i is missing in the recipient list.
- In CTR mode, the encryption counter block Ctn_j is used as a keystream string to encrypt the plaintext block B_j, for $j = 1, \ldots, N$. In OFB and CFB modes, the encrypted block I_j is used as a keystream string to encrypt the plaintext block B_j, for $j = 1, \ldots, N$. In all these three modes, if the ciphertext block C_i is lost, then the recipient makes use of block Cnt_i (for CTR) or I_i (for OFB and CFB) to decrypt ciphertext C_{i+1} for $i = 1, \ldots, N-1$. Therefore, the name with index i is missing in the recipient list and all the subsequent names are very likely to be incorrectly recovered, if CTR, OFB, and CFB modes are used. Those three modes operate like stream ciphers where any loss in the keystream string results in a loss of synchronization.
- In CBC mode, the encryption ciphertext block C_{j-1} is used to encrypt plaintext block C_j, $j = 2, \ldots, N$. If ciphertext block C_i is lost, then the decryption of the subsequent ciphertext blocks is performed as: $B_i = Dec_K\left(C_{i+1}\right) \oplus C_{i-1}$, $B_{i+1} = Dec_K\left(C_{i+2}\right) \oplus C_{i+1}, \ldots, B_{N-1} = Dec_K\left(C_N\right) \oplus C_{N-1}$. Because of a jump in ciphertexts, $B_i = Dec_K\left(C_{i+1}\right) \oplus C_{i-1}$ is very likely to be an incorrect name. Therefore, the name with index i is missing in the recipient list and the names of index greater than i are unlikely to be correctly recovered, if CBC mode is used.

Problem 8.2

Recall that CFB mode processes segments of a bit-length s, which is not greater than that of a block denoted b. CFB mode operates like a stream cipher in which the leftmost s bits of keystream block I_j are XORed with plaintext segment $B_j^{\#}$ to produce the ciphertext segment $B_j^{\#}$. Assuming that b is a multiple of s, let $q = \lceil b/s \rceil$. Keystream blocks are computed as follows:

$I_1 = IV = IV_1 \| IV_2 \| \ldots \| IV_q$, where $IV_{i=1,\ldots,q}$ are s-bits segments of IV.

$I_2 = LSB_{b-s}(I_1) \| C_1^{\#} = IV_2 \| IV_3 \| \ldots \| IV_q \| C_1^{\#}$

$I_3 = LSB_{b-s}(I_2) \| C_2^{\#} = IV_3 \| IV_4 \| \ldots \| C_1^{\#} \| C_2^{\#}$

...

$I_{q+1} = LSB_{b-s}(I_q) \| C_q^{\#} = C_1^{\#} \| C_2^{\#} \| \ldots \| C_q^{\#}$

$I_{q+2} = LSB_{b-s}(I_{q+1}) \| C_{q+1}^{\#} = C_2^{\#} \| C_3^{\#} \| \ldots \| C_q^{\#} \| C_{q+1}^{\#}$

...

1) Error-propagation resistance

In CFB mode, if the ciphertext segment $C_i^{\#}$ is altered, then the plaintext segment $B_i^{\#}$ is unlikely to be correctly recovered. The keystream block I_{i+1}, used to decrypt the subsequent ciphertext segment $C_{i+1}^{\#}$ is computed as: $I_{i+1} = LSB_{b-s}(I_i) \| C_i^{\#}$, which differs from the one used at encryption step. The segment decryptions are unlikely to produce the original plaintext segments as long as the errored ciphertext segment $C_i^{\#}$ is present inside keystream blocks subsequent to I_i. Now, let us see how the segment $C_i^{\#}$ is left-shifted in the subsequent keystream blocks $I_{i+2}, I_{i+3}, \ldots$ until it disappears. Instead of string concatenation, integer representation of block is used for convenience.

$I_{i+1} = LSB_{b-s}(I_i) * 2^s + C_i^{\#}$

$I_{i+2} = LSB_{b-s}(I_{i+1}) * 2^s + C_{i+1}^{\#} = LSB_{b-s}(LSB_{b-s}(I_i) * 2^s + C_i^{\#}) * 2^s + C_{i+1}^{\#}$

In block I_{i+2}, the errored segment $C_i^{\#}$ is left-shifted with s positions.

$I_{i+3} = LSB_{b-s}(I_{i+2}) * 2^s + C_{i+2}^{\#} = LSB_{b-s}(LSB_{b-s}(LSB_{b-s}(I_i) * 2^s + C_i^{\#}) * 2^s + C_{i+1}^{\#}) * 2^s + C_{i+2}^{\#}$

In block I_{i+3}, the errored segment $C_i^{\#}$ is left-shifted with $2s$ positions. The shifting process continues until the segment $C_i^{\#}$ exits on the left. Let $q = \lceil b/s \rceil$. After left-shifting with $q * s$ positions, the ciphertext segment $C_i^{\#}$ is eliminated and the synchronization resumes. Therefore, all the ciphertext segments, from $C_i^{\#}$ to $C_{i+q}^{\#}$, are unlikely to be correctly decrypted.

2) Loss-propagation resistance

After decrypting ciphertext segment $C_{i-1}^{\#}$, the recipient computes keystream block I_i as $I_i = LSB_{b-s}(I_{i-1}) * 2^s + C_{i-1}^{\#}$. If the ciphertext segment $C_i^{\#}$ is lost, then the plaintext segment $B_i^{\#}$ is missing in the plaintext recovered by recipient. Then, the recipient receives ciphertext segment $C_{i+1}^{\#}$, while it was waiting for segment $C_i^{\#}$. Thus, it is unlikely to recover plaintext segment $B_{i+1}^{\#}$. Then, keystream block I_{i+1} is computed as: $I_{i+1} = LSB_{b-s}(LSB_{b-s}(I_{i-1}) * 2^s + C_{i-1}^{\#}) * 2^s + C_{i+1}^{\#}$, in which $C_i^{\#}$ is missing (i.e. there is gap in the sequence of ciphertext segments present in the stream block); thus, it is unlikely to produce plaintext segment $B_i^{\#}$ or $B_{i+1}^{\#}$. After $q = \lceil b/s \rceil - 1$ incorrect decryptions, there is no ciphertext segment gap in subsequent keystream blocks and thus the resynchronization resumes on recipient side, ciphertext segment $C_i^{\#}$ is not treated (because it has not been received), ciphertext segments $C_{i+1}^{\#}$ to $C_{i+q}^{\#}$ are unlikely to decrypt to correct plaintext segments, and the decryption is one-segment behind the encryption, i.e. $C_{i+q+j}^{\#}$ is decrypted as it if was $B_{i+q+j-1}^{\#}$.

Problem 8.3

Let $M_j^1, j = 1, \ldots, n^1$, and $M_j^2, j = 1, \ldots, n^2$, denote blocks of plaintexts M_1 and M_2, respectively. Let $C_j^1, j = 1, \ldots, n^1$, and C_j^2, $j = 1, \ldots, n^2$, denote blocks of ciphertexts C^1 and C^2, respectively; where n_1 and n^2 denote the numbers of blocks of M_1 and M_2, respectively. Without loss of generality, assume that both plaintexts are of a length multiple of that of a block.

Recall that given a plaintext of m blocks, the ciphertext blocks are computed as follows:

If CTR is used, $C_j = B_j \oplus O_j, O_j = Enc_K(Cnt_j), \forall j, 1 \le j \le m$.

If OFB is used, $C_j = B_j \oplus O_j, O_j = Enc_K(I_j), \forall j, 1 \le j \le m, I_1 = IV, I_j = O_{j-1}$.

Therefore, the ciphertext blocks in both modes are computed as $C_j = B_j \oplus O_j$, $\forall\, j,\ 1 \leq j \leq m$. Both modes differ only in how keystream blocks $O_{j=1,\dots,m}$ are computed.

If two plaintexts M_1 and M_2 are encrypted with the same counter or the same IV, then:

$$C_j^1 = B_j^1 \oplus O_j,\ j = 1, \dots, n^1$$
$$C_j^2 = B_j^2 \oplus O_j,\ j = 1, \dots, n^2.$$

Let $m = \min\left(n^1, n^2\right)$. XORing both plaintexts yields:

$$C_j^1 \oplus C_j^2 = \left(B_j^1 \oplus O_j\right) \oplus \left(B_j^2 \oplus O_j\right) = B_j^1 \oplus B_j^2,\ j = 1, \dots, m$$

Therefore, if CTR or OFB modes are used to encrypt two plaintexts with the same counter or the same IV, the adversary can derive the XOR of both plaintexts, which is particularly damaging, if plaintexts are messages in natural language.

Problem 8.4

In this problem, we consider a brute-force attack against OFB mode to disclose the key. The adversary is given a plaintext–ciphertext pair of at least two plaintext blocks.

By design of OFB, $C_1 = B_1 \oplus Enc_K(IV)$, $C_2 = B_2 \oplus Enc_K\left(Enc_K(IV)\right), \dots$, where $B_{i=1,2,\dots}$ are plaintext blocks and $C_{i=1,2,\dots}$, the corresponding ciphertext blocks.

a) Case 1: IV is known to the adversary
From the first ciphertext block and its ciphertext, the following is inferred:

$$C_1 = B_1 \oplus Enc_K(IV)$$

$$C_1 \oplus B_1 = Enc_K(IV) \tag{a}$$

Since the IV is known, the adversary has to find a key such that the encryption of the IV yields $C_1 \oplus B_1$, which is known. With a brute-force attack, a maximum of 2^n keys may be tested, where n denotes the bit-length of the key.

b) Case 2: IV is unknown to the adversary
Using the second ciphertext block and its ciphertext, the following is inferred:

$$C_2 = B_2 \oplus Enc_K\left(Enc_K(IV)\right) \qquad C_2 \oplus B_2 = Enc_K\left(Enc_K(IV)\right)$$

Then, applying the block cipher decryption yields:

$$Dec_K\left(C_2 \oplus B_2\right) = Dec_K\left(Enc\left(Enc_K(IV)\right)\right) = Enc_K(IV) \tag{b}$$

Substitution of (a) in (b) yields:

$$Dec_K\left(C_2 \oplus B_2\right) = C_1 \oplus B_1$$

Next, the adversary has to find a key such that the decryption of the $C_2 \oplus B_2$ yields $C_1 \oplus B_1$, which are known. With a brute-force attack, a maximum of 2^n keys may be tested.

Consequently, making the IV secret does not result in a more complex brute-force attack to disclose the key in OFB mode.

Problem 8.5

The malicious task manager knows that the format of the ciphertext is composed of three blocks C_1, C_2, and C_3, where C_1 is the encryption of the task manager ID, C_2 is the encryption of the participating engineer's ID, and C_3 is the encryption of the number of hours. Since ECB mode is used, the encryption of any engineer's ID produces the same ciphertext block in all the encrypted participation declarations. Let C_{2_mal} be the ciphertext of the malicious engineer's ID. Such a ciphertext bock appear in all the encrypted messages related to the malicious engineer. With C_{2_mal} known, the malicious engineer has just to intercept ciphertexts, between servers, and replace the second ciphertext block of the intercepted ciphertexts by C_{2_mal} and the number of hours will count for him/her.

To discover the ciphertext associated with his/her ID, the malicious engineer knows that task managers used to send participation declarations on Friday before 6:00 p.m., but the server 1 accepts declarations up to Friday midnight. To exploit such a knowledge, he/she sends (for some weeks) his/her declarations late, say on Friday 11:00 p.m., and intercepts the ciphertexts between the servers. After some ciphertext interceptions, he/she can infer, at a high probability, the encryption of his/her ID, which is located in the first block of the ciphertexts. Then, he/she can change the second ciphertext blocks in some messages between servers.

Problem 8.6

Consider the encryption, using CBC-CS1 mode, of a plaintext B of m blocks, where the last block B_m^* is of a bit-length d less than the block length n. Block B_m is padded with $0^{(n-d)}$; then, CBC encryption is applied to m complete blocks to yield ciphertext blocks $C_1, ..., C_m$.

Write C_{m-1} as $C_{m-1} = C_{m-1}^* \| C_{m-1}^{**}$, where C_{m-1}^* is of a bit-length of d and C_{m-1}^{**} of a bit-length of $n - b$.

By design of CBC encryption,

$$C_m = Enc_K \left(B_m \oplus C_{m-1} \right) = Enc_K \left(\left(B_m^* \| 0^{(n-d)} \right) \oplus C_{m-1} \right)$$

$$= Enc_K \left(\left(B_m^* \oplus C_{m-1}^* \| 0^{(n-d)} \oplus C_{m-1}^{**} \right) \right) = Enc_K \left(\left(B_m^* \oplus C_{m-1}^* \| C_{m-1}^{**} \right) \right).$$

In case of non-alteration of the ciphertext, the decryption of the last block using CBC-CS1 is as follows:

$$Dec_K \left(C_m \right) = Dec_K \left(Enc_K \left(\left(B_m^* \oplus C_{m-1}^* \| C_{m-1}^{**} \right) \right) \right) = \left(B_m^* \oplus C_{m-1}^* \| C_{m-1}^{**} \right)$$

Thus, $Z^* = B_m^* \oplus C_{m-1}^*$ and $Z^{**} = C_{m-1}^{**}$.

Then, by addition, $Z^* \oplus C_{m-1}^* = \left(B_m^* \oplus C_{m-1}^* \right) \oplus C_{m-1}^* = B_m^*$. Therefore, the last (incomplete) block is recovered correctly. □

Problem 8.7

We need to prove the correctness of XTS-AES at two levels: block and data unit encryption levels.

1) Correctness of XTS-AES block encryption

In the encryption procedure, the ciphertext is produced as follows:

$C = AES\_Enc \left(K_1, P \oplus A \right) \oplus A$, where $A = AES\_Enc \left(K_2, T \right) \times \alpha^j$

Assuming no alteration of the ciphertext block and given that T and j are the same on both sides, $A = AES\_Enc \left(K_2, T \right) \otimes \alpha^j$ is the same on both sides.

Let P' denote the result of the block decryption procedure. By substitution,

$$P' = AES\_Dec \left(K_1, C \oplus A \right) \oplus A$$

$$= AES\_Dec \left(K_1, \left(AES\_Enc \left(K_1, P \oplus A \right) \oplus A \right) \oplus A \right) \oplus A$$

$$= AES\_Dec \left(K_1, AES\_Enc \left(K_1, P \oplus A \right) \right) \oplus A = \left(P \oplus A \right) \oplus A = P$$

Therefore, the XTS-AES block encryption is correct.

2) Correctness of XTS-AES data unit encryption

- If the length of data unit P is a multiple of 128 bits, then P is split into m 128-bit blocks $(P_0, ..., P_{m-1})$ and an empty block P_m, such that $128m = len(P)$. From the data unit encryption algorithm, we can easily derive that each 128-bit plaintext block is encrypted as a 128-bit ciphertext block. The final ciphertext is $C_0 \| ... \| C_{m-1}$, with $C_i = XTS\_AES\_Block\_Encryption \left(K, P_i, T, i \right)$, $0 \le i \le m - 1$. Since the XTS-AES block cipher is correct, the data unit decryption procedure returns the plaintext blocks $P_0 \| ... \| P_{m-1}$, which is equal to the plaintext P.

- If the last block P_m is not empty and of a bit-length b, less than 128, we need to prove the correctness of the algorithm for the last two blocks. The focus is on step 2.4 in encryption and decryption procedures.

  Let $LMB_b(A)$ and $RMB_b(A)$ denote the leftmost and the rightmost d bits of block A, respectively.

  Let $B\_Enc()$ and B_Dec be abbreviations of $XTS\_AES\_Block\_Encrytion()$ and $XTS\_AES\_Block\_Decrytion$, respectively.

  Assuming no alteration of ciphertext, $b = len\left(P_m \right) = len \left(C_m \right); 0 < b < 128$.

  Data unit Encryption procedure produces the following ciphertext blocks:

  $$C_m = LMB_b \left(B\_Enc \left(K, P_{m-1}, T, m-1 \right) \right)$$

  $$C_{m-1} = B\_Enc \left(K, \left(P_m \| RMB_{128-b} \left(B\_Enc \left(K, P_{m-1}, T, m-1 \right) \right) \right), T, m \right)$$

  Data unit decryption procedure performs the following computations:

  $$P_m' = LMB_b \left(B\_Dec \left(K, C_{m-1}, T, m \right) \right) \tag{a}$$

  $$P_{m-1}' = B\_Dec \left(K, \left(C_m \| RMB_{128-b} \left(B\_Dec \left(K, C_{m-1}, T, m \right) \right) \right), T, m-1 \right) \tag{b}$$

By substitution, (a) becomes: $P'_m =$

$$LMB_b\left(B\_Dec\left(K,\left[\left[B\_Enc\left(K,\left(P_m \| RMB_{128-b}\left(B\_Enc\left(K,P_{m-1},T,m-1\right)\right)\right),T,m\right]\right],T,m\right)\right)$$

$$= LMB_b\left(P_m \| RMB_{128-b}\left(B\_Enc\left(K,P_{m-1},T,m-1\right)\right)\right) = P_m$$

By substitution, (b) becomes:

$$P'_{m-1} = B\_Dec\left(K,\left(\begin{array}{l}\left[LMB_b\left(B\_Enc\left(K,P_{m-1},T,m-1\right)\right)\right]\\ \| RMB_{128-b}\left(B\_Dec\left(K,\left[B\_Enc\left(K,\left(P_m \| RMB_{128-b}\left(B\_Enc\left(K,P_{m-1},T,m-1\right)\right)\right),T,m\right],T,m\right)\right)\end{array}\right),T,m-1\right)$$

$$= B\_Dec\left(K,\left(\left[LMB_b\left(B\_Enc\left(K,P_{m-1},T,m-1\right)\right)\right]\| RMB_{128-b}\left(\left[\left(P_m \| RMB_{128-b}\left(B\_Enc\left(K,P_{m-1},T,m-1\right)\right)\right)\right]\right)\right),T,m-1\right)$$

$$= B\_Dec\left(K,\left(B\_Enc\left(K,P_{m-1},T,m-1\right)\right),T,m-1\right) = P_{m-1}.$$

Therefore, the decryption of the ciphertext produces the initial plaintext. □

Problem 8.8

Eve's chosen-plaintext attack may be performed as follows:
- Using CBC mode, the response P_{Alice} is encrypted as $C_{toBob} = Enc_K\left(IV_0 \oplus P_{Alice}\right)$. Eve intercepts C_{toBob} and IV_0.
- Eve knows that the next IV to be used by Alice is IV_1. She presumes that Alice's response is "Yes" and she wants to confirm her suspicion. She prepares a message $m = IV_1 \oplus IV_0 \oplus' Yes'$ and asks Alice to encrypt the message m.
- Alice encrypts message m using IV IV_1 and sends a ciphertext $C_{toEve} = Enc_K\left(IV_1 \oplus (IV_1 \oplus IV_0 \oplus' Yes')\right)$.
- On reception of C_{toEve}, which is equal to C_{toBob}, Eve easily infers that Alice's response was "Yes", which is a break in confidentiality property.

Notes

1 *Seed* is the initialization parameter of a PRNG. Pseudorandom number generation is addressed in Chapter 16.
2 In cryptography, a codebook is a lookup table for coding and decoding; each word has one string, which replaces it. Like a codebook, ECB mode associates a ciphertext to each plaintext block.
3 Block alteration means presence of bit transformations (e.g. "0" becomes "1" or "1" becomes "0").
4 Capacities required to save ciphertexts on storage devices or to transmit them.
5 Padding is used only to perform ciphertext computation and it does not impact the bit-length of the produced ciphertext.
6 FF2 has not been approved by NIST, because of its vulnerability. FF3-1 is a revision of FF3 mode.
7 It's important to distinguish between symbols and their representation. The same symbol has several representations, depending on the chosen base.
8 The IV value is used once to encrypt/decrypt a set of blocks of the plaintext/ciphertext, while a (different) tweak value is used in each block encryption/decryption. That is a reason to use distinct terms.
9 When the chosen base is greater than 10, a space character is used to separate numerals.
10 "Data unit" as defined above is specific to XTS-AES mode. A data unit does not necessarily correspond to a physical or logical block on a storage device. The mapping between data units and data on storage device is implementation-dependent and is out of the scope of XTS-AES mode.
11 2^{64} limit is for thwarting birthday attack.
12 2^{20} limit is for interoperability of XTS-AES implementations.
13 For any mode of operation, if there are any bit errors in a ciphertext block, then the decryption of that ciphertext block is very unlikely to be correct.
14 Sending IVs or counters results in a vulnerability in the mode of operation.
15 Some modes of operation make use only of the encryption operation of the underlying block cipher to encrypt plaintexts and to decrypt ciphertexts.
16 Modes of operation, which generate a bit string that is XORed with the plaintext (respectively the ciphertext) to produce the ciphertext (respectively the plaintext), provide techniques (in addition to those presented in Chapter 6) to build stream ciphers.

References

1 Goldwasser, S. and Micali, S. (1984). Probabilistic encryption. Journal of Computer and System Sciences 28: 270–299.

2 Dworkin, M. (2001). Recommendation for block cipher modes of operation methods and techniques, special publication 800-38A. NIST. National Institute for Standards and Technology.

3 Dworkin, M. (2019). Recommendation for block cipher modes of operation: methods for format-preserving encryption, special publication 800-38G. NIST. National Institute for Standards and Technology.

4 Dworkin, M. (2010). Recommendation for block cipher modes of operation: three variants of ciphertext stealing for CBC mode, addendum to NIST special publication 800-38A. NIST. National Institute of Standards and Technology.

5 IEEE. (2018). IEEE standard for cryptographic protection of data on block-oriented storage devices, IEEE Std 1619™-2018. Institute of Electrical and Electronics Engineers. IEEE.

6 Liskov, M., Rivest, R., and Wagner, D. (2002). Tweakable block ciphers. Journal of Cryptology 24: 588–613.

9

Block Cipher Modes of Operation for Authentication and Confidentiality

In the previous chapter, we presented the modes of operation of block ciphers to provide confidentiality guarantees. Another security property of prime importance is integrity. Indeed, in the event an adversary alters a message or a storage device content, the decryption operation cannot detect any alteration. Therefore, message authentication codes or other techniques are required to preserve data integrity. To provide confidentiality and integrity guarantees based on block ciphers, the NIST approved a set of modes of operation for block ciphers, which are discussed in this chapter. They include (see Figure 9.1):

- Five modes of operation for confidentiality and authenticity guarantees: CCM, GCM, KW, KWP, and TKW.
- Two modes of operation for authenticity guarantees only: CMAC and GMAC.

All these modes provide capabilities to generate and verify message tags. In addition to approved modes of operation of block ciphers, two other algorithms are useful to authenticate messages:

- AES-GCM-SIV [1] is an extension of GCM, which is resistant to IV misuse.
- ChaCha20-Poly1305 is a scheme recommended to build authenticated encryption for TLS implementation.

Notice that authentication, addressed in this chapter, means message authenticity and not the authentication of the entity sending a message. Entity authentication is addressed in Chapter 15.

9.1   Introduction

Definition 9.1 Data authenticity: *it is a property to indicate that the data originated from its purported source.*

Definition 9.2 Authenticated encryption: *it is a cryptography scheme that provides guarantees to data confidentiality and authenticity verification.*

Definition 9.3 Associated data (*also called* **additional authentication data**): *it may be any bit string (including a MAC address, an IP addresses, a port numbers, a user name, an application name or a protocol title), which is used in data authenticity verification.*

Definition 9.4 Authenticated encryption/decryption with associatedencryption/decryption with associated data"[1] data (AEAD): *it is an authenticated encryption/decryption in which additional data is used to authenticity verification.*

Definition 9.5 Nonce misuse-resistant AEAD: *it is an authenticated-encryption scheme in which encrypting different plaintexts with the same nonce will reveal nothing to adversary.*

Notations: the same notations are used in Chapters 8 and 9.

Cryptography: Algorithms, Protocols, and Standards for Computer Security, First Edition. Zoubir Mammeri.
© 2024 John Wiley & Sons, Inc. Published 2024 by John Wiley & Sons, Inc.

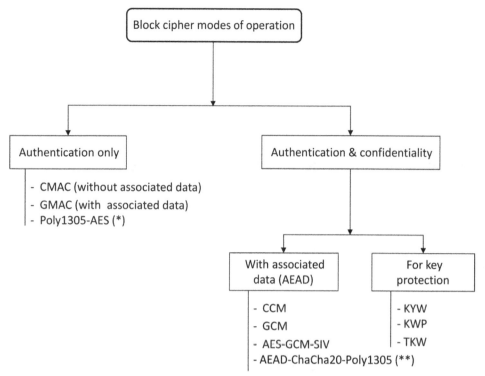

(*) Poly1305-AES is not yet approved as a block cipher mode of operation.
(**) ChaCha20 is a stream cipher, not a block cipher.

Figure 9.1   Block cipher modes of operation for authentication and confidentiality.

9.2   Block Cipher Modes of Operation for Confidentiality and Authentication

9.2.1   Authenticated Encryption and AEAD Algorithms

9.2.1.1   Approaches to Data Authentication

When only confidentiality is provided (using the modes mentioned above), the recipient of a ciphertext performs the decryption whatever the ciphertext content may be. In the event, the ciphertext has been forged by an adversary, the recipient recovers a plaintext that has not been sent by his/her partner, which may result in making inappropriate decisions. Authenticated decryption is a means to verify the integrity of the plaintext before using it.

Dominant approaches to provide data authenticity guarantees make use of *authentication*[2] *tag*, known as *Message Authentication Codes* (MACs). There also is another approach, which relies on spreading the authenticity information along the entire ciphertext (see Key-wrapping modes in Section 9.2.7).

As illustrated by Figure 9.2, there exist three basic approaches to authenticated encryption using a MAC, which differ in when the MAC is generated:

- *Encrypt-and-MAC* approach: a tag is produced using the plaintext and the latter is encrypted without the MAC. The same key is used both in encryption and in tag generation. Both operations may be performed in parallel. The recipient must decrypt the ciphertext and generate the MAC to know if the ciphertext has been altered or not. The MAC is generated only from the plaintext and it is not encrypted, it may leak information about the plaintext.
- *MAC-then-Encrypt* approach: first, the MAC is generated, then the plaintext and the tag are encrypted together. Thus, the encrypted plaintext and tag are combined in a single ciphertext. This approach does not provide integrity to the ciphertext as does the MAC-and-Encrypt approach. Being encrypted together with a plaintext, the MAC does not leak information about the plaintext.
- *Encrypt-then-MAC* approach: first, the plaintext is encrypted, then, a MAC is generated from the ciphertext. Often the encryption and authentication keys are distinct and derived from a master key. This approach provides integrity to both plaintext and ciphertext. The MAC does not leak information about the plaintext.

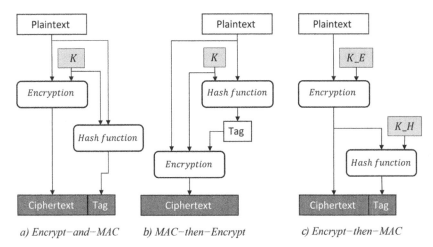

a) *Encrypt−and−MAC*   b) *MAC−then−Encrypt*   c) *Encrypt−then−MAC*

Figure 9.2   Different approaches to authenticated encryption.

Standard algorithms for authenticated encryption (such as CMAC, CCM, and GCM), which are presented in the sequel, are Encrypt-then-MAC algorithms. In order to thwart attacks, it is recommended to always compute the MACs on the ciphertext and to use two distinct keys, one key for encryption and another for MAC generation.

9.2.1.2   Authenticated Encryption with Associated Data Algorithms

The purpose of associated data in encrypted-authentication algorithms is to bind a ciphertext to the context where it is supposed to appear, so that the recipient can detect if a ciphertext is not used in the appropriate context and reject the ciphertext. The associated data does not necessarily have to be stored or transmitted with the ciphertext. Any context-dependent non-secret values (such as MAC address, IP address, TCP port number, user name, application name, or protocol title), that the both involved parties are able to correctly infer, can be used as associated data. In other words, the sender who can encrypt a plaintext and generate a MAC must know in which context the plaintext can be used on the recipient side and the recipient only makes use of the recovered plaintext in the agreed context and not in another. Therefore, a sender who shares a key with the recipient is prevented from accessing services or performing actions not agreed between both parties.

Example 9.1

An agenda management service is available to a group of staff members in a company. To secure communications between the members and the agenda server, a secret key is shared by all group members. To enable each group member access and update his/her agenda entry, an additional authentication data is associated to each member. Therefore, only the member holding the appropriate associated authentication data (say his/her chosen pseudo name) can encrypt and authenticate the data regarding his/her agenda entries.

9.2.1.3   Limits of Authenticated-Decryption Modes

Given a plaintext P_s, the sender encrypts it to C_s and computes a tag T_s. On the recipient side, upon the reception of a ciphertext C'_s and its MAC T'_s, the ciphertext is decrypted to produce a plaintext P_r and then the recipient computes a tag T_r for the plaintext P_r. If $T'_s = T_r$, then the recipient accepts the plaintext P_r. If $T'_s \neq T_r$, then the recipient rejects the ciphertext, because $C'_s \neq C_s$, $T_r \neq T_s$ or both. It is of paramount importance to keep in mind the following limitations when using any authenticated-encryption algorithm:

- If the MAC verification fails, then the received plaintext is definitely distinct from the original plaintext (due to ciphertext alteration) or the ciphertext has not been issued by the legitimate sender holding the shared secret key K. However, if the MAC verification succeeds, it does not necessarily mean that the ciphertext is the original one. Indeed, an attacker can alter the ciphertext and then selects randomly a MAC, which matches the modified ciphertext.

- MAC forgery attacks depend on *Tlen*, the bit-length of the MAC. The probability that the attacker randomly guesses the MAC, which matches the ciphertext he/she modified, is 2^{-Tlen}. The adversary could substitute a ciphertext for another without controlling the content by trying to find a collision (i.e. two distinct ciphertexts with the same MAC). By the birthday paradox, he/she needs to use (i.e. intercepts) at least $2^{\frac{Tlen}{2}}$. Therefore, the level of security is MAC-length-dependent. Standards recommend to use MACs with a length no smaller than 64 bits.

- Another recommendation to prevent attacks is to limit the number of MACs generated with the same key, because in case a large number of tags are generated with the same key, collisions may be observed and their exploitation may be catastrophic. The maximum number of MACs per key depends on each authenticated-encryption algorithm, as discussed in the sequel.

9.2.2 CMAC Mode of Operation

CMAC (Cipher Message Authentication Code) is an algorithm to generate and validate MACs [2]. It makes use of a block cipher (TDEA or AES). Therefore, CMAC is considered as a mode of operation of block ciphers to provide authentication guarantees (and not confidentiality). CMAC is defined with three functions:

1) *CMAC_Subkey_Generation*, which takes a block length b and a key K and returns two subkeys of bit-length b each. Parameter b is equal to 64 if TDEA cipher is used and 128 if AES is used.
2) *CMAC_MAC_Generation*, which computes a tag T given a plaintext M. It looks like CBC encryption mode, but with a single block as output and a special treatment of the last block, using two subkeys.
3) *CMAC_MAC_Verification*, which checks if the tag accompanying a plaintext is valid or not.

The algorithms of CMAC functions are given below. Figure 9.3 depicts the MAC generation procedure of CMAC.

---

function CMAC_Subkey_Generation
    input b: block cipher bit-length ($b = 64$ for TDEA and $b = 128$ for AES)
        K: key (with a bit-length complying with either AES or TDEA)
    output K_1, K_2: subkeys
    1. # R is a binary constant, which only depends on the bit-length block of
       # the underlying block cipher. R starts with sequence of "0" bits of a
       # bit-length of either 59 (for TDEA) or 120 (for AES).
       if $b = 64$, **then** $R = 0^{(59)}11011$ **else** $R = 0^{(120)}10000111$
    2. # L is a block that consists of b "0" bits encrypted with key K
       $L = Enc_K\left(0^{(b)}\right)$
    3. **if** $MSB_1(L) = 0$ **then** $K_1 = L \ll 1$
       else $K_1 = (L \ll 1) \oplus R$
    4. **if** $MSB_1\left(K_1\right) = 0$ **then** $K_2 = K_1 \ll 1$
       else $K_2 = \left(K_1 \ll 1\right) \oplus R$
    5. **return** $\left(K_1, K_2\right)$

---

function CMAC_MAC_Generation
    input b: block cipher bit-length ($b = 64$ for TDEA and $b = 128$ for AES)
        K: key (with a bit-length complying with either AES or TDEA)
        $Tlen$: MAC bit-length; P: plaintext of bit-length $Plen$
    output T: tag of bit-length $Tlen$
    1. # Generate subkeys
       $\left(K_1, K_2\right) = CMAC\_Subkey\_Generation(K, b)$
    2. # n is the number of blocks to process
       if $len(P) = 0$ **then** $n = 1$ **else** $n = \left\lceil \dfrac{len(P)}{b} \right\rceil$
    3. # Split the plaintext into n blocks $P_1, ..., P_{n-1}, P_n^*$ all the blocks but one
       # have the same length of b bits.
       # i.e. $len\left(P_i\right) = b, 1 \leq i < n$ and $0 < len\left(P_n^*\right) \leq b$
       Let $P = P_1 \| P_2 \| ... \| P_{n-1} \| P_n^*$
    4. **if** $len\left(P_n^*\right) = b$ **then** $P_n = K_1 \oplus P_n^*$
       else $j = n * b - Plen - 1; P_n = K_2 \oplus \left(P_n^* \| 1 \| 0^j\right)$
    5. $C_0 = 0^b$
    6. **for** $i = 1$ **to** n **do** $C_i = Enc_K\left(C_{i-1} \oplus P_i\right)$
    7. $T = MSB_{Tlen}\left(C_n\right)$
    8. **return** T

```
function CMAC_MAC_Verification
    input b: block cipher bit-length (b = 64 for TDE and b = 128 for AES)
          K: key (with a bit-length complying with either AES or TDEA)
          Tlen: MAC bit- length; p: plaintext; T: tag of bit-length Tlen
    output V: Decision ("Valid" or "Invalid")
    1. # Compute the tag of plaintext P
       T' = CMAC_MAC_Generation(b,K,Tlen,P)
    2. # Check if both tags are identical or not
       if T = T' then return "Valid" else return "Invalid"
```

9.2.3 CCM Mode of Operation

CCM (Counter with Cipher block chaining-Message authentication code) is an algorithm to provide confidentiality as well as authenticity of data [3]. It combines counter mode encryption (i.e. CTR mode) to provide confidentiality and cipher block chaining (CBC) to provide authenticity assurance. CCM processes blocks with a length of 128 bits. Therefore, it can be used jointly with AES, but not with TDEA whose block length is of 64 bits.

To encrypt, decrypt, and authenticate a set of plaintexts (such a set is called *key span*), CCM requires a secret key K, a block cipher, like AES, with an encryption primitive Enc_K, and a MAC bit-length $Tlen \leq 128$. To encrypt and produce a tag for a plaintext within a key span, CCM makes use of three inputs:

- p: data that need to be encrypted and authenticated. Such data is called *payload*; its bit-length is denoted *Plen*, with $Plen < 2^{67}$.
- A: associated data, which includes some information known to the recipient and that does not need confidentiality, but is used in authentication step. The bit-length of the associated data is denoted *Alen*, with $0 \leq Alen < 2^{67}$.
- N: a nonce, which is a unique value associated with each plaintext; its bit-length is denoted *Nlen*.

9.2.3.1 MAC Generation and Encryption
The tag generation and encryption algorithm is composed of four steps:

1) Represent the inputs (i.e. payload P, associated data A, and nonce N) as 128-bits blocks. Such a formatting operation is described in 9.2.3.3. Let $B_0, ..., B_r$ be the blocks representing the inputs.
2) Encrypt the blocks $B_0, ..., B_r$ and produce a tag T.
3) Use the nonce value and counter indexes to produce formatted counter blocks $Ctr_0, ..., Ctr_m$, where $m = \lceil Plen / 128 \rceil$ denotes the number of blocks of the payload; Section 9.2.3.4 describes the counter formatting function. Then, use CTR mode to produce a ciphertext $C = C_1 \parallel C_2 \parallel ... \parallel C_m$, such that $C_i = P_i \oplus Enc_K(Ctr_i), i = 1, ..., m$. $P_i, i = 1, ..., m$ denote the payload blocks. The last ciphertext block may be incomplete to match the last payload block.

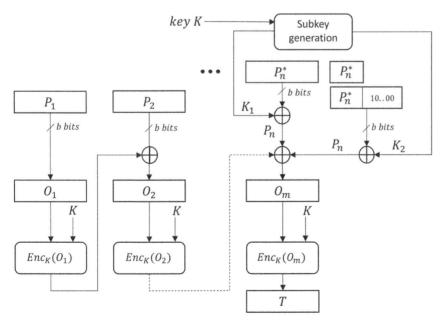

Figure 9.3 Tag generation in CMAC mode of operation.

4) The MAC T is XORed with $Enc_K(Ctr_0)$, so that only the recipient holding the secret key can recover the tag.

The MAC generation and encryption algorithm of CCM is given below and depicted in Figure 9.4.

---

function CCM_MAC_GenenerationAndEncryption
    input K: key (with a bit-length complying with a 128-bit block cipher)
        $Tlen$: MAC bit-length; N: nonce; P: payload of bit-length $Plen$
        A: associated data of bit-length $Alen$, which may be empty.
    output C, Tag: ciphertext and an encrypted tag
    1. # Represent the input (N, A, P) as r 128-bit blocks
      $(B_0, \dots, B_r) = InformationFormatting(N, A, P)$
    2. # Tag computation: encryption of nonce, associated data, and payload
      $Y_0 = Enc_K(B_0)$
      for $i = 1$ **to** r **do** $Y_i = Enc_K(B_i \oplus Y_{i-1})$
      $T = MSB_{Tlen}(Y_r)$ # T is the tag in clear
    3. # Ciphertext computation
      3.1 # Compute $m+1$ formatted counter values (m is the number of
          # blocks in the payload)
          $(Ctr_0, \dots, Ctr_m) = CounterFormatting(m, N)$
      3.2 **for** $j = 0$ **to** m **do** $S_j = Enc_K(Ctr_j)$
      3.3 $S = S_1 \| S_2 \| \dots \| S_m$
      3.4 $CC = P \oplus MSB_{len(P)}(S)$ # Encryption of payload
    4. # Encryption of the tag
      $Tag = T \oplus MSB_{Tlen}(S_0)$
    5. **return** (CC, Tag)

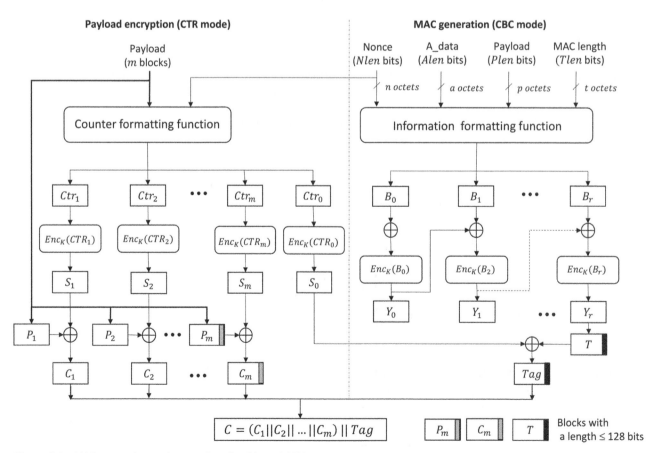

Figure 9.4 MAC generation and encryption algorithm of CCM.

9.2.3.2 MAC Verification and Decryption
MAC verification and decryption algorithm is composed of five steps:

1) Check if the received ciphertext is valid regarding the tag length. If the length of the received ciphertext, *Clen*, is less or equal to that of a valid tag, *Tlen*, the received ciphertext is discarded, because it does not contain any encrypted data.
2) Use the nonce value and counter indexes to produce formatted counter blocks $Ctr_0, ..., Ctr_m$, where m denotes the number of blocks of the payload; $m = \lceil (Clen - Tlen)/128 \rceil$. The ciphertext is interpreted as $C = C_1 \| C_2 \| ... \| C_m \| C_{m+1}$, where C_{m+1} denotes an encrypted tag with a bit-length of *Tlen*. Then, use CTR mode to produce a plaintext $P = P_1 \| P_2 \| ... \| P_m$, such that $P_i = C_i \oplus Enc_K(Ctr_i), i = 1, ..., m$. The last plaintext block may be incomplete to match the last ciphertext block.
3) Decrypt the received tag as $T = C_{m+1} \oplus MSB_{Tlen}(Enc_K(Ctr_0))$.
4) Represent the payload P, associated data A, and nonce N as 128-bits blocks, denoted $B_0, ..., B_r$, using the formatting function. Then, encrypt the blocks $B_0, ..., B_r$ and produce a tag T'.
5) Check if the received and computed tags are identical; and return either "Invalid" or "Valid" plus the payload.

MAC verification and decryption algorithm of CCM are given below.

```
function CCM_MAC_VerificationAndDecryption
    input K: key (with a bit-length complying with a 128-bit block cipher)
          Tlen: MAC bit-length; N: nonce of bit-length Nlen
          C: ciphertext of bit-length Clen; A: associated data of bit-length Alen
    output V: Decision ("Valid" or "Invalid")
           P: plaintext of bit-length Plen
    1. # Check the length of the ciphertext
       if Clen ≤ Tlen, then return "Invalid"
    2. # Payload recovery
       2.1 # Compute m + 1 formatted counter values
           m = ⌈(Clen − Tlen) / 128⌉
           (Ctr₀,...,Ctrₘ) = CounterFormatting(m, N)
       2.2 for j = 0 to m do Sⱼ = Enc_K(Ctrⱼ)
       2.3 S = S₁ ‖ S₂ ‖ ... ‖ Sₘ
       2.4 P = MSB_{Clen−Tlen}(C) ⊕ MSB_{Clen−Tlen}(S)
    3. # Recover the tag included in ciphertext
       T = LSB_{Tlen}(C) ⊕ MSB_{Tlen}(S₀)
    4. # Apply the information formatting function to produce r
       # and encrypt them to produce a tag T' of the received payload
       4.1 (B₀,...,Bᵣ) = InformationFormatting(N, A, P)
       4.2 Y₀ = Enc_K(B₀)
       4.3 for i = 1 to r do Yᵢ = Enc_K(Bᵢ ⊕ Yᵢ₋₁)
       4.4 T' = MSB_{Tlen}(Yᵣ)
    5. # Tag check
       if T' = T, then return ("Valid", P)
       else return "Invalid"
```

9.2.3.3 Information Formatting Function
The formatting function takes three bit-strings (a nonce N, an associated data A, and a payload P) and a tag length and returns a sequence of r 128-bit blocks ($B_0, ..., B_r$) as depicted in Figure 9.5. Let n, a, p, and t denote the byte-length of the nonce, the associated data, the payload, and the tag, respectively. Bit-lengths of all inputs of formatting function are multiple of 8. That is: $n = Nlen/8$, $a = Alen/8$, $p = Plen/8$, and $t = Tlen/8$. Let Q be a byte-string, which represents the payload byte-length and q, the byte-length of string Q. q is a parameter of the formatting function. For example, if $Plen = 8192$ and $q = 3$, then $Q = 1024 = 00000000\,00000100\,00000000$.

Formatting the nonce and control information
The first byte of block B_0 contains four flags: one reserved bit, one bit to indicate presence of associated data, three bits to encode the tag length as $[(t-2)/2]_3$, and three bits to encode the parameter q as $[q-1]_3$. For example, if the tag byte-length t is 16, it is represented as $[(16-2)/2]_3 = 111$.

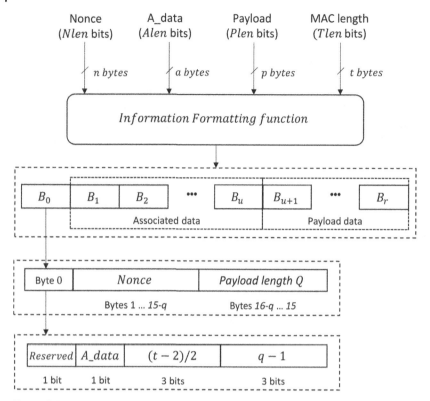

Figure 9.5 Information formatting in CCM mode.

Notice that since $q-1$ is represented on three bits, q cannot be greater than 8. Therefore, the maximum byte-length of payload is $p < 2^{8*q} < 2^{8*8}$.

The remaining 15 bytes of block B_0 are used to represent the nonce and the payload length. The nonce value is represented on $15 - q$ bytes. Notice that the parameter q bounds the nonce space, i.e. the number of distinct nonces is $2^{8*n} < 2^{8*(15-q)}$.

Formatting the associated data
The second bit of the first byte of block B_0 indicates whether associated data is present or not. If $a > 0$, then the associated data and its length are represented on u blocks $B_1, ..., B_u$. The associated-data byte-length a is represented according to three cases:

1) If $0 < a < 2^{16} - 2^8$, then a is represented as $[a]_{16}$, i.e. on two bytes.
2) If $2^{16} - 2^8 \leq a < 2^{32}$, then a is represented as 0xff || 0xfe || $[a]_{32}$, i.e. on six bytes.
3) If $2^{32} \leq a < 2^{64}$, then a is represented as 0xff || 0xff || $[a]_{64}$, i.e. on ten bytes.

Then, a is followed by the associated data. If bytes used to represent the associated data and its length are not a multiple of 128 bits, then a string of 0-bits is appended to fill the last block B_u.

Formatting the payload
The payload is represented as blocks denoted $B_{u+1}, ..., B_r$, where $r = u + \lceil p/16 \rceil$.

9.2.3.4 Counter Formatting Function

The counter formatting function takes the nonce N and $m = \left\lceil \dfrac{Plen}{128} \right\rceil$, which is the number of blocks of the payload data, and returns $m + 1$ 128-bit blocks $Ctr_0, Ctr_1, ..., Ctr_m$ formatted as follows: $Ctr_i = Flags \,||\, Nonce \,||\, i$ as depicted in Figure 9.6. A counter index i, $i = 1, ..., m$ is associated with each payload block i. Ctr_0 is used to encrypt/decrypt the tag. Counter formatting function makes use of the same formatting rules as those of information formatting described in Section 9.2.3.3.

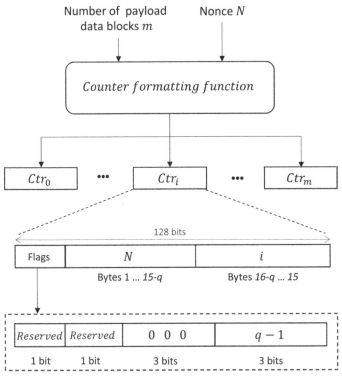

Number of payload
data blocks m Nonce N

Counter formatting function

Ctr_0 ••• Ctr_i ••• Ctr_m

128 bits

Flags	N	i
	Bytes 1 ... 15-q	Bytes 16-q ... 15

Reserved	Reserved	0 0 0	$q-1$
1 bit	1 bit	3 bits	3 bits

Figure 9.6 Counter block formatting in CCM mode.

9.2.4 GCM and GMAC Modes of Operation

GCM and GMAC are modes of operation of symmetric key block ciphers. Galois/Counter Mode (GCM) is an algorithm for authenticated encryption with associated data to be used jointly with a 128-bit block cipher such as AES [4]. GMAC makes use of the GCM operations to provide only data authenticity; it targets applications using non-confidential data, but with integrity requirements. GCM provides assurance of data confidentiality using a variation of counter mode (CTR) and it provides assurance of data authenticity using a hash function, which is defined over an extension field. Therefore, GCM and CCM differ regarding the generation and verification of tags.

9.2.4.1 GCTR Encryption Mode

As mentioned previously, GCM encryption relies on a variation of CTR mode, called GCTR, with two distinguishing features compared to the basic CTR mode: 1) the plaintext is not required to be of a length multiple of that of a block and 2) counter values are computed using a special increment function modulo 2^s defined as follows:

$$Inc_s(X) = MSB_{len(X)-s}(X) \;\|\; \left[int\left(LSB_s(X)\right) + 1 \; mod \; 2^s \right]_s$$

$Inc_s(X)$ increments the rightmost bits of bit string X and the leftmost $len(X) - s$ bits remain unchanged. In AES-GCM, the increment function is instantiated as $Inc_{32}(X)$.

GCTR algorithm is presented below and depicted in Figure 9.7.

function GCTR
    input K: Key (with a bit-length complying with a 128-bit block cipher)
        P: plaintext, a bit string; ICB: initial counter block (128 bits)
    output C: ciphertext
    1. # m is the number of blocks in bit string P . P_m^*, the last block, may be incomplete
        $m = \lceil len(X) / 128 \rceil$; Let $P = P_1 \| P_2 \| \dots \| P_{m-1} \| P_m^*$
    2. # Compute the counter blocks
        $Cnt_1 = ICB$
        for $i = 2$ **to** m **do** $Cnt_i = Inc_{32}\left(Cnt_{i-1}\right)$

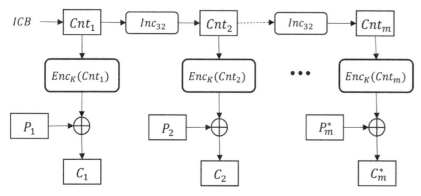

Figure 9.7 GCTR encryption mode.

> 3. # Compute the cipher blocks
> **for** $i = 1$ **to** $m-1$ **do** $C_i = P_i \oplus Enc_K(Cnt_i)$
> $C_m^* = P_m^* \oplus MSB_{len(P_m^*)}(Enc_K(Cnt_m))$
> 4. $C = C_1 \| C_2 \| \dots \| C_{m-1} \| C_m^*;$ **return** C

9.2.4.2 Hash Function of GCM

The tag is computed using the *GHash* function defined as follows:

$$GHash_H(D) = \left(D_1 \otimes H^m\right) \oplus \left(D_2 \otimes H^{m-1}\right) \oplus \dots \oplus \left(D_{m-1} \otimes H^2\right) \oplus \left(D_m \otimes H\right)$$

where H denotes the hash key; and $\otimes$ is the multiplication operation, defined over extension field $F_{2^{128}}$, with the irreducible polynomial $f(x) = x^{128} + x^7 + x^2 + x + 1$. (For more on multiplication over extension fields see Section 3.2.3). $D = D_1 \| D_2 \| \dots \| D_m$ where $D_1, D_2, \dots, D_m$ are 128-bit blocks and $m = len(D)/128$.

GCM standard provides an efficient method to implement the multiplication over the chosen finite field and its irreducible polynomial. As chosen below the multiplication algorithm only makes use of XOR and shift operations, which are very useful to speed the multiplication. The convention for interpreting strings as polynomials is little endian; i.e. the block $U = u_0 u_1 \dots u_{127}$ corresponds to the polynomial $P(U) = u_{127}x^{127} + u_{126}x^{126} + \dots + u_1 x + u_0$.

---

function GCM_Block_Multiplication
    input P, Q: two 128-bit blocks
    output Z: product
    1. Let $p_0 p_1 p_2 \dots p_{127}$ be the bit sequence of block P
    2. $Z_0 = 0^{128}$ # Z_0 is set to a string of 128 "0" bits
       $V_0 = Q; R = 11100001 \| 0^{120}$
    3. **for** $i = 0$ **to** 127 **do**
       if $p_i = 0$ **then** $Z_{i+1} = Z_i$ **else** $Z_i \oplus V_i$
       if $LSB_1(V_i) = 0$ **then** $V_{i+1} = V_i \gg 1$ **else** $V_{i+1} = (V_i \gg 1) \oplus R$
    4. **return** Z_{128}

9.2.4.3 Authenticated Encryption with GCM

To encrypt, decrypt, and authenticate a set of plaintexts (such a set is called *key span*), GCM requires a secret key K, a block cipher, like AES, with an encryption primitive Enc_K, and a MAC bit-length $Tlen \le 128$. To encrypt and produce a tag for a plaintext in the key span, GCM makes use of three inputs:

- P: data that needs to be encrypted and authenticated. Such data is called *payload* and its bit-length is denoted *Plen*. The standard requires that $Plen \le 2^{39} - 256$.
- A: associated authenticated data, which includes some information known to the recipient and which does not need confidentiality, but it is used in the authentication step. The bit-length of the associated data is denoted *Alen*. The associated data may be an empty bit-string. GCM requires that $Alen \le 2^{64} - 1$.

- *IV*: an initialization vector, which is a unique value (i.e. a nonce) associated with each plaintext; its bit-length is denoted *IVlen*. The latter may take a value of 64, 96, 128, or 160. The total number of invocations of the authenticated-encryption algorithm shall not exceed 2^{32}, including all IV lengths, with the same key.

The algorithm of encryption and Tag generation of GCM is given below and also depicted in Figure 9.8.

---

function GCM_Authenticated_Encryption
    input K: key (with a bit-length complying with a 128-bit block cipher)
        P: plaintext; A: associated authentication data
        IV: initialization vector; *Tlen*: tag bit-length ($\leqslant 128$)
    output C: ciphertext (of same length than that of plaintext)
        T: tag (of *Tlen* bits)

1. $H = Enc_K\left(0^{128}\right)$
2. J_0 is computed to serve as the initial value of the counter in CTR mode
    if $len(IV) = 96$, **then** $J_0 = IV \parallel 0^{31} \parallel 1$
    if $len(IV) \neq 96$, **then**
        $s = 128 * \lceil len(IV) \rceil / 128 - len(IV)$
        $J_0 = GHash_H\left(IV \parallel 0^{s+64} \parallel \left[len(IV)\right]_{64}\right)$
3. # Compute the ciphertext C
    $C = GCTR_K\left(Inc_{32}(J_0), P\right)$
4. # u and v denote the lengths of the incomplete ciphertext block and
    # associated data if applicable, respectively
    $u = 128 * \lceil len(C)/128 \rceil - len(C); v = 128 * \lceil len(A)/128 \rceil - len(A)$
5. # Compute and encrypt the tag
    $S = GHash_H\left(A \parallel 0^v \parallel C \parallel 0^u \parallel \left[len(A)\right]_{64} \parallel \left[len(C)\right]_{64}\right)$
    $T = MSB_{Tlen}\left(GCTR_K(J_0, S)\right)$
6. **return** (C, T)

9.2.4.4 Authenticated Decryption with GCM

The operations of the authenticated decryption are similar to those of encryption. Below is the algorithm of the GCM authenticated decryption.

---

function GCM_Authenticated-Decryption
    input K: key (with a bit-length complying with a 128-bit block cipher)
        C: ciphertext; T: tag (of *Tlen* bits); *Tlen*: tag bit-length ($\leqslant 128$)
        A: associated authentication data; IV: initialization vector
    output V: Decision ("Valid" or "Invalid")
        P: plaintext (of the same length than that of ciphertext)

1. $H = Enc_K\left(0^{128}\right)$
2. # J_0 is computed to serve as the initial value of the counter
    if $len(IV) = 96$, **then** $J_0 = IV \parallel 0^{31} \parallel 1$
    if $len(IV) \neq 96$, **then**
        $s = 128 * \lceil len(IV)/128 \rceil - len(IV)$
        $J_0 = GHash_H\left(IV \parallel 0^{s+64} \parallel \left[len(IV)\right]_{64}\right)$
3. # Compute the plaintext P
    $P = GCTR_K\left(Inc_{32}(J_0), C\right)$
4. # u and v denote the length of the incomplete ciphertext block and
    # associated data if applicable, respectively
    $u = 128 * \lceil len(C)/128 \rceil - len(C); v = 128 * \lceil len(A)/128 \rceil - len(A)$
5. # Compute and encrypt the tag
    $S = GHash_H\left(A \parallel 0^v \parallel C \parallel 0^u \parallel \left[len(A)\right]_{64} \parallel \left[len(C)\right]_{64}\right)$
    $T' = MSB_{Tlen}\left(GCTR_K(J_0, S)\right)$
6. **if** $T' = T$, **then return** ("Valid", P) **else return** "Invalid"

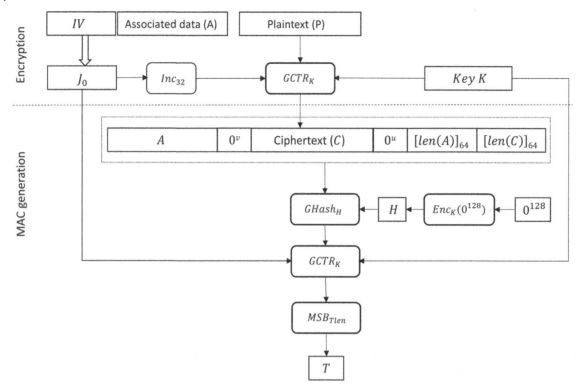

Figure 9.8 GCM authenticated encryption.

9.2.4.5 GMAC Mode

When GCM is used for guaranteeing data authenticity only, the restricted GCM is called GMAC (Galois Message Authentication Code). The same functions are used in both modes as depicted in Figure 9.9.

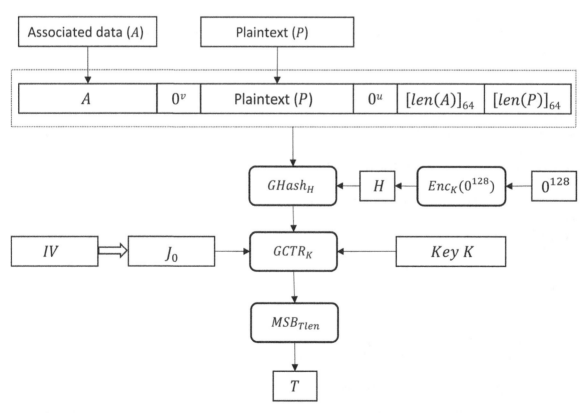

Figure 9.9 GMAC tag generation.

9.2.4.6 Forbidden Attack Against GCM with Repeated IV

GCM mode is vulnerable to an IV value repeated, by mistake, with the same key. The attack against GCM, known as *forbidden attack*, aims to recover the authentication key, denoted H, and then exploits such a finding to forge tags, which will be validated by the recipient. Recall H that is computed as $H = Enc_K\left(0^{128}\right)$ and in consequence, it is assumed to be unknown to adversaries. Notice that the forbidden attack aims to recover the authentication key and not the encryption key. In order to simplify understanding of the attack, consider a scenario where the message sender makes use of AES-GCM to generate 128-bit tags for two one-block messages with the same IV and does not make use of associated data. Since AES is used as the underlying block cipher and the tag bit-length, denoted *Tlen*, is equal to 128, for any integer J and a bit string S:

$$MSB_{Tlen}\left(GCTR_K(J,S)\right) = GCTR_K(J,S)$$

If S is a one-block string, then $GCTR_K(J,S) = S \oplus Enc_K(J)$

Given two plaintexts $M^{(1)}$ and $M^{(2)}$, their encrypted tags $T^{(1)}$ and $T^{(2)}$ are computed as follows:

$$T^{(1)} = GCTR_K\left(J_0,\ S^{(1)}\right) = S^{(1)} \oplus Enc_K\left(J_0\right)$$

$$T^{(2)} = GCTR_K\left(J_0,\ S^{(2)}\right) = S^{(2)} \oplus Enc_K\left(J_0\right)$$

where:

J_0 is the initial counter derived from the IV

$C^{(1)} = GCTR_K\left(J_0+1,\ M^{(1)}\right)$ and $C^{(2)} = GCTR_K\left(J_0+1,\ M^{(2)}\right)$ are the ciphertexts.

$$S^{(1)} = GHash_H\left(C^{(1)} \parallel 0^u \parallel \left[len(A)\right]_{64} \parallel \left[len\left(C^{(1)}\right)\right]_{64}\right)$$

$$S^{(2)} = GHash_H\left(C^{(2)} \parallel 0^u \parallel \left[len(A')\right]_{64} \parallel \left[len\left(C^{(2)}\right)\right]_{64}\right)$$

$S^{(1)}$ and $S^{(2)}$ are the tags, in cleartext. Assuming that plaintexts $M^{(1)}$ and $M^{(2)}$ are one-block each and no associated data is used:

$$S^{(1)} = GHash_H\left(C^{(1)} \parallel [0]_{64} \parallel [1]_{64}\right) = GHash_H\left(C^{(1)} \parallel [1]_{128}\right)$$

$$S^{(2)} = GHash_H\left(C^{(2)} \parallel [0]_{64} \parallel [1]_{64}\right) = GHash_H\left(C^{(2)} \parallel [1]_{128}\right)$$

For both tags, the input of function $GHash_H$ is a two-block string.

Tags $S^{(1)}$ and $S^{(2)}$ are computed with the $GHash_H$ function as follows:

$$S^{(1)} = \left(C^{(1)} \otimes H^2\right) \oplus \left(1 \otimes H^1\right) = \left(C^{(1)} \otimes H^2\right) \oplus H \tag{9.1}$$

$$S^{(2)} = \left(C^{(2)} \otimes H^2\right) \oplus \left(1 \otimes H^1\right) = \left(C^{(2)} \otimes H^2\right) \oplus H \tag{9.2}$$

The encrypted tags and ciphertexts are known to the adversary and both plaintexts are encrypted with the same IV. Thus,

$$T^{(1)} \oplus T^{(2)} = \left(S^{(1)} \oplus Enc_K\left(J_0\right)\right) \oplus \left(S^{(2)} \oplus Enc_K\left(J_0\right)\right) = S^{(1)} \oplus S^{(2)} \tag{9.3}$$

Substitution of (9.1) and (9.2) in (9.3) yields:

$$T^{(1)} \oplus T^{(2)} = \left(C^{(1)} \oplus C^{(2)}\right) \otimes H^2 \tag{9.4}$$

Since the function $GHash_H$ is defined over the extension field $F_{2^{128}}$ with the irreducible polynomial $f(x) = x^{128} + x^7 + x^2 + x + 1$, (9.4) can be rewritten as:

$$H^2 = \left(T^{(1)} \oplus T^{(2)}\right) * \left(C^{(1)} \oplus C^{(2)}\right)^{-1} \mod f(x) \tag{9.5}$$

$\left(C^{(1)} \oplus C^{(2)}\right)$ and $\left(T^{(1)} \oplus T^{(2)}\right)$ are constants; and H is the unknown. Finding the square root of $\left(T^{(1)} \oplus T^{(2)}\right) * \left(C^{(1)} \oplus C^{(2)}\right)^{-1}$ over $F_{2^{128}}$ yields the value of H. Notice that in the binary field, H and $-H$ are the same.

In general, the square root of an element $x \in F_{2^m}$ is defined by: $\sqrt{x} = x^{2^{m-1}}$, if $2^m - 1$ is a prime (see Corollary 3.4). Finally, H is given by the following:

$$H = \left[\left(T^{(1)} \oplus T^{(2)}\right) * \left(C^{(1)} \oplus C^{(2)}\right)^{-1}\right]^{127} mod\, f(x) \tag{9.6}$$

It is worth noticing that in general, $GHash_H$ function yields a polynomial of degree m, which depends on the number of blocks in the plaintext and the associated data. In consequence, the number of roots of the polynomial inferred from $S^{(1)} \oplus S^{(2)}$ may be high, if messages are longer than one block and/or associated data is used; and the adversary may decide which root (i.e. which authentication key H to keep) among a large set to forge tags. To increase the chance of success in choosing the correct authentication key, the adversary may need to collect many pairs of messages encrypted with the same IV, each pair providing a set of roots. Then, combining the roots yielded by all pairs helps to find a single root (i.e. the valid authentication key) that matches all the pairs. Therefore, the forbidden attack against AES-GCM is likely to succeed only if the sender either encrypts plaintexts with small sizes or frequently makes use of the same IV to generate tags.

9.2.5 AES-GCM-SIV Mode

9.2.5.1 What Does Nonce Misuse-resistance Mean?

In the nonce-based algorithms (OFB, CTR, and GCM) described above, it is assumed that the nonce value does not repeat with the same key. Such a requirement may not be fulfilled in practice because of weak randomness of some devices generating nonce values. For example, in CTR mode, if a counter value is repeated (because of a wrong counter value generation), the attacker can easily recover the XOR of two plaintexts. A second example of attack is the forbidden attack of AES-GCM (see Section 9.2.4). Therefore, those algorithms suffer vulnerability when two distinct plaintexts are (wrongly) encrypted with the same[3] key and nonce.

Nonce misuse-resistant AEADs, such as AES-GCM-SIV presented in the sequel, do not suffer the nonce-misuse vulnerability. For this class of AEADs, encrypting two plaintexts with the same nonce value only discloses whether the plaintexts were equal or not. Therefore, these algorithms are suggested in any situations where nonce uniqueness cannot be guaranteed. However, it is worth noticing that there does not yet exist a fully nonce misuse-resistant algorithm in which the nonce may repeat indefinitely without jeopardizing the security. Rather, there are bounds of nonce repetitions to provide some security levels (see Section 10.5.2).

9.2.5.2 Overview of AES-GCM-SIV Mode

AES-GCM-SIV is a nonce-misuse resistant authenticated-encryption mode, which has the property that both privacy and integrity are preserved, even if nonces are repeated. It is an improvement of AES-GCM[4] mode with the following main design differences:

- In AES-GCM, a single key K is used to compute the tag and to encrypt, while in AES-GCM-SIV, the initial key K, called master key, is used to derive two keys, K_hash (used to compute the tag) and K_msg (used to encrypt the plaintext and the tag).
- In AES-GCM, the initial counter value is computed only from the IV, while in AES-GCM-SIV, the encrypted tag is used as an initial counter value, thus providing more randomness.
- While using the same extension field $F_{2^{128}}$, AES-GCM and AES-GCM-SIV use distinct irreducible polynomials. The authors of AES-GCM-SIV showed that the computations are faster with the irreducible polynomial they chose, in particular when operations are implemented in specific hardware.
- The tag is computed with distinct hash functions: *GHash* for AES-GCM and *Polyval* for AES-GCM-SIV.
- AES-GCM authenticates the encoded associated data and the ciphertext, while AES-GCM-SIV authenticates the encoded associated data and the plaintext. In other words, AES-GCM follows the Encrypt-then-MAC approach, while AES-GCM-SIV follows the MAC-then-Encrypt approach.

The principle of AES-GCM-SIV is as follows: two keys, K_hash and K_msg, are derived from a master key K and the initial nonce. The hash key K_hash is applied to the associated data, the plaintext, and the data lengths to generate a hash, which is encrypted with the key K_msg to produce a tag. The plaintext is encrypted with the CTR mode using the key K_msg and the tag as the initial counter value. Therefore, the initial counter value is an effective nonce, which is distinct for every different initial-nonce/plaintext pair. In the event, the initial nonce repeats, the initial counter value will not repeat, if the plaintext does not repeat.

9.2.5.3 Key Derivation and Hash Functions

Key derivation function: the encryption/decryption algorithm begins by deriving two keys, a hash key, denoted K_hash and an encryption key, denoted k_msg, from a master key K and the nonce N. As shown in the AES_GCM_SIV_KeyDerivation function below, the length of the encryption key depends on the length of the master key (i.e. 128 or 256 bits).

---

function AES_GCM_SIV_KeyDerivation

    Input K: key (of a bit-length of 128 or 256)

        N: nonce (96 bits)

    output K_hash: authentication key (128 bits)

        K_msg: encryption key (128 or 256 bits)

    1. **if** $len(K) = 128$ **then** $Nb\_iter = 4$ **else** $Nb\_iter = 6$

    2. **for** $i = 0$ **to** $Nb\_iter - 1$ **do**

        # integers are in little-endian encoding

        $T_i = MSB_{64}\left(AES\_Enc_{K\_msg}\left([i]_{32} \| N\right)\right)$

    3. $K\_hash = T_0 \| T_1$

    4. **if** $len(K) = 128$ **then** $K\_msg = T_2 \| T_3$

        else $K\_msg = T_2 \| T_3 \| T_4 \| T_5$

    5. **return** $\left(K_{hash}, K_{msg}\right)$

Hash function *Polyval*

AES-GCM-SIV hash function is denoted *Polyval* and is defined as follows:

$$Polyval_H(D) = \sum_{i=1}^{m}\left(D_i \otimes H^{m-i+1} \otimes x^{-128(m-i+1)}\right)$$

where H denotes the hash key and $\otimes$ is the multiplication operation defined over extension field $F_{2^{128}}$ with the irreducible polynomial $f(x) = x^{128} + x^{127} + x^{126} + x^{121} + 1$, and $D = D_1 \| D_2 \| ... \| D_m$. $D_1, D_2, ..., D_m$ are 128-bit blocks and $m = len(D)/128$. Notice that x^{-128} can also be written as $x^{127} + x^{124} + x^{121} + x^{114} + 1$ in $F_{2^{128}}$ with $f(x) = x^{128} + x^{127} + x^{126} + x^{121} + 1$.

Differences between $Polyval_H$ and $GHash_H$ functions:

Both functions are defined over extension field $F_{2^{128}}$, but with different irreducible polynomials: $f(x) = x^{128} + x^{127} + x^{126} + x^{121} + 1$ for $Polyval_H$ and $f(x) = x^{128} + x^7 + x^2 + x + 1$ for $GHash_H$. The little-endian representation of the first polynomial is $10^{(120)}10000111$ and that of the second polynomial is $111000010^{(120)}1$. Therefore, those irreducible polynomials are the "reverse", in little-endian representation, of each other. Both functions use little-endian encoding; but they make use of different mappings to/from 128-bit strings and extension field elements. Let $U = U_0U_1U_2U_3U_4U_5U_6U_7U_8U_9U_{10}U_{11}U_{12}U_{13}U_{14}U_{15}$ be a 16-byte string. Let $U_0 = b_0b_1b_2b_3b_4b_5b_6b_7$, ..., $U_{15} = b_{120}b_{121}b_{122}b_{123}b_{124}b_{125}b_{126}b_{127}$, where b_is are bits.

$Polyval_H$ takes the least significant bit (i.e. b_7) to most significant bit (i.e. b_0) of byte U_0 to be the coefficients of x^0 to x^7, while $GHash_H$ takes them to be the coefficients of x^7 to x^0. The same mapping continues until the last byte U_{15} where $Polyval_H$ takes the least significant bit b_{127} to most significant bit b_{120} of byte U_{15} to be the coefficients of x^{120} to x^{127}, while $GHash_H$ takes them to be the coefficients of x^{127} to x^{120}.

Example 9.2

Consider the polynomial $Q(x) = x^{127} + x^{124} + x^{121} + x^{114} + 1$. $Q(x)$ is represented as $01\,00\,00\,00\,00\,00\,00\,00\,00\,00\,00\,00\,00\,00\,04\,92$ in AES-GCM-SIV and as $80\,00\,00\,00\,00\,00\,00\,00\,00\,00\,00\,00\,00\,00\,20\,49$ in AES-GCM.

9.2.5.4 Authenticated Encryption with AES-GCM-SIV

AES-GCM-SIV authenticated encryption takes a master key K of 128 or 256-bit length, a nonce N of 96-bit length, a plaintext P, and associated data A; P and A are byte strings of variable length. It returns a ciphertext C and a 128-bit tag, *Tag*. The AES-128 or AES-256 is used depending on the master key length. The authenticated encryption runs in three main steps:

1) *Key derivation*: from the master key K and the nonce N, two keys are derived: K_hash of 128-bit length and K_msg of 128 or 256-bit length.

2) *Hash generation*: the $Polyval_{K\_Hash}$ hash function takes the hash key K_hash, the padded associated data, the padded plaintext, and the data lengths $len(A)$ and $len(P)$ and returns a hash. The generated hash is encrypted with the encryption key K_msg.

3) *Plaintext encryption*: it is performed with a CTR encryption taking the key K_msg and the encrypted tag as the initial counter value. The CTR mode used in AES-GCM-SIV is very similar to that used in AES-GCM; the minor difference is in counter incrementing due to integer encoding.

The authenticated encryption of AES-GCM-SIV algorithm is given below and is illustrated by Figure 9.10.

---

function AES_GCM_SIV_CTR
    input K_msg: encryption key (of 128 or 256 bits)
        P: plaintext, a bit string no longer than 2^{36} bits
        InitialCtr: initial counter block (128 bits)
    output C: ciphertext (of the same bit-length than the plaintext)
    1. # m is the number of blocks in bit string P. $P_m^{\bullet}$, the last block can be incomplete.
        $m = \lceil len(X)\,/\,128 \rceil$; Let $P = P_1 \parallel P_2 \parallel \ldots \parallel P_{m-1} \parallel P_m^{\bullet}$
    2. # Compute the counter blocks: the initial counter block is the tag
        # with the most significant bit of the last byte set to 1. Then, the
        # counter advances by incrementing the first 32 bits.
    $Cnt_1 = InitialCtr$
    for $i = 2$ **to** m **do**
        # Convert the first four bytes of Cnt_{i-1} from little-endian encoding

---

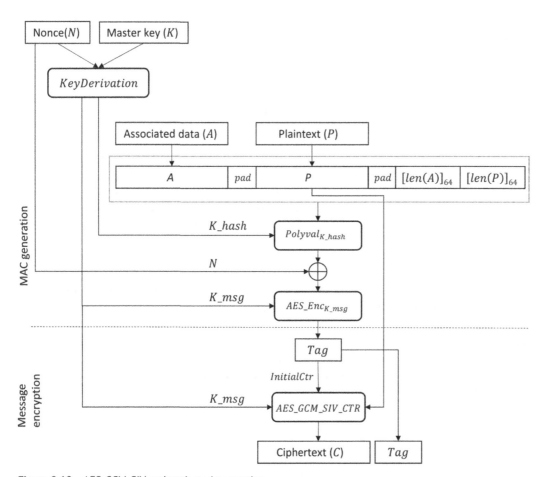

Figure 9.10 AES-GCM-SIV authenticated encryption.

to integer, convert the sum modulo 2^{32} to little-endian
encoding, and update the first four bytes of Cnt_i
$k = LittleEndian\_to\_Integer\left(MSB_{32}\left(Cnt_{i-1}\right)\right)$
$s = Integer\_to\_LittleEndian\left(k+1 \bmod 2^{32}\right)$
$Cnt_i = [s]_{32} \parallel [Cnt_{i-1}]_{96}$
3. # Compute the ciphertext blocks
    for $i = 1$ **to** $m-1$ **do** $C_i = P_i \oplus AES\_Enc_{K\_msg}\left(Cnt_i\right)$
    $C_m^* = P_m^* \oplus MSB_{len(P_m^*)}\left(AES\_Enc_{K\_msg}\left(Cnt_m\right)\right)$
4. $C = C_1 \parallel C_2 \parallel \dots \parallel C_{m-1} \parallel C_m^*$; **return** C

---

function AES_GCM_SIV_AuthenticatedEncryption
    input K: master key (of 128 or 256 bits)
        P: plaintext, a bit string no longer than 2^{36} bits
        A: associated data, a bit string no longer than 2^{36} bits
        N: nonce (of 96 bits)
    output C: ciphertext (of the same bit length than the plaintext)
        Tag: encrypted tag (of a length of 128 bits)
1. # Key derivation
   $(K\_hash, K\_msg) = AES\_GCM\_SIV\_KeyDerivation(K,N)$
2. # Tag computation (note: integers are in little-endian encoding)
   2.1 $L = [len(A)]_{64} \parallel [len(P)]_{64}$
   2.2 # pad the plaintext and associated data to multiple of 128 bits
      $P\_Pad = Right\_pad(P)$; $A\_Pad = Right\_pad(A)$
   2.3 $h = Polyval_{K\_hash}\left(A\_Pad \parallel P\_Pad \parallel L\right)$ # h is the tag in clear
   2.4 # XOR the first twelve bytes of h with the nonce
      for $i = 0$ **to** 11 $h[i] = h[i] \oplus N[i]$
      # Clear the most significant bit of the last byte of h.
      $h[15] = h[15] \& 0X7F$ # "&" denotes the bitwise AND operator
   2.5 # Tag encryption. Notice that AES-GCM-SIV encrypts
      # directly the tag with the AES encryption operation, while
      # the AES-GCM mode encrypts the tag using the CTR mode
      $.Tag = AES\_Enc_{K\_msg}(h)$
3. # Plaintext encryption
   3.1 # The initial counter block is the encrypted tag with the most
      # significant bit of the last byte set to 1.
      # "|" denotes the bitwise OR
      $InitialCtr = Tag$; $InitialCtr[15] = InitialCtr[15] | 0x80$
   3.2 $C = AES\_GCM\_SIV\_CTR(K\_msg, InitialCtr, P)$
4. **return** (C, Tag)

9.2.5.5 Authenticated Decryption with AES-GCM-SIV

The decryption algorithm below makes use of the same functions as the encryption algorithm.

---

function AES_GCM_SIV_AuthenticatedDecryption
    input K: master key (of 128 or 256 bits)
        C: ciphertext, a bit string no longer than 2^{36} bits
        Tag: tag, a bit string of 128 bits
        A: associated data, a bit string no longer than 2^{36} bits
        N: nonce, a bit string of 96 bits
    output P: plaintext (of the same bit-length than the ciphertext)
        V: Decision ("Valid" or "Invalid")
1. # Key derivation

> $(K\_hash, K\_msg) = AES\_GCM\_SIV\_KeyDerivation(K, N)$
> 2. # Decryption of ciphertext using the SIV-CTR mode
>   2.1 $InitialCtr = Tag$; $InitialCtr[15] = InitialCtr[15] | 0x80$
>   2.2 $P = AES\_GCM\_SIV\_CTR(K\_msg, InitialCtr, C)$
> 3. # Computation of the tag associated with the received ciphertext
>   3.1 $L = \left[len(A) * 8\right]_{64} \,\|\, \left[len(P) * 8\right]_{64}$
>   3.2 # pad the plaintext and associated data to multiple of 128 bits
> $P\_Pad = Right\_pad(P)$; $A\_Pad = Right\_pad(A)$
>   3.3 $h = Polyval_{K\_hash}\left(A\_Pad \,\|\, P\_Pad \,\|\, L\right)$ # h is the tag in clear
>   3.4 # XOR the first twelve bytes of h with the nonce
>   **for** i=0 **to** 11 **do** $h[i] = h[i] \oplus N[i]$
>   # Clear the most significant bit of the last byte of h.
> $h[15] = h[15] \& 0x7F$
>   3.5 # Tag encryption
> $T' = AES\_Enc_{K\_msg}(h)$
> 4. **if** $T' = Tag$, **then return** ("Valid", P), **else return** "Invalid"

9.2.6 Poly1305

Poly1305 is a fast algorithm to generate message tags. Initially Poly1305 was proposed under the name Poly1305-AES to be used jointly with AES [5]. Poly1305 is not yet approved by the NIST as a mode of operation of AES. However, it is recommended as one of the schemes to build AEAD algorithms used in TLS [6]. In TLS, the Poly1305 is used jointly with the stream cipher ChaCha20 (see Section 6.2.5); and their combination is referred to as ChaCha20-Poly1305 AEAD.

9.2.6.1 Poly1305-AES

To generate a tag, Poly1305-AES makes use of:

- One-time[5] key of 32 bytes divided into two equal-size keys
- an AES-128 key, denoted s, and an additional 128-bit key, denoted r; $r[0]$, $r[1]$, ..., $r[15]$ denote the bytes of the additional key
- a 128-bit nonce, n
- a message m of variable byte-length

Additional key r

The additional key r is not used to encrypt or decrypt. It is an integer in little-endian encoding, i.e. $r = r[0] + 2^8 r[1] + 2^{16} r[2] + ... + 2^{120} r[15]$. r must be a positive integer with the following restrictions:

- The four most-significant bits of bytes $r[3]$, $r[7]$, $r[11]$, and $r[15]$ must be zeros; i.e. $r[3]$, $r[7]$, $r[11]$, and $r[15]$ take values smaller than 16.
- The two least-significant bits of bytes $r[4]$, $r[8]$, and $r[12]$ must be zeros; i.e. $r[4]$, $r[8]$, and $r[12]$ take values divisible by 4.

r can be obtained by picking a random integer z in interval $[0, 2^{128}($ and applying the "and" operation (denoted $\wedge$) to z in big-endian, using a mask as follows:

$$r = z \wedge \left[\text{0f ff ff fc0f ff ff fc0f ff ff fc0f ff ff ff}\right]_{16}$$

Message conversion and padding

Let m be a message of a byte-length of l; $m[0]$, $m[1]$, ..., $m[l-1]$ denote the bytes of message m. Before computing the tag, conversion and padding operations are applied as follows:

1) Split message m into segments of 16 bytes.
2) Pad each 16-byte segment of message m to a 17-byte segment by appending one byte with the value 1.
3) If the last segment of message m is of a byte-length less than 16, then append a byte with the value 1 and append bytes with the value 0, until the padded segment byte-length reaches 17. Padding with zeros does not affect the value of integers.

The pseudocode of the message conversion and padding is as follows:

```
function ConvertPadMessage
    input m: message of l bytes
    output c: converted message
    1. q = ⌈Blen(m) / 16⌉  # q: number of segments in message m
       # Only the last segment can be incomplete
       # Message segments are interpreted as integers in little-endian
       # encoding. Appending a complete segment with a byte of value 1
       # is equivalent to adding 2^128 to integer representing the segment.
    2. for i = 1 to ⌊Blen(m) / 16⌋  # Blen(m) means the byte-length of m
       # map each 16-byte of message m to a 17-byte segment in c
       2.1 for j = 16 to 1 do: c[i] = c[i] + m[16 * i − j] * 2^{8(16−j)}
       2.2 c[i] = c[i] + 2^128
    3. if (Blen(m) mod 16) ≠ 0, then
       3.1 z = Blen(m) − 16 * q; c[q] = 2^{8*z}
       3.2 for j = 16 to z do: c[q] = c[q] + m[16 * i − j] * 2^{8(16−j)}
    4. return c
```

Tag generation

Given a one-time key (r,k), a nonce n, and a message m, which is transformed to a message c, the tag computation is defined by:

$$Poly1305\text{-}AES(m,(r,s),n) = \left(\left(\sum_{i=1,\ldots,q}\left(c_i * r^{(q-i+1)}\right)\right) \bmod \left(2^{130}-5\right) + Enc_s(n)\right) \bmod 2^{128}$$

Security of Poly1305-AES

Poly1305-AES scheme is designed to ensure that a forged message is rejected with a probability of $1 - \left(14\left\lceil\frac{L}{16}\right\rceil\right) * 2^{-106}$ for a L-byte message, even after having observed 2^{64} legitimate authenticated messages; thus, it is resistant against tag forgery attacks [5].

9.2.6.2 ChaCha20-Poly1305 AEAD

Poly1305, used jointly with ChaCha20, is recommended as one of the building blocks of AEAD to implement TLS protocol. ChaCha20-Poly1305 is an adaptation of the original Poly1305-AES, where the 32-byte encryption key of Chacha20 is used to encrypt/decrypt data and to generate the one-time key (r,k), used to generate the tag.

9.2.6.2.1 Poly1305-mac

To generate a tag for a plaintext m, Poly1305-mac takes the following inputs:

- 32-byte master key K, the key used to encrypt
- 96-bit nonce n
- Message m of arbitrary byte-length

Tag generation follows three steps:

1) One-time key generation: the master key K, the nonce n, and a counter with value 0 are used as input of ChaCha20 to produce a 64-byte keystream block Y. Only the leftmost 32 bytes of the block Y are used: $r = Y[0:15]$ and $s = Y[16:31]$. Then, r is clamped to set to 0 some bits of bytes $r[3]$, $r[4]$, $r[7]$, $r[8]$, $r[11]$, $r[12]$, and $r[15]$, exactly as in Poly1305-AES.
2) Message m is converted and mapped as in Poly1305-AES to yield a padded plaintext c.
3) Tag is computed according the following formula:

$$t = \left(\left(\sum_{i=1,\ldots,q}\left(c_i * r^{(-i+1)}\right)\right) \bmod \left(2^{130}-5\right) + s\right) \bmod 2^{128}$$

Note. Poly1305mac does not encrypt the nonce n, while Poly1305-AES does. Poly1305mac makes use of the nonce to generate a one-time key (r,s), while Poly1305-AES assumes that the one-time key is given as input. In Poly1305mac, the component s of the one-time key is the half of a keystream block generated by ChaCha20; therefore, the encryption of the nonce in Poly1305-AES is equivalent to s in Poly1305mac.

The pseudocode of Poly1305mac scheme is as follows:

```
function Poly1305mac
    input K: 32-byte key; n: 96-bit nonce
          m: message of arbitrary byte-length
    output t: tag of 128 bits
    1. z = ChaCha20(K,0,n) # generate a 64-byte keystream string
    2. r = z[0:15]; s = z[15:31]
    3. r = r ∧ [0f ff ff fc 0f ff ff fc 0f ff ff fc 0f ff ff ff]₁₆ # Clamp r
    4. c = ConvertPadMessage(m)
```

$$5.\, t = \left(\left(\sum_{i=1,\,\ldots,\,q} \left(c_i * r^{(q-i+1)}\right)\right) \bmod \left(2^{130} - 5\right) + s\right) \bmod 2^{128}$$

```
    6. return t
```

9.2.6.2.2 AEAD-ChaCha20-Poly1305

ChaCha20 and Poly1305mac can be combined to build an AEAD, called AEAD-ChaCha20-Poly1305. To encrypt and generate a tag for a plaintext P, AEAD-ChaCha20-Poly1305 takes the following inputs:

- 256-bit encryption key K.
- 96-bit nonce n.
- Plaintext P of arbitrary byte-length of at most (nearly) 256 G bytes.
- Optional additional data A of at most $2^{64} - 1$ bytes.

It performs the following operations:

1) Generate a one-time key (r,s), using the encryption key K and the nonce n.
2) Plaintext P is encrypted by ChaCha20, using key K; the ciphertext is denoted C.
3) A tag t is produced by Poly1305mac, using a byte string *MacData* composed as follows: $MacData = A \parallel$ Append16(A) $\parallel C \parallel$ Append16(C) $\parallel LenA \parallel LenC$ where Append16(Y) is a 0-string, such that the length of $Y \parallel$ Append16(Y) is multiple of 16; $LenA$ is the byte-length of the additional data A, and $LenC$, that of the plaintext P. $LenA$ and $LenC$ are represented on 64 bits, each.

Figure 9.11 illustrates the structure of AEAD-ChaCha20-Poly1305 encryption; and its pseudocode is as follows:

```
function AEAD_ChaCha20_Poly1305Encrypt
    input K: 256-bit key;  n: 96-bit nonce
          P: message of arbitrary byte-length
          A: additional data (optional)
    output C,t: ciphertext and 128-bit tag
    1. C = ChaCha20(K,1,n,P) # encrypt the plaintext
    2. MacData = A || Pad16(A) || C || Pad16(C) || [Blen(A)]₆₄ || [Blen(C)]₆₄
    3. t = Poly1305mac(MacData,K,n)
    4. return (C,t)
```

9.2.7 Key Wrapping Modes

The authenticated-encryption algorithms presented in the previous subsections provide confidentiality and authentication guarantees. In addition to those algorithms, three modes of operation have been approved by NIST as modes to provide confidentiality and authentication guarantees to protect cryptographic keys when exchanged between two parties via an untrusted channel. Indeed, cryptographic keys are of prime importance in any cryptosystem; thus, they require more attention when exchanged. A key wrapping mode enables to encrypt a secret key with another secret key.

The key wrapping modes are stronger than the other modes, which target general data. However, the key protection is achieved at the cost of a lower performance compared to the other authenticated-encryption algorithms. That is the reason why key wrapping modes are only recommended to encrypt/decrypt keys and other highly-critical data.

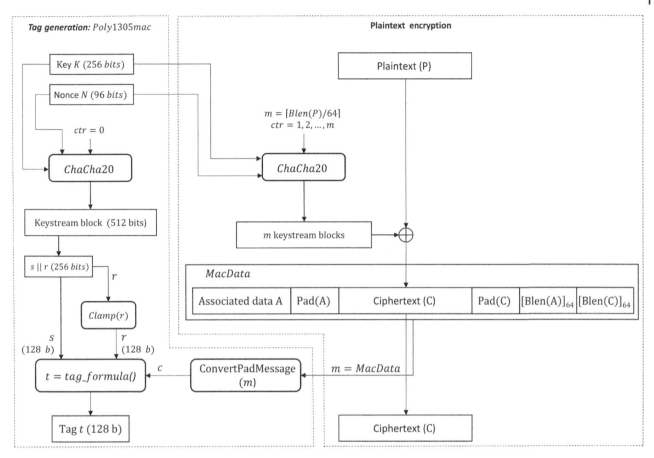

Figure 9.11 Overall structure of ChaCha20-Poly1305 AEAD.

Definition 9.6 Key wrapping: *it is a symmetric cryptographic scheme, which provides confidentiality and integrity guarantees for cryptographic keys when exchanged between parties; i.e. it is a method of encrypting and decrypting keys using symmetric-key cryptography.*

Key wrapping modes differ from the other authenticated-encryption modes presented in previous subsections:

- They do not generate a tag. Rather, they append (on the left of the plaintext) a constant-bit string, which is encrypted together with the plaintext, and then the decryption succeeds only if the constant-bit string is recovered at the beginning of the decryption output.
- They do not provide capacity to use associated data.
- They do not provide capacity to generate signatures. Recall that tags are required to generate signatures.

One may think about key wrapping as a mode of operation where the encryption of each bit of input is dependent on every other bits of input in all the blocks in a non-trivial way. In other words, key wrapping modes are based on the input diffusion.

The three key wrapping modes are called KW (AES Key Wrap), KWP (KW with Padding), and TKW (Triple DEA Key Wrap) [7]. For KW and KWP, the underlying block cipher is AES with the key length of 128, 192, or 256 bits. For TKW, the underlying block cipher is TDEA with the key length of 56 bits.

9.2.7.1 KW and KWP Modes of Operation

KW and KWP are modes of operation of AES block cipher. Therefore, both modes process blocks of a length of 128 bits. Each block is split into two halves called semiblocks.[6] As shown in the encryption and decryption algorithms of KW and KWP modes, the main components of KW mode are its functions denoted W and W^{-1}; wrapping function W performs the encryption and unwrapping function W^{-1} the decryption. KWP is an extension of KW to process plaintexts of arbitrary length.

---

function KW_Authenticated_Encryption
    input K: key (with approved bit-length)
        P: plaintext, a string of n semiblocks $(2 \leq n \leq 2^{54} - 1)$
    output C: ciphertext
    1. $S = 0xA6A6A6A6A6A6A6A6 \parallel P$
    2. $C = W(S)$
    3. **return** C

---

function KW_Authenticated_Decryption
    input K: key (with approved bit-length)
        C: ciphertext, a string of n semiblocks $(3 \leq n \leq 2^{54})$
    output P: plaintext; V: "Valid" or "Invalid"
    1. $S = W^{-1}(C)$
    2. # Check
        2.1 **if** $MSB_{64}(S) \neq 0xA6A6A6A6A6A6A6A6$, **then return** "Invalid"
        2.2 **else** $P = LSB_{64 * (len(C) - 1)}(S)$
        2.3 **return** $(P, \text{"Valid"})$

---

function KWP_Authenticated_Encryption
    input K: key (with approved bit-length)
        P: plaintext, a byte-string of length in $[1..2^{32} - 1]$ bytes
    output C: ciphertext
    1. # Pad the plaintext, so that the byte-string to encrypt is of a
       # length multiple of semiblock byte-length.

$$lenPAD = 8 * \left\lceil \frac{len(P)}{64} \right\rceil - \left\lceil \frac{len(P)}{8} \right\rceil$$

    2. $S = 0xA65959A6 \parallel \left[\left\lceil \frac{len(P)}{8} \right\rceil \right]_{32} \parallel P \parallel 0^{(8 * lenPAD)}$

    3. **if** $len(P) \leq 64$, **then** $C = Enc_K(S)$ **else** $C = W(S)$
    4. **return** C

---

function KWP_Authenticated_Decryption
    input K: key (with approved bit-length)
        C: ciphertext, a byte-string of a length in $\left[2..2^{29} \right]$ semiblocks.
    output P: plaintext of the same length than that of input C
        V: "Valid" or "Invalid"
    1. $n = len(C) / 64$ # n is the number of semiblocks in C
    2. **if** $n = 2$, **then** $S = Dec_K(C)$, **else** $S = W^{-1}(C)$
    3. **if** $MBS_{32}(S) \neq 0xA65959A6$, **then return** "Invalid"
    4. **if** $MBS_{32}(S) = 0xA65959A6$, **then**
        4.1 $Plen = int(LSB_{32}(MBS_{64}(S))$
        4.2 $lenPAD = 8 * (n - 1) - Plen$
        4.3 **if** $lenPAD < 0$ **or** $lenPAD > 7$, **then return** "Invalid"
        4.4 **if** $LBS_{8 * lenPAD}(S) \neq 0^{8 * lenPAD}$, **then return** "Invalid"
        4.5 $P = MSB_{8 * Plen}\left(LSB_{64 * (n-1)}(S) \right)$
        4.6 **return** ("Valid", P)

Wrapping function W takes a string S and splits it into n semiblocks. It makes use of internal variables A^t and R_i^t with $t = 1, \ldots, s$, $s = 6(n - 1)$, $i = 1, \ldots, n$. Wrapping function W runs s steps and in each step t $(t = 1, \ldots, s)$, it performs an AES encryption and it updates variables A^t and R_n^t. The variables R_k^t, with $2 \leq k < n$, are updated using the values of the previous iteration as follows: $R_k^t = R_{k+1}^{t-1}$.

The complete algorithm is given below. Notice that: 1) the encryption starts with A^0, which is equal to the constant value 0x$A6A6A6A6A6A6A6A6$, then the encryption output is propagated to the subsequent iterations, 2) the constant value is the only way to check the authenticity and its encryption is embedded in all the ciphertext bits. Therefore, no tag is generated. Figure 9.12 depicts the operations of wrapping function W for encrypting four semiblocks S_1, S_2, S_3, S_4. Figure 9.13 illustrates a wired representation of wrapping function W with four semiblocks. The wired representation is a structure composed of $6(4-1) = 18$ rectangles connected each other. Each rectangle represents an encryption operation: the two wires on the left represent two semiblocks to encrypt and the wires on the right represent two (intermediate) ciphertext semiblocks. The wires on the top convey the most significant 64 bits and the wires on the bottom the least significant 64 bits of the input or the output of the AES encryption.

---

function W

 input K: key (with approved bit-length)
   S: plaintext, a string of n semiblocks ($n \geq 3$)
 output C: ciphertext of the same length than that of input S
 1. # Variable initialization
  1.1. $s = 6*(n-1)$
  1.2. Let $S = S_1 \| S_2 \| \ldots \| S_n$ # $S_{i=1,\ldots,n}$ are semiblocks of S
  1.3. $A^0 = S_1$
  1.4. **for** $i = 2$ **to** n **do** $R_i^0 = S_i$.
 2. # Compute intermediate ciphertexts
  for $t = 1$ **to** s **do**
  2.1. $A^t = MSB_{64}\left(Enc_K\left(A^{t-1} \| R_2^{t-1}\right)\right) \oplus [t]_{64}$
  2.2. **for** $i = 2$ **to** $n-1$ **do** $R_i^t = R_{i+1}^{t-1}$
  2.3. $R_n^t = LSB_{64}\left(Enc_K\left(A^{t-1} \| R_2^{t-1}\right)\right)$
 3. # Function output
  3.1. $C_1 = A^s$
  3.2. **for** $i = 2$ **to** n **do** $C_i = R_i^s$
  3.3. $C = C_1 \| C_2 \| \ldots \| C_n$; **return** C

The unwrapping function W^{-1} decrypts a ciphertext using the inverse operations of wrapping function W. Its algorithm is given below.

---

function W^{-1}

 input K: key (with approved bit-length)
   C: ciphertext, a string of n semiblocks ($n \geq 3$)
 output P: plaintext of the same length than that of input C
 1. # Initialize the variables
  1.1. $s = 6*(n-1)$
  1.2. Let $C = C_1 \| C_2 \| \ldots \| C_n$ # $C_{i=1,\ldots,n}$ are semiblocks of C
  1.3. $A^s = C_1$
  1.4. **for** $i = 2$ **to** n **do** $R_i^s = C_i$
 2. # Compute intermediate plaintext values
  for $t = s$ **to** 1 **do**
  2.1. $A^{t-1} = MSB_{64}\left(Dec_K\left(\left(A^t \oplus [t]_{64}\right) \| R_n^t\right)\right)$
  2.2. $R_2^{t-1} = LSB_{64}\left(Dec_K\left(\left(A^t \oplus [t]_{64}\right) \| R_n^t\right)\right)$
  2.3. **for** $i = 2$ **to** $n-1$ **do** $R_{i+1}^{t-1} = R_i^t$
 3. # Function output
  3.1. $S_1 = A^0$
  3.2. **for** $i = 2$ **to** n **do** $S_i = R_i^0$
  3.3. $P = S_1 \| S_2 \| \ldots \| S_n$; **return** P

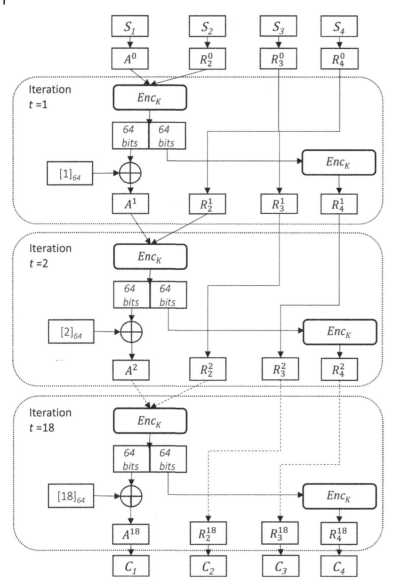

Figure 9.12 Iterative encryption of wrapping function W (with four semiblocks).

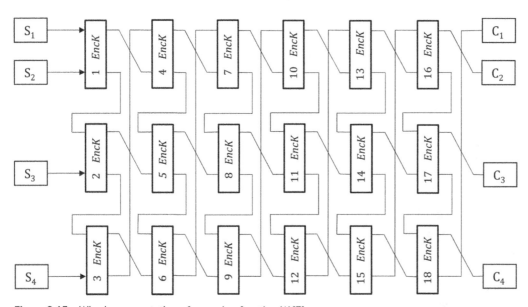

Figure 9.13 Wired representation of wrapping function W [7].

9.2.7.2 TKW Mode of Operation

TKW is a mode of operation of TDEA block cipher. Therefore, it processes blocks of a length of 64 bits. With the exception of the block length and the lengths of plaintext and ciphertext, KW and TKW modes are the same. The algorithms of TKW are given below:

---

function TKW_Authenticated_Encryption
    input K: key (with approved bit-length)
        P: plaintext, a string of n semiblocks $(2 \leq n \leq 2^{28} - 1)$
    output C: ciphertext of the same the bit-length than input P
    1. $S = 0xA6A6A6A6 \parallel P$
    2. $C = TW(S)$; **return** C

---

function TKW_Authenticated_Decryption
    input K: key (with approved bit-length)
        C: ciphertext, a string of n semiblocks $\left(3 \leq n \leq 2^{28}\right)$
    output P: plaintext of the same the bit-length than input C
        V: "*Valid*" or "*InValid*"
    1. $S = TW^{-1}(C)$
    2. **if** $MSB_{32}(S) \neq 0xA6A6A6A6$, **then return** "Invalid"
        else $P = LSB_{32*(len(C)\,-1)}(S)$; **return** ("*Valid*", P)

The wrapping function TW and unwrapping function TW^{-1} are the same as the functions W and W^{-1} where the used semiblock length is 32 instead of 64 and the encryption/decryption primitives are those of TDEA. To build functions TW and TW^{-1}, substitute, in the algorithms described in 9.2.7.1, MSB_{32} to MSB_{64}, LSB_{32} to LSB_{64}, and $[t]_{32}$ to $[t]_{64}$.

9.2.7.3 Security of Key Wrapping Modes

First, wrapping key modes are deterministic; i.e. the ciphertext does not change, if the plaintext does not. Consequently, to prevent attacks based on repetitions of plaintext, it is recommended to include a nonce in each plaintext occurrence.

Second, as previously emphasized in other authenticated-encryption modes, if the authenticity verification fails when applying the key wrapping decryption, then there is no doubt, the ciphertext is not authentic. However, if the authenticity verification succeeds, there is no absolute assurance that the recovered plaintext is authentic, because of forgery attacks. The probability that an adversary would be able to forge a ciphertext that would be wrongly validated by the recipient should be addressed before using key wrapping modes. Recall that the authenticity verification in key wrapping modes is to check if the leftmost substring yielded by the decryption is equal to a constant bit-string (which equals $0xA6A6A6A6A6A6A6A6$ for KW, $0xA65959A6$ for KWP, and $0xA6A6A6A6$ for TKW). Recall also that KWP pads the plaintext bit-length on the right of the constant $0xA65959A6$, which results in a 64-bit string. Therefore, the probability to produce a valid ciphertext is 2^{-64} for KW and KWP and 2^{-32} for TKW. It is worth noticing that TKW mode is vulnerable to forgery attacks.

Third, cryptanalysis of key wrapping modes showed that these modes are vulnerable to attacks based on very long messages. In two very long messages, collisions located at some positions may occur and then may be used to design some attacks. To address such a vulnerability, the plaintext length is limited to 2^{60}, 2^{32}, and 2^{33} bytes for KW, WP, and TKW, respectively.

9.2.8 Security of Authenticated-Encryption Modes

When a block cipher is used for confidentiality and/or authentication, the security goal is to prevent an adversary with limited computational power i) to learn any information on the plaintext, and/or ii) to alter the ciphertext or the plaintext while forging a valid MAC. Summarized below are the main vulnerabilities of authenticated-encryption modes addressed in literature.

9.2.8.1 Block Repetitions and Replay

CMAC aims at providing message authenticity only. It is based on CBC, but without using an IV. Therefore, CMAC mode does not inherently protect against replay attacks. Indeed, the same message with its MAC may be re-sent multiple times by the attacker, and the recipient tag verification process validates all the (re)sent messages. However, since the plaintext is sent in clear, detection of plaintext repetitions does not matter in CMAC.

CCM, GCM, and AES-GCM-SIV are based on CTR and CBC mode with a nonce. Therefore, replay attacks can be easily detected. Since all those three modes make use of a nonce, they hide plaintext repetitions.

9.2.8.2 Chosen-Ciphertext Attacks

With authenticated encryption, the task of adversary becomes (extremely) hard to disclose keys or plaintexts. It is worth noticing that the authenticated encryption can provide security against chosen-ciphertext attacks in which the adversary attempts to gain advantage (such as recovering the key) by submitting chosen ciphertexts to a decryption oracle. Authenticated decryption can easily recognize improperly built ciphertexts and do not decrypt them. Thus, adversary cannot select ciphertexts and receive their plaintexts.

9.2.8.3 Birthday Attacks

MAC forgery attacks depend on *Tlen*, the bit-length of the tag. The probability that the attacker randomly guesses the MAC, which matches the ciphertext he/she modified, is 2^{-Tlen}. The adversary could substitute a ciphertext to another without controlling the content by trying the find a collision (i.e. two distinct ciphertexts with the same tag). By the birthday paradox, the adversary needs to use (i.e. intercepts) at least $2^{\frac{Tlen}{2}}$.

In case of CMAC and GMAC, which are two modes that do not provide confidentiality guarantees, the adversary may alter the plaintext (because it is in cleartext) and forge the tag using birthday attacks.

9.2.8.4 Bit-flipping Attacks

When MACs are of concern, the aim of the bit-flipping attack would be to change a ciphertext or plaintext block and the MAC at some positions in order to change the plaintext recovered by recipient at the same positions. Such type of attacks is very unlikely to succeed in MAC generating modes, because the attacker has no means to know which bits will change in the recovered plaintext when bits are changed in the ciphertext or in the tag.

9.2.8.5 Nonce Misuse

Recall that nonce misuse means that two or more plaintexts are encrypted with the same nonce by mistake. CMAC mode does not use any nonce; therefore, vulnerability to nonce misuse is not relevant. GCM mode is vulnerable to nonce misuse (see Section 9.2.4.6). AES-GCM-SIV provides a solution to make GCM resistant to nonce misuse.

In CCM mode, if two plaintexts are encrypted with the same nonce, the same key and the same parameter q (the byte-length of the byte-length of plaintext), then counter blocks used to encrypt both messages are the same. Therefore, the forbidden attack may be mounted to derive the XOR of two plaintexts.

9.3 Exercises and Problems

9.3.1 List of Exercises and Problems

Exercise 9.1

Consider a user who encrypts and generates tags for files of 1 G bytes using CCM. How many files can he/she process before changing the key? Hint: observe the information formatting function.

Problem 9.1

CMAC is known to be an improvement of CBC-MAC[7] algorithm. Both algorithms perform exactly the same operations until the last plaintext block P_n. In CBC-MAC, the last block P_n is directly encrypted, while in CMAC, it is XORed with a subkey before being encrypted in step 4 of tag generation algorithm. CBC-MAC does not make use of subkeys K_1 and K_2. Assume that the tag bit-length is the same as that of a block and the plaintext length is a multiple of block length (i.e. we consider a tag generator without truncation of the final ciphertext and without padding the last plaintext block). Show that CBC-MAC is vulnerable to the following MAC forgery attack, while CMAC is not: given two plaintexts and their tags, the adversary can generate a forged plaintext with a valid tag without knowing the key.

Problem 9.2

In order to generate 128-bit tags for plaintexts of a bit-length multiple of 128, Bob modifies the standard CMAC by substituting addition mod 997 to XOR operations, i.e. instead of computing $A \oplus B$, as in the original CMAC, he computes $(A + B)$ *mod* 997. Bob tries three MAC schemes:

1) Scheme 1: Bob sends an encrypted 3-block message to the bank including an amount of money to transfer to Eve and the amount is encoded in the second block. Eve intercepts a message containing an amount of \$25. How can Eve increase the amount she will receive, while the final tag does not change?

2) Scheme 2: Bob sends an encrypted 3-block message to the bank including an amount of money to transfer to Eve and the amount is encoded in the third block (i.e. the last block). Eve intercepts a message containing an amount of \$25. How can Eve increase the amount she will receive, while the final tag does not change?

3) Scheme 3: Bob sends an encrypted 3-block message to the bank including an amount of money to transfer to Eve and the amount is encoded in an incomplete third block (i.e. only the five first bits of the third block are used in the plaintext). Eve intercepts a message containing an amount of \$25. How can Eve increase the amount she will receive, while the final tag does not change?

Problem 9.3

Consider the following variant of CMAC intended to generate tags for messages of arbitrary lengths, which are multiples of the block length. The construction uses a block cipher $E : \{0,1\}^k \times \{0,1\}^n \to \{0,1\}^n$, which is assumed to be secure, and computes a tag T for message M as $T = MAC(M,K) = CBC_K(M \parallel l)$, where l is the bit-length of M represented on n bits. Show that the construction is insecure under chosen-plaintext attack; i.e. an adversary who can get tags of some plaintexts can forge a tag.

Problem 9.4

Consider the following variant of CMAC intended to generate tags for messages of arbitrary lengths, which are multiples of the block length. The construction uses a block cipher $E : \{0,1\}^k \times \{0,1\}^n \to \{0,1\}^n$, which is assumed to be secure. The secret key is a pair (K, K'). The construction takes a message M and computes a tag T as follows: $T = MAC(M, (K, K')) = CBC_K(M) \oplus K'$. K' is of a block bit-length n, while K is of a bit-length of k, the cipher key bit-length. CBC is used with an IV of a fixed value 0. Show that the construction is insecure under the chosen-plaintext attack; i.e. an adversary who can get the tags of some plaintexts can forge a tag.

Problem 9.5

This problem addresses vulnerabilities of CMAC when a set of messages is processed with the same key assuming that the tag bit-length is the same as that of a block and the plaintext length is a multiple of block length (i.e. we consider a CMAC without performing truncation of the final ciphertext and without padding the last plaintext block).

1) How many messages are required to have a collision (i.e. two distinct messages with the same tag) following the birthday paradox?

2) Given two messages M and M', which have the same tag $T = CMAC_K(M) = CMAC_K(M')$, how to build more collisions of the form $M \parallel X$ and $M' \parallel X$? Such an attack is called length extension.

3) Use answers to questions 1 and 2 to show how an adversary can forge a pair (message and tag) with an uncontrolled appended content.

Problem 9.6

This problem addresses message number limits in CMAC to prevent collision attacks. Hint: use birthday paradox.

1) In page 13, the CMAC standard [2] recommends the following "the default recommendation is to limit the key to no more than 2^{48} messages when the block size of the underlying block cipher is 128 bits, as with the AES algorithm, and 2^{21} messages when the block size is 64 bits, as with TDEA. Within these limits, the probability of a collision is expected to be less than one in a billion for the AES algorithm, and less than one in a million for TDEA." How the recommended limits (i.e. 2^{48} and 2^{21}) can be substantiated?

2) In most real-world systems, it is recommended that the adversary's advantage should not be greater than 2^{-32}. In particular, the number of tags generated with the same key is such that the probability of tag collision should not be greater than 2^{-32}. What is the limit on message number to tag with AES-CMAC and TDEA-CMAC, both using the same key, such that collision risk does not exceed 2^{-32}?

Problem 9.7

Show that ChaCha20-Poly1305 AEAD does not assure confidentiality protection, if the nonce is reused for two distinct messages.

Problem 9.8

In this problem, we want to show that Poly1305-AES is secure against forgery attacks, even if one-time key (r,s) and nonce n are both reused to compute tags for two distinct plaintexts m and m', both of the same byte-length of 16. To simplify the problem, assume that m' is no less than m. Discuss why forging a plaintext f using m, m', and their tags cannot succeed. For example, try to find a tag for $f = m' - m$, assuming that one-time key (r,s) and nonce n are unknown to the adversary.

9.3.2 Solutions to Exercises and Problems

Exercise 9.1

Payload length is 1 G bytes. $1\,G = 2^{30}$; thus, q the byte-length of the payload length is 4. In formatting function, the nonce is represented on bytes 1 to $15 - q$ of the block B_0. If $q = 4$, then the byte-length of the nonce is 11. Hence, the maximum distinct values of nonces is 2^{11*8}. Since each file requires a distinct nonce, the maximum number of files to encrypt and authenticate with the same key is 2^{88}.

Problem 9.1

With the given assumptions, CBC-MAC may be defined by:

$P_n = P_n^*$ # No subkeys are used in CBC-MAC

$C_0 = 0^b$

for $i = 1$ to n do: $C_i = Enc_K\left(C_{i-1} \oplus P_i\right)$

$T = MSB_b\left(C_n\right) = C_n$, because the tag and block are of the same bit-length

Let (P,T) and (P', T') be two known plaintexts and their tags. Let n and n' denote the number of blocks of plaintexts P and P' respectively. Let $P_1', P_2', \dots P_{n'}'$ denote the blocks of plaintext P'.

1) Under CBC-MAC, the adversary can forge, by concatenation, a plaintext P'' as follows: $P'' = P \parallel \left(P_1' \oplus T\right) \parallel P_1' \parallel \dots \parallel P_{n'}'$.
   Let C_j, $j = 1, \dots, n$ denote the encryptions of blocks of P''.

$$C_1 = Enc_K\left(C_0 \oplus P_1''\right) = Enc_K\left(C_0 \oplus P_1\right) = Enc_K\left(P_1''\right) = Enc_K\left(P_1\right) = T$$

...

$$C_n = Enc_K\left(C_{n-1} \oplus P_n''\right) = Enc_K\left(C_{n-1} \oplus P_n\right) = T$$

$$C_{n+1} = Enc_K\left(T \oplus P_{n+1}''\right) = Enc_K\left(T \oplus \left(P_1' \oplus T\right)\right) = Enc_K\left(P_1' \oplus 0\right)$$

Hence, the encryption of blocks of plaintext P is cancelled. Next, the encryption of plaintext P'' continues exactly as that of plaintext P' and the final tag is T'. Then, the adversary sends (P'',T'), which will be validated by the recipient.

2) Now consider CMAC algorithm. The tag of plaintext P is computed as $T = Enc_K\left(C_{n-1} \oplus \left(K_1 \oplus P_n\right)\right)$.
   Since the last block of plaintext P is not the last block of message P'', the tag of P'' is computed as:

$C_n = Enc_K\left(C_{n-1} \oplus P_n''\right) = Enc_K\left(C_{n-1} \oplus P_n\right) = T_1$, which is distinct from $T = Enc_K\left(C_{n-1} \oplus \left(K_1 \oplus P_n\right)\right)$. Then,

$C_{n+1} = Enc_K\left(T_1 \oplus P_{n+1}''\right) = Enc_K\left(T_1 \oplus \left(P_1' \oplus T\right)\right) = Enc_K\left(P_1' \oplus T_1 \oplus T\right)$, which is distinct from $Enc_K\left(P_1'\right)$. Hence, the encryption of plaintext P'' does not continue as that of P'. The tag of plaintext P'' would be T'', which is distinct from T'. Therefore, the forgery attack cannot succeed under CMAC.

Problem 9.2

1) Scheme 1: the CMAC scheme designed by Bob to generate a 128-bit tag for each 3-block message $P = \left(P_1 \parallel P_2 \parallel P_3^*\right)$ is as follows:

   Bob_MAC_Generation(K,P):

   $\left(K_1, K_2\right) = CMAC\_Subkey\_Generation(K, 128)$

Let *Amt* denote the amount included in the second block of *P*.

By CMAC design, $P_3 = (K_1 + P_3^*) \bmod 997$, when P_3^* is a complete block

$C_0 = 0^{(b)}$

For i $= 1$ *to* 3 *do:* $C_i = Enc_K((C_{i-1} + P_i) \bmod 997)$

Return (C_3)

Assume that Bob has generated a tag *T* for a message *P* that has the value 25 in its second block, i.e. $P_2 = 25$.

$$T = Bob\_MAC\_Generation(K,P) = Enc_K((C_2 + P_3) \bmod 997)$$

$$= Enc_K(((Enc_K((C_1 + 25) \bmod 997)) + P_3) \bmod 997)$$

If Eve increases the amount by 997, the second block becomes $P_2 = 1122$. Thus, the tag of the forged message is:

$$T' = Enc_K(((Enc_K((C_1 + 1122) \bmod 997)) + P_3) \bmod 997).$$

Both tags are the same. Therefore, Eve succeeds in increasing the amount.

2) Scheme 2: the CMAC scheme designed by Bob to generate a 128-bit tag for each 3-block message $P = (P_1 \| P_2 \| P_3^*)$ is as follows:

Bob_MAC_Generation(K,P):

$(K_1, K_2) = CMAC\_Subkey\_Generation(K, 128)$.

Let *Amt* denote the amount included in the third block of *P*.

Let $P_3 = (K_1 + Amt) \bmod 997$

$C_0 = 0^{(b)}$

For i $= 1$ *to* 3 *do:* $C_i = Enc_k((C_{i-1} + P_i) \bmod 997)$

Return (C_3)

Assume that Bob has generated a tag *T* for a message *P* that has the value 25 in its third block, i.e. $P_3 = 25$.
$T = Bob\_MAC\_Generation(K,P) = Enc_k((C_2 + P_3) \bmod 997) = Enc_K((C_2 + Amt + K_1) \bmod 997)$
If Eve increases the amount *Amt* by 997, the third block becomes $P_3 = 1122$; and the tag does not change. Therefore, Eve succeeds in increasing the amount.

3) Scheme 3: the amount of money is included in the third block and encoded, so that it contains only the amount; i.e. the last block of the plaintext is incomplete. That is, Bob's MAC scheme becomes:
Bob_MAC_Generation(K,P):

$(K_1, K_2) = CMAC\_Subkey\_Generation(K, 128)$

Let *Amt* denote the amount included in the third block of *P* denoted P_3^*.

$j = 128 - len(P_3^*)$

$P_3 = K_2 \oplus (P_3^* \| 1 \| 0^j)$

$C_0 = 0^b$

for *i* $= 1$ to 3 *do:* $C_i = Enc_K((C_{i-1} + P_i) \bmod 997)$

Return (C_3)

The tag generated by Bob is:

$$T = Enc_K((C_2 + K_2 + ([25]_5 \| 1 \| 0^{122})) \bmod 997).$$

If Eve increases the amount by *x*, then:

Let *L* denote the bit-length of integer $x + 25$. Hence, the tag of the forged message is:

$$T' = Enc_K((C_2 + K_2 + ([x + 25]_L \| 1 \| 0^{128-L-1})) \bmod 997).$$

Eve can find a value *x*, such that the following holds, and then change the amount:

$$\left([25]_5 \parallel 1 \parallel 0^{122} \right) \left([x+25]_L \parallel 1 \parallel 0^{128-L-1} \right) mod\ 997$$

The conclusion is that the modulo operator is not appropriate to design MAC schemes, as suggested by Bob.

Problem 9.3

As a solution to the problem, we discuss a forgery attack with a 3-block message.

By construction of the proposed MAC scheme:

If $M = B_1 B_2 B_3$ then $T = MAC(M,K) = E_K \left(E_K \left(E_K \left(E_K \left(B_1 \right) \oplus B_2 \right) \oplus B_3 \right) \oplus 3 \right)$,

The steps of the attack are as follows:

- get the tag of message $M_0 = [0]_n$, $T_0 = E_K \left(E_K \left([0]_n \right) \oplus 1 \right)$
- get the tag of message $M_1 = [1]_n$, $T_1 = E_K \left(E_K \left([1]_n \right) \oplus 1 \right)$
- get the tag of message $M_2 = [0]_n \parallel [1]_n \parallel T_0$,

$$T_2 = E_K \left(E_K \left(E_K \left(E_K \left([0]_n \right) \oplus [1]_n \right) \oplus T_0 \right) \oplus 3 \right)$$

$$= E_K \left(E_K \left(\left[T_0 \oplus T_0 \right]_n \right) \oplus 3 \right) = E_K \left(E_K \left([0]_n \right) \oplus 3 \right)$$

- Forge a message $M_{forge} = [1]_n \parallel [1]_n \parallel T_1$ with tag T_2, which matches the forged message, because:

$$MAC \left([1]_n \parallel [1]_n \parallel T_1, K \right) = E_K \left(E_K \left(E_K \left(E_K \left([1]_n \right) \oplus [1]_n \right) \oplus T_1 \right) \oplus 3 \right)$$

$$= E_K \left(E_K \left(\left[T_1 \oplus T_1 \right]_n \right) \oplus 3 \right) = E_K \left(E_K \left([0]_n \right) \oplus 3 \right) = T_2$$

We can apply the previous steps for any pair of blocks M_0 and M_1, and forge a tag.

Problem 9.4

The tag forgery attack may be designed as follows:

i) The adversary gets two tags:

$$T_1 = CBC_K \left(0^{(n)} \right) \oplus K' \text{ and } T_2 = CBC_K \left(0^{(n)} \parallel T_1 \right) \oplus K'$$

By the proposed MAC scheme,

$$T_1 = CBC_K \left(0^{(n)} \right) \oplus K' = E_k \left(0^{(n)} \right) \oplus K'$$

$$T_2 = CBC_K \left(0^{(n)} \parallel T_1 \right) \oplus K' = E_k \left(E_k \left(0^{(n)} \right) \oplus E_k \left(0^{(n)} \right) \oplus K' \right) \oplus K' = E_k \left(K' \right) \oplus K'$$

ii) The adversary can forge T_2, as a valid tag of a message $0^{(n)} \parallel T_1 \parallel T_2$, because:

$$CBC_K \left(0^{(n)} \parallel T_1 \parallel T_2 \right) \oplus K'$$

$$= E_k \left(E_k \left(E_k \left(0^{(n)} \right) \oplus E_k \left(0^{(n)} \right) \oplus K' \right) \oplus \left(E_k \left(K' \right) \oplus K' \right) \right) \oplus K'$$

$$= E_k \left(E_k \left(K' \right) \oplus \left(E_k \left(K' \right) \oplus K' \right) \right) \oplus K' = T_2$$

Problem 9.5

1) With a tag bit-length of b, the number of distinct tags is 2^b. From the birthday paradox (in Section 3.4), we can deduce that if the number of messages (for which the tags have been produced with the same key K) known to the adversary is close to $2^{b/2}$, then there exists a high probability that two distinct messages M and M' have the same tag; i.e. $CMAC_K(M) = CMAC_K \left(M' \right) = T$.

2) Assume that two messages M and M' are known and they have the same tag under the key in use; i.e. $T = CMAC_K(M) = CMAC_K \left(M' \right)$. Let n and n' denote the number of blocks of messages M and M', respectively. Let C_i, $i = 1, ..., n$, and C'_j, $j = 1, ..., n'$, denote the ciphertext blocks computed for messages M and M', respectively. Since any plaintext block is of length b, only the subkey K_1 is used. The tag of both messages is computed as follows:

$$T = Enc_K\left(C_{n-1} \oplus K_1 \oplus M_n\right) = Enc_K\left(C'_{n'-1} \oplus K_1 \oplus M'_{n'}\right)$$

Thus, $C_{n-1} \oplus K_1 \oplus M_n = C'_{n'-1} \oplus K_1 \oplus M'_{n'}$

$$\Rightarrow C_{n-1} \oplus M_n = C'_{n'-1} \oplus M'_{n'} \tag{a}$$

Now, extend both messages with the same bit string X of p blocks.

$M^1 = M \| X$ and $M^2 = M' \| X$

Let $C_i^1, i = 1, \ldots, n + len(X)$, and $C_j^2, j = 1, \ldots, n' + len(X)$, denote the ciphertext blocks computed for messages M^1 and M^2, respectively.

$$C_n^1 = Enc_K\left(C_{n-1}^1 \oplus M_n^1\right) = Enc_K\left(C_{n-1} \oplus M_n\right) \tag{b}$$

$$C_{n'}^2 = Enc_K\left(C_{n'-1}^2 \oplus M_{n'}^2\right) = Enc_K\left(C'_{n'-1} \oplus M'_{n'}\right) \tag{c}$$

From (a)–(c), we deduce: $C_n^1 = C_{n'}^2$.

Then, continuing the encryption of M^1 and M^2 blocks, yields:

$$C_{n+d}^1 = C_{n'+d}^2, \text{ for } d = 1, \ldots, len\left(X\right)$$

Thus, $CMAC_K\left(M \| X\right) = CMAC_K\left(M' \| X\right)$. Any value of X results in a collision discovery.

3) According to the birthday paradox, the attacker needs $2^{b/2}$ messages and their MACs to observe a collision $T = CMAC_K\left(M\right) = CMAC_K\left(M'\right)$. Next, he/she needs to get a message M'' starting with either M or M' and its tag is T''. Using the answer to question 2, the attacker makes a substitution in the first part of M''. If $M'' = M \| X$, then the forged pair is $\left((M \| X), T''\right)$. Otherwise, it is $\left((M \| X), T''\right)$. The forged pair will be validated by the recipient, because it has a valid tag.

Problem 9.6

If one generates tags for 2^{128} messages with AES-CMAC or 2^{64} messages with TDEA-CMAC, the probability of collision (i.e. two messages map to the same tag) is 1. In general, when tag generation is of concern, the number of messages processed with the same key should not exceed a specific limit to make the risk of collision below some desired threshold.

Recall that the generalization of the birthday paradox (see Section 3.4) states that: given any set of M values with a uniform distribution, the probability $Pr(n)$ two values among n values from the set are identical is given by: $n \approx \sqrt{2 * M * Pr(n)}$. We apply the birthday paradox formula to prove the validity of the statement included in the CMAC standard. In this problem, M is the number of distinct tags and n the number of messages required for a collision to occur at a probability of $Pr(n)$.

1) Proof of statement in CMAC standard

The birthday paradox formula can be rewritten as: $Pr(n) \approx \dfrac{n^2}{2M}$. Given a collision risk threshold of P the number n of messages tagged with the same key should be such that $Pr(n) < P$. So, the following inequality must hold:

$$\frac{n^2}{2M} < P \tag{a}$$

- Case 1: If AES-CMAC is used, then the tag space is of 2^{128}. One billion can be approximated by 2^{30}; thus, "less than one in a billion" may be replaced by "$< 2^{-30}$" and the collision risk threshold becomes $P = 2^{-30}$. By making substitutions in inequality (a): $\dfrac{\left(2^{48}\right)^2}{2 * 2^{128}} = \dfrac{1}{2^{33}} < \dfrac{1}{2^{30}}$.

- Case 2: If TDEA-CMAC is used, then the tag space is of 2^{64}. One million can be approximated by 2^{20}; thus, "less than one in a million" may be replaced by "$< 2^{-20}$" and the collision risk threshold becomes $P = 2^{-20}$. By making substitutions in inequality (a): $\dfrac{\left(2^{21}\right)^2}{2 * 2^{64}} = \dfrac{1}{2^{23}} < \dfrac{1}{2^{20}}$.

In both cases, the bound on the collision risk is not exceeded, if the limit on the number of messages is fulfilled. Therefore, the statement in CMAC standard is valid.

2) Limit of message to tag with a collision risk not greater than $= 2^{-32}$

Rearrange inequality (a) as $n < \sqrt{2*M * P}$, then make substitutions.

- Case 1: AES-CMAC: $n < \sqrt{2 * 2^{128} * 2^{-32}} = \sqrt{2} * 2^{48}$
- Case 2: TDEA-CMAC: $n < \sqrt{2 * 2^{64} * 2^{-32}} = \sqrt{2} * 2^{21}$

In conclusion, the statement given in CMAC standard is an undersizing of limits yielded for a collision risk not greater than 2^{-32} in order to provide an easy way to appreciate the impact of message number on the tag collision occurrence.☐

Problem 9.7

Assume that an encryption key K and nonce n are reused to encrypt two plaintexts m and m' of the same byte-length l. If the key K and the nonce n are used twice, the generated keystream string is the same for both executions of ChaCha20. Let Y denote the generated keystream string, using key K and nonce n. Since ChaCha20 is a stream cipher, the produced ciphertexts are $C = m \oplus Y$ and $C' = m' \oplus Y$. From $C \oplus C' = m \oplus m'$, one can derive useful information regarding the plaintexts; thus, confidentiality is compromised.

Problem 9.8

The lengths of both messages m and m' are of 16 bytes. Therefore, the conversion and padding operations result in adding 2^{128} to each plaintext (we omit the little-endian encoding). Two padded plaintexts c and c' are yielded; then, two tags t and t' are computed. Since both initial plaintexts are of a 16-byte-length, tags are computed as:

$$t = \left(\left(c_1 * r^1\right) mod \left(2^{130} - 5\right) + Enc_s(n)\right) mod\ 2^{128}$$

$$= \left(\left(\left(m + 2^{128}\right) * r\right) mod \left(2^{130} - 5\right) + Enc_s(n)\right) mod\ 2^{128}$$

$$t' = \left(\left(c'_1 * r^1\right) mod \left(2^{130} - 5\right) + Enc_s(n)\right) mod\ 2^{128}$$

$$= \left(\left(\left(m' + 2^{128}\right) * r\right) mod \left(2^{130} - 5\right) + Enc_s(n)\right) mod\ 2^{128}$$

Assume that the plaintext that could be forged, using the same one-time key and nonce, is $f = m' - m$. The padded segment yielded from f is $c_f = \left(m' - m\right) + 2^{128}$. The tag of f, computed by the legitimate sender, is the following:

$$t_f = \left(\left(c_f * r^1\right) mod \left(2^{130} - 5\right) + Enc_s(n)\right) mod\ 2^{128}$$

$$= \left(\left(\left(m' - m + 2^{128}\right) * r\right) mod \left(2^{130} - 5\right) + Enc_s(n)\right) mod\ 2^{128}$$

$$t' - t = \left(\left(\left(m' - m\right) * r\right) mod \left(2^{130} - 5\right)\right) mod\ 2^{128}$$

$$t_f = \left(t' - t\right) + \left(\left(2^{128} * r\ mod \left(2^{130} - 5\right) + Enc_s(n)\right) mod\ 2^{128}\right)$$

Since r, s, and n are unknown to the adversary, he/she cannot compute the second component of right part of the last equality. Therefore, Poly1305-AES is secure against the suggested forgery attack.

Notes

1 In literature, the acronym AEAD is expanded as either "Authenticated Encryption with Associated Data" or "Authenticated Encryption with Additional Data," which are the same notion.

2 It is worth noticing that in this chapter, *authentication* refers to *data authenticity* and not to *user authentication* (e.g. with a password or biometrics), which is another aspect of security.

3 Notice that to be standard-complying, applications should not use the same key and nonce to process distinct messages.

4 AES-GCM means GCM mode of operation of AES bock cipher.

5 For each tag to compute, a distinct 32-byte key is used. So, the sender and recipient of tagged messages must agree on a procedure (e.g. a key derivation function) to generate one-time keys from a session key.

6 A *semiblock* is the half of a block, i.e. a 64-bit substring, if AES is used and a 32-bit substring, if TDEA is used.

7 CBC-MAC has not been approved as standard because of its vulnerabilities.

References

1 Gueron, S. and Lindell, Y. (2017). Better bounds for block cipher modes of operation via nonce-based key derivation - report 2017/702. Cryptology ePrint Archive. Cryptology ePrint Archive.

2 Dworkin, M. (2016). Recommendation for block cipher modes of operation: the CMAC mode for authentication, special publication 800-38B. NIST. National Institute for Standards and Technology.

3 Dworkin, M. (2007). Recommendation for block cipher modes of operation: the CCM mode for authentication and confidentiality, special publication 800-38C. NIST. National Institute for Standards and Technology.

4 Dworkin, M. (2007). Recommendation for block cipher modes of operation: Galois/counter mode (GCM) and GMAC, special publication 800-38D. NIST. National Institute for Standards and Technology.

5 Bernstein, D. (2005). The poly1305-AES message-authentication code. *12th International Workshop on Fast Software Encryption*, 32–49. Paris: Springer. LNCS 3357.

6 Rescorla, E. (2018). The transport layer security (TLS) protocol version 1.3, RFC 8446. Internet Engineering Task Force (IETF). Internet Engineering Task Force.

7 Dworkin, M. (2012). Recommendation for block cipher modes of operation: methods for key wrapping, special publication 800-38F. NIST. National Institute for Standards and Technology.

10

Introduction to Security Analysis of Block Ciphers

Modern cryptography security relies on the computational difficulty[1] to break ciphers rather than on the theoretical impossibility to break them. If adversaries have enough resources and time, they can break any cipher. The security analysis of block ciphers and their modes of operation is a wide field in cryptography. One approach to address the security of ciphers is to show how it is hard for adversaries to break ciphers given the resources they can use. The adversaries have access to black boxes (called oracles) associated with the ciphers to attack and they try to guess some information through the exploitation of chosen plaintexts and ciphertexts. Consequently, information inference is probabilistic. The information inferred through querying a black-box is measured in terms of *adversary advantage*. Secure ciphers are those ciphers for which the advantage of adversaries is negligible if their resources and time remain below some limits. The analysis of different scenarios of attacks is an approach to assess the security of ciphers from a probabilistic point of view. In particular, security analysis aims to define bounds beyond which the use of some ciphers may become insecure.

Security analysis is based on oracles, in particular oracles modeling the encryption, decryption, MAC generation, and MAC verification operations. The cipher to analyze is put in the worst conditions; i.e. the adversaries can choose any plaintexts to encrypt or ciphertexts to decrypt or the adversaries choose MACs and then ask the oracle to verify their validity. Therefore, the interception of true plaintexts and ciphertexts is not an issue.

In general, block cipher analysis is defined using two parameters relating to the following questions:

- What is the goal of the adversary: decrypt a ciphertext, learn something about the plaintext from the ciphertext or recover the key?
- What is the amount of resources available to the adversary? The resources are described in terms of computation time and known plaintexts, ciphertexts, and plaintext–ciphertext pairs. In addition, the memory required to store data may be a critical issue.

Security analysis of modes of operation of block ciphers addresses two issues:

- *Privacy*: it should be computationally infeasible for an adversary to derive any information from the ciphertexts unless the key is known. Such a property is called *perfect secrecy* [1].
- *Authenticity*: it should be computationally infeasible for an adversary to forge a valid pair ciphertext-tag unless the key is known.

As mentioned in other chapters, cryptographic standards specify limits for the number of plaintexts to encrypt to not compromise the security. This chapter aims at introducing some security bounds, which link the plaintext limit and the expected security in terms of privacy and authenticity preserving. It is worth noticing that this chapter is far from covering the field of probabilistic security analysis.

10.1 Pseudorandom Functions and Permutations

Pseudorandom functions (PRFs) and pseudorandom permutations (PRPs) are basic tools in cryptography. One of the primary motivations of PRFs and PRPs is to enable the security analysis of block ciphers and their modes of operation [2–4]. This section presents basic definitions relevant to PRFs and PRPs.

10.1.1   Definitions of Random and Pseudorandom Functions and Permutations

Definition 10.1 Function*: a function $f: \mathcal{M} \to \mathcal{R}$ from a set $\mathcal{M}$, called function domain, to a set $\mathcal{R}$, called function range or codomain, assigns to each element of $\mathcal{M}$ one element of $\mathcal{R}$.*

Definition 10.2 Permutation*: a permutation $\pi: \mathcal{M} \to \mathcal{M}$ from a set $\mathcal{M}$, called permutation domain, to the set $\mathcal{M}$, is a bijective function that uniquely assigns to each element of $\mathcal{M}$ one element of $\mathcal{M}$.*

Definition 10.3 Function family*: a function family F is a map $F: \mathcal{K} \times \mathcal{M} \to \mathcal{R}$, where $\mathcal{K}$ denotes the key space, $\mathcal{M}$ the domain of F, and $\mathcal{R}$ its range, which also is called co-domain of F.*

When functions are used in cryptographic algorithm analysis, the elements (or points) of $\mathcal{K}$, $\mathcal{M}$, and $\mathcal{R}$ are bit strings. That is, $\mathcal{K} = \{0,1\}^k$, $\mathcal{M} = \{0,1\}^n$, and $\mathcal{R} = \{0,1\}^L$, where k denotes the key bit-length; n and L denote the bit-length of function input and output, respectively.

Definition 10.4 Instance of a function family*: given a key $K \in \mathcal{K}$, an instance of a function family F, denoted F_K, is a map from each point $x \in \mathcal{M}$ to a point $y \in \mathcal{R}$ such that $F_K(x) \to y$.*

Definition 10.5 Permutation family*: a permutation family P is a collection of permutations with the same domain and range; i.e. $P: \mathcal{K} \times \mathcal{M} \to \mathcal{M}$.*

Definition 10.6 Instance of a permutation family*: given a key $\mathcal{K} \in \mathrm{K}$, an instance of a permutation family P, denoted P_K, is a map from each point $x \in \mathcal{M}$ to a unique point $y \in \mathcal{M}$ such that $y = P_K(x)$ and $P_K(x) \neq P_K(x')$ if $x \neq x', \forall x, x' \in \mathcal{M}$.*

A function family $F: \mathcal{K} \times \mathcal{M} \to \mathcal{R}$ is a collection of functions $F_1, F_2, ..., F_{2^k}$, each with a key in the key space; and a permutation family $P: \mathcal{K} \times \mathcal{M} \to \mathcal{M}$ is a collection of permutations $P_1, P_2, ..., P_{2^k}$, each with a key in the key space $\mathcal{K}$.

The collection of all functions of $\mathcal{M}$ to $\mathcal{R}$ is denoted $Func(\mathcal{M}, \mathcal{R})$; and the collection of all permutations of $\mathcal{M}$ to $\mathcal{M}$ is denoted $Perm(\mathcal{M})$.

Notice the massive difference in size between F and $Func(\mathcal{M}, \mathcal{R})$ sets and between P and $Perm(\mathcal{M})$ sets (see Problem 10.1):

- $|F| = |\mathcal{K}| = 2^k$ and $|Func(\mathcal{M}, \mathcal{R})| = |\mathcal{R}|^{|\mathcal{M}|} = 2^{L*2^n}$
- $|P| = |\mathcal{K}| = 2^k$ and $|Perm(\mathcal{M})| = |\mathcal{M}|! = 2^n!$

Example 10.1

AES-128 block cipher is a family of permutations that make use of 128-bit keys and 128-bit plaintext to produce 128-bit ciphertext blocks. Therefore, it is a family of permutations with $\mathcal{K} = \{0,1\}^{128}$ and $\mathcal{M} = \{0,1\}^{128}$.

AES-128-CMAC is a function family of algorithms that produce tags (i.e. message authentication codes) of *Tlen*-bit length for messages of arbitrary bit-length. Therefore, it is a function family with $\mathcal{K} = \{0,1\}^{128}$, $\mathcal{M} = \{0,1\}^*$, and $\mathcal{R} = \{0,1\}^{Tlen}$.

Definition 10.7 Random function*: given an element x of a domain $\mathcal{M}$, a random function $\varphi: \mathcal{M} \to \mathcal{R}$ is a black-box, which returns a random element y in codomain $\mathcal{R}$. If the same input x is given to a random function φ, at multiple times, the same output y is returned. Given any distinct inputs x_1 and x_2, the output $y_1 = \varphi(x_1)$ and $y_2 = \varphi(x_2)$ are independent.*

Definition 10.8 Random permutation*: given an element x of a domain $\mathcal{M}$, a random permutation $\pi: \mathcal{M} \to \mathcal{M}$ is a black-box, which returns a random element y of $\mathcal{M}$. If an input x is given to a random permutation π, for the first time, the returned output is distinct from all previously returned outputs. If the same input x is given to a random permutation π, at multiple times, the same output y is returned. Given any distinct inputs x_1 and x_2, the outputs $y_1 = \pi(x_1)$ and $y_2 = \pi(x_2)$ are independent and distinct.*

Definition 10.9 Pseudorandom function (PRF)*: a PRF $F: \mathcal{K} \times \mathcal{M} \to \mathcal{R}$ a is a family of functions whose any instance is computationally indistinguishable from a random function of the function family $Func(\mathcal{M}, \mathcal{R})$.*

Definition 10.10 Pseudorandom permutation (PRP)*: a PRP $F: \mathcal{K} \times \mathcal{M} \to \mathcal{M}$ is a family of permutations whose any instance is computationally indistinguishable from a random instance of the permutation family $Perm(\mathcal{M})$. A PRP P is required to be bijective, and to have an efficient inversion function P^{-1}; i.e. $\forall K \in \mathcal{K}, P^{-1}(K, P(K, x)) = x$.*

A pseudorandom function family F (resp. PRP P) is *computationally indistinguishable* from a random function (resp. permutation), if an adversary that has practical computational resources and given access to an instance of the PRF F (resp. PRP P) and to a random function (resp. permutation), with the same domain and codomain; he/she cannot distinguish between the outputs of the PRF (resp. PRP) and those of the random function (resp. permutation).

10.1.2 Indistinguishability and Security of PRFs

Definition 10.11 Oracle: *an oracle of a function f is a (theoretical) black box that responds to every unique query with a (truly) random response chosen uniformly from the output domain of the function.*

The most commonly used approach to evaluate the security (i.e. indistinguishability) of PRFs (and also PRPs) is based on a probabilistic analysis and referred to as *Real-Or-Random* (ROR), which works as a game between a *distinguisher A* (called hereafter *adversary*) of a PRF F and a challenger (see Figure 10.1).

Adversary A is given an interface to access two oracles and it submits one or more queries and receives answers. Before processing the first query, the game challenger, whose strategy is unknown to the adversary, uniformly selects at random a key K from the key space $\mathcal{K}$ and a random binary b. For each submitted query, if $b = 1$, then the query is processed with the instance function F_K (i.e. processed with the oracle of F); and if $b = 0$, then the query is processed with a random function φ selected function from the family $Func(\mathcal{M}, \mathcal{R})$. Upon reception of an answer, the adversary tries to guess which oracle processed its query, i.e. which value was chosen for b. The adversary outputs 1, if it thinks that the query was processed by an instance of PRF F (i.e. the received bit string is a valid ciphertext); and 0 otherwise (i.e. the received bit string is random).

Each adversary query and guess is called *experiment*. For each experiment, a quantity called *PRF-advantage* is computed to measure how the adversary is able to distinguish between the PRF and a random function:

$$ADV_F^{prf}(A) \stackrel{def}{=} \Pr\left[K \xleftarrow{R} \mathcal{K}; A^{F_K} \Rightarrow 1\right] - \Pr\left[\varphi \xleftarrow{R} Func(\mathcal{M}, \mathcal{R}); A^{\varphi} \Rightarrow 1\right]$$

where:

$K \xleftarrow{R} \mathcal{K}$: it denotes the uniform selection at random of a key K from key space $\mathcal{K}$.

$\varphi \xleftarrow{R} Func(\mathcal{M}, \mathcal{R})$: it denotes the selection of a random function φ from all the random functions in $Func(\mathcal{M}, \mathcal{R})$.

A^{F_K}: adversary A is given access to F_K, an instance of the function family F.

A^{φ}: adversary A is given access to φ, a random function from $Func(\mathcal{M}, \mathcal{R})$.

$\Pr[A^{F_K} \Rightarrow 1]$ is the probability that the adversary outputs $b = 1$, given that the query was effectively processed by F_K; i.e. it is the probability of a correct guess.

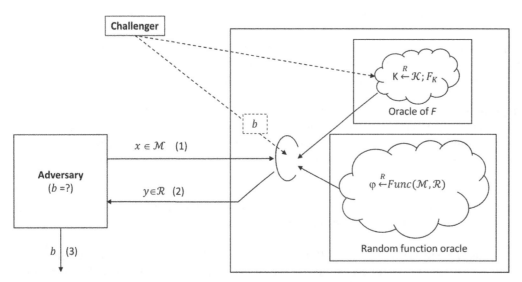

Figure 10.1 General framework for PRF indistinguishability analysis.

$\Pr[A^{\varphi} \Rightarrow 1]$ is the probability that the adversary outputs $b = 1$, given the query was processed by a random function $\varphi \in Func(\mathcal{M}, \mathcal{R})$; it is the probability of a wrong guess.

Note. For a testing session, the adversary queries the interface one or more times depending on the amount of computation time the adversary can use. The challenger randomly selects the parameter b, $b \in \{0,1\}$, one time per session before the adversary starts submitting its queries and b remains unchanged during all the testing session. If $b = 1$, then the challenger uniformly selects a random key K from the key space $\mathcal{K}$. Therefore, all the queries of a session are processed either by the same instance of function family, denoted F_K, or by a random function, denoted φ.

Different adversaries may have different PRF-advantages depending on their number of queries and computation time and how each adversary exploits the received outputs. The security of a function as PRF is measured as:

$$ADV_F^{prf}(t,q) \stackrel{def}{=} \max_A \left(ADV_F^{prf}(A) \right)$$

where q is the maximum number of queries that any adversary can ask; and t is the maximum testing computation time.

Definition 10.12 Secure PRF: *a PRF $F: \mathcal{K} \times \mathcal{M} \to \mathcal{R}$ is (t, q, ε)-secure if the PRF-advantage over all adversaries is negligible i.e. $ADV_F^{prf}(t,q) \leq \varepsilon$, where $\varepsilon \ll 1$ is a context-dependent bound; q and t denote the maximum number of queries and computation time for any adversary, respectively.*

Example 10.2

Let $\mathcal{K} = \{0,1\}^n$ and $\mathcal{M} = \{0,1\}^n$. Consider the function family $\Phi: \mathcal{K} \times \mathcal{M} \times \mathcal{M}$ defined by $\Phi(K, x) = K \oplus x$. Let us show that Φ is not a secure function family. An adversary A queries with two distinct elements x_1 and x_2 and receives two elements $y_1 = f(x_1)$ and $y_2 = f(x_2)$, where f is either an instance of Φ or a random function from $Func(\mathcal{M}, \mathcal{M})$. If f is an instance of Φ, then $y_1 \oplus y_2 = (K \oplus x_1) \oplus (K \oplus x_2) = x_1 \oplus x_2$. The strategy of the adversary A would be to output 1 if $y_1 \oplus y_2 = x_1 \oplus x_2$, and 0 otherwise. The probability that the adversary outputs 1 if the pair (x_1, x_2) was processed by an instance of Φ is equal to 1. The probability that the adversary outputs 1 if the pair (x_1, x_2) was processed by a random function is $\frac{1}{2^n}$, because there exists a single element $v \in \mathcal{M}$ such that $v = y_1 \oplus y_2 = x_1 \oplus x_2$. The adversary advantage is:

$$ADV_\Phi^{prf}(A) = \Pr\left[K \stackrel{R}{\leftarrow} \mathcal{K}; A^{\Phi_K} \Rightarrow 1 \right] - \Pr\left[\varphi \stackrel{R}{\leftarrow} Func(\mathcal{M}, \mathcal{R}); A^{\varphi} \Rightarrow 1 \right] = 1 - \frac{1}{2^n}$$

$1 - \frac{1}{2^n}$ is far from negligible. Therefore, the function family Φ is not secure.

In addition, it is easy to recover the key used by the function family Φ. The adversary submits $x = 0^{(n)}$ and receives $y = K \oplus 0^{(n)}$. Then, the key is recovered as $K = y$.

10.1.2.1 Indistinguishability and Security of PRPs

Since any PRP $P: \mathcal{K} \times \mathcal{M} \to \mathcal{M}$ has an inverse $P^{-1}: \mathcal{K} \times \mathcal{M} \to \mathcal{M}$, the indistinguishability analysis of PRPs should consider two types of adversary attacks: the adversary has an access to the permutation P oracle and/or to the inverse permutation P^{-1} oracle. The first type of indistinguishability analysis is referred to as PRP under chosen-plaintext attack and the second as PRP under Chosen-ciphertext attack.

10.1.2.1.1 *PRP under Chosen-Plaintext-Attack*

The analysis of a PRP P, under Chosen-plaintext-attack (CPA) case, is the same as that of a PRF, with the exception that a collection of permutations are used instead of a collection of functions. Adversary A is given access to the oracle of permutation family P and to the random permutations. When the permutation family oracle is accessed, the adversary submits a plaintext and receives a ciphertext computed with a permutation instance P_K, where K is a random key selected uniformly from the key space $\mathcal{K}$. The test of how the adversary is able to distinguish between an instance of the permutation family and a random permutation from $Perm(\mathcal{M})$ follows the same game as that of a PRF and the *PRP-advantage* under CPA is defined by:

$$ADV_P^{prp-cpa}(A) \stackrel{def}{=} \Pr\left[K \stackrel{R}{\leftarrow} \mathcal{K}; A^{P_K} \Rightarrow 1 \right] - \Pr\left[\pi \stackrel{R}{\leftarrow} Perm(\mathcal{M}); A^{\pi} \Rightarrow 1 \right]$$

where:

$K \xleftarrow{R} \mathcal{K}$: it denotes the uniform selection at random of a key K from key space $\mathcal{K}$.

$\pi \xleftarrow{R} Perm(\mathcal{M})$: it denotes the selection of a random permutation π from all the random permutations in $Perm(\mathcal{M})$.

A^{P_K}: adversary A is given access to P_K, an instance of permutation family P.

$A\pi$: adversary A is given access to π, a random permutation in $Perm(\mathcal{M})$.

$\Pr[A^{P_K} \Rightarrow 1]$ is the probability that the adversary outputs $b=1$, given that the query was effectively processed by P_K. It is the probability of a correct guess.

$\Pr[A^{\pi} \Rightarrow 1]$ is the probability that the adversary outputs $b=1$, given that the query was processed by a random permutation π. It is the probability of a wrong guess.

In a similar way as for PRF, the PRP-advantage over all adversaries asking a maximum of q queries requiring a total computation time no more than t is defined by:

$$ADV_P^{prp-cpa}(t,q) \stackrel{def}{=} \max_A \left(ADV_P^{prp-cpa}(A) \right)$$

Definition 10.13 Secure PRP under CPA: *a PRP $P: \mathcal{K} \times \mathcal{M} \to \mathcal{M}$ is said to be (t,q,ε)-secure under CPA if the PRP-advantage over all adversaries is negligible, i.e. $ADV_P^{prp-cpa}(t,q) \leq \varepsilon$, where $\varepsilon \ll 1$ is a context-dependent bound; q and t denote the maximum number of queries and computation time for any adversary, respectively.*

10.1.2.1.2 PRP under Chosen-Ciphertext Attack

Analysis of a PRP P under Chosen-Ciphertext Attack (CCA) case is similar to that of a PRF with the exception that a collection of permutations is used instead of a collection of functions. Adversary A is given access to the oracles of permutation P_K and its inverse P_K^{-1}. It submits bit-strings (assuming they are ciphertexts) and receives bit-strings.

If $b=1$, then the queries are processed with an instance of P_K^{-1} and the returned bit-strings are valid plaintexts (i.e. if the inputs to the oracle of P_K^{-1} are valid ciphertexts with regard to the key K, then they are decrypted to valid plaintexts). If $b=0$, then the queries are processed with a random inverse permutation and do not yield valid plaintexts. Upon receiving bit-strings, the adversary has to guess if they are valid plaintexts or not.

The *PRP-advantage* under CCA is the measurement of how the adversary is able to distinguish between an instance of the inverse permutation family and a random inverse permutation from $Perm(\mathcal{M})$; it is defined by:

$$ADV_P^{prp-cca}(A) \stackrel{def}{=} \left| \Pr \left[K \xleftarrow{R} \mathcal{K}; A^{P_K, P_K^{-1}} \Rightarrow 1 \right] - \Pr \left[\pi \xleftarrow{R} Perm(\mathcal{M}); A^{\pi, \pi^{-1}} \Rightarrow 1 \right] \right|$$

where:

$K \xleftarrow{R} \mathcal{K}$: it denotes the uniform selection at random of a key K from key space $\mathcal{K}$.

$\pi^{-1}\pi; \xleftarrow{R} Perm(\mathcal{M})$: it denotes the selection, form $Perm(\mathcal{M})$, of a random permutation π and its inverse π^{-1}.

$A^{P_K, P_K^{-1}}$: adversary A is given access to the oracles of permutation instances P_k and P_K^{-1} of permutation family P with the key K.

$A^{\pi^{-1}; \pi}$: adversary A is given access to both random permutation instances π and π^{-1} of permutation family $Perm(M)$

$\Pr[A^{P_K, P_K^{-1}} \Rightarrow 1]$ is the probability of a correct guess.

$\Pr[A^{P_K, P_K^{-1}} \Rightarrow 1]$ is the probability of a wrong guess.

In a similar way as for PRF, the PRP-advantage under CCA over all adversaries asking a maximum of q queries requiring a total computation time no more than t is defined by:

$$ADV_P^{prp-cca}(t,q) \stackrel{def}{=} \max_A \left(ADV_P^{prp-cca}(A) \right)$$

Definition 10.14 Secure PRP under CCA: *a PRP $P: \mathcal{K} \times \mathcal{M} \to \mathcal{M}$ is said to be (t,q,ε)-secure under CCA if the PRP-advantage over all adversaries is negligible, i.e. $ADV_P^{prp-cca}(t,q) \leq \varepsilon$, where $\varepsilon \ll 1$ is a context-dependent bound; q and t denote the maximum number of queries and computation time for any adversary, respectively.*

Definition 10.15 Strong PRP: *PRP P*: $\mathcal{K} \times \mathcal{M} \to \mathcal{M}$ *is said to be a strong PRP if it is CPA-secure and CCA-secure.*

Example 10.3

Consider a block cipher E: $\{0,1\}^3 \times \{0,1\}^2 \to \{0,1\}^2$ defined by the following matrix of permutations:

Key	0	1	2	3
0	0	1	2	3
1	3	0	1	2
2	2	3	0	1
3	1	2	3	0
4	0	3	2	1
5	1	0	3	2
6	2	1	0	3
7	3	2	1	0

Examples of mappings of inputs: $E_0(0) = 0$, $E_1(1) = 0$, $E_5(2) = 3$, $E_7(3) = 0$.

Now, compute the PRP-advantage, under chosen-plaintext attack, an adversary can get depending on the number of queries it can submit.

- One query: the adversary submits x and receives $E_K(x) = y$. Any image y can be returned either by a permutation E_K or by a random permutation at a same probability of $\frac{1}{4}$. The adversary always outputs 1 upon reception of an image y.

  Therefore, the PRP-CPA advantage is $ADV_E^{prp-cpa}(t,1) = 1 - 1 = 0$.
- Two queries: the adversary submits two inputs $x_1 = 0$ and $x_2 = 1$. There exist $4!/2!$ pairs (y_1, y_2) among which eight can be generated by a permutation E_K. If the adversary receives one of the pairs (0,1), (3,0), (2,3),(1,2), (0,3), (1,0), (2,1), (3,2), it outputs 1. The probability that a random permutation returns one of the same eight pairs is $\dfrac{8}{(4!/2!)}$. Thus, the PRP-CPA advantage is $ADV_E^{prp-cpa}(t,2) = 1 - \dfrac{8}{12} = 1/3$.

- Four queries: the adversary submits four inputs $x_1 = 0$, $x_2 = 1$, $x_3 = 2$, $x_4 = 3$. There exist $4!$ results (y_1, y_2, y_3, y_4) among which eight can be generated by a permutation E_K. If the adversary receives one of the quadruplets (0,1,2,3), (3,0,1,2), (2,3,0,1), (1,2,3,0), (0,3,2,1), (1,0,3,2), (2,1,0,3), (3,2,1,0), it outputs 1. The probability that a random permutation returns one of the same eight quadruplets is $\dfrac{8}{(4!)}$. Hence, the PRP-CPA advantage is $ADV_E^{prp-cpa}(t,4) = 1 - \dfrac{8}{24} = 2/3$

10.1.2.2 PRF/PRP Switching Lemma

The usual assumption to make about a block cipher is that it behaves as a PRP. However, it usually turns out to be easier to analyze the security of a block cipher-based algorithm (e.g. authentication algorithm) assuming the block cipher is secure as a PRF. The gap between PRF-based or PRP-based analysis approaches is bridged by Bellare and Rogaway's lemma [5, 6].

Lemma 10.1 PRP-PRF switching lemma:

let n be the bit-length of domain $\mathcal{M}$. If an adversary can ask at most q queries, then:

$$\left| \Pr\left[\varphi \xleftarrow{R} Func(\mathcal{M},\mathcal{M}); A^\varphi \Rightarrow 1 \right] - \Pr\left[\pi \xleftarrow{R} Perm(\mathcal{M}); A^\pi \Rightarrow 1 \right] \right| \leq \frac{q(q-1)}{2^{n+1}}$$

As a consequence, for a permutation E: $\left| ADV_E^{prf}(A) - ADV_E^{prp}(A) \right| \leq \dfrac{q(q-1)}{2^{n+1}}$.

Lemma 10.1 states that the difference between the probability for the adversary to output 1, if it is given access to a random function or to a random permutation is bounded by $\dfrac{q(q-1)}{2^{n+1}}$. Therefore, given n and q, the acceptability of the bound $\dfrac{q(q-1)}{2^{n+1}}$ should be confirmed before interpreting a PRP as PRF in the analysis of block cipher-based algorithms. For example, if $q = 2^{n/2}$, then $\dfrac{q(q-1)}{2^{n+1}} \approx \dfrac{1}{2}$, which is far from being a negligible probability difference.

If q is large, $\dfrac{q(q-1)}{2^{n+1}}$ may be approximated by $\dfrac{q^2}{2^{n+1}} = 0.5 * \dfrac{q^2}{2^n}$. Therefore, a permutation family may have a PRF-advantage advantage that exceeds its PRP-advantage, but not by more than $0.5 * \dfrac{q^2}{2^n}$.

10.2 Security of TDEA and AES

It is commonly admitted in the cryptography field that a block cipher $E: \{0,1\}^k \times \{0,1\}^n \to \{0,1\}^n$, where k and n are the bit-lengths of the key and the block, respectively, is a permutation family E. For example, $AES128: \{0,1\}^{128} \times \{0,1\}^{128} \to \{0,1\}^{128}$ and $AES256: \{0,1\}^{256} \times \{0,1\}^{128} \to \{0,1\}^{128}$ are two permutation families. The inverse to the block cipher E is a permutation family E^{-1} with the same domain. In this book, the instances of permutations families E and E^{-1} are denoted Enc_K (for encryption) and Dec_K (for decryption). In the cryptography field, a PRP isreferred to as block cipher and vice versa. Therefore, the security of a block cipher E can be quantified as the maximum advantage that an adversary A can obtain when trying to distinguish between an instance of a permutation family E and a random permutation with the same domain as seen in Section 10.1.2.1.

The security analysis should address multiple objectives of adversaries. A block cipher is secure, if it prevents CPA, CCA, and key recovery attacks. As far as we know, standard block ciphers have not been proven to be fully secure. The usual method to evaluate the security of a block cipher works as follows: any adversary is given access to a block box, which runs either the block cipher with a randomly selected key or a random permutation. The adversary asks the black box and receives answers; then, it tries to guess in which context its queries are handled. For each addressed attack, a bound on the adversary advantage may be calculated.

The bounds proposed in literature are mainly dependent on the number of queries and computation time available to the adversary. Block ciphers remain secure as long as the bounds are not exceeded. It is worth noticing that many bounds have been proposed and improved over time. This section aims to give some examples of security bounds; however, it is far from covering the topic. Following the same notations as in previous sections, the advantage that an adversary A may have against a block cipher E, by modeling the block cipher either as a permutation family or as a function family, is defined as follows:

$$ADV_E^{prf}(A) \overset{def}{=} \Pr\left[K \overset{R}{\leftarrow} \mathcal{K}; A^{E_K} \Rightarrow 1\right] - \Pr\left[\varphi \overset{R}{\leftarrow} Fact(\mathcal{M},\mathcal{M}); A^{\varphi} \Rightarrow 1\right]$$

$$ADV_E^{prp}(A) \overset{def}{=} \Pr\left[K \overset{R}{\leftarrow} \mathcal{K}; A^{E_K} \Rightarrow 1\right] - \Pr\left[\pi \overset{R}{\leftarrow} Perm(\mathcal{M}); A^{\pi} \Rightarrow 1\right]$$

In [5], the authors proved that given a block cipher E, the difference between maximum advantages over all adversaries that run in time t and submit q queries, depending whether E is interpreted as a PRF or a PRP is bounded as follows:

$$ADV_E^{prf}(t,q) \leq ADV_E^{prp}(t,q) + \frac{q(q-1)}{2^{n+1}}$$

If the adversary is given access to both E (to make a chosen-plaintext attack) and E^{-1} (to make a chosen-ciphertext attack), its advantage is defined by:

$$ADV_E^{\pm prp}(A) \overset{def}{=} \Pr\left[K \overset{R}{\leftarrow} \mathcal{K}; A^{E_K, E_K^{-1}} \Rightarrow 1\right] - \Pr\left[\pi \overset{R}{\leftarrow} Perm(\mathcal{M}); A^{\pi, \pi^{-1}} \Rightarrow 1\right]$$

When AES and DES are attacked by an adversary, which runs in at most t and submits q queries, the following bounds are proposed in literature as conjectures [2, 4]:

$$ADV_{DES}^{prf}(t,q) \leq c_1 * \frac{t/T_{DES}}{2^{55}} + \frac{q^2}{2^{64}} \text{ and } ADV_{AES}^{prf}(t,q) \leq c_1 * \frac{t/T_{AES}}{2^{128}} + \frac{q^2}{2^{128}}$$

T_{DES} (resp. T_{AES}) denotes the time to do one DES (resp. AES) computation on the RAM (Random Access Machine) model[2] of adversary; and c_1 is a constant depending upon the adversary RAM model.

In [6], the following adversary advantage bound is proven for TDES:

$$ADV_{TDES}^{prp}(t,q) \leq 12(2n+k)\frac{q^2}{2^{3k}} + 10.7\left(\frac{q}{2^{k+n/2}}\right)^{2/3} + \frac{12}{2^k}$$

With $n = 64$ and $= 56$, the advantage becomes:

$$ADV_{TDES}^{prp}(t,q) \leq 12(2*64+56)\frac{q^2}{2^{168}} + 10.7\left(\frac{q}{2^{88}}\right)^{2/3} + \frac{12}{2^{56}} \tag{10.1}$$

The first component (i.e. $\frac{2208*q^2}{2^{168}}$) dominates when q is large. The maximal adversary advantage against TDEA is small until the adversary asks about 2^{78} queries, because:

$$ADV_{TDES}^{prp}\left(t,2^{77}\right) \leq \frac{2208*2^{77^2}}{2^{3*56}} = 0.135$$

$$ADV_{TDES}^{prp}\left(t,2^{78}\right) \leq \frac{2208*2^{78^2}}{2^{3*56}} = 0.540$$

Notice that in all the bounds above, if the number of queries exceeds $2^{\frac{n}{2}}$, the adversary advantage exceeds $\frac{1}{2}$; n is the block bit-length.

10.2.1 Security Against Key Recovery Attack

The number of distinct keys is 2^k, where $k \in \{128, 192, 256\}$ for AES, $k = 56$ for DES, and $k = 3*56$ for TDEA. Given a plaintext–ciphertext pair (P,C), a brute-force attack to recover a key requires 2^k steps (i.e. check if $Enc_K(P) = C$, for every key $K \in \{0,1\}^k$). When the security of AES-128 or DES is of concern, the complexity of brute-force attack is below the bound of 2^{80}; the latter marks the computational infeasibility of attacks. Therefore, to make block ciphers resistant to brute-force attacks against the key, the number of blocks encrypted with the same key is limited.

Table 10.1 shows how it is time-consuming to recover a key using a brute-force attack. Assume that an adversary has a plaintext–ciphertext pair and tries to crack the key of a block cipher and it can check[3] $10^6, 10^9$, and 10^{16} keys per second.

One usual approach to modeling the security against key recovery of a block cipher E is similar to that of PRF/PRP security analysis presented in previous subsections. An adversary A is given access to an oracle of E_K, an instance of permutation family E. One game between the challenger and the adversary is as follows: the adversary asks the oracle with a plaintext and receives a ciphertext. Then, it tries to guess the key used by the challenger to encrypt the plaintext. The key-recovery advantage for an experiment is defined by:

$ADV_E^{kr}(A) \overset{def}{=} \Pr[A^{K \xleftarrow{R} K} = (K' = K)]$, which is the probability that the adversary guesses a key K', which is the same than the key K used by the challenger.

Definition 10.16 Secure block cipher under key recovery attack: *a block cipher $E: K \times M \to M$ is said to be $(t,q,)$-secure under key-recovery attack, if the kr-advantage over all adversaries is negligible, i.e. $ADV_E^{kr}(t,q) \leq \varepsilon$, where $\varepsilon \ll 1$ is a context-dependent bound; q and t denote the maximum number of queries and computation time for any adversary.*

In [4], Rogaway proved the following bounds regarding the key-recovery attack when the block cipher is modeled as a PRF or as a PRP:

$$ADV_F^{kr}(t,q) \leq ADV_F^{prf}(t,q) + \frac{1}{2^n} \tag{10.2}$$

$$ADV_F^{kr}(t,q) \leq ADV_F^{prp-cpa}(t,q) + \frac{1}{2^n - q} \tag{10.3}$$

Table 10.1 Time to crack a key vs its bit-length.

Key length	10^6 keys per second	10^9 keys per second	10^{15} keys per second
56 bits	2 284 years	2 284 years	72 sec
128 bits	$1.08*10^{25}$ years	$1.08*10^{22}$ years	$1.08*10^{16}$ years
192 bits	$1.99*10^{44}$ years	$1.99*10^{41}$ years	$1.99*10^{35}$ years
256 bits	$3.67*10^{63}$ years	$3.67*10^{60}$ years	$3.67*10^{54}$ years

Bounds (10.2) and (10.3) mean that if a family of functions is a secure PRF or PRP, then it is also secure against key-recovery attacks. Therefore, if a block cipher is modeled as a PRF or PRP, it is implicitly assumed to be secure against key-recovery attacks.

10.2.2 Birthday Attack Against Block Ciphers

The birthday paradox is used to analyze the security of block ciphers. Such a (statistical) analysis is referred to as birthday attack against bock ciphers. Recall that the principle of the birthday paradox (see Section 3.4) is as follows: given a population of N individuals, the probability to get two individuals with the same birthday exceeds $\frac{1}{2}$ if $\sqrt{N}$ individuals are randomly picked from the population.

Let $E:\{0,1\}^k \times \{0,1\}^n \to \{0,1\}^n$ be a block cipher. The adversary is given access to two oracles, a permutation E_k and a random function. It asks one of the oracles with q distinct elements $x_1, x_2, \ldots, x_q$ and receives $y_1, y_2, \ldots, y_q$ images. If the adversary is given access to a permutation E_k, then all the images are distinct (by virtue of the pseudorandom permutation property). If among the received images, there exist two identical images, then the adversary is given access to a random function. To get two identical elements (or images), at a probability greater than $\frac{1}{2}$ from the function domain $\{0,1\}^n$, $\sqrt{2^n}$ queries are required.

The birthday-based analysis game would be for the adversary to output 1 at a probability of 1, if no identical images are received. The probability that no collision occurs under the random permutation oracle is at most $e^{-\frac{q(q-1)}{2^n}}$ (for more detail on such a probability, see Section 3.4). Hence, the advantage of a birthday-attack adversary when $q = 2^{\frac{n}{2}}$ is at least $1 - e^{-1/2} \approx 0.4$, which is a very high advantage.

Using the upper and lower bounds of collision probability introduced in Section 3.4, the following advantage bound is proposed and proven in [5].

Lemma 10.2

Let $E:\{0,1\}^k \times \{0,1\}^n \to \{0,1\}^n$ be a block cipher and q a number of queries such that $1 \leq q \leq 2^{(n+1)/2}$. Then, the advantage of any adversary making q queries within a computation time not exceeding $q * n$ is $ADV_E^{prf}(t,q) \geq 0.316 * \frac{q(q-1)}{2^n}$.

Conclusion from Lemmas 10.1 and 10.2:

Replacing q by $2^{\frac{n}{2}}$ in lemma 10.1 yields $\left| ADV_E^{prf}\left(t, 2^{\frac{n}{2}}\right) - ADV_E^{prp}\left(t, 2^{\frac{n}{2}}\right) \right| \leq 0.5 - \frac{1}{2^{\left(\frac{n}{2}+1\right)}}$, which may be approximated by 0.5.

Therefore, if the number of queries is at most $2^{\frac{n}{2}}$, PRF-advantage and PRP-advantage of a permutation family do not differ by more than the amount given by the birthday attack (i.e. 0.5). Replacing q by $2^{\frac{n}{2}}$ in lemma 10.2 yields:

$$ADV_E^{prf}(t,q) \geq 0.316 * \left(1 - \frac{1}{2^{n/2}}\right) \approx 0.316.$$

10.3 Security Analysis Modes of Operation of BC for Confidentiality

Notations

$\{0,1\}^*$: any bit string
$\mathcal{K} = \{0,1\}^k$: set of all bit-strings of length k; k is the key bit-length
$\{0,1\}^n$: set of all bit-strings of length n; n is the block bit-length
$(\{0,1\}^n)^+$: one or more n-bit blocks
$(\{0,1\}^s)^+$: one or more s-bit segments, with $s \leq n$ (applicable to CFB only)

Modes of operation of block ciphers, which are presented in detail in Chapter 8, aim to protect data. Therefore, the security analysis of such modes focuses on privacy.

In ECB mode, identical plaintext blocks yield identical ciphertext blocks. Therefore, ECB mode leaks the repetitions in plaintexts; and in consequence, it is not regarded as an interesting mode of operation. In literature, ECB security is mainly addressed from the information leakage point of view. For example, the analysis would infer statistical results such as similarity between two ciphertexts, frequency of repetition in the same ciphertexts, locations of repetitions, etc. Since there are no dependencies between ciphertext blocks corresponding to the same plaintent, ECB mode looks like a repetitive use of a block cipher. Therefore, its security regarding CPA, CCA, and key recovery is similar to that of a block cipher alone.

With the exception of ECB mode, a mode of operation is modeled as permutation family and its inverse:

$$\varepsilon: \mathcal{K} \times \mathcal{V} \times \mathcal{P} \to \mathcal{C}$$

$$\mathcal{D}: \mathcal{K} \times \mathcal{V} \times \mathcal{C} \to \mathcal{P}$$

where: $\mathcal{K}$ denotes the key space, $\mathcal{V}$ the space of IV or of counter, $\mathcal{P}$ and $\mathcal{C}$ the plaintext and ciphertext spaces, respectively. The IV may be a random value, a nonce, or a tweak, depending on the analyzed mode.

Let $\varepsilon_K^v(P) = C$ denote the encryption of plaintext $P \in \mathcal{P}$ using a key $K \in \mathcal{K}$ and a parameter $v \in \mathcal{V}$; and $\mathcal{D}_K^v(C) = P$ denote the decryption of plaintext $C \in \mathcal{C}$ using a key $K \in \mathcal{K}$ and a parameter $v \in \mathcal{V}$. Modes of operation of block ciphers are modeled as permutation families:

$$ECB: \{0,1\}^k \times \left(\{0,1\}^n\right)^+ \to \left(\{0,1\}^n\right)^+$$

$$CBC: \{0,1\}^k \times \{0,1\}^n \times \left(\{0,1\}^n\right)^+ \to \left(\{0,1\}^n\right)^+$$

$$OFB: \{0,1\}^k \times \{0,1\}^n \times \{0,1\}^* \to \{0,1\}^*$$

$$CFB: \{0,1\}^k \times \{0,1\}^n \times \left(\{0,1\}^s\right)^+ \to \left(\{0,1\}^s\right)^+$$

$$CTR: \{0,1\}^k \times \{0,1\}^n \times \{0,1\}^* \to \{0,1\}^*$$

$$XTS: \{0,1\}^{2k} \times \{0,1\}^{128} \times \{0,1\}^* \to \{0,1\}^*.$$ XTS makes use of keys of a bit-length $2k = 256$ or $2k = 512$ and a 128-bit tweak.

Question *assuming the underlying block cipher E is secure at an advantage of $ADV_E^{prf}(t',q')$ or $ADV_E^{prp}(t',q')$, depending on whether the block cipher is modeled as a PRF or a PRP, what are the values parameters t (the computation time), q_e (the number of encryption queries), q_d (the number of decryption queries), μ_e (the total of plaintext bits), and μ_d (the total ciphertext bits) such that the adversary advantage in attacking a symmetric cipher remains small?*

Different ways to address the analysis of the security of modes of operation of block ciphers have been proposed in literature, including Real-or-Random indistinguishability (see Section 10.1.2), Left-or-Right, Find-then-Guess, and Semantic security [2]. In this book, we only focus on the Left-or-Right approach, which is, as far as we know, the most used to derive concrete bounds on indistinguishability of modes of operation for confidentiality.

10.3.1 Left-or-Right Indistinguishability

The idea of the Left-or-Right (LOR) indistinguishability is that the adversary cannot distinguish which plaintext, between two equal bit-length plaintexts, has been encrypted given one ciphertext (see Figure 10.2).

In CPA security analysis session, the adversary submits q_e queries each of the form (m_0^i, m_1^i), where m_0^i and m_1^i are equal-length plaintexts for every query i ($i = 1, \ldots, q_e$). If parameter $b = 0$, then every plaintext m_0^i is encrypted and a ciphertext $c_i = \varepsilon_K(m_0^i)$ is returned; and if $b = 1$, then every plaintext m_1^i is encrypted and a ciphertext $c_i = \varepsilon_K(m_1^i)$ is returned. The game for the adversary, is to guess which plaintext m_0^i (the left) or m_1^i (the right) has been encrypted.

The advantage that an adversary A_{CPA} can get is the difference between the probability that the adversary outputs 1 if it thinks that its queries have been processed with $b = 1$, while it is effectively true and the probability that it outputs 1 if it thinks that its queries have been processed with $b = 1$, while it is false. Formally, the advantage of adversary A_{CPA} is defined by:

$$ADV_\varepsilon^{lor-cpa}\left(A_{CPA}\right) = \Pr\left[output = 1 \text{ } while \text{ } b = 1\right] - \Pr\left[output = 1 \text{ } while \text{ } b = 0\right]$$

In other words, the adversary advantage is measured in terms of the difference between the probabilities to guess which plaintexts have been encrypted, the left or the right ones. Then, the maximal advantage over all CPA adversaries that can run in at most time t and submit a maximum of q_e encryption queries totaling[4] at most μ_e bits is defined by:

$$ADV_\varepsilon^{lor-cpa}\left(t, q_e, \mu_e\right) = \max_{A_{CPA}}\left(ADV_\varepsilon^{lor-cpa}\left(A_{CPA}\right)\right)$$

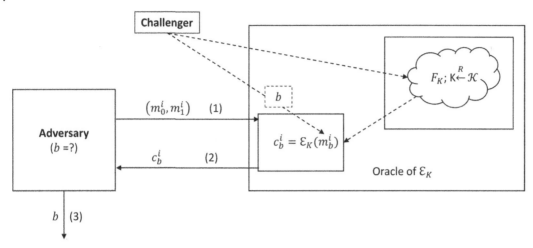

Figure 10.2 Left-or-Right game for distinguishability.

In a CCA security analysis session, in addition to q_e encryption queries, the adversary submits q_d decryption queries each of the form of a bit-string y_i, $i = 1$, ..., q_d, under the assumption that y_i has not been previously returned by the encryption oracle ε_K. Otherwise, the adversary will obviously win the game. Then, if y_i is a valid ciphertext, the decryption oracle returns a plaintext $m_i = \mathcal{D}_K(y_i)$. Otherwise, it returns a null symbol $\perp$. Using the chosen ciphertexts and received plaintexts, the adversary has to guess which value is used for parameter b.

The advantage that a CCA adversary can get is defined as that of CPA; and the maximal advantage over all CCA adversaries that can run in a time t and submit a maximum of q_e encryption queries totaling at most μ_e bits and q_d decryption queries totaling at most μ_d bits is defined by:

$$ADV_{\varepsilon}^{lor-cca}\left(t, q_e, \mu_e, q_d, \mu_d\right) = \max_{A_{CCA}}\left(ADV_{\varepsilon}^{lor-cca}\left(A_{CCA}\right)\right)$$

A mode of operation ε is said to be LOR-CPA secure if $ADV_{\varepsilon}^{lor-cpa}(t, q_e, \mu_e) \leq \beta_{cpa}$ and LOR-CCA secure if $ADV_{\varepsilon}^{lor-cca}(t, q_e, \mu_e) \leq \beta_{cca}$, where β_{cpa} and β_{cca} are negligible bounds.

10.3.2 Some Bounds of Security of Block Cipher Modes of Operation

Below are given some bounds proven in literature. They are very useful to understand why the number of plaintexts encrypted with the same key is limited, in order to not compromise the security. It is worth noticing that the security analysis has mainly focused on CBC and CTR modes for two reasons: they are the most used in practice and the security of OFB and CFB modes may be inferred from those of CBC and CTR.

Security under chosen-plaintext attack
To simplify the bound definitions, we assume that the plaintext bit-length is a multiple of n, the block length of the underlying block cipher. In [2, 5, 7], the following security bounds are proved, where q is the total number[5] of n-bit blocks encrypted using the block cipher E under the same key and μ_e is the total number of bits encrypted with CBC or CTR such that $\mu_e = n * q$. Notice that q_e is at most q and it has no impact on the following bounds.

CBC mode (if the IV is randomly selected and unpredictable by adversary):

$$ADV_{CBC[E]}^{lor-cpa}\left(t, q_e, \mu_e\right) ADV_E^{prf}\left(t, q\right) + \frac{q^2}{2^n} \tag{10.4}$$

CTR mode (if the initial counter value is randomly chosen):

$$ADV_{CTR[E]}^{lor-cpa}\left(t, q_e, \mu_e\right) \leq ADV_E^{prf}\left(t, q\right) + \frac{0.5 * q^2}{2^n} \tag{10.5}$$

Inequalities (10.4) and (10.5) state that the adversary advantage attacking the CBC or CTR modes, under CPA, is at most the advantage when attacking the underlying block cipher E, if it is modeled as a PRF, plus a quantity that depends on the number of encrypted blocks. Notice that CTR mode has a better security bound. If the underlying block cipher is secure and the number of encrypted blocks is low, then both CBC and CTR modes are secure.

Example 10.4

Using the TDES security bound (10.1), given the maximum number of blocks to encrypt under CBC over TDES, the CBC-adversary advantage β can be yielded as follows:

$$\beta = ADV_{CBC[TDES]}^{lor-cpa}\left(t,\ q_e,\mu_e\right) \le ADV_{TDES}^{prf}\left(t,q\right) + \frac{q^2}{2^n}$$

By PRF/PRP switching lemma,

$$\beta = ADV_{CBC[TDES]}^{lor-cpa}\left(t,\ q_e,\mu_e\right) \le ADV_{TDES}^{prp}\left(t,q\right) + \frac{q^2}{2^n} + \frac{q(q-1)}{2^{n+1}}$$

In TDES, $n = 64$ and $k = 56$. Thus, by substitutions:

$$\beta \le 2\left[12(2*64+56)\frac{q^2}{2^{168}} + 10.7\left(\frac{q}{2^{88}}\right)^{\frac{2}{3}} + \frac{12}{2^{56}}\right] + \left(\frac{q^2}{2^{64}} + \frac{q(q-1)}{2^{64+1}}\right)$$

$$= \left(\frac{4416*q^2}{2^{168}} + \frac{21.4*q^{2/3}}{2^{88*2/3}} + \frac{24}{2^{56}}\right) + \left(\frac{q^2}{2^{64}} + \frac{q(q-1)}{2^{65}}\right)$$

If $q = 2^{30}$ (i.e. a total of 16 G bytes are encrypted with the same key), then

$$\beta = \left(\frac{4416*2^{30*2}}{2^{168}} + \frac{21.4*2^{30*2/3}}{2^{88*2/3}} + \frac{24}{2^{56}}\right) + \left(\frac{2^{30*2}}{2^{64}} + \frac{2^{30}(2^{30}-1)}{2^{65}}\right) \approx \frac{1}{2^4}, \text{ which is a high bound.}$$

If $q = 2^{20}$ (i.e. a total of 16 M bytes are encrypted with the same key), then

$$\beta = \left(\frac{4416*2^{20*2}}{2^{168}} + \frac{21.4*2^{20*2/3}}{2^{88*2/3}} + \frac{24}{2^{56}}\right) + \left(\frac{2^{20*2}}{2^{64}} + \frac{2^{20}(2^{20}-1)}{2^{65}}\right) \approx \frac{1}{2^{24}}, \text{ which is a small bound.}$$

Security under Chosen-Ciphertext Attack

CCA attacks are powerful enough to break all the modes of operation of block ciphers including CBC, CFB, OFB, and CTR. As far as we know, only XTS-AES was proven to be a strong PRP (i.e. it is secure under CCA attacks). In [8], the following bound is proven regarding the XTS-AES:

$$ADV_{XTS-AES}^{cca}\left(t,q\right) \le 2*ADV_{AES}^{prp-cca}\left(t',\ q\right) + \frac{q^2}{2^{128}} \tag{10.6}$$

where q denotes the total number of encryption and decryption queries. t and t' are the maximum computation times of adversaries attacking XTS-AES; $t' = t + O(q)$. $O(q)$ denotes "in order of q".

Below are two examples of CCAs against CTR and CBC modes.

1) Recall that CTR encryption of one block B is defined by $C = B \oplus Enc_K\left(Counter\right)$ and the decryption defined by $B = C \oplus Enc_K\left(Counter\right)$. Let $\left(V, C\right)$ denote a ciphertext block C and V the counter value obtained with a query to CTR encryption oracle. Flip a bit in C and get C'; i.e. $C = C_L \parallel c \parallel C_R$ and $C' = C_L \parallel \bar{c} \parallel C_R$ (C_L and C_R are the left and right bits of C, respectively; and c is the flipped bit). Next, query CTR decryption oracle with $\left(V, C'\right)$ and receive an n-bit string B'. If B' differs from B by one bit (the one flipped in the ciphertext), then the adversary infers that it is given access to CTR decryption oracle, because:

$$C = \left(C_L \parallel c \parallel C_R\right) = B \oplus Enc_K\left(V\right)$$

$$\left(C_L \parallel c \parallel C_R\right) \oplus Enc_K\left(V\right) = B = \left(B_L \parallel b \parallel B_R\right)$$

$$C' \oplus Enc_K\left(V\right) = \left(C_L \parallel \bar{c} \parallel C_R\right) \oplus Enc_K\left(V\right) = \left(B_L \parallel \bar{b} \parallel B_R\right) = B'.$$

The probability that the random permutation oracle returns a bit string that differs from B by a single bit at a known position is $1/2^n$. Thus, CCA-adversary advantage is close to 1.

2) Recall that CBC encryption of one block B is defined by $C = Enc_K(B \oplus IV)$ and the decryption defined by $B = Dec_K(C) \oplus IV$. Let (V, C) denote a ciphertext block C and V the IV value obtained with a query to CBC encryption oracle. Flip a bit in V and get V'; i.e. $V = V_L \parallel v \parallel V_R$ and $V' = V_L \parallel \bar{v} \parallel V_R$ (V_L and V_R are the left and right bits of V, respectively; and v is the flipped bit). Next, query CBC decryption oracle with (V', C) and receive an n-bit string B'. If B' differs from B by one bit (the one flipped in the IV), then the adversary infers that it was given access to CBC decryption oracle, because:

$$C = Enc_K(B \oplus V) = Enc_K\left((B_L \parallel b \parallel B_R) \oplus (V_L \parallel v \parallel V_R)\right)$$

$$Dec_K(C) \oplus V' = Dec_K(Enc_K(B \oplus V)) \oplus V' = B \oplus V \oplus V'$$

$$= (B_L \parallel b \parallel B_R) \oplus (V_L \parallel v \parallel V_R) \oplus (V_L \parallel \bar{v} \parallel V_R) = (B_L \parallel \bar{b} \parallel B_R) = B'$$

The probability that the random permutation oracle returns a bit string that differs from B by a single bit at a known position is $1/2^n$. Thus, CCA-adversary advantage is close to 1.

10.4 Security Analysis of Authenticity-only Schemes

Authenticity-only schemes, which include CMAC, GMAC, and HMAC, aim to generate and verify MACs. Therefore, the security analysis of such schemes focuses on authenticity. Authenticity modes of operation, which include CMAC and GMAC standards, are presented in Chapter 9. HMAC is another way to provide authenticity guarantees by using hash functions and not block ciphers; it is presented in Section 5.3.2.1.

10.4.1 Generic Models for Security Analysis of Authenticity Schemes

The main objective of security analysis models of MAC modes is to find bounds on the probability that an adversary can infer some useful information on the MAC modes in order to forge valid tags (i.e. the adversary is able to apply existential forgery attack). Recall that MAC modes aim to authenticate the origin of messages and not to make the information confidential. Therefore, the main purpose of MAC mode security evaluation focuses only on tag forgery. There exist two models of MAC security analysis, one focuses on tag forgery and the other on the MAC function indistinguishability.

10.4.1.1 Game for Tag Forgery Analysis
The basic security analysis model of MAC modes is an oracle with two components: MAC generation and MAC verification (see Figure 10.3). In the initialization step, a key K is uniformly selected at random from the key space $\mathcal{K} = \{0,1\}^k$, where k is the key bit-length. Then, the adversary selects a message $M \in \{0,1\}^*$ and queries the MAC generation component to produce a valid tag $T = F_K(M)$, where F is the MAC mode under analysis. The tag generation query operation is repeated[6] several times. Then, using the collected tags, the adversary tries to forge a tag T' for some message M' that has never been submitted to the tag generation component, and queries the MAC verification component to check if tag T' is valid or not; the oracle returns 1 if the tag is valid and 0 otherwise. The tag verification query operation is repeated several times, until the adversary succeeds in forging a tag or stops.

Given a MAC mode F (such as CMAC, GMAC, or HMAC), the maximum probability of forging a valid tag by an adversary $\mathcal{A}$ is referred to as adversary *mac-advantage* and it is denoted $ADV_F^{mac}(\mathcal{A})$. The resources used by an adversary to forge a tag, by querying the oracle, are represented in terms of the number of tag generation queries, denoted q_{gen}, and that of tag

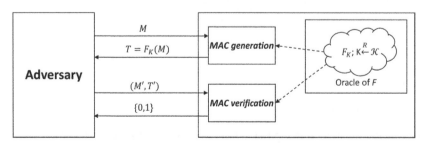

Figure 10.3 Generic oracle for MAC mode security analysis.

verification queries, denoted q_{ver}. The probability of attack success depends on the number of queries; the higher the number of queries, the higher the probability of success. The computation time t required to perform encryptions (Enc_K), decryptions (Dec_K), and tag verifications to answer all the queries is of paramount importance, because it indicates if the attack is computationally feasible or not under the expected probability.

$ADV_F^{mac}(t, q_{gen} + q_{ver}, \mu)$ denotes the probability of tag forgery over all adversaries that ask at most t calls[7] to the underlying block cipher, q_{gen} queries to the MAC generation component, and q_{ver} queries to the MAC-verification component with a maximum of μ bits per query. Formally,

$$ADV_F^{mac}(t,q,\mu) \overset{def}{=} \max_{\mathcal{A}} ADV_F^{mac}(\mathcal{A})$$

$$ADV_F^{mac}(\mathcal{A}) \overset{def}{=} \Pr\left[K \overset{R}{\leftarrow} \mathcal{K}; \ \mathcal{A}^{F_K} \Rightarrow 1\right]$$

where $K \overset{R}{\leftarrow} \mathcal{K}$ denotes a uniform selection at random of a key K; $\Pr\left[K \overset{R}{\leftarrow} \mathcal{K}; \ \mathcal{A}^{F_K} \Rightarrow 1\right]$ means the probability that the adversary $\mathcal{A}$ receives 1 (i.e. it succeeds in forging a tag T' and a message M' such that $T' = F_K(M')$).

A MAC mode is said to be secure if $ADV_F^{mac}(t, q, \mu)$ is below an acceptable probability, which depends on applications.

10.4.1.2 Game for MAC Indistinguishability

With the exception of GMAC, all the MAC modes presented in this book are pseudo random functions (PRFs). Thus, a MAC mode F is a PRF $F: \{0,1\}^k \times \{0,1\}^* \to \{0,1\}^{Tlen}$, where k and $Tlen$ denote the key and tag bit-lengths, respectively.

Then, the security analysis of a MAC mode F may be measured as the maximum advantage that an adversary $\mathcal{A}$ can obtain when trying to distinguish between the oracle of F and a random function. Following the same idea of indistinguishability of function and permutation families introduced in Section 10.1.2 (see Figure 10.1), the principle of MAC indistinguishability is to give the adversary access to two oracles:

1) First oracle denoted F_K: uniformly select a key K at random from key space $\mathcal{K}$ and then process adversary queries with the function F_K.
2) Second oracle φ: select at random a function φ from the set $\Phi: \{0,1\}^* \to \{0,1\}^{Tlen}$ of all random functions that take an input from the message space $\mathcal{M}$ and return a $Tlen$-bit string. Then, all adversary queries are processed with function φ.

Before processing the adversary queries, the challenger uniformly selects at random a parameter $b \in \{0,1\}$. If $b = 1$, the adversary is given access to the oracle F_K; and it receives a valid tag $T = F_K(M)$ for any input message M. If $b = 0$, it is given access the oracle of φ; and it receives a random $Tlen$-bit string for any input message M. Then, the adversary asks with a set of messages selected (according to some strategy) from the message domain $\mathcal{M}$. Then, it receives either a set of valid tags or a set of random $Tlen$-bit strings. Notice that we are talking about chosen-plaintext-attacks. Making exploitation of the received answers, the adversary is requested to guess which oracle is used.

The adversary advantage of a MAC F as a PRF is its ability to distinguish between a MAC function and a random function. The advantage is measured in terms of the difference between the probability it outputs 1 while it has access to oracle of F_K (i.e. probability of a correct guess) and the probability it outputs 1 while it has access to a random function oracle (i.e. probability of a wrong guess). Using the same notations as in Section 10.1.2, the advantage of adversary $\mathcal{A}$ attacking a MAC F as a PRF is defined by:

$$ADV_F^{prf}(\mathcal{A}) \overset{def}{=} \Pr\left[K \overset{R}{\leftarrow} \mathcal{K}; \ \mathcal{A}^{F_K} \Rightarrow 1\right] - \Pr\left[\varphi \overset{R}{\leftarrow} Func\left(\mathcal{M}, \{0,1\}^{Tlen}\right); \ \mathcal{A}^{\varphi} \Rightarrow 1\right]$$

The maximum advantage over all adversaries with computation time at most t and submitting at most q plaintexts with a total of μ bits is defined by:

$$ADV_F^{prf}(t, q, \mu) \overset{def}{=} \max_{\mathcal{A}} ADV_F^{prf}(\mathcal{A})$$

It is commonly accepted that if function family F is secure as a PRF (i.e. F is indistinguishable from a random function), it is secure as a MAC (i.e. attacker cannot forge tags, which are validated by MAC F). That fact is formalized by the following relationship proven in [5]:

$$ADV_F^{mac}(t, q, \mu) \le ADV_F^{prf}(t', q) + \frac{1}{2^{Tlen}} \tag{10.7}$$

where:

q is the number of queries; t and t' denote the computation times of adversary attacking F as a MAC or as a PRF, respectively. t' exceeds t with an amount in order of $Tlen + d$, where d is the bit-length of plaintext. Notice that $\frac{1}{2^{Tlen}}$ is added in (10.7), because even a perfect PRF (i.e. $ADV_F^{prf}(\ldots) = 0$), there is a probability of $\frac{1}{2^{Tlen}}$ that the adversary can randomly choose a valid tag and submit a query, and then receives 1 (i.e. the tag is valid) from the tag verifier.

The maximum adversary advantage to forge a tag is called the *maximum forgery probability*.

10.4.2 Some Security Bounds for MAC Schemes

10.4.2.1 Security Bounds for CMAC

CMAC mode is modeled as a PRF: $CMAC: \{0,1\}^k \times \{0,1\}^* \to \{0,1\}^{Tlen}$. It operates above a block cipher E. Since E is PRP, the adversary advantage includes a PRP advantage. As far as we know, the security of CMAC and its variants are the most addressed in literature. Below are some useful proven bounds on CMAC tag forgery probability; in the three bounds, n denotes the block cipher bit-length:

$$ADV_{CMAC}^{mac}(t, q, \sigma) \leq \frac{4 * \sigma^2 + 1}{2^n} + ADV_E^{prp}(t', q') \quad [9]$$

$$ADV_{CMAC}^{prf}(t, q, m) \leq \frac{l * q^2}{2^n} * \left(12 + \frac{64 * l^3}{2^n}\right) \quad [2]$$

$$ADV_{CMAC}^{prf}(t, q, \sigma) \leq \frac{4 * \sigma * q}{2^n} + \frac{8q(q-1) * m^4}{2^{2n}} \quad [10]$$

where: q denotes the total number of tag generation and verification queries. σ denotes the total number of blocks of all the q queries. l denotes the maximum number of blocks per query. In the tag verification query, one block contains the forged tag. In [9], $q' = \sigma + 1$ and $t' = t + O(\sigma)$. $O(\sigma)$ means "in order of σ".

Example 10.5

In AES-CMAC standard, it is recommended to limit the key to no more than 2^{48} messages for general-purpose applications and to no more than 2^{48} blocks if a higher confidence in security is required. The $ADV_E^{prp}(t', q')$ is negligible, if the number of blocks q' is at most 2^{48}. The third bound of forgery probability may be reduced to $\frac{4 * \sigma * q}{2^n}$, because the second factor is very small.

− If each of 2^{48} messages is 1 G bytes in length, then

$$q = 2^{48}, \sigma = \left(\frac{2^{30}}{16}\right) * 2^{48} = 2^{74}.$$

The best advantage bound is $ADV_{CMAC}^{prf}(t, q, \sigma) \leq \frac{5 * 2^{74} * 2^{48}}{2^{128}} = \frac{5}{64}$, which is a weak security.

− If each of 2^{48} messages is 16 bytes in length, then

$$q = 2^{48}, \sigma = \left(\frac{16}{16}\right) * 2^{48} = 2^{48}.$$

The best advantage bound is $ADV_{CMAC}^{prf}(t, q, \sigma) \leq \frac{5 * 2^{48} * 2^{48}}{2^{128}} = \frac{5}{2^{32}}$, which is a strong security.

− If each of 2^{32} messages is 1 G bytes in length, then

$$q = 2^{32}, \sigma = \left(\frac{2^{30}}{16}\right) * 2^{32} = 2^{58}.$$

The best advantage bound is $ADV_{CMAC}^{prf}(t, q, \sigma) \leq \frac{5 * 2^{58} * 2^{32}}{2^{128}} = \frac{5}{2^{38}}$, which is a very strong security.

10.4.2.2 Security Bounds for HMAC

Hash functions and HMAC are presented in Section 3.5.2.1. HMAC is a family of MAC schemes parameterized with a cryptographic hash function. HMAC instances are denoted HMAC_H, where H may be any hash function including SHA-1, SHA-256, SHA3-512, etc. HMAC does not make use of any block cipher; its security relies on the underlying hash function. A MAC of a message M is computed as follows:

$$HMAC\_H(K, M) = H\left(\left(K' \oplus oPad\right) \| \left(H(K' \oplus iPad \| M)\right)\right) \quad (10.8)$$

where H is the underlying hash function, K' an expanded key derived from a master key K, and $oPad$ and $iPad$ are constant bit strings.

H function takes any bit string (with length multiple of 8) and returns a bit string (called digest) of fixed length $Hlen$. Function H splits up a message into blocks of a fixed length b, which is a parameter of H (e.g. $b = 512$ for SHA-1 and $b = 1024$ for SHA-512) and iterates[8] over them with a compression function h. A compression function h is basic hash function that takes a single b-bit block and a chaining parameter (which may be an IV or the tag of the previous block) and returns a $Hlen$-bit tag; i.e. h is a map: $h: \{0,1\}^{Hlen} \times \{0,1\}^b \rightarrow \{0,1\}^{Hlen}$. Any HMAC variant is a function, i.e.

$$HMAC\_H: \{0,1\}^k \times \{0,1\}^* \rightarrow \{0,1\}^{Hlen}$$

where k denotes the key bit-length and $Hlen$ the tag bit-length (e.g. $Hlen = 160$ if $H =$ SHA-1, $Hlen = 256$ if H is SHA-256, and $Hlen = 512$ if H is SHA3-512).

HMAC security relies on i) the security of the key derivation key (KDF), which computes K' from K and ii) on the security of the underlying hash function H. The KDF used in standard HMAC is a PRG (pseudorandom generator). Therefore, the first condition is omitted when analyzing the security of standard HMAC.

In [11], Bellare proved that HMAC is a PRF under the sole assumption that the compression function of the underlying hash function is a PRF. Standard hash families SHA-1 and SHA-2 (including SHA-224, SHA-256, SHA-384, SHA-512, SHA-512/224, and SHA-512/256) are iterated hash functions and are considered as secure PRFs. SHA-3 is a based on the Keccak permutation and it also is considered as a secure hash function.

Under the assumption that the underlying compression function is a PRF, Bellare proposed the following bound:

$$ADV_{HMAC}^{prf}(\mathcal{A}) \leq ADV_h^{prf}(\mathcal{A}_1) + (q-1)\left(\sigma - \frac{q}{2}\right) * ADV_h^{prf}(\mathcal{A}_2) + \frac{q(q-1)}{2^{Hlen+1}}$$

$\mathcal{A}$ is any adversary that attacks HMAC. $\mathcal{A}$ makes at most q queries with a total of σ blocks (each of b bits); $\sigma = n_1 + n_2 + \ldots + n_q$, where n_i is the number of blocks of query i. $\mathcal{A}_1$ is any adversary that attacks the compression function h used in HMAC. $\mathcal{A}_1$ submits q queries (totalizing σ blocks). $\mathcal{A}_2$ is any adversary, which submits at most two queries (totalizing at most $2m$ blocks) to attack the compression function h. $\mathcal{A}$ and $\mathcal{A}_1$ run at most in t, while $\mathcal{A}_2$ runs at most in $O(m * t_h)$, where $m = \max_i(n_i)$ and t_h is the time for one computation of h.

It is worth noticing that the bound mentioned above is a simplified one of a more accurate bound proposed in [6], which adds an advantage of any adversary that attacks the dual function of compression h. $\bar{h}$ is a dual function of h is defined by $\bar{h}(x,y) = h(y,x)$.

10.5 Generic Models for Security Analysis of Authenticated-Encryption Modes

10.5.1 Generic Modeling of Security of AEAD Modes

Authenticated-encryption modes (i.e. CCM, GCM, and AES-GCM-SIV) are presented in Chapter 9. The security analysis of authenticated-encryption modes focuses both on privacy and on authenticity. Therefore, security analyses of privacy (see section 10.3) and authenticity (see Section 10.4) are used to provide bounds for CCM, GCM, and AES-GCM-SIV. Recall that an authenticated-encryption mode takes a plaintext, an associated data, and an IV and it returns a pair ciphertext–tag. Thus, an authenticated-encryption F can be defined by a function:

$$F: \mathcal{K} \times \mathcal{N} \times \mathbb{A} \times \mathcal{M} \rightarrow \mathcal{C}$$

where $\mathcal{K}$ denotes the key space, $\mathcal{N}$ the IV space, $\mathbb{A}$ the associated data space, $\mathcal{M}$ the plaintext space, and the $\mathcal{C}$ ciphertext-tag space.

The authenticated decryption is defined by:

$$F^{-1}: \mathcal{K} \times \mathcal{N} \times \mathbb{A} \times \mathcal{C} \rightarrow \mathcal{M} \cup \{\perp\}$$

where $\perp$ denotes that the input ciphertext is invalid and the returned result is undefined.

Using the same notations as in previous sections, the privacy advantage and authenticity advantage of an adversary attacking an authenticated-encryption F, over block cipher E, are defined by:

$$ADV_{F[E]}^{priv}(\mathcal{A}) \overset{def}{=} \Pr\left[K \overset{R}{\leftarrow} \mathcal{K}; \ \mathcal{A}^{F_K} \Rightarrow 1\right] - \Pr\left[\pi \overset{R}{\leftarrow} Perm(\mathcal{M}); \ \mathcal{A}^{\pi} \Rightarrow 1\right]$$

$$ADV_{F[E]}^{mac}(\mathcal{A}) \overset{def}{=} \Pr\left[K \overset{R}{\leftarrow} \mathcal{K}; \ \mathcal{A}^{F_K, F_K^{-1}} \Rightarrow 1\right]$$

The maximum privacy advantage and authenticity advantage of any adversary attacking an authenticated-encryption F, which run in at most t and submit q queries with a total[9] of plaintext not exceeding μ are defined by:

$$ADV_{F[E]}^{priv}(t,q,\mu) \overset{def}{=} \max_{\mathcal{A}} ADV_F^{priv}(\mathcal{A})$$

$$ADV_{F[E]}^{auth}(t,q,\mu) \overset{def}{=} \max_{\mathcal{A}} ADV_F^{mac}(\mathcal{A})$$

10.5.2 Some Security Bounds for CCM, GCM, and AES-GCM-SIV

10.5.2.1 Bounds for CCM

CCM authenticated-encryption mode is based on CTR. The most known security analysis of CCM was made by Jonsson [12] who proposed the following bounds:

$$ADV_{CCM[E]}^{priv}\left(t,\left(q_E,q_D\right),l_E\right) \leq ADV_E^{prp}\left(t,q'\right) + \frac{\left(l_E\right)^2}{2^n} \qquad [12]$$

$$ADV_{CCM[E]}^{auth}\left(t,\left(q_E,q_D\right),\left(l_E,\ l_D\right)\right) \leq ADV_E^{prp}\left(t,q'\right) + \frac{\left(l_E+l_D\right)^2}{2^n} + \frac{q_D}{2^{Tlen}} \qquad [12]$$

where: q_E and q_D are the numbers of encryption and decryption (i.e. forgery attempt) queries, respectively; l_E and l_D are total numbers of block cipher calls needed to respond to all encryption and decryption queries, respectively. Each encryption/decryption enquiry is composed of plaintext, associated data, and padding (for detail on CCM format, see Section 9.2.3).

10.5.2.2 Bounds for GCM

The first bounds on GCM privacy and authenticity were proposed by D. A. McGrew and J. Viega, the authors of GMAC, in [13], but in [14], the authors showed that the proof was invalid in some cases and proposed other bounds with a larger security bound roughly by a factor of 2^{22}, then optimized bounds were proposed in [14].

$$ADV_{GMAC[E]}^{Priv}\left(t,q,\left(l_p,l\right)\right) \leq ADV_E^{prp}\left(t',q'\right) + \frac{\left(\frac{l_p}{n}+2q\right)^2}{2^{n+1}} +$$

$$q\left(\left(\frac{l_p}{n}+2q\right)\left[\frac{l_{IV}}{n}+1\right]\frac{1}{2^{n-1}} + \left[\frac{l}{n}+1\right]\frac{1}{2^{Tlen}}\right) \qquad [13]$$

$$ADV_{GMAC[E]}^{auth}\left(t,q,\left(l_p,l\right)\right) \leq ADV_E^{prp}\left(t',q'\right) + \frac{\left(\frac{l_p}{n}+2q\right)^2}{2^{n+1}} +$$

$$q\left(\left(\frac{l_p}{n}+2q+1\right)\left[\frac{l_{IV}}{n}+1\right]\frac{1}{2^{n-1}} + \left[\frac{l}{n}+1\right]\frac{1}{2^{Tlen}}\right) \qquad [13]$$

$$ADV_{GMAC[E]}^{priv}\left(t,\left(q_E,q_D\right),\left(l_p,l\right)\right) \leq \frac{\left(\frac{l_p}{n}+q_E+1\right)^2}{2^{n+1}}$$

$$+ \frac{32 * q_E * \left(\frac{l_p}{n}+q_E\right)\left(\frac{l_{IV}}{n}+1\right)}{2^n} \qquad [14]$$

$$ADV_{GMAC[E]}^{auth}\left(t,\left(q_E,q_D\right),\left(l_p,l\right)\right) \leq \frac{\left(\frac{l_p}{n}+q_E+q_D+1\right)^2}{2^{n+1}} +$$

$$\frac{32\left(q_E+q_D\right)\left(\frac{l_p}{n}+q_E+1\right)\left(\frac{l_{IV}}{n}+1\right)}{2^n} + \frac{q_D\left(\frac{l}{n}+1\right)}{2^{Tlen}} \qquad [14]$$

where:

    q denotes the number of queries (either MAC generation or verification queries);

    q_E and q_D are the numbers of encryption and decryption queries, respectively;

    l_p is total number of plaintext bits;

    l_{IV} is the maximum bit-length of the IV; l is the maximum number of input bits (of ciphertext and associated data) for any query;

    t and t' are computation times of GMAC and PRP E adversaries, respectively;

    q' is the total number of blocks processed by the block cipher E.

10.5.2.3 Some Bounds for AES-GCM-SIV Security

AES-GCM-SIV is the strongest authenticated-encryption mode. It is expected to become dominating AEAD mode in the future. AES-GCM-SIV is a nonce-misuse-resistant algorithm at some extent. That is, the nonce cannot repeat indefinitely without jeopardizing the security of the encryption system. In [15], the authors of AES-GCM-SIV proved the following bound:

$$Adv^{priv}_{GMAC-SIV[AES]}\left(t,N,Q_E,\ Q_D,m\right)\leq\frac{3N}{2^{96}}+\frac{N*Bmax^2}{2^{129}}+\frac{\sum_{i=1}^N\left(Q_E^i\right)^2}{2^{126-m}} \qquad [15]$$

where:

    t denotes the maximum computation time, and N, the number of different nonces in both encryption and decryption queries;

    Q_E^i ($i=1,\ ...,\ N$) denotes the number of encryption queries using the nonce i; thus, $Q_E=\{Q_E^1,...,Q_E^N\}$;

    Q_D^i ($i=1,\ ...,\ N$) denotes the number of decryption queries using the nonce i; thus, $Q_D=\{Q_D^1,...,Q_D^N\}$;

    $Bmax=\max_{i=1,..,N}(B^i)$, where B^i denotes the number of blocks encrypted or decrypted using nonce i. If all messages are of the same length, then $Bmax=\max_{i=1,..,N}(Q_E^i+Q_D^i)*2^m$; 2^m denotes the length (in blocks) of the longest message.

Gueron and Lindell's bound is proved under the assumptions that: i) that the number of queries N is at most 2^{64}, ii) the advantage when attacking AES is negligible, iii) no associated data is included in queries, and iv) $2^m*\sum_i^N Q_D^i<\frac{N*Bmax^2}{2}$.

Example 10.6

Table 10.2 shows examples of combinations of parameters in the adversary's advantage bound, assuming: 1) in each row, the value of the parameter N_E^i is the same for all the nonces and 2) the numbers of encrypted and decrypted messages per

Table 10.2 Example of usage bounds of AES-GCM-SIV.

N	Q_E^i	2^m	$\frac{3N}{2^{96}}$	$\frac{N*Bmax^2}{2^{129}}$	$\frac{\sum_{i=1}^N\left(Q_E^i\right)^2}{2^{126-m}}$
1	2^{31}	2^{16}	$\approx 2^{-94}$	2^{-34}	2^{-47}
2^{25}	2^6	2^{30}	$\approx 2^{-69}$	2^{-32}	2^{-59}
2^{32}	1	2^{30}	$\approx 2^{-62}$	2^{-35}	2^{-62}
2^{32}	2^{10}	2^{24}	$\approx 2^{-62}$	2^{-29}	2^{-50}
2^{32}	2^{15}	2^{16}	$\approx 2^{-62}$	2^{-35}	2^{-48}
2^{42}	2^8	2^{16}	$\approx 2^{-52}$	2^{-39}	2^{-52}
2^{45}	2^{10}	2^{16}	$\approx 2^{-49}$	2^{-32}	2^{-45}
2^{48}	2^{10}	2^{14}	$\approx 2^{-46}$	2^{-33}	2^{-44}
2^{48}	2^8	2^{16}	$\approx 2^{-46}$	2^{-33}	2^{-46}
2^{64}	2^{10}	2^3	$\approx 2^{-30.1}$	2^{-39}	2^{-39}
2^{64}	2^{15}	1	$\approx 2^{-30.41}$	2^{-33}	2^{-31}
2^{64}	2^8	2^8	$\approx 2^{-30.41}$	2^{-33}	2^{-38}
2^{64}	2^{10}	2^{10}	$\approx 2^{-30.41}$	2^{-25}	2^{-32}

N: maximum number of different nonces; Q_E^i: number of messages encrypted with nonce i;
$Bmax$: maximum number of blocks encrypted or decrypted with the same nonce.
$Q_E^i=\max_{i=1,...,N}\left(N_E^i\right)$ for the same row; 2^m: maximum message length (in blocks);

nonce are equal (i.e. $N_E^i = N_D^i, i = 1, ..., Q$). In gray, are some parameter combinations that do not fulfill the NIST recommendation, which states that the adversary's advantage should not be greater than 2^{-32}.

10.6 Problems and Solutions

10.6.1 List of Problems

Problem 10.1

Prove the following cardinalities:
1) $|F| = \mathcal{K} = 2^k$ and $|P| = |\mathcal{K}| = 2^k$, where k is the key bit-length.
2) $|Func(\mathcal{M}, \mathcal{R})| = |\mathcal{R}|^{|\mathcal{M}|} = 2^{L*2^n}$, where $|\mathcal{R}| = L$ and $|\mathcal{M}| = n$.
3) $|Perm(\mathcal{M})| = |\mathcal{M}|! = 2^n!$.

Problem 10.2

Let $E: \{0,1\}^k \times \{0,1\}^n \to \{0,1\}^n$ be a block cipher such that: $E_K(x) = x, \forall K \in \{0,1\}^k, \forall x \in \{0,1\}^n$. Show that E is very secure against key-recovery attack, but it is very insecure against chosen-plaintext attacks. Use the Real-or-Random security analysis model.

Problem 10.3

Let $E: \{0,1\}^k \times \{0,1\}^n \to \{0,1\}^n$ be a secure PRP. Consider the permutation family $E': \{0,1\}^k \times \{0,1\}^{2n} \to \{0,1\}^{2n}$ defined by:
$\forall x \in \{0,1\}^n, \forall x' \in \{0,1\}^n, E_K'(x \,||\, x') = E_K(x) \,||\, E_k(x \oplus x')$. Show that E' is not a secure PRP. Use the Real-or-Random security analysis model.

Problem 10.4

Let $E: \{0,1\}^k \times \{0,1\}^n \to \{0,1\}^n$ be a block cipher. The twofold cascade of E is the block cipher $E^{(2)}: \{0,1\}^{2k} \times \{0,1\}^n \to \{0,1\}^n$ defined by $E_{K_1 || K_2}^{(2)}(x) = E_{K_1}(E_{K_2}(x))$, for all $K_1, K_2 \in \{0,1\}^k$ and all $x \in \{0,1\}^n$. Prove that if E is a secure PRP, $E^{(2)}$ is too. Use the Real-or-Random security analysis model.

Problem 10.5

An adaptive CPA-adversary is the one that exploits the results of past queries $1, ..., q-1$ to decide which plaintext M_q to submit in the query q. For each query i, it receives $f(M_i)$, which is computed using either an instance of permutation family or a random permutation. A non-adaptive adversary is the one that prepares in advance a set of plaintexts $M_1, M_2, ..., M_q$ and then queries the accessible oracle. The adversary gets a set of ciphertexts $f(M_1), f(M_2), ..., f(M_q)$, which have been computed either with an instance of a permutation family or by a random permutation.

1) Show that a 128-bit block cipher, with 128-bit key, defined by $E_k(x) = K \oplus x$ is insecure for an adaptive adversary as well as for a non-adaptive one.
2) Show that a 128-bit block cipher, with 128-bit key, defined by $E_k(x) = K \oplus \text{Rotate}(x, K \bmod 128)$ is insecure for an adaptive adversary as well as for a non-adaptive one. $\text{Rotate}(x, m)$ is a function, which performs an m-bit left-rotation of x.
Use the Real-or-Random security analysis model.

Problem 10.6

Consider an adversary against ECB that submits a pair of plaintexts (M_1, M_2) each of two blocks, $M_1 = [0]_n || [0]_n$ and $M_2 = [0]_n || [1]_n$. Show that ECB is insecure (i.e. the advantage of an adversary is very high). Use the Right-or-Left security analysis model.

Problem 10.7

Consider an adversary against CBC that submits two queries: $(M_0^1 = 0, M_1^1 = 0)$ and $(M_0^2 = 0, M_1^2 = 1)$, where all $M_{i=0,1}^{j=1,2}$ are one-block each. Show that CBC is insecure (i.e. the advantage of an adversary is high), if the IV is predictable. Use the Right-or-Left security analysis model.

Problem 10.8

Consider the case of 2^{48} messages of a length of 2^{16} blocks each. All the messages are encrypted with the same nonce. What is the adversary's advantage in this case? Use Gueron and Y. Lindell's bound (see Section 10.5.2.3).

Problem 10.9

This problem aims to show that AES-GCM-SIV outperforms AES-GCM in terms of the amount of data that can be encrypted. Consider a user encrypting a collection of data with length multiple of 128 bits, while guaranteeing an adversary's advantage bound no greater than 2^{-32}. What is the maximum byte-length of data that can be encrypted with the same key in the following scenarios? Use Gueron and Lindell's bound (see Section 10.5.2.3).

1) A single IV is used to encrypt with the AES-GCM mode.
2) 2^{32} distinct IVs are used to encrypt with the AES-GCM mode. Notice that for AES-GCM standard compliance, the maximum number of IV values used under the same key with AES-GCM should not exceed 2^{32}.
3) A single nonce is used to encrypt with the AES-GCM-SIV mode, assuming that data are fragmented into messages of 2^{30} 128-bit blocks.
4) 2^{32} distinct nonces are used to encrypt with the AES-GCM-SIV mode, assuming that data are fragmented into messages of 2^{30} 128-bit blocks.
5) 2^{62} distinct nonces are used to encrypt with the AES-GCM-SIV mode, assuming that data are fragmented into messages of 2^{8} 128-bit blocks and the maximum nonce repetition is 2^{8} for all nonces.

10.6.2 Solutions to Problems

Problem 10.1

1) Since the bit-length of the key is k, there exist 2^k distinct keys. Therefore, there exist 2^k distinct instances of the function family F and the same applies to permutation family P. Hence, $|F|=|P|=|\mathcal{K}|=2^k$.
2) Let $\mathcal{M}=\{x_1, x_2, ..., x_{2^n}\}$ and $\mathcal{R}=\{y_1, y_2, ..., x_{2^L}\}$ be the domain and codomain of function collection $Func(\mathcal{M}, \mathcal{R})$. If f is a function from $\mathcal{M}$ to $\mathcal{R}$, then each element x_i of $\mathcal{M}$ can be mapped to any of the 2^L elements of $\mathcal{R}$. By the multiplication principle of counting,[10] the total number of functions from $\mathcal{M}$ to $\mathcal{R}$ is $2^L * 2^L *...* 2^L = (2^L)^{2^n}$. For example, $n=2$ and $L=2$. There exist 2^2 mappings for each of the 2^2 input elements. Thus, there are 2^{2*2^2} mappings in total; and therefore, $|Func(2,2)|=256$. For, $n=3$ and $L=2$. There exist 2^2 mappings for each of the 2^3 input elements. Hence, there are 2^{2*2^3} in total; and therefore, $|Func(3,2)|=65536$.
3) Let permutation domain be $\mathcal{M}=\{x_1, x_2, ...,x_{2^n}\}$, $i \neq j \Rightarrow x_i \neq x_j$. Assume that the first permutation π_1 is defined by $\pi_1(x_1)=x_1', \pi_1(x_2)=x_2', ..., \pi_1(x_{2^n}')$, where $\mathcal{M}=\{x_1', x_2', ..., x_{2^n}'\}=\{x_1, x_2, ..., x_{2^n}\}$, then the second permutation π_2 is defined by $\pi_2(x_1')=x_1'', \pi_2(x_2')=x_2'', ..., \pi_2(x_{2^n}')=x_2''$, etc. $\pi_1 \rightarrow \pi_2 \rightarrow \pi_3 ...$ The number of distinct elements to permute is 2^n. In general, the number of permutations of a set of N distinct elements is $N!$. Therefore, the number of permutations of $Perm(\mathcal{M})$ is $(2^n)!$

Problem 10.2

When the adversary queries the oracle of E with a value x, the challenger selects a random key, which is not used to compute $y=E_K(x)$. Therefore, upon reception of y, the adversary has no information in y to help it find the used key. Even though the number of queries is large, no useful information will be inferred by the adversary from the returned results. Therefore, the probability that the adversary guesses the key is $\frac{1}{2^n}$; i.e. $ADV_E^{kr}(.)=\frac{1}{2^n}$. Hence, the block cipher is very secure against key-recovery attacks. However, with a single query, because the adversary knows that $E_K(x)=x$, upon reception of y, if $y=x$, the adversary strategy is to output 1 with a probability of 1. With a probability of $\frac{1}{2^n}$, the adversary outputs 1 while a random function is used and the returned value is such that $y=x$. Therefore, $ADV_E^{prf-cpa}(q,t)=1-\frac{1}{2^n}$, which means that the block cipher E is insecure against chosen-plaintext attacks.

Problem 10.3

The adversary asks the oracle of E' with a pair $(x_1,0)$ and receives y. If an instance E_K' of E' is used, then $y=E_K'(x \parallel 0)=E_K(x) \parallel E_k(x \oplus 0)=E_K(x) \parallel E_K(x)$. Therefore, the strategy of the adversary would be to output 1, if the two halves of y are identical. If the adversary has access to a random permutation, then there is a probability of $\frac{1}{2^n}$ that $y=y_1 \parallel y_1$, $y_1 \in \{0,1\}^n$ has been picked at random. Hence, $ADV_{E'}^{prp-cpa}(q,t)=1-\frac{1}{2^n}$, which is very high. Therefore, E' is an insecure PRP.

Problem 10.4

Twofold cascade of E is also called double-encryption of E. There are two cases to address: $K_1=K_2$ and $K_1 \neq K_2$.

Case: $K_1 = K_2 = K$

The adversary asks the oracle with any point $x \in \{0,1\}^n$ and gets a point $y \in \{0,1\}^n$. Since E is a secure PRP, the adversary cannot distinguish between an instance E_k and a random permutation π. Then, y is submitted to the oracle and the adversary gets a point $y' \in \{0,1\}^n$. Once again, since E is a secure PRP, the adversary cannot distinguish between an instance E_K and a random permutation π. Hence, after two queries, the adversary cannot distinguish between $\pi(\pi(x))$ and $E_K(E_K(x))$. Therefore, $E^{(2)}$ is a secure PRP.

Case: $K_1 \neq K_2$

In this case, the test runs in two sessions, each with a (distinct) key. The adversary asks the oracle with any point $x \in \{0,1\}^n$ and gets a point $y \in \{0,1\}^n$. Since E is a secure PRP, the adversary cannot distinguish between an instance E_{K_2} and a random permutation π_2. Then, y is submitted to the oracle and the adversary gets a point $y' \in \{0,1\}^n$. Since E is a secure PRP, the adversary cannot distinguish between an instance E_{K_1} and a random permutation π_1. Hence, after two queries, the adversary cannot distinguish between $\pi_1(\pi_2(x))$ and $E_{K_1}(E_{K_2}(x))$. Therefore, $E^{(2)}$ is a secure PRP.

Problem 10.5

1) Consider a block cipher $E : \{0,1\}^{128} \times \{0,1\}^{128} \rightarrow \{0,1\}^{128}$ such that $E_K(x) = K \oplus x$.

First, consider an adaptive adversary, which chooses $M_1 = 1$ and queries the oracle and gets y. Then, it asks the oracle with $M_2 = y$ and gets z. If the adaptive adversary has access to the oracle of E, then:

$$z = E_K(y) = K \oplus y = K \oplus E_K(1) = K \oplus K \oplus 1 = 1$$

Therefore, if $z = 1$, then the adversary outputs 1 with a probability of 1. The probability that $z = 1$ is returned by a random permutation, for the second query, is $\dfrac{1}{2^{128}}$. Hence, $ADV_E^{prp-cpa}(t,2) = 1 - \dfrac{1}{2^{128}}$; and the block cipher E is insecure against an adaptive adversary.

Second, consider a non-adaptive adversary, which selects a large set of q (e.g. $q = 2^{20}$) random integers from $\{0,1\}^{128}$ and then queries the oracle. It gets q integers: $y_i = E_K(x_i)$ or $y_i = (x_i)$, for any $i \in [1,q]$, where π is a random permutation. If the adversary is given access to the permutation family E, then for any pair $i, j \in [1, q]$, $i \neq j$, $y_i \oplus y_j = E_K(x_i) \oplus E_K(x_j) = (K \oplus x_i) \oplus (K \oplus x_j) = x_i \oplus x_j$

Therefore, if $y_i \oplus y_j = x_i \oplus x_j$, $\forall i, \forall j \in [1, q], i \neq j$, the adversary outputs 1 with a probability of 1. The probability that a random permutation returns values that match the previous condition is very low. Therefore, the block cipher is insecure, even for a non-adaptive adversary.

2) Consider a block cipher $E : \{0,1\}^{128} \times \{0,1\}^{128} \rightarrow \{0,1\}^{128}$ defined by $E_K(x) = K \oplus \text{Rotate}(x, K \bmod 128)$.

First, consider an adaptive adversary, which chooses two plaintexts $M_1 = 0$ and $M_2 = 1^{(128)}$; i.e. 128 1-bits. It queries the oracle and gets $y_1 = f(0)$ and $y_2 = f(1^{(128)})$. If the adversary is given access to the oracle of E_K, then:

$$y_1 = K \oplus \text{Rotate}(0, K \bmod 128) = K$$

$$y_2 = K \oplus \text{Rotate}(1^{(128)}, K \bmod 128) = K \oplus 1^{(128)}$$

$$y_1 \oplus y_2 = K \oplus K \oplus 1^{(128)} = 1^{(128)}$$

Therefore, if $y_1 \oplus y_2 = 1^{(128)}$, the adversary outputs 1 with a probability of 1. The probability that a random permutation returns two images y_1 and y_2, such that $y_1 \oplus y_2 = 1^{(128)}$, is of $1/2^{128}$. Therefore, the adversary advantage is close to 1, which makes the block cipher insecure.

Second, consider a non-adaptive adversary, which selects a large set of q random integers from $\{0,1\}^{128}$ and then queries the oracle. It gets q integers: $y_i = E_K(x_i)$ or $y_i = (x_i)$, for all $i \in [1, q]$, where π is a random permutation. If the adversary is given access to the permutation family E, then for any pair $i, j \in [1, q], i \neq j$,

$$y_i \oplus y_j = E_K(x_i) \oplus E_K(x_j)$$
$$= K \oplus \text{Rotate}(x_i, K \bmod 128) \oplus K \oplus \text{Rotate}(x_j, K \bmod 128)$$
$$= \text{Rotate}(x_i, K \bmod 128) \oplus \text{Rotate}(x_j, K \bmod 128)$$

Then, the adversary takes any pair (x_i, x_j) and checks if $y_i \oplus y_j = \text{Rotate}(x_i, r) \oplus \text{Rotate}(x_j, r)$, for $r = 0, \dots, 127$. If the test is positive, then the adversary outputs 1 with a probability of 1. The probability that a random permutation returns a pair of values, which matches the previous condition, is very low. Therefore, the adversary advantage is close to 1, which makes the block cipher insecure even for a non-adaptive adversary.

Problem 10.6

The security analysis model to use in this problem is the Right-or-Left model.

After querying with a pair of plaintexts (M_0, M_1), the adversary receives a two-block-ciphertext, $C = C_1 \| C_2$.

If $b = 0$, then $C_1 = Enc_K([0]_n)$ and $C_2 = Enc_K([0]_n)$; i.e. M_0 is encrypted by the oracle.

If $b = 1$, then $C_1 = Enc_K([0]_n)$ and $C_2 = Enc_K([1]_n)$; i.e. M_1 is encrypted by the oracle.

Thus, after receiving the ciphertext C, if $C_1 \neq C_2$, the adversary outputs 1 at a probability of 1; and if it receives C_2 such that $C_1 = C_2$, it outputs 0 at a probability of 1. Since the underlying block cipher is a pseudorandom permutation, the probability that $C_1 = Enc_K(0) = C_2 = Enc_K(1)$ is 0. Hence, the probability that the adversary outputs 1, while the left (i.e. $b = 0$) oracle was accessed, is 0. Therefore, the ECB-CPA-adversary advantage is $1 - 0 = 1$, which means that EBC is insecure.

Problem 10.7

$(M_0^1 = 0, M_1^1 = 0)$ and $(M_0^2 = 0, M_1^2 = 1)$,

The security analysis model to use in this problem is the Right-or-Left model.

Assume that the adversary can predict that the IV to encrypt the first message is $IV_1 = 0$ and that to encrypt the second is $IV_2 = 1$. In the first query, the adversary submits a pair $(0, 0)$ and receives (C_1, IV_1), where $C_1 = Enc_K(0 \oplus IV_1) = Enc_K(0)$, because $M_0^1 = M_1^1 = 0$ (whatever the encrypted block, the result is the same). Then, in the second query, it submits a pair $(0, 1)$ and receives (C_2, IV_2).

If $b = 0$, then $C_2 = Enc_K(M_0^2 \oplus IV_2) = Enc_K(0 \oplus IV_2) = Enc_K(1)$.

If $b = 1$, then $C_2 = Enc_K(M_1^2 \oplus IV_2) = Enc_K(1 \oplus 1) = Enc_K(0) = C_1$. Thus, after the second query, if the adversary receives C_2 such that $C_1 = C_2$, it outputs 1 at a probability of 1; and if the adversary receives C_2 such that $C_1 \neq C_2$, it outputs 0 at a probability of 1. Since the underlying block cipher is a pseudorandom permutation, the probability that $C_1 = Enc_K(0) = C_2 = Enc_K(1)$ is 0. Thus, the probability that the adversary outputs 1, while the left (i.e. $b = 0$) oracle was accessed, is 0. Therefore, the CBC-CPA-adversary advantage is $1 - 0 = 1$, which means that CBC is insecure, if the IV can be predicted.

Problem 10.8

Recall that the adversary's bound provided by Gueron and Lindell's bound is $Adv = \frac{3N}{2^{96}} + \frac{N * Bmax^2}{2^{129}} + \frac{\sum_{i=1}^{N} (Q_E^i)^2}{2^{126-m}}$ (see Section 10.5.2.3).

A single nonce is used to encrypt and decrypt 2^{48} messages. So,

$$N = 1, Q_E^1 = 2^{48}, Q_D^1 = 0, \text{ and } Bmax = (2^{48} + 0) * 2^{16}.$$

Therefore, $Adv = \frac{3}{2^{96}} + \frac{1 * (2^{64})^2}{2^{129}} + \frac{(2^{48})^2}{2^{126-16}} = \frac{3}{2^{96}} + \frac{1}{2} + \frac{1}{2^{14}}$, which is dominated by $\frac{1}{2}$. Thus, encryption of $2^{48} * 2^{16}$ blocks, with the same nonce under AES-GCM-SIV algorithm, is insecure. By the birthday paradox, the adversary can succeed in breaking the ciphering code.

Problem 10.9

1) With one IV, GCTR of AES-GCM mode can generate 2^{32} distinct counter blocks. Hence, in total, 2^{32} blocks (i.e. 2^{36} bytes) can be encrypted.

2) With 2^{32} distinct IVs, used in the AES-GCM mode, a total of $2^{32} * 2^{32}$ blocks (i.e. 2^{68}) bytes can be encrypted.

3) Using Gueron and Lindell's bound (see Section 10.5.2.3), to provide an adversary's advantage bound no greater than 2^{-32}, the inequality $\frac{3 * N}{2^{96}} + \frac{N * Bmax^2}{2^{129}} + \frac{\sum_{i=1}^{N} (Q_E^i)^2}{2^{126-m}} \leq 2^{-32}$ must hold. If only encryptions are considered, then the inequality becomes:

$$\frac{3 * N}{2^{96}} + \frac{N * (\max_{i=1,..,N} (Q_E^i) * 2^m)^2}{2^{129}} + \frac{\sum_{i=1}^{N} (Q_E^i)^2}{2^{126-m}} \leq 2^{-32}.$$

With a single nonce (i.e. $N = 1$) and a message block-length of 2^{30} (i.e. $m = 30$): $\frac{3 * 1}{2^{96}} + \frac{(2^{30})^2 (Q_E^1)^2}{2^{129}} + \frac{(Q_E^1)^2}{2^{126-30}} \leq 2^{-32}$. The dominating factor is $\frac{(2^{30})^2 (Q_E^1)^2}{2^{129}}$. Hence, $(N_E^1)^2 \leq 2^{69-32} \Rightarrow N_E^1 \leq 2^{18.5}$. Therefore, the total data that can be encrypted is $2^{18.5} * 2^{32}$ blocks $\approx 2^{54}$ bytes.

4) With 2^{32} nonces (i.e. $N = 2^{32}$) and a message block-length of 2^{30} (i.e. $m = 30$), the inequality becomes: $\frac{3 * 2^{32}}{2^{96}} + \frac{2^{32} * (2^{30})^2 * (Q_E^i)^2}{2^{129}} + \frac{2^{32} * (Q_E^i)^2}{2^{126-32}} \leq 2^{-32}$. The dominating factor is $\frac{2^{32+2*30} * (Q_E^i)^2}{2^{129}}$. Hence, $(Q_E^1)^2 \leq 2^{37-32} \Rightarrow Q_E^1 \leq 2^{2.5}$. Therefore, the total data that can be encrypted is $2^{32} * 2^{2.5} * 2^{32}$ blocks $\approx 2^{70}$ bytes.

5) With $N = 2^{62}$, $Q_E^i = 2^8$ for all nonces, and a message length of 2^8, the inequality becomes: $\dfrac{3*2^{62}}{2^{96}} + \dfrac{2^{62}*(2^8)^2*(2^8)^2}{2^{129}} + \dfrac{2^{62}*(2^8)^2}{2^{126-8}} = \dfrac{3}{2^{34}} + \dfrac{1}{2^{35}} + \dfrac{1}{2^{40}} \leq 2^{-32}$. Therefore, the total data that can be encrypted is $2^{62} * 2^8 * 2^8$ blocks $\approx 2^{82}$ bytes. Notice that if $N = 2^{64}$ or $N = 2^{63}$, the inequality cannot hold, because $\dfrac{3*2^{64}}{2^{96}} > \dfrac{3*2^{63}}{2^{96}} > \dfrac{1}{2^{32}}$.

Notes

1 The computational difficulty refers to the fact that given practical resources that adversaries can use, the time for an attack to succeed is too long (in centuries or more) to attempt the attack.

2 A random-access machine model is an abstract CPU model used to do some computations.

3 Each key check requires more than 10^3 (which is very optimistic) processor operations. The fastest computer in 2022 has a speed of $442*10^{15}$ operations per second.

4 Notice that the total amount of encrypted bits is $\mu_e/2$, because each query takes two equal-length plaintexts and only one of them is encrypted.

5 q shall not exceed 2^n blocks encrypted with the same key; otherwise, a collision occurs. Indeed, attack, after encrypting 2^n blocks with the same key, the adversary can collect twice a ciphertext, which is known as collision.

6 It is assumed that the adversary does not query the oracle twice with the same value either for tag generation or for tag verification, because querying twice with the same input does not provide new knowledge to the adversary.

7 Notice that the computation time t is specified in terms of encryption and decryption operations of the underlying block cipher, because those operations are the most time-consuming.

8 A hash function, which makes use of a compression function that is iterated on each block, is referred to *iterated hash function*.

9 Some proposed bounds include the total length of associated data in μ.

10 According to the *Multiplication counting principle*, if one event can occur in u ways and a second event can occur in v ways after the first event has occurred, then the two events can occur in $u*v$ ways. In the considered problem, each point of $\mathcal{M}$ may have up to 2^L images in $\mathcal{R}$ independently of the other points.

References

1 Shannon, C.E. (1949). Communication theory of secrecy systems. *Bell System Technical Journal* 28: 656–715.

2 Bellare, M., Piertrzak, K., and Rogaway, P. (2005). Improved security analyses for CBC MACs. In: *Advances in Cryptology – CRYPTO 2005* (ed. V. Shoup), 527–545. Santa Barbara, California: Springer. LNCS 3621.

3 Bellare, M. and Rogaway, P. (2005). *Introduction to modern cryptography, course notes*. University of California at San Diego (US).

4 Rogaway, P. (2011). *Evaluation of some block cipher modes of operation, research report*. Davis University, California (US).

5 Bellare, M., Kilian, J., and Rogaway, P. (2000). The security of the cipher block chaining message authentication code. *Journal of Computer and System Sciences* 61: 362–399.

6 Bellare, M. and Rogaway, P. (2006). Code-based game-playing proofs and the security of triple encryption. In: *25th International Conference on the Theory and Applications of Cryptographic Techniques, Advances in Cryptology*. 409–426. Petersburg, Russia: Springer. LNCS 4004.

7 Bellare, M., Desai, A., Jokipii, E. et al. (1997). A concrete security treatment of symmetric encryption. In: *38th Annual Symposium on Foundations of Computer Science*. 394–403. Florida, US: IEEE Press.

8 Liskov, M. and Minematsu, K. (2008). *Comments on XTS-AES*. [Online]. (Cited 2023 April). Available from: https://csrc.nist.gov/csrc/media/projects/block-cipher-techniques/documents/bcm/comments/xts/xts_comments-liskov_minematsu.pdf.

9 Iwata, T. and Kurosawa, K. (2003). Stronger security bounds for OMAC, TMAC, and XCBC. In: *4th International Conference on Cryptography in India*. 402–515. New Delhi, India: Springer. LNCS 2904.

10 Nandi, M. (2009). Improved security analysis for OMAC as a pseudorandom function. *Journal of Mathematical Cryptology* 3: 133–148.

11 Bellare, M. (2006). New proofs for NMAC and HMAC: security without collision-resistance. In: *26th International Conference on the Theory and Applications of Cryptographic Techniques, Advances in Cryptology – CRYPTO 2006*. 602–619. Santa Barbara, California: Springer. LNCS 4117.

12 Jonsson, J. (2002). On the security of CTR + CBC-MAC. In: *9th Annual International Workshop on Selected Areas in Cryptography*. 76–93. Newfoundland, Canada: Springer. LNCS 2595.

13 McGrew, D.A. and Viega, J. (2004). *The security and performance of the galois/counter mode of operation*. Report 2004/193. Cryptology ePrint Archive.

14 Iwata, T., Ohashi, K., and Minematsu, K. (2012). Breaking and repairing GCM security proofs. In: *32rd Annual Cryptology Conference, Advances in Cryptology - CRYPTO 2012*. 31–49. Santa Barbara, California: Springer. LNCS 7417.

15 Gueron, S. and Lindell, Y. (2017). *Better bounds for block cipher modes of operation via nonce-based key derivation - report 2017/702*. Cryptology ePrint Archive.

11

Introduction to Cryptanalysis Attacks on Symmetric Ciphers

Cryptanalysis is the science and techniques of analyzing and breaking cryptographic algorithms and protocols. There exist hundreds of cryptanalysis attack variants. Cryptanalysis is a very exciting field; and improvements of existing attacks are proposed every year. Cryptanalysis attacks can be categorized according to various criteria, such as:

- Nongeneric vs generic attacks: in the first category, attackers take advantage of vulnerabilities of internal components of attacked ciphers, while they do not in the second category. In general, nongeneric attacks are more efficient than generic ones, as attackers know the internal vulnerabilities of attacked ciphers.
- Statistical vs deterministic attacks: in the first category, the attackers derive some properties of attacked ciphers that can hold with some probabilities and exploit such statistical knowledge to partially or entirely recover keys. In the second category, attackers design models of ciphers in form of equations. Models are used to reduce the search space of keys. Linear and differential cryptanalyses are examples of statistical attacks, while algebraic attacks are deterministic. Linear cryptanalysis together with differential cryptanalysis are the most widely used attacks against block ciphers.
- Known vs chosen information: there exist four main types (or models) of attacks: ciphertext-only, known-plaintext, chosen-plaintext, and chosen-ciphertext attacks.

In Section 2.4.2, a general categorization of cryptanalysis methods is provided to show the main categories of attacks. This chapter aims at introducing some common methods used to attack symmetric ciphers, namely:

- Memory-time trade-off attacks, including Hellman's tables and rainbow chains
- Linear cryptanalysis
- Differential cryptanalysis
- Algebraic cryptanalysis
- Cube attacks
- Divide-and-conquer attacks
- Correlation attacks

This chapter introduces only the basic version of each mentioned attacks. All the basic attacks have been improved and specialized (to address specific ciphers) in literature and many variants exist for each attack. The chapter is not a comprehensive survey.

Examples are used to show how a key can be partially or entirely recovered. It is worth noticing that only simple ciphers (or toy ciphers) are used in examples below. The parameters of our toy-ciphers are such that the reader could check the attacks "by hand." Recovering key bits of real ciphers requires a lot of formulas and time-consuming experimentations.

Three metrics are commonly used to assess the complexities of attacks: computation time, memory to store data (plaintexts, ciphertexts, and others), and the number of known/chosen plaintexts and/or ciphertexts. Those metrics are briefly discussed in this chapter, because huge parameters are often required to describe attack complexities. It is worth noticing that almost all cryptanalysis attacks are academic and cannot be performed, in practice, by normal attackers against real ciphers, because of the huge amount of required resources. However, some security and intelligence agencies could have resources to perform them.

Cryptography: Algorithms, Protocols, and Standards for Computer Security, First Edition. Zoubir Mammeri.
© 2024 John Wiley & Sons, Inc. Published 2024 by John Wiley & Sons, Inc.

11.1 Memory-Time Trade-off Attacks

In general, we can regard Memory-Time Trade-Off (MTTO) attacks as methods searching for a preimage of a one-way function by utilizing a significant memory prepared in a precomputation phase to reduce the time complexity. The latter is decreased by increasing the memory complexity and vice versa. Common MTTO attacks rely on Hellman's and Rainbow tables and their extensions. MTTO attacks may be used under known plaintext, chosen plaintext, or ciphertext-only assumptions.

11.1.1 Hellman's Table-based Attacks

Hellman proposed a table design for inverting one-way functions [1]. In particular, Hellman's tables have been used to break DES cipher. Cryptographic attacks based on Hellman's tables are categorized as MTTO attacks. Hellman's table design is a solution to deploy a probabilistic dictionary attack while taking into account the memory-time trade-off. Hellman's table (HT) design is based on two principles:

1) partially store a reduced attack dictionary,
2) decide a trade-off between two parameters, m (the memory space) and t (the number of table lookup operations).

Therefore, HT-based MTTO attacks in cryptography are probabilistic in nature. Below is described the design of an HT-based MTTO attack to recover a secret key K of n-bit-length, assuming a pair plaintext–ciphertext, (P_0, C_0) of bit-length of l each, is known. If $l > n$, then a reduction function R is used to reduce the length of ciphertext (for example delete the last $l - n$ bits of the ciphertext).

Let $Enc_K(P_0) = C_0$ denote the encryption of plaintext P_0 using key K. A one-way function f is defined by $f(K) = R[Enc_K(P_0)]$. Computing $f(K)$, given K, is equivalent to $R[Enc_K(P_0)]$, with known K and P_0. Therefore, it is easy to compute. However, computing K given $Enc_K(P_0)$ and R is equivalent to cryptanalysis. An HT-based attack is composed of two phases: offline precomputation and key search.

11.1.2 Offline Precomputation

First, the attacker selects the value of two trade-off parameters m (memory space) and t (computation time). Then, he/she chooses m start points, $SP_1, SP_2, ..., SP_m$, randomly in $\{0, 1, ..., N\}$, where $N = 2^n$ and n is the key bit-length, computed as follows (illustrated by Figure 11.1):

---

1. for $i = 1$ to m do
   1.1 $x_{i,0} = SP_i$
   1.2 for $j = 1$ to t do
         $x_{i,j} = f(x_{i,j-1}) = R\left[Enc_{x_{i,j-1}}(P_0)\right]$
   1.3 Let $P_i = f^t(SP_i) = x_{i,t}$ (EP_i: endpoint of the ith chain)
2.1 Discard all intermediate points (to save memory)
2.2 Build a table $HT : \{SP_i, EP_i\}, 1 \leq i \leq m$, sorted on endpoints

---

A matrix row is called a *chain*. The iterative computation of chain $i(0 \leq i \leq m)$ is as follows:

$$x_{i,d} = \begin{cases} SP_i & if \quad d = 0 \\ f(x_{i,d-1}) = R\left[Enc_{x_{i,d-1}}(P_0)\right] & if \quad 1 \leq d \leq t \end{cases} \qquad (11.1)$$

Therefore, chain i contains t encryption keys. With the exception of the start point, a key $x_{i,k}$ is the result of two operations, encryption using key $x_{i,k-1}$, followed by a reduction.

Collisions and false alarms

It may happen that two distinct chains i and j collide, i.e. they yield the same key α located at position k_1 in chain i and at position k_2 in chain j, with $0 < k_1 \leq t$ and $0 < k_2 \leq t$. That is,

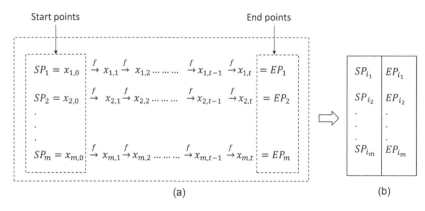

Figure 11.1 (a) Matrix of images under f and (b) Hellman table.

X_i, the set of keys of chain i, is $\left\{ x_{i,0}, x_{i,1}, \ldots, x_{i,(k_1-1)}, \alpha, \ldots, x_{i,t-1}, x_{i,t} \right\}$ and

X_j, the set of keys of chain j, is $\left\{ x_{j,0}, x_{j,1}, \ldots, x_{j,(k_2-1)}, \alpha, \ldots, x_{j,t-1}, x_{j,t} \right\}$

Since a single reduction function R is used, the keys in both chains overlap starting with the position of α. In such a case, the chains merge. For example, if chains i and j collide at positions $k_1 = 5$ and $k_2 = 7$, with $t = 20$, the chains have 14 common keys.

If two chains i and j merge at their endpoints, i.e. $EP_i = x_{i,t} = EP_j = x_{j,t} = y$, but $x_{i,t-1}$ and $x_{j,t-1}$ are distinct, then the same value y has two inverse images, $f^{-1}(y) = x_{i,t-1}$ and $f^{-1}(y) = x_{j,t-1}$. Such a case is referred to as *false alarm*. A false alarm means that when online key search is performed, both chains may be inspected and only one chain will (probably) contribute to find the secret key and the other chain is a wrong track. Notice that false alarms may concern more than two chains.

11.1.3 Key Search

Recall that row i is computed according to formula (11.1). Given a ciphertext C_0 associated with plaintext P_0, the key search is performed column by column:

- Test if key K is in the column $t-1$:
  If there exists a row i, $0 \le i \le m$, such that $EP_i = R[C_0]$, then $EP_i = x_{i,t} = R\left[Enc_{x_{i,t-1}}(P_0)\right]$. Hence, $C_0 = Enc_{x_{i,t-1}}(P_0)$ and maybe $K = x_{i,t-1}$. Check if the guessed key is correct: if $Enc_{x_{i,t-1}}(P_0) \ne C_0$, then try another row, until a correct key is found or all rows are tested.
- If the key is not in the column $t-1$, then test if it is in column $t-2$:
  If there exists a row i, $0 \le i \le m$, such that $x_{i,t-1} = R\left[Enc_{x_{i,t-2}}(P_0)\right]$, then $C_0 = Enc_{x_{i,t-2}}(P_0)$ and maybe $K = x_{i,t-2}$. If the guessed key is not correct, then try another row until a correct key is found or all rows are tested.
- Iteratively, until all the columns are tried or the correct key is found, try columns $t-3$, $t-4$, ..., 1.

The pseudocode for key HT-based search is as follows:

---

1) Let $y_1 = R[C_0]$. C_0 is the known ciphertext.
2) Check if y_1 is an endpoint in *HT*.
3) Case 1: y_1 is an endpoint. So, there exists $i \in \{1,\ldots,m\}$ such that $y_1 = EP_i$. Either $K = x_{i,t-1}$ or EP_i has more than one inverse image.
   - Case 1.1: If there is a single inverse image for EP_i, the attacker needs to rebuild the row i until $x_{i,t-1}$ is reached, because the intermediate computations have been discarded after the precomputation phase. Since endpoints are computed as reduced ciphertexts, the attacker has to check if the guessed key $x_{i,t-1}$ is correct or not. The attack succeeds, if and only if $Enc_{x_{i,t-1}}(P_0) = C_0$. There is a non-null probability that the guessed key is not correct. If the $x_{i,t-1}$ is not the correct key, then continue as in case 2.
   - Case 1.2: If there is a false alarm (i.e. $y_1 = EP_i$, but $Enc_{x_{i,t-1}}(P_0) \ne C_0$), proceed as in case 2.

---

4) Case 2: if y_1 is not an endpoint or there is a false alarm. Then,
   - Compute $y_2 = f(y_1) = R\left[Enc_{y_1}(P_0)\right]$.
   - If y_2 is an endpoint of some row i, which has a unique inverse, then maybe $K = x_{i,t-2}$. Proceed as in case 1.1.
5) If y_2 is not an endpoint or there is a false alarm, iteratively compute $y_3 = f(y_2), y_4 = f(y_3), ..., y_t = f(y_{t-1})$. If for some $2 < k \le t$, y_k is an endpoint with a single inverse image, then check if $x_{i,t-k}$ encrypts correctly the plaintext. If $Enc_{x_{i,t-k}}(P_0) = C_0$, then $K = x_{i,t-k}$. Otherwise, continue the iterative search until y_t is tested.
6) The attack fails if no correct key is found.

Attack success probability

Hellman showed that if all the $m * t$ elements in the matrix in the 0th to $t-1^{th}$ columns are distinct and the secret key K is chosen randomly, the probability of success is $m * t / N$, where N is the cardinality of the key space. Unfortunately, two or several matrix rows starting with distinct points merge and yield common keys. The larger a table, the higher the probability that chains merge with each other. The probability of attack success with a table of m rows and t columns, given in [1], is as follows:

$$\text{Pr}_{SingleTable}(m,t) \ge \frac{1}{N}\sum_{i=1}^{m}\sum_{j=0}^{t-1}\left(1 - \frac{i*t}{N}\right)^{j+1}$$

Hellman showed that:

- For a fixed value of N, there is not much to be gained by increasing m or t beyond the point at which $m * t^2 = N$.
- A typical setting would be $m = t = N^{1/3}$.
- If m is very small compared to N, then $\text{Pr}_{SingleTable}(m,t) \ge \frac{m*t}{N}$.

Note. A single HT results in a maximum of $m*t$ distinct keys among N possible keys, with $N \ge m * t^2$. To increase the probability of attack success, it is recommended to use t tables with a distinct reduction function for each table. Using t reduction functions $(R_1, R_2, ..., R_t)$ results in a probability of success of:

$$\text{Pr}_{tTables}(m,t) \ge 1 - \left(1 - \frac{1}{N}\sum_{i=1}^{m}\sum_{j=0}^{t-1}\left(1 - \frac{i*t}{N}\right)^{j+1}\right)^{t}$$

Complexity of HT-based attacks

Hellman's table is composed of m rows each of two columns (start and end points). With t tables of m chains each and with $m = t = N^{1/3}$, the memory complexity is $N^{2/3}$. If n is the key bit-length, then $t * 2m * n$ bits are required to store the start and end points of t tables. The key search is performed column by column. A key search operation is composed of y_i calculation (i.e. encryption and reduction), test if y_i is in the last column of the HT, and if y_i is an endpoint, test if the key in the column $t - i$ is the secret key. Assume[1] that the false alarm rate is not enough high to dominate the computation. Under such an assumption, the number of encryption and reduction operations for one table is t. Since HT-based attacks make use of t tables, the attack time complexity is t^2. If $t = N^{1/3}$, then the time complexity is $N^{2/3}$.

Brute-force attack to recover a key of 100-bit-length has a complexity time of 2^{100}, thus computationally infeasible. With MTTO attack, the time complexity is $t = \left(2^{100}\right)^{2/3} \approx 2^{67}$, thus computationally feasible.

Example 11.1 The following is a simple example to show how Hellman's table-based attack works. Let the key space size be $N = 64$. Choose a simple encryption, say $Enc_k(P) = P * k \bmod 2N$. Plaintexts and ciphertexts are of 7-bit length.
   Assume that the known plaintext is $P_0 = 57$.

1) Building of Hellman's tables

According to Hellman's recommendation (i.e. $m = t = N^{1/3}$), let $m = t = 4$. Four reduction functions are needed to build four HTs. Let the reduction functions be:

$$R_1(z) = \left\lfloor \frac{z}{2} \right\rfloor \qquad R_2(z) = \left(\left(z \bmod 16\right) * 16 + \left(\left\lfloor \frac{z}{16} \right\rfloor\right)\right) \bmod N$$

$$R_3(z) = |3z - 11| \bmod N \quad R_4(z) : \left|\frac{z}{2}\right| - \left|\frac{z}{7}\right|$$

Let the random start points be:

$$\{15, 32, 17, 36, 24, 11, 48, 61, 57, 10, 4, 42, 63, 19, 54, 26\}.$$

The HT matrices are shown in Table 11.1.

Notice that there exist collisions in HTs 1, 2, and 4 (e.g. chains 3 and 4 in HT 1 have three common values). All endpoints are distinct in all HTs, which makes higher the probability of key search success.

2) Key search in HTs

Three scenarios are considered.

i) Scenario 1: plaintext encrypted with $K = 36$

   Hence, $C_0 = 57 * 36 \bmod 128 = 4$

   o Table 1 exploration

   $y_1 = R_1(C_0) = R_1(4) = 2$. 2 is the endpoint in chain 2 in table 1. $x_{2,3}^1 = 36$ is the correct key.

ii) Scenario 2: plaintext encrypted with $K = 17$

   Hence, $C_0 = 57 * 17 \bmod 128 = 73$

   o Table 1 exploration

   $y_1 = R_1(C_0) = R_1(73) = 36$. 36 is not an endpoint in table 1.

   $y_2 = f_1(y_1) = R_1(57 * 36 \bmod 128) = 2$

   2 is an endpoint in table 1 and $x_{2,2}^1 = 8$. Since $57 * 8 \bmod 128 = 72 \neq C_0$, $x_{2,2}^1$ is not the correct key.

   $y_3 = f_1(y_2) = R_1(57 * 2 \bmod 128) = 57$. 57 is not an endpoint in table 1.

   $y_4 = f_1(y_3) = R_1(57 * 57 \bmod 128) = 24$. 24 is the endpoint in chain 3 of table 1. Since table 1 has no false alarms, the key is $x_{3,0}^1 = 17$, which is the correct key.

Table 11.1 Example of Hellman's tables.

SP_i^1						EP_i^1
j i	0	1	2	3	4
1	15	43	9	0	0
2	32	16	8	36	2
3	17	36	2	57	24
4	36	2	57	24	44

SP_i^2						EP_i^2
j i	0	1	2	3	4
1	24	5	17	20	7
2	11	55	51	53	20
3	48	3	50	34	33
4	61	17	20	7	48

SP_i^3						EP_i^3
j i	0	1	2	3	4
1	57	8	13	36	1
2	10	35	22	39	2
3	4	33	0	11	14
4	42	3	54	7	34

SP_i^4						EP_i^4
j i	0	1	2	3	4
1	63	2	41	12	16
2	19	21	16	6	31
3	54	3	15	31	37
4	26	27	1	20	42

SP_i^b and EP_i^b denote start and end points of Hellman's table b ($b = 1, \ldots, 4$).

iii) Scenario 3: plaintext encrypted with $K = 23$

Hence, $C_0 = 57 * 23 \ mod \ 128 = 31$

○ Table 1 exploration

$y_1 = R_1(C_0) = R_1(31) = 15$. 15 is not an endpoint in table 1.

$y_2 = f_1(y_1) = R_1(57 * 15 \ mod \ 128) = 43$. 43 is not an endpoint in table 1.

$y_3 = f_1(y_2) = R_1(57 * 43 \ mod \ 128) = 9$. 9 is not an endpoint in table 1.

$y_4 = f_1(y_3) = R_1(57 * 9 \ mod \ 128) = 0$. 0 is the endpoint of chain 1 in table 1, but $x_{1,0}^1 = 15$. Since $57 * 15 \ mod \ 128 = 87$ $\neq C_0$, the key is not correct.

End of table 1 exploration.

○ Table 2 exploration

$y_1 = R_2(C_0) = R_2(31) = 49$. 49 is not an endpoint in table 2.

$y_2 = f_2(y_1) = R_2(57 * 49 \ mod \ 128) = 22$. 22 is not an endpoint in table 2.

$y_3 = f_2(y_2) = R_2(57 * 22 \ mod \ 128) = 38$. 38 is not an endpoint in table 2.

$y_4 = f_2(y_3) = R_2(57 * 38 \ mod \ 128) = 39$. 39 is not an endpoint in table 2.

End of table 2 exploration.

○ Table 3 exploration

$y_1 = R_3(C_0) = R_3(31) = 18$. 18 is not an endpoint in table 3.

$y_2 = f_3(y_1) = R_3(57 * 18 \ mod \ 128) = 5$. 5 is not an endpoint in table 3.

$y_3 = f_3(y_2) = R_3(57 * 5 \ mod \ 128) = 12$. 12 is not an endpoint in table 3.

$y_4 = f_3(y_3) = R_3(57 * 12 \ mod \ 128) = 57$. 57 is not an endpoint in table 3.

End of table 3 exploration.

○ Table 4 exploration

$y_1 = R_4(C_0) = R_4(31) = 11$. 11 is not an endpoint in table 4.

$y_2 = f_4(y_1) = R_4(57 * 11 \ mod \ 128) = 41$. 41 is not an endpoint in table 4.

$y_3 = f_4(y_2) = R_4(57 * 41 \ mod \ 128) = 12$. 12 is not an endpoint in table 4.

$y_4 = f_4(y_3) = R_4(57 * 12 \ mod \ 128) = 16$. 16 is the endpoint of chain 1 in table 4, but $x_{1,0}^4 = 63$. Since $57 * 63 \ mod \ 128 = 7 \neq C_0$, the key is not correct.

End of table 4 exploration. Stop the search.

Conclusion: no correct key is recovered in scenario 3. If one visually inspects the four tables, no element equal to 23 is present. Therefore, there is no chance that the correct key can be found in the used tables.

Distinguished points

Rivest suggested an improvement of the original Hellman's tables, cited in [2]. Rivest observed that the number of table lookups (and consequently the attack time) is drastically reduced if the endpoints have some property; for example, endpoints beginning with a fixed number of 0s. Such endpoints are called *distinguished points*. Therefore, instead of performing exactly t computations for each start point, computations continue until an endpoint with the appropriate property is found for each start point. Then, the improved table is used in the online key search as in the original Hellman's algorithm.

11.1.4 Rainbow Chains

Oechslin proposed an improvement to Hellman's tables called *rainbow chains* to reduce the effect of chain collisions [3]. In HTs, when two chains collide at some point, they merge and yield redundant keys. In most cases, rainbow chains do not merge even if they collide.

Rainbow table precomputation

A rainbow table is equivalent to t HTs. Recall that in the Hellman's tables, each table has its own reduction function. Rainbow chains make use of t distinct reduction functions denoted R_1, R_2, ..., R_t in every chain. Therefore, t one-way functions are defined by:

$$f_d(K) = R_d\big[Enc_K(P_0)\big], \text{ for } 0 \le d \le t \tag{11.2}$$

M start points are randomly selected in key space. Let SP_1, SP_2, ..., SP_M be the selected start points. Then, the keys of rainbow chain i $(1 \le i \le M)$ are computed as follows:

$$x_{i,d} = \begin{cases} SP_i & \text{if} \quad d=0 \\ f_d(x_{i,d-1}) = R_d\big[Enc_{x_{i,d-1}}(P_0)\big] & \text{if} \quad 0<d \le t \end{cases} \tag{11.3}$$

Figures 11.2 and 11.3 show the construction of a rainbow table and the difference between t HTs and one rainbow table. The notation $x \xrightarrow{f_d} y$ means $y = R_d\big(Enc_{d-1}(P_0)\big)$. As in Hellman's tables, only start and end points of rainbow chains are saved in memory.

Key search in rainbow table

It is worth noticing that lookup in a rainbow table is a little bit more complex than that in Hellman's table, because t reduction functions are used in every rainbow chain, while the same reduction function is used in all the chains of the same HT.

Given a ciphertext C_0 associated with plaintext P_0, the secret key search is performed column by column starting with column $t-1$ and ending with column 0. Below are the conditions for the secret key K to be in column d, $0 \le d < t$, of chain i:

- Key K is in column $t-1$:

  If $K = x_{i,t-1}$, then $x_{i,t} = R_t\big[Enc_{x_{i,t-1}}(P_0)\big] = R_t\big[Enc_K(P_0)\big] = R_t[C_0]$.

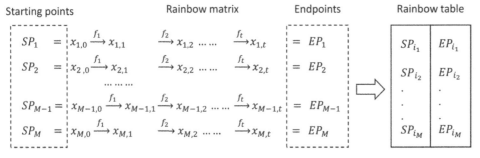

Figure 11.2 Rainbow matrix and table structure.

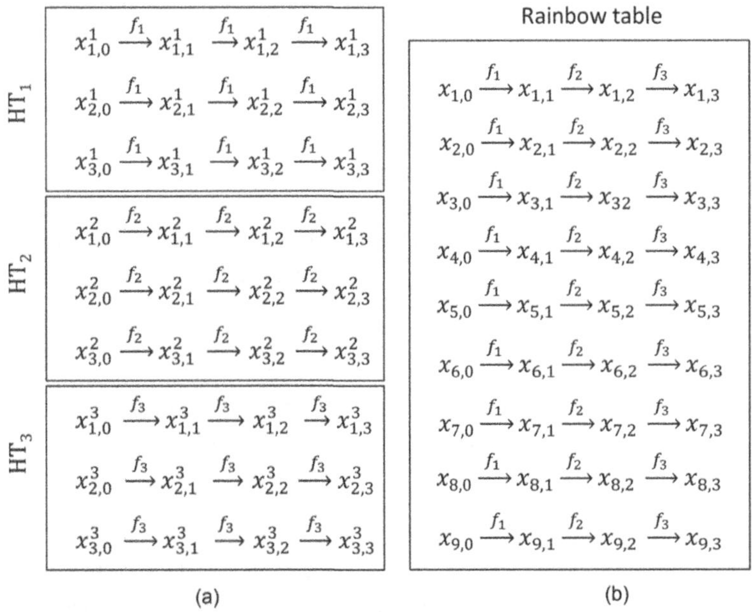

Figure 11.3 (a) Three 3*3 Hellman's tables and (b) one 9*3 Rainbow table.

- Key K is in column $t-2$:

  If $K = x_{i,t-2}$, then $x_{i,t-1} = R_{t-1}\left[Enc_{x_{i,t-2}}(P_0)\right] = R_{t-1}\left[Enc_K(P_0)\right] = R_{t-1}[C_0]$ and $x_{i,t} = R_t\left[Enc_{x_{i,t-1}}(P_0)\right] = R_t\left[Enc_{R_{t-1}[C_0]}(P_0)\right]$

  $= f_t\left(R_{t-1}[C_0]\right) = EP_i$

- Key is in column $t-3$:

  If $K = x_{i,t-3}$, then $x_{i,t-2} = R_{t-2}\left[Enc_{x_{i,t-3}}(P_0)\right] = R_{t-2}\left[Enc_K(P_0)\right] = R_{t-2}[C_0]$,

  $x_{i,t-1} = R_{t-1}\left[Enc_{x_{i,t-2}}(P_0)\right] = R_{t-1}\left[Enc_{R_{t-2}[C_0]}(P_0)\right] = f_{t-1}\left(R_{t-2}[C_0]\right)$

  $x_{i,t} = f_t\left(f_{t-1}\left(R_{t-2}[C_0]\right)\right) = EP_i$

- Iteratively, the condition for key K to be in column d, $0 \le d < t-3$, is:

  If $K = x_{i,d}$, then $x_{i,t} = f_t\left(f_{t-1}\ldots f_{d+1}\left(R_d[C_0]\right)\ldots\right) = EP_i$

---

1) Let $y_1 = R_t(C_0)$. C_0 is the known ciphertext.
2) Check if y_1 is an endpoint in the rainbow table.
3) Case 1: y_1 is an endpoint. So, there exists $i \in \{1,\ldots,M\}$ such that $y_1 = EP_i$.
   Either $K = x_{i,t-1}$ or EP_i has more than one inverse image.
   - Case 1.1: If there is a single inverse image for EP_i, the attacker needs to rebuild the chain i until $x_{i,t-1}$ is reached
   and then check if the guessed key $x_{i,t-1}$ is correct or not. The attack succeeds if and only if $Enc_{x_{i,t-1}}(P_0) = C_0$.
   If $x_{i,t-1}$ is not the correct key, then continue as in case 2.
   - Case 1.2: If there is a false alarm (i.e. $y_1 = EP_i$, but $Enc_{x_{i,t-1}}(P_0) \ne C_0$), proceed as in case 2.
4) Case 2: if y_1 is not an endpoint or there is a false alarm. Then,
   - Compute $y_2 = f_t\left(R_{t-1}[C_0]\right)$
   - If y_2 is an endpoint of some chain i, which has a unique inverse, then maybe $K = x_{i,t-2}$. Proceed as in case 1.1.
5) If y_2 is not an endpoint or there is a false alarm, iteratively compute
   $$y_3 = f_t\left(f_{t-1}\left(R_{t-2}[C_0]\right)\right), y_4 = f_t\left(f_{t-1}\left(f_{t-2}\left(R_{t-4}[C_0]\right)\right)\right), \ldots,$$
   $$y_t = f_t\left(f_{t-1}\left(f_{t-2}\ldots\left(f_2\left(R_1[C_0]\right)\right)\right)\right).$$
   If for some d, $2 < d \le t$, y_d is an endpoint with a single inverse image,
   then check if $x_{i,t-d}$ encrypts correctly the plaintext.
   If $Enc_{x_{i,t-d}}(P_0) = C_0$, then $K = x_{i,t-d}$. Otherwise, continue the iterative search until y_t is tested.
6) The attack fails if no correct key is found.

From the previous conditions, the iterative search in the rainbow table is constructed according to the following pseudocode:

Attack success probability

When two rainbow chains i and j collide at points k_1 and k_2, they merge only if $k_1 = k_2$. Therefore, the probability for two chains of length t to merge is $\frac{1}{t}$. Hence, the probability of attack success, given in [3], is:

$$Pr(M,t) \ge 1 - \prod_{i=1}^{t}\left(1 - \frac{M_i}{N}\right)$$

where $M_1 = M$ and $M_{k+1} = N\left(1 - e^{-\frac{M_k}{N}}\right)$.

If $M = m * t$ and t distinct reductions functions are used in both table types, then the success probability of a rainbow table of size $M * t$ is equivalent to that of t HTs of size $m * t$.

Complexity of rainbow-chain-based attacks

With one table of $M = m * t$ chains and $m = t = N^{1/3}$, the memory complexity of attack is of $N^{2/3}$; the same as that of Hellman's tables. In the worst case, all t columns of the rainbow table have to be tested when searching a secret key. Assume that false alarm rate is not high enough to dominate computation. To test if the secret key is in column $t-1$, $y_1 = R_1 \left[C_0 \right]$ is calculated, which requires one reduction. To test if it is in column $t-2$, $y_2 = f_t \left(R_{t-1} \left[C_0 \right] \right)$ is calculated, which requires one encryption-reduction operation. To test if it is in column 0, $y_t = f_t \left(f_{t-1} \left(f_{t-2} \cdots \left(f_2 \left(R_1 \left[C_0 \right] \right) \right) \right) \right)$ is calculated, which requires $t-1$ encryption-reduction operations. To compute each y_d, $d = 1, \ldots, t$, $\dfrac{t(t-1)}{2}$ encryption-reduction operations are required, which is the half of that needed for Hellman's tables.

In addition to encryption-reduction operations, t table lookup operations are needed to check if each y_i is an endpoint; and t chain reconstruction operations to check if each y_i is the correct key. Since encryption-reduction operation dominate in computation, the complexity of rainbow-table-based attack, with $t = N^{1/3}$, is $\dfrac{t(t-1)}{2} * N^{1/3}$.

Example 11.2 The following is a simple example to show how a rainbow chain-based attack works. Let the key space size be $N = 64$. Choose a simple encryption, say $Enc_k \left(P \right) = P * k \mod 2N$. Plaintexts and ciphertexts are of 7-bit length.
Assume that the known plaintext is $P_0 = 57$.

1) Building of rainbow table

According to Hellman's recommendation (i.e. $m = t = N^{2/3}$), let $m = t = 4$.

Four reduction functions are needed to build the rainbow table. The reduction functions and start points are the same as those used in Example 11.2:

$$R_1 (z) = \left\lfloor \frac{z}{2} \right\rfloor \qquad R_2 (z) = \left((z \bmod 16) * 16 + \left(\left\lfloor \frac{z}{16} \right\rfloor \right) \right) \bmod N$$

$$R_3 (z) = |3z - 11| \bmod N \qquad R_4 (z) = \left\lfloor \frac{z}{2} \right\rfloor - \left\lfloor \frac{z}{7} \right\rfloor$$

The start point set is $\{10, 63, 54, 19, 4, 32, 48, 57, 15, 42, 24, 61, 17, 36, 26, 11\}$.
The rainbow table is shown in Table 11.2:

Table 11.2 Example of rainbow table.

i \ j	0	1 (R_1)	2 (R_2)	3 (R_3)	4 (R_4)
1	10	29	23	18	1
2	63	3	50	27	1
3	54	3	50	27	1
4	19	29	23	18	1
5	4	50	34	43	7
6	32	16	1	32	12
7	48	24	5	12	16
8	57	24	5	12	16
9	15	43	49	48	18
10	42	45	16	37	22
11	24	44	4	33	32
12	61	10	35	22	37
13	17	36	0	11	41
14	36	2	39	2	41
15	26	37	19	38	43
16	11	57	19	38	43

Merges and false alarms are highlighted in gray. For example, chains 2 and 3 merge, because a collision occurred in position $j = 1$ for both chains, while chains 15 and 16 merge, because a collision occurred in position $j = 2$ for both chains. Endpoint 1 has four inverse images, while endpoints 16, 41, and 43 all have two inverse images. Merges and false alarms are frequent when the key space is small, which is the case of this example ($N = 64$).

2) Key search in rainbow table

Three scenarios are considered.

i) Scenario 1: plaintext encrypted with $K = 27$

$C_0 = 57 * 27 \bmod 128 = 3.$

$y_1 = R_4(C_0) = \left\lfloor \frac{3}{2} \right\rfloor - \left\lfloor \frac{3}{7} \right\rfloor = 1.$ 1 is the endpoint of chains 1, 2, 3, and 4. Key is $x_{2,3} = x_{3,3} = 27$, which is the correct key.

Testing keys $x_{1,3}$ and $x_{4,3}$ (both equal to 18) results in incorrect key.

ii) Scenario 2: plaintext encrypted with $K = 5$
Hence, $C_0 = 57 * 5 \bmod 128 = 29.$

$y_1 = R_4(C_0) = \left\lfloor \frac{29}{2} \right\rfloor - \left\lfloor \frac{29}{7} \right\rfloor = 10,$ which is not an endpoint.

$y_2 = f_4(R_3[C_0]) = f_4(\lfloor (3 * 29 - 11) \rfloor \bmod 64) = f_4(12) = R_4(Enc_{12}(P_0)) = 16,$ which is the endpoint of chains 7 and 8.
$x_{7,2} = x_{8,2} = 5,$ which is the correct key.

iii) Scenario 3: plaintext encrypted with $K = 6$
$C_0 = 57 * 6 \bmod 128 = 86.$

$y_1 = R_4(C_0) = \left\lfloor \frac{86}{2} \right\rfloor - \left\lfloor \frac{86}{7} \right\rfloor = 31,$ which is not an endpoint.

$y_2 = f_4(R_3[C_0]) = f_4(\lfloor (3 * 86 - 11) \rfloor \bmod 64) = f_4(55) = R_4(Enc_{55}(P_0)) = R_4(63) = 22,$ which is the endpoint of chain 10; but it is a false alarm.
$y_3 = f_4(f_3(R_2(C_0))) = f_4(f_3(37)) = f_4(R_3(Enc_{37}(57))) = f_4(R_3(61)) = f_4(44) = R_4(Enc_{44}(57)) = 28,$ which is not an endpoint.
$y_4 = f_4(f_3(f_2(R_1(C_0)))) = f_4(f_3(f_2(43))) = f_4(f_3(49)) = f_4(48) = 18,$

which is the endpoint of chain 9; but it is a false alarm.
Stop the search.

Conclusion: no correct key is recovered in scenario 3. If one visually inspects the rainbow table, no element equal to 6 is present. Therefore, there is no chance that the correct key can be found in the table.

11.2 Linear Cryptanalysis

Linear cryptanalysis technique was first introduced by Mitsuru Matsui, who applied it to DES cipher [4]. Using CPU technology of the 1990s, 12-round DES was broken in 50 hours using 2^{33} known plaintexts; and 16-round DES was broken, using 2^{47} known plaintexts.

Linear cryptanalysis is applied to key-alternating block ciphers to either disclose some plaintexts or to recover the cipher key [5]. It may be used in known-plaintext attacks or only-ciphertext attacks. In the following, we only focus on known-plaintext attacks. The probability of attack success depends on the number of known plaintext–ciphertext pairs; in general, this number is large. The basic ideas of linear cryptanalysis are:

- Find relationships, in form of linear approximations, between bits of plaintext, ciphertext, and key.
- Use each linear approximation as distinguisher to predict one bit of information about an unknown plaintext, the cipher key or the last-round key.

Linear cryptanalysis is suitable against key-alternating block ciphers (such as DES and AES) where the key of round i is XORed with the round input to yield the round output, using a transformation function (as shown on Figure 11.4). The

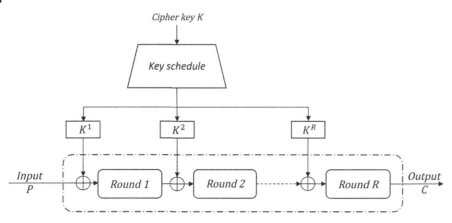

Figure 11.4 Key-iterating block cipher diagram.

relationships are associated with one round, some rounds, or the full cipher. Specifically, linear cryptanalysis tries to linearly approximate the nonlinear components of a block cipher. Recall that s-boxes are the main nonlinear functions used in block ciphers.

11.2.1 Bias and Piling-up Lemma

Linear cryptanalysis is a statistical attack based on the notion of probabilistic bias (or simply bias), which is recalled before we introduce the attack.

Let $X_1, X_2, ..., X_m$ be m independent random binary variables (i.e. $X_i \in \{0,1\}$, $\forall i = 1, ..., m$), such that: $Pr(X_i = 0) = p_i$ and $Pr(X_i = 1) = 1 - p_i$.

The bias of a random binary variable X_i, denoted ε_i, is defined by:

$$\varepsilon_i = Pr(X_i = 0) - \frac{1}{2} = p_i - \frac{1}{2} \tag{11.4}$$

In other words, the bias is the deviation of expected value from $\frac{1}{2}$. ε belongs to interval $\left[-\frac{1}{2}, \frac{1}{2}\right]$. We can easily derive the following properties:

$$Pr(X_i = 0) = \varepsilon_i + \frac{1}{2} \text{ and } Pr(X_i = 1) = \frac{1}{2} - \varepsilon_i$$

A binary function $h : F_2^m \to F_2$, in m binary variables X_i, $i = 1, ..., m$, is linear, if it can be represented as $h(X_1, X_2, ..., X_m) = a_1 X_1 \oplus a_2 X_2 \oplus ... \oplus a_m X_m$, where $a_i \in \{0,1\}$, $\forall i = 1, ..., m$. F_2 denotes the binary field. A function $f : F_2^m \to F_2$, in m binary variables $X_{i=1,...,m}$, is *affine*, if $f(X_1, X_2, ..., X_m) = h(X_1, X_2, ..., X_m)$, or $f(X_1, X_2, ..., X_m) = h(X_1, X_2, ..., X_m) \oplus 1$.

Given two binary variables X and Y, $X \oplus Y = 1$ means that $X \neq Y$.

Piling-up lemma is a principle used to construct linear approximations involving several random binary variables [4]. The lemma states the following:

Lemma 11.1. Piling-up lemma.

Let $X_1, X_2, ..., X_m$ be m independent random binary variables whose values are 0 with probability p_i or 1 with probability $1 - p_i$. Then, the probability that $X_1 \oplus X_2 \oplus ... \oplus X_m$ is equal to 0 is : $\frac{1}{2} + 2^{m-1} \prod_{i=1}^{m} (p_i - 1/2)$.

Alternatively, Piling-up lemma may be stated as:
The bias of a linear binary function in m independent random binary variables $X_1, X_2, ..., X_m$ is related to the product of the biases of the input variables:

$$\varepsilon_{1,...,m} = \varepsilon(X_1 \oplus X_2 \oplus ... \oplus X_m) = 2^{m-1} \prod_{i=1}^{m} \varepsilon(X_i) \tag{11.5}$$

In particular, $\varepsilon_{1,2}$, the bias of two random binary variables, X_1 and X_2, is $\varepsilon_{1,2} = 2\varepsilon_1\varepsilon_2$.

Notice that if any of variables X_i, $i = 1, ..., m$, is unbiased (i.e. $\varepsilon_i = 0$), then $Pr\left(X_1 \oplus X_2 \oplus ... \oplus X_m = 0\right) = \dfrac{1}{2}$. There exists a linear relationship between m variables $X_{i=1,...,m}$, only if the bias $\varepsilon_{1,...,m}$ is not zero.

11.2.2 Constructing Linear Approximation Expressions

First of all, notice that for a given cipher and a set of plaintext–ciphertext pairs, there may or may not exist linear relationships, whose exploitation results in deduction of bit-information about the key. Linear attack success depends on the selected linear approximations and on the randomness in known plaintexts.

Let P and C denote a plaintext and its ciphertext, and K, the cipher key, such that $C = Enc_K(P)$. To simplify, assume that P, C, and K are of the same bit-length of b. Let $P[i_1, i_2, ..., i_p]$, $C[j_1, j_2, ..., j_q]$, and $K[k_1, k_2, ..., k_u]$, denote p bits of plaintext located at positions $i_1, i_2, ..., i_p$, q bits of ciphertext located at positions $j_1, j_2, ..., j_q$, and u bits of key located at positions $k_1, k_2, ..., k_u$. The first form of linear expression is specified as:

$$P[i_1, i_2, ..., i_p] \oplus C[j_1, j_2, ..., j_q] \oplus K[k_1, k_2, ..., k_u] = 0 \tag{11.6}$$

The second linear expression form, which is used in the sequel, is specified as:

$$\begin{aligned}
&(\alpha \cdot P) \oplus (\beta \cdot C) \oplus (\kappa \cdot K) = 0 \\
&= \left(\bigoplus_{i=1,...,b} (\alpha_i \cdot P_i) \right) \oplus \left(\bigoplus_{i=1,...,b} (\beta_i \cdot C_i) \right) \oplus \left(\bigoplus_{i=1,...,b} (\kappa_i \cdot K_i) \right) = 0
\end{aligned} \tag{11.7}$$

where α, β, and κ are called *masks* of plaintext, ciphertext, and key, respectively, such that: $\alpha = \sum_{a \ni \{i_1, i_2, ..., i_p\}} 2^{b-a}$, $\beta = \sum_{a \ni \{j_1, j_2, ..., j_q\}} 2^{b-a}$, and $K = \sum_{a \ni \{k_1, k_2, ..., k_u\}} 2^{b-a}$.

$\alpha_{i=1,...,b}$, $\beta_{i=1,...,b}$, and $\kappa_{i=1,...,b}$ are all binary constants. "." denotes the bit product operation (i.e. AND operation) and $\bigoplus_{i=1,...,b}$ denotes the XOR operation of b binary variables.

Example 11.3 Let P, C, and K be strings of six bits.

$$P[2,3,4,5] \oplus C[1,3,6] \oplus K[5,6] = (P_2 \oplus P_3 \oplus P_4 \oplus P_5) \oplus (C_1 \oplus C_3 \oplus C_6) \oplus (K_5 \oplus K_6)$$

Using three masks, in binary, the expression is rewritten as:

$$\left([011110] \cdot P\right) \oplus \left([101001] \cdot C\right) \oplus \left([000011] \cdot K\right)$$

When $P = [011010]$, $C = [111010]$, and $K = [001010]$, the expression takes the value:

$$\left([011110] \cdot [011010]\right) \oplus \left([101001] \cdot [111010]\right) \oplus \left([000011] \cdot [001010]\right) = 0$$

11.2.2.1 Finding Linear Approximations Associated with an s-box

The main nonlinear components of block ciphers are s-boxes. Therefore, linear cryptanalysis focuses essentially on s-boxes. For simplicity, assume that the input and output of s-boxes are of the same bit-length. The quality of linear expressions combining input and output bits is analyzed and the good ones are kept. Good linear approximations are those which result in a high probability of attack success. To understand how linear expressions can be identified, let us consider the following example.

Example 11.4 Consider an s-box, which takes four bits and outputs four bits, according to the table in Figure 11.5. As you may see the s-box is not a linear function.

Three linear expressions are tried: $X_1 \oplus X_4 = Y_4$, $X_2 \oplus X_3 = Y_4$, and $X_2 \oplus X_3 = Y_1 \oplus Y_2$.

In Table 11.3, incorrect approximations are highlighted in gray.

$$Pr\left(X_1 \oplus X_4 = Y_4\right) = Pr\left(X_1 \oplus X_4 \oplus Y_4 = 0\right) = 12/16. \text{ The bias is } \frac{12}{16} - \frac{1}{2} = \frac{1}{4}.$$

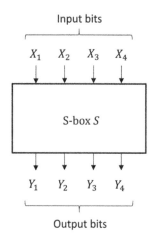

Input bits

X_1 X_2 X_3 X_4

S-box S

Y_1 Y_2 Y_3 Y_4

Output bits

X	0	1	2	3	4	5	6	7	8	9	a	b	c	d	e	f
$S(X)$	c	5	6	b	9	0	a	d	3	e	f	8	4	7	1	2

Figure 11.5 Simple s-box and its table.

Table 11.3 Evaluation of linear expressions.

X_1	X_2	X_3	X_4	Y_1	Y_2	Y_3	Y_4	$Y_4 = X_1 \oplus X_4$	$Y_4 = X_2 \oplus X_3$	$Y_1 \oplus Y_2 = X_2 \oplus X_3$
0	0	0	0	1	1	0	0	0 = 0	0 = 0	0 = 0
0	0	0	1	0	1	0	1	1 = 1	1 = 0	1 = 0
0	0	1	0	0	1	1	0	0 = 0	0 = 1	1 = 1
0	0	1	1	1	0	1	1	1 = 1	1 = 1	1 = 1
0	1	0	0	1	0	0	1	1 = 0	1 = 1	1 = 1
0	1	0	1	0	0	0	0	0 = 1	0 = 1	0 = 1
0	1	1	0	1	0	1	0	0 = 0	0 = 0	1 = 0
0	1	1	1	1	1	0	1	1 = 1	1 = 0	0 = 0
1	0	0	0	0	0	1	1	1 = 1	1 = 0	0 = 0
1	0	0	1	1	1	1	0	0 = 0	0 = 0	0 = 0
1	0	1	0	1	1	1	1	1 = 1	1 = 1	0 = 1
1	0	1	1	1	0	0	0	0 = 0	0 = 1	1 = 1
1	1	0	0	0	1	0	0	0 = 1	0 = 1	1 = 1
1	1	0	1	0	1	1	1	1 = 0	1 = 1	1 = 1
1	1	1	0	0	0	0	1	1 = 1	1 = 0	0 = 0
1	1	1	1	0	0	1	0	0 = 0	0 = 0	0 = 0

$$Pr\left(X_2 \oplus X_3 = Y_4\right) = Pr\left(X_2 \oplus X_3 \oplus Y_4 = 0\right) = 1/2. \text{ The bias is } 0.$$

$$Pr\left(X_2 \oplus X_3 = Y_1 \oplus Y_2\right) = Pr\left(X_2 \oplus X_3 \oplus Y_1 \oplus Y_2 = 0\right) = 12/16. \text{ The bias is } \frac{12}{16} - \frac{1}{2} = \frac{1}{4}.$$

The first and third linear approximations of the s-box are more likely to be correct than the second one. They are good linear approximations; they are written as follows:

$$[1001] \cdot X \oplus [0001] \cdot Y = 0 \text{ (first approximation)}$$

$$[0110] \cdot X \oplus [1100] \cdot Y = 0 \text{ (third approximation)}$$

11.2.2.2 Measuring Quality of Linear Approximations

If b is the bit-length of the input and output of an s-box, we can try 2^b masks for each random variable X (input) or Y (output). Therefore, the number of linear approximations is 2^{2b}. However, only a few linear approximations are good. The idea of linear cryptanalysis is to keep expressions with a large or low probability of occurrence; i.e. keep expressions with a large (or low) bias; the larger the bias, the better the quality of approximation. Expressions that occur with a probability of ½ (or very close to ½) do not provide information useful to perform linear attacks, because those expressions may hold or not with the same probability of ½; their bias is (close to) 0. Expressions with a bias of $\mp\frac{1}{2}$ are perfect. In summary:

- If $\varepsilon = 0$, nothing can be learned.
- If $\varepsilon > 0$, approximation $(\alpha \cdot X) \oplus (\beta \cdot Y) = 0$ is good.
- If $\varepsilon < 0$, approximation $(\alpha \cdot X) \oplus (\beta \cdot Y) \oplus 1 = 0$ is good.

The common method to measure the quality of linear approximations is the *linear approximation table* (LAT), which is a 2^b-by-2^b matrix, where $LAT(\alpha, \beta)$ denotes the number of correct matchings (i.e. $(\alpha \cdot X) \oplus (\beta \cdot Y) = 0$) of the expression using α and β values, minus 2^{b-1}. Formally, the LAT is defined by:

$$LAT(\alpha, \beta) = 2^b * \varepsilon(\alpha, \beta) \tag{11.8}$$

Equation (11.8) is equivalent to $LAT(\alpha, \beta) = |X, Y \in F_2^b |\{\alpha \cdot X = \beta \cdot Y\}| - 2^{b-1}$.

| **Note.** The sum of all elements of a LAT is 0. The sum of all elements of any column or row is either 2^{b-1} or -2^{b-1}.

$LAT(\alpha, \beta)$ equal zero means that the approximation is as good as a random approximation. Therefore, we do not learn anything form zero-elements of a LAT. The larger is the absolute value of a LAT element, the more the linear approximation tells us about the approximated function. Positive elements mean that linear approximation is frequently correct, while negative elements mean that linear approximation is rarely correct. Adding 1 to a linear expression that is rarely correct results in a linear expression that is frequently correct; i.e. if $\alpha \cdot X \oplus \beta \cdot Y = 0$ is rarely correct, then $\alpha \cdot X \oplus \beta \cdot Y \oplus 1 = 0$ is frequently correct.

| **Note.** Designers of block ciphers need to use s-boxes with low values in their LATs, while attackers prefer them with large values. Therefore, to design ciphers resistant against linear cryptanalysis, s-boxes with low LAT values are needed.

Example 11.5 Table 11.4 is the LAT corresponding to the s-box specified in Figure 11.5.

Table 11.4 Example of linear approximation table of an s-box.

α \ β	0	1	2	3	4	5	6	7	8	9	a	b	c	d	e	f
0	8	0	0	0	0	0	0	0	0	0	0	0	0	0	0	0
1	0	0	0	0	0	-4	0	-4	0	0	0	0	0	-4	0	4
2	0	0	2	2	-2	-2	0	0	2	-2	0	4	0	4	-2	2
3	0	0	2	2	2	-2	-4	0	-2	2	-4	0	0	0	-2	-2
4	0	0	-2	2	-2	-2	0	4	-2	-2	0	-4	0	0	-2	2
5	0	0	-2	2	-2	2	0	0	2	2	-4	0	4	0	2	2
6	0	0	0	-4	0	0	-4	0	0	-4	0	0	4	0	0	0
7	0	0	0	4	4	0	0	0	0	-4	0	0	0	0	4	0
8	0	0	2	-2	0	0	-2	2	-2	2	0	0	-2	2	4	4
9	0	4	-2	-2	0	0	2	-2	-2	-2	-4	0	-2	2	0	0
a	0	0	4	0	2	2	2	-2	0	0	0	-4	2	2	-2	2
b	0	-4	0	0	-2	-2	2	-2	-4	0	0	0	2	2	2	-2
c	0	0	0	0	-2	-2	-2	-2	4	0	0	-4	-2	2	2	-2
d	0	4	4	0	-2	-2	2	2	0	0	0	0	2	-2	2	-2
e	0	0	2	2	-4	4	-2	-2	-2	-2	0	0	-2	-2	0	0
f	0	4	-2	2	0	0	-2	-2	-2	2	4	0	2	2	0	0

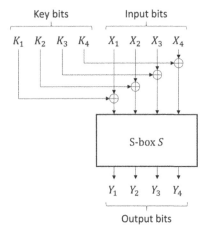

Figure 11.6 Example of a toy-cipher with one round.

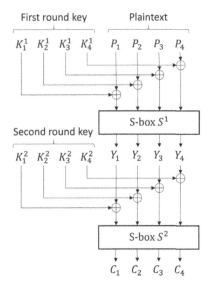

Figure 11.7 Example of a toy-cipher with two rounds.

11.2.2.3 Finding Linear Expressions Associated with an s-box and a Key

Consider the toy-cipher, illustrated by Figure 11.6, which makes use of the s-box defined in Figure 11.5. The key is XORed with the plaintext to yield the input bits of the s-box. Therefore, a linear approximation involving the plaintext, the ciphertext, and the key has the following form:

$$\left(\alpha\cdot\left(P\oplus K\right)\right)\oplus\left(\beta\cdot C\right)=0$$

The form above is equivalent to $\left(\alpha\cdot P\right)\oplus\left(\beta\cdot C\right)=\alpha\cdot K$, meaning that if some information is known about some bits of the plaintext and ciphertext, then some information could be deduced about some bits of the key. For example, if $\left([0110]\cdot P\right)\oplus\left([0001]\cdot C\right)=0=\left([0011]\cdot K\right)$, then $K_3\oplus K_4=0$. Therefore, the 3rd and 4th bits of the key are both equal either to 1 or to 0.

11.2.2.4 Finding Linear Expressions Associated with Two s-boxes and a Key

Consider the toy-cipher, illustrated by Figure 11.7, which makes use of two s-boxes. The cipher has two rounds. Let K^r denote the key of round r and $k^r_{i=1...,4}$, the four bits of k^r. We can express linear expressions of the form:

$$\alpha\cdot\left(P\oplus K^1\right)-\beta^1\cdot Y^1 \tag{11.9}$$

$$\beta^1\cdot\left(Y^1\oplus K^2\right)=\beta^2\cdot C \tag{11.10}$$

where, Y^r, β^r, and K^r denote the output, the output mask, and the key of round r, respectively. Combining equations (11.9) and (11.10) yields:

$$\alpha\cdot P\oplus\beta^2\cdot C=\alpha\cdot K^1\oplus\beta^1\cdot K^2 \tag{11.11}$$

The last linear expression is referred to as *linear full-cipher approximation*. By Piling-up lemma, its bias is $\varepsilon_{1,2}=2*\varepsilon_1*\varepsilon_2$, where ε_1 and ε_2 are biases of expressions (11.9) and (11.10), respectively.

Note. The output of the first round and the input of the second round make use of the same mask. Otherwise, in the approximation, some input bits of the second rounds have no relationship with the plaintext and the key of the first round.

Example 11.6 Consider the cipher illustrated by Figure 11.7. We can use the following two expressions to express a linear approximations to infer some information about the 1st bit of the second key round from the approximation of the 1st and 4th bits of the first round key and the plaintext (as shown by the masks):

$$L^1 := \left([1001]\cdot\left(P\oplus K^1\right)\right)=\left([0001]\cdot Y^1\right)$$

$$L^2 := \left([0001]\cdot\left(Y^1\oplus K^2\right)\right)=\left([0101]\cdot Y^2\right)$$

Combining linear equations L^1 and L^2 yields L^3:

$$L^3 := \left(\left([1001]\cdot\left(P\oplus K^1\right)\right)\oplus\left([0001]\cdot Y^1\right)\right)\oplus\left(\left([0001]\cdot\left(Y^1\oplus K^2\right)\right)\oplus\left([0101]\cdot Y^2\right)\right)=0$$

L^3 can be rewritten as follows: $[1001]\cdot P\oplus[0101]\cdot Y^2=[1001]\cdot K^1\oplus[0001]\cdot K^2$

Now, evaluate the three linear approximations above, assuming that s-boxes S^1 and S^2 are identical. We use the LAT illustrated in Table 11.4, to find the biases.

For the first linear approximation: $LAT(9,1)=4=2^4*\varepsilon_1\Rightarrow\varepsilon_1=1/4$. Hence, the first expression holds with a probability of $P_1=\dfrac{1}{2}+\dfrac{1}{4}=\dfrac{3}{4}$.

For the second linear approximation: $LAT(1,5) = -4 = 2^4 * \varepsilon_2 \Rightarrow \varepsilon_2 = -\frac{1}{4}$. Hence, the second expression holds with a probability of $P_2 = \frac{1}{2} - \frac{1}{4} = \frac{1}{4}$.

For the third linear approximation, we use Piling-up lemma applied to two random binary variables in L^1 and L^2:

$\varepsilon_{1,2} = 2 * \varepsilon_1 * \varepsilon_2 = -\frac{1}{8}$. Hence, the third expression holds with a probability of $P_3 = \frac{1}{2} - \frac{1}{8} = \frac{3}{8}$.

11.2.2.5 Finding Linear Expressions Associated with a Full Cipher

When the cipher is composed of more than two rounds, each using several s-boxes and permutation, the linear expressions can be selected among a large set of combinations. Using Piling-up lemma and LAT of each s-box, the selected s-boxes should be such that the biases of linear full-cipher approximation are the largest. Each linear full-cipher approximation contributes to infer a bit of information on the cipher key (i.e. a relationship between some bits of the cipher key). S-boxes selected to perform linear cryptanalysis are referred to as active s-boxes. Below, we show how to find a linear full-cipher approximation associated with a toy-cipher.

Example 11.7

Notations

> b: bit-length of plaintext, ciphertext, and key
> P_i, $i = 1,...,b$: plaintext bits; C_i, $i = 1,...,b$: ciphertext bits
> R: number of rounds
> d: number of s-boxes per round; m: number of input (or output) bits per s-box
> K^r: key of round r, $r = 1,...,R$; K_i^r, $i = 1,...,b$: bits of K^r
> Y^r: output of round r; Y_i^r, $i = 1,...,b$: bits of Y^r
> $U_{l,j}^r$, $l = 1,...,d$, $j = 1,...,m$: input bits of s-box S_l^r
> $V_{l,j}^r$, $l = 1,...,d$, $j = 1,...,m$: output bits of s-box S_l^r
> $LAT^l(i,j)$: value of the LAT of s-box l at row i and column j.

Consider the cipher illustrated by Figure 11.8, where $b = 16$, $R = 5$, and $d = m = 4$. In each round r, with the exception of the first and last rounds, the output of round $r-1$ is permuted and then XORed with the key of round r to feed s-boxes of round r. A single permutation is used in the entire cipher, with the following mapping:

$$1 \to (3,2) \quad 2 \to (4,1) \quad 3 \to (4,3) \quad 4 \to (4,2) \quad 5 \to (1,2) \quad 6 \to (1,1) \quad 7 \to (2,3) \quad 8 \to (1,4)$$
$$9 \to (3,1) \quad 10 \to (2,4) \quad 11 \to (2,1) \quad 12 \to (1,3) \quad 13 \to (3,3) \quad 14 \to (2,2) \quad 15 \to (4,4) \quad 16 \to (3,4)$$

where $i \to (l,j)$ denotes connection of bit i of permutation input to input bit j of s-box l. In Figure 11.8, thick lines highlight how bits are used to form linear approximation corresponding to rounds. To simplify, all the s-boxes are identical to the one with LAT shown in Table 11.4.

First-round linear approximation (L^1):

$$L^1 := \left(\left(P_2 \oplus K_2^1 \right) \oplus \left(P_3 \oplus K_3^1 \right) \oplus \left(P_4 \oplus K_4^1 \right) \right) \oplus Y_3^1 \oplus Y_4^1 = 0$$

where $Y_3^1 = V_{1,3}^1$ and $Y_4^1 = V_{1,4}^1$. So,

$$L^1 := \left(\left(P_2 \oplus P_3 \oplus P_4 \right) \oplus \left(K_2^1 \oplus K_3^1 \oplus K_4^1 \right) \right) \oplus Y_3^1 \oplus Y_4^1 = 0$$

Let $\Omega_P = P_2 \oplus P_3 \oplus P_4$ and $\Omega_{K^1} = K_2^1 \oplus K_3^1 \oplus K_4^1$. So,

$$L^1 := \Omega_P \oplus \Omega_{K^1} \oplus \left(Y_3^1 \oplus Y_4^1 \right) = 0$$

Let ε^1 denote the bias of linear approximation L^1. Since only s-box S_1^1 is used,

$$\varepsilon^1 = \frac{LAT^1(7,3)}{16} = \frac{4}{16} = \frac{1}{4}.$$

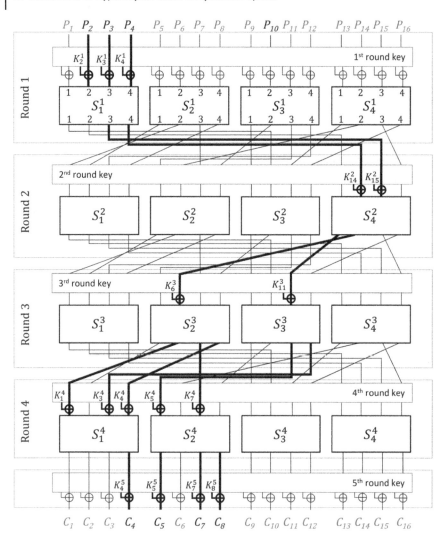

Figure 11.8 Cipher with four rounds, four s-boxes per round, and a permutation.

Second-round linear approximation (L^2):

$$L^2 := \left(U^2_{4,2} \oplus U^2_{4,3}\right) \oplus \left(Y^2_{13} \oplus Y^2_{14}\right) = 0$$

where $Y^2_{13} = V^2_{4,1}$, $Y^2_{14} = V^2_{4,2}$. Thus,

$$L^2 := \left(\left(Y^1_4 \oplus K^2_{14}\right) \oplus \left(Y^1_3 \oplus K^2_{15}\right)\right) \oplus \left(Y^2_{13} \oplus Y^2_{14}\right) = 0$$

Let $\Omega_{K^2} = K^2_{14} \oplus K^2_{15}$. Thus,

$$L^2 := \Omega_P \oplus \Omega_{K^1} \oplus \Omega_{K^2} \oplus \left(Y^2_{13} \oplus Y^2_{14}\right) = 0$$

Let ε^2 denote the bias of linear approximation L^2. Since two s-boxes are used, by Piling-up lemma, $\varepsilon^2 = 2 *$

$$\frac{LAT^1(7,3)}{16} * \frac{LAT^4(6,12)}{16} = 2 * \frac{4}{16} * \frac{4}{16} = \frac{1}{8}.$$

Third-round linear approximation (L^3):

$$L^3 := \left(U_{2,2}^3 \oplus U_{3,3}^3\right) \oplus \left(Y_6^3 \oplus Y_7^3 \oplus Y_8^3 \oplus Y_{11}^3 \oplus Y_{12}^3\right) = 0$$

where $Y_6^3 = V_{2,2}^3$, $Y_7^3 = V_{2,3}^3$, $Y_8^3 = V_{2,4}^3$, $Y_{11}^3 = V_{3,3}^3$, $Y_{12}^3 = V_{3,4}^3$. So,

$$L^3 := \left(\left(Y_{14}^2 \oplus K_6^3\right) \oplus \left(Y_{13}^2 \oplus K_{11}^3\right)\right) \oplus \left(Y_6^3 \oplus Y_7^3 \oplus Y_8^3 \oplus Y_{11}^3 \oplus Y_{12}^3\right) = 0$$

Let $\Omega_{K^3} = K_6^3 \oplus K_{11}^3$. Thus,

$$L^3 := \Omega_P \oplus \Omega_{K^1} \oplus \Omega_{K^2} \oplus \Omega_{K^3} \oplus \left(Y_6^3 \oplus Y_7^3 \oplus Y_8^3 \oplus Y_{11}^3 \oplus Y_{12}^3\right) = 0$$

Let ε^3 denote the bias of linear approximation L^3. Four s-boxes are used; by Piling-up lemma,

$$\varepsilon^3 = 2^3 * \left(\frac{LAT^1(7,3)}{16}\right) * \frac{LAT^4(6,12)}{16} * \frac{LAT^2(4,7)}{16} * \frac{LAT^3(2,3)}{16} = 8 * \frac{4}{16} * \frac{4}{16} * \frac{4}{16} * \frac{2}{16} = \frac{1}{64}.$$

Fourth-round linear approximation (L^4):

$$L^4 := \left(U_{1,1}^4 \oplus U_{1,3}^4 \oplus U_{1,4}^4 \oplus U_{2,1}^4 \oplus U_{2,3}^4\right) \oplus \left(Y_4^4 \oplus Y_5^4 \oplus Y_7^4 \oplus Y_8^4\right) = 0$$

where $Y_1^4 = C_4 \oplus K_4^5$, $Y_5^4 = C_5 \oplus K_5^5$, $Y_7^4 = C_7 \oplus K_7^5$, $Y_8^4 = C_8 \oplus K_8^5$. So,

$$L^4 := \left(\left(Y_6^3 \oplus K_1^4\right) \oplus \left(Y_{12}^3 \oplus K_3^4\right) \oplus \left(Y_8^3 \oplus K_4^4\right) \oplus \left(Y_{11}^3 \oplus K_5^4\right) \oplus \left(Y_7^3 \oplus K_7^4\right)\right)$$

$$\oplus \left(\left(C_4 \oplus K_4^5\right) \oplus \left(C_5 \oplus K_5^5\right) \oplus \left(C_7 \oplus K_7^5\right) \oplus \left(C_8 \oplus K_8^5\right)\right) = 0$$

Let $\Omega_{K^4} = K_1^4 \oplus K_3^4 \oplus K_4^4 \oplus K_5^4 \oplus K_7^4$ and $\Omega_{K^5} = K_4^5 \oplus K_5^5 \oplus K_7^5 \oplus K_8^5$.

Let $\Omega_K = \Omega_P \oplus \Omega_{K^1} \oplus \Omega_{K^2} \oplus \Omega_{K^3} \oplus \Omega_{K^4} \oplus \Omega_{K^5}$

Finally, L^4 becomes

$$L^4 := \left(P_2 \oplus P_3 \oplus P_4\right) \oplus \left(C_4 \oplus C_5 \oplus C_7 \oplus C_8\right) \oplus \Omega_K$$

Let ε^4 denote the bias of linear approximation L^4. Six s-boxes are used; by Piling-up lemma,

$$\varepsilon^4 = 2^5 * \left(\frac{LAT^1(7,3)}{16}\right) * \frac{LAT^4(6,12)}{16} * \frac{LAT^2(4,7)}{16}$$

$$* \frac{LAT^3(2,3)}{16} * \left(\frac{LAT^1(11,1)}{16}\right) * \left(\frac{LAT^2(10,11)}{16}\right)$$

$$= 2^5 * \frac{4}{16} * \frac{4}{16} * \frac{4}{16} * \frac{2}{16} * \frac{-4}{16} * \frac{-4}{16} = \frac{1}{256}.$$

Linear equation L^4 is a full-cipher linear approximation. Since the bias ε^4 is positive, linear equation L^4 holds with a probability of $\frac{1}{2} + \frac{1}{256} = \frac{129}{256}$. Using mask notation, L^4 can be rewritten as:

$$L^4 := [0111\ 0000\ 0000\ 0000] \cdot P \oplus [0001\ 1011\ 0000\ 0000] \cdot C = \Omega_K,$$

where Ω_K is a binary constant that depends on the cipher key.

However, when we want to recover one bit-information about the cipher key (using Matsui's algorithm 1, described in the sequel), we need a linear expression of the form $\pi \cdot P \oplus \sigma \cdot C \oplus \kappa \cdot K = 0$. Therefore, another analysis work must be done. That is, using the key scheduling algorithm of cipher, cryptanalyst needs to express Ω_K (which is a sum of bits of key rounds) as a sum of bits of the first-round key (i.e. the cipher key). That is, he/she needs to find a mask κ such that $\Omega_K = \kappa \cdot K$. When the key scheduling yields round keys using key permutation, it is easy to find the mask κ (as shown in Example 11.8).

11.2.3 General Methodology for Performing Linear Cryptanalysis

General methodology for performing linear cryptanalysis follows three steps:

1) Compute linear approximation tables (LATs) of s-boxes and associate linear expressions to linear components (e.g. permutation tables) of the cipher.
2) Using LATs of s-boxes and Piling-up lemma,
   - Select good linear approximations for each round. There may exist several good linear approximations.
   - Select[2] good full-cipher or partial[3]-cipher linear approximations. There may exist several good linear approximations.
3) Use each linear approximation of a full or a partial cipher and known plaintext–ciphertext pairs to deduce a bit of information about the cipher key, to partially recover the last-round key, or to disclose plaintexts.

There exist two basic algorithms to perform linear cryptanalysis attacks, which were both proposed in the seminal Matsui's paper: deduction of a bit-information about cipher key or recovery of bits of last-round key.

11.2.3.1 Algorithm 1: Deduction of a Bit-information about Cipher Key

In this algorithm, the adversary selects a good full-cipher linear approximation of the form $\pi \cdot P \oplus \sigma \cdot C \oplus k \cdot K = 0$. The selected linear approximation takes into account all rounds and with a large (positive or negative) bias.

The set of known plaintext–ciphertext pairs should be as large as possible, and with random plaintexts. The number of known plaintexts and their randomness have an impact on the probability of correctly guessing one bit-information about the cipher key.

A bit-information means $\kappa \cdot K = 0$ or $\kappa \cdot K = 1$, depending on the bias. Each linear full-cipher approximation provides one bit of the cipher key (if the mask κ has only one 1-bit) or a relationship between some bits of the key (if the mask κ has more than one 1-bit). For example, if we learn that two bits of the key are either 1 or 0, we reduce the exhaustive search by a factor of 2. Several linear full-cipher approximations are needed to recover the entire cipher key. Matsui's algorithm 1 works as follows:

Matsui-Algorithm 1

Let $\left(P^i, C^i\right), i = 1, \ldots, N$, be N known plaintext–ciphertext pairs. All plaintexts are encrypted with the same key.
Linear full-cipher approximation is $\left(\pi \cdot P\right) \oplus \left(\sigma \cdot C\right) \oplus \left(\kappa \cdot K\right) = 0$
Let ε be the bias of the linear full-cipher approximation
$T = 0$
for $i = 1$ **to** N **do if** $\left(\pi \cdot P^i\right) \oplus \left(\sigma \cdot C^i\right) = 0$, **then** $T = T + 1$
if $T > N/2$, **then if** $\varepsilon > 0$, **then** guess $\kappa \cdot K = 0$ **else** guess $\kappa \cdot K = 1$
else if $\varepsilon > 0$, **then** guess $\kappa \cdot K = 1$ **else** guess $\kappa \cdot K = 0$

Example 11.8 Consider the toy-cipher illustrated by Figure 11.9. All arguments are of a bit-length of 4. The cipher runs in two rounds, which make use of the same s-box. The linear approximation table of the used s-box is identical to that given in Table 11.4. The key of the first round is the cipher key; and that of the second round is yielded by a permutation of the first key. The encryption of all plaintexts using all keys is shown in Table 11.5.

Assume that the following plaintext–ciphertext pairs are known:

$$\left(1, 12\right), \left(2, 8\right), \left(4, 9\right), \left(5, 13\right), \left(8, 10\right), \left(12, 11\right), \left(15, 14\right).$$

11.2 Linear Cryptanalysis

Selection and use of the first linear full-cipher approximation

From the LAT of chosen s-box, we select $LAT(10,11)$. Therefore, the linear approximation for the first round is $\left(10\cdot\left(P\oplus K^1\right)\right)\oplus\left(11\cdot Y\right)$, which has a bias of $-1/4$. In bit representation, linear approximation for the first round is:

$$\left(P_1\oplus K_1^1\right)\oplus\left(P_3\oplus K_3^1\right)\oplus Y_1\oplus Y_3\oplus Y_4=0$$

For the second round, we select $LAT(11,1)$. Hence, the linear approximation for the second round is $\left(11\cdot\left(Y\oplus K^2\right)\right)\oplus\left(1\cdot C\right)$, which corresponds to a bias of $-1/4$. In bit representation, linear approximation for the second round is:

$$\left(Y_1\oplus K_1^2\right)\oplus\left(Y_3\oplus K_3^2\right)\oplus\left(Y_4\oplus K_4^2\right)\oplus C_4=0$$

By substitutions and using key permutation, where $K_1^2=K_3^1$, $K_3^2=K_4^1$, $K_4^2=K_1^1$,

$$\left(\left(\left(P_1\oplus K_1^1\right)\oplus\left(P_3\oplus K_3^1\right)\right)\oplus K_3^1\oplus K_4^1\oplus K_1^1\right)\oplus C_4=0$$

which can be rewritten as $10\cdot P\oplus1\cdot C=K_4^1$; it has a bias of $2\left(-\dfrac{1}{4}\right)\left(-\dfrac{1}{4}\right)=\dfrac{1}{8}$.

We apply Matsui's algorithm 1, with N, the number of known plaintexts, of 7:

- Computation of $V(P,C)=10\cdot P\oplus1\cdot C$, for known plaintexts

$V(1,12)=0 \quad V(2,8)=1 \quad V(4,9)=1 \quad V(5,13)=1$

$V(8,10)=1 \quad V(12,11)=0 \quad V(15,14)=0$

- The bias is positive and the count T is equal to 3, which is less than $7/2$. Hence, we guess that $K_4^1=1$.

Selection and use of the second linear full-cipher approximation

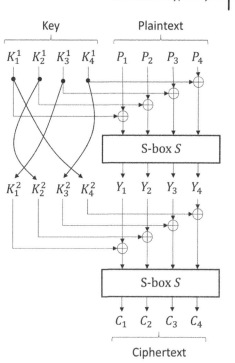

Figure 11.9 Example of a toy-cipher with two s-boxes and a key permutation.

Table 11.5 Ciphertexts for all plaintexts and keys.

P\K	0	1	2	3	4	5	6	7	8	9	a	b	c	d	e	f
0	4	d	1	5	7	a	a	b	6	7	a	b	5	c	4	7
1	0	1	b	4	9	2	5	9	2	c	5	9	6	b	2	1
2	a	e	9	2	1	8	0	1	1	8	f	0	9	0	e	3
3	8	9	7	a	e	4	4	d	e	4	d	3	d	a	f	8
4	e	6	6	d	3	b	f	0	0	9	3	e	a	e	6	d
5	c	8	0	c	5	f	d	3	a	d	8	f	8	9	0	c
6	f	2	5	f	6	7	c	8	c	5	7	4	f	2	1	5
7	7	3	3	b	2	c	e	6	b	6	1	2	7	3	b	4
8	b	4	d	6	c	5	7	4	7	a	2	c	4	d	d	6
9	1	5	c	0	b	6	1	2	9	2	6	7	0	1	c	0
a	2	f	8	9	0	9	3	e	d	3	0	1	2	f	9	2
b	3	7	a	e	a	d	8	f	f	0	4	d	3	7	7	a
c	9	0	e	3	d	3	b	a	3	b	b	a	e	6	8	9
d	d	a	f	8	f	0	9	5	5	f	9	5	c	8	a	e
e	5	c	4	7	8	1	2	c	8	1	c	8	b	4	5	f
f	6	b	2	1	4	e	6	7	4	e	e	6	1	5	3	b

From the LAT of chosen s-box, we select $LAT(15,7)$. Therefore, the linear approximation for the first round is $\left(15 \cdot \left(P \oplus K^1\right)\right) \oplus \left(7 \cdot Y\right)$, which has a bias of $-1/8$. In bit representation, linear approximation for the first round is:

$$\left(P_1 \oplus K_1^1\right) \oplus \left(P_2 \oplus K_2^1\right) \oplus \left(P_3 \oplus K_3^1\right) \oplus \left(P_4 \oplus K_4^1\right) \oplus Y_2 \oplus Y_3 \oplus Y_4 = 0$$

For the second round, we use $LAT(7,3)$. Hence, the linear approximation for the second round is $\left(7 \cdot \left(Y \oplus K^2\right)\right) \oplus \left(3 \cdot C\right)$, which corresponds to a bias of $1/4$.

In bit representation, linear approximation for the second round is:

$$\left(Y_2 \oplus K_2^2\right) \oplus \left(Y_3 \oplus K_3^2\right) \oplus \left(Y_4 \oplus K_4^2\right) \oplus C_3 \oplus C_4 = 0$$

The combination of the linear approximations of both rounds yields the second full-linear approximation:

$$P_1 \oplus P_2 \oplus P_3 \oplus P_4 \oplus C_3 \oplus C_4 = K_1^1 \oplus K_2^1 \oplus K_3^1 \oplus K_4^1 \oplus K_2^2 \oplus K_3^2 \oplus K_4^2$$

Using key permutation, where $K_2^2 = K_2^1$, $K_3^2 = K_4^1$, and $K_4^2 = K_1^1$, the linear approximation becomes: $P_1 \oplus P_2 \oplus P_3 \oplus P_4 \oplus C_3 \oplus C_4 = K_3^1$; and its bias is $2\left(-\frac{1}{8}\right)\left(\frac{1}{4}\right) = -\frac{1}{16}$.

We apply Matsui's algorithm 1, with N, the number of known plaintexts, of 7:

- Computation of $V(P,C) = 15 \cdot P \oplus 3 \cdot C$, for known plaintexts

  $V(1, 12) = 1 \qquad V(2, 8) = 1 \qquad V(4, 9) = 0 \qquad V(5, 13) = 1$

  $V(8, 10) = 0 \qquad V(12, 11) = 0 \qquad V(15, 14) = 1$

- The bias is negative and the count T is equal to 3, which is less than $7/2$. Therefore, we guess that $K_3^1 = 0$.

Selection and use of the third linear full-cipher approximation

From the LAT of chosen s-box, we select $LAT(11,14)$. Thus, the linear approximation for the first round is $\left(11 \cdot \left(P \oplus K^1\right)\right) \oplus \left(14 \cdot Y\right)$, which has a bias of $1/8$. In bit representation, linear approximation for the first round is:

$$\left(P_1 \oplus K_1^1\right) \oplus \left(P_3 \oplus K_3^1\right) \oplus \left(P_4 \oplus K_4^1\right) \oplus Y_1 \oplus Y_2 \oplus Y_3 = 0$$

For the second round, we use $LAT(14,5)$. Thus, the linear approximation for the second round is $\left(14 \cdot \left(Y \oplus K^2\right)\right) \oplus \left(5 \cdot C\right)$, which corresponds to a bias of $1/4$. In bit representation, linear approximation for the second round is:

$$\left(Y_1 \oplus K_1^2\right) \oplus \left(Y_2 \oplus K_2^2\right) \oplus \left(Y_3 \oplus K_3^2\right) \oplus C_2 \oplus C_4 = 0$$

The combination of the linear approximations of both rounds yields the third full-linear approximation:

$$P_1 \oplus P_3 \oplus P_4 \oplus C_2 \oplus C_4 = K_1^1 \oplus K_3^1 \oplus K_4^1 \oplus K_1^2 \oplus K_2^2 \oplus K_3^2$$

Using key permutation, where $K_1^2 = K_3^1$, $K_2^2 = K_2^1$, $K_3^2 = K_4^1$, and $K_4^2 = K_1^1$, the linear approximation becomes: $P_1 \oplus P_3 \oplus P_4 \oplus C_2 \oplus C_4 = K_1^1 \oplus K_2^1$; and its bias is of $2\left(\frac{1}{8}\right)\left(\frac{1}{4}\right) = \frac{1}{16}$.

We apply Matsui's algorithm 1, with N, the number of known plaintexts, of 7:

- Computation of $V(P,C) = 11 \cdot P \oplus 5 \cdot C$, for known plaintexts

  $V(1, 12) = 0 \qquad V(2, 8) = 1 \qquad V(4, 9) = 1 \qquad V(5, 13) = 1$

  $V(8, 10) = 1 \qquad V(12, 11) = 0 \qquad V(15, 14) = 0$

- The bias is positive and the count T is equal to 3, which is less than $7/2$. Therefore, we guess that $K_1^1 \oplus K_2^1 = 1$.

With three full-cipher linear approximations, we know that $K_1^1 \oplus K_2^1 = 1$, $K_3^1 = 0$, and $K_4^1 = 1$. Therefore, the cipher key is either 5 or 9. The latter is the correct key.

11.2.3.2 Algorithm 2: Recovery of the Last-round Key

Algorithm 2 is an efficient alternative to Algorithm 1 in order to recover several bits of the last-round key and a bit-information about cipher key, by using one linear partial-cipher approximation. Then, Algorithm 2 can be rerun using other linear partial-cipher approximations to recover other bits of last-round key and other bits of information about cipher key. Exploitation of results yielded by several executions of Algorithm 2 contributes to recover partially or totally the cipher key. In the sequel, we only focus on a single execution of Algorithm 2, assuming a cipher with R rounds and a structure similar to that illustrated by Figure 11.8 (i.e. with d s-boxes and a permutation).

Linear cryptanalysis follows two steps: linear partial-cipher approximation selection and use of Algorithm 2.

1) *Selection of a linear partial-cipher approximation*

A linear approximation for $R-1$ rounds, with the largest bias ε, is selected. Such an approximation does not include the key of round R; and has the following form:

$$\pi \cdot P \oplus \sigma \cdot U^{R-1} = \left(\pi^1 \cdot K^1\right) \oplus \left(\pi^2 \cdot K^2\right) \oplus \ldots \oplus \left(\pi^{R-1} \cdot K^{R-1}\right) = \kappa \cdot K \tag{11.12}$$

where U^{R-1} and σ denote the input of s-boxes of round $R-1$ and their corresponding mask; and π^i, $i = 2, \ldots, R-1$ denotes the mask of the key of round i. Masks π and π^1 are identical, because the first-round key and plaintext are XORed (without permutation) to feed s-boxes in the first round. Y^{R-1}, the output of s-boxes of round $R-1$, is referred to as intermediate ciphertext, because $Y^{R-1} = C \oplus K^R$.

Once the cipher key is fixed, the sum $\Omega = \left(\pi^1 \cdot K^1\right) \oplus \left(\pi^2 \cdot K^2\right) \oplus \ldots \oplus \left(\pi^{R-1} \cdot K^{R-1}\right)$ is a fix value, either 0 or 1, depending on the cipher key. Therefore, linear expression (11.12) holds with a probability of $\frac{1}{2} + \varepsilon$, if $\Omega = 0$ or $\frac{1}{2} - \varepsilon$, if $\Omega = 1$.

2) *Recovery of bits of the last-round key*

In the cipher structure under consideration, the output of round $R-1$ is XORed with the key of round R to produce the ciphertext. Hence, the basic idea of Algorithm 2 is to find a last-round key candidate, such that the partial decryption of known ciphertexts most likely yields the inputs of s-boxes of round $R-1$. Notice that last-round key candidates refer to varying bits corresponding to active s-boxes in round $R-1$. Pseudocode of Algorithm 2 is as follows:

Matsui-Algorithm 2

1) Let $\left(P^i, C^i\right), i = 1, \ldots, N$, be N known plaintext–ciphertext pairs.

   All the plaintexts are encrypted with the same key.
2) Let R be the number of rounds.
3) Let ε be the bias of selected linear partial-cipher approximation.
4) Let π, σ, and κ denote masks of plaintext, input of s-boxes of round $R-1$, and cipher key, in the selected partial-cipher linear-approximation.
5) Let *ReverseSboxes* denote a function that, given the output of s-boxes in round $R-1$, returns the input of those s-boxes.
6) Let f denote the number of active s-boxes in round $R-1$.
7) Let KC^R be the list of key candidates obtained by varying from 0 to $2^m - 1$ bits at the positions corresponding to each of the f active s-boxes; and the bits corresponding to inactive s-boxes are set to 0.

   m denotes the bit-length of s-box input (and output).

   With f active s-boxes, there exist m^f key candidates.

   Let $KC^R_{(j)}$, $j = 1, 2, \ldots, m^f$ denote the jth last-round key candidate.
8) **for** $j = 1$ **to** m^f **do** $T_j = 0$
9) **for** $i = 1$ **to** N **do**

   $Y^{R-1} = C^i \oplus KC^R_{(j)}$ # partial decryption

   $U^{R-1} = ReverseSboxes\left(Y^{R-1}\right)$ # use backward the s-boxes

   if $\left(\pi \cdot P^i\right) \oplus \left(\sigma \cdot U^{R-1}\right) = 0$, **then** $T_j = T_j + 1$

(Continued)

(Continued)

10) Let $T_{max} = \max_j T_j$ and $T_{min} = \min(T_j$, for every $j)$

11) **if** $|T_{max} - N/2| > |T_{min} - N/2|$, **then**

   adopt the key candidate $K_{(j)}^R$ corresponding to T_{max}

   if $\varepsilon > 0$, **then** guess $\kappa \cdot K = 0$ **else** guess $\kappa \cdot K = 1$

12) **if** $|T_{max} - N/2| < |T_{min} - N/2|$, **then**

   adopt the key candidate $K_{(j)}^R$ corresponding to T_{min}

   if $\varepsilon > 0$, **then** guess $\kappa \cdot K = 1$ **else** guess $\kappa \cdot K = 0$

Example 11.9 Reuse the 3rd linear approximation selected in Example 11.7.

$$L^3 := \Omega_P \oplus \Omega_{K^1} \oplus \Omega_{K^2} \oplus \Omega_{K^3} \oplus \left(Y_6^3 \oplus Y_7^3 \oplus Y_8^3 \oplus Y_{11}^3 \oplus Y_{12}^3\right) = 0.$$

where: $\Omega_P = P_2 \oplus P_3 \oplus P_4$; $\Omega_{K^1} = K_2^1 \oplus K_3^1 \oplus K_4^1$; $\Omega_{K^2} = K_{14}^2 \oplus K_{15}^2$; $\Omega_{K^3} = K_6^3 \oplus K_{11}^3$

By construction of the cipher structure under consideration, the following equations hold:

$$U_1^4 = Y_6^3 \oplus K_1^4 \qquad U_3^4 - Y_{12}^3 \oplus K_3^4 \qquad U_4^4 - Y_8^3 \oplus K_4^4$$

$$U_5^4 = Y_{11}^3 \oplus K_5^4 \qquad U_7^4 = Y_7^3 \oplus K_7^4$$

By substitution in L^3, we obtain the following linear approximation L:

$$\Omega_P \oplus \Omega_{K^1} \oplus \Omega_{K^2} \oplus \Omega_{K^3} \oplus \left(\left(U_1^4 \oplus K_1^4 \oplus U_3^4 \oplus K_3^4 \oplus U_4^4 \oplus K_4^4 \oplus U_5^4 \oplus K_5^4 \oplus U_7^4 \oplus K_7^4\right)\right) = 0$$

Let $\Omega = \Omega_{K^1} \oplus \Omega_{K^2} \oplus \Omega_{K^3} \oplus \Omega_{K^4}$, where $\Omega_{K^4} = K_1^4 \oplus K_3^4 \oplus K_4^4 \oplus K_5^4 \oplus K_7^4$.

Using the mask notation, L can be rewritten as:

$$0x7000 \cdot P \oplus 0xba00 \cdot U^4 \oplus \Omega = 0$$

The set of last-round key candidates is composed of 256 keys, by varying the eight leftmost bits from $0x00$ to $0xff$ and the eight rightmost bits are $0x00$.

Notes

- Linear cryptanalysis attack, as described in this section, is a known-plaintext attack. The randomness of known pairs has an impact on the attack success probability.
- Collected plaintext-ciphertext pairs should be associated with the same key. Otherwise, the linear approximations are likely to be wrong. Collecting plaintexts encrypted with two or more keys, leads to an unsuccessful attack.
- Linear cryptanalysis is a nongeneric attack. Therefore, linear approximations depend on the structure of attacked cipher, i.e. how its components (s-boxes, permutations, and other linear or nonlinear functions) are combined to produce ciphertexts.

11.3 Differential Cryptanalysis

In the beginning of the 1990s, Biham and Shamir applied differential cryptanalysis to successfully break DES [6]. Using the technology of the early 1990s, DES with six rounds was broken in less than 0.3 seconds, DES with eight rounds in two minutes, and DES with 15 rounds in less time than that of an exhaustive search. Attacks against 15 and 16 rounds required 2^{47} chosen plaintexts.

Like linear cryptanalysis, differential cryptanalysis focuses on key-iterating ciphers, in which output bits of s-boxes of round $r-1$ are permuted and then XORed with the rth round key to form the input of s-boxes of round r, as illustrated by Figure 11.8 [5].

Differential cryptography attack is a chosen-plaintext attack that takes advantage of the effect, with high probability, of differences in plaintexts on the differences in the last round input. In this model, the attacker can request a cryptosystem to encrypt plaintexts of his/her choice using the target key (which is not known to the attacker). By analyzing the returned ciphertexts, the attacker can guess the key being used. The best characteristics (represented as differences between inputs and between outputs of each s-box) of individual s-boxes are combined to yield an overall characteristic of the cipher, which in turn enables to recover some bits of the last-round key; and the remaining bits may be recovered by a brute-force attack. The first step of a differential attack is the construction of difference distribution tables associated with s-boxes.

11.3.1 Difference Distribution Table

Recall that in the extended field F_2^n, the difference and the sum are identical (i.e. both are bitwise XOR). For any n-bit integer pair $Z = [Z_1, Z_2, ..., Z_n]$ and $Z^* = [Z_1^*, Z_2^*, ..., Z_n^*]$, the difference is defined by:

$$\Delta Z = Z - Z^* = Z \oplus Z^* = \left[(Z_1 \oplus Z_1^*), (Z_2 \oplus Z_2^*), ..., (Z_n \oplus Z_n^*) \right].$$

Example 11.10 Let $P = [01010010]$ and $\Delta P = [10000001]$. Then, $P^* = P \oplus \Delta P = [11010011]$.

Let $C = Enc(P) = [10001111]$ and $C^* = Enc(P^*) = [01001001]$.

Then, $\Delta C = C \oplus \Delta C^* = [11000110]$.

11.3.1.1 Difference Distribution Table: Construction and Properties

Difference Distribution Table (DDT) of an s-box S is a $2^n \times 2^m$ matrix, where n and m denote the bit-length of s-box input and output, respectively. DDT reveals vulnerabilities of a cipher that could be exploited to perform differential attacks. If some elements of the DDT have large values, then the s-box has vulnerabilities.

Definition 11.1 **Difference set of** α (denoted Δ_α): it is a set of ordered pairs of elements, which have a difference of α. Formally, $\Delta_\alpha = \left\{ (X_1, X_2) \in F_2^n \times F_2^n \mid X_1 \oplus X_2 = \alpha \right\}$. Alternatively, Δ_α can be defined by $\Delta_\alpha = \left\{ (X, X \oplus \alpha) \mid X \in F_2^n \right\}$.

Definition 11.2 **Difference set of s-box S with respect to** α **and** β (denoted $\Delta_{\alpha,\beta}^S$): it is a set of ordered pairs of elements, which have a difference in s-box input of α and a difference in s-box output of β. Formally, $\Delta_{\alpha,\beta}^S = \left\{ (X_1, X_2) \in F_2^n \times F_2^n \mid (X_1 \oplus X_2 = \alpha) \wedge (S(X_1) \oplus S(X_2)) = \beta \right\}$. Alternatively, it can be defined by: $\Delta_{\alpha,\beta}^S = \left\{ (X_1, X_2) \in F_2^n \times F_2^n \wedge (X_1, X_2) \in \Delta_\alpha \mid (S(X_1), S(X_2)) \in \Delta_\beta \right\}$.

Each pair (α, β) is referred to as *differential*. When $\Delta_{\alpha,\beta}^S$ is 0, it is called impossible differential.

Example 11.11 Consider elements of finite field F_2^4. Let $\alpha = 9$. The difference set when $\alpha = 9$ is denoted Δ_9; and it contains the following pairs (in binary representation):

$$\{(0,9), (1,8), (2,11), (3,10), (4,13), (5,12), (6,15), (7,14), (8,1), (9,0), (10,3), (11,2), (12,5), (13,4), (14,7), (15,6)\}.$$

Table 11.6 shows the differences in s-box output, when the difference in input is $\alpha = 9$. The s-box is the same than that of Figure 11.5 and the numbers are in hexadecimal representation. Difference sets of chosen s-box S, with respect to $\alpha = 9$ and $\beta \in \{2,4,6,8,e\}$ are the following:

$$\Delta_{9,2}^S = \{(0,9), (9,0)\} \qquad \Delta_{9,4}^S = \{(3, a), (5,c), (a,3), (c,5)\} \qquad \Delta_{9,6}^S = \{(1,8), (8,1)\}$$

$$\Delta_{9,8}^S = \{(6, f), (f,6)\} \qquad \Delta_{9,c}^S = \{(7, e), (e,7)\} \qquad \Delta_{9,e}^S = \{(2, b), (4, d), (b,2), (d,4)\}$$

Definition 11.3 **Difference distribution table of an s-box** S (denoted $\mathfrak{D}^S$): it is an n-by-m matrix, where the entry indexed by α and β corresponds to the number of pairs which have a difference in s-box input of α and a difference in s-box output of β. Formally, $\mathfrak{D}_{\alpha,\beta}^S = \left| \Delta_{\alpha,\beta}^S \right|$ for $(\alpha, \beta) \in F_2^n \times F_2^m$, where $|.|$ denotes the cardinality of a set.

Table 11.6 Example of computation of input/output differences of an s-box.

X	$X \oplus 9$	$S(X)$	$S(X \oplus 9)$	$S(X \oplus 9) \oplus S(X)$
0	9	c	e	2
1	8	5	3	6
2	b	6	8	e
3	a	b	f	4
4	d	9	7	e
5	c	0	4	4
6	f	a	2	8
7	e	d	1	c
8	1	3	5	6
9	0	e	c	2
a	3	f	b	4
b	2	8	6	e
c	5	4	0	4
d	4	7	9	e
e	7	1	d	c
f	6	2	a	8

$\mathfrak{D}_{a,b}^{S} = 0$ means that it never happens that when the input difference is a, the output difference is b. Table 11.7 shows an example of DDT, where the largest value is 4.

X	0	1	2	3	4	5	6	7	8	9	a	b	c	d	e	f
$S(X)$	c	5	6	b	9	0	a	d	3	e	f	8	4	7	1	2

Table 11.7 Example of DDT of an s-box.

α \ β	0	1	2	3	4	5	6	7	8	9	a	b	c	d	e	f
0	16	0	0	0	0	0	0	0	0	0	0	0	0	0	0	0
1	0	0	0	4	0	0	0	4	0	4	0	0	0	4	0	0
2	0	0	0	2	0	4	2	0	0	0	2	0	2	2	2	0
3	0	2	0	2	2	0	4	2	0	0	2	2	0	0	0	0
4	0	0	0	0	0	4	2	2	0	2	2	0	2	0	2	0
5	0	2	0	0	2	0	0	0	0	2	2	2	4	2	0	0
6	0	0	2	0	0	0	2	0	2	0	0	4	2	0	0	4
7	0	4	2	0	0	0	2	0	2	0	0	0	2	0	0	4
8	0	0	0	2	0	0	0	2	0	2	0	4	0	2	0	4
9	0	0	2	0	4	0	2	0	2	0	0	0	2	0	4	0
a	0	0	2	2	0	4	0	0	2	0	2	0	0	2	2	0
b	0	2	0	0	2	0	0	0	4	2	2	2	0	2	0	0
c	0	0	2	0	0	4	0	2	2	2	2	0	0	0	2	0
d	0	2	4	2	2	0	0	2	0	0	2	2	0	0	0	0
e	0	0	2	2	0	0	2	2	2	2	0	0	2	2	0	0
f	0	4	0	0	4	0	0	0	0	0	0	0	0	0	4	4

Properties of DDT

i) A DDT contains $2^n * 2^m$ elements, which are all positive even integers.

ii) Element[4] $\mathfrak{D}_{0,0}^S$ is 2^n; it is called trivial differential; and it is not used in differential cryptanalysis.

iii) The sum of any matrix row α is $\sum_{\beta=1}^{m} \mathfrak{D}_{\alpha,\beta}^S = 2^n$ (see Problem 11.7).

Definition 11.4 **Difference uniformity of an s-box** *S: it is the highest value (except the value in the first cell) of the s-box DDT; i.e. it is equal to* $\max_{\alpha \neq 0 \wedge \beta \neq 0} \left| \Delta_{\alpha,\beta}^S \right|$.

High values of the differential uniformity are better for attackers, while low values are better for cipher designers. An s-box with a differential uniformity of η is referred to as η–uniform s-box.

11.3.1.2 Difference-Propagation Probability

When there exist large numbers in the DDT, if two randomly selected inputs satisfy the input difference, there is a high probability that the output difference will be satisfied as well. In differential cryptanalysis, attackers exploit the non-uniformity distribution of DDT values. If DDT values are uniformly distributed, differential cryptanalysis attack is not usable to break block ciphers.

Definition 11.5 **Difference-propagation probability of an s-box** *S* **with respect to** α **and** β: *it is the probability that, given an s-box input with a difference of α, the difference of output will be of β Formally,* $Pr^S(\alpha, \beta) = \dfrac{\left| \Delta_{\alpha,\beta}^S \right|}{2^n}$.

In Table 11.7, the highest difference-propagation probability is of $\dfrac{4}{16}$.

> **Notes**
>
> – DEA (or DES) s-boxes are $6 * 4$ matrices. In [6], the largest value of DES s-box DDT is of 14, with an associated probability of $\dfrac{14}{64} \approx 0.22$. Therefore, DEA/DES is vulnerable to differential cryptanalysis attacks.
>
> – AES s-box is a $8 * 8$ matrix. DDT building codes available on the internet showed that the largest AES entry is of 4, with a difference-propagation probability of $\dfrac{4}{256} \approx 0.016$. Therefore, AES is resistant to differential cryptanalysis.

11.3.1.3 Effect of Round Key Addition

Below, we show that adding round keys has no effect on the analysis. Recall that, with the exception of the first and last rounds of the considered cipher structure, output bits of round $r-1$ are permuted and XORed with bits of the rth round key to feed the s-boxes of round r.

Let Y^{r-1} and Z^{r-1} denote a pair of permuted outputs of round $r-1$ (or not permuted when they are plaintexts). Let $Y^{r-1} \oplus Z^{r-1} = \alpha$ be the difference of the pair. The pair of inputs of s-boxes of round r are defined by: $X = Y^{r-1} \oplus K^r$ and $X^* = Z^{r-1} \oplus K^r$, where K^r denotes key of round r.

$$X \oplus X^* = \left(Y^{r-1} \oplus K^r\right) \oplus \left(Z^{r-1} \oplus K^r\right) = Y^{r-1} \oplus Z^{r-1} = \alpha.$$

Therefore, the difference is the same, with or without the round key. In other words, the values of Y^{r-1} and Z^{r-1} will change as they proceed through the XOR with the key, but their relationship (i.e. their difference) to each other will not. Therefore, since the key bits have no effect on the difference in the s-box input, the key is ignored in the overall difference computation process.

11.3.2 Differential Attack Design

The attack runs in three steps: identification of the combination of s-boxes with a high overall difference-propagation probability, selection of random plaintext pairs, and recovery of a subset of the last-round key.

11.3.2.1 First step: Selection of an Overall Difference-Propagation Probability

Once the DDTs of all s-boxes are computed, the highest difference-propagation probabilities (DPPs) of s-boxes are easily distinguishable. Overall-cipher characteristic may be identified by combining different DPPs, using a trial technique or an optimization

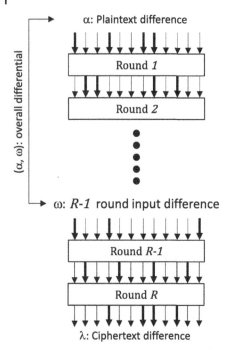

Figure 11.10 Illustration of an overall differential.

technique (such as mixed integer linear programming). Assume that the attacker has selected one or more s-boxes in each round, such that overall-cipher characteristic is the highest. Selected s-boxes are referred to as active s-boxes.

As illustrated by Figure 11.10, the overall differential is denoted (α,ω), where $\alpha = \begin{bmatrix} 100100110000 \end{bmatrix}$ is the difference in plaintext and $\omega = \begin{bmatrix} 100100000001 \end{bmatrix}$, the difference in the input of the last-but-one round. Notice that the computation of the overall differential depends on the structure of the attacked cipher. Therefore, the description below is valid only for ciphers with a structure similar to that shown in Figure 11.11.

The overall-cipher difference-propagation probability, denoted $\mathbb{P}$ is the product of all intermediate DPPs of involved active s-boxes. Formally,

$$\mathbb{P} = \prod_{(\alpha,\beta)\in\Omega} Pr^S\left(\alpha,\beta\right) \tag{11.13}$$

where Ω is the set of differentials of active s-boxes. For example, in Figure 11.11, s-boxes S_2^1, S_1^2, and S_4^3 are selected. With the assumption that each of the selected differentials has a probability of $\frac{1}{4}$, $\mathbb{P} = \left(\frac{1}{4}\right)^3$. That is, if the

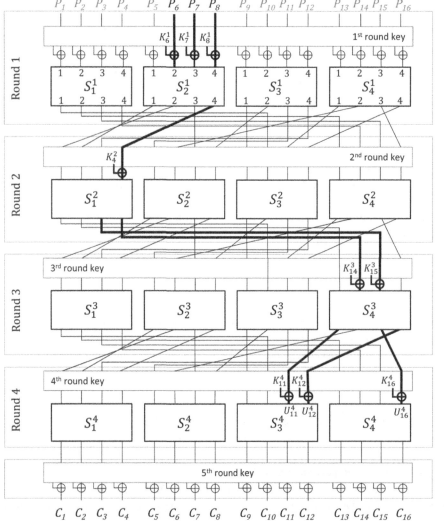

Figure 11.11 Example of scenario for differential cryptanalysis.

difference in plaintexts is $\alpha = \begin{bmatrix} 0000\,0111\,0000\,0000 \end{bmatrix}$, then the difference in the input of the fourth round is $\omega = \begin{bmatrix} 0000\,0000\,0011\,0001 \end{bmatrix}$, with a probability of $\dfrac{1}{64}$.

Example 11.12

Notations

  b: bit-length of plaintext, ciphertext, and key
  $P_i, i = 1,\ldots,b$: plaintext bits; $C_i, i = 1,\ldots,b$: ciphertext bits
  R: number of rounds
  d: number of s-boxes per round
  m: number of input (or output) bits per s-box
  K^r: key of round r, $r = 1,\ldots,R$; K_i^r, $i = 1,\ldots,b$: bits of K^r
  U^r: input difference of s-boxes of round r; U_i^r, $i = 1,\ldots,b$: bits of U^r
  Y^r: output difference of s-boxes of round r; Y_i^r, $i = 1,\ldots,b$: bits of Y^r

Consider the cipher illustrated by Figure 11.11, where $b = 16$, $R = 5$, and $d = m = 4$. In each round r, with the exception of the first and last rounds, the output of round $r-1$ is permuted and then XORed with the key of round r to feed s-boxes of round r. The first and last rounds do not make use of permutation. A single permutation is used in all rounds, with the following mappings:

$1 \rightarrow (3, 2)$	$2 \rightarrow (4, 1)$	$3 \rightarrow (4, 3)$	$4 \rightarrow (4, 2)$	$5 \rightarrow (1, 2)$	$6 \rightarrow (1, 1)$	$7 \rightarrow (2, 3)$	$8 \rightarrow (1, 4)$
$9 \rightarrow (3, 1)$	$10 \rightarrow (2, 4)$	$11 \rightarrow (2, 1)$	$12 \rightarrow (1, 3)$	$13 \rightarrow (3, 3)$	$14 \rightarrow (2, 2)$	$15 \rightarrow (4, 4)$	$16 \rightarrow (3, 4)$

where $i \rightarrow (l, j)$ denotes connection of bit i of permutation input to input bit j of s-box l.

In Figure 11.11, thick lines highlight how bit differences are used to combine difference-propagation probabilities. Notice that in linear cryptanalysis example (in Figure 11.8), thick lines highlight s-box inputs, while in Figure 11.11, they mark the difference in s-box inputs.

To simplify, assume that all s-boxes are identical to the one whose DDT is shown in Table 11.7. A good combination of s-box differentials that we choose is constructed as follows:

- Round 1: s-box S_2^1 is selected. One of its best differentials is $\Delta_{7,1}^{S_2^1}$, with a probability of $4/16$. $\Delta_{7,1}^{S_2^1}$ means that a difference of 7 in input of s-box S_2^1 is likely to result in a difference of 1 in its output. Thus, the rightmost bit of the output s-box S_2^1 is used. Therefore,
  ○ Difference in plaintext is $\Delta P = \begin{bmatrix} 0000\,0111\,0000\,0000 \end{bmatrix}$.
  ○ Difference in input of first-round boxes is $\Delta U^1 = \begin{bmatrix} 0000\,0111\,0000\,0000 \end{bmatrix}$.
  ○ Difference in output of first-round boxes is $\Delta Y^1 = \begin{bmatrix} 0000\,0001\,0000\,0000 \end{bmatrix}$.
- Round 2: the rightmost bit of s-box S_2^1 is connected to 4th bit of s-box S_1^2. Thus, S_1^2 is selected. One of the best differentials of S_1^2 is $\Delta_{1,3}^{S_1^2}$, with a probability of $4/16$. Therefore,
  ○ Difference in input of second-round boxes is $\Delta U^2 = \begin{bmatrix} 0001\,0000\,0000\,0000 \end{bmatrix}$.
  ○ Difference in output of second-round boxes is $\Delta Y^2 = \begin{bmatrix} 0011\,0000\,0000\,0000 \end{bmatrix}$.
- Round 3: the two rightmost bits of s-box S_1^2 are connected to the 2nd and 3rd bits of S_4^3. Thus, s-box S_4^3 is selected; one of its best differential is $\Delta_{6,b}^{S_4^3}$, with a probability of $4/16$. Therefore,
  ○ Difference in input of third-round boxes is $\Delta U^3 = \begin{bmatrix} 0000\,0000\,0000\,0110 \end{bmatrix}$.
  ○ Difference in output of third-round boxes is $\Delta Y^3 = \begin{bmatrix} 0000\,0000\,0000\,1011 \end{bmatrix}$.
- Round 4: the three selected bits of s-box S_4^3 are connected to the 3rd and 4th bits of s-box S_3^4 and to the 4th bit of s-box S_4^4. Therefore,
  ○ Difference in input of fourth-round box is $\Delta U^4 = \begin{bmatrix} 0000\,0000\,0011\,0001 \end{bmatrix}$.

Finally, if the difference in plaintext is $\Delta P = \begin{bmatrix} 0000\,0111\,0000\,0000 \end{bmatrix}$, then the difference in the input of s-boxes in round 4 would be $\Delta U^4 = \begin{bmatrix} 0000\,0000\,0011\,0001 \end{bmatrix}$. That is, the overall differential is

$$(\alpha, \omega) = \left(\begin{bmatrix} 0000\,0111\,0000\,0000 \end{bmatrix}, \begin{bmatrix} 0000\,0000\,0011\,0001 \end{bmatrix} \right)$$

with a probability of

$$Pr\left(\Delta U^4 = \begin{bmatrix} 0000\,0000\,0011\,0001 \end{bmatrix} \mid \Delta P = \begin{bmatrix} 0000\,0111\,0000\,0000 \end{bmatrix} \right) = \frac{1}{4} * \frac{1}{4} * \frac{1}{4} = 2^{-6}$$

Then, exploitation of the overall differential enables to guess eight bits (at positions 9 to 16) of the 5th round key.

11.3.2.2 Second Step: Selection of Chosen Plaintexts

In the first step, an overall differential with a high probability is selected. Let (α, ω) be the selected differential. Since differential cryptanalysis is a chosen-plaintext attack, the attacker randomly selects a plaintext P and requests the cryptosystem to encrypt P and $P + \alpha$ and receives two ciphertexts, C and C^*. The plaintext selection and encryption is repeated until a set, denoted $\mathcal{C}$, of N pairs (C, C^*) is collected.

11.3.2.3 Third Step: Recovery of some Bits of the Last-round Key

In the previous two steps, an overall differential and a set of appropriate chosen plaintexts were selected. The third step aims to guess some bits of last-round key. The method to recover bits of the last-round key can be summarized as follows:

1) Define KCS, the set of candidates for the last-round key, as follows: vary the bits corresponding to the active s-boxes and set to 0 the bits corresponding to inactive s-boxes. In the example of Figure 11.11, the set of key candidates is composed of values from $[0000\,000\,0000\,0000]$ to $[000\,000\,0011\,1111\,111]$, because only the third and fourth s-boxes are active in round 4.

2) For each key candidate KC^i, $i = 1, \ldots, |KCS|$
   - Set a counter T^i to 0.
   - For each ciphertext pair $(C, C^*) \in \mathcal{C}$:
     - partially decrypt C and C^*. When the attacked cipher structure is similar to that of Figure 11.11, partial decryption of a ciphertext means XOR the ciphertext with the key candidate; then, by using backward the active s-boxes, determine their inputs. Formally, the inputs of the s-boxes in round $R - 1$ are defined by:

     $$IC = BoxesReverse\left(C \oplus KC^i\right)$$
     $$IC^* = BoxesReverse\left(C^* \oplus KC^i\right)$$

     where *BoxesReverse* is a function that returns the concatenation of inputs of d s-boxes, given their outputs.

     - In IC and IC^*, set to 0 the bits corresponding to inactive s-boxes and obtain $\overline{IC}$ and $\overline{IC^*}$.
     - If $\overline{IC} \oplus \overline{IC^*}$ matches the selected difference ω, (i.e. $\overline{IC} \oplus \overline{IC^*} = \omega$), then increment counter T^i.

3) Keep the candidate key KC^I with the highest counter, i.e. $T^I = \max_i T^i$.

An attacker can try different overall differentials to guess, as much as possible, bits of the last-round key. If last-round key bits are not entirely recovered, the attacker must perform a brute-force attack to recover the remaining bits.

11.4 Algebraic Cryptanalysis

Algebraic attacks mainly address vulnerabilities of synchronous LFSR-based stream ciphers, which make use of filter functions. Their basic idea is to express plaintext-to-ciphertext relationship as a system of equations. Given a set of plaintext–ciphertext pairs, the attacker tries to solve an equation system to recover the encryption key. Algebraic cryptanalysis is referred to as the process of breaking ciphers by solving polynomial systems of equations [7].

There exist many distinct designs of algebraic attacks to address single-LFSR or multiple-LFSR ciphers under memoryless or with-memory filter functions. For simplicity, only stream ciphers using a single LFSR and memory-less filter functions are considered in the sequel. With this limitation in mind, the basic principle of algebraic attack is to build a system of nonlinear equations, which links the keystream bits to the internal state of the LFSR and then solve the equation system. In general, solving a nonlinear equation system is known to be NP-complete. Hence, each stream cipher structure requires an appropriate ad hoc technique to recover the key. Algebraic attacks are composed of two steps: build and solve a nonlinear equation system. In the sequel, solving nonlinear equation systems is not addressed.

The algebraic attack presented in this section aims to recover the key (i.e. the initialization value of the LFSR), $k = [k_0 k_1 \ldots k_{n-1}]$, from some subset of keystream bits [8]. The attack is a partial known-plaintext attack, which assumes that m bits of the keystream are known to attacker (i.e. attacker knows some bits of a plaintext and their corresponding bits in the ciphertext). Thus, the positions of keystream bits are known. The known bits do not need to be consecutive.

In the algebraic attack proposed by Courtois, the attacked stream cipher is defined by two components: an n-bit LFSR, defined by a connection[5] function L, and a nonlinear function f. LFSR is initialized with a key $k = (k_0, k_1, \ldots, k_{n-1})$. Let $b_t, \ldots, b_1, b_0$ be the keystream bits until the current cycle t and $s_t, \ldots, s_1, s_0$ be the states of LFSR until the current cycle. The stream cipher is defined by:

$$s_0 = (k_0, k_1, \ldots, k_{n-1})$$

$$s_i = L(s_{i-1}), \text{ for } i > 0$$

$$b_i = f(s_i), \text{ for } i \geq 0$$

s_t and b_t denote the current state of LFSR and the last output bit of the cipher, respectively. Keystream bits are computed as follows:

$$\begin{cases} b_0 = f\left(k_{0,}, k_1, \ldots, k_{n-1}\right) \\ b_1 = f\left(L\left(k_{0,}, k_1, \ldots, k_{n-1}\right)\right) \\ \quad \cdots \\ b_t = f\left(L^t\left(k_{0,}, k_1, \ldots, k_{n-1}\right)\right) \end{cases}$$

When m bits of keystream, at positions $i_1, i_2, \ldots, i_m$, are known to the adversary, he/she constructs the following equation system:

$$S = \begin{cases} b_{i_1} = \left(L^{i_1}\left(k_{0,}, k_1, \ldots, k_{n-1}\right)\right) \\ b_{i_2} = f\left(L^{i_2}\left(k_{0,}, k_1, \ldots, k_{n-1}\right)\right) \\ \quad \cdots \\ b_{i_m} = f\left(L^{i_m}\left(k_{0,}, k_1, \ldots, k_{n-1}\right)\right) \end{cases}$$

The degrees of polynomials yielded by function f depend on the known positions $i_1, i_2, \ldots,$ and i_m. Therefore, solving the equation system becomes an issue. Under some assumptions regarding nonlinear function f [8], proposed a method to significantly reduce the degrees of polynomials and then break the stream cipher.

The larger number of equations included in system S, the larger the computation time of nonlinear equation system solver. Therefore, the attacker may need to select a subset of the equations that (hopefully) uniquely determines the key. In addition, there is a non-null probability of failure to recover a unique key, in a reasonable time, if the number of known keystream bits is small.

Example 11.13 Below is a simplified version of algebraic cryptanalysis. Consider the keystream generator shown in Figure 11.12. It is composed of a 4-bit LFSR and a filter function f defined[6] by: $f\left(R_0, R_1, R_2, R_3\right) = \left(R_0 \wedge \neg R_2\right) \vee \left(R_1 \wedge \neg R_3\right)$.

1) Encryption step

Let the key be $k = (0,0,1,1)$. The party, which encrypts a plaintext $P = 10110$ needs to compute the following keystream bits:

$$b_0 = f(0,0,1,1) = 0 \qquad b_1 = f\left((0 \oplus 1),0,0,1\right) = 1$$
$$b_2 = f\left((1 \oplus 1),1,0,0\right) = 1 \qquad b_3 = f\left((0 \oplus 0),0,1,0\right) = 0$$
$$b_4 = f\left((0 \oplus 0),0,0,1\right) = 0$$

Let bits of plaintext be $P_0 = 1, P_1 = 0, P_2 = 1, P_3 = 1, P_4 = 0$. Then, encryption is:

$$C_0 = P_0 \oplus b_0 = 1 \oplus 0 = 1 \qquad C_1 = P_1 \oplus b_1 = 0 \oplus 1 = 1$$
$$C_2 = P_2 \oplus b_2 = 1 \oplus 1 = 0 \qquad C_3 = P_3 \oplus b_3 = 1 \oplus 0 = 1$$
$$C_4 = P_4 \oplus b_4 = 0 \oplus 0 = 0$$

2) Algebraic attack

Consider an adversary who intercepts the ciphertext $C = 11010$ and he/she knows the first two bits of the corresponding plaintext; and also knows that these bits are the ones encrypted with the key to break; i.e. known keystream bit indices are $i_1 = 0$ and $i_2 = 1$. Thus, known keystream bits are $b_0 = 1 \oplus 1 = 0$ and $b_1 = 0 \oplus 1 = 1$.

There are two known keystream bits. Hence, the attacker builds a system of two equations:

$$S = \begin{cases} b_0 = 0 = f\left(k_0, k_1, k_2, k_3\right) \\ b_1 = 1 = f\left(L\left(k_0, k_1, k_2, k_3\right)\right) \end{cases}$$

Use of the first equation:

At the first clock cycle: $\left(R_0, R_1, R_2, R_3\right) = \left(k_0, k_1, k_2, k_3\right)$

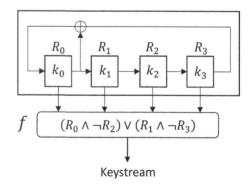

f $\quad (R_0 \wedge \neg R_2) \vee (R_1 \wedge \neg R_3)$

Keystream

Figure 11.12 Example of keystream generator (for algebraic attack).

$$b_0 = f\left(R_0, R_1, R_2, R_3\right) = \left(k_0 \wedge \neg k_2\right) \vee \left(k_1 \wedge \neg k_3\right) = 0 \qquad \text{(a)}$$

Equality (a) holds, if both $\left(k_0 \wedge \neg k_2\right)$ and $\left(k_1 \wedge \neg k_3\right)$ are 0. Therefore, condition c1 must hold:

$$\left(k_0 = 0 \vee k_2 = 1\right) \wedge \left(k_1 = 0 \vee k_3 = 1\right) \qquad \text{(c1)}$$

Use of the second equation:

$$L\left(k_0, k_1, k_2, k_3\right) = \left(\left(k_0 \oplus k_3\right), k_0, k_1, k_2\right)$$

$$b_1 = f\left(R_0, R_1, R_2, R_3\right) = \left(\left(k_0 \oplus k_3\right) \wedge \neg k_1\right) \vee \left(k_0 \wedge \neg k_2\right) = 1 \qquad \text{(b)}$$

Equality (b) holds, if $\left(\left(k_0 \oplus k_3\right) \wedge \neg k_1\right) = 1$ or $\left(k_0 \wedge \neg k_2\right) = 1$. Therefore, condition c2 must hold:

$$\left(k_0 \oplus k_3 = 1 \wedge k_1 = 0\right) \vee \left(k_0 = 1 \wedge k_2 = 0\right) \qquad \text{(c2)}$$

Three solutions satisfy conditions c1 and c2:

$$\left(k_0, k_1, k_2, k_3\right) = \left(0, 0, 0, 1\right)$$
$$\left(k_0, k_1, k_2, k_3\right) = \left(0, 0, 1, 1\right) \; \text{// which is the correct key}$$
$$\left(k_0, k_1, k_2, k_3\right) = \left(1, 0, 1, 0\right)$$

Therefore, the two known keystream bits are not enough to disclose the unique key. More keystream bits are needed.

11.5 Cube Attack

Cube attack scheme was proposed by Dinur and Shamir in 2009 [9]. It is a chosen-plaintext attack that can be used to recover the key of block ciphers, stream ciphers, and MAC algorithms. However, in literature, cube attacks focused especially on stream ciphers. In particular, Trivium stream cipher with a reduced[7] number of initialization rounds was broken in a reasonable number of bit operations: Trivium with 672 and 767 initialization rounds were broken in 2^{19} and 2^{45} bit operations, respectively [9]. In the sequel, we only introduce cube attack against stream ciphers.

11.5.1 Main Idea of Cube Attack

Recall that a stream cipher generates keystream bits after being initialized. Stream cipher initialization step consists in supplying a key and an initialization vector (IV). The latter is public, while the key is secret. The initialization performs some rounds before delivering the first bit of keystream.

The main idea of cube attack may be summarized as follows:

Attacker is given an oracle (i.e. a black box) associated with the targeted stream cipher. He/she queries the oracle by varying some bits of IV and receives one keystream bit for each query. Each output bit of the keystream generator is represented as multivariate polynomial[8] in the bits of the key and IV. Such a polynomial represents a relationship between the selected bits. By modifying IV bits, the attacker can build a system of polynomial equations and then solves it to recover the key.

The attack takes advantage of the existence of a low degree polynomial representation of a single keystream bit as a function of the bits of the key and the IV. These bits are summed over all possible values of a subset of the IV bits to detect linear equations in key bits, which can be efficiently solved. Polynomials are evaluated over binary field F_2.

11.5.2 Polynomial Representation

Let $k_1, k_2, \ldots, k_n$ denote key bits, $v_1, \ldots, v_m$ denote IV bits, and $b \in \{0, 1\}$ denotes one-bit output of the oracle corresponding to the keystream generator. b can be represented as a polynomial P of degree d, over field F_2: $P\left(k_1, k_2, \ldots, k_n, v_1, v_2, \ldots, v_m\right) = b$

P is called *master polynomial*. Since the IV is known to the attacker, IV bits are referred to as *public bits*.

In field F_2, for any binary variable x, $x^i \equiv x \bmod 2$, for $i > 0$. Therefore, by varying variables $\left(k_1, k_2, \ldots, k_n, v_1, v_2, \ldots, v_m\right)$, we can construct polynomials of degree d, composed of a maximum of N terms (i.e. monomials), where N is a sum of combinations:

$$N = \sum_{i=0,\ldots,d} \binom{n+m}{d} \qquad \text{(11.14)}$$

Example 11.14 Let $n = 3$, $m = 3$, and $d = 3$.

By (11.14), the number of terms of $P(k_1, k_2, k_3, v_1, v_2, v_3)$ is $\binom{6}{3} + \binom{6}{2} + \binom{6}{1} + \binom{6}{0} = 42$

$$P(k_1, k_2, k_3, v_1, v_2, v_3) =$$
$$k_1 k_2 k_3 \oplus k_1 k_2 v_1 \oplus k_1 k_2 v_2 \oplus k_1 k_2 v_3 \oplus k_1 k_3 v_1 \oplus k_1 k_3 v_2 \oplus k_1 k_3 v_3 \oplus k_2 k_3 v_1 \oplus$$
$$k_2 k_3 v_2 \oplus k_2 k_3 v_3 \oplus k_1 v_1 v_2 \oplus k_1 v_1 v_3 \oplus k_1 v_2 v_3 \oplus k_2 v_1 v_2 \oplus k_2 v_1 v_3 \oplus k_2 v_2 v_3 \oplus$$
$$k_3 v_1 v_2 \oplus k_3 v_1 v_3 \oplus k_3 v_2 v_3 \oplus v_1 v_2 v_3$$
$$\oplus k_1 k_2 \oplus k_1 k_3 \oplus k_2 k_3 \oplus k_1 v_1 \oplus k_1 v_2 \oplus k_1 v_3 \oplus k_2 v_1 \oplus k_2 v_2 \oplus k_2 v_3 \oplus k_3 v_1$$
$$\oplus k_3 v_2 + k_3 v_3 \oplus v_1 v_2 \oplus v_1 v_3 \oplus v_2 v_3$$
$$\oplus k_1 \oplus k_2 \oplus k_3 \oplus v_1 \oplus v_2 \oplus v_3 \oplus 1$$

Notice that the highest degree of terms is 3.

Let V_I denote a term of polynomial P, such that V_I is the product of IV variables with indices in index subset $I \subseteq \{1, ..., m\}$. That is, $V_I = v_{j_1} * v_{j_1} * ... v_{j_{|I|}}$. For example, if $m = 4$, then $V_{\{1,3\}} = v_1 v_3$ and $V_{\{1,2,3,4\}} = v_1 v_2 v_3 v_4$.

Definition 11.6 **Superpoly:** *Given a polynomial $P(k_1, k_2, ..., k_n, v_1, v_2, ..., v_m)$ and an index subset $I \subseteq \{1, ..., m\}$, polynomial $P_{S(I)}$ is referred to as superpoly of subset I in P if:*

a) $P(k_1, k_2, ..., k_n, v_1, v_2, ..., v_m) = V_I \cdot P_{S(I)} + Q(k_1, k_2, ..., k_n, v_1, v_2, ..., v_m)$

b) $V_I = \prod_{\forall i \in I} v_i$

c) No term in polynomial Q divides the product V_I

d) $P_{S(I)}$ and V_I have no common variables

Definition 11.7 **Maxterm:** *A maxterm of polynomial P is a term V_I, such that the superpoly of I in P is of degree 1, i.e. $P_{S(I)}$ is a linear polynomial, which is not a constant.*

Each index subset I of size j $(j \leq m)$ defines a j-dimensional binary cube, denoted C_I, of 2^j vectors obtained by varying[9] IV variables included in index subset I, and leaving all other variables undetermined. Each vector $w \in C_I$ defines a new derived polynomial, denoted P_w, with $n + m - j$ variables. The variables in index subset I are called cube variables. Summing all derived polynomials in C_I, yields a new polynomial $P_I = \bigoplus_{w \in C_I} P_w$, which matches the following property, proven in [9]:

$$P_I \equiv P_{S(I)} \bmod 2 \tag{11.15}$$

Dinur and Shamir proved that the summation of 2^j polynomials derived from a master polynomial P by varying values of the j IV variables included in index subset I, eliminates terms except those contained in the superpoly of I in P. Hence, the degree of the master polynomial is reduced. In particular, the following theorem is proven in [9]:

If V_I is a maxterm of polynomial P, then P_I yields a linear equation in the remaining variables.

11.5.3 Cube Attack Mounting

Cube attack follows two steps: preprocessing phase (also called offline phase) and key recovery (also called online phase).

11.5.3.1 Preprocessing Phase

Let n denote the bit-length of the key and m that of the IV of a targeted stream cipher. Let $F(K, IV)$ denote the unknown function that, given a key and an IV, returns the first bit of the keystream of the targeted cipher. F also is called oracle. The first step is to select a master polynomial P of degree d. Polynomial P should fulfill at least two conditions: 1) its degree should be low enough to limit the attack computation time and 2) it contains enough terms that are selected among the potential terms of polynomials of degree d in $n + m$ variables. Maxterms are highly preferred[10] to mount a cube attack.

Notes

– Cube attack can be applied to any stream cipher, provided that the first output bit of the keystream generator can be represented by a polynomial of a low degree.

– Methods to select master polynomials are provided in [9]. The proposed methods are too long to be described in this introductory presentation. If the selected master polynomial does not meet some conditions regarding the randomness in its terms, the attack may fail.
– Finding the optimal degree of master polynomial for a given cipher is a hard issue, even if the internal structure of the targeted cipher is known.

To simplify the description of the cube attack, assume that the master polynomial P has enough maxterms and correctly represents the targeted cipher. Each maxterm may be used to yield a linear expression. Let ℓ be the number of index sets to use in the attack. A list $\mathcal{L}$ of linear expressions is built as follows:

1) $h = 1; \mathcal{L} = []$
2) while $h < \ell$:

- Let V_{I_h} be a maxterm not yet considered.
- Find the superpoly $P_{S(I_h)}$ corresponding to index set I_h. Since V_{I_h} is a maxterm, $P_{S(I_h)}$ is a linear expression in variables not included in I_h, with a possible addition of the constant 1.
- Append pair $\left(I_h, P_{S(I_h)}\right)$ to list $\mathcal{L}$.

However, it should be noticed that in practice, it is unlikely to find a master polynomial that correctly characterizes a stream cipher, without information about its internals, to recover the correct key. The authors of the cube attack suggested an offline test-based approach to check the validity of chosen superpoly associated with each index set. The suggested procedure may be described as follows:

1) Choose an index set I and its superpoly $P_{S(I)}$, which is a linear expression.
2) In superpoly $P_{S(I)}$, set to either 0 or 1 all IV variables not included in $P_{S(I)}$.
3) Build a list VC of $2^{|I|}$ IVs, by varying the bits corresponding to variables included in index set I, and fixing the remaining bits as in step 2.
4) Randomly select a large number of key values. Then, for each chosen key k:

- Evaluate $P_{S(I)}$, and obtain a binary value π_k.
- For each IV_i in list VC, query the oracle, with k and IV_i, and receive an output $\rho_i = F(k, IV_i)$
- If $\pi_k \neq \left(\sum_{i=1,\ldots,|VC|} \rho_i\right) \bmod 2$, then the chosen superpoly is not valid and the test procedure stops. Otherwise, go to step 4 and continue the test.

5) If the selected superpoly passes all the tests, it can be used to mount the attack.

11.5.3.2 Key Recovery Phase
Recall that, by property (11.15), for each index set I_h, the summation of derived polynomials, denoted P_{I_h}, is congruent to $P_{S(I_h)} \bmod 2$. Key recovery exploits property (11.15). It may be designed as follows:

1) Build a system of linear equations S as follows:
While list $\mathcal{L}$ is not empty, repeat:

- Withdraw a pair $\left(\mathcal{J}, P_{S(\mathcal{J})}\right)$ from list $\mathcal{L}$.
- By varying all the variables included in index set $\mathcal{J}$, submit $2^{|\mathcal{J}|}$ queries to the oracle and receive $2^{|\mathcal{J}|}$ outputs. Let σ be the sum, in F_2, of all received outputs.
- Build a linear equation $P_{S(\mathcal{J})} = \sigma$ and add it to S.

2) Solve the linear equation system S.

Example 11.15 Below is a cube attack against a toy-cipher, which is composed of a 6-bit LFSR initialized with three key-bits and IV-bits. The output function of the cipher is defined by the following polynomial of degree 6 (unknown to the attacker):

$$F(k_1, k_2, k_3, v_1, v_2, v_3) = k_1 k_2 k_3 v_1 v_2 v_3 \oplus k_1 k_3 v_1 v_2 v_3 \oplus k_2 k_3 v_1 v_2 v_3 \oplus k_1 k_2 v_3 \oplus k_1 k_3 v_1 \oplus k_1 v_1 v_2 \oplus k_2 v_1 v_2 \oplus k_2 v_2 v_3 \oplus k_1 v_1 v_3$$

$$\oplus k_2 v_1 v_3 \oplus k_3 v_1 v_3 \oplus k_3 v_2 v_3 \oplus v_1 v_2 v_3 \oplus v_1 v_2 \oplus v_1 v_3 \oplus v_2 v_3$$

Assume that the secret key to recover is 110.

Phase 1

All the terms of any polynomial of degree 3 in $3+3$ variables are shown in Example 11.14. We select[11] a master polynomial of degree 3 as follows:

$$P(k_1, k_2, k_3, v_1, v_2, v_3) = k_1 k_2 k_3 \oplus k_1 k_2 v_1 \oplus k_1 k_2 v_3 \oplus k_1 k_3 v_1 \oplus k_1 v_1 v_2 \oplus k_2 v_1 v_2 \oplus k_2 v_2 v_3 \oplus k_1 v_1 v_3$$
$$\oplus k_2 v_1 v_3 \oplus k_3 v_1 v_3 \oplus k_3 v_2 v_3 \oplus v_1 v_2 v_3 \oplus k_1 k_2 \oplus k_2 k_3 \oplus k_2 v_1 \oplus k_3 v_2 \oplus v_1 v_2 \oplus v_1 v_3 \oplus v_2 v_3 \oplus k_1 \oplus k_2 \oplus v_2 \oplus v_3 \oplus 1$$

We select three index sets that result in maxterms and we fix to 0 all IV variables used in superpolys.

1) Let index set $I = \{1,2\}$. Hence, $V_I = v_1 v_2$; V_I is a maxterm.
   Master polynomial P can be rewritten as a summation:

   $$P(k_1, k_2, k_3, v_1, v_2, v_3) = v_1 v_2 (k_1 \oplus k_2 \oplus v_3 \oplus 1) \oplus Q_1 (k_1, k_2, k_3, v_1, v_2, v_3)$$

   where $Q_1(k_1, k_2, k_3, v_1, v_2, v_3)$ is a polynomial composed of the remaining terms.
   The superpoly $P_{S(\{1,2\})}$ is $k_1 \oplus k_2 \oplus v_3 \oplus 1$.

   Cube $C_{\{1,2\}}$ is defined by four vectors associated with derived polynomials

   $$P_{v_1 v_2 = 00}(\ldots) = Q_1 (k_1, k_2, k_3, 0, 0, v_3)$$

   $$P_{v_1 v_2 = 10}(\ldots) = Q_1 (k_1, k_2, k_3, 1, 0, v_3)$$

   $$P_{v_1 v_2 = 01}(\ldots) = Q_1 (k_1, k_2, k_3, 0, 1, v_3)$$

   $$P_{v_1 v_2 = 11}(\ldots) = (k_1 \oplus k_2 \oplus v_3 \oplus 1) + Q_1 (k_1, k_2, k_3, 1, 1, v_3)$$

   By property (11.15),

   $$P_{\{1,2\}} = \left(\sum_{v_1 v_2 \in \{00,\ldots,11\}} P_{v_1 v_2}(\ldots) \right) \equiv (k_1 + k_2 \oplus v_3 \oplus 1) \, mod \; 2$$

   By setting v_3 to 0, $P_{S(\{1,2\})} = k_1 \oplus k_2 \oplus 1$.

2) Let index set $I = \{1,3\}$. Hence, $V_I = v_1 v_3$; V_I is a maxterm.
   Master polynomial P can be rewritten as a summation: $P(k_1, k_2, k_3, v_1, v_2, v_3) = v_1 v_3 (k_1 \oplus k_2 \oplus k_3 \oplus v_2 \oplus 1)$
   $\oplus Q_2 (k_1, k_2, k_3, v_1, v_2, v_3)$
   The superpoly $P_{S(\{1,3\})}$ is $k_1 \oplus k_2 \oplus k_3 \oplus v_2 \oplus 1$.
   By property (11.15), $P_{\{1,3\}} \equiv (k_1 \oplus k_2 \oplus k_3 \oplus v_2 \oplus 1) \, mod \, 2$
   By fixing $v_2 = 0, P_{S(\{1,3\})} = k_1 \oplus k_2 \oplus k_3 \oplus 1$.

3) Let index set $I = \{2,3\}$. Hence, $V_I = v_2 v_3$; V_I is a maxterm.
   Master polynomial P can be rewritten as a summation: $P(k_1, k_2, k_3, v_1, v_2, v_3) = v_2 v_3 (k_2 \oplus k_3 \oplus v_1 \oplus 1)$
   $\oplus Q_3 (k_1, k_2, k_3, v_1, v_2, v_3)$
   The superpoly $P_{S(\{2,3\})}$ is $k_2 \oplus k_3 \oplus v_1 \oplus 1$.
   By property (11.15), $P_{\{2,3\}} \equiv (k_2 \oplus k_3 \oplus v_1 \oplus 1) mod \, 2$
   By setting v_1 to 0, $P_{S(\{2,3\})} = k_2 \oplus k_3 \oplus 1$.
   The three superpolys were tested using all the eight keys.

Phase 2

We used a program to simulate the black box $F(K, IV)$, where K is fix and IV is chosen by the attacker.
Use of the first set index $I = \{1,2\}$
Query by varying variables v_1 and v_2 and fixing v_3 to 0.

$$F(K, 000) = 0 \qquad F(K, 100) = 0$$
$$F(K, 010) = 0 \qquad F(K, 110) = 1$$

The first linear equation is:

$$k_1 \oplus k_2 \oplus 1 = F(K,000) \oplus F(K,100) \oplus F(K,010) \oplus F(K,110) = 1 \tag{E1}$$

Use of the second set index $I = \{1,3\}$

Query by varying variables v_1 and v_3 and fixing v_2 to 0.

$$F(K,000) = 0 \qquad F(K,100) = 0$$
$$F(K,001) = 1 \qquad F(K,101) = 0$$

The second linear equation is:

$$k_1 \oplus k_2 \oplus k_3 \oplus 1 = F(K,000) \oplus F(K,100) \oplus F(K,001) \oplus F(K,101) = 1 \tag{E2}$$

Use of the third set index $I = \{2,3\}$

Query by varying variables v_2 and v_3 and fixing v_1 to 0.

$$F(K,000) = 0 \qquad F(K,010) = 0$$
$$F(K,001) = 1 \qquad F(K,011) = 1$$

The first linear equation is:

$$k_2 \oplus k_3 \oplus 1 = F(K,000) \oplus F(K,010) \oplus F(K,001) \oplus F(K,011) = 0 \tag{E3}$$

The system of linear equations E1, E2, and E3 is as follows:

$$\begin{cases} k_1 \oplus k_2 \oplus 1 = 1 \\ k_1 \oplus k_2 \oplus k_3 \oplus 1 = 1 \\ k_2 \oplus k_3 \oplus 1 = 0 \end{cases}$$

The solution to the equation system above is $k_1 = 1$, $k_2 = 1$, and $k_3 = 0$, which corresponds to the key we fixed.

11.6 Other Attacks Against Stream Ciphers

11.6.1 Divide-and-Conquer Attack

Divide-and-conquer attack is a plaintext attack, which aims to reduce the key search space in order to make the key recovery computationally feasible. Its principle is to divide the key space into smaller subspaces and then recover key portions using the subspaces.

Example 11.16 Consider a single-LFSR-based stream cipher, illustrated by Figure 11.13. Let us see how a divide-and-conquer attack can contribute to recover cipher key. The vulnerability of the stream cipher considered in this example is that the filter function makes use only of the odd bits of LFSR.

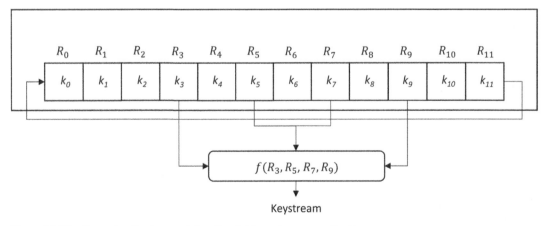

Keystream

Figure 11.13 Example of a stream cipher (for divide-and-conquer attack).

1) An LFSR with 12 bits, denoted R_0, ..., R_{11}, is used jointly with a filter function $f(R_3, R_5, R_7, R_9)$, which produces the keystream .... $s_7 s_6 s_5 s_4 s_3 s_2 s_1 s_0$.

   Initial values of LFSR bits are $R_i = k_i$, for $i = 0, ..., 11$, where k denotes the key.

2) Keystream bits produced in four cycles (without interference of the register feedback) are as follows:
   Cycle 1: $s_0 = f(k_3, k_5, k_7, k_9)$, then LFSR shifts.
   Cycle 2: $s_1 = f(k_2, k_4, k_6, k_8)$, then LFSR shifts.
   Cycle 3: $s_2 = f(k_1, k_3, k_5, k_7)$, then LFSR shifts.
   Cycle 4: $s_3 = f(k_0, k_2, k_4, k_6)$, then LFSR shifts.
   We notice that only odd bits of key (i.e. k_1, k_3, k_5, k_7, k_9) are used to compute the even bits of the keystream (i.e. s_0, s_2) and only even bits of key (i.e. k_0, k_2, k_4, k_6, k_8) are used to compute odd bits of the keystream (i.e. s_1, s_3).

   Function $f(.)$ is known to the adversary as well as a plaintext–ciphertext pair. Instead of testing 2^{12} distinct keys, the adversary divides the search space into three subspaces: one subspace, to find the first five even bits of the key, a second subspace, to find the first five odd bits, and a third subspace, to find the last two bits. Therefore, in total, the adversary tries $(2 * 2^5) * 2^2$ alternatives; and time complexity is reduced from 2^{12} to 2^8.

11.6.2 Correlation Attack

The correlation attack exploits statistical dependencies (i.e. bias) between the keystream bits and some bits of the LFSRs composing a stream cipher. They are especially efficient in attacking filter-based stream ciphers. The principle of a basic correlation attack is as follows:

1) Given the internal structure of a stream cipher, the adversary builds a table of outputs of the filtering function f of the cipher. The table has 2^m entries, where m is the number of inputs of function f. Inputs of function f are specific bits of the n LFSRs composing the cipher. Let $R_{i_1}^1, R_{i_2}^1, ..., R_{i_j}^n$ be the set of inputs of function f, where R_d^r denotes bit d of LFSR r, $r = 1, ..., n$.
2) With an appropriate interception technique, collect l bits of the keystream denoted $s_1, s_2, ..., s_l$; the higher the value of l, the higher the probability to break the cipher.
3) From the table of function f outputs, determine for each bit $s_i \in \{s_1, s_2, ..., s_l\}$ which input bit $R_x^y \in \{R_{i_1}^1, R_{i_2}^1, ..., R_{i_j}^n\}$ has a significant influence on the output s_i. If no bit has an influence greater than 50%, the attack is unlikely to succeed.
4) Use each of the influencing bits to guess the key, bit per bit. The attacker can recover the key partially or entirely. At this step an appropriate (maybe sophisticated) statistical analysis method may be used.

Example 11.17   Recall that the efficiency of correlation attacks depends on the vulnerability of the filtering function and l, the number of known keystream bits. The stronger the bias, the more information is deduced, when analyzing the relationships between inputs and outputs of the filtering function. Let us see how the correlation attack may contribute to recover the key of a simple cipher based on a vulnerable filtering function.

Assume a keystream generator composed of two 6-bit LFSRs R^1 and R^2 initialized with key bits $k_0, k_1, k_2, ..., k_{11}$, as illustrated by Figure 11.14. Filter function f produces keystream bits as follows:

$$f(R_3^1, R_4^1, R_3^2, R_4^2) = ((R_3^1 \wedge R_4^1) \vee (R_3^1 \wedge R_3^2)) \oplus R_4^2$$

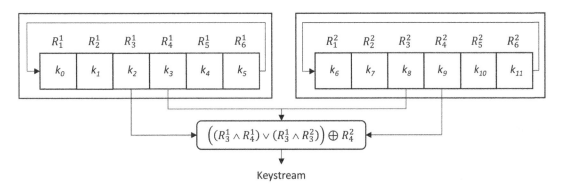

Figure 11.14   Example of a keystream generator (for correlation attack).

The following table shows the outputs of filter function f.

R_3^1	R_4^1	R_3^2	R_4^2	output
0	0	0	0	0
0	0	0	1	1
0	0	1	0	0
0	0	1	1	1
0	1	0	0	0
0	1	0	1	1
0	1	1	0	0
0	1	1	1	1

R_3^1	R_4^1	R_3^2	R_4^2	output
1	0	0	0	0
1	0	0	1	1
1	0	1	0	1
1	0	1	1	0
1	1	0	0	1
1	1	0	1	0
1	1	1	0	1
1	1	1	1	0

From filter function output table, one can see that bit R_4^2 has a significant influence on the output of filter function. In 10 inputs, the output is identical to bit R_4^2. Therefore, under randomly chosen inputs, in average $10/16$ of outputs are the same as bit R_4^2; and therefore, the second register has more influence on the keystream generator output than the first one. Now, assume that the secret key is 011010011010. Then, assume that the adversary has derived (for example, using the message header) the first three bits of the keystream. Let $s_0 = 0$, $s_1 = 1$, and $s_2 = 0$. Both LFSRs shift at each cycle.

Use of keystream bit $s_0 = 0$:

$$s_0 = 0 = f\left(k_2, k_3, k_8, k_9\right)$$

There is a chance of $10/16$ that $R_4^2 = 0$. Thus, guess $k_9 = 0$

Use of keystream bit $s_1 = 1$

$$s_1 = 1 = f\left(k_1, k_2, k_7, k_8\right)$$

There is a chance of $10/16$ that $R_4^2 = 1$. Thus, guess $k_8 = 1$.

Use of keystream bit $s_2 = 0$:

$$s_2 = 0 = f\left(k_0, k_1, k_6, k_7\right)$$

There is a chance of $10/16$ that $R_4^2 = 0$. Thus, guess $k_7 = 0$.

Hence, up to now, three key bits (i.e. k_7, k_8, and k_9) are guessed. Then, use the guessed bits to reduce the key search space:

$$s_0 = 0 = f\left(k_2, k_3, k_8, k_9\right) = \left(\left(k_2 \wedge k_3\right) \vee \left(k_2 \wedge 1\right)\right) \oplus 1$$
$$\Rightarrow \left(k_2 \wedge k_3\right) \vee k_2 \oplus 1 = 0 \Rightarrow k_2 = 1$$
$$s_1 = 1 = f\left(k_1, k_2, k_7, k_8\right) = \left(\left(k_1 \wedge k_2\right) \vee \left(k_1 \wedge 0\right)\right) \oplus 1$$
$$\Rightarrow \left(k_1 \wedge k_2\right) = 1 \Rightarrow k_1 = k_2 = 1$$
$$s_2 = 0 = f\left(k_0, k_1, k_6, k_7\right) = \left(\left(k_0 \wedge k_1\right) \vee \left(k_0 \wedge k_6\right)\right) \oplus 0$$
$$\Rightarrow \left(k_0 \vee \left(k_0 \wedge k_6\right)\right) = 0 \Rightarrow k_0 = 0$$

At this stage, six key bits (i.e. k_3, k_4, k_5, k_6, k_{10}, and k_{11}) are still unrecovered. To recover those bits, we need to test 2^6 candidate keys, instead of 2^{12}, required in case of a brute-force attack.

11.7 Problems and Solutions

11.7.1 List of Problems

Problem 11.1

Use the rainbow table of Example 11.2 and check that

1) The correct key is 2, when $P_0 = 57$ and $C_0 = 114$.
2) The correct key is 17, when $P_0 = 57$ and $C_0 = 73$.

Problem 11.2

Consider a rainbow table with m rows and $t+1$ columns.

1) What is the maximum probability of search success of an n-bit key, if the table has no collisions?
2) What is the memory size required to recover a 128-bit key with a probability of 1/8, assuming no collisions in the table and a maximum computation time of $2^{40}c$? c denotes the computation time to perform an encryption-and-reduction operation and a table lookup.
3) What do you conclude from the answer to question 2?

Problem 11.3

Given $t+1$, the number of columns in a rainbow table and their associated reduction functions, prove that if the key, used to encrypt a plaintext P_0 to a ciphertext C_0, is present in the table (in one or more columns with indices less than t), then that key is found by the key search procedure.

1) $t=1$ (i.e. a single reduction function is used)
2) $t=2$ (i.e. two reduction functions are used)

Problem 11.4

Consider a linear approximation table (TAL) with random binary variables of an arbitrary bit-length b.

1) Prove that $TAL(0,0)=2^{b-1}$.
2) Prove that the sum of all elements of a TAL is 0.

Problem 11.5

Prove that $TAL(\alpha,\beta)0 = 2^b * (\alpha,\beta)$, where b denotes the bit-length of random binary variables, α and β are masks of variable, and $\varepsilon(\alpha,\beta)$, the bias depending on α and β.

Problem 11.6

1) Consider a non-well designed s-box, defined by a linear transformation $Y = \lambda \cdot X \oplus \mu$, where λ and μ are two b-bit constants; and X and Y are random b-bit variables. What is the bias of any linear approximation of the s-box? What can you conclude?
2) Assume that the best bias of any s-box used in a 16-round block cipher is $\frac{1}{4}$. What is the best bias of a linear approximation involving one s-box in each round?

Problem 11.7

Consider the difference distribution table (DDT) of an s-box with an input and output bit-length of n; the latter is an arbitrary integer greater than 1.

1) Prove that every DDT element is even.
2) Prove that the sum of any row of s-box DDT is 2^n.

Problem 11.8

Consider the stream cipher illustrated by Figure 11.15. It has a feedback polynomial $\mathcal{F}(x) = x^3 + x + 1$, which is primitive. Then, assume that the attacker intercepted a ciphertext of 703 bits and he/she knows the three last bits of the plaintext. Show how the attacker can recover the key.

11.7.2 Solutions to Problems

Problem 11.1

1) $P_0 = 57$ and $C_0 = 114$.

$$y_1 = R_4(C_0) = \left\lfloor \frac{114}{2} \right\rfloor - \left\lfloor \frac{114}{7} \right\rfloor = 41, \text{ which is an endpoint of chains 13 and 14.}$$

$x_{14,4-1} = 2$, which is the correct key.

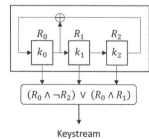

Figure 11.15 Example of stream cipher.

2) $P_0 = 57$ and $C_0 = 73$.

$$y_1 = R_4(C_0) = \left|\frac{73}{2}\right| - \left|\frac{73}{7}\right| = 26, \text{ which is not an endpoint.}$$

$$y_2 = f_4(R_3[C_0]) = f_4(|(3*73-11)| \mod 64) = f_4(16) = R_4(Enc_{16}(P_0)) = R_4(16) = 6, \text{ which is not an endpoint.}$$

$$y_3 = f_4(f_3(R_2(C_0))) = f_4(f_3(20)) = f_4(R_3(Enc_{20}(57))) = f_4(R_3(116)) = f_4(17) = R_4(Enc_{17}(57)) = 26, \text{ which is not an endpoint.}$$

$$y_4 = f_4(f_3(f_2(R_1(C_0)))) = f_4(f_3(f_2(36))) = f_4(f_3(0)) = f_4(11) = 41, \text{ which is the endpoint of chains 13 and 14.}$$

$$x_{13,0} = 17, \text{ which is the correct key.}$$

Problem 11.2
Recall that last column of a rainbow table contains endpoints, which are not keys.

Each test of a key in rainbow chains requires an encryption, a reduction, and a table lookup, which together take a computation time of c.

1) The number of keys is 2^n. If the table has no collision, the maximum number of keys that can be found in the table is $m*t$. Therefore, the maximum probability of key search success is $P = \dfrac{(m*t)}{2^n}$.

2) In this problem, $t = 2^{40}$. If c is one millisecond, then the total computation time is 1 billion seconds (i.e. nearly 34 years).

    The maximum success probability is $\dfrac{1}{8}$. Thus, $\dfrac{1}{8} = \dfrac{(m*t)}{2^{128}} \Rightarrow m = 2^{-3} * 2^{128} * 2^{-40} = 2^{85}$. Each rainbow table entry has two values (start and end points), which represent keys. Therefore, the rainbow table entry size is of $2*128$ bits (i.e. 2^5 bytes). Therefore, the required memory space is 2^{85+5} bytes, which is overmuch large!

3) 128 is the block bit-length of AES. We conclude that MTTO attack against AES is computationally infeasible, because it requires 2^{90} bytes.

Problem 11.3
Let $t+1$ denote the number of columns in a rainbow table, and $R_1, R_2, ..., R_t$, the reduction functions. Let m denote the number of rows in the table.

Let P_0, C_0, and K be the plaintext, the ciphertext, and the key, respectively.

Let $x_{i,0}$, for $i = 1, ..., m$, denote the random start points.

1) Scenario with $t = 1$. Endpoints are defined by $x_{i,1} = R_1\left(Enc_{x_{i,0}}(P_0)\right)$, for $i = 1, ..., m$.

    If key K, such that $x_{i,1} = R_1\left(Enc_{x_{i,0}}(P_0)\right)$, is present in the table, then there exists an endpoint $x_{j,1}$ such that $x_{j,1} = R_1\left(Enc_{x_{i,0}}(P_0)\right) = R_1(C_0)$. Therefore, the first test in the key search procedure returns key K.

2) Scenario with $t = 2$

    There exist two cases: key K arises in the column 1 or in column 0.

    Case 1: key K arises in column 1, i.e. $K = x_{j,1}$ for some j, $(1 \le j \le m)$

    Hence, $x_{j,2} = R_2\left(Enc_{x_{j,1}}(P_0)\right) = R_2\left(Enc_K(P_0)\right) = R_2(C_0)$.

    Therefore, the first test in the key search procedure returns key K.

    Case 2: key K arises in column 0, i.e. $K = x_{j,0}$ for some j, $(1 \le j \le m)$

    Hence, $x_{j,1} = R_1\left(Enc_{x_{j,0}}(P_0)\right) = R_1\left(Enc_{x_K}(P_0)\right) = R_1(C_0)$. Then,

    $$x_{j,2} = R_2\left(Enc_{R_1(C_0)}(P_0)\right)$$

    Since K is not in column $t-1$, the search procedure makes the following computation:

    $$y_2 = f_2(R_1(C_0)) = R_2\left(Enc_{R_1(C_0)}(P_0)\right), \text{ which is an endpoint. Therefore, the second test in the key search procedure returns key } K.$$

Problem 11.4

1) If $\alpha = \beta = 0$, then the number of matchings, m, is:

$$m = \left|\left\{X,Y \in F_2^b \mid 0 \cdot X \oplus 0 \cdot Y = 0\right\}\right| = 2^b$$

Therefore, $Pr(0 \cdot X \oplus 0 \cdot Y = 0) = 1$ and $\varepsilon(0,0) = \dfrac{1}{2}$.

Thus, $LAT(0,0) = 2^b * \varepsilon(0,0) = 2^{b-1}$

2) Prove that the sum of all elements of a TAL is equal to 0.

$$S = \sum_{\alpha=0}^{2^{b-1}}\sum_{\beta=0}^{2^{b-1}} LAT(\alpha,\beta) = 2^b \sum_{\alpha=0}^{2^{b-1}}\sum_{\beta=0}^{2^{b-1}} \varepsilon(\alpha,\beta)$$

For any pair (α,β), the bias is: $\varepsilon(\alpha,\beta) = Pr(\alpha \cdot X \oplus \beta \cdot Y = 0) - \dfrac{1}{2} = \dfrac{n_{(\alpha,\beta)}}{2^b} - \dfrac{1}{2}$

where $n_{(\alpha,\beta)}$ denotes the number of matchings (i.e. $\alpha \cdot x \oplus \beta \cdot y = 0$, where x and y are values of random variables X and Y). By substitution,

$$\sum_{\alpha=0}^{2^{b-1}}\sum_{\beta=0}^{2^{b-1}} \varepsilon(\alpha,\beta) = \left(\frac{\sum_{\alpha=0}^{2^{b-1}}\sum_{\beta=0}^{2^{b-1}} n_{(\alpha,\beta)}}{2^b}\right) - \frac{1}{2} * 2^{2b}$$

When we consider all combinations of values of X, Y, α, and β, there exist 2^{3b} expressions of the form $\alpha \cdot X \oplus \beta \cdot Y$. One half of expressions are equal to 0 and the others to 1. That is,

$$\sum_{\alpha=0}^{2^{b-1}}\sum_{\beta=0}^{2^{b-1}} n_{(\alpha,\beta)} = \frac{2^{3b}}{2}$$

By substitution,

$$\sum_{\alpha=0}^{2^{b-1}}\sum_{\beta=0}^{2^{b-1}} \varepsilon(\alpha,\beta) = \frac{1}{2^b}\left(\frac{2^{3b}}{2}\right) - \frac{1}{2} * 2^{2b} = 0$$

Therefore, the sum S is equal to 0.

Problem 11.5

By definition, $TAL(\alpha,\beta)$ is the number of correct matchings (i.e. $\alpha \cdot X = \beta \cdot Y$) of the linear expression, using α and β values, minus 2^{b-1}. m, the number of correct matchings for a fixed pair (α,β), is defined by:

$$m = \left|\left\{X,Y \in F_2^b \mid \alpha \cdot X \oplus \beta \cdot Y = 0\right\}\right|$$

With a bit-length of b, there exist 2^b linear equations. Therefore, the probability $Pr(\alpha \cdot X + \beta \cdot Y = 0)$ is $m/2^b$ and the bias $\varepsilon(\alpha,\beta)$ is $\dfrac{m}{2^b} - \dfrac{1}{2}$. Then, by substitutions:

$$2^b * \varepsilon(\alpha,\beta) = 2^b\left(\frac{m}{2^b} - \frac{1}{2}\right) = m - 2^{b-1} = LAT(\alpha,\beta)$$ □

Problem 11.6

1) If the s-box is defined by $Y = \lambda \cdot X \oplus \mu$, then the linear approximation of the s-box, for any mask pair (α,β) is

$$\alpha \cdot X \oplus \beta \cdot Y = \alpha \cdot X \oplus \beta \cdot (\lambda \cdot X \oplus \mu) = (\alpha \oplus \beta \cdot \lambda) \cdot X \oplus \beta \cdot \lambda$$

In binary representation,

$$\left(\oplus_{i=1,\ldots,b}\left((\alpha_i\beta_i) \cdot X_i\right)\right) \oplus \left(\oplus_{i=1,\ldots,b}(\beta_i\mu_i)\right)$$ (a)

Once α, β, λ, and μ are fixed, $\left(\oplus_{i=1,\dots,b}\left(\beta_i\mu_i\right)\right)$ is a constant c_0, either 0 or 1; $\alpha_i\beta_i$ is a constant denoted a_i, either 0 or 1, for $i=1, \dots, b$. The relationship can be rewritten as $\left(\oplus_{i=1,\dots,b}\left(a_i \cdot X_i\right)\right)\oplus c_0$. Since the sum of b bits (for all bit combinations) is equally either even or odd,

$$Pr\left(\left(\oplus_{i=1,\dots b}\left(a_i \cdot X_i\right)\right)=0\right)= Pr\left(\left(\oplus_{i=1,\dots b}\left(a_i \cdot X_i\right)\right)=1\right)=\frac{1}{2}$$

$$Pr\left(\left(\oplus_{i=1,\dots b}\left(a_i \cdot X_i\right)\right)\oplus c_0 =0\right)=\frac{1}{2}$$

Therefore, the bias of linear expression (a) is 0. By Piling-up lemma, if a random binary variable Z has a bias of 0, the bias of any variable combination including Z also is 0. We can conclude that linear cryptanalysis cannot be applied to break ciphers using linear s-boxes.

2) By Piling-up lemma, the bias of a linear expression involving 16 s-boxes, all with a bias of ¼, is $2^{15} * \left(\frac{1}{4}\right)^{16}=2^{-17}$.

Problem 11.7

Recall that DDT $\mathfrak{D}^S_{*,*}$ of an n-by-m s-box S has 2^n rows and 2^m columns. When $n=m$, $\mathfrak{D}^S_{*,*}$ is a square matrix. By definition of $\mathfrak{D}^S_{\alpha,\beta} =\left|\Delta^S_{\alpha,\beta}\right|$, such that:

$$\Delta^S_{\alpha,\beta} =\left\{\left(X_1, X_2\right)\in F^n_2 \times F^n_2 \wedge \left(X_1, X_2\right)\in\Delta_\alpha \mid \left(S\left(X_1\right), S\left(X_2\right)\right)\in\Delta_\beta\right\} \tag{a}$$

α, $\left(0 \leq\alpha\leq 2^n -1\right)$, and β, $\left(0 \leq\beta\leq 2^m -1\right)$, are indices of rows and columns of DDT, respectively.

1) Consider any differential (α, β). For any s-box input X, if $\left(X, X\oplus\alpha\right)$ is such that $S(X)\oplus S\left(X\oplus\alpha\right)=\beta$, then also $S\left(X\oplus\alpha\right)\oplus S(X)=\beta$. Therefore, if $\left(X, X\oplus\alpha\right)$ is included in set $\Delta^S_{\alpha,\beta}$, then $\left(X\oplus\alpha, X\right)$ also is included. Thus, the cardinality of the set $\Delta^S_{\alpha,\beta}$, in equation (a), is even. In other words, the elements of each DDT are even positive integers.

2) Consider any row α in DDT. The bit-length of variable X and of α is of n. Therefore, we can build 2^n ordered pairs $\left(X, X\oplus\alpha\right)$. A difference $S(X)\oplus\left(X\oplus\alpha\right)$ is associated with each pair $\left(X, X\oplus\alpha\right)$. Therefore, the number of s-box output differences associated with row α is 2^n. Therefore, the element sum of each DDT row is 2^n.

Problem 11.8

First step: compute the bits of the keystream until the last intercepted bit. Since the considered LFSR has a primitive feedback polynomial, it has seven distinct states. Assume that the initial state is $s_0 =\left(k_0, k_1, k_2\right)=(1,1,0)$. Then,

$$s_1 = L(1, 1, 0)=(1,1,1) \qquad s_2 = L(1, 1, 1)=(0,1,1)$$

$$s_3 = L(0, 1, 1)=(1,0,1) \qquad s_4 = L(1, 0, 1)=(0,1,0)$$

$$s_5 = L(0, 1, 0)=(0,0,1) \qquad s_6 = L(0, 0, 1)=(1,0,0)$$

The LFSR has a period of 7. Since the filter function is memory-less, the keystream bits are computed as follows (where d is any positive integer):

$$b_{0+7d} = f(1,1,0)=\left(1 \wedge \neg 0\right)\vee\left(1\wedge 1\right)=1$$

$$b_{1+7d} = f(1,1,1)=\left(1 \wedge \neg 1\right)\vee\left(1\wedge 1\right)=1$$

$$b_{2+7d} = f(0,1,1)=\left(0 \wedge \neg 1\right)\vee\left(0\wedge 1\right)=0$$

$$b_{3+7d} = f(1,0,1)=\left(1 \wedge \neg 1\right)\vee\left(1\wedge 0\right)=0$$

$$b_{4+7d} = f(0,1,0)=\left(0 \wedge \neg 0\right)\vee\left(0\wedge 1\right)=0$$

$$b_{5+7d} = f(0,0,1)=\left(0 \wedge \neg 1\right)\vee\left(0\wedge 0\right)=0$$

$$b_{6+7d} = f(1,0,0)=\left(1 \wedge \neg 0\right)\vee\left(1\wedge 0\right)=1$$

Second step: the three known plaintext bits are located at positions 700, 701, and 702 (the first position is 0) in the ciphertext; thus, they are encrypted with $b_{0+700} =1$, $b_{1+700} =1$, and $b_{2+700} =0$, respectively. Then, adversary constructs the following equation system:

$$S = \begin{cases} b_0 = 1 = f(k_0, k_1, k_2) \\ b_1 = 1 = f(L(k_0, k_1, k_2)) \\ b_2 = 0 = f(L^2(k_0, k_1, k_2)) \end{cases}$$

Use of the first equation:

At the first clock cycle: $(R_0, R_1, R_2) = (k_0, k_1, k_2)$

$$b_0 = 1 = f(R_0, R_1, R_2) = (k_0 \wedge \neg k_2) \vee (k_0 \wedge k_1) \tag{a}$$

Equality (a) holds if $(k_0 \wedge \neg k_2)$ or $(k_0 \wedge k_1)$ is 1 or both are equal to 1. Therefore, condition c1 must hold:

$$(k_0 = 1 \wedge k_2 = 0) \vee (k_0 = 1 \wedge k_1 = 1) \tag{c1}$$

Use of the second equation:

$$L(k_0, k_1, k_2) = ((k_0 \oplus k_2), k_0, k_1)$$

$$b_1 = 1 = f(R_0, R_1, R_2) = ((k_0 \oplus k_2) \wedge \neg k_1) \vee ((k_0 \oplus k_2) \wedge k_0) \tag{b}$$

Equality (b) holds if $((k_0 \oplus k_2) \wedge \neg k_1) = 1$ or $((k_0 \oplus k_2) \wedge k_0) = 1$. Therefore, condition c2 must hold:

$$(k_0 \oplus k_2 = 1 \wedge k_1 = 0) \vee ((k_0 \oplus k_2) = 1 \wedge k_0 = 1) \tag{c2}$$

Use of the third equation:

$$L^2(k_0, k_1, k_2) = L((k_0 \oplus k_2), k_0, k_1) = ((k_0 \oplus k_2 \oplus k_1), (k_0 \oplus k_2), k_0)$$

$$b_2 = 0 = f(R_0, R_1, R_2) = ((k_0 \oplus k_2 \oplus k_1) \wedge \neg k_0) \vee ((k_0 \oplus k_2 \oplus k_1) \wedge (k_0 \oplus k_2)) \tag{c}$$

Equality (c) holds if both $((k_0 \oplus k_2 \oplus k_1) \wedge \neg k_0)$ and $((k_0 \oplus k_2 \oplus k_1) \wedge (k_0 \oplus k_2))$ are equal to 0. Therefore, condition c3 must hold:

$$((k_0 \oplus k_2 \oplus k_1) = 0 \vee k_0 = 1) \wedge ((k_0 \oplus k_2 \oplus k_1) = 0 \vee (k_0 \oplus k_2) = 0) \tag{c3}$$

Finally, the unique solution that satisfies conditions c1, c2, and c3 is

$$(k_0, k_1, k_2) = (1, 1, 0).$$

Notes

1 If such an assumption holds, only one chain is tested for each column. If the assumption does not hold, i.e. some endpoints have more than a reverse image, multiple chains may be tested for each column, which makes the time complexity analysis harder.

2 At this step, mixed integer linear programming can be used to find the best linear approximations.

3 Partial-cipher means only some consecutive rounds of the cipher are considered.

4 It is obvious that if there is no change in plaintext difference (i.e. $\alpha = 0$), there is no change in the ciphertext difference (i.e. $\beta = 0$), for all the 2^n plaintext pair $(P, P \oplus 0)$.

5 A connection function is the function that updates the state of LFSR bits at each clock cycle. It makes use of the feedback polynomial of LFSR.

6 $\wedge$, $\vee$, and $\neg$ denote AND, OR, and NOT bit operators, respectively.

7 Trivium stream cipher is described in Section 6.2.7.1. The full initialization of Trivium performs $4 * 288 = 1152$ rounds.

8 The polynomial is assumed to be in algebraic normal form (ANF); i.e. it is a summation of binary variable products.

9 Each IV variable in index set I, of size j, takes 0 and 1 values. So, 2^j polynomials are derived from the master polynomial. Each derived polynomial is considered as a vector and the set of vectors form a j-dimensional cube. This geometric representation was the origin of the name of the attack.

10 Terms that are not maxterms can also be used in a cube attack, but more processing is needed to yield linear equations.

11 Notice that most terms in the master polynomial $P()$ are identical to the ones in polynomial $F()$, unknown to attacker. Many tests were performed before finding $P()$ that correctly represents $F()$.

References

1 Hellman, M.E. (1980). A cryptanalytic time-memory trade-off. *IEEE Transactions on Information Theory* 26 (4): 401–406.

2 Denning, D.E. (1982). *Cryptography and Data security*. Addison-Wesley.

3 Oechslin, P. (2003). Making a faster cryptanalytic time-memory trade-off. *23rd Annual International Cryptology Conference - Advances in Cryptology*. Santa Barbara, California: Springer, LNCS 2729, 617–630.

4 Matsui, M. (1993). Linear cryptanalysis method for DES cipher. In: *International Workshop on the Theory and Application of Cryptographic Techniques, Advances in Cryptology* (ed. T. Helleseth), 386–397. Lofthus, Norway: Springer. LNCS 765.

5 Heys, H.M. (2001). *A Tutorial on Linear and Differential Cryptanalysis*. Canada: University of Waterloo.

6 Biham, E. and Shamir, A. (1991). Differential cryptanalysis of DES-like cryptosystems. *Journal of Cryptology* 4 (1): 3–72.

7 Bard, G.V. (2009). *Algebraic Cryptanalysis*. Springer.

8 Courtois, N.T. and Meier, W. (2003). Algebraic attacks on stream ciphers with linear feedback. *Annual International Conference on the Theory and Applications of Cryptographic Techniques*. Warsaw, Poland: Springer, LNCS 2656, 345–349.

9 Dinur, I. and Shamir, A. (2009). Cube attacks on tweakable black box polynomials. *28th Annual International Conference on the Theory and Applications of Cryptographic Techniques*. Cologne, Germany: Springer, LNCS 5479, 278–299.

12

Public-Key Cryptosystems

RSA and Finite Field Cryptography-based Schemes

12.1 Introduction to Public-Key Cryptosystems

In symmetric cryptosystems, the message sender and recipient must share a common secret (i.e. a ciphering key) before encrypting and decrypting messages. The big question is: how to agree on the secret key in first place, particularly if sender and receiver never met? It looks like the "The chicken or egg" dilemma. Trust is required before exchanging the secret key in a secure way. Therefore, symmetric cryptosystems are limited to use in cases where both parties know and trust each other.

The turning point in modern cryptography occurred in 1976–1977, when Diffie and Hellman [1] on one side and Rivest, Shamir, and Adleman [2], on the other, proposed original schemes to secure systems without requiring a unique cipher shared by both parties. The proposed schemes were and are still used to design public-key cryptosystems. The latter provide support to secure communications worldwide between people who do not a priori know each other. The first and still most widely used public-key cryptosystem is with no doubt is the RSA.

Modern cryptography is founded on the idea that the key used to encrypt messages can be made public, while the key used to decrypt messages must be kept private. As such, these systems are known as public-key cryptographic systems (also called asymmetric cryptosystems) and are based on operations easy to process in one direction, but difficult to invert.

Public-key algorithms provide support for confidentiality through message encryption and authentication through message signature (see Figure 12.1). Public-key encryption is founded on the idea that the key used to encrypt messages is made public, while the key used to decrypt is kept private. Public-key signature is based on the idea that the key used to sign messages is private, while the key used to verify signature is made public.

There exist hundreds (or even more) algorithms in the symmetric cryptography world, while there exist only three families of public key algorithms, namely RSA, discrete logarithm-based, and elliptic curve schemes. The first generation of public-key cryptosystems, including RSA, Diffie-Hellman key exchange, Menezes-Qu-Vanstone, and ElGamal cryptosystems are addressed in this chapter. The security of those cryptosystems is based on either integer factorization problem (addressed in Section 12.2.4) or discrete logarithm problem (DLP) in cyclic groups $\mathbb{Z}_p^*$ (addressed in Section 12.3.1). Those problems are known to be computationally infeasible for large numbers. The second generation of public-key cryptosystems is based on elliptic curve theory. They are more powerful than the first generation and are on the way to dominate in the future. The security of elliptic curve cryptosystems is based on discrete logarithm problem in finite fields F_p (addressed in Section 3.2.2).

Public-key cryptography is fundamentally based on the theory of numbers and not on a shared secret without worrying about adversaries listening in the exchanged messages via an insecure network. The strong idea behind the public-key cryptography is a challenge to attackers, which may be phrased as follows: *you, the potential attackers, know the key used to encrypt the messages sent to me, but you cannot decrypt them unless you have algorithms to solve factoring or DLP problems.*

Public-key cryptography makes use of one-way functions, also called trapdoor functions. A one-way function is a function easy to compute if the input is given, but it is computationally infeasible to find the input if the output is given (i.e. given the function image). For example, RSA is based on integer factoring. Computing the product $n = p * q$ given p and q is easy. However, finding p and q given n is computationally infeasible when n is a product of two large random primes.

In summary public-key cryptography is divided into two classes: IFC (Integer Factorization Cryptography) and DLC (Discrete Logarithm Cryptography). The latter is divided into two subclasses: Finite Field Cryptography (FFC) and Elliptic

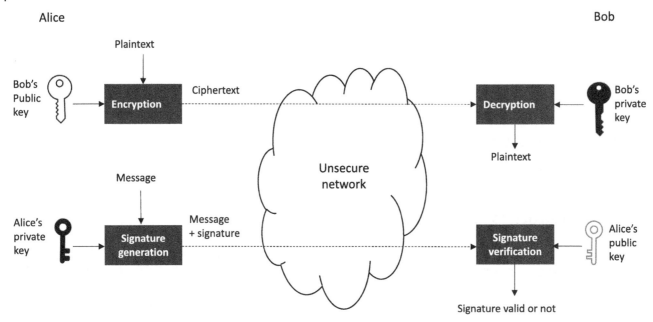

Figure 12.1 Overall scheme of public-key cryptosystems.

Table 12.1 Security services provided by public-key-algorithms.

		Algorithm family	
Service	IFC	FFC	ECC
Key exchange	RSA	DHKE, MQV	ECDH, ECMQV
Encryption	RSA	ElGamal	ECIES
Signature	RSA	DSA, ElGamal	ECDSA, EdDSA

DHKE: Diffie-Hellman Key Exchange, DSA: Digital Signature Algorithm, ECDH: Elliptic Curve Diffie-Hellman key agreement protocol, ECIES: Elliptic Curve Integrated Encryption Scheme, MQV: Menezes-Qu-Vanstone, ECMQV: Elliptic Curve MQV, ECDSA: Elliptic Curve Digital Signature, EdDSA: Edwards-curve DSA.

Curve Cryptography (ECC). DSA is an example of FFC algorithms; ECDSA is an example of ECC algorithms. Other examples of DLC algorithms are the Diffie-Hellman and MQV key agreement algorithms, which have both FFC and ECC forms. The difference between those three classes is the underlying used math. IFC and FFC algorithms are discussed in this chapter and the ECC algorithms in the next one.

Table 12.1 summarizes the services provided by public-key algorithms:

- Encryption service is for guaranteeing confidentiality. In general, public-key cryptosystems are not recommended to encrypt large amounts of data.
- Signature service is for authentication of message origin.
- Key exchange service is the way to use public keys to generate a shared secret between parties. Then, the shared secret is used to derive a symmetric key; and then, parties make use of a symmetric cipher, such as AES, to encrypt and decrypt their messages.

Note. RSA and DLP-based schemes rely on cyclic groups. To address those cryptographic schemes the fundamentals of modular arithmetic and cyclic groups are reminded with examples in Chapter 3.

12.1.1 Attacks Against Public-Key Cryptosystems

Since public-key cryptosystems reveal a part of data used in the encryption or signature schemes, they are vulnerable to man-in-the-middle attacks. For decades, attackers and cryptanalysts have addressed a lot of vulnerabilities to recover the hidden part of those cryptosystems. Identified vulnerabilities have been taken into account to provide a high level of security in the current public-key cryptosystems.

Public-key cryptosystems are considered safe at multiple levels of security strength depending on the length (in bits) of the keys. Public-key standards provide useful guides to select parameter values for each cryptographic algorithm. As discussed in the sequel, when public-key algorithms are used correctly, they are secure enough to prevent all known attacks. However, if a cryptosystem is not complying with standards, it becomes a target for attackers, which, in particular, can easily lead to recovering the private key. Even a brute-force attack, which is inefficient in general, can succeed if the algorithm is not parameterized correctly. The potential attacks depend on the mathematical foundations of each algorithm. In the next sections, some well-known attacks are discussed.

12.1.1.1 Attacks Against Encryption Schemes

Attacks against encryption schemes aim at recovering the private key, disclosing the plaintext or generating illegitimate messages. When used correctly, the standard public-key encryption algorithms are known to be resistant to attacks aiming to recover private keys or plaintexts. Correct use of algorithms mainly includes selection of large prime numbers, padding of messages, and single use of keys to encrypt.

However, the third type of attack, known as existential forgery attack, cannot be thwarted by public-key algorithms. Given the public key and/or some encrypted messages intercepted by the adversary, the latter can forge and encrypt a message without controlling the content of the message. Such an attack may lead the recipient to receive data, which tamper its functions. As the adversary cannot choose the content of the message, his/her objective is jeopardizing the recipient availability.

12.1.1.2 Attacks Against Digital Signature Schemes

In the cyberspace, digital signature is a cryptographic transformation. Consequently, the difficulty in forging signatures is linked to the mathematical foundations used to design digital signature schemes. The latter are far more difficult to forge than hand signatures.

Attacks against digital signature may be categorized into three groups:

1) *Universal forgery*: adversary is able to recover the private key of the signer and then sign any message.
2) *Selective forgery*: adversary is able to create valid signatures on messages of his/her choice.
3) *Existential forgery*: adversary can generate a pair composed of a signature and a message without controlling the message content.

When used correctly, standard public-key signature algorithms are known to be resistant to the first and second types of attacks. Public-key signature algorithms presented in this chapter and the next make signature forgery computationally infeasible even if the signatures of some messages are known to adversary. However, the existential forgery attack remains a threat to public-key cryptosystems. In this type of attack, the adversary intercepts the public key of the signer and some signed messages, then he/she generates a forged signature and derives the message content that matches the forged signature (see an example in Section 12.3.4.3). Notice that the content of the message depends on the forged signature and cannot be controlled by the adversary. The recipient validates the signature and makes use of the received content, which may jeopardize its functions.

Last but not least, potential attacks against digital signatures are identity and private-key theft, which are both out of the scope of algorithms presented in this chapter and the next one. In the first type of attack, the adversary sends his own public key to recipient pretending he/she is the legitimate party and then signs messages. To thwart identity theft, a certificate authority, which acts as a notary, provides assurance regarding the validity of the public key. Certification authority is addressed in Section 15.2. Consequently, in operational cryptosystems, public-key cryptographic algorithms are used jointly with certificate authorities. Private-key theft is a more challenging issue. Either the private key has been really stolen or the malicious owner tries to deny sending a particular message. The solutions to real or alleged private-key theft are not addressed in this book.

12.2 RSA Cryptosystem

The seminal asymmetric ciphering was patented[1] by Rivest, Shamir, and Adleman in 1977 and published in [2]. Named after its coauthors, RSA was the first radically different approach in which the sender and receiver do not need to share a secret key. RSA is based on two keys: a private key known only to its owner and a public key, as the name suggests, known to all. In the last four decades, vulnerabilities of RSA have been intensively addressed and the proposed countermeasures were included in operational RSA cryptosystems. Most of clients and servers in the today's Internet make use of RSA to secure their communications.

Let us consider a scenario in which Bob needs to receive messages from Alice and both partners agree to use the RSA cryptosystem to make their messages confidential. To do so, the steps to follow are:

1) Bob computes two keys (public and private keys).
2) Bob sends his public key to Alice.
3) When Alice has a message to send, she encrypts the message using Bob's public key.
4) When Bob receives the encrypted message, he uses his private key to retrieve the plaintext.

To provide secure systems, RSA must address fundamental questions:

- How Bob can compute public and private keys?
- How Bob can share his public key with Alice?
- A more challenging question: how to make it *computationally infeasible* to derive the private key from the public key (assuming a known key computation algorithm)?

Answers to the first and third questions take their roots in the modular arithmetic (a sub-branch of arithmetic), which is the basis of RSA. However, RSA by itself does not address the second question. It only assumes that the network is reliable, but insecure. Public-key distribution is provided by public-key infrastructures (PKIs), which are addressed in Section 15.2. First, RSA operations (i.e. key generation and distribution, encryption, and decryption) are described, then security and correctness proof are addressed.

12.2.1 RSA Encryption and Decryption

The computations and exchanges to achieve an RSA-based secure communication between Alice and Bob are illustrated by Figure 12.2.

Bob	Alice
Key generation - Select two distinct large prime numbers p and q. - Compute $n = p*q$ and $\phi(n) = (p-1)*(q-1)$ n is the public-key modulus. - Generate an integer e less than $\phi(n)$ and relatively prime to $\phi(n)$, i.e. such that: $GCD(e, \phi(n)) = 1$. e is the public-key exponent. - The public key is (n, e). - Compute the private key d, an integer less than $\phi(n)$ and multiplicative inverse[2] of e *mod* n, i.e. such that: $d*e \equiv 1 \mod \phi(n)$. *Key management* - Private key must be kept secret. - Public key is sent to Alice via a reliable channel, which is not required to be secure (because the key is public).	
	- Receive (n,e) - Let M be a message[3] to send. $M \in \mathbb{N}, M < n$ - *Encryption*: the ciphertext C is computed as follows: $C \equiv M^e \mod n$ - Send (C)
- Receive (C') - *Decryption*: plaintext M' is computed as follows: $M' \equiv (C')^d \mod n$	

Figure 12.2 Illustration of RSA-based communication.

Notes

- Not any integer e can be used as public key. e must be prime with $\phi(n)$. The private key d, which is the multiplicative inverse of e mod $\phi(n)$, exists only if $GCD(e, \phi(n)) = 1$.
- Since $p - 1$ and $q - 1$ are even (because p and q are primes), $e = 2$ cannot be used.
- One may be tempted to use $e = 3$, to reduce the encryption time. However, there are risks in using small values for public key exponent. Some attacks succeed when e is small (see Problem 12.1).

Example 12.1

Key generation (by Bob)	*Encryption (by Alice)*
Bob selects two primes $p = 7$ and $q = 17$	Receive Bob's public key
$n = 7 * 17 = 119$	Let $M = 19$ be the message to
$\phi(n) = (7-1) * (17-1) = 96$	encrypt.
$e = 5 \# GCD(96, 5) = 1$	$C \equiv 19^5 \ mod \ 119 = 66$
$d = 77 \# \ 77 * 5 \equiv 1 \ mod \ 96$	
Bob's public key $= (119, 5)$	*Decryption* (by Bob)
Bob's private key $= 77$	$M \equiv 66^{77} \ mod \ 119 = 19$
Bob's public key is sent to Alice	

12.2.2 Implementation Issues

12.2.2.1 Fast Modular Exponentiation Methods

RSA encryption and decryption are modular exponentiation operations, which are time consuming in operational RSA cryptosystems and complex to do by hand. Imagine you have $1918^{24367} \ mod \ 669984751$ to compute. A naïve method would be to apply an iterative method to compute powers of 1918 from 1 to 24367, and then compute the modulo 669984751. That would take a huge amount of time. Hopefully, there exist fast methods for modular exponentiation computation, which are based on the exploitation of intermediate computations. The most commonly used methods to optimize the RSA computation time are:

- Square-and-multiply method, which may be used for encryption, or decryption, or for both.
- Chinese-remainder-theorem-based method, which may be used for decryption.

The reader should refer to Section 3.3.2 to learn how the square-and-multiply method, called right-to-left binary exponentiation, works. The CRT-based decryption is specific to RSA and is described below.

12.2.2.2 Chinese Remainder Theorem-based RSA Decryption

Chinese remainder theorem (CRT) is a powerful tool to solve congruence equation systems. The CRT is independent of RSA and it is presented in Section 3.3.4. The reader should first learn how the CRT works in general before applying it to implement RSA decryption. As previously described, the decryption of a ciphertext C requires a modular exponentiation: $M \equiv C^d \ mod \ N$, where M is the plaintext, d the private key, and N the RSA modulus. Recall that $N = pq$ and d is the modular inverse of the public key e modulo $(p-1)(q-1)$.

To make RSA decryption faster, the idea of the CRT-based RSA decryption method is to perform two exponentiations $C^{d_p} \ mod \ p$ and $C^{d_q} \ mod \ q$ instead of $C^d \ mod \ pq$ and then make use of CRT to produce a result, which is the plaintext M.

Below is the principle of CRT-based RSA decryption method:

- Since p and q are primes, for any integer $M < N$, if $M \equiv C^d \ mod \ pq$, then $M \equiv C^d \ mod \ p$ and $M \equiv C^d \ mod \ q$ (application of Lemma 3.2).
- Since p and q are primes, they are either coprime to C or one of them (not both) is not coprime to C. The application of the CRT requires at least two congruence equations. Therefore, the CRT-based RSA decryption is used only if both p and q are coprime to C. If p and q are coprime to C, then by Fermat's little theorem:

$$1 \equiv C^{p-1} \ mod \ p \ \text{and} \ 1 \equiv C^{q-1} \ mod \ q.$$

- Exponent d can be written as: $d = i_1(p-1)^{i_2} + d_p = k_1(q-1)^{k_2} + d_q$, where i_1, i_2, d_p, k_1, k_2, and d_q are positive integers and $d_p < p - 1$ and $d_q < q - 1$. Then,

$$M \equiv C^d \ mod \ p \equiv C^{i_1(p-1)^{i_2} + d_p} \ mod \ p \equiv (1)^{i_1 * i_2} \ C^{d_p} \ mod \ p \equiv C^{d_p} \ mod \ p$$

$$M \equiv C^d \bmod q \equiv C^{k_1(q-1)^{k_2}+d_q} \bmod q \equiv (1)^{k_1 * k_2} \ C^{d_q} \bmod q \equiv \ C^{d_q} \bmod q$$

Therefore, the exponents may be significantly reduced. Exponent d_p is bounded by $p-1$ and d_q, by $q-1$.

- The congruence equation system is:

$$\begin{cases} M \equiv C^{d_p} \bmod p \\ M \equiv C^{d_q} \bmod q \end{cases}$$

which can be simplified as:

$$\begin{cases} M \equiv \left(C_p\right)^{d_p} \bmod p, \text{ where } C_p \equiv C \bmod p \\ M \equiv \left(C_q\right)^{d_q} \bmod q, \text{ where } C_q \equiv C \bmod q \end{cases}$$

Let $C^{d_p} \bmod p \equiv M_p$, such that $M_p < p$, and $C^{d_q} \bmod q \equiv M_q$, such that $M_q < q$.

- By virtue of the Chinese remainder theorem, there exists a unique integer $M < p * q$ such that both congruence equations are fulfilled. By Gauss's algorithm (see Section 3.3.4), M is computed as:

$$M \equiv \left(\left(M_p * q * \left(q^{-1} \bmod p\right)\right) + \left(M_q * p * \left(p^{-1} \bmod q\right)\right)\right) \bmod pq$$

The pseudocode of the CRT-based decryption is as follows:

---

function CRT_RSA_Decryption

        input C: Ciphertext; p,q: RSA prime parameters

                  d: private key

        output M: plaintext

    1. # Reduction of bases of C in $\mathbb{Z}_p$ and $\mathbb{Z}_q$

        $C_p = C \bmod p; C_q = C \bmod q$

    2. # Reduction of the exponent d in $\mathbb{Z}_{p-1}$ and $\mathbb{Z}_{q-1}$

        $d_p = d \bmod (p-1); d_q = d \bmod (q-1)$

    3. # Exponentiation in $\mathbb{Z}_p$ and $\mathbb{Z}_q$

        $M_p = C_p^{d_p} \bmod p; M_q = C_q^{d_q} \bmod q$

    4. # CRT-based solution to decryption

        $M = \left(M_p * q * \left(q^{-1} \bmod p\right) + M_q * p * \left(p^{-1} \bmod q\right)\right) \bmod pq$

    5. **return** M

Example 12.2 Let $p = 37$, $q = 89$, $d = 2987$, and $C = 2494$.

The plaintext M is such that $M \equiv 2494^{2987} \bmod 37 * 89$ and by Lemma 3.2, $M \equiv 2494^{2987} \bmod 37$ and $M \equiv 2494^{2987} \bmod 89$. To find the plaintext M using the CRT-based RSA decryption, we proceed as follows:

- Reduce the bases of both congruences as follows:

$$2494 = 67 * 37 + 15 = 28 * 89 + 2$$
$$C_p \equiv 2494 \bmod 37 \equiv (67 * 37 + 15) \bmod 37 \equiv 15$$
$$C_q \equiv 2494 \bmod 89 \equiv (28 * 89 + 2) \bmod 89 \equiv 2$$

- Reduce the exponents:

$$2987 = 82(37 - 1) + 35 = 33(89 - 1) + 83$$
$$d_p = 2987 \bmod (37 - 1) = 35$$

$$d_p = 2987 \ mod \ (89-1) = 83$$

- Exponentiation in $\mathbb{Z}_{37}$ and $\mathbb{Z}_{89}$:

$$15^{8*4} \ mod \ 37 \equiv (7)^4 \ mod \ 37 \equiv 33 \qquad 15^3 \ mod \ 37 \equiv 8$$

$$2^{11} \ mod \ 89 \equiv 1 \qquad\qquad\qquad 2^6 \ mod \ 89 \equiv 64$$

$$M_p = C_p^{d_p} \ mod \ p = 15^{35} \ mod \ 37 \equiv \left(15^{8*4}\right)\left(15^3\right) mod \ 37 \equiv 5$$

$$M_q = C_q^{d_q} \ mod \ q = 2^{83} \ mod \ 89 \equiv (2^{11*7})(2^6) \ mod \ 89 \equiv 64$$

- CRT-based solution to decryption

$$89^{-1} \ mod \ 37 \equiv 5 \qquad\qquad 37^{-1} \ mod \ 89 \equiv 77$$

$$M = \left(\left(5*89*\left(89^{-1} mod \ 37\right)\right) + \left(64*37*\left(37^{-1} mod \ 89\right)\right)\right) mod \ 37*89$$

$$M = \left(\left(5*89*5\right) + \left(64*37*77\right)\right) mod \ 3293 \equiv 153$$

Therefore, the plaintext is 153.

Decryption time reduction

If the decryption $M \equiv C^d \ mod \ pq$ is carried out with the exponent d using the right-to-left binary exponentiation method, $\lceil log_2 \ d \rceil$ iterations[4] are performed. d is less than N, but it may have the same bit-length than that of the modulus N. Therefore, exponentiation C^d requires at most $\lceil log_2 \ pq \rceil$ iterations.

If the CRT-RSA decryption method is used jointly with the right-to-left binary exponentiation method to decrypt, $\lceil log_2 \ d_p \rceil + \lceil log_2 \ d_q \rceil$ iterations are performed. Since d_p and d_q are bounded by p and q respectively, $\lceil log_2 \ d_p \rceil + \lceil log_2 \ d_q \rceil < \lceil log_2 \ p \rceil + \lceil log_2 \ q \rceil = \lceil log_2 \ pq \rceil$. Therefore, there is no gain in terms of iterations in the right-to-left binary exponentiation method. However, CRT-RSA method may result in a reduction of computation time by a factor of 4 if the primes p and q have the same bit-length (which is often the case in operational cryptosystems). Indeed, the regular decryption performs operations over pq while in CRT-RSA decryption performs operations over $\mathbb{Z}_p$ and $\mathbb{Z}_q$, which have nearly the same cardinality. In the right-to-left binary exponentiation method, the most time-consuming operation is the modular multiplication. Consider a computer, which has a basic unsigned multiplication operation, which takes two 32-bit words and returns a 64-bit result. The product $a*b$, with a and b integers less than $2^{32}-1$, requires a single multiplication operation. Now, consider that a and b are less than $2^{64}-1$. Therefore, they may be represented as $a = 2^{32}*a_1 + a_2$ and $b = 2^{32}*b_1 + b_2$, with $a_2 = a \ mod \ 2^{32}$ and $b_2 = b \ mod \ 2^{32}$. To compute $C = a*b$ we need four multiplications: a_1*b_1, a_1*b_2, a_2*b_1, and a_2*b_2 and then do some additions and storage in two 64-bit long words. That is why CRT-RSA decryption may reduce the decryption time by a factor of 4 at least.

12.2.2.3 Why $e = 65537$ Is Often Used in RSA Cryptosystems?

Since the public key exponent e is public, the security of RSA does not rely on the exponent value provided that e is greater or equal to 3 and coprime with $\phi(n)$ and the *padding* technique is used. See Problem 12.1, which shows why e must be different of 1 and 2. However, it is recommended that the exponent selection should be done in such a way that encryption computation is minimized. Recall that encryption is a modular exponentiation. 65537 is the exponent value the most used in operational RSA cryptosystems. First, 65537 is prime and there is no need to check if $GCD(e, \phi(n)) = 1$ holds. Second, and more important, 65537 is equal to $2^{16} + 1$, which makes modular exponentiation faster.

12.2.3 Proof of Correctness of RSA

RSA is correct if the decryption of a ciphertext $C = M^e \ mod \ n$ returns the original plaintext M. Formally, the following must hold:

$$\left(M^e \ mod \ n\right)^d \ mod \ n \equiv M \ mod \ n = M, \forall M \leq n-1 \tag{a}$$

By the modular arithmetic rule (Lemma 3.1), which states: $a^q \ mod \ p \equiv \left(a \ mod \ p\right)^q \ mod \ n$, in which a is replaced by $M^e \ mod \ n$, (a) is rewritten as:

$$M^{ed} \ mod \ n \equiv M \ mod \ n, \ \forall m \leq n \tag{b}$$

Below is the method most used in literature to prove (b); it is based on Fermat's little theorem.

By definition: $e * d \equiv 1 \ mod(p-1)(q-1)$. Therefore, there exists an integer k such that:

$$e * d = 1 + k(p-1)(q-1)$$

By substitution:

$$M^{e*d} \ mod \ n \equiv M^{1+k(p-1)(q-1)} \ mod \ n$$

$$\equiv M * \left(M^{(p-1)}\right)^{k(q-1)} \ mod \ n \equiv M * \left(M^{(q-1)}\right)^{k(p-1)} \ mod \ n$$

If $M = 0$ then $0^{e*d} \ mod \equiv 0 \ mod \ N$.

Let us consider $M > 0$. Since $M < n$ and n is a product of two primes p and q, M can have common dividers with p or with q, but not with both. Thus, three cases are to consider:

Case 1: M is coprime with p and with q.
Case 2: M is coprime with p and not with q.
Case 3: M is coprime with q and not with p.
Cases 2 and 3 are identical.

1) Case 1: M is coprime with p and with q.
   If M is coprime with p, by Fermat's little theorem:

   $$M^{e*d} \ mod \ p \equiv M * \left(M^{(p-1)}\right)^{k(q-1)} \ mod \ p$$

   $$\equiv M * (1)^{k(q-1)} \ mod \ q \equiv M \ mod \ p$$

   If M is coprime with q, by Fermat's little theorem, we have the same as for p:

   $$M^{e*d} \ mod \ q \equiv M * \left(M^{(q-1)}\right)^{k(p-1)} \ mod \ q$$

   $$\equiv M * (1)^{k(p-1)} \ mod \ q \equiv M \ mod \ q$$

   The integer $M^{e*d} - M$ is a multiple of p and q. Since p and q are primes, there exists a positive integer f such that $M^{e*d} - M = f * p * q$. It results that $M^{e*d} - M$ also is a multiple of $n = p * q$. Consequently, $M^{e*d} \ mod \ n \equiv M \ mod \ n$.

2) Case 2: M is coprime with p and not with q.

   Since q is a prime number, M is either 0 or a multiple of q (i.e. $M \equiv 0 \ mod \ q$). By the modular arithmetic exponentiation rule, we have:

   $$M^{e*d} \ mod \ q \equiv (0)^{e*d} \ mod \ q \equiv 0 \ mod \ q \equiv M \ mod \ q$$

   Since M is coprime with p, by Fermat's little theorem,

   $$M^{e*d} \ mod \ p \equiv M * \left(M^{(p-1)}\right)^{k(q-1)} \ mod \ p \equiv M * (1)^{k(q-1)} \ mod \ p$$

   The integer $M^{ed} - M$ is a multiple of p and q. Since p and q are primes and $n = p * q$, $M^{ed} - M$ also is a multiple of $M^{ed} - M$. Consequently, $M^{ed} \equiv M \ mod \ n$. $\square$

12.2.4 RSA Security

Aiming to recover the confidential messages, adversaries need to disclose d, the private key of the recipient. By definition of RSA scheme: $d * e \equiv 1 \ mod \ \phi(n)$. If an adversary could find $\phi(n)$, then he/she could compute d and recover the plaintext. However, if $n = p * q$ is a product of two primes, computing $\phi(n)$ is equivalent to factoring n.

Factoring the RSA modulus n is a particular case of the following well-known problem, which is known to be computationally infeasible for large integers:

> **Integer factorization problem:** given an integer N, find prime factors n_1, n_2, ..., n_k such that $N = \prod_{i=1}^{k} (n_i)^{b_i}$, where $b_i \in \mathbb{N}^*, i = 1, ..., k$.

In case of RSA, the number of integers, which are coprime with n is $(p-1)(q-1)$, which is derived from Euler's totient theorem (Theorem 3.1).

Given n, finding p and q may be solved by naïvely checking all pairs p' and q' in the range $[3..(n-1)]$ to find the pair whose product is equal to n. Thus, the number of tries (in case of brute-force attack) is very high when large primes are used. Another approach is to pick randomly an integer and test if it is a factor of n. Given that there exist $\phi(n)$ integers that are coprime with n, the probability to pick an integer that divides n is $1 - \dfrac{\phi(n)}{n}$; with large prime numbers p and q, such probability is almost zero.

As far as we know and under the current known attacks, RSA security relies on the difficulty to factorize the modulus. No algorithm has been published that can factorize all integers in polynomial time. The general number field sieve (GNFS) is the most efficient algorithm for factoring (very) large integer; its correctness is considered in [3]. The GNFS has a time complexity of:

$$exp\left(\left(\left(\frac{64}{9}\right)^{\frac{1}{3}} + o(1)\right)\left((ln\ n)^{\frac{1}{3}}(ln\ ln n)^{\frac{2}{3}}\right)\right)$$

Such a complexity makes the factorization computationally infeasible for very large numbers. That is the reason why the RSA requires the selection of large prime numbers p and q to generate the keys. If both p and q are not large enough, there exists an efficient algorithm, called Lenstra's elliptic-curve factorization method, which makes use of elliptic curves (discussed in Chapter 13), with a time complexity of $exp\left(\sqrt{log(p) * log(log(p))}\right)$, where p is the smallest factor of the number to factorize. To thwart attacks based on Lenstra's algorithm, it is recommended to use both RSA primes of a bit-length in magnitude of 1000 or more.

For readers interested in prime numbers, the list of 10 000 first prime numbers and the top ten prime numbers are available at: https://tk5.org.

Just for curiosity, the largest prime number was discovered in 2018; it is $2^{82\ 589\ 933} - 1$ (it has 24 862 048 decimal digits).

When the value of the modulus n is not large, some RSA-S[5] had been cracked: RSA-576 cracked in 2003, RSA-640 in 2005, and RSA-768 in 2009. However, it should be noticed that much computation resources were monopolized to crack RSA. Cryptanalysts used either special multiprocessors or clusters interconnected via Internet. For example, RSA-640 was cracked with the equivalent of almost 200 years of computing on a single core 2.2 GHz and RSA-768 with the equivalent of almost 2000 years of computing on a single core 2.2 GHz.

No RSA-S with $S > 768$ has been cracked yet. RSA-2048 is recommended and currently widely used. In conclusion, RSA is considered secure when used with large primes (made of 1024 or more bits). Therefore, users may continue using RA for years before the RSA-2048 would be broken.

| **Note.** It is not yet formally proven that the only way to disclose RSA-encrypted message is by factoring the modulus n.

12.2.5 Optimal Asymmetric Encryption Padding (OAEP)

Low public-key exponent values may make the system vulnerable to some attacks, if the system is not complying with security implementation guidelines. For example, the same message encrypted three times with exponent $e = 3$ and three pairwise coprime moduli can be recovered (see Problem 12.1). Another example of incorrect use of RSA is to send messages represented by low values (see Problem 12.5).

A countermeasure has been proposed by Bellare and Rogaway [4] to address vulnerabilities raised by low values. The proposed method is called Optimal Asymmetric Encryption Padding (OAEP). When implemented, the OAEP enables to use any public-key exponent greater than 2 and any message value less than the modulus. Since 2016, the OAEP support is required to provide security to new applications [5].

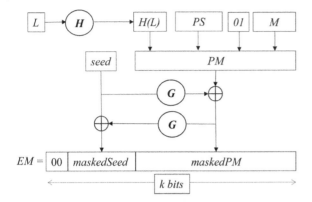

Figure 12.3 OAEP encryption diagram.

Message encoding is a way to message formatting before the RSA encryption is applied. Therefore, short messages are extended with padding data and then encrypted at a high level of security (see Figure 12.3). RSA-OAEP is the combination of basic RSA and OAEP.

RSA-OAEP is parameterized by the choice of a hash function $H()$ and a mask generation function $G()$. In current RSA cryptosystems, OAEP mainly makes use of SHA-256, SHA-384, and SHA-512. Any mask generation function used in RSA-OAEP shall be deterministic (i.e. the output is fully determined by the input). Mask generation function takes a byte string of variable length and returns a string of the desired length. The output should be pseudorandom (i.e. given a part of the output but not the input, it should be infeasible to predict another part of the output). At the time of writing this chapter, only one mask generation function is specified by the RSA standards, which is labeled MGF1. The latter is a hash function. Thus, in current RSA-OAEP cryptosystems, the encoding is based on hash functions; a single hash function may be used for both parameters $H()$ and $G()$ or two distinct hash functions may be used. Below is the description of the RSA-OAEP cryptosystem [5].

RSA-OAEP set up
- Select a hash function $H()$ with output of *hLen* bytes.
- Select a mask generation function $G()$ with output of *maskLen* bytes.
- The identity[6] of the selected functions shall be known to both parties.

RSA-OAEP encoding
- Let k denote the length (in bytes) of the modulus n and *mLen* denote the length of the message M to encrypt. Message length *mLen* is bounded: $mLen \leq k - 2 * hLen - 2$ (because padding bytes and hashes are concatenated with the original message before encryption).
- Select a string label L associated with the message M. In the version PKCS #1 v2.2, L is the empty string.
- Compute: $H(L)$, the hash associated with the label L.
- Generate a padding string PS formed by $k - mLen - 2 * hLen - 2$ zero-bytes. The length of string PS may be zero.
- Make concatenation: $PM = H(L) \| PS \| 0x01 \| M$. (0x01 denotes a byte with value 1).
- Generate a random string *seed* of length *hLen* bytes.
- Compute: $masked\ PM = PM \oplus G(seed, k - hLen - 1)$.
- Compute: $maskedSeed = seed \oplus G(maskedPM, hLen)$.
- Make concatenation: $EM = 0x00 \| maskedSeed \| maskedPM$. The length of the encoded message EM is k (i.e. the modulus length in bytes).

RSA-OAEP encryption
Encryption: $C \equiv EM^e \bmod n$ (e is the public key exponent and EM is the output of the OAEP encoding operation).

RSA-OAEP decryption
- Decryption: $EM \equiv C^d \bmod n$ (d is the private key and C, the ciphertext)
- OAEP decoding (assuming no error in the coding step)
  - Let $EM.maskedSeed$ and $EM.maskedPM$ denote the values of the fields *maskedSeed* and *maskedPM*, respectively, in the byte string EM
  - Compute: $seed = EM.maskedSeed \oplus G(EM.maskedPM, hLen)$
  - Compute: $PM = EM.maskedPM \oplus G(seed, k - hLen - 1)$
  - Extract M from PM byte string.

Example 12.3 In the example, byte values are represented in decimal.
- RSA modulus and key selection
  - 6 is the minimum length to form an OAEP message with one data byte, one padding byte, two one-byte hashes, and two constant bytes (see Figure 12.3). Therefore, the length of the RSA-OAEP modulus n should be of six bytes at least.

- $p = 32\,452\,843$ and $q = 1\,000\,003$ are two primes such that $n = p*q = 32\,452\,940\,358\,529$ has a length of six bytes.
  - Public key exponent selection: $e = 5$
  - Private key selection: $d = 6\,490\,581\,381\,137$
- Hash and mask generation functions and padding string
  - To make the computations easy to check without a specialized library, let $H()$ be the identity function and $G()$ the one-byte-left rotation function that returns the most-right byte(s).
  - Let L be one-byte string with decimal value 65. A single byte is hashed. Hence, $hLen = 1$.
- OAEP encoding
  - Let M be one-byte message with decimal value 10.
  - A single padding zero-byte is included in the OAEP message.
  - $PM = H(L) \,\|\, PS \,\|\, 0x01 \,\|\, M = 65 \,\|\, 00 \,\|\, 01 \,\|\, 00$.
  - Let $seed$ be 21.
  - $maskedPM = PM \oplus G(seed, k - hLen - 1) = PM \oplus G(21, 4)$
    $G(21,\ 4)\ = 00 \,\|\, 00 \,\|\, 21 \,\|\, 00$
    $PM \oplus G(21,4) = 65 \,\|\, 00 \,\|\, 20 \,\|\, 10$
  - $maskedSeed = seed \oplus G(maskedPM, hLen) = (21) \oplus G(maskedPM,\ 1) = (21) \oplus (65) = 84$
  - The resulting encoded message is:
    $EM = 00 \,\|\, 84 \,\|\, 65 \,\|\, 00 \,\|\, 20 \,\|\, 10$
  - EM is converted into an integer as follows:
    $EM = 10 + 20*256 + 0*256^2 + 65*256^3 + 84*256^4 + 0*256^5$
    $EM = 361\,867\,777\,034$
- Encrypion: $C \equiv (361\,867\,777\,034)^5 \bmod n = 9\,420\,165\,225\,441$
- *RSA-OAEP decryption*
  - $EM\,(9\,420\,165\,225\,441)^{6\,490\,581\,381\,137} \bmod 32\,452\,940\,358\,529 = 361\,867\,777\,034$
- OAEP decoding
  - Convert EM into six bytes (in decimal):
    $EM = 00 \,\|\, 84 \,\|\, 65 \,\|\, 00 \,\|\, 20 \,\|\, 10$
  - In the byte string EM:
    $EM.maskedSeed$ is 84
    $EM.markedPM$ is $65 \,\|\, 00 \,\|\, 20 \,\|\, 10$
  - $seed = EM.maskedSeed \oplus G(EM.maskedPM, hLen)$
    $= (84) \oplus G(EM.maskedPM, 1) = (84) \oplus (65) = 21$
  - $PM = EM.maskedPM \oplus G(seed, k - hLen - 1)$
    $= (65 \,\|\, 00 \,\|\, 20 \,\|\, 10) \oplus (00 \,\|\, 00 \,\|\, 21 \,\|\, 00) = 65 \,\|\, 00 \,\|\, 01 \,\|\, 10$
  - Extract M from the most-right byte of PM. Thus, $M = 10$.

12.2.6 RSA Signature

RSA signature scheme is specified in two standards: ANSI standard X9.31 [6] and RFC 8017 [5]. In the ANSI standard, it is called RSA DSA (digital signature algorithm) and RSASSA (Signature Scheme with Appendix) in RFC 8017. There exist some detail differences between the standards, which makes implementations non-interoperable. In the sequel, the focus is on the common principles of RSA signature scheme in both standards.

RSA digital signature is computed with a private key d and a hash function $H()$ and it is verified with the public key (e, n). A signature key pair $((e, n), d)$ shall be used only for signing and not for other purposes.

The standards specify three choices for the size of the modulus n: 1024, 2048, and 3072 bits. The standards recommend that the modulus size and the hash output size must be the same unless an agreement had been made between participating entities to use a stronger hash function.

12.2.6.1 RSA Signature Generation

The signature of message M is generated as follows:

Compute the message hash: $h = H(M)$

Encrypt the hash: $s \equiv h^d \bmod n$, s is the signature

Send the following items to the verifier

(M,s): message and its signature

(e,n): signer's public-key

$H()$: identity of the hash function

12.2.6.2 RSA Signature Verification

The intended recipient, or any other party (since the message content is not encrypted), verifies the signature to determine the authenticity of the message.

Before signature verification, the verifier should receive and accept signer's public-key and the identity of the hash function. Upon reception of a message M' and its signature s', the verification is as follows:

Compute the hash of the received message: $h' = H(M')$

Signature decryption: $h(s')^e \equiv \bmod n$

Verification: if $h' = h$, the signature is valid. Otherwise, reject the message.

As for message encryption, in order to increase the efficiency of signature generation and verification, the public key exponents $e - 3$ and $e - 65537$ are commonly used.

12.2.6.3 Probabilistic Signature Scheme (PSS)

In the PKCS#1 standard, two signature methods are specified: RSASSA-PSS and RSASSA-PKCS1-v1_5. RSASSA-PKCS1-v1_5 and RSA-PKCS1-v1_5 are used interchangeably; and RSASSA-PSS and RSA-PSS also are used interchangeably. RSA-PKCS#1 method is no more recommended; and current and future RSA signature systems are required to use RSA-PSS method.

RSA-PSS method is expected to provide a higher level of security to prevent attacks, which try to discover private keys from intercepted signed messages. The PSS method is similar to the OAEP method introduced in the previous section. PSS is based on adding random padding information to the original message before generating the signature. Below is the description of RSA-PSS.

RSA-PSS set up

- Select a hash function $H()$ with output of *hLen* bytes.
- Select a mask generation function $G()$ with output of *maskLen* bytes. In the current version of the RSA signature standards, it is recommended that the function $G()$ is the same as the hash function $H()$.
- Select a salt length *sLen*. A salt is a random byte string added to the original message. The salt string used in RSA-PSS and the seed string used in RSA-OAEP (section 12.2.5) have the same role, which is creating randomness in messages. Therefore, that the same message content results in distinct messages when encrypted or signed.
- The identity of the selected functions and the salt length shall be known to both parties.

RSA-PSS encoding (see Figure 12.4)

- Let k denote the length (in bytes) of the modulus n. k also is the length of signature s. Let M be the message to sign.
- Compute: $mHash = H(M)$, the hash associated with the message M.
- Generate a random string *salt* of length *sLen* bytes.
- Make concatenations and hashing:
  - $PHsalt = (0000000000000000) \| mHash \| salt$. *PHsalt* is a byte string with length of $8 + hLen + sLen$ bytes.
  - $Hash = H(PHsalt)$
  - Generate a string PS consisting of $k - sLen - hLen - 2$ zero bytes. PS may be the empty string.
  - $Psalt = PS \| 0x01 \| salt$ (the length of $Psalt$ is $k - hLen - 1$)
  - $maskedPsalt = Psalt \oplus G(Hash, k - hLen - 1)$
  - $EH = maskedPsalt \| Hash \| 0xbc$

  EH is the encoded hash and $0xbc$ is a byte with hexadecimal value bc.

RSA-PSS signature generation

- $s \equiv EH^d \mod n$ (d is the private key and EH is the output of the encoding operation)

RSA-PSS signature verification

- Receive the domain parameters (including: $H()$ and $G()$ identities and salt length), signer's public key (e,n), and a message M and its signature s.
- Signature decryption: $EH \equiv s^e \mod n$
- Signature decoding and verification
  - Compute the hash of received message:
    $mHash = H(M)$
  - From EH extract $EH.maskedPsalt$ and $EH.Hash$.
  - $Psalt = EH.maskedPsalt \oplus G(EH.Hash, k - hLen - 1)$
    Extract *salt* value from *Psalt*.
- Let *PHsalt* be a string formed as follows:
  $(00\,00\,00\,00\,00\,00\,00\,00) \| mHash \| salt$.
  - Compute the hash of *PHsalt*: $Hash' = H(PHsalt)$
  - If $Hash' = EH.Hash$, then the signature is valid. Otherwise, it is not valid.

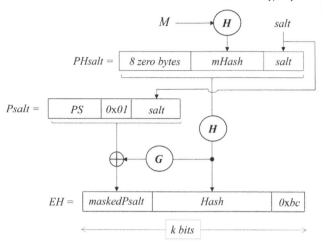

Figure 12.4 PSS encoding method of RSA-PSS.

Example 12.4 In the example, byte values are represented in decimal.
- Consider the following RSA parameters:
  - $p = 702613$ and $q = 1\,000\,003$.
  - $n = p * q = 702\,615\,107\,839$ has a length of five bytes.
  - $k = 5$, k is the byte length of modulus n.
  - Public key exponent selection: $e = 5$.
  - Private key selection: $d = 140\,522\,681\,045$.
- Hash and mask generation functions
  As in example 12.3, to make the computations easy to check without a specialized library, let $H()$ be the identity function and $G()$ the one-byte-left rotation function that returns the most-right byte(s). Let the hash output length be 1 (i.e. $hLen = 1$).
- To use a modulus with length of six bytes, and without loss of generality, the string of eight zeros in *PHsalt* is removed and the padding string *PS* is the empty string.
- PSS encoding
  - Let M be one-byte message with decimal value 10.
  - $H(10) = 10$
  - Let $salt = 77$ (a random value of one byte length)
  - $PHsalt = 10 \| 77$
  - $Hash = H(PHsalt) = 10 \| 77$
  - PS consists of the empty string
  - $Psalt = 01 \| 77$
  - $maskedPsalt = Psalt \oplus G(Hash, 2) = (01 \| 77) \oplus (77 \| 10) = 76 \| 71$
  - $EH = maskedPsalt \| Hash \| 0xbc$
    $= 76 \| 71 \| 10 \| 77 \| 188$ (188 is the decimal representation of $0xbc$)
- *Signature encryption*
  EH in decimal representation:
  $EH = 188 + 77 * 256 + 10 * 256^2 + 71 * 256^3 + 76 * 256^4$
  $= 327\,609\,372\,092$

  $s \equiv EH^d \mod n \equiv 327\,609\,372\,092^{140\,522\,681\,045} \mod 702\,615\,107\,839$
  $= 507\,988\,379\,558$
- *Signature decryption*
  $EH \equiv 507\,988\,379\,558^5 \mod 702\,615\,107\,839 = 327\,609\,372\,092$
  EH representation as a string of five integers:
  $EH = 188 \| 77 \| 10 \| 71 \| 76$

- Signature decoding and verification
  - $H(M) = H(10) = 10$
  - $Psalt = EH.maskedPsalt \oplus G(EH.Hash, k - hLen - 1)$
    $= (76 \| 71) \oplus (77 \| 10) = 01 \| 77$
  - Thus, $salt = 77$
  - Let $PHsalt$ be the string: $mHash \| salt = 10 \| 77$
  - $H(PHsalt) = H(10 \| 77) = EH.Hash$. Thus, the signature is valid.

12.3 Finite Field-based Cryptography

12.3.1 Discrete Logarithm Problem

12.3.1.1 What Is the Discrete Logarithm Problem?

> **Discrete logarithm problem** (DLP): given a cyclic multiplicative group $\mathbb{Z}_p^*$, a generator g of the group $\mathbb{Z}_p^*$, and an element h of $\mathbb{Z}_p^*$, find k such that: $g^k = h \bmod p$.
>
> k is called discrete logarithm.

Recall that in classic mathematics, given two real numbers a and b, $\log_b(a)$, the logarithm of a to base b, is a real number c such that: $b^c = a$. $\log(x)$ is the inverse function of e^x. Analogously, in any cyclic group $\mathbb{Z}_p^*$ with generator g, powers g^k can be defined for all integers k, and $\log_g(h)$, the discrete algorithm of an element $h \in \mathbb{Z}_p^*$, is an integer k such that: $g^k \equiv h \bmod p$.

Example 12.5 Let us consider $\mathbb{Z}_{11}^* = \{1, 2, 3, 4, 5, 6, 7, 8, 9, 10\}$

Element 2 is a generator of $\mathbb{Z}_{11}^*$, since:

$2^0 = 1$	$2^1 = 2$	$2^2 = 4$	$2^3 = 8$
$2^4 = 16 \equiv 5 \bmod 11$	$2^5 = 32 \equiv 10 \bmod 11$	$2^6 = 64 \equiv 9 \bmod 11$	
$2^7 = 128 \equiv 7 \bmod 11$	$2^8 = 256 \equiv 3 \bmod 11$	$2^9 = 512 \equiv 6 \bmod 11$	

Find k such that $2^k \equiv 3 \bmod 11$. It is easy to find k when the powers of 2 calculated a priori; $k = 8$.

12.3.1.2 Attacks Against DLP

One naïve way (also called brute-force attack) to solve the discrete logarithm is to prepare the table of powers of the generator element for all the elements of the cyclic group $\mathbb{Z}_p^*$ (i.e. $|\mathbb{Z}_p^*|$ powers of the generator should be calculated and stored). Therefore, the complexity (in computation or memory capacity) of the brute-force attack is $O(p)$. With today's computers, it is recommended to use cyclic groups with cardinality higher that 2^{90} to make brute-force attack computationally infeasible.

The best known attack algorithms against DLP, which work in arbitrary groups, have a complexity of $O(\sqrt{p})$ and include *Baby-step giant-step* algorithm and *Pollard's rho* algorithm. For both attack algorithms, the set of elements of the cyclic group is partitioned before testing candidate solutions.

Other efficient DLP attacks algorithms exist, under some assumptions, including *Pohlig-Hellman* algorithm (which assumes that the order of the group has a small number of prime factors) and *Index calculus* algorithm (which requires an efficient procedure to select a relatively small subset of elements of the group, in such a way that a significant fraction of elements can be efficiently expressed as products of elements of the selected subset). For more detail on DLP attacks, refer to [7].

In general, DLP is considered computationally intractable. That is, no feasible algorithm is known for computing discrete logarithms when large cyclic fields are used, because the modular exponentiation $g^k = h \bmod p$ is a one-way function. Considering current and near-future CPU technologies, it is recommended to use groups with cardinality higher than 2^{2*80} to make the best known DLP attacks computationally infeasible. In practice, cryptosystems make use of groups with cardinality higher than 2^{1024}.

The most recent record on solving DLP in cyclic groups $\mathbb{Z}_p^*$ was announced in late 2019. Researchers computed the discrete logarithm modulo for 795 bits. The computation took approximately 3100 core-years, using Intel Xeon Gold 6130 CPUs (2.1GHz). Another record on solving DLP in extension fields $GF\left(2^m\right)$ was announced in late 2019. Researchers computed the discrete logarithm modulo for $GF\left(2^{30750}\right)$ using 25 481 219 core hours on clusters based on Intel Xeon architecture.

In the sequel, the most known finite field-based cryptographic algorithms (namely, DHKE, ElGamal, and MQV), are presented.

12.3.2 Diffie-Hellman Key Exchange

The Diffie-Hellman Key Exchange (DHKE[7]) scheme is the first important application of DLP to design a cryptography scheme [1]. In order to describe the DHKE protocol, let us consider a use case in which Alice and Bob generate a shared secret (see Fiure 12.5).

The main purpose of the DHKE protocol is the key exchange between communicating parties. DHKE does not explicitly address how the shared secret can be used for encryption or for digital signature. Therefore, in practice, it is not used for encryption or signature. Other schemes, such as ElGamal encryption and signature algorithms, extended DHKE. It is worth noticing that the encryption with DHKE may be easily implemented as follows:

Encryption: $C = M.S \ mod \ p$; (M is the message to encrypt)
Decryption: $M = C.S^{-1} \ mod \ p$

where: M is the message to encrypt, C the ciphertext, S the shared secret, and S^{-1} is the inverse of element S in the multiplicative group $\mathbb{Z}_p^*$.

Example 12.6 Alice and Bob decide to compute a shared secret using DHKE protocol with $p = 227$, which is prime, and $g = 2$.

Alice chooses her private key to be $Pr_A = 175$. Then, she computes her public key: $Pu_A = 2^{175} \ mod \ 227 = 2^{3*44+43} \ mod \ 227 = \left(171^3 * 199\right) \ mod \ 227 = 201.$

Bob chooses his private key to be $Pr_B = 44$. Then, he computes his public key: $Pu_B = 2^{44} \ mod \ 227 = 171.$
Then, public keys are exchanged between Alice and Bob.
The shared secret computed by Alice is:

$$S = Pu_B^{175} \ mod \ 227 = \left(171\right)^{175} \ mod \ 227 = \left(171^5\right)^{35} \ mod \ 227$$

$$= \left(188^5\right)^7 \ mod \ 227 = \left(129\right)^{5+2} \ mod \ 227 = \left(132\right) * \left(129\right)^2 \ mod \ 227 = 160$$

Bob	Alice
Alice and Bob agree on two public parameters: g (a subgroup generator) and prime P, the modulus of the $\mathbb{Z}_p^*$ group.	
• Pick a private key, Pr_B, an integer such that: $1 \leq Pr_B < p-1$ [8] • Compute the public key Pu_B: $Pu_B = g^{Pr_B} \ mod \ p$ • Send Pu_B to Alice	• Pick a private key, Pr_A, an integer such that: $1 \leq Pr_A < p-1$ • Compute the public key Pu_A: $Pu_A = g^{Pr_A} \ mod \ p$ • Send Pu_A to Bob
Public keys are exchanged via an insecure network.	
• Receive Alice's public key • Compute a shared secret S: $S = S_B = \left(Pu_A\right)^{Pr_B} \ mod \ p$	• Receive Bob's public key • Compute a shared secret S: $S = S_A = \left(Pu_B\right)^{Pr_A} \ mod \ p$
Alice and Bob have generated the same secret S, which can be used, entirely or in part, as a session key of a symmetric cipher to encrypt and decrypt messages.	

Figure 12.5 Illustration of Diffie-Hellman key exchange protocol.

The shared secret computed by Bob is:

$$S = Pu_A^{44} \ mod \ 227 = 201^{44} \ mod \ 227 = \left(201^4\right)^{11} \ mod \ 227$$

$$= \left(25\right)^{5*2+1} \ mod \ 227 = 85^2 * 25 \ mod \ 227 = 160$$

Proof of correctness of DHKE:

The proof of correctness of DHKE is obvious, since the S value computed by both parties is the same:

$$S_A = \left(Pu_B\right)^{Pr_A} \ mod \ p = \left(g^{Pr_B} \ mod \ p\right)^{Pr_A} \ mod \ p = g^{Pr_B * Pr_A} \ mod \ p$$

$$S_B = \left(Pu_A\right)^{Pr_B} \ mod \ p = \left(g^{Pr_A} \ mod \ p\right)^{Pr_B} \ mod \ p = g^{Pr_A * Pr_B} \ mod \ p$$

$$\Rightarrow S_A = S_B = S \qquad \qquad \square$$

Resistance to attacks

Given the public parameters (g, p, Pu_B, and Pu_A), breaking the Diffie-Hellman key exchange scheme means revealing the session key S, which requires solving a problem known as Diffie-Hellman problem.

Diffie-Hellman problem (DHP): given a cyclic multiplicative group $\mathbb{Z}_p^*$, a generator g of the group $\mathbb{Z}_p^*$, and two values $g^x \ mod \ p$ and $g^y \ mod \ p$, x and y are two random values, find $g^{x*y} \ mod \ p$.

Since the session key S is derived from a couple of public and private keys, from either $\left(Pu_B, Pr_A\right)$ or $\left(Pu_A, Pr_B\right)$, the adversary should[9] reveal one of private keys (Pr_B or Pr_A). Unfortunately, for the adversary, revealing a private key, which is defined by a modular exponentiation, requires the adversary to solve the DLP problem, which is known to be computationally infeasible. In such a case, the DHP is equivalent to the DLP. Therefore, solving the Diffie-Hellman problem (DHP) also is computationally infeasible for large values of cyclic group size.

12.3.3 Menezes-Qu-Vanstone Key-exchange Protocol

MQV (Menezes-Qu-Vanstone) key-agreement is one of the numerous extensions to the original Diffie-Hellman key-exchange protocol [8–10]. MQV is designed to work in an arbitrary finite group, either in FFC context or in ECC context. In both cases, MQV provides a countermeasure to some attacks against the DHKE, including the small group attack, discussed in 13.5.3.1. MQV makes use of two key-pairs for each party: a static (i.e. long-term) key-pair and an ephemeral key-pair. The protocol run by Alice and Bob to generate a shared secret is shown in Figure 12.6.

12.3.4 ElGamal Cryptosystem

ElGamal cryptosystem makes use of the DHKE protocol to provide a complete cryptosystem [11]. From the cryptographic foundation point of view, ElGamal scheme is just a reordering of DH communications between parties to implement encryption and signature. The security of ElGamal scheme is equivalent to that of DHKE scheme.

12.3.4.1 ElGamal Encryption

Consider a use case in which Bob needs to receive confidential messages from Alice. The calculations and exchanges are illustrated by Figure 12.7.

Proof of correctness of ElGamal encryption:

The encryption/decryption is correct if $M = C.S^{-1} \ mod \ p$ is true. The proof of correctness is easily established by substitutions as follows:

$$C.S^{-1} \ mod \ p \equiv \left(M * S \ mod \ p\right) * S^{-1} \ mod \ p$$

$$\equiv \left(M * g^{Pr_B * k} \ mod \ p\right) * g^{-\left(Pr_B * k\right)} \ mod \ p$$

$$\equiv M.g^0 \ mod \ p = M \qquad \qquad \square$$

Bob	Alice
Alice and Bob agree on three public parameters: prime p, g (a subgroup generator) and q, the order of the subgroup.	
• Pick a static private key, Pr_B, an integer such that: $1 \le Pr_B < p-1$ • Compute the static public key Pu_B: $Pu_B = g^{Pr_B} \bmod p$ • Send Pu_B to Alice • Pick an ephemeral private key, Pr_B^e, an integer such that: $1 \le Pr_B^e < p-1$ • Compute the ephemeral public key Pu_B^e: $Pu_B^e = g^{Pr_B^e} \bmod p$ • Send Pu_B^e to Alice	• Pick a static private key, Pr_A, an integer such that: $1 \le Pr_A < p-1$ • Compute the static public key Pu_A: $Pu_A = g^{Pr_A} \bmod p$ • Send Pu_A to Bob • Pick an ephemeral private key, Pr_A^e, an integer such that: $1 \le Pr_A^e < p-1$ • Compute the ephemeral public key Pu_A^e: $Pu_A^e = g^{Pr_A^e} \bmod p$ • Send Pu_A^e to Bob
Public keys are exchanged via an insecure network.	
• Receive Alice's public keys • Compute a shared secret Z: $w = \left\lfloor \frac{1}{2} \log_2(q) \right\rfloor$ $T_B = \left(Pu_B^e \bmod 2^w\right) + 2^w$ $S_B = \left(Pr_B^e + T_B * Pu_B\right) \bmod q$ $T_A = \left(Pu_A^e \bmod 2^w\right) + 2^w$ $Z = \left(Pu_A^e * \left(Pu_A\right)^{T_A}\right)^{S_B} \bmod p$	• Receive Bob's public keys • Compute a shared secret Z: $w = \left\lfloor \frac{1}{2} \log_2(q) \right\rfloor$ $T_A = \left(Pu_A^e \bmod 2^w\right) + 2^w$ $S_A = \left(Pr_A^e + T_A * Pu_A\right) \bmod q$ $T_B = \left(Pu_B^e \bmod 2^w\right) + 2^w$ $Z = \left(Pu_B^e * \left(Pu_B\right)^{T_B}\right)^{S_A} \bmod p$
Alice and Bob have generated the same secret Z, which can be used, entirely or in part, as a session key of a symmetric cipher to encrypt and decrypt messages.	

Figure 12.6 Illustration of MQV key exchange protocol.

Bob	Alice
• Select two group parameters: g (a subgroup generator) and prime P, the modulus of $\mathbb{Z}_p^*$ group. • Pick a private key, Pr_B, an integer such that: $2 \le Pr_B \le p-2$ • Compute the public key[10] Pu_B: $Pu_B = g^{Pr_B} \bmod p$ • Send (p, g, Pu_B) to Alice	
	• Receive (p, g, Pu_B) • Pick an integer k[11] such that: $0 \le k \le p-2$ • Compute public key Pu_A: $Pu_A = g^k \bmod p$ • Compute the session key S: $S = \left(Pu_B\right)^k \bmod p$ • Encrypt the message: $C = M * S \bmod p$ • Send $\left(Pu_A, C\right)$ to Bob
• Receive $\left(Pu_A, C'\right)$ • Compute a shared secret S: $S = \left(Pu_A\right)^{Pr_B} \bmod p$ • Decrypt the ciphertext: $M' = C'.S^{-1} \bmod p$	

Figure 12.7 Illustration of ElGamal encryption.

Notes

– The sender should not use the same per-message secret k to encrypt more than one message. If the same value $k0$ is used to encrypt two messages M_1 and M_2, the adversary would be able to discover the content of M_2, assuming he/she had previously intercepted the content, in clear, of message M_1, as follows:

$$C_1 = M_1 * \left(Pu_B\right)^{k0} \bmod p; \quad C_2 = M_2 * \left(Pu_B\right)^{k0} \bmod p; \quad \frac{C_1}{C_2} = \frac{M_1}{M_2} \bmod p$$

From the public information (C_1, C_2, p) and the intercepted message M_1, the adversary can easily discover M_2: $M_2 = M_1 * C_2 * C_1^{-1}$ *mod p*.

In general, if the sender does not change the private key, the adversary has just to capture the plaintext of any message to learn the content of all messages of a session.

- The consequence of encrypting a single message by each private key value is that when the sender transmits, at different times, the same data (for example a password or PIN code), the ciphertexts are different and the adversary will not be able to detect that the same data is sent multiple times.

12.3.4.2 ElGamal Signature

Consider a use case in which Bob sends signed messages, using ElGamal signature scheme, to Alice who checks the authenticity of messages sent by Bob. The calculations and exchanges are illustrated by Figure 12.8.

Example 12.7 Use case: Bob sends a message to Alice who verifies the signature.
Bob operations:

- Use $\mathbb{Z}_{19}^*$ and $g = 10$
- Pick a private key $Pr_B = 16$
- Compute the public key $Pu_B = 10^{16} \ mod 19 = 4$
- Send domain parameters $(p = 19, g = 10, \ Pu_B = 4)$ to Alice
- Choose a message $M = 14$
- Pick a per-message-signature key $K_B = 5$ /* $GCD(5, 19-1) - 1$ */
- Generate signature of M:

$$r = 10^5 \ mod 19 = 3$$

$$s = (14 - 16 * 3)(5^{-1}) \ mod 18 = (2) * (11) \ mod \ 18 = 4$$

- Send $(14, (3, 4))$

Alice's operations

- Receive $(p = 19, g = 10, Pu_B = 4)$
- Receive $(M = 14, (r = 3, s = 4))$
- Verify signature:$v = (4^3 * 3^4) \ mod \ 19 = (7) * (5) \ mod \ 19 = 16$

$g^M \ mod \ p = 10^{14} \ mod 19 = 16 = v$

$\Rightarrow$ The signature is valid.

Bob	Alice
• Select two group parameters: g (a subgroup generator) and prime p, the modulus of the $\mathbb{Z}_p^*$ group. • Pick a private key Pr_B, an integer such that: $2 \le Pr_B \le p-2$ • Compute the public key Pu_B: $Pu_B = g^{Pr_B} \ mod \ p$ • Send (p, g, Pu_B) to Alice	
	• Receive (p, g, Pu_B)
• M: message to sign ($M \le p-2$) • Pick an integer[12] K_B such that: $2 \le K_B \le p-2$ and $GCD(K_B, p-1) = 1$ ([13]) • Generation of signature, a couple (r, s): $r = g^{K_B} \ mod \ p$ $s = (M - Pr_B * r) K_B^{-1} mod(p-1)$ • Send $(M, (r, s))$ to Alice	
	• Receive $(M', (r', s'))$ • Calculate $v = (Pu_B^{r'} * r^{s'}) mod \ p$ • If $v = g^{M'} \ mod \ p$, then "valid signature" else "invalid signature"

Figure 12.8 Illustration of ElGamal signature protocol.

Proof of correctness of ElGamal digital signature

A digital signature service is correct if the result of the verification of a valid signature is "valid signature". The proof of correctness of ElGamal signature may be proven by substitutions as follows:

First, we introduce the following lemma:

Lemma 12.1   "$mod\ p \leftrightarrow mod\ p-1$": for any positive integers a, p, and k, the following holds: $a^k\ mod\ p \equiv a^{k\ mod(p-1)}\ mod\ p$

Lemma proof: For any integers k and p, there exists an integer k_1, such that:

$$k = k_1 * (p-1) + (k\ mod\ (p-1))$$

Therefore, for any integer a, by substitution, we can write:

$$a^k = a^{k_1 *(p-1)+(k\ mod\ (p-1))}$$

$$\Rightarrow a^k\ mod\ p \equiv a^{k_1 *(p-1)+(k\ mod\ (p-1))}\ mod\ p$$

$$a^k\ mod\ p \equiv \left(a^{k_1}\right)^{(p-1)} * a^{(k\ mod\ (p-1))}\ mod\ p$$

Using Little Fermat theorem (i.e. $a^{p-1} \equiv 1\ mod\ p$), the last equality becomes:

$$a^k\ mod\ p \equiv 1 * a^{(k\ mod\ (p-1))}\ mod\ p \equiv a^{k\ mod\ (p-1)}\ mod\ p \qquad \square$$

Second, make substitutions in the formula used by the recipient to verify the signature:

$$v \equiv \left(Pu_B^r * r^s\right) mod\ p$$

$$\equiv \left(\left(g^{Pr_B}\right)^r * \left(g^{K_B}\right)^s\right) mod\ p \qquad\qquad \text{\# substitute } Pu_B \text{ and } r$$

$$\equiv g^{Pr_B *r + K_B *s}\ mod\ p$$

$$\equiv g^{Pr_B *r + K_B *\left((M - Pr_B *r)*K_B^{-1}mod(p-1)\right)}\ mod\ p \qquad\qquad \text{\# substitute } s$$

$$\equiv g^{Pr_B *r + \left((M - Pr_B *r)mod(p-1)\right)}\ mod\ p$$

$$\equiv g^{M\ mod(p-1)}\ mod\ p$$

Using Lemma 12.1 "$mod\ p \leftrightarrow mod\ p - 1$", we have:

$$g^{M\ mod(p-1)}\ mod\ p \equiv g^M\ mod\ p.$$

Therefore, the signature associated with the received message is valid and the result of the signature verification in correct. $\square$

12.3.4.3 ElGamal Digital Signature Security and Potential Attacks

12.3.4.3.1 Security

If the signature scheme is implemented properly (i.e. compliance with single-use of per-message-signature keys), most attacks (including trying to derive private keys from a set of messages with their signatures or trying to generate a valid signature without signer's private key or trying to generate a message given the signatures of other messages) are equivalent to solving the Discrete logarithm problem.

12.3.4.3.2 Potential Attacks Against ElGamal Signature

Attack aiming to disclose signer's private key: a per-message-signature key must be used to sign a single message and must not be reused (in conjunction with the same public key). Otherwise, the adversary will be able to derive the private key of the signer as shown in Problem 12.22.

Attack aiming to forge a signature: the attack also is called *existential forgery*. In the signature scheme presented previously, an adversary can generate legitimate signatures without knowledge of the private key of the legitimate signer, but he/she cannot decide (or control) which content to include in the message. Therefore, there is no potential impact in terms of security, except of denial of service, because the adversary always tries to send specific content such as "send money" or "apply an action on an asset" to win something. Problem 12.23 shows how signature forging may be designed.

12.4 Digital Signature Algorithm (DSA)

The original digital signature scheme of ElGamal results in signatures composed of two items (r and s), each of which has a size of p bits. Consequently, the size of the digital signature is twice the message size. Thus, signing long size messages (such as pictures, scanned documents, and videos) results in significant consumption of resources (bandwidth and memory), which are limited in some mobile and embedded devices. To alleviate such a drawback of ElGamal signature scheme, it is recommended to sign the hash of the message and not the entire message. This recommendation led to the DSA[14] (Digital Signature Algorithm) standard, which is currently one of the three techniques mostly used to sign documents online. The main adaptions of ElGamal signature scheme to yield the DSA standard are addressed in this section. For specific details regarding the implementations of the DSA standard (including how parameters are selected and checked), refer to [12] and Chapter 14.

12.4.1 DSA Domain Parameters

A digital signature is computed using the following domain parameters that should be agreed upon by the two parties before signing:

- p: a prime modulus
- g: a subgroup generator, of order q, in the multiplicative group $\mathbb{Z}_p^*$
- q: the order of generator g (q is a prime divisor[15] of $p-1$). In other words, $g^q \ mod \ p = 1$ (see Problem 12.25).

DSA standard specifies four security strength levels and their associated pairs (L,N), where L and N are the length (in bits) of p and q, respectively:

$$L=1024, N=160 \qquad L=2048, N=224$$
$$L=2048, N=256 \qquad L=3072, N=256$$

To make infeasible the known attacks against the DSA, the minimum security strength requires to make use of a generator g that generates a subgroup of 2^{160} elements from a larger group of 2^{1024}. In addition to domain parameters, the two parties should agree on a hash function, which should have at least a security strength equivalent to the one of the agreed pair (L, N).

12.4.2 DSA-Keys Generation

As in DHKE and ElGamal schemes, the private and public keys of the signer are generated using domain parameters and an approved random bit generator. However, it should be noticed that the DSA private-keys and the per-message-signature keys are picked in the range $\left[1, q-1\right]$ and not in $\left[1, p-1\right]$ as DHKE and ElGamal schemes.

12.4.3 DSA Signature Generation

DSA signature generation is an adaptation of ElGamal signature generation in which the message hash is signed instead of signing the entire message. Formally, DSA signature (r, s) of a message M is defined as follows:

$$r = \left(g^K \ mod \ p\right) mod \ q \qquad (K \text{ is the per-message-signature key})$$
$$Z = leftmost \left(\min \left(N, outlen\right), HASH(M)\right)$$
$$s = K^{-1} * \left(Z + Pr_s * r\right) mod \ q \qquad (Pr_s \text{ is the private key of the signer})$$

$\min\left(N, outlen\right)$ denotes the minimum of the N (the order of the generator) and *outlen* (the bit length of the hash function output).

If $r=0$ or $s=0$, a new value of r shall be recalculated and tried.

12.4.4 DSA Signature Verification

The intended recipient, or any other party (since the message content is not encrypted), verifies the signature to determine the authenticity of the signer. First, the verifier should receive and agree on the DSA domain parameters, the identity of the hash function, and the public key of the signer Pu_s, before any signature verification. Upon reception of a message M' and its signature (r', s'), the verification is as follows:

$$Z = leftmost\left(\min\left(N, outlen\right), HASH(M')\right)$$

$$w = s'^{-1} \ mod \ q$$

$$u_1 = Z * w \ mod \ q$$

$$u_2 = r' * w \ mod \ q$$

$$v = \left(\left(g^{u_1}\right) * \left(Pu_s^{u_2}\right) mod \ p\right) mod \ q$$

If $v = r'$ the signature is Valid. Otherwise, the message is rejected.

12.4.5 Advantages of DSA over ElGamal Signature Scheme

Both schemes are based on the discrete logarithm problem. Therefore, their security is the same. From a mathematical point of view, both schemes have the same foundations. The elements (private and per-message-signature keys) to keep secret and the way they are changed are the same in both schemes. However, the schemes mainly differ from the performance point of view. Table 12.2 summarizes the main differences between ElGamal signature and DSA.

DSA standard specifies four security strength levels (see DSA domain parameters in Section 12.4.1) and the ratio between p and q varies from $\frac{1024}{160} = 6.4$ to $\frac{3072}{256} = 12$. Thus, DSA produces signatures, which are six times smaller, resulting in less memory and less bandwidth than ElGamal scheme. In general, the calculations of modular exponentiations are the slowest parts of the cryptographic systems. DSA signature generation is at least six times faster than ElGamal signature generation. In addition, DSA verification requires two exponentiations rather than three in ElGamal scheme. Thus, DSA signature verification is faster.

The definition of the first component of the signature, r, differs. In DSA, two moduli are applied. In ElGamal scheme, the magnitude of r is at least six times the one of DSA. Therefore, in DSA, r only carries a partial information about the per-message-signature key K. Thus, deriving the per-message-signature key from intercepted signatures would be harder in DSA than in ElGamal scheme.

In DSA, the selection of the generator g fulfills a specific condition, i.e. $g^q \ mod \ p = 1$. With such a condition, some $\mathbb{Z}_p^*$ generator candidates are discarded when selecting the generator g. It is known in cryptanalysis that some attacks, such as Pohlig-Hellman attack, can efficiently compute logarithms is subgroups whose generators have some properties. Thus, by design, DSA is more resistant to attacks than ElGamal scheme.

12.5 Exercises and Problems

12.5.1 List of Exercises and Problems

Exercise 12.1
Let $p = 19$ and $q = 11$ be two primes for RSA settings. Which of the following values are valid public keys: $e_1 = 11$, $e_2 = 4$, $e_3 = 120$, $e_4 = 15311$?

Table 12.2 Differences between ElGamal and DSA schemes.

	ElGamal DS	DSA
Key size (bits)	p	q
Signature size (bits)	$2p$	$2q$
Signed object	Entire message	Message hash
r	$g^k \ mod \ p$	$\left(g^k \ mod \ p\right) mod \ q$
g	No condition	$g^q \ mod \ p = 1$

Exercise 12.2

Compute RSA public and private keys with $p = 7$ and $q = 13$. Then encrypt message $M = 10$ and decrypt the ciphertext.

Exercise 12.3

Use the Extended Euclidean algorithm to find the private key of RSA for the following scenarios:

1) $p = 13$, $q = 11$, and $e = 7$ (e is the public key)
2) $p = 7$, $q = 11$, and $e = 13$

Exercise 12.4

Let RSA parameters be: $p = 101$, $q = 113$, and $e = 6747$.

1) Find the private key d using the Extended Euclidean algorithm to compute the multiplicative inverse (see Section 3.3.1.3.2).
2) Find the plaintext associated with ciphertext 5859 using the right-to-left binary exponentiation method (see Section 3.3.2).

Exercise 12.5

Given the following RSA parameters find the plaintext using the Chinese remainder theorem:
$p = 37$, $q = 131$, private key $d = 3343$, and ciphertext $C = 1819$.
Check the result assuming that public key $e = 7$.

Hint: $6^{31} \bmod 37 \equiv 31$ and $116^{93} \bmod 131 \equiv 30$.

Exercise 12.6

1) In example 12.5, $k = 8$ is given as a discrete logarithm of 3 *mod* 11 when the generator of $\mathbb{Z}_{11}^*$ is 2. Are there any other values for k?
2) Given the cyclic group $\mathbb{Z}_{97}^*$ and $g = 5$ as a generator of $\mathbb{Z}_{97}^*$, find k such that $5^k = 35 \bmod 97$.

Exercise 12.7

Consider ElGamal's signature. Let Bob's private key be 9 and his public key parameters be $(p = 31, g = 7, Pu_B = 8)$.
Compute and verify signatures of messages $M_1 = 25$ and $M_2 = 57$ using ephemeral keys $k_1 = 11$ and $k_2 = 17$, respectively.

Problem 12.1

1) Explain why 1 and 2 cannot be used as public-key exponent values.
2) Imagine that a user sends three times his/her credit card PIN using the same public-key exponent $e = 3$ with different values of the modulus, which are pairwise coprime. For example, the public keys used are $(e = 3, n = 5*11)$, $(e = 3, n = 23*29)$, and $(e = 3, n = 41*101)$. Show that the PIN code can be recovered. Make use of the Chinese remainder theorem.

Problem 12.2

Use the following statements to prove the correctness of RSA:
• Euler's theorem (Theorem 3.4) states that if a and z are two coprime positive integers, then $a^{\phi(z)} \equiv 1 \bmod z$, where is $\phi(z)$ the Euler's totient.[16]
• If z is prime, then $\phi(z) = z - 1$.
• Given three integers x, y, and z, if $z = x * y$, then $\phi(z) = \phi(x) * \phi(y)$.

Problem 12.3

Use the Chinese remainder theorem (Theorem 3.26), Gauss's algorithm, and the following lemma to prove the correctness of RSA.
Lemma:[17] given two distinct primes p and q, $q(q^{-1} \bmod p) + p(p^{-1} \bmod q) = pq + 1$.

Problem 12.4

1) The ciphertext 75 was obtained using $n = 437$ and $e = 3$. In addition the plaintext is supposed to be a number between 3 and 10. Determine which is the valid plaintext without factoring n.
2) Suppose that you know that $516107^2 \equiv 7 \bmod n$ and $187722^2 \equiv 2^2 * 7 \bmod n$. Use this information to factor n.

Problem 12.5

Assume that a sender encrypts messages values between 2 and 9 with $e = 3$ and a very large modulus n. By mistake, he/she relies on a large value of the modulus n. Show that the plaintexts can be recovered.

Problem 12.6

The attacker sends a public key to the recipient, who accepts it as a public key of a legitimate signer. Then, he/she signs messages. How does RSA protect against this attack?

Problem 12.7

Given two messages M_1 and M_2 and their RSA signatures s_1 and s_2, show that the adversary cannot (within a reasonable computation time) forge a signed message with a content of his/her choice.

Problem 12.8

Let Bob's public key be $(5,119)$. Show how Eve can perform an existential forgery attack to send a signed message to Alice.

Problem 12.9

Textbook RSA signature scheme is a simplified design of the RSA signature. It does not use a hash function. Notice that Textbook RSA signature scheme is not used in practice to sign messages. Consider the following attack against a Textbook RSA signature scheme: given a message M and its signature s, the adversary can forge a signature s' without controlling the content of a message M', where: $s' = 2s$ and $M' = 2^e M$ (e is the public key exponent). Prove that the attacker can generate a valid signature.

Problem 12.10

In practice, we use low values for public keys to reduce the encryption time. In this problem, we discuss the impact of using low-value private keys. Assume that the right-to-left binary exponentiation method (RLBEM) is used in both operations (encryption and decryption) and the complexity time is measured in number of iterations performed by the RLBEM. Let RSA parameters be $p = 1009$ and $q = 1013$. The following pairs of keys are given: $(x = 5, \ y = 816077)$, $(x = 13, \ y = 78469)$, $(x = 17, \ y = 180017)$, $(x = 19, \ y = 805339)$, $(x = 25, \ y = 775273)$, $(x = 29, \ y = 386933)$.

1) What do you notice if x represents the public key and y the private key and vice versa?
2) Discuss how the sum of encryption and decryption times is impacted if x is the public key and y is the private key and vice versa.
3) Consider an adversary who suspects, when looking at the value of the public key and the modulus pq, that the sender is using a low-value for the private key, say $d < 100$. Given a known pair plaintext–ciphertext, how the adversary could discover the primes p and q?
4) What is minimum bit-length of the private key to make brute-force attack with known plaintext infeasible to find the private key, assuming that the adversary can perform a maximum of 2^{Ω} square-and-multiply operations?
5) Conclude regarding the use of low-value private keys.

Problem 12.11

1) Show that the product of two RSA ciphertexts is equal to the encryption of the product of the two respective plaintexts. In other words, show that RSA has a multiplicative property.
2) Assume that Bob, Alice, and Eve share a public key (e, n) and Bob owns the private key d. The ciphertexts are known to the three partners. Alice and Bob exchange plaintexts that Eve should not read. To check that Bob possesses the right private key, Eve encrypts messages, using Bob's public key, and asks Bob to decrypt them and return the plaintext. If Bob decrypts correctly the ciphertexts, Eve concludes that he owns the appropriate private key. Unfortunately, such a challenge-based authentication protocol has a weakness. Design an attack based on RSA multiplicative property, which enables Eve to disclose messages sent by Alice.
3) Numeric check: RSA parameters: $p = 101$, $q = 103$, $e = 19$, and $d = 6979$. Assume $x = 40$ and $M_{sec} = 27$ and their respective ciphertexts $C_x = 40^{19} \ mod \ 101 * 103 = 8697$ and $C_{sec} = 27^{19} \ mod \ 101 * 103 = 7408$. Check that Eve recovers the content $M_{sec} = 27$.
4) Why the multiplicative property-based attack, as designed above, cannot succeed in current RSA cryptosystems?

Problem 12.12

Assume that RSA encryption makes use of the right-to-left binary exponentiation method (RLBEM, presented in Section 3.3.2) to compute the modular exponentiation. To simplify, assume that i) the most time-consuming operation in the RLBEM is the modular multiplication and ii) $m^2 * c$ is the runtime[18] of a modular multiplication with m-bit operands, with c a constant depending on the implementation of the modular multiplication and the underlying hardware, and iii) the public key e is $2^{16} + 1$.

1) How does the encryption time increase in the modulus increase?
2) Show the increase ratio between moduli 1024 and 4092.

Problem 12.13

1) $100\,000\,007$ is a prime number. Given the cyclic group $\mathbb{Z}^*_{100\,000\,007}$ and g its generator, what is the worst time it takes to solve the DLP for a computer that calculates and compares every power of the generator g in 1 μs.

2) Let $\mathbb{Z}^*_p$ be a cyclic group with p of 90-bit length. What is the worst time it takes to solve the DLP for a computer that calculates and compares a power of g in 1 μs?

Problem 12.14

Alice and Bob agree to use prime $p=101$ as modulus to generate a shared secret key using the DHKE protocol. Compute the shared secret key in the following:

1) Generator $g=13$, $Pr_A=26$, $Pr_B=4$
2) Generator $g=13$, $Pr_A=12$, $Pr_B=17$
3) Derive a condition that the pairs of private keys (Pr_A,Pr_B) must meet to generate the same secret key under the same generator and modulus.

Problem 12.15

Why private keys used in DHKE protocol must be distinct from 1 and $p-1$, with p the modulus.

Problem 12.16

May it happen that the shared secret key generated with the DHKE protocol be equal to 1 assuming that private keys are distinct from $p-1$?

Problem 12.17

1) Given a modulus p of 2048-bit-length and a generator $g \in \mathbb{Z}^*_p$, which has an order of 2^{256}. What is the maximum value that the private keys can have in DHKE protocol?
2) What is the minimum order of a generator to provide security strength of 256 bits?
3) Assume that two elements $g_1=2$ and $g_2=2^{16}+1$ have the same order *mod* p. Which one of the generators is more secure when used in DHKE protocol?

Problem 12.18

1) Let g be an element of $\mathbb{Z}^*_p$ and p a prime. Prove that if $g=p-1$, then the order of g is 2.
2) Why it is not secure to use a generator $g=p-1$ under modulus p in DHKE protocol?

Problem 12.19

Let p be a safe prime (i.e. such that $p=2q+1$ and q is a prime).

1) Show that the order of any element of cyclic group $\mathbb{Z}^*_p$ is $1, 2, \dfrac{p-1}{2}$, or $p-1$.
2) Discuss the contribution of safe primes in terms of security strength when DHKE protocol is used.

Problem 12.20

Is the DHKE protocol, as defined in this chapter, vulnerable to man-in-the-middle attack?

Problem 12.21

Consider an ElGamal encryption system based on a pseudorandom generator (PRNG) $\pi(i)$, which returns a random integer to be used as a private key. The function $\pi(i)$ may be complex, but it depends only on parameter i and it is public. $\pi(i)$ is used as per-message key for encrypting message i, $i=1,2,3,\ldots$, $\pi(0)$ is the initialization value of the PRNG.

1) Discuss the vulnerability of ElGamal encryption regarding PRNG $\pi(i)$.
2) Suggest a method for enforcing the security even if the adversary may know the initial value (seed) of the PRNG.
3) Conclude on the role of PRNG in ElGamal cryptosystems.

Problem 12.22

Given two messages M_1 and M_2 and their ElGamal signatures (r_1, s_1) and (r_2, s_2). Show that if both messages are signed with the same per-message-signature key, i.e. $r_1=r_2$, the adversary can easily recover the private key of the signer.

Problem 12.23

Assume that an adversary forges a legitimate ElGamal signature, without controlling the content of the generated fake message as follows:

g (generator), p (modulus), and Pu_B (public key of the legitimate signer) are public parameters known to the adversary. The adversary's actions are:

i) Select two positive integers a and b such that:

$a, b < p - 2$ and $DCD(b, p - 1)$ (thus, $b^{-1} mod(p-1)$ exists).

ii) Calculate the signature components:

$r = g^a * (Pu_B)^b \ mod \ p$

$s = -r * b^{-1} mod(p-1)$

iii) Compute the (fake) message:

$M \equiv s * a \ mod(p-1)$

Notice that the message generated by the adversary depends on a and b and cannot be controlled by the adversary to include a specific content.

iv) Send $(M, (r,s))$

Prove that the recipient (Alice) verification will conclude that the signature is valid.

Problem 12.24

1) How many distinct first-components (i.e. r) of ElGamal signature can be generated for a message x given a modulus $p = 17$ and generator $g = 3$.

2) How many distinct first-components (i.e. r) of ElGamal signature can be generated for a message x given a modulus $p = 17$, a generator $g = 2$.

3) How many distinct first-components (i.e. r) of ElGamal signature can be generated for a message x given a modulus p, which is a safe prime, and g a generator of $\mathbb{Z}_p^*$.

4) How many distinct first-components (i.e. r) of ElGamal signature can be generated for a message x given a modulus p, which is a safe prime, and g an element of $\mathbb{Z}_p^*$.

Problem 12.25

Given g a generator of a subgroup of order q in the multiplicative group $\mathbb{Z}_p^*$, prove the following lemma:

Lemma 12.2 (property of DSA generator) states that: if q is a prime divisor of $p - 1$ and g is a generator of DSA subgroup in $\mathbb{Z}_p^*$, then $g^q \ mod \ p \equiv 1$.

Problem 12.26

Prove the correctness of the DSA scheme.

Problem 12.27

Bob is curious about cryptography and asks you why AES keys are of 128 bits, while those of RSA are of 2048 or even more.

12.5.2 Solutions to Exercises and Problems

Exercise 12.1

Given two primes, p and q, an RSA public key e is chosen such that $GCD(e, \varphi(p * q)) = 1$.

$p = 19$ and $q = 11 \Rightarrow \varphi(19 * 11) = 180$

$GCD(11, 180) = 1$. Hence, $e_1 = 11$ is a valid RSA public key.

$GCD(4, 180) = 4$. Hence, $e_2 = 4$ is not a valid RSA public key.

$GCD(120, 180) = 60$. Hence, $e_3 = 60$ is not a valid RSA public key.

$GCD(15311, 180) = 1$. Hence, $e_4 = 15311$ is a valid RSA public key.

Exercise 12.2

$p = 7, q = 13$

Key generation	Encryption
$n = 7 * 13 = 91$	Receive the public key $= (91, 5)$
$\phi(n) = (7-1) * (13-1) = 72$	Let $M = 10$ be the message to encrypt.
$e = 5 \qquad$ # $GCD(72, 5) = 1$	$C = 10^5 \bmod 91 = 82$
$d = 29 \qquad$ # $29 * 5 \equiv 1 \bmod 96$	*Decryption:*
Public key $= (91, 5)$	$M = 82^{29} \bmod 91 = 10$
Private key $= 29$	
Send the public key	

Exercise 12.3

Recall that given two primes p and q, the RSA private key d is the multiplicative inverse of the public exponent e. Formally:

$$e * d \equiv 1 \bmod \varphi(p * q), \text{ where } \varphi(p * q) = (p-1)(q-1)$$
$$e * d \equiv 1 \bmod \varphi(p * q) \Rightarrow \exists k \in \mathbb{N} \mid e * d = 1 + k * \varphi(p * q)$$

Thus, the following property holds:

$$(e * d) + (-k * \varphi(p * q)) = 1$$

Let $k' = -k$

By RSA design, e is coprime with $\varphi(p * q)$, i.e. $GCD(\varphi(p * q), e) = 1$. Thus, the problem to solve becomes

$$(\varphi(p * q) * k') + (e * d) = GCD(\varphi(p * q), e), \text{ where } d \text{ and } k' \text{ are the variables to find.}$$

The Extended Euclidean Algorithm (EEA) enables to solve the equation $ax + by = GCD(a, b)$. When RSA private key computation is of concern, the EEA is used to find d, the private key, and k' such that:

$$\varphi(p * q) * k' + e * d = 1$$

In this exercise, only d is of interest.

1) $p = 13$, $q = 11$, and $e = 7$

   $\varphi(p * q) = (13-1)(11-1) = 120$

   The problem to solve is $120 * k' + 7 * d = GCD(120, 7)$

   First, even if $GCD(120, 7)$ is known, the steps of EEA to find $GCD(120, 7)$ are required to find d. In this scenario, there are two steps to find $GCD(120, 7)$:

   1st step: $120 = 7 * 17 + 1$
   2nd step: $17 = 17 * 1 + 0$

   Second, to find the values of EEA variables d and k', do substitutions starting from the equality of the step whose remainder is 1.

   $$1 = 120 * 1 - 7 * 17 = 120 * 1 + 7 * (-17)$$

   Thus, $d = -17$. In modulo 120, $d = 103$.

2) $p = 7$, $q = 11$, and $e = 13$

   $\varphi(p * q) = (7-1)(11-1) = 60$

   First, the steps of EEA to find $GCD(60, 19)$ are required to find d. In this scenario, there are six steps:

   1st step: $60 = 13 * 4 + 8 \qquad 2^{nd}$ step: $13 = 8 * 1 + 5$
   3rd step: $8 = 5 * 1 + 3 \qquad 4^{th}$ step: $5 = 3 * 1 + 2$
   5th step: $3 = 2 * 1 + 1 \qquad 6^{th}$ step: $2 = 2 * 1 + 0$

   Second, to find the values of EEA variables d and k', do substitutions starting from the equality of the 5th step:

   $$1 = 3 - 2 = (5 - 2) - (2)$$
   $$= (8 - 3 - 2) - (2) = (8 - 5) - (2)$$

$$= \left(\left(60 - 13 * 4 \right) - \left(13 - 8 \right) \right) - \left(2 \right)$$

$$= \left(\left(60 - 13 * 4 \right) - \left(13 - \left(60 - 13 * 4 \right) \right) \right) - \left(2 \right)$$

$$= \left(60 * 2 - 13 * 9 \right) - \left(\left(60 - 13 * 4 \right) - 2 * \left(8 - 5 \right) \right)$$

$$= \left(60 * 2 - 13 * 9 \right) - \left(\left(60 - 13 * 4 \right) - \left(2 * \left(\left(60 - 13 * 4 \right) - \left(13 - \left(60 - 13 * 4 \right) \right) \right) \right) \right)$$

$$= 60 * 5 + 13 * \left(-23 \right)$$

Thus, $d = -23$. In modulo 60, $d = 37$.

Exercise 12.4

Let RSA parameters be $p = 101, q = 113$, and $e = 6747$.

Since RSA parameters p, q, and e are known, it is easy to find the private key d and then decrypt the ciphertext.

1) Find the secret key using the Extended Euclidean algorithm

   RSA modulus $n = 101 * 113 = 11413$ and $\varphi(n) = 100 * 112 = 11200$

   By definition of RSA private key: $d * 6747 \equiv 1 \bmod 11200$.

   The Extended Euclidean algorithm is used to find x and y such that $ax + by = \mathrm{GCD}(a, b)$.

   Let $a = 11200$ and $b = 6747$.

   By definition of RSA public key, $\mathrm{GCD}(11200, 6747) = 1$.

   Application of the Extended Euclidean algorithm:

   $11200 = 6747 * 1 + 4453$

   $6747 = 4453 * 1 + 2294$

   $4453 = 2294 * 1 + 2159$

   $2294 = 2159 * 1 + 135$

   $2159 = 135 * 15 + 134$

   $135 = 134 * 1 + 1$

   Now, do the inverse calculations to retrieve x and y such that $11200x + 6747y = 1$

   $1 = 135 - 134$

   $$= \left(2294 - 2159 \right) - \left(2159 - 15 * \left(2294 - 2159 \right) \right)$$

   $$= \left(2294 \right) - 2 * 2159 + \left(15 * \left(2294 - 2159 \right) \right)$$

   $$= 16 * \left(2294 \right) + \left(-17 \right) * \left(2159 \right)$$

   $$= 33 * \left(6747 - 4453 \right) - 17 * \left(4453 \right)$$

   $$= 11200 * \left(-50 \right) + 6747 * \left(83 \right) = 1$$

   Section 3.3.1.3.2 shows that when $\mathrm{GCD}(a,b) = ax + by$ is solved with a prime and $\mathrm{GCD}(a,b) = 1$, y represents $b^{-1} \bmod a$.

   Therefore, the secret key is $d = 83$.

2) Decryption of the ciphertext 5859 using the right-to-left exponentiation method.

   $C = 5859$

   Decryption: $M \equiv 5859^{83} \bmod 11413$

   The exponent $83 = 64 + 16 + 2 + 1 = 2^6 + 2^4 + 2^1 + 2^0$

   Thus, the right-to-left binary exponentiation runs seven iterations.

   $L = 7$, $k_6 = 1$, $k_5 = 0$, $k_4 = 0$, $k_3 = 0$, $k_2 = 0$, $k_1 = 1$, $k_0 = 1$

   $$b_0 \equiv \left(5859^1 \right)^{2^0} \bmod 11413 \equiv 5859$$

   $$b_1 \equiv \left(5859^1 \right)^{2^1} \bmod 11413 \equiv 8990$$

   $$b_2 \equiv \left(5859^0 \right)^{2^2} \bmod 11413 \equiv 1$$

   $$b_3 \equiv \left(5859^0 \right)^{2^3} \bmod 11413 \equiv 1$$

   $$b_4 \equiv \left(5859^1 \right)^{2^4} \bmod 11413 \equiv 10505$$

$$b_5 \equiv \left(5859^0\right)^{2^5} mod\ 11413 \equiv 1$$

$$b_6 \equiv \left(5859^1\right)^{2^6} mod\ 11413 \equiv 708$$

$$5859^{83}\ mod\ 11413 \equiv 5859 * 8990 * 1 * 1 * 10505 * 1 * 708\ mod\ 11413 \equiv 9192$$

Check: one can easily do computations (using a program of the right-to-left binary exponentiation method) to confirm that:

$1 \equiv 9192^{112}\ mod\ 11413$ and $5859 \equiv 9192^{27}\ mod\ 11413$

Thus, encrypting the plaintext 9192 with the public key 6747 results in

$$C \equiv 9192^{6747}\ mod\ 11413 \equiv 9192^{60*112+27}\ mod\ 11413 = 5859.$$

Exercise 12.5

Let $p = 37$, $p = 131$, $d = 3343$, and $C = 1819$.

The plaintext M is such that $M \equiv 1819^{3343}\ mod\ 37 * 131$ and by Lemma 3.2,

$M \equiv 1819^{3343}\ mod\ 37$ and $M \equiv 1819^{3343}\ mod\ 131$.

To find the plaintext M using the CRT-based RSA decryption, we proceed as follows:

- Reduce the bases of congruences:

$1819 = 37 * 49 + 6 = 131 * 13 + 116$

$C_p \equiv 1819\ mod\ 37 \equiv 6$

$C_q \equiv 1819\ mod\ 131 \equiv 116$

- Reduce the exponents:

$3343 = 92 * (37 - 1) + 31 = 25 * (131 - 1) + 93$

$d_p = 3343\ mod\ (37 - 1) = 31$

$d_q = 3343\ mod\ (131 - 1) = 93$

- Exponentiation in $\mathbb{Z}_{37}$ and $\mathbb{Z}_{131}$:

$M_p = C_p^{d_p}\ mod\ p = 6^{31}\ mod\ 37 \equiv 31$

$M_q = C_q^{d_q}\ mod\ q = 116^{93}\ mod\ 131 \equiv 30$

- CRT-based solution to decryption

$131^{-1}\ mod\ 37 \equiv 13 \qquad 37^{-1}\ mod\ 131 \equiv 85$

$M = \left(\left(31 * 131 * \left(131^{-1}\ mod\ 37\right)\right) + \left(30 * 37 * \left(37^{-1}\ mod\ 131\right)\right)\right) mod\ 37 * 131$

$M \equiv \left(\left(31 * 131 * 13\right) + \left(30 * 37 * 85\right)\right) mod\ 4847 \equiv 1733$

Check: assume that the public key $e = 7$.

$$C \equiv 1733^7\ mod\ 37 * 131 \equiv \left(\left(1733^2\right)^3 * 1733\right) mod\ (37 * 131) \equiv 1819$$

Exercise 12.6

1) Let us consider the group $\mathbb{Z}_{11}^*$ with generator 2. 8 is one of the discrete logarithms of 3, since $2^8 \equiv 3\ mod\ 11$. 18 also is a discrete logarithm of 3, since

$$2^{18}\ mod\ 11 \equiv \left(\left(2^8\ mod\ 11\right) * \left(2^8\ mod\ 11\right) * \left(2^2\ mod\ 11\right)\right) mod\ 11$$

$$\equiv (3) * (3) * (4)\ mod\ 11 = 3$$

By Fermat's little theorem (Theorem 3.5), any $m = 8 + 10k$ is a discrete logarithm of 3 $mod\ 11$, because:

$$2^{8+10k}\ mod\ 11 = \left(\left(2^8\ mod\ 11\right) * \left(2^{(11-1)k}\ mod\ 11\right)\right) mod\ 11$$

$$= (3) * (1)^k\ mod\ 11 = 3\ mod\ 11.$$

However, since $8 + 10k \notin \mathbb{Z}_{11}^*$, for $k > 0$, only 8 is a valid solution in $\mathbb{Z}_{11}^*$.

2) What is the solution to $5^k \equiv 35 \; mod \; 97$?

With the help of a python program, powers of 5 from 1 to 95 have been computed. $k = 32$ is the solution to the DLP. The result can be easily checked with the modular exponentiation[19] as follows:

$$5^2 \equiv 25 \; mod \; 97 \qquad\qquad 5^4 \equiv 25^2 \; mod \; 97 = 43$$

$$5^{16} \equiv 43^4 \; mod \; 97 = 36 \qquad\qquad 5^{32} \equiv 36^2 \; mod \; 97 = 35$$

Exercise 12.7

Bob's public key parameters are $\left(p = 31, g = 7, \; Pu_B = 8\right)$ and his private key is $Pr_B = 9$.

Compute signatures of messages $M_1 = 25$ and $M_2 = 57$ using ephemeral keys $k_1 = 11$ and $k_2 = 17$

$$r_1 = 7^{11} \, mod \; 31 = 20$$

$$s_1 = \left(25 - 9 * 20\right) * 11^{-1} mod \; 30 = \left(-155\right) * 11 \; mod \; 30 = 5$$

$$r_2 = 7^{17} \, mod \; 31 = 18$$

$$s_2 = \left(57 - 9 * 18\right) * 17^{-1} mod \; 30 = \left(57 - 9 * 18\right) * 23 \; mod \; 30 = 15$$

Verification of $M_1 = 25$ and its signature $\left(20, 5\right)$:

$$v = Pu_B^r * r^s \, mod \; p = \left(8^{20} * 20^5\right) mod \; 31 = 25$$

$$g^M \, mod \; p = 7^{25} \, mod \; 31 = 25$$

$v = g^M \, mod \; p$ is satisfied; thus, the signature is valid.

Verification of $M_2 = 57$ and its signature $\left(18, 15\right)$:

$$v = Pu_B^r * r^s \, mod \; p = \left(8^{18} * 18^{15}\right) mod \; 31 = 16$$

$$g^M \, mod \; p = 7^{57} \, mod \; 31 = 16$$

$v = g^M \, mod \; p$ is satisfied; thus, the signature is valid.

Problem 12.1

1) If $e = 1$, then the encryption becomes $C \equiv M^1 \, mod \; n = M$. Thus, with $e = 1$, the plaintext and ciphertext are identical; no confidentiality is assured.

If $e = 2$, then $d * e \equiv 1 \, mod \; \phi(n)$ becomes $2 * d \equiv 1 \, mod \; \phi(n)$. Since p and q are primes, $\phi(n)$ is divisible by 2 and consequently, there is no d such that $2*d$ and $\phi(n)$ are coprime. In other words, $GCD\left(2, \phi(n)\right) \neq 1$. Therefore, the multiplicative inverse of 2 $mod \; \phi(n)$ does not exist.

2) Let M be a message, which is encrypted three times with the same public-key exponent $e = 3$ and with three distinct moduli, which are pairwise coprime. For example, the public keys are $(e = 3, \; n_1 = 5 * 11)$, $(e = 3, \; n_2 = 23 * 29)$, and $\left(e = 3, \; n_3 = 41 * 101\right)$. The ciphertexts are as follows:

$$C_1 \equiv M^3 \, mod \; n_1 \qquad C_2 \equiv M^3 \, mod \; n_2 \qquad C_3 \equiv M^3 \, mod \; n_3$$

Let x be M^3. By substitution:

$$x \equiv C_1 \, mod \; n_1 \qquad x \equiv C_2 \, mod \; n_2 \qquad x \equiv C_3 \, mod \; n_3$$

Then, by transformation (with k_1, k_2, and k_3 positive integers):

$$x = C_1 + k_1 * n_1 \qquad x = C_2 + k_2 * n_2 \qquad x = C_3 + k_3 * n_3$$

Let us take an example with $M = 13$ and the suggested public keys. The ciphertexts are:

$$C_1 \equiv 13^3 \, mod \left(5 * 11\right) = 52 \qquad C_2 \equiv 13^3 \, mod \left(23 * 29\right) = 196$$

$$C_3 \equiv 13^3 \, mod \left(41 * 101\right) = 2197$$

The linear equation system to solve is as follows:

$$x = 52 + k_1 * \left(5 * 11\right)$$

$$x = 196 + k_2 * \left(23 * 29\right)$$

$$x = 2197 + k_3 * \left(41 * 101\right)$$

Since the moduli n_1, n_2, and n_3 are pairwise coprime, and any ciphertext is less than the modulus (i.e. $C_i < n_i, i = 1,2,3$), by the Chinese remainder theorem, there exists one and only one value of x to fulfill the equation system.

There exist multiple methods to solve linear equation systems. The solution to the problem is $k_1 = 39$, $k_2 = 3$, $k_3 = 0$. Consequently, $x = 2197$ and $\sqrt[3]{2197} = 13$. Thus, the message can be recovered from the known ciphertexts and public keys.

Problem 12.2

Let e, d, and n be the RSA public and private key and modulus, respectively.

RSA is correct if the decryption of a ciphertext $C = M^e \bmod n$ returns the original plaintext M. Formally, the following must hold:

$$\left(M^e \bmod n\right)^d \equiv M \bmod n = M, \forall M \leq n-1 \tag{a}$$

Modular arithmetic rule (see Lemma 3.1) states that:

$$a^d \bmod n \equiv \left(a \bmod n\right)^d \bmod n \tag{b}$$

Replacing a by M^e in (b) yields:

$$M^{e*d} \bmod n \equiv \left(M^e \bmod n\right)^d \bmod n \tag{c}$$

Therefore, we need to prove that $M^{e*d} \bmod n \equiv M \bmod n$.

By definition of RSA, p and q are primes and n is equal to $p*q$. By statements 2 and 3, $\phi(n) = \phi(p)*\phi(q) = (p-1)*(q-1)$. By definition of RSA public and private keys: $e*d \equiv 1 \bmod (p-1)(q-1)$.

Thus, there exists a positive integer k such that $e*d = 1 + k*(p-1)(q-1)$

By substitution:

$$M^{e*d} \bmod n \equiv M^{1+k*(p-1)(q-1)} \bmod n \equiv M * M^{k*(p-1)(q-1)} \bmod n$$

$$\equiv M * M^{k*\phi(n)} \bmod n$$

By Euler's theorem: $M * M^{k*\phi(n)} \bmod n \equiv M * 1^k \bmod n = M$

Problem 12.3

Let e, d, and n be the RSA public and private key and modulus, respectively.

RSA is correct if the decryption of a ciphertext $C = M^e \bmod n$ returns the original plaintext M. Formally, the following must hold:

$$\left(M^e \bmod n\right)^d \equiv M \bmod n = M, \forall M \leq n-1 \tag{a}$$

Modular arithmetic rule (see Lemma 3.1) states that:

$$a^d \bmod n \equiv \left(a \bmod n\right)^d \bmod n \tag{b}$$

Replacing a by M^e in (b) yields:

$$M^{e*d} \bmod n \equiv \left(M^e \bmod n\right)^d \bmod n \tag{c}$$

By definition of RSA keys: $e*d \equiv 1 \bmod (p-1)(q-1)$. Thus, there exists an integer k such that: $e*d = 1 + k(p-1)(q-1)$

By substitution: $M^{e*d} \bmod n \equiv M^{1+k(p-1)(q-1)} \bmod n$

$$\equiv M * \left(M^{(p-1)}\right)^{k(q-1)} \bmod n \equiv M * \left(M^{(q-1)}\right)^{k(p-1)} \bmod n$$

We need to prove that: $M^{e*d} \bmod n \equiv M \bmod n$

Since $M < n$ and n is a product of two primes p and q, M can have common dividers with p or with q, but not with both. Hence, three cases are to consider:

Case 1: M is coprime with p and with q.

Case 2: M is coprime with p but not with q.

Case 3: M is coprime with q but not with p.

Cases 2 and 3 are identical from the proof point of view.

1) Case 1: M is coprime with p and with q

   By Fermat's little theorem:

   $$\left(M^{(p-1)}\right)^{k(q-1)} \equiv 1 \ mod \ p$$

   $$\left(M^{(q-1)}\right)^{k(p-1)} \equiv 1 \ mod \ q$$

   Multiplying by M both congruences above yield the following congruence equation system:

   $$S = \begin{cases} M \equiv M^{e*d} \ mod \ p \\ M \equiv M^{e*d} \ mod \ q \end{cases}$$

   The Chinese theorem states that: if k integer numbers $n_i, i = 1, ..., k$ are pairwise coprime and greater than 1, and if k numbers $a_1, ..., a_k$ such that $0 \le a_i < n_i$ for every i, there exists a unique integer $0 \le x < \prod_{i=1}^{i=k} n_i$ such that $x \equiv a_i \ mod \ n_i$ for every i in $(1, ..., k)$. By Gauss's algorithm (see Section 3.3.4),

   $$x \equiv \left(\sum_{i=1}^{k}\left(a_i * N_i * N_i^{-1}\right)\right) mod \ N \tag{d}$$

   In system S, the Chinese remainder theorem parameters are as follows:

   $$k = 2, \ a_1 = a_2 = M^{e*d}, \ n_1 = p, \ n_2 = q, \text{ and } x = M.$$

   Computations in Gauss' algorithm yield:

   $$N = pq, \ N_1 = q, \ N_2 = p, \ N_1^{-1} = q^{-1} \ mod \ p, \text{ and } N_2^{-1} = p^{-1} \ mod \ q$$

   By substitution of system S parameters in equality (d):

   $$M \equiv M^{e*d} * \left(q * \left(q^{-1} \ mod \ p\right) + p * \left(p^{-1} \ mod \ q\right)\right) mod \ pq \tag{e}$$

   To fulfill congruence equation (e), the following must hold:

   $$1 \equiv \left(q * \left(q^{-1} \ mod \ p\right) + p * \left(p^{-1} \ mod \ q\right)\right) mod \ pq \tag{f}$$

   Congruence (f) is true by the lemma provided in this problem. Therefore,

   $M \equiv M^{e*d} \ mod \ pq$, which proves the correctness of RSA decryption.

2) Case 2: M is coprime with p but not with q

   Since q is a prime number, M is either 0 or a multiple of q (i.e. $M \equiv 0 \ mod \ q$). By the modular arithmetic exponentiation rule, we have:

   $$M^{e*d} \ mod \ q \equiv \left(0\right)^{e*d} mod \ q \equiv 0 \ mod \ q \equiv M \ mod \ q$$

   Since M is coprime with p, by Fermat's little theorem:

   $$M^{e*d} \ mod \ p \equiv M * \left(M^{(p-1)}\right)^{k(q-1)} mod \ p \equiv M * \left(1\right)^{k(q-1)} mod \ p = M$$

   The integer $M^{ed} - M$ is a multiple of p and q. Since p and q are primes and $n = p * q$, $M^{ed} - M$ also is a multiple of n. Therefore, $M^{ed} \equiv M \ mod \ n$, which proves the correctness of RSA decryption.

Problem 12.4

1) The ciphertext 75 was obtained using $n = 437$ and $e = 3$. Since the plaintext is supposed to be a value between 3 and 10, we have to check a maximum of eight alternatives:

   If the valid plaintext is 3, then $3^3 \ mod \ 437 \equiv 27$.

   If the valid plaintext is 4, then $4^3 \ mod \ 437 \equiv 64$.

   If the valid plaintext is 5, then $5^3 \ mod \ 437 \equiv 125$.

If the valid plaintext is 6, then $6^3 \bmod 437 \equiv 216$.
If the valid plaintext is 7, then $7^3 \bmod 437 \equiv 343$.
If the valid plaintext is 8, then $8^3 \bmod 437 \equiv 75$.
Thus, the valid plaintext is 8.

2) We know that $516107^2 \equiv 7 \bmod n$ and $187722^2 \equiv 2^2 * 7 \bmod n$. Use this information to factor n. By multiplication and substitution,

$$4 * 516107^2 \equiv 4 * 7 \bmod n$$
$$4 * 516107^2 - 2^2 * 7 \equiv 0 \bmod n$$
$$4 * 516107^2 - 187722^2 \equiv 0 \bmod n$$
$$\left(2 * 516107\right)^2 - 187722^2 \equiv 0 \bmod n$$
$$\left(2 * 516107 + 187722\right) * \left(2 * 516107 - 187722\right) \equiv 0 \bmod n$$

Thus, factorization of n is found.

Problem 12.5

Having $e = 3$, any message M is encrypted as $C \equiv M^3 \bmod n$.

If M is in the range of $[3 .. 9]$, $3^3 \le M^3 \le 9^3$ and the modulus n is large, then

$$M^3 = \left(M^3 \bmod n\right) + 0 * n$$

Given $C \equiv M^3 \bmod N$, there is a unique solution to M, if $M^3 = \left(M^3 \bmod n\right) + 0 * n$, which is $\sqrt[3]{C}$.

For example, $n = 41 * 101$ and $M = 5$ yield $C = 5^3 = 125 = 125 + 0 * n$.

Therefore, $\sqrt[3]{125} = 5$.

Problem 12.6

RSA signature scheme does not protect against stolen public keys. It assumes that a higher level mechanism (i.e. authentication) is used jointly with RSA signature.

Problem 12.7

Recall that RSA signature is the modular exponentiation of the hash of the message to sign. Given two messages M_1 and M_2 and their signatures s_1 and s_2, the adversary may start with the following computations:

$$(s_1 * s_2) \bmod n \equiv \left(H(M_1)^d * H(M_2)^d\right) \bmod n \ (d \text{ is the private key})$$

$$(s_1 * s_2) \bmod n \equiv \left(H(M_1) * H(M_2)\right)^d \bmod n$$

$(s_1 * s_2)$ could be the forged signature. To do so, the adversary must find a message M', such that $H(M') = H(M_1) * H(M_2)$. However, he/she has to find the message associated with the given hash. Such an attack is referred to as preimage attack, which is known to be computationally infeasible, because hash functions are one-way functions.

Problem 12.8

Recall that an existential forgery attack means the adversary can generate a pair composed by a message and its signature without controlling the message content.

Suppose that Bob signed two messages $M_1 = 25$ and $M_2 = 57$ and produced two signatures: $s_1 \equiv 25^d \bmod 119$ and $s_1 \equiv 57^d \bmod 119$.

Then, $(25, s_1)$ and $(57, s_2)$ are sent to Alice.

Eve intercepts $(25, s_1)$ and $(57, s_2)$ and she knows Bob's public key $(5, 119)$. Then, an existential attack may consist in sending $(25 * 57, s_1 * s_2)$ to Alice. Notice that Eve just multiplies the values she received.

Upon reception of $(25 * 57 \ s_1 * s_2)$, Alice verifies signature as follows:

$$(s_1 * s_1)^e \bmod 119 \equiv \left((25 * 57)^d\right)^e \bmod 119 \equiv 25 * 57$$

Therefore, the received forged signed message is accepted by Alice. However, notice that Eve cannot control the content of the forged message.

Problem 12.9

In case of Textbook RSA signature scheme, no hash function is used and the signature of message M is computed as follows:

$$s \equiv M^d \bmod n \qquad (d \text{ is the private key})$$

In the considered attack: $s' \equiv 2s \bmod n$ and $M' \equiv 2^e M \bmod n$

By Textbook RSA signature of message M':

$$s' \equiv (M')^d \bmod n \equiv (2^e M \bmod n)^d \bmod n$$

By modular arithmetic rule $a^k \bmod n = (a \bmod n)^k \bmod n$:

$$s' \equiv (2^e M \bmod n)^d \bmod n \equiv (2^e M)^d \bmod n \equiv 2^{e*d} M^d \bmod n$$

$$2^{e*d} \bmod n \equiv (2^e)^d \bmod n = 2 \text{ and } M^d \bmod n \equiv s$$

Hence, $s' \equiv 2*s \bmod n$.

Therefore, the adversary succeeds in forging an attack against the Textbook RSA signature.

Problem 12.10

1) x is a (very) low value compared to y. If the public key has a low value, its corresponding private key has a high value and vice versa.
2) Let M and C denote the plaintext and ciphertext respectively. Let t_{enc} denote the number of iterations of the encryption operation and t_{dec} that of the decryption operation. Recall that the right-to-left binary exponentiation method computes $a^k \bmod b$ within $\lceil log_2 k \rceil$ square-and-multiply iterations.

    If x is the public key and y the private key, then

    $$t_{enc} = \lceil log_2 x \rceil \text{ and } t_{dec} = \lceil log_2 y \rceil.$$

    If y is the public key and x the private key, then

    $$t_{enc} = \lceil log_2 y \rceil \text{ and } t_{dec} = \lceil log_2 x \rceil.$$

    Therefore, the sum of $t_{enc} + t_{dec}$ is the same, if the public and private keys are swapped.
    There is no gain in terms of the sum of RSA operation times, if we choose low values as private keys.
3) If the adversary knows the public key e and the modulus n and suspects that the private key d is less than 100, he/she tries decryption with, at most, 98 candidate private keys and produces 98 candidate plaintexts among which the known plaintext is used to validate the private key recovery. Keys 1 and 2 are not tested, because key 1 is the identity and 2 is not coprime with $\varphi(pq)$, which is even. Let D be the recovered private key. The adversary finds a candidate value matching $\varphi(pq)$ and then checks it regarding RSA parameters as follows:

    Starting from $\lambda = n - 1$, because $\varphi(pq)$ is not far from n, and until p and q are recovered, check decreasing values of λ:

- If $GCD(e * D, \lambda) \neq 1$, try the next value of λ.

- If $GCD(e * D, \lambda) = 1$, suppose that $\lambda = \varphi(pq)$. Then check:

    $$n = pq \text{ and } \lambda = (p-1)(q-1) = pq - p - q + 1 = n - p - q + 1$$

    $$\Rightarrow p = \frac{n}{q} = n - \lambda - q + 1 \Rightarrow \frac{n}{q} + q = n - \lambda + 1$$

    $$\Rightarrow q^2 - q(n - \lambda + 1) + n = 0$$

    "$n - \lambda + 1$" is a constant. If the solutions to the second-degree equation above are integers, a pair (p, q) is found. Then, check if all RSA parameters are consistent (i.e. $e * D \equiv 1 \bmod \varphi(pq)$). If not consistent, then try the next value of λ.

    Example (just the final attempts of attack are given): assume the private key $d = 13$ has been recovered using a known pair of plaintext–ciphertext. The modulus, $n = 1009 * 1013$, and public key, $e = 78469$, are known to the adversary.

    After some attempts, $\lambda = 1020096$, which meets $78469 * 13 \equiv 1 \bmod 1020096$, is found.

    Make substitutions in the second degree equation above:

    $$q^2 - q(1009 * 1013 - 102096 + 1) + 1009 * 1013$$

    $$= q^2 - 2022q + 1022117$$

    The solutions to equation are $q = 1009$ and $q = 1013$, which means that the primes are recovered.

4) Let m be the bit-length of the private key. Given a pair of plaintext–ciphertext, each tested private key $k \in \left[3, 2^m - 1\right]$ requires $\lfloor log_2\, k \rfloor$ RLBEM iterations. To test all the private keys in range $\left[3, 2^m - 1\right]$, $\sum_{i=3}^{2^m-1} \lfloor log_2\, i \rfloor = \sum_{k=3}^{m} \left(k * 2^{k-1}\right)$ $-(m-1)+3 = 2^m\,(m-1)-m$. RLBEM iterations are needed (the proof of the formula is addressed below). Therefore, to make infeasible a plaintext brute-force attack with a capacity of 2^Ω iterations, $2^m\,(m-1)-m \geq 2^\Omega$, i.e approximately $m\lceil log_2\, m \rceil \geq \Omega$.

5) As a conclusion, the use of low-value RSA private keys is insecure. Therefore, they are prohibited in RSA cryptosystems.

Proof: $\sum_{i=3}^{2^m-1} \lfloor log_2\, i \rfloor = \sum_{k=3}^{m} \left(k * 2^{k-1}\right) - (m-1)+3 = 2^m\,(m-1)-m$

i) Proof by recurrence that $\sum_{i=3}^{2^m-1} \lfloor log_2\, i \rfloor = \sum_{k=3}^{m} \left(k * 2^{k-1}\right) - (m-1)+3$:

$m = 3$: $\quad \sum_{i=3}^{8-1} \lfloor log_2\, i \rfloor = 2 + 2 + 3 + 3 + 3 = 13$

$\qquad \sum_{k=3}^{3} \left(k * 2^{k-1}\right) - (3-1)+3 = 3 * 2^{3-1} - (3-1)+3 = 13$

$m = 4$: $\quad \sum_{i=3}^{16-1} \lfloor log_2\, i \rfloor = 2 * (2) + 4 * (3) + 7 * (4) = 44$

$\qquad \sum_{k=3}^{4} \left(k * 2^{k-1}\right) - (4-1)+3 = 3 * 2^{3-1} + 4 * 2^{4-1} - (4-1)+3 = 44$

Now, assume that the equality holds for $m = n$ $(n > 3)$ and prove that the property holds for $m = n+1$:

$$\sum_{k=3}^{n+1} \left(k * 2^{k-1}\right) - \left((n+1)-1\right)+3$$

$$= \sum_{k=3}^{n} \left(k * 2^{k-1}\right) + (n+1)\left(2^n\right) - \left((n+1)-1\right)+3$$

$$= \left[\sum_{k=3}^{n} \left(k * 2^{k-1}\right) - (n-1)+3\right] + (n+1)\left(2^n\right) - 1$$

$$\sum_{i=3}^{2^{n+1}-1} \lfloor log_2\, i \rfloor = \left(\sum_{i=3}^{2^n-1} \lfloor log_2\, i \rfloor\right) + \left(\sum_{i=2^n}^{2^{n+1}-1} \lfloor log_2\, i \rfloor\right)$$

$$\sum_{i=2^n}^{2^{n+1}-1} \lfloor log_2\, i \rfloor = \lfloor log_2\, 2^n \rfloor + \sum_{i=2^n+1}^{2^{n+1}-1} \lfloor log_2\, i \rfloor = n + \sum_{i=2^n+1}^{2^{n+1}-1} \lfloor log_2\, i \rfloor \qquad (a)$$

In the sum $\sum_{i=2^n+1}^{2^{n+1}-1} \lfloor log_2\, i \rfloor$, i takes $2^n - 1$ values ranging from $2^n + 1$ to $2^{n+1} - 1$ and $\lfloor log_2\, i \rfloor = n+1$. Hence, $\sum_{i=2^n+1}^{2^{n+1}-1} \lfloor log_2\, i \rfloor = (n+1)\left(2^n - 1\right)$ and equation (a) becomes

$$\sum_{i=3}^{2^{n+1}-1} \lfloor log_2\, i \rfloor = \sum_{i=3}^{2^n-1} \lfloor log_2\, i \rfloor + \left(n + (n+1)\left(2^n - 1\right)\right)$$

$$= \left(\sum_{k=3}^{n} \left(k * 2^{k-1}\right) - (n-1)+3\right) + \left(n + (n+1)\left(2^n - 1\right)\right)$$

$$= \left(\sum_{k=3}^{n} \left(k * 2^{k-1}\right) - (n-1)+3\right) + \left((n+1)2^n - 1\right)$$

$$= \left(\sum_{k=3}^{n+1} \left(k * 2^{k-1}\right) - \left((n+1)-1\right)\right) + 3$$

Therefore, $\sum_{i=3}^{2^m-1} \lfloor log_2\, i \rfloor = \sum_{k=3}^{m} \left(k * 2^{k-1}\right) - (m-1)+3$

ii) Proof by recurrence that $\sum_{k=2}^{m} \left(k * 2^{k-1}\right) = 2^m\,(m-1)-4$

$m = 3$: $\quad \sum_{k=3}^{3} \left(k * 2^{k-1}\right) = 3 * 2^2 = 2^3\,(3-1)-4 = 12$

$$m = 4: \quad \sum_{k=3}^{4} \left(k * 2^{k-1} \right) = 3 * 2^2 + 4 * 2^3 = 2^4 (4-1) - 4 = 44$$

Now, assume that the equality holds for $m = n$ $(n > 3)$ and and equation (a) becomes $m = n+1$:

$$\sum_{k=3}^{n+1} \left(k * 2^{k-1} \right) = \sum_{k=3}^{n} \left(k * 2^{k-1} \right) + (n+1) 2^n$$

$$= \left(2^n (n-1) \right) - 4 + \left((n+1) 2^n \right) = 2^n (2n) - 4 = 2^{n+1} (n) - 4$$

Therefore, $\sum_{i=2}^{2^m - 1} \lceil \log_2 i \rceil = \sum_{k=2}^{m} \left(k * 2^{k-1} \right) = 2^m (m-1) - 4.$

Finally, $\sum_{i=3}^{2^m - 1} \lceil \log_2 i \rceil = 2^m (m-1) - m.$ $\qquad \square$

Problem 12.11

1) Let $C_1 \equiv (M_1)^e \bmod n$ and $C_2 \equiv (M_2)^e \bmod n$ be two ciphertexts.

$$C_1 * C_2 \bmod n \equiv \left((M_1^e \bmod n) * (M_2^e \bmod n) \right) \bmod n$$

$$\equiv M_1^e * M_2^e \bmod n \equiv (M_1 * M_2)^e \bmod n$$

Therefore, the product of two RSA ciphertexts is equal to the encryption of the product of the two respective plaintexts.

2) Assume that Eve has intercepted a ciphertext sent by Alice. Let be $C \equiv M_{sec}^e \bmod n$ be the ciphertext known to Eve. M_{sec} is the plaintext to recover by Eve. The attack may be designed as follows:

- Eve chooses an arbitrary plaintext $x \in \mathbb{Z}_n^*$, then computes $C_{arb} \equiv x^e * C \bmod n$
- Eve sends the ciphertext C_{arb} to Bob as a pretext to check if he owns the private key associated with the public key (e, n).
- Bob decrypts the ciphertext and obtains an arbitrary plaintext M_{arb}:

$$M_{arb} \equiv C_{arb}^d \bmod n \equiv \left(x^e * C \right)^d \bmod n$$

$$\equiv \left(x^{e*d} * C^d \right) \bmod n \equiv \left(x^{e*d} \bmod n \right) * \left(C^d \bmod n \right) \bmod n$$

$$\equiv x * M_{sec} \bmod n$$

- Bob returns the plaintext M_{arb} to Eve.
- Eve knows x and M_{arb}; thus, she can compute $M_{sec} \equiv x^{-1} * M_{arb} \bmod n$

3) Numeric check:
- Eve computes: $C_{arb} \equiv 40^{19} * 7408 \bmod 10403 \equiv 1597$
- Eve sends ciphertext 1597
- The plaintext computed by Bob is: $M_{arb} \equiv 1597^{6979} \bmod 10403 \equiv 1080$
- Eve computes:

$$M_{sec} \equiv 40^{-1} * 1080 \bmod 10403 = 3381 * 1080 \bmod 10403 = 27$$

4) The Optimal Asymmetric Encryption Padding (see Section 12.2.5) prevents the attack based on multiplicative property of RSA. Indeed, OAEP encodes each message, using padding bits, before its encryption.

Let $P(M)$ denote the OAEP-encoding of message M. Given two plaintexts M_1 and M_2, RSA with OAEP, encrypts M_1 as $C_1 = \left(P(M_1) \right)^e \bmod n$, M_2 as $C_2 = \left(P(M_2) \right)^e \bmod n$, and $M_1 * M_2$ as $C_3 = \left(P(M_1 * M_2) \right)^e \bmod n$. So, $C_1 * C_2 \bmod n \equiv \left(\left(P(M_1) \right)^e * \left(P(M_2) \right)^e \right) \bmod n \not\equiv \left(P(M_1 * M_2) \right)^e \bmod n$. Therefore, the attack cannot succeed.

Problem 12.12

1) In general, the right-to-left binary exponentiation method (RLBEM) requires $\lceil \log_2 k \rceil$ iterations to find x such that $x \equiv a^k \bmod n$, given a, k, and n. RLBEM iteration is composed of a test, two modular multiplications, and a one-bit-shift.

If only the modular multiplication matters, the encryption time is $2 * \lceil log_2 e \rceil * m^2 * c$, where m denotes the bit-length modulus n. c is a constant that depends on the underlying implementation and hardware.

If the bit-length of the modulus n multiplied by a factor of δ, the encryption time is increased by a factor of

$$\frac{2 * \lceil log_2 \left(2^{16} + 1 \right) \rceil * \left(\delta * m \right)^2 * c}{2 * \lceil log_2 \left(2^{16} + 1 \right) \rceil * m^2 * c} = \frac{17 * \left(\delta * m \right)^2}{17 * m^2} = \delta^2.$$

2) Modulus 4092 is $4 * 1024$. With $\delta = 4$, by substitution in the formula above, the ratio of the encryption time increase is $\delta^2 = 16$. It is worth noticing that increasing the security level of an RSA cryptosystem comes with a significant computation time increase.

Problem 12.13

1) $100\,000\,007$ is prime. Thus, $\mathbb{Z}^*_{100\,000\,007}$ has $100\,000\,006$ elements, which is close to 10^8. Therefore, in case of a brute-force attack, approximately 10^8 powers of the generator should be computed and tested. Consequently, the worst computation time is $1 * 10^8$ μs (i.e. 100 seconds), which is not deterrent for attackers.

2) If the length of p is 90 bits and p is prime, then $\mathbb{Z}^*_p$ has approximately 2^{90} elements. Consequently, the worst computation time is $1 * 2^{90}$ $\mu s = \left(2^{10} \right)^9$ $\mu s = 1024^9 \mu s \approx 10^{27}$ seconds!

Therefore, Brute-force attack is computationally infeasible if the group cardinality is large.

Problem 12.14
Recall that the shared secret key is computed in DHKE protocol as follows:

$$K_{AB} \equiv \left(g^{Pr_A} \right)^{Pr_B} mod \ p \equiv \left(g^{Pr_B} \right)^{Pr_A} mod \ p$$

where Pr_A, Pr_B, g, and p denote party private keys, the generator, and the modulus, respectively.

1) With $p = 101$, $g = 13$, $Pr_A = 26$, $Pr_B = 4$

$$K_{AB} \equiv \left(13^{26} \right)^4 mod \ 101 \equiv \left(13^{104} \right) mod \ 101$$
$$\equiv \left(13^{100} \right) * 13^4 \ mod \ 101$$

By Fermat's little theorem, $K_{AB} \equiv 1^{100} * 13^4 \ mod \ 101 \equiv 79$

2) With $p = 101$, $g = 13$, $Pr_A = 12$, $Pr_B = 17$

$$K_{AB} \equiv \left(13^{12} \right)^{17} mod \ 101 \equiv \left(13^{204} \right) mod \ 101$$
$$\equiv \left(13^{100*2} \right) * 13^4 \ mod \ 101$$

By Fermat's little theorem, $K_{AB} \equiv 1^{200} * 13^4 \ mod \ 101 \equiv 79$

3) Let $\left(Pr_A, Pr_B \right)$ and $\left(Pr'_A, Pr'_B \right)$ be two distinct private key pairs. Both pairs generate the same shared secret key $K_{AB} \equiv g^\alpha \ mod \ p$, with α a positive integer less than $p - 1$, if there exist two positive integers k and k' such that $Pr_A * Pr_B = k * (p - 1) + \alpha$ and $Pr'_A * Pr'_B = k' * (p - 1) + \alpha$, because, by Fermat's little theorem:

$$g^{Pr_A * Pr_B} mod \ p \equiv g^{k*(p-1)+\alpha} \ mod \ p \equiv \left(g^{p-1} \right)^k g^\alpha \ mod \ p \equiv g^\alpha \ mod \ p$$
$$g^{Pr'_A * Pr'_B} mod \ p \equiv g^{k'*(p-1)+\alpha} \ mod \ p \equiv \left(g^{p-1} \right)^{k'} * g^\alpha \ mod \ p \equiv g^\alpha \ mod \ p.$$

In questions 1 and 2, $\left(Pr_A, Pr_B \right) = \left(26, 4 \right)$ and $\left(Pr'_A, Pr'_B \right) = \left(12, 17 \right)$

$$Pr_A * Pr_B = 26 * 4 = 1 * \left(100 - 1 \right) + 4$$
$$Pr'_A * Pr'_B = 12 * 17 = 2 * \left(101 - 1 \right) + 4$$

Problem 12.15

- A private key used in DHKE protocol must be distinct from 1, because of the following:

  If one side, say Bob, picks 1 as his private key, then his public key is $Pu_B \equiv g^1 \bmod p \equiv g$.

  The other side, say Alice, picks a private key Pr_A distinct from 1, then her public key is $Pu_A \equiv g^{Pr_A} \bmod p$.

  Next, the shared secret key is computed as $K_{AB} \equiv \left(g^1\right)^{Pr_A} \equiv g^{Pr_A} \bmod p$. Therefore, the shared secret key is the same as Alice's public key, which is insecure.

- A private key used in DHKE protocol must be distinct from $p-1$, because of the following:

  If Bob picks $p-1$ as his private key, then his public key is $Pu_B \equiv g^{p-1} \bmod p \equiv 1$ (by Fermat's little theorem). Alice picks a private key Pr_A distinct from $p-1$, then her public key is $Pu_A \equiv g^{Pr_A} \bmod p$.

  Next, the shared secret key computed by Bob is $K_{BA} \equiv \left(Pu_A\right)^{p-1} \bmod p \equiv \left(g^{Pr_A}\right)^{p-1} \bmod p \equiv 1$; the shared secret key computed by Alice is $K_{AB} \equiv (1)^{Pr_A} \bmod p \equiv 1$.

  Hence, if a participant uses $p-1$ as private key, then both sides would generate a shared secret key equal to 1, which is equivalent to not using any cipher.

Problem 12.16

The shared secret key generated by the DHKE protocol is defined by:

$K_{AB} \equiv \left(g^{Pr_A}\right)^{Pr_B} \bmod p \equiv g^{Pr_A * Pr_B} \bmod p$, where Pr_A, Pr_B, g, and p denote party private keys, the generator, and the modulus, respectively.

If the private keys are chosen such that $Pr_A * Pr_B = k*(p-1)$, with k a positive integer, then $K_{AB} \equiv g^{Pr_A * Pr_B} \bmod p \equiv \left(g^{p-1}\right)^k \bmod p$.

Since g is coprime to p, by Fermat's little theorem, $K_{AB} \equiv (1)^k \bmod p = 1$.

For example, if $p = 47$, $Pr_A = 23$, and $Pr_B = 2$, then $K_{AB} \equiv g^{23*2} \bmod 47 \equiv 1$.

Problem 12.17

1) Given a group $\mathbb{Z}_p^*$, by definition of element order (see Section 3.2.1)), if an element g has an order of $\Omega(g)$, then $g^{\Omega(g)} \bmod p \equiv 1$. Hence, for any positive integers k and α, with $\alpha < \Omega(g)$, $g^{k*\Omega(g)+\alpha} \bmod p \equiv g^{\alpha} \bmod p$.

In DHKE protocol, the computation of the shared secret key K_{AB} from two private keys Pr_A and Pr_B is as follows: $K_{AB} = g^{Pr_A * Pr_B} \bmod p$.

If $Pr_A = k*\Omega(g)+\alpha$ and $Pr_B = k'*\Omega(g)+\alpha'$, with k and k', two positive integers, and α and α', two positive integers less than $\Omega(g)$, then $K_{AB} = g^{\alpha*\alpha'} \bmod p$.

Increasing a private key value by a multiple of $\Omega(g)$ does not change the resulting shared secret key. Therefore, if a generator g has an order of 2^{256}, then the maximum value that private keys can have is $2^{256}-1$.

2) In DHKE, the security strength depends on the private key value range, which in turn is limited by the order of the generator. Therefore, to provide a security strength of 256 bits to DHKE protocol, the generator should have an order of at least 2^{256}.

First, the generator used in DHKE protocol is public, thus known to the adversary. Second, to recover a private key K, one has to solve a discrete logarithm problem either "find K such that $2^K \equiv h \bmod p$" or "find K such that $\left(2^{16}+1\right)^K \equiv h \bmod p$", with known p and h. Therefore, from the security point of view, the value of the generator (excluding 1 and $p-1$) does not matter. Therefore, it is customary to select a generator g, which makes public and shared key computations easier, usually $g = 2$ or $g = 3$.

Problem 12.18

1) If $g = p-1$, then $(p-1)^k \bmod p$ is either 1 or $p-1$ for any positive integer k:

$$(p-1)^0 \equiv 1 \bmod p$$

$$(p-1)^1 \equiv p-1 \bmod p$$

$$(p-1)^2 = p^2 - 2p + 1 \equiv 1 \bmod p$$

For any $k > 2$, there exist $k_1 \geq 1$ and $k_2 \in \{0,1\}$ such that $k = 2k_1 + k_2$

Hence, $(p-1)^k \equiv \left((p-1)^2\right)^{k_1} * (p-1)^{k_2} \equiv (1)^{k_1} * (p-1)^{k_2} \; mod \; p$.

Therefore, $g = p-1$ generates only two elements; its order is 2.

2) Let $g = p-1$ be the generator used in HDKE protocol. The answer to question 1, shows that $(p-1)^k$ is either 1 or $p-1$. Therefore, the shared secret key generated by DHKE is either 1 or $p-1$ whatever are the chosen private keys. Therefore, the shared secret key is easy to recover from observing the public parameters p and g.

Problem 12.19

1) Lagrange's theorem states that if G is a group and H is a subgroup of G, then $|H|$ divides $|G|$. In addition, any element $a \in G$, with order denoted $\Omega(a)$ generates a subgroup of G; thus, $\Omega(a)$ divides $|G|$.

If p is a prime, then $\left|\mathbb{Z}_p^*\right| = p-1$. If p is a safe prime, then $p-1 = 2q$, with q prime. Hence, dividers of $p-1$ are $\{1, 2, q, p-1\}$. Therefore, any element in $\mathbb{Z}_p^*$ has an order of 1, 2, $q = \dfrac{p-1}{2}$, or $p-1$.

Element 1 generates a subgroup of a single element, which is 1 itself, because $1^k = 1$, for any positive integer k.

Element $p-1$ generates a subgroup of two elements, 1 and $p-1$, because $(p-1)^1 \equiv (p-1) mod \; p$, $(p-1)^2 = p^2 - 2p + 1 \equiv 1 \; mod \; p, ..., (p-1)^{2k} \equiv 1 \; mod \; p$ and $(p-1)^{2k+1} \equiv p-1 \; mod \; p$, for any positive integer k. Hence, the order of 1 is 1 and that of $p-1$ is 2. Therefore, any element in $\{3, 4, ..., p-2\}$ has an order of either $\dfrac{p-1}{2}$ or $p-1$, if p is a safe prime.

2) When DHKE protocol is of concern, parties agree on a generator g to compute a shared secret key. If p is a safe prime, any element g of $\mathbb{Z}_p^* - \{1, p-1)$ has an order of either $\dfrac{p-1}{2}$ or $p-1$. Hence, depending on the shown generator, either $\dfrac{p-1}{2} - 1$ or $p-2$ distinct private keys may be chosen. Therefore, a safe prime p provides a security strength of nearly $2^{log_2(p)}$.

Problem 12.20

Yes, the basic DHKE protocol, as defined in this chapter, is vulnerable to man-in-the-middle attack. Let us show a scenario: Alice and Bob cooperate to generate a shared secret key. Eve intercepts the messages sent by Alice and Bob. Then, instead of the legitimate Alice's public key, Eve makes use of her private key and sends her public key to Bob. Then, the generated shared secret key is known to Eve. Therefore, she can recover the messages sent by Bob to Alice and then either not forward them to Alice or modify them before sending them. To let Alice decrypt the messages, Eve sends her public key to Alice instead of Bob's public key. In this scenario, there are two shared secret keys, one between Bob and Eve and another between Eve and Alice. To prevent DHKE protocol from man-in-the-middle attack, a third trusted party must be used to authenticate the public keys used to generate a shared secret key.

Problem 12.21

1) If the initialization value $\pi(0)$ used by a party B and the public key of partner A are known to adversary who can intercept ciphertexts, then the adversary can easily derive the per-message keys used for encrypting the plaintexts, because she/he knows the PRNG in use. Also, if the adversary knows the kth pair ciphertext-plaintext, he/she can use k to obtain per-message keys used for plaintexts encrypted before and after the kth plaintext, because the PRNG in use is deterministic.

2) The primary technique to make a known PRNG secure when used in a cryptosystem, is to make its seed (i.e. initial value) confidential. Another technique is to randomly discard some returned results of the PRNG before using a value as a private key. For example, use in tandem two PRNGs, one is public and another is private. The second PRNG is periodically used to pick a random integer, which indicates the number of PRNG results to discard before selecting one result as a per-message key. Since the number and the positions of discarded values of the PRNG are unknown to the adversary, he/she cannot reconstruct the series of per-message keys from the construction of the public PRNG.

3) As conclusion, we can say that the security of ElGamal cryptosystem depends not only on the subgroup used to pick private keys but also on the security of the PRNG used to generate random private keys.

Problem 12.22

Let (r_1, s_1) and (r_2, s_2) be the ElGamal signatures of two messages M_1 and M_2. The public key and private keys are denoted by Pu_B and Pr_B, respectively. The per-message-signature key used to sign both messages is K_B. By definition of component r of signature:

$$r_1 = r_2 = r = g^{K_B} \; mod \; p$$

The second components in signatures are:

$$s_1 = \left(M_1 - Pr_B * r\right)K_B^{-1} \ mod \ (p-1)$$
$$s_2 = \left(M_2 - Pr_B * r\right)K_B^{-1} \ mod \ (p-1)$$

Then, by subtraction:

$$s_1 - s_2 = \left(M_1 - M_2\right)K_B^{-1} \ mod \ (p-1)$$
$$\Rightarrow K_B = \frac{M_1 - M_2}{s_1 - s_2} \ mod \ (p-1)$$

s_1, s_2, r_1, r_2, M_1, M_2, and p are public. Therefore, the per-message-signature key K_B can be derived easily. Then, the adversary makes use of the disclosed per-message-signature key and one of the components s_1 or s_2 to derive the private key Pr_B of the signer:

$$Pr_B = \frac{M_1 - \left(s_1 * K_B\right)}{r} \ mod \ (p-1).$$

Problem 12.23

Alice receives $\left(p, \ g, \ Pu_B, \ M, \ (r,s)\right)$ such that:

$$r = g^a * \left(Pu_B\right)^b \ mod \ p$$
$$s = -r * b^{-1} \ mod \ (p-1)$$
$$M \equiv s * a \ mod \ (p-1)$$

She applies the verification procedure as follows:

$$v = \left(Pu_B^r * r^s\right) mod \ p$$

By substitution:

$$v = \left(g^{Pr_B}\right)^r * \left(g^a * Pu_B^b\right)^s mod \ p$$
$$= \left(g^{Pr_B * r}\right) * \left(g^{a + Pr_B * r}\right)^s mod \ p$$
$$= g^{Pr_B * r} * \left(g^{a + Pr_B * b}\right)^{-r * b^{-1} mod \ (p-1)} mod \ p$$

Using the lemma 12.1 "$mod \ p \leftrightarrow mod \ p-1$" (introduced in correctness proof of ElGamal signature) v becomes:

$$v = g^{Pr_B * r} * \left(g^{a + Pr_B * b}\right)^{\left(-r * b^{-1}\right)} mod \ p$$
$$= g^{Pr_B * r} * \left(g^{\left(-a * r * b^{-1}\right) + \left(-Pr_B * b * r * b^{-1}\right)}\right) mod \ p$$
$$= g^{Pr_B * r} * \left(g^{\left(-a * r * b^{-1}\right) + \left(-Pr_B * r\right)}\right) mod \ p$$
$$= g^{\left(Pr_B * r - Pr_B * r\right)} * \left(g^{\left(-a * r * b^{-1}\right)}\right) mod \ p$$
$$= g^{\left(-a * r * b^{-1}\right)} mod \ p$$
$$= g^{s * a} mod \ p$$

Then, Alice tests if $v = g^M \ mod \ p$.

By construction: $M \equiv s * a \ mod \ (p-1)$.

By substitution of v and M, the test becomes:

$$g^{s * a} \ mod \ p = g^{s * a \ mod(p-1)} \ mod \ p?$$

Using Lemma 12.1 "*mod p $\leftrightarrow$ mod p $-$ 1*", the test becomes:

$$g^{s*a} \ mod \ p = g^{s*a} \ mod \ p$$

Therefore, the signature is considered valid.

Problem 12.24

1) According to ElGamal's signature design, the signer must select an ephemeral key k such that $2 \leq k \leq p-2$ and $\text{GCD}(k, p-1) = 1$. Thus, if $p = 17$, then ephemeral keys are selected from $\{3, 5, 7, 9, 11, 13, 15\}$. Compute the first-component (r) of signature for each candidate ephemeral-key, using $g = 3$:

$$r_1 = 3^3 \ mod \ 17 = 10 \qquad r_2 = 3^5 \ mod \ 17 = 5$$

$$r_3 = 3^7 \ mod \ 17 = 11 \qquad r_4 = 3^9 \ mod \ 17 = 14$$

$$r_5 = 3^{11} \ mod \ 17 = 7 \qquad r_6 = 3^{13} \ mod \ 17 = 12$$

$$r_7 = 3^{15} \ mod \ 17 = 6$$

Therefore, the number of distinct first-components of signature that can be associated with a message x, under the given parameters, is 7. Notice that the order of element 3 is 16; thus, it is a generator of the group $\mathbb{Z}_{17}^{*}$.

2) $p = 17$: as in previous case, ephemeral keys are selected from $\{3, 5, 7, 9, 11, 13, 15\}$. Compute the first-component of signature for each candidate ephemeral-key, using $g = 2$:

$$r_1 = 2^3 \ mod \ 17 = 2^{11} \ mod \ 17 = 8$$

$$r_2 = 2^5 \ mod \ 17 = 2^{13} \ mod \ 17 = 15$$

$$r_3 = 2^7 \ mod \ 17 = 2^{15} \ mod \ 17 = 9$$

$$r_4 = 2^9 \ mod \ 17 = 2$$

Therefore, the number of distinct first-components of signature that can be associated with a message x, under the given parameters, is 4. Notice that the order of element 2 is 8 (because $2^8 \ mod \ 17 = 1$). Hence, 2 is a generator of the subgroup of $\mathbb{Z}_{17}^{*}$.

3) If p is a safe prime, then the number of nonzero elements in $\mathbb{Z}_p^{*}$ is $2q$, with $p = 2q+1$ and q a prime. Any ephemeral key in $\mathbb{Z}_p^{*}$ is coprime to $p-1$, i.e. coprime to $2q$. Since q is prime, any odd element in $\mathbb{Z}_p^{*}$ is coprime to $2q$. Therefore, the number of elements that can be used as ephemeral keys is $\dfrac{p-1}{2} - 1$, "-1" is to exclude element 1, which cannot be used as ephemeral key. Since g is a generator of $\mathbb{Z}_p^{*}$, no distinct keys k_1 and k_2, with $2 < k_1 < k_2 < p-1$, could result in the same signature first-component, because $g^{k_1} \not\equiv g^{k_2} \ mod \ p$. Hence, the number of distinct first-components of signature that can be generated for the same message, under the given conditions, is $\dfrac{p-1}{2} - 1$.

4) Let p be a safe prime and g, an element of $\mathbb{Z}_p^{*}$. The order of g is denoted $\Omega(g)$. In the previous question, we considered the case when g is a generator of $\mathbb{Z}_p^{*}$. If g is not a generator of $\mathbb{Z}_p^{*}$, then $\Omega(g) < p-1$. As in previous question, the number of elements in $\mathbb{Z}_p^{*}$ that are coprime to $p-1$ and distinct from 1 is $\dfrac{p-1}{2} - 1$. However, if g is not a generator of $\mathbb{Z}_p^{*}$, any pair of elements k_1 and k_2 such that $k_2 = \Omega(g) + k_1$ results in the same first component of signature $r \equiv g^{k_1} \ mod \ p \equiv g^{k_2} \ mod \ p \equiv \left(g^{\Omega(g)}\right) * \left(g^{k_1}\right) mod \ p \equiv (1) * \left(g^{k_1}\right) mod \ p$. Hence, only odd elements of $\mathbb{Z}_p^{*}$ less than $\Omega(g)$ can result in distinct first-components. Notice that $r \equiv g^1 \ mod \ p \equiv g^{\Omega(g)+1} \ mod \ p$. Element 1 cannot be used as an ephemeral key but element $\Omega(g) + 1$ can be used. Thus, the number of distinct first components of signature that can be generated for the same message, under the given conditions, is $\left\lceil \dfrac{\Omega(g) - 1}{2} \right\rceil$.

Problem 12.25

g is a generator of a subgroup, of order q of the multiplicative group $\mathbb{Z}_p^*$ and q is a prime divisor of $p-1$. Since g is an element of $\mathbb{Z}_p^*$ of order q, by the definition of the element order (see Section 3.2.1), $g^q \bmod p \equiv 1$.

The property can also be proven otherwise as follows:

If q is a prime divisor of $p-1$, then there exists a unique positive integer i such that: $p-1 = i*q$.

Generator g can be rewritten as: $g \equiv h^i \bmod p \equiv h^{\left(\frac{p-1}{q}\right)} \bmod p$, with h a positive integer less than p. Then,

$$g^q \bmod p \equiv \left(h^{\left(\frac{p-1}{q}\right)} \bmod p\right)^q \bmod p \equiv \left(\left(h^{(1/q)}\right)^{(p-1)} \bmod p\right)^q \bmod p$$

By Little Fermat's theorem: $g^q \bmod p \equiv (1)^q \bmod p \equiv 1$. $\qquad\square$

Problem 12.26

DSA scheme is correct if the verification of a legitimate signed message accompanied with its signature results is "Valid signature".

Assume that the received data are p, g, Pub_s, M, and (r,s) generated by the legitimate signer. If M is the authentic message, then the hash computed by the verifier is Z, which is the same as the one computed by the signer. To prove DSA correctness, we make substitutions in the formulas used by the verifier as follows:

$$w = s^{-1} \bmod q = \left(K^{-1} * (Z + Pr_s * r)\right)^{-1} \bmod q$$

$$= K*(Z + Pr_s * r)^{-1} \bmod q$$

$$u_1 = Z * w \bmod q$$

$$u_2 = r * w \bmod q$$

$$v = \left(g^{u_1} * Pub_s^{u_2} \bmod p\right) \bmod q$$

$$= \left(\left(g^{Z*w \bmod q}\right) * \left(\left(g^{Pr_s}\right)^{r*w \bmod q}\right) \bmod p\right) \bmod q$$

$$= \left(g^{((Z + Pr_s * r)*w) \bmod q} \bmod p\right) \bmod q$$

Substitute w in v:

$$v = \left(g^{\left[(Z + Pr_s * r)*\left(K*(Z + Pr_s * r)^{-1}\right)\right] \bmod q} \bmod p\right) \bmod q$$

$$= \left(g^{K \bmod q} \bmod p\right) \bmod q$$

Then, we have to prove that:

$$v = \left(g^{K \bmod q} \bmod p\right) \bmod q = r = \left(g^K \bmod p\right) \bmod q$$

To do so, the following Lemma is needed:

Lemma 12.3 If p and q are two primes, such that q divides $p-1$, and a and b are two positive integers, such that $a \bmod q = b \bmod q$, then $g^a \bmod p = g^b \bmod p$.

Proof: Since $a \bmod q = b \bmod q$, a can be written as: $a = b + j*q$ (j is an integer).

$$g^a \bmod p = g^{b+j*q} \bmod p = g^b * g^{j*q} \bmod p$$

$$= \left[\left(g^b \bmod p\right) * \left(g^q \bmod p\right)^j\right] \bmod p$$

$$= \left(g^b \bmod p\right) * (1) \bmod p \qquad \text{(by Lemma 12.2)}$$

$$= g^q \bmod p = 1 \qquad\qquad\qquad\qquad\qquad\qquad\square$$

Since $K \bmod q = (K \bmod q) \bmod q$, replace in lemma 12.3 a by K and b by $K \bmod q$. Then, from lemma 12.3:

$$g^K \bmod p = g^{K \bmod q} \bmod p$$
$$v = \left(g^K \bmod p\right) \bmod q = \left(g^{K \bmod q} \bmod p\right) \bmod q$$

Then: $v = \left(g^{K \bmod q} \bmod p\right) \bmod q = r = \left(g^K \bmod p\right) \bmod q$, which means that the signature verification is correct. □

Problem 12.27

In block ciphers, the key length is chosen enough long to be resistant to brute-force attack, while in RSA, the modulus and private key have to be enough large to be resistant against factoring. Naïve brute-force attack against AES is of a complexity of 2^{128}. Using the complexity bound proven in [3], the complexity of factoring RSA-2048 modulus is of

$$\exp\left(\left(\left(\frac{64}{9}\right)^{\frac{1}{3}}\right)\left(\left(\ln 2^{2048}\right)^{\frac{1}{3}}\left(\ln \ln 2^{2048}\right)^{\frac{2}{3}}\right)\right) \approx 2^{117}$$

Both complexities result in computationally infeasible attacks. Therefore, RSA keys are much larger than AES keys.

Notes

1 The patent for the RSA algorithm (US patent n° 4405829) was issued on September 1983, exclusively licensed to RSA Security Inc. This patent expired in 2000.
2 By definition of multiplicative inverse, $d \equiv e^{-1} \bmod n$.
3 The value of M must be an integer between 0 and $n-1$, because the encryption and the description functions are *mod ulon*. In case the message to send has a value greater than $n-1$, it must be fragmented into a series of segments and each segment is encrypted separately.
4 An iteration is composed of a test, a multiplication, a division, and a squaring (see the algorithm of the right-to-left binary exponentiation method in Section 3.3.2).
5 RSA-S denotes RSA with modulus on S bits (e.g. RSA-2048 denotes RSA with modulus n, where $n < 2^{2048} - 1$).
6 The identity of a function enables to know the input and output lengths as well as the algorithm to run.
7 The US patent n° 4200770, which describes the DH agreement protocol, was assigned to Hellman, Diffie, and Merkle in 1980. This patent expired in 1997.
8 In order to make the private key unpredictable, in both parties, the generation of private keys shall use standard random number generator, which has been approved to be attack-resistant.
9 The only known attack to reveal the session key is to derive a private key by solving the DLP. Other ways of breaking DHKE are being investigated without publication of breaking success.
10 Unlike the public-key of the message sender, the public-key of the recipient does not need to change during the session to receive multiple encrypted messages.
11 k also is called *per-message secret number*. It is used to generate a public-key of the sender, which has to change for each message to encrypt.
12 K_B also is called *per-message-signature key*. The public key of the message signer may be generated once for a session, but, the key (K_B) to sign must be generated for each message.
13 $GCD\left(K_B, p-1\right)$ is the condition of existence of K_B^{-1} used the signature generation in which the computation is done $\bmod(p-1)$.
14 The US patent n° 5231668, which describes DSA, was assigned to the US department of commerce in 1993. This patent expired in 2011.
15 k is a prime divisor of an integer n, if k is a prime number and it divides n.
16 The Euler's totient function $\phi(n)$ counts the number of integers k such that $1 \le k \le n$ and $GCD(k,n) = 1$.
17 This lemma is proven in Problem 3.9.
18 In literature, other time complexity models of modular multiplication exist. For example, Karatsuba proposed an algorithm to compute modular multiplication with a complexity of $O\left(m^{\log_2(3)}\right) \approx O\left(m^{1.585}\right)$.
19 When a, n, and k are positive integers, then: $a^k \bmod n = (a \bmod n)^k \bmod n$.

References

1 Diffie, W. and Hellman, M.E. (1976). New directions in cryptography. *IEEE Transactions on Information Theory* 22 (6): 644–654.

2 Rivest, R., Shamir, A., and Adleman, L. (1978). A method for obtaining digital signatures and public-key cryptosystems. *Communications of the ACM* 21 (2): 120–126.

3 Crandall, R. and Pomerance, C. (2005). *Prime Numbers: A Computational Perspective*. Springer.

4 Bellare, M. and Rogaway, P. (1994). Optimal asymmetric encryption. In: *Workshop on the Theory and Application of Cryptographic Techniques, Advances in Cryptology*, 92–111. Perugia, Italy: Springer. LNCS 950.

5 Moriarty, K., Kaliski, B., Jonsson, J. et al. (2016). *PKCS #1: RSA Cryptography Specifications Version 2.2, RFC 8017*. Internet Engineering Task Force (IETF).

6 ANSI (1998). *Digital Signatures Using Reversible Public Key Cryptography for the Financial Services Industry (rDSA) - ANS X9.31*. American National Standard Institute.

7 Menezes, A., van Oorschot, P., and Vanstone, S. (2001). *Handbook of Applied Cryptography*. CRC Press.

8 Menezes, A., Qu, M., and Vanstone, S. (1995). Key agreement and the need for authentication. In *Workshop on Public Key Solutions*, Toronto, Canada.

9 Law, L., Menezes, A., Qu, M. et al. (2003). An efficient protocol for authenticated key agreement. *Designs, Codes and Cryptography* 28 (2): 119–134.

10 Barker, E., Chen, L., Roginsky, A. et al. (2018). *Recommendation for Pair-Wise Key-Establishment Schemes Using Discrete Logarithm Cryptography - Special Publication 800-56A (Rev. 3)*. NIST.

11 ElGamal, T. (1985). A public key cryptosystem and a signature scheme based on discrete logarithms. *IEEE Transactions on Information Theory* 31 (4): 469–472.

12 NIST (2013). *Digital Signature Standard (DSS) - FIPS PUB 186-4*. National Institute of Standards and Technology.

13

Public-Key Cryptosystems

Elliptic Curve Cryptography

13.1 Introduction

13.1.1 What Is Elliptic Curve Cryptography?

First, notice that Elliptic curves (EC) have nothing to do with ellipses. Elliptic-curve cryptography (ECC) is a high performance alternative approach to RSA for asymmetric algorithms. Elliptic curve cryptography algorithms entered wide use in 2004. After a slow start, elliptic curve-based algorithms are gaining popularity and the pace of adoption is accelerating. EC cryptosystems have been adopted by Amazon, Google, and many others to secure communications with their customers.

As shown in Table 13.1 (from RFC 5349 [1]), EC cryptosystems amply outperform RSA-based cryptosystems. The table compares the level of security (i.e. resistance to attacks) of symmetric, ECC, and RSA systems depending on the length of keys. We can conclude, at least, that: i) with a key size of $2L$ bits, ECC provides a comparable level of security to symmetric systems with a key size of L bits without the need to share the same secret key, as required by symmetric systems, and ii) ECCs with less than 255-bit keys provide comparable security level to RSA-2048 systems (i.e. RSA with the key size currently in use). RSA-2048 requires eight times bits than ECC with comparable security level. Even more significantly, RSA-512 requires 30 times bits than ECC with comparable security level.

Until 2015, the NSA (National Security Agency, US) recommended 256-bit ECC for protecting classified information up to the secret level and 384-bit for Top secret level. Since 2015, the NSA recommended 384-bit for all classified information. IETF standards have been proposed to support ECC for SSL and TLS [2–4]. In most applications such as OpenSSL and OpenSSH, the key length is 256 bits.

ECC ensures fast encryption speed with a high complexity of decryption to ensure data confidentiality and authentication. Shorter ECC encryption keys use fewer memory and CPU resources. However, the ECC comes with a drawback, which is its complexity of design. ECC uses fairly more difficult mathematical operations based on elliptic curves on finite fields, which are addressed in this chapter.

Public keys in the ECC are *elliptic curve points*, which are pairs of integer coordinates (x, y), laying on elliptic curve over a finite field F_p, while RSA public keys are integers within $\mathbb{Z}_p$.

ECC provides three groups of algorithms, which share the same foundations, the elliptic curves over finite fields:

- ECC key-agreement like EC cofactor Diffie-Hellman (see Section 13.5.3) and EC Menezes-Qu-Vanstone (see Section 13.5.4).
- ECC digital-signature algorithms like the well-known ECDSA (see Section 13.5.5) and EdDSA (see Section 13.5.6).
- ECC encryption algorithms including the ECIES and EEEC (see Section 13.5.7).

First, the foundations of ECC algorithms are addressed and then the three types of algorithms are presented.

Table 13.1 Comparable key sizes (in bits).

Symmetric	ECC	RSA
80	160–223	1024
112	224–255	2048
128	256–383	3072
192	384–511	7680
256	512+	15360

13.1.2 What Is an Elliptic Curve?

The idea of elliptic curves in cryptography was suggested independently by Neal Koblitz [5] and Victor Miller [6].

Definition 13.1: *An **elliptic curve** over a set S (real numbers, integer numbers, etc.), denoted E(S), is the set of solutions* $(x,y) \in S^2$ *to the equation:*[1]

$$y^2 + dxy + ey = x^3 + cx^2 + ax + b \tag{13.1}$$

where a,b,c,d, and e are constants.

Figure 13.1 shows some examples of shape of elliptic curves over real numbers.

The *elliptic curve cryptography* uses elliptic curves over finite fields. This means that the points on the curve are limited to integer coordinates within the field. There are two types of fields to build ECs: prime fields, denoted F_p, where p is a prime, and extension fields, denoted F_{2^m}, where the number of elements is a prime power.

ECs over prime fields and ECs over extension fields differ in their EC equations and in their operations on curve points. The former are not easy to grasp quickly; the latter are still a bit more complex, but they are recommended by the standards of public key cryptosystems like ECDSA (elliptic curve digital signature algorithm).

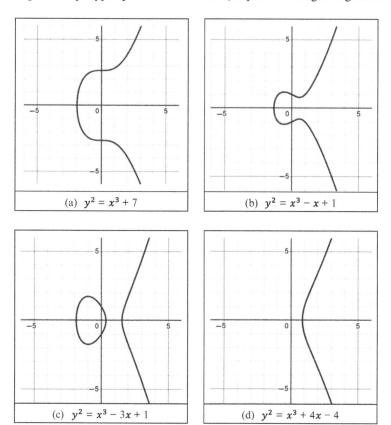

(a) $y^2 = x^3 + 7$

(b) $y^2 = x^3 - x + 1$

(c) $y^2 = x^3 - 3x + 1$

(d) $y^2 = x^3 + 4x - 4$

Figure 13.1 Examples of EC with associated equations.

13.1.3   Order and Point Set of an Elliptic Curve

Definition 13.2:   *The **order** of an EC is the number of points on the EC including a virtual point called point to infinity.*

Notations:

- An elliptic curve is denoted $E(F_p)$ in case of a prime field and $E(F_{2^m})$ in case of an extension field.
- The EC order is denoted $\#E(F_p)$ or $\#E(F_{2^m})$ depending on the field type.

The role of the point to infinity is addressed in the sequel.

> **Note.** Elliptic curves are based on finite fields. To address easily EC-based cryptosystems, the basics of finite fields are reminded with examples and exercises in Chapter 3 (see Section 3.2.2).

13.2   Elliptic Curve Cryptography over Prime Field *Fp*

13.2.1   Definition of Elliptic Curves over Prime Fields: E(F$_p$)

***Definition 13.3 Elliptic curve:*[2]** *it is denoted $E(F_p)$ and formed by the set of solutions $(x, y) \in F_p^{\,2}$ to the equation 13.2 under the condition 13.3.*

$$E : y^2 \equiv x^3 + ax + b \ mod \ p \tag{13.2}$$

$$(a, b \in F_p) \wedge (4a^3 + 27b^2 \not\equiv 0 \ mod \ p) \tag{13.3}$$

F_p is the set of positive integers: $F_p = \{0, 1, 2, ..., p-1\} = \mathbb{Z}_p$.

> **Note.** The equation $y^2 \equiv x^3 + ax + b \ mod \ p$ is called Weierstrass equation. Hence, the elliptic curves defined by the equation are called Weierstrass curves.

Point to infinity

A special point called *point at infinity*, denoted $\mathcal{O}$, is associated with any elliptic curve. It is used to tell that addition of two points cannot lead to a third point (see *vertical point addition* below). Point to infinity (also called *zero element*) is the neutral element of elliptic curve arithmetic. Adding point to infinity to any point P results in that other point, including adding point to infinity to itself: $P + \mathcal{O} = P, \mathcal{O} + \mathcal{O} = \mathcal{O}$.

   Point to infinity is an artificial point of the curve; it is introduced to fill gaps in the table for addition of points on the curve, and it acts as the group neutral element. When two points have the same x-coordinate, their addition results in a point to infinity

Example 13.1   The equation of the elliptic curve used in Bitcoin (denoted *secp256k1*) is $y^2 = x^3 + 7$. When we limit the use of the EC to F_{17}; i.e. the equation becomes: $y^2 \equiv (x^3 + 7) \ mod \ 17$. The points are shown on Figure 13.2.[3] Notice that condition 13.5 is fulfilled since: $(4 * 0^3 + 27 * 7^2) \ mod \ 17 \not\equiv 0 \ mod \ 17$.

- Point $(3, 0)$ belongs to $E(F_{17})$, because $3^3 + 7 - 0 = 34 \equiv 0 \ mod \ 17$.
- Point $(8, 3)$ belongs to $E(F_{17})$, because $8^3 + 7 - 3^2 = 510 = 17 * 30 \equiv 0 \ mod \ 17$.
- Point $(3, 3)$ does not belong to $E(F_{17})$, because $3^3 + 7 - 3^2 = 7 \equiv 7 \ mod \ 17$.

> **Notes**
>
> - The shape of the curve given by $y^2 \equiv x^3 + ax + b \ mod \ p$ over a prime field F_p differs from that of the curve $y^2 \equiv x^3 + ax + b$ (i.e. without specifying a field). For example, the shapes of the curves of the first EC in Figures 13.1 and 13.2 are distinct although they have the same equation $y^2 = x^3 + 7$. The reason is that when the field is finite, say F_p, the points of the initial curve are mapped *modulo p* on a curve where the points have integer coordinates in a square p by p. Let (x, y) be the coordinates of any point on the infinite elliptic curve. Rewrite x and y as $y = y_1 + k_1 p$ and $x = x_1 + k_2 p$, where x_1 and y_1 are two positive integers less than p. Equation 13.4 may be rewritten as $(y_1 + k_1 p)^2 \equiv (x_1 + k_2 p)^3 + a(x_1 + k_2 p) + b \ mod \,$

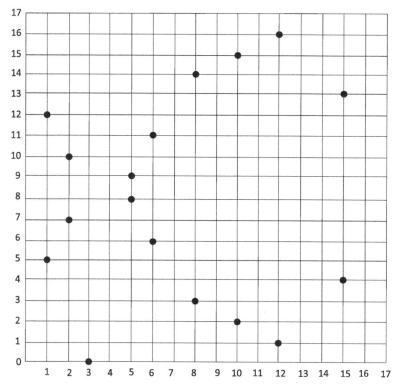

Figure 13.2 Points of elliptic curve E: $y^2 \equiv (x^3 + 7) \bmod 17$.

which can be simplified (using modular arithmetic rules) as $y_1^2 \equiv x_1^3 + ax_1 + b \bmod p$. Consequently, all the points whose coordinates differ by a multiple of the modulus p have the same image point on the EC. For example, all points of EC defined by $y^2 = x^3 + 7$ with coordinates $x = 3 + 17k$ (k is integer) and $y = 0$ are mapped to a single point with coordinates $(3,0)$ on the $EC(F_{17})$.
- The number of points on the elliptic curve over a finite field F_p is different from the number of elements in the field F_p. Since points on the curve $E(F_p)$ have their coordinates in a square p by p, the number of points may be larger than p. Exercise 13.1 shows an example of $EC(F_{23})$, which has 27 points plus the point to infinity.

13.2.2 Operations on Elliptic Curves

A single basic operation can be applied to elliptic curve points, the addition, with four forms: point addition, point doubling, point multiplication by a scalar, and vertical point addition. Note that all operations are *modulo p*.

Point addition

Let $P = (x_P, y_P)$ and $Q = (x_Q, y_Q)$ be two points, such that $x_P \neq x_Q$, on the elliptic curve $E: y^2 \equiv (x^3 + ax + b) \bmod p$. Addition of points P and Q results in a point $R = P + Q$, such that $R = (x_R, y_R)$ where:

$$x_R = \lambda^2 - x_P - x_Q \qquad y_R = \lambda(x_P - x_R) - y_P \qquad \lambda = \frac{y_Q - y_P}{x_Q - x_P}$$

Example 13.2 Figure 13.3 shows an example of point additions:

$$R_1 = P + Q; \; R_2 = P + R_1; \; R_3 = P + R_2$$

To locate point R_1 on the curve; first, a line is drawn between points P and Q. The intersection of the line PQ with the curve is the point $-R_1$. Then, the intersection of the vertical line including point $-R_1$ with the curve results in the point R_1. $-R_1$ and R_1 are symmetrical with respect to the x-axis.

Point doubling

Let $P = (x_P, y_P)$ be a point on the elliptic curve $E: y^2 \equiv (x^3 + ax + b) \bmod p$. The point doubling results in a point $R = P + P = 2P$, such that $R = (x_R, y_R)$ where:

$$x_R = \lambda^2 - 2x_P \qquad y_R = \lambda(x_P - x_R) - y_P \qquad \lambda = \frac{3x_P^2 + a}{2y_P}$$

As there is no second point to add when point doubling, to locate the point $2P$, a tangent to the curve is drawn at point P. Then, from the intersection between tangent and curve, draw a vertical line to locate the point $2P$ (see Figure 13.4).

Addition of vertical points (addition of negative point)

Equation $y^2 = x^3 + ax + b$ yields a symmetric curve. A point with the same x-coordinate has two y-coordinates. If $P = (x, y)$, its negative is denoted $-P$, and defined as $-P = -(x, y) = (x, -y)$.[4]

Addition of point P and its negative results in point to infinity: $P + (-P) = \mathcal{O}$.

Using the graphical representation of the elliptic curve, one can easily observe that when two points P and Q have the same x-coordinate, there is no other point on the line PQ that intersects with the curve, that is why their addition results in point to infinity. For example, in Figure 13.3, $R_1 + (-R_1) = \mathcal{O}$.

Point multiplication by a scalar

Let P be a point over the EC and k an integer, multiplying P by k results in a point $R = k \cdot P = P + P + \cdots + P$. Scalar multiplication is achieved by repeated addition. Notice that a direct multiplication does not exist for elliptic curves, which makes the EC-based cryptography secure (see section 13.4). Figure 13.4 shows an example of multiplication $R = 4 \cdot P$. Multiplying any EC point by 0 returns the point to infinity $\mathcal{O}$; and multiplying $\mathcal{O}$ by any positive integer k returns $\mathcal{O}$.

Note. In literature, two notations exist to denote scalar multiplication: either with a symbol "·" between the scalar and the point (e.g. $8 \cdot P$) or without the symbol (e.g. $8P$). In the sequel, the first notation is used to denote point multiplication and "*" to denote integer multiplication.

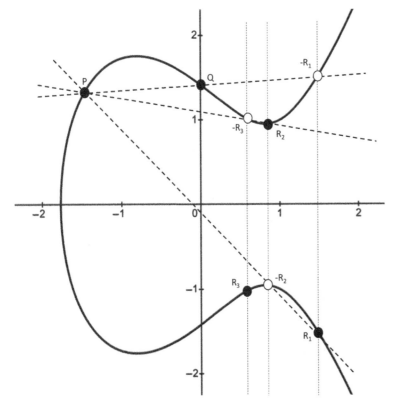

Figure 13.3 Point addition.

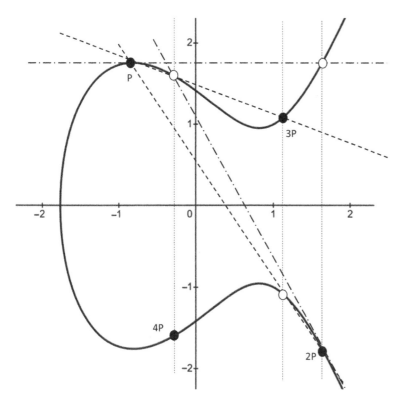

Figure 13.4 Point multiplication by a scalar.

13.2.3 Generator and Cofactor of EC

Every EC over a field F_p is a cyclic group. Consequently, there exists a point $G \in E(F_p)$, such that all the points of the EC are multiples of G.

Definition 13.4: *An element G on an elliptic curve $E(F_p)$ is a **generator** (also called **primitive element**) if and only if any point on the elliptic curve is a multiple of G. Formally:*

$$G \text{ is a generator of } E(F_p) \Rightarrow \forall P \in E(F_p), \exists k \in \mathbb{N}^* \mid k \cdot G = P.$$

In general, not any points on an elliptic curve can generate all the points of the EC. Rather, each point of an EC can generate a subset of points. In group theory, we say that the EC is a group, and the subset of points, a subgroup.

An elliptic curve is a group with N points. If N is prime, then there is only one subgroup that is the same than the entire group. If N is not a prime, then to each integer d that divides N is associated a subgroup of N/d points. For example, if N is divisible only by 2, 4, and 8, there exist subgroups with 2, 4, 8, $N/8$, $N/4$, $N/2$, and N points.

By Lagrange's theorem (Theorem 3.11), all the orders of the subgroups of a group are dividers of the order of the group. If the group order is prime, then any element of the group, with the exception of the neutral element, are generators of the group.

Definition 13.5: *The **order of a point** P on an EC, denoted ord(P), is the number of points, including the point to infinity, which can be generated starting from point P.*

Definition 13.6: *The **cofactor**, denoted h, of a point P is the ratio between the cardinality of the elliptic curve and the order of point P. Formally,* $h = \dfrac{\#E\left(F_p\right)}{ord\left(P\right)}.$

Lemma 13.1 Let E be an elliptic curve with order N and d, a prime divider of N. Then, for any point Q on the curve E, $\dfrac{N}{d} \cdot Q$ is either the point to infinity $\mathcal{O}$ or it has an order of d.

In other words, Lemma 13.1 means that taking a point Q on a curve and multiplying it by the cofactor necessarily yields a point in a subgroup of prime order d. Therefore, that Lemma is important when selecting a base point in elliptic curve cryptography. A base point is a point that can generate all points in a subgroup of the curve. The simplified procedure to select a base point is:

1) Select a prime p and the parameters of the elliptic curve
2) Compute the order of the elliptic curve, denoted $\#E(F_p)$
3) Choose n, the prime order of the curve subgroup
4) Compute the cofactor $h = \dfrac{\#E\left(F_p\right)}{n}$
5) Choose a random point Q on the curve
6) If $h \cdot Q \neq \mathcal{O}$, then Q is a basepoint (of prime order n and cofactor h). Otherwise, go to step 5 and try another point.

In cryptography, we use a base point B, which can generate a subset of n points, such that n is a prime and it divides N, the order of the curve. The cofactor of B is $h = \dfrac{N}{n}$.

If the cofactor is 1, then the used subgroup is the entire group. Any nonzero point on the curve is an elliptic curve generator and any point that satisfies the curve equation is an element of the subgroup. If the cofactor is greater than 1, then the used subgroup of order n is strictly included in the group. A point that satisfies the curve equation belongs to some subgroups and does not belong to other subgroups. Therefore, EC-based cryptographic algorithms must consider this property.

Notes

- Notice there may exist more than one generator for the same elliptic curve.
- If point P is a generator of an elliptic curve, then its cofactor is 1. EC cryptosystems with cofactor larger than 4 are more susceptible to attacks and are undesirable when the size of the subgroups is small.
- In EC-based algorithms, a base point is used to compute the public keys. To face attacks against EC-based cryptosystems, the ideal value of base-point cofactor is 1 (see Section 13.4).

13.2.4 Montgomery and Edwards Curves

Montgomery and Edwards curves are two special categories of EC [7]. Since 2019, both EC categories are recommended by the NIST for digital signature [8, 9]. Those curves are claimed to have better performance and increased side-channel resistance compared to traditional curves described in previous sections.

Definition 13.7 Edwards curve: *it is an elliptic curve over a finite field F_p, denoted $E(F_p)$, with prime p, formed by the set of solutions $(x,y) \in F_p^2$ to the equation (13.4) under the condition (13.5).*

$$E: y^2 + ax^2 = 1 + dx^2y^2 \bmod p \tag{13.4}$$

$$(d \neq 0) \wedge (d \neq a) \tag{13.5}$$

Currently, two Edwards curves exist:

1) Edwards25519 curve, with $p = 2^{255} - 19$, $a = -1$, $d = -121665/121666$, and a cofactor of 8.
2) Edwards448 curve, with $p = 2^{448} - 2^{224} - 1$, $a = 1$, $d = -39081$ and a cofactor of 4.

Definition 13.8 Montgomery curve: *it is an elliptic curve over a finite field F_p, denoted $E(F_p)$, with prime p, formed by the set of solutions $(x,y) \in F_p^2$ to the equation (13.6) under the condition (13.7).*

$$E: By^2 = x^3 + Ax^2 + x \bmod p \tag{13.6}$$

$$B(A^2 - 4) \neq 0 \tag{13.7}$$

Currently, two Montgomery curves exist:

1) Curve25519 curve, with $p = 2^{255} - 19$, $A = 486662$, $B = 1$, and a cofactor of 8.
2) Curve448 curve, with $p = 2^{448} - 2^{224} - 1$, $A = 156326$, $B = 1$, and a cofactor of 8.

The operations applicable to traditional EC are redefined to match Montgomery and Edwards EC models.

13.2.4.1 Operations on Edwards EC Points

Point addition

Let $P = (x_P, y_P)$ and $Q = (x_Q, y_Q)$ be two points on an Edwards elliptic curve. The addition of points P and Q results in a point $R = P + Q$, such that $R = (x_R, y_R)$ where:

$$x_R = \frac{x_P * y_Q + x_Q * y_P}{1 + d * x_P * x_Q * y_P * y_Q} \qquad y_R = \frac{y_P * y_Q - a * x_P * y_Q}{1 - d * x_P * x_Q * y_P * y_Q}$$

Point doubling

Let $P = (x_P, y_P)$ be a point on an Edwards elliptic curve. The point doubling results in a point $R = P + P = 2P$, such that $R = (x_R, y_R)$ where:

$$x_R = \frac{2x_P * y_P}{1 + d * x_P^2 * y_P^2} \qquad y_R = \frac{y_P^2 - a * y_P^2}{1 - d * x_P^2 * y_P^2}$$

Identity element and negative of a point

Point $(0,1)$ is the identity element, because $(x, y) + (0,1) = (x, y)$, $\forall x \in F_p$, $\forall y \in F_p$. Therefore, point is the point to infinity in the Edwards EC mo i.e. $\mathcal{O} = (0,1)$.

If $P = (x, y)$ is a point on an Edwards curve, its negative is denoted $-P$, and defined as $-P = -(x, y) = (-x, y)$.

13.2.4.2 Operations on Montgomery EC Points

Point addition

Let $P = (x_P, y_P)$ and $Q = (x_Q, y_Q)$ be two points, such that $P \neq \pm Q$, on a Montgomery elliptic curve. The addition of points P and Q results in a point $R = P + Q$, such that $R = (x_R, y_R)$ where:

$$x_R = B\lambda^2 - x_P - x_Q - A \text{ and } y_R = \lambda(x_P - x_R) - y_P, \text{ where } \lambda = \frac{y_Q - y_P}{x_Q - x_P}$$

Point doubling

Let $P = (x_P, y_P)$ be a point on a Montgomery elliptic curve, such that $P \neq -P$. The point doubling results in a point $R = P + P = 2P$, such that $R = (x_R, y_R)$, where:

$$x_R = B\lambda^2 - 2x_P - A \text{ and } y_R = \lambda(x_P - x_R) - y_P, \text{ where } \lambda = \frac{3x_P^2 + 2A * x_P + 1}{2B * y_P}$$

Identity element and negative of a point

Point to infinity $\mathcal{O}$ is the identity element; it does not appear on the Montgomery curve (the same as in the traditional ECs).

If $P = (x, y)$ is a point on a Montgomery curve, its negative is denoted $-P$, and defined as $-P = -(x, y) = (x, -y)$.

13.3 Elliptic Curve Cryptography over Extension Fields

Prime power fields, of the form F_{2^m}, also are called extension fields (or extended binary fields); their basics and useful properties of are presented in Section 3.2.4.

It is worth noticing that some cryptographic standards based on finite fields recommended the utilization of extension fields, F_{2^m}, to make computations faster. In 2013, NIST recommended fifteen elliptic curves to support signature with ECDSA among which ten are based on F_{2^m} fields [10].

13.3.1 Definition of EC over Extension Fields

ECDSA, which is the most likely standard to dominate in future cryptosystems, recommends the use of elliptic curves over extension fields [10–12]. The latter provide a foundation to more efficient cryptosystems than those provided by EC over prime fields. However, extension fields come with more complexity in calculations.

Definition 13.9: *An elliptic curve over an extension field F_{2^m}, denoted $E\left(F_{2^m}\right)$, is the set of points (x,y), which are solutions to equation (13.8) under condition (13.9):*

$$E : y^2 + xy = x^3 + ax^2 + b \tag{13.8}$$

$$\left(a, b \in F_{2^m}\right) \wedge \left(b \neq 0 \wedge \ is\_prime(m)\right) \tag{13.9}$$

Note. The elliptic curves defined by the equality (13.8) and condition (13.9) are also referred to as binary Weierstrass curves or simply by binary curves.

Examples of elliptic curves under equation (13.8) over $\mathbb{R}$ (real numbers) are shown in Figure 13.5. Notice that, unlike curves over prime fields, the curves over F_{2^m} fields are not symmetrical regarding the x-axis.

Example 13.3 Let us consider the elliptic curve $E : y^2 + xy = x^3 + 1$ over F_{2^2} with reduction polynomial $f(x) = x^2 + x + 1$, which is irreducible in F_2.

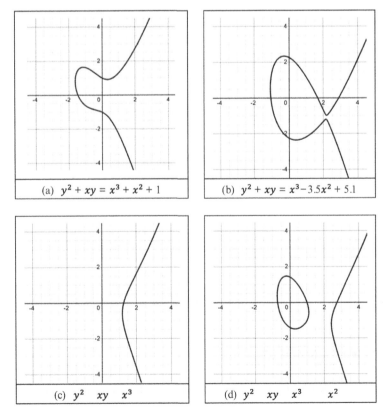

(a) $y^2 + xy = x^3 + x^2 + 1$

(b) $y^2 + xy = x^3 - 3.5x^2 + 5.1$

(c) $y^2 \quad xy \quad x^3$

(d) $y^2 \quad xy \quad x^3 \quad x^2$

Figure 13.5 Examples of EC over real numbers with associated equations.

– Check that $g = x$ is a generator of the group F_{2^2}

$$g^0 \ mod \ f(x) = x^0 \ mod \ f(x) = 1 = (01) = 1$$
$$g^1 \ mod \ f(x) = x^1 \ mod \ f(x) = x = (10) = 2$$
$$g^2 \ mod \ f(x) = x^2 \ mod \ f(x) = x + 1 = (11) = 3$$
$$g^3 \ mod \ f(x) = x^3 \ mod \ f(x) = g^0 \ mod \ f(x)$$
$$g^4 \ mod \ f(x) = x^4 \ mod \ f(x) = g^1 \ mod \ f(x)$$
$$g^5 \ mod \ f(x) = x^5 \ mod \ f(x) = g^2 \ mod \ f(x)$$
$$g^6 \ mod \ f(x) = x^6 \ mod \ f(x) = g^0 \ mod \ f(x)$$

The field F_{2^2} has four elements, i.e. $F_{2^2} = \{(00), (01), (10), (11)\}$

– Find EC points over F_{2^2}. Given that the number of points (x, y) to test is low, $|F_{2^2}| * |F_{2^2}| = 4 * 4$, one naïve method is to check every couple regarding the EC equation. Let us list every point and check if equation (13.8) is satisfied. In Table 13.2, rows in gray denote points on the curve.

13.3.1.1 Operations on Points of Curve $E\left(F_{2^m}\right)$

Rules for point operations are defined for elliptic curves over F_{2^m}. The formulas differ from the ones defined for curves over prime fields (F_p), because the EC equations differ (see equations 13.2, 13.4, 13.6, 13.8).

> **Note.** Operations on EC points, over an extension field F_{2^m}, are done modulo the irreducible polynomial selected for the field F_{2^m}.

Point addition

Let $P = (x_P, y_P)$ and $Q = (x_Q, y_Q)$ be two points, with distinct x-coordinates (i.e. $x_P \neq x_Q$), on the elliptic curve $E: y^2 + xy = x^3 + ax^2 + b$. The addition results in a point $R = P + Q$, such that $R = (x_R, y_R)$ where:

$$x_R = \lambda^2 + \lambda + x_P + x_Q + a \qquad y_R = \lambda(x_P + x_R) + x_R + y_P \qquad \lambda = \frac{y_Q + y_P}{x_Q + x_P}$$

Table 13.2 Example of EC point computation.

x	y	$y^2 + xy$	$x^3 + 1$
(00)	(00)	$(00)^2 + (00)^2 = (00)$	$0^3 + 1 = (01)$
(00)	$(01) = g^0$	$\left(g^0\right)^2 + 0 = (01)$	$0^3 + 1 = (01)$
(00)	$(10) = g^1$	$\left(g^1\right)^2 + 0 = (11)$	$0^3 + 1 = (01)$
(00)	$(11) = g^2$	$\left(g^2\right)^2 + 0 = (10)$	$0^3 + 1 = (01)$
$(01) = g^0$	(00)	$(00)^2 + (00)(01) = (00)$	$g^{0*3} + 1 = 1 + 1 = (00)$
$(01) = g^0$	$(01) = g^0$	$\left(g^0\right)^2 + \left(g^0\right)^2 = (00)$	$g^{0*3} + 1 = 1 + 1 = (00)$
$(01) = g^0$	$(10) = g^1$	$\left(g^1\right)^2 + g^0 g^1 = (01)$	$g^{0*3} + 1 = 1 + 1 = (00)$
$(01) = g^0$	$(11) = g^2$	$\left(g^2\right)^2 + g^0 g^2 = (01 \quad)$	$g^{0*3} + 1 = 1 + 1 = (00)$
$(10) = g^1$	(00)	$(00)^2 + (00)g^1 = (00)$	$g^{1*3} + 1 = g^0 + 1 = (00)$
$(10) = g^1$	$(01) = g^0$	$\left(g^0\right)^2 + g^1 g^0 = (11)$	$g^{1*3} + 1 = g^0 + 1 = (00)$
$(10) = g^1$	$(10) = g^1$	$\left(g^1\right)^2 + g^1 g^1 = (00)$	$g^{1*3} + 1 = g^0 + 1 = (00)$
$(10) = g^1$	$(11) = g^2$	$\left(g^2\right)^2 + g^1 g^2 = (11)$	$g^{1*3} + 1 = g^0 + 1 = (00)$
$(11) = g^2$	(00)	$(00)^2 + g^2 (00) = (00)$	$g^{2*3} + 1 = g^0 + 1 = (00)$
$(11) = g^2$	$(01) = g^0$	$\left(g^0\right)^2 + g^2 g^0 = (10)$	$g^{2*3} + 1 = g^0 + 1 = (00)$
$(11) = g^2$	$(10) = g^1$	$\left(g^1\right)^2 + g^2 g^1 = (10)$	$g^{2*3} + 1 = g^0 + 1 = (00)$
$(11) = g^2$	$(11) = g^2$	$\left(g^2\right)^2 + g^2 g^2 = (00)$	$g^{2*3} + 1 = g^0 + 1 = (00)$

Point doubling

Let $P = (x_P, y_P)$ be a point on the elliptic curve $E: y^2 + xy = x^3 + ax^2 + b$. Point doubling results in a point $R = P + P = 2 \cdot P$, such that $R = (x_R, y_R)$ where:

$$x_R = \lambda^2 + \lambda + a \qquad y_R = x_P{}^2 + (+1)x_R \qquad \lambda = x_P + \frac{y_P}{x_P}$$

Addition of vertical points (addition of negative point)

Under the equation $y^2 + xy = x^3 + ax^2 + b$, the negative of point P is denoted $-P$, and defined as $-P = -(x, y) = (x, x + y)$. As for EC over prime fields, addition of point P and its negative results in point to infinity: $P + (-P) = \mathcal{O}$.

Point multiplication by a scalar

Let P be a point over the EC and k a scalar, multiplying P by k results in a point $R = k \cdot P = P + P + \cdots + P$ (k times). As for EC over prime fields, scalar multiplication of points of $E(F_{2^m})$ is achieved by repeated addition. Multiplying an EC point by 0 returns the point to infinity $\mathcal{O}$ and multiplying point to infinity by a scalar returns the point to infinity. That is:
$\forall P \in E(F_{2^m}), 0 \cdot P = \mathcal{O}$, and $k \cdot \mathcal{O} = \mathcal{O}$ for every integer k.

Example 13.4   Consider again the curve $E(F_{2^2})$ with equation $y^2 + xy = x^3 + 1$ (parameter a of the equation is equal to 0) over the field F_{2^2} with reduction polynomial $f(x) = x^2 + x + 1$ and generator $g = x$. Points of $E(F_{2^2})$ are:

$$E(F_{2^2}) = \{(0,1), (1,0), (1,1), (2,0), (2,2), (3,0), (3,3)\} \cup \{\mathcal{O}\}$$

The order of $E(F_{2^2})$ is 8 and the four points $(2,0), (2,2), (3,0)$, and $(3,3)$ are generators of $E(F_{2^2})$.

13.3.1.2 Fast Scalar Multiplication

Multiplication of a point P by a scalar k is defined by repeated point addition. There is no direct multiplication by a scalar as for real or integer numbers. In the previous subsections, a naïve method to calculate $k \cdot P$ is used: apply one point doubling operation followed by $k - 1$ point additions. Such a method is time consuming, especially when k is a large value, which is used in practice to secure communications (k is of order 2^{256} in current EC implementations). To optimize the computation time of scalar multiplication, fast methods have been proposed taking advantage of the associativity property of cyclic groups. For example:

$$23 \cdot P = P + 22 \cdot P = P + 2(11) \cdot P = P + 2\big(1 + 2\big(1 + 2(2 \cdot P)\big)\big)$$

To calculate $23 \cdot P$, four point doublings and three point additions are required instead of one point doubling followed by 22 point additions under the naïve method. Among the proposed algorithms for fast scalar multiplication in EC cryptosystems, two algorithms are presented below: *left-to-right binary method for point multiplication* and *recursive method for point multiplication*. Many other variations of fast scalar multiplication of EC points do exist [13]. The first point multiplication method is based on the binary representation of the scalar k; its pseudocode is as follows:

```
function Left_to_right_binary_point_multiplication
    input k,P: positive integer and EC point
    output Q: EC point
    1. Let k_{r-1}...k_1k_0 be the binary representation of k, (k_{r-1} = 1)
    2. Q = O
    3. for i = r−1 down to 0 do
          Q = 2 · Q
          if k_i = 1 then Q = Q + P
    4. return Q
```

The pseudocode of the recursive method is as follows:

```
function RPM   # recursive method for point multiplication
          input k,P: positive integer and an EC point
          output Q: EC point
          1. if k = 0 then return (𝒪)  # no point to compute
          2. else if k = 1 then return (P)
              2.1 else if k mod 2 = 1 then
                  return (P + PRM(P, k − 1))  # addition when k is odd
              2.2 else return (2 · RPM(P, k/2))  # doubling when k is even
```

13.3.2   Set and Number of Points of an EC

13.3.2.1   Finding the Set of Points on an EC

Given the EC equation parameters (i.e. a and b) and the cardinality of the field (i.e. p or 2^m), finding the set of all points on an elliptic curve in case of low values of p or m is not a hard problem. One naïve approach is to test every couple of integers (x,y) regarding the EC equation. That is, p^2 or 2^{2m} (x,y)-couples have to be tested and if the equations verified for a given couple, the latter is a point on the EC. However, when the value of p or m is large (the magnitude of p and 2^m is 2^{256} for standard-based cryptosystems), calculation of all points becomes complex. Luckily, EC-based public key protocols do not require to know all the EC points; rather they need to select one random point, called *base point*, on the elliptic curve. EC-based cryptosystems include functions that return a random point on an EC given the EC equation parameters and field cardinality. The examples of sets of EC points given in this chapter are used only for educational purpose.

13.3.2.2   Finding the Exact Number of Points on an EC

Given the EC equation parameters (i.e. a and b) and the field cardinality q (q is either a prime p or a power prime 2^m), finding the exact number of points on an elliptic curve is a hard problem (in term of complexity) in the general case. Many methods to approximate the exact number of points on an EC have been proposed in the literature. Hasse's theorem is the most commonly used way to know the lower and upper bounds of the number of EC points, given the cardinality of the finite field F_q. It states the following:

Theorem 13.1   Hasse's theorem: Let E be an elliptic curve over a finite field F_q, then:

$$\left| \#E\left(F_q\right) - q - 1 \right| \leq 2\sqrt{q}$$

(13.10)

Hasse's theorem tells us that $\#E\left(F_q\right)$ is in the interval $\left[q + 1 - 2\sqrt{q}, \ q + 1 + 2\sqrt{q}\right]$. $\#E\left(F_q\right)$ is roughly equal to the size of F_q. In case of prime fields only, Theorem 13.2 gives the exact number of points of an elliptic curve over a prime field.

Theorem 13.2   Let p be a prime and E an elliptic curve over a finite field F_p, then:

$$\#E\left(F_p\right) = p + 1 + \sum_{x \in F_p} \left(\frac{x^3 + ax + b}{p} \right)$$

(13.11)

where $\left(\dfrac{x^3 + ax + b}{p} \right)$ denotes Legendre symbol (see Section 3.1.7.1), which is equal to 1 if there exists $y \in F_p$ such that $y^2 = x^3 + ax + b \ mod \ p$ and -1, otherwise, with one exception, if $x^3 + ax + b \equiv 0 \ mod \ p$, Legendre symbol is equal to 0.

The idea of Theorem 13.2 is to consider $u = \left(x^3 + ax + b\right) \ mod \ p$ for each $x \in F_p$ and check if u is a square residue (i.e. there exists $v \in F_p$ such that $v^2 \equiv u \ mod \ p$). Therefore, Theorem 13.2 comes with a high cost to compute the number of points.

13.4   Security of EC Cryptosystems

Breaking an EC cryptosystem is equivalent to solving the computational problem known as elliptic curve discrete logarithm problem, which is stated as follows:

> **Elliptic curve discrete logarithm problem** (ECDLP): given two points p and Q on an elliptic curve over a finite field F_q, find an integer k, if it exists, such that $Q = k \cdot P$

In regular algebra, when a product $A * B$ is given and A is known, inferring B is easy. In EC, point $Q = k \cdot P$ is equal to the addition of point $(k-1) \cdot P$ to point P. Therefore, to use a point $Q = k \cdot P$, point $(k-1) \cdot P$ must be calculated, and so on until $2 \cdot P$. Multiplication of an EC point by a scalar k is performed through repeated addition:

$$k \cdot P = Q_k \mid Q_j = Q_{j-1} + P, \quad (2 < j \le k), \ Q_1 = P$$

In addition, since ECs are cyclic groups, if the order of P is n, the following holds:

$$(d * n + k) \cdot P = k \cdot P = Q, \forall d \in \mathbb{N}, k \in \mathbb{N}, k < n$$

Therefore, the attacker should not only find and exploit a single value of k, but a set of values modulo n. To deduce which value of k matches the product $k \cdot P$ and recover the private key k, one needs to calculate all multiples modulo n of the given point P.

To intuitively understand the complexity of inferring k from $k \cdot P$, let us make the analogy with points on a circle. From a point P on the circle move left or right, with a given angle, to a new point P', then repeat the moving on the circle until a point Q is reached, then, from point Q, make a large number d of rotations (each rotation is a series of shifting on the circle) over the circle and then stop. Determining the exact number of shifting, given the start point P and finish point Q, is computationally intractable if the variation of shifting angle and the number of rotations are large.

Consequently, "inferring k given $k \cdot P$" problem becomes computationally infeasible to break operational EC cryptosystems where the bit-length of the order of the chosen base point P and that of the field cardinality are of 256 or more.

At the time of writing this chapter, the last known breaking of EC cryptosystem was made by mathematicians in 2004. A message encrypted with an elliptic curve key algorithm using a 109-bit long key was broken. The effort required 2600 computers and took 17 months.

Table 13.3, from [14], illustrates the computing power needed to solve the EC discrete logarithm problem, with the most efficient method known at the time of writing this chapter, depending on the size of the underlying finite field.

Note. To not jeopardize the security of EC cryptosystems (i.e. to make the key discovery attacks computationally infeasible), the cofactor of the base point G, which is used as parameter in ECC-based algorithms, should be as small as possible, i.e. close to 1. Recall that the cofactor is $h = \dfrac{\#E(F_p)}{ord(G)}$, where $\#E(F_p)$ is that cardinality of the EC and $ord(G)$ is the number of points generated starting from p. If $h = 1$, then the selected base point is a generator of the EC, and consequently all the points of the curve may be used to generate public keys, thus making the space of search too wide, which prevents attacks.

Table 13.3   Computing power required to solve the EC discrete logarithm problem.

Bit-length of the order of base point	Computing power needed (in MIPS years)
162	1.1×10^{12}
224	2.3×10^{21}
256	1.5×10^{26}
384	2.9×10^{45}
521	8.4×10^{65}

(1 MIPS year = the amount of work performed, in one year, by a computer operating at the rate of one million instructions per second).

13.5   Elliptic Curve-based Algorithms

The elliptic curve-based algorithms used in cryptosystems are categorized as key-agreement, message signature, and message encryption algorithms. First, the common features are presented, then how ECs is used for each category of algorithms is addressed.

13.5.1   Security Strength Levels of EC Algorithms

The level of security is measured in bits. It represents the capacity of the EC algorithms to resist to attacks. Each extra bit of security doubles the amount of computation needed by an attacker to compromise security. ECC standards specify four security strength levels and the requirements regarding the parameter n (the order of the base point G):

- Security strength 112: $2^{223} < n < 2^{256}$
- Security strength 128: $2^{255} < n < 2^{384}$
- Security strength 192: $2^{383} < n < 2^{512}$
- Security strength 256: $2^{511} < n$

13.5.2   Domain Parameters

All EC-based algorithms require the selection of domain parameters. Domain parameters are public information exchanged via an insecure network. They are:

- q: the order (or cardinality) of the underlying field F_q. q is either a prime p or a prime power 2^m (with prime m).
- FR: field representation, if $q = 2^m$ (i.e. the underlying field is an extension field). FR includes the degree and coefficients of the reduction polynomial $f(x)$ associated with the field F_{2^m}.
- a and b: coefficients of elliptic curve equation. Both are elements of F_q. There are four EC equations:
  - Basic curves over prime fields: $y^2 = x^3 + ax + b \ mod \ p$.
  - Edwards curves: $y^2 + ax^2 = 1 + dx^2 y^2 \ mod \ p$.
  - Montgomery curves: $By^2 = x^3 + Ax^2 + x \ mod \ p$.
  - Basic curves over extension fields: $y^2 + xy = x^3 + ax^2 + b$.
- (x_G, y_G): coordinates of the base point G.
- n: order of base point G (the order of G is the number of points generated by G). It is the smallest prime number n such that: $n \cdot G = \mathcal{O}$).
- h: the cofactor associated with the base point: $h = \dfrac{|E(Fp)|}{n}$

ANSI and IETF standards provide approved guidelines to select all domain parameters and to verify their validity regarding the required level of security strength [2–4, 7, 14]. It is worth noticing that the parameters selection is of paramount importance to comply with the needed level of security strength. It is highly recommended for EC-based algorithms implementers to use the standard domain parameters.

13.5.3   EC Diffie–Hellman (ECDH) Key-Agreement Protocol

One of the most important variation of the original Diffie-Hellman scheme [15], which is presented in Section 12.3.2, is its combination with elliptic curves over finite fields to provide powerful protocol, the ECDH, to share public keys. ECDH (Elliptic Curve Diffie-Hellman) protocol is recommended as a standard for key-agreement protocol by NIST. The readers interested in detail regarding the protocol may refer to the ANSI standard X9-63 [16]. In sequel, only the principle of the ECDH is described.

ECDH is a key-agreement protocol that enables two parties to generate a shared secret, while using an elliptic curve. The execution of ECDH protocol by two parties, Alice and Bob, is as illustrated by Figure 13.6.

Proof of ECDH correctness:

Bob computes: $S_B = Pr_B \cdot A = ((Pr_B * P_A) \ mod \ n) \cdot G$.
Alice computes: $S_A = Pr_A \cdot B = ((Pr_A * Pr_B) \ mod \ n) \cdot G$.
Since multiplication is commutative over integers, $S_B = S_A$. Thus, both parties compute the same shared secret. Notice that the modulus in the equations above is n (the order of base point G) and not q, the modulus of the field F_q.   □

Bob	Alice
Domain parameters (q, a, b, FR, G, n, and h) are sent by either Bob or Alice and are public.	

• Pick a private key Pr_B, an integer such that $1 \le Pr_B \le n-1$ (5)
 • Compute a point B: $B = Pr_B \cdot G$
  B is the public key of Bob
 • Send (x_B, y_B), the coordinates of point B, to Alice
	• Pick a private key Pr_A, an integer such that $1 \le Pr_A \le n-1$
	 • Compute a point A: $A = Pr_A \cdot G$
	  A is the public key of Alice
	 • Send (x_A, y_A), the coordinates of point A, to Bob

Coordinates of points A and B are public.	
• Receive coordinates of point A • Compute a point S_B on the curve: $S_B = Pr_B \cdot A$	• Receive coordinates of point B • Compute a point S_A on the curve: $S_A = Pr_A \cdot B$
Alice and Bob have computed the same point $S = S_A = S_B = (x_S, y_S)$ Their shared secret is x_S, the x-coordinate of point S.	

Figure 13.6 Elliptic-Curve Diffie-Hellman key-agreement.

The shared information may be used as a symmetric key to encrypt messages exchanged between Alice and Bob.

Note. The shared secret is the x-coordinate of point S. The y-coordinate (y_S) is not a second secret, because if x_S is known, y_S is calculated using the EC equation whose parameters (a and b) are public.

Example 13.5 Let us consider the elliptic curve $E : y^2 = (x^3 + 2x + 2) \, mod \, 17$.
– Check that F_{17} is a prime field:
  ○ 17 is a prime number.
  ○ $F_{17} = \{0, 1, 2, 3, 4, 5, 6, 7, 8, 9, 10, 11, 12, 13, 14, 15, 16\}$
  ○ 0 is the neutral element for addition and each element in F_{17} has an additive inverse in F_{17}: $0 + 0 \equiv 0 \, mod \, 17$, $1 + 16 \equiv 0 \, mod \, 17$
  ○ $2 + 15 \equiv 0 \, mod \, 17$, ..., $16 + 1 \equiv 0 \, mod \, 17$
  ○ 1 is the neutral element for multiplication and each nonzero element in F_{17} has a multiplicative inverse in F_{17}:
  ○ $1^{-1} = 1$; $2^{-1} = 9$, because $2 * 9 \equiv 1 \, mod \, 17$, ...
  ○ $16^{-1} = 16$, because $16 * 16 = 255 \equiv 1 \, mod \, 17$
  ○ F_{17} is a cyclic group for addition and for multiplication operations.
  ○ F_{17} is a prime field.
– Calculate points of the EC over F_{17}:
  Points (x, y), on the elliptic curve $E : y^2 = (x^3 + 2x + 2) \, mod \, 17$ are the following[6]:

$$E(F_{17}) = \{(0, 6), (0, 11), (3, 1), (3, 16), (5, 1), (5, 16), (6, 3), (6, 14), (7, 6), (7, 11), (9, 1), (9, 16),$$
$$(10, 6), (10, 11), (13, 7), (13, 10), (16, 4), (16, 13)\} \cup \{\mathcal{O}\}$$

– Select a base point G
  It is recommended to select the point with the highest order. In this example, all points have the same order equal to 19. The check has been done with an ad hoc program. Below are the scalar multiplications for point $G = (7,6)$. As you may notice point G can generate all points of $E(F_{17})$:

$$
\begin{array}{llll}
G = (\mathbf{7, 6}) & 2 \cdot G = (5,16) & 3 \cdot G = (13,7) & 4 \cdot G = (6,14) \\
5 \cdot G = (0,6) & 6 \cdot G = (10,11) & 7 \cdot G = (16,13) & 8 \cdot G = (3,16) \\
9 \cdot G = (9,16) & 10 \cdot G = (9,1) & 11 \cdot G = (3,1) & 12 \cdot G = (16,4) \\
13 \cdot G = (10,6) & 14 \cdot G = (0,11) & 15 \cdot G = (6,3) & 16 \cdot G = (13,10) \\
17 \cdot G = (5,1) & 18 \cdot G = (7,11) & 19 \cdot G = \mathcal{O}
\end{array}
$$

$$ord((7,6)) = 19 \text{ and } cofactor((7,6)) = \frac{|E(F_{17})|}{ord((7,6))} = \frac{19}{19} = 1.$$

- As the domain parameters (p, a, b, n, G) are public, it does not matter who computes and sends them – Alice or Bob. We assume that Bob computes and sends the domain parameters to Alice who accepts them. That is: $p = 17$, $a = 2$, $b = 2$, $n = 19$, $G = (7,6)$.
- Bob picks 9 as a private key ($K_{Bob} = 9$). He computes point $B = 9 \cdot G = (9, 16)$ and sends it to Alice.
- Alice picks 13 as a private key ($K_{Alice} = 13$). She computes point $A = 13 \cdot G = (10, 6)$ and sends it to Alice.
- Bob receives Alice's point A and calculates point $K_{Bob} \cdot A = 9 \cdot A = 9 \cdot (10,6) = (13,7)$
- Alice receives Bob's point B and calculates point $K_{Alice} \cdot B = 13 \cdot B = 13 \cdot (9,16) = (13,7)$
- Alice and Bob share the same secret, 13, which is the x-coordinate of point $(13, 7)$.

13.5.3.1 Small-Subgroup Attack Against ECDH

Some attacks have been reported in literature and focused mainly on domain parameter selection and not directly on the design of ECDH. In particular, the small subgroup attack is of interest, because it resulted in ECDH extensions including the ECMQV agreement protocol described in next subsection. It works as follows: assume that an active attacker, say Eve, can intercept and modify messages exchanged between Alice and Bob while running the ECDH protocol and assume that n, the order of the subgroup, is $n = c * m$, where c is a small value:

1) Eve intercepts $A = Pr_A \cdot G$, the public key of Alice, and replaces it by $m \cdot A$, then sends it to Bob.
2) Eve intercepts $B = Pr_B \cdot G$, the public key of Bob, and replaces it by $m \cdot B$, then sends it to Alice.
3) Alice computes $S_A = Pr_A \cdot mB = (Pr_A * m * Pr_B) \cdot G$
4) Bob computes $S_B = Pr_B \cdot mA = (Pr_B * m * Pr_A) \cdot G$

Eve impacts the agreement as follows:

- Minor impact: the shared secret is not exactly the one the parties were expecting to generate. Indeed, Alice and Bob agree on $(Pr_A * Pr_B * m) \cdot G$ and not on $(Pr_A * Pr_B) \cdot G$.
- Dramatic impact: the attack forces the shared secret to be one of a small and known subset of EC points, which makes an exhaustive search of the shared secret computationally feasible. Indeed,

$$\exists\, k \in \mathbb{N},\ k' \in \mathbb{N},\ k' < c \mid Pr_A * Pr_B * m = k * (m * c) + k' * m$$
$$(Pr_A * Pr_B * m) \cdot G = (k * (c * m) \cdot G) + (k' * m \cdot G)$$
$$= k * \mathcal{O} + (k' * m \cdot G) = k' * m \cdot G, \text{ because } c * m \text{ is the order of the group.}$$

Varying k' from 1 to c results in a set of points $\{G, 2 \cdot G, ..., (c-1) \cdot G\}$ points. Thus, Alice and Bob agree on a shared point in a tight set when c is a small value.

Example 13.6 shows how the small-subgroup attack may limit the set of shared secret values.

Example 13.6 Alice and Bob agree to use the elliptic curve $E : y^2 \equiv (x^3 + 7)$ over prime field F_{17}. The 18 points of the used EC are:

$$E(F_{17}) = \{(1,5), (1,12), (2,7), (2,10), (3,0), (5,8),(5,9), (6,6), (6,11),$$
$$(8,3), (8,14), (10,2), (10,15), (12,1), (12,16), (15,4), (15,13), \mathcal{O}\}$$

Point $(6, 6)$ is a generator of the group $E(F_{17})$; its order is $n = 18 = 2 * 9$. Assume that selected base point G is point $(6, 6)$. When Eve makes use of the small-subgroup attack, the following actions and computations are performed:

Eve intercepts $A = Pr_A \cdot G$, the public key of Alice, and replaces it by $9 \cdot (A)$, then sends it to Bob.
Eve intercepts $B = Pr_B \cdot G$, the public key of Bob, and replaces it by $(Pr_B * 9)$, then sends it to Alice.
Alice computes $S_A = Pr_A \cdot (9 \cdot B) = (Pr_A * 9 * Pr_B) \cdot G$
Bob computes $S_B = Pr_B \cdot (9 \cdot A) = (Pr_B * 9 * Pr_A) \cdot G$
Let $Z = 9 * (Pr_B * Pr_A - 1)$

If Z is even, then $Z = 18 * Z'$, $Z' \in \mathbb{N}$; therefore,

$$S_A = S_B = Z' \cdot (18 \cdot G) + 9 \cdot G = Z' \cdot \mathcal{O} + 9 \cdot G = 9 \cdot G.$$

If Z is even, then $Z = 18 * Z'' + 9$, $Z'' \in \mathbb{N}$; therefore,

$$S_A = S_B = Z'' \cdot (18 \cdot G) + 18 \cdot G = \mathcal{O}.$$

Alice and Bob have no choice; the only valid shared secret is point $9 \cdot G$. Therefore, Eve can easily disclose confidential messages.

13.5.4 EC Menezes-Qu-Vanstone (ECMQV) Key-Agreement Protocol

MQV (Menezes-Qu-Vanstone) [17, 18] key-agreement is one of the numerous extensions to the original Diffie-Hellman key-exchange protocol. MQV is designed to work in an arbitrary finite group and, in particular, elliptic curve groups. It is recommended by the NIST [19].

ECMQV provides a countermeasure to some attacks against the ECDH, including the small group attack discussed in previous subsection. MQV makes use of two key-pairs for each party: a static (i.e. long-term) key-pair and an ephemeral (i.e. a key-pair used only in the key-agreement transaction) key-pair. The protocol run by Alice and Bob to generate a shared secret is depicted in Figure 13.7.

Proof of ECMQV correctness

$$S_A = h * Sig_A * \left(B' + \overline{B'} \cdot B\right) = h * Sig_A * \left(Pr_B^e \cdot G + \overline{B'} * Pr_B^s \cdot G\right)$$

$$= h * Sig_A * \left(Pr_B^e + \overline{B'} * Pr_B^s\right) \cdot G = h * Sig_A * Sig_B \cdot G$$

$$S_B = h * Sig_B * \left(A' + \overline{A'} \cdot A\right) = h * Sig_B * \left(Pr_A^e \cdot G + \overline{A'} * Pr_A^s \cdot G\right)$$

$$= h * Sig_B * \left(Pr_A^e + \overline{A'} * Pr_A^s\right) \cdot G = h * Sig_B * Sig_A \cdot G$$

Thus, $S_A = S_B = h * Sig_B * Sig_A \cdot G$; i.e. both parties generate the same secret. $\qquad\square$

Bob	Alice
Domain parameters $(q, a, b, \text{FR}, G, n, \text{and } h)$ are sent by either Bob or Alice and are public.	
• Bob generates his static key-pair (Pr_B^s, Pu_B^s) • Pick a private key Pr_B^s, an integer such that $1 \le Pr_B^s \le n-1$ • Compute a point B: $B = Pr_B^s \cdot G$ • Send B to Alice	• Alice generates her static key-pair (Pr_A^s, Pu_A^s) • Pick a private key Pr_A^s, an integer such that $1 \le Pr_A^s \le n-1$ • Compute a point A: $A = Pr_A^s \cdot G$ • Send A to Bob
• Bob generates his ephemeral key-pair (Pr_B^e, Pu_B^e) • Pick an ephemeral private key Pr_B^e, an integer such that $1 \le Pr_B^e \le n-1$ • Compute a point B': $B' = Pr_B^e \cdot G$ • Send B' to Alice	• Alice generates her ephemeral key-pair (Pr_A^e, Pu_A^e) • Pick an ephemeral private key Pr_A^e, an integer such that $1 \le Pr_A^e \le n-1$ • Compute a point A': $A' = Pr_A^e \cdot G$ • Send A' to Bob
Let f denote the bit-length of the subgroup order f; i.e. $f = \lceil log_2(n) \rceil$. For any EC point $R = (x_R, y_R)$, the notation $\overline{R}$ means: $\overline{R} = \left(x_R \bmod 2^{\lceil f/2 \rceil}\right) + 2^{\lfloor f/2 \rfloor}$	
• Compute an implicit signature $Sig_B = (Pr_B^e + \overline{B'} * Pr_B^s) \bmod n$ • Compute the shared secret: $S_B = h * Sig_B * (A' + \overline{A'} \cdot A).$	• Compute an implicit signature $Sig_A = (Pr_A^e + \overline{A'} * Pr_A^s) \bmod n$ • Compute the shared secret: $S_A = h * Sig_A * (B' + \overline{B'} \cdot B).$

Figure 13.7 Elliptic Curve MQV agreement protocol.

13.5.5 Elliptic-Curve Digital-Signature Algorithm (ECDSA)

At the time of writing this chapter, most SSL/TLS certificates are still being signed with RSA keys. However, since the early 2010s, many certificate authorities are involved in the deployment of ECDSA as a new and performant algorithm to digital signature and most modern signature-service clients have implemented support for ECDSA. The latter will probably become the standard in public key industry. The ECDSA is composed of three processes [14]:

- Setup process
- Signature generation process
- Signature verification process

13.5.5.1 Setup Process

Let us consider Alice and Bob as two parties in communication. Alice has a message M to send to Bob. That is, Alice is the *signer* and Bob the *verifier*. In the setup process, the elliptic curve domain parameters (see Section 13.5.2) and the hash function are selected by the signer. ECDSA works on the hash of the message, rather than on the message itself. SHA-256 and SHA-512 are currently recommended by security standards.

Alice makes use of the selected elliptic curve domain parameters to generate a key pair (Pr_A, Pu_A), where Pr_A is Alice's private key, which is a random integer in $\{1, ..., n-1\}$, and $Pu_A = Pr_A \cdot G$ is her public key; G is the base point.

13.5.5.2 ECDSA Signature Generation

The signature generation (also called *signing process*) is done by Alice, the signer, as follows:

1) Generate a new ephemeral key pair (k, Q) as follows:
   - Pick a cryptographically secure random[7] integer k such that $0 < k < n$. n is the order of the base point G.
   - Calculate point $Q = k \cdot G$; (x_Q, y_Q) are the coordinates of EC point Q.
2) Calculate $r = x_Q \bmod n$.
3) If $r = 0$, return to step 1 and try again.
4) Compute the message digest[8] $H = hash(M)$, where $hash()$ is the hash function selected by the signer.
5) Calculate $s = k^{-1} * (H + r * Pr_A) \bmod n$. k^{-1} is the multiplicative inverse of k in the underlying finite field. Notice that, in order to optimize computation time, the signature relates to the hash of the message and not to the entire message.
6) If $s = 0$, then return to step 1 and try again.[9]
7) The pair (r,s) is the signature of message M.

13.5.5.3 ECDSA Signature Verification

Assume that Bob has received, from Alice, the followings items:

- Domain parameters selected by Alice, the public key of Alice Pu_A, and the identity of the hash function
- Message M' and its signature (r', s').

The signature verification process is as follows:

1) If $r' \notin \{1, ..., n-1\}$ or $s' \notin \{1, ..., n-1\}$, stop the verification, because the signature pair is invalid regarding the signature generation procedure.
2) Compute the message digest $H' = hash(M')$.
3) Compute $U_1 = H'(s')^{-1} \bmod n$ and $U_2 = r'(s')^{-1} \bmod n$.
4) Compute the EC point $R = (x_R, y_R) = U_1 \cdot G + U_2 \cdot Pu_A$.
5) If $x_R \bmod n = r'$, the signature is valid. Otherwise, it is invalid.

Example 13.7 Many online tools provide services for playing with ECDSA. The domain parameters of recommended EC are listed in [10]. As far as we know, the most used elliptic curve in EC-based digital signature systems is labeled P-256; its equation is $y^2 = x^3 - 3x + b \bmod p$ over prime field F_p. Notice that parameter a is -3; and parameter b should be selected prior starting signing process.

The domain parameters of the EC P-256 are as follows:

$p = 15792089210356248762697446949407573530086143415290314195533631308867097853951$

$n = 115792089210356248762697446949407573529996955224135760342422259061068512044369$

$b = 5ac635d8\ aa3a93e7\ b3ebbd55\ 769886bc\ 651d06b0\ cc53b0f6\ 3bce3c3e\ 27d2604b$

$x_G = 6b17d1f2\ e12c4247\ f8bce6e5\ 63a440f2\ 77037d81\ 2deb33a0\ f4a13945\ d898c296$

$y_G = 4fe342e2\ fe1a7f9b\ 8ee7eb4a\ 7c0f9e16\ 2bce3357\ 6b315ece\ cbb64068\ 37bf51f5$

The following scenario is provided using *8gwifi.org* tool.

1) Select P-256 as elliptic curve.
2) The randomly produced private key looks like this:

```
-----BEGIN EC PRIVATE KEY-----
MHQCAQEEIFqqEkIem0YXpT1WBsUjXGH/flXMLbScdBNbrOzP4zCWoAcGBSuBBAAKoUQDQgAERVFoufpWA
1h1d7f1Y+DneelWWmoGI5EWuMeDN/xu/Z2UWk1DQ+rXAxCE/Eo1gFb5gpHB1uTNwreW2Ft+4YXUbQ==
-----END EC PRIVATE KEY-----
```

3) The randomly produced public key looks like this:

```
-----BEGIN PUBLIC KEY-----
MFYwEAYHKoZIzj0CAQYFK4EEAAoDQgAERVFoufpWA1h1d7f1Y+DneelWWmoGI5EWuMeDN/xu/
Z2UWk1DQ+rXAxCE/Eo1gFb5gpHB1uTNwreW2Ft+4YXUbQ==
-----END PUBLIC KEY-----
```

4) Message = "Hello ECDSA users".
5) Signature looks like this:

```
MEYCIQCtK/+15PFcTIqDJA21qIocPTCkOCF4SIJ3gLzIh0TdvgIhAMV3egIYolvZmPhwOsAuHAjLFvOfs
sso79tQ9MvI4NSD
```

13.5.5.4 Correctness of ECDSA Algorithm

ECDSA is correct if and only if both following conditions hold:

- C1: If Bob receives the correct message M and its signature (r, s), then the result is "Valid signature".
- C2: If Bob receives either an incorrect message or an incorrect signature, then the result is "Invalid".

To address both conditions, we start from step 4 in signature verification. Since ECs are cyclic groups modulo the order of the EC, *mod n* is omitted in the following proof.

Condition C1

If Bob receives the valid data, then: $M' = M, (r', s') = (r, s)$, and $H' = H$. Using the definition of Pu_A, U_1, and U_2, we can write:

$$R = U_1 \cdot G + U_2 \cdot Pu_A = U_1 \cdot G + U_2 \cdot Pr_A \cdot G$$
$$= \left(H * s^{-1} + r * s^{-1} \cdot Pr_A\right) \cdot G = s^{-1} * \left(H + r * Pr_A\right) \cdot G$$

By definition (step 5 in Signature generation): $s = k^{-1}(H + r * Pr_A)$.

For any element z in a finite field: $z * z^{-1} = 1$. We can write:

$$k * s = k * k^{-1}\left(H + r * Pr_A\right) = H + r * Pr_A$$
$$\Rightarrow k = s^{-1} * \left(H + r * Pr_A\right)$$

We substitute $s^{-1} * (H + r * Pr_A)$ by k in our last definition of R:

$$R = s^{-1}(H + r \cdot Pr_A) \cdot G = k \cdot G$$

$R = k \cdot G$ is the same point as $Q = k \cdot G$ (step 1 in Signature generation). Consequently, ECDSA verification result is correct when the received message and its signature are valid.

Condition C2

If Bob received an incorrect message, then: $H' \neq H$.

If Bob received an incorrect signature, then: $(s, r) \neq (s', r')$. There are three cases to check:

$$H' \neq H \wedge (s,r) = (s', r')$$
$$H' = H \wedge (s,r) \neq (s', r')$$
$$H' \neq H \wedge (s,r) \neq (s', r')$$

We only prove the first case (then, the two others may be easily proven).

H' and H differ; hence, we can write: $H' = H + \delta$.

Using the definition of Pu_A, U_1, and U_2, we can write:

$$R = U_1 \cdot G + U_2 \cdot Pu_A = U_1 \cdot G + U_2 \cdot Pr_A \cdot G$$
$$= \left(H' * s^{-1} + r * s^{-1} \cdot Pr_A \right) \cdot G = \left((H + \delta) * s^{-1} + r * s^{-1} \cdot Pr_A \right) \cdot G$$
$$= \left[s^{-1}(H + r \cdot Pr_A) \cdot G \right] + [s^{-1} * \delta \cdot G]$$

As in Condition 1 proof, we can write:

$$k = s^{-1}(H + r * Pr_A)$$

substitute $s^{-1}(H + r * Pr_A)$ by k in our last definition of R:

$$R = \left[s^{-1}(H + r \cdot Pr_A) \cdot G \right] + \left[s^{-1} * \delta \cdot G \right] = \left[k \cdot G \right] + \left[s^{-1} * \delta \cdot G \right]$$

Point R calculated by Bob differs from point $Q = k \cdot G$ (step 1 in Signature generation). If the hash function has a sufficient level of security strength, there is a very negligible probability that $s^{-1} * \delta \cdot G = 0$. Thus, the result of ECDSA is "Invalid", which is a correct decision. $\square$

13.5.6 Edwards Curve Digital Signature Algorithm (EdDSA)

When the digital signature is produced using an Edwards curve, it is referred to as *Edwards curve digital signature* and denoted EdDSA. Edwards curve model is introduced in Section 13.2.4. EdDSA signatures are recommended, because they are efficient (in terms of computation time) compared to traditional ECDSA signatures.

As in traditional ECs, domain parameters must be selected before generating and verifying EdDSA signatures. Domain parameters of Edwards ECs are the following:

- p: prime.
- a and d: the coefficients of the Edwards curve equation $y^2 + ax^2 = 1 + dx^2 y^2 \bmod p$. Both coefficients are elements in F_p.
- $G = (x_G, y_G)$: base point.
- n: order of base point G.
- h: cofactor associated with the base point: $h = \dfrac{|E(Fp)|}{n}$.

Edwards25519 and Edwards448 curves make use of the hash functions SHA-512 and SHAKE256,[10] respectively.

13.5.6.1 EdDSA Key Pair Generation

Let b denote the bit-length of the private key. $b = 256$, when Edwards25519 curve is used; and $b = 456$, when Edwards448 curve is used.

1) Pick a cryptographically secure random[11] integer k of b bits.
2) Compute the private key hash H:
    - For Edwards25519 curve: $H = SHA\text{-}512(k)$
    - For Edwards448 curve: $H = SHAKE256(k, 912)$
3) Let $(h_0, h_1, ..., h_{2b-1})$ denote the $2b$ bits of the key hash H. Let $H_1 = (h_0, h_1, ..., h_{b-1})$ and $H_2 = (h_b, h_{b+1}, ..., h_{2b-1})$; i.e. H_1 and H_2 are the first and second halves of $H(k)$, respectively.
4) Generate the public key Q:
    - For Edwards25519: set $h_0 = h_1 = h_2 = 0$; $h_{b-2} = 1$; $h_{b-1} = 0$. Then, set t to the modified H_1; i.e. $t = (0,0,0,h_3, ..., h_{b-3}, 1, 0)$
    - For Edwards448: set $h_0 = h_1 = 0$; $h_{b-9} = 1$; and $h_i = 0$, for $b-8 \leq i \leq b-1$. Then, set t to the modified H_1; i.e. $t = (0,0,h_2, ..., h_{b-10}, 1, 0, 0..., 0)$

- Encode t: $s = BitStringToInteger(t)$
- $Q = s \cdot G$ # multiplication of point G by a scalar s
- Encode[12] $Q = Q_{enc} = EncodePoint(Q, b)$

5) Encoded public key Q_{enc} is sent either along with the signed message or separately.

Using steps 4.1 (or 4.2) and 4.3 in key-pair generation procedure, we can see that integer s has the three (or two) least significant bits at 0. Let us focus on the Edwards25519 curve (the same apply to the second curve). We can write s as $s = s' * 8$, where s' the rightmost $b - 3$ bits of s. 8 is the cofactor of the Edwards2219 curve. Notice that s' is distinct from 0, because it has at least a 1-bit. Then, in step 4.4, the public key is computed as $Q = s \cdot G$. By substitution: $Q = (8 * s') \cdot G = 8 \cdot (s' \cdot G)$. By Lemma 13.1, Q is point of prime order n. Therefore, the legitimate signer makes use of public key with an order of n.

13.5.6.2 EdDSA Signature Generation

The signature of a message M is of a bit-length of $2b$; it is composed of two equal-length parts, R and S computed as follows:

1) Compute the private-key hash H:
   - For Edwards25519 curve: $H = SHA\text{-}512(k)$
   - For Edwards448 curve: $H = SHAKE256(k, 912)$
2) Let $(h_0, h_1, \ldots, h_{2b-1})$ denote the $2b$ bits of the key hash H. Let $H_1 = (h_0, h_1, \ldots, h_{b-1})$ and $H_2 = (h_b, h_{b+1}, \ldots, h_{2b-1})$.
3) Compute the part R of the signature using H_2, the second half of the key hash:
   - For Edwards25519: $r = SHA\text{-}512(H_2 \| M)$
   - For Edwards448: $r = SHAKE256(AppendedData \| H_2 \| M, 912)$, where

     $AppendedData = "SigEd448" \| octet(0) \| octet(len(context)) \| context$;

     $octet(a)$ denotes an octet with a value a; $context$[13] denotes a bit-string known to the signer and the verifier; by default,
     $context$ is the empty string.
     $SHAKE256(InputData, 912)$ produces a hash of 456 bits.
   - Compute point $R' = r' \cdot G$, where $r' = BitStringToInteger(r)$. Then, encode point R' as a b-bit-string $R = EncodePoint(R', b)$
4) Compute the part S of the signature using H_1, the first half of the key hash
   - For Edwards25519: set $h_0 = h_1 = h_2 = 0$; $h_{b-2} = 1$; $h_{b-1} = 0$. Then, set t to the modified H_1; i.e. $t = (0, 0, 0, h_3, \ldots, h_{b-3}, 1, 0)$
   - For Edwards448: set $h_0 = h_1 = 0$; $h_{b-9} = 1$; and $h_i = 0$, for $b - 8 \leq i \leq b - 1$. Then, set t to the modified H_1; i.e. $t = (0, 0, h_2, \ldots, h_{b-10}, 1, 0, 0, \ldots, 0)$
   - Encode t: $s = BitStringToInteger(t)$[(14)]
   - For Edwards25519: $W = SHA\text{-}512(R \| Q_{enc} \| M)$
   - For Edwards448: $W = SHAKE256(AppendedData \| R \| Q_{enc} \| M, 912)$
   - $v = \left(r' + BitStringToInteger\left(W\right) * s\right) \bmod n$
     Encode v: $S = IntegerToBitString(v, b)$
5) The EdDSA signature is $Sig = R \| S$

13.5.6.3 EdDSA Signature Verification

Let M denote the signed message and Sig, its signature. Domain parameters and the signer public-key Q_{enc}, are known to the verifier. The signature verification process is as follows:

1) Data decoding:
   - Decode the signer public key Q_{enc} to an EC point Q.
   - Decode the first half of the signature Sig to a point R'.
   - Decode the second half of the signature Sig to an integer v. If $v < n$ continue the verification. Otherwise, reject the received message.
2) Compute the hash:
   - $DataToHash = EncodePoint(R') \| Q_{enc} \| M$
   - For Edwards25519: $u = SHA\text{-}512(DataToHash)$

- For Edwards448: $u = SHAKE256(AppendedData \parallel DataToHash, 912)$, where $AppendedData$ has the same content than that in Signature generation; i.e. $AppendedData = "SigEd448" \parallel octet(0) \parallel octet(len(context)) \parallel context$
- $t = BitStringToInteger(u)$

3) Check:
- For Edwards25519: $c = \log_2(h) = 3$; $h = 8$ is the cofactor of Edwards25519.
- For Edwards448: $c = \log_2(h) = 2$; $h = 4$ is the cofactor of Edwards448.
- If $(2^c * v) \cdot G = 2^c \cdot R' + (2^c * t) \cdot Q$, then accept message M, else reject it.

Proof of EdDSA correctness

To simplify the proof of correctness of the EdDSA scheme, omit the conversion between integers and bit-strings and use a hash function *Hash* that can be either SHA-512 or SHAKE256.

– From key-pair generation procedure, we have: $Q = s \cdot G$
– From the signature generation procedure we have:

$$r = Hash(H_2 \parallel M)$$

$$t = Hash(R \parallel Q_{enc} \parallel M)$$

$$R' = r \cdot G$$

$$S = v = \left(r + Hash\left(R \parallel Q_{enc} \parallel M\right) * s\right) mod\ n$$

– Since the base point G has an order of n, we omit the *mod n* in S. Indeed, for any positive integers a and b, such that $b < n$, we have:

$$\left(a * n + b\right) \cdot G = \left(a * n\right) \cdot G + b \cdot G = \mathcal{O} + b \cdot G = b \cdot G = \left(\left(a * n + b\right) mod\ n\right) \cdot G$$

– Make substitutions in the left part of the equality in the step 3 of the signature verification procedure:

$$(2^c * v) \cdot G = 2^c \left(\left(r + t * s\right)\right) \cdot G = \left(2^c * r\right) \cdot G + 2^c \left(t * s\right) \cdot G$$

$$= 2^c \cdot R' + \left(2^c * t\right) \cdot \left(s \cdot G\right) = 2^c \cdot R' + \left(2^c * t\right) \cdot Q$$

The right part of the equality is the same as the left one. Therefore, if a signature is legitimate, it is validated by the verifier. $\qquad\qquad\qquad\qquad\qquad\qquad\qquad\qquad\qquad\qquad\qquad\qquad\qquad\qquad\qquad\qquad\qquad\qquad\qquad$ □

13.5.6.4 Comment on EdDSA Signature Verification Procedure

The signature verification is based on the test of the condition $(2^c * v) \cdot G = 2^c \cdot R' + (2^c * t) \cdot Q$, where 2^c is the cofactor of the used curve. This signature verification is referred to as batch verification. Another verification condition referred to as cofactor-less verification (or also unbatched verification) may be used; the verifier tests $v \cdot G = R' + t \cdot Q$. Any signature that passes the factor-less verification passes the batched verification. However, not all signatures that pass the batched verification pass the factor-less verification as shown by the following example.

To simply, we omit the encoding. Let $\left(R', S\right)$ be a signature and let U be a point[15] with an order of 2^c (thus, $2^c \cdot U = \mathcal{O}$). Replace $\left(R', v\right)$ by $\left(R' + U, v\right)$. In the batched verification, the check is:

$$(2^c * v) \cdot G = 2^c \cdot \left(R' + U\right) + (2^c * t) \cdot Q = 2^c \cdot R' + 2^c \cdot U + (2^c * t) \cdot Q$$

$$= 2^c \cdot R' + (2^c * t) \cdot Q.$$

Therefore, the signature $\left(R' + U, v\right)$ passes the batched verification. However, it should be noticed that the second part $(2^c * t) \cdot Q$ can only be produced by the (dishonest) signer that owns the private key. Thus, this signature modification has no impact on security, because the second part of the signature is computed by the private key owner. In the cofactor-less verification, the check is:

$$v \cdot G = \left(R' + U\right) + t \cdot Q = R' + U + t \cdot Q \neq R' + t \cdot Q$$

Therefore, the signature $\left(R' + U, v\right)$ does not pass the cofactor-based test.

Because multiplication by 2^c eliminates the 2^c-torsion component, the batch verification, can be thought of as checking validity only in the prime-order subgroup (i.e. it checks only signatures generated by honest private-key owners), while the cofactor-less can be thought of as checking validity in the full group and rejects signatures modified by dishonest private-key owners. It is argued in literature that under specific implementations of the verification test, the batch verification can speed up the verification.

13.5.7 Elliptic Curve Encryption Algorithms

EC encryption algorithms provide public-key-based mechanisms to encrypt messages exchanged over an insecure network. EC encryption schemes are designed, so that it is hard for an attacker to recover plaintexts from their ciphertexts.

A variety of EC-based encryption algorithms have been proposed in literature. In particular, two EC-based encryption schemes are of interest to cryptosystem designers and users: Elliptic Curve Integrated Encryption Scheme (ECIES), which is specified in ANSI X9-63 standard, and the EC-based ElGamal encryption scheme.

13.5.7.1 ECIES Framework

The best known encryption scheme based on elliptic curves is ECIES. ECIES provides capabilities for encryption, key exchange, and digital signature. Hence, it is called *Integrated Encryption Scheme*. Notice there exist different versions of ECIES depending on the standards such as ANSI X9-63 [16], IEEE 1363 [20], and ISO 18033-2 [21]. Differences may prevent interoperability between ECIES implementations. In this chapter, we focus on the common principles of ECIES versions.

The basic idea of the ECIES is as follows: the two parties share elliptic curve domain parameters. Then, each party generates a key pair (private and public keys). From the key pairs and the base point G, both parties calculate the shared secret Z. Then, from the shared secret, the same key derivation function is used to generate two keys one for symmetric encryption and the other for authentication. The messages are encrypted and decrypted with a symmetric cipher. Thus, ECIES is a hybrid scheme that uses a public key system to transport a session key to be used by a symmetric cipher.

13.5.7.1.1 ECIES Functions

As the "I" in the name indicates, ECIES integrates a set of functions: Key-Agreement function (KA), hash function, message authentication code function, Key-Derivation Function (KDF), and symmetric encryption/decryption functions

- *Key-Agreement* function (KA): it is used to exchange the ECC domain parameters and public keys between parties and to compute the shared secret. The most commonly used KA, in current ECIES implementations, is the ECDH protocol (see Section 13.5.3). Other protocols may also be used.
- *Hash function*: it is used to produce hashes in KDF and in MAC function. SHA-256 and SHA-512 functions dominate in current ECIES implementations.
- *Message Authentication Code* (MAC): a MAC accompanying each message is used for authentication. Consequently, ECIES includes mechanisms to provide data integrity as well as message authentication. HMAC-SHA-256, HMAC-SHA-512, CMAC-AES-128, CMAC-AES-192, and CMAC-AES-256 schemes dominate in current ECIES implementations. The key used in MAC scheme is denoted k_2 and it is computed by KDF function.
- *Symmetric Encryption/decryption* scheme: it is used to encrypt and decrypt messages. The most commonly used symmetric scheme, in current ECIES implementations, is the AES standard. The symmetric encryption (and decryption) key, denoted k_1, is computed by KDF function.
- *Key Derivation Function* (KDF): the role of this function is to compute, from the shared secret, a string[16] K composed of two keys: symmetric encryption key (k_1) and MAC key (k_2). The most commonly used KDF is the one defined in the ANSI X9-63 standard [16], which operates as follows [22]:

---

function ANSI_X9.63_KDF
      input Z : shared secret (i.e. the x-coordinate of an EC point)
            keydatalen : size (in bytes) of the symmetric key to generate
            hashlen : size (in bytes) of the hash values computed by the
                selected hash function
            hashmaxlen : constant, which represents the maximum size of
                        output of the selected hash function

output K: bit-string (referred to as *keying material*)

1. # Test of validity of parameters:

    if $|Z| + 4 \geq hashmaxlen$, **then stop**

    if $keydatalen \geq hashlen * (2^{32} - 1)$, **then stop**

2. # Initiate a 4-octet big-endian octet string

    $Counter = 00000001_{16}$

3. **for** i = 1 **to** $\left\lceil \dfrac{keydatalen}{hashlen} \right\rceil$ **do**

    $S_i = HASH(Z \parallel Counter)$; $Counter = Counter + 1$

4. $K = S_1 \parallel S_2 \parallel \ldots \parallel S_{\lceil keydatale/hashlen \rceil}$

5. **return** K

13.5.7.1.2 ECIES Operation

ECIES is composed of three processes: Setup, encryption, and decryption.

Setup process

Before starting ECIES to encrypt/decrypt messages, the two parties should prepare (using a protocol not a part of ECIES) the context of use. The message recipient selects the following items and sends them to the message sender:

- The hash function *HASH* and its output bit-length (*hashlen*), the KDF function, the MAC scheme and its bit-length of the MAC key (*mackeylen*), and the symmetric cipher to encrypt/decrypt data.
- Domain parameters: $T = \{q, a, b, G, FR, n, h\}$.[17]
- The public key of the recipient $Pu_R = Pr_R \cdot G$. The recipient key-pair is a long-term pair (i.e. can be used to decrypt a set a messages).

In case the sender does not agree on the ECIES parameters selected by the recipient, the setup process fails.

ECIES Encryption

function ECIES_Encryption

    input $\{q, a, b, G, FR, n, h\}$: domain parameters

        Pu_R: public key of the recipient (Pu_R is an EC point); M: plaintext

        hashlen: length (in bytes) of the output of the HASH function

        keydatalen: length (in bytes) of the encryption key

        mackeylen : length (in bytes) of the MAC key

    output S: bit-string

1. # Select an ephemeral[18] EC key pair $\left(Pr_S^e, Pu_S^e\right)$, with:

    Pr_S^e is a random integer in $\{1, \ldots, n-1\}$

    $Pu_S^e = Pr_S^e \cdot G$ is an EC point, which represents public key of sender

2. # Compute the shared secret Z

    $Z = Pr_S^e \cdot Pu_R$ # ($Z = (x_z, y_z)$)

    if $Z = \mathcal{O}$, **then go to** step 1

3. # Derive the encryption and MAC keys

    $(k_1, k_2) = KDF\left(x_z\right)$, where:

    k_1 is the encryption key; and it is the *keydatalen* leftmost bytes of the byte string returned by function *KDF*(),

    k_2 is the MAC key and is the *mackeylen* rightmost bytes of the byte string returned by function *KDF*(),

4. # Encrypt the message and compute the encrypted message MAC

    $C = ENC\left(M, k_1\right)$; $T = MAC\left(C, k_2\right)$

5. $S = Pu_S^e \parallel C \parallel T$; **return** S

ECIES decryption

```
function ECIES_Decryption
        input   {q, a, b, G, FR, n, h}: domain parameters
                Pr_R : private key of the recipient
                Pu_S^e : ephemeral public key of the message sender
                C : ciphertext; T : message tag
                hashlen : length (in bytes) of the output of the HASH function
                keydatalen : length (in bytes) of the encryption key
                mackeylen : length (in bytes) of the MAC key
        output M : bit-string
        1. # Compute the shared secret Z
            Z = Pr_R · Pu_S^e      # Z is a point; i.e. Z = (x_z, y_z)
            if Z = O, then Reject the received message and Stop.
        2. # Derive the decryption and MAC keys
            (k_1, k_2) = KDF(x_z), with the same notations as in Encryption process
        3. # Compute and verify the tag
            T' = MAC(C, k_2)
            if T' ≠ T, then Reject the message (authentication failure).
        4. # Decrypt the message
            M = DEC(C, k_1)
        5. return (M)
```

13.5.7.1.3 *Security and Proof of Correctness of ECIES Algorithm*

Breaking ECIES is equivalent to solving the EC discrete logarithm problem. Thus, ECIES is considered secure when used with a base point of a large order. The proof of correctness is easy to establish. First, recall that the domain parameters and all the functions (hash, key derivation, and key encryption/decryption) and their inputs are the same for both parties. Second, the KDF returns the same couple of keys for both parties, because the secret Z used is the same.

The recipient computes (line 1 of pseudocode) the shared secret as $Z_R = Pr_R \cdot Pu_S^e$ and the message sender computes it (line 2 in pseudocode) as $Z_S = Pr_S^e \cdot Pu_R$.

Since $Pu_R = Pr_R \cdot G$ and $Pu_S^e = Pr_S^e \cdot G$, $Z_R = Z_S = Z$.

If the encrypted message C and the associate tag T have been generated by the legitimate message sender, then $T = MAC(C, k_2) = T'$. By definition of symmetric ciphering, we have $DEC(C, k_1) = DEC(ENC(M, k_1), k_1) = M$.

13.5.7.2 **ElGamal Encryption Using EC Cryptography**

The ElGamal Encryption using elliptic curve (EEEC) is an adaptation of the original ElGamal encryption scheme [23] to the elliptic curve context. The core of the EEEC is that the message to encrypt is hidden in an EC point coordinate. It is worth noticing that EEEC is fully-based on public key cryptography, while ECIES makes use of public key cryptography and symmetric cryptography. In other words, EEEC is a pure public key scheme, while ECIES is a hybrid one.

13.5.7.2.1 *Mapping Messages to EC Points*

EEEC scheme applies operations on EC points to encrypt and decrypt messages. Unlike the encryption schemes presented in previous sections and chapters (in which a message is handled as an integer), EEEC requires that the message to encrypt is in the form a point on an elliptic curve. Mapping integers to EC points adds complexity to the encryption scheme. The mapping should be done in such a way that the plaintext is uniquely recovered from the ciphertext.

One naïve method to do mapping is as follows: given a message, represented by an integer M, and a point G on the considered elliptic curve, map M to $M \cdot G$, which is an EC point. Such a mapping can be used if the size of the message is small. However, this type of mapping obviously makes the EC discrete logarithm problem easy to solve.

In general, there is no known polynomial deterministic algorithm for mapping integers to points on an arbitrary elliptic curve. However, there exist some fast probabilistic methods for mapping. In particular, Koblitz proposed some methods, called embedding plaintext methods, to map integers to EC points [5]. The method to choose depends on the cardinality of the field (i.e. F_p or F_{2^m}). Below is the most known mapping method, which is called *probabilistic mapping method*.

The probabilistic mapping method can be used for elliptic curves over F_p, with p a prime, to embed a message M in the x-coordinate of an EC point as follows:

1) Select an integer K smaller than $log_2(p)$.

2) Any message to encode is represented by an integer M such that:

$$0 \leq M + 1 < \frac{p}{K}.$$

3) Pick an integer x, such that: $K * M \leq x < K * (M+1) < p$.

4) If $f(x) = (x^3 + ax + b) \bmod p$ is a square in F_p, then $\left(x, \sqrt{f(x)}\right)$ is a point on the elliptic curve $E(F_p)$. Otherwise, try another integer x until the test is positive or all the values of x in the range have been tested.

5) If M is embedded in x, then, M is easily retrieved from x: $M = \left\lfloor \frac{x}{k} \right\rfloor$.

Notes

- The probabilistic mapping method may fail in finding an x value, which represents the x-coordinate of a point on the elliptic curve.
- The x value yielded by the mapping (if it succeeds) is $x = K * M + c$ (c is an integer, $0 \leq c < K$). Since x represents the coordinate of a point on $E(F_p)$, x is less than p. Thus, the value of any message M to encrypt should be less than $\left\lfloor \frac{P}{K} \right\rfloor$.
- To speed the computations, K should be a power of 2. If $K = 2^L$ (L is an integer), then x is yielded by L left-bit shifts of the integer M. The plaintext L can be decoded simply by dropping the M rightmost bits of x. That is: $M = \frac{x}{2^L}$.
- On one hand, the value of K should be as low as possible, because it impacts the amount of data embedded in plaintexts; the higher the value of K is, the lower the size of messages that can be mapped to EC points is. On the other hand, the lower the value of K is, the lower probability to find an EC point is. The probability of mapping failure is 2^{-K}. See Problem 13.7.

Example 13.8 Let $E(F_{113})$ be an elliptic curve of equation $y^2 = x^3 + 7$.
Let K be 8. Consequently, any message M to map should be such that:

$$0 \leq M \leq \left\lfloor \frac{113}{8} \right\rfloor - 1 = 13$$

Let the message to map be $7 \Rightarrow 8 * 7 \leq x < 8 * (7+1)$.
$x = 60$ fulfills the EC equation: $60^3 + 7 \bmod 113 = 64 = 8^2$. Thus, point $(60, 8)$ is a solution to map message 7. In binary representation, $60 = 111100_2$. The value of first three bits forms the value of M, which is $7 = 111_2$.

- Let $E(F_{113})$ be an elliptic curve of equation $y^2 = x^3 + 7$.

  Let K be 16. Consequently, any message M to map should be such that:

  $$0 \leq M \leq \left\lfloor \frac{113}{16} \right\rfloor - 1 = 6$$

As shown by the following table, some messages have more than one EC point candidates to be embedded, while two messages (0 and 6) have no EC point to be mapped; therefore, they cannot be encrypted under the selected elliptic curve and the probabilistic mapping method.

Value of M	Candidate EC points for mapping
0	No point
1	$(30, 0)$
2	$(34, 10), (37, 6), (39, 1), (40, 7)$
3	$(58, 9), (60, 8)$
4	$(69, 5), (72, 4)$
5	$(80, 2), (81, 3)$
6	No point

13.5.7.2.2 Encryption and Decryption

Below is the operation sequence followed by Alice and Bob to secure their communication, while using the EEEC algorithm.

Bob	Alice

• Select EC parameters: a, b, and p.
• Select a base point G on the elliptic curve; n is the order of G.
• Select an EC key pair $\left(Pr_B, Pu_B\right)$, with:
  Pr_B is a random integer in $\{1,\dots,n-1\}$
  $Pu_B = Pr_B \cdot G$ is an EC point, which is Bob's public key
• Send $\left(a,\ b,\ p,\ G,\ n,\ Pu_B\right)$	

• Receive and accept $\left(a,\ b,\ p,\ G,\ n,\ Pu_B\right)$
   • M is the message to send
   • Select[19] an integer K and map integer M to an EC point μ
   • Select a random value k' in $\{1,\dots,n-1\}$
   • Compute Alice's public key: $Pu_A = k' \cdot G$
   • Compute ciphertext: $C = \mu + k' \cdot Pu_B$
   • Send $\left(Pu_A,\ C,\ K\right)$	

• Receive $\left(Pu_A',\ C',\ K'\right)$ • Retrieve the EC point: $\mu' = C' - Pr_B \cdot Pu_A'$ • From the x-coordinate of point μ' extract M': $M = \left\lfloor \dfrac{x_{\mu'}}{K'} \right\rfloor$	

Example 13.9 Alice and Bob use the elliptic curve $E : y^2 \equiv \left(x^3 + x + 1\right) \bmod 23$. Points of $E\left(F_{23}\right)$ are the following:

$$\{(0,1) \quad (0,22) \quad (1,7) \qquad (1,16) \quad (3,10) \quad (3,13)$$
$$(4,0) \quad (5,4) \quad (5,19) \qquad (6,4) \quad (6,19) \quad (7,11)$$
$$(7,12) \quad (9,7) \quad (9,16) \qquad (11,3) \quad (11,20) \quad (12,4)$$
$$(12,19) \quad (13,7) \quad (13,16) \qquad (17,3) \quad (17,20) \quad (18,3)$$
$$(18,20) \quad (19,5) \quad (19,18) \quad \mathcal{O}\}$$

Any of the following points can be used as generator of the chosen EC:

$$\left\{(0,1),\ (0,22),\ (1,7),\ (1,16),\ (3,10),(3,13),\ (9,7),\ (9,16),\ (18,3),(18,20),\ (19,5),\ (19,18)\right\}.$$

Alice encrypts and Bob decrypts as follows:

– Bob's parameter selection:
  ○ Field cardinality: $p = 23$.
  ○ Elliptic curve: $E : y^2 - (x^3 + x + 1) \bmod 23$, $(a = b = 1)$.
  ○ Base point: $G = (9,16)$, which is a generator; hence, $ord(G) = \left|E\left(F_{23}\right)\right| = 28$.
  ○ Bob's private key: $Pr_B = 3$.
  ○ Bob's public key: $Pu_B = 3 \cdot G = 3 \cdot (9,16) = (1,16)$.
  ○ Send $\left(a,\ b,\ p,\ G,\ n,\ Pu_B\right)$.
– Alice's encryption
  ○ Message to send is $M = 3$.
  ○ Parameter for integer to point mapping: $K = 4$
  ○ Mapping of integer 3 onto the selected EC, with $K = 4$, yields point $\mu = (12,4)$ # (because $4^2 = (12^2 + 12 + 1) \bmod 23$).
  ○ Pick $k' = 4$.
  ○ Alice's public key: $Pu_A = 4 \cdot G = 4 \cdot (9,16) = (13,7)$.
  ○ Compute ciphertext: $C = (12,4) + 4 \cdot (1,16) = (12,4) + (17,3) = (6,\ 4)$.
  ○ Send (Pu_A, C, K).
– Bob's decryption
  ○ Receive (Pu_A, C, K).
  ○ $\mu' = (6,4) - (3 \cdot (13,7)) = (6,4) - (17,3)$.
  ○ By definition, if $P = (x,y)$, the negative point of P, in a prime field, is $-P = (x,-y)$.

    ◦ Thus, $\mu' = (6, 4) + (17, -3) = (6, 4) + (17, 20) = (12, 4)$.

    ◦ Then, $M' = \left\lfloor \dfrac{x_{\mu'}}{K} \right\rfloor = \left\lfloor \dfrac{12}{4} \right\rfloor = 3$, which is the message encrypted by Alice.

13.5.7.2.3 EEEC Security
Breaking EEEC is equivalent to solving the EC discrete logarithm problem. Thus, EEEC is considered secure when used with large size fields.

13.5.7.2.4 Proof of Correctness
To retrieve the EC point generated by the sender, the recipient computes
$\mu' = C' - Pr_B \cdot Pu_A$, which, by substitutions, becomes:
$\mu' = \mu + k' \cdot Pu_B - Pr_B \cdot Pu_A = \mu + (k' \cdot Pr_B \cdot G) - (Pr_B \cdot k' \cdot G) = \mu$
Then, from x-coordinate of point μ', the recipient extracts the message $M = \left\lfloor \dfrac{x_\mu}{k} \right\rfloor$.   □

13.6 Exercises and Problems

13.6.1 List of Exercises and Problems

Exercise 13.1   Points of EC with equation $y^2 \equiv (x^3 + 7) \bmod 17$ are:

$$E(F_{17}) = \{(1, 5), (1, 12), (2, 7), (2, 10), (3, 0), (5, 8), (5, 9), (6, 6), (6, 11), (8, 3), (8, 14),$$
$$(10, 2), (10, 15), (12, 1), (12, 16), (15, 4), (15, 13), \ \mathcal{O}\}$$

1) Show that $(5, 8)$ is not a generator of $E(F_{17})$.
2) Show that $(6, 6)$ is a generator of $E(F_{17})$.

Exercise 13.2   Let the EC equation be $y^2 = x^3 + 4x + 20$ and the prime field be F_{29}. $E(F_{29})$ has 37 points including the point to infinity, $\mathcal{O}$:

$(0, 7)$	$(0, 22)$	$(1, 5)$	$(1, 24)$	$(2, 6)$	$(2, 23)$
$(3, 1)$	$(3, 28)$	$(4, 10)$	$(4, 19)$	$(5, 7)$	$(5, 22)$
$(6, 12)$	$(6, 17)$	$(8, 10)$	$(8, 19)$	$(10, 4)$	$(10, 25)$
$(13, 6)$	$(13, 23)$	$(14, 23)$	$(14, 6)$	$(15, 2)$	$(15, 27)$
$(16, 2)$	$(16, 27)$	$(17, 10)$	$(17, 19)$	$(19, 13)$	$(19, 16)$
$(20, 3)$	$(20, 26)$	$(24, 7)$	$(24, 22)$	$(27, 2)$	$(27, 27)$

All points of $E(F_{29})$ are generators with the exception of the element $\mathcal{O}$. Show that $(8, 19)$ is a generator of $E(F_{29})$.

Exercise 13.3   Let E be an elliptic curve given by $y^2 = x^3 + 1$ over the prime field F_{103}.

1) Check if point with coordinate $x = 2$ is on the curve $E(F_{103})$.
2) Check if point with coordinate $x = 4$ is on the curve $E(F_{103})$.
Hint: use Euler's criterion (Theorem 3.7).

Exercise 13.4

1) Let E be an elliptic curve given by $y^2 = x^3 + x + 1$ over prime field F_{103}. What are the y-coordinates of points with coordinates $x = 0$, $x = 11$, and $x = 73$?
2) Let E be an elliptic curve given by $y^2 = x^3 + x + 1$ over prime field F_{101}. What are the y-coordinates of points with coordinates $x = 0$, $x = 8$, $x = 100$, and $x = 57$?
Hint: use Euler's criterion (Theorem 3.7).

Exercise 13.5 Let E be an elliptic curve over F_{23} with equation $y^2 = \left(x^3 + x + 1\right) mod\ 23$.

1) Find all points on E.
2) Compare the number of found points with the result given by theorem 13.2.

Exercise 13.6 Consider the elliptic curve $E: y^2 + xy = x^3 + 1$ over the field F_{2^2}.
Points of $E(F_{2^2})$ are $\{(0,1), (1,0), (1,1), (2,0), (2,2), (3,0), (3,3)\} \cup \{\mathcal{O}\}$.
The field F_{2^2} has a reduction polynomial $f(x) = x^2 + x + 1$ and a generator $g = x$.
Show that:

1) Point $(1,1)$ is not a generator of $E(F_{2^2})$,
2) Points $(2,2)$ is a generator of $E(F_{2^2})$.

Exercise 13.7 Let E be an elliptic curve with equation $y^2 = x^2 + 2x + 2\ mod\ 17$.

1) Find the points of the elliptic curve E defined with equation $y^2 = x^3 + 2x + 2\ mod\ 17$.

2) Use theorems 13.1 and 13.2 to check that $\#E\left(F_{17}\right) = 19$.

Exercise 13.8 Let $E\left(F_{179}\right)$ be an elliptic curve of equation $y^2 = x^3 + 2x + 7$.
Use the probabilistic mapping method and find an EC point to map the message $M = 11$ assuming that $K = 10$.

Problem 13.1
1) How many point operations are required to compute $128 \cdot P$ with the left-to-right binary method for point multiplication?
2) How many point operations are required to compute $127 \cdot P$ with the left-to-right binary method for point multiplication?

Problem 13.2
1) What is the time complexity of the left-to-right binary method for point multiplication?
2) What is the time complexity of the recursive method for point multiplication?

Problem 13.3 Consider the elliptic curve $E(F_{2^2})$ with equation $y^2 + xy = x^3 + 1$. Point set of $E(F_{2^2})$ is $\{(0,1), (1,0), (1,1), (2,0), (2,2), (3,0), (3,3)\} \cup \{\mathcal{O}\}$.
The field F_{2^2} has a reduction polynomial $f(x) = x^2 + x + 1$ and a generator $g = x$.

1) Calculate $7 \cdot (2,2)$ using the left-to-right binary point multiplication algorithm.
2) Calculate $7 \cdot (2,2)$ using the recursive point multiplication algorithm.

Problem 13.4 Consider an elliptic curve E defined by equation $y^2 = x^3 + 2x + 2\ mod\ 17$. Why all points of the elliptic of curve E are primitive elements (i.e. they are all generators of all the other points of the curve)? Hint: use Lagrange's theorem (Theorem 3.11) and its corollary.

Problem 13.5 Prove Theorem 13.2.

Problem 13.6 In December 2010, the ECDSA private key used by Sony to sign the software for PlayStation 3 console was discovered. The attack worked, because Sony used a static value for k in the signature generation procedure. In this problem, you are asked to design an attack to discover Alice's private key assuming that, by mistake, Alice makes use of the same value of k for all her signed messages.

Problem 13.7 Alice and Bob use the elliptic curve $y^2 = x^3 + x + 1\ mod\ 23$. The EC points are shown in example 13.9.

1) Can Alice and Bob agree to use point $(4,0)$ as value for parameter G?
2) Can Bob select point $(13,7)$ as value for parameter G and then try to use a private key equal to 7?
3) With the selected parameters (i.e. $a = b = 1$ and $p = 23$), what are the messages that Alice can encrypt using the probabilistic mapping method?

13.6.2 Solutions to Exercises and Problems

Exercise 13.1 Points of EC with equation $E: y^2 \equiv (x^3 + 7) \bmod 17$ are:

$$E(F_{17}) = \{(1,5), (1,12), (2,7), (2,10), (3,0), (5,8),(5,9), (6,6), (6,11),$$
$$(8,3), (8,14), (10,2), (10,15), (12,1),(12,16), (15,4), (15,13),\ \mathcal{O}\}$$

1) Check that point $(5,8)$ is not a generator.

Let x_{kP} denote the x-coordinate of point $k \cdot P$ and y_{kP} its y-coordinate. P is point $(5,8)$. The formula of point doubling yields:

$$\lambda = \frac{3 * x_{1P}^2 + a}{2 * y_{1P}} = \frac{3 * 5^2 + 0}{2 * 8} = \frac{75}{16} = 75 * 16^{-1} = 7 * 16 \equiv 10\ \textit{mod}\ 17$$

$$\left(16^{-1} \equiv 16\ \textit{mod}\ 17\right).$$

$$x_{2P} = \lambda^2 - 2 * x_{1P} = 10^2 - 2 * 5 = 90 \equiv 5\ \textit{mod}\ 17$$

$$y_{2P} = \lambda\left(x_{1P} - x_{2P}\right) - y_{1P} = 10(5-5) - 8 = -8 = 9 \equiv \textit{mod}\ 17$$

Then, try to add to P to $2P$ using formula of point addition:

$$\lambda = \frac{y_{2P} - y_{1P}}{x_{2P} - x_{1P}} = \frac{9-8}{5-5} = \frac{1}{0} \Rightarrow P + 2P = 3P = \mathcal{O}\ (\text{point to infinity})$$

$3P$ cannot be calculated. Consequently, $P = (5,8)$ is not a generator for points of $E(F_{17})$.

2) Check how points of EC are generated from point $(6,6)$, which is one of the generators of the EC $E: y^2 = (x^3 + 7)\ \textit{mod}\ 17$:

Start with $P = (6,6)$, then use point doubling and addition formulas:

$$\lambda = \frac{3 * x_{1P}^2 + a}{2 * y_{1P}} = \frac{3 * 6^2}{2 * 6} = 9\ \textit{mod}\ 17$$

$$x_{2P} = \lambda^2 - 2 * x_{1P} = 9^2 - 2 * 6 = 69 \equiv 1\ \textit{mod}\ 17$$

$$y_{2P} = \lambda\left(x_{1P} - x_{2P}\right) - y_{1P} = 9(6-1) - 6 \equiv 39\ \textit{mod}\ 17 = 5$$

$$\lambda = \frac{y_{2P} - y_{1P}}{x_{2P} - x_{1P}} = \frac{5-6}{1-6} = 5^{-1} = 7 \qquad \left(5^{-1} \equiv 7\ \textit{mod}\ 17\right).$$

$$x_{3P} = \lambda^2 - x_{2P} - x_{1P} = 7^2 - 6 - 1 \equiv 42\ \textit{mod}\ 17 = 8$$

$$y_{3P} = \left(x_{1P} - x_{3P}\right) - y_{1P} = 7(6-8) - 6 \equiv -20\ \textit{mod}\ 17 = 14$$

Table 13.4 shows the results of calculations for all EC points. All the EC points are multiple of point $(6,6)$; hence, it is a generator of the EC. The order of the generator $(6,6)$ is $\#E(F_p) = 18$.

Exercise 13.2 Given the EC $E: y^2 = x^3 + 4x + 20$ over the finite field F_{29}, point $(8,19)$ is one of the generators of $E(F_{29})$.
The check is as follows:
Let P denote the point $(8,19)$. The multiples of P are:

$0 \cdot P = \mathcal{O}$	$10 \cdot P = (17,10)$	$20 \cdot P = (19,16)$	$30P = (2,6)$
$1 \cdot P = (8,19)$	$11 \cdot P = (5,7)$	$21 \cdot P = (27,2)$	$31 \cdot P = (10,25)$
$2 \cdot P = (0,7)$	$12 \cdot P = (3,1)$	$22 \cdot P = (14,23)$	$32 \cdot P = (20,3)$
$3 \cdot P = (16,27)$	$13 \cdot P = (24,22)$	$23 \cdot P = (1,5)$	$33 \cdot P = (6,17)$
$4 \cdot P = (6,12)$	$14 \cdot P = (1,24)$	$24 \cdot P = (24,7)$	$34 \cdot P = (16,2)$
$5 \cdot P = (20,26)$	$15 \cdot P = (14,6)$	$25 \cdot P = (3,28)$	$35 \cdot P = (0,22)$
$6 \cdot P = (10,4)$	$16 \cdot P = (27,27)$	$26 \cdot P = (5,22)$	$36 \cdot P = (8,10)$
$7 \cdot P = (2,23)$	$17 \cdot P = (19,13)$	$27P = (17,19)$	$37 \cdot P = \mathcal{O}$
$8 \cdot P = (13,23)$	$18 \cdot P = (15,27)$	$28 \cdot P = (4,10)$	
$9 \cdot P = (4,19)$	$19 \cdot P = (15,2)$	$29 \cdot P = (13,6)$	

Thus, point $(8,19)$ is a generator of the elliptic curve $E(F_{29})$.

Table 13.4 Calculations of multiple points of point (6,6).

k	λ	x_{kP}	y_{kP}	kP
1	–	6	6	$1 \cdot P = (6,6)$
2	9	1	5	$2 \cdot P = (1,5)$
3	7	8	14	$3 \cdot P = (8,14)$
4	4	2	10	$4 \cdot P = (2,10)$
5	16	10	15	$5 \cdot P = (10,15)$
6	15	5	9	$6 \cdot P = (5,9)$
7	14	15	4	$7 \cdot P = (15,4)$
8	13	12	1	$8 \cdot P = (12,1)$
9	2	3	0	$9 \cdot P = (3,0)$
10	2	12	16	$10 \cdot P = (12,16)$
11	13	15	13	$11 \cdot P = (15,13)$
12	14	5	8	$12 \cdot P = (5,8)$
13	15	10	2	$13 \cdot P = (10,2)$
14	16	2	7	$14 \cdot P = (2,7)$
15	4	8	3	$15 \cdot P = (8,3)$
16	7	1	12	$16 \cdot P = (1,12)$
17	9	6	11	$17 \cdot P = (6,11)$
18	$\propto$			$18 \cdot P = \mathcal{O}$

Exercise 13.3 To be on an elliptic curve $E : y^2 = x^3 + ax + b \bmod p$, $x^3 + ax + b$ must be a quadratic residue. Euler's criterion (Theorem 3.7) states that given integers a and p, such that $p > 2$ and a and p are coprime, $a^{\frac{p-1}{2}} \equiv 1 \bmod p$, if there exists r such that $r^2 \equiv a \bmod p$ and $a^{\frac{p-1}{2}} \equiv -1 \bmod p$, otherwise.

Let E be an elliptic curve given by $y^2 = x^3 + 1$ over finite field F_{103}.

1) Does $y^2 = (2)^3 + 1 \bmod 103$ has a solution?

$9^{\frac{103-1}{2}} \bmod 103 = 1$ # (a tool of modular exponentiation is needed).

By Euler's criterion, there exists an integer y such that $y^2 = (2)^3 + 1 \bmod 103$.

It is easy to find $y^2 = 9 \bmod 103$. $y = \pm 3$ is a solution.

Hence, $(2,3)$ and $(2,100)$ are points of the curve $E(F_{103})$.

2) Does $y^2 = (4)^3 + 1 \bmod 103$ has a solution?

$65^{\frac{103-1}{2}} \bmod 103 = 102 = -1 \bmod 103$

By Euler's criterion, there is no integer y such that $y^2 = (4)^3 + 1 \bmod 103$.

Therefore, no point with coordinate $x = 4$ is on the elliptic curve $E(F_{103})$.

Exercise 13.4

1) Let $E : y^2 = x^3 + x + 1$ be an elliptic curve over field F_{103}. Given x-coordinate, to find the y-coordinate, we need to find square roots.

- $x = 0 \Rightarrow y^2 \equiv 1 \bmod 103 \Rightarrow y = \pm 1 \bmod 103$. Hence, points are $(0, 1)$ and $(0, 102)$.
- $x = 11 \Rightarrow 11^3 + 11 + 1 \bmod 103 \equiv 4 \bmod 103 \Rightarrow y = \pm 2 \bmod 103$. Hence, points are: $(11, 2)$ and $(11, 101)$.
- $x = 73 \Rightarrow y^2 \equiv 73^3 + 73 + 1 \bmod 103 \equiv 60 \bmod 103$

In this case, there is no easy way to find the square roots. More work is needed. By Euler's criterion (Theorem 3.7), 60 is a square residue, because $\left(60^{\frac{103-1}{2}}\right)$. Thus, a square root exists. Since $103 \equiv 3 \bmod 4$, by Lemma 3.5,

$$y \equiv \pm\left(60^{\frac{103+1}{4}}\right) \bmod 103 \equiv \pm 36 \bmod 103.$$ Hence, points are $(73, 36)$ and $(73, 67)$.

2) Let $E: y^2 = x^3 + x + 1$ be an elliptic curve over field F_{101}.

- $x = 0 \Rightarrow y^2 \equiv 1 \bmod 101 \Rightarrow y = \pm 1$. Thus, points are: $(0, 1)$ and $(0, 100)$.
- $x = 8 \Rightarrow y^2 \equiv 8^3 + 8 + 1 \bmod 101 \equiv 16 \bmod 101 \Rightarrow y = \pm 4$. Hence, points are: $(8, 4)$ and $(8, 97)$.
- $x = 100 \Rightarrow y^2 \equiv 100^3 + 100 + 1 \bmod 101$
  $y^2 \equiv 100^3 \bmod 101 \equiv (-1)^3 \bmod 101 \equiv -1 \bmod 101 \equiv 100 \bmod 101$
  $\Rightarrow y = \pm 10$. Hence, points are $(100, 10)$ and $(100, 91)$.
- $x = 57 \Rightarrow y^2 \equiv 17 \bmod 101$.

In this case, there is no easy way to find the roots. More work is needed. By Euler's criterion, 17 is a square residue, because $17^{\frac{101-1}{2}} \equiv 1 \bmod 101$. Thus, a square root exists. Since $101 \equiv 1 \bmod 4$, Tonelli-Shanks algorithm (see Section 3.3.5.1) can be used to find the square roots.

The steps of Tonelli-Shanks algorithm are as follows:

$101 = 2^2 * 25 + 1$. Hence, $s = 2$ and $q = 25$.

Find a square nonresidue modulo 101: $u = 2$ is a square nonresidue.

Initialization: $m = 2; c = 2^{25} \bmod 101 = 10$

$t = 17^{25} \bmod 101 = 100; R = 17^{(25+1)/2} \bmod 101 = 65$

Loop:

Iteration 1:

i) $100^{2^1} \equiv 1 \bmod 101$. Hence, $k = 1$
ii) $b \equiv 10^{2^{m-k-1}} \bmod 101 \equiv 10^{2^0} \bmod 101 = 10$
iii) $m = 1$
iv) $c \equiv 10^2 \bmod 101 = 100$
v) $t \equiv 100 * 10^2 \bmod 101 = 1$
vi) $R \equiv 65 * 10 \bmod 101 = 44$

Iteration 2:
vii) $t \equiv 1 \bmod 101$. Hence, stop and return $r = 44$

Check: $(\pm 44)^2 = 17 \bmod 101$.
Therefore, points are: $(57, 44)$ and $(57, 57)$.

Exercise 13.5

1) In general, to find all points over an elliptic curve $E: y^2 = x^3 + ax + b \bmod p$, we need to check for each coordinate $x \in F_p$, if $u = x^3 + ax + b \bmod p$ is a square residue. We make use of Euler's criterion (Theorem 3.7) to check if an integer u is a square root $\bmod p$. Then, for each square residue, we compute the square root (i.e. y). The following table gives the results of calculations. The number of points is $27 + 1$ ($+1$ to count the point to infinity).

x	$u = (x^3 + x + 1)$ $\bmod 23$	$\left(\dfrac{u}{23}\right)$	$y \mid y^2$ $\equiv u \bmod 23$	Points on EC
0	1	1	1, 22	$(0, 1), (0, 22)$
1	3	1	7, 16	$(1, 7), (1, 16)$
2	11	-1		
3	8	1	10, 13	$(3, 10), (3, 13)$
4	0	0	0	$(4, 0)$
5	16	1	4, 19	$(5, 4), (5, 19)$

6	16	1	4, 19	$(6,4), (6,19)$
7	6	1	11, 12	$(7,11), (7,12)$
8	15	−1		
9	3	1	7, 16	$(9,7), (9,16)$
10	22	−1		
11	9	1	3, 20	$(11,3), (11,20)$
12	16	1	4, 19	$(12,4), (12, 19)$
13	3	1	7, 16	$(13,7), (13,16)$
14	22	−1		
15	10	−1		
16	19	−1		
17	9	1	3, 20	$(17,3), (17, 20)$
18	9	1	3, 20	$(18,3), (18, 20)$
19	2	1	5, 18	$(19,5), (19,18)$
20	17	−1		
21	14	−1		
22	22	−1		

2) The value calculated by Theorem 13.2 is:

$$\#E(F_p) = 23 + 1 + \sum_{x \in F_p}\left(\frac{x^3 + ax + b}{p}\right) = 23 + 1 + 4 = 28.$$

The sum of Legendre's symbol associated with x-coordinates in F_{23} is given by the sum of the values in the third column. Therefore, we checked the correctness of Theorem 13.2. For formal proof of Theorem 13.1, see Problem 13.5.

Exercise 13.6

Since $E(F_{2^2})$ has seven points plus the point to infinity, its order is $ord(F_{2^2}) = 8$.

Therefore, every point $P \in E(F_{2^2})$, such that $8 \cdot P = \mathcal{O}$ is a generator of $E(F_{2^2})$.

The elliptic curve has equation $y^2 = xy + x^3 + 1$; thus, $a = 0$.

The field F_{2^2} has a reduction polynomial $f(x) = x^2 + x + 1$ and a generator $g = x$.

The elements, in binary representation, of F_{2^2} are $\{00, 01, 10, 11\}$; they are all powers of the generator $g = x$ under the reduction polynomial $f(x) = x^2 + x + 1$:

$$g^0 \equiv x^0 \ mod \ f(x) = (01)$$

$$g^1 \equiv x^1 \ mod \ f(x) = x^1 = (10)$$

$$g^2 \equiv x^2 \ mod \ f(x) = x^1 + 1 = (11)$$

$$g^3 \equiv x^3 \ mod \ f(x) = 1 \ mod \ f(x) = (01)$$

$$g^4 \equiv x^4 \ mod \ f(x) = x^1 \ mod \ f(x) = (10)$$

$$g^5 \equiv x^5 \ mod \ f(x) = x^1 + 1 \ mod \ f(x) = (11)$$

Representation of elements as powers of the field generator g is very useful for point addition calculation. The coordinates of points are represented as powers of g. Remember that addition of two elements of F_{2^2} is a bitwise XOR operation and the multiplication is the remainder modulo the reduction polynomial $f(x)$.

As shown in Example 13.3, points of $E(F_{2^2})$ are $\{(0,1), (1,0), (1,1), (2,0), (2,2), (3,0), (3,3)\} \cup \{\mathcal{O}\}$.

Let point $P = (x_p, y_p)$ denote the point to check.

1) Check of point $(1,1)$

First, calculate point $Q = (x_q, y_q) = 2 \cdot P = 2 \cdot (1,1) = 2 \cdot (g^0, g^0)$ using the point doubling formulas, i.e.:

$$\lambda = x_P + \frac{y_P}{x_P} \qquad x_{2P} = \lambda^2 + \lambda + a \qquad y_{2P} = x_P^2 + (\lambda + 1)x_{2P}$$

$$\lambda = g^0 + \frac{g^0}{g^0} = g^0 + g^0 = (00)$$

$$x_{2P} = (00)^2 + (00) + 0 = (00) \qquad y_{2P} = (g^0)^2 + ((00) + 1)(00) = g^0$$

That is: $2 \cdot (1,1) = (0,1) = ((00), g^0)$

Now, check $3 \cdot (1,1)$: $3 \cdot (1,1) = (1,1) + 2 \cdot (1,1) = (1,1) + (0,1)$ using the formulas of point addition $(x_P, y_P) + (x_Q, y_Q) = (x_R, y_R)$, i.e.:

$$\lambda = \frac{y_Q + y_P}{x_Q + x_P} \qquad x_R = \lambda^2 + \lambda + x_P + x_Q + a \qquad y_R = \lambda(x_P + x_R) + x_R + y_P$$

$$\lambda = \frac{g^0 + g^0}{(00) + g^0} = 0$$

$$x_{3P} = (00)^2 + (00) + g^0 + (00) = g^0$$

$$y_{3P} = (00)(g^0 + g^0) + g^0 + g^0 = (00)$$

That is: $3 \cdot (1,1) = (1,0) = (g^0, (00))$

Now, check $4 \cdot (1,1)$: $4 \cdot (1,1) = (1,1) + 3 \cdot (1,1) = (1,1) + (1,0)$

$$\lambda = \frac{(00) + g^0}{g^0 + g^0} = \frac{(00) + g^0}{0} \text{ (division by zero).}$$

That is: $4 \cdot (1,1) = \mathcal{O}$, which means that the order of point is 4 and consequently it is not a generator of $E(F_{2^2})$.

2) Check of point $(2,2)$ using the formulas of point doubling and point addition

- $2 \cdot P = 2 \cdot (2,2)$

$$\lambda = g^1 + \frac{g^1}{g^1} = g^2 \qquad x_{2P} = (g^2)^2 + g^2 + 0 = g^0$$

$$y_{2P} = (g^1)^2 + (g^2 + g^0) = g^0$$

$$\Rightarrow 2 \cdot (2,2) = (1,1) = (g^0, g^0)$$

- $3 \cdot P = 3 \cdot (2,2) = (2,2) + (1,1)$

$$\lambda = \frac{g^0 + g^1}{g^0 + g^1} = 1 \qquad x_{3P} = 1 + 1 + g^1 + g^0 = g^2$$

$$y_{3P} = 1(g^1 + g^2) + g^2 + g^1 = (00)$$

$$\Rightarrow 3 \cdot (2,2) = (3,0) = (g^2, 0)$$

- $4 \cdot P = 4 \cdot (2,2) = (2,2) + (3,0)$

$$\lambda = \frac{(00) + g^1}{g^2 + g^1} = \frac{g^1}{g^3} = \frac{g^1}{g^0} = g^1 \qquad x_{4P} = (g^1)^2 + g^1 + g^1 + g^2 = (00)$$

$$y_{4P} = g^1(g^1 + (00)) + (00) + g^1 = g^0$$

$$\Rightarrow 4 \cdot (2,2) = (0,1) = (0, g^0)$$

- $5 \cdot P = 5 \cdot (2,2) = (2,2) + (0,1)$

$$\lambda = \frac{g^0 + g^1}{(00) + g^1} = \frac{g^2}{g^1} = g^2 g^{-1} = g^1 \qquad x_{5P} = \left(g^1\right)^2 + g^1 + g^1 + (00) = g^2$$

$$y_{5P} = g^1\left(g^1 + g^2\right) + g^2 + g^1 = g^2$$

$$\Rightarrow 5 \cdot (2,2) = (3,3) = \left(g^2, g^2\right)$$

- $6 \cdot P = 6 \cdot (2,2) = (2,2) + (3,3)$

$$\lambda = \frac{g^2 + g^1}{g^2 + g^1} = g^0 \qquad x_{6P} = \left(g^0\right)^2 + g^0 + g^1 + g^2 = g^0$$

$$y_{6P} = g^0\left(g^1 + g^0\right) + g^0 + g^1 = (00)$$

$$\Rightarrow 6 \cdot (2,2) = (1,0) = \left(g^0, (00)\right)$$

- $7 \cdot P = 7 \cdot (2,2) = (2,2) + (1,0)$

$$\lambda = \frac{(00) + g^1}{g^0 + g^1} = \frac{g^1}{g^2} = g^1 g^{-2} = g^2 \qquad x_{7P} = \left(g^2\right)^2 + g^2 + g^1 + g^0 = g^1$$

$$y_{7P} = g^2\left(g^1 + g^1\right) + g^1 + g^1 = (00)$$

$$\Rightarrow 7 \cdot (2,2) = (2,0) = \left(g^1, (00)\right)$$

- $8 \cdot P = 8\,(2,2) = (2,2) + (2,0)$

$$\lambda = \frac{(00) + g^1}{g^1 + g^1} = \frac{g^1}{0} \text{ (division by zero)}$$

$$\Rightarrow 8 \cdot (2,2) = \mathcal{O}. \text{ Thus, } ord(2,2) = 8. \text{ Point } (2,2) \text{ is a generator of } E(F_{2^2}).$$

Exercise 13.7

1) Find points of the elliptic curve E: $y^2 = x^3 + 2x + 2 \bmod 17$

   First, compute the quadric residues $mod\,17$

   $(1)^2 \equiv (-1)^2 \equiv (16)^2 \equiv 1 \bmod 17$ $\qquad$ $(2)^2 \equiv (-2)^2 \equiv (15)^2 \equiv 4 \bmod 17$

   $(3)^2 \equiv (-3)^2 \equiv (14)^2 \equiv 9 \bmod 17$ $\qquad$ $(4)^2 \equiv (-4)^2 \equiv (13)^2 \equiv 16 \bmod 17$

   $(5)^2 \equiv (-5)^2 \equiv (12)^2 \equiv 8 \bmod 17$ $\qquad$ $(6)^2 \equiv (-6)^2 \equiv (11)^2 \equiv 2 \bmod 17$

   $(7)^2 \equiv (-7)^2 \equiv (10)^2 \equiv 15 \bmod 17$ $\qquad$ $(8)^2 \equiv (-8)^2 \equiv (9)^2 \equiv 13 \bmod 17$

   Second, compute $f(x) = x^3 + 2x + 2 \bmod 17$ for $x \in [0, 16]$

$f(0) = 2$	$f(1) = 5$	$f(2) = 14$	$f(3) = 1$	$f(4) = 6$
$f(5) = 1$	$f(6) = 9$	$f(7) = 2$	$f(8) = 3$	$f(9) = 1$
$f(10) = 2$	$f(11) = 12$	$f(12) = 3$	$f(13) = 15$	$f(14) = 3$
$f(15) = 7$	$f(16) = 16$			

   Third, keep points such that $f(x)$ is a quadratic residue $mod\,17$. Hence, the 19 points of the elliptic curve with equation $y^2 = x^3 + 2x + 2 \bmod 17$ are

   $$\left\{(0, \pm 6), (3, \pm 1), (5, \pm 1), (6, \pm 3), (7, \pm 6), (9, \pm 1), (10, \pm 6), (13, \pm 7), (16, \pm 4), \mathcal{O}\right\}.$$

2) Theorem 13.1 (Hasse's theorem) bounds the cardinality of an elliptic curve as follows:
$\left|\#E\left(F_q\right)-q-1\right|\le 2\sqrt{q}$. In this exercise $E\left(F_q\right)=19$ and $q=17$.

$\left|19-17-1\right|\le 2\sqrt{17}$. Therefore, Hasse's theorem is satisfied.

When an elliptic curve is defined over a prime finite field, theorem 13.2 provides an accurate value of the cardinality of the elliptic curve as follows:

$$\#E\left(F_p\right)=p+1+\sum_{x\in F_p}\left(\frac{x^3+ax+b}{p}\right) \tag{a}$$

where $\left(\dfrac{u}{p}\right)$ denotes Legendre symbol defined as follows:

$$\left(\frac{u}{p}\right)=\begin{cases}0 & if & GCD(u,p)\ne 1\\ +1 & if & u\ is\ quadratic\ residue\\ -1 & if & u\ is\ quadratic\ nonresidue\end{cases}$$

Compute Legendre symbol for every $x\in F_{17}$:

$\left(\dfrac{0^3+2*0+2}{17}\right)=\left(\dfrac{2}{17}\right)=1$ $\qquad$ $\left(\dfrac{1^3+2*1+2}{17}\right)=\left(\dfrac{5}{17}\right)=-1$

$\left(\dfrac{2^3+2*2+2}{17}\right)=\left(\dfrac{14}{17}\right)=-1$ $\qquad$ $\left(\dfrac{3^3+2*3+2}{17}\right)=\left(\dfrac{35}{17}\right)=\left(\dfrac{1}{17}\right)=1$

$\left(\dfrac{4^3+2*4+2}{17}\right)=\left(\dfrac{6}{17}\right)=-1$ $\qquad$ $\left(\dfrac{5^3+2*5+2}{17}\right)=\left(\dfrac{1}{17}\right)=1$

$\left(\dfrac{6^3+2*6+2}{17}\right)=\left(\dfrac{9}{17}\right)=1$ $\qquad$ $\left(\dfrac{7^3+2*7+2}{17}\right)=\left(\dfrac{2}{17}\right)=1$

$\left(\dfrac{8^3+2*8+2}{17}\right)=\left(\dfrac{3}{17}\right)=-1$ $\qquad$ $\left(\dfrac{9^3+2*9+2}{17}\right)=\left(\dfrac{1}{17}\right)=1$

$\left(\dfrac{10^3+2*10+2}{17}\right)=\left(\dfrac{2}{17}\right)=1$ $\qquad$ $\left(\dfrac{11^3+2*11+2}{17}\right)=\left(\dfrac{12}{17}\right)=-1$

$\left(\dfrac{12^3+2*12+2}{17}\right)=\left(\dfrac{3}{17}\right)=-1$ $\qquad$ $\left(\dfrac{13^3+2*13+2}{17}\right)=\left(\dfrac{15}{17}\right)=1$

$\left(\dfrac{14^3+2*14+2}{17}\right)=\left(\dfrac{3}{17}\right)=-1$ $\qquad$ $\left(\dfrac{15^3+2*15+2}{17}\right)=\left(\dfrac{7}{17}\right)=-1$

$\left(\dfrac{16^3+2*16+2}{17}\right)=\left(\dfrac{16}{17}\right)=1$

Check that 1, 2, 9, 15, and 16 are quadratic residues:

$1^2\equiv 1\ mod\ 17$ $\qquad$ $6^2\equiv 2\ mod\ 17$ $\qquad$ $3^2\equiv 9\ mod\ 17$

$100^2\equiv 15\ mod\ 17$ $\qquad$ $4^2\equiv 16\ mod\ 17$

Make substitution in (a): $\#E\left(F_p\right)=17+1+1=19$.

Exercise 13.8 Let $E\left(F_{179}\right)$ be an elliptic curve with equation $y^2 = x^3 + 2x + 7$.

Find an EC point to map the message $M = 11$ assuming that $K = 10$.

$K = 10 \Rightarrow$ any message M to map should be such that: $0 \leq M < \left\lfloor \dfrac{179}{10} \right\rfloor - 1 = 16$.

Let the message to map be $11 \Rightarrow 10 * 11 \leq x < 10 * (11 + 1)$.

There are three points that fulfill equation $y^2 \equiv (x^3 + 2x + 7) \bmod 179$:

$\left(110^3 + 2 * 110 + 7\right) \bmod 179 = 2^2 \bmod 179$. Thus, point $(110, 2)$ is a mapping solution.

$\left(111^3 + 2 * 111 + 7\right) \bmod 179 = 11^2 \bmod 179$. Thus, point $(111, 11)$ is a mapping solution.

$\left(112^3 + 2 * 112 + 7\right) \bmod 179 = 3^2 \bmod 179$. Thus, point $(112, 3)$ is a mapping solution.

Problem 13.1

1) Representation of 128 in power of 2 results in: $128 \cdot P = 2(2(2(2(2(2(2 \cdot P))))))$. Under Left-to-right point multiplication algorithm, seven point doublings are used. More generally, when k is a power of 2 (i.e. $k = 2^m$), m point doublings are used to compute $k \cdot P$.

2) There are different alternatives to calculate $127 \cdot P$ among which the following ones:
   i) $127 \cdot P$ is rewritten as $127 \cdot P = (128 - 1) \cdot P = 128 \cdot P - P$. Under binary representation multiplication method, seven point doublings and one addition are used. $-P$ is the negative of point P. $-P$ coordinates depend on the underlying field: $-(x, y) = (x, -y)$ if the field is prime and $-(x, y) = (x, x + y)$ if the field is an extension one (i.e. of the form F_{2^m}).
   ii) $127 \cdot P = \left(1 + 2(63)\right) \cdot P = \left(1 + 2\left(1 + 2(31)\right)\right) \cdot P$

$$= \left(1 + 2\left(1 + 2\left(1 + 2(15)\right)\right)\right) \cdot P$$

$$= \left(1 + 2\left(1 + 2\left(1 + 2\left(1 + 2(7)\right)\right)\right)\right) \cdot P$$

$$= \left(1 + 2\left(1 + 2\left(1 + 2\left(1 + 2\left(1 + 2(1 + 2)\right)\right)\right)\right)\right) \cdot P$$

$$= \left(P + 2 \cdot \left(P + 2 \cdot \left(P + 2 \cdot \left(P + 2 \cdot \left(P + 2 \cdot (P + 2 \cdot P)\right)\right)\right)\right)\right)$$

Thereby, calculation of $127 \cdot P$ requires six doublings and six additions.

Problem 13.2

1) In the left-to-right binary method for point multiplication, scalar k is represented as a bit string with r bits such that $k = (k_{r-1} k_{r-2} \dots k_0)$. The number of iterations is r. Therefore, the complexity of the method is $O\left(\log_2(k)\right)$.

2) In the recursive method for point multiplication, scalar k is divided by 2 until it reaches 0 or 1. Therefore, the number of iterations is in $O\left(\log_2(k)\right)$.

Problem 13.3 Consider the elliptic curve $E(F_{2^2})$ with equation $y^2 + xy = x^3 + 1$. Points of $E(F_{2^2})$ are: $\left\{(0, 1), (1, 0), (1, 1), (2, 0), (2, 2), (3, 0), (3, 3)\right\} \cup \{\mathcal{O}\}$.

The field F_{2^2} has a reduction polynomial $f(x) = x^2 + x + 1$ and a generator $g = x$.

1) Calculate $R = 7 \cdot (2, 2)$ using the left-to-right binary point multiplication algorithm. Below are the execution steps:
$P = (2, 2)$
$k = 7 = 111_2;\ k_2 = 1,\ k_1 = 1,\ k_0 = 1$
$Q = \mathcal{O}$
$i = 2$:
   $Q = 2 \cdot Q = \mathcal{O}$

$$k_2 = 1 \Rightarrow Q = Q + P = \mathcal{O} + P = P = (2,2)$$

$i = 1$:

$$Q = 2 \cdot Q = 2 \cdot (2,2)$$
$$k_1 = 1 \Rightarrow Q = Q + P = 2 \cdot (2,2) + P = 3 \cdot (2,2) = (3,0)$$

$i = 0$:

$$Q = 2 \cdot Q = 2 * (3,0) = 6 \cdot (2,2) = (1,0)$$
$$k_0 = 1 \Rightarrow Q = Q + P = (1,0) + (2,2) = 7 \cdot (2,2) = (2,0)$$

Return $(2,0)$.

2) Calculate $7 \cdot (2,2)$ using the recursive point multiplication (RPM) algorithm.

1st function call: $RPM((2,2),7)$

$$k = 7 \Rightarrow k \bmod 2 = 1 \Rightarrow \text{Return } (P + RPM((2,2),6))$$

2nd function call: $RPM((2,2),6)$

$$k = 6 \Rightarrow k \bmod 2 = 0 \Rightarrow \text{Return } (2 \cdot RPM((2,2),3))$$

3rd function call: $RPM((2,2),3)$

$$k = 3 \Rightarrow k \bmod 2 = 1 \Rightarrow \text{Return } (P + RPM((2,2),2))$$

4th function call: $RPM((2,2),2)$

$$k = 2 \Rightarrow k \bmod 2 = 0 \Rightarrow \text{Return } (2 \cdot RPM((2,2),1))$$

5th function call: $RPM((2,2),1)$

$$k = 1 \Rightarrow \text{Return } ((2,2))$$

Starting from the bottom, the substitution of the result returned by the ith call of RPM in the $i\text{-}1^{th}$ RPM call yields the final result, which is $(2,0)$.

Problem 13.4   Given the elliptic curve $E: y^2 = x^3 + 2x + 2 \bmod 17$, why all points of the elliptic are generators?
Recall that the order of a point P of an elliptic curve is the smallest k such that $k \cdot P = \mathcal{O}$ and a point G is a generator, if the order of G is equal to the number of points of the curve including the point $\mathcal{O}$. In general, with the exception of point $\mathcal{O}$, which has an order of 1 (because $1 \cdot \mathcal{O} = \mathcal{O}$), the elements of a group E associated with an elliptic curve have orders in $\left[2, \#E(F_p)\right]$. By Lagrange theorem and its corollary, any element of a group has an order, which divides the cardinality of the group. Since the cardinality of the group associated with the elliptic curve $y^2 = x^3 + 2x + 2 \bmod 17$ is equal to 19, which is a prime, the order of all elements, distinct from $\mathcal{O}$ is 19. Therefore, by definition of a group generator, all points of the elliptic curve, with the exception of $\mathcal{O}$, are generators.

Problem 13.5 *(Proof of Theorem 13.2)*   Let $E: y^2 \equiv x^3 + ax + b \bmod p$ be an elliptic curve over prime field F_p. A prime field has exactly p elements. For any $u \in F_p$, if $\left(u^3 + au + b\right) \bmod p$ is a square residue, then there exists two points (u,w) and $(u,-w)$ on the elliptic curve such that $(\pm w)^2 \equiv \left(u^3 + au + b\right) \bmod p$, with the exception that if $\left(u^3 + au + b\right) \bmod p = 0$, there exists a single point $(u,0)$. Therefore, the number of points associated with any $u \in F_p$ is $1 + \left(\dfrac{u^3 + au + b}{p}\right)$, where $\left(\dfrac{u^3 + au + b}{p}\right)$ is Legendre symbol (see Section 3.1.7.1) of integer $\left(u^3 + au + b\right)$ and p. Recall that, given two integers a and p, with $a \leq p$, Legendre symbol $\left(\dfrac{a}{p}\right)$ is equal to 1, if a is a square residue modulo p; it is equal to –1, if a is a square nonresidue modulo p; and it is equal to 0, if $a \bmod p = 0$. Therefore, considering all the elements of F_p, the number of points on the elliptic curve, denoted $\#E(F_p)$, is given by:

$$\#E(F_p) = 1 + \sum_{u \in F_p}\left[1 + \left(\frac{u^3 + au + b}{p}\right)\right] = 1 + p + \sum_{u \in F_p}\left(\frac{u^3 + a + b}{p}\right)$$

The "1" after sign "=" is used to include the point to infinity $\mathcal{O}$. □

Problem 13.6 Alice signed two messages M_1 and M_2. Let (r_1, s_1) and (r_2, s_2) be ECDSA signatures of messages M_1 and M_2 respectively.

If Alice used the same point $Q = k \cdot G$ to sign both messages, then $r_1 = r_2 = x_Q \bmod n$ (recall that the component r in signature is the x-coordinate of point Q). In messages M_1 and M_2, signatures (r_1, s_1) and (r_2, s_2), point Q, and the hash function are public. Therefore, the attacker can use them.

First, the attacker calculates the hashes: $H_1 = hash(M_1)$ and $H_2 = hash(M_2)$.
Second, using the definition of the component s of signature, the attacker can write:

$$s_1 = k^{-1}(H_1 + r_1 * Pr_A) = k^{-1}(H_1 + x_Q * Pr_A)$$

$$s_2 = k^{-1}(H_2 + r_2 * Pr_A) = k^{-1}(H_2 + x_Q * Pr_A)$$

$$s_1 - s_2 = k^{-1}(H_1 - H_2)$$

Multiplying both sides of previous equality by k, results in

$$k*(s_1 - s_2) = (H_1 - H_2) \Rightarrow k = (H_1 - H_2)*(s_1 - s_2)^{-1}$$

Problem 13.7 Alice and Bob use the elliptic curve $y^2 = x^3 + x + 1 \bmod 23$. The EC points of $E(F_{23})$ are:

$$\{(0, 1) \quad (0, 22) \quad (1, 7) \quad (1, 16) \quad (3, 10) \quad (3, 13)$$
$$(4, 0) \quad (5, 4) \quad (5, 19) \quad (6, 4) \quad (6, 19) \quad (7, 11)$$
$$(7, 12) \quad (9, 7) \quad (9, 16) \quad (11, 3) \quad (11, 20) \quad (12, 4)$$
$$(12, 19) \quad (13, 7) \quad (13, 16) \quad (17, 3) \quad (17, 20) \quad (18, 3)$$
$$(18, 20) \quad (19, 5) \quad (19, 18) \quad \mathcal{O}\}$$

1) Alice and Bob should not use point $(4, 0)$ as parameter G, because the order of point $(4, 0)$ is 2. Point $(4, 0)$ can only generate itself and $\mathcal{O}$ (because the y-coordinate is 0). With $G = (4, 0)$, both public keys are the same and equal to $(4, 0)$, because the single value that Bob can choose as private key and that Alice can choose as ephemeral key k' is 1.
2) If Bob selects point $(13, 7)$ for parameter G, he cannot use a private key higher than 6, because $7 \cdot (13, 7) = \mathcal{O}$ (the order of point $(13, 7)$ is 7).
3) The messages that Alice can encrypt depend only on parameters K and p. Since $p = 23$, the messages that can be encrypted are in the range $[0, 22]$. In addition, the messages, which will be encrypted, depend on the success of the probabilistic mapping method. The table below gives, for each K value, the range of message values that can be tested for mapping, the message values for which the mapping succeeded to find EC points, the mapping success ratio, and the ratio of the numbers l of integers less than p that can be encrypted.

K	Range of M	Mapped values of M	Mapping success rate	Ratio l/p
1	[0, 22]	0, 4, 5, 6, 11, 12, 17, 18	8/23	8/23
2	[0, 10]	0, 2, 3, 5, 6, 8, 9	7/11	7/23
3	[0, 6]	0, 1, 2, 3, 4, 5, 6	1	7/23
4	[0, 4]	0, 1, 2, 3, 4	1	5/23
5	[0, 3]	0, 1, 2, 3	1	4/23
6,7	[0, 2]	0, 1, 2	1	3/23
8:11	[0, 1]	0, 1	1	2/23
12:22	[0, 0]	0	1	1/23

As you may notice, the higher the value of K is, the higher the probability of mapping success is. Conversely, the higher the value of K is, the lower the number of message values to map is.

Notes

1 Elliptic curves used in cryptography are a simplified form of the general equation of elliptic curves. This book is limited to ECs for cryptography.

2 This is the definition of the traditional ECs over finite fields F_p with prime p.

3 The EC points were calculated using a few-lines python code.

4 Note that the same sign "–" is used with different meanings. "–" before a point means the inverse point within the underlying field (it comes from a field operation), while "–" before a y-coordinate means the inverse regarding the y-axis (it comes from the usual interpretation of "minus").

5 For both parties, the generation of private keys shall use standard random number generator, which has been approved to be attack-resistant (see Chapter 16).

6 Points may be calculated with a simple program, given a and b (the coefficients of the curve equation) and p (the modulus of the field).

7 The randomness of selection of k must be approved and k must be kept secret. The values of k have the same security requirements as the private key. If an attacker retrieves two or more messages signed with the same value of k, he/she can derive the private key of the signer.

8 The calculations in the signing process are made *modulo n*. Consequently, the bit size of the hash H must not be greater than the bit size of n (the order of the base point G). In case, the bit size of the hash H is greater than the bit size of n, only the leftmost $\lceil log_2(n) \rceil$ bits of the hash are used in signing and also in verification.

9 The probability that $r = 0$ (or that $s = 0$) is approximately $1/n$.

10 SHAKE256 is a variant of the SHA3 family. $SHAKE256(Data, 912)$ has an output of $912/2 = 456$ bits.

11 The randomness of selection of k must be approved and k must be kept secret.

12 Encoding an EC point is the transformation of point coordinates into a bit-string.

13 For example, use $context = 1$, to sign emails, $context = 2$, to sign pictures, and $context = 3$, to sign videos.

14 s is the same in Key-pair generation and Signature generation.

15 In elliptic curve theory, point U is called a 2^c-torsion point. There may exist several 2^c-torsion points on any elliptic curve with an order divisible by 2^c.

16 The string yielded by a key derivation function is referred to as *keying material*.

17 Edward and Montgomery curves have parameters which differ a little from those of the traditional curves (see Section 13.2.4).

18 To prevent attacks, an ephemeral key-pair is selected for each message to encrypt.

19 If the mapping method fails to find an EC point with the chosen K value, then try another value.

References

1 Zhu, L., Jaganathan, K., and Lauter, K. (2008). *Elliptic Curve Cryptography (ECC) Support for Public Key Cryptography for Initial Authentication in Kerberos (PKINIT), RFC 5349*. Internet Engineering Task Force (IETF).

2 Adamantiadis, A., Josefsson, S., and Baushke, M. (2020). *Secure Shell (SSH) Key Exchange Method Using Curve25519 and Curve448, RFC 8731*. Internet Engineering Task Force (IETF).

3 Nir, Y., Josefsson, S., and Pegourie-Gonnard, M. (2018). *Elliptic Curve Cryptography (ECC) Cipher Suites for Transport Layer Security (TLS) Versions 1.2 and Earlier - RFC 8422*. Internet Engineering Task Force (IETF).

4 Housley, R. (2018). *Use of the Elliptic Curve Diffie-Hellman Key Agreement Algorithm with X25519 and X448 in the Cryptographic Message Syntax (CMS) - RFC 8418*. Internet Engineering Task Force (IETF).

5 Koblitz, N. (1987). Elliptic Curve Cryptosystems. *Mathematics for Computers* 48 (177): 203–209.

6 Miller, V.S. (1985). Use of elliptic curves in cryptography. In: *Annual International Conference on the Theory and Application of Cryptographic Techniques - CRYPTO'85*; Santa Barbara, California: Springer, LNCS 218, 417–426.

7 Langley, A., Hamburg, M., and Turner, S. (2016). *Elliptic Curves for Security, RFC 7748*. Internet Engineering Task Force (IETF).

8 Chen, L., Moody, D., Regenscheid, A. et al. (2019). *Recommendations for Discrete Logarithm-Based Cryptography: Elliptic Curve Domain Parameters, (Draft) SP 800-186*. NIST.

9 Josefsson, S. and Liusvaara, I. (2017). *Edwards-Curve Digital Signature Algorithm (EdDSA) - RFC 8032*. Internet Research Task Force (IETF).

10 NIST. (2013). *Digital Signature Standard (DSS) - FIPS PUB 186-4*. National Institute of Standards and Technology.

11 ANSI. (1998). *Public Key Cryptography for the Financial Services Industry: The Elliptic Curve Digital Signature Algorithm (ECDSA) - ANSI X9.62*. American National Standard Institute.

12 Johnson, D., Menezes, A., and Vanstone, S. (2001). *The Elliptic Curve Digital Signature Algorithm (ECDSA)*. Canada: University of Waterloo.

13 Hankerson, D., Menezes, A., and Vanstone, S. (2004). *Guide to Elliptic Curve Cryptography*. Springer.

14 ANSI. (2020). *Financial services - Public Key Cryptography for the Financial Services Industry: The Elliptic Curve Digital Signature Algorithm - ECDSA - ANSI X9.142*. American National Standard Institute.

15 Diffie, W. and Hellman, M.E. (1976). New directions in cryptography. *IEEE Transactions on Information Theory* 22 (6): 644–654.

16 ANSI. (2001). *Public-Key Cryptography for the Financial Services Industry: Key Agreement and Key Transport Using Elliptic Curve Cryptography - ANSI X9.63*. American National Standard Institute.

17 Menezes, A., Qu, M., and Vanstone, S. (1995). Key agreement and the need for authentication. In: *Workshop on Public Key Solutions*; Toronto, Canada.

18 Law, L., Menezes, A., Qu, M. et al. (2003). An efficient protocol for authenticated key agreement. *Designs, Codes and Cryptography* 28 (2): 119–134.

19 Barker, E., Chen, L., Roginsky, A. et al. (2018). *Recommendation for Pair-Wise Key-Establishment Schemes Using Discrete Logarithm Cryptography - Special Publication 800-56A (Rev. 3)*. NIST.

20 IEEE. (2020). *IEEE Standard Specifications for Public-Key Cryptography, IEEE Std 1363-2000*. Institute of Electrical and Electronics Engineers.

21 ISO/IEC. (2006). *Information technology, Security techniques, Encryption algorithms, Part 2: Asymmetric Ciphers, Draft ISO/IEC 18033-2*. International Organization for Standardization/International Electrotechnical Commission.

22 Certicom. (2009). *Standards for Efficient Cryptography, "SEC 1: Elliptic Curve Cryptography"*. Certicom (Canada).

23 ElGamal, T. (1985). A public key cryptosystem and a signature scheme based on discrete logarithms. *IEEE Transactions on Information Theory* 31 (4): 469–472.

14

Key Management

In previous chapters, we discussed how cryptographic keys might be used. More precisely, symmetric keys are mainly used for data encryption and decryption and for message authentication code generation and verification. Private and public key pairs are mainly used for digital signature generation and verification, for shared secret generation, and for encryption and decryption of keys and data. In addition to those usages of keys, in this chapter, we discuss how existing keys may be used to derive new keys.

Keys are owned and used by entities (e.g. devices, individuals or organizations) that interact with other entities to conduct specific operations in different fields of activities (e.g. e-commerce, e-government services, e-health, etc.). These keys are analogous to the combination of a safe. If adversaries know the combination of a safe, the latter does not provide any security against attacks, even it is very complex. Keys are the most valuable items in computer security; thus, their protection (i.e. confidentiality, integrity, and availability) is of paramount importance. During its lifetime, the key is either in transit (i.e. exchanged between parties), in use (to encrypt, to decrypt, to sign, etc.), or in storage. Key protection[1] shall address all those steps in the key lifetime cycle.

Key management provides the functions for a secure management of cryptographic keys throughout their lifetime. It mainly includes key generation, storage, distribution, recovery, suspension, and withdrawal. This chapter aims at introducing the main mechanisms and protocols for key generation, key agreement, key transport, and key distribution.

Public-key infrastructures (PKIs) are essential services for distribution of public keys. The latter are included in certificates delivered by trusted authorities enabling the recipient to have assurance regarding the holder of a public key. PKIs maintain coherent and valid lists of public keys. PKIs are discussed in Section 15.2.

Randomness is of prime importance to generate robust keys (i.e. keys very difficult to guess with statistical analysis methods). In Chapter 16, we introduce the recommended pseudorandom bit generators.

It is worth noticing that the protocols and functions presented in this chapter are specified in NIST recommendations and RFCs (Request for comments) and used in current secured applications and services.

14.1 Key-Management-related Notions

14.1.1 Types, Security Strengths, and Cryptoperiod of Keys

14.1.1.1 Key Types
Keys are used for providing different forms of services, mainly including:

- Data confidentiality
- Data integrity
- Entity authentication (i.e. provide assurance of the identity of a party)
- Non-repudiation
- Authorization to access protected physical or logical resources
- Support services (e.g. key establishment, key agreement, random number generation, etc.)

Thus, keys may be categorized into several types depending on their use. More precisely, the following key types are used to categorize keys [1]:

- *Symmetric encryption and decryption keys*: they are used with symmetric-key algorithms to provide confidentiality guarantees.
- *Symmetric key-wrapping keys*: they are used to encrypt other keys when they are in transit.
- *Symmetric master/key-derivation keys*: they are used to derive other symmetric keys.
- *Symmetric authentication keys*: they are used with symmetric-key algorithms to provide identity authentication and integrity.
- *Symmetric key-agreement keys*: they are used to establish symmetric keys.
- *Symmetric DRBG[2] keys*: they are used to generate random bits or numbers.
- *Symmetric authorization keys*: they are used to provide privileges to an entity using a symmetric cryptographic algorithm.
- *Private signature-generation keys*: they are used by public-key algorithms to generate digital signatures intended for long-term use.
- *Public signature-verification keys*: they are used by public-key algorithms to verify digital signatures.
- *Private authentication keys*: they are used with public-key algorithms to provide evidence of the sender identity, when establishing an authenticated session or performing some action.
- *Public authentication keys*: they are used with public-key algorithms to verify the identity of the sender, when establishing an authenticated session or performing some action.
- *Private key-transport keys*: they are the private keys of asymmetric-key algorithms and are used to decrypt keys that have been encrypted with the corresponding public key, when establishing symmetric keys.
- *Public key-transport keys*: they are the public keys of asymmetric-key algorithms and are used to encrypt keys when establishing symmetric-keys.
- *Private static key-agreement keys*: they are the long-term private-keys of asymmetric-key algorithms and are used to establish symmetric keys.
- *Public static key-agreement keys*: they are long-term public keys of asymmetric-key algorithms. They are used to establish symmetric keys.
- *Private ephemeral key-agreement keys*: they are the short-term private keys of asymmetric-key algorithms. They are used only once to establish one or more symmetric keys.
- *Public ephemeral key-agreement keys*: they are the short-term public keys of asymmetric-key algorithms. They are used in a single key-establishment transaction to establish one or more symmetric keys.
- *Private authorization keys*: they are the private keys of asymmetric-key algorithms and are used to prove the owner's right to privileges.
- *Public authorization keys*: they are the public keys of asymmetric-key algorithms and are used to verify privileges for an entity that knows the associated private authorization-key.

Usage uniqueness

In general, each key should be used for only one purpose (e.g. confidentiality, integrity authentication, or digital signature), because of, at least, the following two reasons:

1) The use of the same key for two distinct cryptographic applications may weaken the security provided by one or both of the applications.
2) Limiting the use of a key limits the damage that could be done if the key is compromised.

14.1.1.2 Security Strengths

Cryptographic algorithms can provide different security strengths depending mainly on the bit-length of the used keys. Recall that the security strength (also called security level) is defined as a number associated with the amount of operations that is required to break a cryptographic algorithm. The commonly used numbers of security strengths are 80, 112, 128, 192, and 256 bits.

Note. The security strength of 80 bits is no more secure with the current technologies that can be used by attackers. Therefore, the lowest recommended security strength is of 112 bits.

Tables 14.1 and 14.2 provide the security strength of the cryptographic algorithms (i.e. ciphers, digital signature generation, hash functions, MAC generation, etc.) discussed in previous chapters. As you may see, algorithms have comparable security strengths with different key bit-lengths; e.g. RSA with a key bit-length of 3072 has a security strength comparable to that of AES with a key of 128 bits.

Table 14.1 Security strengths of common ciphers. Adapted from [1].

Security strength	Symmetric key algorithms	Asymmetric algorithms		
		DSA, DH, MQV	RSA[3]	ECC-based algorithms
112	3TDEA	$L = 2048, N = 224$	$K = 2048$	$F = 224\text{-}255$
128	AES-128	$L = 3072, N = 256$	$K = 3072$	$F = 256\text{-}383$
192	AES-192	$L = 7680, N = 384$	$K = 7680$	$F = 384\text{-}511$
256	AES-256	$L = 15{,}360, N = 512$	$K = 15{,}360$	$F \geq 512$

DSA: Digital Signature Algorithm, DH: Diffie-Hellman, MQV: Menezes-Qu-Vanstone, ECC: Elliptic Curve Cryptography, L: public-key bit-length, N: private key bit-length, K: RSA modulus bit-length, F: key bit-length.

Table 14.2 Security strengths of common hash and hash-based functions [1].

Security strength	Hash functions for applications requiring collision resistance (e.g. digital signatures)	Hash functions for HMAC, KMAC, KDF, and DRBG
112	SHA-224, SHA-512/224, SHA3-224	
128	SHA-256, SHA-512/256, SHA3-256	SHA-1, KMAC128
192	SHA-384, SHA3-384	SHA-224, SHA-512/224, SHA3-224
≥ 256	SHA-512, SHA3-512	SHA-256, SHA-512/256, SHA-384, SHA-512, SHA3-256, SHA3-384, SHA-512, KMAC-256

HMAC: Hash-based Message Authentication Code, KDF: Key-Derivation Function, KMAC: Keccak-based Message Authentication Code, DRBG: Deterministic Random Bit Generator.

Many applications require multiple cryptographic services (e.g. key establishment, confidentiality protection, integrity protection, digital signature, etc.). A different algorithm and key could be used to provide each service or multiple services could be provided by the same algorithm using the same or different keys. In addition, many services can be provided by more than one algorithm (e.g. digital signature can be provided by either RSA or ECDSA). Some algorithms are inherently efficient by design to perform some specific services, e.g. HMAC is efficient to provide data integrity protection. Therefore, a cryptosystem designer may have to choose a variety of algorithms and their appropriate key bit-lengths. It is worth noticing that the higher the security strength is, the higher the computation time and amount of other resources required to perform security operations are. Therefore, a trade-off between security strength and performance is to be considered when selecting the bit-length of keys.

14.1.1.3 Cryptoperiod

Definition 14.1 Cryptoperiod*: it is the time span during which a specific key is authorized for use by legitimate entities.*

The security provided by a key may be reduced or completely lost with time, because of the progress in cryptanalysis or simply the key becomes suspect (i.e. potential attackers might know some information about the key). The cryptoperiod of a key may be defined in terms of time between the generation of the key and its end of use or in terms of the maximum amount of data protected by the key. An adequately defined key cryptoperiod has the following properties:

i) It limits the number of plaintext and ciphertext pairs encrypted with the same key; and therefore, it limits the amount of information available to attackers to recover the key.

ii) It limits the time for attackers to access resources protected with a key.

In general, short cryptoperiods enhance security. However, frequent changes of keys result in an overhead (due to key generation and distribution) and key-distribution methods are subject to human errors, which might actually increase the risk of key exposure. Therefore, a trade-off between cryptoperiod, overhead, and risk is to be considered by security-system administrators. Table 14.3 summarizes the key types and their respective cryptoperiods suggested by the NIST [1]. Notice that the cryptoperiod may be different, depending on the entity using the key, the originator (i.e. the entity that starts the information exchange) or the recipient.

14.1.2 Key-Management Phases and Functions

As illustrated by Figure 14.1, a cryptographic key follows a series of steps, among which the following are the most addressed in cryptosystems:

- The key is generated using a specific key generation scheme.
- In case of public-key cryptosystems, the public key is registered at a trusted authority.
- The key is stored on a permanent and failure-resistant device.
- The key is made available to legitimate users.
- The key is used to perform cryptographic actions (encryption, decryption, signature generation and verification, etc.).
- The key is suspended, because its cryptoperiod is exceeded or it became compromised.
- The key is archived; and it is no more used in cryptographic operations.
- The key is destroyed and its material is completely removed from the operational cryptosystem.

The key management encompasses a set of functions along with requirements that depend on the characteristics of data protected by each key. For example, top-secret data do not require the same severity level of key management than nonclassified data.

In this chapter, we focus on two fundamental functions: key generation and key establishment. Both functions are present in almost all key management systems. Overall, the key life cycle can be divided into four phases:

1) *Pre-operational phase*: the key is not yet available to perform cryptographic operations. Two main functions compose this phase: key generation and secure key distribution. In addition, for public-key algorithms, a third function is required, the key registration at some trusted authority.
2) *Operational phase*: the key is available for use to encrypt, decrypt, sign, etc. The key shall be stored on a safe device, often including key backup capabilities.
3) *Post-operational phase*: the key is no longer used to encrypt or sign data. Key-related information is archived on separate devices, and may be processed to recover some keys or other information. The keys, at this phase, are archived until no

Table 14.3 Key types, provided services, and cryptoperiods.

Key type	Provided security services([4])	Cryptoperiod (years)
Symmetric encryption key	Confidentiality	≤ 2 (*)
Symmetric key-wrapping key	Support	≤ 2 (*)
Symmetric master/key-derivation key	Support	≤ 1
Symmetric DRBG key	Support	
Symmetric authentication key	Authentication, Integrity	≤ 2 (*)
Symmetric key-agreement key	Support	1 to 2 (**)
Symmetric authorization key	Support	≤ 2
Private signature-generation key	Authentication, Integrity, non-repudiation	1 to 3
Public signature-verification key	Authentication, Integrity, non-repudiation	Several
Private authentication key	Authentication, Integrity	1 to 2
Public authentication key	Authentication, Integrity	1 to 2
Private key-transport key	Support	1 to 2 (***)
Public key-transport key	Support	1 to 2
Private static key-agreement key	Support	1 to 2 (***)
Public static key-agreement key	Support	1 to 2
Private ephemeral key-agreement key	Support	One transaction
Public ephemeral key-agreement key	Support	One transaction
Private authorization key	authorization	≤ 2
Public authorization key	authorization	≤ 2

(*) At most two years for originator; and at most three years more than originator, for recipient.
(**) In some applications (e.g. email) where received messages are stored and decrypted at a later time, the recipient key usage period may exceed the originator-usage period.
(***) In some applications (e.g. email) where received messages are stored and decrypted at a later time, the cryptoperiod of private key may exceed that of the corresponding public key.

longer needed to authenticate data or entities or to decrypt data, previously encrypted with these keys. Public keys should be de-registered.

4) *Destruction phase*: the key is no longer available for any cryptographic operation.

14.2 Key-Generation Schemes

Definition 14.2 Shared secret*: it is a secret value that has been computed using a key-agreement scheme and is used as input to a key-derivation function.*

Definition 14.3 Key generation*: it is a procedure by which a new key is created.*

Definition 14.4 Key derivation*: it is a procedure by which one or more keys are derived from a shared secret.*

Definition 14.5 Key owner*: in the symmetric systems, any entity, which is authorized to share and use a key, is an owner of that key. In asymmetric systems, the party, which creates a pair of keys (private and public keys), is the owner of the private key.*

Definition 14.6 Static key*: a key that is intended for use for a relatively long period (in years) and is typically intended for use in many key-establishment operations.*

Definition 14.7 Ephemeral key*: a cryptographic key that is generated for each execution of a cryptographic process (e.g. key-agreement or key-transport) and that meets other requirements of the key type (e.g. unique to each message or session).*

14.2.1 Key Generation for Symmetric-Key Systems

A symmetric key can be generated by one party and then is communicated to the other party or generated by both parties using a key-agreement protocol. A key can be generated using an approved DRBG, from a password, by combining multiple keys, or by using a key-derivation function. Keys may also be generated using approved key-agreement protocols. Figure 14.2 depicts the main methods to generate keys. Those methods are addressed in more detail in the subsequent sections. In all cases, the key generation shall be based directly or indirectly on an approved DRBG, which guarantees randomness.

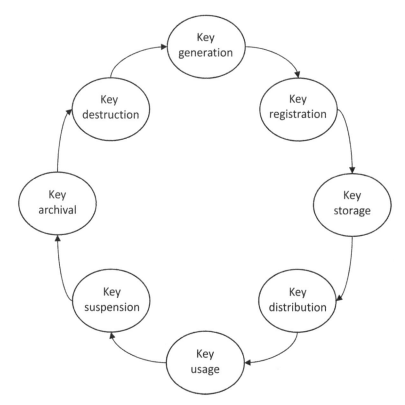

Figure 14.1 Main steps in the life cycle of a cryptographic key.

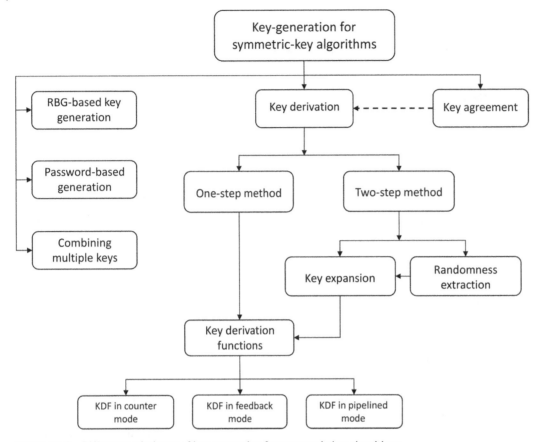

Figure 14.2 Different techniques of key generation for symmetric-key algorithms.

14.2.1.1 Key Generation Using DRBGs

Approved DRBGs (Deterministic random bit generators) may be used to generate symmetric keys or inputs for asymmetric-key-generation algorithms. Approved DRBGs are discussed in Chapter 16. The random bit string, say B, of a bit-length $Blen$, required for the generation of a key K, is obtained as follows [2]:

$$B = U \oplus V$$

where: U is a bit string of $Blen$ bits obtained as the output of an approved DRBG, which shall have at least the security strength of the algorithm/application that will use key K. V is a bit string of $Blen$ bits, which could be all zeroes. U and V are statistically independent of each other. Bit string V may be another key or computed by a hash function or any other function that can increase the randomness of pair (U, V).

The bit-length $Blen$ depends on the algorithm/application that will use the key (see Table 14.1).

14.2.1.2 Key Derived from a Password

In some popular applications (including encryption of data on storage devices), keys are generated from passwords. However, in general, user-generated passwords are less random than is required for cryptographic keys; that is, the number of passwords that are likely to be used to derive a key is significantly smaller than the number of keys that are possible for a given key bit-length. Therefore, passwords shall not be used directly as cryptographic keys.

To enable users generate keys from their passwords, the NIST approved a family of key derivation functions to transform a password into a key [3]. Each password-based key derivation function, denoted PBKDF, is defined by the selection of a pseudorandom function (see Chapter 10 for more on PRFs) and a fixed iteration count C. More precisely, a PBKDF is an HMAC parameterized with a hash function (e.g. SHA-256 or SHA3-384) and a hash bit-length $Hlen$. The PBKDF takes a password P, a salt S, a key bit-length $Klen$; and outputs a key K of the desired bit-length $Klen$. The salt is used as a part of the key in HMAC and it shall be generated using an approved DRBG with a bit-length of at least 128. The number of

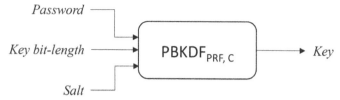

Figure 14.3 General structure of a PBKDF.

iterations, C, shall be as large as possible; 1000 is the minimum recommended value for C. For critical keys, C should be in millions. Figure 14.3 illustrates the generic structure of a PBKDF; and the pseudocode is as follows.

Note. Some functions are generic; and they need specific elements (such as a hash function or some bit-lengths) to build them before any usage. The elements used one time to instantiate a generic function are specified in **parameters** clause. The **input** clause specifies the values used in each function call.

---

function PBKDF
    parameters HMAC: HMAC with an approved hash function
                         $Hlen$: bit-length of hash function used by HMAC
    input P: password; S: salt (it is a part of the key of HMAC)
                 C: iteration count; $Klen$: key bit-length
    output K: key
    1. **if** $Klen > \left(2^{32} - 1\right) * Hlen$ **then return** "Error"
    2. $Len = \lceil Klen / Hlen \rceil$
    3. $r = Klen - \left(Len - 1\right) * Hlen$
    4. **for** i=1 **to** Len **do**
           $T_i = 0$; $U_0 = S \parallel Int(i)$
             for j=1 **to** C **do** $U_j = HMAC\left(P, U_{j-1}\right)$; $T_i = T_i \oplus U_j$
    5. $T = Trunc\left(T_{Len}, r\right)$ # keep the r first bits of T_{Len}
    6. $K = T_1 \parallel T_2 \parallel \ldots \parallel T_{Len-1} \parallel T$; **return** K

Notes
– The process of key generation described above is public. Therefore, when passwords are used to generate cryptographic keys, it is assumed that an attacker is able to perform search attacks (e.g. dictionary attack) on the key generation process. Therefore, the password entropy is a critical issue. To make attacks computationally infeasible, it is recommended i) to use randomly generated passwords instead of user-chosen passwords, ii) the typical password length is of 20 to 30 characters.
– The salt of bit-length $Slen$ allows generating a set of 2^{Slen} keys corresponding to each password, for a fixed iteration count. Using a salt makes it difficult for attackers to prepare a table of potential keys. To make attacks computationally infeasible, the bit-length of the salt should be as large as possible.

14.2.1.3 Key-Generation by Key-Derivation Methods

Two key derivation methods[5] (KDM) are recommended [4], one-step and two-step methods. The second method provides more randomness in the generated key compared to the first method, but it requires more computation time.

14.2.1.3.1 One-Step Key Derivation Method

In one-step key-derivation method, the KDM is parameterized with an auxiliary function, denoted H, which can be a hash function $Hash$, HMAC defined by its hash function, or KMAC. The KDM takes a shared secret Z, a key bit-length, a salt (only if options 2 or 3 are used), and optional fixed data; and yields a key of the desired key bit-length (see Figure 14.4). Auxiliary function H may be defined by one of the following options:

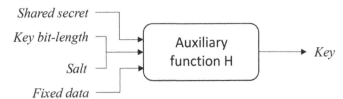

Figure 14.4 General structure of one-step key-derivation method.

1) Option 1: $H(x) = Hash(x)$
2) Option 2: $H(x) = HMAC_{Hash}(Salt, x)$
3) Option 3: $H(x) = KMAC_{128|256}(Salt, x, "KDF")$

where x denotes the input string; *Hash* is one of the recommended hash functions, and "KDF" is a constant bit-string, which represents a sequence of three characters, in 8-bit ASCII. *Salt* is used as key of HMAC or KMAC. A hash function can be used directly (option 1) or as a parameter of a keyed MAC (options 2 and 3).

The hash functions recommended to build the auxiliary function of the KDM are shown in Table 14.4. When used in a KDM, KMAC-128 and KMAC-256 provide a security strength of 128 and 256 bits, respectively. The pseudocode of the one-step key derivation method is the following:

```
function One_Step_KDM
    parameters   H: auxiliary function (hash unction, HMAC or KMAC)
                 Hlen:  bit − length of the output of the function H
    input   Z: shared secret; Klen: bit-length of the key to generate
            FixedData: optional data
    Output K: key
    1. Cnt = 0x00000000 # a 32-bit word with a value of 0
    2. N = ⌈Klen / Hlen⌉
    3. if N > 2³² − 1, then return "Error"
    4. Result(0) = Empty_Bit_String()
    5. for Cnt = 1 to N do
           Cnt = Cnt + 1; K(i) = H(Cnt || Z || FixedData)
           Result(i) = Result(i − 1) || K(i)
    6. K = LeftmostBits(Result(N), Klen)
    7. return K
```

| **Note.** The one-step derivation method is a generalization of the KDF in counter mode (see Section 14.2.1.5).

14.2.1.3.2 Two-Step Key Derivation Functions

As illustrated by Figure 14.5, two-step key-derivation method makes use of two functions: randomness extraction and key expansion. In addition to the shared secret and the key bit-length, the two-step KDM requires a salt and an IV, when the KDF is in feedback mode (see Section 14.2.1.5).

The randomness-extraction function makes use of either HMAC or AES-CMAC mode of operation to generate a tag, which serves as a key-derivation key, denoted *Kdk*, in the second step. The required *Salt* is used as a MAC key in HMAC or in the AES-CMAC. The second step is similar to that of the one-step KDM and it makes use of one of the basic key-derivation functions described in Section 14.2.1.5.

When HMAC is used in the two-step KDM, the recommended hash functions are the same as for the one-step KDM (see Section 14.2.1.5). When AES-CMAC is used to generate the tag, the security strength is of 128 bits regardless of the AES variant used (i.e. 128, 192, or 256), because the output of AES is always of 128 bits.

Table 14.4 Hash functions approved for use in key generation.

Hash function	Hash bit-length	S: security strength[6]
SHA-1	160	$112 \leq S \leq 160$
SHA-224	224	$112 \leq S \leq 224$
SHA-256	256	$112 \leq S \leq 256$
SHA-512/224	224	$112 \leq S \leq 224$
SHA-512/256	256	$112 \leq S \leq 256$
SHA-384	384	$112 \leq S \leq 384$
SHA-512	512	$112 \leq S \leq 512$
SHA3-224	224	$112 \leq S \leq 224$
SHA3-256	256	$112 \leq S \leq 256$
SHA3-384	384	$112 \leq S \leq 384$
SHA3-512	512	$112 \leq S \leq 512$

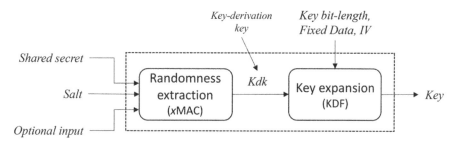

Figure 14.5 General structure of the two-step key derivation method.

The pseudocode of the two-step key-derivation method is the following:

```
function Two_Step_KDM
    parameters   MAC: MAC function (i.e. HMAC or AES-CMAC)
                 Hlen: bit-length of the output of the MAC function
                 KeyExpansion: key expansion function
    input   Z: shared secret;   Klen: bit-length of the key to generate
            Salt: a secret or non-secret byte string
            FixedData: optional bit-string
            IV: initialization vector (used when KDF is in feedback mode)
    output   K: key
    1. Kdk = MAC(Salt, Z)
    2. K = KDF(Kdk, Klen, IV, FixedData)
    3. return K
```

As illustrated by Figure 14.6, the two-step KDM, as described above, can be generalized to produce a set of m keys with arbitrary bit-lengths $(L_1, L_2, ..., L_m)$ using, when applicable, a set of IVs $(IV_1, IV_2, ..., IV_m)$ and a set of fixed data $(FD_1, FD_2, ..., FD_m)$. Then, the yielded keys may be combined to generate a single key (see Section 14.2.1.4).

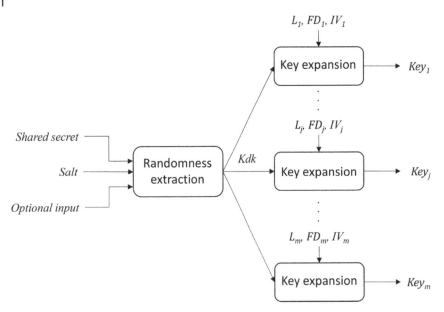

Figure 14.6 KDM for multiple key generation.

14.2.1.4 Key Generated by Combining Multiple Other Keys and Data

A symmetric key can be generated from other existing symmetric keys. Let K_1, K_2, ..., K_n be a list of independently gener-ated keys and D_1, D_2, ..., D_n be a list of additional data, which are not required to be secret. The list of keys and additional data can be combined in different ways to generate a new key K as follows [2]:

- Key concatenating: $K = K_1 \| K_2 \| ... \| K_n$.
- Key-data XORing: $K = K_1 \oplus K_2 \oplus ... \oplus K_n \oplus D_1 \oplus D_2 \oplus ... \oplus D_n$.
- Key extracting: $K = Trunc\left(\left(HMAC_{Hash}(Salt, K_1 \| K_2 \| ... \| K_n)\right), Klen\right)$; *Hash* is a hash function. The function *Trunc* is applied to keep *Klen* bits from the produced tag. *Salt* is used as a key for the HMAC function.

The keys, which are combined, may be generated using any other method of key generation.

14.2.1.5 Key-Derivation Functions

A pseudorandom function (PRF) is the core component for building key-derivation functions. A PRF is computationally indistinguishable from a random function for those observers without knowledge of the key used by the PRF. For more on PRF properties, the reader should refer to Chapter 10. The commonly used PRFs to build KDFs include HMAC, KMAC, and CMAC mode of operation.

Given a PRF, there exist three modes of function for generating a key from another shared key [5]:

- KDF in counter mode, where the distinctive input of the PRF is a counter value used to produce a portion of the final output.
- KDF in feedback mode, where the output of the PRF in each iteration is used in the next iteration to produce a portion of the final output.
- KDF in double-pipelined mode, where the outputs of the PRF in feedback and counter modes are pipelined.

Figure 14.7 illustrates the three modes of KDF. The secret used as input to KDFs is called *key-derivation key*, and denoted K_{in}. The desired key bit-length is denoted *Klen*. In addition, an IV, which is used in the feedback mode, and other fixed data may be used.

> **Note**. All KDFs discussed in this chapter are parametrized with an auxiliary function, which can be a hash function or a keyed-MAC algorithm (i.e. HMAC or KMAC). Therefore, a KDF is a family of functions that mainly differ in their auxiliary functions.

Below are the pseudocodes of the three modes of KDF.

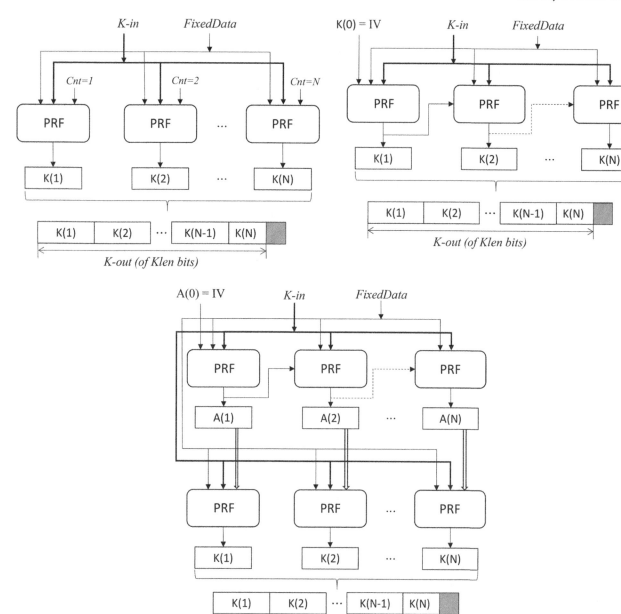

Figure 14.7 Variants of KDFs.

function KDF_in_Counter_mode
    parameters   *PRF* : pseudorandom function (i.e. HMAC, CMAC, ...)
                     Hlen : bit-length of the PRF output
    input K_{in} : key-derivation key (i.e. a shared secret)
              Klen : bit-length of the key to generate
              FixedData : optional bit-string
    output K_{out} : generated key
    1. $N = \lceil Klen / Hlen \rceil$
    2. **if** $N > 2^{32} - 1$, **then return** "Error"
    3. $Result(0) = EmptyBitString()$

4. **for** $Cnt = 1$ **to** N **do**
    4.1 $K(Cnt) = PRF\left(K_{in}, \left([Cnt]_2 \;\|\; FixedData \;\|\; [Klen]_2\right)\right)$
    4.2 $Result(Cnt) = Result(Cnt - 1) \;\|\; K(Cnt)$
5. $K_{out} = LeftmostBits(Result(N), Klen)$
6. **return** K_{out}

---

function KDF_in_Feedback_mode
    parameters   *PRF*: pseudorandom function (i.e. HMAC or CMAC)
                    Hlen: bit-length of the PRF output
    input K_{in}: key-derivation key (i.e. a shared secret)
              Klen: bit-length of the key to generate
              IV: initialization vector, which may be a null bit-string
              FixedData: optional bit-string
    output K_{out}: generated key

1. $N = \left\lceil \dfrac{Klen}{Hlen} \right\rceil$
2. **if** $N > 2^{32} - 1$, **then return** "Error"
3. $Result(0) = EmptyBitString(); K(0) = IV$
4. **for** $i = 1$ **to** N **do**
    4.1 $K(i) = PRF\left(K_{in}, \left(K(i - 1) \;\|\; FixedData \;\|\; [Klen]_2\right)\right)$
    4.2 $Result(i) = Result(i - 1) \;\|\; K(i)$
5. $K_{out} = LeftmostBits(Result(N), Klen)$
6. **return** K_{out}

---

function KDF_in_Double_Pipelined_mode
    parameters   *PRF*: pseudorandom function (i.e. HMAC or CMAC)
                    Hlen: bit-length of the PRF output
    input K_{in}: key-derivation key (i.e. a shared secret)
              Klen: bit-length of the key to generate
              IV: initialization vector, which may be a null bit-string
              FixedData: optional bit-string
    output K_{out}: generated key

1. $N = \left\lceil \dfrac{Klen}{Hlen} \right\rceil$
2. **if** $N > 2^{32} - 1$, **then return** "Error"
3. $Result(0) = EmptyBitString()$
4. $A(0) = IV \;\|\; FixedData \;\|\; [Klen]_2$
5. **for** $i = 1$ **to** N **do**
    5.1 $A(i) = PRF(K_{in}, A(i - 1))$
    5.2 $K(i) = PRF\left(K_{in}, \left(A(i) \;\|\; FixedData \;\|\; [Klen]_2\right)\right)$
    5.3 $Result(i) = Result(i - 1) \;\|\; K(i)$
6. $K_{out} = LeftmostBits(Result(N), Klen)$
7. **return** K_{out}

14.2.2 Key Generation for Asymmetric-Key Cryptosystems

Pairs of public and private keys are generated using the mathematical specifications of the involved algorithms. Recall that the security of public-key-based algorithms relies on the difficulty either to factorize large integers (as mentioned in

Chapter 12) or to find the discrete logarithm for large integers (as mentioned in Chapters 12 and 13). Thus, public-key-based cryptography is divided into two categories:

- Integer Factorization Cryptography (IFC); RSA is the most known and used algorithm in IFC.
- Discrete logarithm Cryptography (DLC), which is divided into two subcategories, Finite-Field Cryptography (FFC) and Elliptic-Curve Cryptography (ECC). The most known and commonly used DLC algorithms are Diffie-Hellman (DH) and Menezes-Qu-Vanstone (MQV) algorithms, which can be used under either FFC or ECC.

In this subsection, we present the methods for generating key-pairs (i.e. public and private key pairs); and in the next subsection, we address how IFC- and DLC-based algorithms can be used to build key-agreement protocols.

14.2.2.1 RSA Key-Pair Generation

RSA is presented in Section 12.2. An RSA key-pair is denoted $\left((N,d),(N,e)\right)$, where N is the modulus, d, the private exponent, and e, the public exponent. $Nb = \lceil log_2 N \rceil$ denotes the bit-length of the modulus N. The commonly used RSA modulus bit-lengths vary from 2048 to 8192. Currently, the maximum value of Nb, which is suggested by the RSA standard for the protection of critical data, is of 15,360.

The parameters used to generate RSA key-pairs should meet the following requirements [6, 7]:

1) Public exponent e: $2^{16} < e < 2^{256}$ and $GCD\left(e, LCM\left(p-1, q-1\right)\right)=1$.

2) Private exponent d: $2^{\frac{Nb}{2}} \le d < LCM\left(p-1, q-1\right)$ and $d*e = 1 \bmod \left((p-1)(q-1)\right)$.

3) Primes p and q: $2^{\frac{Nb-1}{2}} < p < 2^{\frac{Nb}{2}}, 2^{\frac{Nb-1}{2}} < q < 2^{\frac{Nb}{2}}, |p-q| > 2^{\frac{Nb}{2}-100}$. Primes p and q are generated using recommended procedures, which are introduced in Chapter 16.

RSA key-pair generators (RSAKPGs) make use of an approved DRBG. Two families of RSAKPGs are recommended [7]: RSAKPG1 (with a fixed exponent e) and RSAKPG2 (with a random exponent e). Each family has three variants, which differ only in the format of the output representation: in the basic format, the output is (N,d); in the prime-factor variant, the output is (p,q,d); and in the CRT (Chinese[7] remainder theorem), the output is $(N,e,d,p,q,dP,dQ,qInv)$, where $dP = d \bmod (p-1)$, $dQ = d \bmod (q-1)$, and $qInv = q^{-1} \bmod p$. In the sequel, we only describe the basic variant.

> **Note.** Because of potential errors in implementation that may have undesirable impacts on the security, the consistency of the generated key-pair must be checked using a simple verification as follows: take some integer $m, 0 < m < N-1$, and verify $m = \left(m^{ed}\right) \bmod N$. If the verification fails, an indication of "Inconsistency" is returned and the key-pair generation operation shall be re-run.

14.2.2.1.1 RSAKPG1 Family

RSAKPG1 generators make use of a *fixed* public-exponent. Three RSA key-pair generator variants compose the RSAKPG1 family: *rsakpg1-basic*, *rsakpg1-prime-factor*, and *rsakpg1-crt*. The pseudocode of the basic variant of RSAKPG1 is as follows:

```
function rsakpg1_basic
    input   Nb: modulus bit-length; S: expected security strength
            e: public exponent
    output  (N,d),(N,e): private and public keys
    1. Check parameter validity
        1.1 if (e not odd or not in [65537, 2^256 − 1]) then return "Error"
        1.2 if (S > Nb), then return "Error"
        1.3 if (S not in [112, 256]), then return "Error"
    2. Generate two primes p and q # using a prime generation procedure
    3. Determine the private exponent d, such that
       d*e = 1 mod (LCM(p − 1)(q − 1))
    4. N = p * q
    5. Key-pair consistency verification
       if (InconsistencyFound), then return "Inconsistency"
    6. Destroy any copies of primes p and q
    7. return (N,d),(N,e) # private and public keys.
```

14.2.2.1.2 RSAKPG2 Family

RSAKPG2 generators make use of a *random* public exponent. Three RSA key-pair generator variants compose the RSAKPG2 family: *rsakpg2-basic*, *rsakpg2-prime-factor*, and *rsakpg2-crt*. The pseudocode of the basic variant of RSAKPG2 is as follows:

```
function rsakpg2_basic
    input   Nb: modulus bit-length; S: expected security strength
            elen: bit-length of the public exponent e
    output  (N,d),(N,e): private and public keys
    1. Check parameter validity
        1.1 if (not (17 ≤ elen ≤ 256)) then return "Error"
        1.2 if (S > Nb), then return "Error"
        1.3 if (S not in [112,256]) then return "Error"
    2. Generate an odd exponent e in the interval [2^(elen−1) +1, 2^elen −1]
       By using an approved DRBG
    3. Generate two primes p and q # using a prime generation procedure
    4. Determine the private exponent d, such that
       d * e = 1 mod (LCM (p−1)(q−1))
    5. N = p * q
    6. Key-pair consistency verification
       if (InconsistencyFound), then return "Inconsistency"
    7. Destroy any copies of primes p and q
    8. return (N,d,e) # private and public keys
```

14.2.2.2 Key-Pair Generation for DH and MQV

Diffie-Hellman (DF) and Menezes-Qu-Vanstone (MQV) are the most used cryptographic algorithms based on prime finite fields (see Sections 12.2–12.3).

14.2.2.2.1 FFC Domain Parameter Selection

The selection of domain parameters is of prime importance for the security of finite-field cryptography-based schemes as well as for elliptic-curve cryptography based schemes. A finite field with p elements $\{0, 1, ..., p-1\}$ is denoted F_p (see mathematical notations and notions relating to prime finite fields in Section 3.2.2). $F_p - \{0\}$ is denoted F_p^*.

Public keys recommended to perform key establishment using finite-field cryptography are restricted to a cyclic subgroup of F_p^* with prime order q, such that q divides $p-1$. An element $g \in F_p^*$ is a generator of F_p^* if any element $a \in F_p^*$ can be written as a power of g modulo p; i.e. $\forall a \in F_p^*, \exists k \in \mathbb{N} \,|\, a \equiv g^k \bmod p$.

Domain parameters required in FFC-based schemes are the following:

- p: a safe prime denoting the size of the finite field F_p.
- g: a subgroup generator of the cyclic group F_p^*.
- q: a prime denoting the order of the subgroup generated by g.
- Optional parameters used in some specific prime and generator selection procedures.

Testing integer primality is addressed in Section 16.3.2. There does not exist an algorithm, which can test the primality of any large integer in a reasonable time, but there exist probabilistic algorithms that can test if an integer is not prime. If an integer is not confirmed (at a given probability) to be non-prime, it is probably prime. Hence the notion of probable primes used in cryptographic algorithms (see Section 16.3.2.2).

Two methods are recommended to select FFC domain parameters:

1) *Generation of domain parameters using recommended safe-primes*: the first method to select domain parameters is as follows:
   - Choose p out of the same primes[8] recommended in [8–10] and shown in Table 14.5.
   - Choose $q = (p-1)/2$; since p is a safe prime, q is a prime.
   - Choose $g = 2$, which makes implementation efficient.

Table 14.5 Safe-primes approved for use in key-agreement schemes.

Safe prime	Security strength S
$2^{2048} - 2^{1984} + \left\lfloor 2^{1918} * e + 560316 \right\rfloor * 2^{64} - 1$	$S = 112$
$2^{2048} - 2^{1984} + \left\lfloor 2^{1918} * \pi + 124476 \right\rfloor * 2^{64} - 1$	$S = 112$
$2^{3072} - 2^{3008} + \left\lfloor 2^{2942} * e + 2625351 \right\rfloor * 2^{64} - 1$	$112 \leq S \leq 128$
$2^{3072} - 2^{3008} + \left\lfloor 2^{2942} * \pi + 1690314 \right\rfloor * 2^{64} - 1$	$112 \leq S \leq 128$
$2^{4096} - 2^{4032} + \left\lfloor 2^{3966} * e + 5736041 \right\rfloor * 2^{64} - 1$	$112 \leq S \leq 152$
$2^{4096} - 2^{4032} + \left\lfloor 2^{3966} * \pi + 240904 \right\rfloor * 2^{64} - 1$	$112 \leq S \leq 152$
$2^{6144} - 2^{6080} + \left\lfloor 2^{6014} * e + 15705020 \right\rfloor * 2^{64} - 1$	$112 \leq S \leq 176$
$2^{6144} - 2^{6080} + \left\lfloor 2^{6014} * \pi + 929484 \right\rfloor * 2^{64} - 1$	$112 \leq S \leq 176$
$2^{8192} - 2^{8128} + \left\lfloor 2^{8062} * e + 4743158 \right\rfloor * 2^{64} - 1$	$112 \leq S \leq 200$
$2^{8192} - 2^{8128} + \left\lfloor 2^{8062} * \pi + 10965728 \right\rfloor * 2^{64} - 1$	$112 \leq S \leq 200$

e is the base of natural logarithm and $\pi = 3.14...$

2) *Generation of domain parameters using ad hoc probable or provable primes*: the second method to select domain parameters is summarized as follows [6]:

   – Probable primes can be generated using a hash function H, such as SHA-256, a *Counter*, which specifies the number of repetitions of the hash function, and a *Seed* (a random integer, which must be unique for each set of parameter domain).
   – Provable primes can be generated using Shawe-Taylor's algorithm [11], as discussed in Section 16.3.4.1.
   – Once two primes p and p are generated, select a generator g using the following algorithm.

Below is a simple recommended method for finding a finite field generator:

```
function Generator_Selection
    input   p, q: two FFC domain parameters
    output  g: generator of a finite field F_p
    1. u = (p-1)/q # u is an integer, because by definition of FFC
       # domain parameters q divides p - 1
    2. Pick a random integer h, 2 ≤ h < (p-1)
    3. g = h^u mod p
    4. if (g > 1), then return g
    5. else go to step 2
```

14.2.2.2.2 FFC Key-Pair Generation Methods

Two methods are recommended for generating static or ephemeral key-pairs in FFC.

1) Key-pair generation using extra random bits (FFC-KPGERB): it makes use of a DRBG to select the key-pair.
2) Key-pair generation by testing candidates (FFC-KPGTC): it picks a random number and then checks whether it can produce a valid private key.

The pseudocodes of both key-pair generation methods are as follows:

```
function FFC_KPGERB   # Key-pair generation using extra random bits
    input   p, q, g: FFC domain parameters
            PrLen: maximum bit-length of the private key
            S: required security strength
```

output   *Pr, Pu*: private and public keys
1. # Check parameter validity
    1.1 **if** $(S > SecurityStrength(p)$ *or* $S > SecurityStrength(q))$,
        then return "Error"
    1.2. **if** $\big((PrLen < 2 * S)$ *or* $(PrLen > len(q))\big)$, **then return** "Error"
2. $B = DRBG(PrLen + 64)$ # Obtain a string of $PrLen + 64$ bits from a DRBG
3. $c = BitStringToIntger(B)$ # type conversion
4. $M = \min\big(2^{PrLen}, q\big)$
5. $Pr = (c \bmod (M - 1)) + 1$; $Pu = g^{Pr} \bmod p$
6. **return** (Pr, Pu)

---

function FFC_KPGTC   # Key-pair generation by testing candidates
    input   *p, q, g*: FFC domain parameters
        PrLen: maximum bit-length of the private key
        S: required security strength
    output *Pr, Pu*: private and public keys
1. # Check parameter validity
    1.1 **if** $(S > SecrityStrength(p)$ *or* $S > SecurityStrength(q))$,
        then return "Error"
    1.2. **if** $\big((PrLen < 2 * S)$ *or* $(PrLen > len(q))\big)$,
        then return "Error"
2. $B = DRBG(PrLen)$ # Obtain a string of $PrLen$ bits from a DRBG
3. $c = BitStringToIntger(B)$ # type conversion
4. $M = \min\big(2^{PrLen}, q\big)$
5. **if** $(c > M - 2)$, **then go to** step 2
6. $Pr = c + 1$; $Pu = g^{Pr} \bmod p$
7. **return** (Pr, Pu)

14.2.2.3 ECC Key-Pair Generation

14.2.2.3.1 ECC Domain Parameter Selection
ECC domain parameters are the following (for more detail, see Chapter 13):

- q: the order (or cardinality) of finite field F_q. q is either a prime or a prime power 2^m (with prime m).
- *FR*: field representation if $q = 2^m$ (i.e. the underlying field is an extension field). *FR* includes the degree and coefficients of the reduction polynomial $f(x)$ associated with the field F_{2^m}.
- a and b: coefficients of elliptic curve equation ([9]).
- $G = (x_G, y_G)$: coordinates of the base point G.
- n: order of base point G.
- h: cofactor associated with the base point.
- *Others*: other parameters may be required when specific procedures are used to generate some random values.

The recommended elliptic curves are shown in Table 14.6. The complete domain parameters of recommended ECs are specified in [6, 12]. The irreducible polynomial is specified only for ECs over extension fields F_{2^m}.

14.2.2.3.2 ECC Key-Pair Generation Methods
The two methods recommended in ECC-based algorithms are similar to those for FFC-based algorithms; but they differ in the types of their parameters (input as well as output):

1) Key-pair generation using extra random bits (ECC-KPGERB), which makes use of a DRBG to select the key-pair.

Table 14.6 Elliptic curves approved by the NIST for key-agreement.

Elliptic curves over prime fields

NIST [10, 11] EC name	Prime q	Cofactor[12]	Security strength S
P-224	$2^{224} - 2^{96} + 1$	1	$112 \leq S \leq 128$
P-256	$2^{256} - 2^{224} + 2^{192} + 2^{96} - 1$	1	$112 \leq S \leq 128$
P-384	$2^{384} - 2^{128} - 2^{96} + 2^{32} - 1$	1	$112 \leq S \leq 224$
P-521	$2^{521} - 1$	1	$112 \leq S \leq 256$
W-25519	$2^{255} - 19$	8	$112 \leq S \leq 128$
W-448	$2^{448} - 2^{224} - 1$	4	$112 \leq S \leq 192$
Edwards-25519	$2^{255} - 19$	8	$112 \leq S \leq 128$
Edwards-448	$2^{448} - 2^{224} - 1$	4	$112 \leq S \leq 224$
E448[13]	$2^{448} - 2^{224} - 1$	4	$112 \leq S \leq 192$
Curve-25519	$2^{255} - 19$	8	$112 \leq S \leq 128$
Curve-448	$2^{448} - 2^{224} - 1$	4	$112 \leq S \leq 192$

Elliptic curves over extension fields F_{2^m} ([14])

	Irreducible polynomial[15]	*Cofactor*	*Security strength*
K-233	$x^{233} + x^{74} + 1$	4	$112 \leq S \leq 128$
K-283	$x^{283} + x^{12} + x^{7} + x^{5} + 1$	4	$112 \leq S \leq 128$
K-409	$x^{409} + x^{8} + 1$	4	$112 \leq S \leq 192$
K-571	$x^{571} + x^{10} + x^{5} + x^{2} + 1$	4	$112 \leq S \leq 256$
B-233	$x^{233} + x^{74} + 1$	2	$112 \leq S \leq 128$
B-283	$x^{283} + x^{12} + x^{7} + x^{5} + 1$	2	$112 \leq S \leq 224$
B-409	$x^{409} + x^{87} + 1$	2	$112 \leq S \leq 192$
B-571	$x^{571} + x^{10} + x^{5} + x^{2} + 1$	2	$112 \leq S \leq 256$

2) Key-pair generation by testing candidates (ECC-KPGTC), which picks a random number and then checks whether it can produce a valid private key.

The pseudocodes of both key-pair generations are as follows:

```
function ECC_KPGERB   # Key-pair generation using extra random bits
    input q, G, n: ECC domain parameters
           PrLen: maximum bit-length of the private key
           S: required security strength
    output   Pr: private key (an integer); Pu: public key (an EC point)
    1. # Check parameter validity
       if (S cannot be supported with the domain parameters),
       then return "Error"
    2. L = len(n) + 64
    3. B = DRBG(L) # Obtain a string of L bits from a DRBG
    4. c = BitStringToIntger(B)
    5. Pr = (c mod (n − 1)) + 1
    6. Pu = Pr.G # EC point multiplication by a scalar
    7. return (Pr, Pu)
```

```
function ECC-KPGTC        # Key-pair generation by testing candidates
    input   q,G,n: ECC domain parameters
            PrLen: maximum bit-length of the private key
            S: required security strength
    output Pr: private key (an integer); Pu: public key (an EC point)
    1. # Check parameter validity
        if (S cannot be supported with the domain parameters),
            then return "Error"
    2. L = len(n)
    3. B = DRBG(L) # Key-pair generation by testing candidates
    4. c = BitStringToIntger(z)
    5. if (c > n − 2) then go to step 3
    6. Pr = c + 1
    7. Pu = Pr.G # EC point multiplication by a scalar
    8. return (Pr,Pu)
```

14.3   Key-Establishment Schemes

14.3.1   Overall View of Key-Establishment Schemes

The key establishment is the process by which two (or more) parties establish shared keys. As shown in Figure 14.8, there are two categories of key-establishment protocols: generate-then-send approach or follow-key-agreement approach. In the first category, the key is generated by one party, using methods discussed in Section 14.2.1 (for symmetric keys) and Section 14.2.2 (for asymmetric keys); and, then, transmits (or distributes) the generated key to the other party. In case of a symmetric

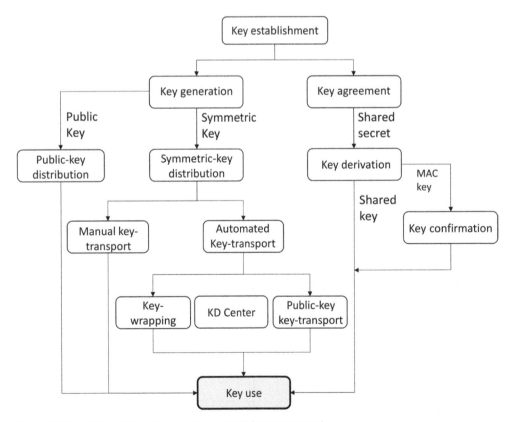

Figure 14.8   Main building-blocks of key-establishment protocols.

key, the latter is securely transmitted to the other party manually or using a key-wrapping or a key-transport protocol. In case of a public key, the latter is not secret and it is directly sent to the other party or embedded in a digital certificate delivered by a trusted party. Digital certificates are discussed in Section 15.1.

In the second category, both parties provide to information, which jointly establish a shared secret key. A key derivation function is then used to derive a secret key from the shared secret. Key-derivation functions are discussed in Section 14.2.1.5.

Definition 14.8 Key establishment: it is the process by which two (or more) parties establish a shared secret key. The execution of the key-establishment scheme is referred to as key-establishment transaction.

Definition 14.9 Key agreement: it is the process by which the resultant secret key is obtained from the information contributed by both parties. The execution of the key-agreement scheme is referred to as key-agreement transaction.

Definition 14.10 Key transport: it is the process by which one party (the sender) selects and encrypts or wraps a key and then distributes it to another party (the recipient). The execution of the key-transport scheme is referred to as key transaction.

Definition 14.11 Key distribution: it is the process by which a key, from an entity that either owns, generates, or otherwise acquires the key is transmitted to another entity that is intended to use the key. The process may be either manual or by using a key transport protocol.

Definition 14.12 Perfect Forward Secrecy (PFS): it is a property of key agreement protocols that change the session key for each user-initiated session, so that if one session key is compromised, only the data encrypted with such a key is vulnerable; and the data encrypted with any other session key will not be affected.

In the public-key-based key-establishment schemes, the following actions should be performed before starting a key-establishment process:

- Selection of the FFC or ECC domain parameters to use (for recommended values of domain parameters, see Section 14.2.2).
- Generation (and maybe registration) and distribution of the public keys.
- Selection of a key-derivation function and its parameters (see Section 14.2.1.5).
- Selection of a hash function or a MAC algorithm and the associated parameters (tag bit-length, MAC key bit-length, and maybe additional fixed data), when a key-confirmation is required (see Section 14.3.3.1.1).

One usual approach is that the initiator of a key-establishment transaction selects and validates all the parameters; and the other party accepts the proposed parameters.

The output of a key-establishment transaction, called *Keying material*, is either a secret key or a bit-string from which a secret key and other information are extracted.

> **Note.** The key-establishment schemes aim to establish keys and other cryptographic elements (e.g. initialization vectors, etc.), the whole is called *keying material*. The focus in this chapter is on the shared keys. Thus, by default, the keying material is limited to a secret key K, which may be used for providing confidentiality assurance and authentication, and a MAC key, *MacKey*, which is used only during the agreement process to confirm the possession of private keys. Thus, in subsequent pseudocodes, $KeyingMaterial = (K, MacKey)$.

Symmetric-key distribution
There exist two main solutions:

1) *Peer-based generation and distribution*: once a symmetric key is generated by one party, it is made available to other party either manually[16] or using an automated key-transport protocol. The latter may be either a key-wrapping protocol such as KW or KWP, which are addressed in detail in Section 9.2.6, or a public-key key-transport protocol, such as RSA-KTS-OAEP, which is addressed in Section 14.3.3.2.2.
2) *Use of a key distribution center*: a server is used to generate and distribute (session) keys to end-users associated with the server (see Section 14.3.2).

Public-key distribution
For security reasons, the following two recommendations shall be observed when using public-key-based schemes to protect data or services:

- One key-pair shall be used for one usage.
- To be trusted, a public key shall have a certificate associated with it. It is highly recommended that public keys should be distributed by a trusted third-party. This issue is addressed in Section 15.2.

The distribution of the public key shall provide assurance to the recipient that:

- The public key is valid (e.g. the public key satisfies the required mathematical properties).
- The purpose/usage of the public key is known (e.g. for RSA digital signatures or for elliptic-curve key-agreement).
- All the domain parameters associated with the public key are known and the recipient agrees to use them.
- The public-key owner actually possesses the corresponding private key. This last requirement may be checked by the recipient through a key-confirmation procedure (see Section 14.3.3.1).

14.3.2 Key-Establishment Using a Key Distribution Center

Definition 14.13 Key distribution center (KDC): *it is a solution to generate and distribute keys to entities that need to communicate with each other but do not share keys except with the center. Entities that have a keying relationship with a KDC are called* ***subscribers***.

A KDC may have two or more levels. At the bottom of the hierarchy, there are entities, called subscribers, that need to securely exchange data. At the top, a central server is used. When the number of subscribers is large or when fault tolerance is an issue or for other organizational or security reasons, there may exist intermediate servers. Without loss of generality, we focus, in the sequel, on two-level KDCs, i.e. subscribers are connected to one server. Each subscriber shares a key with the server. To enable establishing a secure session between two subscribers, a session key is generated by the server and distributed to the subscribers. Therefore, the KDC is a solution to simplify the key management when the subscribers cannot generate and distribute their public keys or when using a symmetric key for each pair of subscribers, which would result in a huge number of symmetric keys. For example, the KDC-based approach would be appropriate in a virtual private network or in an IoT network where the *things* cannot (because of their limited computation resources) make use of public keys.

As illustrated in Figure 14.9, each subscriber S_i shares two keys with the server [13]:

1) A key-wrapping key KWK_i, which is used to wrap (i.e. protect) a session key generated by the server when the key is transmitted to the subscriber *s*;
2) A data-authentication key DAK_i, which is used by the server and the subscriber S_i to send authenticated-messages and to authenticate received messages.

In general, key-wrapping and data-authentication keys are configured manually on the server and the subscribers. Key-wrapping keys are used by algorithms, such as AES key wrap, AES key wrap with padding, and Triple DEA key wrap (see Section 9.2.7). Data-authentication keys are used by algorithms such as CMAC and GMAC, which are discussed in Chapter 9. There exist two approaches to select the authentication and wrapping algorithms. In the first approach, the authentication and wrapping algorithms are fixed on all the components of the KDC (i.e. the server and subscribers) before requesting any session key generation. In the second approach, the subscriber that requests a new session key includes, in its request, information to indicate which algorithms (out of those available) to use and their parameters (e.g. the key bit-length and the hash output bit-length). Then, the provided inputs are either accepted or rejected by the KDC server or by the other subscriber(s). Notice that the second approach is more flexible than the first one, but it is more complex to implement. Without loss of generality, we assume in the sequel that the first approach is used.

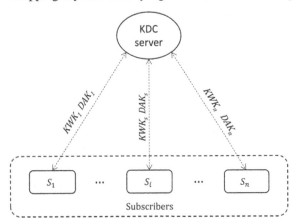

Figure 14.9 Relationships between the server of KDC and its subscribers.

Notes
- All subscribers must trust the KDC server. The latter must be protected against attacks. If the KDC server is compromised, all messages can be easily discovered.
- The availability of the KDC server is an issue. If the KDC server becomes faulty or inaccessible to some subscribers, some or all subscribers cannot establish session keys.

Session key establishment

When a subscriber S_i needs to securely communicate with another subscriber S_j, and it does not share a session key with S_j or needs to change the current session key shared with S_j, the following operations are performed:

1) Subscriber S_i sends an authenticated message M_1 to request a session key. The message M_1 includes, at least, the IDs of subscribers S_i and S_j and a tag computed by the subscriber S_i using the key DAK_i, which it shared with the server.
2) The server receives the message M_1 and authenticates it, using the key DAK_i that it shares with subscriber S_i. If the authentication succeeds, the process continues; otherwise, no session key is delivered to subscriber S_i, an error notification is returned and the process is stopped.
3) The server makes use of derivation function to generate a new session key $SK_{i,j}$.
4) The server makes use of a key-wrapping algorithm and the key-wrapping keys KWK_i and KWK_j to protect two copies of the session key $SK_{i,j}$. Depending on the implantation of the KDC, there are two options[17] to continue the process.
5) Option 1 (illustrated in Figure 14.10a):

    5.1   The server builds an authenticated message M_2 (using the key DAK_i) that includes the session key $SK_{i,j}$ wrapped with the key KWK_i and an authenticated message M_3 (using the key DAK_j) that includes the session key $SK_{i,j}$ wrapped with the key KWK_j. Then, the message M_2 is sent to subscriber S_i; and the message M_3 to subscriber S_j.

    $$M_2 = A\left(DAK_i, W\left(KWK_i, SK_{i,j}\right)\right), \quad M_3 = A\left(DAK_j, W\left(KWK_j, SK_{i,j}\right)\right)$$

    where A and W are the agreed authentication and wrapping algorithms, respectively.

    5.2   The subscriber S_i (resp. S_j) receives the message M_2 (resp. M_3) and authenticates the message using its key DAK_i (resp. DAK_j). If the authentication fails, the subscriber S_i (resp. S_j) returns an error notification and the process is stopped. Otherwise, the subscriber S_i (resp. S_j) extracts the wrapped session key from the message M_2 (resp. M_3), and makes use of the agreed key-wrapping algorithm to obtain the session key $SK_{i,j}$. An authenticated acknowledgment is sent by the subscriber S_i (resp. S_j) to the server:

    $$SK_{i,j} = W^{-1}\left(KWK_i, W\left(KWK_i, SK_{i,j}\right)\right)$$

    $$\left(\text{resp. } SK_{i,j} = W^{-1}\left(KWK_j, W\left(KWK_j, SK_{i,j}\right)\right)\right)$$

    5.3   Upon receipt of the acknowledgment from the subscriber S_j, the server sends an authenticated acknowledgment to the subscriber S_i to confirm that the subscriber S_j has received the session key.

    5.4   When the subscriber S_i receives the acknowledgment from the server, the key-establishment process successfully terminates.

6) Option 2 (illustrated in Figure 14.10b):

    6.1   The server builds an authenticated message M_2 (using the key DAK_i) that includes two copies of the session key $SK_{i,j}$ wrapped with the keys KWK_i and KWK_j. Then, the message M_2 is sent to the subscriber S_i.

    $$M_2 = A\left(DAK_i, \left(W\left(KWK_i, SK_{i,j}\right) \| W\left(KWK_j, SK_{i,j}\right)\right)\right)$$

    6.2   The subscriber S_i receives the message M_2 and authenticates the message using its key DAK_i. If the authentication fails, an error notification is returned and the process is stopped. Otherwise, the subscriber S_i extracts the part $W\left(KWK_i, SK_{i,j}\right)$ from the message; then, using its wrapping key KWK_i, the subscriber S_i unwraps the wrapped session-key and obtains the session key $SK_{i,j}$ in cleartext. The subscriber S_i sends an authenticated acknowledgment to the server. Then, subscriber S_i extracts $W\left(KWK_j, SK_{i,j}\right)$ from M_2 and sends it to subscriber S_j.

    6.3   Using its wrapping key KWK_j, the subscriber S_j unwraps the wrapped session-key and obtains the session key $SK_{i,j}$ in cleartext. Then, it sends an acknowledgment to subscriber S_i.

    6.4   When the subscriber S_i receives the acknowledgment from subscriber S_j, the key-establishment process successfully terminates.

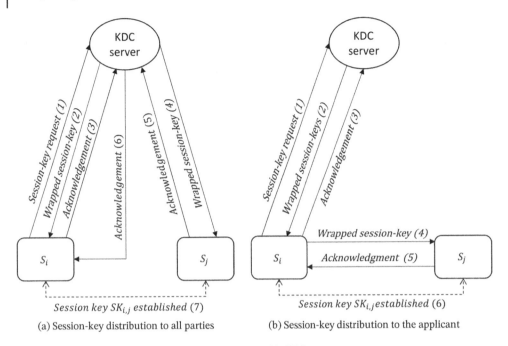

(a) Session-key distribution to all parties

(b) Session-key distribution to the applicant

Figure 14.10 Diagrams of session-key distribution with KDC.

Note. One of the most known and currently used KDCs is with no doubt Kerberos. The latter is presented in Section 15.4.

14.3.3 Key-Establishment Using Public-Key-based Schemes

As previously mentioned, key-establishment includes key-agreement and key-transport. As shown in Figure 14.11, there exist only two recommended schemes for key-transport (namely, KTS-OAEP and key-wrapping modes KW and KWP), while there exist several key-agreement schemes: two schemes are based on RSA, ten on Diffie-Hellman protocol, and four on Menezes-Qu-Vanstone protocol.

Key-establishment may involve two or more parties. Without loss of generality, we assume, in the sequel, that only two parties are involved. The party, which starts the key-establishment process, is called the *initiator* of the key-establishment transaction; and the other party, the *recipient*.

In all the key-agreement and key-transport schemes described in this chapter, the key-pair (i.e. private and public keys) of a party is generated either by that party or by a trusted party. Then, the public key of each partner may be distributed to the other party either directly by the public-key owner or included in a certificate issued by an authority trusted by both parties. Thus, in the diagrams that will follow, the terms *Distribute* and *Obtain* public keys and dashed arrows are used in instead of *Send*, *Receive*, and solid arrows.

Notes

- To prevent attacks against implementations of cryptographic algorithms, it is recommended to destroy any sensitive copies of secrets and other parameters used during the execution of key-establishment transactions.
- The static (also referred to as long-term) public keys of the parties involved in key-agreement schemes are assumed to be generated and distributed (directly or via a trusted party) before starting agreement transactions.
- Once a shared secret Z is generated, it is provided as input to a key-derivation function to yield a shared key. Thus, any key-agreement transaction includes the agreed KDF and its parameters.

14.3.3.1 Common Mechanisms and Functions

14.3.3.1.1 Key-Confirmation

In all the public-key based key-establishment schemes, the recipient may trust or not the public key of the other party. To provide assurance about the public key used in a key-establishment scheme, an operation, called *key-confirmation*, may be required. Using the key-confirmation, one party (or both) get(s) assurance that the other party has generated the shared secret using its private key, which must correspond to the public key used in the transaction. In other words, using the key-confirmation, the recipient has assurance that its partner effectively owns the key-pair used in the key-agreement

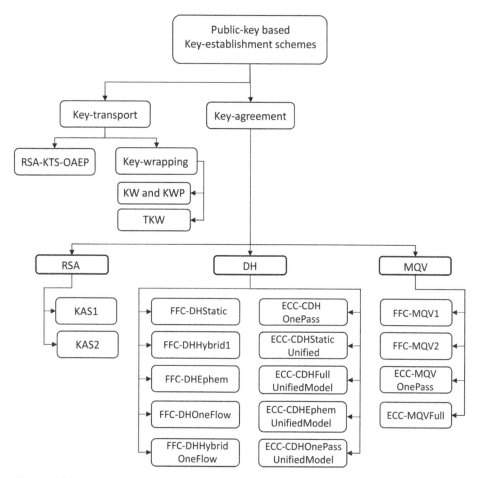

Figure 14.11 Recommended public-key-based key-establishment schemes.

or key-transport transaction. The key-confirmation may be unilateral (i.e. only one party requires the verification of key-pair possession) or bilateral (both parties require the verification key-pair possession). A bilateral key-confirmation is composed of two instances of the unilateral key-confirmation; thus, both parties can detect an error in the key-agreement process. Key-confirmation makes use of a MAC algorithm among the recommended algorithms (see Table 14.4).

14.3.3.1.2 *Common Conversion Functions*
The following conversion functions are common to many schemes.

```
function BitStrToInteger (S, z)
        # Convert a bit-string S to integer z
function IntegerToByteStr (z, S)
        # Convert an integer z to a bit-string S
function FieldElementToInteger (A, Z)
        # Convert an element A of finite field to an integer z
function FieldElementToByteStr (A, S)
        # Convert an element A of finite field to a byte-string S
```

MAC algorithms recommended in key-establishment schemes are shown in Table 14.7.

14.3.3.2 Key-Establishment Schemes Using RSA

14.3.3.2.1 *Key-Agreement Schemes Using RSA*
Two main families of key-agreement schemes (KASs) are recommended to establish a key between two parties X and Y [7]. Both KAS families may be used with or without key-confirmation. They differ mainly in the number, one or two, of key-pairs that are used.

Table 14.7 MAC algorithms recommended in key-establishment schemes [14].

	Hash bit-length	Security strength S
HMAC SHA-1	160	$112 \leq S \leq 160$
HMAC SHA-224	224	$112 \leq S \leq 224$
HMAC SHA-256	256	$112 \leq S \leq 256$
HMAC SHA-512/224	224	$112 \leq S \leq 256$
HMAC SHA-512/256	256	$112 \leq S \leq 256$
HMAC SHA-384	384	$112 \leq S \leq 384$
HMAC SHA-512	512	$112 \leq S \leq 512$
HMAC SHA3-224	224	$112 \leq S \leq 224$
HMAC SHA3-256	256	$112 \leq S \leq 256$
HMAC SHA3-384	384	$112 \leq S \leq 384$
HMAC SHA3-512	512	$112 \leq S \leq 512$
KMAC-128	$(^{18})$	$112 \leq S \leq 128$
KMAC-256		$112 \leq S \leq 256$
AES-128-CMAC	512	$112 \leq S \leq 128$
AES-192-CMAC	256	$112 \leq S \leq 192$
AES-256-CMAC	384	$112 \leq S \leq 256$

Before starting the key-agreement, both parties must agree on the key-derivation function to use and its associated hash function. In addition, if a confirmation is required, the parties must agree on a MAC algorithm and the parameters to use (i.e. bit-lengths of the MAC key and MAC tag). The agreement on the MAC parameters to use is out of the scope of the KASs. Both KASs make use of two operations, *RSASVE_GENERATE* (RSA Secret-Value Encapsulation) and *RSASVE_RECOVER*:

1) *RSASVE_GENERATE*(N,e): this operation enables one party to generate a shared secret Z, and to encrypt it with the public key of the other party. The operation makes use of a DRBG to produce a random bit-string with the same bit-length than that of the modulus N. The output of this operation is a pair (Z,C), a shared secret and its ciphertext.
2) *RSASVE_RECOVER* (N,d): this operation enables the ciphertext recipient to decrypt the received message with its private key in order to recover the shared secret Z.

The pseudocode of *RSASVE_GENERATE* and *RSASVE_RECOVER* operations is the following:

```
function RSASVE_GENERATE
    input   (N,e): public key
    output  Z,C: shared secret and its ciphertext
    L = ⌈len(N) / 8⌉ # byte-length of the modulus
    Z = DRBG(L) # generate L random bytes
    z = BitStrToInteger(Z)
    if not(1 < z < (N − 1)), then go to step 2
    c = RSAEncrypt(N, e, z)
    C = IntegerToBitStr(c)
    return (Z,C)
```

```
function RSASVE_RECOVER
    input   C,(N,d): ciphertext and private key
    output  Z: shared secret
    L = ⌈len(N) / 8⌉ # byte-length of the modulus
    c = BitStrToInteger(Z)
    z = RSADecrypt(N, d, c)
    Z = IntegerToBitStr(z)
    return Z
```

14.3.3.2.1.1 Key-Agreement Scheme #1 (KAS1)

KAS1 makes use of a single key-pair. KAS1 family consists of two variants: basic-KAS1 (without key-confirmation) and Uni-Cnf-KAS1 (with unilateral key-confirmation). Both variants are depicted in Figure 14.12.

Let X denote the party, which initiates the key agreement and Y, the recipient. Let Pr_Y and Pu_Y denote the static private and public keys of the party Y, respectively.

The steps of the agreement scheme Basic-KAS1 are as follows:

1) Party X generates a secret Z and encrypts it using Pu_Y; the encrypted secret is denoted C; i.e. $(Z, C) = RSASVE\_GENERATE(N,e)$.
2) C is exchanged between the parties.
3) Party Y recovers the shared secret using the operation $RSASVE\_RECOVER$ and its private key (N,d); i.e. $Z = RSASVE\_RECOVER(C,N,d)$
4) Party Y generates[19] a nonce $Nonce_Y$ and sends it to party X.
5) Both parties use the shared secret Z, the nonce $Nonce_Y$, and an agreed key-derivation function KDF (and may be other additional parameters depending on the KDF) to derive a new key K and a MAC key, if the key-confirmation is required. That is,

$$KeyingMaterial = \left(K\left[,MacKey\right]\right) = KDF\left(Z, Nonce_Y, \ldots\right) \quad (20)$$

6) The shared secret Z is destroyed by both parties.

In Uni-Cnf-KAS1 variant, a MAC algorithm, a MAC bit-length, $TagLen$, and the IDs of parties are included in key-agreement transaction. After Basic-KAS1, the following steps are performed:

7.1 Party Y computes a tag T_Y; and party X, a tag T_X, using the same information (i.e. C, $Nonce_Y$, and may be other additional parameters) and the same MAC algorithm, with the same parameters (i.e. $MacKey$ and $TagLen$):

$$S_Y = \text{"KC\_1\_Y"} \| ID_Y \| ID_X \| Nonce_X \| C \| \ldots \quad (21)$$

$$T_X = MAC\left(MacKey, TagLen, S_Y\right)$$

$$T_Y = MAC\left(MacKey, TagLen, S_Y\right)$$

Party X		Party Y
Selection of IFC domain parameters and a KDF		
Obtain Pu_Y	$\leftarrow$	Generate static key-pair $\left(Pr_Y, Pu_Y\right)$: $Pr_Y = (N,d)$, $Pu_Y = (N,e)$ Distribute Pu_Y
Basic key-agreement scheme #1 (Basic-KAS1)		
1. $(Z,C) = RSASVE\_GENERATE(N,e)$ 2. Send C 3. 4. Receive $Nonce_Y$ 5. Generate keying material: $KeyingMaterial = KDF\left(Z, Nonce_Y\right)$ 6. Destroy Z	$\rightarrow$ $\leftarrow$	1. 2. Receive C 3. $Z = RSASVE\_RECOVER\left(C,N,d\right)$ 4. Generate and send nonce $Nonce_Y$ 5. Generate a keying material: $KeyingMaterial = KDF\left(Z, Nonce_Y\right)$ 6. Destroy Z
Uni-Cnf-KAS1 (unilateral key-confirmation provided by party Y)		
7.1. Compute a tag T_X: $\quad S_Y = \text{"KC\_1\_Y"} \| ID_Y \| ID_X \| Nonce_Y \| C$ $\quad T_X = MAC\left(MacKey, S_Y, TagLen\right)$ 7.2. Receive T_Y 7.3. If $T_X \neq T_Y$, then return "Error" 7.4. Destroy $MacKey$	 $\leftarrow$	7.1. Compute a tag T_Y: $\quad S_Y = \text{"KC\_1\_Y"} \| ID_Y \| ID_X \| Nonce_Y \| C$ $\quad T_Y = MAC\left(MacKey, S_Y, TagLen\right)$ 7.2. Send T_Y 7.3. 7.4. Destroy $MacKey$

Figure 14.12 Flow diagram of key-agreement scheme #1 (KAS1).

Note. In Tables 14.12-14.28, some steps are included without any performed operation; they aim to provide symmetry in party's behavior.

where ID_X and ID_Y are the IDs of parties X and Y, respectively. *MacKey* is extracted from the output of the KDF. Partner X does not need to send a tag, because it does not own a public key to verify.

7.2 The tag T_Y is exchanged between the parties.

7.3 Verification by party X: If $T_X \neq T_Y$, then a KAS error is raised. Otherwise, the key-confirmation succeeds.

7.4 Both parties destroy the key *MacKey* used to generate the tags.

14.3.3.2.1.2 Key-Agreement Scheme #2 (KAS2)

KAS2 makes use of two key-pairs; thus, both parties equally contribute to the shared secret construction, which is used to generate a new key. KAS2 family consists of three variants: BasicKAS2 (without key-confirmation), Uni-Cnf-KAS2 (with key-confirmation by one party), and Bil-Cnf-KAS2 (with bilateral key-confirmation). KAS2 variants are depicted in Figure 14.13. Basic-KAS2 steps are as follows:

1) Party X generates the first part of the shared secret, denoted Z_X, and encrypts it using Pu_Y; the encrypted secret is denoted C_X; i.e. $(Z_X, C_X) = RSASVE\_GENERATE(N_Y, e_Y)$.

2) C_X is exchanged between the parties.

3) Party Y recovers the first part of shared secret using the operation $RSASVE\_RECOVER$ and its private key (N_Y, d); i.e. $Z_X = RSASVE\_RECOVER(C_Y, N_Y, d_Y)$.

4) Party Y generates the second part of the shared secret, denoted Z_Y, and encrypts it using Pu_X; the encrypted secret is denoted C_Y; i.e. $(Z_Y, C_Y) = RSASVE\_GENERATE(N_X, e_X)$.

5) C_Y is exchanged between the parties.

6) Party X recovers the shared secret using the operation $RSASVE\_RECOVER$ and its private key (N_X, d_X); i.e. $Z_Y = RSASVE\_RECOVER(C_Y, N_X, d_X)$.

7) Both parties form the shared secret Z, as $Z = Z_X \parallel Z_Y$.

8) Both parties use the shared secret Z and an agreed key-derivation function KDF (and may be other additional parameters depending on the KDF) to derive a new key K. They derive a MAC key, if the key-confirmation is required; *KeyingMaterial* $= KDF(Z, \ldots)$.

9) The shared secrets Z, Z_X, and Z_Y are destroyed.

Party X		Party Y
Selection of IFC domain parameters and a KDF		
Generate a static key-pair (Pr_X, Pu_X): $Pr_X = (N_X, d_X)$, $Pu_X = (N_X, e_X)$ Distribute Pu_X Obtain Pu_Y	$\rightarrow$ $\leftarrow$	Generate a static key-pair (Pr_Y, Pu_Y): $Pr_Y = (N_Y, d_Y)$, $Pu_Y = (N_Y, e_Y)$ Obtain Pu_X Distribute Pu_Y
Basic Key-agreement scheme #2 (Basic-KAS2)		
1. Generate the first part of the shared secret: $(Z_X, C_X) = RSASVE\_GENERATE(N_Y, e_Y)$ 2. Send C_X 3. 4. 5. Receive C_Y 6. $Z_Y = RSASVE\_RECOVER(C_Y, N_X, d_X)$ 7. Shared secret $Z = Z_X \parallel Z_Y$ 8. *KeyingMaterial* $= KDF(Z, \ldots)$ 9. Destroy Z, Z_X, Z_Y	$\rightarrow$ $\leftarrow$	1. 2. Receive C_X 3. $Z_X = RSASVE\_RECOVER(C_X, N_Y, d_Y)$ 4. Generate the second part of the shared secret: $(Z_Y, C_Y) = RSASVE\_GENERATE(N_X, e_X)$ 5. Send C_Y 6. 7. Shared secret $Z = Z_X \parallel Z_Y$ 8. *KeyingMaterial* $= KDF(Z, \ldots)$ 9. Destroy Z, Z_X, Z_Y
Unilateral or bilateral key-confirmation may be added		

Figure 14.13 Flow diagram of key-agreement scheme #2 (KAS2).

Unilateral or bilateral confirmation may be added to the basic KAS2 to build the Uni-Cnf-KAS2 and Bil-Cnf-KAS2 respectively. Bil-Cnf-KAS2 is the double instantiation of Uni-Cnf-KAS1 steps. The key-confirmation steps are depicted in Figure 14.14.

Unilateral key-confirmation provided by party X		
1. Compute a tag T_X: $\quad S_X = \text{"KC\_1\_X"} \parallel ID_X \parallel ID_Y \parallel C_X \parallel C_Y$ $\quad T_X = MAC(MacKey, S_X, TagLen)$ 2. Send T_X 3. 4. Destroy *MacKey*	$\rightarrow$	1. Compute a tag T_Y: $\quad S_X = \text{"KC\_1\_X"} \parallel ID_X \parallel ID_Y \parallel C_X \parallel C_Y$ $\quad T_Y = MAC(MacKey, S_X, TagLen)$ 2. Receive T_X 3. If $T_X \neq T_Y$, then return "Error" 4. Destroy *MacKey*
Unilateral key-confirmation provided by Y		
1. Compute a tag T_X: $\quad S_Y = \text{"KC\_1\_Y"} \parallel ID_Y \parallel ID_X \parallel C_Y \parallel C_X$ $\quad T_X = MAC(MacKey, S_Y, TagLen)$ 2. Receive T_Y 3. If $T_X \neq T_Y$, then return "Error" 4. Destroy *MacKey*	$\leftarrow$	1. Compute a tag T_Y: $\quad S_Y = \text{"KC\_1\_Y"} \parallel ID_Y \parallel ID_X \parallel C_Y \parallel C_X$ $\quad T_Y = MAC(MacKey, S_Y, TagLen)$ 2. Send T_Y 3. 4. Destroy *MacKey*
Bilateral key-confirmation		
1. Compute tag T_X: $\quad S_X = \text{"KC\_2\_X"} \parallel ID_X \parallel ID_Y \parallel C_X \parallel C_Y$ $\quad T_X = MAC(MacKey, S_X, TagLen)$ 2. Send tag T_X 3. Receive tag T_Y 4. Compute tag T_X^Y: $\quad S_Y = \text{"KC\_2\_Y"} \parallel ID_Y \parallel ID_X \parallel C_Y \parallel C_X$ $\quad T_X^Y = MAC(MacKey, S_Y, TagLen)$ 5. If $T_Y \neq T_X^Y$, then return "Error" 6. Destroy *MacKey*	$\rightarrow$ $\leftarrow$	1. Compute tag T_Y: $\quad S_Y = \text{"KC\_2\_Y"} \parallel ID_Y \parallel ID_X \parallel C_Y \parallel C_X$ $\quad T_Y = MAC(MacKey, S_Y, TagLen)$ 2. Receive tag T_X 3. Send tag T_Y 4. Compute tag T_Y^X: $\quad S_X = \text{"KC\_2\_X"} \parallel ID_X \parallel ID_Y \parallel C_X \parallel C_Y$ $\quad T_Y^X = MAC(MacKey, S_X, TagLen)$ 5.If $T_X \neq T_Y^X$, then return "Error" 6. Destroy *MacKey*

Figure 14.14 Flow diagram of key-confirmation alternatives for KAS2.

14.3.3.2.2 *Key-Transport Schemes Using RSA*

In the key-transport schemes (KTSs), the initiator of the transaction selects a key and then sends it to the recipient. It is recommended to use the Optimal Asymmetric Encryption Padding (OAEP) procedure to encrypt the key and the additional inputs [7]. The OAEP procedure is described in Section 12.2.5. Therefore, OAEP is added as a suffix to RSA-based KTS. KTS-OAEP family has two variants, Basic-KTS-OAEP (without key-confirmation) and Uni-Cnf-KTS-OAEP (with unilateral key-confirmation). KTS-OAEP specifies only a unilateral key-confirmation, because a single key-pair is used in the transaction. The material used to perform key-confirmation in KTS is the same as in KASs.

The keying material (i.e. the secret key and the MAC key, if a key-confirmation is required) is encrypted with *RSA-OAEP-Encrypt* operation and decrypted with *RSA-OAEP-Decrypt*. Notice that the modulus N of the key-pair of the transaction initiator must be at least equal to the key to transport, because the ciphertext of the key is yielded *modulo N*.

Both KTS-OAEP variants are depicted in Figure 14.15. The steps of Basic KTS-OAEP scheme are as follows:

1) Party X selects the key K to transport and the optional input A.
2) Party X encrypts the key K and optional input A using public key Pu_Y. The encrypted secret is denoted C; i.e.
$\quad C = RSA\text{-}OAEP\text{-}Encrypt(Pu_Y, K, A)$.
3) Ciphertext C is exchanged between parties.
4) Party Y recovers the key K; it recovers the *MacKey*, if a unilateral key-confirmation is required.
$\quad (K, MacKey) = RSA\text{-}OAEP\text{-}Decrypt((N, d), C)$

Party X		Party Y
Selection of IFC domain parameters and a KDF		
Obtain Pu_Y	←	Generate a static key-pair (Pr_Y, Pu_Y): $Pr_Y = (N,d)$, $Pu_Y = (N,e)$ Distribute Pu_Y
Basic-KTS-OAEP		
1. Select key K to transport and optional data A 2. $C = RSA\text{-}OAEP\text{-}Encrypt(Pu_Y, K, A)$ 3. Send C 4.	→	1. 2. 3. Receive C 4. $(K, MacKey) = RSA\text{-}OAEP\text{-}Decrypt((N,d), C)$
Uni-Cnf-KTS-OAEP (key-confirmation provided by party Y)		
5.1 Compute the tag T_X: $\quad S_Y = "KC\_1\_Y" \,\|\, ID_Y \,\|\, ID_X \,\|\, Null \,\|\, C$ $\quad T_X = MAC(MacKey, S_Y, TagLen)$ 5.2 Receive T_Y 5.3 if $T_X \neq T_Y$, then return "Error" 5.4 Destroy $MacKey$	←	5.1 Compute the tag T_Y: $\quad S_Y = "KC\_1\_Y" \,\|\, ID_Y \,\|\, ID_X \,\|\, Null \,\|\, C$ $\quad T_Y = MAC(MacKey, S_Y, TagLen)$ 5.2 Send tag T_Y 5.3 5.4 Destroy $MacKey$

Figure 14.15 Flow diagram of Key-transport scheme (KTS-OAEP).

In Uni-Cnf-KTS, the following steps are performed after the Basic-KTS-OAEP:

5.1 Party X computes a tag T_X and party Y, a tag T_Y, using the same information (i.e. C, and may be other additional parameters) and the same MAC algorithm, with the same parameter (i.e. $MacKey$ and $Taglen$):

$$T_X = MAC(MacKey, S_Y, TagLen)$$
$$T_Y = MAC(MacKey, S_Y, TagLen)$$
$$S_Y = Null \,\|\, C \,\|\, \ldots$$

5.2 If $T_X \neq T_Y$, then an Error notification is returned.
5.3 Both parties destroy the MAC key used to generate tags.

14.3.3.3 DLC-based Key-Agreement Schemes

14.3.3.3.1 DLC-based Primitives for Shared-Secret Generation

Four primitives are used to compute a shared secret based either on FFC or on ECC:

- Primitive FFC-DH: computes a shared secret using Diffie-Hellman algorithm based on the finite-field cryptography (see Section 12.3.2).
- Primitive ECC-CDH: computes a shared secret using EC cofactor Diffie-Hellman algorithm based on the elliptic-curve cryptography (see Section 13.5.3).
- Primitive FFC-MQV: computes a shared secret using Menezes-Qu-Vanstone algorithm based on the finite-field cryptography (see Section 12.3.3).
- Primitive ECC-MQV: computes a shared secret using Menezes-Qu-Vanstone algorithm based on the elliptic-curve cryptography (see Section 13.5.4).

The four primitives are used in the next subsection to build key-agreement schemes. Before calling these primitives, the domain parameters should be selected and the required key-pairs generated. The output of the primitives is a shared secret that will be used in a subsequent step to generate a secret key and, when needed, other keying material.

Pseudocodes of the primitives are as follows:

```
primitive FFC_DH
        input   p, g: two domain parameters (a prime p and a generator g)
            xₐ: private key of the party running the primitive
            y_B: public key of the other party
```

output Z: shared secret (a byte-string)
1. ErrorIndication = False; $Z =$ ""
2. $z = y_B^{x_A} \bmod p$
3. **if** $\big((z \le 1) \vee (z = p - 1)\big)$, **then** ErrorIndication = True
4. **else** $\{Z = IntegerToString(z);$ Destroy $z\}$
5. **return** (ErrorIndication, Z)

---

primitive ECC_CDH
    input G: base point
      h: cofactor of base point G
      x_A: the private key of the party running the primitive
      Ω_B: the public key of the other party (EC point)
    output Z: shared secret (byte-string)
    1. ErrorIndication = False; $Z =$ ""
    2. $P = (h * x_A) \cdot \Omega_B$ # Compute an EC point P $(^{22})$
    3. **if** $(P = \mathcal{O})$, **then** ErrorIndication = True $(^{23})$
    4. **else** $\{z = x\_coordinate(P); Z = IntegerToString(Z);$ Destroy $z\}$
    5. **return** (ErrorIndication, Z)

---

primitive FFC_MQV
    input
      p, q, g: three domain parameters (two primes and a generator)
      x_A: static private key of the party running the primitive
      y_B: static public key of the other party
      r_A: ephemeral private key of the party running the primitive
      t_A: ephemeral public key of the party running the primitive
      t_B: ephemeral public key of the other party
    output Z: shared secret (a byte-string)
    1. ErrorIndication = False; $Z =$ ""
    2. $w = \left\lceil \dfrac{1}{2} \log_2(q) \right\rceil$
    3. $T_A = (t_A \bmod 2^w) + 2^w$
    4. $S_A = (r_A + T_A * x_A) \bmod q$
    5. $T_B = (t_B \bmod 2^w) + 2^w$
    6. $z = \left(t_B * (y_B)^{T_B} \right)^{S_A} \bmod p$
    7. **if** $((z \le 1) \vee (z = p - 1))$, **then** ErrorIndication = True
    8. **else** $\{Z = Integer(z);$ Destroy $T_A, T_B, S_A,$ and $z\}$
    9. **return** (ErrorIndication, Z)

---

primitive ECC_MQV
    function $V(R, f)$
        input R: EC point
        output U: integer
        1. $x_R = x\_coordinate(R)$
        2. $U = \left(FieldElementToInteger(x_R) \bmod 2^{\lceil f/2 \rceil} \right) + 2^{\lceil f/2 \rceil}$
        3. **return** U
    input
      G: base point; h: cofactor of base point G
      n: order of base point G
      x_A^s: static private key of the party running the primitive

Ω_B^s: the static public key of the other party

x_A^e: ephemeral private key of the party running the primitive

Ω_A^e: ephemeral public key of the party running the primitive

Ω_B^e: the ephemeral public key of the other party

output Z: shared secret (a byte-string)

1. ErrorIndication = False; $Z = ""$
2. $f = \lceil log_2(n) \rceil$ # f is the bit-length of n, the subgroup order
3. $S_A = \left(x_A^e + V\left(\Omega_A^e\right) * x_A^s\right) \bmod n$
4. $P = h * S_A * \left(\Omega_B^e + V\left(\Omega_B^e\right) * \Omega_B^s\right) \bmod n$
5. **if** $(P = \mathcal{O})$, **then** ErrorIndication = True
6. **else** $\{z = x\_coordinate(P); Z = IntegerToByteStr(z); Destroy \, z\}$
7. **return** (ErrorIndication, Z.)

14.3.3.3.2 *Key-Agreement Categories and Common Steps*

Fourteen DLC-based key-agreement schemes (KASs) are recommended [14]: ten Diffie-Hellman-based schemes and four Menezes-Qu-Vanstone-based schemes. DLC-based KASs are grouped into two categories: agreement schemes based on FFC (Finite Field Cryptography) and those based on ECC (Elliptic Curve Cryptography). Another distinctive feature of DLC-based KASs is the number of static and ephemeral keys that are used (see Figure 14.16). The most robust (but the most resource consuming) schemes are the ones in which each partner participates in the key-agreement with its static and ephemeral keys. The lightest schemes are those in which only ephemeral keys are used; hence, trust between parties is required before performing key-agreement transactions. As shown in Figure 14.17, DLC-based KASs are built using six steps (not all the steps are required in all key-agreement schemes):

- Selection of the (FFC or ECC) domain parameters and a key-derivation function and its parameters. This step is out of the scope of the key-agreement transaction.
- Generation and distribution of the static public key(s), if required. This step is out of the scope of the key-agreement transaction.
- Generation and exchange of ephemeral public key(s), if required.
- Computation of a shared secret. This step is mandatory.

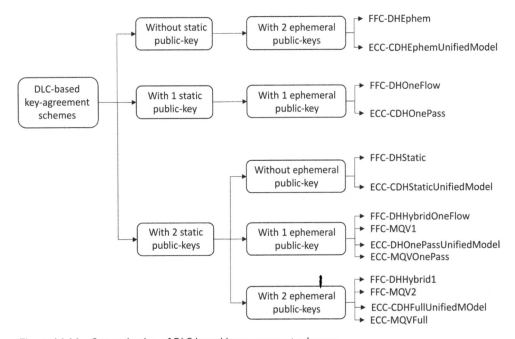

Figure 14.16   Categorization of DLC-based key-agreement schemes.

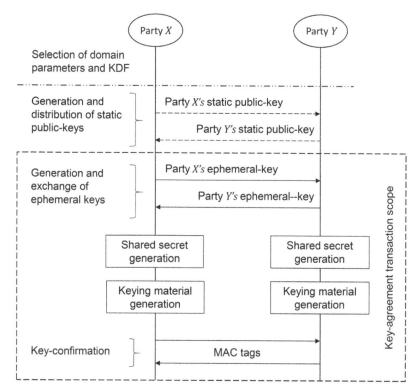

Figure 14.17 Main steps of DLC-based key-agreement schemes.

- Derivation of keying material, which includes a secret shared key and a MAC key (to generate tags used in key-confirmation step). This step is mandatory.
- Key-confirmation, which enables one party to provide to the other party assurance about its used public key.

14.3.3.3.3 Key-Confirmation

Key-confirmation may be included in most of the DLC-based key-agreement transactions to provide assurance that a party possesses the static private key associated with the static public key used in the key-agreement process. Like RSA-based KASs, DLC-based KASs can specify unilateral (when only a single static public key is used) or bilateral (if a pair of static public keys are used) key-confirmation.

The parameters (MAC algorithm and MAC bit-length) and operations (generation and exchange of tags) used in key-confirmation in DLC-based KASs are the same than those used in RSA-based KASs (Section 14.2.2.1). The only difference is in the values used in tag generation. The MAC key (denoted *MacKey*) used to generate the tags is extracted from the output of the KDF by both parties. There exist four key-confirmation schemes:

1) 2e-2s key-confirmation scheme is applicable when two ephemeral and two static public keys are used. Each of the parties participates with an ephemeral key, denoted $Ephem_X$ or $Ephem_Y$. The 2e-2s key-confirmation scheme is depicted in Figure 14.18.
2) 1e-2s key-confirmation scheme is applicable when only one party, say X, makes use of an ephemeral public key and two static public keys are used. Party Y participates in the key-confirmation by a nonce, instead of an ephemeral key. The 1e-2s key-confirmation is depicted in Figure 14.19.
3) 1e-1s key-confirmation scheme is applicable when the party X has an ephemeral public key and the party Y has a static public key. No bilateral key-confirmation is provided, because there is a single static public key in this scheme. Party X participates with a nonce. The 1e-1s key-confirmation is depicted in Figure 14.20.
4) 0e-2s key-confirmation scheme is applicable when no ephemeral public key is used and two static public keys are used. The 0e-2s key-confirmation is depicted in Figure 14.21.

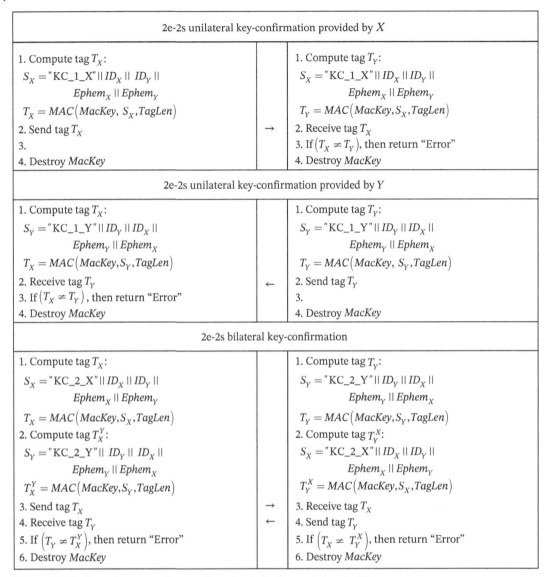

Figure 14.18 Flow diagrams of key-confirmation in 2ephemeral-2static KASs.

1e-2s unilateral key-confirmation provided by X		
1. Receive $Nonce_Y$ 2. Compute tag T_X: $\quad S_X = \text{"KC\_1\_X"} \| ID_X \| ID_Y \|$ $\quad\quad\quad Ephem_X \| Nonce_Y$ $\quad T_X = MAC\big(MacKey,\ S_X, TagLen\big)$ 3. Send tag T_X 4. 5. Destroy *MacKey*	$\leftarrow$ $\rightarrow$	1. Generate and send nonce $Nonce_Y$ 2. Compute tag T_Y: $\quad S_X = \text{"KC\_1\_X"} \| ID_X \| ID_Y \|$ $\quad\quad\quad Ephem_X \| Nonce_Y$ $\quad T_Y = MAC\big(MacKey, S_X, TagLen\big)$ 3. Receive tag T_X 4. If $\big(T_X \neq T_Y\big)$, then return "Error" 5. Destroy *MacKey*

Figure 14.19 Flow diagrams of key-confirmation in 1-ephemeral-2static KASs.

1e-2s unilateral key-confirmation provided by Y		
1. Compute tag T_X: $$S_Y = \text{"KC\_1\_Y"} \| ID_Y \| ID_X \| \\ Null \| Ephem_X$$ $$T_X = MAC(MacKey, S_Y, TagLen)$$ 2. Receive tag T_Y 3. If $T_X \neq T_Y$, then return "Error" 4. Destroy *MacKey*	$\leftarrow$	1. Compute tag T_Y: $$S_Y = \text{"KC\_1\_Y"} \| ID_Y \| ID_X \| \\ Null \| Ephem_X$$ $$T_Y = MAC(MacKey, S_Y, TagLen)$$ 2. Send tag T_Y 3. 4. Destroy *MacKey*
1e-2s bilateral key-confirmation		
1. Receive $Nonce_Y$ 2. Compute tag T_X: $$S_X = \text{"KC\_2\_X"} \|\| ID_X \| ID_Y \| \\ Ephem_X \| Nonce_Y$$ $$T_X = MAC(MacKey, S_X, TagLen)$$ 3. Send tag T_X 4. Receive tag T_Y 5. Compute tag T_X^Y: $$S_Y = \text{"KC\_2\_Y"} \| ID_Y \| ID_X \| \\ Nonce_Y \| Ephem_X$$ $$T_X^Y = MAC(MacKey, S_Y, TagLen)$$ 6. If $\left(T_Y \neq T_X^Y\right)$, then return "Error" 7. Destroy *MacKey*	$\leftarrow$ $\rightarrow$ $\leftarrow$	1. Generate and send nonce $Nonce_Y$ 2. Compute tag T_Y: $$S_X = \text{"KC\_2\_Y"} \| ID_Y \| ID_X \| \\ Nonce_Y \| Ephem_X$$ $$T_Y = MAC(MacKey, S_Y, TagLen)$$ 3. Receive tag T_X 4. Send tag T_Y 5. Compute tag T_Y^X: $$S_X = \text{"KC\_2\_X"} \| ID_X \| ID_Y \| \\ Ephem_X \| Nonce_Y$$ $$T_Y^X = MAC(MacKey, S_X, TagLen)$$ 6. If $\left(T_X \neq T_Y^X\right)$, then return "Error" 7. Destroy *MacKey*

Figure 14.19 (Cont'd)

1e-1s unilateral key-confirmation provided by Y		
1. Compute tag T_X: $$S_Y = \text{"KC\_1\_Y"} \| ID_Y \| ID_X \| Null \\ \| Ephem_X$$ $$T_X = MAC(MacKey, S_Y, TagLen)$$ 2. Receive tag T_Y 3. If $\left(T_X \neq T_Y\right)$, then return "Error" 4. Destroy *MacKey*	$\leftarrow$	1. Compute tag T_Y: $$S_Y = \text{"KC\_1\_Y"} \| ID_Y \| ID_X \| Null \\ \| Ephem_X$$ $$T_Y = MAC(MacKey, S_Y, TagLen)$$ 2. Send tag T_Y 3. 4. Destroy *MacKey*

Figure 14.20 Flow diagram of key-confirmation in 1-ephemeral-1static KASs.

0e-2s unilateral key-confirmation provided by X ([24])		
1. Receive $Nonce_Y$ 2. Compute tag T_X: $$S_X = \text{"KC\_1\_X"} \| ID_X \| ID_Y \| \\ Nonce_X \| Nonce_Y$$ $$T_X = MAC(MacKey, S_X, TagLen)$$ 3. Send tag T_X 4. 5. Destroy *MacKey*	$\leftarrow$ $\rightarrow$	1. Generate and send nonce $Nonce_Y$ 2. Compute tag T_Y: $$S_X = \text{"KC\_1\_X"} \| ID_X \| ID_Y \| \\ Nonce_X \| Nonce_Y$$ $$T_Y = MAC(MacKey, S_X, TagLen)$$ 3. Receive tag T_X 4. If $\left(T_X \neq T_Y\right)$, then return "Error" 5. Destroy *MacKey*

Figure 14.21 Flow diagrams of key-confirmation in 0-ephemeral-2static KASs.

0e-2s unilateral key-confirmation provided by Y		
1. Compute tag T_X: $$S_Y = "KC\_1\_Y" \| ID_Y \| ID_X \| Null$$ $$\| Nonce_X$$ $$T_X = MAC(MacKey, S_Y, TagLen)$$		1. Compute tag T_Y: $$S_Y = "KC\_1\_Y" \| ID_Y \| ID_X \| Null$$ $$\| Nonce_X$$ $$T_Y = MAC(MacKey, S_Y, TagLen)$$
2. Receive tag T_X 3. If $(T_X \ T_Y)$, then return "Error" 4. Destroy $MacKey$	←	2. Send tag T_Y 3. 4. Destroy $MacKey$

0e-2s bilateral key-confirmation		
1. Receive $Nonce_Y$	←	1. Generate and send nonce $Nonce_Y$
2. Compute tag T_X: $$S_X = "KC\_2\_X" \| ID_X \| ID_Y \|$$ $$Nonce_X \| Nonce_Y$$ $$T_X = MAC(MacKey, S_X, TagLen)$$		2. Compute tag T_Y: $$S_Y = "KC\_2\_Y" \| ID_Y \| ID_X \|$$ $$Nonce_Y \| Nonce_X$$ $$T_Y = MAC(MacKey, S_Y, TagLen)$$
3. Send tag T_X		3. Receive tag T_X
4. Receive tag T_Y	→	4. Send tag T_Y
5. Compute tag T_X^Y: $$S_Y = "KC\_2\_Y" \| ID_Y \| ID_X \|$$ $$Nonce_Y \| Nonce_X$$ $$T_X^Y = MAC(MacKey, S_Y, TagLen)$$	←	5. Compute tag T_Y^X: $$S_X = "KC\_2\_X" \| ID_X \| ID_Y \|$$ $$Nonce_X \| Nonce_Y$$ $$T_Y^X = MAC(MacKey, S_X, TagLen)$$
6. If $(T_Y \neq T_X^Y)$, then return "Error" 7. Destroy $MacKey$		6. if $(T_X \neq T_Y^X)$, then return "Error" 7. Destroy $MacKey$

Figure 14.21 (Cont'd)

Each key-confirmation scheme may have three alternatives: unilateral key-confirmation provided by party X, unilateral key-confirmation provided by party Y, or a bilateral key-confirmation.

14.3.3.3.4 *Diagrams of the DLC-based Key-Agreement Schemes*
Diagrams of some KASs are shown in Figures 14.22–14.28. The other KASs are specified in similar ways. For sake of simplicity, the optional parameters, marked by "..." in KDF, are not included. Only the steps performed in a key-agreement transaction are numbered.

Party X		Party Y
Selection of the FFC domain parameters and a KDF		
1. Generate an ephemeral key-pair (Pr_X^e, Pu_X^e): $Pu_X^e = g^{Pr_X^e} \bmod p$		1. Generate an ephemeral key-pair (Pr_Y^e, Pu_Y^e): $Pu_Y^e = g^{Pr_Y^e} \bmod p$
2. Send ephemeral public key Pu_X^e	→	2. Receive Pu_X^e
3. Receive Pu_Y^e	←	3. Send ephemeral public key Pu_Y^e
4. Compute the shared secret: $$(EI, Z) = FFC\_DH(Pr_X^e, Pu_Y^e)$$		4. Compute the shared secret: $$(EI, Z_1) = FFC\_DH(Pr_Y^e, Pu_X^e)$$
5. If $(not(EI))$: 5.1. Derive the keying material: $$KeyingMaterial = KDF(Z, ...)$$ 5.2. Destroy Z		5. If $(not(EI))$: 5.1. Derive the keying material: $$KeyingMaterial = KDF(Z, ...)$$ 5.2. Destroy Z
No key-confirmation can be added		

Figure 14.22 Diffie-Hellman-based key-agreement scheme FFC-DHEphem.

Party X	Party Y
Selection of the ECC domain parameters and a KDF	
1. Generate an ephemeral key-pair $\left(Pr_X^e, \Omega u_X^e\right)$: $\Omega u_X^e = Pr_X^e.G$	1. Generate an ephemeral key-pair $\left(Pr_Y^e, \Omega u_Y^e\right)$: $\Omega u_Y^e = P_Y^e.G$
2. Send ephemeral public key Ωu_X^e →	2. Receive Ωu_X^e
3. Receive Ωu_Y^e ←	3. Send ephemeral public key Ωu_Y^e
4. Compute the shared secret: $(EI, Z) = ECC\_CDH\left(Pr_X^e, \Omega u_Y^e\right)$	4. Compute the shared secret: $(EI, Z) = ECC\_CDH\left(Pr_Y^e, \Omega u_X^e\right)$
5. If $\left(not(EI)\right)$: 5.1. Derive the keying material: $KeyingMaterial = KDF(Z,...)$ 5.2. Destroy Z	5. If $\left(not(EI)\right)$: 5.1. Derive the keying material: $KeyingMaterial = KDF(Z,...)$ 5.2. Destroy Z
No key-confirmation can be added	

Figure 14.23 scheme: ECC-CDHEphemeralUnifiedModel.

Party X	Party Y
Selection of the FFC domain parameters and a KDF	
Generate a key-pair $\left(Pr_X, Pu_X\right)$: $Pu_X = g^{Pr_X} \bmod p$ Distribute static public key Pu_X → Obtain Pu_Y ←	Generate a static key-pair $\left(Pr_Y, Pu_Y\right)$: $Pu_Y = g^{Pr_Y} \bmod p$ Obtain Pu_X Distribute static public key Pu_Y
1. Generate and send nonce $Nonce_X$ → 2. Compute the shared secret: $(EI, Z) = FFC\_CDH\left(Pr_X, Pu_Y\right)$ 3. If $\left(not(EI)\right)$: 3.1 Derive the keying material: $KeyingMaterial = KDF\left(Z, Nonce_X\right)$ 3.2. Destroy Z	1. Receive $Nonce_X$ 2. Compute the shared secret: $(EI, Z) = FFC\_CDH\left(Pr_Y, Pu_X\right)$ 3. If $\left(not(EI)\right)$: 3.1. Derive the keying material: $KeyingMaterial = KDF\left(Z, Nonce_X\right)$ 3.2. Destroy Z
Unilateral or bilateral 0e-2s key-confirmation may be added	

Figure 14.24 Diffie-Hellman-based key-agreement scheme DHStatic.

Party X	Party Y
Selection of the ECC domain parameters and a KDF	
Generate a static key-pair $\left(Pr_X, \Omega u_X\right)$: $\Omega u_X = Pr_X.G$ Distribute static public key Ωu_X → Obtain Ωu_Y ←	Generate a static key-pair $\left(Pr_Y, \Omega u_Y\right)$: $\Omega u_Y = Pr_Y.G$ Obtain Ωu_X Distribute static public key Ωu_Y
1. Generate and send nonce $Nonce_X$ → 2. Compute the shared secret: $(EI, Z) = ECC\_CDH\left(Pr_X, \Omega u_Y\right)$ 3. If $\left(not(EI)\right)$: 3.1 Derive the keying material: $KeyingMaterial = KDF\left(Z, Nonce_X\right)$ 3.2. Destroy Z	1. Receive $Nonce_X$ 2. Compute the shared secret: $(EI, Z) = ECC\_CDH\left(Pr_Y, \Omega u_X\right)$ 3. If $\left(not(EI)\right)$: 3.1 Derive the keying material: $KeyingMaterial = KDF\left(Z, Nonce_X\right)$ 3.2.Destroy Z
Unilateral or bilateral 0e-2s key-confirmation may be added	

Figure 14.25 Diffie-Hellman-based key-agreement scheme ECC-CDHStaticUnifiedModel.

Party X		Party Y
Selection of the ECC domain parameters and a KDF		
Generate a static key-pair $(Pr_X, \Omega u_X)$: $\Omega u_X = Pr_X.G$ Distribute static public key Ωu_X Obtain Ωu_Y	$\dashrightarrow$ $\leftarrow\dashv$	Generate a static key-pair $(Pr_Y, \Omega u_Y)$: $\Omega u_Y = Pr_Y.G$ Obtain Ωu_X Distribute static public key Ωu_Y

1. Generate an ephemeral key-pair $(Pr_X^e, \Omega u_X^e)$: $\Omega u_X^e = Pr_X^e.G$
 2. Send ephemeral public key Ωu_X^e
 3. Compute the first part of the shared secret: $(EI_1, Z_1) = ECC\_CDH(Pr_X, \Omega u_Y)$
 4. Compute the second part of the shared secret: $(EI_2, Z_2) = ECC\_CDH(Pr_X^e, \Omega u_Y)$
 5. If $(not(EI_1) \wedge not(EI_2))$:
   5.1 $Z = Z_2 \parallel Z_1$
   5.2 Derive the keying material:
     $KeyingMaterial = KDF(Z,...)$
   5.3. Destroy Z, Z_1, Z_2
	$\rightarrow$	1.
		
		 2. Receive Ωu_X^e
		 3. Compute the first part of the shared secret: $(EI_1, Z_1) = ECC\_CDH(Pr_Y, \Omega u_X)$
		 4. Compute the second part of the shared secret: $(EI_2, Z_2) = ECC\_CDH(Pr_Y, \Omega u_X^e)$
		 5. If $(not(EI_1) \wedge not(EI_2))$:
		   5.1 $Z = Z_2 \parallel Z_1$
		   5.2 Derive the keying material:
		     $KeyingMaterial = KDF(Z,...)$
		   5.3. Destroy Z, Z_1, Z_2

Unilateral or bilateral 1e-2s key-confirmation may be added		

Figure 14.26 Diffie-Hellman-based key-agreement scheme ECC-DHOnePassUnifiedModel.

Party X		*Party Y*
Selection of the ECC domain parameters and a KDF		
Generate a static key-pair $(Pr_X, \Omega u_X)$: $\Omega u_X = Pr_X.G$ Distribute static public key Ωu_X Obtain Ωu_Y	$\dashrightarrow$ $\leftarrow\dashv$	Generate a static key-pair $(Pr_Y, \Omega u_Y)$: $\Omega u_Y = Pr_Y.G$ Obtain Ωu_X Distribute static public key Ωu_Y

1. Generate an ephemeral key-pair $(Pr_X^e, \Omega u_X^e)$: $\Omega u_X^e = Pr_X^e.G$
 2. Send ephemeral public key Ωu_X^e
 3. Compute the shared secret:
 $(EI, Z) =$
 $ECC\_MQV(Pr_X, \Omega u_Y, Pr_X^e, \Omega u_X^e, \Omega u_Y)$
 4. If $(not(EI))$:
   4.1. Derive the keying material:
     $KeyingMaterial = KDF(Z,...)$
   4.2. Destroy Z
	$\rightarrow$	1.
		
		 2. Receive Ωu_X^e
		 3. Compute the shared secret:
		 $(EI, Z) =$
		 $ECC\_MQV(Pr_Y, \Omega u_X, Pr_Y, \Omega u_Y, \Omega u_X^e)$
		 4. If $(not(EI))$:
		   4.1. Derive the keying material:
		     $KeyingMaterial = KDF(Z,...)$
		   4.2. Destroy Z

Unilateral or bilateral 1e-2s key-confirmation may be added		

Figure 14.27 MQV-based key-agreement scheme ECC-MQVOnePass.

Party X		Party Y
Selection of the ECC domain parameters and a KDF		
Generate a static key-pair $(Pr_X, \Omega u_X)$: $\Omega u_X = Pr_X.G$		Generate a static key-pair $(Pr_Y, \Omega u_Y)$: $\Omega u_Y = Pr_Y.G$
Distribute static public key Pu_X	$\dashrightarrow$	Obtain Pu_Y
Obtain Pu_Y	$\dashleftarrow$	Distribute static public key Pu_Y
1. Generate an ephemeral key-pair $\left(Pr_X^e, \Omega u_X^e\right)$: $\Omega u_X^e = Pr_X^e.G$		1. Generate an ephemeral key-pair $\left(Pr_Y^e, \Omega u_Y^e\right)$: $\Omega u_Y^e = Pr_Y^e.G$
2. Send ephemeral public key Ωu_X^e	$\rightarrow$	2. Receive Ωu_X^e
3. Receive Ωu_Y^e	$\leftarrow$	3. Send ephemeral public key Ωu_Y^e
4. Compute the first part of the shared secret: $(EI_1, Z_1) = ECC\_CDH(Pr_X, u_Y)$		4. Compute the first part of the shared secret: $(EI_1, Z_1) = ECC\_CDH(Pr_Y, u_X)$
5. Compute the second part of the shared secret: $(EI_2, Z_2) = ECC\_CDH\left(Pr_X^e, u_Y^e\right)$		5. Compute the second part of the shared secret: $(EI_2, Z_2) = ECC\_CDH\left(Pr_Y^e, u_X^e\right)$
6. If $\left(not(EI_1) \wedge not(EI_2)\right)$: 6.1 $Z = Z_2 \parallel Z_1$ 6.2 Derive the keying material: $KeyingMaterial = KDF(Z, ...)$ 6.3. Destroy Z, Z_1, Z_2		6. If $\left(not(EI_1) \wedge not(EI_2)\right)$: 6.1. $Z = Z_2 \parallel Z_1$ 6.2. Derive the keying material: $KeyingMaterial = KDF(Z, ...)$ 6.3. Destroy Z, Z_1, Z_2
Unilateral or bilateral 2e-2s key-confirmation may be added		

Figure 14.28 Diffie-Hellman-based key-agreement scheme: ECC-CDHFullUnifiedModel.

14.4 Problems and Solutions

14.4.1 List of Problems

Problem 14.1

Bob needs to generate two RSA key-pairs to communicate with Alice and Charlie. He selects two moduli N_1 and N_2, which have a common factor. Show that such a strategy is extremely dangerous.

Problem 14.2

Assume that Alice and Bob are members of a private network in which all the RSA public keys have a modulus in the interval $\left[2^{2047}, 2^{2048} - 1\right]$ and the same public exponent $e = 3$. Alice decides to use the following scheme to generate a 256-bit AES key to encrypt/decrypt data exchanged with Bob:

- Alice selects a random integer $K \ni \left[0, 2^{256} - 1\right]$.
- She computes $C = K^e \mod N_B$, where N_B denotes the modulus of Bob's public key; and she sends C to Bob.
- Upon receipt of message C, Bob decrypts the message to obtain the key K; $K = C^{d_B} \mod N_B$, where d_B denotes the private key of Bob.
- Then, both parties send and receive messages, encrypted and decrypted using AES-256 with the key K.

1) Show that, using the encrypted message C, a malicious member in the private network can recover the AES key generated by Alice.
2) Suggest an idea to Alice to make her protocol secure.

Problem 14.3

Discuss why it is recommended, when using RSA, to select large primes p and q such that $|p - q| > 2^{\frac{len(n)}{2} - 100}$.

Problem 14.4

Consider a virtual network of 1000 hosts, which need to secure their communications using symmetric keys. The first solution is to associate a permanent symmetric key with each pair of hosts; the second is to use a KDC to generate session keys, on-demand. Assume that any host can exchange data simultaneously with at most two other peers.

1) What is the number of permanent and session keys in both solution?
2) Discuss the advantages of the second solution compared to the first one.
3) Assume that all hosts include two encryption algorithms, AES-CBC and AES-GCM. Which algorithm do you recommend to secure communications between hosts?

Problem 14.5

In this problem, we discuss some properties and weaknesses of the KDC-based establishment scheme described in Section 14.3.2.
1) Can Eve obtain a session key on behalf of Bob; and then communicate with Alice who does not trust her?
2) Is the scheme vulnerable to replay attacks? If yes, suggest a solution to prevent replay attacks.

Problem 14.6

Alice and Bob receive from a third party a key K, of m bits, to secure their exchanges. They make use of a dedicated protocol to guarantee that they effectively share the same key. Alice generates an m-bit random integer N_A; then, she computes and sends to Bob a message including the integer $C_A = N_A \oplus K$. Then, upon reception of the integer C_A, Bob XORes C_A with the shared key and sends the $C_B = C_A \oplus K$. Next, Alice makes the verification. Then, Bob initiates the same key verification operation than that of Alice.
1) Show that the protocol above enables both parties to confirm that they share the same key.
2) Show that the protocol used by Alice and Bob enables Eve, who passively listens to communications between Alice and Bob, to easily recover their secret key.

Problem 14.7

Alice and Bob agree to use the Diffie-Hellman protocol with prime p and generator g. They perform the following actions:
- Alice generates a random integer x and computes her public key $Ku_A = g^x \bmod p$; and sends it to Bob.
- Bob generates a random integer y and computes his public key $Ku_B = g^y \bmod p$; and sends it to Alice.
- Upon receiving Bob's public key, Alice computes the shared key $K = Ku_B^x \bmod p$.
- Upon receiving Alice's public key, Bob computes the shared key $K = Ku_A^y \bmod p$.
- Then, Alice and Bob exchange messages encrypted using the key K.
- Which of security properties are guaranteed: confidentiality, integrity, or/and authenticity?

Problem 14.8

Discuss why key-agreement scheme without static public key is not recommended.

Problem 14.9

Alice and Bob use one of the following methods to derive session keys from a master key *Kmst*. The used hash function has an output bit-length of *Hlen*.
Derivation 1: $SK_1 = H(Kmst)$; $SK_i = H(SK_{i-1})$, for $i \geq 2$.
Derivation 2: $SK_1 = H(Kmst)$; $SK_i = H\left(SK_{i-1} \oplus \left(i \bmod 2^{Hlen}\right)\right)$, for ≥ 2.
Derivation 3: $SK_1 = H(Kmst)$; $SK_i = H\left(SK_{i-1} \oplus Kmst\right)$, for 2.
Assume that Eve knew the key-derivation methods used by Alice and Bob and she recovered the session key SK_m, for some $m > 2$. Which of the three methods minimizes the plaintexts that Eve can recover in sessions with index lower than m and those with index greater than m?

Problem 14.10

1) Discuss some reasons to show that asymmetric cryptography is not appropriate to encrypt large data (e.g. several concatenated large-files).
2) How one can do to encrypt and send a large amount of data, if only the public key of the recipient is available?

Problem 14.11

Alice and Bob established a session key $K_{A,B}$ using the Diffie-Hellman scheme with a modulus p of 1024 bits. They hesitate to use one of the methods suggested below to encrypt a large amount of data to be sent from Alice to Bob. They ask you which one of the methods minimizes the plaintexts that Eve can recover, assuming that Alice will encrypt a plaintext of 128 bits known to Eve; the position of the plaintext in the data is known to Eve. Assume that the known plaintext is located in one AES block or in two DEA blocks. It is assumed that Eve has reasonable computation and storage resources to run a computationally feasible brute-force attack. In addition, the methods of encryption are known to Eve.
1) Use of AES-128 with a key K defined by:
   i) $K = leftmost\left(K_{A,B}, 128\right)$

   ii) $K = rightmost\left(K_{A,B}, 128\right)$

   iii) $K = H\left(K_{A,B}\right)$, where H is a hash function of an output bit-length of 128.

2) Use of DEA (i.e. DES) with a key defined by:

   i) $K_i = leftmost\left(K_{A,B}, 56\right) + i \bmod 2^{56}$; the index i starts with 0 and it is incremented after encrypting 100 plaintext blocks.

   ii) $K_i = Hash\left(K_{A,B}\right) + i$; the index i starts with 0 and it is incremented after encrypting 100 plaintext blocks. H is a hash function of an output bit-length of 56.

   iii) $K_i = Hash\left(K_{A,B} + i\right)$; the index i starts with 0 and it is incremented after encrypting 100 plaintext blocks. H is a hash function of an output bit-length of 56.

Problem 14.12

In 1979, Shamir proposed an original secret sharing scheme to enable a group of members to share a secret, which is represented by n pieces. Notice that the pieces are not fragments of the secret. At least k, $k < n$, pieces are required to reconstruct the secret. Less than k pieces cannot reconstruct the secret. Shamir's secret sharing scheme works as follows:

- *Let D be the data representing the secret.*
- *D is represented by n pieces, denoted D_1, D_2, ..., D_n.*
- *Pick a random prime p bigger than both D and n.*
- *Pick a polynomial Q(x) of degree $k-1$*
  $$Q(x) = a_0 + a_1 x + a_2 x^2 + \ldots + a_{(k-1)}x^{(k-1)}$$
  where all the coefficients a_is are integers. a_0 is required to be equal to D and the other coefficients are randomly chosen in the interval $\left[0, p-1\right]$.
- *The pieces are computed as follows:*
  $$D_1 = Q(1) \bmod p, \; D_2 = Q(2) \bmod p, \; ..., \; D_n = Q(n) \bmod p$$
- *The pieces and their indices are distributed among the group members; i.e. each group member holds one or several pairs $\left(D_i, i\right)$. The same piece may be held by one or more members.*
- *Reconstitution of the secret:*
  Given a subset of k distinct pieces and their indices, the coefficients of the polynomial Q(x) are computed. Then, compute $D = a_0$.

The correctness of Shamir's relies on the fact that given k points $\left(x_i, y_i\right)$, with distinct x_i's, there exists one and only one polynomial $Q(x)$, of degree k, such that $y_i = Q\left(x_i\right)$, $i = 1, ..., k$. Shamir showed that by using $n = 2k - 1$, one gets a very robust scheme.

   Consider that the staff members in a bank make use of Shamir's scheme to share the combination of a safe, say $D = 1723$. To compute the pieces, the following values are chosen: $n = 6$, $k = 3$, and $p = 1999$. The chosen polynomial $Q(x)$ is of degree 2 and is defined by $1723 + 1500x + 1001x^2$.

1) Show how the piece values are computed.
2) Take three pieces and their indices, then reconstruct the safe combination.

14.4.2 Solutions to Problems

Problem 14.1

Given two moduli N_1 and N_2, it is easy to find their greatest common divider, $GCD\left(N_1, N_2\right) = p$. Since any RSA modulus is a product of only two primes, if the first prime is found, then it is very easy to find the second. Therefore, any observer who has access to Bob's public keys can easily disclose the private keys he is using.

Problem 14.2

1) The malicious member in the network knows that the modulus of any public key is in the interval $\left[2^{2047}, 2^{2048} - 1\right]$ and its public exponent is $e = 3$. Any key K, randomly selected by Alice, has a value less than 2^{256}. Thus, $K^3 < 2^{256*3} < 2^{2047} \leq N_B < 2^{2048} \Rightarrow K^3 \bmod N_B = K^3 = C$. Therefore, using C, the attacker can derive the secret key shared by Alice and Bob, i.e. $K = C^{\frac{1}{3}}$.

2) To make Alice's protocol secure, one suggestion would be to generate a random integer n in the interval $\left[1, 2^{2048} - 1\right]$. Then, she computes and sends $C = n^e \bmod N_B$. Next, n is recovered by Bob. Then, Alice and Bob use the rightmost 256 bits of n as their AES-256 key.

Problem 14.3

Let RSA modulus N be of large bit-length, say 2048. Imagine an attacker who assumes that one of the primes, p or q, say p, is of a short bit-length, say m bits. Then, the attacker can test a maximum of 2^m integers to factorize N; and then discloses the second prime and the private key. The attack succeeds using reasonable resources, if m is less than 80; even if the bit-length of the modulus is very large, it does not prevent the recovery of the private key if one of the primes is small. When the modulus N is of a bit-length of 2048 or even more (e.g. 3072 or 4096) and p and q primes are selected such that $|p - q| > 2^{\frac{len(N)}{2} - 100}$, the bit-lengths of both primes is in magnitude of 1000 or even more, which makes the attack above computationally infeasible.

Lenstra's elliptic curve factorization method is the most efficient method to factorize large integers, when one of their prime factors is small.

Problem 14.4

1) In the first solution, $1000 * 999 / 2$ permanent keys are required.
   In the second solution, 1000 authentication keys and 1000 wrapping keys are required; in total, 2000 permanent keys are required. Wrapping keys are used to transport session keys. Since each host can exchange at most with two other peers, a maximum of 1000 session keys may be used.
2) In the first solution, the number of keys (keys to configure, store, and communicate to all parties) is large. In addition, if a key shared between two parties is compromised, all the plaintexts exchanged between the parties can be recovered and a manual reconfiguration of the key is required to protect the future exchanges. In the second solution, there are less keys to store, to change manually, and to secure. Session keys are generated on-demand and hosts can change them to prevent attacks making exploitation of a huge plaintexts encrypted with the same key. If the ith session key is compromised, only the plaintexts encrypted with the ith session key can be recovered.
3) AES-CBC provides only confidentiality guarantees, while AES-GCM provides authenticity and confidentiality. In both solutions, to prevent attacks that alter the ciphertexts, we recommend the use of AES-GCM. In general, when a KDC is used, it is recommended that subscribers use session keys with authenticated-encryption algorithms to preserve confidentiality and integrity.

Problem 14.5

1) The session-key request includes the IDs of the parties that need to obtain a session key and a tag computed with the authentication key shared between the request-originator and the server. In addition, the session key is wrapped using the wrapping-key of the request originator. Therefore, unless Eve knows the authentication and wrapping keys of Bob, she cannot impersonate Bob to generate a session key, shared with Alice, with Bob being the originator of the request.
2) The KDC scheme is vulnerable to replay attacks as shown by the following example. Bob establishes a first session key with Alice. To limit the amount of data encrypted with the same session key, Bob requests a new session key for each data block to send to Alice. Eve intercepts the first authenticated message containing the first wrapped session-key. Then, each time Bob requests a new session key, Eve intercepts the request and replies with the message that contains the first session key. Notice that Eve cannot know the value of the session key, but she compels Alice and Bob to use the same session key for a long time and maybe she can infer some information about the ciphertexts she intercepts. To prevent replay attacks, one solution is to use a nonce in each key request; the same nonce is included in the message returned by the server. Since both messages (i.e. the request and the response) are authenticated and they include a nonce, the replay attack cannot succeed.

Problem 14.6

1) The key verification process run by Alice and Bob enables to confirm the key possession by both parties:
   First verification operation: Alice sends $C_A = N_A \oplus K$; Bob sends $C_B = C_A \oplus K = N_A$; Alice receives N_A, which is the random number she generated and concludes that Bob possesses the key K.
   Second verification operation: Bob sends $C'_B = N_B \oplus K$; Alice sends $C'_A = C'_B \oplus K = N_B$; Bob receives N_B, which is the random number he generated and concludes that Alice possesses the key K.
2) The protocol used by Alice and Bob is insecure when their exchanges can be intercepted. If Eve receives the messages C_A and C_B, she derives the secret key by: $C_A \oplus C_B = N_A \oplus K \oplus N_A = K$.

Problem 14.7

No security properties are guaranteed with the proposed actions, because of the man-in-the-middle-attack. An attacker who can intercept the first message (which contains a public key) sent by Alice or Bob, can reply to the sender using his own public key, which results in a shared key computed between a legitimate party and the attacker.

Problem 14.8

In general, static public keys are distributed by a trusted third party or each static public key is included in the sender's digital certificate to prove that the name of the entity on the certificate owns the private key associated with the public key. A key-agreement is a process to establish a secret key between two parties to exchange confidential data. If no static public key is used, both parties cannot trust each other. Therefore, it is not recommended to use a key-agreement without static public keys. Otherwise, any interested attacker can apply a man-in-the-middle attack and compromise the confidentiality of transmitted data. For example, consider the following scenario:

Bob wants to establish a secret key with Alice. He generates an ephemeral key-pair and sends his ephemeral public key to Alice. Eve intercepts the message sent by Bob and replies with her ephemeral public key. Then, Bob and Eve compute a shared secret, which contains a secret key K. Next, Bob encrypts his messages using the key K, which is known to Eve. Therefore, no transmitted data by Bob remains confidential to Eve.

Problem 14.9

Since the hash function H is not invertible, Eve cannot recover any session key before session m, whatever the key-derivation method from the three.

In Derivation 1, once the key of session m is recovered, Eve can derive the session keys of all the subsequent sessions, because the hash function is public. The same applies to Derivation 2, because the $SK_{m+1} = H\left(SK_m \oplus (m+1) \bmod 2^{Hlen}\right)$, where all elements (i.e. SK_m, m, $Hlen$, and H) are known to Eve.

In Derivation 3, once the key of session m is recovered, Eve cannot derive the session keys of the subsequent sessions, because the key SK_m is XORed with $Kmst$ before hashing. Therefore, Eve cannot recover SK_{m+1} only from SK_m; she needs $Kmst$.

Problem 14.10

1) There are mainly two reasons, which are extensively discussed in literature. The first is that for the same security strength, the asymmetric encryption is known to be very slow compared to symmetric encryption, in particular when symmetric encryption is achieved by hardware. The second reason is that the symmetric encryption preserves the length of the plaintext, while some asymmetric encryption algorithms, such as RSA-OAEP, need to extend the original plaintext with padding bits to prevent some attacks, when the very short messages are encrypted (see Problem 12.5).

2) If only the recipient public key is available, the sender encrypts data using this public key and the recipient decrypts using his/her private key. Alternatively, the sender can generate a symmetric key K, encrypts it with the recipient public key, and sends it to the data recipient. Then, the sender encrypts the data using the symmetric key K, which is known to the recipient.

Problem 14.11

When Alice and Bob use the Diffie-Hellman scheme with a modulus p of 1024, they establish a session key of a bit-length of 1024, which is larger than the keys used by AES or DEA. Therefore, only a piece of the session key can be used to encrypt with either AES or DEA. There exist many ways to derive a block cipher key from a session key. In practice, key-derivation functions are used. Let us focus on the methods suggested in this problem.

1) Use of AES: it is admitted that brute-force attack against AES-128 is computationally infeasible using the current technologies. Since the session key $K_{A,B}$ is unknown to Eve, the three proposed methods provide the same security strength. From the known plaintext, Eve cannot recover the AES key to disclose other plaintexts. Notice that the third method makes use of a hash function, which does not increase the security strength.

2) Use of DEA: it is known that DEA key recovery using brute-force attack is computationally feasible, because 2^{56} keys can be tested with an acceptable computation time.

   i) The first method enables to change the DEA key after 100 blocks, which seems introducing unpredictability in DEA keys. When ciphertext, at the position of the known plaintext, is intercepted, Eve runs a brute-force attack (i.e. she tests a maximum of 2^{56} keys) to recover the DEA key used to encrypt the known plaintext. Since the formula of DEA key updating is linear and known to Eve, she can recover the previous (by modular subtraction) and the next (by modular addition) DEA keys. Therefore, she can disclose all the plaintexts. Therefore, this method is insecure.

   ii) When the second method is used, Eve can recover the key, which served to encrypt the plaintext she knew; let this key be K_p. Then, since the key of the *i*th group of 100 blocks is yielded from the previous key plus one, Eve can disclose the keys before and after the key K_p. The hash function does not help to secure the messages.

   iii) When the third method is used, Eve can recover the key K_p, which served to encrypt the plaintext she knew. Then, she can decrypt a maximum of 100 consecutive plaintexts that have been encrypted using the key K_p.

However, even if the DEA-key updating formula is known to Eve, she cannot recover the other keys, because the hash function is not invertible. From $K_p = H(K_{A,B} + p)$, Eve cannot derive $K_{A,B} + p$ in order to compute $K_{A,B} + p - 1$ or $K_{A,B} + p + 1$; and then disclose the keys after and before key K_p. Therefore, the third method can be considered as partially secure.

Problem 14.12

1) Computation of the secret pieces:

$$D_1 = Q(1) \bmod 1999 = 1723 + 1500 * 1 + 1001 * 1 = 226$$

$$D_2 = Q(2) \bmod 1999 = 1723 + 1500 * 2 + 1001 * 4 = 731$$

$$D_3 = Q(3) \bmod 1999 = 1723 + 1500 * 3 + 1001 * 9 = 1239$$

$$D_4 = Q(4) \bmod 1999 = 1723 + 1500 * 4 + 1001 * 16 = 1750$$

$$D_5 = Q(5) \bmod 1999 = 1723 + 1500 * 5 + 1001 * 25 = 265$$

$$D_6 = Q(6) \bmod 1999 = 1723 + 1500 * 6 + 1001 * 36 = 782$$

2) Take three pieces and their indices, say $(731, 2)$, $(1239, 3)$, and $(265, 5)$. Build the following equation system:

$$731 = a_0 + 2a_1 + 4a_2 \bmod 1999 \tag{a}$$

$$1239 = a_0 + 3a_1 + 9a_2 \bmod 1999 \tag{b}$$

$$265 = a_0 + 5a_1 + 25a_2 \bmod 1999 \tag{c}$$

Then, we get:

$$1239 - 731 = 508 = a_1 + a_2 5 \bmod 1999 \tag{d}$$

$$1239 - 265 = 974 = -2a_1 - 16a_2 \bmod 1999 \tag{e}$$

Then, from (d) and (e), we get:

$$508 * 2 + 974 = -6a_2 \bmod 1999$$

$$a_2 = -1990 * 6^{-1} \bmod 1999 = -1990 * 1666 \bmod 1999 = 1001$$

Then, from (d), we get:

$$508 = a_1 + 1001 * 5 \bmod 1999$$

$$a_1 = 508 - 1001 * 5 \bmod 1999 = 1500$$

Finally, from (a), we get:

$$D = a_0 = 731 - 2 * 1500 - 4 * 1001 \bmod 1999 = 1723$$

Therefore, the entire safe combination is reconstructed.

Notes

1 Protection may be provided manually, in an automated fashion, or by some combination of manual and automated methods. This book does not focus on manual protection of keys (including trusted courier, bags, safes, etc.).

2 DRBG stands for Deterministic Random Bit Generator. Chapter 16 addresses in detail the approved DRBGs.

3 The following formula is useful to compute $S(n)$, the maximum security strength of RSA with a modulus of a bit-length of n:

$$S(n) = \left[1.923 * \sqrt[3]{n * \ln(2)} * \sqrt[3]{\left[\ln\left(n * \ln(2)\right) \right]^2} - 4.69 \right] / \ln(2). \quad S(n) \text{ is rounded to a standard value (i.e. 112, 128, 192, ...)}.$$

4 Support services mainly include key-agreement, key-transport, and random number generation.

5 Sometimes, "key derivation method" and "key derivation function" are used interchangeably.

6 The security strength is the same whether the hash function is used in option 1 or in option 2. It also is the same when used in the two-step key derivation method.

7 The Chinese Remainder Theorem (CRT) is presented in Section 3.3.4 and the RSA-CRT-based decryption is described in Section 12.2.2.2. RSA implementations are faster when the CRT is used for decryption.

8 p is a safe prime if $(p-1)/2$ is also a prime.

9 Parameters a and b are used in traditional elliptic curves. Edwards and Montgomery curves make use of other parameters (see Section 13.2.4).

10 Other names may be used in Internet RFCs, but the specification is the same.

11 P224, P-256, P-384, P-521, W-25519, and W-448 are names of Weierstrass (i.e. traditional) curves. Curve25519 and Curve448 are names of Montgomery curves. E488 is an Edwards curve.

12 The number of EC points that can be generated by the selected base point is the number of points (x,y) that match the EC equation divided by the cofactor.

13 Curves E448 and Edwards-448 differ in the value of parameter d.

14 Since 2019, binary curves are deprecated, because of their limited adoption in industry [12, 15].

15 Some ECs have the same irreducible polynomial, but differ in other domain parameters.

16 "Manual key-transport" refers to a variety of methods to let the other party know the key, including face-to-face exchange, suitcase, email, phone, etc. In general, all those methods are not recommended.

17 Option 1 results in more activities performed by the KDC server, while option 2 results in more activities by the subscriber that originates a session-key transaction.

18 KMAC generates tags of variable bit-length. In practice, the bit-length should be close to either 128 or 256.

19 Notice that in KAS1, the party X generates the shared secret Z, while the party Y generates the nonce $Nonce_Y$. Therefore, both parties do not equally contribute to the shared secret, which is used to generate a new secret key.

20 The output of the KDF is split into two parts: a shared key K and a MAC key $MacKey$ (used to generate tags when required). "[,]" means optional.

21 "..." means that other optional parameters may be used.

22 "*" denotes integer multiplication, while "·" denotes the multiplication of an EC point by a scalar.

23 $\mathcal{O}$ denotes the point to infinity.

24 $Nonce_X$ used in 0e-2s key-confirmation alternatives is the same as the one used in KDF.

References

1 Barker, E. (2020). *Recommendation for Key Management: Part 1 - General - Special Publication 800-57 Part 1 (Rev. 5)*. NIST.

2 Barker, E., Roginsky, A., and Davis, R. (2020). *Recommendation for Cryptographic Key Generation - Special Publication 800-133 (Rev. 2)*. NIST.

3 Turan, M.S., Barker, E., Burr, W. et al. (2010). *Recommendation for Password-Based Key Derivation, Part 1: Storage Applications, Special Publication, 800-132*. NIST.

4 Barker, E., Chen, L., and Davis, R. (2020). *Recommendation for Key-Derivation Methods in Key-Establishment Schemes - Special Publication 800-56C*. NIST.

5 Chen, L. (2009). *Recommendation for Key Derivation Using Pseudorandom Functions, Special Publication 800-108*. NIST.

6 NIST (2013). *Digital Signature Standard (DSS) - FIPS PUB 186-4*. National Institute of Standards and Technology.

7 Barker, E., Chen, L., Roginsky, A. et al. (2019). *Recommendation for Pair-Wise Key Establishment Using Integer Factorization Cryptography - Special Publication 800-56B (Rev. 2)*. NIST.

8 Barker, E. and Kelsey, J.J. (2015). *Recommendation for Random Number Generation Using Deterministic Random Bit Generators - Special Publication 800-90A (Rev. 1)*. NIST.

9 Kivinen, T. and Kojo, M. (2003). *More Modular Exponential (MODP) Diffie-Hellman groups for Internet Key Exchange (IKE), RFC 3526*. Internet Engineering Task Force (IETF).

10 Gillmor, D. (2016). *Negotiated Finite Field Diffie-Hellman Ephemeral Parameters for Transport Layer Security (TLS), RFC 7919*. Internet Engineering Task Force (IETF).

11 Shawe-Taylor, J. (1986). Generating Strong Primes. *Electronic Letters* 22 (16): 875–877.

12 Chen, L., Moody, D., Regenscheid, A. et al. (2019). *Recommendations for Discrete Logarithm-Based Cryptography: Elliptic Curve Domain Parameters, (Draft) SP 800-186*. NIST.

13 Barker, E. and Barker, W.C. (2018). *Recommendation for Key Establishment Using Symmetric Block Ciphers - Special Publication 800-71*. NIST.

14 Barker, E., Chen, L., Roginsky, A. et al. (2018). *Recommendation for Pair-Wise Key-Establishment Schemes Using Discrete Logarithm Cryptography - Special Publication 800-56A (Rev. 3)*. NIST.

15 NIST (2019). *Digital Signature Standard (DSS) - FIPS PUB 186-5 (Draft)*. National Institute of Standards and Technology.

15

Digital Certificate, Public-Key Infrastructure, TLS, and Kerberos

There exist two approaches to establish trust between communicating entities: trust based on public keys and trust based on symmetric keys. The first category is used to secure communications between clients and servers over Internet, while the second is used in private networks where clients and servers share symmetric keys with a central entity, called Key Distribution Center.

In the first category, to perform cryptographic operations (e.g. message decryption or signature verification), users of a public key require confidence that the associated private key (used to encrypt or sign) is owned by the legitimate remote entity (person, system, or organization). This confidence is obtained thanks to digital certificates, which are delivered by trusted third parties, called Certificate authorities (CAs).

To better understand the notions relating to digital certificates in the computer-based society, let us take the following example: imagine someone who wants to sell a painting to somebody, who can afford it. The seller claims that the painting is made by a known painter and his/her signature is at the bottom of the painting. The painter's signature is publicly known. The painting is (very) expensive. The question is: will the buyer take the seller at his/her word? Of course not. He/she requires a certificate (a document), which proves that the signature on the painting is that of the painter. The buyer will not trust any certificate; rather, he/she asks the seller to provide a certificate signed by a known authority in the art field, and whom the buyer trusts. Transactions in the digital world (in particular e-commerce transactions) require the same caution.

Public-key infrastructures are the frameworks, which provide certification management functions (creation, granting, revocation, renew, cancellation, and storage of digital signatures). They are of paramount importance to establish trust between partners that do not a priori trust each other in the open digital world. Today, digital certificates are used by billions of end-entities, including web servers and their clients, in many applications, such as calls and conferences via VPNs, cloud servers, and Internet-of-things devices. The main protocol to secure communications over the internet is with no doubt TLS (Transport Layer Security), which is the underlying security layer of the well-known HTTPS.

This chapter aims to discuss the notions of digital certificate, CA (certificate authority), PKI (public-key infrastructure), and TLS.

A second alternative to establish trust among peers that have only symmetric keys is to use a key distribution center, like Kerberos, to generate and distribute shared keys (called session keys) inside private networks. The last section of this chapter aims at introducing the main notions and operations of Kerberos.

15.1 Digital Certificate: Notion and X.509 Format

Definition 15.1 Digital certificate *(or **public-key certificate**): it is an electronic document used to prove the ownership of a public key.*

Definition 15.2 X.509 certificate*: it is a digital signature compliant with the ISO/ITU-T X.509 standard.*

Definition 15.3 Owner *(of a certificate): it is an entity that is identified as the subject in a public-key certificate; it may be an individual, a device, a computer, an organization, a company, or something else.*

Definition 15.4 Certificate authority *(CA): it is a trusted third party, which signs and issues digital certificates used to prove the ownership of public keys.*

Cryptography: Algorithms, Protocols, and Standards for Computer Security, First Edition. Zoubir Mammeri.
© 2024 John Wiley & Sons, Inc. Published 2024 by John Wiley & Sons, Inc.

The certificate authority is an organization, a company or a governmental agency that issues digital signatures to confirm that the private keys associated with the public keys included in the certificates belong to the entities noted in the certificates. A CA issuing a certificate is trusted by all parties that use the public key included in the certificate. If an entity Y trusts a CA, which delivered a certificate C_X to entity X associated with public key Pu_X, then the entity Y can verify that the public key Pu_X is owned by the entity X identified in the certificate C_X.

15.1.1 Types of Digital Certificates

There exist different types of digital certificates depending on their usages. Currently, the most issued certificate types are: SSL, software signing, and client certificates.

15.1.1.1 TLS (Transport Layer Security) Certificates

TLS certificates are also called SSL (Secure Socket Layer) certificates and sometimes referred to as SSL/TLS certificates. In the internet, to be trusted, any server (web server, application server, email server, etc.) should own a TLS certificate. The purpose of these certificates is to ensure that the communications between the client and the server are secured. The distinctive mark of servers that make use of TLS certificates is "S", which stands for "secure" in HTTPS. Therefore, TLS certificates are of paramount importance to secure the internet. TLS protocol is addressed in more detail in Section 15.3.

15.1.1.2 Code (or Software) Signing Certificates

They are used to sign software, codes, or any other form of files that are downloaded over the internet. The code/software signature is generated by the code/software developer before publishing (or sending to clients) the code/software. The purpose of code/software certificates is to enable code/software users to obtain guarantees on the origin of the code/software. Code/software signing certificates also act as a proof that the file hasn't been altered during transfer.

15.1.1.3 Client Certificates

They are also called digital IDs; and are used to identify one end-entity (a device or an individual) to another. Client certificates are used to prove the connection is trusted by both parties. The number of client certificates is increasing every date to enable signed emails, electronic payments, and many other forms of transactions. In particular, to prevent some attacks made via emails, users who need a strong security should require the certificate of any message sender before processing the message.

15.1.2 X.509 Standard Format

A digital certificate is a data structure that contains an entity identity, a public key (including the associated set of domain parameters and the algorithm that can use the public key), the identifier, and the signature of the trusted authority that issued the certificate to bind an entity ID to a public key, and possibly other information.

The standard format of certificates in Internet domains is the X.509 format, which is defined by the following fields [1], illustrated by Figure 15.1:

- *Version number*: the version of the X.509 standard used to generate the certificate. The current version is the third. Notice that the 3rd version number field contains 2, because the numbering is V1(0), V2(1), and V3(2).
- *Serial number*: a unique serial number assigned by the CA to the certificate.
- *Signature algorithm ID*: the name of the algorithm (e.g. RSA with SHA-256 or ECDSA with SHA-512) used to sign the certificate.
- *Issuer name*: the name[1] of the CA, which signed and issued the certificate.
- *Validity period*: time interval (i.e. not-before and not-after dates) during which the certificate is valid.
- *Subject name*: name of the entity (i.e. individual, system or organization) to which the certificate is issued and who/which will use the certificate.
- *Subject public-key information*: this field carries the public key that is associated with the certificate and the algorithm with which the key is used (e.g. RSA, Diffie-Hellman or elliptic curve Diffie-Hellman).
- *Extensions*: this optional field allows a CA to include private information in the certificate, for example:
  - Alternative names of the CA, if it has several names.
  - Alternative names of the subject, if it has multiple names.
  - CA public-key used to sign the certificate when the CA owns several public keys.
  - Usages (signing, encrypting, etc.) of the public key in the certificate.

Standard Version V3
Certificate serial number
CA Signature algorithm (identifier and parameters)
CA (Issuer) name
Period of validity
Subject name
Algorithm to use the public-key
Public-key value
Extensions (optional)
Issuer unique Identifier (optional)
Subject unique Identifier (optional)
CA signature

Figure 15.1 Fields of X.509 certificate format.

Version number	V3
Serial number:	00:EE:90:29:A6:43:6D:7A:8A:09:27:16:8C:23:70:A4:30
Signature algorithm ID:	Hash function = sha256 Encryption algorithm = RSA
Issuer name	Country = US Organization = Google Trust Services
Validity period	Not before = Mon, 30 May 2022 09:54:30 GMT Not after = Mon, 22 Aug 2022 09:54:29 GMT
Subject name	www.google.com
Subject public key	Algorithm = Elliptic Curve, Key size = 256Curve = P-256Public key value = 04:95:7F:89:52:E9:A9:DE:D9:5B:D3:3D:23:54:FF:03:FF:F1: 70:BB:A2:59:04:B5:D8:75:5D:A2:1B:D4:46:FD:C3:AF:E3:E 3:05:8B:69:7C:D6:B8:DE:CA:99:C7:15:BD:BA:4F:8A:72:A7: AE:B9:48:F8:9E:60:98:C1:E9:06:F7:D8
Extensions	Key usages = Digital signature, server authentication CRL Endpoints = Distribution point http://crls.pki.google/gts1c3/zdATt0Ex_Fk.crl
Signature	Hash = SHA-2560A:F0:03:67:5E:AE:A4:74:0D:05:1C:48:08:2D:D5:BA:D 4:7F:60:37:22:04:BA:3C:1B:4C:0E:01:B3:B3:38:F7

Figure 15.2   Example of X.509 certificate.

- – CRL distribution points (CDP): when a user, service, or computer presents a certificate, the verifying application or service must determine whether the certificate has been revoked before its validity period has expired. The CDP extension provides one or more URLs where the application or service can retrieve the certificate revocation list (CRL).
  - – A certification path, which includes the chain of certification (i.e. the CAs used to issue a certificate to the CA under consideration). See Section 15.2.4.
- • *Issuer unique identifier*: (optional and not recommended field) it enables the reuse of the issuer name over time.
- • *Subject unique identifier*: (optional and not recommended field) it enables the reuse of the subject name over time.
- • *Signature of the CA*: to sign a certificate, the CA computes the hash of the fields of the certificate and then encrypts it with its private key. Thus, the authenticity of the certificate can be verified using the public key of the CA. Any entity, which trusts a CA, knows the public key of that CA. Certificate verifier first decrypts the signature using the CA public-key, then it hashes the fields of the certificate, using the same hash function than that used by the CA, and then compares the hashes.

Figure 15.2 illustrates one of the digital certificates issued to the domain `www.google.com` (in 2022). Google is its own certificate authority.

A certificate has a validity period. Therefore, certificate-using clients can cache certificates, while being valid, and verify them once, which limits unnecessary resource-consuming exchanges.

15.2   Public-Key Infrastructure

Definition 15.5 Public key infrastructure (PKI): *it is framework that is used to issue, maintain, and revoke digital certificates.*

There exist two categories of PKIs: private and public PKIs.

1) Private PKI: it involves the security of exchanges between entities within an organization or a company. Private certificates are issued by internal CAs and are trusted only inside the organization/company.
2) Public PKI: it issues certificates for public servers and users to perform e-banking, e-commerce, and many other types of transactions.

Public PKIs belong either to private companies or to governmental agencies/services. Examples of public CAs (operational in 2022) include: Comodo, DigiCert, Geant Vereniging, GlobalSign, Verisign, and Google Trust Services. It is very likely that if you check the list of certificates available in your computer (and used by the web browser or other networking-applications), at least one of the CAs above is present in your list.

15.2.1 Components of a PKI

Definition 15.6 Trust anchor: *it is an authoritative entity for which trust is assumed. All certificates are delivered on behalf of the trust anchor and the security provided by a PKI depends upon the authenticity and integrity of the trust anchor. Trust anchor certificates are often distributed as self-signed certificates.*

From a functional perspective, a PKI includes the following components (not all of them are mandatory):

- Certificate authority that stores, issues, and signs the digital certificates.
- Registration authority (RA): it operates on behalf of a CA. It receives and checks the validity of the information submitted by the end-entities, which need to register their public keys and obtain certificates.
- A repository: a system or a collection of distributed systems that stores certificates and CRLs (certificate revocation lists) and serves as a means of distributing these certificates and CRLs to end-entities.
- Validation authority (VA): allows end-entities to check if a certificate has been revoked. VA has access to a certificate revocation list to check certificate validity.
- A directory in secure location in which CA private-keys are stored.
- A certificate policy stating the PKI requirements concerning its procedures. Its purpose is to allow end-entities to analyze the PKI trustworthiness. In general, only PKIs with a strong and verifiable certificate policy are recommended to end-entities.

> **Notes**
>
> - Depending on the number of PKI subscribers (i.e. the end-entities) and their particularities (geographic locations, required level of security, frequency of certificate validation requests, etc.), a PKI may be composed of one CA or a set of CAs (one of them is the root CA), one or a set of registration authorities, and one or a set of validation authorities.
> - In this chapter, the PKI components are addressed from the functional point of view only. Depending on the number of end-entities that use a PKI and their geographical locations and the applications they use, a single computer may implement all the components or a computer is dedicated to each component or a distributed system is dedicated to each component or to a group of components.

15.2.2 Certificate Authority Hierarchy

Definition 15.7 Root CA: *it is the topmost CA (i.e. the trust anchor) of any certification hierarchy. A root CA is a CA that issues the certificates that are used by its subordinate CAs to sign other certificates. Root CA certificates are self-signed certificates. For security reasons, the root CA is isolated from network access, and is often kept in an offline state.*

Definition 15.8 Issuing CA: *it is a CA that issues certificates to end-entities (i.e. owners of public keys).*

Definition 15.9 Intermediate CA: *it is any CA between the root CA and the issuing CAs.*

A huge number of entities (individuals, systems, and organizations) around the world need certificates to be trusted by their partners in a large variety of transactions (e.g. e-commerce, e-administration, etc.). A single CA used to issue and verify certificates for all entities connected to internet is not appropriate for many reasons, including:

- Performance: a single CA would have to process millions of requests (verification of public keys, certification of new public keys, etc.) per second, which would result in a worldwide bottleneck. Any transaction using a public key would take a long time.
- Fault-tolerance: in the event the unique CA is down (or in maintenance), all the internet (and intranets) may be blocked.
- Security: a unique CA would be a perfect target for attackers to break its private keys or to block it, using DDoS attacks.
- Sovereignty: the country hosting the unique CA would prevent other countries or companies to perform transactions requiring public keys.

Because of the reasons above, public-key certification, either inside a company or a country or worldwide, is based on hierarchized structures. Well-designed CA structures have several benefits:

- Separate administrative controls for different organizational and geographic units.
- In large organizations, it may be appropriate to delegate the responsibility for issuing certificates to several CAs. Therefore, the certification activities and resources are shared among different CAs.
- To optimize performance (in particular the response time of certification verification requests), it may be important for a CA to be physically located in the same geographic areas as those of the entities to whom it is issuing certificates.
- The ability to deploy specific security protection for each CA.

The number of levels of CAs in a CA hierarchy depends on the structure of the considered context (i.e. a small organization, a worldwide company, a country, etc.). Notice that adding CA levels to a hierarchy means increasing the number of certificates, which increases the validation time of certificates. Generally, there exist four types of hierarchies, which are denoted by the number of levels: one-tier, two-tier, three-tier hierarchies, and four or more tiers. Any CA hierarchy starts with a root CA. Under the root CA, intermediate CAs can be used. The root CA issues intermediate CA certificates; and the intermediate CAs issue one level down certificates or sign end-entity certificates.

One-tier hierarchy: a single CA is used as a root CA and as issuing CA. Any end-entity that trusts the root CA trusts any certificate issued in the CA hierarchy. One CA level is commonly used during development and testing phases. However, it is not recommended for operational use, because it violates the best practices of separating the security policy of the root CA (i.e. isolate the root CA from the network) and the CAs that issue end-entity certificates. In addition, one-tier hierarchy is not fault-tolerant.

Two-tier hierarchy: this is the simplest hierarchy that can be used in practice. In this hierarchy, there are a root CA and one or several issuing CAs. Such a hierarchy provides flexibility and scalability. An issuing CA may be dedicated to a geographic zone, a category of end-entities, or a category of applications (business, education, etc.).

Three-tier hierarchy: in this hierarchy, policy tiers are placed between the root CA and the issuing CAs. The role of policy tiers is to issue certificates to issuing CAs depending on the types of end-entity certificates they can issue. The policy tiers can also be used to revoke compromised issuing CAs. Notice that this type of hierarchy is the most commonly deployed in practice. Figure 15.3 illustrates a three-level certificate hierarchy.

Four or more tier hierarchy: in this hierarchy, four or more levels of CAs may be required to strengthen administrative delegations. Such a hierarchy may be used in very large companies or to certify public-keys worldwide.

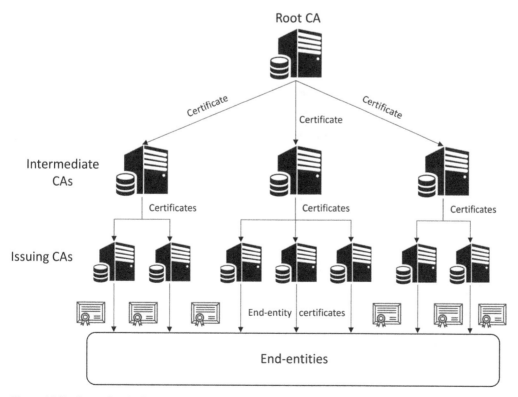

Figure 15.3 Example of a 3-level CA hierarchy.

The certification hierarchy in Figure 15.3 is a 3-level hierarchy. The PKI can be used by a worldwide company where one intermediate CA is assigned to region (Europe, America, Africa, and Asia) and an issuing CA is assigned to each country.

15.2.3 Registration of a Public-Key and Certificate Acquisition

The process of creation of a new certificate follows steps, illustrated by Figure 15.4:

1) A user, say U, creates a new pair of keys (private and public keys) complying with the mathematical rules of the cryptographic algorithm to use (i.e. RSA, Diffie-Hellman, elliptic curves, etc.)
2) User U stores on a secure location his/her/its private key.
3) User U selects a CA, say C; the selection is based on various criteria such as the cost of subscription, the prominence of the PKI of CA, etc. In general, the name of the CA to select is already present in the list of trusted CAs available to user U. Otherwise, a process of trust chain verification may be performed (i.e. user U must find a chain of trust in which the CA C is present).
4) A certificate request, which includes the public key to register, the ID of user U, the domain name of the user institution or company, the planned usages of the certificate, and other information (such as the country, the city, etc.) is provided to the CA C or to its registration authority R. In the following steps, assume that an RA R is associated with CA C.
5) The RA R checks the information included in the certificate request. At this stage, the RA obtains the assurances about the ID of user U and the possession of the private key associated with the public key to register. A proof of possession (POP) is a procedure that is commonly used by RAs to obtain assurance of private-key possession during key registration. For example, the RA asks user U to encrypt his/her/its ID and other data chosen by the RA; and sends them to the RA. If the user U owns the submitted public key, he/she/it correctly replies to the RA challenge, and the process of registration continues. Alternatively, the RA may ask the user U to sign his/her/its certificate request using the appropriate private key. Then, if the signature is validated by the RA, using user U's public key, the process of registration continues. Notice that other methods exist to provide guarantees to the RA regarding the information provided by user U (e.g. verification of the submitted domain name, etc.).
6) If the verification of the certificate request succeeds, the RA R forwards the relevant information to the CA C to issue the certificate to user U.

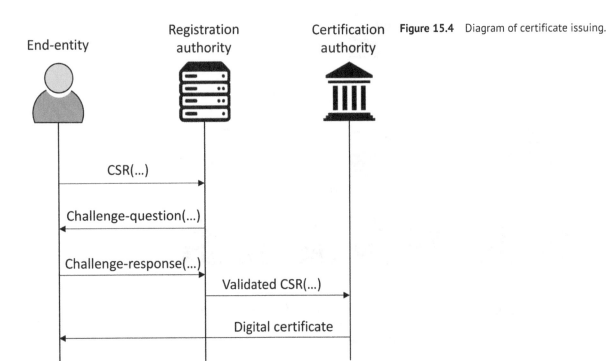

Figure 15.4 Diagram of certificate issuing.

CSR: Certificate signing request

7) The CA C generates a certificate, including the information confirmed by the RA R and the validity period. It signs the certificate and records in its repository. Then, the certificate, generally complying with X.509 standard, is delivered to user U.

8) User U receives the certificate and can use it to perform secured operations.

15.2.4 Chain of Trust and Trust Models

Definition 15.10 Chain of trust (*or* ***path of trust***): *it is the list of certificates used to authenticate an end-entity.*

A chain (or path) of trust begins with the certificate of uppermost CA, i.e. the root CA, and finishes with the certificate of an end-entity. Figure 15.5 illustrates an example of chain of trust composed of four certificates: the end-entity $User_1$ has a certificate signed by the CA CA_2. The certificate of CA_2 is signed by the CA CA_1 and finally the certificate of CA_1 is singed by CA_0 whose certificate is self-signed. Thus, the chain of trust is $CA_0 \rightarrow CA_1 \rightarrow CA_2 \rightarrow User_1$.

Definition 15.11 Model of trust*: it refers to the mechanism or method used to trust the signer of a certificate.*

The question here is: how an entity that receives a certificate signed by a CA can trust the signing CA? To answer the question, various models of trust have been proposed, each appropriate to a particular context of certificate use. The commonly used models include the following ones:

Single-CA model: in an organization or a company, a single CA is used and any certificate signed by the CA is trusted by all end-entities. In the event the unique CA is corrupted, the security of exchanges in the entire organization/company is compromised.

Hierarchical trust model: the end-entities trust delegated (i.e. intermediate) CAs that, in turn, trust an upper-level CA until the root-CA. The whole security depends on the root-CA honesty.

Oligarchy-based trust model: multiple trust anchors are used and they sign each other (forming a mesh trust network). To trust a certificate of an end-entity, the latter shall have a trust path, which terminates at more than one trust anchors.

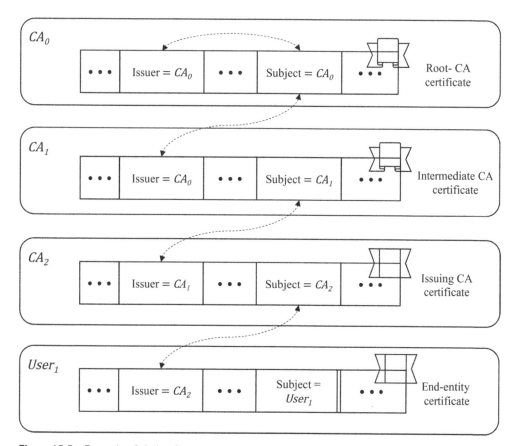

Figure 15.5 Example of chain of trust.

Notes

- Whatever the context, the trust in certificates is only as good as the trust in the underlying trust anchors.
- Roaming users should be aware that they are implicitly trusting all software on the host systems that they use. In particular, when they are traveling abroad, they should have concerns about trust-anchor certificates used by web browsers, when they use systems in airports, hotels, conferences, etc.

15.2.5 Validation of Certificates and Trust Paths

Assume that a user U receives a certificate C_X containing the issuer name X and the subject name U. The received certificate may be a forged or an invalid certificate. To obtain guarantees of authenticity and validity, before using the received certificate, the user U should verify the validity of the certificate and its trust path.

Validation of a trust path
The aim of the trust path validation is to verify that each certificate in the certificate chain, from the root CA to the CA A, is worth of trust. The recursive path-validation process can be summarized as follows:

1) The verification process starts with the certificate of CA A. The fields of CA A's certificate are verified following the certificate validation process discussed below. If any error is notified, the trust path is declared invalid.
2) Extract the issuer of CA A's certificate, say B, and perform the same verification for the CA B than that done for CA A. If any error is notified, the trust path is declared invalid.
3) While the verified CA is not the root-CA, replace A by B and perform step 2.

Validation of a certificate C_X signed by a CA A
Before performing the following steps, user U finds the public key of the CA A in his/her/its certificate repository (such a repository contains the certificates known to the user). If he/she/it cannot find the public key of CA A in the repository, he/she/it must obtain it via other CAs known to him/her/it. Once the public key of the CA A, denoted Pk_A, is known, the following verifications are undertaken:

1) *Verification of certificate integrity*
   - Using the CA's public key Pk_A, decrypt the CA's signature and obtain a hash H.
   - Using the hash function, whose name is included in the certificate, and the fields of the signature C_X, compute a hash H'. If both hashes, H and H', are identical, the certificate validation continues. Otherwise, the certificate C_X is rejected and an error is returned.
2) *Verification of certificate validity*: if the current date is not between the Not-before and Not-after dates included in the certificate C_X, reject the certificate and return an error.
3) *Verification of the certificate revocation status*:
   - To obtain guarantees that the certificate has not been revoked, user U sends a request to the validation authority (VA), if it exists in the considered PKI, or any server that distributes the CRL.
   - The VA/server inspects its CRL and sends a response to the requesting user to confirm/infirm the validity of the certificate C_X.
   - If the certificate C_X is found in the CRL, the user U rejects the certificate and the verification process stops.
4) *Verification of public-key usages*: the user U verifies if the list of usages (included in the extension field of certificate C_X) are consistent with the operations he/she/it is expecting to perform with the public key in the certificate.

15.2.6 Digital-Certificate Revocation

When a certificate is issued, it is expected to be used for its entire validity period. However, various circumstances (e.g. the public-key owner changes his/her/its name, the owner of a public key leaves his/her company, or the corresponding private key became comprised) may cause a certificate to become invalid before its expiration date. Therefore, when a certificate becomes invalid, the CA that issued a certificate needs to revoke the certificate as soon as possible to prevent usage of the invalid certificate.

The revocation of certificates may be initiated either by a CA (for example, when the CA signing private key is compromised) or by the public-key owner (for example, when the user is no more confident in his/her/its private key).

To let the potential users of public keys know the status of the certificates, each CA periodically[2] updates the list of invalid certificates; the list is called certificate revocation list (CRL). The CRL is signed by the issuing CA and made available to interested users. Therefore, an entity, which needs to verify the public key validity, checks if the certificate sent by a remote end-entity is in the most recent CRL known to him/her/it. Any CRL includes timestamps to indicate when each certificate was invalidated by the CA. CRL timestamps should be used by end-entities to check if some transactions performed before their invalidity timestamps are suspicious (e.g. detect transactions performed using stolen private keys). Each revoked certificate remains recorded in the CRL until its expiration date, after which the certificate is removed from the CRL.

15.3 Transport Layer Security (TLS 1.3)

SSL[3] (Secure Socket Layer) was introduced by Netscape in 1991 to secure communications over Internet. When the SSL protocol, which is proprietary to Netscape, was standardized by the IETF, it was renamed Transport Layer Security (TLS). TLS is the most used protocol to secure communications between web servers and their clients. TLS is also widely used to secure emails and file transfers. Common protocols such as HTTPS, SMTPS, and FTPS make use of TLS to secure communications. Since 2018, almost all websites make use of TLS, which provides authentication, confidentiality, and integrity to communicating entities.

TLS 1.3 is the most recent version of the standard; it was finalized by IETF in 2018 [2]. TLS 1.0 and 1.1 were deprecated in 2021 and they are no more supported by current systems. TLS 1.2 is still in use. Some reported vulnerabilities of TLS 1.2 were addressed in TLS 1.3 to enhance security. Compared to TLS 1.2, the TLS 1.3 introduced some enhancements including:

- Addition of encryption mechanisms when establishing a connection handshake between a client and server;
- The number of steps required to complete a handshake is reduced, which results in faster handshake process;
- Several cryptographic algorithms (e.g. 3DES and CBC) used to encrypt data were removed, as they were not recommended for secure transport;
- Several hashing algorithms (e.g. RC4, MD5, and SHA-1) used to generate hashes were removed, as they were vulnerable to some reported attacks.
- Authentication can make use of elliptic curve signatures (i.e. ECDSA and EdDSA) or symmetric pre-shared keys. DSA was deprecated.
- All public-key-based key-exchange mechanisms used in TLS 1.3 provide forward secrecy.[4]

In the sequel, the main features and (sub)protocols of TLS 1.3 are introduced. As we only focus on TLS 1.3, TLS implicitly refers to TLS 1.3.

15.3.1 TLS Certificates

The authentication of parties provided by TLS is based on X.509 digital certificates. Certificate authorities (such as Digicert) issue three types of SSL/TLS certificates: domain validated, organization validated, and extension validation certificates. The type of a server certificate is a label of trust in the owner of the public key.

Domain validated (DV) certificates
They are at the lowest level of validation. The CA just verifies that the domain name does exist and the email of the applicant is valid. Therefore, the CA cannot be sure who is truly behind the submitted public key. It takes a few minutes, for the applicant, to receive a DV certificate. In general, DV certificates are appropriate for business or other actions that require to quickly receive certificates, at low cost and without the effort of submitting company documents.

Organization validated (OV) certificates
They are granted to a company or an institution. The CA checks the registration of the company, its address, its business, the applicant name, phone, and authority, etc. It may take a few days before receiving an OV certificate. OV certificates provide assurance to website visitors about who is behind the site.

Extended validation (EV) certificates
They are the highest industry standard for authentication. EV certificates are issued after a rigorous verification of all types of businesses, including companies, government entities, institutions, and organizations. To receive and EV certificate, the applicant provides many documents to the CA and it may take several days to process the application before issuing an EV certificate. In particular, EV certificates have helped increase consumer confidence in e-commerce. All the steps required for a CA before issuing an EV certificate follow standardized guidelines and include:

- Verifying the legal, physical, and operational existence of the entity.
- Verifying that the identity of the entity matches official records.
- Verifying that the entity has exclusive right to use the domain specified in the EV certificate.
- Verifying that the entity has properly authorized the issuance of the EV certificate.
- Performing yearly audits to ensure the integrity of the issuance process.

Most of the current browsers (e.g. Firefox, Google Chrome, and Apple Safari) identify EV certificates and activate the browser interface security enhancements.

Notes

- For some operations (such as e-banking or e-shopping), users should only trust severs with EV certificates.
- The category of TLS is a label of trust in the certification process. It comes with a cost. The pricing of TLS certificates can vary wildly from a certificate provider to another. To give you an idea, a certificate costs from tens to thousands of dollars per year.

15.3.2 TLS 1.3 Protocols

TLS is composed of four (sub)protocols: handshake protocol, record protocol, alert protocol, and 0-RTT protocol. In the TLS handshake phase, the parties (i.e. the client and the web server) negotiate the version of TLS and the cryptographic algorithms to use, establish a shared secret for symmetric encryption, and authenticate each other using their public keys. In the record phase, the parties encrypt and decrypt messages using the shared key, and verify the integrity of received data. Errors are handled with the Alert protocol. When the client and the server have pre-shared keys, TLS enables the transmission of data without authentication; such a protocol is referred to as 0-RTT protocol. Handshake and record protocols are the most used; in the following, we provide an overview of both protocols.

15.3.2.1 Handshake Protocol
The parties exchange `Hello` messages in order to:

- Select the cryptographic algorithms to use.
- Establish the shared keying material (i.e. a secret key for encryption/decryption and a hash key for generating MACs).
- Authenticate the server to the client, and optionally the client to the server.

The first (and most important) messages in TLS are `ClientHello` and `ServerHello`. Both messages have the same structure, shown in Figure 15.6:

- TLS versions (1.2 or 1.3) that the client can support or the version the server supports.
- A random nonce to prevent replay attacks.
- A list of extensions, some of them are mandatory.
- Options (used, in particular, for compatibility with TLS 1.2).

Any TLS extension contains a list of items that are ordered according to the sender's preferences (most preferred choice first). In a `ClientHello` message, which is a request, any extension indicates items supported by the client. In a `ServerHello` message, which is a response, the extension indicates, in general, the item that will be used by the server to protect the current connection. For example, the client includes a list of ciphers in a `ClientHello` message; and the server includes the cipher that it selected in the `ServerHello` message.

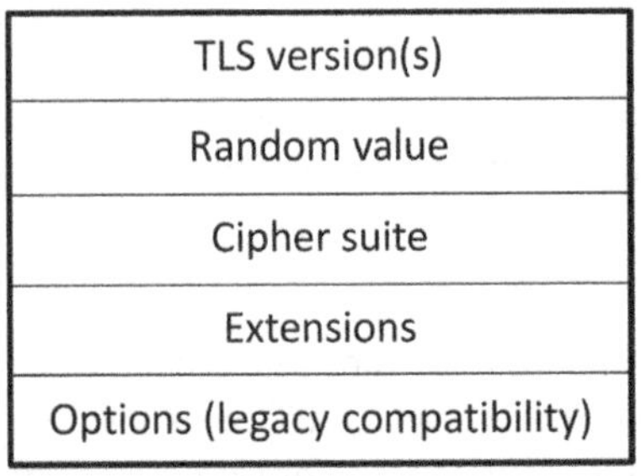

The most used extensions are the following:

| TLS version(s) |
| Random value |
| Cipher suite |
| Extensions |
| Options (legacy compatibility) |

Figure 15.6 Structure of `Hello` messages.

- *Supported groups* extension: it indicates the supported mathematical groups (i.e. finite fields and elliptic curves).
- *Key share* extension: it indicates the supported key exchange protocols.
- *Pre-shared key* extension: it indicates the pre-shared keys known to the client and server before starting the current handshake.
- *Signature algorithms* extension: it indicates the supported signature algorithms.
- *Certificate authorities* extension: it indicates which certificate authorities are supported. This extension is used to indicate the known trust anchors.

- *Early data indication* extension: it allows the client to send application data encrypted with the pre-shared symmetric key, without performing the authentication.

Figure 15.7 illustrates the steps of basic full handshake, where $E_{SK}()$ means encryption using the shared key.

Notes

– In Figure 15.7, gray boxes indicate that the authentication of the client is not mandatory. Indeed, many people accessing web servers do not have certificates; thus, they cannot be authenticated.
– A Hello message may be transmitted in a single record or split into two or many records.

15.3.2.1.1 *Cryptographic-Algorithms Negotiation*

In the ClientHello message, the client includes the following extensions: list of supported cipher suites (for confidentiality and integrity protection), list of supported groups, list of signature algorithms, and list of pre-shared symmetric keys (optional).

- *Supported cipher suites*: the ciphers supported by the client are specified in form of pairs, AEAD (Authenticated encryption with Associated data) algorithm, and a hash function. TLS 1.3 protocol accepts the following pairs:
  – (AES-128-GCM, SHA256); GCM is presented in Section 9.2.4.
  – (AES-256-GCM, SHA384).
  – (AES-128-CCM, SHA256); CCM is presented in Section 9.2.3.
  – (AES-128-CCM-8,[5] SHA256).
  – (ChaCha20, Poly1305); ChaCha20-Poly1305 is presented in Section 9.2.6.2.2.
- *Supported groups* extension: the client includes an ordered list of the names of the groups that it supports for key exchange. The names of elliptic curves (e.g. x25519 and x448) and finite field groups (e.g. ffdhe2048) are included using this extension.

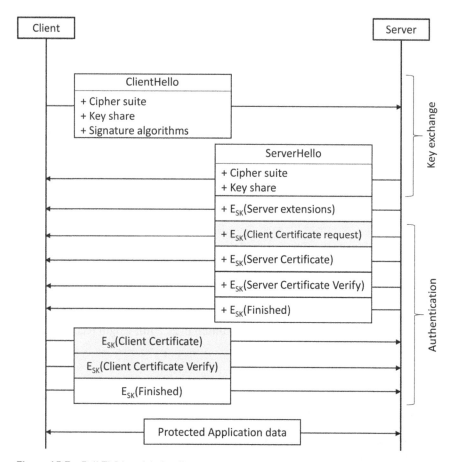

Figure 15.7 Full TLS handshake diagram.

- *Key-share* extension: the client may include one of the following:
  - An empty string to indicate that the client wants to know the list of key-share options supported by the server; in this case an additional round is needed to agree on the key-share;
  - An ordered list of supported key sharing protocols; and for each protocol, the parameters of the field used to generate a shared key are specified. They may be either Diffie-Hellman parameters (i.e. public key, generator, and prime *p*) or Elliptic curve Diffie-Hellman parameters (i.e. name of an elliptic curve, e.g. P-284 or Edwards25519, and the public key of the client).
- *Signature algorithms* extension: it indicates which algorithms to be used in digital signatures. TLS 1.3 protocols accept the following signature algorithms:
  - RSA with SHA256, SHA384 or SHA512
  - ECDSA with SHA256, SHA384 or SHA512 # ECDSA is presented in Section 13.5.5
  - EdDSA[6] (Edwards's curves 25519 and 448). # EdDSA is presented in Section 13.5.6
- *Pre-shared-key* extension: it contains a list of pre-shared keys. The latter may be established in previous TLS connections between the client and the server and then used to establish a new connection; or may be computed and shared using other protocols (out of band). In this mode, referred to as PSK (Pre-Shared Key), the client and the server may use an existing key, without performing authentication.

If the server supports at least one choice in each list suggested by the client, it responds with a `ServerHello` message that contains the server-selected algorithms. The server computes the shared keying material, which is then used to encrypt the remaining parts of the handshake. On the other side, when the client receives the server response, it computes the shared keying material using the same algorithms than those included in the `ServerHello` message.

If there is no overlap between the received lists and the lists supported by the server, the handshake is aborted. Under some conditions, the server can send a `HelloRetryRequest` message to ask the client change some of its choices.

15.3.2.1.2 Authentication

Authentication of the server is mandatory, while that of the client is optional (because not all clients own certificates).

- *Authentication to the client*: using the shared key included in the Key-share extension of the `ServerHello`, the server sends two extensions: `Certificate` (that contains the encrypted server certificate) and `CertificateVerify` (that is a signature over all the previous items of the handshake using the server private-key). `CertificateVerify` extension is used to provide explicit proof that the sender possesses the private key corresponding to its certificate. If the client validates the signature included in the `CertificateVerify`, then the server is trusted. Finally, an encrypted extension `Finished` is sent.
- *Authentication to the server*: when the server needs to authenticate the client, it sends an encrypted `CertificateRequest` extension. Then, as in the previous case, the client makes use of the shared key to send two encrypted extensions `Certificate` (that includes the client certificate) and `CertificateVerify`. If the server validates signature included in the `CertificateVerify`, then the client is trusted. Finally, an encrypted extension `Finished` is sent by the client.

15.3.2.2 Record Protocol

Record protocol is used to provide confidentiality and integrity of transmitted data. The same protocol is used to protect handshake, application data, and alert messages.

The record layer fragments data into records with a maximum length of 2^{14} bytes. Any record to transmit is encrypted and decrypted with an AEAD algorithm agreed between client and server. To prevent some attacks, a nonce is included in each encrypted record.

To keep the security of encryption below an acceptable security margin, a maximum of $2^{24.5}$ full-length records may be encrypted on a given connection using AES-GCM.

15.3.2.3 Alert Protocol

Alert protocol provides indication regarding errors and incapacities to establish or maintain a secure connection between parties. The alerts include the following (the list is not comprehensive):

- Not supported TLS version, Handshake failure, Unknown pre-shared key identifier.
- Bad certificate, Unsupported certificate, Expired Certificate, Revoked Certificate, unknown CA.
- Bad record MAC, Record exceeding the limit size.

15.4 Kerberos

Kerberos[7] is a network authentication protocol, developed at the MIT (Massachusetts Institute of Technology), which is used to verify the identity of users or hosts, called clients, which need to connect to applications servers, which do not trust each other. Application servers include Web, email, print, and file servers. The fundamental design approach of Kerberos is to provide a secure system whose unique service is to authenticate users to multiple application/service servers. Therefore, it frees applications and service servers from having to perform their own authentication. With Kerberos, passwords are no more transmitted to authenticate a user.

Kerberos is supported in all major operating systems (i.e. Microsoft Windows, Apple Mac OS, and Linux) and platforms (such as Oracle and Amazon Web services). The current version of Kerberos is the 5th version, published in RFC 4210 [3].

Kerberos is a kind of key-distribution center, which relies on symmetric keys. Kerberos is the most used KDC to authenticate users to access resources in private networks. In theory, it can be adapted to operate with public keys. However, to date there is no operational Kerberos implementation based on public keys.

This section aims at introducing the main principles and features of Kerberos. For specific details, refer to Kerberos RFCs [3], and its updates.

Definition 15.12 **Authentication**: *it is the process of verifying the identity claimed by a user, a device, or a system.*

Definition 15.13 **Session key**: *a temporary encryption key shared between two entities, with a lifetime limited to the duration of a single login "session."*

Definition 15.14 **Session sub-key**: *it is a temporary encryption key used by a client and a server, selected and exchanged using the session key; its lifetime is limited to a single association (e.g. transfer of a file, messages downloading from a mail box, etc.).*

Definition 15.15 **Ticket**: *it is a record that enables a client authenticate itself to a server; it contains the client's identity, a session key, a timestamp, and other information, all encrypted using the private key of the server.*

15.4.1 Kerberos Principles

Kerberos KDC is a trusted third party, which provides services to establish trust between clients (i.e. users, hosts, devices, etc.) and application servers. Clients and servers may belong to the same domain or to multiple domains. For example, a worldwide company may have multiple interconnected domains, each with a Kerberos KDC. In the Kerberos dialect, clients and application servers are called *principals* and the domains, *realms*.[8]

As illustrated by Figure 15.8, Kerberos KDC is composed of three main elements: an authentication server, a ticket-granting service, and a database. Each principal shares a symmetric key with the Kerberos authentication server. The names of principals and the keys they share with Kerberos are introduced in the database either manually or with an automated tool, both out of the scope of Kerberos. The authentication server authenticates the clients; and the ticket-granting service provides tickets to clients to access application servers.

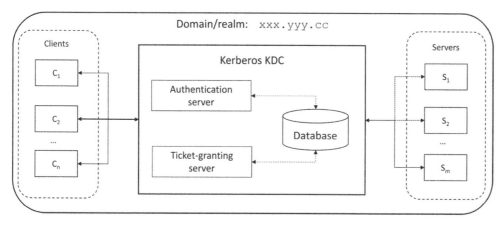

Figure 15.8 General structure of Kerberos KDC and its subscribers.

Kerberos protocol consists of several sub-protocols to provide two-step[9] and three-step authentications, each with several options, for intra-domain or inter-domain usages. In this chapter, we focus only on the most used sub-protocol, precisely the three-step authentication in intra-domain, where a client logs into a local system and then accesses one or several application servers in the same domain. As illustrated by Figure 15.9, the simplified description of Kerberos authentication proceeds as follows.

Step 1: authentication to Kerberos server
- *Authentication server request*: at the initiation of a login session, the client, which wishes to access some servers, sends an authentication request to Kerberos authentication server (KAS). The authentication server request includes the names of the client and the ticket-granting server, all in cleartext, because no sensitive information is included.
- *Authentication server response*: upon receiving an authentication server request, the KAS verifies that the client name is in the KDC database and retrieves its (private[10]) key. If the request-originator client is registered in the database, the KAS generates a random session key, which will be shared between the client and the TGS. Then, the KAS builds a response message composed of three parts: the client name and realm in cleartext, a ticket to the TGS, and a part (encrypted using the client key) containing the session key along with other data. The ticket generated at this step is denoted TGT[11] (Ticket-Granting Ticket) and is used in the next step to obtain tickets to access application servers. The TGT includes the session key and other data; all encrypted using the TGS key. Only the request-originator client can recover the session key included in the response message and only the TGS can check to which client the TGT is granted. When the client receives the response, the initial authentication terminates; the client is logged into the local system. Notice that the client key is used only at this initial authentication step, which provides a better protection to client keys.

Step 2: service ticket acquisition
- *Service ticket request*: once the client receives a TGT and a session key and it wishes to access an application server, it sends a service ticket request to the TGS. In particular, the request includes the TGT received from the KAS and the client name along with other data, encrypted using the session key.
- *Service ticket response*: upon receiving a service ticket request, the TGS verifies that the application server is in the KDC database and retrieves its key. It also verifies that the client has received the session key. If the requested application server is registered in the database and the client has been authenticated by the KAS, the TGS builds a service ticket, which includes the session key extracted from the TGT along with the client name and other data. The service ticket is encrypted with the application server key; thus, only the latter can check to which client the ticket is granted. The format

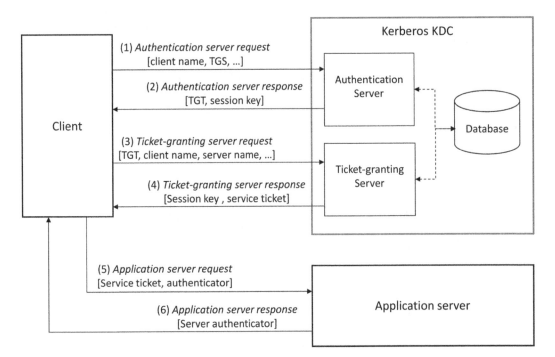

Figure 15.9 Overview of Kerberos authentication process.

of the response message sent by the TGS to the client is almost identical to that of the response message sent by the KAS to the client as above. The difference is that the TGS makes use of the session key (and not the client key) to encrypt the second part of the response message.

Step 3: Mutual client/server authentication

- *Application server request*: upon receiving a service ticket, the client can authenticate to the application server whose name is included in the service ticket. The client builds a message including the service ticket and an authenticator. The latter contains the name and realm of the client along with other data, all encrypted with the session key. The authenticator is used by the application server to verify that the client, which sent the request, possesses the session key included in the service ticket (i.e. the client is the principal to whom the ticket was issued).
- *Application server response*: upon receiving an application service request, the application server verifies that the client possesses the session key. Then, it builds a response message, which includes some values sent by the client, all encrypted using the session key. Upon receiving the response message, the client decrypts the message using the session key and compares the values included in the response to those in its request. If both values are identical, the client has the proof that the application server is the one that holds the key registered in the KDC database; i.e. the mutual authentication is confirmed.

15.4.2 Message Formats and Authentication Steps of Kerberos

15.4.2.1 Ticket and Authenticator Formats

A ticket is delivered either by the Kerberos authentication server or by the Ticket-Granting Server (TGS). The ticket format is the same. As illustrated by Figure 15.10a, a Kerberos ticket contains the following fields:

- *Realm*: name of realm in which the ticket is issued
- *Server name*: it is a name of either the TGS or an application server to access
- *Encrypted part*: the following items are encrypted using the key of the server to access (i.e. either the TGS or an application server)
  - *Session key*: random secret key to share between the client and either the TGS or the application server.
  - *Client realm*: the name of the realm in which the client is registered.
  - *Client name*: the name of the client to whom the ticket is granted.
  - *Authentication time*: time of initial authentication for the named client.
  - *Start time*: time after which the ticket is valid.
  - *End time*: time after which the ticket expires.
  - *Max renew time*: maximum expiration time of a renewable ticket.
  - *Flags*: ticket flags (e.g. *Initial flag* indicates that the ticket is issued by Kerberos authentication server and *Renewable* indicates that the ticket may be renewed).
  - *Options*: optional data.

As previously mentioned, an authenticator is a set of data items encrypted using the session key. It enables the message receiver to verify that the message sender holds the session key. If the values included in a ticket are identical to those included in the authenticator, the message receiver has assurance that the message sender holds the session key. As illustrated by Figure 15.10b, an authenticator contains the following fields:

- *Realm of the client*.
- *Name of the client*.
- *Client time*: the time when the client builds the request in the current exchange
- *Other optional data*: sub-key used by the client, sequence number to detect replays in messages exchanged between the client and the application server, etc.

15.4.2.2 Protocol Actions and Message Description

Below are provided messages and actions details to show how the three-step authentication is performed. To simplify the presentation, optional parameters in requests and responses are only denoted by "..." and some protocol details are omitted. We consider the case of a single realm; and the client and application server do not need a key (called sub-key) in addition to the session key.

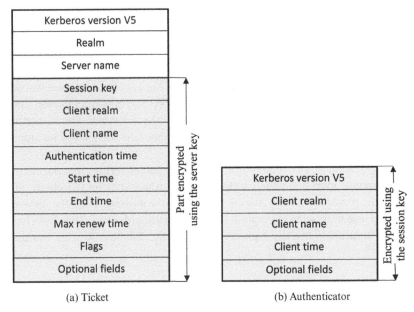

Figure 15.10 Kerberos ticket and authenticator formats.

Notations

Cname, Crealm: client name and realm.

Sname, Srealm: application server name and realm. When only a single domain is considered, *Crealm* and *Srealm* are the same.

StartTime: time after which the granted authentication is valid.

EndTime: time after which the granted authentication is no more valid.

TimeStamp: time[12] at which Kerberos issued the response.

CtimeStamp: time at which the client issued the request.

Nonce: random number, unique for each request.

Cipher: block cipher to be used.

$E_{K_C}(P)$: encryption of P using the key of the client C.

$E_{K_S}(P)$: encryption of P using the key of the application server S.

$E_{K_{SK}}(P)$: encryption of P using the session key.

$E_{K_{TGS}}(P)$: encryption of P using the TGS key.

…: flags and optional items.

15.4.2.2.1 First Step: Client Authenticates to Kerberos Authentication Server

The first step is composed of the following actions.

1) The client prepares and sends to the KAS a request, *KRB_AS_Req*, that includes the client name, the not-before and not-after dates desired by the client, a nonce, and the block cipher desired by the client. The last parameter is used only when multiple block ciphers are supported by Kerberos and the application server. Currently only AES variants can be used. Notice that in the *KRB_AS_Req*, the requested server is implicitly the TGS.

$$KRB\_AS\_Req = (Cname, StartTime, EndTime, Nonce, Cipher, …)$$

2) Upon reception of a *KRB_AS_Req* message, the KAS performs the following:
   - Verify that the requesting client is in the database. If no, return an error.
   - Verify that the nonce is distinct from those nonces included in requests previously received from the requesting client. If no, return an error.
   - From the database, retrieve the key of the requesting client; let K_C denote the client key.
   - Generate a random session key *SK*, which matches the key bit-length of the block cipher desired by the client.
   - Build a message *KRB_AS_Rep* composed of three parts: the first part is the name and the realm of the client (in cleartext), the second part is a TGT (encrypted with the TGS key), and the third is an encryption of the parameters from the request.

$$KRB\_AS\_Rep = ((Crealm, Cname), TGT, EncPart)$$

$$\text{where } TGT = \left(\begin{array}{c} Srealm, Sname, \\ E_{K_{TGS}}(Cname, Crealm, TimeStamp, StartTime, EndTime, ...) \end{array} \right)$$

$$EncPart = E_{K_c}(SK, Nonce, TimeStamp, Starttime, EndTime, Srealm, Sname, ...)$$

Note that the values of *Nonce*, *StartTime*, and *EndTime* are the same in both messages *KRB_AS_Req* and *KRB_AS_Rep*. *Srealm* and *Sname* are those of the TGS.

– Send the message *KRB_AS_Rep* to the client.

3) Upon receiving a message *KRB_AS_Rep*, the client decrypts the encrypted part of the message using its key K_C. If one of the values of *Nonce*, *StartTime*, and *EndTime* is not identical to one included in the *KRB_AS_Req*, an error in raised. Otherwise, the client concludes that the sender of *KRB_AS_Rep* knows its key. Then, the client saves the TGT and the session key *SK*. The authentication of the client by the KAS is finished.

15.4.2.2.2 Second Step: Getting an Application Server Ticket

When the client needs to access an application server, the following actions are performed to get an application server ticket.

1) The client prepares and sends to the TGS a request *KRB_TGS_Req* that includes the client name, the server name and realm, the not-before and not-after dates desired by the client to use the application server ticket, the block cipher desired by the client, and the TGT received in step 1. That is,

$$KRB\_TGS\_Req = \left| \begin{array}{c} Cname, Sname, Srealm, StartTime, EndTime, \\ Nonce, Cipher, TGT, ... \end{array} \right|$$

2) Upon reception of a *KRB_TGS_Req* message, the TGS performs the following:

– Decrypt the TGT and compare its values with those included in the *KRB_TGS_Req*. Then, check the validity period of the TGT. If any test fails, an error indication is returned.

– Retrieve in the database the key of the application server requested by the client. Let K_s denote the application server key.

– Generate an application server ticket *AST*, then build a three-part TGS response *KRB_TGS_Rep* in a similar way than for *KRB_AS_Rep*; i.e.

$$KRB\_TGS\_Rep = ((Crealm, Cname), AST, EncPart),$$

$$\text{where } AST = \left(\begin{array}{c} Srealm, Sname, \\ E_{K_{SK}}(Cname, Crealm, TimeStamp, StartTime, EndTime, ...) \end{array} \right)$$

$$EncPart = E_{SK}(SK, Nonce, TimeStamp, Starttime, EndTime, Srealm, Sname, ...)$$

Note that the values of *Nonce*, *Start Time*, and *EndTime* are the same in both messages *KRB_TGS_Req* and *KRB_TGS_Rep*. *Srealm* and *Sname* are those of the application server requested by the client.

3) Upon receiving a message *KRB_TGS_Rep*, the client decrypts the encrypted part of the message using the session key. If one of the values of *Nonce*, *Start Time*, and *End Time* is not identical to one included in the *KRB_TGS_Req*, an error is raised. Otherwise, the client concludes that the sender of *KRB_TGS_Rep* is the TGS. Then, the client saves the application server ticket *AST*.

15.4.2.2.3 Third Step: Mutual Client/Server Authentication

In the third step, the following actions are performed.

1) The client prepares a server request *KRB_AP_Req*, which includes the ticket *AST* and an authenticator using the session key; i.e.

$$KRB\_AP\_Req = (AST, Authenticator)$$

$$\text{where } Authenticator = E_{K_{SK}}(Crealm, Cname, CtimeStamp, SeqNumber, ...)$$

2) Upon reception of a request *KRB_AP_Req*, the application server performs the following actions:
   - Decrypt the ticket *AST* using its key K_S.
   - From the ticket, get the session key and the name and realm of the sender.
   - Decrypt the authenticator using the session key.
   - If the data (i.e. client name and realm and other information) included in the authenticator is not identical to that included in the ticket *AST*, an error is returned to the client. Otherwise, the application server successfully authenticates the client.
   - The application server builds a response message *KRB_AP_Rep*, which includes the timestamp and sequence number from the *KRB_AP_Req* message, all encrypted using the session key:

$$KRB\_AP\_Rep = E_{K_{SK}}(CtimeStamp,\ SeqNumber, \ldots)$$

3) Upon reception of a response message *KRB_AP_Rep*, the client decrypts the message using the session key. If the content of the message matches the data included in the request message *KRB_AP_Req*, the mutual authentication successfully terminates.

15.4.3 Advantages, Limits, and Security of Kerberos

Advantages. There are many advantages in using Kerberos, in particular the following:
- Kerberos enables secured exchanges between principals that do not trust each other.
- Kerberos separates authentication from services. The application servers do not know, or ask for, the client passwords.
- A single client authentication to Kerberos server is enough to access all Kerberos-authenticated services. Therefore, Kerberos provides a *Single sign-on* service to clients.
- Protecting user information is simplified, since all user authentication information is stored on one centralized authentication server.
- Kerberos concentrates the maintenance of secrets (i.e. stored keys) in a small number of places (that can be protected appropriately) rather than distributing them all over the network.

Limits. The following issues should be considered when using Kerberos:
- The names of all the principals are registered in the database. They must be unique in each realm. The clients must know the names of the application servers they need to access. Any change in names may result in authentication failures. Consider for example, a client that received a ticket to access an application server *S* for a period of one year. Then, the server name is changed to S'. After the name change, the client is no more authenticated by the server, because the ticket became invalid.
- The database is the main vulnerability point of Kerberos. It must be protected using appropriate procedures that are not part of Kerberos.
- Any denial-of-service attack against Kerberos results in a denial-of-service attack against all the principals using Kerberos.
- Kerberos generates and securely transmits the session key to the client and server. Once obtained, the session key must be protected by the client and the server without actions from Kerberos. In particular, clients may be attacked to recover the session key and then attackers disclose the private communications.
- Validity check of ticket period relies on synchronized clocks in the whole system. Clock synchronization is required, but not provided by Kerberos. Any desynchronization (at some drift) may result in invalid tickets. Therefore, any participants (clients, application servers, and Kerberos) must use the appropriate time services (e.g. Network Time Protocol).
- As an authentication service, Kerberos provides a means of verifying the identity of principals on a network. Authentication is usually useful primarily as a first step in the process of authorization, determining whether a client may use a service, which objects the client is allowed to access, and the type of access allowed for each object. Kerberos does not, by itself, provide authorization. Possession of an application server ticket provides only authentication of the client to that service, and not how the client can use the resources of the application server (i.e. read, write, delete, ... objects).
- Kerberos does not, by itself, provide integrity and confidentiality of data exchanged between a client and an application server. Additional mechanisms (such as HMAC or authenticated-encryption algorithms) should be agreed between the parties before sending data.

Security. Researchers have been investigating Kerberos since it was first published. Weaknesses have been discovered in specific Kerberos implementations, as well as in the protocol itself. Those weaknesses have been addressed, and Kerberos remains fundamental for authentication in the private networks. Kerberos has been widely implemented for decades, and it is considered a mature and safe protocol for authenticating users. Kerberos uses strong cryptography, including secret-key encryption, to protect sensitive data. Therefore, Kerberos protocol is currently considered secure.

15.5 Exercises and Problems

15.5.1 List of Exercises and Problems

Exercise 15.1

Consider a PKI with a single CA, which acts as root-CA and issuing CA. It signs and sends three certificates to three collaborative users U_1, U_2, and U_3. User U_1 wants to send a signed document to user U_2. Then, user U_2 updates the document, signs it, and then sends it to user U_3. The hash function used by the collaborating users is known before the start of the document update. Explain how the digital certificates are used to protect the integrity of the document.

Exercise 15.2

Is a registration authority an intermediate CA?

Exercise 15.3

1) Imagine that Eve knew Bob's public key and certificate. Can she use the known information to exchange data with Alice pretending to be Bob?
2) Can Eve change Bob's certificate and include her public key in place of that of Bob, and then sends the certificate to Alice?

Exercise 15.4

Alice and Bob obtained digital certificates from a CA. Then, they authenticated to each other and exchanged some data encrypted with a session key established using the Diffie-Hellman protocol, and stopped their session. Eve intercepted all the ciphertexts exchanged between Alice and Bob; and she recovered the private key used by the CA to generate Alice and Bob's certificates.

1) Can Eve disclose plaintexts exchanged between Alice and Bob in the closed session?
2) Can Eve disclose plaintexts to be exchanged in a future session?

Exercise 15.5

Users in domains D_1 and D_2 have CA C_1 and CA C_2 as trust anchors, respectively. Both domains are acquired by a company, which owns a domain D_3 and has CA C_3 as trust anchor. What are the steps that the users in the three domains must follow to communicate with each other?

Exercise 15.6

1) Can Kerberos protect against denial-of-service attacks?
2) Can Kerberos protect against replay attacks?
3) Can Kerberos guarantee the integrity of data exchanged between principals?
4) Can Kerberos protect application server resources against unauthorized accesses?

Problem 15.1

Some people may be attacked, because they consider that any website with HTTPS and a padlock icon belongs to an honest entity. In addition, some people do not carefully read, letter by letter, the names of secured websites. Suggest a use case of fraudulent website where an attacker owning an authentic digital certificate, delivered by a trusted authority, can obtain confidential data from un-warned or naïve people.

Problem 15.2

Assume that the secret keys of Kerberos clients are derived from their passwords, which are entered securely in the database, i.e. passwords cannot be intercepted during transfer. Show a scenario where an attacker can obtain tickets to access application servers.

Problem 15.3

This problem aims to discuss a simple way to include public keys into Kerberos. Consider a modification of Kerberos, which provides a two-step validation: the Kerberos authentication server delivers application-server tickets to clients. Instead of using private keys stored on Kerberos database, each principal has a certificate delivered by an authority trusted by Kerberos. The modified Kerberos frees principals from checking the validity of certificates. Suggest a public-key-based protocol to deliver tickets and session keys. List some of the drawbacks of public-key-based Kerberos.

15.5.2 Solutions to Exercises and Problems

Exercise 15.1

Steps to update the document:

- The three users exchange their certificates. Certificate validation is immediate, because all users trust the same root-CA, which signed their certificates.
- User U_1 computes a hash H_1 of the document D_1; encrypts H_1 with his/her private key; obtains a signature S_1; and sends a message M_1 containing $D_1 \parallel S_1$ to user U_2.
- User U_2 receives the message M_1. He/she extracts the public key of user U_1 from U_1's certificate. He/she decrypts the signature S_1 using U_1's public key and obtains a bit-string H_1'. He/she computes a hash H_1'' of the document D_1. If $H_1' = H_1''$, then the collaboration continues. Otherwise, the document has been altered during transfer; and the collaboration is stopped.
- User U_2 updates the document D_1 to yield a document D_2. He/she computes a hash H_2 of the document D_2, encrypts it using his/her private key, obtains a signature S_2, and finally sends a message M_2 that contains $D_2 \parallel S_2$ to user U_3.
- User U_3 receives the message M_2. He/she extracts the public key of user U_2 from U_2's certificate. He/she decrypts the signature S_2 using U_2's public key and obtains a bit-string H_2'. He/she computes a hash H_2'' of the document D_2. If $H_2' = H_2''$, then the collaboration successfully terminates. Otherwise, the document has been altered during transfer; and the collaboration fails.

Exercise 15.2

No. An intermediate CA is a CA that is not a root-CA and it issues certificates to lower level CAs or end-entities. An RA assists a CA to check and validate the information included in certificate requests submitted by end-entities.

Exercise 15.3

1) No. Bob's public key as well as his certificate is not secret. To decrypt the data encrypted by Alice using Bob's public key, Eve needs Bob's private key.
2) No. Recall that the CA signature is a signed hash of the user public key plus other data. Bob's certificate is signed using the CA's private key. If Bob's public key is changed, the signature on the certificate becomes invalid.

Exercise 15.4

1) Certificates do not include private keys. Therefore, the session key established by Alice and Bob using their private keys cannot be recovered by Eve with the help of the CA private-key. Thus, she cannot disclose the plaintexts exchanged in the closed session.
2) Using the CA private-key, Eve can generate and sign on behalf of the CA a certificate with Bob as the owner name, but with her public key. Then, when the new session is to be setup between Alice and Bob, Eve can mount a man-in-the-middle attack and replace Bob's messages by her messages. Alice will receive a valid certificate with Bob's name. Then, Alice will encrypt her messages with Eve's public key and not with that of Bob.

Exercise 15.5

- CA C_3 issues a certificate to domain D_1 and another to domain D_2.
- All users in domains D_1 and D_2 get the public key of CA C_3. Then, they add C_3 as their trust anchor.
- When any pair of users in the three domains want to communicate, they exchange their certificates signed by CA C_3.

Exercise 15.6

1) No. Kerberos is not resistant to denial-of-service. DoS are common attacks against systems and are out of the scope of Kerberos.
2) Yes. Each client request includes a nonce and/or a timestamp, which are checked by Kerberos to prevent replay attacks.
3) No. Kerberos provides a session key to be used by the principals (i.e. client and server) to encrypt their messages. However, the encryption alone cannot provide integrity guarantees; other mechanisms are required (e.g. use of HMAC of authenticated-encryption algorithms as those discussed in Chapter 9).
4) No. Kerberos provides assurance to application servers that the clients who received tickets have been authenticated. The authentication does not specify which type of access (i.e. read, write, append, delete, etc.) is granted to clients when accessing server resources.

Problem 15.1

We suggest the following scenario. An attacker legally obtains a certificate for a domain `bnpparisbas.com`, and mounts a website identical to that of `https//:bnpparibas.com`, a French bank. Then, he sends messages using some emailing list, asking customers of BNP Paribas to use an included link to do some operations on their accounts. People who have no accounts at BNP Paribas ignore the message, but some of the BNP Paribas customers may click on the link provided in the email and perform the requested operations. If they check the certificate, they can see the name of `bnpparisbas.com` and they do not pay attention to the "s" after "`pari`", which does not exist in the authentic domain name of BNP Paribas. Therefore, a digital certificate plus a secured website do not necessarily mean an honest website.

Problem 15.2

It is known that Kerberos is vulnerable to attacks based on password guessing. If the passwords used by clients are weak, attackers can disclose them, using dictionary attacks, derive their secret keys (because the derivation function of keys from passwords is known), and then can authenticate to Kerberos and obtain application server tickets. Therefore, it is recommended to use strong passwords and change them periodically.

Problem 15.3

The suggested protocol is as follows:

- The client obtains the certificate of the application server, then sends a ticket request including his/her certificate and that of the application server.
- The modified Kerberos checks the validity of both certificates (maybe asking the authority, which delivered the certificates).
- Modified Kerberos generates a random session key and a ticket (that includes the session key and client name) encrypted with the public key of the application server. The session key is encrypted using the public key of the client. Then, a message, including the encrypted session key and the ticket, is sent to the client.
- The client decrypts the first part of the message to recover the session key. Then, he/she prepares an authenticator (which includes authentication-data, e.g. a timestamp and/or a name) encrypted using the session key. Then, he/she sends a request to the application server. The request includes some of authentication data (in cleartext), the authenticator, and the ticket.
- Upon reception of a client request, the application server decrypts the ticket using his/her private key and recovers the session key. Then, he/she decrypts the authenticator to confirm that the sender knows the session key. Finally, a response is sent to the client. The response includes some of the authentication data of the client encrypted with the session key.
- The client receives the server response and decrypts the message to confirm that the responding server holds the appropriate private key used to encrypt the ticket.

Drawbacks of public-key-based Kerberos include:

- Public-key cryptography is a relatively expensive operation.
- Checking the validity of certificates requires much more work than checking just if a principal is registered in the local database of Kerberos.
- Principals are required to pay to receive and renew their certificates.

Notes

1 The issuer and subject names are commonly represented using an X.500 or Lightweight Directory Access Protocol (LDAP) format.

2 It may take time before an invalid certificate is added to the CRL. The period of CRL updating may be an hour, a day, a week …; it depends on each CA and the usages of the public-keys certified by that CA.

3 Since 2015, all SSL versions are deprecated. Today, when people use the term SSL, they talk about TLS. The reason of still using SSL or SSL/TLS is that the term SSL persists in minds as it was a guarantee of security over Internet.

4 Forward secrecy is a feature of key agreement schemes, which provide the property that session keys are not compromised if the private keys used in the key agreement become compromised.

5 AES-128-CCM and AES-128- CCM-8 are identical with an exception: AES-128- CCM-8 uses eight octets for authentication, instead of the full 16 octets used by AES-128-CCM.

6 The name of the hash function is not specified, because implicitly Edwards's curve 25519 is used with SHA512 and the curve with SHAKE256.

7 The name *Kerberos* was derived from the Greek mythology; it is a name of a three-head dog that protected the gates of hells.

8 The term *realm* is used to make the analogy between the protection of digital systems and that of the realms in the spirit of the Greek mythology of the three-head dog.

9 In the two-step authentication, the client must authenticate to the Kerberos authentication server for each application server to access.

10 It is a symmetric key; therefore, "private" is omitted in the sequel.

11 The TGT (also called initial ticket) generated by Kerberos is similar to the certificate issued by a certificate authority when a public key is used. It is used to prove that the client holding the TGT was authenticated and it can share, with the application server, the session key included in the TGT to encrypt and decrypt messages.

12 Kerberos makes use of absolute time. So, the clocks of the entities (Kerberos, clients, and application servers) must be synchronized (with a bounded difference between clocks).

References

1 Cooper, D., Santesson, S., Farrell, S. et al. (2008). *Internet X.509 Public Key Infrastructure Certificate and Certificate Revocation List (CRL) Profile - RFC 5280*. Internet Engineering Task Force (IETF).

2 Rescorla, E. (2018). *The Transport Layer Security (TLS) Protocol Version 1.3, RFC 8446*. Internet Engineering Task Force (IETF).

3 Neuman, C. (2005). *The Kerberos Network Authentication Service (V5), RFC 4120*. Internet Engineering Task Force (IETF).

16

Generation of Pseudorandom and Prime Numbers for Cryptographic Applications

As emphatically underlined in previous chapters, random numbers (RNs) and prime numbers (PNs) play a fundamental role in cryptography. In particular, cryptographic keys and nonces used in some cryptographic algorithms shall appear as entirely random bit-strings for observers (i.e. attackers).

In general, there exist two basic strategies for generating random numbers: non-deterministic and deterministic strategies. In the first category, a physical process is used to generate bit sequences, while in the second category, an algorithm is used. Non-deterministic RN generators produce true RNs, while deterministic RN generators produce pseudo RNs. The second category of RN generators is the most dominant in computer-based systems and are built using deterministic random bit generators (DRBGs). The latter are algorithms that output random bit-strings, which mainly depend on an initial input called *seed*. Therefore, the outputs of DRBGs are pseudorandom bit-strings instead of true random ones. Even if the algorithm of a DRBG is known, when the seed is picked from a (very) large set and kept secret, the DRBG output is very likely to be unpredictable and looks like a random value.

Pseudorandom bit-strings are also called pseudorandom numbers and DRBGs are referred to as Pseudo Random Number Generators (PRNGs). The first part of this chapter addresses basic and recommended algorithms to generate pseudo RNs.

The security of IFC (Integer Factorization Cryptography) and DLC (Discrete Logarithm Cryptography)-based algorithms fundamentally relies on prime numbers. Unlike for PRNs, there does not exist algorithms that deterministically generate, with certainty, large prime numbers. A practical alternative to true primes is to use integers that are not proven to be composite. The second part of this chapter presents the recommended algorithms to support prime number generation based on primality testing.

It is worth noticing that since the security of cryptographic algorithms depends on PRNGs, if a PRNG can be made predictable for attackers, it can be used as a backdoor to compromise confidentiality and integrity of protected data. The same threat applies to the algorithms used to select prime numbers.

16.1 Introduction to Pseudorandom Number Generation

16.1.1 Basic Notions and Definitions

Definition 16.1 Ideal random bit-string: *it is a bit-string in which each bit is unpredictable and unbiased, with a value that is independent on the values of the other bits in the sequence.*

Definition 16.2 Random number sequence: *it is a random sequence of numbers, which has no order and does not follow an intelligible pattern or combination. For external observers, a random sequence of numbers appears like a digitalization of noise.*

Definition 16.3 Random number generator: *it is an algorithm (or a circuit) which outputs a sequence of statistically independent and unbiased numbers.*

Definition 16.4 Truly random number generator (TRNG): *it is a process, which relies on physical observations (e.g. coin flipping, lottery, thermal noise of an equipment, natural phenomena, etc.) to generate numbers.*

Properties of truly random numbers
TRNs are characterized by two fundamental properties:

1) *Uniform distribution:* i.e. all the numbers in a required range often occur with the same probability.
2) *Independence:* if one knows some or all the numbers up to a certain point in a random number sequence, he/she should not be able to predict the next one(s).

TRNGs have some limitations, including:

- They require extra hardware, which has a cost.
- In general, they are not fast enough to generate RNs at a high rate required by some applications or services.
- Their output is not reproducible to support the testing of cryptographic applications and algorithms.
- If attackers have access to the physical phenomenon used by a TRNG, the entire security of a system may be compromised.

Definition 16.5 Seed: *it is the initial value provided to a random number (or bits) generator to output a sequence of* pseudorandom numbers (or bit-strings).

In practice, TRNGs are used only to generate seeds (i.e. initial inputs) for software pseudorandom number generators, which are capable of generating RNs at high rates.

Definition 16.6 Pseudorandom number generator *(PRNG): it is a deterministic algorithm which, given a truly random number, called seed, outputs a sequence of numbers, which appear as being random.*

Definition 16.7 Pseudorandom Bit Generator *(PRBG) (also called **Deterministic Random Bit Generator** (DRBG)): it is a deterministic[1] algorithm which, given a truly random binary sequence of length k, called seed, outputs a binary sequence of length L which appears to be random. The output of a PRBG is called a pseudorandom bit sequence.*

A DRBG can be used to generate (uniformly distributed) random numbers. For example, a random integer in the interval $[0, n]$ can be obtained by generating a random bit sequence of length $\lfloor log_2 (n) \rfloor + 1$, and converting it to an integer; if the resulting integer exceeds n, one option is to discard it and generate a new random bit sequence. The other option is to pick the *modulo n* of the DRBG output.

Definition 16.8 Period *of a PRNG/PRBG: any PRNG/PRBG repeats a specific pattern of random numbers (or bits). The period of a PRNG/PRBG measures the number of output numbers (or bits) after which the PRNG/PRBG begins to repeat itself.*

16.1.2 Entropy

In cryptography, the unpredictability of secrets (such as cryptographic keys) is essential. If X is a random variable associated with a secret, then the probability that a secret value is guessed correctly is related to the entropy of the random variable X. If a process used to generate secret items has a small entropy (i.e. it is so poor that it can only generate a small number of different random numbers), the cryptographic items (such as session keys, nonces, and initialization vectors) become predictable. Therefore, entropy is of paramount importance to design secrets. Basics of entropy are presented in this section.

Definition 16.9 Entropy: *it is the amount of information provided by an observation of a random variable. It reflects the uncertainty associated with predicting the variable value. The larger the value of entropy, the greater the uncertainty in predicting the value of an observation.*

16.1.2.1 Source of Entropy

An entropy source is a combination of an analogue noise source (e.g. thermal noise or device vibration noise), a conditioner, and a health testing, which together generate random bit-strings to be used as seeds by pseudorandom bit generators. Figure 16.1 illustrates the components of an entropy source:

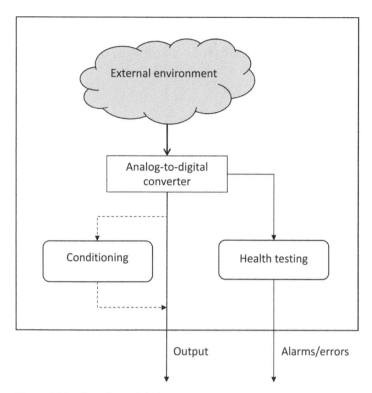

Figure 16.1 Generic model of entropy source.

- *Analogue noise source*: an analogue signal is sampled and digitalized. Notice that without a genuine noise, adding other deterministic components in the chain of random bit generation would not help in producing unpredictable numbers, because the algorithms used in number generation are public, in general.
- *Conditioning component*: it is an optional deterministic function responsible for reducing bias and/or increasing the entropy rate of the resulting output bits. In general, keyed-hash and encryption functions are used as conditioning components.
- *Health testing* of a noise source aims to detect failures of the noise source (e.g. no change in the signal due to a hardware failure) or to detect a deviation from the expected output during the correct operation of the noise source (e.g. no variation in a physical phenomenon as expected).

Noise sources can be divided into two categories: physical and digital noise sources. The following physical phenomena may be used as physical noise sources:

- The sound from a microphone or a video input from a camera.
- The air turbulence within a sealed disk drive, which causes random fluctuations in read latency times of disk drive sector.
- The frequency instability of a free running oscillator.
- Elapsed time between emission of particles during radioactive decay.
- Thermal noise from a semiconductor diode or resistor.

The following may be used as digital noise sources:

- The system time measured at a fine granularity.
- The current value of a portion of the random access memory.
- The position of a PC mouse.
- A portion of a file (e.g. in Linux, the file `/dev/random` contains information collected from device drivers, which can be used to generate random numbers).

16.1.2.2 Entropy from a Statistical Point of View

There are many possible measures of entropy, but the central notion of information theory for expressing the uncertainty about a random variable is the Shannon's entropy [1].

Definition 16.10 Shannon's entropy: *it is a measure of the average uncertainty of a random variable X. Formally, the Shannon's entropy is defined as follows: let X be a random variable, which takes its values in a set $S = \{x_1, x_2, ..., x_N\}$, with probability $\Pr(X = x_i) = p_i$, $i \in [1, N]$, the entropy of the random variable X, denoted $H(X)$, is defined by [1]:*

$$H(X) = -\sum_{i=1}^{N} \left(p_i * log_2(p_i) \right)$$

It also is the minimum number of bits required on the average to describe a value x_i of the random variable X.

Example 16.1

- Let X be a random variable that takes its values in the Latin alphabet. If all the letters are equiprobable, then $H(X) = log_2(26) = 4.70$. Therefore, five bits are required to represent each value of the variable X.
- Let Y bet a random variable, which takes its values in a set of passwords. Assume that a password is composed of eight equiprobable characters: five letters (upper or lower cases) || two decimal digits || one special character out of eight. There exist 52^5 arrangements of 5 letters out of 52, 10^2 arrangements of two digits out of 10, and eight arrangements of one special character out of eight. Therefore, the cardinality N of the distinct passwords is $N = 52^5 * 10^2 * 8 = 3041 \approx 6322560028^{38.14}$. Hence,

$$H(X) = -\sum_{i=1}^{N} \frac{1}{N} \left(log_2 \left(\frac{1}{N} \right) \right) = log_2(N) = 38.14$$

Definition 16.11 Joint entropy *of two random variables X and Y: it measures the uncertainty of a joint event "X and Y." It is denoted $H(X,Y)$ and defined by:*

$$H(X,Y) = -\sum_{i=1}^{N}\sum_{j=1}^{M} \left(p_{i,j} * log_2(p_{i,j}) \right)$$

where $p_{i,j} = Pr\left(X = x_i, Y = y_j\right)$ and N and M are the numbers of values of X and Y, respectively.

Definition 16.12 Conditional entropy: *it quantifies the amount of information needed to describe the outcome of a random variable Y given the value of a random variable X is known. It is written as $H(Y \mid X)$ and defined by:*

$$H(Y \mid X) = -\sum_{i=1}^{N}\sum_{j=1}^{M} p_{i,j} * log_2 \left(\frac{p_{i,j}}{p_i} \right)$$

where $\dfrac{p_{i,j}}{p_i}$ is the conditional probability. The conditional entropy of Y if $X = x_i$ is defined by:

$$H(Y \mid X = x_i) = -\sum_{j=1}^{M} \left(Pr\left(\left(Y = y_j \mid X = x_i\right)\right) * log_2 \left(Pr\left(\left(Y = y_j \mid X = x_i\right)\right)\right)\right)$$

Properties of entropy

Let X and Y be two random variables, which take N and M distinct values, respectively. The following properties hold:

 i. $0 \le H(X) \le log_2 N$, which means that there is an upper bound to the entropy.
 ii. $H(X) = 0$, if and only if $\exists i \in [1, N] \mid p_i = 1$. $H(X) = 0$ means that we are certain of the variable value that will be observed.
 iii. $H(X) = -\left(\dfrac{1}{N}\right)\sum_{i=1}^{n} log_2 \left(\dfrac{1}{N}\right) = log_2 N$, if and only if $p_i = p_j = \dfrac{1}{N}$, $\forall i, \forall j \in [1, N]$, which is the most uncertain situation to predict the value of the random variable.
 iv. Any change toward equalization of the probabilities $p_1, p_2, ..., p_N$ increases the entropy $H(X)$. $H(X)$ reaches it maximal value when all the probabilities are equal.
 v. $H(X, Y) \le H(X) + H(Y)$. The uncertainty of a joint event is less than or equal to the sum of the individual uncertainties.

vi. $H(Y \mid X) = H(X, Y) - H(X)$ or alternatively, $H(X, Y) = H(X) + H(Y \mid X)$.

vii. $H(Y \mid X) = 0$, if and only if the value of Y is completely determined by the value of X. $H(Y \mid X) = H(Y)$, if and only if Y and X are independent. Uncertainty of Y is never increased, if X is known.

Definition 16.13 Min-entropy *of a random variable X that takes values from a set $S = \{x_1, x_2, \ldots, x_N\}$, with probability $\Pr(X = x_i) = p_i$, $i = 1, \ldots, N$, is denoted $H\_min(X)$ and defined by: $H\_min(X) = \min_{i=1,\ldots,N}(-\log_2 p_i) = -\log_2 max_{i=1,\ldots,N} \, p_i$.*

The min-entropy is the negative logarithm of the probability that X is determined correctly with only one guess of the form "is X equal to x_i?"

Properties of min-entropy

i. The maximum possible value for the min-entropy of a random variable with N distinct values is $\log_2 N$ that is reached when the random variable has a uniform probability distribution.

ii. If a random variable X has a min-entropy of h, then the probability of observing (or guessing) any particular value of X is no greater than 2^{-h}.

Definition 16.14 Hartley's entropy: *it is also called max-entropy; and it is a simple measurement that only relies on the cardinality of the set of possible values of the variable. Let N denote the cardinality of the values of a variable X. The Hartley's entropy of X is defined by: $HH(X) = \log_2(N)$.*

Hartley's entropy assumes the distribution of values of the random variable is uniform. Therefore, the Shannon's entropy is a generalization of that of Hartley, because when all the values are identically distributed, i.e. $p_i = p_j = \frac{1}{N}, \forall i \in [1, N], \forall j \in [1, N]$, the Shannon's entropy formula becomes:

$$H(X) = -\sum_{i=1}^{N}\left(\frac{1}{N} * \log_2\left(\frac{1}{N}\right)\right) = -N * \frac{1}{N} * \log_2\left(\frac{1}{N}\right) = \log_2(N)$$

> **Note.** The most used model of entropy in cryptography is the min-entropy, which measures the lower bound on the entropy. The min-entropy is never greater than the Shannon's entropy, which measures the average unpredictability of the outcomes.

16.1.3 Some Popular PRNGs (not to use in Cryptography)

The following three PRNGs are well known and used, in particular in simulation and testing applications. However, they are not used in cryptography field, because the prediction of the PRNG output is easy.

16.1.3.1 Middle-Square Algorithm

Take a first random number X_0 (generated by an entropy source) of n digits, square it, and then pick the n digits in the middle of X_0^2 and obtain a new random number X_1, then square X_1 and pick the n digits in the middle of X_1^2 and obtain X_2, etc. The sequence of numbers generated by the Middle-square algorithm is defined by:

$$X_i = Middle\_digits\_of\left(X_{n-1}^2, n\right), i > 0$$

where X_0 is a selected seed. If some X_i has less than $2n$ digits, it is padded, on the left, with 0s to get a number with $2n$ digits. The generated sequence of numbers in the interval $[0, 10^n - 1]$ appear as a sequence of random numbers.

Example 16.2

– Let $X_0 = 89$.

   $X_0^1 = 7921$; hence, $X_1 = 92$. $X_1^2 = 8464$; hence, $X_2 = 46$.
   $X_2^2 = 2116$; hence, $X_3 = 11$. $X_3^2 = 0121$; hence, $X_4 = 12$.

  The sequence continues as follows: $14, 19, 36, 29, 84, 5, 2, 0, 0, 0, \ldots 0$.
  The PRNG stops producing distinct values when it reach $X_{12} = 0$.

- Let $X_0 = 2916$

$X_0^2 = 2916^2 = 08503056$; thus, $X_1 = 5030$.
$X_1^2 = 5030^2 = 25300900$; thus, $X_2 = 3009$.
$X_2^2 = 3009^2 = 09054081$; thus, $X_3 = 0540$.
$X_3^2 = 0540^2 = 00291600$; thus, $X_4 = 2916 = X_0$.

Therefore, the second PRNG has a period of 4, which is a very low value.

16.1.3.2 Linear Congruential Generator

The current golden standard for the generation of random numbers is the linear congruential generator (LCG). The LCG has four inputs: the modulus m, the multiplier a, the increment b, and the seed X_0. The LCG random number sequence is defined by:

$$X_i \equiv (aX_{i-1} + b) \bmod m, \, i > 0$$

One of the most known and used LCGs was proposed by Park and Miller in 1988; it is referred to as MINSTD. The original version of Park and Miller's LCG was defined by a modulus $m = 2^{31} - 1 = 2147483647$, a multiplier $a = 7^5 = 16807$, and an increment $b = 0$. Some implementations use $a = 48,271$ or $a = 69621$. Park and Miller's LCG has a (full) period of $m - 1$. It is worth noticing that the `rand()` function of ISO C standard is based on Park and Miller's LCG.

Another known LCG is the one used by the `drand48()` function of Linux (complying with POSIX 1.-2001), where the random number sequence is defined by: $X_i = (25214903917 * X_{i-1} + 11) \bmod 2^{48}$. The values returned by `drand48()` are nonnegative double-precision, floating-point values uniformly distributed over the interval $[0, 1)$.

Example 16.3 Let LCG parameters be $X_0 = 19$, $m = 101$, $a = 13$, and $b = 11$. The numbers generated with the selected parameters are:

19, 56, 32, 23, 7, 1, 24, 20, 69, 100, 99, 86, 18, 43, 65, 48, 29, 85, 5, 76, 90, 70, 12, 66, 61, 97, 60, 84, 93, 8, 14, 92, 96, 47, 16, 17, 30, 98, 73, 51, 68, 87, 31, 10, 40, 26, 46, 3, 50, 55, 19, 56, 32, 23, 7, 1, 24, 20, 69, 100, 99, 86, 18, 43, 65, 48, 29, 85, 5, 76, 90, 70, 12, 66, 61, 97, 60, 84, 93, 8, 14, 92, 96, 47, 16, 17, 30, 98, 73, 51, 68, 87, 31, 10, 40, 26, 46, 3, 50, 55.

First, notice that all the numbers appear in double. Therefore, they are uniformly distributed. Second, notice that when the seed (i.e. 19) repeats, all the following numbers repeat. Therefore, the generated sequence has a cycle of 50 numbers; and it should not be used when more than 50 random numbers are required.

Notes

- In general, LCGs have greater cycle periods than Middle-square algorithms, which makes them preferred PRNGs.
- The period of an LCG may be the same than that of its modulus.
- Because of their predictability, LCGs should not be used as building blocks of cryptosystems (see Problem 16.1).

16.1.3.3 Mersenne Twister PRNG

Currently, the most respected PRNG is called Mersenne Twister (MT); it was proposed by Matsumoto and Nishimura in 1998 [2]. Its period is of $2^{19937} - 1$, which means that approximately 10^{5980} random numbers may be generated without sequence repetition. There exist standard implementations of the MT19937 in many programming languages (such as Python) and libraries (such as C++, Mathematica, and Statistical Package for the Social Sciences).

Note. For interested readers, Park and Miller discussed some properties to design and implement good random number generators [3].

16.1.4 PRNGs for Cryptography: Notions and Design Principles

16.1.4.1 Properties of PRNGs for Cryptography

Definition 16.15 Cryptographically secure PRNG (CSPRNG): it is a PRNG suitable to cryptographic applications and services. Numbers generated by a CSPRNG shall be statistically indistinguishable from pure random numbers and unpredictable for an adversary that does not know the seed.

In other words, a pseudorandom number sequence is cryptographically secure, if it is difficult for an attacker, with limited computational resources, to predict the next number(s) from the numbers already in his/her possession. A minimum security requirement for PRNG is that the length k of the random seed should be sufficiently large, so that a search over 2^k elements (i.e. the entire seed space of possible seeds) is computationally infeasible, which prevents brute-force attacks.

16.1.4.2 General Guidelines for the Design of PRBGs for Cryptography
In practice, different approaches can be used to build a CSPRNG:

- Block ciphers running in some suitable modes such as CTR.
- Stream ciphers[2] (with an adequate period).
- Hash functions and keyed-hash functions.
- Combination of the above building blocks.

The NIST recommendation is to use Deterministic Random Bit Generators (DRBGs) to generate PRNs, as discussed in the next section. A DRBG generates bit-strings that are converted into numbers. Therefore, in the context of this chapter, DRBGs are equivalent to PRNGs. In [4–6], useful recommendations are provided to help DRBG developers. Below is a summary of the proposed guidelines. For more detail, refer to the complete recommendations.

16.1.4.2.1 Entropy Input
A DRBG takes an entropy input and other inputs (personalized string, nonce, etc.) to generate a sequence of pseudo-random bit strings. As shown in Figure 16.2, there exist three main alternatives to deliver an entropy input depending on noise source quality:

- A single source of noise is used (see Figure 16.2a): when a noise source delivers outputs, which are close to true-random bit-strings, the outputs of noise source can be directly used as input to the DRBG.
- A single source of noise is used jointly with conditioning function (see Figure 16.2b): when a noise source delivers outputs, which are not close to true-random bit-strings, the outputs are processed by a conditioning function to reduce the bias in the noise and then the outputs of the conditioning function are used as input to the DRBG. Recall that a conditioning function can be an encryption or a hash function.
- Multiple sources are used jointly with a conditioning function (see Figure 16.2c): when the entropy of a single noise source is not enough to deliver entropy input with the required length, multiple noise sources can be used and their outputs are concatenated to form an entropy bit-string, with a sufficient length, which then is processed with a conditioning function to generate the entropy input to the DRBG.

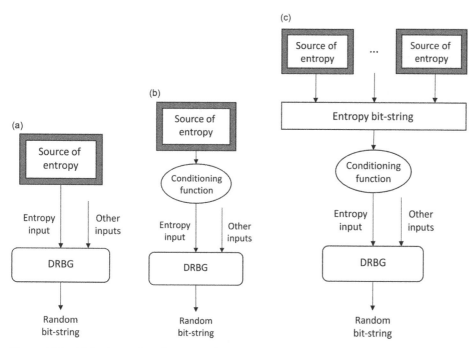

Figure 16.2 Main alternatives for entropy input.

When DRBGs recommended by the NIST are considered, the conditioning function may be one of the following:

- HMAC algorithm (see Section 5.3.2.1)
- AES-CMAC (see Section 9.2.2)
- AES-CBC-MAC[3]
- An approved hash function (see Table 16.1)
- `Hash_DerivationFunction` (see Section 16.2.2)
- `BC_DerivationFunction` (see Section 16.2.4)

16.1.4.2.2 Validation of Entropy Noise

In order to design an entropy source that provides an adequate amount of entropy per output bit-string, the developer must be able to accurately estimate the amount of entropy that can be provided by sampling the used noise source. The validation of an entropy source presents many challenges, because it depends on the environment of the security system and details of implementation. The general approach to validate a source of a DRBG is to sample the noise source and use statistical tests, such as Chi-square test, to assess the IID property of the outputs. The samples from a noise source are independent and identically distributed (IID), if each sample has the same probability distribution as every other sample, and all samples are mutually independent. The IID assumption significantly simplifies the process of entropy estimation. When the IID assumption does not hold, i.e. the samples are either not identically distributed or are not independently distributed (or both), estimating entropy is more difficult and requires other advanced methods. The recommended solution to reduce the imperfection (i.e. the bias) of a source of noise is to include a conditioning function. For more detail on recommended methods for testing entropy sources, refer to [5].

16.1.4.2.3 Full Entropy

It is recommended that the bit-strings used as entropy input of DRBGs are full entropy bit-strings. A bit-string has the full entropy property, if the amount of entropy is essentially the same as its length.

Definition 16.16 Full entropy bit-string: *it is a bit-string in which each bit is with a uniform distribution and independent of every other bits of that bit-string. A bit-string of n bits is said to have full entropy, if the bit-string is estimated to contain at least $(1-)n$ bits of entropy, where ε is a very small value (e.g. $\varepsilon \leq 2^{-64}$), which represents the upper bound on bias.*

In [6], it is considered that when a process (which may be a noise source, a noise source with conditioning function, or a combination of multiple noise sources) has an input with an entropy of at least $2n$, the process is sufficient to generate full entropy bit-strings of n bits.

16.1.4.2.4 Reseeding DRBGs

In general, in cryptography, the period of a PRNG is not an issue, if it is large (e.g. in magnitude of 2^{64}). However, in CSPRBGs, it is recommended to reseed the generation process (i.e. change the seed), for the following reasons:

1) Prevent against attackers being able to figure out numbers that were output before the internal state of the PRBG becomes compromised. Reseeding, is an efficient operation (with no extra cost), which protects against backtracking attacks. When entropy source is available on-demand, the DRBG is said to support *prediction resistance*.

Table 16.1 Recommended values and hash functions for DRBGs.

	SHA-224 and SHA-512/244	SHA-256 and SHA-512/256	SHA-384	SHA-512
Maximum provided security strength (^{5})	112	128	192	256
Seed bit-length	440	440	888	888
Maximum entropy-input bit-length	2^{35}	2^{35}	2^{35}	2^{35}
Maximum number of bits per generation-request	2^{19}	2^{19}	2^{19}	2^{19}
Maximum number of generation-requests between two reseed operations	2^{48}	2^{48}	2^{48}	2^{48}
Maximum personalization string bit-length	2^{35}	2^{35}	2^{35}	2^{35}
Maximum additional input string bit-length	2^{35}	2^{35}	2^{35}	2^{35}

2) To include fresh signals from the current source of entropy or to add new sources of entropy to the system in order to improve the randomness of the seed.

Reseeding is optional, but recommended, and it may be

- Explicitly requested by a consuming cryptographic application or service.
- Performed when prediction resistance is requested by a consuming application.
- Triggered when a predetermined number of pseudorandom outputs have been produced or a predetermined number of *generate* requests have been made (i.e. at the end of the seed life).
- Triggered by external events (e.g. whenever a new entropy is available).

As discussed in the next section, the NIST recommends to reseed a DRBG after some amount of generated bit-strings (see Tables 16.1 and 16.2).

16.1.4.2.5 Other Inputs of DRBGs

DRBGs used in practice are standard; and the sources of entropy rely on public algorithms. Therefore, most operational cryptographic applications and services make use of the same components to generate random numbers, which may result in a backdoor. In addition to entropy input, it is highly recommended to add other user-chosen inputs to DRBGs used in cryptography to enforce their resistance to attacks. In particular, DRBGs recommended by the NIST have three optional parameters: a personalization string, a nonce, and an additional input.

- *Personalization string*: it is intended to introduce additional input into the initialization of a DRBG. This personalization string might contain values unknown to attackers or values that tend to differentiate a DRBG instance from all others. Ideally, a personalization string is set to some bit string that is as unique as possible. Appropriate contents for the personalization bit-string include: device serial numbers, user identification, network addresses, protocol version identifiers, per-module or per-device values, random numbers generated with other PRNGs, and timestamps. A combination of the previous items can be used to form a personalization bit-string. The personalization string is used during the instantiation of the DRBG.
- *Nonce*: a nonce may be required in the construction of a seed during a DRBG instantiation in order to provide a security cushion to block certain attacks. Each nonce shall be unique to the cryptographic module in which instantiation is performed, but need not be secret. When used, the nonce shall be considered to be a critical security parameter. A nonce may be composed of one (or more) of the following components (other components may also be appropriate): a random value that is generated anew for each nonce, using an approved random bit generator; a timestamp of sufficient resolution, so that it is different each time it is used; a monotonically increasing sequence number; or combination of a timestamp and a monotonically increasing sequence number. When provided, the nonce is used in the DRBG instantiation and reseeding operations.
- *Additional input*: it is an optional input provided to reseeding operations and random bit-string generation requests and it aims to add randomness to the current state of the DRBG, so that each bit-string is generated using internal state of the DRBG and a user randomly-selected input.

Table 16.2 Recommended values for block-cipher-based DRBGs.

	3TDEA	AES-128	AES-192	AES-256
Maximum provided security strength	112	128	192	256
Seed bit-length	232	256	320	384
Maximum number of bits per request (^{6})	$\min(2^{13}, B)$	$\min(2^{19}, B)$	$\min(2^{19}, B)$	$\min(2^{19}, B)$
Max. number of requests between 2 reseed operations	2^{32}	2^{48}	2^{48}	2^{48}

	3TDEA or AES-(128, 192, 256)	
	With derivation function	Without derivation function
Maximum entropy-input bit-length	2^{35}	Seed bit-length
Maximum personalization string bit-length	2^{35}	Seed bit-length
Maximum additional input string bit-length	2^{35}	Seed bit-length

16.1.4.2.6 Conversion of a Bit-String into Integers

DRBGs generate bit-strings with a required bit-length of L, while algorithms (such as Diffie-Hellman) need random numbers in a range of $[1, n-1]$ to generate keying material. As depicted in Figure 16.3, to generate a random number from the output of a DRBG, a conversion operation is required. Currently, two conversion methods are recommended [7]: modular reduction and discard method.

16.1.4.2.6.1 Modular Reduction

DRBG output, a value in $[0, 2^L - 1]$, is reduced to an integer in the interval $[1, n-1]$, while ensuring that any bias introduced in the conversion is negligible, using the following procedure:

---

function ModularConversion
    input X: bit-string generated by a DRBG
           n: $n-1$ represents the maximum value of valid result
           ε: upper bound on bias (in general, $\varepsilon \leq 2^{-64}$)
    output Res: integer in range $[1, n-1]$
    1. $L = len(X); N = 2^L$
    2. **if** $(N < n)$, **then return** "Invalid" (# the bit-length of the output of the
          DRBG is not enough)
    3. $r = N \bmod (n-1); \rho = r / (n-1)$
    4. **if** $\big((2\rho(1-\rho)(n-1) > \varepsilon {*} N)\big)$, **then return** "Invalid"
    5. $z = BitStringToInteger(X)$ # Bit-string to integer conversion.
    6. $Res = (z \bmod n-1) + 1$
    7. **return** Res # Res is in range $[1, n-1]$

16.1.4.2.6.2 Discard Method

This method converts a probability distribution on $[0, n-1]$ into a probability distribution on $[0, 2^L - 1]$ and accepts an output value only if it is in both intervals, $[0, n-1]$ and $[0, N-1]$, using the following procedure:

---

function DiscardMethod
    input X: bit-string generated by a DRBG
           n: $n-1$ represents the maximum value of valid result; $n \geq 2$
    output Res: integer in range $[1, n-1]$
    1. $L = len(X); N = 2^L$
    2. **if** $\big((n \geq N) or (n < 2)\big)$, **then return** "Invalid"
    3. $z = BitStringToInteger(X)$ # Bit-string to integer conversion
    4. **if** $(z > n - 2)$, **then return** "Invalid"
    5. $Res = z + 1$
    6. **return** Res # Res is in the range $[0, n-1]$

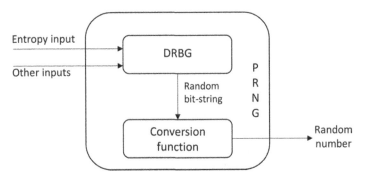

Figure 16.3 PRNG = DRBG + conversion function.

16.1.4.2.7 Conceptual Interface

Conceptually, a DRBG can be viewed as a black-box that can be accessed by users[4] requesting random bit-strings through an interface defined by at least four operations:

1) `Instantiate` function: it initializes the internal status of the DRBG, using the entropy input, the personalization string, and, optionally, a nonce. It builds the seed.
2) `Reseed` function: it acquires a new entropy input and combines it with the current internal state and any additional input that is provided to create a new seed and a new internal state.
3) `Generate` function: it enables the consuming application to query the DRBG to obtain a new rand bit-string.
4) `Health testing` function: it provides useful information to check if the DRBG continues to operate correctly or not.

16.2 Pseudorandom Bit Generators Recommended for Cryptography

In [4], the NIST recommends three models of DRBGs: hash-function-based, HMAC-based, and block-cipher-based DRBGs. The three models share common notions: inputs, internal state (i.e. variables that represent the current state of the DRBG), and access interface functions.

16.2.1 Common Mechanisms and Processes

16.2.1.1 Security Strength

If the seed is kept secret, the bits generated by the DRBG will be unpredictable, up to the instantiated security strength of the DRBG. The three specified DRBGs support four security strengths: 112, 128, 192, or 256 bits. The security strength is requested during the DRBG instantiation, and the `Instantiate` function obtains the appropriate amount of entropy for the requested security strength (see values in Tables 16.1 and 16.2). If the available entropy input does not have the required security strength, the instantiation fails. The maximum security strength supported by a specific DRBG instantiation depends on the DRBG implementation and on the amount of entropy used to feed the DRBG. In order to provide a security strength of S bits, the bit-length of the entropy input shall be of at least S. Once instantiated, a DRBG G is called to generate bit-strings with a bit-length L specified by the consuming application. The security strength of the output of a bit-length L is $SL(G, L) = min(L, DRBG\_SL(G))$, where $DRBG\_SL(G)$ denotes the maximum security strength level that the DRBG G can provide. Therefore, applications that require a certain security strength must request random bit-strings of a bit-length at least equal to the required security strength.

> **Note.** Using a random bit-string yielded by a concatenation of m outputs, each of L bits, of a DRBG with a maximum strength level of 128 bits, will not result in a security strength of $m * 128$ bits, but of $min(128, m * L)$.

16.2.1.2 Instantiating a DRBG

Any DRBG shall be instantiated before requesting random bit-strings. The instantiation process performs the following actions:

- If the security strength required by the consuming application is greater than the maximum security strength that can be provided by the DRBG, then return an error. Otherwise, set the *DRBG_instance_security_strength* to the lowest security strength greater than or equal to the required security strength from the set {112, 128, 192, 256}. *DRBG_instance_security_strength* is one of the constants of the internal state of the DRBG.
- If the lengths of some parameters do not comply with the limits (as specified in Tables 16.1 and 16.2), then return an error.
- Get the entropy input from the entropy source. If the used source of entropy does not have the capacity to deliver outputs with a bit-length that can provide the *DRBG_instance_security_strength*, then return an error.
- When the `Instantiate` function makes use of a nonce, obtain a nonce with a security strength of at least *DRBG_instance_security_strength* / 2.
- Use the `Instantiate` function to compute the initial state of the DRBG.

16.2.1.3 Reseeding a DRBG

Reseeding a DRBG does not change its *DRBG_instance_security_strength*. The reseeding process performs the following actions:

- If the lengths of some parameters do not comply with the limits (as specified in Tables 16.1 and 16.2), then return an error.
- Get the entropy input from the entropy source. If the used source of entropy does not have the capacity to deliver outputs with a bit-length that can provide the *DRBG_instance_security_strength*, then return an error.
- Use the `Reseed` function to compute the new internal state of the DRBG.

16.2.1.4   Internal State of a DRBG

Any DRBG instance has an internal state, which, in general, includes two categories of elements: common elements and specific elements. Elements common to all the three DRBG models include:

- Constants: the maximum security strength that can be provided by the DRBG instance (denoted *DRBG_instance_security_strength*), the bit-length of the seed (denoted *SeedLen*), the maximum bits per `generate` request, and the maximum number of `generate` requests before reseeding.
- Variable *ReseedCounter*, which indicates the number of random bit-strings generated since the instantiation of the DRBG or since the last reseeding action. It is reinitialized to 1 when the DRBG is reseeded.

16.2.1.5   Description Format of DRBG Functions

In the following subsections, the description of the DRBG functions are provided in sufficient detail with the following notation and restrictions:

- The specification of DRBG functions includes a clause **parameters**, which specifies the fixed values or functions used to build the DRBG functions before calling them, while the clause **input** specifies the values used in each function call.
- In the description of the DRBG functions, the test of cases of invalid calls (such as: the requested bit-length is greater than the fixed maximum value, the maximum number of requests is exceeded, etc.) are not included, assuming that the function calls are valid. Therefore, some specific details are omitted.

16.2.2   Hash-based DRBGs

Currently, two DRBGs based on hash functions are recommended: Hash-DRBG and HMAC-DRBG; their security strength is, at most, the same as the security strength of the hash function for pre-image resistance (see Table 16.1).

The recommended values and functions for hash-DRBG usage are provided in Table 16.1 [4].

> **Notes**
>
> – SHA-1 is deprecated for its insecurity and not recommended in DRBGs.
> – SHA3 is not recommended in [4]. However, it may be used to build (not NIST-approved) DRBGs.

A hash-based DRBG is characterized by its hash function. Its internal state consists of the common elements and two specific variables:

- V: a variable of the same bit-length than that of the seed. It changes each time a new random bit-string is generated;
- C: a variable of the same bit-length than that of the seed. It changes only when the DRBG is instantiated or reseeded.

Hash-DRBG instantiation

function Hash_DRBG_Instantiate
    parameters *Hash, Hlen*: hash function and its output bit-length
               SeedLen: bit-length of the seed
    input *EntropyInput*: bit-string generated by the entropy source
        Nonce: nonce; *PersonalizationString*: optional bit-string
    output $(V, C, ResedCounter)$: initial internal state of DRBG
    1. $Str\_Instantiate = EntropyInput \,||\, Nonce \,||\, PersonalizationString$
    2. $Seed = Hash\_DerivationFunction(Str\_Instantiate, SeedLen)$
    3. $V = Seed$
    4. $C = Hash\_DerivationFunction((0x00 \,||\, V), SeedLen)$
    5. $ReseedCounter = 1$
    6. **return** $(V, C, ReseedCounter)$

function *Hash_DerivationFunction*
    parameters *Hash, Hlen*: hash function and its output bit-length
            SeedLen: bit-length of the seed
    input *StrInput*: bit-string to hash; *ReqStrLen*: requested bit-length
    output *ResStr*: bit-string
    1. $Str = EmptyString()$; $m = \lceil ReqStrLen / Hlen \rceil$; $count = \text{0x01}$
    2. **for** j=1 **to** *m* **do**
        Str = Str || *Hash(count* || *ReqStrLen* || *StrInput)*
        count = count + 1
    3. $RndStrGen = leftmost\,(Str, ReqStrLen)$
    4. **return** *RndStrGen*

Hash-DRBG reseeding

function Hash_DRBG_Reseed
    parameters *SeedLen*: bit-length of the seed
    input $(V, C, ReseedCounter)$: current internal state of DRBG
        EntropyInput: bit-string generated by the entropy source
        AdditionalInput: optional bit-string
    output $(V, C, ReseedCounter)$: new internal state of DRBG
    1. $Str\_reseed = \text{0x01}$ || V || *EntropyInput* || *AdditionalInput*
    2. $Seed = Hash\_DerivationFunction(Str\_reseed, SeedLen)$
    3. $V = Seed$; $C = Hash\_DerivationFunction((\text{0x00}$ || $V), SeedLen)$
    4. $ReseedCounter = 1$
    5. **return** $(V, C, ReseedCounter)$

Hash-DRBG bit-string generation

function Hash_DRBG_Generate
    parameters *SeedLen*: bit-length of the seed
    input $(V, C, ReseedCounter)$: values of the current state of DRBG
        ReqStrLen: number of requested bits
        AdditionalInput: optional input bit-string
    output *RndStr*: returned random bit-string
        $(V, C, ReseedCounter)$: new internal state of DRBG
    1. **if** $(len\,(AdditionalInput) > 0)$, **then**
        $w = Hash\,(\text{0x02}$ || V || $AdditionalInput)$; $V = (V + w) \bmod 2^{SeedLen}$
    2. $RndStr = HashGen(ReqStrLen, V)$; $H = Hash(\text{0x03}$ || $V)$
    3. $V = (V + H + C + ReseedCounter) \bmod 2^{SeedLen}$
    4. $ReseedCounter = ReseedCounter + 1$
    5. **return** $(RndStr, V, C, ReseedCounter)$

function HashGen
    parameters *Hash, Hlen*: hash function and its output bit-length
            SeedLen: bit-length of the seed
    input *ReqStrLen*: number of requested bits
        V: variable in the internal state of DRBG
    output *RndStrGen*: returned random bit-string
    1. $m = \lceil ReqStrLen / Hlen \rceil$; $D = V$; $W = emptyString()$
    2. **for** j=1 **to** *m* **do**
        $W = W$ || $Hash(D)$; $D = (D + 1) \bmod 2^{SeedLen}$
    3. $RndStrGen = leftmost\,(W, ReqStrLen)$
    4. **return** *RndStrGen*

The overall structure of hash-based DRBGs is depicted in Figure 16.4; the pseudocodes of the DRBG functions are given below.

16.2.3 HMAC-based DRBGs

HMAC-DRBG iterates on an approved keyed hash function (see the list in Table 16.1).

In addition to the common elements, the internal state of an HMAC-DRBG instance includes two variables:

- Variable V: bit-string of the same bit-length than that of the used hash function.
- Variable Key: key of the same bit-length than that of the used hash function. Such a key changes from time to time; but it must change when a new random bit-string is generated.

The overall structure of HMAC-DRBGs is depicted in Figure 16.5; the pseudocodes of the DRBG functions are given below.

HMAC-DRBG instantiation

function HMAC_DRBG_Instantiate
    parameters *Hash*, *Hlen*: hash function and its output bit-length
    input   *EntropyInput*: random bit-string from the entropy source
            Nonce: a unique bit-string
            PersonalizationString: optional bit-string
    output $(V, Key, ReseedCounter)$: initial internal state of DRBG
    1. $Str\_Instantiate = EntropyInput \parallel Nonce \parallel PersonalizationString$
    2. $Key = 0^{(Hlen)}$ # a bit-string of *Hlen* 0-bits
    3. $V = 0x01010\ldots0101$ # a bit-string of *Hlen* alternating 0-1 bits
    4. $(Key, V) = HMAC\_DRBG\_Update(Str\_Instantiate, Key, V)$
    5. $ReseedCounter = 1$
    6. **return** $(V, Key, ReseedCounter)$

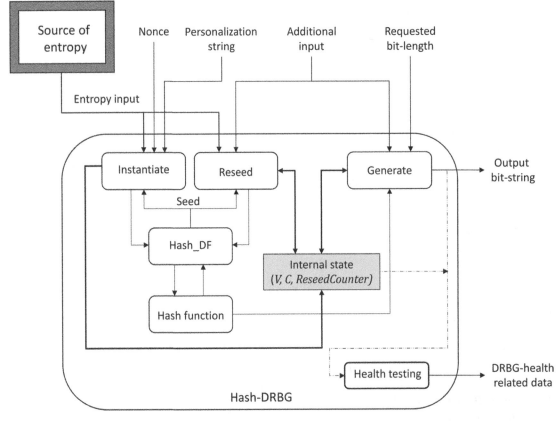

Figure 16.4 Overall structure of Hash-DRBG.

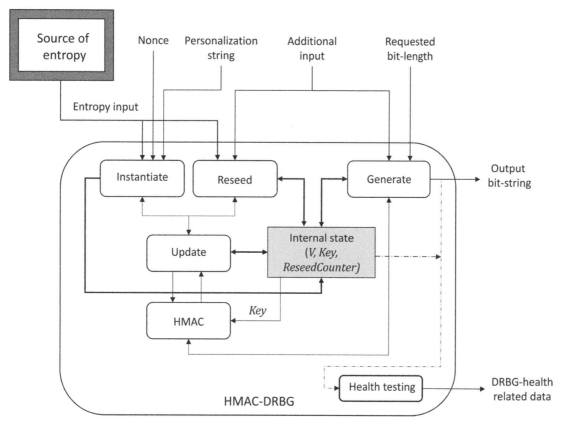

Figure 16.5 Overall structure of HMAC-DRBG.

---

function HMAC_DRBG_Update

    parameters *Hash, Hlen*: hash function and its output bit-length

    input *ProvidedData*: optional bit-string

        Key: current value of the key used in HMAC algorithm

        V: current value of variable *V*

    output *Key*: new value of the key; *V*: new value of variable *V*

    1. $Key = HMAC(Key, (V \| 0x00 \| ProvidedData)); V = HMAC(Key, V)$

    2. **if** $(len(ProvidedData) = 0)$, **then return** (Key, V)

    3. **else**

        $Key = HMAC(Key, V \| 0x01 \| (ProvidedData)); V = HMAC(Key, V)$

        return (Key, V)

HMAC-DRBG reseeding

function HMAC_DRBG_Reseed

    parameters *Hash, Hlen*: hash function and its output bit-length

    input $(V, Key, ReseedCounter)$: current internal state of DRBG

        EntropyInput: random bit-string from the entropy source

        AdditionalInput: optional bit-string

    output $(V, key, ReseedCounter)$: new internal state of DRBG

    1. $Str\_Reseed = EntropyInput \| AdditionalInput$

    2. $(Key, V) = HMAC\_DRBG\_Update(Str\_Reseed, Key, V)$

    3. $ReseedCounter = 1$

    4. **return** $(V, Key, ReseedCounter)$

HMAC-DRBG bit-string generation

function HMAC_DRBG_Generate

    parameters *SeedLen*: bit-length of the seed

    input $(V, Key, ReseedCounter)$: current internal state of DRBG

        ReqStrLen: number of requested bits

        AdditionalInput: optional input

    output *RndStr*: returned random bit-string

        $(V, Key, ReseedCounter)$: new internal state of DRBG

    1. **if** $(len(AdditionalInput) > 0)$, **then**

        (Key,V) = HMAC_DRBG_Update(AdditionalInput, Key, V)

    2. $Str = EmptyString()$

    3. **while** $(len(Str) < ReqStrLen)$ **do**

        $V = HMAC(Key, V)$; $Str = Str \parallel V$

    4. $RndStr = leftmost(Str, ReqStrLen)$

    5. $(Key, V) = HMAC\_DRBG\_Update(AdditionalInput, Key, V)$

    6. $ReseedCounter = ReseedCounter + 1$

    7. **return** $(RndStr, Key, V, ReseedCounter)$

16.2.4 Block Cipher-based DRBGs

CTR (CounTeR) mode of operation of block ciphers, which is introduced in Section 8.5, is used to build CTR-DRBGs. Recommended CTR-DRBGs make use of the encryption primitive of either 3-key TDEA or AES. Therefore, their security strength is, at maximum, the same as the security strength of the underlying block cipher (see Table 16.2).

Two methods are proposed to build CTR-DRBGs:

1) When the source of entry provides a full entropy, there is no need to use a block cipher derivation function.
2) If the source of entropy cannot provide a full entropy, a derivation function is used to provide the needed randomness.

In addition to the common elements, internal state of CTR-DRBG includes two variables:

- Variable V: bit-string of the same bit-length than that of the block length of the underlying block cipher (i.e. 64 bits for TDEA and 128 for AES).
- Variable *Key*: key of the same bit-length than that of by the underlying block cipher (i.e. 56 bits for TDEA, and 128, 192 or 256 for AES) used to encrypt.

Limits on CTR-DRBG parameters are summarized in Table 16.2. The overall structure of CTR-DRBGs is depicted in Figure 16.6; and pseudocodes of DRBG functions are given below.

CTR-DRBG instantiation

function CTR_DRBG_Instantiate

    parameters *DF_used*: boolean, which indicates if a derivation

                function is used in the implementation of DRBG

        BC.Encrypt: encryption primitive of AES or TDEA

        BlkLen: block bit-length of the used block cipher

        KeyLen: key bit-length of the used block cipher

        SeedLen: seed bit-length

    input *EntropyInput*: random bit-string from the entropy source

        Nonce: nonce (used only if *DF_used* is true)

        PersonalizationString: optional bit-string

    output $(V, Key, ReseedCounter)$: new internal state of DRBG

    1. $L = len(PersonalizationString)$

    2. **if** (DF_used), **then**

        Str_Instantiate = EntropyInput || Nonce || PersonalizationString

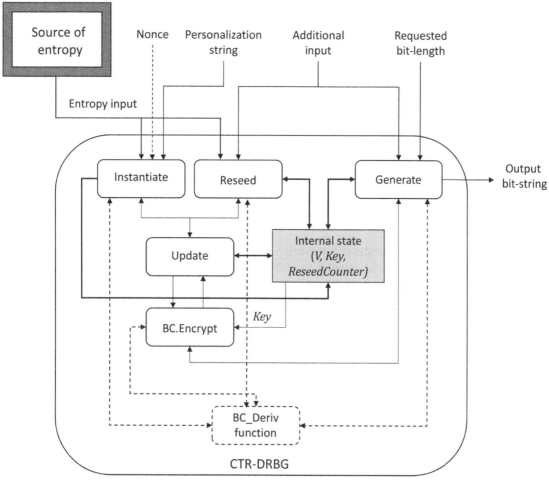

Figure 16.6 Overall structure of CTR-DRBG.

$Str\_Instantiate = BC\_DerivFunction(Str\_Instance, SeedLen)$
else
    $PersonalizationString = PersonalizationString \parallel 0^{((SeedLen-L))}$
    $Str\_Instantiate = EntropyInput \oplus PersonalizationString$
3. $Key = 0^{(KeyLen)}$ # a bit-string of $KeyLen$ 0-bits
4. $V = 0^{(BlkLen)}$ # a bit-string of $BlkLen$ 0-bits
5. $(Key, V) = CTR\_DRBG\_Update(Str\_Instantiate, Key, V)$
6. $ReseedCounter = 1$
7. **return** $(V, Key, ReseedCounter)$

function CTR_DRBG_Update
    parameters $BC.Encrypt$: encryption primitive of either TDEA or AES
                       $BlkLen$: block bit-length of the used block cipher
                       $KeyLen$: key bit-length of the used block cipher
                       $CtrLen$: a value between 4 and $BlkLen$, which specifies how the
                       input V is incremented (full or partial increment). See step 2.1.
                       $SeedLen$: seed bit-length
    input $ProvidedData$: optional bit-string
             Key: current value of the key used to encrypt
             V: current value of variable V of DRBG
    output Key: new value of the key
             V: new value of variable V

1. $Str = EmptyString()$
2. **while** $\left(len\left(Str\right) < SeedLen\right)$ **do**
   2.1 **if** $\left(CtrLen < BlkLen\right)$ **then**
      $inc = (rightmost(V, CtrLen) + 1) \, mod \, 2^{CtrLen}$
      $V = leftmost\left(V, BlkLen - CtrLen\right) \| inc$
      else $V = \left(V + 1\right) mod \, 2^{BlkLen}$
   2.2 $Str = Str \| BC.Encrypt\left(Key, V\right)$
3. $Str = leftmost\left(Str, SeedLen\right) \oplus ProvidedData$
4. $Key = leftmost\left(Str, KeyLen\right); V = rightmost\left(Str, BlkLen\right)$
5. **return** $\left(Key, V\right)$

CTR-DRBG reseeding

function CTR_DRBG_Reseed

parameters   *DF_used*: boolean, which indicates if a derivation
                    function is used in the implementation of DRBG
              SeedLen: seed bit-length

input $\left(V, Key, ReseedCounter\right)$: variable values of the current state
      EntropyInput: random bit-string from the entropy source
      AdditionalInput: optional bit-string

output $\left(Key, V, ReseedCounter\right)$: new internal state of DRBG

1. $L = len\left(AdditionalInput\right)$
2. **if** $\left(DF\_used\right)$, **then**
    $Str\_Reseed = EntropyInput \| AdditionalInput$
    $Str\_Reseed = BC\_DerivFunction\left(Str\_Reseed, SeedLen\right)$
  else
    $AdditionalInput = AdditionalInput \| 0^{\left(SeedLen - L\right)}$
    $Str\_Reseed = EntropyInput \oplus AdditionalInput$
3. $\left(Key, V\right) = CTR\_DRBG\_Update\left(Str\_Reseed, Key, V\right)$
4. $ReseedCounter = 1$
5. **return** $\left(V, Key, ReseedCounter\right)$

CTR-DRBG bit-string generation

function CTR_DRBG_Generate

    parameters *DF_used*: boolean, which indicates if a derivation function
               is used in the implementation of DRBG
              SeedLen: bit-length of the seed
    input $\left(V, Key, ReseedCounter\right)$: current internal state of DRBG
       ReqStrLen: number of requested bits
       AdditionalInput: optional input
    output *RndStr*: returned random bit-string
       $\left(V, Key, ReseedCounter\right)$: new internal state of DRBG
1. $L = len\left(AdditionalInput\right)$
2. **if** $\left(L > 0\right)$, **then**
    2.1 **if** $\left(DF\_used\right)$, **then**
      $AdditionalInput = BC\_DerivFunction\left(AdditionalInput, SeedLen\right)$
      else $AdditionalInput = AdditionalInput \| 0^{\left(SeedLen - L\right)}$
    2.2 $\left(Key, V\right) = CTR\_DBRG\_Update\left(AdditionalInput, Key, V\right)$
    else $AdditionalInput = 0^{\left(SeedLen\right)}$
3. $Str = EmptyString()$
4. **while** $\left(len\left(str\right) < ReqStrLen\right)$ **do**

4.1 **if** $\left(CtrLen < BlkLen \right)$, **then**

$\qquad inc = \left(rightmost \left(V, CtrLen \right) + 1 \right) mod \; 2^{CtrLen}$

$\qquad V = \left(\left(leftmost \left(V, BlkLen - CtrLen \right) \right) + 1 \right) \| \; inc$

$\qquad$ **else** $V = \left(V + 1 \right) mod \; 2^{CtrLen}$

4.2 $Str = Str \| BC.Encrypt \left(Key, V \right)$

5. $RndStr = leftmost \left(Str, ReqStrLen \right)$

6. $\left(Key, V \right) = CTR\_DBRG\_Update \left(AdditionalInput, Key, V \right)$

7. $ReseedCounter = ReseedCounter + 1$

8. **return** $\left(RndStr, Key, V, ReseedCounter \right)$

---

function BC_DerivFunction # Block cipher derivation function

$\qquad$ **parameters** $\quad$ *BC.Encrypt*: encryption primitive of AES or TDEA

$\qquad\qquad\qquad\qquad$ *BlkLen*: bit-block length of the underlying block cipher

$\qquad$ **input** *ProvidedData*: bit-string; *ReqStrLen*: number of requested bits

$\qquad$ **output** *RndStr*: returned random bit-string

1. $L = len \left(ProvidedData \right) / 8 \quad$ # *L* is a 32-bits integer

2. $N = ReqStrLen / 8 \quad$ # *N* is a 32-bits integer

3. $S = L \| N \| ProvidedData \| 0x80$

4. **while** $\left(\left(len \left(S \right) mod \; BlkLen \right) \neq 0 \right)$ **do** $S = S \| 0x00$

5. $Str = EmptyString()$

6. $i = 0$

7. $K = leftmost \left(0x00010203 \ldots 1D1E1F, KeyLen \right)$

8. **while** $\left(len \left(Str \right) < KeyLen + BlkLen \right)$ **do**

$\qquad$ 8.1 $IV = i \| 0^{BlkLen - len(i)}; \; S\_tmp = IV \| S$

$\qquad$ 8.2 $chain = 0^{(BlkLen)}; \; n = len \left(S\_tmp \right) / BlkLen$

$\qquad$ 8.3 # starting from the leftmost bits, split *S_tmp* into *n* blocks of

$\qquad\qquad$ *BlkLen* bits:

$\qquad\qquad \left(B_1, B_2, \ldots, B_n \right) = Split\_in\_blocks \left(S\_tmp, BlkLen \right)$

$\qquad$ 8.4 **for** $i = 1$ ***to*** n **do** $\{ B = chain \oplus B_i; \; chain = BC.Encrypt \left(B \right) \}$

$\qquad$ 8.5 $Str = Str \| chain; \; i = i + 1$

9. $Key = leftmost \left(Str, KeyLen \right)$

10. # pick bits at positions from *KeyLen* + 1 to *KeyLen* + *BlKLen* in *str*

$\qquad Z = select\_bits \left(Str, KeyLen + 1, Kelen + BlkLen \right)$

11. $str = EmptyString()$

12. **while** $\left(len \left(Str \right) < ReqStrLen \right)$ **do**

$\qquad Z = BC.Encrypt \left(Key, Z \right); \; Str = Str \| Z$

13. $RndStr = leftmost \left(Str, ReqStrLen \right)$

14. **return** $RndStr$

16.3 Prime Number Generation

Public-key cryptographic algorithms (such as RSA, Diffie-Hellman, and MQV algorithms) require prime numbers to select their domain parameters (i.e. public and private keys and other parameters). The first approach is to use true primes, also called provable primes. As discussed in this section, generating provable primes may be very time consuming. The second approach is to use numbers that are very likely to be primes; such numbers are referred to as probably-primes.

In the previous section, we discussed methods for generating large random numbers. Since there are no guarantees that a random number is prime, we need to test if a randomly generated number is prime before using it. The problem of determining whether a given number is prime has become a challenge for centuries. With the event of computer-based systems, the issue had become more challenging, because larger and larger prime numbers are required to strengthen the security of infrastructures and services. This section aims at introducing some basics of prime numbers and the NIST-recommended methods to generate primes for use in Diffie-Hellman, Menezes-Qu-Vanstone, and RSA algorithms.

16.3.1 Basics and Facts about Primes

16.3.1.1 Definition of Some Prime Categories of Interest for Cryptography

Definition 16.17 Provable prime (or **true prime**): *it is a prime that is confirmed using a deterministic algorithm.*

Definition 16.18 Probably prime (or **pseudoprime**): *a large odd integer p is said to be probably prime if there is a high probability that it is prime. An integer p is probably prime if it has not been demonstrated to be either composite or prime.*

Definition 16.19 Safe prime and **Sophie Germain prime**: *a prime p is said to be safe prime, if there exists a prime q, called Sophie Germain prime, such that $p = 2q + 1$.*

Example 16.4
11 is a safe prime, because $11 = 2 * 5 + 1$.
83 is a safe prime, because $83 = 2 * 41 + 1$.
381 is a safe prime, because $381 = 2 * 191 + 1$.

Definition 16.20 Mersenne prime: *a prime p is said to be a Mersenne prime, if there exists a positive integer m, such that $p = 2^m - 1$.*

Definition 16.21 Strong prime: *it is an integer p satisfying the following conditions:*

- *p is chosen at random using a PRNG.*
- *p is a large prime.*
- *$p - 1$ has a large prime factor p_1.*
- *$p + 1$ has a large prime factor p_2.*
- *$p_1 - 1$ has a prime factor p_3.*

Example 16.5 Below are two strong primes (not usable in cryptography)

– 127 is a (non-cryptographic) strong prime, because
  $127 - 1 = 126$ has a prime factor of 7.
  $127 + 1 = 128$ has a prime factor of 2.
  $7 - 1 = 6$; and 6 has a prime factor of 3.
– 331 is a (non-cryptographic) strong prime, because
  $331 - 1 = 330$ has a prime factor of 11.
  $331 + 1 = 332$ has a prime factor of 83.
  $11 - 1 = 10$; and 10 has a prime factor of 5.

Currently, the method recommended to generate provable primes for FFC and IFC algorithms is based on Shawe-Taylor's algorithm, which generates strong primes (see Section 16.3.4).

16.3.1.2 Distribution of Prime Numbers

The prime number theorem is well-known in mathematics and tells us the following:

Theorem 16.1 *(Prime number theorem)*

For an integer $n > 1$, the number of primes not greater than n, denoted $\pi(n)$, may be approximated by $\frac{n}{ln(n)}$; i.e. $\lim_{n \to \infty} \left(\frac{\pi(n)}{\frac{n}{ln(n)}} \right) = 1$, where ln denotes the natural logarithm.

Thus, for a large integer n, the probability that a random integer, not greater than n, is prime is approximately $\frac{1}{\log(n)}$; and the average gap between consecutive prime numbers out of the first n integers is approximately $ln(n)$.

Example 16.6 Recall that for a prime p to be used to generate keys of RSA with a modulus of 2048 bits, it shall fulfill the condition $2^{\frac{2048-1}{2}} \leq p < 2^{2048/2}$. The number of primes that can be used for p is approximated, using the prime number theorem, by:

$$\pi\left(2^{\frac{2048}{2}}\right) - \pi\left(2^{\frac{2047}{2}}\right) = \frac{2^{\frac{2048}{2}}}{ln\left(2^{\frac{2048}{2}}\right)} - \frac{2^{\frac{2047}{2}}}{ln\left(2^{\frac{2047}{2}}\right)} = \frac{2^{\frac{2048}{2}}}{\frac{2048}{2} * ln(2)} - \frac{2^{\frac{2047}{2}}}{\frac{2047}{2} * ln(2)}$$

$$= \frac{1}{ln(2)} * \left(\frac{2^{\frac{2048}{2}}}{2^{10}} - \frac{2^{\frac{2047}{2}}}{2^{10} - \frac{1}{2}}\right) \cong \frac{2^{\frac{2047}{2}}}{ln(2) * 2^{10}} * \left(2^{\frac{1}{2}} - 1\right) = 2^{\frac{2027}{2}} * 0.597$$

16.3.2 Methods for Primality Testing

Two methods are used for primality testing of numbers used in cryptographic algorithms: probabilistic and deterministic tests. Deterministic primality testing algorithms either confirm, with certainty, that an integer is a prime or output "Failure", if the specified number of tries is exceeded. They are computationally intensive and require that tested integers have some properties, which makes them unusable in practice when the numbers to be tested are randomly generated and of bit-lengths of hundreds or thousands (e.g. RSA primes p and q are required to have bit-lengths greater than 1023). The second category of primality tests are probabilistic in nature; they either confirm, with certainty, that the tested integer is composite or they stop the algorithm, with a conclusion "the tested integer is probably prime."

16.3.2.1 Deterministic Methods for Primality Testing

First of all, it is worth noticing that deterministic primality testing methods are computationally intensive and/or applicable under specific assumptions. In this subsection, we introduce the three best known deterministic tests of primality.

16.3.2.1.1 Generating Primes Using Sieve-of-Eratosthenes Method and Trial Division Test

a) *Generating primes using the sieve-of-Eratosthenes method*
The sieve of Eratosthenes is an ancient deterministic method for finding prime numbers up to a given n greater than 1. It is one of the methods recommended to generate a list of primes. The idea behind the method is that a number is prime, if none of the smaller prime numbers divides it. The list of primes are computed as follows:

1) Build an initial set $S = \{2, 3, 4, ..., n\}$.
2) For $p = 1$ to $\lfloor \sqrt{n} \rfloor$: discard any element $z \in S$ such that $z = k * p$, where k is an integer greater than 1.
3) The final set s contains only primes.

The time complexity of sieve of Eratosthenes method is of $O(n \log \log n)$.

b) *Trial division method for primality testing*
The basic method for testing if an integer is a prime is called *trial division primality testing*. It is applicable to any positive integer. It is of a naïve design:

1) Let z be the integer to be tested.
2) Using the sieve of Eratosthenes method (or another method), build a table of primes less than $\sqrt{n}$.
3) Declare z prime, if no integer in the prime table divides it.

16.3.2.1.2 Lucas-Lehmer Test

When the integer p to be tested can be written as $p = 2^m - 1$, i.e. p is a Mersenne number, the following test, called Lucas-Lehmer test, is known to be efficient for testing, with certainty, if p is a prime. The test is based on a known fact that a Mersenne number $p = 2^m - 1$ can be prime only for prime m. Lucas-Lehmer primality test may be defined by the following function:

```
function Lucas-Lehmer_Primality_Test
    input p = 2^m − 1, number to be tested
    output "Prime" or "Not prime"
    1. s_0 = 4
    2. for i = 1 to m − 2 do s_i = (s²_{i−1} − 2) mod p
    3. if (s_i = 0), then return "Prime"
    4. else return "Not prime"
```

Example 16.7 Consider $p = 2^7 - 1$ and apply Lucas-Lehmer test to check if p is a prime. The generated sequence is: $s_0 = 4$, $s_1 = 14$, $s_2 = 67$, $s_3 = 42$, $s_4 = 111$, $s_5 = 0$. Hence, $2^7 - 1 = 127$ is a prime.

16.3.2.1.3 Lucas's Primality Test

In 1876, Edouard Lucas turned Fermat's little theorem (Theorem 3.5) into a primality test. He proved the following theorem:

Theorem 16.2 *(Lucas's primality test)*
Let n be a positive integer. If there exists an integer a, $1 < a < n$, such that:

$$a^{n-1} \equiv 1 \bmod n$$

and for every prime factor q of $n-1$, $a^{(n-1)/q} \not\equiv 1 \bmod n$, then n is a prime.

Lucas's test is considered as the basis of modern primality tests; it outputs "Prime" only if the tested integer is prime. However, it requires too much time to find the integer a (if it exists), when n is a large integer.

16.3.2.1.4 Pocklington-Lehmer Primality Test

Pocklington-Lehmer primality test was proposed in 1927 and it is based on the following theorem:

Theorem 16.3 *(Pocklington-Lehmer test of primality)*
Let n be a positive integer such that $n - 1 = F * R$, where F and R are coprime, $F > R$, and the prime factorization of F is known. If for each prime factor p of F, there exists an integer a_p, $1 < a_p < n$, such that:

$$a_p^{n-1} \equiv 1 \bmod n \text{ and } GCD\left(a_p^{(n-1)/p} - 1, n\right) = 1, \text{ then } n \text{ is a prime.}$$

It is worth noticing that the NIST recommends the Pocklington-Lehmer primality test to generate provable primes.

Example 16.8 We make use of Pocklington-Lehmer theorem to check the primality of $n = 547$, which is known to be prime.

- Factor $547 - 1$ as $(2 * 3 * 13) * 7$; i.e. $F = (2 * 3 * 13)$ and $R = 7$. F and R fulfill the theorem requirements.
- Using a tool, which provides GCD and modular exponentiation functions, we try different integers a for $p = 13$, which is a prime factor of F:

Start with $a = 2$:

$$2^{546} \equiv (2)^{(2*3*7)*13} \bmod 547 \equiv (475)^{13} \bmod 547 = 1$$

$$GCD\left(2^{\frac{546}{13}} - 1, 547\right) = 1$$

Conditions of the theorem are met. Therefore, we stop the search and confirm that 547 is a prime.

16.3.2.2 Probabilistic Methods for Primality Testing

The two well-known algorithms for probabilistic primality testing are addressed below. Miller-Rabin primality test is the one recommended by the NIST.

16.3.2.2.1 Fermat's Primality Test and Carmichael Numbers

The following theorem, which is an alternate statement of Fermat's little theorem, provides a fast method to check if an integer is not a prime.

> **Theorem 16.4** *(alternate statement of Fermat's little theorem)*
> If $a^{p-1} \not\equiv 1 \bmod p$ for some a coprime to p, then p is not prime.

Theorem 16.4 enables to answer the question: Isn't an integer x prime? The inverse statement of Theorem 16.4 is not always true. That is, if $a^{p-1} \equiv 1 \bmod p$, for some a coprime to p, then p is not always prime, as shown by the following counterexamples. When $a^{p-1} \equiv 1 \bmod p$, while composite, a is called a Fermat *liar* for p.

Example 16.9 $2^{10} \equiv 1 \bmod 341$; hence, $(2^{10})^{34} \equiv (1)^{34} \bmod 341 = 1$, but 341 is not prime, as it is equal to $31 * 11$. Therefore, 2 is a Fermat liar for 341.

$5^{80} \equiv 1 \bmod 561$; thus, $(5^{80})^7 \equiv (1)^7 \bmod 561 = 1$, but 561 is not prime, as it is equal to $17 * 11 * 3$. Therefore, 5 is a Fermat liar for 561.

One of the seminal works on primality testing was proposed by Fermat. The latter came up with the following algorithm, which is a direct application of Theorem 16.4:

> **Fermat's primality test**
> To test whether an integer p is prime or composite, choose an integer a at random and compute $a^{p-1} \bmod p$. Then,
> 1. **if** $a^{p-1} \not\equiv 1 \bmod p$, **then** declare p composite.
> 2. **if** $a^{p-1} \equiv 1 \bmod p$, **then** declare p *probably prime*, and optionally take another integer a and redo the test.

Fermat's primality test is not efficient to declare with a low probability that an integer n is prime. However, it was a starting idea for many primality tests in literature. Since, by design, a random integer a is picked for testing, the algorithms that improved Fermat's test are probabilistic in nature. A number of iterations should be fixed in advance to stop the algorithm, if the input p is not declared composite. That is why the result of the test is "Probably prime". In the sequel, the focus is on the most referenced and used primality test, the one proposed by Miller and Rabin [8, 9].

Definition 16.22 Carmichael number: *an integer n is said to be Carmichael number if there exists an integer a coprime to n such that $a^{n-1} \equiv 1 \bmod n$.*

Example 16.10 561 is a Carmichael number, because $561 = 3 * 11 * 17$.

If we take any $a < 561$ and a coprime to 561, $a^{560} \equiv 1 \bmod 561$. For example, $2^{560} \equiv 1 \bmod 561$. However, $3^{560} \equiv 375 \bmod 561$, because 3 is not coprime with 561.

Property of Carmichael numbers: any Carmichael number n is composite and will pass Fermat's primality test, for any number a coprime to n.

As numbers become very large, Carmichael numbers become very rare. For example, it is shown in [10] that there exist approximately 20 million Carmichael numbers between 1 and 10^{21}. Hence, the probability to pick a Carmichael number, from the interval $[1, 10^{21}]$, is very low (i.e. approximately $5 * 10^{-13}$). Therefore, for randomly chosen odd integer n with hundreds of digits, the probability for n to be a Carmichael number is zero for practical purpose. Such a property limits the number of false positives yielded by Fermat's primality test.

16.3.2.2.2 Miller-Rabin Primality Test

The basic idea of Miller-Rabin primality test is that given a positive integer p, if we randomly pick k integers less than p and if all of them are coprime with p, then it is very likely that p is a prime. Miller-Rabin primality test is probabilistic in nature; hence, it is prone to decision errors. The probability that a composite integer is declared probably prime depends on the number of iterations (i.e. the number of the tested random integers). Rabin [9] proved that the probability that a composite number p is erroneously asserted to be probably prime is smaller than 2^{-2k}, if k random integers less than p are tested. The interpretation of such a probability means that if the test is applied to 2^{2k} randomly chosen integers, the expected wrong answers is 1.

Miller-Rabin test for primality takes advantage of the following fact:

> **Lemma 16.1**[7] If $a^{(n-1)/2} \not\equiv \pm 1 \bmod n$, with n coprime to a, then n must be composite.

Below is the pseudocode of Miller-Rabin primality test.

---

function Miller_Rabin_Primality_Test
    input p: integer to be tested; $p > 1$
        Nb_iterations: maximum number of iterations to perform
    output Decision: "Probably prime" or "Composite"
    1. Find a, the largest integer such that 2^a divides $p - 1$
    2. $m = \dfrac{p-1}{2^a}$; $L = len(p)$

    3. **for** $i = 1$ **to** *Nb_iterations* **do**
        3.1 Using a random number generator, obtain a random
            integer b with a bit-length of L
        3.2 **if** (($b \leq 1$) or($b \geq p - 1$)), **then go to** step 4.1
        3.3 $V = b^m \bmod p$
        3.4 **if** (($V = 1$) or ($V = p - 1$)), **then go to** step 4.7
        3.5 **for** $j = 1$ **to** $a - 1$ **do**
            $V = V^2 \bmod p$
            if ($V = p - 1$), **then go to** step 4.7
            if ($V = 1$), **then return** ("Composite")
            continue
        3.6 **return** ("Composite")
        3.7 **continue**
    4. **return** ("Probably prime")

Example 16.11   Primality test of 1729 with one iteration
– Assume that the selected random value is $b = 57$
   Step 1:
       $1729 = 2^6 * 27 + 1$. Thus, $a = 6$ and $m = 27$
   Step 4: (1st iteration)
       4.1 Let $b = 57$ be the selected random value
       4.3 $V = 57^{27} \bmod 1729 = 190$
       4.5.1 $j=1$: $V = 190^2 \bmod 1729 = 1520$
       4.5.1 $j=2$: $V = 1520^2 \bmod 1729 = 456$
       4.5.1 $j=3, 4, 5$: $V = 456^2 \bmod 1729 = 456$.
       4.6 Return Composite
– Assume that selected random value is $b = 712$
   Step 1:
       $1729 = 2^6 * 27 + 1$. Thus, $a = 6$ and $m = 27$
   Step 4: (1st iteration)
       4.1 Let $a = 712$ be the selected random value
       4.3 $V = 712^{27} \bmod 1729 = 818$
       4.5.1 $j=1$: $V = 818^2 \bmod 1729 = 1$
       Return "Composite"
Comment: in both scenarios, the result is correct, because $1729 = 7 * 13 * 19$.

16.3.3 Generation of Probably-Prime Pair

The algorithms introduced below generate probably-prime pair that comply with the FFC and IFC domain parameter requirements (see Sections 14.2.2.1–14.2.2.2).

16.3.3.1 Generation of Probably-Prime Pair for DH and MQV

The function below, recommended in [11], provides a solution to generate a pair of integers p and p, that are probably-prime, to be used in Diffie-Hellman and Menezes-Qu-Vanstone protocols. It makes use of a hash function, a DRBG, and Miller-Rabin primality test. $DRBG.generate\left(bl\right)$ denotes the invocation of the underlying DRBG to generate an integer of a bit-length of bl. In addition to the probably-prime pair, the function optionally may return a *Seed* and a *Counter* that can be used as an FFC domain parameters to check the compliance to standard of generated parameters.

---

function Generate_Probably_Prime_Pair_FFC

    parameters *Hash*, *Hlen*: hash function and its output bit-length

    input Len_p, Len_q: requested bit-lengths of primes p and q, respectively

                  SeedLen: seed bit-length, where $SeedLen \geq Len_q$

    output p, q: generated probably-primes

                  Seed: seed computed when generating the primes (optional)

                  Ctr: counter computed when generating the primes

1. $n = \left\lceil \dfrac{Len_p}{Hlen} \right\rceil - 1; b = Len_p - 1 - (n * Hlen)$

2. $Seed = DRBG.generate\left(SeedLen\right); U = Hash\left(Seed\right) \bmod 2^{Len_q - 1}$

3. $q = 2^{Len_q - 1} + U + 1 - (U \bmod 2)$

4. **if** $\left(Miller\_Rabin\_Primality\_Test\left(q\right) = \text{"} Probably\ prime\text{"}\right)$,

    then go to step 3

5. $Offset = 1$

6. **for** $Counter = 0$ **to** $(4 * Len_p - 1)$ **do**

    6.1 **for** $j = 0$ **to** n **do** $V_j = \left(Hash\left(Seed + Offset + j\right) \bmod 2^{SeedLen}\right)$

    6.2 $W = \left(\sum_{j=0}^{n-1}\left(Vj * 2^{j*Hlen}\right)\right) + \left(\left(V_n \bmod 2^b\right) * 2^{n*Hlen}\right)$

    6.3 $X = W + 2^{Len_p - 1}; c = X \bmod 2 * q$

    6.4 $p = X - (c - 1)$ # $p \equiv 1 \bmod 2 * q$, which is required for FFC domain parameters

    6.5 **if** $\left(p < 2^{Len_p - 1}\right)$ **go to** step 8.8

    6.6 **if** $\left(Miller\_Rabin\_Primality\_Test\left(q\right) = \text{"} Probably prime\text{"}\right)$,

    then go to step 10

    6.7 $Offset = Offset + n + 1$

7. **go to** step 3

8. **return** $(p, q, Seed, Counter)$

Notice that the function above stops only when a probably-prime pair is found, while the other functions presented in the sequel have a limit in the number of tries and may fail in producing valid outputs [11] does not provide evidence that the algorithm terminates within a reasonable time.

16.3.3.2 Generation of Probably-Prime Pair for RSA

The function below, recommended in [11], provides a solution to generate a pair of integers, p and q, that are very likely to be primes, to be used in RSA. It makes use of a hash function, a DRBG, and Miller-Rabin primality test. The inputs are the bit-length of the modulus (i.e. 2048, 3072, 4092, etc.) and the public exponent.

---

function Generate_Probably_Prime_Pair_RSA

    input   *ModLen*: bit-length of the modulus $p * q$; e: public exponent

    output *status*: "Success" or "Failure"; p, q: generated probably-primes

1. # Generate p

    1.1 $i = 0; p = DRBG.generate\left(\frac{ModLen}{2}\right)$

    1.2 **if** $\left(Not\left(Odd(p)\right)\right)$, **then** $p = p + 1$

1.3 **if** $\left(p < 2^{(ModLen-1)/2}\right)$ **then go to** step 1.2

1.4 **if** $(GCD(p-1, e) = 1),$ **then**

    if $(Miller\_Rabin\_Primality\_Test(q) = "Probably\ prime"),$

    then go to step 2

1.5 $i = i + 1$

1.6 **if** $(i \geq 5 * Modlen/2),$ **then return** $("Failure", 0, 0)$

    else go to step 1.2

2. # Generate q

   2.1 $i = 0; q = DRG.generate\left(\frac{ModLen}{2}\right)$

   2.2 **if** $\left(Not\left(Odd\left(q\right)\right)\right),$ **then** $q = q + 1$

   2.3 **if** $\left(q < 2^{(ModLen-1)/2}\right)$ **go to** step 2.2

   2.4 **if** $\left(\left|p - q\right| < 2^{\left(\frac{ModLen}{2} - 100\right)}\right)$ **go to** step 2.2

   2.5 **if** $\left(GCD\left(q - 1, e\right) = 1\right),$ **then**

      if $\left(Miller\_Rabin\_Primality\_Test\left(q\right) = "Probably\ prime"\right),$

      then return $\left("Success", p, q\right)$

   2.6 $i = i + 1$

   2.7 **if** $\left(i \geq 5 * Modlen / 2\right),$ **then return** $\left("Failure", 0, 0\right)$

    else go to step 2.2

Note. The algorithm above may fail in finding a pair of probably primes.

Minimum number of iterations

When Miller-Rabin test is used, the accuracy (i.e. the probability that a number is erroneously declared probably-prime) depends on the number of iterations and the bit-length of the integer to be tested. The NIST recommends that the minimum number of iterations is of 40.

16.3.4 Generation of Provable Primes

16.3.4.1 Shawe-Taylor Algorithm

Shaw-Taylor proposed an efficient algorithm to generate strong primes [12]. When the algorithm succeeds (it may fail to generate a prime), the generated number is guaranteed to be a true prime. Shawe-Taylor's algorithm is recommended by the NIST for generating provable primes to be used in cryptographic algorithms (precisely, DH, MQV, and RSA) [11]. Shawe-Taylor's algorithm is a recursive function, which takes a seed and a bit-length of the prime to be generated, and it provides the following outputs: a status, which indicates if a prime has been found or not, a provable prime (if any), and a counter (i.e. the number of tries before finding a prime). To make it easy to understand the principle of Shawe-Taylor's function, assume that all the calls are successful. Shawe-Taylor's function proceeds as follows:

- Let *ReqLen* denote the bit-length of the prime to generate.
- First case: *ReqLen* < 33:
  There is a single call to the function, which performs as follows: a random integer c is generated and its primality is tested using the trial division primality test (see Section 16.3.2.1.1). Then, an output, which depends on the primality test, is returned.
- Second case: $33 \leq ReqLen \leq 62$:
  There are two calls to the function, which generate two primes. That is, the function is called with a requested bit-length of *ReqLen*, which is greater than 32. Then, the function is recursively called with a requested bit-length of $\lceil ReqLen / 2 \rceil + 1,$

which is less than 33, and it returns a prime (if any), denoted c_0. Then, an integer $2*t*c_0+1$ is generated. The value of t is chosen such that c is guaranteed to be less than 2^{ReqLen}. Finally, the primality of c is tested using Pocklington-Lehmer primality test and an output is returned.

- Third case: $63 \leq ReqLen$:
The first call generates a prime $c_1 = 2*t_1*c_2+1$, of a bit-length of $ReqLen$. The second call generates a prime $c_2 = 2*t_2*c_3+1$, of a bit-length of $\lceil ReqLen/2 \rceil + 1$.

The third call generates a prime $c_3 = 2*t_3*c_4+1$, of a bit-length of $\left\lceil \dfrac{\left\lceil \frac{ReqLen}{2} \right\rceil + 1}{2} \right\rceil + 1$. If $\left\lceil \dfrac{\left\lceil \frac{ReqLen}{2} \right\rceil + 1}{2} \right\rceil$ is less than 32, then c_4

is the first fully-generated prime. Otherwise, the division process of the initial requested bit-length, $ReqLen$, continues.

Test of primality used by Shawe-Taylor's algorithm:

1) When the requested bit-length of the prime to generate, denoted $ReqLen$, is greater than 62, the output of Shawe-Taylor's algorithm is defined by $c = 2*t*c_0+1$, where c_0 is a prime in the interval $[2^{\lceil ReqLen/2 \rceil}, 2^{\lceil ReqLen/2 \rceil+1}-1]$ (see steps 11 and 15.2.4 in the pseudocode below).

2) In steps 15.4.1 and 15.4.2 of the pseudocode below, the Pocklington-Lehmer primality test (see Section 16.3.2.1.4) is applied to $n-1 = F*R$, where $n = c$, $F = c_0$, and $R = 2*t$. F is coprime to $2*t$, because c_0 is a prime. $F > 2*t$ (i.e. $c_0 > \sqrt{c}$), because c_0 is in the interval $[2^{\lceil ReqLen/2 \rceil}, 2^{\lceil ReqLen/2+1 \rceil}-1]$ and c is in the interval $[2^{ReqLen-1}, 2^{ReqLen}-1]$.

The pseudocode of Shawe-Taylor's algorithm is as follows:

```
function Shawe_Taylor_Provable_Prime
    parameters   Hash, Hlen: hash function and its output bit-length
    input    ReqLen: requested bit-length of the prime to be generated
             InputSeed: seed
    output status: "Success" or "Failure"; p: generated provable-prime
           pSeed: a seed computed during prime generation
           pGenCtr: counter incremented during prime generation
```
1. if $(ReqLen \geq 33)$, then go to step 11
   # Case where the generated prime can be tested using
   # Trial-Division test
2. $pSeed = InputSeed$; $pGenCtr = 0$
3. $c = Hash(pSeed) \oplus Hash(pSeed+1)$
4. $c = 2^{ReqLen-1} + (c \bmod 2^{ReqLen-1})$
5. $c = (2*\lfloor c/2 \rfloor)+1$ # c is guaranteed to be of bit-length of $ReqLen$
6. $pGenCtr = pGenCtr+1$
7. $pSeed = pSeed+2$
8. if $(Trial\_Division\_Primality\_Test(c) = Prime)$, then return
      ("Success", c, $pSeed$, $pGenCtr$)
9. if $(pGenCtr > 4*ReqLen)$, then return ("Failure", 0, 0, 0)
10. go to step 3
   # Case where a long bit-length prime is required.
11. $(status, c_0, pSeed, pGenCtr) =$
      $Shawe\_Taylor\_Provable\_Prime(\lceil ReqLen/2 \rceil+1, InputSeed)$
12. if $(status = "Failure")$, then return ("Failure", 0, 0, 0)
13. $Nb\_iterations = \lceil ReqLen/Hlen \rceil - 1$
14. $OldCtr = pGenCtr$
15. # Generate an integer c in range $[2^{ReqLen-1}, 2^{ReqLen}-1]$ and
      test its primality using a random integer a in range $[2, c-2]$
    15.1.1 $x = 0$
    15.1.2 for $i = 0$ to $Nb\_iterations$ do

$$x = x + \left(Hash \left(pSeed + i \right) * 2^{i*Hlen} \right)$$

15.1.3 $x = 2^{ReqLen-1} + \left(x \bmod 2^{ReqLen-1} \right)$

\# Generate a candidate prime c using a random integer x and the prime c_0 generated for bit-length of $\lceil ReqLen / 2 \rceil + 1$

15.2.1 $pSeed = pSeed + Nb\_iterations + 1$

15.2.2 $t = \lceil x / (2 * c_0) \rceil$

15.2.3 **if** $\left((2*t*c_0 + 1) > 2^{ReqLen} \right)$, **then** $t = \left\lceil 2^{ReqLen-1} / (2*c_0) \right\rceil$

15.2.4 $c = 2*t*c_0 + 1$

15.2.5 $pGenCtr = pGenCtr + 1$

\# Choose an integer a in $[2, c-2]$

15.3.1 $a = 0$

15.3.2 **for** $i = 0$ **to** $Nb_{iterations}$ **do**
$$a = a + \left(Hash(pSeed + i) * 2^{i*Hlen} \right)$$

15.3.3 $a = 2 + \left(a \bmod (c-3) \right)$

15.3.4 $pSeed = pseed + Nb\_iterations + 1$

\# Use of Pocklington-Lehmer primality test to check if c is prime

15.4.1 $z = a^{2*t} \bmod c$

15.4.2. **if** $\left((GCD(z-1, c) = 1) \text{ and } (1 = z^{c_0} \bmod c) \right)$, **then**
    return $("Success", c, pSeed, pGenCtr)$

16. **if** $(PgenCtr > (4 * ReqLen + OldCtr))$, **then return** $("Failure", 0, 0)$

17. $t = t + 1$

18. **go to** step 15.2.3

16.3.4.2 Generation of Provable-Prime Pair for DH and MQV

The recommended method, for generating a pair of provable primes p and q to be used as FFC domain parameters is composed of three steps:

1) Phase 1: generate a random number, denoted *FirstSeed*, which is then used to generate a prime.
2) Phase 2: use Shawe-Taylor's algorithm to generate two primes q and p_0. The latter shall be of the half bit-length of prime p.
3) Phase 3: use primes q and p_0 to compute $\left(2 * \left\lfloor \frac{x}{2*q*p_0} \right\rfloor * p_0 \right) * q + 1$, where x is a random number in range $[2^{Len_p - 1}, 2^{Len_p}]$. Recall that in FFC domain parameters, prime q divides $p - 1$. The primality of the computed p is confirmed using Pocklington-Lehmer primality test.

The complete pseudocode of the recommended method is as follows:

function Generate_Provable_Prime_Pair_FFC
    parameters *Hash, Hlen*: hash function and its output bit-length
    input Len_p, Len_q: requested bit-length of primes p and q, respectively
        SeedLen: seed bit-length used to generate pseudorandom
        numbers, where $SeedLen \geq Len_q$
    output *status*: "Success" or "Failure"; p, q: generated provable primes
        pSeed, qSeed, pGenCtr, qGenCtr: optional outputs, which can
        serve as random numbers for other FFC domain parameters
    \# Phase 1: first seed generation
    1. \# Generate a first seed generation with a value $\geq 2^{Len_q - 1}$
        1.1 $FirstSeed = 0$
        1.2 **while** $\left(FirstSeed < 2^{Len_q - 1} \right)$ **do**
            $FirstSeed = DRBG.generate(SeedLen)$
    \# Phase 2: generation of two primes q and p_0
    2. \# Use Shawe-Taylor algorithm to obtain a prime q and two numbers
        2.1 $(status, q, qSeed, qGenCtr) =$

$$Shawe\_Taylor\_Provable\_Prime\left(Len_q, FirstSeed\right)$$

2.2 **if** $\left(status = "Failure"\right)$, **then return** "Failure"

3. # Use Shawe-Taylor algorithm to obtain a prime p_0, with half bit-length of prime p

3.1 $\left(status, p_0, pSeed, pGenCtr\right) =$
$$Shawe\_Taylor\_Provable\_Prime\left(\left\lceil\frac{Len_p}{2}+1, qSeed\right\rceil\right)$$

3.2 **if** $\left(status = "Failure"\right)$, **then return** "Failure"

Phase 3: using p_0 and q, generate a prime p that fulfills FFC requirements

4. $Nb_{iterations} = \left\lceil\frac{Len_p}{Hlen}\right\rceil - 1$

5. $OldCtr = pGenCtr$

6. # Generate a pseudorandom number x in range $\left[2^{Len_p-1}, 2^{Len_p}\right]$

6.1 $x = 0$

6.2 **for** $i = 0$ **to** $Nb\_iterations$ **do**
$$x = x + \left(Hash\left(pSeed + i\right) * 2^{i*Hlen}\right)$$

6.3 $x = 2^{Len_p-1} + (x \bmod 2^{Len_p-1})$

7. # Generate a candidate prime p in range $\left[2^{Len_p-1}, 2^{Len_p}\right]$

7.1 $pSeed = pSeed + Nb\_iterations + 1$

7.2 $t = \left\lceil x / (2 * q * p_0)\right\rceil$

7.3 **if** $\left((2 * t * q * p_0 + 1) > 2^{Len_p}\right)$, **then** $t = \left\lceil 2^{Len_p-1} / \left(2 * q * p_0\right)\right\rceil$

7.4 $p = 2 * t * q * p_0 + 1$

7.5 $pGenCtr = pGenCtr + 1$

8. # Choose an integer a in $\left[2, p-2\right]$

8.1 $a = 0$

8.2 **for** $i = 0$ **to** $Nb\_iterations : a = a + \left(Hash\left(pSeed + i\right) * 2^{i*Hlen}\right)$

8.3 $a = 2 + \left(a \bmod \left(p - 3\right)\right)$

9. $pSeed = pSeed + Nb\_iterations + 1$

10. # Use random integer a and Pocklington-Lehmer primality test to check if p is prime

10.1 $z = a^{2*t*q} \bmod p$

10.2 **if** $\left(\left(GCD\left(z-1, p\right) = 1\right) \text{ and } \left(1 = z^{p_0} \bmod p\right)\right)$, **then**
$$return \left("Success", p, q, pSeed, qSeed, pGenCtr, qGenCtr\right)$$

11. **if** $\left(pGenCtr > \left(4 * Len_p + OldCtr\right)\right)$, **then return** $\left("Failure", 0, 0\right)$

12. $t = t + 1$

13. **go to** step 7.3

| **Note**. The algorithm above may fail to find two primes that fulfill the FFC domain parameter requirements.

16.3.4.3 Generation of Provable-Prime Pair for RSA

To generate a prime pair that fulfills the RSA requirements, two calls to a function that generate a single prime are performed. The algorithm may fail in generating a pair of RSA primes. The public exponent e is assumed to be known before trying to generate primes p and q; and the modulus bit-length $nLen$ is assumed to be valid.

function Generate_Provable_Prime_Pair_RSA

  input $nLen$: intended bit-length of the modulus $n = p * q$
      e: public exponent
  output $status$: "Success" or "Failure"; p, q: generated provable primes
  # Phase 1: seed generation
        1.1 $SecurityStrength$ = security strength associated to a modulus of $nLen$ bits
        1.2 $Seed = DRBG.generate\left(2 * SecurityStrength\right)$

```
# Phase 2: generation of prime p
    2.1 (status, p, pSeed) =
        Generate_Provable_RSA_Prime(nLen/2, Seed, e)
    2.2 if (status = "Failure"), then return ("Failure", 0, 0)
    2.3 tmpSeed = pSeed
# Phase 3: generation of prime q
    3.1 (status, q, qSeed) = Generate_Provable_RSA_Prime(nLen/2, tmpSeed, e)
    3.2 if (status = "Failure"), then return ("Failure", 0, 0)
    3.3 tmpSeed = qSeed
# Phase 4: test of compliance with RSA parameter requirements
    4.1 if (|p − q|) ≤ 2^((nLen/2) − 100), then go to step 3.1
    4.2 return ("Success", p, q)
```

The function *Generate_Provable_RSA_Prime* generates one prime of a bit-length of L in two steps:

1) Phase 1: Generate a prime p_0 using Shawe-Taylor's algorithm. p_0 is of the bit-length of $\lceil L/2 \rceil + 1$.

2) Phase 2: compute a random integer x in the interval $\left[\sqrt{2} * 2^{pLen-1}, 2^{pLen} - 1 \right]$ and compute t using x and p_0; then, using the Pocklington-Lehmer test, check if $p = 2 * t * p_0 + 1$ is a prime.

```
function Generate_Provable_RSA_Prime
        # Note. The pseudocode below is a simplification of a more general
        function specified in reference [11] to generate strong primes
    parameters Hash, Hlen: hash function and its output bit-length
    input   pLen: intended bit-length of the RSA prime to be generated
            InputSeed: a seed value
            e: public exponent
    output status: "Success" or "Failure"; p: generated provable-prime
            pSeed: seed computed during provable-prime generation; it
            will be used as input to generate the second RSA-prime
    # Phase 1: Generate a prime p_0 of bit-length of ⌈pLen / 2⌉ + 1
    1. (status, p_0, pSeed, pGenCtr) =
        Shawe_Taylor_Provable_Prime(⌈pLen/2⌉ + 1, inputSeed)
    2. if (status = "Failure"), then return ("Failure", 0, 0)
    # Phase 2: generate a strong prime p of a bit-length of pLen
    3. Nb_iterations = ⌈pLen / Hlen⌉ − 1
    4. pGenCtr = 0
    5. # Generate a random integer x in range [√2 * 2^(pLen−1), 2^(pLen) − 1]
        5.1 x = 0
        5.2 for i = 0 to Nb_iterations do x = x + (Hash(pSeed + i) * 2^(i*Hlen))
        5.3 x = ⌈√2 * 2^(pLen−1)⌉ + (x mod (2^(pLen) − ⌈√2 * 2^(pLen−1)⌉))
    6. pSeed = pSeed + Nb_iterations + 1
    7. t = ⌈(2 * p_0 + x) / (2 * p_0)⌉
    8. if ((2 * (t − 1) * p_0 + 1) > 2^(pLen)), then
        t = ⌈((2 * p_0) + √2 * 2^(pLen−1)) / (2 * p_0)⌉
    9. p = 2 * (t − 1) * p_0 + 1
    10. pGenCtr = pGenCtr + 1
    # By definition of an RSA-prime p, GCD(p − 1, e) = 1
    11. if (GCD(p − 1, e) = 1), then
    # Choose an integer a in [2, p − 2] and test primality of p
```

11.1 $a = 0$

11.2 **for** $i = 0$ **to** *Nb_iterations* **do**

   $a = a + (Hash(pSeed + i) * 2^{i*Hlen})$

11.3 $a = 2 + (a \bmod (p - 3))$

11.4 $pSeed = pSeed + Nb\_iterations + 1$

\# Test the primality of p using the Pocklington-Lehmer test

11.5 $z = a^{2 \cdot (t-1)} \bmod p$

11.6 **if,** $\left((GCD(Z - 1, p) = 1) \text{ and } (1 = z^{P_0} \bmod p)\right)$, **then**

   return (*"Success"*, p, $pSeed$)

12. **if** $\left(pGenCtr > (5 * pLen)\right)$, **then return** (*"Failure"*, 0, 0)

13. $t = t + 1$

14. **go to** step 8

| **Note.** The algorithm above may fail to find a prime that fulfills the RSA domain parameter requirements.

16.4 Exercises and Problems

16.4.1 List of Exercises and Problems

Exercise 16.1

Let X be a one-character random variable that takes its values in a set composed of 26 uppercase Latin letters, 10 decimal digits, and 8 special characters. Let $pr_c, pr_v, pr_d,$ and pr_s denote the probability of selection of a consonant, a vowel, a digit, and a special character, respectively.

What is the entropy of random variable X assuming that $Pr_c = 2Pr_v = 4Pr_d = 10Pr_s$?

Exercise 16.2

Consider a function F that generates an output of one decimal digit and the observed sequence is $\{1, 2, 7, 0, 4, 6, 3, 5, 9, 8\}$, which repeats indefinitely. Can F satisfy the properties of a cryptographically-secure PRNG?

Exercise 16.3

This exercise aims to highlight the sensitivity of LCGs in terms of the period of the longest generated number sequence, when selecting its seed.

1) Consider an LCG with parameters $m = 256$, $a = 25$, and $b = 16$.

   What is the period of the LCG as defined above when the seed is selected as follows: $X_0 = 255$, $X_0 = 2$, $X_0 = 6$, $X_0 = 10$, $X_0 = 0$?

2) Consider an LCG with parameters $m = 255$, $a = 25$, and $b = 16$. What do you observe if $X_0 = 0$ or if $X_0 = 4$?

Exercise 16.4

Make use of Miller-Rabin test for primality to check the primality under the following scenarios:

1) $n = 19$ assuming the picked random values are $\{3, 7, 17\}$

2) $n = 113$ assuming the picked random values are $\{107, 76, 2\}$

Exercise 16.5

How many prime numbers of a bit-length of 1024 are there?

Problem 16.1

How can an attacker, who knew five successive random numbers generated by a linear congruential generator, break such an LCG (i.e. he/she can find the LCG parameters)?

Problem 16.2

What is the category (i.e. safe prime and strong prime) of primes generated by the function `Shawe_Taylor_Provable_Prime`? Use the pseudocode of the function in Section 16.3.4.1.

Problem 16.3

By the prime number theorem, we know that the probability of an integer $z \in [2, N]$ to be prime is $\frac{1}{ln(N)}$. Consider m RSA public-keys, with moduli of at most 2^{2048}; and all used primes are no greater than 2^{1024}.

1) Assume that all used primes are generated by a truly PRNG (pseudorandom number generator). Then, estimate the probability that there exist, at least, two RSA keys, out of the m known keys, that have a prime factor in common.
2) Assume that you know 100 million public-keys generated using the same PRNG Π; and you find out that 1000 moduli share a common prime factor. What can you conclude?

16.4.2 Solutions to Exercises and Problems

Exercise 16.1

Let X be a one-character random variable that takes its values in a set composed of 26 uppercase Latin letters (20 consonants and 6 vowels), 10 decimal digits, and 8 special characters. All the 20 consonants have the same selection probability, and the same applies to vowels, digits, and special characters. Therefore,

$$20Pr_c + 6Pr_v + 10Pr_d + 8Pr_s = 1.$$

If we assume that $Pr_c = 2Pr_v = 4Pr_d = 10Pr_s$, then:

$$Pr_c\left(20 + \frac{6}{2} + \frac{10}{4} + \frac{8}{10}\right) = Pr_c(26.3) = 1 \Rightarrow Pr_c = 0.038$$

The entropy of random variable X is:

$$H(X) = -\sum_{i=1}^{46}\left(p_i * log_2(p_i)\right)$$

$$= -\left(\begin{array}{l}\sum_{i=1}^{20}\left(Pr_c * log_2(Pr_c)\right) + \sum_{i=1}^{6}\left(Pr_v * log_2(Pr_v)\right) \\ + \sum_{i=1}^{10}\left(Pr_d * log_2(Pr_d)\right) + \sum_{i=1}^{6}\left(Pr_s * log_2(Pr_s)\right)\end{array}\right)$$

$$= -\left(\begin{array}{l}20 * Pr_c * log_2(Pr_c) + 6 * Pr_v * log_2(Pr_v) + \\ 10 * Pr_d * log_2(Pr_d) + 8 * Pr_s * log_2(Pr_s)\end{array}\right)$$

$$= -\left(\begin{array}{l}20 * Pr_c * log_2(Pr_c) + 6 * \frac{Pr_c}{2} * log_2\left(\frac{Pr_c}{2}\right) + \\ 10 * \frac{Pr_c}{4} * log_2\left(\frac{Pr_c}{4}\right) + 8 * \frac{Pr_c}{10} * log_2\left(\frac{Pr_c}{10}\right)\end{array}\right)$$

$$= 5.122$$

Exercise 16.2

The function F, which generates a cyclic sequence of $\{1, 2, 7, 0, 4, 6, 3, 5, 9, 8\}$, fulfills the first condition of PRNG, i.e. the outputs are independent and identically distributed. However, it does not fulfill the property of unpredictability, because the output can be easily predicted, when the first period is known. Therefore, F is not appropriate to be used in cryptographic applications.

Exercise 16.3

1) Consider an LCG with parameters $m = 256$, $a = 25$, and $b = 16$. Below are the longest sequences generated, depending on the initial value of the seed X_0:
   - $X_0 = 255$ results in a longest sequence of 32 numbers: {255, 247, 47, 167, 95, 87, 143, 7, 191, 183, 239, 103, 31, 23, 79, 199, 127, 119, 175, 39, 223, 215, 15, 135, 63, 55, 111, 231, 159, 151, 207, 71}
   - $X_0 = 2$ results in a longest sequence of four numbers: {2, 66, 130, 194}
   - $X_0 = 6$ results in a longest sequence of eight numbers: {6, 166, 70, 230, 134, 38, 198, 102}
   - $X_0 = 10$: results in a longest sequence of a single number: {10}, i.e. no new number can be generated.
   - $X_0 = 0$: results in a longest sequence of 16 numbers: {0, 16, 160, 176, 64, 80, 224, 240, 128, 144, 32, 48, 192, 208, 96, 112}.
2) Consider an LCG with parameters $m = 255$, $a = 25$, and $c = 16$. What do you observe if $X_0 = 0$?

– When $X_0 = 0$, the sequence that repeats is {16, 161, 216, 61, 11, 36, 151, 221, 186, 76, 131, 231, 181, 206, 66, 136, 101, 246, 46, 146, 96, 121, 236, 51}. We observe that the number 0 is not generated. In this case, 0 is called a tail, which does not repeat in the cycle of the PRNG.

– When $X_0 = 4$, the sequence which repeats is {116, 111, 241, 176, 81, 1, 41, 21, 31, 26, 156, 91, 251, 171, 211, 191, 201, 196, 71, 6, 166, 86, 126, 106}. We observe that the number 4 is not generated. In this case, 4 is a tail.

Exercise 16.4

Check of primality using Miller-Rabin test.

1) $n = 19$ with random values $\{3, 7, 17\}$. The algorithm runs in a maximum of three iterations.
Step 1:
  $19 = 2^1 * 9 + 1$. Hence, $s = 1$ and $m = 9$
Step 4: (1st iteration)
  4.1 Let $a = 3$ be the selected random value
  4.3 $V = 3^9 \bmod 19 = 18$
  4.5 Since $s = 1$, "for j from 1 to $s - 1$" is skipped
Step 4: (2nd iteration)
  4.1 Let $a = 7$ be the selected random value
  4.3 $V = 7^9 \bmod 19 = 1$
  4.4 Go to Step 4.7
Step 4: (3rd iteration)
  4.1 Let $a = 17$ be the selected random value
  4.3 $V = 17^9 \bmod 19 = 1$
  4.5 Go to Step 4.7
Step 5: return "Probably prime".

2) $n = 113$ with random values $\{107, 76, 2\}$. The algorithm runs in a maximum of three iterations.
Step 1:
  $113 = 2^4 * 7 + 1$. Hence, $s = 4$ and $m = 7$
Step 4: (1st iteration)
  4.1 Let $a = 107$ be the selected random value
  4.3 $V = 107^7 \bmod 113 = 78$
  4.5.1 $j=1$: $V = 78^2 \bmod 113 = 95$
  4.5.1 $j=2$: $V = 95^2 \bmod 113 = 98$
  4.5.1 $j=3$: $V = 98^2 \bmod 113 = 112 = 113 - 1 \Rightarrow$ *go to 4.1*
Step 4: (2nd iteration)
  4.1 Let $a = 76$ be the selected random value
  4.3 $V = 76^7 \bmod 113 = 71$
  4.5.1 $j=1$: $V = 71^2 \bmod 113 = 69$
  4.5.1 $j=2$: $V = 69^2 \bmod 113 = 15$
  4.5.1 $j=3$: $V = 15^2 \bmod 113 = 112 = 113 - 1 \Rightarrow$ *go to 4.1*
Step 4: (3rd iteration)
  4.1 Let $a = 2$ be the selected random value
  4.3 $V = 2^7 \bmod 113 = 15$
  4.5.1 $j=1$: $V = 15^2 \bmod 113 = 112 = 113 - 1 \Rightarrow$ *go to 4.1*
Step 5: return "Probably prime."
Comment: the result is correct, because 113 is a true prime.

Exercise 16.5

By the Prime number theorem (Theorem 16.1), there roughly exist $n/ln(n)$ prime numbers no greater than n. Therefore, there exist $2^{1024}/ln(2^{1024})$ prime numbers of bit-length of 1024 bits. $2^{1024}/(1024 * ln(2)) = 2^{1014}/ln(2) \, 10^{300}$.

Problem 16.1

Recall that the ith, $i \geq 1$, output of an LCG is defined by $X_i (aX_{i-1} + b) \bmod m$, where a, b, and m are the parameters of the LCG and X_0, the seed.

When an LCG is used for generating random numbers, the attacker only needs to know five successive outputs to disclose with certainty the LCG parameters and then predict the next outputs of the LCG. Let us take an example.

Assume that the attacker knows five successive outputs: 73, 42, 20, 50, and 55.
The attacker builds and solves the following 3-equation system:

$$42 \equiv (73a + b) \bmod m \tag{a}$$
$$20 \equiv (42a + b) \bmod m \tag{b}$$
$$50 \equiv (20a + b) \bmod m \tag{c}$$

First, eliminate parameter b:
   Subtract equation (a) from (b) and obtain: $22 \equiv 31a \bmod m$ (d)
   Subtract equation (c) from (b) and obtain: $-30 \equiv 22a \bmod m$ (e)
Find the modulus m:
   Multiply equation (d) by 22 and equation (e) by 31:
   Equation (d) becomes: $22 * 22 \equiv 22 * 31a \bmod m$ (d')
   Equation (e) becomes: $31 * (-30) \equiv 31 * 22a \bmod m$ (e')
   Subtract (e') from (d'), and obtain: $22 * 22 + 31 * 30 = 1414 \equiv 0 \bmod m$.
   Hence, m divides $14 * 101$. Therefore, $m \in \{14, 101, 1414\}$. We discard $m = 14$, because the left part of the equations has values greater than 14. We need to check $m = 101$ and $m = 1414$.
Find a using equation (a) when $m = 101$:
   $a = 22 * 31^{-1} \bmod 101 = 22 * 88 \bmod 101 = 17$
Finally, find b using equation (a):
   $b \equiv \left(42 - (73 * 17)\right) \bmod 101 = 13$.
   Check using the fifth value: $17 * 50 + 13 \bmod 101 = 55$.
If we take $m = 1414$ and use the method above, the parameters a and b would be $a = 360$ and $b = 720$. These parameter values match the congruence system above. However, when we compute the next value, i.e. $(50 * 320 + 760) \bmod 1414$, the output would be 1116, which is different from the fifth known value, i.e. 55. Thus, the valid modulus is 101.

Problem 16.2

Recall that a prime p is a safe prime if it satisfies condition (a) below; and it is a strong prime, if it fulfills the following three conditions:

   $p - 1$ has a large prime factor p_1 (a)
   $p_1 - 1$ has a large prime factor p_3 (b)
   $p + 1$ has a large prime factor p_2 (c)

Let L denote the requested bit-length. To generate primes for FFC- and IFC-based algorithms, the required bit-length L is too large that the prime generated by Shawe-Taylor's algorithm is guaranteed to be large. Shawe-Taylor's function is recursive. For example, to generate a prime of a bit length of $L = 1024$, Shawe-Taylor's function is called with the following bit-lengths: $L_1 = 1024$, $L_2 = 1024/2 + 1 = 513$, $L_3 = \lceil 513/2 \rceil + 1 = 258$, $L_4 = 258/2 + 1 = 130$, $L_5 = 66$, $L_6 = 34$, and $L_7 = 18$.

Let $c^{(L)}$ denote the output of Shawe-Taylor's function for a requested bit-length of L. $c^{(L)}$ is computed in step 15.2.4, as follows: $c^{(L)} = 2 * t^{(L)} * c^{(L/2+1)} + 1$. Using Pocklington-Lehmer test, the output (i.e. $c^{(L)}$) of each Shawe-Taylor's function call is guaranteed to be a prime.

- $c^{(L)} - 1 = 2 * t^{(L)} * c^{(\lceil L/2 \rceil + 1)}$; thus, $c^{(L)}$ has a prime factor $c^{(\lceil L/2 \rceil + 1)}$. Thus, condition (a) is satisfied. Therefore, $c^{(L)}$ is a safe prime.
- $c^{(\lceil L/2 \rceil + 1)} - 1 = 2 * t^{(\lceil L/2 \rceil + 1)} * c^{(\lceil (\lceil L/2 \rceil + 1)/2 \rceil + 1)}$; thus, $c^{(\lceil L/2 \rceil + 1)}$ has a prime factor $c^{(\lceil (\lceil L/2 \rceil + 1)/2 \rceil + 1)}$. Thus, condition (b) is satisfied.
- The third condition is much more complex to check; and it is not addressed here.

Problem 16.3

1) By the prime number theorem, the number of primes, denoted n, in the interval $[2, 2^{1024} - 1]$ is $n \approx \frac{2^{1024}}{\ln(2^{1024})} = \frac{2^{1024}}{1024 * \ln(2)} \approx \frac{2^{1024}}{710}$.
   To generate m RSA public-keys, a maximum of $2m$ primes are required (because RSA modulus is a product of two primes). If among $2m$ primes, two (or more) values are identical, then there exists at least two RSA keys that share a common prime factor. We randomly pick the first prime out of n primes. Then, when we randomly pick the second prime, there is a probability of $1/n$ that the new prime is identical to the first one. Then, when we randomly pick the third prime, there is a probability of $2/n$ that the new prime is identical to one of the two old primes, etc. Finally, when we randomly pick the last prime, there is a probability of $(2m - 1)/n$ that the new prime is identical to one of the $2m - 1$ old primes. Therefore, the

probability to have at least two identical primes is $P = \frac{1}{n} + \frac{2}{n} + \ldots + \frac{2m-1}{n} = \frac{(2m-1+1)(2m-1)}{n} \approx \frac{2*m^2}{n}$. Notice that we can obtain the same result by applying the formula of birthday paradox, which states that the probability of a collision among k integers randomly picked out of a set of L integers is $P(k) \approx \frac{k^2}{2L}$.

2) By the answer to the first question, if a truly PRNG is used to generate 100 million RSA public-keys, the probability to have two RSA keys that share a common prime factor is $\frac{(10^8)^2}{2^{1024}}$, which is by far smaller than that provided by PRNG Π, which is of $\frac{\frac{10^3}{710}}{10^8}$. Therefore, we can conclude that PRNG Π is faulty; it lacks randomness.

Notes

1 *Deterministic* means that given a seed value, the generator will always produce the same output sequence.

2 As far as we know, the NIST has not yet recommended CSPRNGs, which are mainly based on stream ciphers.

3 CMAC is an improvement of CBC-MAC. Some weaknesses of CBC-MAC have been addressed in literature; and CBC-MAC is not considered secure, under specific usage conditions (see some problems discussed in Chapter 9).

4 In this chapter, user requesting DRBG outputs is referred to as "consuming application".

5 The required minimum entropy bit-length is the same than that of the highest security strength that can be provided.

6 $B = (2^{CtrLen} - 4) * BlkLen$; *CtrLen* is a building parameter of CTR-DRBGs.

7 See Problem 3.19 for proof of Lemma 16.1.

References

1 Shannon, C. (1948). A mathematical theory of communication. *Bell System Technical Journal* 27: 379–423, 623–656.

2 Matsumoto, M. and Nishimura, T. (1998). Mersenne Twister: a 623-dimensionally equidistributed uniform pseudo-random number generator. *ACM Transactions on Modeling and Computer Simulation* 8 (1): 3–30.

3 Park, S. and Miller, K. (1988). Random number generators: good ones are hard to find. *Communications of the ACM* 31 (10): 1192–1201.

4 Barker, E. and Kelsey, J. (2015). *Recommendation for Random Number Generation Using Deterministic Random Bit Generators - Special Publication 800-90A (Rev. 1)*. NIST. National Institute for Standards and Technology.

5 Turan, M., Barker, E., Kelsey, J., and et, A. (2018). *Recommendation for the Entropy Sources Used for Random Bit Generation, Special Publication 800-90B*. NIST. National Institute for Standards and Technology.

6 Barker, E. and Kelsey, J. (2016). *Recommendation for Random Bit Generator (RBG) Constructions - Second draft SP 800-90C*. NIST. National Institute of Standards and Technology.

7 NIST (2019). *Digital Signature Standard (DSS) - FIPS PUB 186-5 (Draft)*. National Institute of Standards and Technology.

8 Miller, G.L. (1975). Riemann's hypothesis and tests for primality. *7th ACM Annual Symposium on Theory of Computing*, 234–239. Albuquerque, NM, US: ACM.

9 Rabin, M.O. (1980). Probabilistic algorithm for testing primality. *Journal of Number Theory* 12 (1): 128–138.

10 Pinch, R. (2007). The carmichael numbers up to 10^21. *Proceedings of Conference on Algorithmic Number Theory*, 129–131. Turku, Finland: TUCS General Publication.

11 NIST (2013). *Digital Signature Standard (DSS) - FIPS PUB 186-4*. National Institute of Standards and Technology. Institute for Standards and Technology.

12 Shawe-Taylor, J. (1986). Generating strong primes. *Electronic Letters* 22 (16): 875–877.

Appendix: Multiple Choice Questions and Answers

A.1 Questions

A.1.1 Basic Definitions of Security and Cryptography

---

1. Any item of value in information security is known as

   a) Program   *b)* Data   *c)* Asset   *d)* Secret file

---

2. Which of the following best describes cryptography?

   a) It is a set of methods for defeating attacks
   b) It is the art and science of disclosing secrets
   c) It enables to securely exchange messages
   d) It is art and science of secret writing

---

3. Verifying that data received was sent by the specified sender is a test of

   a) Integrity   *b)* Authentication   *c)* Authenticity   *d)* Identity

---

4. Which of the following is the best source to pick a random text?

   a) Birthdays   *b)* City names   *c)* Books   *d)* People first names

---

5. The weakness in a risk mitigating action is referred to as:

   a) Exposure   *b)* Vulnerability   *c)* Attack   *d)* Risk

---

6. Sending unsolicited contents is an act of

   a) Spoofing   *b)* Spamming   *c)* Cracking   *d)* Sniffing

---

7. Which of the following is the property of information being disclosed only to authorized people?

   a) Integrity   *b)* Privacy   *c)* Confidentiality   *d)* Availability

---

8. What term is used in security to refer to potential danger regarding a system if an adversary exploits a vulnerability of the system?

   a) Risk   *b)* Threat   *c)* Danger   *d)* Security problem

---

9. In the internet, the main security issue is

   a) Which service provider to subscribe to   *b)* Which server to connect to
   c) Who to trust   *d)* Which resources to hide

---

10. Which of the following defines the best cryptanalysis?

    a) It is a set of methods for defeating attacks   *b)* It is the science of breaking codes
    c) It enables to securely exchange messages   *d)* It is art and science of secret writing

---

11. The mouse pointer moves on your PC screen without you touching the mouse. What do you do?

    a) Unplug the mouse   *b)* Turn your computer off
    c) Disconnect your PC from the network   *d)* Run an antivirus

---

Cryptography: Algorithms, Protocols, and Standards for Computer Security, First Edition. Zoubir Mammeri.
© 2024 John Wiley & Sons, Inc. Published 2024 by John Wiley & Sons, Inc.

12. What is a botnet?

    a) A set of system vulnerabilities

    b) A set of computers connected to Internet used to make attacks

    c) A set of computers to protect company assets

    d) A network to prevent denial-of-service attacks

13. Which of the following refers to a weakness in security systems?

    a) Vulnerability   *b)* Threat   *c)* Intrusion   *d)* Attack

14. Which of the following best describes accountability?

    a) Recording actions on the assets   *b)* Making profit

    c) Ensuring consistent and correct access to data

    d) Making individuals aware of what is expected from them to protect company assets

15. Which of the following terms is not used in security?

    a) Attack   *b)* Bug   *c)* Vulnerability   *d)* Threat

16. Which one of the following refers to the technique used for verifying the integrity of messages?

    a) Message encryption   *b)* Message padding

    c) Message signature   *d)* Message digest

17. Which one of the following is also referred to as malicious software?

    a) Malware   *b)* Illegitimate-ware   *c)* Illegal-ware   *d)* Malicious-ware

18. In the CIA Triad, which one of the following properties is not involved?

    a) Confidentiality   *b)* Authenticity   *c)* Availability   *d)* Integrity

19. What security function should be used by online retailers to prevent repudiation of customers' transactions?

    a) Secure encryption algorithm   *b)* Strong secret shared with customers

    c) Digital signature verification   *d)* Customer identification

20. What type of attack an adversary exerts when he/she captures messages during a session?

    a) Trojan horse   *b)* Man-in-the-middle

    c) Denial of service   *d)* Signature forging

21. What type of attack an adversary can exert when he/she has access to a set of ciphertexts?

    a) Chosen-ciphertext   *b)* Chosen-plaintext

    c) Known-ciphertext   *d)* Known-plaintext and known-ciphertext

22. Which of the following is not a passive attack?

    a) Eavesdropping   *b)* Sniffing   *c)* Traffic analysis   *d)* Virus

23. Which of the following is not an active attack?

    a) Denial of service   *b)* Spoofing   *c)* Sniffing   *d)* Password cracking

24. Which of the following methods is the most efficient to defend against brute-force attack?

    a) Use of frequency of letters in codes to build the private key

    b) Use of statistical analysis of ciphertext variation to eliminate weak ciphertexts

    c) Use of large space for keys to make the time to mount an attack in magnitude of millions of years

    d) Use of public-key cryptosystem to share a secret

25. Which of the following is not categorized as a security threat?

    a) Modification   *b)* Interception   *c)* Receiving   *d)* Forging

26. Which of the following is not categorized as an attack?

    a) Spoofing   *b)* Encryption   *c)* Denial of service   *d)* Phishing

27. Which of the following is correct?

    a) Steganography is the science of encryption

    b) Cryptanalysis is the science and art of transforming messages to make them secure and immune to attacks

    c) Cryptography is the science and art of transforming messages to make them confidential

    d) Steganography is based on cryptanalysis

28. Which of the following does not refer to integrity protection?

    a) Intentional data file manipulation
    b) Unauthorized file update
    c) Unauthorized file read
    d) Accidental file deleting

29. Which of the following best describes man-in-the-middle attack?

    a) Attack is designed and mounted by man
    b) The attacker impersonates as a legitimate party to replace him/her in communication
    c) The attacker takes the identity of both parties in communication
    d) The attacker sends to and receives from both legitimate parties

30. A malicious program that makes a copy of itself in different locations is known as

    a) Virus
    b) Logic bomb
    c) Worm
    d) Ransomware

31. Encryption and decryption together form

    a) Signature algorithm
    b) Secret
    c) A pair of keys
    d) Cipher

32. What is denial of service?

    a) Trying to break a code
    b) Attempting to hack a database
    c) Pretending to be a user known to the system
    d) Blocking service access

33. An action attempting to disclose secrets is called

    a) Damage
    b) Vulnerability
    c) Attack
    d) Threat

34. Which term best describes a trapdoor?

    a) Black hole
    b) Backdoor
    c) Virus
    d) Secret

35. What is the purpose of the non-repudiation service?

    a) Enable confidential communications
    b) Enable authentication and integrity
    c) Prohibit a signer to deny messages he/she sent
    d) Enable availability of service

36. Inclusion of a secret in texts, images, and videos is known as

    a) Message alteration
    b) Stenography
    c) Steganography
    d) Identity theft

37. Which cryptography approach is most often used in business over Internet?

    a) Encrypted file systems
    b) Public-key cryptosystems
    c) Symmetric cryptosystems
    d) Strong passwords

38. There exist two families of message encryption algorithms

    a) AES and RSA
    b) Symmetric and asymmetric algorithms
    c) Block and stream ciphers
    d) Substitution and rotating algorithms

39. Which of the following statements is not correct?

    a) Unconditionally secure cipher is unbreakable whatever the used resources
    b) Computationally secure and computationally infeasible refer to the same property of cryptographic algorithms
    c) To break a computationally secure cipher, too much time and resources would be required
    d) To break an unconditionally secure cipher, a high level of mathematics expertise is required

40. Which statement is not correct?

    a) Symmetric and asymmetric encryptions provide similar security levels
    b) Symmetric and asymmetric encryptions are fundamentally different in design
    c) Symmetric and asymmetric encryptions use keys
    d) Weaknesses of symmetric and asymmetric encryptions are the same

41. Which of the following is the best method to protect passwords?

    a) Encrypted password file
    b) File with limited access rights
    c) File containing password hashes
    d) Encrypted password file with hash

42. An attack based on an exhaustive test of all solutions rather than on an efficient strategy exploiting vulnerabilities of the target is known as

    a) Cryptanalysis
    b) Birthday paradox
    c) Denial of service
    d) Brute-force attack

43. What is the greatest challenge to the security in symmetric cryptosystems?

    a) Using a strong cipher 　　　　　　　　*b)* Protection of the secret key
    c) Authentication of the partner 　　　　　*d)* The validity of signatures

44. Which of the following is not correct?

    a) The private key is used to sign messages
    b) The public key is used to encrypt messages
    c) The public key is used to verify signatures
    d) The public key is used to decrypt messages

45. Which of the following is not a threat?

    a) Intrusion detection 　　*b)* Replay 　　*c)* Repudiation 　　*d)* Masquerade

46. What is the name of the key used for encryption/decryption and known to two parties?

    a) Public key 　　*b)* Secret key 　　*c)* Signature 　　*d)* Private key

47. What is a cipher?

    a) An algorithm that encrypts data
    b) An algorithm that decrypts data
    c) An algorithm that encrypts and decrypts data
    d) An algorithm that generates public keys

48. What is the work factor in cryptography?

    a) It is the amount of time to encrypt
    b) It is the amount of effort required to break down a cryptosystem
    c) It is the amount of time to decrypt
    d) It is the amount of time to sign

49. In a company, security management focuses on the protection of

    a) Database 　　*b)* Equipment 　　*c)* Software 　　*d)* Assets

50. A timely review of login files is a method to attack

    a) Avoidance 　　*b)* Detection 　　*c)* Prevention 　　*d)* Mitigating

51. Hiding a secret in an image is known as

    a) Digital signing 　　*b)* Hashing 　　*c)* Encryption 　　*d)* Steganography

52. Cryptography does not focus on

    a) Authenticity 　　*b)* Integrity 　　*c)* Availability 　　*d)* Confidentiality

53. Which of the following best describes a honeypot?

    a) An intrusion prevention system 　　　*b)* An access control method
    c) A device to capture information about attacks
    d) A system providing fake services and used to collect information about attacks

54. Which of the following best describes a hijacking?

    a) An attack in which the attacker collects confidential data
    b) An attack in which the attacker takes control of a computer
    c) An attack in which the attacker deletes the entire database
    d) An attack in which the attacker discloses the private key

55. Which of the following action is not a characteristic of viruses?

    a) Copy a file 　　*b)* Corrupt or delete a file 　　*c)* Hash a file 　　*d)* Encrypt a file

56. Cryptanalysis is used to

    a) Design ciphers 　　　　　　　　*b)* Protect data
    c) Assess resource consumption of cryptographic algorithms
    d) Find weaknesses in cryptographic algorithms

57. What is the inverse of confidentiality?

    a) Reliability 　　*b)* Availability 　　*c)* Disclosure 　　*d)* Alteration

58. Which of the following terms is not used to refer to an attacker in the security field?

    a) Hacker 　　*b)* Enemy 　　*c)* Adversary 　　*d)* Intruder

59. Which of the following best describes non-repudiation?

    a) The sender can verify that his/her message is received
    b) The receiver has a proof that the sender sent the message
    c) The receiver can verify the identity of the sender
    d) Sender and receiver are trusted parties

60. Which of the following best describes *Meet in the middle attack*?

    a) An attack where the timing required for the attack via brute force is reduced
    b) An attack where the adversary uses several computers to decrypt, thus reducing the attack computation time
    c) An attack where messages are intercepted and then either relayed or substituted with other messages
    d) An attack where some plaintext–ciphertext pairs are known.

61. What is a weak key?

    a) A short key
    b) A Key used when the required level of security is low
    c) A key that produces short ciphertexts
    d) A key that is easy to break

62. Which of the following does not describe a computationally infeasible problem?

    a) It takes too much time to be solved
    b) It is a hard problem
    c) It is a complex problem
    d) It has no solution

63. Which of the following security properties is threatened by a buffer overflow attack?

    a) Integrity   *b)* Availability   *b)* Confidentiality   *b)* Authenticity

64. What is a linear congruent generator an example of?

    a) A random number generator
    b) A prime number generator
    c) A pseudorandom number generator
    d) A random bit-string generator

65. Using current technologies, an attack is computationally infeasible if the number of tests to do is

    $a) < 2^{60}$ $b)$ between 2^{60} and 2^{80} $c) \geq 2^{90}$ $d) \geq 2^{128}$

66. Against what type of attack does nonce protect?

    a) Replay   *b)* Signature forging   *c)* Key recovery   *d)* Plaintext recovery

67. What is message padding?

    a) Encryption   *b)* Extension with specific bits   *c)* Signature   *d)* Message digest

A.1.2 Symmetric Cryptosystems

68. Assume an affine cipher with key $K = (5,7)$ and a modulus of 26. Which one of the following letters is the ciphertext of the plaintext B?

    a) K *b)* T *c)* E *d)* Q

69. What weakness is present in a ciphertext produced by substitution alone?

    a) It has a length distinct from that of the plaintext
    b) It is hard to break
    c) It maintains letter frequency
    d) It is too simple to implement

70. In which mode of operation of block ciphers each plaintext block has one and only one corresponding ciphertext?

    a) CBC   *b)* ECB   *c)* Hash function   *d)* HMAC

71. Which algorithm has supplanted DES?

    a) RS   *b)* Diffie-Hellman   *c)* AES   *d)* Elliptic curve encryption

72. How long is the ciphertext corresponding to an 88-bit plaintext if encrypted with a block cipher?

    a) 128   *b)* 88   *c)* 256   *d)* 89

73. How long is the ciphertext corresponding to an 88-bit plaintext if encrypted with AES?

    a) 128   *b)* 256   *c)* 88   *d)* 512

74. What is maximum key space of AES?

    $a) 2^{56}$ $b) 2^{256}$ $c) 2^{1024}$ $d) 2^{2048}$

75. Which of the following pair of number of rounds and key length is not correct regarding AES?

    a) NbRounds=10, KeyLen=128
    b) NbRounds=14, KeyLen=256
    c) NbRounds=16, KeyLen=256
    d) NbRounds=12, KeyLen=192

76. Which of the following is one of the main drawbacks of symmetric systems?

a) Key length   *b)* Key distribution   *c)* Key storage   *d)* Key generation

77. Which of the following is said to be unbreakable by brute-force attack?

a) RSA   *b)* One-time pad   *c)* AES   *d)* TDEA

78. Both AES and TDEA are

a) Stream ciphers   *b)* Byte ciphers   *c)* Block ciphers   *d)* Public-key ciphers

79. Which of the following mode is not a mode of operation of block ciphers?

a) RSA   *b)* CBC   *c)* CFB   *d)* CTR

80. Which of the following best describes Vigenere's cipher?

a) Transposition   *b)* Mono-alphabetic   *c)* Poly-alphabetic   *d)* Additive cipher

81. Which of the following characteristics is not good for a stream cipher?

a) Statistically unbiased   *b)* Long period
c) Keystream not linearly related to the key   *d)* Statistically predictable

82. Which of the following ciphers makes use of two distinct keys to encrypt and to decrypt?

a) Symmetric   *b)* Asymmetric   *c)* Stream   *d)* Block

83. How long would be the ciphertext of a 100 bit message encrypted with a stream cipher?

a) 156 bits   *b)* 228 bits   *c)* 90 bits   *d)* 100 bits

84. Which of the following modes of operation of AES can be used as a stream cipher?

a) ECB   *b)* OFB   *c)* CBC   *d)* XTS

85. Which pair of words in the following list refers to the labor needed to encrypt or decrypt a plaintext?

a) Stream encryption, block decryption   *b)* Symmetric, asymmetric
c) Confusion, diffusion   *d)* Block encryption, stream decryption

86. In which of the following categories TDEA is included?

a) Stream ciphers   *b)* MAC algorithms   *c)* Hashing algorithms   *d)* Block ciphers

87. What is the maximum key space of TDEA?

a) 2^{56} *b)* 2^{168} *c)* 2^{128} *d)* 2^{256}

88. Which of the following is not a mode of operation of block ciphers?

a) ECB   *b)* CEB   *c)* CBC   *d)* CFB

89. Which of the following is not a parameter of block ciphers?

a) Number of rounds   *b)* Key length   *c)* Block length   *d)* Message length

90. Which of the following transformations is not applied in AES?

a) SubBytes   *b)* ShiftRows   *c)* MixColumns   *d)* PermuteKey

91. Which of the following transformations does not (at some level) contribute to diffusion in AES?

a) SubBytes   *b)* ShiftRows   *c)* AddRoundKey   *d)* MixColumns

92. Which of the following operations most contribute to confusion in DEA?

a) Permutation   *b)* S-boxes   *c)* Round key scheduling   *d)* Key expansion

93. Which of the following is correct?

a) Rijndael is a symmetric cipher, while AES is an asymmetric cipher
b) Rijndael is a stream cipher, while AES is a block cipher
c) AES is the standard version of Rijndael
d) Rijndael is Feistel structure-based, while AES is not

94. Which of the following operations most contributes to diffusion in DEA?

a) Permutation   *b)* S-boxes   *c)* Round key scheduling   *d)* Key expansion

95. Which of the following transformations most contribute to diffusion in AES?

a) SubBytes   *b)* ShiftRows
c) AddRoundKey   *d)* MixColumns and ShiftRows

96. Which of the following encryption methods is considered unbreakable?

    a) RSA   *b)* Elliptic curve encryption   *c)* DEA   *d)* One-time pad

97. Which of the following mode is the most appropriate to encrypt (very) short data?

    a) CFB (cipher feedback)   *b)* ECB (electronic codebook)

    c) CTR (counter)   *d)* OFB (output feedback)

98. Which of the following is a step before establishing an encrypted session using TDEA or AES?

    a) Key storage   *b)* Key exchange   *c)* Round key generation   *d)* Key expansion

99. Vigenere's cipher is an example of

    a) Polyalphabetic cipher   *b)* Additive cipher

    c) Block cipher   *d)* Transposition cipher

100. Which of the following characteristics is not good for a stream cipher?

    a) Keystream not linear to the key   *b)* Long periodic

    c) Keystream statistically predictable   *d)* Can be implemented in hardware

101. What are CBC and AES-XTS?

    a) Block ciphers   *b)* Public-key ciphers

    c) Stream ciphers   *d)* Modes of operation of block ciphers

102. Which of the following modes is a Format Preserving Encryption mode?

    a) FF1   *b)* AES-XTS   *c)* AES   *d)* CBC

103. For which of the following reasons, the One-time Pad is not recommended for parties that frequently exchange messages?

    a) It is not secure   *b)* It is impractical

    c) It consumes a lot of bandwidth   *d)* It degrades performances

104. To which of the following notions, does the property of synchronism of a stream cipher refer?

    a) Speed of encryption   *b)* Error recovery

    c) Error propagation   *d)* Speed of decryption

105. Which of the following best describes an S-box of DEA?

    a) It takes six bits and permutes them   *b)* It takes six bits and returns the four first bits

    c) It takes six bits and returns four bits   *d)* It takes six bits and rotate them

106. Which of the following best describes the role of an S-box of DEA?

    a) Compression   *b)* Permutation   *c)* Diffusion   *d)* Expansion

107. Which of the following statements is not correct?

    a) Using diffusion, the statistical structure of plaintext is dissipated in the ciphertext.

    b) Diffusion and confusion are achieved by permutation.

    c) In confusion, the relationship between the key and the plaintext is made complex.

    d) Diffusion is achieved by permutation and confusion by substitution.

108. Which of the following modes of operation cannot be used as a stream cipher?

    a) CBC (Cipher Block Chaining)   *b)* CTR (Counter)

    c) OFB (Output FeedBack)   *d)* CFB (Cipher FeedBack)

109. Which of the following modes of operation leaks repetitions in plaintexts?

    a) CBC (Cipher Block Chaining)   *b)* ECB (Electronic CodeBook)

    c) OFB (Output FeedBack)   *d)* CFB (Cipher FeedBack)

A.1.3 Hash Functions, MAC, and Digital Signatures

110. Which of the following algorithms can be used to verify message integrity?

    a) AES   *b)* SHA-1   *c)* DES   *d)* RSA

111. Message authentication code is also referred to as

    a) Cryptographic code   *b)* Cyclic redundancy check

    c) Cryptographic check bits   *d)* Cryptographic checksum

112. What is the type of mapping of a hash function?

    a) One-to-one   *b)* Many-to-one   *c)* Many-to-many   *d)* One-to-many

113. Who generates the message digest?

    a) Sender   *b)* Receiver   *c)* Sender and receiver   *d)* Network administrator

114. In which algorithms, secret key is not used?

    a) Signature algorithms   *b)* MAC algorithms
    c) Hashing algorithms   *d)* Encryption algorithms

115. Which services are provided by HMAC?

    a) Integrity and authenticity   *b)* Availability and confidentiality
    c) Integrity and confidentiality   *d)* Authenticity and availability

116. Which of the following does not have the same meaning as message hash?

    a) Digest   *b)* Ciphertext   *c)* Cryptography checksum   *d)* Fingerprint

117. What is not required from hash function?

    a) It can be applied to message of any size   *b)* It cannot be easily inversed

    c) It can produce an output of any size   *d)* It can be easily implemented

118. What requirements a digital signature algorithm should not satisfy?

    a) The signature algorithm supports non-repudiation service
    b) The signature depends on the message and sender key
    c) It is easy to save a copy of signature for use in the future
    d) It is difficult to forge signatures

119. Which of the following best describes a digital signature?

    a) Message hash   *b)* MAC   *c)* Encrypted message   *d)* Encrypted hash

120. Which of the following is not provided by digital signature?

    a) Confidentiality   *b)* Integrity   *c)* Authentication   *d)* Hash encryption

121. Which key is used to sign digital certificates?

    a) User's public key   *b)* Certificate Authority public-key
    c) User's private key   *d)* Certificate Authority private-key

122. For which of the following, the digital certificate is not used?

    a) User authentication   *b)* Identity verification

    c) Message confidentiality   *d)* Protection against repudiation

123. In which hash function, the Keccak function is used?

    a) SHA-1   *b)* SHA-3   *c)* SHA-256   *d)* SHA-512

124. Which of the following is provided by digital signatures?

    a) Confidentiality   *b)* Authentication   *c)* Authorization   *d)* Integrity

125. Which of the following is used for integrity and authenticity?

    a) AES   *b)* ECDSA   *c)* SHA-3   *d)* Diffie-Hellman

126. What is the magnitude of hash function output size (in bits)?

    a) Tens   *b)* One hundred   *c)* Hundreds   *d)* Thousands

127. What is highest hash bit-length of current SHA standards?

    a) 160   *b)* 1024   *c)* 2048   *d)* 512

128. What is the complexity of the best generic attack to find hash collision?
    n denotes the bit-length of hash function output

    a) $n * n$ *b)* $2^n / 2$ *c)* 2^n *d)* $2^{n/2}$

129. Which of the following algorithms cannot be implemented with multiple bit strengths?

    a) SHA-1   *b)* AES   *c)* SHA-2   *d)* SHA-3

130. Which of the following best describes a digital signature?

    a) The receiver decrypts the message with his/her private key

    b) The sender encrypts the message with his/her private key

    c) The sender encrypts the message hash with his/her private key

    d) The sender encrypts the message hash with his/her public key

131. SHA-256 is an example of

    a) Encryption algorithm

    b) Hash algorithm

    c) Key exchange algorithm

    d) Encryption and hash algorithm

132. Trusted software vendors associate signatures with their products for enabling customers to

    a) Set up the software

    b) Easily maintain the software

    c) Check the software performance

    d) Verify that the software has not been altered

133. Why the initialization vector of hash function is fixed?

    a) Sender and recipient can share the initiation vector as a secret

    b) It guarantees that the sender and recipient use the same values to start hash function

    c) It is an arbitrary choice in hash functions

    d) It provides a higher level of security strength

134. A hash function generates a 384-bit hash. How many random messages are needed in average to find a collision with brute-force attack?

    a) 384

    b) 2^{384}

    c) 2^{192}

    d) $384 * 2^{192}$

135. Which of the following is not an attack against hash functions?

    a) Collision attack

    b) Third preimage attack

    c) Preimage attack

    d) Second preimage attack

136. Do collision-resistant and collision-free refer to the same property of hash functions?

    a) Yes, because "collision-resistant" is the same as "collision-free"

    b) No, because collision-free functions do not exist

    c) Yes, because collision-resistance is enough to have collision-free

    d) No, because it is difficult to design collision-free hash functions

137. Using the birthday paradox, how many image tests it takes to find a collision on a hash function with output length of *n* bits, with a probability of 0.50?

    a) $2^n / 2$

    b) 2^n

    c) $n * 2^{\left(\frac{n}{2}\right)}$

    d) $2^{\left(\frac{n}{2}\right)}$

138. Which of the following methods is the strongest to ensure message integrity?

    a) Hash message, append the hash to message, then encrypt the whole

    b) Encrypt the message with a secret key

    c) Sign the message

    d) Append a hash to the message

139. An attack based on the probability that two messages have the same hash is referred to as

    a) Length extension attack

    b) Birthday attack

    c) Known-plaintext attack

    d) Cryptographic attack

140. MAC does not provide non-repudiation service because

    a) No key is used

    b) MAC is not a public-key-based service

    c) The secret may be known to more than one user

    d) The recipient cannot forge a valid MAC

141. The underlying structure of the SHA-3 algorithm is referred to as

    a) Construction layer

    b) Hashing construction

    c) Sponge construction

    d) Digest construction

142. Trying to find a password that hashes to a known hash is

    a) Preimage attack

    b) Second preimage attack

    c) Collision attack

    d) Birthday attack

143. Trying to modify a signed message is

a) Preimage attack   b) Second preimage attack

c) Collision attack   d) Birthday attack

144. Sheets, planes, and slices refer to

a) SHA-1   b) State array of SHA-3

c) SHA-2   d) Symmetric cipher-based MAC

145. Which of the following statements is not correct?

a) One-way function is enough to generate signatures

b) One-way function may be used to generate short MACs

c) One-way function is not enough to generate signatures

d) One-way function is not enough to generate MACs

A.1.4 Public-Key Cryptosystems

146. Which of the following algorithm does not belong to the public-key family?

a) DSA   b) DHKE   c) AES   d) ECIES

147. What is the most common use of Diffie-Hellman algorithm?

a) To secure the exchange of keys   b) To generate signatures

c) To encrypt and decrypt messages   d) To provide certificates

148. Which of the following is the ciphertext of plaintext 5 if RSA modulus is 209 and the public key is e=17?

a) 418   b) 80   c) 34   d) 85

149. Which of the following cannot be used as a public key?

a) 3   b) 2   c) 7   d) 11

150. What is the discrete logarithm problem?

a) Given a large integer N, find all prime dividers of N.

b) Given an integer a and a large integer N, find an integer z such that $z^2 \equiv a \bmod N$.

c) Given two integers a and b and a large prime p, find an integer z, such that $a^z \equiv b \bmod p$.

d) Given an integer a and a large prime p, find an integer z, such that $a * z \equiv 1 \bmod p$.

151. Consider the integer factorization problem and the discrete logarithm problem. Which of the following is not correct?

a) They have the same computational complexity

b) They make cryptographic algorithms hard to break

c) They are the basis of public-key cryptography

d) One of them is the basis of elliptic curve cryptography

152. Which of the following public-key encryption is based on the difficulty of factoring large numbers?

a) AES cipher   b) Elliptic curve encryption   c) ElGamal encryption   d) RSA

153. Which statement describes asymmetric ciphers?

a) They are slow compared to stream ciphers

b) They have a key bit-length ranging from 56 to 256

c) They include AES and TDEA

d) They use a shared secret key

154. In what way does RSA fundamentally differ from AES?

a) It uses a single key   b) It uses two keys

c) It is based on a symmetric algorithm   d) It cannot produce a signature

155. Which one of the following is not an elliptic curve recommended in standards?

a) Edwards curve   b) Montgomery curve   c) Rabin curve   d) Weierstrass curve

156. Which one of the following is not a signature algorithm?

    a) EdDSA   *b)* Sig-RSA   *c)* ECDSA   *d)* DSA

157. In which protocol, handshake is used?

    a) Diffie-Hellman   *b)* Kerberos   *c)* ECDSA   *d)* TLS

158. Which of the following terms is not used in PKIs?

    a) Verification CA   *b)* Root CA   *c)* Intermediate CA   *d)* Issuing CA

159. Which term does not apply to elliptic curves?

    a) Order   *b)* Inverse point   *c)* Cofactor   *d)* Generator

160. Given a prime p, a generator $g \in Z_p^*$, and four integers a, b, X, and Y, such that $X = g^a \bmod p$ and $Y = g^b \bmod$, which of the following is the shared key in Diffie-Hellman key exchange protocol?

    a) $X * Y \bmod p$ *b)* $g^{a*b} \bmod p$ *c)* $g^{a+b} \bmod p$ *d)* $X^b * Y^a \bmod p$

161. Which of the following is correct regarding symmetric and asymmetric systems execution time?

    a) They have similar execution time
    b) Decryption in asymmetric systems is faster than in symmetric systems
    c) Decryption in symmetric systems is twice faster than in asymmetric systems
    d) Decryption in symmetric systems is by far faster than in asymmetric systems

162. Given a prime $p = 17$, a generator $g = 3$, and two private keys $a = 5$ and $b = 5$, which of the following is the shared secret yielded by the Diffie-Hellman key exchange protocol?

    a) $3 * 5 * 5 \bmod 17 = 7$ *b)* $3^5 \bmod 17 = 5$

    c) $3^{5*5} \bmod 17 = 14$ *d)* $3^{5+5} \bmod 17 = 8$

163. Which of the following is not an objective of random padding in RSA?

    a) Repeated encryptions of the same message results in different ciphertexts.
    b) Prevent attacks against short messages.
    c) Scrambling occurs even if the message is short.
    d) Make ciphertext a multiple of some block bit-length.

164. Which parameter is used neither in RSA nor in Diffie-Hellman?

    a) Generator   *b)* Cofactor   *c)* Prime pair   *d)* Key pair

165. Which of the following is not provided by ElGamal system?

    a) Encryption   *b)* MAC   *c)* Digital signature   *d)* Decryption

166. Which of the following is not correct regarding public-key cryptosystems?

    a) It is computationally infeasible to derive a private key from the public key
    b) It is easy to generate a signature given the public key
    c) It is computationally infeasible to recover the plaintext from the ciphertext and the public key
    d) It is easy to decrypt a ciphertext given the private key

167. Which of the following is not correct regarding RSA?

    a) Key pair can be used for encryption and decryption
    b) Security depends on assumption that the discrete logarithm problem is a hard problem
    c) The security depends on the chosen prime numbers
    d) The complexity of decryption is generally more complex than encryption

168. Which of the following public-key encryption is not based on the difficulty of solving the discrete logarithm problem?

    a) Diffie-Hellman algorithm   *b)* RSA

    c) ElGamal encryption   *d)* Elliptic curve encryption

169. Which of the following items is not an input to AEAD algorithms?

    a) Tag   *b)* Associated data   *c)* Plaintext   *d)* Nonce

170. Which of the following is not an AEAD algorithm?

    a) GMAC   *b)* GCM   *c)* CCM   *d)* AES-GCM-SIV

A.1.5 Key Management, PKI, and Certificates

171. Under what circumstance a certificate might be revoked? *a)* The certificate owner's private key has been compromised *b)* The certificate owner's public key has been compromised *c)* The certificate not-before-date is not yet reached *d)* The certificate not been used since issued
172. What does salt mean in cryptographic algorithms? *a)* Random value   *b)* Nonce   *c)* Key prefix   *d)* Message digest
173. Which type of key is not used in Kerberos? *a)* Private key   *b)* Public key   *c)* Session key   *d)* Shared key
174. Messages between parties are encrypted using a key, often referred to as *a)* Session key   *b)* Static key   *c)* Connection key   *d)* Temporary key
175. Which of the following is not a requirement for digital certificates? *a)* Any entity can read the certificate to determine the name and the public key of the certificate owner *b)* Only authorized entities can send requests to check the certificate validity *c)* Any entity can ask the validation authority to check the certificate validity *d)* Only the CA can issue a digital certificate
176. Which of the following best describes two-factor authentication? *a)* Use of profession   *b)* Use of animal name and a random number *c)* Use of birth city   *d)* Use of preferred song and beach
177. What is the purpose of biometrics in access control? *a)* User authentication   *b)* User identification *c)* User rights management   *d)* User certification
178. To obtain a certificate from a certificate authority, the user must present *a)* Proof of identity   *b)* Public and private keys *c)* Password and public key   *d)* Proof of identity and public key
179. Kerberos vs Key distribution center (KDC) *a)* KDC makes use of Kerberos   *b)* Kerberos is a component of KDC *c)* They are two distinct notions   *d)* Kerberos = implementation of KDC
180. Which of the following services is provided by Kerberos? *a)* Authorization   *b)* Protection against denial of service *c)* Protection against password guessing   *d)* Authentication
181. Which of the following does not provide data integrity over Internet? *a)* TLS   *b)* Kerberos   *c)* HTTPS   *d)* EdDSA
182. Which of the following is not correct? *a)* Both PKI and KDC are based on asymmetric keys *b)* Both PKI and KDC require trusted tiers *c)* KDC is based on symmetric keys *d)* Both PKI and KDC provide authentication services
183. Which of the following type of key is not used in cryptographic algorithms? *a)* Dynamic key   *b)* Private key   *c)* Static key   *d)* Ephemeral key
184. Which of the following attacks is prevented by digital signatures? *a)* Denial-of-service   *b)* Forgery attack   *c)* Password theft   *d)* Repudiation

A.1.6   Math and Pseudorandom Number Generation

---

185. Which of the following integers is not a prime power?

    a) 32   *b)* 18   *c)* 81   *d)* 103

---

186. Which of the following integers is not a safe prime?

    a) 23   *b)* 47   *c)* 101   *d)* 107

---

187. Which of the following integers has no multiplicative inverse in $\mathbb{Z}_{30}^{*}$?

    a) 7   *b)* 25   *c)* 17   *d)* 29

---

188. Which of the following is Euler's totient $\phi(n)$, when $n = 1111$?

    a) 1000   *b)* 100   *c)* 121   *d)* 111

---

189. Of which of the following congruences -5 is a square root?

    a) 2 *mod* 17   *b)* 2 *mod* 19   *c)* 2 *mod* 23   *d)* 2 *mod* 29

---

190. Which of the following polynomials is irreducible over binary field F_2?

    a) $x^2 + 1$ *b)* $x^2 + x$ *c)* $x + 1$ *d)* $x^2 + x + 1$

---

191. Which of the following is an extension field?

    a) F_2 *b)* F_3 *c)* F_8 *d)* F_5

---

192. Which of the following values is the order of the group $< \mathbb{Z}_{21}^{*}, \times >$?

    a) 20   *b)* 12   *c)* 13   *d)* 15

---

193. 2^{100} *mod* $101 =$

    a) 7   *b)* 1   *c)* 3   *d)* 7

---

194. A primitive polynomial is also called

    a) Singular Polynomial   *b)* Non-factorizable Polynomial

    c) Perfect Polynomial   *d)* Irreducible Polynomial

---

195. What is the GCD of $x^3 + x + 1$ and $x^2 + 1$ over F_2?

    a) x *b)* x^2 *c)* 1   *d)* $x + 1$

---

196. What is the GCD of $x^3 + 2x^2 + x - 1$ and $x^2 + 1$ over F_3?

    a) $x^2 + 1$ *b)* x^2 *c)* 1   *d)* $x + 1$

---

197. Consider a prime $p = 3$ *mod* 4 and a prime $a \in \mathbb{Z}_p$. Which of the following is equivalent to a square root of $a \bmod p$?

    a) $a^{\frac{p+1}{3}}$ *mod* p *b)* a^{p-1} *mod* p *c)* $a^{\frac{p-1}{2}}$ *mod* p *d)* $a^{\frac{p+1}{4}}$ *mod* p

---

198. Which of the following is a bad source of entropy to random number generators?

    a) Number of key strokes per minute   *b)* Outdoor temperature

    c) Number of cars in a car park   *d)* Number of students in a classroom

---

199. Which of the following statements is false? x is an element of $\mathbb{Z}_n$

    a) If $x^{-y} \equiv y$ *mod* n, then y is the multiplicative inverse of x

    b) If $x * y \equiv 1$ *mod* n, then y is the multiplicative inverse of x

    c) The multiplicative inverse of x exists iff $gcd(x, n) = 1$

    d) If $x = 0$, then the multiplicative inverse of x does not exist

---

200. Which of the following is the entropy of a variable X that takes N uniformly distributed values?

    a) $\log_{10}(n)$ *b)* $\log_2(n)$ *c)* $n / \log_2(n)$ *d)* $\log(\log(n))$

A.2 Answers

1. *c*	41. *c*	81. *d*	121. *d*	161. *d*
2. *d*	42. *d*	82. *b*	122. *c*	162. *c*
3. *c*	43. *b*	83. *d*	123. *b*	163. *d*
4. *c*	44. *d*	84. *b*	124. *b*	164. *b*
5. *b*	45. *a*	85. *c*	125. *b*	165. *b*
6. *b*	46. *b*	86. *d*	126. *c*	166. *b*
7. *c*	47. *c*	87. *b*	127. *d*	167. *b*
8. *b*	48. *b*	88. *b*	128. *d*	168. *b*
9. *c*	49. *d*	89. *d*	129. *a*	169. *a*
10. *b*	50. *c*	90. *d*	130. *c*	170. *a*
11. *c*	51. *d*	91. *d*	131. *b*	171. *a*
12. *b*	52. *c*	92. *b*	132. *d*	172. *a*
13. *a*	53. *d*	93. *c*	133. *b*	173. *b*
14. *d*	54. *b*	94. *a*	134. *c*	174. *a*
15. *b*	55. *c*	95. *d*	135. *b*	175. *b*
16. *d*	56. *d*	96. *d*	136. *b*	176. *d*
17. *a*	57. *c*	97. *b*	137. *d*	177. *a*
18. *b*	58. *b*	98. *b*	138. *a*	178. *d*
19. *c*	59. *b*	99. *a*	139. *b*	179. *d*
20. *b*	60. *c*	100. *c*	140. *c*	180. *d*
21. *c*	61. *d*	101. *d*	141. *c*	181. *b*
22. *d*	62. *d*	102. *a*	142. *a*	182. *a*
23. *c*	63. *b*	103. *b*	143. *b*	183. *a*
24. *c*	64. *c*	104. *c*	144. *b*	184. *d*
25. *c*	65. *c*	105. *c*	145. *a*	185. *b*
26. *b*	66. *a*	106. *a*	146. *c*	186. *c*
27. *c*	67. *b*	107. *d*	147. *a*	187. *b*
28. *c*	68. *d*	108. *a*	148. *b*	188. *a*
29. *b*	69. *c*	109. *b*	149. *b*	189. *c*
30. *c*	70. *b*	110. *b*	150. *c*	190. *d*
31. *d*	71. *c*	111. *d*	151. *a*	191. *c*
32. *d*	72. *b*	112. *b*	152. *d*	192. *b*
33. *c*	73. *a*	113. *a*	153. *a*	193. *b*
34. *d*	74. *b*	114. *c*	154. *b*	194. *d*
35. *c*	75. *c*	115. *a*	155. *c*	195. *c*
36. *c*	76. *b*	116. *b*	156. *b*	196. *a*
37. *b*	77. *b*	117. *c*	157. *d*	197. *d*
38. *b*	78. *c*	118. *c*	158. *a*	198. *d*
39. *d*	79. *a*	119. *d*	159. *b*	199. *a*
40. *d*	80. *c*	120. *a*	160. *b*	200. *b*

Index

Note: *Italic* page numbers refer to figure and **Bold** page numbers reference to tables. Page numbers followed by 'n' refer to notes.

Cryptography: Algorithms, Protocols, and Standards for Computer Security, First Edition. Zoubir Mammeri.
© 2024 John Wiley & Sons, Inc. Published 2024 by John Wiley & Sons, Inc.

Greek scytale 34

group 10, 13, 15, 34, 37, 48, 51, 60, 63, 66–72, 79, 81, 92, 95, 119, 124–126, 137, 163, 273, 283, 381–383, 394–396, 400, 402, 404, 405, 408, 416–418, 420, 421, 424, 426, 429, 430, 433, 434, 436, 438–440, 442, 446, 461, 478, 503, 505, 512, 518, 519

h

hackers 2, 12, 13, 33
handshake protocol 518–520
hardware availability 7
hardware integrity 6, 7
Hartley's entropy 535
hash code 142
hash-DRBG 542–544
hash function 19, 39, 40, *41*, 42, 43, 48, 142–171, 207, 289, 290, 294–296, 326, 328, 329, 336n8, 390–392, 400, 401, 403, 412, 413, 441, 443, 445–448, 462, 466, 470–472, **473,** 474, 479, 483, 488, 502, 503, 505, 506, 507n6, 511, 516, 519, 527, 530n6, 537, 538, **538,** 542–545, 555, 557, 558, 560
health testing of a noise source 533
Hellman's tables 338, 339, 341, **342,** 343, 344, *344,* 346
Hierarchical trust model 515
HMAC 41, 158–161, 165, 171, 326, 328–329, 467, 470–476, 526, 528, 538, 545
HMAC-DRBG 542, *544,* 544–546, *545*
honeypot 16, 20, 24–25

i

identification 3, 19, 124–126, 130–132, 363, 539
identity authentication 7, 8, 19, 466
index calculus 394
indistinguishability 316–320, 323–324, 326, 327–328
information-theoretic secure cipher 117
information-theoretic security 43, 44
initialization vector (IV) 125, 145–146, 170–171, 173, 175, 187, 188, 190, 194–197, 203, 249–250, 252–253, 255, 257, 269–277, 279, 279n8, 281, 291, 293–294, 305, 307, 323, 324, 326, 329, 331–333, 335, 368–371, 380n9, 472–474, 476, 483, 532, 549
initial permutation 211–213, **213,** 235, 237
instance of a function family 315
instance of a permutation family 315, 320, 332
integer factorization 60, 381
integer factorization cryptography (IFC) 37, 381, 382, 477, 531, 550, 554
integer factorization problem 381, 389
Integrated Encryption Scheme 446
integrity 4, 6–7, 19, 29, 30, 33, 34, 39–41, *41,* 42, *42,* 48, 57n4, 135, 140, 142, 143, 145, 157–159, 161, 163–165, 168, 175, 184, 247, 269, 273, 274, 281, 282, 289, 294, 301, 446, 465–467, 502, 504, 512, 516–520, 526–528, 531

intermediate CA 512–515, 527, 528
International Organization for Standardization (ISO) 182, 446, 509, 536
Internet Engineering Task Force (IETF) 158, 182, 193, 205n10, 424, 437, 517
intrusion detection 20, 23
intrusion detection system (IDS) 17, 19, 20, 22–24, *23,* 26
intrusion prevention 20, 25
Intrusion Protection Systems (IPSs) 20, 24
intrusion signatures 22, 23
inverse permutation 213, **214,** 317, 318
invertible element 60, 63, 79, 95, 200
InvMixColumns 223, 224, 227, 233–234, 236, 245
InvShiftRows 223, 224, 226–227, *227,* 233
InvSubBytes 223, 224–226, **225, 226,** 232–233, 236, 244
irreducibility 73, 80, 89–91, 107, 108
irreducibility test 90
irreducible polynomial 72–73, 75, 77–80, 96, 97, 111, 113, 229, 231, 290, 294, 295, 433, 480, 507n15
ISO/IEC 184, 194
issuing CA 512–514, 516, 527
iterated block cipher 222
iterated hash functions 329, 336n8
IT security 1, 3–4, *4,* 7, 15–16, 18, 20, 29, 33
IV misuse 281

j

Jefferson's wheel cipher 35, *35*
joint entropy 534

k

Kasumi 209
KDF in counter mode 472, 474, 475–476
KDF in double-pipelined mode 474, 476
KDF in feedback mode 474, 476
Keccak 152, 160, 171n9
Keccak[c] 157
Keccak-p 152, **153,** 157, 170, 171n10
Keccak_p permutation 152, 155, 157, 171n10, 329
Kerberos 486, 509–530
Kerberos ticket 523, *524*
Kerckhoffs, A. 43, 52–54
key agreement 382, 396, 424, 465, 466, **481,** 482, 483, 486, 487, 489, 495, 505, 506n4
key-agreement function (KA) 446
key-agreement protocols 37, 43, 45, 437–440, 465, 469, 477, 483
key-agreement scheme #1 (KAS1) *489,* 489–490, 507n19
key-agreement scheme #2 (KAS2) *490,* 490–491, *491*
key-agreement schemes (KASs) 469, **479,** 483, 486, 487–488, 491, 492–501, *494,* 495, *495–501,* 502, 529n4
key-agreement transaction 483, 486–489, 494, 495, 498
keyboard 14, 15, 122–124, 126, 127